AN EXEGETICAL SUMMARY OF
HEBREWS

AN EXEGETICAL SUMMARY OF HEBREWS

Second Edition

J. Harold Greenlee

SIL International

Second Edition

Library of Congress Catalog Card Number: 2008923535
ISBN: 978-155671-209-8

Printed in the United States of America

Copies of this and other publications
of SIL International may be obtained from

International Academic Bookstore
SIL International
7500 West Camp Wisdom Road
Dallas, TX 75236-5699, USA

Voice: 972-708-7404
Fax: 972-708-7363
academic_books@sil.org
www.ethnologue.com

PREFACE

Exegesis is concerned with the interpretation of a text. Exegesis of the New Testament involves determining the meaning of the Greek text. Translators must be especially careful and thorough in their exegesis of the New Testament in order to accurately communicate its message in the vocabulary, grammar, and literary devices of another language. Questions occurring to translators as they study the Greek text are answered by summarizing how scholars have interpreted the text. This is information that should be considered by translators as they make their own exegetical decisions regarding the message they will communicate in their translations.

The Semi-Literal Translation

As a basis for discussion, a semi-literal translation of the Greek text is given so that the reasons for different interpretations can best be seen. When one Greek word is translated into English by several words, these words are joined by hyphens. There are a few times when clarity requires that a string of words joined by hyphens have a separate word, such as "not" (μή), inserted in their midst. In this case, the separate word is surrounded by spaces between the hyphens. When alternate translations of a Greek word are given, these are separated by slashes.

The Text

Variations in the Greek text are noted under the heading TEXT. The base text for the summary is the text of the fourth revised edition of *The Greek New Testament,* published by the United Bible Societies, which has the same text as the twenty-sixth edition of the *Novum Testamentum Graece* (Nestle-Aland). The versions that follow different variations are listed without evaluating their choices.

The Lexicon

The meaning of a key word in context is the first question to be answered. Words marked with a raised letter in the semi-literal translation are treated separately under the heading LEXICON. First, the lexicon form of the Greek word is given. Within the parentheses following the Greek word is the location number where, in the author's judgment, this word is defined in the *Greek-English Lexicon of the New Testament Based on Semantic Domains* (Louw and Nida 1988). When a semantic domain includes a translation of the particular verse being treated, **LN** in bold type indicates that specific translation. If the specific reference for the verse is listed in *A Greek-English Lexicon of the New Testament and Other Early Christian Literature* (Bauer, Arndt, Gingrich, and Danker 1979), the outline location and page number is given. Then English equivalents of the Greek word are given to show how it is translated by commentators who offer their own translations of the whole text and, after a semicolon, all the versions in the list of abbreviations for translations. When reference is made to "all versions," it refers to only the versions in the list of translations. Sometimes further comments are made about the meaning of the word or the significance of a verb's tense, voice, or mood.

The Questions

Under the heading QUESTION, a question is asked that comes from examining the Greek text under consideration. Typical questions concern the identity of an implied actor or object of an event word, the antecedent of a pronominal reference, the connection indicated by a relational word, the meaning of a genitive construction, the meaning of figurative language, the function of a rhetorical question, the identification of an ambiguity, and the presence of implied information that is needed to understand the passage correctly. Background information is also considered for a proper understanding of a passage. Although not all implied information and background information is made explicit in a translation, it is important to consider it so that the translation will not be stated in such a way that prevents a reader from arriving at the proper interpretation. The question is answered with a summary of what commentators have said. If there are contrasting differences of opinion, the different interpretations are numbered and the commentaries that support each are listed. Differences that are not treated by many of the commentaries often are not numbered, but are introduced with a contrastive 'Or' at the beginning of the sentence. No attempt has been made to select which interpretation is best.

In listing support for various statements of interpretation, the author is often faced with the difficult task of matching the different terminologies used in commentaries with the terminology he has adopted. Sometimes he can only infer the position of a commentary from incidental remarks. This book, then, includes the author's interpretation of the views taken in the various commentaries. General statements are followed by specific statements, which indicate the author's understanding of the pertinent relationships, actors, events, and objects implied by that interpretation.

The Use of This Book

This book does not replace the commentaries that it summarizes. Commentaries contain much more information about the meaning of words and passages. They often contain arguments for the interpretations that are taken and they may have important discussions about the discourse features of the text. In addition, they have information about the historical, geographical, and cultural setting. Translators will want to refer to at least four commentaries as they exegete a passage. However, since no one commentary contains all the answers translators need, this book will be a valuable supplement. It makes more sources of exegetical help available than most translators have access to. Even if they had all the books available, few would have the time to search through all of them for the answers.

When many commentaries are studied, it soon becomes apparent that they frequently disagree in their interpretations. That is the reason why so many answers in this book are divided into two or more interpretations. The reader's initial reaction may be that all of these different interpretations complicate exegesis rather than help it. However, before translating a passage, a translator needs to know exactly where there is a problem of interpretation and what the exegetical options are.

ABBREVIATIONS AND BIBLIOGRAPHY

Commentaries and Reference Books

Alf Alford, Henry. *The Epistle to the Hebrews, and the Catholic Epistles of St. James and St. Peter.* The Greek Testament, Vol. 4. London: Rivingtons, 1859.

BAGD Bauer, Walter. *A Greek-English Lexicon of the New Testament and Other Early Christian Literature.* Translated and adapted from the 5th German edition, 1958, by William F. Arndt and F. Wilbur Gingrich. 2d English ed. revised and augmented by F. Wilbur Gingrich and Frederick W. Danker. Chicago: University of Chicago Press, 1979.

Blm Bloomfield, S. T. *The Greek Testament.* Vol. 2., 3d ed. London: Longman, Orme, Brown, Green, & Longmans, 1839.

EBC Morris, Leon. "Hebrews." In vol. 12 of *The Expositor's Bible Commentary*, edited by Frank E. Gaebelein. Grand Rapids: Zondervan, 1981.

EGT Dods, Marcus. "The Epistle to the Hebrews." In vol. 4 of *The Expositor's Greek Testament*, edited by W. Robertson Nicoll, n.d. Reprint. Grand Rapids: Eerdmans, 1980.

GNC Hagner, Donald A. *Hebrews.* A Good News Commentary, edited by W. Ward Gasque. San Francisco: Harper and Row, 1983.

HNTC Montefiore, Hugh. *A Commentary on the Epistle to the Hebrews.* Black's New Testament Commentaries (Harper's New Testament Commentary in USA), Henry Chadwick, general editor. London: Adam & Charles Black, 1964.

Hu Hughes, Philip Edgcumbe. *A Commentary on the Epistle to the Hebrews.* Grand Rapids: Eerdmans, 1977.

Hwt Hewitt, Thomas. *The Epistle to the Hebrews.* Grand Rapids: Eerdmans, 1970.

ICC Moffatt, James. *A Critical and Exegetical Commentary on the Epistle to the Hebrews.* The International Critical Commentary, edited by Alfred Plummer. Edinburgh: T. & T. Clark, 1924.

Lg Moll, Carl Bernhard. *The Epistle to the Hebrews.* Commentary on the Holy Scriptures, vol. 11, edited by John Peter Lange. 1870. Translated by A. C. Kendrick, whose additional notes are indicated by Lg(K). Grand Rapids: Zondervan, 1960.

LN Louw, Johannes P., and Eugene A. Nida. *Greek-English Lexicon of the New Testament Based on Semantic Domains.* 2 vols. New York: United Bible Societies, 1988.

Lns Lenski, R. C. H. *The Interpretation of The Epistle to the Hebrews and The Epistle of James.* Minneapolis: Augsburg, 1966.

Mil Miller, Neva F. *The Epistle to the Hebrews; An Analytical and Exegetical Handbook.* Dallas: Summer Institute of Linguistics, 1988.

My Lünemann, Göttlieb. *Critical and Exegetical Hand-book to the Epistle to the Hebrews.* Meyer's Commentary on the New Testament, edited by Heinrich August Wilhelm Meyer. Translated by Maurice J. Evans, with supplementary notes by Timothy Dwight indicated by My(D). New York and London: Funk and Wagnalls, 1890.

NCBC Wilson, Robert McLelland. *Hebrews.* New Century Bible Commentary, edited by Matthew Black. Grand Rapids: Eerdmans, 1987.

NIC Bruce, F. F. *The Epistle to the Hebrews.* New International Commentary on the New Testament. Grand Rapids: Eerdmans, 1990.

NIGTC Ellingworth, Paul. *The Epistle to the Hebrews*. The New International Greek Testament Commentary, edited by I. Howard Marshall and W. Ward Gasque. Grand Rapids: Eerdmans, 1993.

NTC Kistemaker, Simon J. *Exposition of the Epistle to the Hebrews*. New Testament Commentary. Grand Rapids: Baker, 1984.

TH Ellingworth, Paul, and Eugene A. Nida. *A Translator's Handbook on the Letter to the Hebrews*. New York: United Bible Societies, 1983.

TNTC Guthrie, Donald. *The Letter to the Hebrews*. Tyndale New Testament Commentaries, edited by Leon Morris. Grand Rapids: Eerdmans, 1983.

WBC Lane, William L. *Hebrews 1–8, 9–13*. 2 vols. Word Biblical Commentary. Dallas: Word, 1991.

Wst Westcott, Brooke Foss. *The Epistle to the Hebrews: The Greek Text with Notes and Essays*. 3d ed. London: Macmillan, 1909.

GREEK TEXT AND TRANSLATIONS

GNT The Greek New Testament. Edited by B. Aland, K. Aland, J. Karavidopoulos, C. Martini, and B. Metzger. 4th ed. London, New York: United Bible Societies, 1993.

CEV The Holy Bible, Contemporary English Version. New York: American Bible Society, 1995.

KJV The Holy Bible, Authorized (or King James) Version, 1611.

NAB The New American Bible. Camden, New Jersey: Thomas Nelson, 1971.

NASB The New American Standard Bible. Nashville, Tenn.: Holman, 1977.

NIV The Holy Bible, New International Version. Grand Rapids: Zondervan, 1984.

NJB The New Jerusalem Bible. Garden City, New York: Doubleday, 1985.

NLT The Holy Bible, New Living Translation. Wheaton, Ill.: Tyndale House, 1996.

NRSV The Holy Bible, New Revised Standard Version. New York: Oxford University Press, 1989.

REB The Revised English Bible. Oxford: Oxford University Press and Cambridge University Press, 1989.

TEV Good News Bible, Today's English Version. 2d ed. New York: American Bible Society, 1992.

TNT The Translator's New Testament. London: British and Foreign Bible Society, 1973.

GRAMMATICAL TERMS

act.	active
fut.	future
impera.	imperative
indic.	indicative
infin.	infinitive
mid.	middle
opt.	optative
pass.	passive
perf.	perfect
pres.	present
subj.	subjunctive

EXEGETICAL SUMMARY OF HEBREWS

DISCOURSE UNIT: 1:1–10:18 [Mil, TNTC]. The topic is the mediator of the New Covenant compared with the mediators of the Old Covenant [Mil], the superiority of Christianity [TNTC].

DISCOURSE UNIT: 1:1–5:10 [Lg]. The topic is the Son, the perfect Mediator, exalted above all.

DISCOURSE UNIT: 1:1–2:18 [Lg, NIC, NIGTC, NTC, WBC; REB]. The topic is Jesus elevated above the OT mediators [Lg], the finality of Christianity [NIC, NIGTC], the superiority of Jesus and his saviorhood and priesthood [NTC], Jesus as divine and human [REB], God's revelation through his Son [WBC].

DISCOURSE UNIT: 1:1–2:4 [Lns]. The topic is the supremacy of the Son.

DISCOURSE UNIT: 1:1–14 [NASB, NIV]. The topic is God's final word in his Son [NASB], the Son's superiority to angels [NIV].

DISCOURSE UNIT: 1:1–4 [EBC, GNT, Hwt, Lg, NCBC, NIC, NIGTC, NTC, TNTC, WBC, Wst; CEV, NAB, NIV, NJB]. The topic is the introduction [EBC, Hwt, NTC; NAB], the prologue [NCBC], the superiority of God's new revelation [NIV], God's final revelation in the Son [Lg, NIC, NIGTC, TNTC, WBC], the finality of Christianity [Wst], the greatness of God's Son [NJB].

DISCOURSE UNIT: 1:1–3 [GNC, Hu, Lns, Mil; NLT, TEV]. The topic is God's definitive revelation [GNC], God's word given through his Son [GNT; TEV], the mediator of the New Covenant is God's Son, who is superior to the prophets [Mil], Christ's superiority to the prophets [Hu], Christ's supremacy [Lns], Jesus Christ, God's Son [NLT].

1:1 In-many-parts/times/ways[a] and in-many-manners[b] in-the-past[c] God having-spoken to-the fathers[d] by/in[e] the prophets

LEXICON—a. πολυμερῶς (LN **63.19; 67.11; 89.81**) (BAGD p. 687): 'in many parts' [**LN** (63.19)], 'in many portions' [Lns, Mil; NASB], 'many times' [**LN** (67.11); NLT, TEV], 'at many times' [CEV, NIV], 'at many moments' [NJB], 'at various days' [NIC], 'at various times' [WBC], 'at sundry times' [KJV], 'in many ways' [BAGD, LN (89.81)], 'in many different ways' [LN (89.81)]. The phrase πολυμερῶς καὶ πολυτρόπως 'in many portions and in many manners' is translated 'in a great many different ways' [**LN** (89.81)], 'in many and various ways' [NRSV, TNT], 'in many and varied ways' [REB], 'in fragmentary and varied ways' [NAB], 'in fragmentary and varied fashion' [HNTC].

b. πολυτρόπως (LN **58.29; 89.82**) (BAGD p. 690): 'in many ways' [LN (58.29, 89.82), Lns, Mil, NIC, WBC; CEV, NASB, NLT, TEV], 'in various ways' [BAGD; NIV, NRSV, TNT], 'in varied ways' [NAB,

REB], 'by many means' [NJB], 'in diverse manners' [KJV]. The reference is to diversity of manner or mode of presentation [Alf, Blm, EGT, Hu, Hwt, My].

c. πάλαι (LN **67.24**) (BAGD p. 605): 'in the past' [HNTC, WBC; NIV, NJB, TEV, TNT], 'in time past' [KJV], 'in times past' [NAB, REB], 'in earlier times' [NIC], 'in olden times' [Lns], 'long ago' [BAGD, LN, Mil; CEV, NASB, NLT, NRSV], 'formerly' [BAGD]. The reference is to the OT revelations [TH, Wst].

d. πατήρ (LN 10.20) (BAGD 1.b. p. 635): 'father' [HNTC, Lns, NIC, WBC; KJV, NAB, NASB], 'forefather' [BAGD, LN, Mil; NIV, REB, TNT], 'ancestor' [BAGD, LN; CEV, NJB, NLT, NRSV, TEV]. The reference is to the ancestors of the Jews [Alf, GNC, HNTC, Hwt, Lg, My, NCBC, TH], OT believers in general [EBC, ICC].

e. ἐν with dative object (LN 83.13; 90.6): 'by' [HNTC, LN, NIC; KJV, NRSV, TNT], 'through' [WBC; NAB, NIV, NJB, NLT, REB, TEV], 'in' [LN, Mil; NASB], 'in the person of' [Lns]. The phrase ὁ θεὸς λαλήσας ἐν τοῖς προφήταις 'God having spoken by/in the prophets' is translated 'God's prophets spoke his message' [CEV].

QUESTION—What is meant by πολυμερῶς 'parts/times/ways'?

1. It pertains to the many parts of God's communication [Alf, Blm, EGT, HNTC, Hu, Lg, LN (63.19), Lns, Mil; NAB, NASB]: in many parts and in many ways God spoke. The former revelations were fragmentary [EGT, HNTC; NAB], given piecemeal, bit by bit [EGT]. For each act of instruction God chose from various modes to bring home the various aspects of truth [Wst].
2. It pertains to the many occasions on which God spoke [LN (67.11), My, NIC, TNTC, WBC; CEV, KJV, NIV, NJB, NLT, REB, TEV]: at many times and in many ways God spoke. Different occasions stretched over all OT history as God spoke in many manners: visions, angelic communications, prophetic messages, and events [TNTC].
3. It pertains to the many ways in which God spoke [BAGD, ICC, LN (89.81), NIGTC; NRSV, REB, TNT]: in very many ways God spoke. The phrase πολυμερῶς καὶ πολυτρόπως 'in many ways and many manners' is used for intensifying the statement: 'in a great many different ways' [LN (89.81); NIGTC].

QUESTION—What relationship is indicated by the aorist participle λαλήσας 'having spoken'?

The aorist tense indicates that the speaking was completed [Hu, NIGTC, TH]; it points forward to the following finite verb in the next verse [Lns].

1. The participle is semantically parallel to ἐλάλησεν 'he spoke' in the following verse [TH, TNTC; NAB, NIV, NJB, NRSV, TEV, TNT]: God spoke to the fathers and/but he also spoke to us.
2. The participle is temporal [Mil, My; NASB]: after God spoke to the fathers, he spoke to us. God's speaking through the prophets is contrasted with his speaking through Christ in the following verse [Mil].

3. The participle may be concessive [NTC]: although he spoke to the fathers by the prophets, he spoke to us by his Son.

QUESTION—What is implied by the use of the article in the phrase τοῖς πατράσιν 'the fathers'?

1. It implies 'our' fathers [Hu, ICC; CEV, NAB, NIV, NJB, NLT, NRSV, REB, TEV, TNT]: God spoke to our fathers.
2. It implies that not all of the readers were descendants of the fathers [NIGTC, TH]: God spoke to the fathers of the Jews. Some gentiles were among the readers [NIGTC].

QUESTION—What relationship is indicated by the phrase ἐν τοῖς προφηταῖς 'by/in the prophets'?

1. It is instrumental [NIGTC]: God was speaking to the fathers 'through' [Blm, TH, WBC; NAB, NIV, NJB, NLT, REB, TEV] or 'by' [HNTC, NIC, NTC; KJV, NRSV, TNT] the prophets. God caused his prophets to speak on his behalf [TH]. The definite article indicates that the prophets are known to the readers [NIGTC].
2. It means that God was speaking 'in' the prophets [Alf, EGT, Hwt, ICC, Lg, Lns, My, Wst]. The reference is to the element in which the speaking took place [Alf]; God was dwelling in them [Hwt, My] as their enabling power [Wst].

QUESTION—Who are referred to by the term τοῖς προφήταις 'the prophets'?

1. They were the OT prophets [TH].
2. They include the authors of all the OT books [GNC].
3. They were the authors of the canonical prophetic writings plus Moses and others through whom God spoke [EBC, HNTC, Hwt, ICC, Lns, Mil, My, NCBC, NIC, NTC, Wst].
4. It includes those who spoke for God even down to John the Baptist [Alf].

1:2 in[a] (the) last[b] of-the these days he-has-spoken to-us by/in[c] (a) son,

LEXICON: a. ἐπί with genitive object (LN 67.33) (BAGD I.2. p. 286): 'in' [BAGD, Mil, NIC, WBC; all versions except TNT], 'at' [HNTC; TNT], 'at the time of' [LN], 'at . . . during' [Lns]. The sense is temporal [Lns, WBC].

b. ἔσχατος (LN 61.13) (BAGD 3.b. p 314): 'last' [BAGD, LN], 'final' [LN; NLT]. The phrase ἐπ' ἐσχάτου τῶν ἡμερῶν 'in the last of these days' is translated 'in these last days' [Mil, NIC; KJV, NASB, NIV, NRSV, TEV], 'in this final age' [WBC], 'in this, the final age' [NAB, REB], 'at the end of this age' [HNTC; TNT], 'at the end, during these days' [Lns], 'in our time, the final days' [NJB], 'now at last' [CEV].

c. ἐν with dative object: 'by, in'. See this word in 1:1.

QUESTION—How is this clause related to the preceding clause?

It is contrasted with 'in the past' in 1:1 [Mil, My] and many translations begin this verse with the relation word 'but' [NIC, WBC; CEV, NIV, NJB, NLT, NRSV, REB, TEV]. There is both contrast and continuity in reference to God's speaking in the two eras [NTC, WBC]. The two verses compare

God's speaking and give three points of contrast: (1) in the past – in these last days (2) to the fathers – to us (3) by the prophets – by his Son [NIGTC, TH, WBC]. There is also a contrast between 'many times and ways' with an implicit 'once' (implied by the singular υἱῷ 'a Son') [TH]. However, the points of contrast are not to be exaggerated [NIGTC].

QUESTION—What is meant by the phrase ἐπ' ἐσχάτου τῶν ἡμέρων τούτων 'in the last of these days'?

1. It refers to the close of the present age [Alf, ICC, Lg, My, NIGTC, TH, Wst], since ἐσχάτου 'last' is neuter and does not modify the feminine ἡμέρων 'days' [NIGTC]. Τούτων 'these' indicates that the last days have already begun [NIGTC].
2. It refers to the beginning of a new era [EBC, GNC], the Messianic age [EBC, NTC], the turning point in God's plan and his final word of fulfillment through the Son [GNC].
3. It means the end of the old age (with the death of Christ [Mil]) and the beginning of the new age [Hwt, Lg, Mil, My, NCBC, TNTC].
4. There is a double temporal sense—at the end of the OT period, and during these recent days [Lns].

QUESTION—To whom does ἡμῖν 'to us' refer?

It refers to the Christian church in general since the writer was not directly addressed by the Son [Wst]. It refers to all who have heard or will hear the message, directly from Christ or indirectly through others [Alf], all believers [Hwt, NIGTC], the people of the present age [My], the Christian Church [ICC]. It includes the readers [TH].

QUESTION—What is implied by υἱῷ 'son' without a definite article?

It is qualitative, focusing on his relationship or his essential nature [Alf, EBC, EGT, Hwt, Lg, Lns, Mil, My, NCBC, NIGTC, TH, WBC, Wst]. It also indicates a contrast with the preceding phrase τοῖς προφήταις 'the prophets' [NIGTC]. This person is not merely a prophet, but a Son [TH]. It implies the superiority of the Son [TNTC]. It is the equivalent of a proper name [NTC].

whom he-placed[a] (as) heir[b] of-all-things,

LEXICON: a. aorist act. indic. of τίθημι (LN 37.96) (BAGD I.2.aα. p. 816): 'to place' [Lns], 'to appoint' [LN, Mil, NIC, WBC; all versions except NAB, TEV], 'to make' [BAGD, HNTC; NAB], 'to choose' [TEV]. The reference is to appointment [EGT]. The aorist tense indicates a definite point of time, namely at the beginning [Alf], in eternity past [ICC, My]; or it is timeless [TNTC].

b. κληρονόμος (LN 57.139) (BAGD 2.a. p. 435): 'heir' [BAGD, LN, Lns, Mil, NIC, WBC; all versions except TEV, TNT], 'rightful owner' [HNTC]. This noun is also translated as a verbal phrase: 'to possess at the end' [TEV], 'to enter into possession of' [TNT]. The entire clause is translated 'and everything will someday belong to the Son' [CEV], 'God promised everything to the Son as an inheritance' [NLT].

QUESTION—Why is this and the following clauses mentioned?

They emphasize the exalted status of the Son [NCBC, NIC, NTC]. They show why God's revelation through his Son is the highest he can give [NIC].

QUESTION—What is meant by the Son being an heir?

This word refers to lawful possession [EBC, NIGTC] without indicating the reason for the possession [EBC]. It means that the Son will come into possession of what rightfully belongs to him [TH]. The Son has possessed the universe since its beginning [HNTC], from eternity [Hwt, Lns, Mil, TNTC]. He received his inheritance as a man when he had completed his saving work [Lns]. It refers to his universal lordship [EGT], to his office as mediator [Hu]. He was appointed heir because of his sonship [Alf, Blm, GNC, Hu, Wst]. His inheritance is redeemed humanity and the renewed universe [Hu].

through[a] whom also/yet he-made[b] the ages;[c]

LEXICON: a. διά with genitive object (LN 90.4): 'through' [HNTC, LN, Lns, Mil, NIC, WBC; all versions except CEV, KJV], 'by' [LN; CEV, KJV].

b. aorist act. indic. of ποιέω (LN 42.29) (BAGD I.1.a.β. p. 681): 'to make' [LN, Lns, NIC; KJV, NASB, NIV, NJB, NLT, TNT], 'to create' [BAGD, HNTC, Mil, WBC; CEV, NAB, NRSV, REB, TEV], 'to fashion' [LN].

c. αἰών (LN **1.2**) (BAGD 3. p. 28): 'age' [Mil; NJB], 'eon' [Lns], 'universe' [HNTC, LN, NIC; CEV, NAB, NIV, REB, TEV, TNT], 'the universe and everything in it' [NLT], 'world' [BAGD, Mil, WBC; KJV, NASB, NRSV].

QUESTION—What relationship is indicated by διά 'through'?

It refers to Christ as the personal agent of God [Alf, EBC, Lns, Mil, NIC, Wst], Christ as the effective creator [Blm], as the instrumental cause [Hwt, NIGTC] or means [Mil], although God is the ultimate creator [EBC].

QUESTION—What is καί 'also/yet' connected with?

1. It is connected with ἐποίησεν 'he made' [Alf, ICC, Lg(K), Lns, TH, Wst], emphasizing the fact of creation [TH, Wst]: through whom he also made the world. It marks the correspondence this has with the preceding clause: the Son was to possess what he had been instrumental in making [ICC]. It points out how proper it was to commit everything to Christ [EGT]; it was because God had made the Son the heir [Lns].
2. It connects this clause with the preceding clause in an adversative sense [WBC]: he was appointed heir, yet he was the one through whom God made the world.

QUESTION—What is the meaning of τοὺς αἰῶνας 'the ages'?

1. It refers to the universe [Alf, Blm, HNTC, Lns, My, NIC, NTC; CEV, NAB, NIV, NLT, REB, TEV, TNT]. It is totally comprehensive, including time, space, and the universe with all it contains [Alf, Lns, My, NIC, NTC], the heavens and earth and all created things in them [Blm].

2. It refers to the world [BAGD, Hu, Mil, NIGTC, TH, WBC; KJV, NASB, NRSV]. It means the world and everything in it [TH]. It is the world in its historical perspective [Hu].
3. It is temporal, including all the periods of time [Hwt, Mil, Wst] and everything manifested in them [EBC].
4. It includes both the created world and the periods of time [TNTC].

1:3 who, being[a] (the) radiance[b] of-the glory[c] and (the) exact-representation[d] of-the real-being[e] of-him,

LEXICON: a. pres. act. participle of εἰμί (LN 13.1): 'to be' [HNTC, LN, Lns, Mil; all versions except TEV, TNT], not explicit [NIC, WBC]. The phrase ὢν ἀπαύγασμα τῆς δόξης . . . αὐτοῦ 'being the radiance of the glory of him' is translated 'he radiates God's glory' [TNT], 'he reflects the brightness of God's glory' [TEV], 'the Son reflects God's own glory' [NLT], 'God's Son has all the brightness of God's own glory' [CEV]. The present tense indicates timelessness [Alf], continuous state and action [Lns, My(D)], the Son's eternal nature [EGT, Hu, Wst].

b. ἀπαύγασμα (LN **14.48**) (BAGD p. 82): 'radiance' [BAGD, **LN,** Mil, WBC; NASB, NIV, REB], 'brightness' [CEV, KJV, TEV], 'reflection' [HNTC, LN; NAB, NJB, NRSV], 'effulgence' [Lns, NIC]. This noun is also translated as a verb: 'to reflect' [NLT, TEV], 'to radiate' [TNT]. It refers to the rays of light coming from God [EGT, GNC, Hu, Hwt, Lns, Mil, My(D), NIC, NIGTC, NTC, TNTC, Wst; NASB, NIV, REB, TNT], the result of shining forth [Lg, NTC]. It means reflection [HNTC, ICC; NAB, NJB, NRSV, TEV], reflected radiance [My]. It means the expression [Alf, GNC] or perfect likeness [Blm] of God.

c. δόξα (LN 14.49; 79.18) (BAGD 1.a. p. 203): 'glory' [HNTC, LN (79.18), Lns, Mil, NIC, WBC; all versions], 'splendor' [BAGD, LN (79.18)], 'brightness' [BAGD, LN (14.49)], 'radiance' [BAGD, LN (14.49)], 'shining' [LN (14.49)]. It refers to God's majesty [Blm, EBC, Lg], to all that belongs to him as God [EGT, Lns, Mil], his eternal nature [HNTC], the full manifestation of his attributes [Wst].

d. χαρακτήρ (LN **58.62**) (BAGD 1.b. p. 876): 'exact representation' [BAGD, HNTC, LN, Mil, WBC; NAB, NASB, NIV], 'exact likeness' [TEV], 'exact imprint' [NRSV], 'very image' [NIC], 'express image' [KJV], 'impress' [Lns; NJB], 'stamp' [REB]. The phrase ὃς ὢν . . . χαρακτὴρ τῆς ὑποστάσεως αὐτοῦ 'who, being . . . the exact representation of his real being' is translated 'he shows us exactly what God's nature is' [TNT], '(he) is like him in every way' [CEV], 'everything about him represents God exactly' [NLT]. It means an exact representation [Blm, EBC, EGT, GNC, HNTC, Hu, Hwt, ICC, Mil, My, NIC, NTC, TH, TNTC, WBC, Wst], a presentation of representative traits [Wst], but a separate person [NTC]. It is stronger than ἀπαύγασμα 'radiance' [NIGTC].

e. ὑπόστασις (LN **58.1**) (BAGD 1. p. 847): 'real being' [BAGD, **LN**], 'being' [HNTC, Lns, NIC; NAB, NIV, NJB, TEV], 'very being' [NRSV, REB], 'essence, substance' [LN], 'nature' [LN, Mil, WBC; NASB, TNT], 'person' [KJV]. It means essential being [Alf, EBC, ICC, Lg, Lns, NIC, NIGTC, Wst] or nature [EGT]. It is a parallel to 'glory' [NTC].

QUESTION—What is the function of the participial phrases 'being the radiance . . . and sustaining everything'?

They tell why the Son is fit to make a cleansing of sins. Along with the following participial phrase 'having made a purification of sins', they give the reason for the Son's taking his seat at the right hand of God [My]. They are concessions to the following contraexpectation [WBC]: although being the radiance . . . sustaining everything, yet he made purification for sins.

QUESTION—What relationship is indicated by the participle ὤν 'being' and the following participle φέρων 'carrying'?

1. They indicate the reason for the Son's taking his seat at God's right hand [My]: because he is the radiance and the exact representation of God, he sat down at God's right hand.
2. They indicate concession [WBC]: although he is the radiance and the exact representation of God, he nevertheless made purification.

QUESTION—How are the two nouns related in the genitive construction ἀπαύγασμα τῆς δόξης 'radiance of the glory'?

Δόξης 'glory' is an objective genitive, stating what is radiated [Mil]. It means that the Son reveals God's glory [Blm, EBC]. It implies the unity of the Son with the Father [Hu].

QUESTION—How are the two nouns related in the genitive construction χαρακτὴρ τῆς ὑποστάσεως 'exact representation of the real being'?

Ὑποστάσεως 'real being' is an objective genitive, stating what is represented [Mil]. It means that the Son perfectly represents God's person and attributes [Blm, EBC]. By seeing the Son, one sees what the Father is like [NIC]. This phrase repeats more explicitly the sense of the preceding phrase [GNC, WBC], further representing the deity of the Son [Lns]. It implies that the Son is distinct from the Father [Hu].

QUESTION—What is αὐτοῦ 'of him' connected with?

It is connected with both δόξης 'glory' and ὑποστάσεως 'real being' [My, TH].

and sustaining[a] everything[b] by-the word[c] of-his power,[d]

LEXICON: a. pres. act. participle of φέρω (LN **13.35**) (BAGD 1.b. p. 855): 'to sustain' [HNTC, **LN**, WBC; NAB, NIV, NJB, NLT, NRSV, REB, TEV], 'to maintain' [LN], 'to uphold' [KJV, NASB, TNT], 'to hold together' [CEV], 'to bear' [Lns], 'to bear up' [BAGD], 'to bear along' [Mil, NIC]. The meaning is to uphold [Lg, Lns, My, NIGTC, NTC, TH, Wst], to carry toward their proper goal [EBC, Hu, Hwt, Lg, Lns, Mil, NIC, NTC, TH, Wst], to govern [EGT, HNTC, NCBC] and to sustain [NCBC, NTC, TNTC].

b. πᾶς (LN 59.23; 63.2) (BAGD 2.b.β. p. 633): 'everything, whole, total, entire' [LN (63.2)], 'all' [LN (59.23)]. The phrase τὰ πάντα 'the everything' is translated 'all things' [BAGD, HNTC, Mil, NIC; KJV, NAB, NASB, NIV, NJB, NRSV], 'all the existing things' [Lns], 'the universe' [BAGD, Mil, WBC; CEV, NLT, REB, TEV, TNT]. Τὰ πάντα is all inclusive [NTC]; it is the common expression for the totality of all things [Alf, EBC, Wst], hence the universe [Alf, Blm] considered as a whole [EBC, Wst].

c. ῥῆμα (LN 33.9; 33.98) (BAGD 1. p. 735): 'word' [HNTC, LN, Mil, NIC, WBC; all versions except NJB, NLT], 'uttered word' [Lns], 'statement' [LN], 'commandment' [BAGD], 'command' [BAGD; NJB, NLT], 'order' [BAGD], 'direction' [BAGD]. It is a message, not a single word [TH]. It focuses on the action of speaking [NTC].

d. δύναμις (LN 76.1) (BAGD 1. p. 207): 'power' [HNTC, LN, Lns; KJV, NASB, REB], 'mighty power' [NLT]. This noun is also translated as an adjective: 'powerful' [BAGD, Mil, WBC; NAB, NIV, NJB, NRSV, TEV, TNT], 'mighty' [CEV]; as a participle: 'enabling' [NIC].

QUESTION—How are the two nouns related in the genitive construction τῷ ῥήματι τῆς δυνάμεως 'the word of the power'?

1. Δυνάμεως 'power' is an attribute of 'word' [Blm, EBC, Hu, Mil, NIGTC, NTC, TH; CEV, NAB, NIV, NJB, NRSV, TEV]: 'the powerful word', or 'enabling word' [NIC].
2. It is the utterance which proceeds from his power [Alf, HNTC, Lns, Wst]: the word which shows his power.

QUESTION—To whom does αὐτοῦ 'his' refer?

It refers to the Son [Alf, Lg, My, Wst].

having-made (a) purification[a] of-the sins he-sat-down[b] at[c] (the) right-hand[d] of-the Majesty[e] in[f] (the) high[g](places),

TEXT—Some manuscripts add δι' ἑαυτοῦ or δι' αὐτοῦ 'through himself' before καθαρισμόν 'cleansing'. GNT omits this phrase with a B rating, indicating that the text is almost certain. The phrase is included by Blm, Hwt, Lg, and KJV.

LEXICON: a. καθαρισμός (LN 53.28) (BAGD 2. p. 387): 'purification' [BAGD, HNTC, LN, Mil, NIC, WBC; NASB, NIV, NRSV, REB], 'cleansing' [Lns, Mil], 'forgiveness' [TEV]. The phrase καθαρισμὸν ποιησάμενος 'a purification having made' is translated 'cleansed' [NAB], 'purged' [KJV, NJB], 'when he had made it possible for man to be cleansed' [TNT], 'washed away' [CEV], 'he died to cleanse us from the stain of sin' [NLT]. It refers to the removal of sins [EBC], of guilt [EGT]. It refers to the completed work of redemption [Lg].

b. aorist act. indic. of καθίζω (LN 17.12) (BAGD 2.a.α. p. 390): 'to sit down' [BAGD, LN, Lns, Mil, NIC, WBC; CEV, KJV, NASB, NIV, NLT, NRSV, TEV, TNT], 'to take one's seat' [HNTC; NAB, NJB, REB]. The aorist tense refers to a single act [Mil, NIGTC] following the completion of redemption [My, NIGTC, TNTC]. It implies that the Son had satisfactorily completed his work [EGT, NIC, TNTC]. It refers to taking the seat of authority [Wst] following his resurrection [WBC]. Honor is also implied [TNTC]. This verb does not imply rest, but rather ceaseless activity [Hu, Lg, Lns] in accomplishing redemption [Lg].

c. ἐν with dative object (LN 83.23) (BAGD I.1.c. p. 258): 'at' [BAGD, HNTC, LN, Lns, NIC, WBC; all versions except KJV], 'on' [Mil; KJV], 'in the place of honor at' [NLT].

d. δεξιός (LN 8.32; 87.36) (BAGD 2.a. p. 174): 'right hand' [BAGD, HNTC, LN, Lns, Mil, NIC, WBC; all versions except CEV, TEV], 'right side' [CEV, TEV], 'right' [BAGD]. The feminine form implies the understood noun 'hand' [Mil].

e. μεγαλωσύνη (LN **12.5**) (BAGD p. 497): 'majesty' [BAGD, Lns]. With the article it is translated 'Majesty' [HNTC], 'the Majesty' [BAGD, **LN,** Mil, NIC**;** KJV, NAB, NASB, NIV, NRSV], 'the Majestic One' [LN], 'the majestic God' [NLT], 'the divine Majesty' [WBC; NJB], 'God's Majesty' [REB], 'God, the Supreme Power' [TEV], 'Almighty God' [TNT], 'the glorious God' [CEV]. This word (with the following phrase 'in the high places' [TNTC]) is a periphrastic reference to God [EBC, HNTC, Hu, ICC, Lg, Mil, NIC, NIGTC, NTC, TH, TNTC, WBC]. It refers to the majesty of God [EGT, Lns, Wst] and both affirms God's majesty and heightens the sense of the glory of the Son [WBC].

f. ἐν with dative object (LN 83.13): 'in (heaven)' [LN; CEV, NAB, NIV, TEV, TNT], '(God) of heaven' [NLT], 'on (high)' [HNTC, Lns, Mil, NIC, WBC; KJV, NASB, NJB, NRSV, REB].

g. ὑψηλός (LN **1.13**) (BAGD 1. p. 850): 'high' [BAGD, HNTC, LN, Lns, Mil, NIC, WBC; KJV, NASB, NJB, NRSV, REB], 'heaven' [BAGD, **LN;** CEV, NAB, NIV, NLT, TEV, TNT]. The reference is to heaven [Blm, EBC, Mil, My, WBC], the residence of God [Mil], above all created beings [Hu]. The plural implies the highest of several heavens [My].

QUESTION—What relationship is indicated by the aorist participle ποιησάμενος 'having made'?

The aorist tense implies the completion of the cleansing [Alf, EBC, EGT, HNTC, Hu, Lns, NTC, TNTC, WBC, Wst] before he 'sat down' [Alf, EGT, Hu, Mil]. The middle voice implies the Son's action on his own part [HNTC, Lg, Lns, Mil, NTC, Wst], in himself [WBC]. The participle is temporal [GNC, HNTC, Lg, Lns, My; all versions except TNT]: when/after he had made a cleansing, he sat down. It expresses a necessary prerequisite to sitting at God's right hand [EGT]. Some translate with two indicatives [Mil, My(D), NIC, WBC], further amplifying the reference to the Son [Mil]: he made a cleansing and then sat down.

QUESTION—How are the two nouns related in the genitive construction καθαρισμὸν τῶν ἁμαρτιῶν 'a purification of sins'?

1. It means that sins were purified [HNTC, Wst]: he purified their sins. The emphasis is on the gracious results for sinners [HNTC]. The cleansing is for sins in general, not particular sins [HNTC, Wst].
2. It means that sinners were purified [EBC, My, NCBC, TH, WBC; NAB, NJB, NLT, REB, TEV, TNT]: he purified them from their sins. What was purified was mankind [My, TH; NAB, TEV, TNT]. The background to this is that the Jews were defiled by their sins and they had to be cleansed by the sprinkling of the blood from a sacrifice upon the altar [WBC].This means that they were forgiven or set free from their sins; Christ made it possible for their sins to be forgiven [TH].

QUESTION—What is meant by the phrase δεξιᾷ τῆς μεγαλωσύνης 'the right hand of the Majesty'?

The reference is to the place of honor [EBC, GNC, HNTC, Hu, Hwt, My, NIC, NTC, TH, TNTC, WBC, Wst; NLT], authority [GNC, ICC, Mil, TH, WBC], power [GNC, My, NIGTC, WBC]. It implies that he is reigning [EGT, Hu, Hwt, Lns, NTC]. This is related to the Son's position as king, priest, and intercessor [Wst]. However, no diminution of God's position is implied [WBC]; a degree of subordination by the Son to the Father is also implied [Hu, NIGTC].

QUESTION—What is the phrase ἐν ὑψηλοῖς 'in the heights' connected with?

1. It is connected with ἐκάθισεν 'he sat down' [HNTC, ICC, Lg, Lns, Mil, My, WBC, Wst; TEV]: he sat down in the high places. This phrase emphasizes the Son's heavenly exaltation, ruling with the power and authority of the Father [WBC].
2. It is connected with μεγαλωσύνης 'Majesty' [Alf, EBC, EGT, My(D); NLT]: the Majesty in the high places.

DISCOURSE UNIT: 1:4–2:18 [Hu, Mil; TEV]. The topic is the Son's superiority to the angels [Hu, Mil; TEV].

DISCOURSE UNIT: 1:4–14 [GNC, Lns, Mil; NLT, TEV]. The topic is the greatness of the Son [TEV], Christ being is greater than the angels [NLT], as deity [GNC], in his exaltation [Lns], in his name and in his sovereignty [Mil].

1:4 by-so-much[a] better[b] having-become[c] than-the angels by-as-much-as[d] he-has-inherited[e] a-more-excellent[f] name/title[g] beyond[h] them.

LEXICON—a. τοσοῦτος (LN **78.52**) (BAGD 2.b.γ. p. 823): 'by so much' [BAGD, Lns], 'so much' [Mil, NIC; KJV], 'as much as' [LN], 'as much' [HNTC; NASB, NIV, NRSV], 'to the degree that' [**LN**], 'as far' [WBC; NAB, NJB, REB], 'far' [NLT, TNT], 'much' [CEV], not explicit [TEV]. This word is intensive [NIGTC].

b. κρείττων (LN **87.28**) (BAGD 1. p. 449): 'better' [BAGD, LN, Lns; KJV, NASB], 'greater' [**LN,** Mil; CEV, NLT, TEV, TNT], 'superior to' [HNTC, LN, NIC; NAB, NIV, NRSV], 'higher in rank' [BAGD], 'above'

[NJB, REB]. The phrase κρείττων γενόμενος 'having become better' is translated 'having been exalted' [WBC]. The superiority relates to position and power [Mil, My, TH, Wst], and is a difference of kind, not of degree [Wst].

c. γίνομαι (LN 13.48): 'to become' [HNTC, LN, Mil, NIC; NASB, NIV, NRSV, TNT], 'to get to be' [Lns], 'to be' [CEV, NJB, NLT], 'to be made' [KJV, TEV], 'to be raised' [REB], not explicit [NAB].

d. ὅσος (LN **78.52**) (BAGD 3. p. 586): 'by as much as', 'as much as' [LN], 'just as' [NLT, TEV], 'to the same degree' [LN], 'to the degree that' [Mil], 'to that extent' [**LN**], 'by how much' [Lns], 'as' [BAGD, HNTC, NIC, WBC; all versions except NLT, TEV, TNT], not explicit [TNT]. It expresses proportion [Alf].

e. κληρονομέω (LN 57.131) (BAGD 2. p. 435): 'to inherit' [Lns, Mil, NIC, WBC; NAB, NASB, NIV, NJB, NRSV, REB], 'to obtain by inheritance' [KJV], 'to have by right' [HNTC], 'to receive, to be given' [LN], 'to acquire, to obtain, to come into possession of' [BAGD]. The phrase κεκληρονόμηκεν ὄνομα 'he has inherited a name' is translated 'the name that God gave him' [NLT, TEV], 'the name he was given' [CEV], 'received the name of Son' [TNT]. This word refers to the Son's abiding possession (as a gift from God [NIGTC, TH]) with no reference to the death of the giver [EBC]. The perfect tense indicates the future age [NIGTC], a present abiding state from eternity past [Alf, EBC, HNTC, Hu, Lg, Lns, My, NIC], the eternal counsel which was realized when the Son's redemptive work was completed [Wst]. It refers to the OT reference to the Messiah as Son, although he was eternally Son [EGT, Lg, Lns, Mil]; it refers to both of these concepts [My(D)].

f. διάφορος (LN 58.40) (BAGD 2. p. 191): 'excellent' [BAGD], 'outstanding' [BAGD], 'different' [LN]. The comparative degree διαφορώτερος is translated 'more excellent' [BAGD, Mil; KJV, NASB, NRSV], 'more superior' [Lns], 'superior' [NIC, WBC; NAB, NIV, REB], 'greater' [CEV, NLT, TEV], 'higher' [NJB], 'more exalted' [HNTC]. The superiority is of kind, not of degree [HNTC]. The comparative form enhances the idea of dignity which the positive form conveys [Lg, Lns, My].

g. ὄνομα (LN 33.126) (BAGD I.2.a and I.4.a. p. 571): 'name' [BAGD, HNTC, LN, Lns, Mil, NIC, WBC; all versions except NJB, REB], 'title' [NJB, REB]. This word is emphatic by its position at the close of the sentence [ICC, NIGTC, TH].

h. παρά with accusative object (LN 78.29) (BAGD III.3. p. 611): 'beyond' [BAGD, LN], 'than' [HNTC, Lns, Mil; CEV, KJV, NASB, NJB, NLT, NRSV, TEV, TNT], 'more than' [BAGD, LN], 'to a greater degree than' [LN], 'in comparison to' [BAGD], 'to' [NIC, WBC; NAB, NIV, REB]. The sense is comparative [Alf, Blm, Lg, Lns, Mil, My, NIGTC].

QUESTION—What is the function of this verse?

It begins the argument to establish the Son's superiority to the angels [GNC, My, NCBC] and the description of the Son's qualifications [My]. It is also closely connected with 1:3 [NCBC]. It forms a bridge between the preceding description of the Son's greatness and the following comparison of the Son with the angels [NIGTC, TH, TNTC, Wst].

QUESTION—What relationship is expressed by the words τοσούτῳ . . . ὅσῳ 'by so much . . . by as much as'?

They express a comparison of degree [Mil, NTC]: greater by so much . . . to the degree that. . . . It is a comparison expressed as a proportion [TH].

QUESTION—What relationship is indicated by the aorist participle γενόμενος 'having become'?

The aorist tense refers to the Son's exaltation as a single event [NIGTC, TH]. The participle refers to the Son's position after his purification of sins and his ascension to God's right hand [Alf, EGT, GNC, Hu, Hwt, Lg, My, Wst]: he became much greater after his work of redemption. He was eternally superior to the angels [EBC, GNC, Hu], but the reference here is in respect to his work of putting away sins [EBC, Lns]. It refers to his human and divine nature [Alf], only to his human nature [Wst]; he had set his position aside during his incarnation [GNC, Hu].

1. The participle indicates the result of his purification of sins and taking his seat [Alf, EBC, EGT, Hu, Hwt; NIV, NJB, TNT]: he made a purification of sins and took his seat at God's right hand; as a result he became better than the angels.
2. The participle indicates the reason for the Son's exaltation at God's right hand [Mil]: he was seated at God's right hand because he had become better than the angels.
3. The participle identifies the Son as superior to the angels [GNC, NIC; TEV] and the aorist tense indicates action simultaneous to the verb ἐκάθισεν 'he sat down' [NIC]: he sat down . . . and was shown to be superior to the angels.

QUESTION—What is meant by ὄνομα 'name/title'?

1. The name 'Son' is better than the name 'angel' [Alf, Blm, EGT, GNC, HNTC, Hu, Lg, Lns, My, NIC, TH, TNTC; TNT]. The name 'Son' is his from eternity [HNTC].
2. The position he has is better than the position the angels have [ICC, NCBC, NTC, Wst]. The name is not 'Son' (although sonship is its principal aspect [ICC]) but rather to his being designated as Son [NTC], to all that Christ is found to be [NCBC, Wst].

DISCOURSE UNIT: 1:5–3:6 [EBC]. The topic is the excellence of Christ.

DISCOURSE UNIT: 1:5–2:18 [Hwt, NIGTC, NTC, TNTC, Wst; NAB, NJB]. The topic is the Son's superiority to angels [EBC, Hwt, NIGTC, NTC, TNTC, Wst; NAB, NJB] and his office as mediator of the new revelation [Wst].

DISCOURSE UNIT: 1:5–14 [EBC, GNT, HNTC, Hwt, Lg, NCBC, NIC, NIGTC, NTC, TNTC, WBC, Wst; CEV, NJB]. The topic is the Son's superiority to angels [GNT, HNTC, Hwt, Lg, NCBC, NIC, NIGTC, NTC; CEV] in his nature [TNTC], proved from Scripture [Hwt, Wst; NJB], and his elevation as Son [Lg], the Messianic enthronement of the Son [NAB], the exalted position of the Son [WBC], the Son of God [NIGTC].

1:5 For[a] to-which of-the angels did-he-say at-any-time,[b] "My son you-are, I today have-begotten[c] you"?

LEXICON—a. γάρ (LN 89.23): 'for' [HNTC, LN, Lns, Mil, NIC, WBC; KJV, NASB, NIV, NLT, NRSV, TEV], 'because' [LN], 'then' [NJB], not explicit [CEV, NAB, REB, TNT].

b. ποτέ (LN 67.9) (BAGD 1. p. 695): 'at any time' [LN; KJV], 'at some time' [LN], 'at some time or other' [BAGD], 'ever' [HNTC, LN, Lns, Mil, NIC, WBC; NAB, NASB, NIV, NJB, NRSV, REB]. The phrase τίνι εἶπεν ποτέ 'to whom did he say at any time?' is translated 'God never said' [CEV, TEV, TNT], 'God never said (to any angel) what he said to Jesus' [NLT]. This word indicates time [Lg, Mil, My] and refers to all of previous history [EGT].

c. perf. act. indic. of γεννάω (LN 23.58) (BAGD 1.b. p. 155): 'to beget' [BAGD, HNTC, LN, Lns, Mil, NIC; KJV, NAB, NASB, NRSV], 'to father' [NJB], 'to be the father of' [LN], 'to become someone's father' [BAGD, WBC; CEV, NIV, NLT, REB, TEV, TNT].

QUESTION—What relationship is indicated by γάρ 'for'?

It indicates the grounds for the preceding comments concerning the Son's superiority to the angels [Alf, Blm, GNC, HNTC, Hu, Hwt, Mil, My, NIC, NTC, TH, TNTC, WBC]: the Son is superior to the angels, since the following comments prove this. It shows that what has just been said is a fulfillment of the OT [Wst]. The word order shows that the emphasis is upon τίνι 'to whom' and τῶν ἀγγέλων 'of the angels' [Lg]; the definite article with 'angels' indicates angels as a class [NTC].

QUESTION—Why is the passage from Psalm 2:7 quoted?

It refers to the exaltation of the Son [Blm, Lg(K)], the Son's great dignity [EBC], his special Sonship [Lg]. It is quoted to prove the eternal generation of the Son [HNTC]. It refers to the Son's incarnation and his redemptive work [Lns].

QUESTION—What is the function of the question in this verse?

It is a rhetorical question expecting a negative response [BAGD, Hu, Lns, Mil, My, NIGTC, NTC, TH, WBC, Wst; CEV, TEV, TNT]: he never said this to any angel. It also introduces the quotations that follow [WBC].

QUESTION—Who is the implied subject of εἶπεν 'he said'?

The implied subject is God [Alf, EGT, Lg, My, NIGTC, TH, TNTC, WBC, Wst; CEV, NAB, NIV, NJB, NLT, NRSV, REB, TEV, TNT]: did God ever say?

QUESTION—To whom does σύ 'you' refer?

The negative statement comes out as addressed to an angel: God never said to an angel, 'You are my son' [CEV, TEV, TNT]. However, it is implied that God actually spoke these words to someone. God's words are quoted from Psalm 2:7 [Hu, NIC, NIGTC, TH] and there in a narrow sense he addressed the descendants of David [Alf, Lns, Mil], David [TNTC], Solomon [Lg, My, NTC, WBC], a king of Israel [EGT, GNC, Hwt]. However, in a wider sense, God was addressing the coming Messiah [Hu, NIC, NIGTC, NTC, WBC]. God was not addressing an angel when he said, 'You are my son'; rather, he was speaking to Jesus, the Messiah [Hu, NIGTC; NLT]. The word σύ 'you' is emphatic [Mil, NTC, TH].

QUESTION—What is meant by 'today I have begotten you'?

It adds emphasis to the preceding statement [EGT]. It merely fills out the quotation [ICC]. It focuses on the fact of the father-son relationship, not upon a time relationship [TH, TNTC]. It is used figuratively with the meaning of making someone to be a son [Alf]. Here it refers to the Son's divine nature [Blm], his eternal Sonship [Hwt, NTC]. It does not refer to the beginning of life, but the entrance into an office [EGT]. It refers to the time of the Son's victory and vindication when the Son resurrected, ascended to heaven, and was glorified so that all could see his superiority to angels [Hu]. It was the time of the Father's acceptance of the Son's redeeming work when the Son was placed on his eternal throne [Lns, TH, WBC]. The perfect tense indicates a completed state [NTC].

QUESTION—What is implied by ἐγώ 'I'?

It is emphatic [Alf, Lns, Mil, NTC]: I and no other.

QUESTION—What is implied by σήμερον 'today'?

1. It refers to the eternal generation of the Son [Alf, My], God's eternal day [Hwt].
2. It refers to the Son's human nature in time, the time of his exaltation to God's right hand [Blm, EGT, GNC, Hu, NIC, NIGTC], to the Son's earthly work [NTC].
3. It is largely irrelevant here; it was quoted simply because it was a part of the OT passage [EBC, HNTC, ICC, NCBC].
4. It refers to an official installation [Mil].

and again[a], "I shall-be to-him as[b] father, and he-himself shall-be to-me as[b] son"?

LEXICON—a. πάλιν (LN 67.55) (BAGD 3. p. 607): 'again' [BAGD, HNTC, LN, Lns, Mil, NIC; KJV, NAB, NASB, NIV, NJB, NLT, NRSV, REB], 'furthermore' [WBC]. The phrase καὶ πάλιν 'and again' is translated 'Neither has God said to any of them' [CEV], 'Nor did God say about any angel' [TEV], 'or' [TNT].

b. εἰς with accusative object (LN 13.51) (BAGD 8.a.β. p. 230): 'as' [Mil]. The phrase εἰμί εἰς is translated 'to be into' [LN], 'to become' [LN], 'to be' [HNTC, Lns, NIC, WBC; all versions], the equivalent of a predicate nominative [BAGD, Lns, NIGTC, WBC]. The sense is 'for' [Alf].

QUESTION—What relationship is indicated by the phrase καὶ πάλιν 'and again'?

It introduces a second grounds for the comment in 1:4 [Mil, My, NTC]. It begins an additional quotation [TH], this time from 2 Sam. 7:14 [Hu, NIC, NIGTC, NTC, TH, WBC] and a parallel passage at 1 Chron. 17:13 [Hu, NIGTC, NTC, TH]. It shows that the Son's relationship to the Father is superior to the angels' relationship [HNTC]. It connects this part of the verse more closely to the first part of this verse than to the following verse; the word εἶπεν 'he said' is to be supplied, but now God is speaking about the Son rather than to him [NIGTC].

QUESTION—What is implied by the forms ἐγώ 'I' and αὐτός 'he himself'?

They are emphatic and intensive [Mil]: *I . . . he himself.*

QUESTION—To whom does αὐτῷ 'him' and αὐτός 'he himself' refer?

They refer to Jesus here, in the Psalm they refer to Solomon [Alf, Blm, EBC, GNC, Hu, Hwt, Lns, My, NCBC, NIC, NTC, TNTC], to David's descendants [EGT, HNTC].

1:6 and/but when again the firstborn[a] he-brings-into[b] into[c] the world[d] he-says, "And all angels of-God let-worship[e] him."

LEXICON—a. πρωτότοκος (LN 10.43) (BAGD 2.a. p. 726): 'firstborn' [BAGD, HNTC, LN, NIC; all versions except CEV, KJV, NLT, TNT], 'first-born Son' [WBC; CEV, TNT], 'first-begotten' [Mil; KJV], 'honored Son' [NLT]. This word is a title of the Messiah [Blm]. It refers to Christ's special relationship with the Father [EBC, EGT, HNTC, ICC] and his honor and dignity [EGT, GNC, Hu, Hwt, Lg, Lns, Mil], his superiority [ICC, Lns, TNTC, WBC], his importance [TH]. It implies the Son's supremacy over the universe and mankind [Alf, Wst]. It refers to his existence before all creation and the fact that the creation is his heritage [NIC]. The principal point is the Son's human nature and his work as redeemer and judge [Lns]. The Son is the firstborn with respect to Christians, who are also sons of God [My].

b. aorist act. subj. of εἰσάγω (LN 15.173; 15.194) (BAGD p. 232): 'to lead into' [BAGD, LN (15.173); NAB], 'to bring into' [HNTC, Mil, NIC, WBC; CEV, NASB, NIV, NJB, NRSV], 'to bring in' [BAGD, LN (15.194), Lns; KJV], 'to present' [NLT, REB], 'to send into' [TEV, TNT]. The reference is to a future event [Alf, EGT, Mil, My] or events, at an undetermined time or times [Wst]. It refers to the event of Christ's enthronement [NIGTC]; it is when the Father puts the Son in possession of his inheritance [Alf, Mil]. The aorist tense refers to a single act [Lns, Mil, NTC], and the subjunctive mood implies a future event [Lns, Mil].

c. εἰς with accusative object (LN 84.22): 'into' [HNTC, LN, Lns, Mil, NIC, WBC; all versions except REB], 'to' [NLT, REB].

d. οἰκουμένη (LN 1.39) (BAGD 1.a. p. 561): 'world' [BAGD, HNTC, LN, NIC; all versions], 'earth' [LN], 'the inhabited earth' [BAGD, Lns], 'the world of mankind' [Mil], 'the heavenly world' [WBC]. The reference is to the earth [Alf], the inhabited earth [Lg, Lns, Wst], the habitable earth [My], the world of mankind [EGT, NTC], the inhabited universe including the realm of the angels [NCBC, NIC], the heavenly world [NIGTC, TH, WBC] in which the Son is enthroned and exalted [NIGTC, WBC].

e. aorist act. impera. of προσκυνέω (LN 53.56) (BAGD 2.a. p. 717): 'to worship' [BAGD, HNTC, LN, Lns, Mil, NIC, WBC; all versions except NJB, REB], 'to fall down and worship' [BAGD, LN], 'to pay homage' [NJB, REB], 'to do obeisance to' [BAGD].

QUESTION—What is the meaning of δέ 'and/but'?

1. It introduces a somewhat different point [ICC, Lns, NIGTC]: and. It marks the transition from the reference to the Son to the reference to the angels [NIGTC].
2. It expresses contrast [Alf, TH, Wst; TEV]: but. A stronger proof than the preceding is about to be mentioned [Alf].

QUESTION—What is πάλιν 'again' connected with and how does this relate to εἰσαγάγῃ 'he brings'?

1. Πάλιν 'again' is connected with λέγει 'he says' and means that this a further proof text [Blm, EBC, GNC, HNTC, ICC, NCBC, NIC, NTC, TH, TNTC, WBC; KJV, NAB, NIV, NJB, NLT, NRSV, REB; and probably CEV, TEV, TNT which omit it]: and again he says. . . . It is parallel with πάλιν 'again' in 1:5 [ICC].

1.1 Εἰσαγάγῃ 'he brings' refers to the incarnation of Jesus [HNTC, ICC, NTC, TNTC; TEV, TNT]: when he brings Jesus into the world at his birth.

1.2 Εἰσαγάγῃ 'he brings' refers to the prophecies concerning Christ's first advent [Blm]: when Scripture ushers in Christ's first advent.

1.3 Εἰσαγάγῃ 'he brings' refers to the Son's enthronement and exaltation as sovereign [EBC, NCBC, NIC, NIGTC, WBC]: when God exalts him as sovereign. When Christ entered the heavenly world after his sacrificial death, he received the angels' homage [NIGTC, WBC]. This is the same world of 2:5 [NIGTC, WBC].

2. Πάλιν 'again' is connected with εἰσαγάγῃ 'he brings into' [Alf, EGT, Hwt, Lg, Lns, Mil, My, Wst; NASB]: when he brings again. . . . Εἰσαγάγῃ 'he brings' refers to the second coming of Christ [Alf, EGT, Hwt, Lg, Lns, Mil, My, Wst]: when he brings him again at the second coming.

QUESTION—What relationship is indicated by λέγει 'he says'?

1. The present tense relates to a future statement regarded as already fulfilled [Wst]. It refers to what God said when he enthroned the Son after the Son's earthly work [TH]. It refers to prophecy that is recorded in Scripture and still unfulfilled [EGT].

2. It refers to God speaking through the prophets in the past [Blm]: God said through the prophets.

QUESTION—What is the function of this quotation?

It shows that the Son is superior to the angels because the angels are commanded to worship him [EBC, GNC, HNTC, Lns, NIC, NIGTC, TNTC]. The OT reference to 'him' is to God [GNC, ICC, NCBC, NIC, NTC]. By referring it to the Son, here his deity [NTC] and thus his superiority over the angels is implied [GNC, Hu, TNTC].

1:7 And on-the-one-hand[a] with-reference-to/to[b] the angels he-says, "The-(one) making[c] his angels/messengers[d] winds/spirits[e] and his servants[f] flames[g] of-fire,"

LEXICON—a. μέν (LN 89.136): 'on the one hand' [LN, Lns, Mil], not explicit [HNTC, NIC, WBC; all versions]. The sense is 'indeed' [Alf]. It is contrasted with the δέ 'on the other hand' in the following verse [EGT, Lg, Lns, Mil, My, NTC].

b. πρός with accusative object (LN 89.7, 90.58): 'with reference to' [Mil], 'in reference to' [WBC], 'with regard to' [LN (89.7), NIC], 'in regard to' [Lns], 'in speaking of' [NIV], 'when speaking of' [TNT], 'of' [HNTC; KJV, NAB, NASB, NRSV, REB], 'about' [CEV, TEV], 'to' [LN (90.58); NJB], not explicit [NLT].

c. pres. act. participle of ποιέω (LN 13.9) (BAGD I.1.b.ι. p. 682): 'to make' [BAGD, HNTC, LN, Lns, Mil, NIC, WBC; all versions except CEV, NJB, NLT], 'to appoint' [CEV, NJB], 'to call' [NLT]. This word indicates that angels are created [Hwt, Wst].

d. ἄγγελος (LN 12.28; 33.195) (BAGD 2.a. p 7): 'angel' [LN (12.28); all versions except NJB, NLT], 'messenger', [LN (33.195); NJB, NLT].

e. πνεῦμα (LN **14.4**) (BAGD 1.a. p. 674): 'wind' [BAGD, HNTC, LN, Lns, Mil, NIC, WBC; all versions except KJV, NLT], 'swift as the wind' [NLT], 'spirit' [KJV]. The meaning is 'wind' [Alf, Blm, Lns, My, Wst].

f. λειτουργός (LN 35.23) (BAGD 1. p. 471): 'servant' [BAGD, LN, WBC; CEV, NIV, NJB, NLT, NRSV, TEV, TNT], 'minister' [HNTC, Mil, NIC; KJV, NAB, NASB, REB], 'official' [Lns]. This is another name for angels [My].

g. φλόξ (LN 2.4) (BAGD p. 862): 'flame'. This noun is plural here and is translated as a plural: 'flames' [Mil, WBC; NIV, NJB, NRSV, REB, TEV, TNT]; as a singular: 'flame' [BAGD, HNTC, LN, Lns, NIC; KJV, NASB, NJB]; as an adjective: 'flaming' [CEV, NAB, NLT].

QUESTION—What relationship is indicated by καί 'and'?

It coordinates the preceding verse with 1:7–12 [NIGTC]. It deals with the relationship between God and the angels [NIGTC]; it begins a further proof of the inferiority of the angels to the Son [Blm, HNTC, Hu, Lg, Lns, NIGTC, WBC], contrasting them as servants [Lg, Lns, My, NTC] to the Son [Hu] as ruler [Alf, Lns, My], the contrast being expressed in the following verse [Hwt, My, TH]. It shows that angels are created [HNTC, Hu, NTC, TH,

TNTC] and that they do not command but obey [HNTC, Hu, NTC]. The angels are subordinate; the Son is creator and Lord [TH, TNTC]. The angels are changeable [GNC, HNTC, ICC, Lg, My, NIC, NTC, WBC] or temporary [EBC], reducible to wind and fire [EBC], but the Son is unchangeable [GNC, ICC, My, WBC], eternal [EBC, NIC]. They are merely God's messengers [Hwt, Lns, NIGTC].

QUESTION—What is meant by πρός 'with reference to, to'?

1. It means 'in reference to' [Alf, BAGD, Blm, EGT, HNTC, Lg, Mil, My, NIC, NIGTC, NTC, WBC, Wst; all versions except NJB]; speaking about the angels, he says, "The one making his angels winds . . ."
2. It means 'to' [NJB]; he says to the angels, "The one making his messengers winds . . ."

QUESTION—Who is the speaker of λέγει 'he says'?

The speaker is God [Hwt, Lns, My, NIGTC, TH; CEV, TEV]. God is also the actor of ὁ ποιῶν 'the one making' [NIGTC].

QUESTION—How are the accusative nouns related in this quotation from Psalm 104:4?

1. The articular nouns τοὺς ἀγγέλους 'the angels' and τοὺς λειτουργούς 'the servants' are objects of ὁ ποιῶν 'the one making', and the anarthrous nouns πνεύματα 'winds' and φλόγα 'flames' are predicates [Alf, Blm, EGT, GNC, Hu, Lg, Lns, My, NTC, TH, TNTC, WBC; all versions except NJB]; the verb 'to be' is implied in both phrases [Mil]: who makes his angels to be winds and who makes his ministers to be flames of fire. This is the sense of the Septuagint [Blm]. It is also the sense of the quoted OT passage [Alf]; the Hebrew is ambiguous [Blm]. The translation of ἀγγέλους must be 'angels', to carry on the point of the passage [Mil]; it should be translated 'messengers', the basic meaning of the word [Lns]. The two parts of the quotation are essentially the same in meaning [TH].
2. 'Winds' and 'flames' are the objects, and 'the angels' (= 'messengers') and 'the ministers' are predicates [NIGTC; NJB]: who makes winds his messengers and flames of fire his servants. The Septuagint cannot carry the other interpretation [NIGTC].

QUESTION—What is the meaning of the quotation?

1. God may change the angels into winds and flames [EGT, GNC, ICC, Lg, WBC]. As created beings, angels are subject to God's will and can be transformed into the elemental forces of wind and fire; this is in contrast with the Son who is above the created order and does not change [ICC, WBC].
2. The angels act in the winds and assume the form of flames [Alf, Hu, Wst]. The angels' function is intermittent as are wind and fire through which they act [Hu].
3. The angels are compared with wind and fire [Blm, GNC, HNTC, Hu, Lns, NIC, NTC; NLT]. The point of comparison between angels and winds is that they are swift [Lns, NIC; NLT] or forceful [NTC]. The point of comparison between angels and fire is that they are strong [NIC] or

destructive [Lns, NTC]. Angels are like wind and fire in that they are insubstantial and changeable [HNTC].

QUESTION—How are the two nouns related in the genitive construction πυρὸς φλόγα 'flames of fire'?

1. The flames consist of fire [Mil]: flames made of fire.
2. 'Flames' describe the fire [CEV, NAB, NLT]: flaming fire.

1:8 but with-regard-to/to[a] the son, "Your throne,[b] God, (is) into[c] the age[d] of-the age,[d]

LEXICON—a. πρός with accusative object: 'with regard to, to'. See this word at 1:7.

b. θρόνος (LN 6.112; 37.71; 37.72) (BAGD 2.c. p. 364): 'throne' [BAGD, HNTC, LN (6.112, 37.71, 37.72), Lns, Mil, NIC, WBC; all versions except CEV, TEV], 'rule, authority' [LN (37.71)], 'place of authority/ruling' [LN (37.72)], 'kingdom' [TEV]. The phrase ὁ θρόνος σου 'your throne' is translated 'you will rule as King' [CEV].

c. εἰς with accusative object (LN **67.95;** 84.22): 'into' [LN (84.22)], 'for' [Lns]. The phrase εἰς τὸν αἰῶνα τοῦ αἰῶνος 'into the age of the age' is translated 'forever' [LN (67.95); CEV], 'forever and ever' [HNTC, LN (67.95), Mil, NIC, WBC; all versions except CEV], '(to) eternity' [BAGD]. This phrase implies unchangeableness [WBC].

d. αἰών (LN 67.143) (BAGD 1.b. p. 27): 'age' [BAGD, LN], 'eon' [Lns].

QUESTION—What relationship is indicated by δέ 'but'?

It indicates a contrast [Blm, NIC; all versions] of the Son's status to that of the angels [TNTC, WBC].

QUESTION—What is meant by πρός 'with reference to, to'?

1. It means 'in reference to' [Blm, HNTC, Hu, ICC, Lg, Lns, Mil, NTC, WBC, Wst; all versions except KJV, NJB]: he says about the Son . . .
2. It means 'to' [NIC, NIGTC, TH; KJV, NJB]: he says to the Son . . ." While the meaning 'God spoke about the angels' is suitable for 1:7, the meaning 'God spoke to the Son' is suitable here because God is speaking to the Son in the quotation [TH].

QUESTION—Why is this quotation from Psalm 45:6–7 included here?

It shows that the Son is addressed in the OT as both God and Lord and indicates that the Son is eternal [NIGTC]. It indicates the unending lordship of the Son [EGT, Hu, Hwt, ICC, Lns, NCBC, NIC, NTC, WBC, Wst]. The purpose of the quotation is to show the Son's lordship, not his deity [EGT, WBC]. It also emphasizes the deity of the Son [NTC].

QUESTION—What is the function of ὁ θεός 'God'?

1. It is a vocative [Alf, Blm, EBC, GNC, HNTC, Hu, Hwt, Lg(K), Lns, Mil, My, NCBC, NIC, NTC, TH, TNTC, WBC; all versions]: your throne, O God, is forever. This ascription indicates the deity of the Son [NTC]. That the Son shares the quality of deity with the Father intensifies the statement about his eternal rule [WBC]. In Psalm 45:6, the addressee is a royal bridegroom and this language is the hyperbole of an oriental court;

however, a king in the line of David was a representative of God and this description would be fully realized with the coming of the Messiah [NIC, TNTC].

2. It is the subject (or the predicate) [ICC, Wst]: God is your throne/your throne is God. His throne was founded on God, the immovable Rock [Wst]. It could also mean that his throne was divine, or it represents God [ICC].

and the scepter[a] of-the straightness[b] (is the) scepter[a] of-your kingdom.[c]

TEXT—Some manuscripts omit the definite article with the first ῥάβδος 'scepter' and add it before the second ῥάβδος, thus reading 'a scepter of righteousness is the scepter'. GNT does not deal with this variant. 'The scepter . . . scepter' is clearly read by Lns, Mil, WBC, Wst, and NJB; 'scepter . . . the scepter' is clearly read by Alf, Blm, ICC, KJV, and NAB.

TEXT—Instead of σου 'your' some manuscripts read αὐτοῦ 'his'. GNT reads σου 'your' with a B rating, indicating that the text is almost certain. Αὐτοῦ 'his' is read by HNTC, Wst; NASB, NJB, and REB.

LEXICON—a. ῥάβδος (LN 6.218; **37.53**) (BAGD p. 733): 'scepter' [BAGD, HNTC, **LN**, Lns, Mil, NIC, WBC; all versions except CEV, TEV, TNT], 'rod' [LN]. This entire phrase is translated 'with righteousness you rule over your kingdom' [**LN**], 'you rule over your people with justice' [TEV], 'your royal scepter stands for justice' [TNT], 'your royal power brings about justice' [CEV], 'your royal power is expressed in righteousness' [NLT].

b. εὐθύτης (LN **88.19**) (BAGD p. 321): 'straightness', 'straightforwardness' [Lns], 'uprightness' [HNTC, LN], 'righteousness' [LN, Mil, NIC, WBC; KJV, NIV, NLT], 'justice' [CEV, NJB, REB, TEV, TNT]. This noun is also translated as an adjective: 'righteous' [BAGD, **LN**; NAB, NASB, NRSV]. Εὐθύτης 'straightness' is a synonym of δικαιωσύνη 'righteousness' (1:9) [NIGTC].

c. βασιλεία (LN 1.82; 37.64) (BAGD 1. p. 134): 'kingdom' [HNTC, LN (1.82), Mil, WBC; KJV, NAB, NASB, NIV, NJB, NRSV, REB], 'kingship' [NIC], 'reign' [LN (37.64)], 'royal rule' [BAGD, Lns], 'royal power' [CEV, NLT].

QUESTION—What relationship is indicated by καί 'and'?

It introduces the parallel line to the preceding first line of the quotation [ICC]. It is included because this part of the quotation brings out the additional point that the Son rules with royal power while the angels are mere servants [NIGTC]. It is not translated by CEV, KJV, NAB, NJB, NLT, TEV, or TNT.

QUESTION—What is the relationship between the two parts of this clause?

1. The first phrase is the subject; the second phrase is the predicate [HNTC, Hu, NIGTC; KJV, NAB, NASB, NIV, NRSV]: the scepter of righteousness is the scepter of your kingdom.

2. The first phrase is the predicate; the second phrase is the subject [Alf; NJB, REB]: the scepter of your/his kingdom is a scepter of righteousness.

QUESTION—How are the two nouns related in the genitive construction ἡ ῥάβδος τῆς εὐθύτητος 'the scepter of straightness'?

Εὐθύτητος 'straightness' is a genitive of quality [BAGD, Mil, NCBC, WBC; NAB, NASB, NRSV]: a straight/righteous scepter. The king holds the scepter in his hand to administer justice [NTC].

QUESTION—How are the two nouns related in the genitive construction ῥάβδος τῆς βασιλείας 'scepter of the kingdom'?

Βασιλείας 'kingdom' is an objective genitive [Mil]: the scepter/rule over the kingdom.

1:9 You-have-loved[a] righteousness[b] and have-hated[c] lawlessness;[d]

LEXICON—a. aorist act. indic. of ἀγαπάω (LN 25.43; 25.104) (BAGD 2. p. 5): 'to love' [BAGD, HNTC, LN (25.43), Lns, Mil, NIC, WBC; all versions], 'to cherish' [BAGD], 'to take pleasure in' [LN (25.104)]. The aorist tense of this and the following verbs apply to Christ's entire earthly life [Alf, Hu, TH, Wst], to his customary attitude [Blm, NTC].

b. δικαιοσύνη (LN 88.13) (BAGD 2.b. p. 196): 'righteousness' [BAGD, LN, Lns, Mil, NIC, WBC; KJV, NASB, NIV, NRSV], 'uprightness' [BAGD; NJB] 'justice' [CEV, NAB], 'right' [HNTC; REB, TNT], 'what is right' [NLT, TEV]. It means the fulfilling of God's law [Mil].

c. aorist act. indic. of μισέω (LN 88.198) (BAGD 2. p. 522): 'to hate' [BAGD, HNTC, LN, Lns, Mil, NIC, WBC; all versions except NJB], 'to detest' [BAGD, LN; NJB].

d. ἀνομία (LN 88.139) (BAGD 1. and 2. p. 72): 'lawlessness' [BAGD (1.), LN, Lns, Mil, NIC, WBC; NASB] 'lawless deed' [BAGD 2.], 'iniquity' [KJV], 'wickedness' [NAB, NIV, NRSV], 'evil' [CEV, NJB], 'wrong' [HNTC; REB, TNT], 'what is wrong' [NLT, TEV].

QUESTION—How is this clause related to its context?

It shows what is meant by εὐθύτητος 'straightness' in the preceding verse [Blm]. It indicates the reason why Christ was exalted [NIGTC]. This refers to Christ's earthly ministry [Hwt, My, Wst].

on-account-of[a] this God, your God, has-anointed[b] you (with) oil[c] of-gladness[d] above[e] your companions."[f]

LEXICON—a. διά with accusative object (LN 89.26): 'on account of' [LN], 'because of' [LN, Mil]. The phrase διὰ τοῦτο 'on account of this' is translated 'therefore' [HNTC, NIC, WBC; KJV, NAB, NASB, NIV, NLT, NRSV, REB], 'this is why' [NJB, TNT], 'that is why' [TEV], 'for this reason' [Lns], 'and so' [CEV].

b. aorist act. indic. of χρίω (LN 37.107) (BAGD 1. p. 887): 'to anoint' [BAGD, HNTC, LN, Lns, Mil, NIC; KJV, NAB, NASB, NJB, NLT, NRSV], 'to exalt by anointing' [WBC], 'to appoint' [LN]. The phrase ἔχρισέν σε . . . ἔλαιον ἀγαλλιάσεως 'has anointed you with the oil of gladness' is translated 'has chosen you and has given you the joy of an honor' [TEV], 'called you and gave you the joy of being anointed king' [TNT], 'I have chosen you and I appointed you and made you happier than . . .' [CEV]. The phrase ἔχρισέν σε . . . παρὰ τοὺς μετόχους σου 'has anointed you above your companions' is translated 'has set you above your companions (fellows [REB]) by anointing you' [NIV, REB]. The anointing occurred at the Son's exaltation in heaven [Alf, Hu, Hwt, My, NIC, Wst]. It refers to the fullness of bliss which he has enjoyed long before his earthly ministry [Lg]. The anointing consists in the application of justice by the Son, which fills him with joy [NTC]. It reflects the joy of festive occasions [TNTC].

c. ἔλαιον (LN 6.202) (BAGD 2. p. 248): 'oil' [BAGD, HNTC, LN, Lns, Mil, NIC, WBC; all versions except CEV, TEV, TNT], not explicit [CEV, TEV, TNT].
d. ἀγαλλίασις (LN 25.132) (BAGD p. 3): 'gladness' [BAGD, Lns, Mil; KJV, NAB, NASB, NJB, NRSV], 'extreme gladness' [LN], 'exultation' [HNTC, NIC], 'joy' [WBC; NIV, NLT, REB, TEV].
e. παρά with accusative object (LN 78.29) (BAGD III.3. p. 611): 'above' [HNTC, WBC; KJV, NAB, NASB], 'beyond' [LN, Lns, Mil; NRSV], 'more than' [LN, NIC; CEV, NLT], 'to a greater degree than' [LN], 'far greater than' [TEV], 'than' [CEV], 'as none' [NJB], 'and not' [BAGD; TNT]. This word is comparative [Mil, WBC] and implies the inferiority of its object, 'companions' [Alf, EGT, Mil, WBC].
f. μέτοχος (LN **34.8**) (BAGD 2. p. 514): 'companion' [BAGD, **LN**, Mil, NIC, WBC; NASB, NIV, NRSV, TEV, TNT], 'partner' [BAGD, LN], 'fellow' [HNTC; KJV, NAB, REB], 'associate' [Lns], 'friend' [CEV], 'rival' [NJB], 'anyone else' [NLT]. The reference is to other heavenly beings, the angels [Alf, GNC, HNTC, ICC, Mil, My], to earthly rulers [Lg, My(D); NAB], to human saints [Lns, NIC, NTC]; the reference is general [EGT, Hu, Hwt, Wst], but especially to angels [Hwt], not limited to angels [Hu].

QUESTION—What does διὰ τοῦτο 'on account of this' refer to?

It means because of his love of righteousness and hatred of evil [Alf, EGT, Hwt, Lg, Lns, Mil, My, NTC, Wst].

QUESTION—How are the two references to God in this clause related?

1. The first reference is the subject of the verb; the second is in apposition with it [Alf, Blm, ICC, Lns, Mil, My(D), TH, WBC, Wst; all versions except REB]: God, i.e., your God, has anointed you. It is God, who has made himself known as Christ's God by the blessings he has given him [Wst].
2. The first reference is a vocative; the second is the subject of the verb [EBC, EGT, GNC, HNTC, Lg(K), My, NIC, NIGTC; REB]: O God, your God has anointed you. The Son is here addressed as God [GNC], thus proving his divinity [HNTC].

QUESTION—What was the purpose of anointing Christ?

1. It was a mark of showing favor at a festive occasion [EGT, ICC, Lns, NIC, TNTC, Wst]. It is a metaphor referring to bliss [ICC].
2. It was to appoint him to rule [Hu, WBC]. God has assigned Christ a superior office than that which angels have [WBC]. The occasion was Jesus' entry into heavenly glory [Hu].
3. The purpose is not in focus [EGT, Hu, NTC, Wst]. Carrying out his justice fills him with joy and this constitutes his anointing [NTC].

QUESTION—How are the two nouns related in the genitive construction ἔλαιον ἀγαλλιάσεως 'oil of gladness'?

1. The oil is a symbol of gladness [Alf, EGT, Lns]: the oil which is gladness.
2. 'Αγαλλιάσεως 'gladness' refers to the quality of the occasion of the anointing [Mil]: it was a joyous occasion when God anointed you.

QUESTION—Who are Christ's companions here?

1. They are angels [ICC, WBC]. This reinforces the comparison between Christ and the angels. The angels also participate in carrying out God's will and are Christ's companions in this sense [WBC].
2. They are believers [NIC, NTC, TH]. They are the 'many sons' of 2:10 [NIC]. This is the same word which occurs as 'partners' in 3:1, 14 [NIC, TH].
3. They are both believers and angels [NIGTC, TNTC, Wst]. There is no limitation to any class of beings [Wst]. In the psalm, this referred to other kings, but here it refers to his companions at the feast [TNTC]. In the heavenly Jerusalem both angels and believers share with Christ [NIGTC].

QUESTION—What relationship is indicated by the phrase παρὰ τοὺς μετόχους σου 'above your companions'?

1. It means that the companions are anointed, but less so than the Son [Alf, HNTC, Lns, Mil, NIC, NTC, TH, WBC, Wst; KJV, NAB, NASB, NJB, NLT, NRSV, TEV]. His companion's joy is great because they accompany him, but his is still greater [NIC].
2. It means that the Son is anointed but the companions are not [My; TNT].

1:10 And, "You, according-to[a] beginnings,[b] Lord, laid-the-foundation-of[c] the earth, and the heavens[d] are works[e] of your hands;

LEXICON—a. κατά with accusative object (LN 67.33) (BAGD II.2.a. p. 406): 'according to, at' [BAGD, LN], 'in' [BAGD, HNTC, Mil, NIC, WBC; KJV, NASB, NIV, NLT, NRSV, TEV, TNT], 'down in' [Lns]. The phrase κατ' ἀρχάς 'according to beginnings' is translated 'of old' [NAB, REB], 'long ago' [NJB], and is an idiom for 'in the beginning' [Mil; CEV]. The plural here refers to periods of time [NTC]. This preposition implies 'from the beginning and onward in time' [Lg].

b. ἀρχή (LN 67.65) (BAGD 1.c. p. 112): 'beginning' [BAGD, HNTC, LN, Lns, Mil, NIC, WBC; CEV, KJV, NASB, NIV, NLT, NRSV, TEV, TNT]. It means before anything existed [TH].

c. aorist act. indic. of θεμελιόω (LN 7.42) (BAGD 1. p. 356): 'to lay the foundation of' [BAGD, HNTC, WBC; CEV, KJV, NASB, NIV, NJB, NLT, TNT], 'to lay down the foundation of' [Mil], 'to lay a foundation' [LN], 'to found' [BAGD, Lns, NIC; NRSV], 'to establish' [NAB], 'to create' [TEV]. The phrase σὺ . . . τὴν γῆν ἐθεμελίωσας 'you laid the foundation of the earth' is translated 'by you were earth's foundations laid' [REB], which is an idiom for the act of creation [NTC]. This verb refers to the first act of creation [Blm].

d. οὐρανός (LN 1.5) (BAGD 1.e. p. 594): 'heaven' [BAGD, HNTC, Lns, Mil, NIC, WBC; all versions], 'sky' [LN]. Here this word includes all creation except earth [Mil].

e. ἔργον (LN 42.12) (BAGD 3. p. 308): 'work' [BAGD, HNTC, Lns, Mil; all versions except CEV, TEV, TNT], 'workmanship' [LN]. The phrase ἔργα τῶν χειρῶν σου 'works of your hands' is translated 'your handiwork' [NIC]. The phrase ἔργα τῶν χειρῶν σού εἰσιν οἱ οὐρανοί 'the heavens are works of your hands' is translated 'with your own hands you made the heavens' [TEV, TNT], 'your hands made the heavens' [WBC], and 'created the heavens' [CEV].

QUESTION—What relationship is indicated by καί 'and'?

It introduces a new quotation [Alf, Lg, Lns, Mil, My, NIC, WBC, Wst]. This connecting word shows that the quotation is intended to show that God is speaking to the Messiah here [NIC, NIGTC, NTC, TNTC, WBC, Wst]. It connects the following quotation with that in 1:8 [Blm]. Therefore the following quotation likewise refers to Christ [Blm].

QUESTION—Why is this quotation from Psalm 102:25–27 (LXX) mentioned?

It is quoted as proof of the Son's unchangeable power and majesty [Alf, Hu, My(D), WBC, Wst], that he is eternal [EBC, GNC, ICC, Lns], that he is God's agent in creation [EBC, Hu, NCBC, WBC], that he is the creator [Hwt, ICC, Mil, NTC], that he is supreme over creation [EBC] and the sustainer of the universe [NTC].

QUESTION—Why is the position of σύ 'you' changed from its position in the OT passage?

Σύ 'you' is forefronted for emphasis [My, NTC, TH, WBC, Wst] and for clarity [Lns]. This pronoun associates this quotation with the preceding one which closes with σου 'you' [WBC], to contrast the Son with the angels [NTC].

QUESTION—Who does the author imply is the addressee as he applies this quotation?

The psalm originally was addressed to God [EBC, EGT, GNC, HNTC, Hu, Hwt, Lg, Lns, My, NCBC, NIC, NTC, TNTC, WBC, Wst]. But the author of Hebrews takes it as addressed to the Son (the Messiah) [Blm, EBC, EGT, GNC, HNTC, Hu, Hwt, ICC, Lg, Mil, My, NCBC, NIC, NTC, TNTC]. The reference to Christ is justified by the psalm's promise that God will be manifested as Savior of his people [EGT] through the Messiah [Lg, Wst]. It was right to transfer to the Son what was applied to God since the writer has already written about the eternal character of his throne [TNTC]. It was through the Son that the universe was made [NIC]. Words not directly addressed to the Son find their fulfillment in him [Wst]. The Septuagint added the word 'Lord' and this was taken by the author as a reference to Christ [Hu, NTC]. This psalm was recognized as Messianic even in pre-Christian times [EGT, Mil] and the psalm was originally directed to the Messiah, not to God [Blm].

QUESTION—Who does the author imply is the speaker as he applies this quotation?

In the Hebrew, the psalmist addresses God [Blm, NIC, WBC, Wst]. In the Septuagint, God is speaking at this point in order to answer the psalmist [NIC, TNTC, WBC]. In this book, the author's use of the connector καί 'and' implies that God is continuing to speak [NIC, NTC, TNTC, WBC, Wst]. This connection is filled out in translations: 'Again he says' [TNT], 'He also says' [WBC; NIV], 'He also said' [TEV].

1. God is the speaker [NIC, TNTC].
2. The Psalmist is the speaker [Blm].

QUESTION—How are the two nouns related in the genitive construction ἔργα τῶν χειρῶν σου 'works of your hands'?

Χειρῶν is a genitive of agency [Mil]: works which your hands performed. 'Hands' is a metonymy, referring to the person whose hands they are [Mil]. The reference to hands implies power [Blm]; it implies direct involvement [TH].

1:11 they-themselves will-perish,[a] but you remain,[b]

LEXICON—a. fut. mid. indic. of ἀπόλλυμι (LN **13.96;** 20.31) (BAGD 2.a.β. p. 95): 'to perish' [HNTC, Lns, Mil, NIC, WBC; KJV, NAB, NASB, NIV, NLT, NRSV, REB], 'to cease to exist' [**LN**], 'to come to an end' [LN (13.96)], 'to disappear' [LN (13.96); CEV, TEV], 'to pass away' [BAGD; NJB], 'to be destroyed' [LN (20.31); TNT], 'to be ruined' [BAGD, LN (20.31)]. The idea is not their being annihilated, but their being changed (12:26–28) [Wst].

b. pres. act. indic. of διαμένω (LN **13.89**) (BAGD p. 186): 'to remain' [BAGD, HNTC, LN, NIC, WBC; all versions except CEV], 'to remain permanently' [Mil], 'to continue to exist' [**LN**], 'to continue on' [Lns], 'to last forever' [CEV]. The prefixed preposition δια- implies permanent endurance [Alf, Lg, Mil, My, NTC, Wst]. The present tense reflects the Son's eternity [Blm, Mil, NTC, WBC], his permanent state [NIGTC, TH]; it is required to express the eternal present existence of God and applied to the Son here [Mil, NTC] and is required by the present tense 'you are the same' in 1:12 [Blm].

QUESTION—Why is this verse mentioned?

It is a continuation of the preceding quotation [Mil], stating the unchangeableness of the Son in the changing universe [Hwt, ICC, NTC, TH, WBC].

QUESTION—To what does αὐτοί 'they themselves' refer?

It is an emphatic form, contrasted with the emphatic σύ 'you' [Lns, Mil]: *they . . .* but *you.*

1. It includes both heaven and earth [Blm, EBC, NIGTC, TNTC, WBC], implying the entire world [Blm]. The gender of the pronoun agrees with the nearer antecedent οὐρανοί 'heavens' [Blm].
2. It refers only to 'heavens' [Alf, Mil, My, Wst], as required by the next figure [Alf], as representing the whole world [Wst].
3. Αὐτοί includes both heaven and earth, but πάντες 'all' in the following line refers only to the heavens [Lns]: the heavens and earth will perish and the heavens will grow old.

and they-all as (a) garment[a] will-become-old,[b]

LEXICON—ἱμάτιον (LN 6.162; 6.172) (BAGD 1. p. 376): 'garment' [BAGD, HNTC, Mil; KJV, NAB, NASB, NIV, NJB], 'clothing' [LN (6.162), WBC; NRSV], 'old clothing' [NLT], 'clothes' [CEV, REB, TEV, TNT], 'cloak' [LN (6.172), NIC], 'coat' [LN (6.172)], 'robe' [LN (6.172); Lns]. This is the outer cloak [Mil].

b. fut. pass. indic. of παλαιόω (LN **67.104**) (BAGD 2. p. 606): 'to become old' [BAGD, **LN**; NASB, TNT], 'to grow old' [HNTC, **LN**, Lns; NAB], 'to wax old' [KJV], 'to deteriorate' [LN], 'to wear out' [Mil, NIC, WBC; CEV, NIV, NJB, NLT, NRSV, REB, TEV].

QUESTION—What relationship is indicated by καί 'and'?

It introduces the expansion of the idea of ἀπολοῦνται 'they will perish' [Blm, Lns]: they will perish; that is, they will become old like a garment.

QUESTION—What relationship is indicated by the phrase ὡς ἱμάτιον 'as a garment'?

It expresses a comparison [Mil, WBC; KJV, TNT] used to illustrate the temporal character of the heavens [Mil, WBC]: they will grow old as a garment does.

1:12 and as (a) cloak[a] you-will-roll-up[b] them,

LEXICON—a. περιβόλαιον (LN 6.163; **6.172**) (BAGD p. 646): 'cloak' [BAGD, HNTC, **LN**, Mil, NTC, WBC; NAB, NJB, NRSV, REB, TNT], 'coat' [LN (6.172); TEV], 'old coat' [NLT], 'robe' [LN (6.172); CEV, NIV], 'mantle' [Lns, NIC; NASB], 'clothing' [LN (6.163)], 'apparel' [LN (6.163)], 'vesture' [KJV]. It is an outer garment, a wrap-around [Alf, Lg, My]. It is a general term for any type of covering, and is synonymous with ἱμάτιον 'garment' [NIGTC].

b. fut. act. indic. of ἑλίσσω (LN 79.120) (BAGD p. 251): 'to roll up' [BAGD, HNTC, LN, Lns, Mil, WBC; CEV, NAB, NASB, NIV, NJB, NLT, NRSV, TNT], 'to fold up' [NIC; KJV, REB, TEV]. The implication is removal to be replaced by others [Alf, Blm, EBC], to be laid aside [Lg, NTC, WBC] as being of no further use [TH, TNTC].

QUESTION—What is implied by ὡσεὶ περιβόλαιον ‘as clothing’?

It is a comparison, implying to treat them as if they were clothing [Mil]. As easily as someone changes from one cloak for another, so the Son will change one order of creation for another [NIGTC].

as (a) garment[a] also they-will-be-altered;[b]

TEXT—Some manuscripts omit ὡς ἱμάτιον ‘as a garment’. GNT includes this phrase with a B rating, indicating that the text is almost certain. Only Alf, Blm, Lg, My, and KJV omit this phrase.

LEXICON—a. ἱμάτιον: ‘garment’. See this word in 1:11.

b. fut. pass. indic. of ἀλλάσσω (LN 57.142; 58.43) (BAGD 1. p. 39): ‘to be altered’ [BAGD, LN (58.43)], ‘to be changed’ [BAGD, HNTC, LN (58.43), NIC, WBC; all versions except CEV, NLT], ‘to fade away’ [NLT], ‘to be exchanged’ [LN (57.142), Lns, Mil], ‘to change’ [CEV]. The meaning is to be exchanged for another garment [Alf, Mil].

but you are the same and your years[a] will-fail[b] not.”

LEXICON—a. ἔτος (LN 67.167) (BAGD p. 316): ‘year’ [BAGD, HNTC, LN, Lns, Mil, NIC; KJV, NAB, NASB, NIV, NJB, NRSV, REB]. The phrase καὶ τὰ ἔτη σου οὐκ ἐκλείψουσιν ‘and your years will not fail’ is translated ‘and your life never ends’ [TEV], ‘you will never die’ [TNT], ‘you will never grow old’ [WBC; NLT], ‘you will live forever’ [CEV].

b. fut. act. indic. of ἐκλείπω (LN **13.39**) (BAGD p. 242): ‘to fail’ [Lns, NIC; KJV], ‘to cease, to die out’ [LN], ‘to end’ [NIV, NRSV, TEV], ‘to be unending’ [NJB], ‘to come to an end’ [BAGD, HNTC, **LN**; NASB], ‘to have an end’ [Mil; NAB, REB].

QUESTION—What is implied by the phrase ‘your years will not fail’?

It means that the Son will never die [NIGTC]; it implies the eternity of the Son [Blm, Mil, NTC].

1:13 But to/with-regard-to[a] whom of-the angels has-he-said at-any-time, “Sit at[b] my right-hand,[c] until I-place[d] your enemies[e] (as) a-footstool[f] of-your feet”?

LEXICON—a. πρός with accusative object (LN 89.7; 90.58): ‘to’ [LN (90.58), Lns, Mil, NIC, WBC; all versions], ‘with regard to’ [LN (89.7)], ‘of’ [HNTC].

b. ἐκ with genitive object (LN 87.34) (BAGD 2.b. p. 175): ‘at’ [BAGD, HNTC, Lns, NIC, WBC; all versions except KJV], ‘on’ [LN, Mil; KJV].

c. δεξιός (LN 82.8) (BAGD 2.b. p. 175): ‘right hand’ [HNTC, NIC, WBC; all versions except CEV, TEV], ‘right’ [BAGD, LN, Lns, Mil], ‘right side’ [LN; CEV, TEV].

d. aorist act. sub. of τίθημι (LN 85.32) (BAGD I.2.a.α. p. 816): ‘to place’ [LN, Lns], ‘to put’ [LN; TEV], ‘to set’ [Mil], ‘to make’ [BAGD, HNTC, Mil, NIC, WBC; all versions except TEV].

e. ἐχθρός (LN 39.11) (BAGD 2.b.β. p. 331): ‘enemy’ [HNTC, LN, Lns, Mil, NIC; all versions], ‘foe’ [WBC].

f. ὑποπόδιον (LN 6.117; 37.7) (BAGD p.847): 'footstool' [HNTC, LN (6.117), Lns, Mil, NIC; CEV, NASB, NIV, NLT, NRSV, TEV, TNT]. The phrase ὑποπόδιον τῶν ποδῶν σου 'a footstool of your feet' is translated 'your footstool' [WBC; KJV, NAB, NJB, REB]. The phrase ἕως ἂν θῶ τοὺς ἐχθρούς σου ὑποπόδιον τῶν ποδῶν σου 'until I place your enemies as a footstool of your feet' is translated 'until I put all your enemies under your feet' [LN (37.7)], 'until I put you in control of your enemies, until I cause you to rule over your enemies' [LN (37.7)].

QUESTION—Why is the introduction to the quotation mentioned?

It sets the following quotation apart from the preceding quotation and forms a parallel with 1:5a [NIGTC].

QUESTION—What relationship is indicated by δέ 'but'?

It indicates a contrast [Mil, NIGTC] with the references to the Son which began in 1:8 [Alf, EGT] as contrasted with the following reference to angels [NIGTC]; it introduces a parallel reference to 1:5 [EGT]; it makes a correlation between what follows and the preceding quotations [WBC].

QUESTION—Why is this quotation from Psalm 110:1 mentioned?

It provides another indication of the superiority of the Son to angels [Blm, ICC]. It is the climax of the argument [Lns, NIC, NTC, WBC], summarizing all that has been said concerning the superiority of the Son over the angels [WBC]. It shows that the Son's enthronement is by God's invitation [WBC]. The author interprets it as being addressed by God to the Son [Alf, EBC, EGT, Hwt, Lg, NIGTC, TH] to imply the superiority of the Son to angels [GNC, Hu], the Son's full sovereignty with God [Hwt, Lg].

QUESTION—What is implied by the question expressed in this verse?

It is a rhetorical question [WBC] implying a negative response [Lns, NIGTC, NTC, TH; TEV, TNT]: God never said the following quotation to any angel. It implies that God did say this to the Son [EGT, NIGTC, TH, WBC; NLT].

QUESTION—What is implied by the phrase 'Sit at my right hand'?

It implies being enthroned with God [Blm, Hu, Lg, TNTC] in authority and reigning [GNC, Hu, Lg, My, NIGTC]. To sit at God's right hand implies superior dignity [EBC, EGT, GNC, HNTC, NTC, TH, TNTC], supremacy over the angels [NIGTC], since the angels stand in God's presence [EBC, NIC, TNTC]. The present tense implies continued sitting [Lns, Mil, Wst] as distinct from taking his seat [Wst]; it implies that the subjugation of the enemies has been provided for and will be completed [Mil]. The phrase does not imply constant sitting without activity [NTC, TH].

QUESTION—What is meant by placing enemies as a footstool of one's feet?

It refers to the custom of a conqueror placing his feet on the neck of his conquered enemy [Alf, Hwt, Lg, Lns, Mil, My, NTC, TH]. It is a figure implying complete subjection [Blm, EBC, EGT, Hwt, My, NTC, TNTC] and humbling of the enemies [NLT]. Here the phrase indicates the Son's universal sovereignty rather than destruction of enemies [NIGTC].

QUESTION—What is meant by ἕως 'until'?

The phrase ἕως ἂν θῶ 'until I place' expresses contingent time [Mil], implying that this full subjection had not yet taken place [Hu, Hwt, Mil]. However, this phrase does not mean that the Son's rule would cease after his enemies had been conquered [Hwt]. It is uncertain whether Christ continues to sit after the enemies are put under his feet [TH]. It should not be taken to mean that there is a limit to the time Christ rules, since in 1:8 it says his rule is forever. However, there is a sense in which Christ finishes his work and hands over the reins of government to the Father (1 Cor. 15:24–28) [Hu].

1:14 Are-they not all ministering[a] spirits, being-sent[b] for[c] service[d] on-account-of[e] the-(ones) being-about to-inherit[f] salvation?[g]

LEXICON—a. λειτουργικός (LN **35.24**) (BAGD p. 471): 'ministering' [HNTC, Mil, NIC; KJV, NAB, NASB, NIV, NJB, REB], 'officiating' [Lns], 'serving' [LN, WBC], 'that render service' [**LN**], 'to be servants' [NLT], 'in holy service' [BAGD], 'in the divine service' [NRSV], 'in the service of God' [TNT], 'who serve God' [TEV], not explicit [CEV]. This word is emphatic [My].

b. pres. pass. participle of ἀποστέλλω (LN 15.66) (BAGD 1.b.γ. p. 98): 'to be sent' [HNTC, LN, NIC; CEV, NAB, NIV, NJB, NLT, NRSV, TEV, TNT], 'to be sent out' [BAGD; NASB, REB], 'to be sent forth' [Mil; KJV], 'to be sent away' [BAGD], 'to be commissioned' [Lns, WBC]. The present tense indicates habitual action [Alf, Lg, Mil, My], continuous action [EGT, HNTC, Lns], action as the occasion arises [Wst]. This word indicates that the angels have no intrinsic dignity [Blm, EGT, ICC] but only delegated authority [Blm, EGT].

c. εἰς with accusative object (LN 89.57) (BAGD 4.d. p. 229): 'for' [BAGD, Lns, Mil], 'for the purpose of' [LN], 'to' [NIC, WBC; CEV, KJV, NAB, NASB, NIV, NJB, NLT, NRSV, TEV, TNT], 'on' [HNTC], 'in' [REB]. It expresses purpose [Mil].

d. διακονία (LN 35.19; 35.21) (BAGD 1. p. 184): 'service' [BAGD, HNTC, LN (35.19), Mil, NIC, WBC; REB], 'ministry' [LN (35.21), Lns]. This noun is also translated as a verb: 'to serve' [CEV, NAB, NIV, NJB, NRSV], 'to render service' [WBC; NASB], 'to do service' [NIC], 'to minister' [KJV], 'to help' [TEV, TNT], 'to care for' [NLT]. This word is used for spiritual ministry [EGT]. It focuses on ministry for God rather than service to people [Alf, My], ministry to God (to Christ [Lns]) for the benefit of Christians [Hwt, Lg, Lns, My(D), Wst], ministry to Christians [Blm, EBC, GNC, HNTC, NIC, TH, TNTC] in regard to salvation [HNTC].

e. διά with accusative object (LN 90.38): 'for' [HNTC, LN, NIC; KJV, NLT], 'for the sake of' [LN, Lns, Mil; NASB, NJB, NRSV, REB], 'on behalf of' [LN] 'for the benefit of' [LN], 'to' [WBC], not explicit [CEV, NAB, NIV, TEV, TNT].

f. pres. act. infin. of κληρονομέω (LN 57.131; 57.138) (BAGD 2. p. 434): 'to inherit' [HNTC, LN (57.138), Lns, NIC, WBC; NAB, NASB, NIV, NJB, NRSV], 'to be an heir' [KJV], 'to be going to be (saved)' [CEV], 'to acquire' [BAGD], 'to obtain' [BAGD, Mil], 'to come into possession of' [BAGD], 'to enter into' [TNT], 'to receive' [LN (57.131); NLT, REB, TEV], 'to be given' [LN (57.131)]. It refers to obtaining possession by whatever means [EBC], possession by gift and based on a previous promise and not merit [HNTC], receiving from God a gift for permanent possession [NIGTC].

g. σωτηρία (LN 21.25) (BAGD 2. p. 801): 'salvation' [BAGD, HNTC, LN, Lns, Mil, NIC, WBC; all versions except CEV]. This noun is also translated as a verb: 'to be saved' [CEV]. The reference is to final salvation [Alf, EBC, HNTC, ICC, Mil, My, NCBC, NIC].

QUESTION—Why is this verse mentioned?

It expresses the conclusion (summary [Lg, TH], climax [NTC]) of the comparison between the Son and the angels [Blm, Hu, ICC, Lg, My, NCBC, NTC] and also a preparation for the following passage [NCBC, NIGTC, TH], giving a description of the angels' function [GNC]. It tells why God could not and did not say to any angel what he said in the preceding verse [Lns, My]; all the angels are no more than ministering spirits [Blm, EBC] for Christian believers [EBC].

QUESTION—What is the function of this question?

It is a rhetorical question expecting an affirmative response [Blm, Lns, Mil, NIGTC, NTC, TH, WBC], as the emphatic negative οὐχί 'not' indicates [Blm, Lns, Mil, NIGTC, NTC]: all the angels are ministering spirits. There is emphasis on πάντες 'all' [EBC, EGT, Hu, ICC, Lg, Lns, Mil, My, NIC, NTC, TNTC, Wst] as the opposite of 'none' implied by πρὸς τίνα 'to whom' in the preceding verse [Lns].

QUESTION—What is the participial phrase ἀποστελλόμενα 'being sent' and its modifiers connected with, and what is its function?

It expands the meaning of λειτουργικά 'ministering' [Blm]: their ministering involves being sent forth for ministry to those who are to inherit salvation.

1. It is translated as a predicate modifier [Blm, NIC; all versions except REB, TEV]: they are ministering spirits, and they are sent forth for ministry.
2. It is translated as an attributive modifier [TEV]: they are ministering spirits who are sent forth for ministry.

QUESTION—To whom does the phrase τοὺς μέλλοντες κληρονομεῖν σωτηρίαν 'the ones being about to inherit salvation' refer?

It refers to faithful Christians [Blm], the people of God [HNTC], with respect to their future expectation [HNTC]. The present participle μέλλοντες 'being about' implies the concept of 'destined' [EGT]; with the following infinitive it implies the prior arrangement for an event yet future [Mil, NIGTC]; it is merely a periphrastic form of the future tense [Lns]. In the present context it refers to what must or will occur [NTC]

DISCOURSE UNIT: 2:1–18 [NTC]. The topic is Jesus as Savior and High Priest.

DISCOURSE UNIT: 2:1–9 [EBC]. The topic is Christ as the author of the great salvation.

DISCOURSE UNIT: 2:1–4 [GNC, GNT, HNTC, Hwt, Lg, Lns, Mil, NCBC, NIC, NIGTC, TNTC, WBC, Wst; CEV, NAB, NASB, NIV, NJB, NLT, TEV]. The topic is an exhortation [NJB], the first exhortation [NIGTC], an exhortation and a warning [Hwt, Mil], a call to be faithful [GNC; NAB], the great salvation [GNT; CEV, TEV], the need to be diligent [HNTC], the need to give heed [NASB], an exhortation against drifting [TNTC; NLT], a warning to pay attention [NIV], a warning against neglecting so great salvation [Lns], a warning against neglecting the message brought by the Son [WBC, Wst], the danger of neglect [NCBC], an admonition concerning the law and the gospel [NIC].

2:1 On-account-of[a] this it-is-necessary more-abundantly[b] for-us to-give-heed[c] to-the-(things) having-been-heard,[d]

LEXICON—a. διά with accusative object (LN 89.26): 'on account of' [LN], 'because of, by reason of' [LN], 'in view of' [NAB]. The phrase διὰ τοῦτο 'on account of this' is translated 'therefore' [HNTC, NIC, WBC; KJV, NIV, NRSV], 'then' [NJB], 'so' [NLT], 'for this reason' [Lns, Mil; NASB, TNT], 'that is why' [REB, TEV], not explicit [CEV].

b. περισσοτέρως (LN 78.31) (BAGD 1. p. 651): 'more abundantly', 'more attentively' [NJB], 'the more earnestly' [Lns], 'more greatly' [LN], 'all the more firmly' [TEV]. This is also translated as an adjective: 'greater' [NRSV], 'closer' [TNT], 'the closest' [WBC], 'full' [CEV]; as an adjectival phrase: 'more earnest' [KJV], 'so much more' [BAGD], 'far more' [Mil], 'all the more' [HNTC; NAB, REB], 'more careful' [NIC; NIV], 'very carefully' [NLT], 'much closer' [NASB]. It expresses manner [Mil].

c. pres. act. infin. of προσέχω (LN **31.47**) (BAGD 1.a.β. p. 714): 'to give heed to' [BAGD, Lns; KJV], 'to pay heed to' [REB], 'to pay attention to' [BAGD, HNTC, Mil, NIC, WBC; NASB, NIV, NRSV, TNT], 'to give attention to' [CEV], 'to attend to' [NAB], 'to turn one's mind to' [NJB], 'to hold on to' [LN; TEV], 'to listen to' [NLT]. The meaning is to pay close attention [EBC, Hwt] and to act upon what is heard [EBC, ICC, TH]. It implies that it is a familiar message [ICC]. The present tense indicates continuing action, implying that they were doing so at present [NIGTC].

d. aorist pass. participle of ἀκούω (LN 24.52) (BAGD 1.b.α. p. 32): 'to be heard' [BAGD, LN, Lns]. The participle is neuter, referring to 'things' [Alf]. The phrase τοῖς ἀκουσθεῖσιν 'the things having been heard' is translated 'what has been heard' [BAGD], 'what we have been told' [HNTC; CEV, REB], 'what we have been taught' [NJB], 'what we have heard' [NIC, WBC; NAB, NASB, NIV, NRSV, TNT], 'the things which we have heard' [Mil; KJV], 'the truths we have heard' [NLT, TEV].

QUESTION—What relationship is indicated by διὰ τοῦτο 'on account of this'?

It indicates a conclusion based on the demonstrated superiority of the Son over the angels [Alf, Blm, EBC, GNC, HNTC, Hwt, Lg, Lns, Mil, My, NIC, WBC, Wst], and that God has spoken through the Son [EGT]: since God has spoken through the Son, who is so superior, we should give heed. It connects what follows with the argument of all of chapter 1 [NIGTC, TH]. It indicates the logical connection between theology and practice [Hu]. It begins a practical exhortation (a strong warning [Lns]) based on the preceding argument [Hu, Lns, Mil, My]. It argues that since Christ is so great, they must heed his words [NTC].

QUESTION—What is meant by δεῖ 'it is necessary'?

It implies a moral necessity [Alf, My], a logical necessity [EGT, Lg, WBC, Wst], necessity in general [Lns, Mil]. It is what believers must logically do because of the evidence from Scripture and ultimately because they will be lost if they do not give heed [NIGTC]. The reason is the superiority of the Son [Alf, EGT, My, TH] or the danger of drifting [Lns]. Eternal issues are at stake and must be earnestly dealt with [Hu].

QUESTION—What is περισσοτέρως 'more abundantly' connected with?

1. It is connected with προσέχειν 'to give heed' [Alf, EGT, GNC, Mil, My, WBC, Wst; all versions]: to give heed more abundantly.
2. It refers to both δεῖ 'it is necessary' and προσέχειν 'to give heed' [Blm]: it is more abundantly necessary to give heed more abundantly.

QUESTION—What is implied by the comparative degree of the adverb περισσοτέρως 'more abundantly'?

1. The adverb has comparative meaning [Alf, EGT, Lns, My, NIC, NIGTC, NTC, TH, Wst; all versions]. It means to pay closer attention than did the Israelites [NIGTC]. It means to pay closer attention than they would if the Son were not superior to the angels [Alf, EGT, My, TH, Wst], if mere angels had given the message instead of Christ [TH].
2. The comparative form has superlative meaning [Hu, ICC, TNTC, WBC, Wst]: we should give the very closest attention.

QUESTION—Who is meant by ἡμᾶς 'us'?

It refers to Christians in general, to all who had heard the message [EGT, NIGTC, Wst], including the author [EGT, ICC, NIGTC, NTC, TH]: we Christians must give heed. This word is not emphatic here, since it is required to show who must give heed [NIGTC].

QUESTION—Who are the hearers referred to by the participial phrase τοῖς ἀκουσθεῖσιν 'the things having been heard'?

The participle is neuter, referring to the things heard [NIGTC]. The hearers are the persons addressed by the author [Alf, EBC, GNC, HNTC, ICC, Lns], and the author himself [EBC, HNTC, ICC, NTC]. The comment implies that the author also had heard the gospel through others [EBC, HNTC, ICC]. However, the author is not included in those who are in danger of drifting away; he includes himself only to soften the warning [Lns]; he includes himself as also subject to the danger [NTC].

QUESTION—What are the things they have heard?

What these things are is identified in 2:3 [Mil, NIGTC]; the reference is to the gospel teachings [Blm, EBC, Hu, Lg, TH], the salvation message proclaimed (by God [Lg, Lns]) through the Lord Jesus [EGT, Hwt, ICC, Lg, Lns, My] (indirectly [NIGTC]) and his immediate followers [ICC, My], through the prophets and the New Testament messengers [Lns]. This does not exclude reading the OT [NIGTC].

lest-perhaps[a] we-should-drift-away.[b]

LEXICON—a. μήποτε (LN 89.62) (BAGD 2.b.α. p. 519): 'lest perhaps' [Mil], 'lest' [LN; NAB, NASB], 'lest at any time' [KJV], 'lest ever' [Lns], 'in order that not' [BAGD, LN], 'so that not' [LN, WBC; CEV, NIV, NJB, NRSV, TEV, TNT], 'so as not' [NIC], 'in case' [HNTC], 'for fear of' [REB], 'or' [NLT]. It introduces a negative purpose [NIGTC]; it means 'lest perhaps' [EGT, Lg]. The -ποτε suffix generalizes the μή 'not' [Alf]; it makes the word emphatic [NIGTC]. This word implies a general continuing possibility [Lns]. This word softens the warning given, but shows the author's concern [Mil].

b. aorist pass. subj. of παραρρέω (LN **31.69**) (BAGD p. 622): with active meaning 'to drift away' [BAGD, HNTC, **LN**, Mil, NIC; CEV, NAB, NASB, NIV, NJB, NLT, NRSV], 'to drift off course' [WBC], 'to drift from one's course' [REB, TNT], 'to flow by' [BAGD], 'to let (something) slip' [KJV]; with passive meaning 'to be drifted past' [Lns], 'to be carried away' [TEV]. The meaning is to drift away from what has been heard [Alf, Blm, EBC, GNC, Hu, Hwt, ICC, Lg, Lns, Mil, My, NIGTC, TNTC], from the faith [LN], to gradually give up what they believed [LN]. Some treat this as a live metaphor of letting the current carry a ship away through carelessness and unconcern [EGT, Hu, ICC, Lns, NIC, WBC]. Others consider the metaphor to be dead [NIGTC].

QUESTION—Why is this clause mentioned?

It expresses the negative purpose of giving heed to the message [TH], the danger (the consequence [Mil]) of failing to heed the message [Lg, Mil], the danger of drifting away from the message [EBC, HNTC], the danger of abandoning their faith [NIC], the danger of losing sight of the reality of salvation [WBC]: we must give careful heed, lest we should drift away from it. The implied danger is indifference or carelessness [HNTC, Hu, Hwt, Lg, Mil, NCBC], disobedience [NCBC], and difficulties [Hwt].

2:2 For[a] if the word[b] having-been-spoken through[c] angels became firm[d]

LEXICON—a. γάρ (LN 89.23): 'for' [HNTC, LN, Lns, Mil, NIC, WBC; KJV, NAB, NASB, NIV, NRSV, REB], 'because' [LN], not explicit [CEV, NJB, NLT, TEV, TNT].

b. λόγος (LN 33.98) (BAGD 1.b.α.): 'word' [HNTC, LN, Lns, Mil, NIC; KJV, NAB, NASB, REB], 'word of the Law' [TNT], 'message' [CEV,

NIV, NJB, NLT, NRSV, TEV], 'statement' [LN], 'speaking' [BAGD], 'what was once spoken' [WBC]. 'Word' is used instead of νόμος 'law' in keeping with the focus on God's speaking [ICC].

c. διά with genitive object (LN 90.4) (BAGD A.III.2.a. p. 180): 'through' [HNTC, LN, Mil, NIC, WBC; NAB, NASB, NJB, NLT, NRSV, REB, TNT], 'by means of' [BAGD, Lns], 'by' [LN; CEV, KJV, NIV, TEV].

d. βέβαιος (LN **28.43**, **31.90**) (BAGD 2. p. 138): 'firm' [Lns], 'binding' [NIV, TNT], 'authoritative' [HNTC], 'valid' [BAGD, WBC; NRSV], 'trustworthy' [**LN** (31.90)], 'dependable' [LN (31.90)], 'reliable' [LN (31.90); NJB], 'certain' [LN (28.43)], 'unchanged' [NAB], 'unalterable' [Mil; NASB], 'securely established' [NIC], 'verified' [LN (28.43)], 'steadfast' [KJV]. The phrase ἐγένετο βέβαιος 'became firm' is translated 'had such force' [REB], 'known to be true' [**LN** (28.43)], 'shown to be true' [**LN** (28.43); TEV], 'proved to be true' [CEV], 'has always proved to be true' [NLT]. The sense is that that word was fully carried out [Blm], its threats were fulfilled [Lns], it could not be violated without punishment [Alf, EGT, GNC, My], it was binding and valid [EBC, Hu, WBC] because it was spoken by God [WBC], it was authoritative and reliable [HNTC, TH], securely grounded in God's character [Mil], made firm by the penalties upon its violators [Hwt].

QUESTION—What relationship is indicated by γάρ 'for'?

It indicates the first of two grounds for what was stated in 2:1 [Mil, NIGTC]. It introduces an argument, arguing from a weaker to a stronger point [Alf, Blm, EBC, EGT, GNC, Hu, ICC, Lg, My].

QUESTION—What relationship is indicated by εἰ 'if' and the indicative verbs ἐγένετο 'became' and ἔλαβεν 'received'?

It is a condition of fact which here assumes that the condition is true [Mil, NIGTC, WBC; CEV, NLT]: if this is true. It is also the grounds for the conclusion given in 2:3 [Mil, WBC; CEV]: since we know this is true, we cannot escape, having neglected so great a salvation.

QUESTION—To what does 'the word spoken through angels' refer?

It refers to the law of Moses [Alf, Blm, EBC, EGT, GNC, HNTC, Hu, Hwt, ICC, Lg, Lns, My, NTC, TH, WBC, Wst]. The aorist tense of the participle refers to the giving of the law on Mt. Sinai [Lns].

QUESTION—What is implied by διά 'through' in the phrase 'the word spoken through angels'?

1. It means the word spoken *by* angels [CEV, KJV, NIV, TEV].
2. It indicates that the agency of the angels is intended [EGT, HNTC, Hu, ICC, Lns, NIC, NIGTC, NTC, TH, WBC, Wst; NAB, NASB, NJB, NLT, NRSV, REB, TNT]: the word spoken through angels. This implies that it was spoken by God through the angels [Hu, Lns, NIGTC, NTC, WBC; NLT]. God gave the law to Moses through angels and thus to the Jewish ancestors [TH]. It was a common belief of first century Judaism that the law was given through the mediation of angels [EGT, HNTC, ICC, Wst]. This was based on the Septuagint version of Deut. 33:2 (the angels were

with God at his right hand) and Psalm 68:18 [HNTC, ICC, NIC, NIGTC, WBC]. The attendance of angels at the revelation on Sinai was taken to show their ministration [NTC, Wst].

and every transgression[a] and disobedience[b] received just[c] recompense,[d]

LEXICON—a. παράβασις (LN 36.28) (BAGD p. 612): 'transgression' [BAGD, HNTC, LN, Lns, Mil, NIC; KJV, NAB, NASB, NRSV], 'violation' [NIV, REB], 'violation of the law' [NLT], 'infringement' [NJB, WBC], 'overstepping' [BAGD]. The phrase πᾶσα παράβασις καὶ παρακοή 'every transgression and disobedience' is translated 'those who did not follow it or obey it' [TEV], 'anyone who broke it or disobeyed it' [TNT], 'all who disobeyed or rejected it' [CEV]. This word implies failure to walk in the proper path [Alf, HNTC, Lns], the violation of a specific command [EGT, Mil, My, Wst], doing anything forbidden by the law [Hwt, Lg, NTC]. This and the following noun are essentially synonymous [TH]. Both nouns imply willful rejection of God's will [WBC].

b. παρακοή (LN 36.27) (BAGD p. 618): 'disobedience' [BAGD, HNTC, LN, Mil, WBC; all versions except CEV, NLT, TEV, TNT], 'disobedient act' [NIC], 'act of disobedience' [NLT], 'unwillingness to hear' [BAGD], 'refusal to hear' [Lns]. It also implies obstinacy [Blm], neglecting to obey [EGT, Mil, WBC], disobedience of a lawful command [HNTC, Wst], not doing something commanded by the law [Hwt, ICC, Lg], lack of attention to a command [My], unwillingness to listen to God [WBC]. It refers to the motive behind the act [NTC].

c. ἔνδικος (LN 88.15) (BAGD p. 263): 'just' [BAGD, HNTC, LN, Lns, Mil, NIC; KJV, NASB, NIV, NRSV], 'right' [LN], 'proper' [NJB, REB], 'due' [NAB], 'deserved' [TEV]. The phrase ἔλαβεν ἔνδικον μισθαποδοσίαν 'received just punishment' is translated 'was duly punished' [TNT], 'were punished as they deserved' [CEV], 'were punished' [NLT]. The sense is that the punishment was based on what is right [Mil, NCBC, NIGTC]. It was appropriate to the sin [WBC].

d. μισθαποδοσία (LN 38.17) (BAGD p. 523): 'recompense' [LN, Mil; NASB], 'recompense of reward' [KJV], 'requital' [NIC], 'punishment' [NAB, NIV, NJB, TEV], 'penalty' [BAGD, LN; NRSV, REB], 'payment in full' [Lns], 'retribution' [HNTC]. The reference is to specific punishments for specific acts [Alf, HNTC].

QUESTION—What is the function of this clause?

1. It gives the second part of the condition [KJV, NAB, NASB, NIV, NRSV, TEV]: if the word was reliable, and if disobedience received just punishment.
2. It describes the extent of the reliability of the word [NJB, REB, TNT]: if the word was so reliable that disobedience brought punishment.

2:3 how (shall) we escape,[a] having-neglected[b] so-great[c] salvation,[d]

LEXICON—a. fut. mid. indic. of ἐκφεύγω (LN 21.14) (BAGD 2.a. p. 247): 'to escape' [BAGD, HNTC, LN, Lns, Mil, WBC; all versions except NJB, REB], 'to go unpunished' [NJB]. The phrase πῶς ἡμεῖς ἐκφευξόμεθα 'how shall we escape' is translated 'what escape will there be for us' [NIC], 'what escape can there be for us' [REB]. The reference is to escaping appropriate recompense [HNTC, Mil], God's punishment [NIGTC], the final judgment [EGT, Lg, Mil, TH].

b. aorist act. participle of ἀμελέω (LN **30.50**) (BAGD p. 44): 'to neglect' [**LN,** Lns, Mil, NIC; KJV, NASB, NJB, NRSV], 'to disregard' [BAGD, LN, Mil, WBC], 'to ignore' [HNTC; NAB, NIV, REB], 'to pay no attention to' [TEV], 'to take no notice of' [TNT], 'to be indifferent to' [NLT], 'to refuse' [CEV]. This word implies total disregard and contempt [Blm, EGT], apathy or contempt [Mil]; it means neglect and considering it unworthy of notice [Hwt]; it means merely neglect [EBC, Lns], indifference [Lns, WBC]. The aorist looks at one's life as a whole [EGT].

c. τηλικοῦτος (LN 78.36) (BAGD 2. p. 814): 'so great' [BAGD, LN, Lns, Mil, NIC; KJV, NASB, NRSV, REB], 'as great' [WBC; NAB], 'such great' [HNTC], 'such a great' [NIV, NJB, TEV], 'so important' [BAGD; TNT], 'so mighty' [BAGD], 'this great' [CEV, NLT]. It indicates that the gospel is so much superior to the OT law [NIGTC]. It is great because of its source [EGT, Wst] and its assured truth [EGT], because it was accomplished by Jesus [EGT, GNC, HNTC], because of its purpose, its origin, its motive [Mil], and its means [EGT, Mil]. Its greatness is shown by the following three proofs (2:3b–4) [ICC, Wst]. This word distinguishes the salvation of the gospel from other salvations offered in ancient times [EBC].

d. σωτηρία (LN 21.25, 21.26) (BAGD 2. p. 801): 'salvation' [BAGD, HNTC, LN, Lns, Mil, NIC, WBC; all versions except CEV, REB], 'deliverance' [REB], 'way of being saved' [CEV]. It refers to the gospel of salvation [NTC], the message [NIGTC].

QUESTION—What is implied by this question?

It is a rhetorical question, implying a negative answer [Mil, NIGTC, TNTC, WBC]: we shall not escape. There is no escape possible [WBC].

QUESTION—What is indicated by the pronoun ἡμεῖς 'we'?

It is emphatic [Alf, Hwt, Mil, My]. It refers to Christians in general [Alf] together with the author himself [Hwt, NIGTC], in contrast with those of the OT who had only the Law [EBC, GNC, Mil, My].

QUESTION—What relationship is indicated by the aorist participle ἀμελήσαντες 'having neglected'?

It is conditional [Alf, EGT, GNC, HNTC, Hwt, Lns, Mil, My, NIGTC, NTC, TH, TNTC, WBC; all versions]: if we neglect. The consequence is indicated by the preceding rhetorical question [Mil]. The aorist tense implies completion [Lns] at the future time indicated [Alf]; it refers to the act which would make the escape impossible [Lg, My]; it looks at life as a single whole [EGT].

which, having-received[a] (a) beginning to-be-spoken through[b] the Lord,

LEXICON—a. aorist act. participle of λαμβάνω (LN 90.48) (BAGD 2. p. 465): 'to receive' [Lns], 'to make' [LN], 'to have' [BAGD]. The phrase ἥτις ἀρχὴν λαβοῦσα λαλεῖσθαι 'which, having received a beginning to be spoken' is translated 'announced first' [NAB], 'first announced' [WBC], 'which at the first began to be spoken' [KJV], 'which was first announced' [NIV], 'after it was at the first spoken' [NASB], 'it was first announced' [NJB], 'this salvation was first announced' [NIC], 'which very salvation was first proclaimed' [Mil], 'this deliverance was first announced' [REB], 'it was declared at first' [NRSV]. This entire phrase is translated 'the Lord himself first announced this salvation' [TEV], 'the Lord himself was the first to tell about it' [CEV], 'that was announced by the Lord Jesus himself' [NLT], 'God announced it first through the Lord himself' [TNT], 'it was announced by the Lord, with whom it originated' [HNTC]. The aorist tense of this participle indicates the point at which the action began [Lns]. The present tense of the infinitive λαλεῖσθαι refers to the process of the Lord's speaking [Lns]; it refers to the present preaching and implies that this is based on Christ's preaching [Wst].

b. διά with genitive object (LN 90.4): 'through' [LN, Lns, Mil, NIC, WBC; NASB, NRSV, REB, TNT], 'by' [HNTC, LN; KJV, NAB, NIV, NJB]. The preposition expresses mediation [Hu, Mil] and agency [Mil]. Christ was the agent, but the message originated with God [Alf, EBC, EGT, Hu, Lg, Mil]. Διά τοῦ κυρίου 'through the Lord' is parallel with δι' ἀγγέλων 'through angels' in 2:2 [Hu, NIGTC, WBC].

QUESTION—What relationship is indicated by the aorist participle λαβοῦσα 'having received'?

1. It is treated as a finite verb (by itself or combined with ἀρχήν 'beginning') expressing action prior to the following verb [HNTC, Mil, NIC; all versions except NAB, NASB]: it began to be spoken and then was confirmed to us.
2. It is treated as a participle indicating a state or action prior to the following verb [WBC; NAB]: first spoken through the Lord, it was confirmed to us.
3. It is treated as a temporal participle (by itself or combined with ἀρχήν 'beginning') [Lns; NASB]: after it was first spoken to us, it was confirmed to us.

QUESTION—Who is meant by τοῦ κυρίου 'the Lord'?

It is Christ [Alf, EGT, GNC, HNTC, Hu, Hwt, Mil, NIC, TH, TNTC, WBC, Wst; NLT]. The title 'Lord' indicates the Son's supreme dignity [Hwt].

it-was confirmed[a] to[b] us by[c] the-(ones) having-heard,

LEXICON—a. aorist pass. indic. of βεβαιόω (LN 28.44, **31.91**) (BAGD 1. p. 138): 'to be confirmed' [HNTC, LN (28.44), Mil; KJV, NAB, NASB, NIV], 'to be verified' [LN (28.44)], 'to be attested' [NRSV], 'to be guaranteed' [BAGD, WBC; NJB], 'to be made firm' [Lns], 'to be delivered with assurance' [NIC], 'to be passed on' [NLT]. It is also translated in the active voice: 'to establish in belief' [LN (31.91)]. This entire phrase is translated 'those who heard him confirmed it to us' [REB, TNT], 'and those who heard him proved to us that it is true' [TEV], 'the people who heard the message proved to us that it was true' [CEV], 'those who heard him caused us to be able to believe it' [**LN** (31.91)]. The aorist tense implies a completed action [NTC].

b. εἰς with accusative object (LN 90.59): 'to' [HNTC, LN, Mil, NIC, WBC; all versions except KJV], 'unto' [KJV], 'for' [LN, Lns]. This preposition here implies the transmission of the message to the hearers [Alf]; it implies an interval of time between the first preaching and the author's hearing of it [Wst].

c. ὑπό with genitive object (LN 90.1): 'by' [HNTC, LN, Lns, Mil, NIC, WBC; KJV, NAB, NASB, NIV, NJB, NLT, NRSV]. It indicates agency [Mil].

QUESTION—To whom does τῶν ἀκουσάντων 'the ones having heard' refer?

It refers to those who directly heard Jesus [EBC, EGT, Hu, ICC, Mil, NIGTC, NTC, TH, Wst; all versions except NASB], who heard the gospel Jesus taught [Alf, HNTC, Lns, My]. It refers to the twelve apostles of Jesus [Lns, Mil, TNTC] and other reliable witnesses [TNTC], and others who accompanied Jesus in his earthly ministry, death, and resurrection [Mil]. It indicates that the author and his readers did not hear the message directly from Jesus but had to depend on the sure testimony of those who had heard it [EBC, EGT, GNC, HNTC, Hu, ICC, Lns, Mil, My, NCBC, NIC, NTC, TH, TNTC, Wst].

QUESTION—What is meant by ἐβεβαιώθη 'it was confirmed'?

Those who heard Jesus passed on his message to the author and his readers and their teaching was reliable. It does not mean that their testimony made Jesus' teaching more reliable [NIGTC]. They guaranteed its accuracy [WBC]. Those who had heard Jesus testified as eyewitnesses to the truth of the events and message connected with Jesus [NTC]. The salvation itself was shown to be real or true in the experience of those who heard the message [Hu, TH, Wst].

2:4 God bearing-witness-at-the-same-time-together-with[a] (them/it) both[b] by-signs[c] and[b] by-wonders[d] and by-various[e] mighty-works[f] and by-distributions[g] of-(the)-Holy Spirit according-to[h] his will?[i]

LEXICON—a. pres. act. participle of συνεπιμαρτυρέω (LN **33.268**) (BAGD p. 787): 'to bear witness at the same time together with, to witness together with' [LN], 'to add one's witness to' [HNTC, **LN**], 'to add one's own witness' [TNT], 'to add one's witness at the same time to' [TEV], 'to bear witness (to) also' [KJV], 'to bear witness with' [Mil; NASB], 'to give witness to' [NAB], 'to confirm one's witness' [NJB], 'to plainly endorse one's witness' [WBC], 'to confirm the message at the same time'

[NIC], 'to testify to also' [NIV], 'to testify at the same time' [BAGD], 'to add one's testimony' [NRSV, REB], 'to support with additional testimony' [Lns], 'to show that one's message is true' [CEV], 'to verify the message' [NLT]. The prefixed preposition συν- means 'to join in' [Alf, Lns, NIGTC], 'together with' [Hu, NTC], meaning that God joined in the witness [EBC]; the prefixed preposition ἐπι- means 'to' [Alf], 'in addition to' [Hu, Lns, NIGTC], 'upon' [NTC], meaning that God added his testimony [Lns]. The present tense indicates continuing action by God [NIGTC, NTC, WBC]. God bore witness to the truth of their witness [Hu, ICC, NIC, WBC] by doing miracles along with their preaching of the message [NIC]. God bore witness along with theirs to the truth of the message [TH, TNTC, Wst]. This word is emphatic by word order; it is a genitive absolute [NIGTC].

b. τε . . . καί (LN 89.102) (BAGD 3.a. p. 807): 'both . . . and' [LN, Lns, Mil; KJV, NASB], '. . . and' [BAGD, HNTC, NIC, WBC; NIV, NJB, NLT, NRSV, REB], not explicit [NAB, TNT]. The phrase σημείοις τε καὶ τέρασιν καὶ ποικίλαις δυνάμεσιν 'by signs and by wonders and by various mighty works' is translated 'by performing all kinds of miracles and wonders' [TEV], 'by working all kinds of powerful miracles and wonders' [CEV]. These two words closely unite the two nouns σημείοις 'signs' and τέρασιν 'wonders' [EGT, Lg, Mil, NIGTC, NTC] and show that both words refer to the same things [EGT, NTC].

c. σημεῖον (LN 33.477) (BAGD 2.a. p. 748): 'sign' [HNTC, LN, Lns, Mil, NIC, WBC; all versions except CEV, TEV], 'miracle' [BAGD, LN; CEV]. This word refers to something that attests a spiritual truth [Alf, EGT, Hwt, Lns], that reveals God's nature and purpose [GNC, HNTC]. It focuses on the meaning of the miracles [EBC, TH]; they are signs of God's working [Hu, Lg, NIGTC].

d. τέρας (LN 33.480): 'wonder' [HNTC, Lns, Mil, NIC, WBC; all versions except NAB, NJB], 'portent' [LN], 'sign' [LN], 'miracle' [NAB], 'marvel' [NJB]. This word refers to something marvelous that cannot be explained by ordinary laws [Alf, EBC, Hu, Lg, Mil]. It focuses on the marvelous aspect [EBC, Hwt, Lg], something intended to attract attention [EGT, Mil, TH], something that causes astonishment [HNTC, Hu, Lns].

e. ποικίλος (LN 58.45) (BAGD 1. p. 683): 'various' [HNTC; NASB, NIV, NLT, NRSV, TNT], 'varied' [NAB], 'a variety of' [NIC], 'of various kinds' [BAGD, LN, Mil], 'diversified' [BAGD, LN], 'divers' [KJV], 'manifold' [BAGD, Lns], 'of all kinds' [NJB], 'all kinds of' [CEV, TEV], 'of many kinds' [WBC; REB]. This word shows the variety of the miracles [Hu, NIGTC]. It modifies only δυνάμεσιν 'mighty deeds' [Alf, EGT, HNTC, Mil, My, NIC, NIGTC; all versions except NJB, TEV]; it modifies all three nouns [TH; CEV, TEV].

f. δύναμις (LN 76.7) (BAGD 4. p. 208): 'mighty work' [HNTC, NIC], 'mighty deed' [LN], 'deed of power' [BAGD], 'act of power' [NAB], 'work of power' [TNT], 'power' [Lns], 'miracle' [BAGD, LN, Mil,

WBC; KJV, NASB, NIV, NJB, NLT, NRSV, REB], 'wonder' [BAGD]. This noun is also translated as an adjective: 'powerful' [CEV]. It emphasizes the power involved [Hu, Lg, Mil, NIGTC, TH, Wst]. It means miraculous powers [Blm, EBC, Lns, NIGTC], acts that show God's power [HNTC, Hwt, NIGTC].

g. μερισμός (LN **57.89**) (BAGD 2. p. 505): 'distribution' [BAGD, LN], 'distribution of the gift(s)' [WBC; NAB], 'gift(s) distributed' [**LN,** Mil, NIC**;** NIV, NRSV, REB], 'distributing the gift(s)' [NJB, TEV, TNT], 'gift' [HNTC; KJV, NASB], 'apportioning' [Lns]. This noun is also translated as a verb: 'to give' [CEV, NLT]. It refers to the action of dividing [NIGTC].

h. κατά with accusative object (LN 89.8): 'in accordance with' [LN], 'in accord with' [Lns], 'according to' [HNTC, Mil, NIC, WBC; KJV, NASB, NIV, NRSV, TEV], 'at' [REB]. The phrase κατὰ τὴν αὐτοῦ θέλησιν 'according to his will' is translated 'just as he wanted them' [LN], 'as he willed' [NAB], 'as he saw fit' [TNT], 'in the various ways he wills' [NJB], 'whenever he chose to do so' [NLT], 'to anyone he chose to' [CEV]. This preposition expresses manner [Mil].

i. θέλησις (LN **25.1**) (BAGD p. 354): 'will' [BAGD, HNTC, Mil, NIC, WBC; KJV, NASB, NIV, NRSV, REB, TEV], 'volition' [Lns]. This word refers to the act of willing [EBC, Lns, NIGTC, NTC, Wst].

QUESTION—What relationship is indicated by the four dative nouns, 'signs', 'wonders', 'mighty works', and 'distributions'?

They are instrumental, indicating the means by which God added his witness [Lns, Mil, WBC; NAB, NASB, NIV]: by signs, by wonders, by mighty works, and by distributions. Signs, wonders, and mighty works are to be taken as a unit and different kinds of manifestations are not in focus [Hu].

QUESTION—How are the two nouns related in the genitive phrase πνεύματος ἁγίου μερισμοῖς 'distributions of the Holy Spirit'?

1. The genitive case is objective [Alf, EBC, EGT, HNTC, ICC, Lg, My, NCBC, NIC, NIGTC, TH; CEV, NJB, NLT, TEV, TNT]: God distributed the Holy Spirit. This means that the Holy Spirit was distributed with a variety of endowments [NIC, NIGTC]. God caused people to have what the Holy Spirit gave them [TH]. This phrase can be translated 'distributing the gifts of the Holy Spirit' [NIC, NIGTC; NJB, NLT, TEV, TNT].
2. The genitive case is subjective; it is the Holy Spirit who distributes [Hu, Lns, NTC, WBC; REB]: gifts distributed by the Holy Spirit. These are the types of gifts listed in 1 Cor. 12 [Hu].

QUESTION—What is the phrase κατὰ τὴν αὐτοῦ θέλησιν 'according to his will' connected with?

1. It is connected only with μερισμοῖς 'distributions' [Alf, Lg, My; NLT, REB, TEV, TNT]: distributions according to his will.

2. It is connected with all four dative nouns [Lns, NIGTC, NTC, WBC, Wst]: signs, wonders, mighty works, and distributions, all according to his will.

QUESTION—To whom does αὐτοῦ 'his' refer?

It refers to God [Alf, EBC, EGT, HNTC, Hu, Hwt, ICC, Lg, My, NCBC, NIGTC, NTC, WBC, Wst]: according to God's will. This word is emphatic by word order [ICC].

DISCOURSE UNIT: 2:5–4:13 [Lns]. The topic is the incarnate Son's suffering.

DISCOURSE UNIT: 2:5–18 [GNT, Lns, Mil, NIGTC, Wst; CEV, NAB, NIV, NJB, NLT, TEV]. The topic is the pioneer of salvation [GNT], the one who leads mankind to salvation [CEV, TEV], redemption through Christ, not through angels [NJB], mankind's destiny fulfilled through Jesus' sufferings [Wst], the Son's exaltation through abasement [NAB], the necessity for the Son to partake of our physical nature in order to deliver us [Lns], Jesus, the Man [NLT], Jesus made like his human brothers [NIV], the Son of Man leads mankind toward future world lordship [Mil], the path to glory [NIGTC].

DISCOURSE UNIT: 2:5–13 [Hwt, Lg]. The topic is the Son's superior position not being canceled by his earthly humiliation [Hwt, Lg].

DISCOURSE UNIT: 2:5–10 [GNC, HNTC; TEV]. The topic is the exaltation of Jesus [HNTC], Christ's superiority to angels even in his humanity [GNC], the one who leads us to salvation [TEV].

DISCOURSE UNIT: 2:5–9 [NCBC, NIC, TNTC, WBC]. The topic is Jesus' supremacy [NCBC], the Son's humiliation and glory [NIC, TNTC, WBC].

DISCOURSE UNIT: 2:5–8 [Lns; NASB]. The topic is God subjecting all things to mankind [Lns; NASB].

2:5 For[a] not to-angels did-he-subject[b] the coming[c] inhabited-world,[d] concerning[e] which we-are-speaking.

LEXICON—a. γάρ (LN 89.23): 'for' [HNTC, LN, Lns, Mil; KJV, NAB, NASB, REB], 'because' [LN], 'now' [WBC; NRSV], 'and furthermore' [NLT], not explicit [NIC; CEV, NIV, NJB, TEV, TNT].

b. aorist act. indic. of ὑποτάσσω (LN 37.31) (BAGD 1.a. p. 848): 'to subject to' [BAGD, HNTC, LN, Lns, NIC, WBC; NASB, NIV, NRSV, REB, TNT], 'to make subject to' [NAB], 'to put in subjection' [KJV], 'to bring to subjection' [BAGD], 'to give control to' [Mil], 'to put under' [NJB], 'to put under the power of' [CEV]. The phrase οὐ ἀγγέλοις ὑπέταξεν 'not to angels did he subject' is translated 'God has not placed the angels as rulers over' [TEV], '(the future world) will not be controlled by angels' [NLT]. The aorist tense refers to the time when the subjection was made [Alf] and indicates God's firm decision not to put angels in control of the future world [NIGTC]. The subject of this verb is God [EGT, My,

NIGTC, TH, TNTC, Wst]. This verb shows that the initiative was God's [TNTC].

c. pres. act. participle of μέλλω (LN 67.62) (BAGD 2. p. 501): 'coming' [NIC; NRSV], 'to come' [BAGD, HNTC, Lns, WBC; all versions except NRSV], 'to be about to' [LN]. This participle is translated as an adjective: 'future' [Mil; CEV, NLT]. This word is a periphrastic form for the future tense [Mil].

d. οἰκουμένη (LN **1.39**) (BAGD 3. p. 561): 'inhabited world', 'inhabited earth' [Lns], 'world' [BAGD, HNTC, LN, Mil, NIC; all versions], 'heavenly world' [WBC]. The reference is to an inhabited world [BAGD, EGT, LN, Lns, Mil, TH, TNTC, Wst].

e. περί with genitive object (LN 89.6, 90.24): 'concerning' [LN (89.6, 90.24), Lns; NASB], 'about' [HNTC, LN (90.24), Mil, WBC; NIV, NJB, NRSV, TNT], 'of' [LN (90.24), NIC; NAB, TEV], 'whereof' [KJV], 'in relation to' [LN (89.6)], 'with regard to' [LN (89.6)], not explicit [CEV]. The phrase περὶ ἧς λαλοῦμεν 'concerning which we speak' is translated 'which is our theme' [REB], 'we are talking about' [NLT].

QUESTION—What relationship is indicated by γάρ 'for'?

1. It indicates the grounds for the argument of the preceding verses [EGT] beginning with 2:2 [Alf].
2. It indicates the second grounds for the exhortation in 2:1 [Mil]: we ought to give heed, for . . .
3. It indicates the grounds for 1:14 [Hwt, Lns]: the angels are ministering spirits, since it is not to them that the coming world is subjected. It also introduces a new subject [Lns].
4. It indicates the grounds for the exhortation to dedication to salvation through the Son [Lg].
5. It links the present discussion with the preceding discussion concerning the Son's supremacy [NIC, NIGTC, NTC, WBC; NLT]. It is another reason to emphasize the Son's superiority [NIC].
6. It opens a new stage in the discussion [ICC, TH].

QUESTION—What is implied by the word order of ἀγγέλοις 'angels'?

It is emphatic by forefronting [Alf, Mil], the emphasis of this verse being on angels [My]; it was not to *angels*. This noun without the article focuses on angels as to their nature [My]. This phrase does not imply that the world was not made subject to anyone [EBC]. The contrast is found in the following verses [Mil]. God has subjected this present world to angels (Deut. 32:8 LXX) but not the coming the world [EGT, HNTC, NIC, NIGTC, NTC].

QUESTION—What does the phrase τὴν οἰκουμένην τὴν μέλλουσαν 'the coming world' refer to?

It refers to the future world which believers to some extent now enjoy [NIGTC], the new order inaugurated by Christ [TNTC] in his earthly life [Alf, Blm, GNC, Mil], death, and resurrection [Blm, GNC, Mil], at his ascension to heaven [NCBC, NIC, NTC, WBC], the Messianic age [EBC, Hu, Lg, My] which has begun but is not yet completed [My, NCBC, NIC], the world of mankind as God destined it to be [EGT], which makes the OT dispensation obsolete [EGT]. It will be completely fulfilled [GNC, Hu] in Christ's second coming [Blm, NIC], in his reign in glory [Alf]. It is the world order which will follow the days of the Messiah [HNTC]. The participle μέλλουσαν 'coming' is a recognized word to refer to that age [Alf]. The participle is used because the old dispensation was still in existence as long as the Temple and the Jewish state existed [Blm].

QUESTION—What is implied by the phrase περὶ ἧς λαλοῦμεν 'concerning which we are speaking'?

It indicates the continuity between 1:5–14 and the present passage [WBC]. This phrase refers to the entire epistle [Wst].

QUESTION—What is implied by λαλοῦμεν 'we are speaking'?

The present tense refers to present time for the author [Alf, NIGTC]: concerning which I am now speaking. It refers to the theme of the whole epistle [My]. The first person plural refers only to the author [ICC, My, NIGTC, TH]: I am speaking in this epistle.

2:6 But somewhere someone testified[a] saying,

LEXICON—a. aorist mid. (deponent = act.) indic. of διαμαρτύρομαι (LN 33.223) (BAGD 2. p. 186): 'to testify' [BAGD, LN, WBC; KJV, NASB, NIV, NRSV], 'to testify solemnly' [Lns, Mil], 'to witness' [NJB], 'to bear witness' [BAGD, NIC], 'to declare' [LN], 'to declare solemnly' [HNTC], 'to assert' [LN]. The phrase διεμαρτύρατο τις 'someone testified' is translated 'this is testified to' [NAB], 'someone says to God' [CEV], 'in the Scriptures it says' [NLT]. This entire phrase is translated 'there is somewhere this solemn assurance' [REB], 'as it is said somewhere in the Scriptures' [TEV], 'someone says, somewhere in the Scriptures' [TNT]. The sense is to affirm or assert positively [Alf, ICC, Lns], to assert solemnly [NIGTC]. It is reinforced by the prefix δια- ('thoroughly') [Mil], indicating that the quotation is to be taken very seriously [EBC].

QUESTION—What relationship is indicated by δέ 'but'?

1. It indicates a positive contrast to the preceding negative statement [Alf, Lg, Mil, My, NTC, TH]. There is an implied ellipsis, "the situation is quite different, because . . ." [Alf], "God has put the world in subjection to Christ, because . . ." [Blm].
2. It has a general and noncontrastive sense [Lns].

QUESTION—What is implied by the indefinite words πού τις 'somewhere someone'?

They imply that the author assumed that his readers knew and would recognize the quotation [Alf, Blm, EGT, Hwt, Lns, Mil, My]. The indefinite phrase is intentional for rhetorical effect [Alf, EGT, Lg, My]. These words do not indicate that the author is quoting from memory, since the words agree exactly with the passage in the Greek OT [Alf, Lg, My]. The author regards all of the Bible as being God's word and he does not emphasize the identity of the human author of the quotation [EBC, HNTC, Hu, ICC,

NCBC, NIC, NIGTC, NTC, TNTC, WBC]. Before the introduction of chapter and verse divisions, it was not possible to cite exact references [NCBC]. His exact quotation shows that he knew the source of the words [EBC].

"What is (a) man[a] that you-remember[b] him, or (a) son[c] of-man that you-care-for[d] him?

LEXICON—a. ἄνθρωπος (LN 9.1; 9.24) (BAGD 2.d. p. 68): 'man' [BAGD, HNTC, LN (9.24), Lns, Mil, NIC, WBC; KJV, NAB, NASB, NIV, NLT, REB, TNT], 'human being' [BAGD, LN (9.1)]. This singular noun is translated as a plural to indicate that it refers to mankind: 'human beings' [NJB, NRSV, TEV], 'humans' [CEV]. It refers to human beings in general [Alf, Blm, EBC, HNTC, TH].

b. pres. mid. (deponent = act.) indic. of μιμνήσκομαι (LN 29.7; 29.16) (BAGD 1.c. p. 522): 'to remember' [BAGD, HNTC, LN (29.16, 29.7), Lns; NASB, REB, TNT], 'to think of' [BAGD; NLT, TEV], 'to bear in mind' [NIC], 'to be mindful of' [KJV, NAB, NIV, NRSV], 'to take thought for' [WBC], 'to spare a thought for' [NJB], 'to be concerned about' [BAGD, Mil], 'to care about' [CEV], 'to care for' [BAGD]. The meaning is to care for [Alf], to bear in mind [Blm, EBC] for the purpose of helping [EBC].

c. υἱός (LN 10.30): 'son' [HNTC, Lns, NIC, WBC; KJV, NAB, NASB, NIV, NLT, TNT], 'male descendant' [LN]. The phrase υἱὸς ἀνθρώπου 'a son of man' is translated 'a man' [REB], 'a son of Adam' [Mil], 'a child of Adam' [NJB]. This singular noun is translated as a plural: 'mortals' [NRSV], 'mere human beings' [TEV], 'weaklings such as we' [CEV]. This phrase emphasizes the quality of humanness [EBC].

d. pres. mid. (deponent = act.) of ἐπισκέπτομαι (LN 35.39) (BAGD 3. p. 298): 'to care for' [WBC; NAB, NIV, NJB, NLT, NRSV, REB, TEV], 'to take care of' [LN], 'to look after' [LN, Mil], 'to be concerned about' [CEV, NASB], 'to show concern for' [TNT], 'to show one's care for' [LN], 'to have regard for' [HNTC], 'to consider' [NIC], 'to visit' [KJV], 'to look in upon' [Lns]. The reference is to God's visitation to bring salvation [BAGD, NTC]. This verb means to favor and protect [Blm], to help and care for [EBC, Mil].

QUESTION—What is implied by this rhetorical question?

1. It implies surprise that God graciously honors undeserving human beings [Alf, EGT, Hwt, Lg, My, TH, Wst]: it is wonderful and unexpected that God cares for human beings. The Psalmist is surprised at the high position of man which he goes on to state [EGT, Lns, NIC]. It implies that mankind seems insignificant in comparison with the universe [Alf, Hwt, Lg, My, Wst] but is nevertheless exalted by God [GNC, Hu, Mil, My, NTC].

2. It implies that human beings must be greatly valued by God for him to honor them as he has [ICC]: what great value God must place on human beings to care for them as he does.
3. Both ideas are involved. Compared to the heavenly bodies, a person is a speck of dust, but his value lies in being created in the image of God and being given authority to rule God's creation [Hu, NTC, TNTC, WBC]. This pertains to man's ideal state, which he lost in the fall [TNTC]. It refers to mankind and also to Christ [Hu], since Jesus is the true realization and restorer of humanity [Hu, WBC].

QUESTION—What relationship is indicated by ἤ 'or'?

It introduces the second member of a parallel reference, not a different referent [Alf, Mil, My, NCBC, TH], and refers to the same referent with different words. 'Son of man' refers to human beings in general, just as does ἄνθρωπος 'man' in the first phrase [Alf, EBC, EGT, HNTC, Hwt, Mil, My, NCBC, TH, Wst]

QUESTION—How is the phrase υἱὸς ἀνθρώπου 'a son of man' related to the NT phrase ὁ υἱὸς τοῦ ἀνθρώπου 'the Son of man'?

1. The usage here is very different from Jesus' reference to himself as 'the Son of Man' [EBC, Mil, WBC, Wst], because this quoted phrase from the OT has no definite articles while the NT phrase has the definite article with each of the two nouns [WBC, Wst].
2. It is the same phrase that Jesus used of himself [GNC, My, NCBC, TNTC].

2:7 You-lowered[a] him some little[b] in-comparison-to[c] angels,

LEXICON—a. aorist act. indic. of ἐλαττόω (LN **87.68**) (BAGD 1. p. 248): 'to lower', 'to make lower' [BAGD, HNTC, Lns, NIC, WBC; all versions except NJB, REB], 'to make less' [Mil; NJB], 'to cause to be less' [LN], 'to make subordinate' [REB], 'to make inferior' [BAGD]. The aorist tense indicates a definite act in past ages [Hwt].

b. βραχύς (LN 59.14; **78.43**) (BAGD 2. p. 147): 'little' [LN (59.14)], 'somewhat' [LN (78.43)]. The phrase βραχύ τι 'some little' is translated 'a little' [Lns, NIC; KJV, NIV], 'only a little' [Mil], 'for a little while' [WBC; NAB, NASB, NLT, NRSV, TEV, TNT], 'for a short while' [HNTC; NJB, REB], 'for a short time' [BAGD], 'for a while' [CEV]. The phrase ἠλάττωσας αὐτὸν βραχύ τι 'you lowered him some little' is translated 'you caused him to be somewhat less' [**LN** (78.43)].

c. παρά with accusative object (LN 78.29) (BAGD III.3. p. 611): 'in comparison to' [BAGD], 'than' [Lns, Mil, NIC, WBC; CEV, KJV, NAB, NIV, NLT, TEV, TNT], 'more than' [BAGD, LN], 'beyond' [BAGD, LN], 'to a greater degree than' [LN], 'to' [REB].

QUESTION—To whom does αὐτόν 'him' refer?

1. It refers to mankind [Alf, EBC, EGT, HNTC, Hwt, ICC, Lg, Lns, Mil, NCBC, NTC, TH, WBC, Wst; NRSV, TEV]. This is his condition before the Fall [Lg].

2. It refers to Jesus, the Son of Man [GNC, Hu, My, NIC]. In Psalm 8:5, the Psalmist was considering mankind in general, but the writer of Hebrews interprets this to mean Jesus, the Son of Man in a unique sense [Hu, NIC].

QUESTION—What is meant by βραχύ τι 'some little'?

1. It means a small degree [Alf, Blm, EBC, EGT, Lg, Lns, Mil, Wst; KJV, NIV]: you made him a little lower than the angels. It refers to a lesser rank [Hwt, LN (78.43)].
2. It means a short time [HNTC, Hu, Hwt, ICC, LN, My, NTC, TH, WBC; all versions except KJV, NIV]: you made him lower than the angels for a little time. Although in Psalm 8:5 it means that mankind in general was lower in degree, here the writer of Hebrews interpreted it to mean a short time [Hu, LN (78.43), NTC, TH].

QUESTION—In what way was he lower than the angels?

Man was less important, had less power or authority than the angels [TH]. Man was equal with the angels when he shared immortality with them, but he was made lower when sin brought mortality [NTC]. Christ was made lower by his incarnation [Hu].

with-glory[a] and honor[b] you-crowned[c] him,

TEXT—Following αὐτόν 'him' at the end of this phrase, some manuscripts add καὶ κατέστησας αὐτὸν ἐπὶ τὰ ἔργα τῶν χειρῶν σου 'and appointed him over the works of your hands'. GNT omits this phrase with a B decision, indicating that the omission is almost certain. This phrase is added only by Lns and KJV.

LEXICON—a. δόξα (LN 79.18; 87.4) (BAGD 1.a. p. 203): 'glory' [HNTC, LN (79.18), Lns, Mil, NIC, WBC; all versions], 'honor' [LN (87.4)], 'brightness' [BAGD], 'splendor' [BAGD, LN (79.18)], 'radiance' [BAGD]. It is one's essential dignity [Wst].

b. τιμή (LN 87.4) (BAGD 2.b. p. 598): 'honor' [BAGD, HNTC, LN, Lns, Mil, NIC; all versions], 'splendor' [WBC], 'respect' [BAGD]. The combination of this and the preceding noun emphasizes man's exalted position in creation [EBC]. It is the outward splendor of glory [Wst].

c. aorist act. indic. of στεφανόω (LN 87.13) (BAGD 2. p. 767): 'to crown' [BAGD, HNTC, Lns, Mil, NIC, WBC; all versions], 'to honor' [BAGD, LN], 'to exalt' [LN].

QUESTION—What does 'glory and honor' refer to?

This is a reference to being given the position of king over creation [NTC, TNTC]. It is dominion over all lesser creation as announced in Gen. 1:26 [NIC]. It is sharing in Christ's rule [Hu].

2:8 you-subjected[a] everything under[b] his feet."

LEXICON—a. aorist act. indic. of ὑποτάσσω (LN 37.31) (BAGD 1.a. p. 848): 'to subject' [BAGD, LN, Lns, NIC; NRSV, TNT], 'to put in subjection' [HNTC, Mil, WBC; KJV, NASB, REB], 'to subordinate' [BAGD], 'to bring under control' [LN], 'to put (under)' [NAB, NIV, NJB]. This entire phrase is translated 'you gave him authority over all things' [NLT], 'you made them rulers over all things' [TEV], 'you have put everything under our power' [CEV]. The aorist tense points to a single event [NTC]. See this word at 2:5.

b. ὑποκάτω (LN **37.8;** 83.51) (BAGD p. 844): 'under' [BAGD, HNTC, LN (**37.8,** 83.51), Lns, Mil, WBC; all versions except NLT, REB, TEV], 'beneath' [NIC; REB], 'below' [BAGD]. The phrase ὑποκάτω τῶν ποδῶν αὐτοῦ 'under his feet' is translated '(you have) put him in control of all things' [**LN** (37.8)].

QUESTION—What is implied by the phrase ὑποκάτω τῶν ποδῶν αὐτοῦ 'under his feet'?

It implies complete supremacy [EBC, Mil]: you have given him complete supremacy over everything. He rules over everything that exists [TH]. Even the angels are subject to man [NTC].

For/now[a] in[b] subjecting[c] to-him the all-things he-left nothing unsubjected[d] to him.

TEXT—Some manuscripts omit the first αὐτῷ 'to him' of this clause. GNT retains this word in brackets with a C decision, indicating that the editorial committee had difficulty in deciding the correct reading. This word is included by all commentaries except NIGTC and by all versions.

LEXICON—a. γάρ: 'for' [Mil; KJV, NASB, NJB, REB], 'now' [WBC; NLT, NRSV], not explicit [HNTC, Lns, NIC; CEV, NAB, NIV, TEV, TNT].

b. ἐν with dative object (LN 67.33; 89.76) (BAGD III.1.b. p. 260): 'in' [NIC, WBC; NAB, NASB, NIV, NJB, NRSV, REB], 'in that' [BAGD, Lns, Mil; KJV], 'while' [BAGD], 'when' [LN (67.33)], 'at the time of' [LN (67.33)], 'by' [HNTC, LN (89.76)], not explicit [CEV, TNT]. This entire phrase is translated 'It says that God made them "rulers over all things"; this clearly includes everything' [TEV], 'when it says "all things," it means nothing is left out' [NLT].

c. aorist act. infin. of ὑποτάσσω: 'to subject'. See this word in a. in the preceding section.

d. ἀνυπότακτος (LN 37.32) (BAGD 1. p. 76): 'unsubjected' [Lns, Mil, NIC; NAB], 'not subjected' [TNT], 'not subject' [HNTC, LN; NASB, NIV], 'not subject to' [**LN**], 'not made subject' [BAGD; REB], 'not put under' [KJV], 'not left out of one's power' [CEV], 'uncontrolled' [LN], 'not controlled by' [LN], 'out of one's control' [WBC], 'outside one's control' [NRSV], 'that man could not be in control of' [LN], 'independent' [BAGD], not explicit [NLT, TEV]. The phrase οὐδὲν ἀφῆκεν αὐτῷ ἀνυπότακτον 'he left nothing unsubjected to him' is translated 'God left nothing that man could not be in control of' [**LN**]. This word means 'not able to be subjected' [NIGTC].

QUESTION—What relationship is indicated by γάρ 'for'?

1. It indicates the grounds for the statement in 2:5 that God did not subject the universe to angels [Alf, Mil, Wst; KJV, NASB, NJB, REB]: God did not subject the world to angels, since he promised to do this for mankind.

2. It explains the preceding quotation [Blm, EBC, Hu, Mil, My, NIGTC, WBC; NLT, NRSV, and probably CEV, NAB, NIV, TEV, TNT]. It is an explanatory amplification of it [Mil], an implication from it [EBC]. It underscores the statement 'you subjected everything under his feet' [WBC].

QUESTION—What relationship is indicated by the infinitive phrase ἐν τῷ ὑποτάξαι 'in subjecting'?

It indicates the grounds for the following statement that nothing was left unsubjected [Mil]: since he subjected everything, he left nothing unsubjected.

QUESTION—What is implied by the phrase τὰ πάντα 'the all things'?

The definite article τά makes πάντα 'all things' all-inclusive, including all of creation [NIGTC, NTC]; the phrase means the universe [Alf].

QUESTION—Who is the subject of the infinitive ὑποτάξαι 'to subject' and the verb ἀφῆκεν 'he left'?

It is God [Alf, Blm, Lg, My, NIGTC; NAB, NASB, NIV, NRSV, REB, TEV]: in God's subjecting . . . he left nothing unsubjected.

QUESTION—To whom does αὐτῷ 'to him' refer?

1. It refers to mankind in all three occurrences in this verse [Alf, EBC, HNTC, ICC, Lg, Lns, Mil, NCBC, Wst; NRSV, TEV]. The promised sovereignty over the world will be given in the new order [Wst].
2. It refers to mankind and Christ [GNC, NIC, NIGTC, NTC, WBC]. The unfulfilled condition causes us to see that the promise is not to mankind in general but to Jesus who fulfilled God's plan [WBC]. Christ is the representative man [NIC].
3. It refers to Christ [Hu, Hwt, My, TNTC]. All things are under Jesus' control, but since his incarnation it does not appear to be so [TNTC].

But now not-yet do-we-see the everything subjected[a] to-him;

LEXICON—a. perf. pass. participle of ὑποτάσσω: 'to be subjected'. See this word above in this verse.

QUESTION—What relationship is indicated by δέ 'but'?

It indicates a contrast between the statement in the quoted psalm and the present situation [NIGTC].

QUESTION—What is implied by this verse?

The use of οὔπω 'not yet' implies that the author expects the prophecy to be fulfilled [EBC, WBC].

1. Νῦν 'now' is temporal [Blm, EBC, HNTC, Lg, Mil, My, NIGTC, TH, WBC, Wst]: now at the present time. It implies that the prophecy has not been completely fulfilled [EBC], but so much has been fulfilled that the rest will surely follow [Blm, Lg].
2. Νῦν 'now' is logical [Lg(K), NIC]: as matters stand we do not see . . .

DISCOURSE UNIT: 2:9–18 [Lns; NASB]. The topic is Jesus briefly humbled [NASB], bringing mankind to glory by Jesus' suffering [Lns].

2:9 but we-see the-(one)-lowered[a] some little in-comparison-to[b] angels, Jesus,

LEXICON—a. perf. pass. participle of ἐλαττόω: 'to be lowered'. See this word in 2:7. The perfect tense of the participle focuses on his lowered state [Alf, NIGTC] into human nature, and that he still retains it [Hu, Mil, Wst].

b. παρά with accusative object: 'in comparison to'. See this word in 2:7.

QUESTION—What relationship is indicated by δέ 'but?

It indicates a strong contrast with what precedes [Alf, ICC, TH]. The prophecy is not fulfilled in mankind, but it is fulfilled in the man Jesus [EBC, WBC]. It is a contrast of circumstance [Mil]. It shows that the quotation is true in spite of the negative circumstance just mentioned [My, Wst] by applying the quotation to Jesus [NCBC]: although not all things are yet subject to Christ, we do see him exalted after his death; so the subjection of all things to him must follow. It tells why Jesus was made lower and exalted; it was for mankind's sake [ICC]. It shows that Jesus has fulfilled the part of the psalm referring to his being lowered [NIGTC].

QUESTION—What does this phrase refer to?

It refers to the temporary lowly state of Jesus on earth [WBC, Wst].

QUESTION—What is the meaning of βραχύ τι 'some little'?

1. It refers to degree [Blm, EGT, HNTC, Hwt, Lns, Mil; KJV, NIV]: made a little lower in degree. He was ranked lower because of his human nature [TH].
2. It refers to time [GNC, Hu, ICC, Lg, NIGTC, TH, WBC; all versions except KJV, NIV]: made lower for a short time. It is in emphatic position in the sentence, emphasizing the brevity of the time [WBC].

QUESTION—What is implied by the word Ἰησοῦν 'Jesus'?

It is in apposition with the participle τὸν ἠλαττωμένον 'the one lowered' [Lg, My]; the use of his personal name points to his humanity [EBC, GNC, Lg, TNTC, WBC, Wst], to the historical fact of his death [NTC]; it shows that only in Jesus is the quotation fulfilled [Lg]. This is the first occurrence of the personal name of Jesus [NIGTC].

1. It is emphatic by word order [EBC, GNC, NCBC, NIGTC, WBC, Wst] to arouse attention [WBC].
2. It is not emphatic by word order and only identifies 'the one lowered' [Alf, My]: the one lowered, namely Jesus.

because-of/in-order-to[a] the suffering[b] of-the death

LEXICON—a. διά with accusative object (LN 89.26): 'because of' [LN, Lns, WBC; NASB, NRSV], 'because' [Mil; NAB, NIV, NJB, NLT, REB, TEV, TNT], 'by reason of, on account of' [LN], 'through' [HNTC], 'in order to' [NIC], 'for' [KJV], not explicit [CEV].

b. πάθημα (LN 24.78) (BAGD 1. p. 602): 'suffering' [BAGD, HNTC, LN, Lns, WBC; KJV, NASB, NRSV]. The phrase διὰ τὸ πάθημα τοῦ θανάτου 'on account of the suffering of death' is translated 'because of the death he suffered' [TEV, TNT], 'because he suffered death' [NAB, NIV, NLT, REB], 'because of his having suffered death' [Mil], 'because he submitted to death' [NJB], 'in order to suffer death' [NIC]. This word emphasizes the suffering involved in his death [HNTC].

QUESTION—What relationship is indicated by διά 'because of, in order to'?

1. It indicates the reason for being crowned [Alf, Blm, EBC, GNC, HNTC, Hu, Lg, Lns, Mil, My, NCBC, NIGTC, TH, TNTC, WBC, Wst; all versions except KJV]: because he suffered death, he was crowned with glory and honor. This phrase is emphatic by forefronting [Alf]. These two phrases form the center of a chiastic structure [WBC].
2. It indicates the purpose for being made lower [EGT, ICC, NIC; KJV]: he was made lower than the angels in order to suffer death.

QUESTION—How are the two nouns related in the genitive construction πάθημα τοῦ θανάτου 'suffering of death'?

1. Θανάτου 'of death' is an objective genitive [ICC, Mil; NAB, NIV, NLT, REB, TEV, TNT]: he experienced death.
2. It is a genitive of apposition [WBC]: his suffering consisted of death.

crowned[a] with-glory[b] and honor,[c]

LEXICON—a. perf. pass. participle of στεφανόω: 'to be crowned'. See this word in 2:7.

b. δόξα: 'glory'. See this word in 2:7.

c. τιμή: 'honor'. See this word in 2:7.

QUESTION—What is this phrase connected with?

1. It is connected with the preceding phrase [Alf, Blm, GNC, HNTC, Hu, Lg, Lns, Mil, My, NCBC, NIC, TH, TNTC, WBC; all versions except KJV]: because he suffered death he was crowned with glory and honor. It is part of the predicate of βλέπομεν 'we see' [My].
2. It is connected with the first phrase of the verse [KJV]: we see Jesus crowned with glory and honor.
3. It is connected with the following clause [EGT]: he was crowned with glory and honor so that his death would be effective for everyone.
4. It is parenthetical, included to complete the quotation from the Psalm [ICC].

QUESTION—When was Jesus "crowned with glory and honor"?

1. It occurred when God exalted him to his right hand after his resurrection [Alf, HNTC, Mil, NTC, WBC].
2. The crowning was in his earthly life, at his baptism and at the Transfiguration; it was this that made his death effective for every person [EGT].

in-order-that[a] by-(the)-grace[b] of-God he-might-taste[c] death in-behalf-of[d] everyone.

TEXT—Instead of χάριτι 'by the grace', some manuscripts read χωρίς 'apart from'. GNT reads χάριτι 'grace' with an A decision, indicating that this text is certain. Only HNTC and NIGTC read χωρίς 'apart from', but it is favorably considered by NIC.

LEXICON—a. ὅπως (LN 89.59) (BAGD 2.a.α. p.576): 'in order that' [BAGD, LN, Lns, NIC], 'so that' [HNTC, LN, Mil, WBC; NIV, NJB, NRSV, REB, TEV], 'that' [KJV, NAB, NASB, TNT], not explicit [CEV, NLT].

b. χάρις (LN 25.89; 88.66) (BAGD 2.a. p.877): 'grace' [BAGD, LN (88.66), Lns, Mil, NIC, WBC; all versions except CEV, NAB, REB], 'graciousness, kindness' [LN (88.66)], 'favor, goodwill' [BAGD, LN (25.89)], 'wonderful kindness' [CEV]; different text [HNTC]. The phrase χάριτι θεοῦ 'by the grace of God' is translated 'through God's gracious will' [NAB], 'by God's gracious will' [REB].

c. aorist mid. (deponent = act.) of γεύομαι (LN 90.78) (BAGD 2. p. 157): 'to taste' [HNTC, Lns, NIC, WBC; KJV, NAB, NASB, NIV, NLT, NRSV], 'to experience' [LN, Mil; REB], 'to come to know' [BAGD]. The phrase γεύσηται θανάτου 'he might taste death' is translated 'he should die' [TEV], 'he might die' [TNT], 'he died' [CEV]. The phrase γεύσηται θανάτου ὑπὲρ παντός 'he might taste death in behalf of everyone' is translated 'his experience of death should benefit all humanity' [NJB]. This verb means to come to know [EBC], to experience fully [Hu] in all its dreadful bitterness [Lns, NTC, WBC], emphasizing the entrance into death and its sufferings [Alf, EBC, EGT, Hwt, Lg]. It is a more emphatic expression for dying [My].

d. ὑπέρ with genitive object (LN 90.36) (BAGD 1.a.ε. p. 838): 'in behalf of' [BAGD], 'on behalf of' [HNTC, LN], 'for the sake of' [BAGD, LN; NAB], 'for' [BAGD, LN, Lns, Mil, NIC, WBC; all versions except NAB, NJB]. He died in order to benefit or help everyone [TH].

QUESTION—What relationship is indicated by ὅπως 'in order that'?

1. It indicates the purpose for being made lower [GNC, Hu, Lns, TH, WBC; NAB, TEV]: he was made lower than the angels in order that he might taste death. These two phrases are part of a chiastic structure [WBC].
2. It indicates the purpose for being crowned [EGT, Hwt]; he was crowned with glory and honor in order that his death might be effective for everyone [Alf, Blm, EGT].
3. It indicates the purpose for both being made lower and being crowned [Alf, Blm, HNTC, Mil, NCBC, NIC, TNTC, Wst; TNT]. Because Christ suffered death and because his suffering resulted in his exaltation, his death avails for all [NIC]. The glory following his death marked its universal efficacy [Wst].

QUESTION—What is the phrase χάριτι θεοῦ 'by the grace of God' connected with?

It tells the means by which Christ's work of salvation was accomplished [EBC, GNC, Mil, My, NCBC, WBC; TNT]: by God's gracious work, Christ tasted death for everyone. It gives the reason Christ tasted death [CEV]: because of God's grace, Christ tasted death for everyone. It tells how

Christ's death was for everyone's advantage [Lns]. It means God's grace to mankind [EGT].

QUESTION—What is implied by the phrase ὑπὲρ παντός 'in behalf of every one'?

This phrase is emphatic by word order [EGT, Lg, NIGTC], emphasizing that Christ's triumph was for mankind's benefit, not merely for himself [EGT].

1. Παντός 'every' is masculine, referring to human beings only [Alf, Blm, EGT, GNC, HNTC, Hu, Hwt, ICC, Lg, Lns, My, NIC, NTC, TNTC, Wst; all versions]. It is singular, emphasizing each person [Alf, Hwt, My, TNTC, Wst]; it is equivalent to a plural, 'all persons' [Hu].
2. Παντός 'every' is neuter, meaning 'everything' [NIGTC].

DISCOURSE UNIT: 2:10–18 [EBC, NCBC, NIC, TNTC, WBC]. The topic is the true man [EBC], Jesus the high priest in his humanity and suffering [NCBC], the Son of Man as Savior and his people's high priest [NIC], Christ's work in behalf of mankind [TNTC], the solidarity of the Son with mankind [WBC].

2:10 For[a] it-was-fitting[b] for-him, on-account-of[c] whom the all-things (exist) and through[d] whom the all-things (exist),

LEXICON—a. γάρ (LN 89.23): 'for' [HNTC, LN, Lns, Mil; KJV, NASB], 'because' [LN], 'indeed' [NIC; NAB], 'and' [NLT], not explicit [WBC; CEV, NIV, NJB, NRSV, REB, TEV, TNT].

b. imperf. act. indic. of πρέπω (LN 66.1) (BAGD p. 699): 'to be fitting' [BAGD, HNTC, LN, Lns, Mil, NIC; all versions except CEV, KJV, NLT, TEV], 'to be right' [LN; NLT, TEV], 'to be appropriate' [WBC], 'to be becoming' [KJV], 'to do the right thing' [CEV]. It was appropriate for God [GNC, Lns, Mil, WBC] and his character [Alf, EBC, EGT, Hwt, My, NCBC, TNTC, WBC, Wst] and also suitable [Alf, EGT, Lns, My, TNTC], and inevitable [ICC]. It was not a matter of chance [EBC, EGT, HNTC]. It was appropriate to God's gracious purpose [ICC]. It was appropriate that Christ should suffer [HNTC, ICC, NIGTC], since suffering is part of human experience [HNTC]. It relates to the preceding phrase 'by the grace of God' in 2:9 [WBC].

c. διά with accusative object (LN 90.44): 'on account of' [LN, Lns], 'because of' [LN], 'for' [HNTC, NIC, WBC; KJV, NAB, NASB, NIV, NJB, NRSV, REB]. The phrase δι' ὅν 'on account of whom' is translated 'for whose sake' [Mil]. The phrase δι' ὃν τὰ πάντα καὶ δι' οὗ τὰ πάντα 'on account of whom all things exist and through whom all things exist' is translated 'who creates and preserves all things' [TEV], 'who made everything and for whom everything was made' [NLT], 'who created all things for his own purposes' [TNT], 'everything belongs to God, and all things were created by his power' [CEV]. This preposition refers to fulfilling God's purpose [My].

d. διά with genitive object (LN 90.4): 'through' [HNTC, LN, Lns, Mil, NIC, WBC; NAB, NASB, NIV, NJB, NRSV, REB], 'by' [LN; KJV], not explicit [CEV, NLT, TEV, TNT]. It indicates the originator [EBC, My].

QUESTION—What relationship is indicated by γάρ 'for'?

1. It indicates the reason Jesus had to die [Alf, EGT, HNTC, Hu, ICC, Mil, NCBC]: he suffered death because it was fitting for God to perfect Jesus through suffering. Jesus' sufferings and death were a part of God's eternal plan [EBC, Lns, NCBC].
2. It explains what is involved in the previous statement about Jesus' incarnation and his tasting death for everyone by God's grace [Hu, NIGTC, WBC, Wst].

QUESTION—To whom does αὐτῷ δι᾽ ὃν τὰ πάντα καὶ δι᾽ οὗ τὰ πάντα 'him on account of whom all things exist and through whom all things exist' refer?

It refers to God [Alf, Blm, Hu, ICC, Lns, My, NCBC, NIC, NIGTC, NTC, TH, TNTC, WBC, Wst; all versions except KJV, NASB]. This phrase designates God as over all things, the supreme Lord, Creator, and Preserver [Blm], the author and the goal [EBC, Hwt, Lns], the reason and cause [EGT, My], the reason and agent [Mil, WBC], the first and final cause [Mil], the final cause and the efficient cause [Hu, Lg, NCBC, NIC, Wst]. This phrase shows that Christ's death was part of God's eternal purpose [ICC].

QUESTION—What is the meaning of τὰ πάντα 'the all things'?

It means the sum total of all things, the universe [Alf, My]. See this phrase at 1:2.

leading[a] many sons[b] into[c] glory[d]

LEXICON—a. aorist act. participle of ἄγω (LN 15.165) (BAGD 1.c. p. 14): 'to lead' [BAGD, LN, Mil, NIC; CEV], 'to bring' [HNTC, LN, Lns, WBC; all versions except CEV].

b. υἱός (LN 9.46; 36.39) (BAGD 1.c.γ. p. 834): 'son' [BAGD, HNTC, LN (9.46), Lns, Mil, NIC, WBC; KJV, NAB, NASB, NIV, NJB, REB, TNT], 'child' [CEV, NLT, NRSV, TEV], 'follower' [LN (36.39)], 'disciple' [LN (36.39)]. The sonship is not only by creation [Alf], but also by adoption [Alf, Hu].

c. εἰς (LN 84.22) (BAGD 4.a. p. 229): 'into' [LN, Mil], 'to' [HNTC, Lns, NIC, WBC; all versions except CEV, KJV, TEV], 'unto' [KJV]. The phrase εἰς δόξαν 'into glory' is translated 'to share his glory' [CEV, TEV]. It indicates the goal [BAGD].

d. δόξα (LN 1.15) (BAGD 1.b.β.. p. 203): 'glory' [HNTC, LN, Lns, Mil, NIC, WBC; all versions]. It refers to being in the next life [BAGD; WBC]; it refers to God's bliss and majesty, which believers partake of in part in this life and fully in the next life [Alf], participation in Christ's glory [Lns], the Messianic blessedness and glory [My], the splendor of eternal salvation [EBC, HNTC, Lns, Mil] and ruling with Christ [Mil].

QUESTION—Who is the actor of this phrase?

1. It is God [Alf, Blm, EBC, EGT, GNC, HNTC, Hu, Hwt, Lg, Lns, Mil, NCBC, NIC, NIGTC, TH, TNTC, WBC; NLT], either as the subject of the preceding phrase, the accusative participle ἀγαγόντα 'leading' irregularly modifying the dative αὐτῷ 'him' [Alf, Blm, EBC, EGT, Lg,

Mil, My, NIC] when followed by an infinitive [EGT, NIC], or as the unexpressed subject of the following infinitive τελειῶσαι 'to perfect' [ICC, Lg, Lns, WBC]: God, in bringing many sons into glory. The reference to sons supports this connection [EGT].

2. It is Jesus [CEV]: Jesus led many of God's children to be saved and to share in his glory.

QUESTION—What relationship is indicated by the use of the participle ἀγαγόντα 'leading'?

1. It indicates purpose [EBC, GNC, HNTC, Mil, NIC, TH, WBC; all versions except NAB]: it was fitting for God to perfect Jesus through suffering in order to bring many sons into glory. This phrase is the principal thought of the verse, and the perfecting of Christ was the means for doing this [TH].
2. It indicates a temporal circumstance [Blm; NAB]

2.1 It refers to the time when God acted [NAB]: it was fitting for God to perfect Jesus through suffering when he brought many sons into glory.

2.2 It refers to the time of God's decree to act [Blm]: it was fitting for God to perfect Jesus through suffering after God had decreed to bring many children into glory.

QUESTION—What is indicated by the aorist tense of ἀγαγόντα 'leading'?

1. It is timeless [EBC, EGT, HNTC, Wst], indicating the act as a completed action [Alf, EBC], a simple event [EBC, EGT, ICC, Lns]: bringing, as he did. This is the most basic meaning of the aorist tense of participles.
2. It indicates simultaneous action [Lg, NIC, TNTC], at the same time as τελειῶσαι 'to perfect' [NIGTC]. This participle expresses the principal action of the clause [NIGTC].
3. It indicates past time, referring to God's action from the beginning of Christ's incarnation [My].
4. It anticipates the future completion of Christ's work of salvation [Hu, WBC].

QUESTION—What is implied by πολλούς 'many'?

It indicates a large number [My, TH, WBC, Wst]. It is in contrast with the one Son [EGT, ICC, Mil, NCBC, NIGTC]. This word is inclusive, not exclusive; it does not mean 'many, but not all' [NCBC, NIGTC, TH]. The reference is to believers [NIGTC]. It is in primary contrast with the one God and secondarily with the one Son [NIGTC]. It implies that not everyone will respond to the offer of salvation [HNTC].

to-perfect[a] the originator[b] of-their salvation[c] through[d] suffering.[e]

LEXICON—a. aorist act. infin. of τελειόω (LN 88.38) (BAGD 2.a. p. 809; 3. p. 810): 'to perfect' [LN, Mil, NIC; NASB], 'to make perfect' [HNTC, LN, WBC; all versions except NASB, NLT], 'to make (him) a perfect (leader)' [NLT], 'to make complete' [Lns], 'to bring to (one's) goal, to consecrate, to initiate' [BAGD].

b. ἀρχηγός (LN **36.6**; **68.2**) (BAGD 3. p. 112): 'originator' [BAGD, LN (68.2)], 'initiator' [LN (68.2)], 'founder' [BAGD, LN (**68.2**)], 'founding leader' [LN (36.6); NLT], 'pioneer leader' [LN (**36.6**)], 'pioneer' [NIC; NRSV, REB], 'leader' [HNTC; NAB, NJB, NLT], 'captain' [KJV], 'leader-captain' [Mil], 'champion' [WBC], 'author' [Lns; NASB, NIV], 'one who institutes' [LN (**68.2**)]. The phrase τὸν ἀρχηγὸν τῆς σωτηρίας αὐτῶν 'the originator of their salvation' is translated 'him who leads them to salvation' [TNT], 'Jesus is the one who leads them to salvation' [TEV], 'Jesus led many of God's children to be saved' [CEV], 'leader, one fit to bring them into their salvation' [NLT]. The meaning is originator [Alf, EBC, Hwt, Lg, Mil, My, NCBC], author [Hwt, Lg, My], the cause [Blm, Lg, My], leader [Mil, NCBC] as both guide and commander [NCBC], a pathfinder who opens the way for others [EBC, ICC, NIC, NIGTC, TH, TNTC, Wst], a leader who commands by showing the way [HNTC], a leader who first acts and then brings his followers to the goal [Hu, My(D)].

c. σωτηρία (LN 21.25, 21.26) (BAGD 2. p. 801): 'salvation' [BAGD, HNTC, LN (21.25; 21.26), Lns, Mil, NIC, WBC; all versions].

d. διά with genitive object (LN 89.76) (BAGD A.III.1.a. p. 180): 'through' [BAGD, HNTC, LN, Mil, NIC, WBC; all versions except CEV], 'by' [CEV], 'by means of' [BAGD, Lns].

e. πάθημα (LN 24.78) (BAGD 1. p. 602): 'suffering' [BAGD, LN]. The plural form of this noun is used here; it is translated as a plural: 'sufferings' [HNTC, Mil, NIC; KJV, NASB, NRSV, REB, TNT]; it is translated as a singular: 'suffering' [Lns, WBC; CEV, NAB, NIV, NJB, NLT, TEV]. It refers to death and its attendant sufferings [Blm]; it refers to all of the sufferings of life and death [EGT, Mil]; it refers only to his death [NIGTC, TH]. It is the means by which Christ is perfected [Lg, NIGTC].

QUESTION—In what sense was Christ perfected?

It means making Christ perfectly equipped to be the leader of salvation [Mil, NCBC, NIC, TH, WBC] through human experience [EGT], to be an effective high priest for mankind [Hu, NIGTC], through his sufferings [HNTC, Hu, Hwt, ICC, Lns]. It also means his becoming a real savior by his perfect sacrifice [Lg, NIGTC]. It refers to the result of his suffering [EBC, NTC] which completed his identification with mankind [GNC], which enabled him to be the savior of mankind [NIC, NTC, TNTC]. It was accomplished through his fellowship with persons who believed in him [Lg]. It refers to his atonement for the sins of the people [NIGTC, NTC]. It means to bring Christ to his final glory, as expressed by 'crowned with glory and honor' in 2:9 [Alf, My]. There is no implication of his needing to be perfected morally [EBC, GNC, HNTC, TH]. It means full moral perfection of his humanity [Wst] through his sufferings [EGT], completed by his resurrection triumph over death [Wst].

QUESTION—How are the two nouns related in the genitive construction ἀρχηγὸν τῆς σωτηρίας 'originator of salvation'?

The genitive is the object [Alf, Mil; TEV]: he provided their salvation.

DISCOURSE UNIT: 2:11–18 [GNC, HNTC]. The topic is the benefits of Christ's humanity [GNC], the full humanity of Jesus [HNTC].

2:11 for[a] both the-(one) making-holy[b] and the-(ones) being-made-holy[c] (are) all from[d] one;[e]

LEXICON—a. γάρ (LN 89.23) (BAGD 1.b. p. 151): 'for' [BAGD, HNTC, LN, Lns, Mil, NIC, WBC; KJV, NASB, NJB, NRSV, REB, TNT], 'because' [LN], 'so now' [NLT], not explicit [CEV, NAB, NIV, TEV].

b. pres. act. participle of ἁγιάζω (LN 53.44; 88.26) (BAGD 2. p. 8): 'to make holy' [LN (88.26), Mil; CEV, NIV, NLT], 'to sanctify' [BAGD, Lns; KJV, NASB, NRSV], 'to cleanse from sin' [TNT], 'to consecrate' [BAGD, HNTC, LN (53.44), WBC; NAB, REB], 'to dedicate' [BAGD]. The phrase ὁ ἁγιάζων 'the one making holy' is translated 'the sanctifier' [NIC], 'consecrator' [NJB], 'he purifies people from their sins' [TEV]. It means to set apart for God [EGT, NIGTC, TH, WBC] by purification of the nature [EGT, NIGTC, WBC], to sanctify and restore to God by removing the impurity resulting from sin [HNTC, Hwt]. It means to set apart for salvation [TNTC]. It refers to the expiation of sins [Blm]. It refers to the total experience of setting people apart for God and making them holy, from new birth to glorification [EBC, Hu] by purification from defilement [Hu, Mil, WBC] producing moral fitness [Mil]. It refers to the securing of fellowship by believers with God through the expiation of their sins, and dedication to God [Lg].

c. pres. pass. participle of ἁγιάζω: 'to be made holy'. See this word in b. above. The phrase οἱ ἁγιαζόμενοι 'the ones being made holy' is translated 'consecrated' [NJB], 'those who are made pure' [TEV]. This word relates to the transformation and consecration of Christ's people [Alf, NIGTC].

d. ἐκ with genitive object (LN 89.3; 90.16): 'from' [LN, Lns], 'of' [WBC; KJV]. The phrase ἐξ ἑνὸς πάντες 'are all from one' is translated 'are all from one Father' [NASB], 'are all from the same Father' [TNT], 'all have the same Father' [TEV], 'have the same Father' [NLT], 'have one and the same Father' [NAB], 'all have one Father' [Mil; NRSV], 'have a common parent' [HNTC], 'are of the same family' [NIV], 'all belong to the same family' [CEV], 'are all of the same stock' [NJB], 'are all of one stock' [REB], 'all come from one stock' [NIC].

e. εἷς (LN 60.10; 63.4): 'one' [LN, Lns; KJV], 'one origin' [WBC].

QUESTION—What relationship is indicated by γάρ 'for'?

1. It indicates the grounds for mentioning 'many sons' in 2:10 [Blm, ICC, My]: I say 'many sons', for the Son and the sanctified ones are all sons of one Father.

2. It indicates the reason why it was fitting to perfect Jesus through sufferings [EGT, Mil, NIGTC, WBC]: it was fitting, because Jesus and the sanctified ones are brothers.

QUESTION—What relationship is indicated by the two attributive participles ὁ ἁγιάζων 'the one making holy' and οἱ ἁγιαζόμενοι 'the ones being made holy'?

1. They are used like nouns [Alf, EGT, ICC, Lg, Lns, My, NIGTC] in a timeless sense [EGT, HNTC, ICC, Lg, NIGTC]: the sanctifier and the sanctified ones.
2. The present tense indicates a continuing process [NTC, Wst] in individuals and in the Church [Wst]: the one continually making holy . . . the ones continually being made holy.

QUESTION—Who is the one making holy?

This attributive participle refers to Jesus [Hu, ICC, NIGTC, NTC, TH, WBC; CEV, NLT].

QUESTION—What is πάντες 'all' connected with?

It is connected with both ὁ ἁγιάζων 'the one making holy' and οἱ ἁγιαζόμενοι 'the ones being made holy' [Alf, Hu, Hwt, Lns, My, NIGTC, WBC, Wst; all versions]: both the sanctifier and the sanctified ones all have the same source. It is emphatic by word order [Lns].

QUESTION—To whom does οἱ ἁγιαζόμενοι 'the ones being made holy' refer?

1. It refers to believers in Christ [My, NIGTC, TNTC].
2. It includes both OT as well as NT saints [Lns].

QUESTION—To whom does ἑνός 'one' refer?

1. It is masculine [Alf, Blm, EBC, EGT, GNC, HNTC, Hwt, Lg, Lns, Mil, My, NCBC, NIC, TH, TNTC, WBC, Wst; NAB, NASB, NIV, NLT, NRSV, TEV, TNT].
1.1 It refers to God [Alf, Blm, EGT, GNC, HNTC, Hwt, Lg, Mil, My, NCBC, NIC, TH, TNTC, WBC, Wst; NAB, NASB, NLT, NRSV, TEV, TNT]: are from the same Father, God.
1.2 It refers to Adam [EBC, Lns]. It is Christ's common descent with man from Adam that enables him to call them brothers [EBC].
1.3 It refers to the human family [NIV]: from the same human family.
2. It is neuter [Hu; NJB, REB]: are from the same stock.

on-account-of[a] which cause[b] not he-is-ashamed[c] to-call them brothers,[d]

LEXICON—a. διά with accusative object (LN 89.26): 'on account of' [LN], 'because of' [LN], 'by reason of' [LN], 'for' [HNTC, Lns, Mil; KJV, NASB, NRSV]. The phrase δι' ἣν αἰτίαν 'on account of which cause' is translated 'that is why' [NIC, WBC; CEV, NJB, NLT, REB, TEV, TNT], 'therefore' [NAB], 'so' [NIV].

b. αἰτία (LN 89.15) (BAGD 1. p. 26): 'cause' [BAGD, LN, Lns; KJV], 'reason' [BAGD, HNTC, LN, Mil; NASB, NRSV].

c. pres. mid. (deponent = act.) of ἐπαισχύνομαι (LN 25.193) (BAGD 3. p. 282): 'to be ashamed' [BAGD, HNTC, Lns, Mil, NIC; all versions except REB], 'to be ashamed of' [LN], 'to shrink from' [REB], 'to blush' [WBC]. The subject of this verb is Jesus [Alf]. The present tense is timeless, implying scripture's permanent witness [NIGTC].

d. ἀδελφός (LN 10.49): 'brother' [HNTC, LN, Lns, Mil, NIC, WBC; all versions except NRSV, TEV]. The plural form is translated 'brothers and sisters' [CEV, NLT, NRSV], 'his family' [TEV].

QUESTION—What relationship is indicated by the phrase δι' ἣν αἰτίαν 'on account of which cause'?

It indicates the result of the preceding comment [Alf, ICC, Mil, NIC, NIGTC, Wst]: because of their common fatherhood, Jesus is not ashamed to call them brothers.

QUESTION—What is meant by οὐκ ἐπαισχύνεται 'he is not ashamed'?

It signifies an affirmation by negating the opposite [GNC, TH]: he is willing to call them brothers. It means that he is proud to call them brothers [Mil, TNTC], or at least that he is happy or content to do so [TH]. It implies the great superiority of Christ to mankind [Blm, Hwt, ICC, Lg, My, TH], since there would be no question of shame in calling people his brothers if he were on their level [Blm, Hwt]. He shares so much with them that he can call them his brothers with no risk of losing his status [TH]. He might have been ashamed of mankind who had fallen from their created state [EGT], who deserved judgment [Hu]. Because of his atoning work for them, he is not ashamed of them [NTC]. He will not be ashamed of them at his second coming [WBC].

QUESTION—To whom does αὐτούς 'them' refer?

It refers to οἱ ἁγιαζόμενοι 'the sanctified ones' [Alf, EBC, HNTC, My]: Jesus is not ashamed to call the sanctified ones 'brothers'.

2:12 saying, "I-will-proclaim[a] your name[b] to-my brothers,[c]

LEXICON—a. fut. act. indic. of ἀπαγγέλλω (LN 33.198) (BAGD 2. p. 79): 'to proclaim' [BAGD, HNTC; NASB, NJB, NRSV, TNT], 'to announce' [Lns; NAB], 'to declare' [Mil, NIC, WBC; KJV, NIV, NLT], 'to make known' [REB], 'to tell' [LN; CEV, TEV].

b. ὄνομα (LN 33.126) (BAGD 1.4.b. p. 571): 'name' [BAGD, HNTC, LN, Lns, Mil, NIC, WBC; all versions except NLT, REB, TEV], 'fame' [REB]. This noun is also translated as a phrase: 'what you have done' [TEV], 'the wonder of your name' [NLT]. It means to proclaim God's revealed character [EBC].

c. ἀδελφός: 'brother'. See this word in 2:11.

QUESTION—What relationship is implied by the present participle λέγων 'saying'?

It is in apposition with the infinitive καλεῖν 'to call' as a restatement; but none of the commentaries deal with this point: that is, he says, etc. The quotation confirms the truth of the preceding comment concerning the relationship that Jesus has with Christians as brothers [Blm, EBC, EGT, GNC, HNTC, Hwt, Mil, My, NIC, NIGTC, NTC, TNTC, WBC].

QUESTION—Who is implied as the one making this statement?

It is Jesus [EBC, EGT, My, NCBC, NIC, TH, WBC] in his earthly ministry [Blm, GNC, Hu, Hwt, NTC], or in his exalted state [NIC], at his second coming [WBC]. Jesus is speaking to God [TH; CEV, TEV], in the words of Psalm 22:22 [NTC].

in[a] (the) midst[b] of-(the)-assembly[c] I-will-sing-praise[d] to-you."

LEXICON—a. ἐν with dative object (LN 83.13): 'in' [HNTC, LN, Lns, Mil, NIC, WBC; all versions except CEV, NLT, TNT]. The phrase ἐν μέσῳ 'in the midst' is translated 'among' [NLT]. This entire clause is translated 'I will join the congregation in singing your praise' [TNT], 'I will sing your praises when they come together to worship' [CEV].

b. μέσος (LN 83.9, 83.10) (BAGD 2. p. 507): 'midst' [HNTC, LN (83.9; 83.10), Lns, Mil, NIC; KJV, NAB, NASB, NRSV, REB], 'middle' [BAGD, LN (83.10)], 'presence' [WBC; NIV], 'full' [NJB], not explicit [TEV].

c. ἐκκλησία (LN 11.78) (BAGD 3. p. 240): 'assembly' [LN, Lns; NAB, NJB, REB], 'congregation' [BAGD, HNTC, Mil, NIC, WBC; NASB, NIV, NRSV, TNT], 'meeting' [TEV], 'church' [KJV], 'all your people' [NLT]. In the OT quotation, the 'assembly' refers to the people of Israel [Mil, TH], but here the writer is thinking of the assembly of Christian brothers [Blm, EBC, Hu, NCBC, NIC, NTC, TH, WBC, Wst].

d. fut. act. indic. of ὑμνέω (LN 33.113) (BAGD 1. p. 836): 'to sing praise' [HNTC, Lns, Mil, NIC; KJV, NAB, NASB, TNT], 'to sing praises' [NIV], 'to sing the praise of' [BAGD], 'to sing hymns of praise to' [BAGD], 'to sing a hymn' [LN], 'to sing a song of praise' [LN], 'to praise' [WBC; NJB, NLT, NRSV, REB, TEV], 'to worship' [CEV].

QUESTION—What is implied by this clause?

It implies that Christ is participating in the worship of God along with believers [EGT, Mil] as a manifestation of his brotherhood with them [EGT, GNC, Mil]. This clause is a poetic parallel to the preceding clause [Mil, NCBC, TH]. This line of poetry is included to fill out the quotation, but the main point is in the first line where Jesus associates himself with his brothers [ICC].

2:13 and again,[a] "I shall-be having-trusted/trusting[b] in[c] him,"

LEXICON—a. πάλιν (LN 67.55, 89.97): 'again' [HNTC, LN (67.55, 89.97), Lns, Mil, NIC; KJV, NASB, NIV, NRSV, REB, TNT], 'also' [LN (89.97)], not explicit [NAB]. The phrase καὶ πάλιν 'and again' is translated 'he also says' [WBC; TEV], 'he also said' [CEV, NLT], 'or in the text' [NJB]. This phrase introduces the second amplification of 2:11 [Mil, My, NIGTC].

b. perf. act. participle of πείθω (LN 31.82) (BAGD 2.a. p. 639): 'to trust' [Lns], 'to trust in' [BAGD, LN], 'to put one's trust in' [NLT], 'to rely on' [LN], 'to depend on' [BAGD, LN], 'to put confidence in' [BAGD], 'to have complete confidence in' [LN]. The phrase ἐγὼ ἔσομαι πεποιθώς 'I shall be having trusted/trusting' is translated 'I will put my trust' [Mil; all versions except CEV, NJB, REB], 'I will place my trust' [NIC], 'I will keep my trust' [HNTC], 'I will keep my trust fixed' [REB], 'I will trust' [WBC; CEV], 'I shall put my hope' [NJB]. Ἐγώ 'I' is emphatic [ICC, Lg, Mil, TH, TNTC, WBC, Wst]; it shows that the Messiah is speaking [Lns, Mil].

c. ἐπί with dative object (LN 83.46) (BAGD II.1.b.γ. p. 287): 'in' [HNTC, Mil, NIC; all versions except REB], 'on' [BAGD, LN; REB], 'upon' [LN], not explicit [Lns, WBC].

QUESTION—What is meant by καὶ πάλιν 'and again'?

It further emphasizes the point of Christ's brotherhood with mankind [EBC, My, NCBC, TNTC, Wst]. This quotation joins the previous quotation in showing Jesus' kinship with his brothers by stating that he, like them, has faith in God [Blm, EGT, HNTC, Hu, Hwt, ICC, Lg, Lns, My, TH, TNTC, WBC].

QUESTION—What is implied by this quotation from Isa. 8:17?

It implies Christ's trust in God [Blm, EGT, GNC, HNTC, Hu, Lg, Lns, Mil, My, NIC, NIGTC, NTC, TH, WBC] as a Son [Mil] and his acknowledgment of the Father's goodness [Blm]. It is faith in God when in the midst of judgments [Wst]. By applying the words of Isaiah to Jesus, the writer is assuming the office of prophet for Christ [Alf].

QUESTION—What is the meaning of the verb phrase ἔσομαι πεποιθώς 'I shall be having trusted/trusting'?

1. This phrase is a periphrastic future perfect tense, implying a state of trust [HNTC, Mil, NIGTC; REB]: I shall be in a condition resulting from having trusted.
2. The phrase ἔσομαι πεποιθώς is used as a periphrastic future tense [ICC, Lns, Mil, NIC, NTC, WBC; all versions except REB]: I shall be trusting. The perfect participle πεποιθώς is always used as a present participle [Lns].

and again, "Behold,[a] I and the children whom God has-given[b] to-me."

LEXICON—a. ἰδού (LN 91.13): 'behold' [Lns, Mil; KJV, NASB], 'listen' [LN], 'look' [LN; NJB], 'here am I' [NIC]. The phrase ἰδοὺ ἐγώ 'behold, I' is translated 'here am I' [HNTC, WBC; NAB, NIV, NRSV, REB, TNT], 'here I am' [CEV, NLT, TEV]. This word implies the Son's readiness to obey the Father [EGT].

b. aorist act. indic. of δίδωμι (LN 57.71) (BAGD 3. p. 193): 'to give' [HNTC, LN, Lns, NIC; all versions], 'to entrust' [BAGD, Mil].

QUESTION—What is implied by καὶ πάλιν 'and again'?

Even though it is a continuation of the preceding quotation, this phrase is included because the writer is making a different point [EBC, EGT, HNTC, Hu, Lg, Lns, My, NCBC, NIC, TH, Wst]: and again, a different point.

QUESTION—What is implied by this quotation from Isa. 8:18?

Christ is identifying himself with the children God has given him [Lg, Lns, NIC, WBC]. It implies that the Messiah and the children are ready to do God's will [Mil]: here we are to do your will.

QUESTION—What is the meaning of the phrase ἰδοὺ ἐγώ 'behold, I'?

It implies an ellipsed 'here am (I)' [HNTC, Mil, NIC, WBC; CEV, NAB, NIV, NRSV, REB, TEV, TNT]: behold, here am I.

QUESTION—To whom do the 'children' belong?

The word παιδία 'children' is a diminutive, implying affection [Lns]: dear children.

1. They belong to God [Alf, EBC, EGT, HNTC, Hu, ICC, Mil, My, NCBC, NIGTC], and he gives them to Jesus [Alf, EBC, Hu, My]; he entrusts them to Jesus [EGT, HNTC, Mil, NIGTC]. Jesus and believers are God's children and fellow sons of God [ICC].
2. They are children of Adam, and God gives them to Jesus [Lns]. Again this brings our the fact that both Jesus and his brothers have the same human nature [Lns].
3. They are Christ's children [Blm, NIC, TH, WBC, Wst]. The believers represent Christ on earth and thus are called his children [NIC]. Jesus is the head of the new humanity [WBC]. The people God gave to Jesus are like children to him [TH].

DISCOURSE UNIT: 2:14–18 [Hwt, Lg]. The topic is the Son's superior state not lessened by his suffering [Hwt], implications of the incarnation [Lg].

2:14 Since therefore[a] the children have-shared[b] blood[c] and flesh,[d] he-himself also similarly[e] partook[f] of-the same (things),

LEXICON—a. οὖν (LN 89.50): 'therefore' [HNTC, LN, Mil; NRSV], 'then' [Lns, NIC; KJV, NASB], 'now' [NAB, TNT], not explicit [WBC; CEV, NIV, NJB, NLT, REB, TEV].

b. perf. act. indic. of κοινωνέω (LN **9.15;** 57.98) (BAGD 1.a. p. 438; 1.a. p. 22; 4. p. 744): 'to share' [BAGD, HNTC, LN (57.98), WBC; NASB, NJB, NRSV, REB], 'to share as their common lot' [Mil], 'to be a sharer' [NIC], 'to be a partaker' [KJV], 'to be a man of' [NAB], 'to have' [NIV], 'to have in common' [TNT] 'to be in fellowship' [Lns]; as a plural: 'to be people of' [CEV, TEV]. The phrase κεκοινώνηκεν αἵματος καὶ σαρκός 'have shared blood and flesh' is translated 'are human beings' [LN (9.15)], 'are human beings—made of flesh and blood' [NLT]. The phrase refers to their partaking of human nature [Blm], their sharing with one another in the established order of nature [Alf, Lg, My; TNT], to their becoming partners with Christ in human nature [Hwt]. The perfect tense implies a still existing state [Alf, EGT, Hu, Lg, Lns, Mil, My, NTC, WBC, Wst]. This word implies that there is more to their beings than just the physical [Lns].

c. αἷμα (LN 8.64) (BAGD 1.a. p. 22): 'blood' [BAGD, HNTC, LN, Lns, Mil, NIC; all versions except NJB]. The phrase αἵματος καὶ σαρκός 'blood and flesh' is translated 'human nature' [BAGD; NJB], 'mortal human nature' [WBC], 'mortal nature' [BAGD]. This phrase refers to the two principal elements of mankind's outward nature [My].

d. σάρξ (LN 8.63) (BAGD 4. p. 744): 'flesh' [BAGD, HNTC, LN, Lns, Mil, NIC; all versions except NJB], 'human nature, mortal nature, earthly descent' [BAGD], not explicit [WBC; NJB].

e. παραπλησίως (LN **64.9**) (BAGD p. 621): 'similarly' [BAGD, HNTC], 'likewise' [BAGD, Lns, NIC; KJV, NAB, NASB, NRSV], 'closely resembling' [LN], 'equally' [NJB], 'in the same way' [TNT], 'in just the same way' [Mil], not explicit [CEV, REB]. The phrase παραπλησίως μετέσχεν τῶν αὐτῶν 'he similarly partook of the same things' is translated 'he became very much like them' [**LN**], 'Jesus himself became like them' [TEV], 'he shared in their humanity' [WBC; NIV], 'Jesus also became flesh and blood by being born in human form' [NLT]. The combination of the adverb παραπλησίως 'similarly' and τῶν αὐτῶν 'the same things' give a double emphasis [Hu]; it strengthens the verb [Lns]. The phrase καὶ αὐτὸς παραπλησίως 'he himself also similarly' is very emphatic [NIGTC].

f. aorist act. indic. of μετέχω (LN 57.6) (BAGD p. 514): 'to partake' [HNTC, NIC; NASB], 'to share' [BAGD, Lns, WBC; NIV, NRSV, TNT], 'to share in' [LN; NJB, REB], 'to take part' [KJV], 'to take on' [Mil]. The phrase μετέσχεν τῶν αὐτῶν 'he partook of the same things' is translated 'Jesus had a full share in ours' [NAB], 'Jesus shared their human nature' [TNT], 'Jesus became one of us' [CEV], 'Jesus also became flesh and blood by being born in human form' [NLT]. The aorist tense refers to the act of the incarnation [Alf, EGT, GNC, Hu, Lg, Lns, Mil, My, NIC, NTC, TNTC, WBC, Wst] without implying that the sharing of humanity ended [Lns]; the identification with humanity continues [Wst]; the incarnation has ended in his glorification [My, Wst]. This verb has the same meaning as κοινωνέω 'to share' above [ICC, NIC, NTC, TNTC, WBC]. The change from the perfect tense κεκοινώνηκεν 'have shared' to the aorist tense μετέσχεν 'he partook' implies that after the conclusion of Christ's earthly life, he no longer has a flesh-and-blood body [NIGTC].

QUESTION—What relationship is indicated by οὖν 'therefore'?

It indicates a conclusion from the preceding argument [Alf, Mil, NCBC, NIGTC, WBC]. It introduces the substantiation of the comment in 2:11 [Alf, TH], the development of the thought of 2:10 [My], the implications of the Son's solidarity with mankind [NCBC, WBC].

QUESTION—What relationship is indicated by ἐπεί 'since'?

It indicates the grounds for the following conclusion [Mil, NIGTC, WBC]: since the children have a human nature, therefore Jesus took it as well. A general principle is followed by a conclusion [NIGTC]:

QUESTION—What is implied by the definite article of the noun phrase τὰ παιδία 'the children'?

It means that the children referred to here are those mentioned in the preceding verse [Alf, Blm, GNC, Hu, Lg, Lns, NIGTC, TH, WBC, Wst]: the children just previously mentioned. The children are Christ's spiritual children [Blm].

QUESTION—What is implied by the phrase αἵματος καὶ σαρκός 'blood and flesh'?

This phrase refers to mankind [Hwt], to mankind's whole physical and sensuous nature [Alf], to human earthly nature [HNTC, Lg, Lns, NCBC, TH, WBC] by its two principal elements [Lg]; it emphasizes the frailty of mankind [HNTC, TH, WBC]. 'Blood' may be mentioned before 'flesh' because of the prominence of blood later in the epistle [HNTC, Lg, NCBC], because blood is the symbol of life [Wst]. There is no significance in the word order [Hu].

QUESTION—What is meant by παραπλησίως 'similarly'?

It indicates general similarity [Alf]; it means in the same manner and in reality, not in mere appearance [Blm]; it means in absolutely the same manner [EGT, Mil], total similarity [Hu, ICC, TH, WBC] with no difference intended [Mil, NTC], quantitative and qualitative similarity [Wst]. It implies both the actual humanity of Christ and also his distinction from other human beings [Lg, My]. It refers to the manner of his becoming like mankind, namely by birth [NIC].

QUESTION— What is the implied reference of τῶν αὐτῶν 'the same'?

It refers to αἵματος καὶ σαρκός 'blood and flesh' [Alf, Lns, My, NIGTC; NLT, TEV, TNT]: he partook of the same things, namely, flesh and blood.

in-order-that[a] through[b] the death he-might-destroy[c] the-(one) having the power[d] of-the death, this is the devil,

LEXICON—a. ἵνα (LN 89.59) (BAGD I.1.e. p. 377): 'in order that' [BAGD, LN; Lns], 'for the purpose that' [LN], 'that' [BAGD, HNTC; KJV, NAB, NASB], 'so that' [Mil, NIC, WBC; NIV, NJB, NRSV, REB, TEV], 'his purpose was' [TNT], 'for' [NLT], not explicit [CEV].

b. διά (LN 89.76) (BAGD A.III.1.a. p. 180): 'through' [BAGD, HNTC, LN, NIC; KJV, NASB, NRSV, TEV], 'by means of' [BAGD, Lns, Mil], 'by' [WBC; NAB, NIV, NJB]. The phrase διὰ τοῦ θανάτου 'through the death' is translated 'by dying' [REB], 'only as a human being could he die, and only by dying could he . . .' [NLT], not explicit [CEV, TNT].

c. aorist act. subj. of καταργέω (LN 13.100) (BAGD 2. p. 417): 'to destroy' [BAGD; CEV, KJV, NIV, NRSV, TEV], 'to put an end to' [LN], 'to bring to nought' [NIC], 'to rob of power' [NAB], 'to break the power' [WBC; NLT, REB], 'to render powerless' [Mil; NASB], 'to put out of commission' [Lns], 'to set aside' [NJB], 'to depose' [HNTC; TNT]. The meaning is to render powerless [NIGTC, TH] as if not existing [Hwt,

Mil]. The aorist tense indicates a single act [NTC], Christ's death [NIGTC].

d. κράτος (LN **76.6**) (BAGD 4. p. 449): 'power' [BAGD, HNTC, LN, NIC, WBC; all versions except NAB, REB], 'might' [Lns], 'sovereignty, rule' [BAGD], 'dominion' [Mil]. The phrase τὸν τὸ κράτος ἔχοντα τοῦ θανάτου 'the one having the power of death' is translated 'the prince of death' [NAB], 'him who had death at his command' [REB].

QUESTION—What relationship is indicated by ἵνα 'in order that'?

It indicates the purpose of the incarnation, which was to destroy the devil [EGT, GNC, HNTC, Hu, Lns, Mil, WBC].

QUESTION—What is implied by τοῦ θανάτου 'the death'?

1. It implies the death of the Son [Alf, Hu, Mil, NIGTC, TH, WBC; NAB, NJB, TEV].
2. It focuses on the concept of death [Lns, My, Wst]: the thing called death.

QUESTION—What does the present tense of the participle ἔχοντα 'having' indicate?

1. It refers to the person holding the power [Alf, Lg]: the devil, who has the power.
2. It refers to the state at the time of the leading verb [KJV]: destroy him who at that time held the power of death.

QUESTION—What is the meaning of the phrase 'having the power of death'?

Because Satan was the author of sin and death in Eden, it is implied that he figuratively has the power of death [EBC, GNC, HNTC, Hwt], both temporal and eternal [Blm]. Satan holds the power of death only in a secondary sense to God's power; he holds it because God has sentenced to death those who reject God and turn to Satan's realm [Hu], because he seduced mankind to rebel against God [WBC]. His power is only over unredeemed mankind [TNTC].

QUESTION—How are the two nouns related in the genitive construction τὸ κράτος τοῦ θανάτου 'the power of death'?

It means power to cause death [EGT, ICC, NIGTC, TH], power over death [NIGTC; TEV], having lordship in the area of death [ICC]. The genitive noun indicates the area over which the power is exercised [EGT, Mil].

2:15 and might-free[a] these (people), as-many-as[b] in-fear of-death through[c] all the living[d] were subject-to[e] slavery.[f]

LEXICON—a. aorist act. subj. of ἀπαλλάσσω (LN 37.127): 'to free' [Lns; NAB, NIV, NRSV], 'to set free' [LN; NJB, TEV], 'to release' [HNTC; TNT], 'to liberate' [WBC; REB], 'to deliver' [Mil, NIC; KJV, NASB, NLT], 'to rescue' [CEV]. This word is used especially of freeing from slavery [Blm, EGT, Mil].

b. ὅσος (LN 59.7) (BAGD 2. p. 586): 'as many as' [BAGD, LN, Lns, Mil], 'who' [HNTC, NIC, WBC; all versions except CEV], 'all of us who' [CEV]. It is synonymous with ὅς 'who' [ICC]. It implies the inclusion of all of those referred to [Alf, EGT, Lg]; it identifies the preceding τούτους 'these persons' [NIGTC].

c. διά with genitive object (LN 67.140) (BAGD A.II.1.a. p. 179): 'through' [Mil], 'throughout' [HNTC, LN]. The phrase διὰ παντὸς τοῦ ζῆν 'through all the living' is translated 'throughout the lifetime' [BAGD], 'all their lifetime' [KJV], 'all their life' [REB], 'all their lives' [WBC; NASB, NIV, NJB, NLT, NRSV, TEV, TNT], 'their whole life long' [NAB], 'their life long' [Lns], 'lifelong' [NIC], 'who live each day' [CEV].

d. pres. act. infin. of ζάω (LN 23.88) (BAGD 1.a.α. p. 336): 'to live' [LN; CEV]. This verb is also translated as a noun: 'life' [HNTC, Lns, WBC; all versions except CEV, KJV], 'lifetime' [BAGD, Mil; KJV]. This articular infinitive is used as a noun [Alf, Blm, EBC, Lns, My].

e. ἔνοχος (LN **37.5**) (BAGD 1. p. 267): 'subject to' [BAGD, HNTC, LN, Lns; KJV, NASB], 'liable to' [NIC]. The phrase ἔνοχοι ἦσαν δουλείας 'were subject to slavery' is translated 'were slaves' [TEV], 'had been slaves' [NAB], 'lived as slaves' [NLT], 'were held in slavery' [Mil, WBC; NIV, NRSV], 'had been held in slavery' [NJB, TNT], 'had been in servitude' [REB], not explicit [CEV]. It implies actual involvement [Alf, Blm], a permanent enslavement [HNTC, Hu].

f. δουλεία (LN 37.26) (BAGD 2. p. 205): 'slavery' [BAGD, LN, Lns, Mil, WBC; NASB, NIV, NJB, NRSV, TNT], 'servitude' [HNTC; REB], 'bondage' [KJV, NIC], 'subservience' [LN], not explicit [CEV].

QUESTION—Why is this clause mentioned?

1. It expresses a second purpose of the incarnation [HNTC, Lns, Mil, NIC, TH, WBC; all versions except TEV]: in order that he might destroy the devil and in order that he might set these people free.
2. It expresses the result of the preceding thought [My, NIGTC; TEV]: in order that he might destroy the devil and therefore might set these people free. It expresses the positive results of Christ's work [NIGTC].

QUESTION—What is τούτους 'these people' connected with?

It refers to (and emphasizes [Alf, My]) the following word ὅσοι 'as many as' [Alf, HNTC, Lg, Mil, My, NIC, WBC; all versions].

1. It refers to people in general [Alf, Lg, Lns], everyone who was thus held in bondage [Mil], to unredeemed mankind [My]: these people, namely as many as . . .
2. It refers to παιδία 'children' in 2:14 [Blm]: the children, as many as . . .

QUESTION—What relationship is indicated by the dative φόβῳ 'in fear'?

It is a dative of cause [EGT, Mil, My]: because of fear.

QUESTION—How are the two nouns related in the genitive construction φόβῳ θανάτου 'fear of death'?

It is an objective genitive [Alf, Mil]: they feared death. The death is both physical and spiritual [Blm].

2:16 For[a] not indeed[b] does-he-take-hold[c] of-angels but he-takes-hold[c] of-(the)-seed[d] of-Abraham.

LEXICON—a. γάρ (LN 89.23): 'for' [HNTC, LN, Lns, Mil, WBC; KJV, NASB, NIV, NJB, NRSV, TEV], 'because' [LN], not explicit [NIC; CEV, NAB, NLT, REB, TNT].

b. δήπου (LN **91.7**) (BAGD p. 179): 'indeed' [LN], 'surely' [BAGD, **LN**; NAB, NIV], 'assuredly' [NASB], 'certainly' [Lns], 'of course' [BAGD, HNTC, WBC], 'clearly' [REB, TNT], 'it is clear that' [NRSV, TEV], 'quite obviously' [Mil], 'verily' [KJV], 'then' [LN], 'you see' [NIC], 'we all know' [NLT], not explicit [NJB]. It implies decision and confidence applied universally [Alf]; it indicates a strong affirmation and assumes knowledge which the readers already have [EBC, NIGTC]; it assumes that the readers agree with the statement [EGT, ICC, Mil, My, TH, WBC, Wst].

c. pres. mid. (deponent = act.) of ἐπιλαμβάνομαι (LN **30.42; 35.1**) (BAGD 2.c. p. 295): 'to take hold' [NIC], 'to take hold to help' [WBC], 'to take helpful hold' [Lns], 'to take upon oneself to help' [Mil], 'to help' [BAGD, HNTC, **LN** (35.1); NIV, REB, TEV], 'to give help' [NASB], 'to come to help' [CEV, NAB, NLT, NRSV, TNT], 'to undertake to help' [Mil], 'to be concerned about' [LN (**30.42**)], 'to be concerned for' [LN (30.42)], 'to be concerned with' [BAGD], 'to take an interest in' [BAGD], 'to take on oneself' [KJV], 'to take to oneself' [NJB]. This verb is repeated for emphasis [NIGTC], for rhetorical effect [ICC] to emphasize the parallel [WBC]. The present tense refers to Christ's continual help [Lg, Lns, My, NIGTC, Wst].

d. σπέρμα (LN 10.29) (BAGD 2.b. p. 761): 'seed' [Lns; KJV], 'offspring' [HNTC, LN, Mil, NIC], 'children' [BAGD; NAB], 'descendants' [BAGD, LN, WBC; CEV, NIV, NLT, NRSV, REB, TEV, TNT], 'posterity' [BAGD, LN], 'line' [NJB]; as a singular noun: 'descendant' [NASB].

QUESTION—What relationship is indicated by γάρ 'for'?

It indicates a summary or conclusion of 2:10–15 [NIGTC]. It explains the reason for the incarnation (2:14) [Alf, Mil, My, NCBC, NIC, Wst]: he came to help Abraham's descendants. This verse functions as a parenthetical comment [ICC, WBC].

QUESTION—What is the meaning of ἐπιλαμβάνεται 'he takes hold'?

1. It means to take hold of to help [Alf, Blm, EGT, HNTC, ICC, Lg, Lns, Mil, My, NCBC, NIC, NTC, TH, WBC, Wst; all versions except KJV, NJB]: he did not help the angels; rather, he helped the descendants of Abraham. It has the idea of help and deliverance [NIC].
2. It means that he took on human nature [EBC, Hu; KJV]: he did not take on the nature of angels; instead, he took on the nature of the descendants of Abraham.
3. It means both taking on human nature and helping mankind [Hwt].

QUESTION—What is the significance of the absence of the definite article with 'angels' and 'seed'?

The absence of the definite article with 'angels' indicates angels as a class [Lg, My, NIGTC]. The absence of the definite article with 'seed of Abraham' indicates mankind as a class [My, NIGTC]. It refers to the character rather than to a specific person [Wst].

QUESTION—What is the meaning of the phrase σπέρματος Ἀβραάμ 'seed of Abraham'?

1. It refers to the Jewish race [Alf, EBC, Lg, Lns, My, TH].
2. It includes both Jews and Gentiles [Blm, GNC, HNTC, Hu, Hwt, ICC, Mil, My(D), NIC, NTC, TNTC, WBC, Wst]. It means the spiritual descendants of Abraham [Hwt, NTC, Wst]. They are the 'many sons' in 2:10 [NIC].

2:17 Therefore[a] he-ought[b] with-regard-to[c] everything to-be-made-like[d] the brothers,

LEXICON—a. ὅθεν (LN 84.11) (BAGD 3. p. 555): 'therefore' [BAGD, NIC; NAB, NASB, NLT, NRSV, REB], 'wherefore' [KJV], 'hence' [BAGD, Lns], 'from which' [LN], 'for this reason' [HNTC, Mil; NIV], 'this means that' [WBC; TEV], 'this is why' [TNT], not explicit [CEV, NJB].

b. imperf. act. indic. of ὀφείλω (LN 71.25; 71.35) (BAGD 2.a.β. p. 599): 'ought' [BAGD, LN (71.25)], 'must' [BAGD, LN (71.35)], 'to be obliged' [Lns], 'to be under obligation' [LN (71.25)], 'to behoove' [KJV], 'to be essential' [WBC; NJB], 'to have to' [LN (71.35), Mil; all versions except KJV, NJB], 'to be necessary' [LN (71.35); NIC; NLT], 'to be incumbent upon (one)' [HNTC]. This verb is also translated 'it behooved him' [KJV]. It refers to moral obligation [Alf, EBC, Hwt, NIGTC, WBC], an inner compulsion [TH], necessity based on the nature of the case [EGT, Mil, My].

c. κατά with accusative object (LN 89.4) (BAGD II.6. p. 407): 'with regard to' [LN], 'in relation to' [LN], 'in' [KJV, NAB, NASB], not explicit [CEV]. The phrase κατὰ πάντα 'according to everything' is translated 'in all respects' [BAGD, Lns, Mil, NIC; TNT], 'in every respect' [HNTC, WBC; NLT, NRSV], 'in every way' [NIV, REB, TEV], 'completely' [NJB]. This phrase is emphatic by word order [ICC, Lns, WBC]; it strengthens the verb ὁμοιωθῆναι 'to be made like' [NIGTC]. It refers to all things necessary to real human nature (except for sin) [Alf, Blm, EGT, GNC, Hu, Hwt, ICC, Lns, My, NIC, NTC, TNTC, WBC], absolute similarity [HNTC], with the exception that his birth, his sinless life, and his death were different from mankind's [Hwt]; it emphasizes the extent of the similarity [Mil]. He shared in their circumstances, trials, sorrows, and pain [TNTC, Wst].

d. aorist pass. infin. of ὁμοιόω (LN 64.4) (BAGD 1. p. 567): 'to be made like' [HNTC, Lns, Mil, NIC, WBC; KJV, NASB, NIV, NJB, REB, TNT], 'to become like' [BAGD; NAB, NRSV, TEV], 'to be like' [LN; NLT], 'to resemble, to be similar to' [LN], 'to be' [CEV]. The meaning is to be made like [HNTC, Lg, Lns, Mil, NIC, NTC, TNTC, WBC; KJV, NASB, NIV, NJB, REB, TNT]; it means to *become* like [NAB, NRSV, TEV]; it means to *be* like [Alf]. The aorist tense implies that the likeness occurred at a specific time [Alf].

QUESTION—What relationship is indicated by ὅθεν 'therefore'?

1. It indicates a conclusion based on 2:16 [Blm, EGT, Hu, Lns, NTC, TH]: since he helps men, therefore he had to be made like them.
2. It introduces a summary of 2:10–16 [NCBC, NIGTC, WBC]: this means that he had to be made like his brothers.
3. It introduces a restatement of 2:14 [ICC, TNTC].

QUESTION—To whom does τοῖς ἀδελφοῖς 'the brothers' refer?

It includes both the race of Israel and all mankind [Alf, TH], the community of believers [WBC]. With the article, it refers to the brothers previously mentioned [NIGTC].

in-order-that[a] he-might-become a-merciful[b] and faithful[c] high-priest (in) the (things) pertaining-to[d] the God,

LEXICON—a. ἵνα (LN 89.59): 'in order that' [LN, Mil, WBC; NIV], 'in order to' [Lns; TEV], 'so that' [LN; CEV, NJB, NLT, NRSV, REB], 'that' [HNTC, LN; KJV, NAB, NASB], 'so as' [NIC]. This entire clause is translated 'that he might serve God as a high priest with compassion and faithfulness' [TNT]. It introduces one purpose for Christ's becoming a high priest [EBC, EGT, Mil, Wst], his purpose in becoming united with mankind [WBC].

b. ἐλεήμων (LN 88.77) (BAGD p. 250): 'merciful' [BAGD, HNTC, LN, Lns, Mil, NIC, WBC; all versions except NJB, TNT], 'sympathetic' [BAGD], 'compassionate' [NJB], 'with compassion' [TNT]. This word refers to Christ's relationship to mankind [Blm, HNTC, Hu, Hwt, Lg, Lns, NTC, Wst]. It is emphatic by word order [EBC, ICC, Lns]. It defines Christ's motivation as high priest [Hu]. It is the quality which enables him to become a faithful high priest [My].

c. πιστός (LN 31.87) (BAGD 1.a.α. p. 664): 'faithful' [BAGD, HNTC, LN, Lns, Mil, NIC, WBC; all versions except NJB, TNT], 'trustworthy' [LN; NJB], 'dependable' [LN], 'reliable' [BAGD, LN], 'with faithfulness' [TNT]. This word refers to Christ's faithfulness to God [Blm, HNTC, Hu, Hwt, Lg, Lns, Mil, NIGTC, NTC, TH]. The meaning is that he was true to God and to mankind in his office [Alf, EGT]; he was trustworthy [Alf, Blm, EGT, Wst]; he faithfully executed his office [Hu, My, NTC, TNTC]; he faithfully endured temptation [ICC]. The meaning is that he trusted in God [EBC].

d. πρός with accusative object (LN 89.7) (BAGD III.5.b. p. 710): 'pertaining to' [Lns, Mil; NASB], 'with regard to' [LN], 'in' [KJV]. The phrase τὰ πρὸς τὸν θεόν 'the things pertaining to God' is translated 'that which concerns God' [BAGD], 'with reference to what concerns God' [BAGD], 'in service to God' [NIV], 'in his service to God' [TEV], 'in the service of God' [WBC; NRSV], 'so that he could serve God' [CEV], 'before God' [NLT, REB], 'before God on their behalf' [NAB], 'for their relationship to God' [NJB], 'in relation to God' [HNTC], 'where their responsibility to God is concerned' [NIC]. This phrase refers to mankind's relations to God [EGT, HNTC, NCBC, Wst], to Christ's mediation for the people to God [Hu, NCBC].

QUESTION—What is implied by γένηται 'he might become' with reference to his priesthood?

1. It means 'to become' [Alf; NASB, NIV, NJB] and refers to the fact that Christ's priesthood was not fully inaugurated until he returned to heaven [Alf].
2. It simply means 'to be' [HNTC; KJV, NAB, NLT, NRSV, REB, TEV].

QUESTION—What is ἐλεήμων 'merciful' connected with?

1. It is parallel to πιστός 'faithful' [Alf, Blm, EGT, GNC, HNTC, Hu, ICC, Lg, Mil, NIGTC, NTC, TNTC, Wst; all versions]: a merciful and faithful high priest.
2. It stands alone [Lns, My]: be merciful, and be a faithful high priest. The καί 'and' means 'and as a result' [My].

QUESTION—What is the phrase τὰ πρὸς τὸν θεόν 'the things pertaining to God' connected with?

1. It is connected with the entire phrase ἐλεήμων καὶ πιστὸς ἀρχιερεύς 'a merciful and faithful high priest' [Alf, Lg]: a merciful and faithful high priest in the things pertaining to God.
2. It relates only to πιστός 'faithful' [EGT, Lns, Mil, TNTC]: a faithful high priest in the things pertaining to God.

for-the-purpose-of[a] the expiating/propitiating[b] the sins of-the people.

LEXICON—a. εἰς with accusative object (LN 89.57): 'for the purpose of' [LN], 'for' [CEV], 'in order to' [LN, Mil], 'so as' [Lns], 'so that' [TEV], 'with a view to' [NIC], 'then' [NLT]. The phrase εἰς τὸ ἱλάσκεσθαι 'for the purpose of expiating' is translated 'to make expiation' [REB], 'to expiate' [HNTC; NAB], 'able to expiate' [NJB], 'to make propitiation' [Mil, WBC; NASB], 'to make reconciliation' [Mil; KJV], 'and that he might make atonement' [NIV], 'to make a sacrifice of atonement' [NRSV], 'and so take away' [TNT]. This phrase expresses the purpose of Christ's priesthood [Blm, EGT, Mil, NTC], the purpose of his faithfulness in the things pertaining to God [Lns].

b. pres. mid. (deponent = act.) of ἱλάσκομαι (LN **40.9**) (BAGD 2. p. 375): 'to expiate' [BAGD, HNTC, Lns; NAB, NJB], 'to make expiation' [REB], 'to make propitiation' [Mil, WBC; NASB], 'to make reconciliation' [Mil; KJV], 'to make atonement' [NIC; NIV], 'to make a sacrifice of atonement' [NRSV], 'to offer a sacrifice that would take away the sins' [NLT], 'to take away' [TNT]; as a passive voice: 'to be forgiven'

[**LN**; TEV]. This verb is also translated as a noun: 'forgiveness' [CEV]. The present tense implies the continuous effect of Christ's work [EGT, Lns, NIGTC, NTC, Wst].

QUESTION—What is the meaning of ἱλάσκεσθαι 'to expiate/propitiate'?

1. The meaning is to expiate (to atone for) sins [HNTC, Lns, NCBC, NIC, NIGTC; NAB, NJB, REB] so as to bring forgiveness [Blm, HNTC, ICC, Lg, Mil, NCBC, NIC, TH, Wst; TEV]; it means to take away sins [TNT]. Propitiation is not a biblical concept [HNTC, Lg, Lns, NCBC].
2. The meaning is to propitiate God [EBC, Hu, TNTC, WBC]. The accusative noun phrase τὰς ἁμαρτίας 'the sins' means 'with respect to the sins' [WBC].

2.1 The propitiation was to remove God's wrath against sinners [EBC]; it was to remove God's wrath against sin [Hu].

2.2 It was not to remove God's wrath, for God himself provided the propitiation [TNTC]; through Christ's work God propitiated himself [Hu].

3. The meaning is to make reconciliation [Hwt; KJV].
4. The meaning is to make atonement [NIV], a sacrifice of atonement [NRSV].

QUESTION—To whom does τοῦ λαοῦ 'of the people' refer?

1. It refers to the Jewish people [Alf, Mil, My].
2. It refers to the Jewish people but also to the Gentiles [Lns, Wst], to all of God's people [TH].
3. It refers to the people for whom Christ died [EBC], the whole family of God [HNTC], the Christian community [NIGTC, WBC], God's elect people [NTC].

2:18 For[a] in[b] that/what[c] he-himself has-suffered[d] having-been-tempted/tested,[e] he-is-able to-help[f] the-(ones) being-tempted/tested.[g]

LEXICON—a. γάρ (LN 89.23): 'for' [HNTC, LN, Lns, Mil, NIC; KJV, NASB, NJB], 'because' [LN], not explicit [WBC; CEV, NAB, NIV, NLT, NRSV, REB, TEV, TNT].

b. ἐν with dative object (LN 89.26; 89.76) (BAGD IV.6.d. p. 261): 'in' [HNTC, Lns, Mil; KJV], 'by' [LN 89.76], 'because' [BAGD], 'because of' [LN 89.26], not explicit [CEV]. The phrase ἐν ᾧ 'in that' is translated 'since' [NIC; NAB, NASB, NLT], 'because' [WBC; NIV, NRSV, REB, TEV, TNT], 'wherein' [Mil]. The phrase ἐν ᾧ πέπονθεν αὐτὸς 'in that he himself has suffered' is translated 'the suffering he himself passed through' [NJB].

c. ὅς (LN 92.27): 'that' [HNTC, Lns; KJV], 'which' [LN], 'what respects' [Mil], not explicit [CEV].

d. perf. act. indic. of πάσχω (LN 24.78) (BAGD 3.a.α. p. 634): 'to suffer' [BAGD, HNTC, LN, Lns, Mil; all versions except NJB, NLT, REB], 'to go through suffering' [NLT], 'to suffer death' [WBC]. The phrase πέπονθεν πειρασθείς 'has suffered having been tempted/tested' is translated 'endured trial and suffering' [NIC], 'has passed through the test of suffering' [REB], 'he was tested through what he suffered' [NAB]. The perfect tense indicates a lasting effect [Mil, NTC, Wst], the fact that his past sufferings resulted in present and continuing compassion and understanding [Hu]. It refers to his sufferings throughout his life on earth, including the cross [EBC, Lns, NIGTC]; it refers especially to the sufferings that led to the cross [ICC].

e. aorist pass. participle of πειράζω (LN 88.308) (BAGD 2.b. p. 640): 'to be tempted' [HNTC, LN, Lns, Mil; CEV, KJV, NASB, NIV, TEV], 'to go through temptation' [NLT], 'to be tested' [NAB, NRSV, TNT], 'to be tried' [BAGD], 'to be made trial of' [BAGD], 'to be put to the test' [BAGD, WBC; NJB]. The aorist tense refers to the fact of his suffering [Lns, Wst].

f. aorist pass. infin. of βοηθέω (LN 35.1) (BAGD 2. p. 144): 'to help' [BAGD, HNTC, Lns, NIC, WBC; all versions except KJV, NASB], 'to come to the aid of' [BAGD, Mil; NASB], 'to succor' [KJV]. The aorist tense focuses on the act of coming to help [Wst].

g. pres. pass. participle of πειράζω (LN 88.308) (BAGD 2.b. p. 640): 'to be tempted' [HNTC, LN, Lns, Mil; CEV, KJV, NAB, NASB, NIV, NLT, TEV], 'to be tested' [WBC; NRSV, TNT], 'to be put to the test' [NJB], 'to endure trial' [NIC]. The phrase τοῖς πειραζομένοις 'the ones being tempted/tested' is translated 'those who are in the midst of their test' [REB]. The present tense refers to repeated and continuing temptations [Lg, Lns, Mil, NTC, Wst].

QUESTION—What relationship is indicated by γάρ 'for'?

It indicates the reason that Christ's becoming like the brothers enabled him to become a merciful and faithful high priest [Alf, EBC, EGT, GNC, Mil, My, TNTC]: it is because he was tempted/tested as the brothers were that he is able to help them. It indicates the author's pastoral concern [NIGTC]. It clarifies 4:17 by making explicit that Christ's dealing with sin is based on his death [NIGTC].

QUESTION—What is the meaning of the phrase ἐν ᾧ 'in that'?

1. It is causal [EGT, Hu, ICC, Lg, My, NIC, NIGTC, TNTC, WBC; all versions except KJV]: because he was tempted/tested.
2. It refers to the area in which he was tempted/tested [Alf, Wst; KJV]: in the thing in which he was tempted/tested. The implication is that Christ's sympathy is as far-reaching as his experience, including the whole range of human life [Wst].

QUESTION—What is implied by αὐτός 'he himself'?

It is emphatic, implying that it was contrary to what was expected [EBC]: he himself suffered. It is connected with πειρασθείς 'having been tempted/tested', emphasizing that he himself has been tempted [Lns, My]. It is connected closely with both 'he has suffered' and 'having been tempted' [Wst]. These words receive the emphasis [My].

QUESTION—What relationship is indicated by the aorist participle πειρασθείς 'having been tempted/tested'?

1. It expresses the means of the suffering [Blm, ICC, Mil; NAB, NRSV, TNT]: he suffered by means of being tempted/tested. The suffering consisted of temptations [Mil].
2. It expresses an action parallel to 'suffered' [HNTC, NIC, TH; TEV]: he suffered and was tempted.
3. It expresses the cause of the suffering [EGT]: he suffered because he was tempted.
4. It expresses the time when he suffered [NIV, NJB]: he suffered when he was tempted.
5. It expresses the area in which he suffered [Alf; NASB]: he was tempted in what he suffered. All of Christ's sufferings were a temptation [Alf].
6. It identifies the test [REB]: the test of suffering.

QUESTION—What is the meaning of the two participles πειρασθείς 'having been tempted' and τοῖς πειραζομένοις 'the ones being tempted'?

1. Both have a negative sense, referring to temptation [EBC, EGT, HNTC, Hu, ICC, Lns, Mil, TH; KJV, NASB, NIV, TEV]: having been tempted . . . the ones who are being tempted. Jesus was tempted to avoid the suffering that ended in his crucifixion and people are tempted to give up their faith to avoid hardships [ICC].
2. The first refers to testing in a neutral sense; the second has the negative sense of tempting [NAB]: having been tested . . . the ones who are being tempted.
3. Both have the neutral sense of testing [Blm, NIC, WBC; NJB, NRSV, REB, TNT]: having been put to the test . . . being put to the test.
4. Both primarily indicate testing, with tempting as an included secondary meaning [NIGTC].
5. The temptations were those of all of his earthly life [NCBC, NIC, NTC], especially his temptations in the wilderness by Satan at the beginning of his ministry [NTC].

QUESTION—What is implied by δύναται 'he is able'?

It means more than that he helps; because he has suffered, he is *able* to help [EBC, My, NIGTC, Wst]. The present tense indicates his continuing ability [Lns, NIGTC].

DISCOURSE UNIT: 3:1–5:10 [NIGTC, WBC; NAB, NJB, REB]. The topic is the Son's character as high priest [WBC], Jesus as the faithful high priest [REB], the faithful and compassionate high priest [NIGTC; NAB, NJB].

DISCOURSE UNIT: 3:1–4:16 [Wst]. The topic is Moses, Joshua, and Jesus, founders of the old and new economies.

DISCOURSE UNIT: 3:1–4:13 [Hu, Hwt, Lg, Mil, NIC]. The topic is Christ the Son as superior to Moses [Hu, Hwt, Lg, Mil] and to Joshua [Lg]; the true home of God's people [NIC].

DISCOURSE UNIT: 3:1–19 [Lns, NTC, TNTC; NLT]. The topic is a warning against hardening their hearts [Lns], the superiority of Jesus to Moses [NTC, TNTC], Jesus greater than Moses [NLT].

DISCOURSE UNIT: 3:1–11 [NASB]. The topic is Jesus our high priest.

DISCOURSE UNIT: 3:1–6 [EBC, GNC, GNT, HNTC, Hwt, Lg, Lns, Mil, NCBC, NIC, NIGTC, NTC, TNTC, WBC, Wst; NAB, NIV, NJB, TEV]. The topic is the faithfulness of Christ [NIGTC], Jesus superior to Moses [EBC, GNC, GNT, NIC; NAB, NIV, NJB, TEV], the Son and Builder superior to the servant [Hwt], an exhortation to be faithful to Christ based on his superiority over Moses [Lg], Jesus in comparison with Moses [Lns, Mil, NCBC, NTC], Son, not servant [HNTC], Jesus the Son and Moses the servant [TNTC, Wst], Jesus a high priest worthy of our trust because he is the faithful Son of God [WBC].

3:1 Therefore,[a] holy[b] brothers, partakers[c] of-a-heavenly[d] calling,[e]

LEXICON—a. ὅθεν (LN 84.11) (BAGD 3. p. 555): 'therefore' [BAGD, HNTC, Mil, NIC; NAB, NASB, NIV, NRSV, REB], 'wherefore' [KJV], 'hence' [BAGD, Lns], 'for which reason' [BAGD], 'for this reason' [WBC], 'that is why' [NJB], 'from which' [LN], 'and so' [NLT, TNT], 'so' [CEV], not explicit [TEV].

b. ἅγιος (LN 53.46; 88.24) (BAGD 1.b.α. p. 9): 'holy' [BAGD, LN, Lns, Mil, NIC, WBC; CEV, KJV, NAB, NASB, NIV, NJB, NRSV], 'consecrated' [HNTC], 'in the family of God' [REB], 'whom God has set apart for himself' [TNT]. The phrase ἀδελφοὶ ἅγιοι 'holy brothers' is translated 'members of a holy brotherhood' [NIC], 'Christian friends' [TEV], 'dear friends who belong to God' [NLT].

c. μέτοχος (LN 34.8) (BAGD 1. p. 514): 'partaker' [Mil, NIC; KJV, NASB], 'partner' [LN; NRSV, REB], 'companion' [LN], 'sharer' [Lns], 'those who share' [HNTC; NAB, NIV, NJB], not explicit [CEV, NLT, TEV]. This noun is also translated as a verb: 'to share' [BAGD, WBC; TNT]. It further identifies the 'holy brothers' [Mil] and strengthens the reference [My]. The sharing is among fellow Christians [NIGTC, TH].

d. ἐπουράνιος (LN 1.12; **12.17**) (BAGD 1.a.δ. p. 306): 'heavenly' [BAGD, HNTC, LN (1.12), Lns, Mil, NIC, WBC; KJV, NAB, NASB, NIV, NJB, NRSV, REB], 'pertaining to heaven, in heaven' [LN (1.12)], 'the life of heaven' [TNT], 'from God' [**LN** (12.17)]. This adjective is also translated as a noun: 'God' [CEV, TEV]. The phrase κλήσεως ἐπουρανίου μέτοχοι 'partakers of a heavenly calling' is translated 'who are bound for heaven' [NLT]. It means that the calling has a heavenly source [Blm, EGT, Lg, My], it is of a heavenly nature [HNTC, NIC], it comes from God [EBC, Hu, Lns, Wst; CEV, TEV]. Christ from heaven calls Christians to heaven [NIGTC]. It indicates that Christians are called to heaven [HNTC, Hu], into God's presence [WBC]. It refers to perfection in heaven [Hu]. It is heavenly in origin, in quality, and in its goal [Mil].

e. κλῆσις (LN 33.312; 33.313) (BAGD 1. p. 435): 'calling' [BAGD, HNTC, LN (33.313), Lns, Mil, NIC, WBC; KJV, NAB, NASB, NIV, NRSV, REB], 'call' [BAGD; NJB], not explicit [NLT]. This noun is also translated as a verb: 'to be called' [TEV, TNT], 'to choose' [CEV]. It is a call from God [Hu, TH, TNTC] to come into his presence [WBC]. It is God's call to his kingdom [My, NTC] through the Gospel message [Blm].

QUESTION—What relationship is indicated by ὅθεν 'therefore'?

It indicates a conclusion from the preceding thought [Alf, EGT, Hu, Hwt, Lg, Lns, Mil, My, NIGTC, NTC, TH, WBC, Wst], the reason for considering Jesus [Alf, EGT]. It refers to 2:5–18 [Lns, Wst].

QUESTION—What is meant by the phrase ἀδελφοὶ ἅγιοι 'holy brothers'?

The reference is to the brotherhood of believers [Alf, Blm, GNC, Lg]. The phrase indicates affection and consecration [EBC, HNTC], familiarity and respect [TNTC]. They are personally dear to the writer [EBC], closely related through their common faith [HNTC]. The word 'holy' implies separation from the world [EGT], chosen and set apart by God [Hu], dedicated to God [EGT, HNTC, Mil, NCBC, NIC, WBC], and set apart for God's service [EBC, HNTC]. It also implies separation from sin [Hwt, NTC] making them fit to enter God's presence [NTC], an obligation to share God's holy character [Mil]. It refers to the ideal, not necessarily already attained [TNTC, Wst]. It refers to the collective destiny for the body of believers rather than present reality [HNTC, Lg(K), NCBC]. The phrase is emphatic [NIGTC].

QUESTION—How are the two nouns related in the genitive construction κλήσεως ἐπουρανίου μέτοχοι 'partakers of a heavenly calling'?

The genitive noun κλήσεως 'calling' tells what they partake of, but none of the commentaries mention this point: they share a heavenly calling.

consider[a] the apostle[b] and high-priest[c] of-our confession[d] Jesus,

TEXT—Some manuscripts add Χριστόν 'Christ' before Ἰησοῦν 'Jesus'. GNT does not deal with this variant. 'Christ' is added by only KJV.

LEXICON—a. aor. act. impera. of κατανοέω (LN **30.4**) (BAGD 3. p. 415): 'to consider' [BAGD, LN, Mil, NIC; KJV, NASB, NRSV], 'to consider thoroughly' [Lns], 'to observe' [WBC], 'to think of' [REB, TEV], 'to think on' [HNTC], 'to think about' [CEV, NLT, TNT], 'to fix one's eyes on' [NAB], 'to fix the eyes of one's spirit upon' [BAGD], 'to fix one's thoughts on' [NIV], 'to turn one's mind to' [NJB]. It means to consider attentively [Alf, Blm, Hu, NCBC, NIGTC, NTC, TNTC, Wst] so as to see the significance [EGT, GNC, Hwt, Lg, Mil, My] and to hold fast to [My]. The prefixed κατα- is an intensifier [Lns, NTC].

b. ἀπόστολος (LN 53.74) (BAGD 2. p. 99): 'apostle' [LN, Lns, Mil, NIC, WBC; all versions except NLT, TEV], 'envoy' [HNTC], 'special messenger' [LN], 'God's messenger' [NLT], 'whom God sent' [TEV]. It indicates that Jesus represents God among mankind [GNC, NIC], that Jesus was sent by God [EGT, GNC, HNTC, Hu, Lns, NTC, Wst] with authority to speak for God [ICC, NTC]. It refers primarily to the incarnation [HNTC]. It indicates the authority for the 'heavenly calling' [Wst].

c. ἀρχιερεύς (LN 53.89) (BAGD 2.a. p. 113): 'high priest' [HNTC, LN, Lns, Mil, NIC, WBC; all versions]. It refers primarily to his atoning death [HNTC]. It indicates that Jesus represents mankind to God [GNC, NIC]. It indicates the source for their being called 'holy' [Wst].

d. ὁμολογία (LN 33.274) (BAGD 2. p. 568): 'confession' [BAGD, LN, Lns, Mil, WBC; NASB, NRSV], 'profession' [KJV], 'profession of faith' [NJB]. The phrase τῆς ὁμολογίας ἡμῶν 'of our confession' is translated 'whom we confess' [NIC; NIV], 'whom we declare to be' [NLT], 'of the faith we profess' [REB, TEV], 'of the faith which we profess' [HNTC], 'whom we acknowledge in faith' [NAB], 'of our religion' [TNT], 'the one we call' [CEV]. It refers to the content of the faith we confess [Alf, GNC, HNTC, ICC, My, NCBC, NIGTC, TH, WBC, Wst; NJB, REB, TEV, TNT], to the act of confessing our Christian faith [HNTC, ICC; NJB], to the person whom we confess, Jesus [EGT, NIC, TNTC; NAB, NIV]. It means an open acknowledgment of our faith [HNTC]. They confess Jesus [Lns, Mil; NAB, NIV]. They acknowledge their allegiance to him [TNTC]. They confess that Jesus is Lord [NTC]. They acknowledge that Jesus is the Son of God [WBC].

QUESTION—What are they to consider about Jesus?

They are to consider the fact that Jesus, who is the apostle and high priest of our calling, was faithful to God [ICC, Lns, WBC; NRSV]. They are to consider Jesus' claim to be the superior high priest [TNTC]. They are to consider Jesus as being their faithful apostle and high priest [Wst].

QUESTION—How are the nouns related in the genitive construction τὸν ἀπόστολον καὶ ἀρχιερέα τῆς ὁμολογίας 'the apostle and high priest of the confession'?

The genitive noun ὁμολογίας 'confession' expresses the reference to which ἀπόστολον 'apostle' [Wst] and ἀρχιερέα 'high priest' refer [TH, Wst]: the apostle and high priest who are involved in our confession. The fact that the one definite article covers both 'apostle' and 'high priest' shows that both nouns refer to Jesus [Alf, EGT, Lns, Mil, My, WBC, Wst] and indicates that Jesus is both apostle and high priest [WBC]. This phrase identifies Jesus [Mil]. Jesus has two functions: he represents God to humans as apostle and he represents humans to God as high priest [NIC]. Another view is that 'apostle' and 'high priest' are a hendiadys, expressing one thought [NIGTC]: a sent high priest.

QUESTION—What is implied by the word order of Ἰησοῦν 'Jesus'?

It is emphatic by its position at the close of the clause [GNC, Mil, NCBC, WBC], by its use without other titles [NIGTC]. It also links this verse with the following verse [NIGTC], marks the beginning of the following argument of the superiority of Jesus to Moses [Mil].

3:2 being faithful[a] to-the-(one) having-appointed/made[b] him as[c] Moses also in[d] all his house.[e]

TEXT—Some manuscripts omit ὅλῳ 'all'. GNT includes this word within brackets in its text with a C decision, indicating that the committee had difficulty in deciding whether to include or omit this word. 'All' is omitted by GNC, HNTC, Hu, ICC, NIGTC, TH, TNTC, WBC, REB and TEV.

LEXICON—a. πιστός (LN 31.87) (BAGD 1.a.α. p. 664): 'faithful' [BAGD, HNTC, LN, Lns, Mil, NIC, WBC; all versions except NJB], 'trustworthy' [LN; NJB], 'dependable' [BAGD, LN], 'reliable' [LN]. This word is emphatic [Hu] by word order [Ed].

b. aor. act. participle of ποιέω (LN 37.106) (BAGD I.1.a.β. p. 681): 'to appoint' [HNTC, Mil, NIC, WBC; all versions except TEV], 'to assign to a task' [LN 37.106], 'to choose to do (a) work' [TEV], 'to make one what one is' [Lns], 'to make' [BAGD]. The agent is God [NIGTC].

c. ὡς (LN 64.12): 'as' [HNTC, LN, Mil, WBC; KJV, NASB, REB], 'even as' [Lns], 'just as' [NIC; CEV, NIV, NLT, NRSV, TEV, TNT], 'just like' [NJB], 'like' [LN], not explicit [NAB]. It introduces a comparison [Mil] of Jesus with Moses [NIGTC, Wst]; it introduces the similarity of Jesus and Moses in this regard [Hu].

d. ἐν with dative object (LN 83.13): 'in' [HNTC, LN, Lns, Mil, NIC, WBC; all versions except NLT]. The phrase 'in all his house' is translated 'and was entrusted with God's entire house' [NLT]. It introduces the place in which the faithfulness occurred [Mil, My].

e. οἶκος (LN 7.2; 10.8) (BAGD 2. p. 561): 'house' [LN 7.2, Lns, Mil, NIC, WBC; KJV, NASB, NIV, NLT, NRSV, TEV], 'household' [BAGD, HNTC, LN (10.8); NAB, NJB, REB, TNT], 'family' [BAGD, LN (10.8)], 'God's people' [CEV]. The meaning is the family [Blm, Hu, ICC, Lg, NIC, NTC], the people [EBC, GNC], the organized society [EGT, Wst].

QUESTION—What relationship is indicated by the participle ὄντα 'being'?

1. It further describes Jesus [Alf, EGT, HNTC, Hu, Lns, NCBC, Wst; all versions except NLT, NRSV].

1.1 It is used in a (nonrestrictive) attributive sense to describe the Son further [EGT; KJV, NAB]: Jesus, who was faithful.

1.2 With its predicate πιστόν 'faithful', it describes the characteristic which they were to consider concerning Jesus [Lns, Wst]: consider Jesus, as being faithful.

1.3 It is expressed as a separate statement [HNTC; CEV, NASB, NIV, NJB, REB, TEV, TNT]: consider Jesus; he was faithful.

2. It indicates a reason for considering Jesus [Mil; NLT]: consider Jesus, because he was faithful.

3. It is used as the predicate of an indirect statement [ICC, Lns, WBC; NRSV]: consider that Jesus was faithful.

QUESTION—What does the present tense of the participle ὄντα 'being' imply? It implies the Son's general character [Alf, My]: he is faithful. It includes his earthly life and his continuing high-priestly office [My, NTC].

QUESTION—What is the meaning of ποιήσαντι 'having appointed/made'?

1. It refers to the Son's appointment to his task [GNC, Hu, ICC, My(D), TH, WBC; all versions except TEV] as apostle and high priest [EBC, EGT, HNTC, Hwt, Mil, NCBC, NIC, NTC, Wst]. God made (constituted [Blm, TNTC]) him apostle and high priest [Alf, Blm, Lns]. God chose him for his task [TEV].
2. It refers to God's placing him in history [Lg].
3. It means that God created him, either in his generation as Firstborn or in his incarnation [My].

QUESTION—What is the phrase ἐν ὅλῳ τῷ οἴκῳ 'in all the house' connected with?

1. It is connected with Moses [Alf, Blm, EBC, EGT, GNC, HNTC, Hwt, ICC, Lg, Lns, Mil, My, NIC, NTC, TH, TNTC; all versions].
1.1 Moses was faithful in God's house [Alf, Blm, EBC, EGT, GNC, HNTC, Hwt, ICC, Lg, Mil, My, NIC, NTC, TH, TNTC; NAB, NASB, NIV, REB, TEV, TNT].
1.2 Moses was faithful in his own house [Lns].
2. It is connected with Jesus [Wst]: Jesus was faithful in God's house.
3. It is connected with τῷ ποιήσαντι αὐτόν 'the one having appointed him' [WBC]: God appointed Jesus in his house.

3:3 For/But[a] this-person has-been-considered-worthy[b] of-more glory[c] beyond[d] Moses,

LEXICON—a. γάρ (LN 89.23): 'for' [LN, Lns, Mil, WBC; KJV, NASB], 'because' [LN], 'yet' [NRSV], 'but' [CEV, NAB, NJB, NLT, REB, TNT], 'in fact' [NIC], not explicit [HNTC; NIV, TEV].

b. perf. pass. indic. of ἀξιόω (LN 65.18) (BAGD 1.a. p. 78): 'to be considered worthy' [BAGD, LN, WBC], 'to be counted worthy' [HNTC; KJV, NASB, REB, TNT], 'to be counted as worthy' [Lns], 'to be deemed worthy' [NIC], 'to be regarded as worthy' [LN], 'to be found worthy' [Mil; NIV], 'to be considered as deserving' [BAGD], 'to be considered as meriting' [LN]. The passive voice is also translated as active: 'to be worthy of' [NAB, NRSV, TEV], 'to deserve' [CEV, NJB, NLT]. This word implies both Christ's being considered worthy and his being bestowed with the worthiness at his exaltation to God's right hand [Alf, Wst]. The perfect tense implies that the worthiness continues [Mil, NIGTC, Wst], beginning with Christ's exaltation [NIGTC]. The agent is God [NIGTC].

c. δόξα (LN 33.357; 87.4): 'glory' [HNTC, Lns, NIC, WBC; KJV, NASB, NJB, NLT, NRSV], 'honor' [LN 87.4, Mil; CEV, NAB, NIV, REB, TEV, TNT], 'praise' [LN 33.357]. The reference is to the glory of the respective positions of Christ and Moses [Lg].

d. παρά with accusative object (LN 78.29) (BAGD III.3. p. 611): 'beyond' [BAGD, LN], 'more than' [BAGD, LN; NLT], 'to a greater degree than' [LN], 'than' [HNTC, Lns, Mil, NIC, WBC; all versions except NLT], 'in comparison to' [BAGD]. This construction indicates a comparison [Alf, NIGTC], implying a greater degree [NIGTC].

QUESTION—What relationship is indicated by γάρ 'for/but'?

1. It indicates the reason [KJV, NASB] for considering Jesus [Alf, Blm, EGT, Lg, Mil, My, NIGTC, TNTC, WBC, Wst]: fix your attention on Jesus, for he is far more exalted than Moses. It is indirectly connected with the whole preceding argument concerning Christ's supremacy [NIGTC].
2. It indicates a contrast with the preceding verse [CEV, NAB, NJB, NLT, NRSV, REB, TNT]: Jesus and Moses are similar, but Jesus is worthy of more honor. This introduces the first contrast between Jesus and Moses [TH].
3. It explains the significance of the titles of Jesus mentioned in 3:1 and explains what must be noted in considering his faithfulness [Lns].

QUESTION—Who does οὗτος 'this person' refer to?

It refers to the person being discussed, Jesus [Alf, Blm, EBC, EGT, HNTC, Hu, Hwt, ICC, Lg, Mil, My, NIC, NIGTC, NTC, TH, TNTC, WBC, Wst; NASB, NIV, NLT, NRSV, REB, TEV, TNT]. It is emphatic by its unusual word order [NIGTC].

QUESTION—What time relationship is implied by the perfect tense verb ἠξίωται 'has been considered worthy'?

1. It focuses on a state continuing at the time when this epistle was written [Wst; NAB, NLT, NRSV, TEV, TNT]: he is now in that state of worthiness.
2. It focuses on a state existing at a time prior to the writing of this epistle [Alf, Lns, NIC; KJV, NASB, NIV, REB]: he was previously placed in that state of worthiness.

QUESTION—What is implied by πλείονος 'more'?

1. It implies a greater degree [EGT, GNC, Mil, NIC, NIGTC, NTC, WBC; NIV, REB, TEV, TNT]: a higher level of honor.
2. It implies a greater quantity [Alf, EBC, HNTC, Hwt, Lns, Wst; KJV, NASB, NRSV]: more honor.

in accordance with[a] as-much-as[b] the-(one) having-built/founded[c] it has more honor[d] than-the house/household;

LEXICON—a. κατά with accusative object (LN 89.8) (BAGD II.5.a.δ.): 'in accordance with' [LN], 'by' [Lns, Mil; NASB]. The phrase καθ' ὅσον 'in accordance with as much as' is translated 'inasmuch as' [BAGD, NIC; KJV], 'in so far as' [BAGD], 'in the same measure as' [WBC], 'to the extent that' [HNTC], 'just as' [CEV, NIV, NJB, NLT, NRSV, TNT], 'as' [NAB, REB], 'in the same way' [TEV].

b. ὅσος (LN 59.19; 78.52) (BAGD 3. p. 586): 'as much as' [LN 59.19; 78.52], 'so much as' [Lns, Mil], 'to the degree that' [LN 78.52], 'just so much' [NASB].

c. aor. act. participle of κατασκευάζω (LN 45.1) (BAGD 2. p. 418): 'to build' [BAGD, LN; KJV, NLT, TEV], 'to construct' [BAGD, Lns], 'to establish' [Mil],. The phrase ὁ κατασκευάσας 'the one having built' is translated 'the builder' [NIC, WBC; CEV, NASB, NIV, NJB, NRSV], 'the founder' [HNTC; NAB, REB, TNT]. The builder is Jesus prior to his incarnation [NIGTC].

d. τιμή (LN 87.4) (BAGD 2.b. p. 817): 'honor' [BAGD, HNTC, LN, Lns, Mil, NIC, WBC; CEV, KJV, NASB, NIV, NRSV, REB, TEV], 'respect' [BAGD, LN]. The phrase πλείονα τιμὴν ἔχει 'has more honor' is translated 'is more honorable' [NAB], 'is more honored' [NJB], 'is more than' [TNT], 'deserves more praise' [NLT]. Here it is synonymous with δόξα 'glory' earlier in the verse [NIGTC].

QUESTION—What relationship is indicated by the phrase καθ' ὅσον 'in accordance with as much as'?

1. It expresses a comparison [Lns, NIC, NTC, TH; CEV, NAB, NIV, NJB, NLT, NRSV, REB, TEV, TNT]: just as the builder/founder has more honor than the house.
2. It expresses degree [HNTC, Mil, WBC; NASB]: by as much as the builder/founder has more honor than the house.

QUESTION—What is meant by ὁ κατασκευάσα…τού οἴκου 'the one having built/founded . . . the house/household'?

1. It means the one who built the house [Hu, NTC, TNTC, WBC, Wst; CEV, KJV, NASB, NIV, NJB, NLT, NRSV, TEV]: the one having built the house.
2. It means the one who founded the household [Alf, Blm, HNTC, ICC, Lns, Mil, NCBC, NIC; NAB, REB, TNT]: the one having founded the household.

QUESTION—What is the implied comparison between Christ and Moses?

Although both were head of their respective households [Blm] and Moses occupied an important position [Hwt, Lns, NIC, Wst], nevertheless Christ was Son [Blm, NIC]. Christ was builder of his house [Blm, EBC, EGT, GNC, Hu, Hwt, Mil, My, NTC, TH], founder of the household [HNTC, ICC, Lg, NIC, NTC], while Moses was a servant in his house [Blm, Hu, Mil, My, NIC, NTC], is associated with the house [GNC, Wst] and is no more than a member of the household [EBC, EGT, HNTC, Hu, Hwt, ICC, Lg, Lns, My, NIC, NTC, TH]. Moses was faithful, as was Jesus [Alf, Lns, NCBC, NTC, WBC, Wst]. The basis of the comparison is glory [WBC].

3:4 For[a] every house[b] is-built[c] by[d] someone,

LEXICON—a. γάρ (LN 89.23) (BAGD 2. p. 152): 'for' [HNTC, LN, Lns, Mil, NIC, WBC; KJV, NASB, NIV, NLT, NRSV], 'for, you see' [BAGD], 'because' [LN], 'of course' [CEV, NJB, TEV], not explicit [NAB, REB, TNT].

b. οἶκος (LN 7.2): 'house' [LN, Lns, NIC, WBC; all versions except TNT], 'household' [HNTC, Mil; TNT].

c. pres. pass. indic. of κατασκευάζω (LN **45.1**)(BAGD 2. p. 418): 'to be built' [BAGD, **LN**, NIC, WBC; CEV, KJV, NASB, NIV, NJB, NRSV, TEV], 'to be constructed' [BAGD, LN, Lns], 'to be founded' [HNTC; NAB, TNT], 'to be established' [Mil]. The phrase κατασκευάζεται ὑπό τινος 'is built by someone' is translated 'has a builder' [NLT], 'has its founder' [REB]. The present tense indicates a general truth [Lns].

d. ὑπό with genitive object (LN 90.1): 'by' [HNTC, LN, Lns, Mil, NIC, WBC; all versions except NLT, REB].

QUESTION—What relationship is indicated by γάρ 'for'?

1. It expands and justifies the reference to ὁ κατασκευάσας 'the one having built' in 3:3 [Alf, NIGTC]. It illustrates and clarifies the preceding comments concerning the founding of God's house [Mil, My, TNTC, WBC]. The conjunction γάρ 'for' shows that this verse is connected with the preceding verse, and the conjunction καί 'and' introducing the following verse shows that the reason given in 3:4 is continued into 3:5–6 [WBC]. It is incidental but not parenthetical, since αὐτοῦ 'his' in the following verse refers back to θεός 'God' in this verse [My]. It states a well-known general truth [Hu, TNTC, Wst].
2. It is parenthetical [Blm, EBC, GNC, Hu, NTC; NRSV]. This verse is not necessary to the argument [GNC].

but[a] the-(one) having-built[b] everything (is) God.

LEXICON—a. δέ (LN 89.94; 89.124): 'but' [LN, Mil, NIC, WBC; all versions except CEV, REB, TEV], 'and' [HNTC, LN; CEV, REB, TEV], 'moreover' [Lns].

b. aor. act. participle of κατασκευάζω (LN 45.1) (BAGD 2. p. 418): 'to build' [LN, NIC; CEV, KJV, NJB, TEV], 'to construct' [LN, Lns], 'to establish' [Mil], 'to make' [NLT]. The phrase ὁ κατασκευάσας 'the one having built' is translated 'the builder' [BAGD, WBC; NASB, NIV, NRSV], 'the founder' [HNTC; NAB, REB, TNT].

QUESTION—What relationship is indicated by δέ 'but'?

It indicates a change of subject [NTC], a contrast [EBC] between the preceding individual statement and the following general statement [Alf]. It guards against any misunderstanding that there may be many builders [Hu].

QUESTION—What is the subject of this clause?

1. The subject is θεός 'God' and the predicate is ὁ κατασκευσάας 'the one having built' [Alf, EBC, EGT, GNC, Hu, Hwt, ICC, Lg, Mil, My, NCBC, NIC, NTC, TH, TNTC, WBC, Wst; NAB, NIV, NJB, NLT, TEV, TNT]: God is the one who built everything. The subject θεός 'God' is emphatic by its final position in the clause [Mil].
2. The subject is ὁ κατασκευσάας 'the one having built', referring to Christ, and the predicate is θεός 'God', stating the deity of Christ [Blm, HNTC, Lns]: Christ, who created all things, is God.

3:5 And[a] Moses on-the-one-hand (was) faithful[b] in[c] all his house[d] as[e] (a) servant[f]

LEXICON—a. καί (LN 89.92): 'and' [LN, Lns; KJV], 'and so' [Mil], 'now' [WBC; NASB, NRSV, TNT], 'indeed' [REB, NIC], 'then' [HNTC], 'it is true that' [NJB], not explicit [CEV, NAB, NIV, NLT, TEV].

b. πιστός (LN 31.87) (BAGD 1.a.α. p. 664; 2. p. 665): 'faithful' [BAGD, HNTC, LN, Lns, Mil, NIC, WBC; all versions except NJB], 'trustworthy' [BAGD, LN; NJB], 'dependable' [BAGD, LN], 'reliable' [LN]. It implies carrying out responsibilities reliably [NIGTC, TH]; it means 'appointed' as well as 'faithful' [WBC].

c. ἐν with dative object (LN 83.13): 'in' [HNTC, LN, Lns, Mil, NIC, WBC; all versions]. Moses managed God's household as a servant who was a part of that household [NIC].

d. οἶκος (LN 7.2): 'house' [LN (7.2), Lns, NIC; KJV, NASB, NIV, NLT, NRSV, TEV], 'household' [HNTC, LN (10.8), Mil, WBC; NAB, NJB, REB, TNT], 'God's people' [CEV]. In Num. 12:7, 'house' refers to God's people, the household of God [WBC].

e. ὡς (LN 64.12): 'as' [HNTC, LN, Lns, Mil, NIC, WBC; all versions except CEV], 'like' [LN], not explicit [CEV]. It introduces the area in which the faithfulness occurred [Mil, My].

f. θεράπων (LN **35.20**) (BAGD p. 359): 'servant' [BAGD, HNTC, LN, Lns, Mil, NIC, WBC; all versions]. It is a general term applicable to anyone who is subservient to another person [Alf, Blm, NTC], an honored servant [EBC, EGT, Lg, Mil, WBC] in an intimate and confidential relationship with his master [Hwt, WBC], one who offers his service rather than being in servitude [HNTC, Lg, Lns, Mil, NIGTC, NTC, TNTC, Wst]. The emphasis is on the subservience [EBC]. It is contrasted with υἱός 'son' in the following verse [Blm, ICC].

QUESTION—What relationship is indicated by καί 'and'?

It introduces an additional reason for expecting to find Jesus to be faithful [EGT]. It is a second proof of Jesus' superiority over Moses [ICC, TNTC]. It introduces the explanation and summarization of 3:2–4 [Mil]. It further clarifies [Mil, My, NTC], repeats [NTC], extends and explains [WBC] the previous comment concerning the faithfulness of Jesus, the superiority of Jesus [WBC, Wst], contrasting Moses and Jesus [NIGTC, NTC, TH]. It is a new argument [TNTC], contrasting the positions of a servant and a Son [NIGTC, TNTC]. The καί 'and indeed' indicates a more sharply defined comparison [My].

QUESTION—What relationship is indicated by μέν 'on the one hand'?

1. It balances (contrasts [Mil]) the present statement about Moses with the following statement, introduced by δέ 'but', concerning Christ [Lns, Mil, My].
2. It implies an inferior status for Moses in contrast with the following δέ 'but' in reference to Christ in the following verse [Alf].

QUESTION—To whom does αὐτοῦ 'his' refer?

It refers to God [Alf, EBC, HNTC, Hwt, Lg, Mil, My, NIC, NIGTC, TH, WBC, Wst; all versions except possibly KJV]: in all God's house.

for[a] (a) testimony[b] of-the-(things) which-were-going-to-be spoken,[c]

LEXICON—a. εἰς with accusative object (LN 89.57) (BAGD 4.d. p. 229): 'for' [BAGD; KJV, NASB], 'for the purpose of' [LN], 'as' [HNTC], 'in regard to' [Lns], not explicit [CEV, NIV, NRSV, REB, TEV, TNT]. The phrase εἰς μαρτύριον 'for a testimony' is translated 'acting as witness' [NJB], 'charged with the task of witnessing' [NAB], 'serving by way of testimony' [NIC], 'his work was an illustration of' [NLT]. This word indicates the purpose [Mil, WBC].

b. μαρτύριον (LN 33.262; 33.264) (BAGD 1.a. p. 494): 'testimony' [HNTC, Lns, NIC; KJV, NASB], 'witness' [BAGD, LN (33.262); NJB], 'witness' (as the message) [LN (33.264)], 'testimony' [NIC], 'illustration' [NLT]. This noun is also translated as a verb phrase: 'to witness' [NAB], 'to bear witness' [BAGD, Mil, WBC; REB, TNT], 'to testify' [NIV, NRSV], 'to speak' [TEV], 'to tell' [CEV].

c. fut. pass. participle of λαλέω (LN 33.70): 'to be spoken' [HNTC, LN, Lns, NIC; KJV, NAB, NASB, NRSV], 'to be said' [LN; CEV, NIV], 'to be told' [LN], 'to be revealed' [NJB]. The phrase τῶν λαληθησομένων 'the things which were going to be spoken' is translated 'the words that God would speak' [REB], 'the things that God would say in the future' [TEV], 'the truths God would reveal later' [NLT], 'what God would say in the future' [TNT], 'what would be spoken in the future' [Mil], 'to be spoken in the future' [WBC], 'what would be said in the future' [CEV]. The future tense refers to what was future to Moses [My(D)] but past from the author's and his readers' perspective [GNC]. The passive clearly implies that the speaker is God [Hu, TH; TEV, TNT]. Promise as well as condemnation are included [NIGTC].

QUESTION—What is the phrase εἰς μαρτύριον 'for a testimony' connected with?

It is connected with the preceding clause as a whole [Alf, Blm, EGT, HNTC, Hu, Mil, TH], with θεράπων 'servant' [My]: the faithful service of Moses was for the purpose of being a testimony. It implies the purpose of teaching [Blm].

QUESTION—How are the noun μαρτύριον 'testimony' and the participle τῶν λαληθησομένων 'the things which were going to be spoken' related?

The participle expresses the contents of the noun [Hu, Mil]: the testimony consisted of the words later spoken.

QUESTION—To what does τῶν λαληθησομένων 'the things which were going to be spoken' refer?

1. The reference is to the gospel that Christ would announce to the people [Alf, EBC, GNC, HNTC, Hu, Hwt, ICC, Lg, Mil, My(D), NCBC,

NIGTC, NTC, TNTC, WBC, Wst; TEV]. Moses testified to the gospel that Jesus later proclaimed [NIC, NTC, TNTC, WBC].

2. The reference is to what Moses would later say to the Israelites as God's prophet [EGT, Lns, Mil, My].

3:6 but Christ as[a] son over[b] his house;

LEXICON—a. ὡς: 'as'. See this word in 3:5.

b. ἐπί with accusative object (LN 37.9) (BAGD III.1.b.α. p. 288): 'over' [BAGD, HNTC, LN, Lns, Mil, NIC, WBC; all versions except CEV, NLT, TEV], 'with responsibility for' [LN], 'in charge of' [CEV, NLT, TEV].

QUESTION—What relationship is indicated by δέ 'but'?

It indicates contrast [Hu, NTC, WBC, Wst; all versions]. The contrast concerns the distinctions between servant and son and between the prepositional phrase in the house and over the house [Hu, NTC, WBC, Wst].

QUESTION—What predicate is to be supplied in this clause?

1. "Is faithful" ("is trustworthy" [NJB]) is to be supplied [Alf, ICC, Lns, My, WBC; NIV, NJB, REB, TEV].

1.1 "Is faithful" is used independently of the following phrase [Alf; NJB]: but Christ is faithful, as a son is over his house.

1.2 "Is faithful" is related to the following phrase [ICC, Lns, WBC; NIV, REB, TEV].

1.2.1 It tells how he is faithful [ICC, Lns, WBC; REB, TEV]: Christ is faithful as Son set over God's house.

1.2.2 It expresses the result of his capacity as son [My]: Christ as Son is faithful over God's house.

2. "Was faithful" is to be supplied [HNTC, Mil, Wst; NAB, NASB, NRSV, TNT].

2.1 It tells how he was faithful [NAB, NASB]: Christ was faithful as Son, placed over God's household.

2.2 It tells the area of his faithfulness [NRSV]: Christ was faithful over God's house as a son.

3. "Is" is to be supplied following Χριστὸς δέ 'but Christ' [Hwt; CEV]: but Christ is Son over his house.

4. "Was" is to be supplied following υἱός 'son' [Lg]: Christ as a son was over his house.

QUESTION: To whom does αὐτοῦ 'his' refer?

1. It refers to God [Alf, EBC, GNC, HNTC, ICC, Lg, Mil, My, NIGTC, TH, WBC, Wst; CEV, NAB, NIV, NRSV, TEV, TNT]: over God's house.

2. It refers to Christ [Hwt; KJV]: over Christ's house.

QUESTION—To whom does τὸν οἶκον 'the house' refer?

It refers to God's people, the church, believers [EBC, EGT, GNC, HNTC, Hu, NIC, NTC, Wst].

whose house/household are we, if-indeed[a] the confidence[b] and the boast[c] of-the hope[d] we-hold-fast.[e]

TEXT: Instead of οὗ 'whose' some manuscripts have ὅς 'which'. GNT reads οὗ with an A decision, indicating that the text is certain. The reading ὅς 'which' is taken by WBC, NAB, and REB.

TEXT: Some manuscripts insert μέχρι τέλους βεβαίαν 'firm to the end' before κατάσχωμεν 'we hold fast'. GNT omits this phrase with a B decision, indicating that the text is almost certain. 'Firm to the end' is read by Blm, EGT, Lg, Lns, My, KJV, and NASB.

LEXICON: a. ἐάνπερ (LN 89.68): 'if indeed' [LN], 'if surely' [LN], 'if only' [REB, TNT], 'if' [HNTC, Lns, Mil, NIC; CEV, KJV, NAB, NASB, NIV, NLT, NRSV, TEV], 'as long as' [NJB], 'supposing that' [WBC].

b. παρρησία (LN 25.158) (BAGD 3.b. p. 630): 'confidence' [BAGD, Mil, NIC, WBC; KJV, NAB, NASB, NRSV, TNT], 'assurance' [Lns], 'boldness' [BAGD, HNTC, LN], 'courage' [BAGD, LN; NIV, TEV], 'fearlessness' [BAGD]. The phrase τὴν παρρησίαν κατάσχωμεν 'we hold fast the confidence' is translated 'we fearlessly maintain' [NJB]. The phrase τὴν παρρησίαν καὶ τὸ καύχημα τῆς ἐλπίδος κατάσχωμεν 'the confidence and the boast of the hope we hold fast' is translated 'we are fearless and keep our hope high' [REB], 'we keep on being brave and don't lose hope' [CEV], 'we keep up our courage and remain confident in our hope in Christ' [NLT]. This word refers to the profession of faith mentioned in 3:1 [Blm]. They must be courageous in the midst of persecution [NTC]. It implies the boldness that underlies frankness of speech [EGT, Mil], the freedom to speak to everyone [NTC], the believer's boldness before God [WBC], openness [Hu, Mil] and confidence [Hu, ICC, Lg, Lns, Mil, My], holding on to what is already possessed [NIGTC].

c. καύχημα (LN 33.368; 33.371) (BAGD 1. p. 426): 'boast' [BAGD, HNTC, Lns; NASB], 'boasting' [LN (33.368)], 'object of boasting' [BAGD], 'what one boasts about' [LN (33.371)], 'pride' [Mil; NRSV, TNT], 'confidence' [TEV], 'rejoicing' [KJV], not explicit [CEV, NLT]. This noun is also translated as a verb: 'to boast' [WBC; NAB, NIV], 'to glory in' [NJB]. It refers to the object of boasting [Alf, EBC, Lns, Mil, My, NIGTC], the result of glorying [Lg].

d. ἐλπίς (LN 25.59; 25.61; 25.62) (BAGD 2.b. p. 253): 'hope' [BAGD, HNTC, LN (25.59; 25.61), Lns, NIC; all versions except TEV], 'what we hope for' [Mil], 'what is hoped for' [LN (25.61)], 'the basis for hope, the reason for hope' [LN (25.62)]. The phrase τῆς ἐλπίδος 'of the hope' is translated 'in what we hope for' [TEV]. It refers to our assured glory in God's kingdom [Lns, Mil, My].

e. aor. act. subj. of κατέχω (LN 57.1) (BAGD 1.b.β. p. 423): 'to hold fast' [BAGD, Lns, Mil; KJV, NAB, NASB], 'to hold firm' [NRSV], 'to hold on to' [HNTC; NIV], 'to retain' [BAGD], 'to keep' [TNT], 'to keep up'

[NLT, TEV], 'to keep on being' [CEV], 'to maintain' [NIC], 'to possess' [LN].

QUESTION—To whom does οὗ 'whose' refer?

1. It refers to God [Alf, EBC, EGT, Lg; NASB, NLT]: we are God's house/household.
2. It refers to Christ [KJV]: we are Christ's house.
3. With a different text, ὅς 'which', referring to the house [WBC; NAB, REB]: which house we are.

QUESTION—To whom does ἡμεῖς 'we' refer?

It refers to the author [Alf, Lns, My(D), TH] and his Hebrew readers [Alf], the NT church [Lns, Mil, My(D), TH]. It is emphatic [Lns, Mil, WBC], emphasizing the identity of believers in Jesus as the church [Mil], emphasizing the corporate concept of the church as God's house [WBC], linking Christians with OT believers [NIGTC].

QUESTION—Why is the clause introduced by ἐάνπερ 'if indeed' mentioned?

It implies that perseverance is necessary to attain the goal [EGT, GNC, HNTC, Hu, Hwt, Mil, My(D), NIC, NTC, Wst]. They must be consistent with their profession [TNTC]. Here, the fact that they hold fast shows that they are God's people [Hu, NIC, TH].

QUESTION: How is the genitive noun ἐλπίδος 'hope' related to the two nouns παρρησίαν 'confidence' and καύχημα 'boast'?

1. It is related only to καύχημα 'boast' [Blm, EBC, Hu, Lns, NIC, NIGTC, NTC, TNTC, WBC, Wst; NAB, NASB, NIV, NJB, REB, TEV] and tells what is being boasted about [Blm, EBC, Hu, Lns, NIC, NIGTC, NTC, WBC; NAB, NIV, NJB, TEV]: if we hold fast to our confidence and to our hope in what we boast about.
2. It is related to both nouns [ICC, Mil, My, TH; NRSV, TNT]: if we hold fast to our confidence and pride in our hope. The principal factor is παρρησίαν 'confidence' [My].

2.1 The hope is the object of the confidence and pride [ICC, TH; TNT].
2.2 The confidence and the pride belong to the hope [NRSV].

DISCOURSE UNIT: 3:7–4:16 [NIGTC]. The topic is rest for God's people.

DISCOURSE UNIT: 3:7–4:13 [EBC, GNT, Wst; NAB, NJB, TEV]. The topic is the promised rest [EBC], rest for God's people [GNT; TEV], how to enter God's land of rest [NJB], promise and people under the two dispensations [Wst], a warning from the unfaithfulness of Israel [NAB].

DISCOURSE UNIT: 3:7–4:7 [Mil]. The topic is an exhortation to follow Jesus into the promised rest and a warning against becoming unfaithful like Israel of old.

DISCOURSE UNIT: 3:7–19 [GNC, HNTC, Hwt, Lg, NCBC, NIC, NTC, TNTC, WBC, Wst; NIV]. The topic is an exhortation inspired by Israel's exodus from Egypt [GNC], the failure of God's people under the leadership of Moses [TNTC], the second warning: the danger of unbelief of God's word [WBC], a warning against unbelief [NTC; NIV], a warning based on Israel in the wilderness [HNTC], a second warning [Hwt], an exhortation to heed the OT warning that unbelievers will not enter God's kingdom [Lg], a warning that rejecting Jesus is more serious than rejecting Moses [NIC], lost in the wilderness [NCBC], faith is the necessary grounds for enjoying God's blessing [Wst].

DISCOURSE UNIT: 3:7–14 [Lns]. The topic is a warning not to harden their hearts.

DISCOURSE UNIT: 3:7–11 [EBC]. The topic is the scriptural basis for the promised rest [EBC].

3:7 Therefore,[a] just-as the Holy Spirit says,

LEXICON—a. διό (LN 89.47): 'therefore' [HNTC, LN, Lns, NIC; NASB, NRSV, REB], 'wherefore' [Mil; KJV, NAB], 'so then' [LN, WBC; TEV], 'so' [NIV], 'for this reason' [LN], 'for this very reason' [LN], 'that is why' [NJB, NLT], not explicit [CEV, TNT].

QUESTION—What relationship is indicated by διό 'therefore'?

1. It indicates the consequence of the necessity if holding fast to be Christ's household [Alf, Blm, EGT, Hu, Lg, Mil, My, NTC, TH, TNTC, WBC, Wst]: we are Christ's household if we hold fast to our confidence and hope; therefore we should . . . It is the conclusion to this first part of the epistle [Blm]. It is a new step in the argument [TH].
2. It indicates the consequence of Christ's superiority [My(D)]: Christ is greater than Moses, therefore we should . . .

QUESTION—What is the implied verb of the clause introduced by διό 'therefore'?

1. It is μὴ σκληρύνητε 'do not harden' in 3:8 [Blm, EBC, ICC, NIGTC, WBC]: therefore . . . don't harden your hearts.
2. It is βλέπετε 'take heed' in 3:12 [Alf, EGT, Hu, Hwt, Lns, Mil, My, NTC, Wst]: therefore . . . take heed. The quotation in 3:7–11 is parenthetical [NTC].

QUESTION—Why is the phrase 'just as the Holy Spirit says' mentioned?

It gives added emphasis to the quotation that follows [EGT, Hu], emphasizing the divine authority of the command [HNTC, Hu, Hwt, TNTC], emphasizing the author's high view of Scripture [WBC]. The author focuses on God's authorship as important rather than the human authors [EGT, GNC, Mil, NCBC, NIC, NTC, Wst].

QUESTION—What is implied by the present tense of λέγει 'says'?

It implies that the Holy Spirit is still speaking [Hwt, Lns]. The OT message (Psalm 95:7–11) is still speaking to the readers of this epistle [NCBC, NTC]. It emphasizes the importance of the message and the peril of disobeying it [Hwt, TNTC].

"Today[a] if you-should-hear[b] his voice,

LEXICON—a. σήμερον (LN 67.205): 'today' [HNTC, LN, Lns, Mil, NIC, WBC; all versions]. This word refers to whatever day in which the quoted

Psalm was used [Alf, EGT] and to the second great day of redemption [EGT]; it refers here to the time of the present exhortation [Blm, EBC, Mil, TNTC]; it refers to the time of salvation brought in by Christ [My]. It is emphatic by word order [EBC, HNTC, Lns, Mil, NCBC], emphasizing the urgency of the warning [HNTC, NCBC, Wst].

b. aor. act. subj. of ἀκούω (LN 24.52; 31.56) 'to hear' [HNTC, LN (24.52), , Lns, Mil, WBC; all versions except NJB, NLT, TNT], 'to heed' [LN (31.56)], 'to listen to' [LN (31.56), NIC; NJB, NLT, TNT].

QUESTION—What is implied by ἐάν 'if'?

1. It implies that they will hear God's voice [GNC, Hwt, TH, TNTC]: when you hear his voice.
2. It implies uncertainty about hearing God's voice: [EGT, NIC, NTC, WBC, Wst; all versions]: if you hear his voice.

2.1 The uncertainty is whether or not they are willing to listen [NIC, NTC; NJB]: if only you would listen to him.

2.2 The uncertainty is whether or not God will again speak [EGT]: if God should still be pleased to speak.

QUESTION—What is implied by the genitive case of τῆς φωνῆς 'the voice' as the predicate of ἀκούσητε 'you should hear'?

1. It refers to the person who is to be heard [Lns]: if you should hear God speaking.
2. It refers to the message [TH]: if you hear what God is saying.

3:8 do-not harden[a] your hearts[b] as in[c] the rebellion[d]

LEXICON—a. aor. act. subj. (with imperative meaning) of σκληρύνω (LN **88.226**) (BAGD 1.a. p. 756): 'to harden' [BAGD, HNTC, Lns, Mil, NIC, WBC; KJV, NAB, NASB, NIV, NJB, NLT, NRSV], 'to make obstinate, to make stubborn' [LN]. The phrase μὴ σκληρύνητε τὰς καρδίας ὑμῶν 'do not harden your hearts' is translated 'to cause the hearts to be obstinate' [**LN**], 'do not grow stubborn' [REB], 'do not be stubborn' [CEV, TEV, TNT]. The reference is to persons hardening their own hearts [Alf, EGT, Hwt, NTC, Wst]. It refers to stubbornness and willful disobedience [Blm, NCBC], refusal to listen or understand [NTC, TH]. The verb is a subjunctive of prohibition [EGT, Lns, Mil], expressing an exhortation [Mil].

b. καρδία (LN 26.3) (BAGD 1.b.γ. p. 404): 'heart' [BAGD, HNTC, LN, Lns, Mil, NIC, WBC; KJV, NAB, NASB, NIV, NJB, NLT, NRSV], 'inner self' [LN]. It is not only the seat of the feelings, but of the mind and will also [Lns]. It refers to the whole inner being [EGT, Mil].

c. ἐν with dative object (LN 67.33; 67.136; 83.13): 'in' [HNTC, LN (83.13), Lns, Mil, NIC, WBC; KJV, NIV, NRSV], 'at' [NAB, NJB], 'at the time of' [LN (67.33)], 'during' [LN (67.136)], 'when' [NASB, NLT, TEV, TNT], not explicit [CEV].

d. παραπικρασμός (LN **39.40**) (BAGD p. 621): 'rebellion' [BAGD, Mil, NIC, WBC; NIV, NJB, NRSV, REB], 'revolt' [NAB], 'provocation'

[KJV], 'exasperation' [HNTC], 'embitterment' [Lns]. The phrase ἐν τῷ παραπικρασμῷ 'in the rebellion' is translated 'when you rebelled' [LN; TNT], 'when they rebelled' [NLT, TEV], 'when they provoked me' [NASB], 'don't rebel' [CEV]. The definite article with this noun points to the specific instance referred to in 3:10 [Blm], when there was a lack of water [Alf, EBC]. It represents the location of Meribah in the OT passage [Alf, EGT, GNC, HNTC, Hu, Hwt, Lg, NCBC, NIC, NTC].

QUESTION—What relationship is indicated by ὡς 'as'?

It introduces a comparison to reinforce the preceding exhortation [Mil]: don't harden your hearts in the way they did in the rebellion. The Israelites' hearts were unyielding and embittered against God because of the wilderness hardships [Lns].

QUESTION—Who is the implied object of τῷ παραπικρασμῷ 'the rebellion'?

The rebellion was against God [Alf, Blm, Hu, LN, TH, TNTC; NASB, TEV, TNT]. It includes the incidents in Exod. 15:22–25, 17:1–7, and 32:1 [TNTC].

in/as-on[a] the day of-the testing[b] in[c] the wilderness,

LEXICON—a. κατά with accusative object (LN **67.33**) (BAGD II.2.a. p. 406): 'in' [BAGD, NIC; KJV, NAB, NASB], 'at' [NJB, REB], 'on' [HNTC, Lns, WBC; NRSV], 'during' [Mil; NIV], not explicit [CEV]. The phrase κατὰ τὴν ἡμέραν 'in the day' is translated 'at the time' [LN], 'when' [NLT], 'that day' [TEV, TNT].

b. πειρασμός (LN 27.46) (BAGD 3. p. 641): 'testing' [BAGD, HNTC, LN, NIC, WBC; NAB, NIV, NJB, NRSV, REB], 'trial' [NASB], 'temptation' [Lns, Mil; KJV]. The phrase τοῦ πειρασμοῦ 'of the testing' is translated 'when they put him to the test' [TEV], 'when you put him to the test' [TNT], 'when they tested God's patience' [NLT].

c. ἐν with dative object (LN 83.13): 'in' [HNTC, LN, Lns, Mil, NIC, WBC; all versions]. It introduces the place where the event occurred [Mil].

QUESTION—What relationship is indicated by κατά 'in, as on'?

1. It indicates time [Alf, HNTC, Lg, Lns, Mil, NIC, Wst; all versions]: the rebellion at the day of testing.
2. It indicates comparison [EGT]: the rebellion as on the day of testing. The meaning is 'according to the manner of' [EGT].

QUESTION—How is the phrase κατὰ τὴν ἡμέραν 'in the day' related to other phrases?

It is subordinate to παραπικρασμῷ 'rebellion', indicating the time of the rebellion [Alf, Lg, Mil, My]. It refers to the incident at Massah in the OT passage [Alf, EGT, GNC, HNTC, Hu, Hwt, Lg, NCBC, NIC, NTC]. It refers to the second instance of complaining against Moses and Aaron because of the lack of water [Alf]. The day refers to the day they refused to enter the promised land (Num. 14:11, 21–22) [WBC]. Perhaps it refers to the beginning day of the testing that lasted for forty years [TNTC]. It means the time of testing from the first year through the fortieth year [HNTC, ICC, NTC, TNTC].

1. The two nouns refer to the same incident [Blm, EBC, EGT, Hu, Lg, Lns, Mil, NTC, TH, WBC], where the Israelites complained because of lack of water [Hu, Mil, NTC].
2. The two nouns refer to two incidents [Alf, HNTC, Hwt, TNTC, Wst].

QUESTION—Who is the implied object of τοῦ πειρασμοῦ 'the testing'?

1. God was tested [Blm, EBC, EGT, HNTC, Hu, My, NIC, TH, WBC, Wst; NLT, TEV, TNT]: the day they tested God. They tested God by trying to see how long God's patience would hold out [NIC, TH]. They refused to trust God until he would do all that they demanded him to do [Hu].
2. The people were tested [CEV]: the day they were tested in the desert.

3:9 where/when[a] your fathers tested[b] (me) by[c] testing[d] and/although they saw my deeds[e]

TEXT—Some manuscripts add με 'me' following ἐπείρασεν 'tested'. GNT does not deal with this variant. Only Blm, EGT, and KJV clearly have με 'me' in their Greek text, although others add 'me' by interpretation.

TEXT—Instead of ἐν δοκιμασίᾳ 'by testing' some manuscripts read ἐδοκίμασέν με 'they tested me'. GNT does not deal with this variant. Only Blm, KJV clearly read ἐδοκίμασεν με 'they tested me'. It is not clear whether HNTC; NAB, NIV, NJB, NRSV, REB, TEV, TNT follow this reading or whether they are giving a stylistic rendering of 'by testing'.

LEXICON—a. οὗ (LN 83.5; 92.28): 'where' [HNTC, LN (83.5; 92.28), Lns, Mil, NIC, WBC; NASB, NIV, NRSV, REB], 'there' [NLT, TEV, TNT], 'in which' [LN (92.28)], 'when' [KJV, NAB, NJB], not explicit [CEV]. It introduces an interpretative comment on the preceding thought [Mil].

b. aor. act. indic. of πειράζω (LN 27.46) (BAGD 2.e. p. 640): 'to test' [LN], 'to put to the test' [BAGD, WBC], 'to try' [BAGD; NASB], 'to make trial of' [BAGD], 'to tempt' [Lns, Mil; KJV]. The phrase ἐπείρασεν ἐν δοκιμασίᾳ 'tried by testing' is translated 'put me to the test and tried me' [TEV], 'tried me and put me to the test' [NIC], 'tested and tried (me)' [LN (**27.46**)], 'tested and tried me' [NAB, NIV], 'tried and tested me' [TNT], 'tried me and tested me' [REB], 'challenged me, and put me to the test' [NJB], 'tested and tried' [HNTC], 'put to the test' [BAGD], 'put me to the test' [NRSV], 'tried my patience' [NLT], 'tested God' [CEV]. It means that they tested God to discover whether he notices sin and will punish it [BAGD].

c. ἐν with dative object (LN 89.76): 'by' [LN, Mil; NASB], 'in' [Lns].

d. δοκιμασία (LN **27.45**) (BAGD p. 202): 'testing' [BAGD, LN, Lns; NASB]. This noun is translated as a phrase: 'putting me to the test' [Mil]; different text 'to prove' [KJV]. The phrase ἐν δοκιμασίᾳ 'by testing' is translated 'through their distrust' [WBC].

e. ἔργον (LN 42.11): 'deed' [HNTC, LN], 'act' [LN], 'work' [Lns, Mil, NIC; KJV, NAB, NASB, NRSV], 'miracle' [NLT], 'judgment' [WBC].

The phrase τὰ ἔργα μου 'my deeds' is translated 'the things I did' [REB], 'what I did' [NIV, TEV], 'what I could do' [NJB]. The phrase εἶδον τὰ ἔργα μου 'saw my deeds' is translated 'watched me at work' [TNT]. The reference is to God's penal judgments [Alf, ICC, WBC], God's punishments for them during forty years [TH], his miracles and other helps for them [Lns, NTC; NLT], his acts of protection and preservation in Egypt and in the wilderness [Blm], his wonderful acts of mercy and of judgment [EGT, Wst].

QUESTION—What is meant by οὗ 'where/when'?

1. It indicates place [Alf, Blm, EGT, HNTC, ICC, Lg, Lns, Mil, My, NIC, NTC, WBC, Wst; NASB, NIV, NLT, NRSV, REB, TEV, TNT]: in the wilderness *where* your ancestors tested me.
2. It indicates time [KJV, NAB, NJB]: in the wilderness *when* your ancestors tested me.

QUESTION—What relationship is indicated by καί 'and/although', and what is meant by τὰ ἔργα 'works'?

1. Καί introduces an added thought [Alf, EBC, EGT, HNTC, ICC, Lns, NIC, TH, Wst; CEV, KJV, NAB, NASB, NIV, NJB, TNT]: and in addition they saw.
   1.1 The works are punishments from God [Alf, ICC, TH]: your ancestors tested God and, as a result, experienced punishment from God.
   1.2 The works are the good things God did for them [Lns, NTC]: your ancestors tested God and saw the good things God did to help them. The works are miracles such as the pillars of fire and cloud, water from the rock, manna, and prolonging the wear of their clothes [NTC] and other acts of God's leading them [Lns].
   1.3 The works are all that God did [Wst]. This refers to both his wonderful acts of mercy and his acts of judgment [EGT, Wst] which were all parts of his loving discipline [Wst].
2. Καί introduces a concession [BAGD, Blm, Hu, Mil, My, NIGTC, WBC; NLT, NRSV, REB, TEV], an unexpected fact [Mil]: although they saw. It means 'and yet' and shows that the fact was surprising and unexpected [BAGD (I.2.g. p. 392)].
   2.1 The works are the good things God did for them [Blm; NLT]: your ancestors tested God even though they saw the good things he did to help them.
   2.2 The works are punishments from God [NIGTC, WBC]: your ancestors tested God even though they saw how God punished them for it.

QUESTION—What is the phrase τὰ ἔργα μου 'my works' connected with?

1. It is connected with εἶδον 'they saw' [Alf, Blm, EGT, Hu, ICC, Lns, Mil, My, NIC, WBC; all versions]: they saw my works.
2. It is connected with the entire preceding clause [EBC, Wst]: they both tested and saw my works.

3:10 for-forty years;

QUESTION—What is this phrase connected with?

It is connected with the preceding phrase [Alf, EBC, EGT, Hu, ICC, Lg, Lns, Mil, My, NIC, TH, WBC, Wst; all versions]: they saw my works for forty years. The accusative case indicates the extent of the time [Mil]. In the original Hebrew text, this phrase goes with the following phrase, but here it indicates the duration of the time they saw God's works [ICC, Wst].

therefore[a] I-became-angry[b] at-this generation[c]

TEXT—Instead of ταύτῃ 'this' some manuscripts read ἐκείνῃ 'that'. GNT does not deal with this variant. 'That' is read by Blm, KJV, NAB, NIV, NJB, NRSV, REB, but some of these latter are probably translating stylistically rather than reading ἐκείνῃ 'that' in their Greek text.

LEXICON—a. διό (LN 89.47): 'therefore' [HNTC, LN, NIC; NASB, NRSV, REB], 'wherefore' [Lns; KJV], 'for this reason' [LN], 'for that reason' [WBC], 'because of this' [NAB], 'that is why' [Mil; NIV, TNT], 'and so' [TEV], 'so' [NLT], 'then' [CEV].

b. aor. act. indic. of προσοχθίζω (LN 88.172) (BAGD p. 717): 'to become angry' [Mil; TNT], 'to be angry' [BAGD, LN, WBC; NASB, NIV, NLT, NRSV, TEV], 'to be angered' [NAB], 'to be incensed' [REB], 'to be provoked' [BAGD, LN], 'to be vexed' [NIC], 'to be revolted' [HNTC], 'to be disgusted' [Lns], 'to become highly displeased' [Mil], 'to get tired of' [CEV], 'to be grieved' [KJV]. The phrase προσώχθισα τῇ γενεᾷ ταύτῃ 'I became angry at this generation' is translated 'that generation sickened me' [NJB]. It means to be greatly displeased with someone [EGT, Wst].

c. γενεά (LN 10.4; 11.4) (BAGD 2. p. 154): 'generation' [BAGD, HNTC, Lns, Mil, NIC, WBC; KJV, NAB, NASB, NIV, NJB, NRSV, REB], 'people' [Mil; TEV], 'people of the same kind' [LN (10.4)], 'people of that time' [TNT], 'those of the same generation' [LN (11.4)], 'those of the same time' [LN (11.4)], 'them' [CEV, NLT]. The emphasis is upon the kind of people with whom God is displeased rather than upon a particular time [Mil].

QUESTION—What relationship is indicated by διό 'therefore'?

It indicates the result of the Israelites' testing God [HNTC, Lns, Mil, NIC, TNTC, WBC; all versions except CEV]. God's anger only arises from a just cause [TNTC]. It clarifies the connection with what precedes [Hwt, NIGTC]. This makes clear that the phrase τεσσεράκοντα ἔτη 'forty years' belongs with what precedes instead of with what follows as in the OT text [Alf, NIGTC]. It shows the relationship between the people's sin and God's displeasure [Lns]. It draws attention to the words following [TH] and introduces the obvious conclusion [Mil].

QUESTION—What is implied by the use of ταύτῃ 'this (generation)' instead of ἐκείνῃ 'that' as in the Septuagint?

It is used to include the present generation of Jews along with those of the OT [Alf, NIC], to make more imminent God's threat of wrath [HNTC]. It is not intended to include the readers of the epistle [Lg].

and I-said, 'Always[a] they-go-astray[b] in-the heart,[c]

LEXICON—a. ἀεί (LN 67.86) (BAGD 3. p. 19): 'always' [HNTC, LN, Lns, Mil, NIC, WBC; all versions except REB], 'continually' [BAGD], 'constantly' [BAGD], 'for ever' [REB]. 'Always' means the τεσσεράκοντα ἔτη 'forty years' [Blm]. This word is governed by πλανῶνται 'they go astray' [Lg, My].

b. pres. pass. indic. of πλανάω (LN 31.67) (BAGD 2.c.α. p. 665): 'to go astray' [BAGD, Mil, NIC, WBC; NASB, NIV, NRSV], 'to go astray from' [LN], 'to be astray' [REB], 'to stray from the truth' [LN], 'to wander from the truth' [LN], 'to turn away (from me)' [NLT], 'to err' [Lns; KJV], 'to be misled' [BAGD], 'to be deluded' [BAGD], 'to be disloyal' [TEV]. The phrase πλανῶνται τῇ καρδίᾳ 'they go astray in the heart' is translated 'they have been of erring heart' [NAB], 'their thoughts are wrong' [TNT], 'they are deliberately going astray' [HNTC], 'they are disloyal' [TEV], 'they never show good sense' [CEV], 'fickle hearts' [NJB].

c. καρδία (LN 26.3): 'heart' [LN, Lns, Mil, NIC; all versions except CEV, TEV, TNT], 'mind, inner self' [LN], not explicit [CEV, TEV, TNT]. It refers to the whole inner being [EBC, Lns], the personal character [Wst], to the will and intellect [HNTC, Lns, TH], the affections [Blm].

QUESTION—What relationship is indicated by καί 'and'?

It indicates the result of the preceding thought [Mil]: I became angry and so I said.

QUESTION—What is implied by this clause?

God is represented as speaking to himself, as the following use of αὐτοί 'they' shows [TH]. It implies that their case is hopeless [Lns].

and[a] they did-not know[b] my ways,'[c]

LEXICON—a. δέ (LN 89.94; 89.124): 'and' [LN (89.94); CEV, KJV, NAB, NASB, NIV, NRSV, TEV], 'moreover' [Lns], 'but' [LN (89.124), WBC], not explicit [HNTC, Mil, NIC; NJB, NLT, REB, TNT]. It restates the preceding charge in different terms [Lns].

b. aor. act. indic. of γινώσκω (LN 27.2; 28.1; 32.16) (BAGD 3.a. p. 161): 'to know' [HNTC, LN (28.1), Lns, WBC; KJV, NAB, NASB, NIV, NRSV], 'to understand' [BAGD, LN (32.16); CEV, TNT], 'to comprehend' [BAGD], 'to discern' [REB], 'to grasp' [NJB], 'to learn' [LN (17.2), Mil, NIC]. This entire phrase is translated 'and refuse to obey my commands' [TEV], 'they refuse to do what I tell them' [NLT]. The aorist tense implies that they did not know before they went astray [Alf]. This word implies not desiring to know [Blm, EBC], willful ignorance [HNTC, Hu], disobedience, not ignorance [GNT, Lns].

c. ὁδός (LN 41.16) (BAGD 2.b. p. 554): 'way' [BAGD, HNTC, Lns, Mil, NIC, WBC; all versions except NLT, TEV], 'way of life' [BAGD, LN], 'way to live' [LN], 'way of acting' [BAGD], 'conduct' [BAGD], 'what God wants them to do' [CEV].

QUESTION—Where does the quotation introduced by καὶ εἶπον 'and I said' end?

1. It ends at the end of this clause [Mil, NIC; CEV, NAB, NASB, NIV, NJB, NLT, NRSV, TEV, TNT].
2. It ends with καρδίᾳ 'heart' in the preceding clause [EGT, HNTC, Lns, WBC]. This is shown by the author's insertion of the phrase αὐτοὶ δέ 'but they' [EGT].

QUESTION—How is this phrase related to the preceding phrase?

1. It expresses a second charge against them [Hwt, Mil, TNTC]: they always go astray, and they have not known my ways. Their habit of straying contributed to their lack of knowledge [TNTC].
2. It states the same charge in different terms [Lns, TH].

QUESTION—How are the noun and pronoun related in the genitive phrase τὰς ὁδούς μου 'my ways'?

The phrase means the ways God wanted them to walk in [Alf, Lns]: my ways for them to live.

3:11 as/therefore[a] I-swore[b] in[c] my anger:[d] 'If[e] they-shall-enter into[f] my rest.'"[g]

LEXICON—a. ὡς (LN 64.12; **89.52**) (BAGD IV.2. p. 898): 'as' [LN (64.12), NIC; NASB, NRSV], 'accordingly' [LN (**89.52**)], 'thus' [NAB], 'so' [HNTC, WBC; KJV, NIV, NLT, REB, TNT], 'so that' [BAGD, Lns, Mil], 'so that as a result' [LN (**89.52**)], 'and then' [NJB], not explicit [CEV, TEV]. It implies justification of the following oath [EGT].

b. aorist act. indic. of ὀμνύω (LN 33.463) (BAGD p. 566): 'to swear' [BAGD, LN, Lns, NIC; KJV, NAB, NASB, NJB, NRSV, TNT], 'to take an oath' [BAGD], 'to make an oath' [LN], 'to declare on oath' [NIV], 'to declare by an oath' [WBC], 'to declare an oath' [Mil], 'to vow' [HNTC; REB], 'to make a vow' [NLT], 'to make a solemn promise' [TEV], 'to tell' [CEV].

c. ἐν with dative object (LN 13.8; 89.84): 'in' [HNTC, LN (13.8), Lns, Mil, NIC, WBC; all versions except CEV, NLT, TEV], 'with' [LN (89.84)]. The phrase ἐν τῇ ὀργῇ μου 'in my anger' is translated 'I was angry' [NLT, TEV], 'God became angry' [CEV]. This word introduces the reason he swore this [Mil].

d. ὀργή (LN 88.173) (BAGD 2.a. p. 579): 'anger' [BAGD, HNTC, LN, Mil, WBC; NAB, NIV, NJB, NRSV, REB, TNT], 'wrath' [BAGD, Lns, Mil, NIC; KJV, NASB], 'fury' [LN], 'indignation' [BAGD]. This is the usual word for God's wrath, and implies God's settled opposition to all that is evil [EBC] when his patience has been exhausted [HNTC, Lns].

e. εἰ (LN 89.65) (BAGD IV. p. 219): 'if' [BAGD, LN]. The phrase εἰ εἰσελεύσονται 'if they shall enter' is translated 'they shall not enter' [Lns, Mil, NIC; KJV, NASB], 'they will not enter' [NRSV], 'they shall certainly not enter' [BAGD; WBC], 'they shall never enter' [HNTC; NAB, NIV, REB], 'they will never enter' [NLT, TEV], 'you will never enter' [CEV], 'that they would never enter' [NJB], 'they would never come in' [TNT].

f. εἰς with accusative object (LN 84.22): 'into' [LN, Lns, Mil, NIC; KJV, NAB], not explicit [HNTC, WBC; CEV, NASB, NIV, NJB, NLT, NRSV, REB, TEV]. The phrase εἰς τὴν κατάπαυσίν μου 'into my rest' is translated 'and rest with me' [TNT].

g. κατάπαυσις (LN 23.81) (BAGD 2. p. 416): 'rest' [HNTC, LN, Lns, Mil, NIC, WBC; KJV, NAB, NASB, NIV, NRSV, REB], 'place of rest' [BAGD; CEV, NJB, NLT], 'land where I would have given them rest' [TEV]. It implies a different rest than that in the land of Canaan [Alf, My], the state of rest for Christians [GNC, ICC, Mil] patterned after the rest which God entered after the completion of creation [Wst], the heavenly Canaan [Blm, Lns], a spiritual state of relaxation in God's presence free from striving [EBC], the eternal Messianic blessed state [My].

QUESTION—What relationship is indicated by ὡς 'as/therefore'?

1. It indicates a comment in conformity with the disobedience [Alf, Wst; NRSV]: in conformity with the fact that they were disobedient, I correspondingly swore . . .
2. It indicates a result [BAGD, HNTC, LN, Lns, Mil, My, WBC; KJV, NAB, NIV, NJB, REB, TNT]: they were disobedient, therefore I swore . . .

QUESTION—What is implied by the form of this oath?

It implies a strong negation of the thought [Alf, HNTC, Lg, My, NIC, TH, TNTC, WBC; all versions]. It is a conditional clause with the clause expressing the consequence suppressed [Lg, Mil, My, TNTC]. When used by people, it implies a suppressed preceding thought such as, "May God do so to me (if . . .)" [Alf, EGT]; used by God, it implies something such as "I am not God (if . . .)" [EBC, Mil]. When God speaks, it means to declare with unchangeable words [TH]. It implies that the Israelites to whom this was directed were irrevocably excluded from the future life [HNTC, Hwt, NCBC], from entry into the earthly Canaan; but pointing forward to God's promised eternal rest for his people [Hu].

DISCOURSE UNIT: 3:12–19 [EBC; NASB]. The topic is the failure of some to enter the rest [EBC], the danger of unbelief [NASB].

3:12 See-to-it,[a] brothers, lest-perhaps[b] there-will-be in[c] someone of-you an-evil[d] heart[e] of-unbelief/unfaithfulness[f] in[g] the turning-away[h] from[i] (the) living[j] God,

LEXICON—a. pres. act. impera. of βλέπω (LN 27.58): 'to see to it' [Lns, NIC; NIV, REB], 'to watch out for' [LN; CEV], 'to beware' [HNTC, LN], 'to take heed' [KJV], 'to take care' [Mil; NAB, NASB, NJB, NRSV], 'to be careful' [WBC; NLT, TEV, TNT].

b. μήποτε (LN 89.62) (BAGD 2.a.γ. p. 519): 'lest perhaps' [Mil], 'perhaps' [Lns], 'lest' [BAGD, HNTC, LN; KJV, NAB, NASB], 'in order that not' [LN], 'so that not' [LN], 'that not' [BAGD, NIC], 'don't let' [CEV]. The phrase μήποτε ἔσται ἔν τινι ὑμῶν 'lest perhaps there will be in someone of you' is translated 'that none of you may have' [NRSV], 'that none of you have' [TEV], 'that none of you has' [NIV], 'that none of you ever has' [NJB], 'that no one among you has' [WBC; REB], 'that none of you' [TNT], 'make sure that . . . not' [NLT]. The ποτε implies possibility [EGT, Lg, My].

c. ἐν with dative object (LN 83.13): 'in' [HNTC, LN, Lns, Mil, NIC; KJV, NASB]. The phrase ἔσται ἔν τινι ὑμῶν 'there will be in someone of you' is translated 'any of you have' [NAB].

d. πονηρός (LN 88.110) (BAGD 1.b.β. p. 691): 'evil' [BAGD, HNTC, LN, Mil, NIC, WBC; CEV, KJV, NAB, NASB, NLT, NRSV, TEV], 'wicked' [BAGD, LN, Lns; NJB, REB, TNT], 'sinful' [NIV].

e. καρδία (LN 26.3) (BAGD 1.b.δ. p. 404): 'heart' [BAGD, HNTC, LN, Lns, Mil, NIC, WBC; all versions except CEV, NAB, TNT], 'spirit' [NAB], 'thoughts' [CEV], 'mind' [LN], not explicit [TNT]. The phrase καρδία πονηρὰ ἀπιστίας 'an evil heart of unbelief' is translated 'through wicked disbelief' [TNT]. It includes the whole inner life [NIGTC].

f. ἀπιστία (LN 31.105) (BAGD 2.b. p. 85): 'unbelief' [Lns, NIC; KJV], 'disbelief' [TNT], 'doubts' [CEV]. This noun is also translated as an adjective: 'unfaithful' [NAB], 'faithless' [REB]; as a participle: 'unbelieving' [BAGD, HNTC, Mil, WBC; NASB, NIV, NJB, NLT, NRSV, TEV], 'not believing' [LN]. It means to refuse to believe [NCBC, TH, WBC], to reject the belief previously held [Hu, Lns]. It is an unbelief that leads to apostasy [ICC, NTC]. It is disloyalty and failure to believe [NIC], mistrust, unreliability [NTC], and disobedience [NTC, TH].

g. ἐν with dative object (LN 89.5; 89.48; 90.23): 'in' [LN (89.5, 90.23), Lns; KJV, NASB], 'with regard to' [LN (89.5)], 'with the result that' [LN (89.48)], 'so that as a result' [LN (89.48)], 'with respect to' [LN (90.23)], 'with reference to' [LN (90.23)], not explicit [NLT]. The phrase ἐν τῷ ἀποστῆναι 'in the turning away' is translated 'and fall away' [NAB], 'that turns away' [WBC; NIV, NRSV], 'that you will turn away' [TEV], 'that would lead you to depart' [Mil], 'as to turn away' [NJB], 'should fall away' [TNT], 'which results in apostasy' [HNTC], 'deserting' [NIC], 'of a deserter' [REB]. It indicates the element in which the unbelief is exhibited [Alf].

h. aor. act. infin. of ἀφίστημι (LN **34.26**) (BAGD 2.a. p. 127): 'to turn away' [LN, WBC; CEV, NIV, NJB, NLT, NRSV, TEV], 'to fall away' [BAGD; NAB, NASB, TNT], 'to apostatize' [Lns], 'to desert' [NIC], 'to depart' [Mil; KJV]. This verb is also translated as a noun: 'deserter' [REB]. It refers to apostasy [Alf, Blm, EGT, GNC, HNTC, Hu, Lg, Lns, Mil], to rebellion [EBC, NIC] against the truth [GNC], against God [GNC, Hu], deliberate rejection [TH, WBC]. The aorist tense indicates definiteness [Lns].

i. ἀπό with genitive object (LN 89.122): 'from' [HNTC, LN, Lns, Mil, WBC; all versions], not explicit [NIC].

j. pres. act. participle of ζάω (LN 23.88) (BAGD 1.a.ε. p. 336): 'to live' [BAGD, HNTC, LN, Lns, Mil, NIC, WBC; all versions]. This word emphasizes the loss involved by unbelief [ICC], a contrast with lifeless idols of heathenism [Alf, EGT]. It emphasizes God's dynamic character [GNC, Lg, TNTC]. It implies God's power to punish [HNTC] and the certainty of punishment [Hwt, ICC, Lg, Lns, My, NCBC], that he keeps his promises [Lns], especially as the one who has fulfilled his promises by appointing Christ as he did Moses [Lg]. The absence of definite articles with θεοῦ ζῶντος 'living God' calls attention to God's character [WBC, Wst], to his power [NTC], to the concept of 'living' [TNTC].

QUESTION—How is this verse related to what precedes?

1. It is connected with διό 'therefore' in 3:7 [Alf, EGT, Hu, Hwt, Lns, Mil, My, NTC, Wst]: therefore . . . see to it. The quotation is parenthetical [NTC] and enforces the preceding by illustration [Wst].
2. It is a new sentence, not dependent on διό 'wherefore' in 3:7 [Blm, EBC, HNTC, ICC, TH, TNTC, WBC]. It reinforces the preceding exhortation [Blm, Hu]. It is a commentary on the preceding comments [GNC, TNTC], an application [ICC, NCBC, NTC, WBC, Wst], an exhortation [Mil, NTC], an explanation [TH].

QUESTION—What is meant by βλέπετε 'see to it'?

Βλέπετε μήποτε 'see to it lest (perhaps)' (plus the future indicative ἔσται 'shall be' [Lg]) indicates a fear of the possibility of such an occurrence [Alf, Hwt, Lg, Lns, Mil, My]. It is a warning [Lg, Lns, My, WBC], and implies the reality and urgency of the admonition [Hwt, NTC, Wst]. The author is not suggesting that the corruption already exists [NIGTC].

QUESTION—What relationship is indicated by the clause introduced by μήποτε 'lest perchance'?

1. It expresses the content of seeing to it [NIC, WBC; NIV, NJB, NRSV, REB, TEV, TNT]: see to it that there not be an evil heart of unbelief.
2. It expresses the purpose of taking heed [NAB, NASB]: take heed in order that there not be an evil heart of unbelief.

QUESTION—How are the two nouns related in the genitive construction καρδία ἀπιστίας 'a heart of unbelief'?

1. The genitive ἀπιστίας 'unbelief' expresses the characteristic quality of the heart [Alf, EGT, ICC, Lg, Lns, Mil, NCBC, TH, WBC, Wst]: an unbelieving heart. Unbelief is the principal idea of the passage [Alf].
2. It expresses the basis of πονηρά 'evil' [My]: a heart that is evil because of unbelief.

QUESTION—What is the meaning of ἀπιστία 'unbelief, unfaithfulness'?

1. It means not believing [BAGD, HNTC, LN, Lns, Mil, NIC, TH, WBC; all versions except NAB, REB]: an evil heart that refuses to believe.
2. It means being unfaithful [NAB, REB]: an evil heart that is unfaithful.

QUESTION—What relationship is indicated by the infinitive phrase ἐν τῷ ἀποστῆναι 'in turning away'?

1. It makes a comment concerning the unbelieving heart [WBC; NIV, NRSV]: an unbelieving heart that turns away.
2. It identifies the unbelief [Lns, My]: unbelieving as shown by apostatizing.
3. It indicates degree or extent of the unbelief [NJB, TEV]: so unbelieving as to turn away.
4. It expresses the possible result of the disbelieving heart [HNTC, Mil, NIGTC, NTC, TNTC; TNT]: should fall away as a result of disbelief.
5. It expresses the evidence of the unbelief [Wst]: unbelieving as demonstrated in the falling away.

3:13 but[a] encourage[b] yourselves[c] at-the-time-of[d] each day,

LEXICON—a. ἀλλά (LN 89.125; 91.2): 'but' [LN (89.125), Mil, NIC, WBC; KJV, NASB, NIV, NRSV], 'but rather' [HNTC], 'instead' [LN (89.125)], 'rather' [REB], 'instead' [TEV], 'yea' [Lns], not explicit [CEV, NAB, NJB, NLT, TNT].

b. pres. act. indic. of παρακαλέω (LN 25.150) (BAGD 2. p. 617): 'to encourage' [BAGD, HNTC, LN, Mil, NIC, WBC; CEV, NAB, NASB, NIV, NJB, REB, TNT], 'to exhort' [BAGD; KJV, NRSV], 'to admonish' [Lns], 'to warn' [NLT], 'to help' [TEV]. The second person plural refers to the entire community [Mil]. It implies comfort that will strengthen and encourage [Hwt]. Encouragement includes warning and reproof [WBC]. It means to admonish one another [ICC]. The present tense implies continuing encouragement [NIGTC].

c. ἑαυτοῦ (LN 92.24): In the plural, 'yourselves' [LN, Lns], 'one another' [Mil, NIC, WBC; all versions], 'each other' [HNTC; NLT]. The meaning is reciprocal, 'one another' [Alf, Blm, EBC, EGT, GNC, HNTC, Hu, Hwt, Lg, Mil, My, NIC, NIGTC, NTC, TH, WBC, Wst; all versions]; it is reflexive, meaning each to encourage himself, 'yourselves' [Lns].

d. κατά with accusative object (LN 67.33) (BAGD II.2.c. p. 406; ἡμέρα 2. p. 346): 'at the time of' [LN]. The phrase καθ' ἑκάστην ἡμέραν 'at the time of each day' is translated 'every day' [BAGD, Lns, WBC; NJB, NLT, NRSV, TEV, TNT], 'each day' [CEV], 'daily' [KJV, NAB, NIV], 'day by day' [HNTC, Mil, NIC; REB], 'day after day' [NASB]. The inclusion of ἑκάστην 'each' adds emphasis [NIGTC]. This preposition has a distributive meaning [Mil]; it is temporal [Mil], indicating continuous action [EBC, Wst] and emphasizes the continuation implied by βλέπετε 'see to it' in 3:12 [Lns].

QUESTION—What relationship is indicated by ἀλλά 'but'?

It indicates an alternative to the warning in 3:12 [REB, TEV], a contrast with the preceding negative comment [NIGTC]. It expresses an exhortation based on the preceding warning, with contrast used to highlight the admonition [Mil]. It tells how to avoid falling away [EGT, Hu, NCBC]. It combines comfort and exhortation [Lg].

while[a] it-is-called[b] the Today,[c]

LEXICON—a. ἄχρις οὗ (LN **67.139**) (BAGD 2.a. p. 129): 'while' [KJV, NAB], 'as long as' [BAGD, HNTC, LN, Lns, Mil; all versions except KJV, NAB], 'so long as' [NIC, WBC]. The reference is to the time during which something can be done, 'while' [EGT, Mil, NIGTC].

b. pres. pass. indic. of καλέω (LN 33.131) (BAGD 1.a.δ. p.399): 'to be called' [BAGD, HNTC, LN, Lns, Mil, NIC, WBC; KJV, NASB, NIV, NLT, NRSV]. The passive voice is also translated as an active voice: 'to be' [NAB], 'to last' [NJB], 'to sound in one's ears' [REB], 'to apply' [TEV, TNT].

c. σήμερον (LN 67.205) (BAGD p. 749): 'today' [BAGD, HNTC, LN, Lns, Mil, NIC, WBC; all versions].

QUESTION—What is the meaning of this clause?

It means as long as the period called 'today' lasts [Mil, My, NIC], the day of grace [Alf, Hu, Lg, Lns, My, TNTC] before the Lord's return [Alf, Lg, My, WBC, Wst], the time while there is still opportunity to hear God's invitation [Blm, EGT, ICC, NCBC, WBC], so long as God still speaks to people through this Psalm [HNTC, Lg, TH, WBC, Wst], so long as God leaves open the promise [NIGTC], the period of one's earthly life [NTC, Wst]. Every day is a new 'today' [GNC]. It implies urgency, since 'today' will not always last [EBC, GNC, Hu, Hwt].

QUESTION—What relationship is indicated by the definite article τό 'the'?

1. With the neuter article, τὸ σήμερον 'the today' means 'the word "Today"' [Alf, EGT, NIGTC; CEV, REB, TEV], the 'today' mentioned in the Psalm [Mil, NIGTC; TNT].
2. The article makes 'today' specific [NJB]: this today.
3. The article refers to the quotation [NTC]: the quotation 'Today'.

in-order-that[a] not anyone of[b] you may-be-hardened[c] by-deceitfulness[d] of-the sin

LEXICON—a. ἵνα (LN 89.59): 'in order that' [HNTC, LN; TEV], 'for the very purpose that' [LN], 'so that' [Mil, WBC; NAB, NIV, NJB, NLT, NRSV, REB], 'and ensure that' [TNT]. The phrase ἵνα μή 'in order that not' is translated 'lest' [Lns, NIC; KJV, NASB], 'if you don't' [CEV].

b. ἐκ with genitive object (LN 63.20): 'of' [HNTC, Lns, Mil, NIC; all versions except NAB, TNT], 'one of' [LN], 'among' [WBC], 'one among' [LN], not explicit [NAB, TNT]. The phrase ἐξ ὑμῶν 'of you' is emphatic [ICC]; it implies 'of your number' [Lns].

c. aor. pass. subj. of σκληρύνω (LN 88.225) (BAGD 2. p. 756): 'to be hardened' [BAGD, HNTC, Lns, Mil, NIC, WBC; KJV, NASB, NIV, NJB, NLT, NRSV], 'to become hardened' [BAGD], 'to grow hardened' [NAB], 'to be stubborn' [LN], 'to become stubborn' [TEV], 'to be made stubborn' [CEV, REB, TNT], 'to be obstinate' [LN]. It is a passive voice of permission, 'to let oneself be hardened' [WBC], a passive voice with middle voice meaning, implying hardening themselves [ICC]. The aorist subjunctive implies that the hardening had not yet occurred [Hu]. It is possible that some had already been deceived [Hwt].

d. ἀπάτη (LN 31.12) (BAGD 1. p. 82): 'deceitfulness' [BAGD, HNTC, NIC; KJV, NASB, NIV, NRSV], 'deceit' [Lns, Mil; NAB], 'deception' [LN], 'enticement' [Mil], 'lure' [NJB], 'wiles' [REB], 'delusive attractiveness' [WBC]. The phrase ἀπάτῃ τῆς ἁμαρτίας 'by deceitfulness of sin' is translated 'be deceived by sin' [NLT, TEV], 'is seduced by sin' [TNT], 'sin may fool' [CEV]. The dative case indicates deceitfulness as the means of the hardening [Lns], the agent of the hardening [NTC].

QUESTION—What relationship is indicated by ἵνα 'in order that' ?

It expresses the purpose of the mutual encouragement [Mil].

QUESTION—How are the two nouns related in the genitive construction ἀπάτῃ τῆς ἁμαρτίας 'deceitfulness of sin'?

The definite article indicates sin as a power [Lns, Wst]. Sin is personified here as if it could itself act [HNTC, Hu, Hwt, Mil, My, NCBC, NTC, TNTC, WBC].

1. The genitive ἁμαρτίας 'sin' is subjective [EBC, HNTC, Hu, Hwt, ICC, Mil, NIGTC, NTC, TNTC, WBC]: sin deceives.
2. Sin is the source of the deceitfulness [Alf]: deceitfulness arising from sin.

3:14 —for[a] we-have-become partakers/partners[b] of/with-the Christ,

LEXICON—a. γάρ (LN 89.23): 'for' [HNTC, LN, Lns, Mil, NIC, WBC; KJV, NASB, NLT, NRSV, REB, TEV, TNT], 'because' [LN; NJB], not explicit [CEV, NAB, NIV].

b. μέτοχος (LN 34.8) (BAGD 1. p. 514): 'partaker' [KJV, NASB], 'participator' [Mil], 'partner' [HNTC, LN, NIC, WBC; NAB, NRSV, REB, TEV, TNT], 'sharer' [Lns], 'companion' [LN]. This word is also translated as a participle: 'sharing' [BAGD]. The phrase μέτοχοι γεγόναμεν 'we have become partakers/partners' is translated 'we have come to share' [NIV], 'we will share in all that belongs to (Christ)' [NLT], 'we have been granted a share' [NJB], 'we became his people' [CEV].

QUESTION—What relationship is indicated by γάρ 'for'?

It indicates the grounds for the warning of 3:12 [Alf, HNTC, ICC, Lg, Lns, Mil, My, Wst]: don't fall away, for. . . . It implies that God's call is still in effect [ICC]. It refers back to 3:6, repeating the warning expressed there [Blm, EGT], which is the subject of the exhortation in 3:13 [Blm]. It contrasts the mention of hardening of the heart with the position of those who are established in Christ [TNTC]. This verse is parenthetical [GNT, HNTC, TNTC].

QUESTION—What does γεγόναμεν 'we have become' indicate?

The perfect tense means that the relationship began in the past and continues in the present [HNTC, Hu, Lns, NIGTC, WBC]. It implies that they did not possess this relationship by nature; it was acquired [Lg, Mil, My]; it is a blessing conferred [Wst]. The first person plural 'we' includes the author and his hearers [Mil].

QUESTION—How are the two nouns related in the genitive construction μέτοχοι τοῦ Χριστοῦ 'partakers/partners of Christ'?

1. 'Christ' is the object of partaking [Alf, Blm, EBC, Hu, Lns, My, NIGTC, NTC, Wst; KJV, NASB, NIV]: we participate in Christ. We participate in the fullness of Christ's life [Wst]. The definite article with 'Christ' indicates Christ as the one who was the hope of the fathers [Wst].
2. It means having a personal interest in Christ [ICC].
3. It means that they were participants with Christ [EGT, HNTC, Lg, Mil, NCBC, NIC, TH, TNTC, WBC; NAB, NLT, NRSV, REB, TEV, TNT]; we are partners with Christ. They share in their participation in the heavenly kingdom [NIC, TNTC].

if-indeed[a] we-hold-fast[b] the beginning[c] of-the confidence[d] firm[e] until[f] (the) end[g]—

LEXICON—a. ἐάνπερ (LN **89.68**) (BAGD I.3.c. p. 211): 'if indeed' [BAGD, HNTC, **LN**, Lns], 'if surely' [LN], 'if only' [BAGD; NAB, NRSV, REB, TNT], 'only if' [NJB], 'only if indeed' [Mil], 'if' [NIC; KJV, NASB, NIV, NLT, TEV], 'supposing that' [BAGD, WBC], not explicit [CEV]. The -περ intensifies the 'if' [Lns, TNTC]. The meaning is 'provided that', stronger than 'if' [ICC, NIGTC]. With the subjunctive mood, it implies the possibility of not fulfilling the condition [Lg]. It is an open condition [NIGTC]. It assumes that the readers would continue in faith [TNTC].

b. aor. act. subj. of κατέχω (LN 57.1) (BAGD 1.b.β. p. 423): 'to hold fast' [BAGD, Lns; NASB], 'to hold tightly' [CEV], 'to hold' [HNTC, Mil, WBC; KJV, NRSV, TEV, TNT], 'to retain' [BAGD], 'to maintain' [NIC], 'to possess' [LN], 'to keep' [REB], 'to keep the grasp' [NJB], 'to be faithful' [NLT].

c. ἀρχή (LN 67.65; 68.1) (BAGD 1.b. p. 111): 'beginning' [BAGD, LN, Lns, NIC; KJV, NASB]. The phrase ἀρχὴν τῆς ὑποστάσεως 'beginning of the confidence' is translated 'our first confidence' [NRSV], 'our initial confidence' [REB], 'that confidence with which we began' [NAB], 'the confidence we had at first' [NIV], 'the confidence we had at the beginning' [TEV, TNT], 'the confidence which we had at the start' [HNTC], 'of our first confidence' [NJB], 'original conviction' [BAGD], 'the original ground of hope' [Mil], 'the basic position we had at the beginning' [WBC], 'we were sure about Christ when we first became his people' [CEV], 'trusting God when we first believed' [NLT]. It refers to their initial belief [Alf, Blm, EBC, GNC, HNTC, Hu, Hwt, ICC, Lg, Lns, Mil, My, NIC, NIGTC, NTC, TH; NAB, NIV, NRSV, REB, TEV, TNT], an active beginning which can develop [Wst].

d. ὑπόστασις (LN **31.84**) (BAGD 2. p. 847): 'confidence' [HNTC, LN, Lns; all versions except NASB], 'trust' [**LN**], 'assurance' [LN; NASB], 'steadfastness' [NIC], 'frame of mind' [BAGD]. It is a confidence based on faith [My], a confident frame of mind [NIGTC].

e. βέβαιος (LN 31.90, 71.15) (BAGD 2. p. 138): 'firm' [BAGD, HNTC, Lns, Mil, NIC; NASB, NJB, NRSV, REB, TNT], 'certain, sure' [LN (71.15)], 'steadfast' [KJV], 'dependable, reliable, trustworthy' [LN (31.90)]. This word is also translated as an adverb: 'firmly' [WBC; NLT, TEV]. The phrase βέβαιαν κατάσχωμεν 'firm we hold fast' is translated 'we hold firmly' [NIV], 'we maintain' [NAB]. Τὴν ἀρχὴν . . . βέβαιαν means '(hold) the beginning as firm' [Lns].

f. μέχρι (LN 67.119) (BAGD 1.b. p. 515): 'until' [BAGD, LN; CEV, NASB, NIV], 'unto' [KJV], 'to' [HNTC, Lns, Mil, NIC, WBC; NAB, NJB, NLT, NRSV, REB, TEV, TNT].

g. τέλος (LN 67.66) (BAGD 1.d.β. p. 812): 'end' [BAGD, HNTC, LN, Lns, Mil, NIC, WBC; all versions]. It is not specified whether it is the close of a person's life or the close of the age [Wst]. The reference is to the Lord's return [Alf, Mil], entrance into God's final rest [WBC], the end of their life [TH].

QUESTION—How are the two nouns related in the genitive construction τὴν ἀρχὴν τῆς ὑποστάσεως 'the beginning of the confidence'?

The genitive tells what was begun [Mil]: we began having the confidence.

DISCOURSE UNIT: 3:15–19 [Lns]. The topic is not failing to enter into God's rest.

3:15 in[a] the being-said, "Today if you should-hear his voice, do-not harden your hearts as in the rebellion."[b]

LEXICON—a. ἐν with dative object (LN 67.33; 89.5): 'in' [HNTC, LN (89.5), Lns; NJB], 'when' [LN (67.33), NIC; NAB, REB], 'while' [KJV, NASB], 'as' [WBC; NIV, NRSV], 'with regard to' [LN (89.5)], 'in the case of' [LN (89.5)], 'seeing that' [Mil]. The phrase ἐν τῷ λέγεσθαι 'in the being said' is translated 'this is what the scripture says' [TEV], 'Scripture says to us also' [TNT], 'the Scriptures say' [CEV], 'but never forget the warning' [NLT].

b. The quoted sentence is the same as at 3:7b–8a.

QUESTION—How is this verse related to other clauses?

1. It is connected with what precedes [Alf, EBC, HNTC, ICC, Mil, NCBC, NTC, WBC, Wst; CEV, KJV, NASB, NIV].

1.1 It is connected with the preceding clause [Alf, EBC] and gives the reason for the comment there [Alf]: if we hold fast . . . for it is said . . .

1.2 It is connected with 3:13–14 [ICC, Mil] as a closing [Mil].

1.3 It is connected with 3:13, and 3:14 is parenthetical [HNTC, Wst]: encourage each other, as it is said . . .

1.4 It summarizes 3:12–14 [WBC].

2. It is connected with what follows [Blm, Lg, Lns, My, NIC, NIGTC; NAB, NJB, REB].

2.1 It introduces the following verse [Blm, Lg, My] in the sense of a condition whose consequence is expressed in 3:16 [Lg]; it also confirms the warning expressed in 3:12–13 [Blm].

2.2 It is connected with 4:1, 3:16–19 being a digression restating what was previously implied [Lg(K)].

3. It is an independent statement [TH; TEV, TNT].

3:16 For/Now[a] who having-heard rebelled?[b]

TEXT—Instead of the interrogative τίνες 'who?' some manuscripts read τινές 'some'. GNT does not deal with this variant. Only KJV reads 'some'.

LEXICON—a. γάρ (LN 89.23; 91.1): 'for' [LN, Mil, WBC; KJV, NASB], 'because' [LN], 'now' [NRSV], 'and' [HNTC; NLT], not explicit [Lns, NIC; CEV, NAB, NIV, NJB, REB, TEV, TNT].

b. aor. act. indic. of παραπικραίνω (LN **39.40**) (BAGD 2. p. 621): 'to rebel' [LN, Mil, NIC, WBC; CEV, NIV, NJB, NLT, REB, TEV, TNT], 'to be rebellious' [BAGD; NRSV], 'to be disobedient' [BAGD], 'to revolt' [NAB], 'to provoke' [KJV, NASB], 'to cause exasperation' [HNTC], 'to make embitterment' [Lns]. This verb carries forward the sense of παραπικρασμῷ 'rebellion' in 3:15, probably referring to the rebellion at Kadesh [WBC].

QUESTION—What relationship is indicated by γάρ 'for/now'?

1. It indicates the reason why the OT Israelites were excluded [Alf, Blm, Mil], which is revealed in the implied answer to the rhetorical questions [Ed]: don't harden your hearts; for they who rebelled under Moses were excluded from God's rest. It strengthens the interrogation and confirms the comment of 3:14 [My]. The warning is that initial confidence is not enough, for they who fell in the wilderness had begun in faith [EGT, Mil].

2. It is the weakest kind of transition [HNTC, Lns, NIGTC, TH; NLT, NRSV].

QUESTION—What relationship is indicated by the aorist participle ἀκούσαντες 'having heard'?

1. It is temporal [Alf, EGT; NAB]: when they had heard, they rebelled.

2. It is concessive [Mil, NIGTC, TH, WBC; NRSV, REB]: although they heard, yet they rebelled. It indicates that they did hear; the aorist tense indicates time preceding the rebellion [NIGTC, WBC].
3. It is parallel to παρεπίκραναν 'rebelled' [NIV, NJB, TEV, TNT]: they heard and they rebelled.

But/Certainly[a] (was it) not all the-(ones) having-come-out from[b] Egypt through[c] Moses?

LEXICON—a. ἀλλά (LN 91.2; 91.11) (BAGD 2. p. 38; 3. p. 38): 'but' [LN (91.2)], 'certainly' [LN (91.11)], 'surely' [BAGD; NJB, REB], 'indeed' [Mil; NASB], 'really' [WBC], 'howbeit' [KJV], 'yea' [Lns], not explicit [HNTC, NIC; CEV, NAB, NIV, NLT, NRSV, TEV, TNT].

b. ἐκ with genitive object (LN 84.4): 'from' [LN], 'out from' [LN], 'out of' [LN; NLT], 'of' [HNTC, Lns, Mil, NIC; CEV, KJV, NASB, TEV, TNT].

c. διά with genitive object (LN 90.4) (BAGD A.III.2.a. p. 180): 'through' [BAGD, LN, Lns], 'by' [LN; KJV, NASB, TEV], 'under' [HNTC; TNT], 'under the leadership of' [Mil], 'with' [CEV]. The phrase διὰ Μωϋσέως 'through Moses' is translated 'under Moses' leadership' [BAGD, NIC]. The phrase οἱ ἐξελθόντες διὰ Μωϋσέως 'the ones having come out through Moses' is translated 'those whom Moses led out' [NJB], 'those whom Moses had led out' [REB], 'those Moses led out' [WBC; NIV, NLT], 'whom Moses had led out' [NAB], 'those who left under the leadership of Moses' [NRSV].

QUESTION—What is the form of this clause?

1. For those who read τίνες 'who?' in the preceding clause.

1.1 This is a second rhetorical question [Alf, Blm, EBC, EGT, GNC, HNTC, Hu, Hwt, ICC, Lg, Lns, Mil, My, NCBC, NIC, NTC, TH, TNTC, WBC, Wst; CEV, NAB, NASB, NIV, NLT, NRSV]: For who rebelled? Was it not all who came out, etc.? This question indicates the reply to the first one [Mil, My, NTC, TH, TNTC, WBC].

1.2 This is a statement in reply to the preceding rhetorical question [NJB, REB, TEV, TNT]: For who rebelled? All who came out, etc.

2. For those who read τινές 'some' in the preceding clause, the verse consists of two statements [KJV]: For some rebelled; but it was not all who came out, etc.

QUESTION—What relationship is indicated by ἀλλά 'but'?

1. It indicates a negation of the uncertainty implied in the preceding question [Alf, My, Wst]: such a question is not necessary; it was all, etc.
2. It negates the possible response "Was it only some?" to the preceding question [EGT, ICC, Mil]: no, it was all. Joshua and Caleb as exceptions are ignored [EGT].
3. It indicates a rhetorical confirmation [Lns, WBC; NASB, NJB, REB]: indeed.

QUESTION—What relationship is implied by οὐ 'not' in this question?
It indicates that an affirmative reply is presumed [Blm, EBC, GNC, Lg, Mil, My]: it *was* all who came out.
QUESTION—What relationship is implied by πάντες 'all'?
It is inclusive, the few exceptions not being considered [Alf, EBC, EGT, Hu, ICC, Lg, NIC, TNTC, WBC, Wst]: all who came out. It also implies that all had heard God's voice [WBC].
QUESTION—What is implied by οἱ ἐξελθόντες 'the ones having come out'?
It indicates that those who rebelled were the ones who had had the privilege of being rescued from Egypt [GNC, Lg, Mil, NIC, Wst]. It implies their own actions and their faith at the time [Wst].
QUESTION—What relationship is implied by the phrase διὰ Μωϋσέως 'through Moses'?
It implies that they acted on their own volition and started out well [EBC]. It indicates Moses as the agent and guide [My, NIC, NIGTC], the instrument of their deliverance [Wst]. The people were under his leadership [HNTC, Mil, WBC; NRSV, TNT]. Since Moses was the intermediate agent, it implies that God was the actual leader [Mil, NIGTC].

3:17 And[a] with-whom was-he-provoked[b] for-forty years?
LEXICON—a. δέ (LN 89.94): 'and' [HNTC, LN, Mil, NIC, WBC; NASB, NIV, NJB, NLT, REB], 'but' [KJV, NRSV], 'moreover' [Lns], not explicit [CEV, NAB, TEV, TNT]. This word implies a slight contrast with the preceding thought [Alf].
b. aor. pass. indic. of προσοχθίζω (LN **88.172**) (BAGD p. 717): 'to be provoked' [**LN**], 'to be provoked to anger' [Mil], 'to be angry' [BAGD, LN, WBC; NAB, NASB, NIV, NJB, NRSV, TEV, TNT], 'to be made angry' [CEV, NLT], 'to be vexed' [NIC], 'to be indignant' [REB], 'to be revolted' [HNTC], 'to be offended' [BAGD], 'to be disgusted' [Lns], 'to be grieved' [KJV].
QUESTION—Why is this verse mentioned?
This and the two following verses imply the fate of the readers if they imitate the actions of the Israelites after the exodus from Egypt [Blm]. It continues the reason for the exhortation of 3:15 [Mil]; it further develops the thought of 3:16 [My].
QUESTION—To what does this clause refer?
It refers to the continuing wrath of God during this period [EBC, EGT, GNC, HNTC, Hu, Lns, WBC], the continuing rebellion [GNC, Hwt, Mil, My, NTC, TNTC, Wst].

(Was it) not with-the-(ones) having sinned,[a] whose corpses[b] fell[c] in[d] the wilderness?[e]
LEXICON—a. aor. act. participle of ἁμαρτάνω (LN 88.289): 'to sin' [HNTC, LN, Lns, Mil, NIC, WBC; all versions].
b. κῶλον (LN **8.8**) (BAGD p. 461): 'corpse' [BAGD, HNTC, LN, Mil, NIC; NAB], 'carcass' [Lns; KJV], 'dead body' [BAGD, **LN**; NJB], 'body'

[WBC; NASB, NIV, NLT, NRSV, REB]. The phrase ὧν τὰ κῶλα ἔπεσεν 'whose corpses fell' is translated 'who fell down dead' [TEV], 'who fell dead' [TNT], 'the ones that died' [CEV].

c. aor. act. indic. of πίπτω (LN 15.118; 23.105) (BAGD 1.b.α. p. 659): 'to fall' [HNTC, LN (15.118), Lns, Mil, NIC, WBC; KJV, NAB, NASB, NIV, NJB, NLT, NRSV], 'to lie where one falls' [REB], 'to fall dead' [BAGD; TEV, TNT], 'to die' [LN (23.105); CEV]. This word implies death [TH]. It means to fall dead [NIGTC], to be stretched out dead [My].

d. ἐν with dative object (LN 83.13): 'in' [HNTC, LN, Lns, Mil, NIC, WBC; all versions].

e. ἔρημος (LN 1.86) (BAGD 2. p. 309): 'wilderness' [BAGD, HNTC, LN, Lns; KJV, NASB, NLT, NRSV], 'desert' [BAGD, LN, Mil, NIC, WBC; CEV, NAB, NIV, NJB, REB, TEV, TNT]. It refers to land not cultivated or inhabited [EBC].

QUESTION—What is the form of this clause?

1. It is a rhetorical question [Alf, EBC, EGT, HNTC, Lns, Mil, My, NIC, WBC; CEV, KJV, NAB, NASB, NIV, NLT, NRSV].
2. It is a statement [NJB, REB, TEV, TNT].

QUESTION—What is implied by the phrase 'whose corpses fell in the wilderness'?

It implies sudden and violent death [Blm, My].

1. It indicates the result of their sinning [Mil, TNTC].
2. It characterizes 'the ones having sinned' [My, Wst].

QUESTION—What is implied by οὐχί 'not'?

It implies an affirmative reply [EBC, Lns, Mil, NIGTC]: it *was* with those who sinned.

3:18 And[a] to-whom did-he-swear[b] not to-be-going-to-enter/that they-would- not -enter into[c] his rest[d] if[e] not to-the-(ones) having-disobeyed?[f]

LEXICON—a. δέ (LN 89.94): 'and' [HNTC, LN, Mil, NIC, WBC; CEV, KJV, NASB, NIV, NLT, NRSV, REB, TNT], 'moreover' [Lns], not explicit [NAB, NJB, TEV].

b. aor. act. indic. of ὀμνύω: 'to swear'. See this word at 3:11.

c. εἰς with accusative object: 'into'. See this word at 3:11.

d. κατάπαυσις (LN **23.81**): 'rest'. See this word at 3:11. The phrase εἰς τὴν κατάπαυσιν αὐτοῦ 'into his rest' is translated 'and rest with him' [LN; TNT]. The reference is to the Promised Land [Hu, GNC, Hu] but its true fulfillment goes beyond earthly rest [GNC]; the author extends the meaning for his readers to God's heavenly rest [Blm, Hu].

e. εἰ (LN 89.65; 89.131): 'if' [HNTC, LN (89.65), Mil, NIC, WBC; NIV, NRSV, REB]. The phrase εἰ μή 'if not' is translated 'except' [LN (89.131)], 'but' [Lns; KJV, NAB, NASB], 'surely' [NJB, TNT], not explicit [CEV, NLT, TEV].

f. aor. act. participle of ἀπειθέω (LN 31.107; 36.23) (BAGD 2. p. 82): 'to disobey' [BAGD, LN (36.23), Lns, Mil, NIC; CEV, NIV, NLT, TNT], 'to be disobedient' [BAGD, HNTC; NASB, NRSV], 'to refuse to obey' [WBC], 'to rebel' [TEV], 'to believe not' [KJV, NJB], 'to refuse to believe' [LN (31.107); REB]. The participial phrase τοῖς ἀπειθήσασιν 'the ones having disobeyed' is translated 'the disobedient' [NAB]. The reference is to disobedience [Alf, EBC, EGT, GNC, NTC, TH, TNTC, WBC, Wst].

QUESTION—What relationship is indicated by δέ 'and'?

It continues the grounds for the exhortation expressed in 3:15 [Mil].

QUESTION—What relationship is indicated by the phrase εἰ μὴ τοῖς ἀπειθήσασιν 'if not to the ones having disobeyed'?

It indicates the response to the question in the first part of the verse [Lns, TNTC]: To whom . . . ? It was to those who disobeyed.

QUESTION—What is the implied subject of the future infinitive εἰσελεύσεσθαι 'to be going to enter'?

The implied subject is the persons against whom the oath is declared [Alf, EBC, GNC, Hu, Mil, TH, Wst; all versions]: he swore that they would not enter.

3:19 and[a] we-see[b] that not they-were-able to-enter on-account-of[c] unbelief.[d]

LEXICON—a. καί (LN 89.87) (BAGD I.2.f. p. 392): 'and' [LN], 'and then' [BAGD, LN], 'and so' [BAGD, Lns, Mil; NASB], 'so' [HNTC; KJV, NIV, NJB, NLT, NRSV, TNT], 'so then' [WBC], 'then' [NIC; REB, TEV], 'moreover' [NAB], not explicit [CEV].

b. pres. act. indic. of βλέπω (LN 24.7, 32.11) (BAGD 7.b. p. 144): 'to see' [HNTC, LN (24.7, 32.11), Lns, Mil, NIC, WBC; all versions], 'to perceive' [LN (32.11)], 'to recognize' [LN (32.11)], 'to understand' [LN (32.11)], 'to discover' [BAGD], 'to find' [BAGD]. The meaning is that they could infer this from the preceding account [Blm]; it implies that the author is confident that his readers will understand [Lns, TNTC]. The use of the first person plural here opens the way for the following discussion [NIGTC].

c. διά with accusative object (LN 89.26): 'on account of' [LN], 'because of' [HNTC, LN, Lns, Mil, NIC, WBC; KJV, NASB, NIV, NLT, NRSV], 'because' [Mil; CEV, TEV, TNT]. The phrase οὐκ ἠδυνήθησαν εἰσελθεῖν δι' ἀπιστίαν 'they were not able to enter on account of unbelief' is translated 'it was their unbelief that kept them from entering' [NAB], 'it was unbelief that prevented their entering' [REB], 'it was their refusal to believe which prevented them from entering' [NJB].

d. ἀπιστία (LN 31.97) (BAGD 2.b. p. 85): 'unbelief' [BAGD, HNTC, LN, Lns, Mil, NIC, WBC; KJV, NAB, NASB, NIV, NLT, NRSV, REB], 'lack of belief' [BAGD], 'refusal to believe' [NJB]. This noun is also translated as a verb phrase: 'to not believe' [Mil; TEV, TNT], 'to not have faith' [CEV]. This word is emphatic by its final position in the clause [EBC, ICC, My, TH].

QUESTION—What relationship is indicated by καί 'and'?

1. It indicates the conclusion of the preceding argument [EBC, HNTC, Hwt, Mil, NIC, NIGTC, TH, Wst; all versions] which began with 3:12 [Alf, ICC, Lns, TNTC, WBC], with 3:15 [My, NCBC], with 3:16 [NTC].
2. It simply introduces a fact [Lg].

QUESTION—What is meant by οὐκ ἠδυνήθησαν 'they were not able'?

It means that their unbelief made them unable to enter [EBC, EGT]; it was a moral impossibility [HNTC, Wst]. Their unbelief made them unfit for God's rest [Blm, Hu] and made it impossible for God to give it to them [Blm].

DISCOURSE UNIT: 4:1–16 [Lns; NASB]. The topic is the promise that those who believe will enter God's rest [Lns], rest for the believer [NASB].

DISCOURSE UNIT: 4:1–14 [WBC]. The topic is rest as a sabbath celebration for God's people.

DISCOURSE UNIT: 4:1–13 [GNC, Hwt, NTC, TNTC, Wst; NIV, NLT]. The topic is the promised rest for God's people [NLT], the remaining promise of rest [GNC, Wst], God's sabbath-rest for his people [NIV], the gospel of rest [Hwt], the superiority of Jesus to Moses; an invitation to enter God's rest [NTC], the superiority of Jesus to Joshua [TNTC]

DISCOURSE UNIT: 4:1–11 [HNTC, NCBC, NIGTC]. The topic is God's people and the rest [HNTC, NCBC], from warning to promise [NIGTC].

DISCOURSE UNIT: 4:1–10 [EBC, Lg, NIC, TNTC]. The topic is that Christians enter God's rest [EBC], God's promise of entering his rest remains for Christians [Lg], the greater rest that Joshua could not secure [TNTC], God's promised rest may be lost [NIC].

DISCOURSE UNIT: 4:1–5 [Lns]. The topic is the rest promised to people of faith.

4:1 Therefore[a] let-us-fear[b] lest-ever[c] a-promise being-left-behind[d] to-enter into[e] his rest[f] anyone of[g] you should-appear[h] to-have-fallen-short.[i]

LEXICON—a. οὖν (LN 89.50): 'therefore' [HNTC, LN, Mil, NIC, WBC; KJV, NAB, NASB, NIV, NRSV, REB], 'then' [LN, Lns; NJB], 'so' [LN; NLT], 'now' [TEV, TNT], not explicit [CEV].

b. aorist pass. (deponent = act.) subj. of φοβέομαι (LN 25.252) (BAGD 1.a. p. 863): 'to fear' [LN, Lns, NIC, WBC; KJV, NASB, REB, TNT], 'to tremble with fear' [NLT], 'to be afraid' [BAGD, LN], 'to be fearful' [NAB], 'to beware' [NJB], 'to be on guard' [HNTC], 'to take care' [CEV, NRSV, TEV], 'to be careful' [NIV], 'to be very careful' [Mil]. The first person plural 'let us' here softens the warning [Mil, My] and shows the author's unity with his readers [Hu, My, NTC, Wst], all of them being responsible for the spiritual welfare of the church [NTC]. It is then necessarily changed to the second person 'you' later in the verse [Alf]. This word is emphatic by its word order [EBC, NIGTC, TNTC, WBC].

c. μήποτε (LN 89.62) (BAGD 2.a.β. p. 519): 'lest ever', 'lest perhaps' [Lns], 'lest perchance' [Mil], 'lest' [BAGD, LN, NIC; KJV, NAB, NASB], 'in order that not' [LN], 'so that not' [LN], 'that not' [BAGD], 'for fear that' [HNTC], 'that' [WBC; NLT, REB, TNT]. The phrase μήποτε . . . τις 'lest ever . . . anyone' is translated 'that . . . none' [CEV, NIV, NRSV, TEV]. The phrase μήποτε . . . δοκῇ τις ἐξ ὑμῶν 'lest ever . . . anyone of you should appear' is translated 'none of you must think' [NJB]. It indicates anxiety [Lns]. It is only indefinite, not including the sense 'at any time' [Alf]; -ποτε adds the sense of possibility [EGT, Mil].

d. pres. pass. participle of καταλείπω (LN **13.92**) (BAGD 2.f. p.413): 'to be left behind', 'to be left' [**LN**, Lns; KJV], 'to be left open' [NIC], 'to be offered' [TEV], 'to be opened' [BAGD]. This is also translated in the active voice: 'to remain' [NASB], 'to remain open' [HNTC, WBC; REB], 'to still hold' [NAB], 'to still hold good' [Mil], 'to still be good' [CEV], 'to still stand' [NIV, NLT, TNT], 'to never lapse' [NJB]. The meaning is that the promise is still offered [Blm, EBC, EGT, GNC, Hu, Hwt, ICC, Lg, Lns, My, NIC, TH, TNTC, WBC, Wst]. The participial phrase καταλειπομένης ἐπαγγελίας 'a promise being left' is a genitive absolute [Alf, ICC, Lns, Mil] (i.e., it is grammatically independent in its clause). The present tense indicates time concurrent with the main verb φοβηθῶμεν 'let us fear' [Mil].

e. εἰς with accusative object (LN 84.22): 'into' [LN, Lns, Mil; KJV, NAB], not explicit [HNTC, NIC, WBC; CEV, NASB, NIV, NJB, NLT, REB, TNT]. The phrase εἰσελθεῖν εἰς 'to enter into' is translated 'that we may receive' [TEV].

f. κατάπαυσις: 'rest'. See this word in 3:19. The author uses this word to refer to far more than the entry into Canaan [EBC, Hu, NIC]; it refers to a spiritual rest [NTC], a heavenly rest [Blm, Hu, Lns, My, WBC], the rest into which God entered [Alf], the rest that belongs to God [Lg].

g. ἐκ with genitive object (LN 63.20): 'of' [HNTC, Lns, Mil, NIC; all versions], 'one of, one among' [LN], 'among' [WBC].

h. pres. act. subj. of δοκέω (LN 31.29) (BAGD 2.a. p. 202): 'to appear', 'to have the appearance' [BAGD], 'to seem' [BAGD, WBC; KJV, NASB, NRSV], 'to turn out' [NIC], 'to think' [HNTC, LN; NJB, TNT], 'to imagine' [LN, Lns], 'to suppose, to believe' [LN], not explicit [CEV, NLT]. The active voice is also translated as a passive voice: 'to be judged' [NAB], 'to be found' [Mil; NIV, REB, TEV]. The meaning is the appearance of the actual condition [Lg, NTC], to be found to be in a certain situation [Alf]. It makes the expression more delicate [My]; it softens the force of the following infinitive [Alf, Blm, EBC, Lg(K), NIGTC, Wst], to avoid saying specifically that any of the readers have missed or will miss the promise [EBC]. It means that even the appearance of failure is to be avoided [Wst].

i. perf. act. infin. of ὑστερέω (LN 13.21; 65.51) (BAGD 1.a. p. 849): 'to fall short' [NIC; NIV], 'to come short' [KJV, NASB], 'to fail to reach'

[BAGD; NRSV], 'to fail to get there' [NLT], 'to fail to attain, to not attain' [LN (13.21)], 'to fail to receive' [TEV], 'to be excluded' [WBC], 'to miss' [BAGD], 'to miss one's opportunity' [REB], 'to miss the opportunity to reach' [HNTC], 'to miss one's chance' [TNT], 'to miss out' [CEV], 'to be excluded' [BAGD, Mil], 'to lose one's chance' [NAB], 'to be behind' [Lns], 'to come too late' [NJB], 'to lack benefits' [LN (65.51)]. The perfect tense indicates an abiding state at the time of the verb δοκῇ 'should appear' [Mil, My, Wst], for which state the person is responsible [Mil].

QUESTION—What relationship is indicated by οὖν 'therefore'?

1. It indicates a conclusion based on the preceding facts [HNTC, Mil, NIC, NIGTC, WBC; KJV, NAB, NASB, NIV, NRSV, REB]: therefore. It begins an (allegorical [Blm]) application of the historical events referred to [Blm, Hu, My, NIGTC, WBC]. Since God's promise still applies to us (3:13–14) and those who rebelled were punished (3:15–19), we should therefore be warned [TH].
2. It is resumptive [Lns, NTC; probably NLT, TEV, TNT]. It resumes and enlarges upon the exhortation of 3:12–14 [NTC].

QUESTION—What is it that they are to fear?

1. They should fear failing to enter the rest [Alf, EBC, GNC, Hu, Hwt, ICC, Mil, My, NCBC, NIC, NTC, TH, TNTC, WBC, Wst; CEV, NASB, NIV, NLT, NRSV, REB, TEV]: let us fear lest any of you fail to enter the rest.
2. They should fear to disobey God, lest they should miss the opportunity of entering the rest [NAB]: let us be fearful of disobeying, lest you miss the opportunity of entering the rest.
3. They should fear thinking that they have missed their opportunity [EGT, HNTC; NJB, REB, TNT]: let us fear that any of you should think he has missed his opportunity.
4. They should fear thinking that the rest was promised to Israel and that they have missed it by becoming a Christian [Lns]: let us fear that someone should think that he has missed the rest by becoming a Christian.
5. This is a general caution, and the rest of the verse is an assurance that the rest is available [NJB]: let us beware; none of you must think that he has come too late to receive the promised rest.

QUESTION—What relationship is indicated by the participial form καταλειπομένης 'being left'?

1. It is temporal [HNTC; NAB, NASB, NRSV, REB, TNT]: while it is still left.
2. It indicates a reason [Mil, NTC; NIV, NJB, NLT]: since it is left.
3. It is concessive [Lns]: although it is left.

QUESTION—What is the meaning of δοκῇ ὑστερηκέναι 'should appear to have fallen short'?

1. It means to be found at the last judgment to have missed the promised rest [Alf, EBC, GNC, Hu, Hwt, ICC, Lg, Mil, My, NCBC, NIC, NIGTC,

NTC, TNTC, Wst], excluded by their unbelief [Alf], through their own fault [Hwt, Mil].

2. It means to think that one has come too late [EGT, HNTC; TNT]. The author is encouraging his readers that they were not born too late to receive the promised rest [EGT].
3. It means to think that one has lost God's rest by becoming a Christian [Lns].

4:2 For[a] also we-have-been evangelized[b] just-as[c] those-persons-also;

LEXICON—a. γάρ (LN 89.23): 'for' [HNTC, LN, Lns, Mil, NIC, WBC; KJV, NASB, NIV, NLT, NRSV, REB, TEV], 'because' [LN], not explicit [CEV, NAB, NJB, TNT]. The addition of καί 'also' before γάρ 'for' emphasizes the connection with the preceding thought [NIGTC].

b. perf. pass. (or deponent = act.) participle of εὐαγγελίζω (LN 33.215) (BAGD 2.b.β. p. 317): 'to be evangelized', 'to have the gospel preached to someone' [KJV, NIV], 'to have good news preached to someone' [WBC; NASB, TNT], 'to have the good news preached to someone' [REB], 'to have the good news proclaimed to someone' [Mil], 'to have the Good News announced to someone' [NLT], 'to have the good news come to someone' [NRSV], 'to be told glad tidings' [Lns], 'to be told the good news, to have the gospel announced' [LN], 'to receive the gospel' [NJB], 'to hear the good news' [HNTC, NIC; NAB, TEV], 'to hear the message' [CEV]. This periphrastic perfect indicative ἐσμεν εὐηγγελισμένοι 'we have been evangelized' indicates that the effects of hearing the message are lasting [NIGTC, TH, Wst]. It implies that the message was complete and adequate for a proper response [Hu, WBC]. The writer includes himself by using the first person plural 'we' [TNTC]. The reference is to good news in general [HNTC, ICC, Mil, NIC, WBC; NAB, NASB, NRSV, REB]; it refers to the gospel [Lns; KJV, NIV, NJB].

c. καθάπερ (LN 64.15) (BAGD p. 387): 'just as' [BAGD, HNTC, LN, Lns, Mil, WBC; CEV, NASB, NIV, NLT, NRSV, REB, TEV, TNT], 'exactly as' [NJB], 'as' [LN, NIC; NAB], 'as well as' [KJV]. It expresses a comparison [Mil]. The phrase καθάπερ κἀκεῖνοι 'just as those people also' is emphatic, referring to all the Israelites who came out of Egypt in the Exodus [TH], linking one generation of God's people with another [NIGTC].

QUESTION—What relationship is indicated by γάρ 'for'?

The point is not to contrast the former people with the present readers; rather, the emphasis is on the verb [Alf, My, NTC, Wst], and the reference to both groups is indicated [Alf, Blm, EGT, HNTC, Hwt, My, NIC, TH, Wst].

1. It indicates the grounds for the statement in 4:1 that the promise is still true [Alf, My]: the promise is still true, because the good news has been announced to us also.
2. It states that the promised rest is still available to the readers [NIGTC, TNTC].

3. It expresses the grounds for the exhortation in 4:1 to be careful [Mil, WBC].
4. It tells why the readers should not believe that they have fallen behind by leaving Judaism and becoming Christians [Lns].

but the word of-the hearing[a] did-not profit[b] those-persons

LEXICON—a. ἀκοή (LN **24.52;** 24.57) (BAGD 2.b. p. 31): 'hearing' [LN (24.52), Lns], 'what is heard' [LN (24.57)], 'message' [LN (24.57); CEV]. The phrase τῆς ἀκοῆς 'of the hearing' is translated 'which they heard' [WBC; NAB], 'they heard' [NASB], 'preached' [KJV]. The phrase ὁ λόγος τῆς ἀκοῆς 'the word of hearing' is translated 'the message they heard' [Mil; NIV, NRSV, REB], 'the message which they heard' [HNTC, **LN**, NIC], 'the preaching that they heard' [TNT], 'hearing the message' [NJB], 'what God told them' [NLT]. This entire phrase is translated 'they heard the message, but it did them no good' [TEV].

b. aorist act. indic. of ὠφελέω (LN 35.2) (BAGD 1.a. p. 900): 'to profit' [Lns, Mil; KJV, NAB, NASB], 'to help' [BAGD, LN], 'to benefit' [BAGD, HNTC, WBC; NRSV], 'to be of value (to)' [NIV], 'to be (of) good (to)' [TNT], 'to be of use (to)' [BAGD], 'to do someone good' [NIC; CEV, NJB, NLT, REB, TEV].

QUESTION—How are the two nouns related in the genitive construction ὁ λόγος τῆς ἀκοῆς 'the word of hearing'?

1. The genitive ἀκοῆς 'of hearing' is a qualitative genitive [ICC, Lns, Mil, NTC, WBC]: the heard word. It describes 'word' [WBC].
2. The genitive ἀκοῆς 'of hearing' is a descriptive genitive, implying that the message was given for the purpose of being heard [Hu].
3. The genitive ἀκοῆς 'of hearing' expresses the recipient and the event [HNTC, Mil, NIC; NIV, NRSV, REB, TNT]: the message they heard.
4. The genitive ἀκοῆς 'of hearing' is in apposition to λόγος 'word' [Alf]: the word; that is, the message which they heard.

QUESTION—To what does ὁ λόγος τῆς ἀκοῆς 'the word of hearing' refer?

It refers to the NT gospel message [Blm]; it refers to the word of God made known by proclamation at any time [Lg].

not united[a] with/in-the faith[b] in/with-the-(ones) having-heard.[c]

TEXT—Instead of the masculine accusative plural συγκεκερασμένους 'united' referring to ἐκείνους 'those persons', some manuscripts read the masculine nominative singular συγκεκερασμένος 'united' referring to λόγος 'word'. GNT reads the accusative plural with a B decision, indicating that the text is almost certain. The accusative plural is read by Alf, Mil, NIGTC, WBC, NJB, and NRSV. The nominative singular is read by Blm, EGT, GNC, HNTC, Hu, Hwt, ICC, Lg, Lns, My, NIC, CEV, KJV, NAB, NASB, NIV, NLT, REB, TEV, and TNT.

LEXICON—a. perf. pass. participle of συγκεράννυμι (LN 62.2) (BAGD 2. p. 773): 'to be united' [BAGD, Mil; NASB, NRSV], 'to be put together' [LN], 'to be blended' [HNTC], 'to be mixed' [KJV], 'to be combined'

[NIC; REB]. The passive voice is also translated as an active voice: 'to combine' [NIV]; as a middle voice: 'to mix itself' [Lns]. This entire phrase is translated 'because they did not share the faith of those who did listen' [NJB], 'because they did not share the faith of those who listened' [WBC], 'because when they heard it, they did not accept it with faith' [TEV], 'for they did not receive it in faith' [NAB], 'because, although they heard it with their ears, they did not believe it in their hearts' [TNT], 'they failed to believe what they heard' [CEV], 'they didn't believe what God told them' [NLT].

b. πίστις (LN 31.85) (BAGD 2.d.β. p. 663): 'faith' [HNTC, LN, Lns, Mil, NIC; all versions except CEV, NLT, TNT]. This noun is also translated as a verb: 'to believe' [CEV, NLT, TNT]. If the nominative singular συγκεκερασμένος 'mingled' is read, this dative is instrumental [BAGD]. It means wholehearted trust in God [EBC]. Specifically, it refers to believing that God's promise is reliable [WBC], believing that God would give them rest [TH]. For the readers, it is faith in God's final word spoken through the Lord [WBC].

c. aorist act. participle of ἀκούω (LN 24.52; 31.56; 36.14): 'to hear' [LN (24.52), Lns, Mil; KJV, NASB, NIV, REB], 'to heed' [LN (31.56)], 'to listen' [NJB, NRSV], 'to listen to' [LN (31.56)], 'to accept' [LN (31.56)], 'to pay attention to and obey' [LN (36.14)]. This participle is also translated as a noun: 'hearer' [HNTC, NIC].

QUESTION—What relationship is indicated by this participial phrase?

It indicates the reason why the word did not profit the people [Blm, EGT, HNTC, ICC, Lg, Mil, WBC; all versions except KJV].

QUESTION—What is indicated by the dative forms in this clause?

1. If the accusative plural of the participle is read, it means that the people in general were not united in faith with the few (specifically, Caleb and Joshua [WBC]) who truly heard and obeyed [Mil, NIGTC, WBC; NJB, NRSV]: they were not joined in faith with those who (truly) heard.
2. If the nominative singular of the participle is read, it means that the people in general did not believe the word they heard [Blm, EGT, HNTC, ICC, Lg; NAB, NASB, NIV, REB, TEV, TNT]: the word was not united with faith in those who heard. They did not accept the word with faith [TEV].

2.1 The dative τῇ πίστει 'with faith' is governed by the preposition συν- 'together with' compounded with the preceding participle [Hu, Lg]; the dative τοῖς ἀκούσασιν 'in the ones who heard' is a dative of reference, indicating the persons referred to [Hu, Lg]: not combined with faith in those who heard.

2.2 The dative τῇ πίστει 'with faith' is a dative of means, indicating how it should have been combined [Lns]; the dative τοῖς ἀκούσασιν 'in the ones who heard' is a dative governed by the prefixed preposition συν- 'together with' [Lns]: 'by means of faith' is not combined with 'those who heard'.

QUESTION—To whom does the participial phrase τοῖς ἀκούσασιν 'the ones having heard' refer?

It refers to people of various times who have heard the message in faith [Alf]: those who have heard with faith at various times.

4:3 For/Then[a] we-the-(ones) having-believed[b] enter into[c] the rest,[d]

TEXT—Some manuscripts omit τήν 'the' before κατάπαυσιν 'rest'. GNT includes 'the' with a C decision, indicating that the committee had difficulty in making their decision. This article is omitted by NIGTC, KJV, and NJB.

LEXICON—a. γάρ (LN 89.23; 91.1): 'for' [LN, Lns, Mil, WBC; KJV, NASB, NLT, NRSV], 'because' [LN (89.2)], 'now' [NIV], 'then' [LN (91.1); TEV], 'on the other hand' [TNT], not explicit [HNTC, NIC; CEV, NAB, NJB, REB].

b. aorist act. participle of πιστεύω (LN 31.85, 31.102) (BAGD 2.b. p. 661): 'to believe' [HNTC, LN (31.85), Lns, Mil, NIC, WBC; KJV, NAB, NASB, NIV, NLT, NRSV, TEV], 'to have faith' [CEV, NJB, REB], 'to believe (in)' [BAGD], 'to be a believer' [LN (31.102); TNT], 'to be a Christian' [LN (31.102)].

c. εἰς with accusative object: 'into'. See this word in 4:1.

d. κατάπαυσις: 'rest'. See this word in 4:1.

QUESTION—What relationship is indicated by γάρ 'for, now'?

1. It indicates the grounds for the preceding statement [Alf, Mil]: it did not benefit those people because they did not join those who heard with faith, since we who have faith enter into the rest.
2. It indicates the grounds for 4:1 [ICC, Wst]: I say confidently that a promise has been left to us, for we who have believed are now entering that rest.
3. It indicates transition to the next point [NIC, TH; NIV, TEV].

QUESTION—What is implied by the aorist participle οἱ πιστεύσαντες 'the ones having believed'?

It is emphatic by its word order [Alf, Lns, My, TH]; it stresses the requirement of faith [EBC]. It indicates a specific group of persons distinct from those who refused to believe [Alf, Blm, My, Wst]; it identifies the 'we' of the verb εἰσερχόμεθα 'we enter' [NIGTC]. The aorist tense refers to those who have believed [Lg, Lns], at the time of conversion [Hu, Mil, TNTC, Wst]; it refers to those who will have believed at the time of entering the rest [Alf, My].

QUESTION—What is implied by the present tense of εἰσερχόμεθα 'we enter'?

This word is emphatic by word order [Alf, EGT, ICC, My(D), WBC]; the first person plural includes the author with his readers [NIGTC].

1. It implies that they were in the process of entering [EGT, GNC, HNTC, Hu, Lg, Lns, NCBC, NTC, TNTC, WBC, Wst; NJB, TNT].
2. It implies that they were to enter in the future [Alf, Blm, ICC, My, NIGTC, TH]. It indicates that they were certain to enter [ICC, My].

3. It refers to each believer's individual experience of entering God's rest, having a stabilized spiritual life on earth [Mil].

QUESTION—What is implied by τὴν κατάπαυσιν 'the rest'?

With the article τήν 'the', it refers to the previously mentioned rest [Alf], the rest in heaven [Blm]. It is both a future expectation and a present reality [GNC].

just-as/for[a] he-has-said, "As I-swore in my anger, 'If they-shall-enter into my rest,'"[b]

LEXICON—a. καθώς (LN 64.14, 89.34): 'just as' [LN (64.14), Mil, WBC; CEV, NAB, NASB, NIV, NRSV, TEV], 'even as' [Lns], 'as' [HNTC, NIC; KJV, NJB], 'because' [LN (89.34)], 'inasmuch as' [LN (89.34)], 'of which' [REB], not explicit [NLT, TNT].

b. This quotation is the same as in 3:11.

QUESTION—What relationship is indicated by καθώς 'just as'?

1. It indicates congruence, meaning that the following quotation corresponds to what God had said previously also [GNC, Lg, Lns, TH]; it corresponds to the preceding quotation of this same passage in 3:11 [Hu].
2. It introduces the grounds for the preceding thought [My].

QUESTION—Who is the speaker implied in εἴρηκεν 'he said'?

1. God is the speaker [EBC, HNTC, Lns, Mil, My, NIC, TH, WBC, Wst; all versions except NJB, TNT]. The perfect tense indicates the permanence of what God has said [EBC, Lns, Mil, TH].
2. Scripture is the speaker [NIGTC; TNT].

QUESTION—What relationship is indicated by ὡς 'as'?

1. It introduces a comparison with what follows [NIC; KJV, NASB, NRSV, REB]: in accordance with what I swore, so they shall not enter into my rest.
2. It introduces a consequence of what precedes [HNTC, Lns, Mil, WBC; NIV]: those who heard did not combine it with faith, therefore I swore that they shall not enter into my rest.

QUESTION—What is meant by εἰ εἰσελεύσονται 'if they shall enter'?

It is an idiom implying a strong negative [Hwt, Lg, WBC]: they shall not enter.

QUESTION—What is the meaning of τὴν κατάπαυσίν μου 'my rest'?

1. It is the rest which God enjoys [Blm, EBC, ICC, NIC, TNTC, WBC, Wst; TNT], a rest of completion and not of inactivity [TNTC].
2. It is the rest which God grants to his people [Mil; TEV].

although/namely[a] the works[b] having-come-to-exist[c] from[d] (the) foundation[e] of-(the) world.[f]

LEXICON—a. καίτοι (LN **89.72**) (BAGD p. 396): 'although' [LN, Mil; KJV, NASB], 'though' [NRSV, TNT], 'even though' [HNTC, **LN**; CEV, NLT, TEV], 'and yet' [BAGD, NIC, WBC; NIV], 'yet' [NAB, REB], 'now' [NJB], not explicit [Lns].

b. ἔργον (LN 42.42) (BAGD 1.a. p. 307): 'work' [LN], 'deed' [BAGD], 'task' [LN]. This plural noun is translated as a plural: 'works' [HNTC, Lns, Mil, NIC; KJV, NASB, NRSV]; as a singular: 'work' [WBC; NAB, NIV, NJB, REB, TEV, TNT], 'everything' [CEV], 'his place of rest' [NLT]. With the definite article, the phrase τῶν ἔργων 'the works' means God's works [Blm, My].

c. aorist pass. (deponent = act.) participle of γίνομαι (LN 13.80): 'to come to exist' [LN], 'to exist' [Lns], 'to be formed' [LN], 'to be finished' [HNTC, Mil, NIC; all versions], 'to be completed' [WBC], 'to be ready' [CEV, NLT].

d. ἀπό with genitive object (LN 67.131): 'from' [HNTC, LN, Mil; KJV, NASB], 'since' [LN, Lns, NIC, WBC; NIV], 'ever since' [TNT], 'at' [NJB, NRSV]. The phrase ἀπὸ καταβολῆς κόσμου 'from the foundation of the world' is translated 'from the time he created the world' [TEV], 'when he created the world' [NAB], 'ever since the world was created' [REB], 'from the time of creation' [CEV], 'since he made the world' [NLT]. It indicates time [Mil, My, WBC].

e. καταβολή (LN 42.37) (BAGD 1. p. 409): 'foundation' [BAGD, HNTC, Lns, Mil, NIC, WBC; KJV, NASB, NRSV], 'creation' [LN; CEV, NIV, TNT], 'beginning' [NJB]. This noun is also translated as a verb: 'to make' [NLT], 'to create' [NAB, TEV], 'to be created' [REB].

f. κόσμος (LN 1.1, 1.39) (BAGD 2. p. 445): 'world' [BAGD, HNTC, LN (1.39), Lns, Mil, NIC, WBC; all versions except CEV], 'earth' [LN (1.39)], 'universe' [LN (1.1)], 'cosmos' [LN (1.1)], not explicit [CEV].

QUESTION—What relationship is indicated by καίτοι 'although/namely'?

1. It indicates a concession [EGT, Lg, Lns, Mil, My, NIC, NIGTC, TH, WBC, Wst]: he said that they would not enter his rest, although his works were completed. The reason they did not enter God's rest was not that the rest was unavailable, since his rest was in effect since the beginning of the world [EGT, NIC, WBC]. God excluded that generation from his rest, yet it existed and was available for some [NIGTC]. It also introduces the thought of the following verses [My(D), WBC].
2. The introductory word καίτοι means 'namely' and this clause describes the rest referred to [Blm]: they shall not enter into my rest, namely the rest I enjoyed after completing creation.

4:4 For[a] he/it-has-said somewhere[b] concerning[c] the seventh (day) thus,[d]

LEXICON—a. γάρ (LN 89.23): 'for' [HNTC, LN, Lns, Mil, NIC, WBC; KJV, NAB, NASB, NIV, NRSV, TEV, TNT], 'because' [LN; NLT], 'in fact' [CEV], not explicit [REB]. The phrase εἴρηκεν γάρ που 'for he/it has said somewhere' is translated 'as one text says' [NJB].

b. πού (LN 83.7) (BAGD 1. p. 696): 'somewhere' [BAGD, HNTC, LN, Lns, Mil, NIC, WBC; CEV, NAB, NASB, NIV, REB, TNT], 'somewhere in the Scriptures' [TEV], 'in a certain place' [KJV], 'in one place' [NRSV], not explicit [NLT].

c. περί with genitive object (LN 90.24): 'concerning' [LN; NASB], 'about' [HNTC, LN, Mil, WBC; NIV, NRSV, TEV, TNT], 'in reference to' [NAB], 'referring to' [NJB], 'regarding' [Lns, NIC], 'with regard to' [Mil], 'of' [KJV, REB], not explicit [CEV, NLT].

d. οὕτως (LN 61.10) (BAGD 2. p. 598): 'thus' [Lns; NASB], 'in this way' [BAGD, Mil], 'in this manner' [WBC], 'in these words' [NIV], 'on this wise' [KJV], 'as follows' [BAGD, HNTC, LN; NRSV], 'the following' [LN], 'saying' [NLT], not explicit [CEV, NAB, NJB, REB]. The phrase εἴρηκεν οὕτως 'he/it has said thus' is translated 'this is said' [TEV], 'this is what Scripture says' [TNT], 'this is what Scripture has said' [NIC]. It points forward to the following quotation [NIGTC].

QUESTION—What relationship is indicated by γάρ 'for'?

It confirms (amplifies [Lns], explains [NCBC]) what was said in the preceding verse [Alf, EGT, Mil, My, Wst].

QUESTION—What is meant by πού 'somewhere'?

It indicates that the passage was well known and does not imply uncertainty as to where it is located [Hu, Lg, Wst]. The reference is to Gen. 2:2 [EGT, GNC, HNTC, ICC, Mil, My, TH]. Although most commentators refer this to Gen. 2:2, one says that it indicates indefiniteness because the quotation is found in three OT passages (Gen. 2:2; Exod. 20:11; 31:17) [Lns]. This manner of reference is characteristic of the author [NIC]; it focuses attention on the words rather than the location [NTC, TNTC].

QUESTION—Who is the implied subject of the verb εἴρηκεν 'he/it has said'?

1. The subject is God [Alf, EBC, GNC, HNTC, Lg, Lns, Mil, My, NIGTC, WBC; KJV, NASB, NIV]: God has spoken.
2. The subject is Scripture [NIC, TH; CEV, NAB, NJB, NLT, NRSV, REB, TNT]: Scripture has spoken. The quotation is from Gen. 2:2, which is in the form of a narrative, not an utterance of God [NIC].

QUESTION—What is indicated by the phrase περὶ τῆς ἑβδόμης 'concerning the seventh (day)'?

'Εβδόμη 'seventh' modifies the implied word ἡμέρας 'day' [Mil].

1. It indicates the passage of scripture referred to by πού 'somewhere' [Blm]: he has spoken somewhere, that is, in the passage concerning the seventh day.
2. It does not indicate the scripture passage [EBC]: he has spoken about the seventh day somewhere.

"And God rested on the seventh day from[a] all his works."[b]

LEXICON—a. ἀπό with genitive object (LN 89.122): 'from' [HNTC, LN, Lns, Mil, NIC, WBC; all versions except CEV, NJB]. The phrase ἀπὸ πάντων τῶν ἔργων αὐτοῦ 'from all his works' is translated 'after all the work he had been doing' [NJB]. The entire clause is translated 'by the seventh day, God had finished his work, and so he rested' [CEV].

b. ἔργον: 'work': see this word in 4:3. The works are God's initial creation [Mil].

QUESTION—What is implied by the aorist tense of κατέπαυσεν 'he rested'?
It means that at the end of the six days creation was completed and God entered a rest from creating [EBC, HNTC, Hwt, NTC, TH]; God began to rest on the seventh day and continues to rest, but this is not a rest of inactivity [Alf, Hwt].

4:5 And in[a] this (passage/matter) again,[b] "If they-shall-enter into my rest."[c]

LEXICON—a. ἐν with dative object (LN 83.13): 'in' [LN, Lns, Mil, NIC, WBC; KJV, NAB, NASB, NIV, NRSV, REB]. The phrase ἐν τούτῳ 'in this (passage)' is translated 'the passage above says' [NJB], 'this same matter is spoken of' [TEV], 'Scripture also says' [TNT], 'this saying' [HNTC], 'in the other passage God said' [NLT], 'we also read that he later said' [CEV].
b. πάλιν (LN 67.55) (BAGD 3. p. 607): 'again' [HNTC, LN, Lns, Mil, NIC; all versions except REB, TNT], 'furthermore' [BAGD, WBC], 'thereupon' [BAGD], 'also' [TNT], not explicit [REB].
c. This quotation is the same as in 3:11 and 4:3.

QUESTION—What is the meaning of τούτῳ 'this'?
1. It refers to the present passage which is being dealt with (4:3) [Alf, GNC, Mil, My, NIC, NTC, Wst; all versions except TEV]: in the above passage.
2. It refers to the same matter being discussed in a second quotation [EGT, Lns, TH; TEV]: this same matter about rest is mentioned again.

QUESTION—What is the meaning of πάλιν 'again'?
1. It means that the author is making a second point [Lns, NIGTC, Wst; NAB].
2. It means that the author is repeating a quotation [My, TNTC]: in the same passage again.
3. It means that God/Scripture repeats the warning in another passage [EBC; TEV, TNT]: in another passage also. It also introduces a second point to the argument [EBC]; the quotation in 4:4 implied that there was a rest [EBC]; the quotation in the present verse shows that the Israelites did not enter the rest [EBC]. The quotation in the present verse shows that God had a rest [EGT].
4. It means 'on the other hand', indicating that the following passage explains the preceding one, emphasizing the fact that no one has yet entered the rest [Alf].

DISCOURSE UNIT: 4:6–11 [Lns]. The topic is an exhortation to strive to enter God's rest.

4:6 Since[a] therefore[b] it-is-left[c] for-some to-enter into[d] it,

LEXICON—a. ἐπεί (LN 89.32) (BAGD 2. p. 284): 'since' [HNTC, LN, Lns, Mil, NIC, WBC; NAB, NASB, NRSV], 'seeing' [KJV], 'clearly' [TNT], not explicit [NLT, TEV]. The phrase ἐπεὶ οὖν 'since therefore' is translated 'since, then' [BAGD], 'this means that' [CEV]. The phrase ἐπεὶ ἀπολείπεται 'since it is left' is translated 'it remains the case' [NJB]. The phrase ἐπεὶ οὖν ἀπολείπεται 'since therefore it is left' is translated 'it still remains' [NIV], 'this implies' [REB]. This entire phrase is translated 'there are, then, others who are allowed to receive it' [TEV].

b. οὖν (LN 89.50): 'therefore' [LN, Mil, WBC; KJV, NAB, NASB, NRSV], 'then' [HNTC, LN, Lns, NIC; NJB, TEV, TNT], 'so' [NLT], not explicit [CEV].

c. pres. pass. indic. of ἀπολείπω (LN **13.140**) (BAGD 2. p. 94): 'to be left', 'to be left to' [LN], 'to be left open' [NIC], 'to be reserved' [BAGD], 'to be let' [LN], 'to be there' [NLT]. The passive voice is also translated as an active voice: 'to remain' [HNTC, Lns, Mil; KJV, NAB, NASB, NIV, NRSV], 'to be still open' [TNT], 'to be still good' [CEV], 'to be certain' [BAGD, Mil], 'to allow' [**LN**]. This verb is translated impersonally: 'the fact remains' [WBC]. The meaning is that it remains, not having been used up [Alf, EGT, Lg, NIGTC]. The present tense indicates continuing validity [NTC].

d. εἰς with accusative object: 'into'. See this word in 4:3.

QUESTION—What relationship is indicated by ἐπεί 'since'?

This word indicates the conclusion to the preceding argument [Lns, NIGTC] (the following οὖν 'therefore' introduces the conclusion stated in 4:7); it introduces the two conditions expressed in this verse [NIGTC]. It summarizes the preceding argument [GNC, Mil, WBC]; it repeats the argument of 4:2b [GNC]. It (with 4:7 [NCBC]) states the implication from the declaration that the former people could not enter the rest [Alf, Blm, EGT, Hu, ICC, NCBC, WBC]: therefore some will enter. The declaration that unbelievers would not enter implies that believers will enter [Blm, Hwt, TNTC, Wst], since it is impossible that God's plan for people to enter his rest should fail to be fulfilled [EBC, EGT, GNC, Hwt, My, TNTC, Wst].

and the-(ones) earlier[a] having-been-told-the-good-news[b] did-not enter because-of[c] disobedience,[d]

LEXICON—a. πρότερος (LN 67.18) (BAGD 1.bα. p. 722): 'earlier' [BAGD], 'formerly' [LN, Lns, Mil, WBC; NASB, NIV, NLT, NRSV], 'previously' [BAGD; NIC], 'beforehand' [BAGD], 'first' [CEV, KJV, NAB, NJB, REB, TEV, TNT], 'in the first place' [HNTC]. This word is emphatic by its position [NTC].

b. aorist pass. participle of εὐαγγελίζω (LN 33.215) (BAGD 2.b.β. p. 317): 'to be told the good news' [LN], 'to have good news preached' [BAGD; NASB], 'to have good news proclaimed' [WBC], 'to be given the glad tidings' [Lns], 'to have the gospel preached' [BAGD; NIV], 'to have the gospel announced' [LN], 'to be preached' [KJV]. The passive voice is also translated as an active voice: 'to hear the good news' [HNTC, Mil, NIC; NLT, REB, TEV, TNT], 'to receive the good news' [NRSV], 'to hear the gospel' [NJB], 'to hear about it (the promise)' [CEV]. The participial phrase οἱ εὐαγγελισθέντες 'the ones having been told the good news' is translated 'those to whom it was announced' [NAB].

c. διά with accusative object (LN 89.26): 'because of' [HNTC, LN, Lns, Mil, NIC, WBC; CEV, KJV, NAB, NASB, NIV, NLT, NRSV, TEV], 'on account of, by reason of' [LN], 'by' [NJB], 'through' [REB], not explicit [TNT].

d. ἀπείθεια (LN 31.107, 36.23) (BAGD p. 82): 'disobedience' [BAGD, HNTC, LN (36.23), Lns, NIC, WBC; NASB, NIV, NRSV], 'unbelief' [KJV, NAB, REB], 'refusal to believe' [LN (31.107); NJB]. The noun is also translated as a verb: 'to disobey' [Mil; CEV, NLT], 'to not believe' [TEV], 'to disbelieve' [TNT]. The meaning is disobedience [Alf, EBC, GNC, Lg, TH, Wst], but it approaches the meaning of disbelief [EBC].

4:7 again[a] he-designates[b] a-certain day, "Today,"

LEXICON—a. πάλιν (LN 67.55): 'again' [HNTC, LN, Lns, NIC, WBC; CEV, KJV, NASB, NIV, NRSV], 'once again' [TNT], 'once more' [NAB, REB], 'anew' [Mil]. The phrase πάλιν τινὰ ὁρίζει ἡμέραν 'again he designates a certain day' is translated 'God fixed another day' [NJB], 'God sets another day' [TEV], 'God set another time' [NLT]. This word is emphatic by its position [Alf]. It means 'once more' [TH]. The reference is to the time of David [EGT, HNTC, Hu]. This word modifies ὁρίζει 'he designates' [Alf, Blm, EGT, Lg, Lns, Mil, NIC, NIGTC, NTC, TNTC, WBC; NAB, NASB, NIV, NRSV, REB, TNT], meaning that God again designated a time [Mil].

b. pres. act. indic. of ὁρίζω (LN 30.83) (BAGD 1.a.α. p. 580): 'to designate', 'to set' [BAGD; NAB, NIV, NLT, NRSV, REB, TEV], 'to fix' [BAGD, Lns, NIC; NASB, NJB], 'to mark out' [Mil], 'to decide' [LN], 'to determine' [BAGD, LN], 'to appoint' [BAGD, HNTC, WBC; TNT], 'to limit' [KJV], not explicit [CEV]. This verb refers to God's sovereign decree [GNC].

QUESTION—Why is this verse mentioned?

It states the conclusion drawn from the preceding comment in 4:6 [Lns, Mil, My] and states the grounds for the exhortation of 4:11 [Mil].

QUESTION—What is the significance of the word σήμερον 'today'?

This word is the point of the passage, emphasizing that there is still the opportunity to enter [EBC, GNC], that the promise was still open when the OT passage was written [Hu, Hwt, NIC]. The writer assumes that this word extends to his own times [EGT, GNC]. The writer directs attention to the word used in the following quotation [Alf, Lg, Lns, Mil, My; TNT]: "Today," saying . . . , "Today . . ." It emphasizes the present availability of the promise [Mil]. It indicates that God calls this later time 'today' [EGT, Hu, NTC; NIV, TEV]. It indicates that this later time is another 'today' [Blm, HNTC, NIC; NJB]. It identifies τινὰ ἡμέραν 'a certain day' [NIGTC, Wst]: a certain day, namely, today.

saying in[a] David after[b] so-long[c] time, just-as[d] it-has-been-said-before,[e] "Today if you-should-hear his voice, do-not harden your hearts."[f]

LEXICON—a. ἐν with dative object (LN 83.13, 90.6) (BAGD I.1.d. p. 258): 'in' [BAGD, LN (83.13), Mil, NIC, WBC; KJV, TNT], 'by' [BAGD, HNTC, LN (90.6)], 'in the person of' [Lns], 'through' [NAB, NASB, NIV, NJB, NLT, NRSV, TEV], '(quoted) from' [REB], not explicit [CEV].

b. μετά with accusative object (LN 67.48) (BAGD B.II.1. p. 510): 'after' [BAGD, LN, Lns, Mil, NIC; KJV, NASB]. The phrase μετὰ τοσοῦτον χρόνον 'after so long time' is translated 'so long afterward' [HNTC], 'long afterward' [NAB], 'a long time later' [NIV, NLT], 'many years later' [TEV, TNT], 'so many years later' [REB], 'so much later' [WBC], 'much later' [CEV, NRSV], not explicit [NJB].

c. τοσοῦτος (LN **59.18**) (BAGD 1.a.α. p. 823): 'so long' [BAGD, Lns, Mil; KJV, NASB], 'such a long lapse of' [NIC], 'so much' [**LN**], 'so great' [LN]. The reference is to the time between Joshua and David [Alf, ICC, Mil, My, NIGTC, NTC, WBC]; it refers to the forty years mentioned earlier [Blm].

d. καθώς (LN 64.14): 'just as' [LN; NASB], 'even as' [Lns], 'as' [HNTC, Mil, NIC; KJV, NIV], 'the same way as' [LN]. The phrase καθὼς προείρηται 'just as it has been said before' is translated 'the words we have quoted' [NAB], 'in the words already quoted' [NLT, NRSV, REB], 'in the text already quoted' [WBC; NJB], 'in the scripture already quoted' [TEV], 'and using the words quoted above' [TNT], 'just as I have already said' [CEV]. The reference is to the previous quotation [NIGTC].

e. perf. pass. indic. of προλέγω (LN **33.86**) (BAGD 2.b. p. 705): 'to be said before' [NIC; NASB, NIV], 'to be said already' [LN; CEV], 'to be said above' [**LN**], 'to be said before' [Lns, NIC], 'to be mentioned before' [Mil], 'to be said' [KJV], 'to be quoted above' [LN], 'to be quoted already' [WBC; NJB, NLT, NRSV, REB, TEV], 'to be quoted before' [HNTC]. The reference is to the author's preceding quotation of this passage [Alf, EGT, GNC, HNTC, ICC, Lg, Mil, My, NIGTC]. The perfect tense implies the permanent validity of God's promise [NTC].

f. This quotation is the same as in 3:7–8.

QUESTION—What is the meaning of the phrase ἐν Δαυίδ 'in David'?

1. God spoke by David as his instrument [Blm, EBC, HNTC, NTC], he spoke in the person of David [Hwt, Lns, My, TNTC, Wst]: God spoke through David.
2. The reference is to the Psalms, attributed to David [Alf, ICC, Mil, NIC, WBC]: God spoke in David's writings.

QUESTION—What is implied by this quotation?

It shows that the promise was still open at the time this OT passage was written and was not fulfilled by the Israelites' entrance into Canaan [Blm, EGT, GNC, Lns, Mil, NIC]. The author is not concerned with the significance of the promise in David's day; he assumes that the quotation extends to him and his readers [HNTC, Lns].

QUESTION—What is σήμερον 'today' in this part of the verse connected with?

1. It is connected with μὴ σκληρύνητε 'do not harden' [Alf, Mil, NTC, WBC; NAB, NIV, NRSV]: don't harden your heart today.
2. It is connected with ἀκούσητε 'hear' [CEV, NJB, NLT, TEV, TNT]: if you should hear today.

DISCOURSE UNIT: 4:8–13 [Mil]. The topic is that a Sabbath rest remains available.

4:8 For[a] if Joshua had-given-rest[b] (to) them, not would-he-have-been-speaking concerning[c] another day after[d] these-things.

LEXICON—a. γάρ (LN 89.23): 'for' [HNTC, LN, Lns, Mil, WBC; KJV, NASB, NIV, NRSV], 'because' [LN], 'now' [NIC; NAB], not explicit [CEV, NJB, NLT, REB, TEV, TNT].

b. aorist act. indic. of καταπαύω (LN **23.85**) (BAGD 1.b.β. p. 416): 'to give rest' [HNTC, **LN**, Lns, Mil, NIC, WBC; CEV, KJV, NASB, NIV, NRSV, REB, TNT], 'to give the rest that God had promised' [TEV], 'to bring to a place of rest' [BAGD], 'to lead into the place of rest' [NAB], 'to lead into this place of rest' [NJB], 'to cause to rest' [LN], 'this new place of rest (where Joshua) led them' [NLT]. This verb is transitive here [My, Wst]; it means to lead the people into the rest being discussed [Alf], the true rest [Blm].

c. περί with genitive object (LN 89.6; 90.24): 'concerning' [LN (89.6; 90.24), Mil], 'with regard to, in relation to' [LN (89.6)], 'about' [HNTC, LN (90.24), Lns; CEV, NIV, NLT, NRSV, TEV], 'of' [LN (90.24), NIC, WBC; KJV, NAB, NASB, NJB, REB, TNT].

d. μετά with accusative object (LN 67.48): 'after' [LN, Mil, NIC; NASB]. The phrase μετὰ ταῦτα 'after these things' is translated 'afterward' [Lns; KJV, NAB], 'afterwards' [REB], 'later' [HNTC; NIV, NJB, NLT, NRSV, TEV], 'later on' [WBC], not explicit [CEV, TNT].

QUESTION—What relationship is indicated by γάρ 'for'?

It indicates the grounds for the preceding argument [Alf, Mil, My]; it adds an additional argument [NCBC]. The point is to show that God's rest is far more than the entrance into Canaan under Joshua [Lns, NIC, TNTC, Wst]. No earthly rest can be God's rest [Wst]. It is a contrary-to-fact condition [EBC, Lns, Mil, NIGTC, NTC, TH, WBC]: if Joshua had given . . . (which he didn't), God would not have been speaking . . . (which he did).

QUESTION—What is implied by the Greek word Ἰησοῦς, which is translated both 'Jesus' and 'Joshua'?

No parallel between Joshua and Jesus is intended [Alf, ICC, NIGTC], but the readers would have observed it [Alf]. The author and his readers would have understood the parallel between the two leaders whose names are represented by the same Greek word [EBC, GNC, NCBC, NIC, NTC].

Naming Joshua here by the same Greek name as Jesus indicates Joshua as somewhat of a type of Jesus [HNTC].

QUESTION—Who is the speaker of ἐλάλει 'he would have been speaking'?

The speaker is God [Alf, Blm, EBC, EGT, HNTC, Hu, Lg, Mil, My, NIC, NIGTC, TH, TNTC, WBC; all versions except KJV which is unclear]: God would not have been speaking. The imperfect tense indicates repeated speaking [Lg, NIGTC, NTC] and the permanent validity of God's promise [NTC]. The Holy Spirit spoke through David [Hwt].

QUESTION—What is the phrase μετὰ ταῦτα 'after these things' connected with?

1. It is connected with ἐλάλει 'he would have been speaking' [Alf, EBC, EGT, HNTC, Hu, Lg, Lns, Mil, My, Wst; all versions except TNT]: he would not have been speaking after these things. It means after the entrance into Canaan [NIGTC].
2. It is connected with ἄλλης ἡμέρας 'another day' [Blm, Hwt]: another day after this.

4:9 Therefore[a] there-remains[b] (a) Sabbath-rest[c] for-the people of-God.

LEXICON—a. ἄρα (LN 89.46) (BAGD 4. p. 104): 'therefore' [KJV, NAB, NASB, NJB, REB], 'consequently' [BAGD, LN, Mil, WBC], 'accordingly' [Lns], 'so' [BAGD, HNTC, LN; NLT, TNT], 'so then' [NIC; NRSV], 'then' [LN; NIV], 'as a result' [BAGD, LN], 'as it is, however' [TEV], 'we may safely infer, then' [Mil], not explicit [CEV].

b. pres. pass. indic. of ἀπολείπω (LN 85.65) (BAGD 2. p. 94): 'to remain' [BAGD, HNTC, Lns, Mil, WBC; KJV, NAB, NASB, NIV, NRSV, TEV], 'to remain open' [NIC], 'to be still open' [TNT], 'to be left' [LN], 'to be reserved' [NJB], 'to be still waiting' [NLT], 'to await' [REB], not explicit [CEV]. It remains as yet unfulfilled and available [Alf, My(D), NIGTC].

c. σαββατισμός (LN **67.185**) (BAGD p. 739): 'Sabbath rest' [BAGD, HNTC, LN, Mil, NIC; NAB, NASB, NIV, NRSV, REB, TNT], 'Sabbath' [Lns], 'Sabbath observance' [BAGD], 'Sabbath celebration' [WBC], 'a Sabbath when we will rest' [CEV], 'seventh-day rest' [NJB], 'rest like God's resting on the seventh day' [TEV], 'rest' [KJV], 'period of rest' [**LN**], 'a special rest' [NLT]. It is a higher designation than the preceding κατάπαυσις 'rest' [Alf, My(D)]; it gives a more precise description of the promised rest [WBC]. It implies that this rest is a symbol of the rest in heaven [Blm, Hu, ICC, Lns, My(D), NIC, Wst]. It identifies this promised rest with God's rest on the seventh day of creation [EGT, GNC, Hu, Lg(K), Mil, NCBC, NIC, NTC] and which is available for believers in this life [Mil] when they yield themselves fully to Christ [Wst]. It is a rest for the souls of believers [EBC], a spiritual rest involving ceasing from sinning, and fully realized in heaven [NTC].

QUESTION—What relationship is indicated by ἄρα 'therefore'?

It indicates the conclusion from the preceding exegesis [HNTC, Hu, Lg, Mil, NCBC, NIC, NIGTC, TNTC, WBC, Wst; all versions], of the preceding thought [EBC], of 4:3–8 [Lns, TH], of the comment in 4:6 [Alf], of 4:7–8 [My], the conclusion from 4:2–3 [Blm]. It repeats the conclusion stated in 4:6a [WBC].

QUESTION—How are the two nouns related in the genitive construction τῷ λαῷ τοῦ θεοῦ 'the people of God'?

It means the people whom God has chosen [NTC]. It includes both Jews and Gentiles who believe [NIGTC, TNTC] and distinguishes them from the unbelieving Israelites [TNTC].

4:10 For[a] the-(one) having-entered into[b] his rest himself also has-rested from[c] his works just-as[d] the God from[c] his-own (works).

LEXICON—a. γάρ (LN 89.23): 'for' [HNTC, LN, Lns, Mil, NIC, WBC; KJV, NASB, NIV, NLT, NRSV, TEV, TNT], 'because' [LN], 'since' [NJB], 'and' [NAB], not explicit [CEV, REB].

b. εἰς with accusative object (LN 84.22): 'into' [LN, Lns, Mil; KJV, NAB], not explicit [HNTC, NIC, WBC; all versions except KJV, NAB].

c. ἀπό with genitive object (LN 89.122): 'from' [HNTC, LN, Lns, Mil, NIC, WBC; all versions except NJB], 'after' [NJB].

d. ὥσπερ (LN 64.13) (BAGD 2. p. 899): 'just as' [BAGD, LN, Mil; CEV, NIV, NLT, TEV, TNT], 'as' [BAGD, HNTC, LN, NIC, WBC; KJV, NAB, NASB, NJB, NRSV, REB], 'even as' [Lns].

QUESTION—What relationship is indicate by γάρ 'for'?

It indicates the grounds for calling God's rest a Sabbath rest in the preceding verse [Blm, EGT, Lg(K), Lns, My, NIC, WBC, Wst]: it is a Sabbath rest, because he who enters it ceases from his work as God did. It describes what the rest means [EBC, Hwt, TNTC]. It further explains 4:9 [NIGTC], that a rest is available [Mil].

QUESTION—What is meant by ὁ εἰσελθών 'the one having entered'?

It refers to one act of entering [Mil, NTC, Wst] after completing one's task [Mil], action at the same time as the leading verb κατέπαυσεν 'he has rested' [NIGTC, Wst].

1. It refers to believers entering the rest in this life [EBC, GNC, Mil, NTC, TNTC], although the full revelation comes in the next life [EBC, GNC, NTC].
2. It refers generally to believers past, present, and future who die [Lns].
3. The time of entering is not in focus [NIGTC, TH].

QUESTION—To whom does αὐτοῦ 'his' refer in the phrase τὴν κατάπαυσιν αὐτοῦ 'his rest'?

1. It refers to God [EGT, Hu, Hwt, Lns, Mil, My, NIC, NIGTC, NTC, TH, TNTC, WBC, Wst; all versions except CEV, KJV, NJB]: God's rest.
2. It refers to Jesus [Alf]: Jesus' rest.

QUESTION—What does the phrase κατέπαυσεν ἀπὸ τῶν ἔργων αὐτοῦ 'has ceased from his works' refer to?

It means entering into the peace and security of God's rest in this life but fully realized in heaven [GNC, NTC]. It means rest in heaven from the toils and tribulations of life [Hu, Hwt, ICC, My], rest in heaven after we have completed our work assigned by God [Lns, NIC, TH]. Those who enter the rest in heaven will experience the completion of their work [WBC]. It means to be committed to carry out God's purpose for oneself [Mil]. The works are not specified [NIGTC].

QUESTION—What is meant by ἰδίων 'his own'?

It makes clear that the reference is to God's works rather than to the works of someone else [Alf, NIGTC, TH], since the preceding αὐτοῦ 'his' refers to believers. It is somewhat emphatic [ICC, TH].

DISCOURSE UNIT: 4:11–13 [EBC, Lg, NIC, TNTC]. The topic is that the remarkable nature of God's word should deter us from resisting it [Lg], an exhortation to enter the rest [EBC, NIC, TNTC].

4:11 Therefore[a] let-us-be-diligent[b] to-enter into[c] that rest,[d]

LEXICON—a. οὖν (LN 89.50): 'therefore' [HNTC, LN, Mil, WBC; KJV, NASB, NIV, NRSV], 'consequently' [LN], 'accordingly' [LN], 'so' [LN], 'so then' [LN], 'then' [LN, Lns, NIC; NJB, REB, TEV, TNT], not explicit [CEV, NAB, NLT].

b. aorist act. subj. of σπουδάζω (LN 68.63) (BAGD 2. p. 763): 'to be diligent' [Lns; NASB], 'to do one's best' [LN; CEV, NLT, TEV], 'to do one's utmost' [TNT], 'to endeavor' [LN], 'to strive' [HNTC; NAB], 'to strive earnestly' [Mil], 'to make every effort' [NIC, WBC; NIV, NRSV, REB], 'to press forward' [NJB], 'to labor' [KJV]. By using the first person plural, the author includes himself with his readers [EBC, Hu, NIGTC]. The aorist tense implies becoming diligent [WBC].

c. εἰς with accusative object: 'into'. See this word in 4:10.

d. κατάπαυσις: 'rest'. See this word in 4:10.

QUESTION—What relationship is indicated by οὖν 'therefore'?

It indicates an exhortation [Alf, Blm, EGT, GNC, HNTC, Hu, Hwt, Lns, Mil, My, NIGTC, NTC, TH, TNTC, WBC, Wst]: since the promise remains, let us be diligent to enter that rest. It is a conclusion [Blm, Mil] drawn from the argument in 4:3–7 [Alf, My(D)], from 3:7 onward [My].

QUESTION—What is implied by the phrase ἐκείνην τὴν κατάπαυσιν 'that rest'?

It refers to the rest mentioned in 4:10 [Alf, GNC, Hu, Lg, My, NIGTC], God's rest of great blessedness [Wst].

in-order-that[a] not anyone/someone might-fall[b] in[c] the same example[d] of-the disobedience.[e]

LEXICON—a. ἵνα (LN 89.59): 'in order that, in order to, for the purpose of, for the purpose that' [LN], 'so that' [HNTC, LN, Mil, NIC; CEV, NAB, NIV, NRSV, REB, TEV]. The phrase ἵνα μή 'in order that not' is translated 'lest' [Lns; KJV, NASB], 'otherwise' [WBC], 'for' [NLT]. This entire clause is translated 'or some of you might copy this example of refusal to believe and be lost' [NJB], 'we must not fail through being disobedient as they were' [TNT].

b. aorist act. subj. of πίπτω (LN 15.118; 20.60) (BAGD 2.a.β. p. 660): 'to fall' [BAGD, HNTC, LN (15.118), Lns, Mil, NIC; KJV, NAB, NASB, NIV, NLT, NRSV, REB], 'to fail' [TEV, TNT], 'to be completely ruined' [BAGD], 'to perish' [WBC], 'to be destroyed' [LN (20.60)], 'to be lost' [NJB], 'to miss going there' [CEV]. It means to perish [WBC], to be destroyed [NIGTC], completely ruined spiritually and eternally [NTC]; the aorist tense indicates a final and fatal fall [Lns]. The writer is thinking of the Israelites whose bodies fell in the wilderness [NTC, TH].

c. ἐν with dative object (LN 13.8; 83.13; 89.26; 89.76): 'in' [LN (13.8, 83.13), Lns], 'in imitation of' [NAB], 'by' [LN (89.76); NIV, REB], 'because of' [LN (89.26)], 'through' [HNTC, NIC, WBC; NASB], 'after' [Mil; KJV]. The phrase ἐν τῷ αὐτῷ ὑποδείγματι 'in the same example' is translated 'as theirs' [NRSV], 'as they did' [CEV, TEV], 'as the people of Israel did' [NLT].

d. ὑπόδειγμα (LN 58.59) (BAGD 1. p. 844): 'example' [BAGD, LN, Mil, NIC, WBC; KJV, NAB, NASB, NIV, NJB, REB], 'model' [BAGD], 'pattern' [BAGD], 'type' [Lns], 'kind' [HNTC], not explicit [CEV, NLT, NRSV, TEV]. This word refers to the effect of the Israelites' failure [Lg].

e. ἀπείθεια: 'disobedience'. See this word at 4:6.

QUESTION—What relationship is indicated by ἵνα 'in order that'?

1. It indicates the negative purpose of the preceding exhortation [Mil]: in order that you may not fall. It warns against unbelief [Mil] and implies its terrible consequences [Blm, NIGTC, WBC].
2. It indicates result [WBC]: otherwise you will fall.

QUESTION—What is the meaning of the phrase ἐν τῷ αὐτῷ ὑποδείγματι τῆς ἀπειθείας 'in the same example of unbelief'?

1. It means in imitation of Israel's unbelief [NTC; KJV, NAB, NASB, NIV, NJB, REB].
2. It means by means of the same kind of disobedience as Israel's [HNTC, Hu, NIC, NIGTC; NRSV, TNT].
3. It means because of the lack of faith [GNC; TEV].
4. It means to be situated in the same type of disobedience as Israel's [Lg, Lns].
5. It means to fall into so as to be in [Alf, My] the same kind of unbelief as Israel's [Alf, Hwt, ICC, My, TNTC].
6. It means to perish in the same manner because of unbelief [Blm, EGT, Mil].

DISCOURSE UNIT: 4:12–14 [HNTC]. The topic is God's sword.

DISCOURSE UNIT: 4:12–13 [Lns, NCBC]. The topic is the word of God [NCBC], an exhortation not to underestimate God's word [Lns].

4:12 For[a] the word of the-God (is) living[b] and effective[c]

LEXICON—a. γάρ (LN 89.23): 'for' [HNTC, LN, Lns, Mil, NIC, WBC; KJV, NASB, NIV, NLT, TNT], 'because' [LN], 'indeed' [NAB, NRSV], not explicit [CEV, NJB, REB, TEV].

b. pres. act. participle of ζάω (LN 23.88) (BAGD 4.b. p. 337): 'to live' [LN, Lns, Mil, NIC, WBC; NAB, NASB, NIV, NRSV], not explicit [BAGD]. This participle is also translated as an adjective: 'alive' [HNTC; CEV, NJB, REB, TEV, TNT], 'living' [NLT], 'quick' [KJV]. It means that it has living power [Alf, HNTC, Mil, My, NIGTC, NTC; NLT] and energy for action [Wst] and speaks vitally from God [Mil]. It has life in itself [Lg]; it is dynamic [EBC, HNTC], it remains in effect [EGT] and God is not disobeyed with impunity [ICC]. It is alive because God is the living God [GNC, Hu, Hwt, Lns, Mil, TNTC]. It is emphatic by forefronting [Alf, Lg, Lns, Mil, NIGTC, NTC, WBC] and dominates the following descriptions [Lns]. The present tense indicates a continuing state, but the commentaries do not mention this point.

c. ἐνεργής (LN **13.124**) (BAGD p. 265): 'effective' [BAGD, **LN**, Lns, WBC; NAB], 'active' [BAGD, HNTC, Mil, NIC; all versions except KJV, NAB, NLT], 'powerful' [BAGD; KJV], 'able to make things happen' [**LN**], 'power' [NLT]. It is energizing power [Alf, Hu, Lns, NIGTC, NTC] still in force [EGT], effective and powerful [NIGTC, NTC], divine activity from God [Mil, TNTC]. It can never be made ineffective [GNC], it is dynamic [EBC, ICC], operative and efficient [Lg, My], it will accomplish its purpose [HNTC, NIC, TH]. It actively challenges everyone who does not meet its demands [TNTC]. This word adds force to the preceding ζῶν 'living' [Alf].

QUESTION—What relationship is indicated by γάρ 'for'?

1. It indicates the reason for seeking diligently to enter God's rest [Alf, EGT, GNC, Mil, My, WBC] since no unbelief can escape God's sight [Blm, HNTC, Hu, TNTC].
2. It indicates the conclusion of the preceding comments [NIGTC, NTC].
3. It justifies the preceding warning [Lg, NCBC], the warning in chapter 3 and the promises in 4:1–11 [Lns].

QUESTION—What is meant by ὁ λόγος τοῦ θεοῦ 'the word of God'?

It means the word that was spoken by God [NIGTC]. It is God's message to people [TNTC]. It refers to God's spoken or written word [Alf, EBC, HNTC, Hu, Hwt, ICC, Lg, Mil, My, NIC, TH, TNTC, Wst], God's spoken word [GNC], of condemnation and of promise [ICC] through Scripture [Hwt, Lg, Lns], especially God's word expressed through Jesus [EBC, ICC, Wst]. It is the expression of God's power [Alf]. It refers to God's promises and offers [EGT]. It refers only to the warning words of God [Blm, My(D)] in the OT and NT [NIGTC]. It refers to Ps. 95:7b–11 quoted in 3:7–4:11 [WBC].

and sharper[a] above[b] every two-edged[c] sword

LEXICON—a. τομός (LN **79.96**) (BAGD p. 822): 'sharper' [BAGD, HNTC, LN, Lns, Mil, NIC, WBC; all versions except NJB, REB]. This adjective is also translated as a verb phrase: 'it cuts more incisively' [NJB], 'it cuts more keenly' [REB].

b. ὑπέρ with accusative object (LN 78.29) (BAGD 2. p. 839): 'above', 'beyond' [LN, Mil], 'to a greater degree than' [LN], 'more than' [LN], 'than' [BAGD, HNTC, Lns, NIC, WBC; all versions]. It introduces a comparison [Mil] which is emphatic [Mil, NIGTC].

c. δίστομος (LN 79.94) (BAGD p. 200): 'two-edged' [HNTC, LN, Lns, NIC; all versions except CEV, NIV, NLT, TEV], 'double-edged' [BAGD, LN, Mil, WBC; CEV, NIV, TEV], 'sharpest' [NLT]. It means that it never fails to cut; it has no blunt edge [Hu].

QUESTION—What is implied by this phrase?

It expresses a comparison, indicating the effectiveness of God's judgments on the soul [Blm, GNC], the power of God's word to penetrate through the person [HNTC, Hwt, TNTC]. It means that God's word is more powerful and penetrating than any man-made instrument [Hu].

and piercing[a] as-far-as[b] division[c] of-soul[d] and spirit,[e] and/both of-joints[f] and of-marrow,[g]

LEXICON: a. pres. pass. (deponent = act.) participle of διϊκνέομαι (LN **15.32**) (BAGD p. 195): 'to pierce' [BAGD, Lns, NIC; KJV, NASB, NRSV, REB], 'to penetrate' [BAGD, HNTC, Mil, WBC; NAB, NIV], 'to penetrate through' [LN], 'to cut' [NLT], 'to cut through' [CEV], 'to cut all the way through' [TEV], 'to seek out' [NJB], 'to go deep enough' [TNT]. The prefixed preposition δια- adds the sense of thoroughness [Mil]. The present tense indicates characteristic action, but the commentaries do not mention this point. This word describes λόγος 'word (of God)' [NIGTC, TH, WBC].

b. ἄχρι with genitive object (LN 84.19) (BAGD 1.b. p. 128): 'as far as' [BAGD, Lns; NASB], 'up to' [LN], 'even to' [Mil; KJV, NIV], 'to' [HNTC, LN; TEV], not explicit [NJB]. The phrase ἄχρι μερισμοῦ 'as far as division' is translated 'to divide' [TNT], 'it divides' [NIC], 'until it divides' [NRSV], 'so deeply that it divides' [REB], 'and divides' [NAB], 'so as to separate' [WBC], 'deep into' [NLT], 'until it discovers' [CEV]. It refers to space, not time [NIGTC].

c. μερισμός (LN **63.24**) (BAGD 1.a. p. 505): 'division' [Lns; NASB], 'dividing' [NIV], 'dividing point' [HNTC], 'dividing asunder' [KJV], 'separation' [BAGD, Mil], not explicit [CEV, NLT]. The phrase μερισμοῦ ψυχῆς καὶ πνεύματος 'division of soul and spirit' is translated 'the place where soul is divided from spirit' [NJB], 'where soul and spirit meet' [TEV], 'the point where soul and spirit meet' [**LN**], 'the point where soul and spirit come together' [**LN**]. This word refers to the (progressive [NTC]) action of division or separation [Mil, My, NTC], to the result of a process [NIGTC]; it means division [ICC]. The action is done by the word of God [My].

d. ψυχή (LN 23.88, 26.4) (BAGD 1.e. p. 894): 'soul' [HNTC, Lns, Mil, NIC, WBC; all versions except NLT], 'heart, inner self, mind, life' [LN], not explicit [NLT]. It refers to the inner aspects of earthly life [Lns, Mil, My, TNTC]; it refers to human beings [HNTC].

e. πνεῦμα (LN 26.9) (BAGD 3.a. p. 675): 'spirit' [BAGD, HNTC, LN, Lns, Mil, NIC, WBC; all versions except NLT], 'inner being' [LN], not explicit [NLT]. It is the seat of God's renewing operation in human life [Lns], the spiritual life [Mil, My], man's life in relation to God [TNTC], the aspect of the person which can respond to God's Spirit [TH].

f. ἁρμός (LN **8.59**) (BAGD p. 107): 'joint' [BAGD, HNTC, LN, Lns, Mil, NIC, WBC; all versions except NLT], not explicit [NLT].

g. μυελός (LN **8.62**) (BAGD p. 528): 'marrow' [BAGD, HNTC, LN, Lns, Mil, NIC, WBC; all versions except NLT], not explicit [NLT].

QUESTION—What relationship is indicated by καί 'and'?

1. It continues the buildup of emphatic descriptions of the word of God [Alf]: living, active, sharper . . . , penetrating . . .
2. It furnishes the proof of the preceding comment [My].

QUESTION—What is the meaning of this phrase?

1. It means that God's word penetrates to the innermost parts of our being [EBC, EGT, HNTC, Hu, ICC, Lg, Lns, Mil, My, NCBC, NIC, NIGTC, TH, TNTC, WBC, Wst], and our entire being is accessible to God [EBC] for examination by him [Mil]. The reference to 'soul' and 'spirit', 'joints' and 'marrow', add to the description of the power of God's word to penetrate to the center of one's being, both physical and spiritual [Hu].

1.1 'Joints' and 'marrow' are figurative equivalents of 'soul' and 'spirit' [ICC, TH], and this phrase is a rhetorical reference to mankind's whole mental nature [ICC]. God's word penetrates to the very core of a person so that nothing in the personality is hidden from it [TH].

1.2 'Joints' and 'marrow' are subordinate to 'soul' and 'spirit' [Lg]: separating soul and spirit, also joints and marrow.

1.3 'Joints' and 'marrow' represent the inner relationship between soul and spirit [Mil, My].

1.4 It means that God's word divides within soul, spirit, joints, and marrow [NIGTC, Wst], soul and spirit representing the non-material elements, joints and marrow the material elements [Wst].

1.5 It means that God's word separates soul from spirit and joints from marrow [NIC; NRSV, TNT].

2. It means that God's word reveals in its true nature every aspect of human life and spirit; 'joints' and 'marrow' refer to both 'soul' and 'spirit', indicating the full aspects of both soul and spirit [Lns].
3. It means that the word of God pierces and divides both the 'joints' and the 'marrow' (speaking figuratively) of the 'soul' and of the 'spirit' [Alf].

4. It means that God's word separates mankind's lower animal life from his higher spiritual life [Hwt].

and (is) able-to-judge[a] of-thoughts[b] and intentions[c] of-(the)-heart;[d]

LEXICON—a. κριτικός (LN **56.23**) (BAGD p. 453): 'to be able to judge' [BAGD, LN, WBC; NASB, NRSV], 'qualified to judge' [Mil], 'keen to judge' [Lns], 'able to discern' [BAGD]. This adjective is also translated as a noun: 'discerner' [KJV]; as a verb: 'to judge' [NAB, NIV, TEV, TNT], 'to pass judgment on' [NJB], 'to discern' [HNTC, NIC], 'to discriminate' [REB], 'to discover' [CEV], 'to expose what one really is' [NLT]. It describes λόγος 'word (of God)' [TH, WBC].

b. ἐνθύμησις (LN 30.15) (BAGD p. 266): 'thought' [LN, NIC, WBC; KJV, NASB, NIV, NRSV, TNT], 'reflection' [BAGD, Mil; NAB], 'consideration' [Lns], 'emotion' [NJB], 'purpose' [REB], 'desire' [CEV, NLT, TEV], 'feeling' [HNTC]. The reference is to feelings [EBC], meditations [Lns], considerations [Mil], affections [Wst]; it refers to the moral and emotional nature [Lg(K)].

c. ἔννοια (LN **30.66**) (BAGD p. 267): 'intention' [LN; NASB, NRSV], 'intent' [HNTC; KJV, TNT], 'thought' [BAGD, Lns; CEV, NAB, NJB, NLT, REB, TEV], 'conception' [Mil], 'attitude' [NIV], 'insight' [BAGD], 'purpose' [**LN**, NIC], 'deliberation' [WBC]. It refers to ideas [Alf], to thoughts [EBC] that result from the meditations [Lns, Mil], to the exercise of the reason [Wst]. The reference is to the intellectual nature [Lg(K)].

d. καρδία (LN 26.3): 'heart' [HNTC, LN, Lns, Mil, NIC, WBC; all versions except NJB, NLT, TNT], 'inner self' [LN], 'mind' [LN; TNT]. This noun is also translated as an adjective: 'secret' [NJB], 'innermost' [NLT]. It is the center of the personality [HNTC, Hu], of the inner life [Mil], of the personal and moral life [Wst].

QUESTION—What is the meaning of this phrase?

It means that God's word passes judgment on mankind's feelings and thoughts [EBC, Hu, Lns, Mil], it tests mankind's desires and intentions [EGT], it is competent to give judicial supervision of the thoughts and intentions [Lg, My, NIC, NIGTC, Wst], it discerns mankind's thoughts and intentions [NTC], it reveals the true nature of thoughts and desires [TH]. The word is personified here [ICC, NIGTC].

4:13 and there-is not (a) creature[a] not-manifest[b] before[c] him,

LEXICON—a. κτίσις (LN 42.38) (BAGD 1.b.α. p. 455): 'creature' [BAGD, Lns; KJV, NASB, NRSV], 'created being' [NIC], 'created thing' [HNTC; NJB], 'thing created' [Mil], 'what has been created' [LN]. The phrase οὐκ ἔστιν κτίσις 'there is not a creature' is translated 'nothing in creation' [WBC], 'nothing in all creation' [NIV, TNT], 'nothing' [CEV, NAB, NLT, REB, TEV]. It includes both visible and invisible things [Alf], every created person and thing [Lns].

b. ἀφανής (LN **28.68**) (BAGD p. 124): 'not manifest' [KJV], 'unexposed' [Lns], 'invisible' [BAGD, HNTC; TNT], 'concealed' [NAB], 'hidden'

[BAGD, **LN,** Mil, NIC, WBC; CEV, NASB, NIV, NJB, NRSV]. The phrase ἀφανὴς ἐνώπιον αὐτοῦ 'not manifest before him' is translated 'can hide from him' [NLT, REB] 'can be hid from God' [TEV]. 'that people can keep God from seeing' [**LN**], 'that people can prevent God from knowing about' [**LN**]. It means 'hidden' [NIGTC].

c. ἐνώπιον (LN 83.33) (BAGD 4. p. 270): 'before' [BAGD, LN, Lns; NRSV], 'in front of' [LN], 'to' [HNTC; TNT], 'from' [NIC; CEV, NAB, NJB, NLT, REB, TEV]. The phrase ἐνώπιον αὐτοῦ 'before him' is translated 'from God's sight' [WBC; NIV], 'from his sight' [NASB], 'in his sight' [KJV], 'to God's view' [Mil].

QUESTION—What relationship is indicated by καί 'and'?

1. It confirms the preceding comment by transferring what was said concerning God's word to God himself [Blm]. It makes plain what was meant in the preceding thought [GNC, Hu]. The same truth as before is expressed in a different figure [EBC].
2. It expresses an additional thought [EGT], a second grounds for the exhortation of 4:11 [Mil].

QUESTION—To whom does αὐτοῦ 'him' refer?

1. It refers to God [Alf, Blm, EGT, HNTC, ICC, Lns, My, NIGTC, WBC, Wst; all versions]: before God. There is a natural movement from the word of God to God himself here [Hu, Hwt, Lg, Mil, My, NIGTC, NTC, TH, Wst] as is made clear by the final clause of the verse [Lg], by the phrase τοῖς ὀφθαλμοῖς αὐτοῦ 'his eyes' [My].
2. It refers to God's word [NIC]: before God's word.

but all-things (are) naked[a] and laid-bare[b] to-the eyes of-him, to[c] whom to-us (is) the word.[d]

LEXICON—a. γυμνός (LN **28.62**) (BAGD 4. p. 168): 'naked' [HNTC, **LN**, Lns; KJV, NLT, NRSV, TNT], 'uncovered' [BAGD, Mil, WBC; NIV, NJB], 'bare' [BAGD, NIC; NAB, REB], 'exposed' [TEV], 'not hidden, easily known' [LN], 'open' [NASB]. The first clause is translated 'He sees through everything' [CEV]. It implies something previously hidden now laid bare [Mil], exposed [NIGTC, TNTC] for examination [NIGTC].

b. perf. pass. participle of τραχηλίζω (LN **28.61**) (BAGD p. 824): 'to be laid bare' [BAGD; NASB, NIV, NRSV], 'to be exposed' [**LN,** Mil, NIC, WBC; NAB, NLT, REB, TNT], 'to be easily known' [LN], 'to be opened' [KJV], 'to be stretched fully open' [NJB], 'to be laid open' [Lns], 'to lie open' [TEV]. This participle is also translated as an adjective: 'prostrate' [HNTC]. It means to prostrate [Alf, HNTC, NCBC] and bring under subjugation [Alf]; it means with the head laid back as in preparation for the slaughter of an animal [Blm, Lns, My], with the head laid back so as to expose the face to view [EGT, Lg, TNTC] by God [TNTC, WBC]; it takes on the general meaning of being exposed to view [My, WBC], laid bare [TNTC]. It is synonymous with γυμνός 'naked' and with οὐκ ἀφανής 'not manifest' [Hu]. The perfect tense implies a state resulting from a preceding action [Lns].

c. πρός with accusative object (LN 89.7): 'to' [HNTC, Mil, NIC, WBC; all versions except KJV, NASB], 'with regard to' [LN], 'with' [KJV, NASB], 'facing' [Lns].

d. λόγος (LN 89.18) (BAGD 2.e. p. 478): 'word' [Lns], 'reason' [LN]. The phrase πρὸς ὃν ἡμῖν ὁ λόγος 'with regard to whom to us is the word' is translated 'to whom we must render an account' [NAB, NRSV], 'to whom we must render account' [HNTC; REB], 'to whom we must give account' [Mil, WBC; NIV, TNT], 'to whom we must give account of ourselves' [NJB], 'to whom our account must be rendered' [NIC], 'and it is to him that we must all give an account of ourselves' [TEV], 'with whom we have to reckon' [BAGD], 'with whom we have to do' [BAGD; KJV, NASB], 'and we will have to tell him the truth' [CEV], 'this is the God to whom we must explain all that we have done' [NLT].

QUESTION—What relationship is indicated by δέ 'but'?

It indicates a strong contrast with what precedes [Alf, Lg, My, WBC]: nothing is hidden; on the contrary, all things are exposed to him. The two clauses are parallel [NIGTC].

QUESTION—How is the last clause related to the preceding clause?

1. The last clause is to be separated from the preceding clause [Alf; TEV]: with him we have to do. To make it closely connected with the preceding clause should have called for ἐκείνου 'that one's' instead of αὐτοῦ 'his' immediately preceding [Alf].
2. The last clause is closely related to the preceding clause [Blm, HNTC, Lns, Mil, My, NIC, WBC; all versions except TEV]: the eyes of him with whom we have to do.

QUESTION—What is meant by πρὸς 'with respect to'?

The relative pronoun ὃν 'whom' refers to the preceding αὐτοῦ 'him' [Mil, My], i.e., to God [NIGTC]; this clause identifies God as judge [Mil].

1. It refers to giving an account to God [Blm, EBC, GNC, HNTC, Hu, ICC, Mil, NCBC, NIC, NIGTC, NTC, TNTC, WBC, Wst; all versions except KJV, NASB]: to whom we must give an account.
2. It refers to dealings with God [Alf, Hwt, Lg, Lns, My, TH; KJV, NASB]: with whom we have to do.

DISCOURSE UNIT: 4:14–10:18 [Hu, Mil]. The topic is Christ's superiority to Aaron [Hu, Mil].

DISCOURSE UNIT: 4:14–9:14 [TNTC]. The topic is a superior high priest.

DISCOURSE UNIT: 4:14–6:20 [Lns, NIC]. The topic is the high priesthood of Jesus [NIC], Jesus our compassionate high priest [Lns].

DISCOURSE UNIT: 4:14–5:11 [EBC]. The topic is a great high priest.

DISCOURSE UNIT: 4:14–5:10 [GNC, GNT, Hwt, Lg, Lns, Mil, NTC; CEV, NAB, NIV, NJB, NLT, TEV]. The topic is the high priesthood of Jesus [GNC, GNT, NTC; CEV, NIV, NLT, TEV], Jesus our compassionate high priest [Hwt; NAB, NJB], the Son being compassionate to our weaknesses because of his own suffering [Lns], Jesus having the requirements to be a high priest [Mil].

DISCOURSE UNIT: 4:14–16 [EBC, Hwt, Lg, NCBC, NIC, NTC, TNTC, Wst; TEV]. The topic is our confidence [EBC], an encouragement for the readers [NTC], a transition to the doctrine of Christ's high priesthood [Wst], Jesus our sympathetic high priest [Hwt, NCBC, TNTC; TEV], Christ's high priesthood being an encouragement to believers [NIC].

4:14 Therefore,[a] having a-great[b] high-priest (now) passed-through[c] the heavens,[d] Jesus the son of God, let-us-hold-fast[e] the confession.[f]

LEXICON—a. οὖν (LN 89.50): 'therefore' [LN, Mil, WBC; NIV, REB], 'consequently' [LN], 'accordingly' [LN], 'so' [LN; TNT], 'so then' [LN], 'then' [HNTC, LN, Lns, NIC; KJV, NAB, NASB, NRSV, TEV], 'that is why' [CEV, NLT], not explicit [NJB].

b. μέγας (LN 87.22) (BAGD 2.b.α. p. 498): 'great' [BAGD, HNTC, LN, Lns, Mil, NIC, WBC; all versions except NJB], 'important' [LN], 'supreme' [NJB]. It refers to Christ's uniqueness [GNC], his superiority over Moses [Blm] and over the Aaronic priests [Blm, EBC, HNTC, Lg, Lns, TNTC], to his having passed through to God's presence [EGT, ICC, Mil, My] and to his designation as the Son of God [EGT, Mil], his exaltation [My, NIC], his excellence [WBC], his dignity [Wst]. Since 'high priest' means 'great priest', the addition of 'great' here implies exaltation [NIC], a position higher than the Aaronic high priests [Hu, Hwt, NIC, NTC]. This word is somewhat redundant [NCBC].

c. perf. act. participle of διέρχομαι (LN 15.17, 15.32) (BAGD 1.a. p. 194): 'to pass through' [HNTC, Mil, NIC; NAB, NASB, NRSV, REB, TNT], 'to go through' [BAGD, LN (15.32), Lns; NIV], 'to go through to' [NJB], 'to go on to' [LN (15.17)], 'to go into' [WBC; CEV, TEV], 'to go to' [NLT], 'to pass into' [KJV].

d. οὐρανός (LN 1.11) (BAGD 1.e. p. 594): 'heaven' [BAGD, HNTC, LN, Lns, Mil, NIC; all versions except NJB, TEV], 'highest heaven' [NJB], 'the very presence of God' [TEV]. This plural noun is translated as a singular: 'heaven' [WBC]. The singular and plural forms of this word are used interchangeably [Hu, TH].

e. pres. act. subjunctive of κρατέω (LN 18.6) (BAGD 2.e.β. p. 448): 'to hold fast' [BAGD, HNTC, Lns, WBC; KJV, NAB, NASB, NRSV, REB, TNT], 'to hold firm' [NJB], 'to hold firmly' [Mil; NIV, TEV], 'to hold on to' [CEV], 'to hold' [LN], 'to cling to and never stop (trusting)' [NLT], 'to maintain' [NIC]. The first person plural subjunctive is an exhortation [TH]. The present tense implies continuation [Lns, Mil, WBC]. It means to continue to hold on to [BAGD, HNTC, Lns, Mil, NIC, NIGTC, TNTC, WBC; all versions]; it means to lay hold of [NCBC], to grasp and cling to

[Wst]. The first person plural 'us' includes the author with his readers [Lns, NTC, TH].

f. ὁμολογία (LN 33.274) (BAGD 2. p. 568): 'confession' [BAGD, LN, Lns, Mil, NIC, WBC; NASB, NRSV], 'profession' [KJV], 'profession of faith' [NAB]. The phrase τῆς ὁμολογίας 'the confession' is translated 'the faith we profess' [NIV, REB, TEV], 'our profession of faith' [NJB], 'what we profess' [HNTC], 'our religious faith' [TNT], 'what we have said about him' [CEV], 'to trust him' [NLT]. The reference is to confessing the Christian faith [Alf, EGT, Lg, My, TH], believing in the heart and acknowledging it to others [Hu, NTC]; it refers to a firm formula and tradition [Mil, WBC].

QUESTION—What relationship is indicated by οὖν 'therefore'?

1. It resumes the topic concerning the high priesthood of Jesus, mentioned in 2:17 [NTC, Wst], 2:17–18 [TNTC], 2:17–3:1 [Hu], commenced in 3:1 [Blm, EGT], briefly mentioned in 3:1 [NTC]. It resumes what was said before [Mil, My, NIGTC] and begins a new section [My]. It merely introduces a new topic [Lns].
2. With the two following verses, it indicates an exhortation based on the preceding argument [Alf, Mil, My, NIGTC], including all of 1:1–3:6 [My, NIGTC]: in view of these things, let us hold fast. It is also transitional [Alf].
3. It indicates a conclusion and is connected with the participial phrase 'having a great high priest' [Lg, My; NLT]: therefore we have a great high priest.

QUESTION—What is implied by the phrase 'having a great high priest'?

1. It implies that Christ's high priesthood has previously been mentioned [My, NIGTC, TH].
2. It implies that the author is refuting the claim of some Jews that Christianity had no priesthood similar to the Aaronic priesthood [Hwt].

QUESTION—What relationship is indicated by the participial form ἔχοντες 'having'?

It indicates the grounds for the following exhortation [HNTC, Lg, Mil, NIC, NIGTC, NTC, WBC; all versions]: since we have a great high priest, let us hold fast the confession. The plural refers to Christians in general [NIGTC]. The present tense indicates a continuing state, but the commentaries do not mention this point [Ed]. It is emphatic [Wst].

QUESTION—What relationship is indicated by the participial form διεληλυθότα 'passed through'?

The perfect tense indicates a state resulting from a preceding action [Mil, NTC]: he has passed through the heavens and is now in God's presence. Christ has passed *through* the heavens (the first and second heavens to the third heaven [Blm]) *to* God's throne [Alf, Blm, EBC, EGT, HNTC, Hu, Hwt, Lns, My, NCBC, NIC, NIGTC, NTC, WBC, Wst], implying the completion of the work of redemption and access to God [Blm]. He went beyond the limits of time and space, thus guaranteeing his greatness and uniqueness

[Hu, Wst]. The translations show that the participle is attributive, making a statement concerning the high priest's activity, although none of the commentaries discuss this point [HNTC, Lns, Mil, NIC, WBC; all versions]: a great high priest who has passed through the heavens.

QUESTION—Why is the phrase 'Jesus the Son of God' mentioned?

It is an emphatic apposition to 'a great high priest' [My]; 'Jesus' is emphatic [NIGTC]. The two titles are placed together to reflect Christ's two natures with their assurance of sympathy and power [EGT, Wst].

1. The reference here to Ἰησοῦν 'Jesus' includes an implied reference to and contrast with the Ἰησοῦς 'Joshua' mentioned in 4:8 [Alf]; it (also [Alf]) emphasizes the majesty of Jesus the high priest [Alf, EBC] and adds great weight to the following exhortation [Alf].
2. There is no connection with 'Joshua' in 4:8 [My, NIGTC]. The personal name 'Jesus' implies his humanity [GNC, HNTC, Hu, Hwt, Lns], his historical identity [TNTC], his understanding and sympathy for mankind [Mil], all of his earthly ministry [NTC]. 'Son of God' implies his deity [HNTC, Hu, Hwt, Lns, TNTC], his exaltation and his unique relationship to God [GNC, Mil], his dignity [EGT, My] and his access to the Father [EGT]. It is the same incarnate Jesus who is now our transcendent Lord in heaven [Hu]. Joining the reference to the two natures of Jesus was an encouragement to the readers to hold fast the confession [Hwt].

DISCOURSE UNIT: 4:15–5:10 [WBC]. The topic is a high priest, the compassionate Son of God, worthy of our faith.

DISCOURSE UNIT: 4:15–16 [HNTC]. The topic is Christ's compassion.

4:15 For[a] we-have not (a) high-priest not being-able[b] to-sympathize[c] with-our weaknesses,[d]

LEXICON—a. γάρ (LN 89.23): 'for' [HNTC, LN, Lns, Mil, WBC; KJV, NAB, NASB, NIV, NJB, NRSV], 'because' [LN], not explicit [NIC; CEV, NLT, REB, TEV, TNT].

b. pres. pass. (deponent = act.) participle of δύναμαι (LN 74.5): 'to be able' [HNTC, LN, Lns, Mil, WBC; NAB, NIV, NRSV, REB], 'to be capable' [NJB], not explicit [CEV, NLT]. The phrase μὴ δυνάμενον 'not being able' is translated 'who cannot' [NIC; NASB, TEV, TNT], 'which cannot' [KJV].

c. aorist act. infin. of συμπαθέω (LN **25.57**) (BAGD p. 779): 'to sympathize with' [BAGD, HNTC, Lns, Mil, NIC; NAB, NASB, NIV, NRSV, REB, TNT], 'to have sympathy with' [BAGD], 'to have sympathy for' [LN], 'to feel sympathy for' [**LN;** TEV], 'to feel with' [WBC; NJB], 'to show sympathy with' [BAGD], 'to be sympathetic toward' [LN], 'to be touched with the feeling of' [KJV], 'to understand' [CEV, NLT].

d. ἀσθένεια (LN 74.23) (BAGD 2. p. 115): 'weakness' [BAGD, HNTC, LN (74.23), Lns, Mil, WBC; all versions except KJV, NAB], 'frailty' [NIC], 'infirmity' [KJV], 'limitation' [LN (74.23)], 'timidity' [BAGD, LN]. This noun, which is plural here, is translated as a singular: 'weakness' [NAB]. The meaning is weakness [Hu, Hwt, TH, TNTC] in any form [Hwt, TNTC], physical, moral, or spiritual weakness [Alf, Mil, My], intellectual and moral weakness [NIGTC], moral weakness [EGT], weaknesses that are the sources of temptation [ICC, WBC], the misery resulting from frailty [Blm]. This plural noun may imply unintentional violations of the law of Moses [NIGTC].

QUESTION—What relationship is indicated by γάρ 'for'?

1. It indicates the grounds for holding fast the confession in 4:14 [Alf, Blm, Mil, My, TNTC].
2. It confirms the thought of 4:14 [EGT].
3. It restates the truth of 2:11–14 [ICC].
4. It continues the declaration of the high priesthood of Christ from the preceding comments [Lg, Mil].
5. It counteracts any inference that Christ's exalted position would hinder his identification with human weakness [TNTC, WBC, Wst].

QUESTION—What relationship is indicated by the participial form δυνάμενον 'being able'?

1. Most translations indicate that it is attributive, making a statement about the high priest [EGT, HNTC, Mil, NIC, WBC; all versions except NJB, REB]: a high priest who is not able. The present tense indicates a continuing state of being able, but none of the commentaries mention this [Ed].
2. It is not attributive [Alf]: a high priest unable.

but[a] (one)-tempted/tested[b] in-relation-to[c] every (thing) in-accordance-with[d] (a) likeness[e] apart-from[f] sin.

LEXICON—a. δέ (LN 89.124) (BAGD 1.d. p. 171): 'but' [HNTC, LN, Lns, Mil, WBC; KJV, NAB, NASB, NIV, NJB, NRSV, REB], 'rather' [BAGD], 'on the contrary' [TEV], not explicit [NIC; CEV, NLT, TNT]. It is adversative [Lg, Lns, NIGTC] and carries forward a heightening of the thought [Lg, NIGTC].

b. perf. pass. participle of πειράζω (LN 88.308) (BAGD 2.b. p. 640): 'to be tempted' [HNTC, LN, Mil; CEV, KJV, NAB, NASB, NIV, TEV], 'to face temptation' [NLT], 'to be tested' [WBC; NRSV, REB, TNT], 'to be tried' [BAGD, Lns], 'to be put to the test' [BAGD; NJB], 'to be made trial of' [BAGD], 'to endure trial' [NIC]. The perfect tense indicates that his past experience of being tempted has continuing results [NIGTC, WBC, Wst].

c. κατά with accusative object (LN 89.4) (BAGD II.6. p. 407): 'in relation to' [LN], 'with regard to' [LN], 'in all respects' [Lns]. The phrase κατὰ πάντα 'in relation to everything' is translated 'in all respects' [BAGD, NIC], 'in every respect' [HNTC, WBC; NRSV], 'in every way' [Mil; CEV, NAB, NIV, REB, TEV, TNT], 'in exactly the same way' [NJB], 'in all points' [KJV], 'in all things' [NASB], 'all' [NLT]. The phrase refers to all things [Alf], every respect [Hu, TNTC], the entire range of human experience [HNTC].

d. κατά with accusative object (LN 89.8) (BAGD II.5.b.β. p. 407): 'in accordance with, in relation to' [LN]. The phrase καθ' ὁμοιότητα 'in accordance with a likeness' is translated 'in like manner as we' [Lns], 'in a similar manner' [BAGD], 'in quite the same way as we are' [WBC], 'just like (we are tempted)' [Mil], 'like ourselves' [NIC], 'as ourselves' [NJB], 'as we are' [NASB, NRSV, REB, TNT], 'just as we are' [NIV], 'like as we are' [KJV], 'similarly to us' [HNTC], 'that we are' [CEV, NAB, TEV], 'the same we do' [NLT].

e. ὁμοιότης (LN **64.3**) (BAGD p. 567): 'likeness' [BAGD, LN], 'similarity' [BAGD, LN]. The phrase καθ' ὁμοιότητα 'in accordance with a likeness' is translated 'in a way similar' [**LN**], 'in quite the same way' [BAGD].

f. χωρίς with genitive object (LN 89.120) (BAGD 2.b.β. p. 890): 'apart from' [LN; NJB], 'without' [BAGD, HNTC, LN, Mil, WBC; NASB, NIV, NRSV, REB], 'except for' [Lns], 'free from' [NIC]. The phrase χωρὶς ἁμαρτίας 'apart from sin' is translated 'yet never sinned' [NAB], 'but did not sin' [TEV], 'but/yet he did not sin' [CEV, NLT, TNT].

QUESTION—What is meant by πεπειρασμένον 'tempted/tested'?

Most translations indicate that it is attributive, making a statement about the high priest [HNTC, Lg, Mil, WBC, Wst; NAB, NASB, NIV, NRSV, REB, TEV]: a high priest who has been tempted/tested.

1. It means tempted to do evil [HNTC, LN, Mil, My, NIGTC, NTC, TNTC, WBC, Wst; CEV, KJV, NAB, NASB, NIV, NLT, TEV].
2. It means tested [Lns, NIC; NJB, NRSV, REB, TNT].
3. It includes both trials and temptations [Blm].

QUESTION—What relationship is indicated by the phrase καθ' ὁμοιότητα 'in accordance with a likeness'?

1. It means in the same way we are [Alf, Blm, Hu, Mil, My, NCBC, NTC, TNTC, WBC; all versions].
2. It means because of his likeness to us [EGT, Lg, NIC].
3. It means both of the above [EBC].

QUESTION—What relationship is indicated by the phrase χωρὶς ἁμαρτίας 'apart from sin'?

1. It means without committing any sin [BAGD, Blm, EGT, GNC, Hu, Hwt, ICC, Mil, My, NCBC, NIC, NIGTC, NTC, WBC; CEV, NAB, NLT, REB, TEV, TNT], referring especially to temptations to disobey God or to apostasy [ICC].
2. It means in all respects except for the temptations that result from having sinned [Wst].
3. Both meanings are included [EBC, HNTC].
4. It means that his participation in human sufferings was without any hint of sinful emotion [Lg]; there was no sin in his life with which temptations could make contact [Alf, Lns]. His temptations were therefore more

severe than ours [Lns, Mil] because he resisted temptation to the extreme instead of yielding as human nature often does [Mil].

4:16 Therefore[a] let-us-come with[b] confidence[c] to-the throne[d] of-the grace,[e]

LEXICON—a. οὖν (LN 89.50) (BAGD 1.b. p. 593): 'therefore' [BAGD, HNTC, LN, Mil, WBC; KJV, NASB, NRSV, REB], 'consequently' [BAGD, LN], 'accordingly' [BAGD, LN], 'then' [BAGD, LN, Lns; NIV, NJB, TEV], 'so then' [LN], 'so' [LN, NIC; CEV, NAB, NLT, TNT].

b. μετά with genitive object (LN 89.79) (BAGD A.III.1. p. 509): 'with' [BAGD, LN, Lns, Mil, NIC, WBC; NASB, NIV, NRSV, TNT]. The phrase προσερχώμεθα μετὰ παρρησίας 'let us come with confidence' is translated 'let us have no fear in approaching' [NJB], 'let us have confidence and approach' [TEV], 'we should come bravely' [CEV].

c. παρρησία (LN **25.158**) (BAGD 3.b. p. 630): 'confidence' [Mil, NIC; NASB, NIV, TEV, TNT], 'boldness' [LN, Lns; NRSV], 'bold frankness' [WBC], 'courage' [LN], 'joyful heart' [BAGD]. The phrase μετὰ παρρησίας 'with openness' is translated 'boldly' [**LN;** KJV, NLT, REB], 'confidently' [HNTC; NAB], 'bravely' [CEV], 'have no fear' [NJB]. This phrase states the manner of approaching the throne [Mil]. This word means sure (bold and joyful [Lg], trusting [NIGTC], inner [TH]) confidence [ICC, Lg, NIGTC, NTC, TH], freedom to speak without fear [TNTC, WBC].

d. θρόνος (LN 6.112, **37.72**) (BAGD 1.b. p. 364): 'throne' [BAGD, HNTC, LN (6.112, **37.72**), Lns, Mil, NIC, WBC; all versions]. The phrase τῷ θρόνῳ τῆς χάριτος 'the throne of grace' is translated 'the place from which grace is dispensed' [LN (**37.72**)]. This word implies royalty [TNTC].

e. χάρις (LN 25.89, 88.66) (BAGD 2.a. p. 877): 'grace' [BAGD, HNTC, LN (88.66), Lns, Mil, NIC, WBC; all versions except CEV, NLT], 'graciousness' [LN (88.66)], 'gracious care' [BAGD], 'gracious help' [BAGD], 'kindness' [LN (88.66)], 'favor' [BAGD, LN (25.89)], 'goodwill' [BAGD, LN (25.89)], not explicit [TEV]. This noun is also translated as an adjective: 'merciful' [CEV], 'gracious' [NLT].

QUESTION—What relationship is indicated by οὖν 'therefore'?

It indicates an exhortation based on the preceding statement [Blm, EGT, Lg, Mil, My, NIGTC, TNTC, WBC].

QUESTION—What is implied by the verb προσερχώμεθα 'let us come'?

It has the implication of approaching an authority figure [ICC] or a deity [Alf, Mil, NIGTC], approaching to have fellowship [My]. The first person plural 'let us come' implies that Christians need no earthly priests for access to God [EBC]. The readers are urged to approach God rather than to draw back [Hu]. The present tense implies continuing to come [Lns], to come repeatedly [WBC] as a daily spiritual exercise [Hwt], to come anytime [Mil], that they are already coming [NTC], that the opportunity is still open [WBC]: let us come continually/repeatedly.

QUESTION—How are the two nouns related in the genitive construction τῷ θρόνῳ τῆς χάριτος 'the throne of grace'?

It means the throne from which grace is bestowed by God [EGT, HNTC, Lg, NIGTC, TNTC, WBC], through Christ [Lg], by Christ [Mil]. Some take it to be a personification: grace is enthroned [ICC, Lg].

QUESTION—What is the throne?

It is the throne of God [Alf, Mil, My, NIC, NIGTC, TH, WBC; TEV] in heaven [Lg] where the glorified Savior sits [Hwt, Mil, Wst]; it is the revelation of God's majestic presence [NCBC, Wst]. It implies the kingship of the Son, who sits at God's right hand, and 'grace' refers to Christ's priesthood [NTC]. It is an allusion to the mercy-seat in the OT ark of the covenant, where God was represented as enthroned [Blm, GNC, NIC]. The term implies God's love for mankind [EBC].

in-order-that[a] we-may-receive mercy[b] and may-find[c] grace[d] for[e] timely[f] help.[g]

LEXICON—a. ἵνα (LN 89.59) (BAGD I.1.c. p. 377): 'in order that' [BAGD, LN, Lns; REB], 'for the purpose that' [LN], 'so that' [LN, Mil, WBC; NIV, NRSV], 'that' [BAGD, HNTC; KJV, NASB, TNT]. The phrase ἵνα λάβωμεν 'in order that we may receive' is translated 'in order to receive' [NIC], 'to receive' [NAB, NJB], 'there we will receive' [NLT, TEV], 'there we will be treated with' [CEV].

b. ἔλεος (LN 88.76) (BAGD 2.b. p.250): 'mercy' [BAGD, HNTC, LN, Lns, Mil, NIC, WBC; all versions except CEV], 'kindness' [CEV]. This word is the response to physical or emotional wretchedness [Lg]; it is the love that helps the wretched [Lns].

c. aorist act. subj. of εὑρίσκω (LN 13.17) (BAGD 3. p. 325): 'to find' [HNTC, LN, Lns, Mil, NIC; all versions], 'to obtain' [BAGD, WBC], 'to attain to' [LN].

d. χάρις (LN 25.89, 88.66) (BAGD 2.a. p. 877): 'grace' [BAGD, HNTC, LN (88.66), Lns, Mil, NIC, WBC; all versions except CEV, NAB, TNT], 'through his grace' [TNT], 'graciousness' [LN (88.66)], 'gracious care' [BAGD], 'gracious help' [BAGD], 'kindness' [LN (88.66)], 'favor' [BAGD, LN (25.89); NAB], 'goodwill' [BAGD, LN (25.89)], 'undeserved (kindness)' [CEV]. This word relates to a favorable inclination to those who have no claim to the favor [Lg]; it is the love that pardons the guilty [Lns].

e. εἰς with accusative object (LN 89.57) (BAGD 4.e. p. 229): 'for' [Lns, Mil, NIC], 'for the purpose of' [LN], 'that' [TNT], 'into' [BAGD], 'to' [BAGD, HNTC; KJV, NASB, NIV, NJB, NLT, NRSV, REB, TEV], not explicit [WBC; CEV, NJB]. This word indicates purpose [Mil].

f. εὔκαιρος (LN 67.6) (BAGD p. 321): 'timely' [Lns, Mil, NIC], 'well-timed' [BAGD], 'suitable' [BAGD], 'in time of need' [BAGD; NAB, TNT], 'at the right time' [WBC], 'favorable' [LN]. The phrase εἰς εὔκαιρον βοήθειαν 'for timely help' is translated 'to give us timely help'

[REB], 'to help in time of need' [HNTC; KJV, NASB, NRSV], 'to help us in our time of need' [NIV], 'to help us when we need it' [NLT], 'to help us just when we need it' [TEV], 'when we are in need of help' [NJB], 'at the right time when we are in need of help' [WBC], 'and we will find help' [CEV]. It means 'seasonable' [ICC].

g. βοήθεια (LN **35.1**) (BAGD p. 144): 'help' [BAGD, Lns, Mil, NIC, WBC; CEV, NAB, NJB, TNT]. This noun is also translated as a verb: 'to help' [HNTC; KJV, NASB, NIV, NLT, NRSV, TEV], 'to give help' [REB]. The phrase εἰς εὔκαιρον βοήθειαν 'for timely help' is translated 'to help us at the proper time' [LN].

QUESTION—What relationship is indicated by ἵνα 'in order that'?

It indicates the purpose of coming to the throne of grace [Lg, Mil].

QUESTION—How are the phrases λάβωμεν ἔλεος 'that we may receive mercy' and χάριν εὕρωμεν 'that we may find grace' related?

The aorist tenses imply receiving and finding at each approach to the throne [Mil].

1. They are two concepts.

1.1 'Receive mercy' relates to forgiveness of sin; 'find grace' relates to receiving assistance [EGT, HNTC, Mil, NCBC, NTC, Wst]. Mercy precedes grace [EGT].

1.2 'Receive mercy' relates to help when we fail; 'find grace' relates to help in our service for God [EBC].

2. The two phrases are similar in meaning [Alf, Blm, NIGTC, TH], are synonymous [My], as the chiastic structure of the two phrases suggests [NIGTC].

QUESTION—What is χάριν 'grace' connected with?

1. It is the predicate of εὕρωμεν 'we may find' [Alf, HNTC, Hu, ICC, Lns, Mil, My, NIC, NTC, TH, WBC, Wst; all versions except NAB]: we may receive mercy and find grace for help.
2. It is the second predicate of λάβωμεν 'we may receive' [NAB]: we may receive mercy and grace, and may find help.

QUESTION—What is the phrase εἰς εὔκαιρον βοήθειαν 'for timely help' connected with?

1. It is connected to both 'receive mercy' and 'find grace' [Alf, Lns, NIGTC, Wst]: that we may both receive mercy and find grace for timely help.
2. It is connected only to χάριν εὕρωμεν 'may find grace' [HNTC, Hu, Mil, NCBC, NIC, WBC; KJV, NASB]: that we may receive mercy, and that we may find grace for timely help.
3. It is connected only with εὕρωμεν 'may find' [NAB]: that we may find help in time of need.

QUESTION—What is meant by εὔκαιρον βοήθειαν 'timely help'?

It means help at the time of need [Blm, EBC, EGT, HNTC, Hu, ICC, Lg, Lns, Mil, My, NIC, NTC, TNTC, WBC, Wst; all versions]. It means help in weakness and temptation [Lg]. It means help while the throne of grace is still available [Alf].

DISCOURSE UNIT: 5:1–7:28 [Wst]. The topic is Christ's high priesthood.

DISCOURSE UNIT: 5:1–14 [NASB]. The topic is the perfect High Priest.

DISCOURSE UNIT: 5:1–10 [NCBC, NIGTC, TNTC, Wst]. The topic is the qualifications for becoming high priest [NCBC], Christ fulfilling the characteristics of a high priest [Wst], Jesus the merciful high priest [NIGTC], Christ as high priest compared with Aaron [TNTC].

DISCOURSE UNIT: 5:1–4 [EBC, HNTC, Hwt, NIC]. The topic is the required qualities of a high priest [EBC, Hwt, NIC], the appointment to high priesthood [HNTC].

DISCOURSE UNIT: 5:1–3 [Lg, NTC]. The topic is Christ's qualification to be high priest because he can sympathize with human weakness [Lg], the ennoblement of the high priest [NTC].

5:1 For[a] every high-priest from-among[b] men being-selected[c] on-behalf-of[d] men is-appointed[e] (in) the-things pertaining-to[f] God,

LEXICON—a. γάρ (LN 89.23): 'for' [HNTC, LN, Lns, Mil, WBC; KJV, NASB, REB], 'because' [LN], 'now' [NLT], not explicit [NIC; CEV, NAB, NIV, NJB, NRSV, TEV, TNT].

b. ἐκ with genitive object (LN 89.3, 90.16): 'from among' [HNTC, Lns, Mil, WBC; all versions except CEV, NLT, TEV], 'from' [LN (89.3, 90.16), NIC; TEV], not explicit [CEV, NLT]. It indicates source [Mil]. This prepositional phrase is emphatic by word order [Alf].

c. pres. pass. participle of λαμβάνω (LN **30.86**) (BAGD 1.f. p. 464): 'to be selected' [BAGD, LN (30.86), WBC; NIV], 'to be chosen' [BAGD, HNTC, **LN** (30.86), Mil; NLT, NRSV, TEV, TNT], 'to be taken' [Lns, NIC; KJV, NAB, NASB, NJB, REB], not explicit [CEV]. The present tense refers to repeated action [Mil], continuing action [Wst]. The passive voice implies that a man could not appoint himself [NTC], rather, it is God's action [NIGTC, NTC, TH].

d. ὑπέρ with genitive object (LN 90.36): 'on behalf of' [LN, NIC, WBC; NASB, NRSV, TEV, TNT], 'in behalf of' [Mil], 'to act on behalf of' [NJB], 'for the sake of' [LN], 'for the benefit of' [Lns], 'for' [LN; KJV], 'to represent' [HNTC]. The phrase ὑπὲρ ἀνθρώπων 'on behalf of men' is translated 'their representative' [NAB, REB], 'to represent them' [NIV], 'to represent other human beings' [NLT], 'to help others' [CEV]. This prepositional phrase is emphatic by word order [Alf].

e. pres. pass. indic. of καθίστημι (LN 37.104) (BAGD 2.b. p. 390): 'to be appointed' [BAGD, HNTC, LN, Lns, Mil, NIC, WBC; CEV, NASB, NIV, NJB, REB, TEV, TNT], 'to be chosen' [NLT], 'to be ordained' [KJV], 'to be put in charge of' [LN; NRSV], 'to be placed in charge of' [LN]. The phrase ὑπὲρ ἀνθρώπων καθίσταται 'is appointed on behalf of men' is translated 'and is made their representative' [NAB]. The passive voice indicates that he does not appoint himself [Hu, NTC] but is appointed by God [NIGTC, NTC, TH, TNTC]. The present tense refers to a general truth [Lns].

f. πρός with accusative object (LN 89.7) (BAGD III.5.b. p. 710): 'pertaining to' [KJV, NASB, NRSV], 'with regard to' [LN], 'with reference to' [Lns], 'relating to' [Mil], 'related to' [NIV], 'in relation to' [HNTC], 'before' [NAB, REB], not explicit [CEV]. The phrase τὰ πρὸς τὸν θεόν 'the things pertaining to God' is translated 'that which concerns God' [BAGD], 'with reference to what concerns God' [BAGD], 'in relationships with God' [NJB], 'where their responsibility to God is concerned' [NIC], 'to serve before God' [TNT], 'to serve God' [TEV], 'in the service of God' [WBC], 'in their dealings with God' [NLT].

QUESTION—What relationship is indicated by γάρ 'for'?

It substantiates what was said in 4:15 [Alf, EGT, My, NIGTC, TNTC, WBC, Wst] and introduces the grounds for the exhortation of 4:16 [EGT, Lns, Mil]. This section shows that the conditions required of any high priest were met by Christ [WBC].

QUESTION—What relationship is indicated by the participle λαμβανόμενος 'being taken'?

1. It describes the high priest [WBC; KJV, NASB, NRSV]: every high priest who is taken from among men.
2. It indicates a reason for appointing a high priest [Alf, EGT, Lg, Mil, My]: every high priest, since he is chosen from among men, is appointed on their behalf.
3. It is treated as a verb parallel to the following verb καθίσταται 'is appointed' [GNC, HNTC, NIGTC; NAB, NIV, NJB, REB, TEV, TNT]: every high priest is taken from among men and is appointed. This is not regular Greek grammar.

QUESTION—What is the phrase ὑπὲρ ἀνθρώπων 'on behalf of men' connected with?

1. It is connected with καθίσταται 'is appointed' [Alf, Blm, EGT, GNC, HNTC, Hwt, My, NIC, NIGTC, TH, WBC; all versions]: he is appointed on behalf of men.
2. It is connected with 'taken from among men' [Lns]: he is taken from among men for the benefit of men.

QUESTION—What relationship is indicated by the phrase τὰ πρὸς τὸν θεόν 'in the things pertaining to God'?

It is an adverbial accusative [EGT, ICC, Lg, Lns, Mil, NIGTC], an accusative of respect [WBC]: he is appointed with reference to the things relating to God. It indicates the area of reference of the appointment [Mil].

in-order-that[a] he-might-offer[b] both gifts[c] and sacrifices[d] concerning[e] sins,

LEXICON—a. ἵνα (LN 89.59) (BAGD I.1.a. p. 376): 'in order that' [BAGD], 'in order to' [LN; NASB, TNT], 'for the purpose of' [LN], 'so that' [LN, Mil], 'that' [BAGD; KJV], not explicit [CEV, NLT]. The phrase ἵνα προσφέρῃ 'in order that he might offer' is translated 'to offer' [HNTC, Lns, NIC, WBC; NAB, NIV, NJB, NRSV, REB, TEV].

b. pres. act. subj. of προσφέρω (LN 57.80) (BAGD 2.a. p. 720): 'to offer' [BAGD, HNTC, Lns, NIC, WBC; all versions except NLT], 'to offer up' [Mil], 'to present' [BAGD], 'to present to, to bring to' [LN], 'to present (gifts) . . . to offer (sacrifices)' [NLT]. The present tense indicates repeated action [Mil].

c. δῶρον (LN 57.84) (BAGD 2. p. 211): 'gift' [HNTC, LN, Lns, Mil, NIC, WBC; all versions except TEV], 'present' [LN], 'offering' [BAGD; TEV].

d. θυσία (LN 53.20) (BAGD 2.a. p. 366): 'sacrifice' [BAGD, HNTC, LN, Lns, Mil, NIC, WBC; all versions], 'offering' [BAGD].

e. ὑπέρ with genitive object (LN 90.24) (BAGD 1.b. p. 838): 'concerning' [LN], 'for' [HNTC, Mil, NIC; all versions except CEV], 'for the purging of' [WBC], 'in behalf of' [Lns], 'in order to atone for' [BAGD, My], 'in order to remove' [BAGD], 'because of' [CEV]. Here it indicates atonement for sins [Alf, Mil, My], removal of sins [Lns].

QUESTION—What relationship is indicated by ἵνα 'in order that'?

1. It indicates the purpose of the appointment to high priestly office [Blm, EGT, Lg, Mil, TH, WBC]: he is appointed in order that he might offer gifts and sacrifices.
2. It is in apposition to τὰ πρὸς τὸν θεόν 'the things pertaining to God' [Lns, My]: he is appointed in reference to the things pertaining to God, namely to offer gifts and sacrifices.

QUESTION—How are the two words δῶρα 'gifts' and θυσίας 'sacrifices' related?

Together the terms are comprehensive of all offerings [Blm, EBC, EGT, HNTC, Hu, ICC], all offerings for sins [NCBC, NIC].

1. They are essentially synonymous in usage [Alf, ICC, NCBC, NIGTC, NTC].
2. The two terms are distinct [Lns, Mil, My, WBC]. 'Gifts' refers to inanimate offerings not involving blood [Blm, Hwt, Lg, TNTC], thank-offerings and worship offerings [Mil], meal offerings [TNTC, Wst], gifts and sacrifices in general [My]. 'Sacrifices' refers to offerings involving blood [Blm, Lg, My, TNTC, Wst], animal sacrifices [Hwt], sin-offerings [Mil]. Blood sacrifices are especially in mind in this passage [My].

QUESTION—What is the phrase ὑπὲρ ἁμαρτιῶν 'concerning sins' connected with?

1. It refers to both 'gifts' and 'sacrifices' [Alf, HNTC, Hu, NIC, NIGTC, NTC, TNTC, WBC], since these two nouns are bound together by τε 'both' [Alf]: gifts and sacrifices, both of which are for sins.
2. It refers only to θυσίας 'sacrifices' [Mil, Wst]: sacrifices for sins.
3. It is connected with προσφέρῃ 'he may offer' [EGT, Lg], with the clause as a whole [My]: in order that he may offer for sins gifts and sacrifices.

5:2 being-able to-moderate-(his)-feelings-with[a] the-(ones)-being-ignorant[b] and going-astray,[c]

LEXICON—a. pres. act. infin. of μετριοπαθέω (LN **88.65**) (BAGD p. 515): 'to moderate one's feelings' [BAGD], 'to be moderate with' [Lns], 'to deal gently with' [BAGD, HNTC, **LN**, Mil, WBC**;** NASB, NIV, NLT, NRSV], 'to bear gently with' [TNT], 'to be gently disposed toward' [LN], 'to be gentle with' [TEV], 'to deal patiently with' [NAB], 'to bear patiently with' [REB], 'to have compassion on' [KJV], 'to deal considerately with' [NIC], 'to sympathize with' [NJB], 'to feel sorry for' [CEV]. It implies forbearance [Blm, ICC, WBC], moderation [EGT, Hwt, Lns, Mil, My, TNTC, Wst], magnanimity [HNTC, Hu] and sympathy based on shared experience [HNTC], a middle attitude between indifference and anger [EBC], between being insensitive and too sensitive [Hwt, Lg, NCBC, NIC, WBC]. The present tense indicates a general truth [NIGTC].

b. pres. act. participle of ἀγνοέω (LN 28.13) (BAGD 4. p. 11): 'to be ignorant' [Mil; NIV, NJB, NLT, TEV, TNT], 'to be ignorant of, not to know, to be unaware of' [LN (28.13)], 'to do wrong' [BAGD], 'to sin (in ignorance)' [BAGD]. This participle is also translated as an adjective: 'ignorant' [HNTC, Lns, NIC; KJV, NASB, NRSV, REB], 'foolish' [CEV]. The phrase τοῖς ἀγνοοῦσιν 'the ones being ignorant' is translated 'those who sin through ignorance' [WBC]. The phrase τοῖς ἀγνοοῦσιν καὶ πλανωμένοις 'the ones being ignorant and going astray' is translated 'erring sinners' [NAB]. This verb implies sinning [ICC].

c. pres. pass. participle of πλανάω (LN 31.67) (BAGD 2.c.α. p. 665): 'to go astray' [BAGD, WBC; NIV, NJB], 'to stray from the truth' [LN], 'to err' [HNTC, Lns, NIC; REB, TNT], 'to be wayward' [Mil; NLT], 'to be out of the way' [KJV], 'to make mistakes' [TEV], 'to be misled' [BAGD], 'to be deluded' [BAGD]. This participle is also translated as an adjective: 'wayward' [NRSV], 'misguided' [NASB], 'sinful' [CEV]. This verb implies sinning [ICC]. It means that they no longer believe the truth and have begun to believe what is false [LN].

QUESTION—What relationship is indicated by the participle δυνάμενος 'being able'?

1. It indicates the reason the high priest is able to make the offerings and sacrifices [Alf]: he is able to make the offerings because he can deal gently with those who sin. It also further expands the concept that he is taken from among men [Alf].
2. It gives a further grounds, in addition to his being taken from among men, for the conclusion to be drawn later that Christ is a valid high priest [Mil].
3. Various translations and commentaries interpret this as an additional comment concerning high priests, although none of the commentaries specifically discuss this point [EBC, GNC, HNTC, Hu, Mil, WBC; all versions]: in addition, he is able to deal gently.

4. It further describes the high priest [Alf, EGT, Hwt, My]: one who is able to deal gently. It implies willingness [Blm]. It indicates a necessary requirement [NIC].
5. It indicates the manner of his actions [Lns]: he acts as being able to deal gently.

QUESTION—What is implied by the two participles in the phrase τοῖς ἀγνοοῦσιν καὶ πλανωμένοις 'the ones being ignorant and going astray'?

Both words are milder than 'sinning', and suggest the feeling of a sinner toward fellow-sinners [Alf]. The two terms are nearly synonymous [Blm]. Both participles refer to the same persons [HNTC, ICC, NCBC, NIC, NIGTC, NTC, TH, WBC], as the single article indicates [NIGTC, NTC, WBC]. The present tenses imply repeated actions [Mil]. The phrase is nearly a hendiadys, meaning sinning through ignorance [ICC, Lns, NCBC, NIC, TH, WBC]. The high priest could deal compassionately with those who sinned through ignorance or error, but intentional and rebellious sin would require exclusion from the congregation [Hu, NIC, NTC, TNTC, WBC, Wst].

since[a] he-himself also is-laid-around-with[b] weakness,[c]

LEXICON—a. ἐπεί (LN 89.32) (BAGD 2, p. 284): 'since' [BAGD, HNTC, LN, Lns, Mil, NIC, WBC; NASB, NIV, NRSV, REB, TEV, TNT], 'because' [BAGD; NJB, NLT], 'for' [BAGD; NAB], 'for that' [KJV], not explicit [CEV].

b. pres. mid. (deponent = act.) of περίκειμαι (LN **13.6**, 85.54) (BAGD 2.b. p. 648): 'to be laid around with', 'to be encompassed with' [Lns], 'to be compassed with' [KJV], 'to be placed around' [LN (85.54)], 'to be put around' [LN (85.54)], 'to be beset by' [NIC; NAB, REB], 'to be beset with' [HNTC, Mil; NASB], 'to be subject to' [BAGD, NTC, WBC; NIV, NJB, NRSV, TNT], 'to have' [CEV]. The phrase περίκειται ἀσθένειαν 'is laid around with weakness' is translated 'he was weak in many ways' [**LN** (13.6)], 'he is weak in many ways' [TEV].

c. ἀσθένεια (LN 74.23) (BAGD 1.c. p. 115): 'weakness' [BAGD, HNTC, LN, Lns, Mil, WBC; CEV, NAB, NASB, NIV, NLT, NRSV, REB, TNT], 'limitations of weakness' [NJB], 'limitation' [LN], 'infirmity' [KJV], 'incapacity' [LN], 'frailty' [NIC]. It includes moral weakness [EBC]; it means moral weakness [Alf, Lg, Mil, My] which leads to susceptibility to sin [Alf, ICC, Mil] and actual sin [My], the result of human depravity [Hu]. The accusative case expresses the thing to which the verb refers [EGT].

QUESTION—What relationship is indicated by ἐπεί 'since'?

It indicates the reason for the preceding statement [EGT, Lns, Mil, My] (or grounds for making the statement [NIGTC]): he is able to moderate his feelings with those who are ignorant and going astray, because he himself is subject to weakness.

5:3 and because-of[a] it he-must,[b] just-as[c] for[d] the people, thus also for[d] himself[e] to-offer[f] for[g] sins.

LEXICON—a. διά with accusative object (LN 89.26, 90.44): 'because of' [LN (89.26, 90.44), Mil, NIC; NASB, NRSV, REB, TNT], 'on account of' [LN]. The phrase δι' αὐτήν 'because of it' is translated 'on this account' [HNTC], 'by reason hereof' [KJV], 'for this reason' [Lns], 'so' [NAB], 'this is why' [NIV], 'that is why' [WBC; CEV, NJB, NLT], 'because he is himself weak' [TEV].

b. pres. act. indic. of ὀφείλω (LN 71.35) (BAGD 2.a.β. p. 599): 'must' [BAGD, LN, NIC; CEV, NAB, NRSV, TEV], 'to be obligated' [BAGD, Mil; NASB], 'to be obliged' [HNTC, Lns; TNT], 'to be under obligation' [WBC], 'to be bound' [REB], 'to have to' [LN; NIV, NJB, NLT], 'to be necessary' [LN], 'ought' [BAGD; KJV]. It means duty [TH], moral obligation [WBC], moral necessity [Lg], obligation [NTC] or necessity [Alf, My, NTC] based on the nature of the case [My, Wst]. It is a requirement under the Mosaic law due to the 'weakness' mentioned [Lg, NIGTC]. It was the duty of a priest to do so [TH], and this was required on the Day of Atonement [TNTC, WBC]. The present tense implies a general truth [Hu, WBC]; it may also imply that the temple was still standing and the high priests were still making offerings [Hu].

c. καθώς (LN 64.14): 'just as' [LN, WBC; TNT], 'as' [Lns; KJV, NASB], 'as well as' [HNTC, NIC; NAB, NIV, NJB, NRSV, REB], 'in the same way as' [Mil], 'not only' [TEV], not explicit [CEV, NLT].

d. περί with genitive object (LN 90.39): 'for' [HNTC, Lns, Mil, NIC, WBC; all versions], 'on behalf of' [LN]. The meaning is 'on behalf of' [EBC].

e. αὐτός (LN 92.11): 'himself' [HNTC, Lns, NIC; KJV, NAB, NASB, NJB, REB, TNT], 'him' [LN]. This personal pronoun 'him' is here used as a reflexive pronoun 'himself' [NIGTC]. The phrase περὶ αὐτοῦ 'for himself' is translated 'for his own sins' [Mil, WBC; CEV, NIV, NLT, NRSV, TEV].

f. pres. act. infin. of προσφέρω: 'to offer.' See this word in 5:1.

g. περί with genitive object (LN 89.6) (BAGD 1.g. p. 644): 'for' [Lns, Mil, WBC; CEV, KJV, NLT, TEV], 'in relation to, with regard to, concerning' [LN], 'to take away, to atone for' [BAGD]. The phrase προσφέρειν περὶ ἁμαρτιῶν 'to offer for sins' is translated 'to make sin offerings' [NAB, NJB, REB, TNT], 'to offer sacrifices for sins' [NASB, NIV, NRSV],

QUESTION—What relationship is indicated by καί 'and'?

It introduces a new point [NIGTC]. It is a continuation (the logical consequence [My]) of the last clause of the preceding verse [Lns, My], amplifying the reference to weakness given there [Mil, NIGTC]: he is encompassed with weakness and because of the weakness he must offer a sin offering for himself. This verse is an incidental comment [My]. It refers to OT priests and does not include Christ [NTC], since Christ did not need to offer a sacrifice for himself [Blm, GNC, NCBC, TNTC].

QUESTION—To what does αὐτήν 'it' refer?

It refers to the high priest's weakness mentioned in 5:2 [Alf, Blm, Lns, Mil, My, NIC, NIGTC, TH, TNTC, Wst]: because of his weakness.

QUESTION—What relationship is indicated by καθὼς . . . οὕτως καί 'just as . . . thus also'?

The two parts connect and introduce the two parts of a comparison [Mil]: just as for the people so also for himself.

QUESTION—What is implied by the word order of the phrase καὶ περὶ αὑτοῦ 'for himself also'?

It is emphatic by its position preceding the infinitive προσφέρειν 'to offer' [NIGTC].

QUESTION—What is the implied object of προσφέρειν 'to offer'?

A sin offering that is offered for the people's sins is the implied object [HNTC, Hu, NIC, NIGTC; NAB, NASB, NJB, REB, TNT]. The phrase προσφέρειν περὶ ἁμαρτιῶν 'to offer for sins' is translated 'to offer sacrifices for sins' [NASB, NIV, NRSV, TEV], 'to make sin offerings' [HNTC; NAB, NJB, REB, TNT], 'to bring a sin offering' [NIC].

DISCOURSE UNIT: 5:4–10 [Lg, NTC]. The topic is Christ, called by God to a Melchizedek priesthood [Lg], Christ's fulfillment of the office of high priest [NTC].

5:4 And not for-himself (does) anyone take the honor[a]

LEXICON—a. τιμή (LN 87.4) (BAGD 2.d. p. 818): 'honor' [LN, Lns, NIC; all versions except REB, TNT], 'place of honor' [BAGD], 'office' [BAGD, HNTC, WBC; REB, TNT], 'honorable office' [Mil]. The reference is to the honor of the office of high priest [Alf, Blm, EGT, ICC, Mil, NIGTC, WBC, Wst]. It means the position or office of high priest [TH].

QUESTION—What is this verse connected with?

It is connected with 5:1 [Alf, EGT, Hu, Lg, My] and further explains it [Hu], stating another qualification for being high priest [EGT, Hwt, Lg, Lns, Mil, My, NIC, TH, Wst]. Verses 2–3 are subordinate to verse 1 [Alf].

QUESTION—What is implied by the word order of ἑαυτῷ 'to himself'?

It is emphatic by forefronting [Alf, NIGTC].

QUESTION—What is implied by the present tense of λαμβάνει 'takes'?

It indicates customary action [Blm].

but being-called[a] by God just-as[b] indeed Aaron also.

TEXT—Some manuscripts insert the definite article ὁ 'the' before the participle καλούμενος 'being called'. GNT does not mention this variant. KJV possibly reads this definite article, although this participle can be attributive here without the article, since its antecedent τις 'anyone' is indefinite.

LEXICON—a. pres. pass. participle of καλέω (LN 33.312) (BAGD 2. p. 399): 'to be called' [BAGD, HNTC, LN, Lns, Mil, NIC, WBC; all versions except CEV, NJB, TEV]. The passive voice is also translated as active: 'to choose' [CEV]. The phrase ἀλλὰ καλούμενος 'but being called' is translated 'it needs a call' [NJB]. The phrase ἀλλὰ καλούμενος ὑπὸ τοῦ θεοῦ 'but being called by God' is translated 'it is only by God's call' [TEV]. The present tense indicates action from time to time [Mil].

b. καθώσπερ (LN **64.15**) (BAGD p. 391): 'just as'. The phrase καθώσπερ καί 'just as indeed' is translated 'just as' [BAGD, HNTC, LN, Mil, WBC; NIV, NLT, NRSV, REB, TEV, TNT], 'even as' [Lns; NASB], 'as' [NIC; KJV, NAB, NJB], not explicit [CEV]. This word is emphatic [Lg, Mil, NIGTC, NTC, TH], 'precisely according as' [Lg].

QUESTION—What relationship is indicated by the participle καλούμενος 'being called'?

1. It is temporal [Alf, EGT, HNTC, ICC, Mil, WBC; NAB, NASB, NRSV, TNT]: when he is called.
2. It is an attributive modifier [NIC; KJV]: he who is called.
3. It indicates a requirement [NIV, NJB]: he must be called.
4. It expresses an additional comment [REB, TEV]: he is called.

QUESTION—What is meant by the reference to Aaron?

It refers only to Aaron himself [Lg, TNTC]. Καί 'even' means 'especially' Aaron, the founder of the levitical priesthood [NIGTC].

DISCOURSE UNIT: 5:5–11[EBC]. The topic is Christ's qualifications to be high priest.

DISCOURSE UNIT: 5:5–10 [HNTC, Hwt, NIC]. The topic is Jesus as high priest [HNTC], Christ's qualifications for the high priesthood [NIC].

5:5 Thus[a] Christ also[b] (did) not glorify[c] himself to-become high-priest

LEXICON—a. οὕτως (LN 61.9): 'thus' [LN, Lns], 'so' [HNTC, LN, Mil; KJV, NASB, NIV, NRSV, REB, TNT], 'in this way' [LN; TEV], 'in the same way' [NIC, WBC], 'that is how' [CEV], 'that is why' [NLT], 'and' [NJB], not explicit [NAB]. It indicates manner [My, TH], referring back to Aaron in 5:4 [TH], comparing Christ with Aaron [WBC]. It refers back to καθώσπερ in 5:4 [NTC, WBC].

b. καί (LN 89.93): 'also' [HNTC, LN, Lns, Mil, NIC; KJV, NASB, NIV, NRSV, TNT], 'even' [NAB], not explicit [WBC; CEV, NJB, NLT, REB, TEV]. It implies Christ in addition to the other high priests [Alf].

c. aorist act. indic. of δοξάζω (LN 87.8) (BAGD 2. p. 204): 'to glorify' [Lns, Mil; KJV, NAB, NASB, NRSV], 'to raise to glory' [BAGD], 'to honor' [LN], 'to take the honor' [WBC], 'to exalt' [NIC; NLT]. The phrase οὐχ ἑαυτὸν ἐδόξασεν 'did not glorify himself' is translated 'did not take upon himself the honor' [TEV, TNT], 'did not take upon himself the glory' [HNTC; NIV], 'did not confer on himself the glory' [REB], 'not just because he wanted the honor' [CEV]. This entire phrase is translated 'and so it was not Christ who gave himself the glory of becoming high priest' [NJB]. This word refers to being raised to the office of high priest [Alf].

QUESTION—What relationship is indicated by οὕτως 'thus'?

1. It indicates the conclusion [Mil] of the superiority of Christ's priesthood [Blm], implying conformity with the pattern of Christ's humility and calling [Hu].
2. It introduces the comparison of Christ with reference to Aaron in 5:4 [WBC].
3. It introduces the transition from the emphasis on Christ's sonship from the beginning of the epistle to his high priesthood as the principal emphasis in chapters 7 through 10 [NIGTC].

QUESTION—What is implied by the use of Χριστός 'Christ' instead of Ἰησοῦς 'Jesus'?

Some think that the Son is being considered here in his position as Messiah rather than in his personal aspect [Lg, WBC] and it implies his appointment by God [WBC]. However, others think that the word 'Christ' is never used in this letter as a messianic title [NIGTC]. It emphasizes his perfect obedience to God in his work [EBC, Wst].

QUESTION—What relationship is indicated by the infinitive γενηθῆναι 'to become'?

It is passive voice, implying having been made high priest by someone [Mil].

1. It explains ἐδόξασεν 'glorified' [Hwt, ICC, WBC]: he did not glorify himself—i.e., to become a high priest.
2. It indicates the purpose of glorifying himself (which he did not follow) [My]: what he did not do was to glorify himself in order to become a high priest.
3. It indicates the result of glorifying himself (which he did not follow) [Alf]: what he did not do was to glorify himself so as to result in his becoming a high priest.

but[a] the-(one)-having spoken to him, "My Son you are, I today have-begotten[b] you";

LEXICON—a. ἀλλά (LN 89.125): 'but' [HNTC, LN, Lns, Mil, WBC; KJV, NASB, NIV, NJB, NRSV], 'instead' [LN; TEV], not explicit [NIC; CEV, NAB, NLT, REB, TNT].

b. perf. act. indic. of γεννάω (LN 23.58) (BAGD): 'to beget' [BAGD, HNTC, LN, Lns, Mil, NIC; KJV, NAB, NASB, NRSV], 'to become one's father' [WBC; CEV, NIV, NLT, REB, TEV, TNT], 'to be the father of' [LN], 'to father' [NJB]. See this word and phrase at 1:5.

QUESTION—What relationship is indicated by ἀλλά 'but'?

It indicates contrast [NIGTC, TH; KJV, NASB, NIV, NRSV, TEV]: Christ did not, but God did.

QUESTION—What is the implied principal verb of this clause?

1. It is the implied phrase ἐδόξασεν αὐτόν 'glorified him' [Blm, EGT, HNTC, Hu, ICC, Lg, My, NCBC, NIC; REB]: he did not glorify himself to become a high priest, but the one who spoke this to him glorified him in this way.

2. It is based on the implied phrase 'appointed him' [NAB, NLT, NRSV, TNT]: 'he was appointed by the one who said . . .' [NRSV], 'he was made high priest by God who said . . .' [TNT], 'he was chosen by God, who said . . .' [NLT], 'he received it from the one who said . . .' [NAB].
3. The participial phrase ὁ λαλήσας 'the one having spoken' is treated as an indicative verb and made the main verb [CEV, NIV, TEV]: but God said to him, etc.

QUESTION—Who is the implied actor of ὁ λαλήσας 'the one having spoken'?

It was God who spoke [Alf, EGT, HNTC, Hu, Hwt, Mil, My, NIGTC, TH, TNTC, WBC, Wst; CEV, NAB, NIV, NLT, REB, TEV, TNT]. The speaking was prior to the glorifying, before the creation of the world [My].

QUESTION—Why is the quotation from Psalm 2:7 mentioned?

It deals with Christ's appointment to royal power [NIC, WBC, Wst], not with his parentage [WBC]. It indicates the fitness of Christ for the high priestly office [Hwt]; it shows that God who had named Jesus as his son was the one who had appointed him high priest [GNC, HNTC, ICC, Lg, Mil, NIGTC] since only the Son of God can be high priest at God's right hand [HNTC]. It unites Christ's sonship with his high priesthood [Hu, TNTC].

QUESTION—Where is the emphasis in the quotation?

It is on υἱός 'Son' and σύ 'you' in the first part and on ἐγώ 'I' and σε 'you' in the second part [Mil]: *My Son you* are; *I* today have begotten *you.*

QUESTION—Why is the second part of the quotation mentioned?

It restates and amplifies the first half of the quotation [Mil].

QUESTION—What is meant by σήμερον 'today'?

It refers to the day when Christ was enthroned [NCBC, NIC]; it refers to a particular moment in eternity [HNTC].

5:6 just-as[a] also in[b] another (place) he-says,

LEXICON—a. καθώς (LN 64.14): 'just as' [HNTC, LN, Mil; NAB, NASB], 'as' [NIC; KJV, NRSV, REB], 'even as' [WBC], 'even' [Lns], 'and' [NIV, NJB, NLT], not explicit [CEV, TEV, TNT].

b. ἐν with dative object (LN 83.13): 'in' [LN, Lns, Mil, NIC, WBC; all versions]. The phrase ἐν ἑτέρῳ 'in another place' is translated 'elsewhere' [HNTC].

QUESTION—What is the function of this clause?

This clause proves that Jesus did not become a priest on his own initiative, but that God directly appointed him [WBC]. It shows that there is another priestly order apart from the Levitical priesthood [NIC]. The same person, God, who called Christ 'Son' is the very one who called him priest [Mil]. The speaker is God [NIGTC, TNTC], whose words are recorded in another place in Scripture [TH].

"You (are) a-priest into[a] the age according-to[b] the order[c] of-Melchizedek,"

LEXICON—a. εἰς with accusative object (LN 67.95, 84.22): 'into' [LN (84.22)], 'for' [Lns]. The phrase εἰς τὸν αἰῶνα 'into the age' is translated 'forever' [HNTC, LN (67.95), Mil, NIC, WBC; all versions].

b. κατά with accusative object (LN 89.8) (BAGD II.5.b.α. p. 407): 'according to' [Lns; NAB, NASB, NRSV], 'in accordance with' [BAGD, LN, Mil], 'similarly to' [BAGD], 'after' [NIC; KJV], 'in' [HNTC; NIV, REB, TEV, TNT], 'of' [NJB]. The phrase κατὰ τὴν τάξιν 'according to the order' is translated 'just like' [WBC; CEV], 'in the line of' [NLT].

c. τάξις (LN **58.21**) (BAGD 4. p. 804): 'order' [Lns, Mil, NIC; all versions except NLT], 'rank' [HNTC], 'line' [NLT], 'kind, type' [LN], 'nature' [BAGD]. The phrase τὴν τάξιν Μελχισέδεκ 'the order of Melchizedek' is translated 'the kind of priest that Melchizedek was, like Melchizedek' [**LN**], 'just like Melchizedek' [BAGD].

QUESTION—What is the function of this quotation from Psalm 110:4?

Together with the preceding quotation in 5:5 [Hu, Hwt], it shows that Christ's office of high priest was an appointment by God [Hu, Hwt, Mil, WBC, Wst] and not appropriated by himself [WBC]. It shows that the Son of God has also been appointed high priest [My, NIC]; only as Son could he do his atoning work, later described [GNC]. It shows the author's concern to associate the titles of Son and high priest [Hu, WBC]; Christ held both positions [Wst]. It further refers to the similarity of Christ to Melchizedek, both of whom were both king and priest, rather than to Aaron [GNC, Lns].

QUESTION—What is implied by the use of the word ἱερεύς 'priest' instead of ἀρχιερεύς 'high priest'?

It means the same as high priest [My, TH]; the author does not distinguish carefully between 'priest' and 'high priest' [ICC].

QUESTION—What is implied by the reference to Melchizedek?

It indicates a universal priesthood not limited to the Jewish Aaronic order [Hu, Wst].

QUESTION—What is meant by τάξις 'order'?

1. It refers to rank [Alf, EGT, ICC, Mil; all versions] or order, even though there was no succession involved [Hwt, ICC].
2. It refers to similarity [BAGD, Blm, EBC, LN, My, NIGTC, TH, WBC]: according to the likeness of Melchizedek. It does not refer to order, since there was no succession of this priesthood [EBC]. The similarity is the type of priesthood [Lg, NIGTC] and character [My].

QUESTION—What is implied by εἰς τὸν αἰῶνα 'for ever'?

It implies permanent effectiveness [NIGTC], that it cannot be improved upon [TNTC], that it had no successor [TNTC, Wst]; no successor was needed nor possible [HNTC, Wst].

5:7 who in[a] the days of-his flesh[b]

LEXICON—a. ἐν with dative object (LN 67.136): 'in' [HNTC, Lns, Mil, NIC; KJV, NAB, NASB, NRSV, TEV, TNT], 'in the course of' [LN; REB], 'during' [LN, WBC; NIV, NJB], 'while' [CEV, NLT].

b. σάρξ (LN **23.90**) (BAGD 4. p. 743): 'flesh' [Lns, NIC; KJV, NAB, NASB, NRSV], 'life' [LN], 'earthly life' [HNTC; REB], 'life on earth' [Mil, WBC; NIV, NJB, TEV], 'human life' [TNT], 'human nature, mortal nature, earthly descent' [BAGD]. The phrase ἐν ταῖς ἡμέραις τῆς σαρκὸς αὐτοῦ 'in the days of his flesh' is translated 'while Jesus was on earth' [CEV, NLT]. It implies the frailty and suffering of human life [Blm, EBC, HNTC, NIC], the general conditions of earthly life [Wst].

QUESTION—What verb is ὅς 'who' connected with?

It is connected with ἔμαθεν 'learned' (5:8) [Lg] and ἐγένετο 'became' (5:9) [EGT, ICC, Mil, My, NIGTC, Wst]: who . . . learned . . . and became . . .

QUESTION—To what does the phrase 'in the days of his flesh' refer?

It refers to his earthly life [Blm, Hu, Hwt, Lg, Lns, Mil, My, NCBC, NIGTC, TH]: in his life on earth he learned obedience. This phrase is in contrast with 'having been perfected' in 5:9 [Wst]. It refers specifically to his agony in the Garden of Gethsemane [GNC].

both prayers[a] and supplications[b] to the-(one)-being-able to-save him from[c] death with[d] strong[e] crying[f] and tears[g] having-offered-up,[h] and having-been-heard[i]

LEXICON—a. δέησις (LN 33.171) (BAGD p. 172): 'prayer' [BAGD, HNTC, LN, Mil, WBC; all versions except CEV], 'plea, request' [LN], 'entreaty' [BAGD, NIC], 'petition' [Lns], not explicit [CEV]. It is the general term for prayer [TNTC], for a request [Wst]. It implies the need underlying the petition [HNTC, Mil].

b. ἱκετηρία (LN **33.172**) (BAGD p. 375): 'supplication' [BAGD, HNTC, LN, Lns, Mil, NIC; KJV, NAB, NASB, NRSV, TNT], 'petition' [NIV, REB], 'entreaty' [NJB], 'earnest entreaty' [WBC], 'plea' [**LN**], 'pleading' [NLT], 'request' [TEV], 'prayer' [BAGD]. This noun is also translated as a verb: 'to beg' [CEV]. It implies a suppliant attitude [HNTC], a desperate need [Hwt, Wst], an urgent entreaty [My, TNTC]. It is stronger than δέησις 'prayer' [Blm, EGT, Lns, Mil, My, NIGTC]; the two words combined add emphasis [Blm, EGT, Lns, Mil, My]. The plurals imply the long duration or repetition of the suffering and the prayers [HNTC, Lg, My]. The two words are essentially synonymous [NIGTC]; they refer to petitions for oneself [TH]. These two words indicate dependence on God [EBC].

c. ἐκ with genitive object (LN 84.4) (BAGD 1.c. p. 234): 'from' [BAGD, HNTC, LN, Lns, NIC, WBC; all versions except NLT], 'out from' [LN], 'out of' [LN, Mil; NLT].

d. μετά with genitive object (LN 89.79, 89.123) (BAGD A.III.1. p. 509): 'with' [HNTC, LN (89.79, 89.123), Mil, NIC, WBC; all versions], 'together with' [Lns], 'combined with' [LN (89.123)], 'in' [BAGD, LN (89.79)]. It introduces an attendant circumstance [Mil].

e. ἰσχυρός (LN 78.16) (BAGD 2. p. 383): 'strong' [Lns; KJV], 'intense' [LN], 'fervent' [WBC], 'great' [LN], 'loud' [BAGD, HNTC, Mil, NIC; all versions except KJV]. It means 'vehement' [Blm], 'loud' [TH].

f. κραυγή (LN 25.138) (BAGD 1.b. p. 449): 'crying' [BAGD, LN, Lns; CEV, KJV, NASB], 'cry' [HNTC, Mil, NIC, WBC; all versions except

CEV, KJV, NASB]. This refers to shouting out, not weeping [TH]. It was a cry of anguish [ICC]. It is a loud noise associated with intense prayer and may be an inarticulate cry [NIGTC].

g. δάκρυον (LN 8.73) (BAGD p. 170): 'tear' [BAGD, HNTC, LN, Lns, Mil, NIC, WBC; all versions]. This plural noun is translated 'weeping' [BAGD].

h. aorist act. participle of προσφέρω (LN 15.192, 57.80) (BAGD 2.b. p. 720): 'to offer up' [Mil, NIC; KJV, NASB, NIV, NJB, NRSV, REB], 'to offer' [BAGD, HNTC, WBC; NAB, NLT, TNT], 'to present' [BAGD, LN (57.80)], 'to bring' [BAGD, LN (15.192, 57.80), Lns], 'to make to' [TEV], not explicit [CEV]. Some think that it includes the concept of sacrifice [Blm, EGT, HNTC, NIGTC, NTC, WBC, Wst]; others think that it does not include the idea of sacrifice [NIC, TH]. It is dependent on ἔμαθεν 'he learned' in 5:8 [Mil, NIGTC].

i. aorist pass. participle of εἰσακούω (LN 24.60) (BAGD 2.a. p. 232): 'to be heard' [BAGD, HNTC, Lns, Mil, NIC, WBC; all versions except NJB, TEV], 'to be heeded' [LN], 'to be listened to' [LN], 'to win a hearing' [NJB]. The passive voice is also translated as an active voice with God as the subject: 'to listen' [CEV], 'to hear' [NLT, TEV]. It implies that God answered him [TH].

QUESTION—What did Christ pray for and how did God answer his prayer?

1. Christ prayed that he might not have to die on the cross, with the additional prayer that God's will be done [Alf, EGT, GNC, HNTC, Hu, ICC, Lg(K), Lns, NIC, NIGTC, NTC, TNTC, Wst]. This is implied by the description of God as the one who is able to save from death [Hu, NIGTC, NTC]. God answered by proceeding to accomplish his will that Jesus must die for mankind [NIGTC, NTC, TNTC], by resurrecting Jesus [Hu, NTC], by giving him courage to face death [ICC], by teaching Jesus that every detail of his life and suffering contributed to the work he came to fulfill [Wst]. He was freed from his fear of death although his request for deliverance from death was not answered [HNTC].
2. He prayed that he might not die in Gethsemane so that he could accomplish salvation by dying on the cross. God answered by keeping him from dying there in the garden [Hwt].
3. He prayed that he might be glorified (John 12:27; 17:5). God answered by exalting him to his right hand after his resurrection [WBC].

QUESTION—What is meant by saving him ἐκ θανάτου 'from death'?

1. It means to enable him to avoid dying [Alf, EGT, GNC, HNTC, Hu, ICC, Lg(K), Lns, NIC, NTC, TH], but only if it was God's will [Lns].
2. It means to restore him to life following his death [My, NIGTC, Wst].

QUESTION—What relationship is indicated by the participial form προσενέγκας 'having offered up'?

1. It is translated as a finite verb [all versions except KJV], but none of the commentaries mention this [Ed]: he offered up . . . and was heard . . .
2. It indicates manner [Lg]: by offering up.

3. It indicates concession [Mil]: although he offered up.
4. It is temporal [Wst; KJV]: after he had offered up.

because-of/from[a] (his) piety/fear,[b]

LEXICON—a. ἀπό with genitive object (LN 89.25) (BAGD V.1. p. 87): 'because of' [BAGD, LN, Mil, NIC, WBC; NAB, NASB, NIV, NLT, NRSV, REB, TNT], 'by' [NJB], 'for' [Lns], not explicit [CEV]. The phrase ἀπὸ τῆς εὐλαβείας 'because of/from his piety/fear' is translated 'in that he feared' [KJV], 'was set free from fear' [HNTC].

b. εὐλάβεια (LN **53.7**) (BAGD p. 321): 'piety' [NASB], 'reverence' [LN; NAB, NJB], 'godly reverence' [Mil], 'reverence for God' [NLT], 'reverent submission' [NIV, NRSV], 'devotion' [REB], 'humble devotion' [NIC], 'awe' [BAGD], 'godly fear' [Lns, WBC; TNT], 'fear of God' [BAGD]. This noun is also translated as a verb phrase: 'to worship God truly' [CEV]. It refers to the cautious reverence of a pious person in approaching God [Alf, Wst], conscientiousness in relationships with God [Lg], reverent submission to God's will [EGT, ICC, Mil, NIGTC, WBC]. It refers to his reverent submission to his Father's will [Alf, EBC, GNC, Hu, NIGTC, NTC], his reverent fear of God [ICC, Lns]; it refers to his fear of his imminent death [Blm, HNTC].

QUESTION—What relationship is indicated by ἀπό in the phrase ἀπὸ τῆς εὐλαβείας 'because of/from his piety/fear' ?

1. It indicates the reason he was heard [Hu, Hwt, ICC, Lg, Mil, My, NIC, NIGTC, NTC, TH, WBC; CEV, NAB, NASB, NIV, NLT, NRSV, TEV, TNT]: he was heard by God because of his piety.
2. It indicates what God delivered him from in answer to his prayer [Blm, HNTC]: he was heard (and delivered) from his fear (of death).

5:8 although[a] being Son, he-learned the obedience from[b] (the things) which he-suffered,[c]

LEXICON—a. καίπερ (LN **89.71**) (BAGD p. 394): 'although' [BAGD, HNTC, LN, Mil, WBC; NASB, NIV, NRSV], 'even though' [**LN**; NLT, TEV], 'though' [LN, Lns, NIC; KJV, NAB, NJB, REB, TNT]. Concession is indicated by translating this clause as a statement followed by the conjunction 'but still' [CEV]. It modifies the participle ὤν 'being' [Alf, My, NIGTC, TH, WBC] and emphasizes its concessive use [EGT, NIGTC].

b. ἀπό with genitive object (LN 89.25, 90.15): 'from' [HNTC, LN, Lns, WBC; NAB, NASB, NIV, NLT, TNT], 'by' [LN, NIC; KJV], 'through' [NJB, NRSV, REB, TEV], 'as a result of' [Mil], 'because of' [LN (89.25)], not explicit [CEV].

c. aorist act. indic. of πάσχω (LN 24.78, 90.66) (BAGD 3.b. p. 634): 'to suffer' [HNTC, LN (24.78, 90.66), Lns, Mil, NIC, WBC; CEV, KJV, NAB, NASB, NIV, NLT, NRSV, TNT], 'to experience' [LN (90.66)], 'to endure' [BAGD].

QUESTION—Why is this verse mentioned?

It expands the significance of the preceding verse [NCBC]. The emphasis is on ἔμαθεν 'he learned' [NTC].

QUESTION—What is implied by the present tense of the participle ὤν 'being'?

1. It may refer to the state at the time of the leading verb ἔμαθεν 'he learned', but none of the commentaries mention this: although he was Son at the time when he learned obedience.
2. It refers to his eternal status [NIGTC]: although he was eternally Son.

QUESTION—What relationship is indicated by υἱός 'son' without the definite article?

It emphasizes the quality of sonship [EBC, Hwt]: Son is what he was. Without the article it is nevertheless definite, similar to the usage with a proper name [Blm]. The article is absent because 'Son' is a predicate [Lns]. It means that he was the Son [Blm, Lns, NIC, WBC]: although he was the Son. It is natural that a son learns obedience by suffering, but Jesus was not an ordinary son—he was the Son of God—and still was not granted exemption from suffering [NIC, WBC].

QUESTION—What is meant by the phrase ἔμαθεν τὴν ὑπακοήν 'he learned obedience'?

Although he was already and always obedient [Hu, Hwt, ICC, Mil, My, NCBC, NIC, NTC, Wst], he learned by experience how difficult it is to obey God's will in the midst of trials [Blm]; he learned obedience by obeying [EBC, ICC, My]; he learned the deeper level of perfect obedient submission through suffering [EGT, GNC, HNTC, Hwt, Lns, Mil, NCBC, NIC, NTC, TNTC, Wst], by accepting his death on Calvary [Hu, WBC] in his agony in Gethsemane [Hu]. It does not imply that previously he was disobedient or rebellious [Hwt].

1. The definite article implies the particular obedience that was required [EGT, Lns, NTC, WBC]; that is, his death on the cross [WBC].
2. The definite article indicates obedience as a specific virtue [My].

QUESTION—What is the implied antecedent of ὧν 'which'?

It is the understood object of the preposition ἀπό 'from' [Mil, My, NIGTC; KJV, NASB]: from the things which he suffered. The pronoun ὧν 'which' is the object of the verb ἔπαθεν 'he suffered'; it is attracted from its normal accusative case to the genitive case of its unexpressed antecedent [Mil, My, NIGTC].

QUESTION—To what does ὧν ἔπαθεν 'the things which he suffered' refer to?

1. It refers to his sufferings during his entire earthly life [Alf, NIC, NIGTC], Gethsemane being the most significant example [Alf, NIGTC].
2. It refers to his death [WBC].

5:9 and having-been-perfected[a] he-became to-all the-(ones)-obeying him (the) cause[b] of-eternal salvation,

LEXICON—a. aorist pass. participle of τελειόω (LN 88.38) (BAGD 2.a. p. 809; 3. p. 810): 'to be perfected' [LN; NAB, NJB, REB], 'to become perfected'

[Mil], 'to be made perfect' [HNTC, LN, NIC, WBC; CEV, KJV, NASB, NIV, NRSV, TEV, TNT], 'to be made complete' [Lns], 'to be brought to one's goal, to be brought to accomplishment, to be consecrated' [BAGD]. This passive is also translated as active with God as the subject: 'to qualify one to be a perfect High Priest' [NLT].

b. αἴτιος (LN **89.15**) (BAGD 1. p. 26): 'cause' [BAGD, HNTC, LN, Lns; TNT], 'source' [BAGD, **LN,** Mil, NIC, WBC; all versions except CEV, KJV, TNT], 'reason' [LN], 'author' [KJV]. This noun is also translated as a verb: 'he can save' [CEV]. It means the originator [EGT]; it is the same as ἀρχηγός 'author' in 2:10 [NTC].

QUESTION—What relationship is indicated by the participial form τελειωθείς 'having been perfected'?

The aorist tense refers to Christ's death [NIGTC, NTC] and exaltation as a single event prior to ἐγένετο 'he became' [NIGTC].

1. It is temporal [GNC, WBC; NAB, NJB, TEV, TNT]: when he was perfected.
2. It indicates the means of his becoming the source of salvation [Mil, NTC, TNTC]: by means of becoming perfected.

QUESTION—What is meant by τελειωθείς 'having been perfected'?

1. It refers to his being brought to the goal of learning and suffering, through death [GNC, HNTC, Hu, Lg].
2. It means being perfected as the cause of salvation, through his death [Lns, NCBC] which was the result of his obedience [NCBC].
3. It refers to the perfection of having suffered [EBC, NTC, TH, TNTC, WBC] in obedience [TNTC], in completion of his task [NTC, WBC].
4. It refers to his having completed the qualifications for his high priesthood through his human life and sufferings [EGT, Mil, TH, WBC] and the completion of his moral discipline in his death [EGT].
5. It refers to his having completed, by his obedience, death, and glorification, the qualifications for becoming high priest [Hwt, NIC] and Savior [NIC].
6. It refers to his resurrection and glorification, when his triumph began [Alf].
7. It refers to his consecration in glory [Blm, My].
8. It refers to the moral development which made it possible for him to offer a perfect self-sacrifice [ICC].

QUESTION—How is the clause beginning with ἐγένετο 'he became' related to other clauses?

1. It expresses the result of his sufferings that brought about his being perfected [EBC, WBC]: he suffered and was perfected; as a result he became the source of salvation.
2. It expresses the result of ἔμαθεν 'he learned' in 5:8 [Mil]: he learned . . . and as a result he became . . .
3. It expresses the result of his having been perfected [NIC]: as a result of having been perfected he became . . .

QUESTION—To what does ἐγένετο 'he became' refer?

The aorist tense indicates that the action is completed [Wst].

1. It refers to his resurrection and glorification [My]: by his resurrection and glorification, he became the cause of salvation.
2. It refers to the time when he became high priest [TNTC].

QUESTION—What does the present tense of the participle τοῖς ὑπακούουσιν 'the ones obeying' indicate?

1. It indicates continuous obedience [Hu, Lns, Wst]: the ones who continually obey him.
2. It refers to the successive obedience by each person [Mil]: the continuing succession of persons who obey him.

QUESTION—To whom does αὐτῷ 'him' refer?

It refers to Jesus [Alf, Lns, Mil]: to those who obey Jesus.

QUESTION—How are the two nouns related in the genitive construction αἴτιος σωτηρίας 'cause of salvation'?

The genitive σωτηρίας 'salvation' tells what was caused [Mil]: he caused salvation.

5:10 having-been-designated[a] by[b] God high-priest according-to[c] the order[d] of-Melchizedek.

LEXICON—a. aorist pass. participle of προσαγορεύω (LN **33.127**) (BAGD 2. p. 711): 'to be designated' [BAGD, Lns, Mil, WBC; NAB, NASB, NIV, NRSV, REB], 'to be called' [BAGD, LN; KJV], 'to be named' [BAGD; HNTC], 'to be acclaimed' [NIC; NJB]. The passive voice is also translated as active with God as subject: 'to designate' [NLT], 'to declare' [TEV], 'to name' [TNT], 'to choose' [CEV].

b. ὑπό with genitive object (LN 90.1): 'by' [HNTC, LN, Lns, Mil, NIC, WBC; NAB, NASB, NIV, NJB, NRSV, REB], 'of' [KJV].

c. κατά with accusative object: 'according to'. See this word at 5:6.

d. τάξις: 'order'. See this word at 5:6.

QUESTION—What relationship is indicated by the participial form προσαγορευθείς 'having been designated' ?

1. It indicates the reason Christ can provide salvation [ICC, Mil, My; CEV]: he became the cause of eternal salvation because he has been designated high priest.
2. It is translated as a finite verb [NIV, NJB, NLT, REB, TEV, TNT]: he became . . . and was designated high priest.

QUESTION—What is meant by προσαγορευθείς 'having been designated'?

It means being called [TH], named [Alf, My, NIGTC, TNTC], appointed [LN], proclaimed and constituted [Blm]. It implies his appointment and inauguration [Alf]. It refers to having a title conferred [EBC, TNTC] by addressing the conferee with the title [Mil, Wst]. It refers to formally ascribing a title of honor [EGT, WBC, Wst]. This occurred at his exaltation [Alf, Hwt, Mil]. It occurred both from eternity and following his death and exaltation [Hu]. It occurred prophetically in the quoted Psalm [Lns, My] and was fulfilled on Calvary [Lns].

DISCOURSE UNIT: 5:11–10:39 [NIGTC, TH, WBC; NAB]. The topic is Christ's high priesthood [NIGTC, WBC], Christ's priesthood and sacrifice [NAB].

DISCOURSE UNIT: 5:11–10:18 [NJB]. The topic is Christ's authentic priesthood.

DISCOURSE UNIT: 5:11–9:22 [REB]. The topic is Jesus and Melchizedek.

DISCOURSE UNIT: 5:11–8:13 [Lg]. The topic is Christ's exaltation as priest-king, an antitype of Melchizedek.

DISCOURSE UNIT: 5:11–6:20 [Hwt, Lg, Mil, NIGTC, NTC, TNTC, Wst; NAB]. The topic is a challenging interlude [TNTC], an exhortation to remember what God has promised [NIGTC], an exhortation to spiritual renewal [NAB], spiritual progress [Hwt], progress in patient effort [Wst], an exhortation to spiritual maturity and a warning against falling away [Mil], warning, consolation, and exhortation [Lg], exhortations [NTC].

DISCOURSE UNIT: 5:11–6:12 [GNT, NCBC, NTC, WBC; CEV, NIV, NLT, TEV]. The topic is an additional admonition [NCBC], a warning against spiritual immaturity [WBC], a warning against turning away from the faith [GNT, NTC; CEV, NIV, TEV], a call to spiritual growth [NLT].

DISCOURSE UNIT: 5:11–6:3 [GNC, HNTC]. The topic is the importance of Christian maturity [GNC], food for adults [HNTC].

DISCOURSE UNIT: 5:11–14 [Hwt, Lg, Lns, NIC, NTC; NJB, TEV]. The topic is an admonition concerning spiritual immaturity [NIC], a concern for slow learners [NTC], spiritual infancy [Hwt], the readers' spiritual deficiency [Lg], a rebuke for the readers [Lns], a warning not to abandon the faith [TEV], Christian life and theology [NJB].

5:11 Concerning[a] whom/which much (is) the word[b] to-us and difficult-to explain[c] to-say,

LEXICON—a. περί with genitive object (LN 89.6, 90.24): 'concerning' [LN (89.6, 90.24), Mil, NIC; NASB], 'about' [HNTC, LN (90.24), WBC; CEV, NAB, NIV, NLT, NRSV, REB, TEV, TNT], 'regarding' [Lns], 'in relation to' [LN (89.6)], 'with regard to' [LN (89.6)], 'of' [KJV], 'on' [NJB].

b. λόγος (LN 33.98) (BAGD 1.a.ζ p. 478): 'word, statement' [LN]. The phrase πολὺς ἡμῖν ὁ λόγος 'much is the word to us' is translated 'we have much to say' [BAGD, HNTC, WBC; NAB, NASB, NIV, NRSV, REB, TNT], 'there is much we have to say' [NIC; TEV], 'there is much for us to say' [Lns], 'there is much for us to discuss' [Mil], 'we have many things to say' [KJV, NJB], 'there is so much more we would like to say' [NLT], 'much more could be said' [CEV]. It refers to the author's discussion [Alf, Mil].

c. δυσερμήνευτος (LN **33.149**) (BAGD p. 209): 'difficult to explain, hard to interpret' [LN], 'hard to explain' [BAGD; NLT]. The phrase δυσερμήνευτος λέγειν 'difficult to explain to say' is translated 'difficult to explain' [HNTC, **LN**; NAB, NJB, REB], 'hard to explain' [BAGD, Mil; CEV, NASB, NIV, NRSV, TEV, TNT], 'difficult to expound' [Lns], 'hard to explain intelligibly' [WBC], 'hard to be uttered' [KJV], 'hard to interpret' [NIC].

QUESTION—To whom or what does οὗ 'whom/which' refer?

1. It refers to a person [Alf, EGT, HNTC, Lns, Mil, My, NCBC, NIC, NIGTC, Wst; KJV, NASB, REB].

1.1 It refers to Melchizedek [Alf, EGT, HNTC, Lns, Mil, NCBC, NIC; NASB, REB].

1.2 It refers to Christ [My, NIGTC].

2. It refers to a topic [Blm, Hu, ICC, Lg, NTC, TH, WBC; NAB, NIV, NJB, NRSV, TEV, TNT], to Christ's priesthood [Blm, Hu, ICC, Lg, TH, WBC].

QUESTION—What is λόγος 'word' connected with?

It is connected with both πολύς 'much' and δυσερμήνευτος 'difficult to explain' [Alf, Lg, Lns, Mil, My]: our topic is much and difficult to explain.

QUESTION—To whom does the plural pronoun ἡμῖν 'us' refer?

1. It refers only to the author [Alf, ICC, NIGTC, TH]: I have much to say.

2. It includes the author and his readers together [Lns].

QUESTION—To what does δυσερμήνευτος 'difficult to explain' refer?

1. It refers to the author [Alf, EGT, HNTC, Hu, ICC, Lg, My, NIGTC, Wst; all versions]: difficult for me to explain.

2. It refers to the readers [NIC]: it is difficult for you to understand.

3. It means that the material is difficult in itself [WBC].

QUESTION—What is the infinitive λέγειν 'to say' connected with?

It is connected with δυσερμήνευτος 'difficult to explain' [ICC, Lns, My, WBC]: it is difficult to explain in saying. This is made clear by the addition of λέγειν 'to say' [Wst].

since[a] you-have-become dull[b] in-the hearing.[c]

LEXICON—a. ἐπεί (LN 89.32) (BAGD 2. p. 284): 'since' [BAGD, HNTC, LN, Lns, NIC, WBC; NASB, NRSV], 'for' [BAGD, LN; NAB], 'because' [BAGD, LN, Mil; NIV, NJB, TEV, TNT], 'so' [NLT], 'seeing' [KJV], 'now that' [REB], not explicit [CEV].

b. νωθρός (LN **32.47**, 88.249) (BAGD p. 547): 'dull' [HNTC; KJV, NASB, NRSV, TNT], 'sluggish' [BAGD, Lns, NIC, WBC], 'lazy' [BAGD, LN]. The phrase νωθροὶ ταῖς ἀκοαῖς 'dull in the hearing' is translated 'deaf' [NAB], 'slow to understand' [**LN**, Mil; CEV, TEV], 'slow at understanding' [NJB], 'slow to learn' [NIV, REB], 'you don't seem to listen' [NLT].

c. ἀκοή (LN 24.52, 24.53) (BAGD 1.c. p. 31): 'hearing' [HNTC, LN (24.52, 24.53), Lns, NIC; KJV, NASB], 'ability to hear' [LN (24.53)], 'understanding' [WBC; NRSV, TNT], 'ear' [BAGD]. This word means the ear in reference to hearing [Lns]; the plural implies each person's two ears [Alf] and also the plurality of the readers [Alf, My]; it refers to hearing [NIGTC], to the sense of hearing [Mil, My]; it refers to intelligent hearing [EGT].

QUESTION—What relationship is indicated by ἐπεί 'since'?

It indicates the reason why the matter is difficult to explain to the readers [Alf, ICC, Mil, My, WBC, Wst]: it is difficult to explain because you have become dull in hearing.

QUESTION—What is implied by the perfect tense of the verb γεγόνατε 'you have become'?

It implies that they were previously in a better spiritual condition but are now in a state of dullness [Hu, Lg, Lns, Mil, My, NIGTC, TH, Wst]: you have become dull in your hearing.

DISCOURSE UNIT: 5:12–6:20 [EBC]. The topic is the danger of apostasy.

DISCOURSE UNIT: 5:12–14 [EBC]. The topic is failure to make spiritual progress.

5:12 For even being-duty-bound[a] to-be teachers on-account-of[b] the time,

LEXICON—a. pres. act. participle of ὀφείλω (LN 71.25) (BAGD 2.a.β. p. 599): 'to be duty-bound', 'ought' [BAGD, HNTC, LN, Lns, Mil, NIC, WBC; KJV, NASB, NIV, NLT, NRSV, REB, TNT], 'should' [CEV, NAB, NJB]. This entire phrase is translated 'there has been enough time for you to be teachers' [TEV]. It refers to their duty [EGT, TH], their obligation [TNTC].

b. διά with accusative object (LN 89.26) (BAGD B.II.1. p. 181): 'on account of' [LN], 'because of' [LN, NIC], 'by reason of' [LN], 'due to' [Lns], 'according to' [BAGD], 'for' [KJV]. The phrase διὰ τὸν χρόνον 'on account of the time' is translated 'by this time' [BAGD, HNTC, Mil, WBC; all versions except CEV, KJV, NLT, TEV], 'by now' [CEV], 'you have been Christians a long time now' [NLT]. The reference is to the length of time they have been believers [Alf, Blm, EBC, EGT, GNC, Hu, Lns, Mil, My, NCBC, NIC, NIGTC, NTC, Wst].

QUESTION—What relationship is indicated by γάρ 'for'?

1. It indicates the grounds for the preceding criticism [Mil, My, NIGTC, TH, TNTC]: you have become dull in hearing; that is true since you again need to be taught.
2. It (with καί 'even' [NTC]) adds to the preceding criticism [Lns, NIC, NTC]: you have become dull in hearing; indeed, you again need to be taught.

QUESTION—What relationship is indicated by the participial form ὀφείλοντες 'being duty-bound'?

It refers to the subject of the following verb ἔχετε 'you have' [WBC]: you ought.

1. It is temporal [Lg(K), My, NIC; KJV, TNT]: when you ought. The preceding καί 'even' intensifies the meaning [My].
2. It indicates a concession [Alf, Blm, EGT, GNC, HNTC, Mil, NIGTC, WBC; NAB, NASB, NIV, REB, TEV]: although you ought to be teachers, yet you need someone to teach you.
3. It indicates a contrast [CEV, NLT, TNT]: you ought to be teachers, but you need someone to teach you.

QUESTION—What is meant by διδάσκαλοι 'teachers'?

1. It means merely that the Christians in general should have mature spiritual understanding and should be able to instruct newer believers [EBC, EGT, HNTC, Hu, ICC, NIC, NIGTC, NTC, TH, WBC]. It does not imply teaching as an occupation [NCBC, NIC].
2. It refers to a small group who were equipped to be teachers but lacked the spiritual perception for teaching the Christian faith [TNTC].

again you-have need of-the someone to-teach you the rudiments[a] of-the beginning[b] of-the oracles[c] of-the God,

TEXT—Instead of τινά 'someone', some manuscripts read τίνα 'which', and some read τινα without an accent, which can be interpreted with either meaning. GNT reads τινά 'someone' with a C decision, which indicates that the committee had difficulty in deciding between the two readings. Τίνα 'which' is read by only Blm, Lg, and KJV.

LEXICON—a. στοιχεῖον (LN **58.19**) (BAGD 1. p. 769): 'element' [BAGD, Lns; NJB], 'elementary concept' [LN], 'basic principle' [**LN**], 'fundamental principle' [BAGD]. The phrase τὰ στοιχεῖα τῆς ἀρχῆς 'the rudiments of the beginning' is translated 'the first principles' [KJV], 'the very first principles' [TNT], 'the elementary principles' [NASB], 'the elementary truths' [WBC; NIV], 'the basic elements' [NAB, NRSV], 'the first lessons' [TEV], 'the ABC' [HNTC; REB], 'the preliminary ABC' [NIC], 'the very ABC's' [Mil]. The phrase τὰ στοιχεῖα τῆς ἀρχῆς τῶν λογίων τοῦ θεοῦ 'the rudiments of the beginning of the oracles of God' is translated 'the simple truths about God's message' [**LN**], 'the simplest things about what God as said' [CEV], 'the very elements of the truths of God' [BAGD], 'the basic things a beginner must learn about the Scriptures' [NLT]. These are the basic truths [Alf, Mil, NIC, NIGTC, NTC], such as repentance and faith [Blm, Mil], upon which more mature truths must be based [Alf]. It refers to the first letters of the alphabet [HNTC].

b. ἀρχή (LN **58.19**, 58.20) (BAGD 1.b. p. 111): 'beginning' [BAGD, Lns], 'elementary aspect' [**LN** (58.19)], 'simple truth' [LN], 'principle' [NJB].

The phrase στοιχεῖα τῆς ἀρχῆς 'rudiments of the beginning' is translated 'elementary principles' [BAGD]. It means the initial stages [EGT].

c. λόγιον (LN **33.97**) (BAGD p. 476): 'oracle' [HNTC, LN, Mil, NIC; KJV, NAB, NASB, NRSV, REB], 'saying' [BAGD, LN, Lns; NJB]. This plural noun is translated as a singular: 'message' [**LN**; TEV], 'revelation' [WBC; TNT], 'word' [NIV]. It indicates teachings based on divine revelations [Alf, EBC, ICC, TH], all of God's word [HNTC], God's message of salvation spoken through the Son [EGT], the message of Christianity [Blm, Hu, Lg, My, NIGTC, TNTC] spoken as God's word [My]. It refers to Judaism as the readers' spiritual infancy [Hwt], to what God has said in the OT [Lns, Wst]; to scripture, which at this time would be primarily the OT but possibly including the words of Jesus [NCBC].

QUESTION—What is implied by πάλιν 'again'?

If they do not even know these basic truths, someone has to teach them again [NTC]. It implies regression to a lower spiritual condition [NIGTC, TNTC].

QUESTION—How is the genitive infinitive related to the noun in the phrase χρείαν τοῦ διδάσκειν ὑμᾶς 'need to teach you'?

The infinitive tells what the need is [Alf, EGT, Lns, Mil, My, WBC; KJV, NASB]: a need to teach you. This phrase marks the contrast with what they should be, namely, teachers [EBC].

QUESTION—What is the function of τινά 'someone' or τίνα 'which'?

1. Reading τινά as masculine accusative singular 'someone', it is the subject of τοῦ διδάσκειν 'to teach' [Alf, GNC, HNTC, ICC, Lns, Mil, My, NIC, NIGTC, TH, WBC, Wst; all versions except CEV, KJV]: someone to teach you. 'Someone' implies reproach, indicating that anyone could teach them [Alf, My]. The readers needed to know the content of the teachings, not to know what the teachings were [Wst].
2. Reading τίνα as neuter nominative plural 'which', it is the subject of the clause it introduces [Blm, Lg(K); KJV]: teach you what the rudiments are.

QUESTION—How are the genitive nouns related in the phrase τὰ στοιχεῖα τῆς ἀρχῆς τῶν λογίων τοῦ θεοῦ 'the rudiments of the beginning of the oracles of God'?

1. Regarding τῆς ἀρχῆς 'of the beginning'.

1.1 Τῆς ἀρχῆς 'the beginning' modifies τὰ στοιχεῖα 'the rudiments' adjectivally [NIC]: the beginning rudiments.

1.2 Τῆς ἀρχῆς 'the beginning' shows that τὰ στοιχεῖα 'the rudiments' are the very beginning of the divine knowledge [Alf]: the rudiments that are the beginning.

1.3 Τῆς ἀρχῆς 'the beginning' is strengthened by τὰ στοιχεῖα 'the rudiments' [EGT, Hu, My]

1.3.1 It means the very rudiments of the beginning [EGT, HNTC, Hu, TH].

1.3.2 It means the very first primary rudiments [My, WBC].

1.3.3 'Αρχή 'beginning' is a redundant repetition of στοιχεῖα 'rudiments' [NCBC, NIGTC].

1.4 Τῆς ἀρχῆς 'the beginning' refers to the beginning of the time during which the oracles were taught [EGT]: the time when the oracles began to be taught.

2. Regarding τῶν λογίων 'of the oracles'.

2.1 The genitive τῶν λογίων 'of the oracles' is the whole of which τῆς ἀρχῆς 'the beginning' is a part [Alf]: the elementary parts of the oracles.

2.2 Ἀρχῆς 'beginning' is used adjectivally with λογίων 'oracles' [NTC]: elementary oracles.

2.3 Τὰ στοιχεῖα 'the rudiments' is a part of τῶν λογίων 'of the oracles' (this is not stated but is implied by the interpretations of 1:1–1:3 above [Ed]) [Alf, EGT, HNTC, Hu, My, NIC, NIGTC, WBC]: the rudimentary part of the oracles.

3. Regarding τοῦ θεοῦ 'of God'. The genitive τοῦ θεοῦ 'of God' indicates the source of τῶν λογίων 'the oracles' [Alf]: the oracles that come from God.

and you-have-become having need of-milk and not of-solid[a] food.

LEXICON—a. στερεός (LN 79.7) (BAGD 1. p. 766): 'solid' [BAGD, HNTC, LN, Lns, Mil, NIC, WBC; all versions except KJV], 'strong' [BAGD; KJV].

QUESTION—What is implied by γεγόνατε 'you have become'?

It implies that their condition had deteriorated from their previous state [EBC, My, NIGTC, Wst]. It implies that they were now in the stage indicated [WBC].

QUESTION—What relationship is indicated by the participial form ἔχοντες 'having'?

1. It is a predicate to γεγόνατε 'you have become' [Lns]: you have come to have need, etc.

2. It describes the readers [Blm, WBC; KJV]: you have become people who have need, etc.

QUESTION—What is meant by γάλακτος 'milk'?

It refers to the elementary instruction in the faith [Blm, My, NIC, NIGTC], including the matters mentioned in 6:1–2 [NIGTC, Wst]; it is essential as a first stage [TNTC, Wst].

QUESTION—What is meant by στερεᾶς τροφῆς 'solid food'?

'Solid food' refers to the more profound truths of Christianity [Blm, My, NIC], especially the high priesthood of Christ [My, NIGTC].

5:13 For[a] every the-(one) partaking[b] of-milk (is) inexperienced-in[c] (the) word[d] of-righteousness,[e]

LEXICON—a. γάρ (LN 89.23): 'for' [HNTC, LN, Lns, Mil; KJV, NASB, NRSV, TNT], 'because' [LN], 'and' [NLT], not explicit [NIC, WBC; CEV, NAB, NIV, REB, TEV]. This entire clause is translated 'truly, no one who is still living on milk can digest the doctrine of saving justice' [NJB].

b. pres. act. participle of μετέχω (LN **23.2**, 23.2fn3) (BAGD p. 514): 'to partake of' [LN (23.3 fn3), Lns, Mil; NASB], 'to have a share in' [LN (23.3 fn3)], 'to use' [KJV], 'to drink' [**LN**], 'to have to drink' [TEV], 'to live on' [BAGD, HNTC, WBC; CEV, NIV, NJB, NLT, NRSV, REB, TNT]. This active participle is also translated as a passive: 'to be fed on' [NIC]. The phrase ὁ μετέχων 'the one partaking' is translated 'whose food is' [NAB].

c. ἄπειρος (LN **28.15**) (BAGD 1. p. 83): 'inexperienced in' [LN, Lns], 'inexperienced with' [WBC], 'without any experience in' [**LN**; TEV], 'without experience of' [HNTC, Mil], 'with no experience of' [REB], '(has) no experience of' [TNT], 'unskillful in' [KJV], 'unskilled in' [NIC; NRSV], 'unacquainted with' [BAGD, LN], 'not acquainted with' [NIV], 'not accustomed to' [NASB], 'not know much about' [NLT], 'not really know' [CEV], 'ignorant of' [NAB]. It means to have no skill in [Alf, EBC, ICC, Lg(K)], to lack experience in [TH, TNTC, Wst], to have no experience in [EGT, Lg]. It is emphatic by its forefronted word order [My]. It implies insufficient knowledge [My], not ignorance [My, TNTC].

d. λόγος (LN 33.98) (BAGD 1.b.β. p. 478): 'word' [BAGD, LN, NIC; KJV, NAB, NASB, NRSV], 'teaching' [WBC; NIV], 'message' [LN; TNT], 'statement' [LN], 'principle' [Mil], 'discourse' [HNTC], 'doctrine' [NJB], 'discussion' [Lns], 'matter' [TEV], not explicit [CEV, NLT, REB]. This word refers to scripture in its Christian interpretation of ethical matters [NIGTC].

e. δικαιοσύνη (LN 88.13) (BAGD 4. p. 197): 'righteousness' [BAGD, LN, Mil, NIC, WBC; KJV, NASB, NIV, NRSV, TNT], 'saving justice' [NJB], 'that sanctifies' [NAB], 'between right and wrong' [HNTC]. The phrase λόγου δικαιοσύνης 'word of righteousness' is translated 'right discussion' [Lns], 'what is right' [CEV, NLT, REB], 'the matter of right and wrong' [TEV].

QUESTION—What relationship is indicated by γάρ?

It indicates a reason for the comments in 5:11–12 [Alf, Blm, EBC, TNTC], the final part of 5:12 [EGT, Mil, My, NCBC, NIGTC, NTC], and especially the difficulty of explaining to the readers [Alf].

QUESTION—What is meant by 'partaking of milk'?

It means making milk one's food, as babies do [Alf, Blm, EGT, Hu, ICC, Lns, My, TH, WBC, Wst]. The application is that those who can understand only the basic elements of the gospel are babies in understanding [Blm, EGT], in understanding the word of righteousness [EGT].

QUESTION—How is the genitive noun λόγου 'word' related in the genitive construction ἄπειρος λόγου 'inexperienced in the word'?

It expresses the area of the inexperience [WBC, Wst] and means a principle [Mil, NIC]: without experience in the principle of righteousness.

QUESTION— How are the two nouns related in the genitive construction λόγου δικαιοσύνης 'word of righteousness'?

1. It means the teaching which deals with righteousness [Alf, Blm, WBC, Wst; NIV]: teaching righteousness.
2. It means perceiving and teaching righteousness [Mil].
3. 'Righteousness' tells what the 'word' does [NAB]: the word that sanctifies.
4. 'Righteousness' is used adjectivally with λόγου 'word' [Lns, NIGTC]: right discussion.
5. The phrase means 'what is right' [CEV, NLT, REB], 'the matter of right and wrong' [TEV].
6. The phrase ἄπειρος λόγου δικαιοσύνη 'inexperienced in the word of righteousness' refers to moral weakness, fear of martyrdom by violent death [WBC].

QUESTION—What is meant by δικαιοσύνη 'righteousness'?

1. It means salvation through Jesus, i.e. justification [Alf, Blm, Hu, Wst]; it means the gospel [Hwt, My].
2. It means right conduct expected of believers [EBC, EGT].
3. It means moral truth [HNTC, ICC], dealing with right and wrong [HNTC, Mil, NTC, TH; TEV].
4. It refers to both ethical judgment and understanding of the Christian faith [NCBC, NIGTC, TNTC].
5. It means simply 'what is right' [Lns; CEV, NLT, REB].

for[a] he-is (an) infant;[b]

LEXICON—a. γάρ (LN 89.23): 'for' [HNTC, LN, Lns, Mil, WBC; KJV, NAB, NASB], 'because' [LN], not explicit [NIC; CEV, NIV, NJB, NLT, NRSV, REB, TEV, TNT].

b. νήπιος (LN 9.43) (BAGD 1.b. p. 537): 'infant' [BAGD, HNTC, NIC, WBC; NIV, NRSV, REB, TNT], 'baby' [CEV, NJB], 'babe' [Mil; KJV, NASB], 'small child' [LN], 'child' [Lns; NAB, TEV], 'minor' [BAGD], 'a person not far along in the Christian life' [NLT].

QUESTION—What relationship is indicated by γάρ 'for'?

It indicates the reason for the preceding statement [Mil, NIGTC], or a restatement of it [NIGTC].

5:14 but of-mature[a] (people) is the solid[b] food,

LEXICON—a. τέλειος (LN **9.10**, 88.100) (BAGD 2.a.β. p. 809): 'mature' [HNTC, LN (88.100), Lns, Mil, NIC; CEV, NAB, NASB, NIV, NLT, NRSV, TNT], 'adult' [BAGD, **LN** (9.10), WBC; NJB, REB, TEV], 'of full age' [KJV]. The reference is to disciplined and experienced believers [HNTC], morally and religiously mature people [NIGTC], competent and responsible Christians [Hu], persons who have progressed to the ability to understand deeper spiritual truths [Blm, Hwt], those who have made the proper progress from spiritual infancy [TNTC]; it is used relatively [Hu]. It is emphatic by forefronting [My].

b. στερεός: 'solid'. See this word at 5:12.

QUESTION—How is the genitive adjective related to the noun in the genitive construction τελείων στερεὰ τροφή 'of mature people is the solid food'?

1. The genitive adjective τελείων 'of mature people' tells for whom the solid food is intended [Alf, HNTC, Mil, NIC, WBC; all versions except KJV]: solid food is for mature people.
2. The genitive adjective tells who eats the solid food [Mil]: solid food is eaten by mature people.
3. The genitive adjective tells to whom the solid food belongs [Lns; KJV]: solid food belongs to mature people.

the-(ones) having the senses[a] trained[b] by/because-of[c] the practice[d] for-the-purpose-of/so-that/to[e] differentiation[f] both of-good and of-evil.

LEXICON—a. αἰσθητήριον (LN **32.28**) (BAGD p. 25): 'sense' [Lns, NIC; KJV, NASB], 'perception' [HNTC; REB, TNT], 'faculty' [BAGD, Mil, WBC; NAB, NRSV], 'capacity to understand' [LN], 'mind' [NJB], not explicit [NIV, NLT, TEV]. This word refers to the soul's inner organs of sense [Alf, EGT, Lg(K), My, NIGTC, Wst], the internal senses [Blm], spiritual sensitivity [Hu], the intellectual faculties [Mil, TNTC].

b. perf. pass. participle of γυμνάζω (LN 36.11) (BAGD p. 167): 'to be trained' [BAGD, HNTC, LN, Lns, Mil, NIC, WBC; CEV, NAB, NASB, NJB, NRSV, REB, TNT], 'to be exercised' [KJV], 'to be able' [TEV]. It is middle voice, indicating acting on oneself: 'to train oneself' [NTC; NIV, NLT]. It refers to exercise which results in a specific ἕξις 'state' [NIGTC].

c. διά with accusative object (LN 89.26, 89.76): 'by' [WBC; NAB, NIV, NJB, NRSV, TNT], 'because of' [LN (89.26), Mil; NASB], 'on account of' [LN (89.26)], 'by reason of' [LN (89.26), Lns; KJV], 'in virtue of' [HNTC], 'through' [LN (89.76), NIC; TEV], not explicit [CEV, NLT].

d. ἕξις (**LN 42.10**) (BAGD p. 276): 'practice' [BAGD, LN, Mil, NIC; NAB, NASB, NJB, NRSV, TEV, TNT], 'use' [KJV], 'constant use' [WBC; NIV], 'long use' [REB], 'condition' [HNTC, Lns], not explicit [CEV, NLT]. It refers to habit [Alf, Blm], to the normal condition or disposition [EGT, HNTC, Lns] resulting from previous practice [HNTC, Wst], to a characteristic state [NIGTC], to experience acquired through practice [Mil, My, NIC], to facility [ICC] or practice [ICC, WBC], to constant practice [NTC].

e. πρός with accusative object (LN 89.60, 89.44, 90.25) (BAGD III.3.c p. 710): 'for the purpose of' [LN (89.60)], 'for' [BAGD, Lns], 'result in' [LN (89.44)], 'to' [HNTC, LN (90.25), Mil, NIC, WBC; all versions].

f. διάκρισις (LN 30.112) (BAGD 1. p. 185): 'differentiation' [BAGD], 'discrimination' [Lns], 'distinguishing' [BAGD], 'ability to judge' [LN], 'ability to decide' [LN], 'ability to make judgments' [LN]. The phrase πρὸς διάκρισιν 'toward differentiation' is translated 'to distinguish' [HNTC, Mil, NIC, WBC; NAB, NIV, NJB, NRSV, TEV, TNT], 'to discern' [KJV, NASB], 'to discriminate' [REB], 'to know' [CEV], 'to recognize' [NLT]. It refers to a process of distinguishing [NTC].

QUESTION—Why is this phrase mentioned?

It further identifies the τελείων 'mature people' [Alf, Blm, EGT, Hu, Lns, Mil, My, TNTC] in contrast with the persons described in the preceding verse [NIGTC].

QUESTION—What relationship is indicated by διά 'by/because of'?

1. It indicates the means by which they became mature [Blm, NIC, TNTC; NAB, NIV, NJB, NRSV, REB, TEV]: they have their senses trained by practicing.
2. It indicates the reason for their maturity [Alf, EGT, Lg(K), Mil; KJV, NASB]: they have their senses trained because of practice.

QUESTION—What relationship is indicated by πρός 'for the purpose of, so that, to'?

1. It indicates the purpose for the training [Alf, Lns, Mil, My]: they have their senses trained in order to differentiate between good and evil.
2. It indicates the result of the training [EGT, HNTC, Hwt, NIGTC]: they have their senses trained so that they differentiate between good and evil.
3. It indicates the content of the training [NCBC, NIC, TH, WBC; all versions]: they have their senses trained to differentiate between good and evil.

QUESTION—How are the two genitive adjectives related to the noun in the genitive construction διάκρισιν καλοῦ τε καὶ κακοῦ 'differentiation of both good and evil'?

The genitive adjectives καλοῦ 'good' and κακοῦ 'evil' tell what is differentiated [HNTC, Mil, NIC, WBC; all versions]. The meaning is to discern both good and evil [Hwt, Lns, Mil; KJV, NASB], to distinguish good from evil [EBC, EGT, HNTC, Hwt, Lns, NIC, TH, TNTC, WBC; all versions except KJV, NASB]. The reference is to good and bad doctrines [Alf, EGT, Hu], truth and error [Blm], moral discrimination [ICC], right and wrong, not moral values [My].

DISCOURSE UNIT: 6:1–8 [NIC; NASB, NJB]. The topic is the peril of falling away [NASB], the impossibility of a second beginning [NIC], an explanation of the author's intention [NJB].

DISCOURSE UNIT: 6:1–3 [EBC, Hwt, Lg]. The topic is an exhortation on the need to make progress [EBC, Hwt], an exhortation to strive for spiritual maturity and perfection [Lg].

6:1 Therefore having-left[a] the teaching[b] of-the beginning[c] of-the Christ let-us-move-on[d] to[e] the maturity,[f]

LEXICON—a. aorist act. participle of ἀφίημι (LN 15.48, 68.43) (BAGD 3.b. p. 126): 'to leave' [HNTC, LN (15.48), Lns, NIC; KJV, NASB, NIV], 'to leave standing' [WBC], 'to leave behind' [Mil; NJB, NRSV, TEV, TNT], 'to go beyond' [NAB], 'to give up' [BAGD, LN (68.43)], 'to stop' [LN

(68.43)] 'to stop discussing' [REB], 'to stop going over again and again' [NLT], 'to start thinking about more than just . . .' [CEV]. The meaning is to leave behind in order to pass on to something else [Alf, EGT, Mil, My, NIGTC, WBC, Wst].

b. λόγος (LN 33.51, 33.98, 33.99) (BAGD 1.b.β. p. 478): 'teaching' [WBC; NAB, NASB, NJB, NRSV], 'message' [LN (33.98), NIC; TNT], 'treatise' [LN], 'doctrine' [HNTC; KJV], 'discussion' [Lns], 'speaking' [BAGD, LN (33.99)]. This singular noun is also translated as a plural: 'teachings' [NIV], 'lessons' [TEV], 'doctrines' [Mil], 'the things we were taught' [CEV]. The phrase τὸν λόγον τοῦ Χριστοῦ 'the teaching of Christ' is translated 'Christianity' [NLT, REB].

c. ἀρχή (LN **58.20**, 68.1) (BAGD 1.b. p. 111): 'beginning' [LN (68.1), Lns], 'preliminary stage' [NIC], 'simple truth' [**LN** (58.20)]. This singular noun is also translated as a plural: 'principles' [KJV], 'rudiments' [REB], 'elementary aspects' [**LN** (58.20)], 'elementary stages' [TNT], 'the basics' [NLT]. It is also translated as an adjective: 'first' [TEV], 'initial' [NAB], 'elementary' [BAGD, HNTC, Mil, WBC; NASB, NIV, NJB], 'basic' [CEV, NRSV]. It is emphatic by word order [NIGTC].

d. pres. mid./pass. subj. of φέρω (LN **13.58**) (BAGD 3.c. p. 855): 'to move on' [BAGD], 'to move on to' [**LN**], 'to advance' [HNTC; NAB, REB], 'to go on' [KJV, NIV, NJB, NLT, NRSV, TNT], 'to go forward' [TEV], 'to press on' [Mil, NIC; NASB], 'to try to become' [CEV], 'to progress' [LN]; with middle voice meaning: 'to bring oneself' [Lns]; with passive voice meaning: 'to be carried forward' [WBC]. It is passive voice, suggesting God as the mover [EBC, Hu, NIGTC, TNTC, WBC, Wst]; it is middle voice, with reflexive meaning [NTC]. The present tense implies continuous surrender to God's influence [Wst]. The first person plural implies that the author includes himself with his readers [NIGTC, NTC, TH, Wst].

e. ἐπί with accusative object (LN 84.17): 'to' [LN, Lns, Mil, NIC, WBC; NAB, NASB, NIV, NJB, TEV, TNT], 'toward' [HNTC, LN; NRSV, REB], 'unto' [KJV], not explicit [CEV, NLT].

f. τελειότης (LN 88.37, **88.101**) (BAGD p. 809): 'maturity' [BAGD, HNTC, **LN** (88.101), Lns, Mil, WBC; NAB, NASB, NIV, REB], 'mature teaching' [TEV], 'advanced teaching' [TNT], 'perfection' [BAGD, LN (88.37), NIC; KJV, NRSV], 'completion' [NJB]. This noun is also translated as an adjective: 'mature' [CEV], 'mature in one's understanding' [NLT].

QUESTION—What relationship is indicated by διό 'therefore'?

It indicates an exhortation [TH]. It is translated with 'let us' [all versions except CEV], or 'we must' [CEV]. It is grounded on the fact that they should be able to understand deeper concepts [Blm, ICC], they ought to have advanced beyond the basic teachings [EGT, Mil]. To continue in the elementary teachings would be of no help to his readers; therefore the author intends to give them mature teachings to take them out of their immaturity

[EBC, NIC]. The readers (and the author himself [Alf]) must advance [Alf, HNTC, My, NCBC, NIGTC, TH, Wst; CEV]. They must do this in order to recover the ground they have lost [HNTC], in order not to lose their present spiritual standing [NCBC]. The readers must advance in spiritual maturity, and the author must advance in mature teaching [Wst]. They were not infants, but were experienced and prepared to receive the solid food. The section 5:11–14 is irony, not the actual situation [WBC].

QUESTION—What relationship is indicated by the participle ἀφέντες 'having left'?

It is treated as a finite verb parallel to the following verb φερώμεθα 'let us move on' [EGT, HNTC, Mil, NIC, NTC, TNTC, WBC; NAB, NIV, NJB, NLT, REB, TEV, TNT]: let us leave . . . and move on . . . The aorist tense indicates a single act prior to moving on [Lns]. The author includes himself with his readers [NIGTC].

QUESTION—How are the nouns related in the genitive construction τὸν τῆς ἀρχῆς λόγον 'the teaching of the beginning'?

1. The noun ἀρχῆς 'beginning' is an attribute of λόγον 'teaching' [HNTC, Mil, My, WBC; CEV, NAB, NASB, NIV, NJB, NRSV, TEV]: the beginning teaching. It means the basic teachings [NRSV], the elementary teachings [HNTC, LN, Mil, WBC; NASB, NIV, NJB].
2. The noun ἀρχῆς 'beginning' is the object of τὸν λόγον 'the teaching' [Blm, Lns; NLT, REB]: teaching the rudiments.

QUESTION—What is the genitive noun phrase τοῦ Χριστοῦ 'of Christ' connected with?

1. It expresses the content of the teaching [ICC, Mil, My, TH; CEV, NAB, NASB, NIV, NJB, NRSV]: the teaching about Christ. It means the elementary teachings about Christ [Mil, My; NAB, NASB, NIV, NJB, NRSV].
2. It further describes the teaching [HNTC; TEV]: the Christian teaching. It means the first lessons about the Christian message [TEV].
3. It refers to the Christian faith [NLT, REB]: the rudiments of Christianity.

QUESTION—Who are included in the word φερώμεθα 'let us move on'?

1. It includes both the readers and the author [Alf, EBC, Hu, ICC, Lg, Lns, My, NIGTC, NTC, Wst]: let us (you and I) move on.
2. It refers to the readers alone [Hwt]: I urge you to move on.
3. It refers the author alone [Blm]: I want to move on in my teaching.

QUESTION—What is meant by τελειότητα 'maturity'?

1. It refers to maturity of the believers [Hu, Hwt, Lg, Mil, My, NIC, NTC, TNTC, WBC; CEV, KJV, NAB, NASB, NIV, NLT, NRSV, REB] and of the author as well [Hu, Lg]: let us move on to your/our maturity. It is an action by God [Hu, WBC], not gradual development [WBC].
2. It refers to mature teachings [Blm, EGT, GNC, HNTC, Hu, ICC, Lns, NIGTC, TH, Wst; NJB, TEV, TNT]: let us move on to discuss mature teachings. Mature teachings are those that are appropriate for those who

are mature Christians [TH]. Mature teachings are the means of their coming to spiritual maturity [Hu, Lns, NIGTC, Wst].

not again laying-down[a] (a) foundation[b] of-repentance[c] from[d] dead[e] works[f] and faith toward[g] God,

LEXICON—a. pres. mid. participle of καταβάλλω (LN **85.49**) (BAGD 2. p. 408): 'to lay down, to lay' [BAGD, HNTC, LN, Lns, Mil, NIC, WBC; KJV, NAB, NASB, NIV, NRSV, REB, TEV], 'to go over' [NJB]. The phrase μὴ πάλιν θελμέλιον καταβαλλόμενοι 'not again laying down a foundation' is translated 'we have already taught you the fundamental things and we need not do it again' [TNT], 'we shouldn't need to keep talking about' [CEV], 'surely we don't need to start all over again with the importance of' [NLT]. The subject of this participle is the readers [Alf, My], united with the author [Alf]. The present tense implies repeated actions [Mil].

b. θεμέλιος/θεμέλιον (LN **89.12**) (BAGD 2.a. p. 356): 'foundation' [BAGD, HNTC, LN, Lns, Mil, NIC, WBC; KJV, NAB, NASB, NIV, NRSV, REB, TEV], 'basis' [**LN**], 'fundamental doctrines' [NJB], 'fundamental things' [TNT], not explicit [CEV, NLT].

c. μετάνοια (LN 41.52) (BAGD p. 512): 'repentance' [BAGD, LN, Lns, Mil, NIC, WBC; KJV, NAB, NASB, NIV, NRSV, REB], 'renunciation' [HNTC]. This noun is also translated as a verb phrase: 'to turn' [CEV], 'to turn away' [BAGD; NJB, NLT, TEV], 'to give up' [TNT].

d. ἀπό with genitive object (LN 89.122): 'from' [LN, Lns, Mil, NIC, WBC; all versions except TNT], 'of' [HNTC]. It implies separation [Mil].

e. νεκρός (LN 23.121, 65.39) (BAGD 1.b.β. p. 534): 'dead' [BAGD, HNTC, LN (23.121), Lns, Mil, NIC; KJV, NAB, NASB, NJB, NRSV], 'useless' [LN (65.39); TEV], 'futile, vain' [LN (65.39)], 'that lead to death' [WBC; NIV]. The phrase νεκρῶν ἔργων 'dead works' is translated 'the deadness of our former ways' [REB], 'conduct which leads to death' [TNT], 'deeds that bring death' [CEV], 'evil deeds' [NLT]. It means to be devoid of power [Alf].

f. ἔργον (LN 42.11) (BAGD 1.c.β. p. 308): 'work' [HNTC, Lns, Mil, NIC, WBC; KJV, NAB, NASB, NRSV, TEV], 'deed' [BAGD, LN; CEV, NLT], 'act' [LN; NIV], 'action' [NJB], 'conduct' [TNT], 'ways' [REB].

g. ἐπί with accusative object (LN 84.17) (BAGD III.1.b.ε. p. 289): 'toward' [HNTC, LN, Lns, Mil; KJV, NASB, NRSV], 'in' [BAGD, NIC, WBC; CEV, NAB, NIV, NJB, NLT, REB, TEV, TNT]. This word indicates the direction of the faith referred to [EGT, HNTC, Lns, Mil, TNTC, Wst; KJV, NASB, NRSV].

QUESTION—Why is this phrase mentioned?

It explains the preceding clause [My]; it is the negative counterpart of the preceding clause [NIGTC, WBC]: let us move on; i.e., let us not lay a foundation again.

QUESTION—What is implied by πάλιν 'again'?

It implies that the foundation must be laid, but not afterward repeated [Alf, GNC].

QUESTION—How are the nouns related in the genitive construction θεμέλιον μετανοίας . . . καὶ πίστεως 'foundation of repentance . . . and faith'?

Μετανοίας 'repentance' and πίστεως 'faith' are the contents of θεμέλιον 'foundation' [Alf, EGT, Hu, ICC, Lns, Mil, My, NCBC, NIC, NIGTC, TH, TNTC, WBC, Wst; NAB, NJB, NRSV, REB]: the foundation consisting of repentance and faith. The reference is to the doctrines concerning these concepts [Blm]; it refers to actual repentance and faith [My, Wst]. These two nouns are the first of three related pairs included in the foundation [Hu, ICC, Mil, My, NCBC, NIC, NIGTC, TNTC, Wst]; this pair deals with the believer's relationship to God [Hwt], with the character of vital faith [TNTC, Wst]. The absence of definite articles with these two nouns implies quality—such things as repentance and faith [My].

QUESTION—What is the meaning of νεκρῶν ἔργων 'dead works'?

1. It means works that are useless [Alf, EGT, GNC, HNTC, Lg, Lns, My, TNTC, Wst; REB, TEV]: repentance from useless works. It refers to Jewish works of the law [Alf, TNTC, Wst], which lost their provisional vitality when Christ's work was fulfilled [Wst]. It refers to fruitless works, not sinful works [My, TNTC]. People must repent of relying on good works to save them [TNTC].
2. It means works that lead to death [Blm, EBC, GNC, Hu, ICC, Mil, NCBC, NIC, NIGTC, NTC, WBC; CEV, NIV, TNT]: repentance from works that bring death. They are evil deeds that result in spiritual death [EBC, GNC, ICC, Mil, NCBC, NIC, NIGTC]. It refers to works not based on faith and which lead to death [Blm, Hu].

QUESTION—What relationship is indicated by πίστεως ἐπὶ θεόν 'faith toward God'?

It indicates true trust in God [EGT, HNTC, Hu] who spoke concerning Christ in the OT [Lns], God as revealed in Christ [NTC]; it is the equivalent of faith in Christ [Hu, NIC].

6:2 of-teaching/a-doctrine[a] of baptisms/washings[b] and laying-on of-hands, and of-resurrection of-(the)-dead and of-eternal judgment.

TEXT—Instead of the genitive singular διδαχῆς 'of teaching' some manuscripts have the accusative singular διδαχήν 'teaching'. GNT reads the genitive singular with an A decision, indicating that the genitive is certain. The difference between these two readings is not always clear from the translation. The genitive διδαχῆς 'of teaching' is clearly read by Alf, Blm, EGT, Lg, Lns, Mil, My, Wst, KJV, NASB, TEV; the accusative διδαχήν 'teaching' is clearly read by EBC, HNTC, ICC, NIC, WBC.

LEXICON—a. διδαχή (LN 33.224, 33.236) (BAGD 2, p. 192): 'teaching' [BAGD, LN (33.224, 33.236), Mil, NIC; NJB, TEV], 'instruction' [HNTC; NAB, NASB, NIV, NLT, NRSV, REB], 'catechetical instruction' [WBC], 'doctrine' [LN (33.236), Lns; KJV]. This noun is also translated as a verb: 'to teach' [CEV, TNT].

b. βαπτισμός (LN 53.31, **53.41**) (BAGD p. 132): 'baptism' [BAGD, **LN** (53.41), Lns, Mil; all versions except NASB, REB], 'washing' [LN (53.31); NASB], 'ablution' [NIC], 'purification' [LN (53.31)], 'cleansing rites' [WBC; REB], 'water rites' [HNTC]. It is emphatic by forefronting [Wst].

QUESTION—What is the noun διδαχῆς 'of teaching/doctrine' (or διδαχήν 'a teaching/doctrine') related to?

1. It gives a further content of the θεμέλιον 'foundation' in 6:1 [Alf, EGT, Lg, Mil, My; NAB, NASB, NJB, NRSV, TEV]: a foundation of teaching. It is the third element of the basic teachings [Lns]. This includes some (not necessarily all) who read the genitive διδαχῆς 'of teaching'.
2. Taking the reading containing the accusative διδαχήν 'teaching', it is parallel to θεμέλιον 'foundation' in 6:1 [EBC, HNTC, NIC, WBC; TNT]: not laying again a foundation, not laying again a teaching.

QUESTION—What is meant by διδαχῆς 'teaching/doctrine'?

1. It refers to the activity of teaching the following topics [NIC; CEV, NAB, NASB, NIV, NLT, NRSV, REB, TNT]: teaching baptisms, etc.
2. It refers to the doctrine about the following topics [BAGD, WBC; KJV, NJB, TEV]: the doctrine concerning baptisms, etc.

QUESTION—What is the content of διδαχῆς 'teaching/doctrine'?

1. The content is the rest of the verse [Alf, EBC, EGT, HNTC, Lg, Lns, My, NIC, NTC, TH, TNTC, WBC, Wst; NJB, REB].
2. The content is both 'baptisms' and 'laying on of hands' [TEV, TNT].
3. The content is only 'baptisms' [Mil]; the word θεμέλιον 'foundation' governs the following words [Mil]: not again laying down a foundation of repentance, of teachings about baptisms, of laying on of hands, of resurrection, and of eternal judgment.

QUESTION—To what does the plural βαπτισμῶν 'baptisms/washings' refer and what was taught?

1. It refers to various Jewish washing ceremonies [Alf, EBC, EGT, GNC, Hu, Lg, My, NCBC, NIC, NTC, TNTC, Wst]. The plural form shows that several ritual cleansing acts are intended [TNTC]. With the cleansing ceremonies, some include both John's and Christian baptism [Alf, EGT, Hu, My, NTC]. The plural implies a contrast between Christian baptism and all other religious washings known to the readers [NTC]. Instructions would be about how the cleansing by Christ's blood, symbolized by baptism, now abrogated Jewish cleansing rites and also possibly instruction about the differences between Christian baptism, Jewish proselyte baptism, John's baptism, and Jesus' baptism, and the work of the Holy Spirit [EGT, Hu].
2. It refers to differences between the baptisms by John and Christian baptism [HNTC].

3. It refers to instruction about the differences between Jewish and Christian baptisms [Blm, NIGTC, WBC], and perhaps also John's and the Qumran community's baptisms [NIGTC].
4. It refers to Christian baptisms, the plural referring to the baptisms received by the various believers [Lns].

QUESTION—What is meant by the phrase ἐπιθέσεως χειρῶν 'laying on of hands'?

It refers to the various OT and NT rites involving this act, and especially following Christian baptism [Alf, ICC], to the laying of hands on the convert at baptism [Blm, EBC, EGT, TH], as a symbol of the impartation of the Holy Spirit [EBC, EGT, GNC, Hwt, Mil, My, NCBC, NIC, NIGTC], of the impartation of spiritual gifts [Blm, TNTC], of giving or restoring strength for service [Wst]. It refers to various uses, including commissioning for service [GNC, ICC, NCBC], to setting apart in general [Lg], for blessing [ICC, Lns, Wst], and for healing [GNC, NCBC].

QUESTION—What does ἀναστάσεως 'resurrection' refer to?

1. It refers to the resurrection generally, including all persons [Alf, Blm, EGT, Hu, Lg, My, NCBC, NIGTC, NTC, TH]. The following reference to judgment implies that this is the general resurrection of both the righteous and the unrighteous [NIGTC].
2. It refers to the resurrection of the righteous [Mil].

QUESTION—What is meant by κρίματος 'judgment'?

It refers to the verdict rendered [Mil, TH, Wst].

1. It is neutral in meaning, including both favorable and unfavorable judgments [Alf, Blm, Lg, My, NCBC, NTC, TH].
2. It refers to the condemnation of sinners [Hu, Mil].

QUESTION—What is the meaning of αἰωνίου?

It means that it remains valid forever [Blm, Lns, TH], its effects are eternal [Blm, EGT, Hu, NIGTC]. It qualifies the judgment as being from God [NIGTC, TH].

6:3 And this we-will-do, if-indeed[a] God permits.

TEXT—Instead of the indicative mood ποιήσομεν 'we will do', some manuscripts read the subjunctive mood ποιήσωμεν 'let us do'. GNT reads the indicative mood with an A decision, indicating that the indicative form is certain. The exhortation 'let us do' is read by only Alf, Lg, My, and CEV.

LEXICON—a. ἐάνπερ (LN **89.68**) (BAGD I.3.c. p. 211): 'if indeed' [BAGD, **LN,** Lns, Mil], 'if surely' [LN], 'if only' [BAGD], 'if, that is' [WBC], 'if' [HNTC; CEV, KJV, NASB, NRSV, REB, TEV, TNT], 'supposing that' [BAGD]. The phrase ἐάνπερ ἐπιτρέπῃ ὁ θεός 'if indeed God permits' is translated 'God permitting' [NIC; NAB, NIV], 'God willing' [NJB, NLT]. It is a hypothetical condition [Alf], a condition of expectancy [Lns]. The suffix -περ 'indeed' implies that the condition expressed by the clause is in harmony with the preceding thought [Alf].

QUESTION—To what does τοῦτο 'this' refer?

1. It refers to going on to maturity [Alf, EGT, Lg, Lns, Mil, My, NIGTC, TH; CEV, NLT]: we will go on to maturity. That the author will give more advanced teaching is implied [NIGTC].
2. It refers to the more advanced teaching [Blm, GNC, HNTC, Hwt, ICC]: we will move on to more advanced teaching.
3. It means the author will give mature teaching, and he as well as the readers will go on to spiritual maturity [NIC].

QUESTION—Who is meant by 'we' in ποιήσομεν 'we will do'?

1. The author is stating what he and his readers determine to do [EBC, EGT, GNC, Lns, NIGTC, NTC, TH, TNTC]: we will do this.
2. The author is stating what he intends to do [Blm, HNTC]: I will do this, i.e., move on to the more advanced teaching.
3. If the subjunctive 'let us do' is read, it is an exhortation to the readers [Alf, Lg; CEV]: let us do this.

QUESTION—Why does he add 'if indeed God permits'?

It expresses his concern [EBC, EGT, GNC, Hwt, Lg, Lns, My, NIC, NTC, TH, TNTC, WBC]. It recognizes the difficulty of the task [EGT], and implies that the condition will encounter opposition [WBC]. The advance can only be made with God's help [EBC, EGT, GNC, Lg(K)] and God must open the readers' hearts [NTC]. It means that the author needs God's help in conveying his message to the readers, and the readers need God's help in overcoming their dullness in understanding [Lns]. It implies the need of making every plan subordinate to God's will [Hwt, My]. It implies the possibility of falling away [Lg]. It is added as a pious comment [ICC].

DISCOURSE UNIT: 6:4–12 [GNC]. The topic is the seriousness of apostasy.

DISCOURSE UNIT: 6:4–8 [EBC, HNTC, Hwt, Lg]. The topic is no second beginning [EBC], the danger of being permanently excluded [HNTC], the third warning [Hwt], the impossibility of renewing those who have fallen away [Lg].

6:4 For (it is) impossible the-(ones) once having-been-enlightened,[a] and having-tasted[b] the heavenly[c] gift and having-become partakers[d] of-(the)-Holy Spirit

LEXICON—a. aorist pass. participle of φωτίζω (LN 14.39) (BAGD 2.b. p. 873): 'to be enlightened' [HNTC, Lns, Mil, NIC; KJV, NAB, NASB, NIV, NLT, NRSV, REB], 'to be given light' [BAGD], 'to be brought into the light' [WBC; NJB], 'to receive the light of God' [TNT], 'to be illuminated' [BAGD, LN], 'to be shined upon' [LN], 'to be in God's light' [TEV], 'to have seen the light' [CEV].

b. aorist mid. (deponent = act.) indic. of γεύομαι (LN **90.78**) (BAGD 2. p. 157): 'to taste' [Lns, Mil, NIC; all versions except CEV, NLT, TNT], 'to have a taste' [HNTC], 'to experience' [LN, WBC; NLT, TNT], 'to obtain' [BAGD], 'to receive' [CEV]. It means to partake of personally and knowingly [Alf], to know by experience [EGT, My]. It is emphatic by word order [Alf].

c. ἐπουράνιος (LN 12.17) (BAGD 1.a.δ. p. 306): 'heavenly' [BAGD, Lns, Mil, NIC; KJV, NAB, NASB, NIV, NRSV, REB], 'from heaven' [WBC; CEV, NJB], 'of heaven' [HNTC; NLT], 'heaven's' [TEV], 'from God' [LN], 'God's' [TNT]. It relates to the heavenly world [HNTC, NCBC, TNTC]; it refers to its source in Christ who came from heaven [My] and heaven as its realization [My, Wst]; it refers to God [NIGTC, TH].

d. μέτοχος (LN 34.8) (BAGD 1. p. 514): 'partaker' [Lns, Mil; KJV, NASB], 'sharer' [NAB], 'companion, partner' [LN], 'sharing in, participating in' [BAGD]. This noun is also translated as a verb: 'to partake' [NIC], 'to share' [CEV, NIV, NLT, NRSV, REB], 'to have a share' [HNTC], 'to receive a share' [WBC]. The phrase μετόχους γενηθέντας 'having become partakers' is translated 'received a share' [NJB, TNT], 'received their share' [TEV]. This word is emphatic by word order [Alf].

QUESTION—What relationship is indicated by γάρ 'for'?

1. It indicates the grounds for 'not laying again a foundation' in 6:1 [Blm, EGT, NIGTC].
2. It indicates the grounds for 'let us go on to maturity' in 6:1 [My] and 'this we will do' in 6:3 [My, WBC].
3. It indicates the grounds for 'this we will do' [ICC, Lg].
4. It indicates the grounds for the contents of 6:1–3 [Alf, EGT, Hwt] and 5:11–14 [Hwt].
5. It indicates the grounds for the comment 'if God wills' [Wst].
6. It indicates the reason the author will not continue to deal with elementary teaching, because if they have forgotten it they cannot begin again [HNTC].
7. It explains the reason success might not be possible for some [Lns, Mil]; converts may so fall that they cannot be brought back to repentance [Lns], that God may not permit renewal (as implied in 6:3) [Mil].

QUESTION—What is meant by ἀδύνατον 'impossible'?

It is connected with ἀνακαινίζειν 'to renew' in 6:6 [ICC, Mil, WBC]: it is impossible to renew (them). It is emphatic by word order [NTC, WBC, Wst].

1. It means actually impossible [Alf, Hu, Lg, My, NIGTC, TH, TNTC, WBC].
2. It means the highest degree of moral impossibility, yet not utterly without hope if there is repentance proportionate to the sin [Blm].
3. It means that in human experience it is virtually impossible [NIC, Wst]. However, it is not impossible for God [NIC].

QUESTION—What is τούς 'the (ones)' connected with?

It is connected with the five following participles [Blm, EGT, GNC, WBC; all versions except KJV, NIV], the four following participles [Lns, NTC, TNTC; KJV, NIV], indicating that one group of persons is being described by all these features [EGT, GNC, Hu, ICC, Lns, Mil, My, NIC, NTC, TNTC]. This long participial phrase is the predicate of ἀνακαινίζειν 'to renew' in 6:6 [EGT, Lns, WBC]: to renew those who have been illuminated, etc. This phrase precedes its verb for emphasis [Wst].

QUESTION—To whom is this long participial phrase directed?

1. They are the persons to whom the author is writing [Alf, EBC, EGT, GNC, Hu, ICC, Lg, Lns, My, NCBC, NIGTC, TH, WBC], but addressed indirectly [NTC].
2. They are persons other than those to whom the author is writing [Hwt, Mil, NTC], although the warning applies to the readers as well [NTC].
2.1 It refers to actual persons [Mil].
2.2 It is a hypothetical situation [Hwt, TNTC].

QUESTION—Who are the persons referred to?

1. It describes persons who have become believers [Alf, Blm, EBC, EGT, GNC, HNTC, Hu, ICC, Lg, Lns, Mil, My, NCBC, NIC, NIGTC, TH, WBC].
2. It refers to persons who have only had some instruction in Christian principles and had some experiences similar to those of Jewish people [Hwt].

QUESTION—What is meant by ἅπαξ 'once'?

It refers to the time of the events described by the following participles [Alf]: they who once were illuminated, etc. It implies that there need not be nor can there be a repetition of the actions [Alf, EGT, Lg]; it means a once for all experience [EGT, Hu, Hwt, ICC, Mil, NCBC, NIC]; it implies only that once should have sufficed [My]. It emphasizes the completeness and sufficiency of the illumination [Wst].

1. It modifies the four following participles through γευσαμένους 'having tasted' in 6:5 [EGT, Hu, Lns, My, WBC].
2. It modifies only φωτισθέντας 'having been enlightened' [Mil, NIC, NIGTC, NTC, Wst].

QUESTION—What does the aorist tense of the following participles indicate?

They imply completed actions [NCBC, NIGTC].

1. They refer to successive steps in the spiritual life prior to the action of the main verb [Alf].
2. They all refer to a single experience of grace [Hu].

QUESTION—What is meant by φωτισθέντας 'having been enlightened'?

It refers to leaving the darkness of the previous life and being illuminated by the gospel [Alf, EGT, Lns, Mil, TH, Wst], receiving the knowledge of the truth of the gospel [ICC, Lg, My, NIGTC, WBC]. It refers to being brought to Jesus, the light of the world [EBC, Hu]. It refers to receiving some initial revelation of Christ [TNTC]. It refers both to baptism [Blm, HNTC] and the accompanying teaching [Blm].

QUESTION—What is the relationship between φωτισθέντας 'having been illuminated' and the following participles?

1. There is a close connection between φωτισθέντας 'having been illuminated' and γευσάμενους 'having tasted' [Lg, Mil, My, NTC], as τε 'and' indicates [Lg, Mil, My, NTC].

2. The two following participles are expansions of φωτισθέντας 'having been illuminated' [Wst], which is supported by τε 'and' [Wst].
3. The three following participles are expansions of φωτισθέντας 'having been illuminated' [ICC, TNTC, WBC], as τε 'and' indicates.

QUESTION—What is implied by γευσαμένους 'having tasted'?

It means to experience something [Hu, Mil, NIGTC, WBC] fully [NIGTC] in a real and personal way [WBC, Wst] by possessing it [Blm, Lg]. It is the full experience of conversion [GNC, Mil]. This word does not imply a diminished experience [Hu, Mil]. However, the experience is only partial and a beginning [HNTC, Wst], as implied by the genitive case of the object of the tasting (τῆς δωρεᾶς τῆς ἐπουρανίου 'the heavenly gift') [Wst]. It is emphatic by position [Lg].

QUESTION—What is meant by τῆς δωρεᾶς τῆς ἐπουρανίου 'the heavenly gift'?

1. It refers broadly to what they received in their new life in Christ [Alf, Hu, Lns, My, NIC, NTC], to a specific gift [TH], to the whole gift of redemption [EGT, GNC, ICC, NCBC, WBC, Wst], to God's gift in general [EBC], to the whole Christian life.
2. It refers to the gift of the Holy Spirit [Blm].

QUESTION—What is implied by 'having become partakers of the Holy Spirit'?

1. It means receiving the Holy Spirit [GNC, TH, WBC], sharing in the Holy Spirit [Alf, TNTC], participating in the Holy Spirit [NIGTC, Wst], partaking of the Holy Spirit [EGT, Lns, NCBC, NIC] by the laying on of hands [Mil] and the gaining of a personal character [Wst].
2. It refers to receiving the charismatic gifts of the Holy Spirit [Hu].

6:5 and good[a] having-tasted[b] (the) word[c] of-God and powers[d] of-(the)-coming[e] age[f]

LEXICON—a. καλός (LN 88.4) (BAGD 2.c.b. p. 400): 'good' [BAGD, LN, Mil; CEV, KJV, NAB, NASB, TEV], 'excellent' [Lns], 'praiseworthy' [LN]. This adjective is also translated as a noun: 'goodness' [HNTC, NIC, WBC; NIV, NJB, NLT, NRSV, REB, TNT].

b. aorist mid. (deponent = act.) of γεύομαι: 'to taste'. See this word in 6:4.

c. ῥῆμα (LN 33.98) (BAGD 1. p. 735): 'word' [BAGD, HNTC, LN, Mil, NIC, WBC; all versions except CEV, NJB], 'utterance' [Lns], 'message' [LN; CEV, NJB].

d. δύναμις (LN 76.1) (BAGD 4, p. 208): 'power' [HNTC, LN, Lns, Mil, WBC; all versions except REB, TNT], 'spiritual power' [REB, TNT], 'deed of power' [BAGD], 'mighty work' [NIC], 'wonder' [BAGD], 'miracle' [BAGD].

e. pres. act. participle of μέλλω (LN 67.62) (BAGD 2. p. 501): 'to come' [BAGD, HNTC, Mil, NIC, WBC; all versions except CEV], 'to be about to come' [Lns], 'to be about to' [LN]. This participle is also translated as an adjective: 'future' [BAGD; CEV].

f. αἰών (LN 67.143) (BAGD 2.b. p. 27): 'age' [BAGD, HNTC, LN, Mil, NIC, WBC; all versions except CEV, KJV, NJB], 'era' [LN], 'eon' [Lns], 'world' [CEV, KJV, NJB].

QUESTION—What is καλόν 'good' connected with?

1. It modifies only ῥῆμα 'word' [Alf, Blm, EBC, EGT, GNC, HNTC, Hu, Hwt, ICC, Lg, Lns, Mil, My, NIC, NIGTC, NTC, TH, TNTC, WBC, Wst; all versions].

1.1 It is attributive to ῥῆμα 'word' [Alf, Hu, Lg, Lns, Mil, My, TH; CEV, KJV, NAB, NASB]: having tasted the good word.

1.2 It is in the predicate position [EGT, ICC, NIC; TEV] and states a quality of ῥῆμα 'word' [HNTC, NIC, NTC, TNTC, WBC, Wst; NIV, NJB, NRSV, REB, TNT]: having tasted the goodness of the word, or, having tasted that the word is good.

2. It modifies δυνάμεις 'powers' as well as ῥῆμα 'word' [EGT, TNTC]: having tasted that the word of God is good and that the powers of the coming age are good.

QUESTION—How are the two nouns related in the genitive construction θεοῦ ῥῆμα 'word of God'?

God is the one who expresses the word [Alf, BAGD, EBC]. He is the source of the word [TH].

QUESTION—To what does θεοῦ ῥῆμα 'word of God' refer?

It refers to any word from God to mankind [EBC], to some specific utterance [HNTC, Wst], to the message of salvation [GNC], to the good news of the gospel [Hu], to the fulfillment of God's promises now realized [Mil], to Christian teaching [TH], to the experience of God at conversion [TNTC].

QUESTION—What is meant by καλὸν θεοῦ ῥῆμα 'good word of God'?

It indicates the wholesome and soul-preserving quality spoken by God in the gospel [Alf], God's OT promise of blessing and salvation as fulfilled in the gospel [Blm, EGT, My].

QUESTION—To what does μέλλοντος αἰῶνος 'coming age' refer?

1. It refers to the new age which began at Christ's first coming [Alf, GNC] and will be consummated at his second coming [EGT, Hu, My].

2. It refers to the new age which will begin at Christ's second coming [Blm, EBC, NIC, NTC, TNTC, WBC, Wst]. Many of the powers associated with that age are already operating in their midst [EBC, Hu, NIC, WBC]. We experience the powers that belong to the future age, but not in their fullness [NTC, TNTC].

QUESTION—What is meant by the δυνάμεις 'powers' of the coming age?

It refers to the spiritual powers given by the Holy Spirit to arm Christians for their spiritual conflict [Alf], to present manifestations of the Holy Spirit [HNTC], to the miraculous works done by the Holy Spirit [My], to the power to work miracles given by the Holy Spirit [EGT], to special powers available to mankind in the coming Messianic age [EBC], to the miracles and mighty works experienced by these Christians when the gospel first reached them [Mil, NIC, NIGTC], to powers belonging to the future age but occurring in this age as well [NTC, TNTC, Wst], to the powerful assurances of future life [Blm]. They are the signs, wonders, and miracles that accompanied the preaching of the gospel as mentioned in 2:4 [EGT, Hu, ICC, NTC].

6:6 and having-fallen-away,[a]

LEXICON—a. aorist act. participle of παραπίπτω (LN **34.26**) (BAGD p. 621): 'to fall away' [BAGD, HNTC, LN, Lns, Mil, NIC, WBC; all versions except CEV, NLT, TEV], 'to commit apostasy' [BAGD], 'to abandon one's faith' [TEV], 'to turn away' [CEV], 'to turn away from God' [NLT].

QUESTION—What relationship is indicated by the participial form παραπεσόντας 'having fallen away'?

1. It continues the description of the group which was begun by τούς 'the (ones)' in 6:4 [Alf, Blm, EGT, HNTC, ICC, Lg, Lns, My, NIGTC, WBC, Wst; all versions except KJV, NIV]: the ones having been enlightened . . . , and . . . , and . . . , and having fallen away. It implies an action subsequent to the preceding participles [NIGTC]. The καί 'and' preceding this participle emphasizes the unusual action described by this participle [NIGTC].
2. It is conditional [Hwt, Mil, NIC, TNTC; KJV, NIV] and hypothetical [Hwt, Lg(K)], a contrary-to-fact condition [Hwt]: if they fall away/if it were possible for them to fall away. (This rendering clearly violates the syntax of the participial phrase; καί 'and' connects this participle as a parallel to the preceding participles; hence the rendering 'if' is impossible.)

QUESTION—What is meant by falling away?

It means having fallen away from the condition described by the preceding participles in this participial phrase [EGT]. The aorist tense indicates a (deliberate [Mil]) single completed act [Lg, Mil, TNTC, WBC]. It is a real warning regarding an actual danger [Mil, NIC, NIGTC, NTC]. It is a hypothetical case which is a real possibility [EGT, TNTC], which will not, in fact, occur [Hu, Hwt, Lg(K)].

1. These were Christians who gave up their faith [Alf, Blm, EGT, HNTC, Lg, Lns, Mil, My, NCBC, NIC, NIGTC, NTC, TH, WBC, Wst] by committing apostasy [Blm, GNC, HNTC, Hu, Lg, Mil, NCBC, NIC, NIGTC, NTC, TNTC, WBC, Wst]. The reference is to Hebrew converts who reject their confidence in Christ [Alf]. They were Christians in the fullest sense [Lns]. They had an elementary but inadequate grasp of the faith [ICC].
2. These were church members who did not have true Christian faith [GNC, Hu]. If they fall away, it shows that they were not truly Christians [GNC, Hu], they had not grasped even the basic principles of the Christian faith [Hu].

again to-renew[a] to[b] repentance,

LEXICON—a. pres. act. infin. of ἀνακαινίζω (LN **13.67**) (BAGD p. 55): 'to renew' [BAGD, Lns, Mil, NIC; KJV, NASB], 'to bring back' [HNTC, LN; CEV], 'to bring' [NLT, REB], 'to restore' [BAGD, WBC; NRSV]. This active voice is also translated as a passive voice: 'to be brought back' [NIV, TEV]. This entire phrase is translated 'to make them repent again' [NAB], 'to be made to repent again' [TNT], 'for them to be brought to the freshness of repentance a second time' [NJB]. It implies renewal of the conditions expressed by the first four participles of the preceding participial phrase [EGT]; it refers to renewal of conversion and baptism [GNC]. The present tense indicates progression [NTC], continual effort [Wst].

b. εἰς with accusative object (LN 84.22) (BAGD 4.a. p. 229): 'to' [HNTC, Mil, NIC, WBC; NASB, NIV, NJB, NLT, NRSV, REB, TEV], 'into' [LN], 'unto' [Lns; KJV], not explicit [CEV]. The phrase εἰς μετάνοιαν 'to repentance' is translated 'to repent' [TEV]. It expresses result [My, Wst].

QUESTION—How is this phrase related to other phrases?

The infinitive ἀνακαινίζειν 'to renew' tells what is ἀδύνατον 'impossible' in 6:4 [Alf, EGT, GNC, Lns, Mil, NTC; NAB, NJB, NRSV, REB] and the predicate of this infinitive is the long participial phrase beginning with τούς 'the (ones)' in 6:4 [Alf, EGT, GNC, Lns; NAB, NRSV, REB]: it is impossible to renew the ones having been enlightened . . .

QUESTION—What is πάλιν 'again' connected with?

It is connected with ἀνακαινίζειν 'to renew' [Alf, EGT, HNTC, Lg, My, TH; KJV, NASB, NJB, NRSV, REB]: to renew again. It is emphatic by forefronting [ICC].

crucifying[a] to-themselves the Son of God and exposing-(him)-to-shame.[b]

LEXICON—a. pres. act. participle of ἀνασταυρόω (LN **20.77**) (BAGD p. 61): 'to crucify' [HNTC, Mil, NIC; NAB, REB], 'to crucify again' [BAGD, LN, WBC; NASB, NJB, NRSV, TEV, TNT], 'to crucify all over again' [NIV], 'to crucify afresh' [KJV], 'to recrucify' [Lns], 'to nail to the cross again' [NLT], 'to do the same as nailing to a cross' [CEV]. The present tense indicates a continuing attitude [EBC, HNTC, Lns, NTC, Wst], continuing consequences [NIGTC]. It refers to the same event as παραπεσόντας 'having fallen away' [NIGTC].

b. pres. act. participle of παραδειγματίζω (LN **25.200**) (BAGD p. 614): 'to put to shame' [LN], 'to put to open shame' [KJV, NASB], 'to expose to public shame' [**LN,** NIC, WBC; TEV], 'to subject to public disgrace' [NIV], 'to hold up to public shame' [NLT], 'to make a public exhibition' [NJB], 'to hold up to contempt' [BAGD, Mil; NAB, NRSV, TNT], 'to expose to mockery and contempt' [HNTC], 'to hold up to mockery' [REB], 'to expose to public ignominy' [Lns], 'to insult in public' [CEV]. The present tense indicates a continuing attitude [EBC, HNTC, Lns, NTC,

Wst], continuing consequences [NIGTC]. It refers to the same event as παραπεσόντας 'having fallen away' [NIGTC].

QUESTION—What relationship is indicated by the participial forms ἀνασταυροῦντας 'crucifying' and παραδειγματίζοντας 'exposing him to shame'?

1. They indicate the reason why such people cannot be renewed to repentance [Alf, EGT, GNC, HNTC, ICC, Lns, Mil, My, NIC, NIGTC, NTC, WBC, Wst; all versions]: it is impossible to renew them to repentance because they are crucifying the Son of God again and exposing him to shame. Παραδειγματίζοντας 'exposing him to shame' continues the action of ἀνασταυροῦντας 'crucifying again' [Alf]; it expresses an additional reason [Mil]. 'Crucifying again' refers to the wrong done to Christ; 'exposing him to shame' refers to the effect of influencing others to turn away from Christ [Wst].
2. They are temporal [Lg]: it is impossible to renew them to repentance while they are crucifying the Son of God again and exposing him to shame.

QUESTION—What is meant by ἀνασταυροῦντας 'crucifying'?

1. The prefix ἀνα- means 'again' and this means to crucify again, a second time [Alf, BAGD, Blm, GNC, Lg, LN, Lns, My, NIGTC, NTC, TNTC, Wst; all versions except NAB, REB].
2. The prefix ἀνα- means 'up' and this means to crucify up on the cross [EGT, NIC].
3. It means simply to crucify [EBC, HNTC, ICC, Mil; NAB, REB].

QUESTION—What relationship is indicated by ἑαυτοῖς 'to themselves'?

The dative case implies a negative benefit, a loss or hurt to themselves [Lg, Mil, My, NIC, NIGTC, NTC, WBC, Wst]; it means with reference to themselves [Alf, Blm, EBC, EGT, Hwt, Lg(K)], for themselves [NIC], in their own selves [HNTC, TH]; it is their own action [ICC]; it means that they must take the responsibility for their action [TNTC].

6:7 For[a] ground the-(one) having-drunk[b] the rain coming often upon[c] it and producing[d] vegetation[e] useful[f] for-those for-the-benefit-of[g] whom also it-is-being-cultivated,[h]

LEXICON—a. γάρ (LN 89.23): 'for' [HNTC, LN, Lns, Mil, WBC; KJV, NASB], 'because' [LN], not explicit [NIC; all versions except KJV, NASB].

b. aorist act. participle of πίνω (LN **14.35**) (BAGD 2.a p. 658): 'to drink' [BAGD, Lns; KJV, NASB], 'to drink in' [HNTC, Mil; NAB, NIV, REB, TEV], 'to drink up' [NIC; NJB, NRSV, TNT], 'to soak up' [LN, WBC; NLT], 'to absorb' [**LN**], not explicit [CEV]. It implies that the soil has absorbed the rain [Alf, EGT]. The aorist tense indicates that this participle is prior to the following participles τίκτουσα 'producing' and ἐκφέρουσα 'bearing' [Alf, EGT, My, Wst].

c. ἐπί with genitive object (LN 83.46) (BAGD I.1.a.β. p. 286): 'upon' [BAGD, HNTC, LN, Lns, Mil, WBC; KJV, NASB, REB], 'on' [BAGD, LN, NIC; NAB, NIV, NJB, NLT, NRSV, TEV, TNT], not explicit [CEV]. The genitive case with this preposition indicates that the rain comes upon it and lies on the soil [Alf, Lg(K), Wst] ready to be absorbed into it [Alf, Wst].

d. pres. act. participle of τίκτω (LN **23.194**) (BAGD 2. p. 816): 'to produce' [LN, NIC; NIV, NRSV, TNT], 'to bring forth' [BAGD, Mil; KJV, NAB, NASB], 'to bear' [HNTC, Lns; NLT], 'to yield' [WBC; NJB, REB], 'to grow' [TEV], 'to make grow' [CEV]. The present tense refers to continued producing [Lns]. This participle is coordinate with the preceding participle ἡ πιοῦσα 'the one having drunk' [Lg(K)].

e. βοτάνη (LN **3.14**) (BAGD 1. p. 145): 'vegetation' [BAGD, HNTC, Mil; NAB, NASB], 'crop' [WBC; CEV, NIV, NLT, NRSV, REB, TNT], 'plant' [LN]. This singular noun is translated as a plural: 'plants' [Lns, NIC; TEV], 'herbs' [KJV], 'crops' [NJB].

f. εὔθετος (LN 65.32; 66.3) (BAGD p. 320): 'useful' [HNTC, LN (65.32), Mil, WBC; CEV, NAB, NASB, NIV, NRSV, TEV, TNT], 'usable' [BAGD, LN (66.3)], 'suitable' [BAGD, LN (66.3), Lns], 'fit' [BAGD, LN (66.3)], 'meet' [KJV], 'serviceable' [NIC], 'of value' [LN (65.32)], 'good' [NLT], 'that are wanted' [NJB]. The phrase εὔθετον ἐκείνοις δι' οὓς καὶ γεωργεῖται 'useful for those for the benefit of whom also it is being cultivated' is translated 'for the use of those who cultivate it' [REB].

g. διά with accusative object (LN 90.38): 'for the benefit of' [LN], 'for the sake of' [LN, Mil; NASB], 'on behalf of' [LN], 'on account of' [Lns, NIC], 'for' [HNTC, LN, WBC; NAB, NIV, NRSV, TEV], 'by' [KJV]. The phrase δι' οὓς καὶ γεωργεῖται 'for the benefit of whom also it is being cultivated' is translated 'who grew them' [NJB], 'who farm it' [TNT], 'to farmers' [CEV], 'for the farmer' [NLT].

h. pres. pass. indic. of γεωργέω (LN **43.1**) (BAGD p. 157): 'to be cultivated' [LN, Mil, NIC, WBC; NAB, NRSV, TEV], 'to be tilled' [BAGD, HNTC, Lns; NASB], 'to be dressed' [KJV]. 'to be farmed' [LN; NIV], 'to be gardened' [LN], not explicit [CEV, NLT]. The passive voice is also translated as active: 'to cultivate' [REB], 'to grow' [NJB].

QUESTION—What relationship is indicated by γάρ 'for'?

It indicates an illustration (an explanation [Hu, NCBC, WBC], the confirmation [My]) of the preceding comment [Alf, GNC, Hwt, ICC, Lns, Mil, NIGTC, NTC, TNTC, Wst], and the grounds [Mil], to show opposite results from similarly favorable conditions [Mil, My].

QUESTION—What is implied by the absence of the definite article with γῆ 'ground'?

It emphasizes 'ground' as a quality [EGT]. It is qualified by the participles and adjectives which follow [NTC].

QUESTION—What relationship is indicated by the participial phrase 'the one having drunk the rain often coming upon it'?

1. With the definite article it is attributive, describing or identifying the land referred to [Alf, EGT, Mil, WBC; all versions except REB].
2. It is temporal, telling when it receives God's blessing [HNTC; REB]: when it has drunk. (The definite article with the participle does not permit this interpretation; perhaps the temporal clauses are intended only as a means of showing that both refer to the same field.)

QUESTION—How are the phrases of this verse related?

1. The phrase 'ground which has drunk the rain which often falls on it' governs both of the following participial phrases, τίκτουσα βοτάνην . . . 'producing vegetation . . .' and ἐκφέρουσα ἀκάνθας . . . 'bearing thorns . . .' [Alf, EBC, EGT, Lns, My, WBC; NAB, NASB, NRSV, TEV, TNT]: ground bearing suitable vegetation receives blessing, but producing thorns is rejected. The definite article with the first participle governs the two following participles as well [Lns]. The illustration in this and the following verse refer to the same field [Alf, EBC, HNTC, Lns, Mil, My(D), NIGTC, WBC; NAB, NASB, NRSV, REB, TEV, TNT], to different parts of the same field [NTC].
2. This phrase governs only the following participial phrase 'producing vegetation'; ἐκφέρουσα ἀκάνθας 'bearing thorns' refers to a different field [Blm, Hwt, NIC; CEV, KJV, NIV, NJB, NLT].

QUESTION—What does the present tense of the participle ἐρχόμενον 'coming' indicate?

It indicates repeated action [Lns]: the rain which repeatedly comes upon it.

QUESTION—What relationship is indicated by the phrase καὶ τίκτουσα βοτάνην 'and producing vegetation'?

It expresses the result of having drunk the rain [Mil].

QUESTION—What are ἐκείνοις 'those' and εὔθετον 'suitable' connected with?

1. 'Εκείνοις 'those' is connected with εὔθετον 'suitable' [Blm, EBC, EGT, Lns, Mil, NIC, Wst; all versions]: suitable for those persons.
2. 'Εκείνοις 'those' is connected with τίκτουσα 'producing' [Alf, ICC]: producing for those persons.
3. Εὔθετον 'suitable' is connected with βοτάνην 'vegetation' [HNTC, NTC, TH]: suitable vegetation.

QUESTION—To whom does δι' οὓς 'for the benefit of whom' refer?

1. It refers to the owners of the field and implies that the cultivators are working for the benefit of those owners [Alf, EGT, Lg, Lns, My, NIGTC; NAB, NASB, NIV, NJB, NRSV, TEV] or the intended consumers of the crop [EGT]: useful for those for whom the field is cultivated. The spiritual reference is to God and Christ [My].
2. It refers to those who cultivate the soil [TH; CEV, KJV, NJB, NLT, REB, TNT]: useful for those who cultivate the field.
3. It refers to both cultivators and owners [EBC, Mil, TNTC, Wst].

receives/shares-in[a] blessing[b] from[c] God;

LEXICON—a. pres. act. indic. of μεταλαμβάνω (LN **90.63**) (BAGD 1. p. 511): 'to receive' [BAGD, HNTC, Mil; KJV, NAB, NASB, NIV, NJB, NRSV, REB], 'to share' [WBC], 'to share in' [BAGD], 'to have a share in' [NIC], 'to partake of' [Lns], 'to experience' [LN], 'to have' [NLT]. This entire phrase is translated 'God blesses' [TEV, TNT], 'God will bless that field' [CEV].

b. εὐλογία (LN 33.356, 33.470) (BAGD 5. p. 323): 'blessing' [HNTC, LN (33.370), Lns, NIC, WBC; all versions except CEV, TEV, TNT], 'praise' [LN (33.356)], 'rich bounty' [BAGD]. This singular noun is translated as a plural: 'blessings' [Mil]. This refers to God's general blessing on creation, not a special blessing [HNTC]; the blessing is the continual rain [NTC]; it is increased fruitfulness [Blm, Wst].

c. ἀπό with genitive object (LN 90.7, 90.15): 'from' [HNTC, LN (90.15), Lns, Mil, WBC; KJV, NASB, NRSV, REB], 'of' [NAB, NIV, NLT], 'by' [LN (90.7)], not explicit [CEV, TEV, TNT]. The phrase ἀπὸ τοῦ θεοῦ 'from God' is translated as a possessive: 'God's' [NJB]; as the subject of the verb 'to bless' [CEV, TEV, TNT].

QUESTION—What is meant by μεταλαμβάνει 'receive/share in'?

1. It means to receive [Alf, BAGD, Blm, EBC, EGT, HNTC, Hu, Hwt, Lns, Mil, NCBC, NIGTC, NTC, TH, TNTC; all versions].
2. It means to share with others [BAGD, Lg(K), My, NIC, WBC, Wst].

6:8 but bearing[a] thorns and thistles, (it is) rejected[b] and near[c] (a) curse,[d]

LEXICON—a. pres. act. participle of ἐκφέρω (LN **23.194**) (BAGD 3. p. 246): 'to bear' [Mil; KJV, NAB, NLT, REB], 'to bring forth' [NIC], 'to produce' [BAGD, HNTC, Lns, WBC; CEV, NIV, NRSV, TNT], 'to yield' [NASB], 'to grow' [LN; NJB, TEV].

b. ἀδόκιμος (LN **65.13**) (BAGD p. 18): 'rejected' [Lns, Mil; KJV], 'disapproved' [Mil], 'worthless' [BAGD, HNTC, NIC; all versions except KJV, NLT, TEV], 'worth nothing' [**LN**; TEV], 'valueless' [LN], 'of no value' [LN], 'useless' [WBC; NLT]. It means unfit for cultivation [Blm].

c. ἐγγύς (LN 67.61, 83.26) (BAGD 3. p. 214): 'near' [LN], 'near to' [Mil], 'nigh' [Lns], 'under' [Mil]. The phrase κατάρας ἐγγύς 'near a curse' is translated 'a curse hangs over it' [HNTC, WBC; REB], 'soon cursed' [NAB], 'in danger of being cursed' [NIV], 'close to being cursed' [BAGD; NASB], 'near to being cursed' [NJB], 'on the verge of being cursed' [NRSV], 'on the point of being cursed' [NIC], 'nigh unto cursing' [KJV], 'almost cursed' [BAGD], 'in danger of being cursed by God' [TEV], 'likely to fall under God's curse' [CEV], 'under God's curse' [TNT], 'the farmer will condemn that field' [NLT]. This phrase expands the implication of ἀδόκιμος 'rejected' [Blm, My].

d. κατάρα (LN 33.474) (BAGD p. 417): 'curse' [HNTC, Lns, Mil, WBC; CEV, NIV, REB, TNT], 'cursed' [BAGD, LN], 'accursed' [LN], 'cursing'

[KJV]. This noun is also translated as a verb: 'to be cursed' [BAGD, NIC; NAB, NASB, NJB, NRSV, TEV], 'to condemn' [NLT].

QUESTION—How is this phrase related to the preceding verse?

1. It refers to the same field as the preceding verse [Alf, EBC, HNTC, Lns, Mil, My(D), NIGTC, WBC; NAB, NASB, NRSV, REB, TEV, TNT].
2. It refers to a different part of the same field [NTC].
3. It refers to a different field [Blm, Hwt, NIC; CEV, KJV, NIV, NJB, NLT].

QUESTION—What relationship is indicated by the participle ἐκφέρουσα 'bearing'?

1. It is attributive, describing the field referred to [Blm; CEV, KJV, NIV, NJB]: which bears thorns.
2. It is conditional [Alf, EGT, Hu, Mil, NCBC, TH, Wst; NAB, NASB, NLT, NRSV, REB, TEV, TNT]: if it bears thorns.
3. It is temporal [Lg(K)]: while it bears thorns.

QUESTION—What is implied by ἐγγύς 'near'?

1. It means not yet, but certain to occur [EBC, EGT, GNC, HNTC, Hu, Hwt, ICC, Lns, NIGTC, Wst].
2. It softens the meaning, implying that the threat is present but the fate may still be avoided [Alf, My, TH, TNTC].

of-which the end[a] (is) for[b] burning.[c]

LEXICON—a. τέλος (LN 67.66, 89.40) (BAGD 1.c. p. 811): 'end' [BAGD, HNTC, LN (67.66, 89.40), Lns, Mil; CEV, KJV, NRSV], 'outcome' [LN (89.40)], 'result' [LN (89.40)]. This entire phrase is translated 'and finally is burned' [NAB], 'and it ends up being burned' [NASB], 'in the end it will be burned' [NIV], 'in the end it will be burned over' [WBC], 'it will end by being burnt' [NJB], 'it ends by being burnt' [REB], 'and will at last be burned' [NIC], 'and will be destroyed by fire' [TEV], 'and will finish in flames' [TNT], '(the farmer) will burn it' [NLT].

b. εἰς with accusative object (LN 78.51, 89.48): 'for' [Lns], 'to the point of' [LN (78.51)], 'as a result' [LN (89.48)]. The phrase εἰς καῦσιν 'for burning' is translated 'burning' [HNTC], 'to be burned' [Mil; KJV], 'to be burned over' [NRSV], 'to be set on fire' [CEV], 'to burn' [NLT]. This word expresses result [Mil]. The phrase εἰς καῦσιν 'for burning' is equivalent to καῦσις 'burning' [EGT].

c. καῦσις (LN **14.63**) (BAGD p. 425): 'burning' [BAGD, HNTC, LN, Lns] 'burned over' [BAGD].

QUESTION—To what does ἧς 'which' refer?

It refers to γῆ 'land' in 6:7 [Alf, EGT, HNTC, Lns, Mil, My, NIGTC, Wst]: the outcome of the land is for burning.

QUESTION—To what does καῦσιν 'burning' refer?

1. It refers to destruction [Alf, EBC, EGT, GNC, Hu, Hwt, ICC, Lg, Lns, My, NCBC, NIC, NIGTC, WBC, Wst; TEV]. The land will never bear crops and so the thorns are kept down by burning [NIC].

2. It refers to burning off the thorns and making the land suitable for cultivation [Blm, HNTC, NTC].

DISCOURSE UNIT: 6:9–20 [Hwt; NASB, NJB]. The topic is comfort and hope based on God's promise [Hwt], words of hope and encouragement [NJB], better things for the believers [NASB].

DISCOURSE UNIT: 6:9–12 [EBC, HNTC, Lg, NIC]. The topic is an exhortation to persevere [EBC, NIC], the hope of an inheritance [HNTC, Lg].

6:9 But we-are-persuaded[a] concerning[b] you, beloved-ones, the better-things and holding[c] salvation,

LEXICON—a. perf. pass. indic. of πείθω (LN 33.301) (BAGD 4. p. 640): 'to be persuaded' [LN, Lns, Mil; KJV, NAB], 'to be convinced' [BAGD, LN, NIC; NASB, REB], 'to be confident' [HNTC; NIV, NLT, NRSV], 'to feel sure' [TEV], 'to be sure' [CEV, NJB], 'to remain sure' [WBC], 'to have no doubt' [TNT]. It implies certainty [EBC], conviction that the readers are genuine in their faith [Hwt], that they will not fall into the negative results warned against [Lg]; it implies only a good hope [Blm]. It is emphatic by its position [TNTC]. The perfect tense of this verb implies a state resulting from having become persuaded [Lns, Mil, NIGTC, TNTC], the result of conviction by proof [Alf], that the author has overcome previous doubts [EGT, Wst]. The first person plural 'we' refers only to the author and means 'I' [EBC, EGT, Hu, ICC, Lg, NIGTC, NTC, TH]; it includes others as well as the writer [Lns].

b. περί with genitive object (LN 89.6): 'concerning' [LN, Lns; NASB], 'about' [TEV, TNT], 'with regard to' [LN], 'in regard to' [NAB], 'in relation to' [LN], 'of' [KJV], not explicit [CEV]. The phrase περὶ ὑμῶν 'concerning you' is translated 'in your regard' [NAB], 'in your case' [HNTC, Mil, WBC; NIV, NRSV], 'that you are meant for' [NLT]. This phrase is emphatic by word order [EGT, My]. The phrase περὶ ὑμῶν τὰ κρείσσονα 'concerning you the better things' is translated 'you are in a better state' [NJB, REB], 'that you are in a better condition' [NIC].

c. pres. mid. participle of ἔχω (LN 18.6, 90.51) (BAGD III.1. p. 334): 'to hold' [LN (18.6)], 'to belong to' [BAGD; NRSV, TEV], 'to accompany' [Mil, WBC; KJV, NASB, NIV], 'to go along with' [NIC], 'to come with' [NLT], 'to be connected with' [HNTC], 'to be in keeping with' [Lns], 'to point to' [NAB], 'to be on the way to' [NJB], 'to make for' [REB], 'to lead to' [TNT], 'to produce' [LN (90.51)], 'that people do when . . .' [CEV]. It means to hold close to [Lns, NTC, TNTC], to be connected with [Blm, My], to attain to [My], to belong to [Lg, Mil, NIGTC] or to obtain [NIGTC], to partake of the nature of [Alf], to accompany [EBC, Lg, Wst], to pertain to and promote[ICC].

QUESTION—What relationship is indicated by δέ 'but'?

The introductory δέ indicates a contrast with the preceding comments [NIGTC]. It is an affectionate encouragement and shows that he does not consider that his readers have committed apostasy [EGT, Mil, NIC, NTC, TNTC, Wst]. It softens the effect of the preceding warning and indicates that the author has good hope for his readers [Blm, EBC, My], assuring them that they are to receive better things that relate to their salvation [NTC]. He does not believe they will fall away [EBC, GNC]; he is confident of them [NCBC] that they are firm in the faith, although there are spiritual dangers [Hu]; he is deeply concerned for them but has good hope [ICC].

QUESTION—What is the function of ἀγαπητοί 'beloved'?

It indicates affection [HNTC, Hu, ICC, Lns, Mil, NCBC, TNTC, Wst] and confidence [Hu], the author's tender concern for his readers [EBC, EGT, GNC] and reassurance [EGT] that he does not intend to cause his readers to despair [Hwt]. It softens the severity of the preceding warning [WBC, Wst].

QUESTION—What is meant by τὰ κρείσσονα 'the better things'?

It refers to the better outcome [Alf], a fruitful spiritual life [Hwt], God's blessings and promises [NIGTC], better than the negative prospects just previously mentioned [EBC, EGT, My] and that their condition is better than the comparison to the field just mentioned [My]. It is better in contrast with the apostates mentioned [TNTC]. The definite article implies the better of two opposite courses of action [Alf]; it refers κρείσσονα 'better' back to the good produce mentioned in 6:7 [NIGTC, WBC]. These 'better things' will be identified in 6:10 [Mil].

QUESTION—What relationship is indicated by καί 'and'?

It introduces an explanation of τὰ κρείσσονα 'the better things' [ICC, My(D), WBC; CEV, NIV, NLT]: the better things; that is, the things that accompany salvation. The definite article τά 'the' preceding κρείσσονα 'better things' governs ἐχόμενα 'holding' also [Lg(K), Lns, My(D)]: the things which are better and pertain to salvation.

even though/if even we-speak thus.

QUESTION—What is the meaning of this clause?

It expresses a concession to what precedes [Mil]: in spite of what we have said.

QUESTION—What is indicated by the present tense of λαλοῦμεν 'we speak'?

It refers to habitual speaking [Alf].

6:10 For God (is) not unjust,[a] to-forget[b] your work[c] and the love which you-have-shown[d] for[e] his name,[f]

TEXT—Some manuscripts add τοῦ κόπου 'the labor' before τῆς ἀγάπης 'the love', giving the rendering 'the labor of the love'. GNT does not deal with this variant. Only Blm and KJV add 'the labor'.

LEXICON—a. ἄδικος (LN 88.20) (BAGD 1, p. 18): 'unjust' [BAGD, HNTC, LN, Mil, WBC; NAB, NASB, NIV, NJB, NRSV, REB, TNT], 'unrighteous' [LN, Lns, NIC; KJV], 'unfair' [NLT, TEV]. The negative phrase 'not unjust' is translated 'always fair' [CEV]. This word has the sense of being unmerciful [Blm].

b. aorist mid. (deponent = act.) infin. of ἐπιλανθάνομαι (LN 29.14, 29.17) (BAGD 2, p. 295): 'to forget' [HNTC, LN (29.14), Lns, Mil, NIC; all versions except CEV, NRSV], 'not to recall' [LN (29.14)], 'to neglect' [BAGD, LN (29.17)], 'to overlook' [BAGD, LN (29.17), WBC; NRSV], 'to care nothing about' [BAGD], 'to forget to do' [LN (29.17)]. This word is also translated positively: 'he will remember' [CEV]. The aorist tense refers to the forgetfulness considered as a whole [Alf], as a fact [Lg, My].

c. ἔργον (LN 42.42) (BAGD 1.c. b. p. 308): 'work' [HNTC, LN, Lns, Mil, NIC, WBC; KJV, NAB, NASB, NIV, NRSV, TEV, TNT], 'deed' [BAGD], 'accomplishment' [BAGD], not explicit [CEV]. The collective singular is used for the plural [BAGD]. The phrase τοῦ ἔργου ὑμῶν 'your work' is translated 'all you have done' [NJB], 'what you have done' [REB], 'how hard you have worked' [NLT]. The reference is to deeds of kindness, the singular considering these deeds as a whole [NIGTC], to Christian activities [EGT, Mil], to obedient Christian life as a whole [Alf, Lg].

d. aorist mid. indic. of ἐνδείκνυμι (LN 28.51) (BAGD 1. p. 262): 'to show' [BAGD, HNTC, LN, Mil; all versions except NJB, REB], 'to demonstrate' [LN, WBC], 'to display' [Lns, NIC], 'to have' [NJB]. The phrase καὶ τῆς ἀγάπης ἧς ἐνεδείξασθε 'and the love which you have shown' is translated 'what you have done for love' [REB]. The middle voice implies personal involvement [Alf].

e. εἰς with accusative object (LN 90.23): 'for' [HNTC, Lns, NIC; NJB, NLT, NRSV, TEV, TNT], 'concerning' [LN], 'with regard to' [WBC], 'toward' [KJV, NASB], 'for (love) of' [REB], 'for his sake' [Mil; NRSV], not explicit [CEV, NAB, NIV].

f. ὄνομα (LN 9.19, 33.126) (BAGD I.4.c.β. p. 572): 'name' [HNTC, LN (33.126), Lns, Mil, NIC; KJV, NASB, NJB, REB], 'person' [LN (9.19)], 'him' [BAGD, WBC; NAB, NIV, NLT, TEV, TNT], not explicit [CEV]. The phrase εἰς τὸ ὄνομα αὐτοῦ 'for his name' is translated 'for his sake' [BAGD; NRSV].

QUESTION—What relationship is indicated by γάρ 'for'?

It introduces the reasons for the author's good hope for his readers [Blm, EBC, ICC, Lg, Lns, Mil, My, NIGTC, TNTC], based on God's righteous character [Blm, EBC, Hwt, Lg, Lns, Mil, My, TNTC], and the readers' deeds [Blm, Hwt, ICC, Lg, TNTC]. The double negative οὐ . . . ἄδικος 'not unrighteous' comprises an emphatic positive, 'he is very righteous' [NIGTC]

QUESTION—What relationship is indicated by the infinitive form ἐπιλαθέσθαι 'to forget' ?

1. It states the way in which the unrighteousness would be shown [Alf, HNTC; NASB, NJB], the conceived result of the unrighteousness [Blm, ICC], the explanation of the unrighteousness [NIGTC]: he is not unrighteous, so that he would forget.
2. It states the degree of the negated unrighteousness [Mil; NJB, REB]: he is not so unrighteous as to forget.

QUESTION—To what does ἧς 'which' refer?

It refers to ἀγάπης 'love' [EBC, EGT, ICC, Mil, NTC, TNTC, Wst; NJB, TEV, TNT]: the love which you have shown.

QUESTION—What relationship is indicated by the prepositional phrase εἰς τὸ ὄνομα αὐτοῦ 'for his name'?

1. It indicates the object of the love.

1.1 God's name is the beneficiary [HNTC, Lg, Lns, My, NIC; NJB, REB]: love for his name. God's name means God himself as he reveals himself [Lns].

1.2 God's benefit is the object [Hu; NRSV]: love for his sake.

2. It indicates reference.

2.1 To his name [Alf; KJV, NASB]: with reference to his name.

2.2 To him [WBC; TNT]: with reference to him. It is the equivalent of 'him' [EBC, GNC, HNTC, TH, TNTC; NAB, NIV, NLT, TEV]: which you have shown him.

having-ministered[a] to-the saints[b] and ministering.[c]

LEXICON—a. aorist act. participle of διακονέω (LN 35.19, 35.37) (BAGD 4. p. 184): 'to minister' [Lns, Mil; KJV, NASB], 'to serve' [LN (35.19), NIC, WBC; NRSV], 'to render service' [REB], 'to help' [BAGD; CEV, NIV], 'to take care of' [LN (35.37)], 'to care for' [NLT], 'to support' [BAGD]. The phrase διακονήσαντες καὶ διακονοῦντες 'having ministered and ministering' is translated 'by your service, past and present' [NAB], 'in your past and present service' [TNT], 'by your past service and indeed by your present service' [HNTC], 'in the help you gave and are still giving' [TEV], 'or the services you have done, and are still doing' [NJB]. The reference is to practical actions [NIGTC].

b. ἅγιος (LN 11.27, 88.24) (BAGD 2.d.β p. 10): 'holy' [LN (88.24)]; in the plural: 'saints' [BAGD, HNTC, Lns, Mil; KJV, NASB, NRSV], 'holy people' [NIC; NAB], 'his people' [LN (11.27); CEV, NIV, TNT], 'holy people of God' [NJB], 'Christians' [NLT, TEV].

c. pres. act. participle of διακονέω: 'to minister'. See this word in a. above.

QUESTION—What relationship is indicated by the participial forms διακονήσαντες 'having ministered' and διακονοῦντες 'ministering'?

The aorist participle 'having ministered' refers to past service [Alf, EBC, GNC, HNTC, Hu, Lns, Mil, My, NIC, NTC, TH, WBC; all versions except NRSV, REB]; the present participle 'ministering' refers to present service [Alf, EBC, GNC, HNTC, Hu, Lns, Mil, My, NIC, NTC, TH, WBC; all versions].

1. They indicate the means by which their love has been shown [HNTC, Lns; NAB, NLT]: the love you have shown by ministering.

2. They indicate the manifestation of their love [Mil; NASB, NRSV, REB, TEV, TNT]: the love you have shown, which consists in ministering.

3. They indicate an attendant circumstance of showing their love [WBC; NIV]: the love you have shown as you minister.

4. They are parallel to 'work' and 'love' [NJB]: your work, your love, and your services.

6:11 But we-desire[a] each of-you to-show[b] the same diligence[c] with-regard-to/for-the-purpose-of[d] the full-assurance/realization[e] of-the hope[f] to[g] (the) end.

LEXICON—a. pres. act. indic. of ἐπιθυμέω (LN **25.12**) (BAGD p. 293): 'to desire' [BAGD, Lns, Mil; KJV, NASB], 'to desire very much' [**LN**], 'to wish' [CEV], 'to be eager' [TNT], 'to long' [HNTC], 'to long for' [BAGD, LN], 'to want' [WBC; NIV, NRSV], 'to like dearly' [REB]. This verb is also translated as a phrase: 'our desire is that' [NIC; NAB, NJB], 'our great desire is that' [NLT, TEV]. This word reflects the writer's affection for his readers [ICC, Mil, NIC]. The first person plural 'we' refers only to the author [NIGTC, NTC, TH]; it includes Christians in general [TNTC].

b. pres. mid. infin. of ἐνδείκνυμι (LN 28.51) (BAGD 1. p. 262): 'to show' [BAGD, HNTC, LN, Mil; all versions except NLT, TEV], 'to demonstrate' [BAGD, LN, WBC], 'to display' [Lns, NIC], 'to keep up' [TEV]. The phrase τὴν αὐτὴν ἐνδείκνυσθαι 'to show the same diligence' is translated 'to keep right on loving others' [NLT]. The present tense indicates continuous action [GNC, Lns, Mil; NJB, TNT].

c. σπουδή (LN 25.74) (BAGD 2. p. 763): 'diligence' [BAGD, Lns, Mil; KJV, NASB, NIV, NRSV], 'earnestness' [BAGD], 'earnest concern' [WBC], 'eagerness' [BAGD, HNTC, LN, NIC; TEV], 'zeal' [Mil; NAB, TNT], 'enthusiasm' [NJB], 'keenness' [REB], 'devotion' [LN]. This noun is also translated as a verb: 'to be eager' [CEV]. It indicates diligent action [NIGTC].

d. πρός with accusative object (LN 78.51, 89.7, 89.60) (BAGD III.5.b. p. 710): 'with regard to' [BAGD, LN (89.7); WBC], 'for the purpose of' [LN (89.60)], 'in order to' [NLT], 'as far as . . . is concerned' [BAGD], 'to' [KJV], 'unto' [Lns], 'for' [NIC], 'so as to realize' [Mil; NASB, NRSV], 'to the point of' [LN (78.51)], not explicit [CEV]. The phrase πρὸς τὴν πληροφορίαν 'toward the full assurance' is translated 'in order to make sure' [NIV], 'fully assured' [NAB]. The phrase πρὸς τὴν πληροφορίαν τῆς ἐλπίδος 'with regard to the full assurance of the hope' is translated 'until your hope is fully realized' [REB], 'so that the things you hope for will come true' [TEV]. The phrase πρὸς τὴν πληροφορίαν τῆς ἐλπίδος ἄχρι τέλους 'with regard to the full assurance of the hope up to the end' is translated 'for the full and final realization of your hope' [HNTC], 'till the ultimate fulfillment of your hope' [NJB]. This preposition indicates purpose [Mil], action directed toward an object [NIGTC].

e. πληροφορία (LN 31.45) (BAGD p. 670): 'full assurance' [BAGD, Lns, Mil; KJV, NASB, NRSV], 'realization' [HNTC, WBC], 'full conviction' [BAGD], 'certainty' [BAGD], 'complete certainty' [LN], 'fulfillment'

[NIV, NJB], 'how strong' [CEV], 'to make certain . . . will come true' [NLT].

f. ἐλπίς (LN 25.61, 25.62) (BAGD 2.b. p. 253): 'hope' [BAGD, HNTC, LN, Lns, Mil, NIC, WBC; all versions except NAB, NLT, TEV], 'that which is hoped for' [LN (25.61)], 'what is hoped for' [LN (25.61); NLT], 'that for which you hope' [NAB], 'the things you hope for' [TEV], 'the basis for hope' [LN (25.62)], 'the reason for hope' [LN (25.62)]. It refers to what is hoped for [NIGTC, TH], which is what God has promised [NIGTC]. The definite article with this noun here indicates the Christian hope of glory [Lns].

g. ἄχρι with genitive object (LN 67.119) (BAGD 1.a p. 128): 'to' [BAGD, Lns; NIV, NRSV, REB, TEV], 'unto' [KJV], 'right on to' [NIC], 'until' [BAGD, LN, Mil, WBC; NASB], 'till' [NAB], 'as long as life lasts' [NLT], 'how lasting' [CEV]. It indicates time [Mil].

QUESTION—What relationship is indicated by δέ 'but'?

1. It indicates contrast [Alf, EGT, NIGTC, WBC; REB]: but. Paul introduces a slight reproof in contrast with the preceding encouraging comment [Alf]. Some have shown the zeal that Paul desires, but he desires that each individual have such a zeal [EGT]. The author gives a warning not because he believes they are already under the curse, but to encourage them to hold to their faith to the end [NIGTC].
2. It indicates a transition in the thought [Mil, My; KJV, NASB, NRSV, and probably CEV, NAB, NIV, NLT, TEV, TNT which do not translate this word]: and.

QUESTION—What is indicated by ἕκαστον ὑμῶν 'each of you'?

It emphasizes the individuals [EBC, HNTC, Hu, Lns, Mil, My, NTC, Wst] in contrast with the body of believers as a whole [EGT]: each one of you. No one of them is excluded [EBC, Lns]. It also indicates the writer's affection [ICC, My]. It does not imply a division in the group [NIGTC].

QUESTION—What is meant by τὴν αὐτὴν σπουδήν 'the same diligence'?

1. It means the same diligence regarding their hope that they have shown in the past [EBC, Hu, WBC] in their love by ministering to the saints [Alf, Blm, EGT, ICC, Lg, Lns, My, NCBC, TH, Wst] and in their love for God's name [Lns].
2. It means that each person should show equal diligence in ministering in love to the saints [NTC].

QUESTION—What is meant by πληροφορίαν 'full assurance'?

1. It refers to full assurance [Alf, Blm, GNC, Hu, Hwt, Lg, Lns, Mil, My, NTC, Wst; KJV, NAB, NASB, NRSV].
2. It refers to full development [EBC, EGT, HNTC, ICC, NCBC, NIC].
3. It includes both of the above, but with full development more prominent here [NIGTC].

QUESTION—What is meant by the genitive construction τὴν πληροφορίαν τῆς ἐλπίδος 'the full assurance of the hope'?

It refers to the hope becoming fully possessed [NIGTC]. The implication is that this assurance was lacking [TNTC].

QUESTION—What is the phrase ἄχρι τέλους 'up to the end' connected with?

This phrase is emphatic by its position [NIGTC, TH].

1. It refers to showing the same diligence [EBC, EGT, Lns, Mil, NTC; NAB, NIV, REB, TEV]: to show the same diligence to the end.
2. It refers to the fulfillment of the hope [EGT, My, TH]: the fulfillment of the hope until the end.
3. It is connected with the entire sentence [Alf]: we desire that you should do this to the end.

QUESTION—What is meant by τέλους 'end'?

1. It is the end of the life of each one [Lns].
2. It is the return of the Lord [Alf, My, WBC].
3. It is the end of the period of trial and discipline [Wst].
4. It refers to the time when the hope had completed its work [EGT].

6:12 in-order-that/so-that not you-may-become sluggish,[a] but imitators[b] of-the-(ones) through[c] faith and patience[d] inheriting[e] the promises.

LEXICON—a. νωθρός (LN **88.249**) (BAGD p. 547): 'sluggish' [BAGD, HNTC, Lns, Mil, NIC, WBC; NASB, NRSV], 'lazy' [BAGD, LN; CEV, NAB, NIV, TEV], 'slothful' [KJV], 'lax' [REB], 'careless' [NJB], 'spiritually dull and indifferent' [NLT]. The phrase ἵνα μὴ νωθροὶ γένησθε 'in order that you may not become lazy' is translated 'and that you should never slack off' [TNT]. This word is in contrast with σπουδήν 'diligence' in 6:11 [NIGTC, TH, TNTC].

b. μιμητής (LN 41.45) (BAGD 1. p. 522): 'imitator' [BAGD, HNTC, LN, Lns, Mil, WBC; NASB, NRSV], 'follower' [KJV]. This noun is also translated as a verb phrase: 'to imitate' [NIC; NAB, NIV, REB], 'to take as one's model' [NJB], 'to be like' [TEV, TNT], 'to follow the example of' [CEV, NLT]. This word implies more than merely being followers [EBC].

c. διά with genitive object (LN 89.76): 'through' [HNTC, LN, Lns, Mil, NIC; all versions except NJB, TEV], 'by' [LN; NJB], 'by means of' [LN], 'with' [WBC], 'because of' [NLT]. The phrase διὰ πίστεως καὶ μακροθυμίας 'through faith and patience' is translated 'who believe and are patient' [TEV], 'who had faith and were patient' [CEV]. It indicates means [Mil].

d. μακροθυμία (LN **25.167**) (BAGD 1. p. 488): 'patience' [HNTC, LN, Mil; all versions except CEV, NJB, TEV], 'steadfastness' [BAGD; NIC], 'steadfast endurance' [WBC], 'perseverance' [NJB], 'long-suffering' [Lns]. This noun is also translated as a verb phrase: 'to be patient' [CEV, TEV].

e. pres. act. participle of κληρονομέω (LN **57.131**) (BAGD 2. p. 434): 'to inherit' [HNTC, Lns, Mil, NIC, WBC; KJV, NAB, NASB, NIV, NLT, NRSV], 'to receive' [**LN**], 'to acquire' [BAGD], 'to obtain' [BAGD], 'to gain possession of' [LN], 'to come into possession of' [BAGD], 'to be given' [LN], 'to be heirs of' [NJB]. The phrase τῶν κληρονομούντων τὰς ἐπαγγελίας 'the ones inheriting the promises' is translated 'those who receive the promised inheritance' [REB], 'those who receive what God has promised' [TEV], 'those who are now taking possession of God's promises' [TNT], 'until God kept his promise to them' [CEV]. The meaning is to have possession, without specifying the means [EBC]. The present tense implies continuation [Lg], repetition [Lns], during many generations [NIGTC]; it refers to inheriting at any time [Alf, HNTC, Hu, My; KJV, NASB, NIV, NRSV, REB, TEV]; it indicates status [Alf]; it refers to inheriting at present [EGT, Lg, Lns, Mil, NIC; NAB, TNT].

QUESTION—What relationship is indicated by ἵνα 'in order that, so that'?

1. It indicates purpose [EBC, HNTC, ICC, Lns, Mil, WBC, Wst; NRSV]: we desire that each of you show diligence so that you may not become lazy.
2. It indicates result [NIGTC; CEV, NLT]: we desire that each of you show diligence; then you will not become lazy.
3. It expresses the writer's desire [NIV, REB, TEV], the continuation of his desire [NJB, TNT]: we don't want you to become lazy, but to imitate . . .
4. It indicates an additional exhortation [NAB]: don't grow lazy, but imitate . . .

QUESTION—What relationship is indicated by δέ 'but'?

It introduces a strong contrast to what precedes [Alf, Mil, TH, WBC]: not lazy, but instead imitators.

QUESTION—What is the implied object of πίστεως 'faith'?

The object is God [EBC]: faith in God.

QUESTION—What is meant by κληρονομούντων τὰς ἐπαγγελίας 'inheriting the promises?

It means receiving what was promised, not receiving the words of the promises [Blm, EGT, Hwt, ICC, Lg, Lns, My, NIC, TH, Wst; REB, TEV]. It refers to the OT saints [Blm, Hu, Hwt, NIC, NIGTC, NTC, TNTC, Wst], including Abraham [Alf, NIGTC, NTC], Christians [EBC, HNTC, Lns, NTC, TNTC, Wst], saints of all times [Alf, Blm, EGT].

DISCOURSE UNIT: 6:13–20 [EBC, GNC, GNT, HNTC, NCBC, NIC, NIGTC, NTC, WBC; CEV, NIV, NLT, TEV]. The topic is the certainty of God's promise [EBC, GNT, NIC; CEV, NIV, TEV], holding on to God's promise [NTC], the promise and the oath [HNTC, NCBC, NIGTC], the unchangeability of God's purpose [GNC], the basis for confidence [WBC], God's promise bringing hope [NLT].

DISCOURSE UNIT: 6:13–15 [Lg, NTC]. The topic is the promise given to Abraham [NTC], Abraham's example [Lg].

6:13 For God having-promised to Abraham,

QUESTION—What relationship is indicated by γάρ 'for'?

1. It indicates the grounds for the preceding statement [Mil, My]: endurance leads to receiving the promised blessings since this is proved in Abraham's case.
2. It introduces an expansion of the discussion of the certainty of God's promises [Blm, GNC]. It connects the statement in 6:12 with the example of Abraham [NIGTC; NLT].

QUESTION—What relationship is indicated by the aorist participle ἐπαγγειλάμενος 'having promised'?

1. It is temporal and relates to the same time as the verb ὤμοσεν 'he swore' [Alf, Lg(K), Mil, NIGTC, NTC, WBC]: when he promised, he swore. The promise and the oath occur together [NIGTC].
2. It relates to time preceding ὤμοσεν 'he swore' [Lg, My, Wst]: after he promised, he swore.

since by[a] no-one greater he-had to-swear,[b] he-swore by himself

LEXICON—a. κατά with genitive object (LN 90.29) (BAGD I.2.a. p. 405): 'by' [BAGD, HNTC, LN, Lns, Mil, NIC, WBC; all versions except CEV, TEV], 'in the name of' [LN], not explicit [CEV, TEV].

b. aorist act. infin. of ὀμνύω (LN 33.463) (BAGD p. 566): 'to swear' [BAGD, LN, NIC, WBC; all versions except CEV, NLT, TEV], 'to make a vow' [TEV], 'to make an oath' [LN], 'to take an oath' [BAGD; NLT], 'to make a promise' [CEV].

QUESTION—What relationship is indicated by ἐπεί 'since'?

It indicates the reason why God swore by himself [Mil].

QUESTION—What is meant by this phrase?

It means that God pledged his deity to fulfill his promise [Blm], that God could as soon cease to exist as fail to fulfill his promise [EGT]. The oath added fuller assurance, even though God's word is certain in itself [Hwt].

6:14 saying, "If indeed[a] blessing I-will-bless you and multiplying[b] I-will-multiply[c] you;"

LEXICON—a. εἰ μήν (LN **91.8**) (BAGD p. 220): 'certainly' [BAGD, **LN**], 'surely' [BAGD, LN, Lns; KJV, NLT], 'truly' [NIC], 'yes' [WBC]. The phrase εἰ μὴν εὐλογῶν εὐλογήσω σε 'if indeed blessing I will bless you' is translated 'I will indeed bless you' [HNTC; NAB], 'surely I will bless you' [Mil], 'I will surely bless you' [NASB, NIV, NRSV], 'I will certainly bless you' [TNT], 'yes, I will certainly bless you' [WBC], 'truly I will bless you greatly' [NIC], 'I will shower blessings on you' [NJB], 'I promise that I will bless you' [TEV], 'I vow that I will bless you abundantly' [REB], 'I, the Lord, will bless you' [CEV]. This phrase introduces the content of the oath [Mil]; it implies assurance [EGT, GNC, WBC], and μήν 'certainly' strengthens a vow [EGT]. It implies a formula such as 'if I do not (bless and multiply you) then may I not (be God)' [Mil].

b. pres. act. participle of πληθύνω (LN **59.69**) (BAGD 1.a. p. 669): 'to multiply' [HNTC, Lns; KJV, NAB, NASB]. The phrase πληθύνων πληθυνῶ σέ 'multiplying I will multiply you' is translated 'I will multiply you greatly' [NIC], 'surely I will multiply you' [Mil], 'I will surely multiply you' [BAGD; NASB, NRSV], 'I will indeed multiply you' [HNTC], 'I will multiply your descendants into countless millions' [NLT], 'I will give you many descendants' [NIV, NJB, TNT], 'I will give you numerous descendants' [WBC], 'I promise that I will give you many descendants' [TEV], 'I vow that I will multiply your descendants' [REB], 'I will cause the number of your descendants to increase' [LN], 'I will bless you with many descendants' [CEV]. It refers to having many descendants [TH].

c. fut. act. indic. of πληθύνω: 'to multiply'. See this word in b. above.

QUESTION—What relationship is indicated by the participial form λέγων 'saying'?

It is appositional to ὤμοσεν 'he swore' in 6:13, but none of the commentaries mention this point: he swore; that is, he said.

QUESTION—What relationship is implied by the two participle-plus-verb phrases, εὐλογῶν εὐλογήσω 'blessing I will bless' and πληθύνων πληθυνῶ 'multiplying I will multiply'?

It is an emphatic expression, derived from a Hebrew form [Blm, EBC, GNC, Hu, Hwt, Lns, Mil, My, NIC, NIGTC, NTC, TH, WBC, Wst], emphasizing the meaning of the verb [Lns, Mil, NIC, NIGTC, WBC] and certainty [EBC, WBC]: I will surely bless . . . I will surely multiply. Taken literally, the participles indicate means [Mil]: by blessing I will bless, by multiplying I will multiply.

6:15 and thus[a] having-been-patient[b] he-obtained[c] the promise.[d]

LEXICON—a. οὕτως (LN 61.9): 'thus' [HNTC, LN, Lns, NIC, WBC; NASB, NRSV, REB], 'so' [LN, Mil; KJV, NAB, NIV, TNT], 'in this way' [LN], 'because of that' [NJB], 'then' [CEV, NLT], not explicit [TEV]. The reference is to his being thus upheld by God's promise [EGT, Lg, Wst] and oath [EGT, Lg].

b. aor. act. participle of μακροθυμέω (LN **25.168**) (BAGD 1. p. 488): 'to be patient' [LN; TEV, TNT], 'to be very patient' [CEV], 'to remain patient' [LN], 'to have patience' [BAGD], 'to endure patiently' [Mil; KJV, NRSV], 'to wait patiently' [HNTC, **LN**; NASB, NIV, NLT], 'to show steadfastness' [NIC], 'to persevere' [NJB], 'to exercise longsuffering' [Lns]. This participle is also translated as a temporal clause: 'after patient waiting' [NAB, REB], 'after steadfast endurance' [WBC]. The reference is to the entire period following God's giving his promise [Lg(K)].

c. aor. act. indic. of ἐπιτυγχάνω (LN **57.60**) (BAGD p. 304): 'to obtain' [BAGD, HNTC, **LN**, Lns, Mil, NIC; KJV, NAB, NASB, NRSV, REB, TNT], 'to receive' [WBC; NIV, NLT, TEV], 'to receive fulfillment'

[NJB], 'to acquire' [LN], 'to be given' [CEV]. It means to get actual possession [Alf]. The aorist tense implies a single past event [TH].

d. ἐπαγγελία (LN 33.288) (BAGD 2.c. p. 280): 'promise' [BAGD, HNTC, LN, Lns, Mil, NIC, WBC; KJV, NASB, NJB, NRSV, REB], 'what was promised' [BAGD; NIV], 'what God had promised' [CEV, NAB, NLT, TEV, TNT]. It refers to the thing promised [Alf, Blm, EBC, EGT, GNC, HNTC, Lns, Mil, My, NIC, NIGTC, NTC, TH, WBC; NAB, NIV, NJB, TEV, TNT], the beginning of that fulfillment being the birth of Isaac [Alf, Blm, EBC, EGT, HNTC, My, NIGTC, NTC, Wst], his receiving back Isaac [Lg, Mil, NIC, WBC, Wst] followed by a reinforced promise of many descendants [WBC]. It refers to his receiving the oath which guaranteed fulfillment of what was promised [Lg, Mil]. It refers to his eternal salvation in Christ, which he received at his death [Lns].

QUESTION—What is οὕτως 'thus' connected with?

1. It is connected with ἐπέτυχεν 'he obtained' [Alf, Lg, Lns, My, NIGTC, Wst; CEV, KJV, NAB, NASB, NIV, NRSV, REB]: thus he obtained.
2. It is connected with μακροθυμήσας 'having been patient' [EBC; NLT, TNT]: thus he was patient.
3. It is connected with the preceding promise [NJB]: because God gave his promise and oath, he thus persevered and received.

QUESTION—What relationship is indicated by the participial form μακροθυμήσας 'having been patient'?

1. It is temporal, the aorist tense indicating an attitude prior to the leading verb [HNTC, Lns, WBC; KJV, NAB, NIV, NLT, REB]: after he had patiently endured, he obtained.
2. It indicates the reason for the leading verb [Mil, My; TEV]: because he was patient, he obtained.
3. It is parallel to the leading verb [Lg(K); NJB, TNT]: he patiently endured and obtained.

DISCOURSE UNIT: 6:16–20 [Lg; NTC]. The topic is an exhortation to hold fast to the promise [Lg], the heirs to the promises [NTC].

6:16 For men swear by[a] the greater,[b]

TEXT—Some manuscripts add μέν 'indeed' following ἄνθρωποι 'men'. GNT does not deal with this variant. Only Lg, Alf (both in brackets), and KJV add this word.

LEXICON—a. κατά with genitive object: 'by'. See this word in 6:13.

b. μείζων (LN 87.28): 'greater' [LN, Lns; KJV], 'one who is greater than themselves' [TNT], 'one greater than themselves' [HNTC; NASB], 'the one greater than themselves' [Mil], 'someone greater than themselves' [WBC; NAB, NIV, NLT, NRSV], 'someone greater than ourselves' [TEV], 'something greater than themselves' [NJB], 'the name of someone or something greater than themselves' [CEV], 'what is greater than themselves' [NIC; REB]. This word is masculine [Alf, Blm, EBC, EGT, Hwt, Mil, My, NTC, TNTC, Wst; NAB, NASB, NIV, NRSV, TEV,

TNT]; it refers to God [Alf, Blm, GNC, HNTC, Hu, Hwt, ICC, Lns, My, NCBC], who could punish any falsehood [Blm, EBC]; it refers to someone greater than the person taking the oath, someone of truth and power who could enforce it [EGT]. It is neuter or general [NJB, REB].

QUESTION—What relationship is indicated by γάρ 'for'?

It indicates the reason for and the purpose of (the grounds of [Mil]) the divine oath [Hwt, Lg, Mil], the grounds for the comment in 6:13 [My]. It introduces a comparison between swearing by men and by God [TH].

QUESTION—What is implied by ἄνθρωποι 'men'?

It is emphatic by word order [Alf]. This noun without the definite article refers to men as to their nature [Wst].

and for-them the oath (is) (the) end[a] of-all contradiction[b] for[c] confirmation;[d]

LEXICON—a. πέρας (LN **61.15**) (BAGD 2. p. 644): 'end' [BAGD, LN, Lns, Mil, NIC, WBC; all versions except REB, TEV], 'conclusion' [**LN**]. 'beyond the reach of' [HNTC]. This entire phrase is translated 'and the vow settles all arguments' [TEV], 'when anyone wants to settle an argument' [CEV], 'and making a statement on oath sets a limit to what can be called in question' [REB], 'and without question that oath is binding' [NLT], 'and in all their disputes, an oath constitutes the conclusion for establishing (evidence)' [LN]. This word is emphatic by its position [NIGTC].

b. ἀντιλογία (LN **33.445**, 33.456) (BAGD 1. p. 75): 'contradiction' [BAGD, LN], 'contradictory statements' [LN (33.445)], 'contrary statement' [Lns], 'dispute' [BAGD, HNTC, **LN (33.445)**, Mil, NIC; NASB, NJB, NRSV, TNT], 'argument' [WBC; CEV, NAB, NIV, TEV], 'strife' [KJV]. It refers to contradiction [Alf, Blm, EGT, Lg, My, Wst], dispute or quarrel [ICC, NIGTC].

c. εἰς with accusative object (LN 89.57): 'for' [KJV], 'for the purpose of' [LN, Mil], 'for purposes of' [NIC], 'as' [NASB, NRSV], 'serves as' [WBC], not explicit [NJB].

d. βεβαίωσις (LN **28.44**) (BAGD p. 138): 'confirmation' [BAGD, Mil, WBC; KJV, NASB, NJB, NRSV], 'validation' [NIC]. The phrase εἰς βεβαίωσιν 'for confirmation' is translated 'gives firmness' [NAB], 'gives an assurance' [TNT], 'provides a confirmation' [HNTC], 'confirms what is said' [NIV], 'by making known that something is true and certain' [LN], 'as far as making a thing firm is concerned' [Lns].

QUESTION—What is meant by this phrase?

It means that an oath confirms the matter under discussion and brings agreement by all parties involved [Alf, EGT, Lns, NTC, TH, WBC, Wst]. It means that it is guaranteed by a high authority [EBC, NCBC]. Πάσης 'all' is emphatic [NIGTC]; it indicates complete effectiveness [EGT]. It implies that an oath taken in God's name was absolutely binding [GNC]. It implies that even a human oath settles a matter [EGT, Lns, NCBC].

QUESTION—What is the function of the definite article in ὁ ὅρκος 'the oath'?

1. The definite article specifies the oath in the situation referred to [Alf], the oath sworn by God [Lns]. 'The oath' is emphatic by its position at the end of the clause [Lns].
2. The definite article is generic, indicating oaths in general [EGT, Lg, NIGTC].

QUESTION—What is the phrase εἰς βεβαίωσιν 'for confirmation' connected with?

1. It is connected with πέρας 'end' [Alf, Blm, Hu, Lg(K), TNTC]: final for the purpose of confirmation.
2. It is connected with ὁ ὅρκος 'the oath' [Mil, WBC; KJV, NASB, NJB, NRSV]: the oath given for confirmation.
3. It is connected with the entire clause [My, NIC].

6:17 in[a] which God, more-abundantly[b] desiring[c] to-show[d] to-the heirs of-the promise the unchanging-(thing)[e] of-his will,[f] interposed[g] by-(an)-oath,

LEXICON—a. ἐν with dative object (LN 89.5) (BAGD IV.6.d. p. 261): 'in' [LN], 'in the case of' [LN], 'with regard to' [LN]. The phrase ἐν ᾧ 'in which' is translated 'because' [BAGD, WBC], 'wherefore' [HNTC], 'wherein' [Lns; KJV], 'in this matter' [NIC], 'in the same way' [NASB, NJB, NRSV], 'so' [CEV], 'and so' [REB], 'that is why' [TNT], not explicit [NAB, NIV, NLT, TEV].

b. περισσότερος (LN 78.31) (BAGD 3. p. 651): 'more abundantly' [Lns; KJV], 'even more' [NASB], 'more fully' [HNTC], 'very clear' [NIV, TEV], 'abundantly clear' [TNT], 'perfectly sure' [NLT], 'even clearer' [NAB], 'even more clearly' [BAGD; NJB, NRSV, REB], 'even more convincingly' [NIC], 'especially plain' [WBC], 'excessive' [LN], 'for certain' [CEV]. This neuter adjective is used as an adverb [EGT, ICC, NIGTC], meaning 'abundantly' [EGT], 'more emphatically' [My], 'all the more' [NIGTC]. It is emphatic [WBC]. It modifies the infinitive ἐπιδεῖξαι 'to show' [EGT, ICC, My, NIGTC, Wst; NAB, NIV, NJB, NRSV, REB, TEV, TNT]; it modifies the participle βουλόμενος 'desiring' [Lns, TNTC].

c. pres. mid. (deponent = act.) participle of βούλομαι (LN 25.3, 30.56) (BAGD 2.b. p. 146): 'to desire' [LN (25.3); NASB, NRSV, REB], 'to want' [LN (25.3), WBC; CEV, NIV, NJB, TEV, TNT], 'to wish' [BAGD, HNTC, NIC; NAB], 'to be willing' [BAGD], 'to will' [LN (25.3); KJV], 'to intend' [LN (30.56), Lns], 'to plan' [LN (30.56)], not explicit [NLT]. It implies reference to the future [NIGTC]. It is a strong word indicating a deliberate act of the will [EBC, TNTC]; it has to do with a purpose with regard to something else [Wst].

d. aor. act. infin. of ἐπιδείκνυμι (LN 24.25, 72.5) (BAGD 2.b. p. 291): 'to show' [HNTC, LN (24.25), Lns, NIC; KJV, NASB, NJB, NRSV, REB], 'to prove' [LN (72.5); CEV], 'to give proof' [BAGD], 'to show to be true'

[LN (72.5)], 'to give evidence' [NAB]. 'to make' [WBC; NIV, TEV, TNT], not explicit [NLT].

e. ἀμετάθετος (LN **13.61**) (BAGD 1. p. 45): 'unchanging' [LN; NIV], 'unchangeable' [NRSV], 'immutable' [REB], 'irrevocable' [WBC]. This adjective is also translated as a noun: 'unchangeableness' [BAGD, HNTC, NIC; NASB], 'immutability' [Lns; KJV]. The phrase τὸ ἀμετάθετον τῆς βουλῆς αὐτοῦ 'the unchanging thing of his will' is translated 'that his purpose would not change' [NAB], 'that he would not change his purpose' [TNT], 'that he would never change his purpose' [TEV], 'that he would never change his mind' [NLT], 'how unalterable his plan was' [NJB], 'that his promise could not be broken' [CEV]. The meaning is that what he wills is unchangeable [Alf, Blm, EGT, GNC, HNTC, Hwt, Lns, Mil, My, NCBC, NIC, WBC; KJV, NASB, NRSV, REB], unchanging [EBC; NIV].

f. βουλή (LN 30.57) (BAGD 2.b. p. 145): 'will' [HNTC], 'plan' [LN; NJB], 'intention' [LN], 'purpose' [LN, NIC; NAB, NASB, NIV, NJB, NRSV, REB, TEV, TNT], 'counsel' [Lns; KJV], 'resolve' [BAGD, WBC], 'mind' [NLT]. This noun is a cognate of the verb βούλομαι 'to desire' [EBC, NIGTC], and the two words are used together for emphasis [NTC]; it implies intention and decision [NIGTC].

g. aor. act. indic. of μεσιτεύω (LN **31.21**) (BAGD p. 506): 'to interpose' [Lns; NASB], 'to bring about an agreement' [LN], 'to cause an agreement' [LN], 'to guarantee' [BAGD, HNTC; NAB, NRSV, REB], 'to confirm' [WBC; KJV, NIV, TNT], 'to convey' [NJB], 'to communicate' [NIC]. The phrase ἐμεσίτευσεν ὅρκῳ 'he interposed by an oath' is translated 'he added his vow' [TEV], 'he made a vow' [CEV], 'God bound himself with an oath' [NLT], 'so he used a vow to help bring about the agreement and make it certain' [**LN**]. The meaning is that God placed himself as the higher authority involved as a mediator [Alf, Blm, My, Wst], as the guarantor of the promise [EBC, EGT, Hu, NCBC, NIGTC, NTC], by means of an oath [Blm, EGT]; he came between himself and his promise [Lg(K), Wst]; he added his oath to his promise [GNC] as a guarantee of the fulfillment of the promise [Hwt].

QUESTION—What relationship is indicated by the phrase ἐν ᾧ 'in which'?

It is connected with ἐμεσίτευσεν ὅρκῳ 'he interposed by an oath' [My, NIGTC].

1. It indicates a conclusion [EGT, HNTC, Lg, My, TNTC; CEV, REB]: therefore.
2. It indicates a reason [ICC, NIGTC, WBC; TNT]: that is why.
3. It indicates a related circumstance [Alf, Lg(K), Lns, Mil, NIC, Wst; KJV]: in this matter/in a similar matter.
4. It indicates manner [NASB, NJB, NRSV]: in the same way.

QUESTION—What relationship is indicated by the participial form βουλόμενος 'desiring'?

1. It indicates reason [Mil; NIV, REB, TNT]: because he wanted.

2. It is temporal [CEV, NJB, NRSV]: when he wanted.
3. It expresses an independent statement [NIC, WBC; TEV]: he wanted.

QUESTION—How are the two nouns related in the genitive construction τοῖς κληρονόμοις τῆς ἐπαγγελίας 'the heirs of the promise'?

The genitive τῆς ἐπαγγελίας 'of the promise' tells what the heirs were to receive [Mil; NLT, TEV, TNT]: the persons who were to inherit what was promised.

QUESTION—To whom does τοῖς κληρονόμοις τῆς ἐπαγγελίας 'the heirs of the promise' refer?

1. It refers to OT believers and Christians [HNTC, Hu, TH, Wst], to all of Abraham's spiritual descendants (and Abraham himself [Lns]) [EBC, EGT, Hwt, ICC, Lns, NCBC, TNTC], the immediate reference being to the author's readers [Wst].
2. It refers to Christians of all times [Mil, NIC, NTC, WBC].
3. It refers only to Christians of the author's time [NIGTC].

QUESTION—How are the adjective and noun related in the genitive construction τὸ ἀμετάθετον τῆς βουλῆς 'the unchanging (thing) of (his) will'?

The genitive τῆς βουλῆς 'the will' tells what is ἀμετάθετον 'unchangeable' [Mil; NAB, NJB, REB, TEV, TNT]: his will is unchangeable.

QUESTION—What relationship is indicated by the dative ὅρκῳ 'by an oath'?

It indicates the means by which God acted [Alf, Blm, Lns, Mil]: he acted by means of an oath.

6:18 in-order-that[a] through[b] two unchangeable[c] things,[d]

LEXICON—a. ἵνα (LN 89.59): 'in order that' [HNTC, LN, Lns, Mil; NASB], 'for the purpose that' [LN], 'so that' [LN, WBC; NAB, NIV, NJB, NRSV], 'that' [KJV], 'his purpose was that' [NIC]. The phrase ἵνα διά 'in order that through' is translated 'here, then, are' [REB], 'there are' [TEV], 'so God used' [TNT], 'so God has given' [NLT], not explicit [CEV, NLT].

b. διά with genitive object (LN 89.76): 'through' [HNTC, LN; NJB, NRSV], 'by' [WBC; KJV, NAB, NASB, NIV], 'by means of' [Lns, Mil, NIC].

c. ἀμετάθετος: 'unchangeable'. See this word in 6:17.

d. πρᾶγμα (LN 13.105) (BAGD 1. p. 697): 'thing' [BAGD, HNTC, Lns, Mil, NIC; all versions except NJB, REB], 'factor' [NJB], 'fact' [WBC], 'happening' [LN], 'event' [LN], 'act' [REB]. The meaning is primarily 'word', but with 'event' implied [NIGTC]; it refers to the event of God's making his promise [TH]; it refers to facts [NTC, WBC].

QUESTION—What relationship is indicated by ἵνα 'in order that'?

It indicates God's purpose in giving his oath [EBC, EGT, Lns, Mil, My, NIGTC], the purpose of doubly establishing God's truthfulness [Hu]; result is also implied [NIGTC].

QUESTION—To what does δύο πραγμάτων ἀμεταθέτων 'two unchangeable things' refer?

They are God's promise and his oath [Alf, Blm, EBC, GNC, HNTC, Hu, Hwt, Lns, Mil, My, NCBC, NIC, NIGTC, NTC, TH, WBC, Wst; CEV, NLT]; his nature and his oath [TNTC].

in[a] which-(things) (it is) impossible for-God to-lie,

TEXT—Some manuscripts omit the definite article τόν before θεόν 'God'. GNT places this word in brackets, indicating doubt, but with no letter rating. This article is omitted by Alf, Blm, EBC, EGT, HNTC, My, NIC, Wst; it is included by NTC. It is not clear whether others omit or include this word.

LEXICON—a. ἐν with dative object (LN 89.5): 'in' [HNTC, LN, Lns, Mil, NIC, WBC; all versions except TEV, TNT], 'about' [LN; TEV, TNT], 'in the case of' [LN], 'with regard to' [LN], not explicit [CEV, NLT].

QUESTION—Why is this clause mentioned?

It tells why the two things just mentioned are unchangeable [Blm]: they are unchangeable because it is impossible for God to lie. It emphasizes the unchangeability of God's promise and his oath [WBC].

QUESTION—What relationship is indicated by ἐν οἷς 'in which things'?

It means in connection with the fulfillment of the two things referred to [My].

QUESTION—What is indicated by the noun θεόν 'God'?

Without the definite article the emphasis is on God's nature [EBC, HNTC, NIC, Wst]: it is impossible for the one having the nature of God to lie.

strong[a] encouragement[b] we-might-have, the-(ones) having-fled-for-refuge[c] to-grasp[d] the hope lying-before[e] (us);

LEXICON—a. ἰσχυρός (LN **78.16**) (BAGD 2. p. 383): 'strong' [BAGD, HNTC, Lns, Mil, NIC, WBC; KJV, NASB], 'vigorous' [NJB], 'great' [LN], 'powerful' [REB], 'new' [NLT]. The phrase ἰσχυρὰν παράκλησιν ἔχωμεν 'strong encouragement we might have' is translated 'we may be greatly encouraged' [NIV], 'we might be strongly encouraged' [NAB, NRSV], 'we are greatly encouraged' [TEV, TNT], 'we were greatly encouraged' [**LN**], 'his promise should greatly encourage us' [CEV]. This word is emphatic by word order; the παράκλησις 'encouragement' is 'strong' because it is founded on God's promise and oath [Blm].

b. παράκλησις (LN 25.150) (BAGD 1. p. 618): 'encouragement' [HNTC, LN, Lns, Mil, NIC; NASB, NJB, REB], 'courage' [NLT], 'incentive' [WBC], 'consolation' [KJV]. This noun is also translated as a verb: 'to be encouraged' [NAB, NIV, NRSV, TEV, TNT], 'to encourage' [CEV]. The phrase ἰσχυρὰν παράκλησιν 'strong encouragement' is translated 'greatly encouraged' [BAGD]. The meaning is encouragement [Alf, Lg, My, NCBC, NIGTC, Wst], consolation [Blm].

c. aorist act. participle of καταφεύγω (LN **21.15**) (BAGD 2. p. 420): 'to flee for refuge' [HNTC, Mil, NIC, WBC; KJV, NASB, NLT], 'to take refuge' [BAGD, **LN**; NAB, NRSV, TNT], 'to flee to safety' [LN], 'to find safety'

[TEV], 'to find refuge' [Lns], 'to lay claim to (one's) protection' [REB], 'to flee' [NIV, NJB], 'to run to God for safety' [CEV]. This verb implies fleeing for refuge [Alf, NIGTC, NTC, TH] to Christ for salvation [Hu, Hwt, My, NTC], to escape completely [NTC]. This participle with its article is attributive [NIGTC, TH, TNTC, WBC, Wst] and identifies 'we' in the verb ἔχωμεν 'we might have' [Mil, NIGTC, TH, TNTC, WBC, Wst; all versions except NAB, REB], including the author with the readers [NTC]. The full realization of the refuge is future for the readers [NIGTC].

d. aorist act. infin. of κρατέω (LN 18.6) (BAGD 2.e.β. p. 448): 'to grasp' [NJB, REB], 'to lay hold' [Mil; KJV, NASB], 'to take hold' [NIC; CEV, NIV], 'to seize' [LN; NAB, NRSV], 'to hold' [LN], 'to hold on' [NLT], 'to hold fast' [BAGD, HNTC, Lns, WBC; TNT], 'to hold firmly' [TEV]. The aorist tense refers to laying hold [EBC, EGT, Hu, ICC, Lg(K), TH, TNTC; all versions except TEV, TNT] as a single action [Alf, EGT] referring to the whole Christian state [Alf, NTC]; it refers to holding fast [HNTC, Lg, My; TEV, TNT], to both laying hold and holding fast [NIGTC, Wst].

e. pres. mid. (deponent = act.) of πρόκειμαι (LN 13.76) (BAGD 2. p. 707): 'to lie before' [HNTC, LN], 'to lie ahead' [LN], 'to be set before' [BAGD, Mil, NIC; KJV, NASB, NRSV, REB, TNT], 'to be placed before' [NAB, TEV], 'to be placed in front of' [WBC], 'to be right in front of' [CEV], 'to be offered' [NIV], 'to be held out to' [NJB], 'to be proffered' [Lns], not explicit [NLT]. It is attributive, indicating the hope which lies before us [NAB].

QUESTION—What relationship is indicated by the infinitive κρατῆσαι 'to grasp'?

1. It is connected with καταφυγόντες 'having fled' [EGT, Lg, Lns, Mil, NIC, NTC; KJV, NASB, NIV, REB].

1.1 It indicates the purpose of fleeing (implied but not specifically stated by a number of translations and commentaries): having fled in order to grasp.

1.2 It indicates the result of fleeing [Lns]: having fled with the result of grasping.

1.3 It indicates the means of fleeing [REB]: having fled by grasping.

1.4 It indicates what is meant by having fled [NASB]: having fled in grasping.

2. It is connected with παράκλησιν 'encouragement' [ICC, LN, My, TH], indicating its content [HNTC, NCBC, TNTC, WBC; NAB, NJB, NRSV, TEV, TNT]: encouragement to grasp.

QUESTION—What is the meaning of ἐλπίδος 'hope'?

1. It refers to the thing hoped for [Alf, Blm, EGT, HNTC, ICC, Lns, TH, WBC], the gift of salvation through Christ [WBC].
2. It refers to looking forward to a realization [EBC, Hu, Lg, My, TNTC].
3. It includes both of the above [My(D), Wst].

6:19 which we-have as (an) anchor of-the soul

QUESTION—What is ἥν 'which' connected with?

It is connected with ἐλπίδος 'hope' in 6:18 [Alf, Blm, EGT, HNTC, Lns, Mil, My, NCBC, NIC, TH, TNTC, WBC, Wst; all versions]: which hope we have.

QUESTION—What is meant by ἔχομεν 'we have'?

1. It means to have in possession [Alf, My, NIGTC; KJV, NASB, NIV, NJB, NRSV, REB]: we possess this hope.
2. It means to hold fast [Blm].

QUESTION—To what does τῆς ψυχῆς 'the soul' refer?

It refers to life as a whole [EBC, GNC, HNTC, Hu, NCBC, NTC, WBC].

QUESTION—What is meant by having an anchor of the soul?

This is a metaphor. Hope is compared with an anchor and the point of similarity is stability [NTC, WBC, Wst] or security [Hu, NIGTC, NTC, TH, TNTC].

both safe[a] and secure[b] and entering into the inner-(part)[c] of-the curtain,[d]

LEXICON—a. ἀσφαλή (LN 21.10): 'safe' [HNTC, LN, Mil, WBC; REB, TEV], 'secure' [LN, NIC], 'sure' [Lns, Mil; KJV, NAB, NASB, NRSV, TNT], 'firm' [CEV, NIV], 'strong' [NLT], not explicit [NJB].

b. βέβαιος (LN 31.90) (BAGD 1. p. 138): 'secure' [BAGD, WBC; NIV, REB], 'dependable' [LN], 'reliable' [LN], 'trustworthy' [LN; NLT], 'sure' [HNTC; TEV], 'steadfast' [Mil; KJV, NASB, NRSV], 'steady' [CEV], 'firm' [Lns, Mil; NAB, TNT], 'stable' [NIC], not explicit [NJB]. This word and ἀσφαλή 'safe' are almost synonymous [TH, TNTC, WBC] and are combined redundantly for emphasis [GNC, TH]; they are separated from their noun ἄγκυραν 'anchor' for emphasis [WBC].

c. ἐσώτερος (LN **7.35, 83.15**) (BAGD p. 314): 'inner part' [**LN (**83.15)], 'inner side' [NIC], 'inner part behind' [Lns], 'inner sanctuary behind' [NIV], 'that within' [KJV]. The phrase εἰς τὸ ἐσώτερον 'into the inner part' is translated 'within' [**LN (**7.35); NASB], 'beyond' [NAB], 'right through inside' [NJB], 'the sanctuary behind' [REB], 'into the inner sanctuary' [HNTC], 'the inner sanctuary behind' [WBC], 'the inner shrine behind' [NRSV], 'into the inner shrine beyond' [Mil]. The phrase εἰς τὸ ἐσώτερον τοῦ καταπετάσματος 'into the inner part of the curtain' is translated 'through the curtain into the inner sanctuary' [TNT], 'through the curtain of the heavenly temple into the inner sanctuary' [TEV], 'behind the curtain and into the most holy place' [CEV], 'through the curtain of heaven into God's inner sanctuary' [NLT]. The phrase τὸ ἐσώτερον τοῦ καταπετάσματος 'the inner part of the curtain' is translated 'what is inside (= *behind*) the curtain' [BAGD], 'the inner sanctuary' [**LN** (83.15)].

d. καταπέτασμα (LN 6.160) (BAGD p. 416): 'curtain' [BAGD, LN, WBC; CEV, NIV, NJB, NLT, NRSV, REB, TEV, TNT], 'sanctuary curtain' [NIC], 'veil' [LN, Lns; KJV, NAB, NASB], 'drape' [LN]. The phrase τὸ ἐσώτερον τοῦ καταπετάσματος 'the inner part of the curtain' is translated 'the inner sanctuary behind the curtain' [BAGD], 'the holy of holies' [BAGD]. It is the veil at the entrance to the holy of holies [Alf, Blm, EBC, EGT, Lns, My, NCBC, NIC, NIGTC, Wst].

QUESTION—What is this phrase connected with?

1. It describes the hope [EBC, GNC, Lg(K), NIGTC, Wst; CEV, NASB, NLT, TNT]: the hope safe and secure and which enters.
2. It describes the anchor [Alf, EGT, Hu, ICC, Lns, My, NIC, TNTC]: an anchor safe and secure and which enters. Since the anchor is the hope, in reality it is our hope that is safe and secure [NIC].
3. 'Safe and secure' refer to 'anchor'; 'entering' refers to 'hope' [HNTC, Mil; NAB, NRSV]: an anchor safe and secure, and hope which enters. (This division is forbidden by καί 'and' which makes 'entering' parallel to 'safe and secure'.)

QUESTION—What relationship is indicated by the participle εἰσερχομένην 'entering'?

The present tense implies continuing action [NIGTC, Wst].

1. It is attributive [Blm, EGT, Mil; KJV, NASB, NRSV]: hope/anchor which enters.

1.1 It describes ἐλπίδος 'hope' [Blm, Hu, Mil, WBC; CEV, NASB, NLT, NRSV].

1.2 It describes ἄγχυραν 'anchor' and indicates why the anchor is 'safe and secure' [EGT]: an anchor which enters, and is safe and secure because it enters.

2. It states an additional circumstance [HNTC; NAB, NIV, REB, TEV]: and hope enters.

QUESTION—How are the adjective and noun related in the genitive phrase τὸ ἐσώτερον τοῦ καταπετάσματος 'the inner part of the curtain'?

The meaning is the inner part behind the curtain [BAGD, Hu, Lns, Mil, My, NCBC, NTC, TH, WBC], the holy of holies (in heaven [Lns]) [Hu, Lns, My, TNTC, WBC, Wst] as (a symbol of [My]) the very presence of God [EGT, GNC, My, Wst].

6:20 where (as) forerunner[a] on-behalf-of[b] us has-entered Jesus,

LEXICON—a. πρόδρομος (LN **36.9**) (BAGD p. 704): 'forerunner' [BAGD, HNTC, **LN**, Lns, Mil, NIC, WBC; KJV, NAB, NASB, NJB, NRSV, REB], 'who went before us' [NIV]. The phrase πρόδρομος εἰσῆλθεν 'as forerunner has entered' is translated 'went on ahead of us' [**LN**], 'went in before us' [TNT], 'has gone in there before us' [TEV], 'has gone there ahead of us' [CEV], 'has already gone in there' [NLT]. It implies preparing the way for others [EBC, GNC, HNTC, Hu, ICC, Mil, My, NCBC, NIC, NIGTC, NTC, TNTC, WBC]. It is emphatic by forefronting [Lg(K), Mil].

b. ὑπέρ with genitive object (LN 90.36) (BAGD 1.a.ε. p. 838): 'on behalf of' [HNTC, LN, Mil, NIC, WBC; NAB, NIV, NJB, NRSV, REB, TEV,

TNT], 'for' [BAGD, LN; KJV, NASB, NLT], 'for the sake of' [LN], 'in behalf of' [BAGD, Lns], not explicit [CEV].

QUESTION—How are the two nouns πρόδρομος 'forerunner' and Ἰησοῦς 'Jesus' related?

1. Πρόδρομος 'forerunner' is the predicate (as the omission of the definite article shows [Alf]) to Ἰησοῦς 'Jesus', and Ἰησοῦς 'Jesus' is the subject of the verb [Alf, EGT, HNTC, Lns, Mil, NCBC, NIC, WBC; all versions except KJV]: Jesus has entered as forerunner.
2. Πρόδρομος 'forerunner' is the subject and Ἰησοῦς is the predicate [KJV]: a forerunner, Jesus, has entered.

QUESTION—What is the phrase ὑπὲρ ἡμῶν 'on behalf of us' connected with?

1. It is connected with εἰσῆλθεν 'he entered' [HNTC, Lg, Lns, Mil, My, NCBC, NIGTC, WBC; KJV, NAB, NIV, NLT, REB, TEV, TNT]: he entered on behalf of us.
2. It is connected with πρόδρομος 'forerunner' [Alf, EGT; NRSV]: forerunner on behalf of us.

QUESTION—What is implied by the use of the personal name 'Jesus'?

It focuses on the human Jesus [EGT, Hu, NTC, Wst]. It is emphatic by its word order [Lg(K), Lns, NIGTC, TH, Wst].

according-to[a] the order[b] of-Melchizedek having-become high-priest into[c] the age/forever.

LEXICON—a. κατά with accusative object (LN 89.8): 'according to' [Lns; NAB, NASB, NRSV], 'in accordance with' [LN, Mil], 'in relation to' [LN], 'in' [HNTC; NIV, REB, TEV, TNT], 'after' [NIC; KJV], 'of' [NJB], not explicit [NLT]. The phrase κατὰ τὴν τάξιν 'according to the order' is translated 'like' [LN], 'just like' [BAGD, WBC; CEV].

b. τάξις (LN 58.21) (BAGD 4. p. 804): 'order' [Lns, Mil, NIC; all versions], 'rank' [HNTC], 'kind' [LN], 'nature' [BAGD].

c. εἰς with accusative object (LN 67.95, 84.22): 'into' [LN (84.22)]. The phrase εἰς τὸν αἰῶνα 'into the age/forever' is translated 'forever' [HNTC, LN (67.95), Lns, Mil, NIC, WBC; all versions except NLT], 'eternal' [NLT].

QUESTION—What is implied by the word order of the phrase 'according to the order of Melchizedek'?

It is emphatic by forefronting [Alf, My, NIGTC, Wst].

QUESTION—What is indicated by the aorist tense of the participle γενόμενος 'having become'?

1. It indicates action prior to εἰσῆλθεν 'he entered' [HNTC, Lns, NTC]: he became high priest before he entered.
2. It indicates the same action as the verb εἰσῆλθεν 'he entered' [NIGTC, WBC]. His entry into heaven is identical with his appointment as high priest [NIGTC]; they go together [WBC].

3. It indicates action subsequent to the verb εἰσῆλθεν 'he entered' [Lg(K), Wst]: he became high priest after he entered. However, his previous atoning death was a priestly action [Wst].
4. It indicates completion of his mission and a continuing activity [NTC].

QUESTION—What relationship is indicated by the participle γενόμενος 'having become'?

1. It indicates reason [EGT, Mil, NTC; TNT]: because he has become high priest.
2. It indicates an additional circumstance [NIV, TEV]: and he has become high priest.
3. It is attributive, describing Jesus [NIC]: who has become high priest.

DISCOURSE UNIT: 7:1–10:18 [Hwt]. The topic is Christ's priesthood, ministry, and sacrifice.

DISCOURSE UNIT: 7:1–28 [EBC, GNT, Hwt, Lg, Lns, Mil, NCBC, NIC, NIGTC, NTC, TNTC, Wst; CEV, NAB, NASB]. The topic is Melchizedek [EBC], Melchizedek's priesthood [GNT], the priestly order of Melchizedek [NCBC, NIC, TNTC; CEV], Christ's high-priesthood foreshadowed by Melchizedek [Wst; NAB, NASB], Jesus as high priest in the order of Melchizedek [Lns, NIGTC, NTC], Christ's Melchizedekian priesthood being superior to the Levitical priesthood [Mil], Christ's eternal and perfect high-priesthood [Lg], the superiority of Christ's priesthood [Hwt].

DISCOURSE UNIT: 7:1–25 [Wst]. The topic is Christ's priesthood according to the order of Melchizedek.

DISCOURSE UNIT: 7:1–14 [GNC; NLT, TEV]. The topic is the enigma of Melchizedek and his priesthood [GNC], Melchizedek the priest [TEV], Melchizedek compared to Abraham [NLT].

DISCOURSE UNIT: 7:1–10 [EBC, Lg, NIGTC, NTC, WBC; NIV]. The topic is Melchizedek [NIGTC], Melchizedek the priest [NIV], Melchizedek, king and priest [NTC, WBC], the greatness of Melchizedek [EBC], the triple superiority of Melchizedek, as a type of Christ, to the Levitical priests [Lg].

DISCOURSE UNIT: 7:1–3 [HNTC, Hwt, Lns, Mil, NIC, NTC; NJB, TEV]. The topic is Melchizedek [HNTC; NJB, TEV], the scriptural information concerning Melchizedek [Lns, NTC], Melchizedek the priest-king [NIC], the characteristics of the priesthood of Melchizedek [Hwt].

7:1 For this Melchizedek, king of Salem, priest of God the Most-High,

QUESTION—What relationship is indicated by γάρ 'for'?

It introduces the explanation of the reference to Melchizedek in 6:20 [Blm, EGT, Mil, My, NIC, NIGTC, Wst]. It links 7:1–3 with 6:20 [TH]. It introduces a reference to the Genesis narrative concerning Melchizedek [WBC].

QUESTION—To what does 'Salem' refer?

1. It refers to Jerusalem [Blm, Hu, Mil, My, NTC, TH, TNTC], the Canaanite Jerusalem [GNC].
2. It does not refer to Jerusalem, but possibly to the Salem mentioned in John 3:23 [Alf] or the ancient city of Shechem [WBC].

QUESTION—To whom does τοῦ θεοῦ τοῦ ὑψίστου 'God the Most High' refer?
It refers to the one true God [Alf, Hwt, Lns, My, NIC, NTC, Wst], the God of the Bible [HNTC, NCBC], the God of Israel [GNC], the God whom Abraham worshipped [Hu, NTC, WBC]. It does not mean the highest among other gods as though there were many [Hu, Hwt, Lns, TH, Wst]. It indicates God's exalted character [TNTC, WBC, Wst].

QUESTION—How is this phrase related to following phrases?
Verses 1–3 form one sentence, the one verb being μένει 'he remains' in 7:3 [Alf, Blm, EGT, ICC, Lg, Lns, Mil, My, TH, WBC, Wst; KJV, NASB] and all that precedes this verb modifies the subject 'Melchizedek' [Blm, EGT, Lns, Mil]. Verses 1–3 are translated as several sentences or clauses [CEV, NAB, NIV, NJB, NLT, NRSV, REB, TEV, TNT] (to adapt to English style [WBC]): he was king . . . he met . . . his name means . . . he remains . . .

the-(one) having-met Abraham returning from[a] the slaughter/defeat[b] of the kings and having-blessed him,

LEXICON—a. ἀπό with genitive object (LN 84.3): 'from' [HNTC, LN, Lns, Mil, NIC, WBC; all versions except TNT], 'away from' [LN], 'after' [TNT]

b. κοπή (LN **20.74**) (BAGD p. 443): 'slaughter' [HNTC, LN, Lns, Mil, NIC; KJV, NASB], 'defeat' [BAGD, **LN,** WBC; NAB, NIV, REB], 'battle in which he defeated' [TEV]. This noun is also translated as a gerund: 'defeating' [NJB, NRSV, TNT], 'killing' [CEV], 'winning a great battle against' [NLT].

QUESTION—What is meant by κοπή 'slaughter, defeat'?

1. The meaning is 'slaughter' [EGT, HNTC, Lns, Mil, NIC; CEV, KJV, NASB].
2. The meaning is 'defeat' [Alf, BAGD, Blm, LN, WBC; NAB, NIV, REB].

QUESTION—What relationship is indicated by the participle εὐλογήσας 'having blessed'?
It is parallel to ὁ συναντήσας 'the one having met' [Alf, HNTC, ICC, Lns, Mil, My, NIC, WBC, Wst; KJV, NAB, NASB, NIV, NJB, NRSV, REB, TEV, TNT].

1. It is attributive [Alf, ICC, Lns, Mil, My, NIC, Wst; KJV, NASB]: who met . . . and blessed.
2. It is translated as a parallel statement [HNTC, WBC; NAB, NIV, NJB, NRSV, REB, TEV, TNT]: he met . . . and blessed.

QUESTION—What is meant by εὐλογήσας 'having blessed'?

It refers to a priestly blessing [Blm, Hwt, Lns, My, TH, WBC, Wst]. He prayed that God would show favor to Abraham [TH]. It indicated that Melchizedek had a position superior to that of Abraham [TNTC].

7:2 to-whom also Abraham apportioned[a] (a) tenth[b] from[c] all (things),

LEXICON—a. aorist act. indic. of μερίζω (LN **57.90**) (BAGD 2.b. p. 504): 'to apportion' [BAGD, HNTC, Mil, NIC; NAB, NASB, NRSV], 'to allot' [WBC], 'to parcel out' [Lns], 'to give as one's share' [REB], 'to give' [LN; CEV, KJV, NIV, NJB, NLT, TEV, TNT]. This verb emphasizes the action of giving a tithe [ICC, NIGTC]. It was a formal act [Alf, Blm] of thanksgiving to God through Melchizedek [GNC]. It recognized Melchizedek to be God's representative [NTC]. It brought out the importance of Melchizedek's priesthood [GNC] and showed that Melchizedek was more important than Abraham [TH, TNTC, Wst].

b. δεκάτη (LN **60.66**) (BAGD 2.b. p. 174): 'tenth' [BAGD, LN, Lns; CEV, NIV, NJB, NLT], 'one tenth' [NIC; NAB, NRSV, TEV], 'tenth part' [Mil; KJV, NASB, TNT], 'tenth share' [WBC], 'tithe' [BAGD, HNTC; REB]. The amount was intentional [Blm].

c. ἀπό with genitive object (LN 63.20): 'from' [Lns, Mil], 'of' [HNTC, NIC, WBC; all versions], 'a part of' [LN].

QUESTION—What is implied by καί 'also'?

It implies that in addition to receiving a blessing from Melchizedek, Abraham *also* recognized Melchizedek's priesthood by giving him the tithe [Lns].

QUESTION—To what does πάντων 'all (things)' refer?

It refers to the things Abraham had seized from the defeated army [Alf, Blm, EBC, EGT, GNC, Hwt, Lns, Mil, My, Wst; NAB, NASB, TEV, TNT].

first on-the-one-hand being-interpreted[a] "king of-righteousness,"[b]

LEXICON—a. pres. pass. participle of ἑρμηνεύω (LN **33.145**) (BAGD 2. p. 310): 'to be interpreted' [LN], 'to be by interpretation' [KJV], 'to be translated' [BAGD, **LN**]. This verb is also translated as a phrase: 'by interpretation' [Lns], 'by the interpretation of his name' [NJB], 'his name is to be interpreted' [NIC], 'by the translation of his name' [Mil; NASB], 'translated, his name means' [WBC], 'his name means' [HNTC; NAB, NIV, NLT, NRSV, REB], 'the name means' [TNT], 'the meaning of Melchizedek's name is' [CEV, TEV]. This participle modifies the understood 'Melchizedek' [NIGTC].

b. δικαιοσύνη (LN 88.13) (BAGD 2.b. p. 196): 'righteousness' [BAGD, HNTC, LN, Lns, Mil, NIC, WBC; KJV, NASB, NIV, NRSV, REB, TEV, TNT], 'justice' [CEV, NAB, NLT], 'saving justice' [NJB].

QUESTION—Why is this phrase mentioned?

1. This and the following phrase give further descriptions of Melchizedek [Alf, EBC, HNTC, Lg, Lns, TH, Wst; all versions]. The phrases are parenthetical [Blm].

1.1 It begins the interpretation of the event concerning Melchizedek [Alf, EBC, Lg, TH, Wst].

1.2 It begins the further description of Melchizedek, this phrase emphasizing his kingship, the following phrase his position [Lns].

2. This and the following phrase express reasons [EGT, Mil].

2.1 It begins the reason why Abraham gave Melchizedek a tithe of the spoils [Mil]: he gave the tithe because Melchizedek was king.

2.2 It begins the reason for Melchizedek's abiding forever (7:3) [EGT]. This phrase bases the reason on Melchizedek's name, the following clause on his position [EGT].

QUESTION—What relationship is indicated by πρῶτον μέν 'first on the one hand'?

It separates the preceding historical comment from the interpretation which follows [WBC].

QUESTION—What relationship is indicated by the participle ἑρμηνευόμενος 'being interpreted'?

It expresses the means by which Melchizedek is designated 'king of righteousness' [Mil]: by being interpreted he is described as king of righteousness.

QUESTION—How are the two nouns related in the genitive construction βασιλεὺς δικαιοσύνης 'king of righteousness'?

The genitive noun 'righteousness' describes the king's quality [Lns, Wst] which results in a righteous rule [Lns, NTC, TH, Wst]: he rules righteously.

then[a] on-the-other-hand also "king of-Salem,"

LEXICON—a. ἔπειτα (LN 67.44) (BAGD 2.b. p. 284): 'then' [BAGD, HNTC, Lns, NIC, WBC; NASB, NIV], 'later' [LN], 'after that' [KJV], 'next' [NRSV, REB], 'in the second place' [Mil], not explicit [CEV, NJB, NLT, TNT]. The phrase ἔπειτα δέ 'then on the other hand' is translated 'he was' [NAB]. The phrase ἔπειτα . . . ὅ ἐστιν 'then . . . which is' is translated 'because he was . . . his name also means' [TEV]. This word means second in the series of descriptions [Mil]. The verb 'he is called' is implied [NIGTC].

which is "king of-peace,"

QUESTION—Why is this clause mentioned?

1. It gives the interpretation of the preceding phrase [My, NIGTC]: which means "king of peace."
2. It continues the description of Melchizedek [Mil].

QUESTION—How are the two nouns related in the genitive construction βασιλεὺς εἰρήνης 'king of peace'?

1. The genitive noun 'peace' means that his rule brings peace [TH].
2. 'Peace' is the name of the place where the king reigns [Lns, TNTC, Wst], and 'peace' characterizes his reign [Wst].

7:3 without-father, without-mother, without-genealogy,[a]

LEXICON—a. ἀγενεαλόγητος (LN **10.27**) (BAGD p. **8**): 'without genealogy' [BAGD, Mil; NASB, NIV, NRSV], 'without a genealogy' [NIC], 'without genealogical line' [Lns], 'without descent' [KJV], 'without ancestry' [NAB], 'without record of ancestors' [LN]. This adjective is translated as a phrase: 'he has no ancestry' [NJB], 'he has no ancestors' [REB], 'he has no lineage' [HNTC]. This entire phrase is translated 'there is no record of his father, mother, or ancestors' [TNT], 'there is no record of Melchizedek's father or mother or of any of his ancestors' [NLT, TEV], 'his father, mother, and line of descent are unknown' [WBC], 'we are not told that he had a father or mother or ancestors' [CEV].

QUESTION—Why is this phrase mentioned?

This phrase shows the contrast between Melchizedek's priesthood and that of the Levitical priests [My, WBC]. The Levitical priesthood required a recorded line of descent in order to be appointed to priesthood [WBC]. This and the two following participial phrases show that Melchizedek's priesthood is independent and single [Mil, WBC].

QUESTION—What is meant by ἀπάτωρ ἀμήτωρ 'without father, without mother'?

1. It means that his parents are not recorded in scripture [Blm, EBC, EGT, GNC, Hu, Hwt, Lns, My, NCBC, NIC, TH, WBC] and that the absence of their mention is inspired and significant [EBC, GNC, Hu, Hwt, NIC]. He did not inherit priestly dignity from parents [EGT].
2. It means that the biblical narrative, apart from the actual facts, implies supernatural origin [HNTC].

QUESTION—What is meant by ἀγενεαλόγητος 'without genealogy'?

It refers to ancestry, not posterity [Alf]; it refers to both ancestry and successors [Lns].

1. It means that scripture is silent concerning his genealogy [GNC, Hu, ICC, My, NIC, TH, WBC, Wst] and that the silence is inspired and significant [EBC, GNC, Hu, Hwt, NIC]. He had no recorded line of descent [WBC].
2. It means that he was not of priestly lineage [Blm, EGT].

having neither beginning of-days[a] **nor end of-life,**

LEXICON—a. ἡμέρα (LN 67. 178) (BAGD 4.b. p. 347): 'day' [HNTC, LN, Lns, Mil, NIC; KJV, NAB, NASB, NIV, NRSV]. This entire phrase is translated 'without either beginning or end of life' [BAGD], 'and his life has no beginning or ending' [NJB], 'his life has no beginning and no end' [REB], 'no beginning or end to his life' [NLT], 'no record of his birth or of his death' [TEV], 'no reference to his birth or death' [TNT], 'and there is no record of his birth or of his death' [WBC], 'we are not told that he had . . . beginning or end' [CEV].

QUESTION—What is meant by this participial phrase?

1. It means that scripture makes no mention of his birth or death [EGT, GNC, Hu, Hwt, ICC, My, Wst], nor of the beginning or end of his priesthood [EGT, GNC, Hu, Hwt, ICC, Wst].
2. It means that his priesthood had no predecessor or successor [Lns].
3. It implies that Melchizedek did not have a beginning and end of life as ordinary people do [Alf]; the silence of the biblical narrative, apart from the historical facts, implies that Melchizedek is eternal [HNTC, NCBC].

QUESTION—What is this phrase connected with?

1. It further describes Melchizedek [Lns, Mil; KJV, NJB] this Melchizedek . . . having neither beginning nor end of life.
2. It is translated as an independent proposition [REB, TEV, TNT]: he has neither beginning nor end of life.
3. It refers to the final phrase of this verse [HNTC, NIC, WBC; NAB, NASB, NIV, NRSV]: having neither beginning nor end of life, he remains a priest, etc. This and the following clause state the positive counterpart to the preceding negative comment [HNTC].

but likened[a] to-the son of-God,

LEXICON—a. perf. pass. participle of ἀφομοιόω (LN **64.4**) (BAGD p. 127): 'to be made similar' [BAGD, **LN**], 'to be made like' [BAGD, Lns; KJV, NASB], 'to be made to resemble' [HNTC, WBC], 'to be made conformable' [NIC]. The passive voice is also translated as active: 'to resemble' [BAGD, **LN**, Mil; NRSV], 'to be like' [CEV, NJB, TEV, TNT], 'to become like' [BAGD], 'to bear the likeness of' [REB], 'to resemble' [NLT]. This participle is also translated as a preposition: 'like' [NAB, NIV]. It means merely 'like' God's Son and does not mean 'made (by God) like' his Son [NIGTC]. The perfect tense indicates a continued state [Lns, NTC]. The prefixed ἀφ- makes this word emphatic [NTC]. The passive voice implies that God is the actor [WBC]. It means that by the picture thus drawn (by the use of this participle rather than the adjective ὅμοιος 'like' [Wst]), he appears to be like the Son of God [EGT], based on the biblical picture rather than in the actual reality [Wst].

QUESTION—What relationship is indicated by this participial phrase?

1. It further describes Melchizedek [Alf, Blm, EBC, EGT, GNC, HNTC, Hu, Hwt, Lns, Mil, NIC; KJV] as a type of the eternal Christ [My, NIC, NTC, Wst]: this Melchizedek . . . likened to the Son of God.
   1.1 It relates directly to the immediately preceding phrase [Blm, EGT, Hwt, My]: having neither beginning of days nor end of life, but likened to the Son of God.
   1.2 It expresses the conclusion from the earlier phrases of this verse [Alf, Lns, TNTC]: because he is without father . . . he is likened to the Son of God.
2. It is translated as an independent proposition [NJB]: he is likened to the Son of God.

3. It refers to the following phrase [HNTC, NIC, TH, WBC; CEV, NIV, NLT, REB, TEV].
 3.1 It states a comparison [TH; NIV, NLT, TEV, TNT]: he is like the Son of God in the fact that he remains a priest forever.
 3.2 It is an accompanying circumstance [HNTC, NIC, WBC; REB]: he remains a priest forever and he bears the likeness of the Son of God.

(he)-remains (a) priest into the continuous (time).[a]

LEXICON—a. διηνεκής (LN **67.95**) (BAGD p. 195): 'continuous' [BAGD], 'uninterrupted' [BAGD]. The phrase εἰς τὸ διηνεκές 'into the continuous (time)' is translated 'forever' [BAGD, **LN**; CEV, NAB, NIV, NJB, NLT, NRSV, TEV], 'for all time' [HNTC; REB, TNT], 'in perpetuity' [Lns, NIC], 'perpetually' [Mil; NASB], 'continually' [KJV], 'continuously' [WBC]. This phrase indicates continuation without ceasing, permanence [EBC, EGT, Lg, Lns, Mil, WBC, Wst], with neither beginning nor end [NIGTC]. This phrase modifies μένει 'he remains' [Mil].

QUESTION—Why is this clause mentioned?

It states the main point of the three verses, 7:1–3 [EGT, NIGTC], which is to emphasize the permanence of the Melchizedekian priesthood [EGT] and ultimately of Christ's priesthood [TNTC], to show how Melchizedek is like the Son of God [TH]; this is the conclusion from the silence of Scripture concerning his death [ICC, WBC], concerning the end of his priesthood [My, Wst].

DISCOURSE UNIT: 7:4–10 [HNTC, Hwt, Lns, NIC; NJB]. The topic is the superiority of Melchizedek [HNTC, Lns, NIC], the superiority of Melchizedek's priesthood [Hwt], Melchizedek received tithes from Abraham [NJB].

7:4 Now[a] **observe/you-observe**[b] **how-great this-person (is),**

LEXICON—a. δέ (LN 89.94): 'now' [Lns, Mil; KJV, NASB, NJB, REB], 'then' [NLT, TEV], 'and' [LN], 'just' [NIV], not explicit [HNTC, NIC, WBC; CEV, NAB, NRSV, TNT]. It introduces the other aspect of the point being discussed [Lg, Lns, Mil, NIGTC, TH]; it indicates a fresh beginning [Wst].

b. pres. act. impera./indic. of θεωρέω (LN **32.11**) (BAGD 2.a. p. 360): 'to observe' [BAGD; NASB], 'to behold' [Lns], 'to notice' [BAGD; CEV], 'to consider' [HNTC, Mil, WBC; KJV, NLT, REB, TNT], 'to perceive' [BAGD, LN], 'to recognize' [LN], 'to see' [LN, NIC; NAB, NRSV, TEV], 'to understand' [**LN**], 'to think' [NIV, NJB]. It implies giving careful attention [NTC, Wst].

QUESTION—What mood is the verb θεωρεῖτε 'observe/you observe'?

1. It is imperative [Alf, EGT, GNC, HNTC, Hu, Hwt, ICC, Lg, Lns, Mil, My, NIC, NTC, TNTC, WBC, Wst; all versions except TEV]: observe.
2. It is indicative [LN; TEV]: you see.

QUESTION—What is meant by πηλίκος 'how great'?

It refers to personal exaltation and dignity [Alf, Lg, My, TH]: how great in dignity. It is an exclamation [TH, WBC].

QUESTION—What verb should be supplied with οὗτος 'this person'?

1. The verb should be a past tense [Alf, EGT, Mil, WBC; KJV, NASB, NIV, NJB, NLT, TEV]: this person was.
2. The verb should be present tense [GNC, HNTC, Lns, NIC; CEV, NRSV, REB, TNT]: this person is.

to-whom also Abraham gave a-tenth[a] from[b] the booty[c]—the patriarch.

LEXICON—a. δεκάτη: 'tenth'. See this word in 7:2.

b. ἐκ with genitive object (LN 63.20): 'from' [REB], 'out of' [Lns], 'of' [HNTC, Mil, NIC, WBC; all versions except REB], 'a part of' [LN]. It indicates source [Mil].

c. ἀκροθίνιον (LN **57.244**) (BAGD p. 34): In the plural: 'booty' [BAGD; NAB], 'spoils' [BAGD, Mil, NIC; KJV, NRSV, TNT], 'plunder' [NIV], 'all he got in the battle' [TEV], 'what he had taken in battle' [NLT], 'what he had taken from his enemies' [CEV], 'best of the booty' [**LN**], 'finest spoils' [LN], 'best spoils' [HNTC], 'finest of the spoil' [REB], 'choice spoils' [Lns], 'choicest spoils' [NASB], 'choicest spoils of war' [WBC], 'finest plunder' [NJB], 'most valuable plunder' [LN]. This word serves to add emphasis to the importance of Melchizedek [WBC].

QUESTION—Why is this clause mentioned?

It is a relative clause supporting the comment about Melchizedek's greatness [Lns, Mil, NCBC, NTC, TH, TNTC, WBC]: how great he is, since Abraham gave him a tithe.

QUESTION—What relationship is indicated by καί 'also'?

It adds emphasis to δεκάτην 'tenth' [Alf, Lg, My]: he went so far as to give a tenth to him. 'Tenth' is emphatic by its position [Lns].

QUESTION—To what does ἀκροθινίων 'booty' refer?

1. This word refers to the booty as a whole [Alf, BAGD, Blm, GNC, Hu, ICC, Mil, NIC, NIGTC; CEV, KJV, NAB, NIV, NLT, NRSV, TEV, TNT]: he gave a tenth of all the booty. This word explains πάντων 'everything' in 7:2 [ICC].
2. This word refers to the best of the booty [EBC, Hwt, Lg, LN, Lns, My, TH, WBC, Wst; NASB, NJB, REB].

2.1 Abraham gave a tenth of all the booty, consisting of the choicest of the spoils [Hwt, Lg, My, TH]: he gave a tenth of all, consisting of the best of the booty.

2.2 Abraham gave a tenth of all the booty, selected from the choicest of the spoils [Lns, Wst; REB]: he gave a tenth of all, selected from the best of the booty.

2.3 Abraham gave a tenth of the best of the spoils [EBC, LN, WBC; NASB, NJB]: he gave a tenth of the best of the booty.

QUESTION—What relationship is indicated by the position of ὁ πατριάρχης 'the patriarch'?

It is emphatic by being placed at the end of the Greek clause [Alf, EBC, EGT, GNC, Hu, ICC, Mil, My, NIGTC, NTC, TH, TNTC, WBC, Wst]: no less than Abraham—the patriarch. The definite article implies 'the great patriarch' [Hu, NIGTC]. It implies the still higher greatness of Melchizedek [Lns, Mil, NIGTC, WBC].

7:5 And[a] on-the-one-hand the-(ones) from[b] the sons of-Levi receiving[c] the priesthood have (a) commandment[d] to-collect-a-tenth-from[e] the people[f] according-to[g] the law,[h]

LEXICON—a. καί (LN 89.92): 'and' [LN, Lns, Mil; KJV, NASB, NRSV, TEV], 'now' [NIC, WBC; NIV, NLT], not explicit [HNTC; CEV, NAB, NJB, REB, TNT]. This entire phrase is translated 'the law provides that the priests of the tribe of Levi should receive tithes from the people' [NAB].

b. ἐκ with genitive object (LN 89.3): 'from' [LN; Lns], 'of' [LN, Mil; KJV, NASB]. The phrase οἱ ἐκ τῶν υἱῶν Λευί 'the ones from the sons of Levi' is translated 'the descendants of Levi' [WBC; CEV, NIV, NLT, REB], 'those descendants of Levi' [NIC; NRSV, TEV], 'those of the descendants of Levi' [HNTC; TNT], 'any of the descendants of Levi' [NJB].

c. pres. act. participle of λαμβάνω (LN 57.125): 'to receive' [HNTC, Lns, Mil, NIC, WBC; KJV, NASB, NRSV, TNT], 'to accept' [LN]. The phrase οἱ τὴν ἱερατείαν λαμβάνοντες 'the ones receiving the priesthood' is translated 'who succeed to the priestly office' [REB], 'who are admitted to the priesthood' [NJB], 'who become priests' [NIV], 'who are priests' [CEV, TEV], 'the priests' [NLT].

d. ἐντολή (LN 33.330): 'commandment' [LN, Lns, Mil, WBC; KJV, NASB, NRSV]. The phrase ἐντολὴν ἔχουσιν 'have a commandment' is translated 'are obliged' [NJB], 'are required' [REB], 'are commanded' [NLT, TEV], 'are authorized' [HNTC; TNT], 'are entitled' [NIC]. The phrase ἐντολὴν ἔχουσιν κατὰ τὸν νόμον 'have a commandment according to the law' is translated 'the law requires' [NIV], 'the law teaches that they must' [CEV]. It refers to a specific law regarding tithes [NIGTC, WBC].

e. pres. act. infin. of ἀποδεκατόω (LN **57.115**) (BAGD 2. p. 89): 'to collect a tenth from' [NASB, NIV], 'to collect one tenth from' [TEV], 'to collect a tenth part from' [TNT], 'to collect a tithe (one tenth) from' [BAGD; NLT], 'to collect tithes from' [HNTC; NRSV], 'to take tithes from' [Mil; NJB], 'to exact tithes from' [LN], 'to exact a tenth from' [WBC], 'to take tithes of' [KJV], 'to collect the tenth' [**LN**], 'to collect tithes' [LN], 'to receive tithes' [NAB], 'to tithe' [Lns; REB]. The phrase ἀποδεκατοῦν τὸν λαόν 'to collect a tenth from the people' is translated 'to be paid tithes by the people' [NIC], 'even Abraham's descendants must give a tenth' [CEV].

f. λαός (LN 11.12) (BAGD 1.c.γ. p. 466): 'people' [BAGD, HNTC, Lns, Mil, NIC, WBC; all versions except CEV, TEV], 'people of God' [LN], 'people of Israel' [TEV], 'Abraham's descendants' [CEV]. This is the term used for God's people, Israel [Mil, NIGTC], the majority of the people apart from the priests [NIGTC].

g. κατά with accusative object (LN 89.8) (BAGD II.5.a.α. p. 407): 'according to' [BAGD, HNTC, NIC; KJV, TNT], 'in accordance with' [BAGD, LN, Mil, WBC], 'in conformity with' [BAGD], 'corresponding to' [BAGD], 'in' [NASB, NRSV], 'by' [Lns; NJB, REB, TEV]. The phrase κατὰ τὸν νόμον 'according to the law' is translated 'the law teaches' [CEV], 'are commanded in the law' [NLT].

h. νόμος (LN 33.55) (BAGD 3. p. 542): 'law' [Lns, Mil, NIC, WBC; KJV, NAB, NIV, NRSV, REB], 'Law' [HNTC, LN; NASB, NJB, TEV, TNT], '(Mosaic) law' [BAGD], 'the law of Moses' [CEV, NLT]. It refers to the Mosaic law [EBC, WBC].

QUESTION—What relationship is indicated by καί 'and'?

This word introduces a different aspect of the subject [EGT]. It introduces the discussion of the implications of Abraham's giving a tithe to Melchizedek [Lns]. It is explanatory [My, NIGTC], restating the thought of 7:4 more specifically [NIGTC, Wst]. It indicates the justification of πήλικος 'how great' in the preceding verse [Alf].

QUESTION—What relationship is indicated by μέν 'on the one hand' (in this verse) and δέ 'on the other hand' (in the following verse)?

They balance the comparison and contrast between the Levitical priests and Melchizedek [Lns, Mil, My, WBC].

QUESTION—To whom does οἱ ἐκ τῶν υἱῶν Λευί 'the ones from the sons of Levi' refer?

1. It refers to Aaron's family [Alf, Blm, EGT, Hu, Hwt, Lns, My, NCBC], but only to the priests and not the entire tribe of Levi [Alf, Blm, EGT, HNTC, Hu, Hwt, Lns, Mil, My].
2. It refers to the entire tribe of Levi [NTC, TH].

QUESTION—What relationship is indicated by the participle λαμβάνοντες 'receiving'?

1. It is governed by the preceding definite article οἱ 'the-(ones)' and is attributive [HNTC, Mil, NIC, NIGTC, WBC; all versions except NAB]: those descendants of Levi who received priesthood. The source of their receiving an appointment to priesthood is God [NIGTC].
2. It is not governed by the preceding definite article, and it is temporal [Alf, Wst]: when descendants of Levi receive the priesthood.

QUESTION—What is the phrase κατὰ τὸν νόμον 'according to the law' connected with?

1. It is connected with ἐντολὴν ἔχουσιν 'they have a commandment' [Blm, EBC, Hwt, My, NIGTC, NTC, TH, TNTC, WBC, Wst; all versions except KJV, TNT]: they have a commandment according to the law.

2. It is connected with ἀποδεκατοῦν τὸν λαόν 'to collect a tenth from the people' [Alf, EGT, Mil]: to collect tithes according to the law. It indicates manner [Mil].

this is, the brothers[a] of-them,

LEXICON—a. ἀδελφός (LN 11.25): 'brother' [LN, Lns, Mil, NIC, WBC; KJV, NASB, NIV, NJB], 'brother Israelite' [NAB], 'fellow-Israelite' [HNTC, TH; TNT], 'fellow Jew' [LN], 'fellow-countryman' [REB], 'one's own relative' [CEV, NLT], 'people' [TEV]. This plural noun is translated 'kindred' [NRSV]. It refers to all of Abraham's descendants [Mil, NIGTC].

QUESTION—Why is this phrase mentioned?

It identifies the people referred to [Mil, My, NIGTC], emphasizing the unusual fact that equals receive tithe from equals [My, WBC]. It indicates that the right to collect these tithes was within one race [Alf, Lg].

even-though[a] having-come-out[b] from[c] the loins[d] of-Abraham;

LEXICON—a. καίπερ (LN 89.71) (BAGD p. 394): 'even though' [LN; NAB, NIV, NLT, TEV], 'although' [BAGD, HNTC, LN, Lns, NIC, WBC; NASB, NJB, REB], 'though' [LN, Mil; KJV, NRSV, TNT], 'even' [CEV]. It indicates that the following statement is true although remarkable [Lns].

b. perf. act. participle of ἐξέρχομαι (LN 15.40, **23.60**) (BAGD 1.b.α. p. 275): 'to come out' [LN (15.40), Lns, Mil; KJV], 'to go out' [BAGD]. The phrase ἐξεληλυθότας ἐκ τῆς ὀσφύος 'Αβραάμ 'having come out from the loins of Abraham' is translated 'are Abraham's offspring' [NIC], 'having descended from (Abraham)' [BAGD], 'are descended from Abraham' [WBC; NASB, NIV, NJB, NRSV], 'all of them are descendants of Abraham' [NAB], 'they too are descendants of Abraham' [HNTC; REB], 'they are also descendants of Abraham' [TEV], 'they also are descended from Abraham' [TNT], 'Abraham's descendants' [CEV], 'Abraham had been their father' [**LN** (23.60)]. The phrase τοὺς ἀδελφοὺς αὐτῶν...ἐξεληλυθότας ἐκ τῆς ὀσφύος 'Αβραάμ 'the brothers of them . . . having come out from the loins of Abraham' is translated 'their own relatives' [NLT].

c. ἐκ with genitive object (LN 84.4, 90.16): 'from' [LN (84.4, 90.16)], 'out from' [LN (84.4)], 'out of' [LN (84.4), Lns, Mil; KJV]. It indicates source [Mil].

d. ὀσφύς (LN 8.43) (BAGD 2. p. 587): This singular noun is translated as a plural: 'loins' [LN, Lns, Mil].

QUESTION—Why is this phrase mentioned?

It indicates that Abraham's descendants paid tithes to their own relatives [Alf, GNC, HNTC, Hu, Lg, My, NIC], further emphasizing the unusual fact of equals receiving tithes from their equals [My]; it further identifies 'the people' [NIGTC], emphasizing the dignity of the Israelites and the authority of the Levitical priests [NIGTC].

1. It implies that those who received the tithes were not inherently superior to those who paid them [EBC, EGT].
2. It implies the superiority of those who received the tithes [HNTC, Lg, My, NTC, WBC, Wst], but only within the family of Abraham [HNTC], and only to show in the following verse their inferiority to Melchizedek [My, WBC]; it implies preeminence without altering the equality of all the people [Wst].

QUESTION—What relationship is indicated by the participle ἐξεληλυθότας 'having come out'?

With the preceding καίπερ 'although', it is concessive [Blm, HNTC, Mil, NIC, WBC; all versions]: although they have come out.

QUESTION—What is the participle ἐξεληλυθότας 'having come out' connected with?

It refers to τοὺς ἀδελφούς 'the brothers' [Alf, Blm, HNTC, Mil, NIC, WBC; NASB, NIV, NJB, NRSV, REB, TEV]: the brothers have come out.

7:6 on-the-other-hand the-(one) not having-(his)-genealogy-traced[a] from[b] them has-collected-a-tenth-from[c] Abraham

LEXICON—a. pres. pass. participle of γενεαλογέω (LN **10.25**) BAGD p. 154: 'to have one's genealogy traced' [NASB], 'to have one's genealogy counted' [Mil], 'to have one's descent traced' [BAGD, HNTC; TNT], 'to have one's descent counted' [KJV], 'to be descended' [**LN**; TEV]. The passive voice is also translated as active: 'to trace one's descent' [WBC; NIV], 'to reckon one's genealogy' [Lns], 'to be in the lineage' [LN]. The phrase γενεαλογούμενος ἐξ αὐτῶν 'not being descended from them' is translated 'who does not belong to their ancestry' [NRSV], 'who was not of their ancestry' [NAB], 'who was not even related to Levi' [NLT], 'who was not of the same descent' [NJB], 'who does not belong to their genealogy' [NIC], 'though he does not share their ancestry' [REB], 'although (Melchizedek) wasn't a descendant of Levi' [CEV], 'they were not his forefathers' [LN].

b. ἐκ with genitive object (LN 89.3): 'from' [HNTC, LN, Lns, Mil, WBC; KJV, NASB, NIV, TEV, TNT], 'of' [NAB]. It indicates source [Mil].

c. perf. act. indic. of δεκατόω (LN **57.115**) (BAGD p. 174): 'to collect a tenth from' [WBC; NASB, NIV, NLT], 'to collect one tenth from' [**LN**; TEV], 'to receive a tenth part from' [TNT], 'to collect tithes' [LN], 'to collect tithes from' [BAGD; NRSV], 'to receive a tithe from' [HNTC], 'to receive tithes from' [BAGD], 'to receive tithes of' [KJV, NAB], 'to exact tithes from' [LN], 'to take tithes from' [Mil], 'to take one's tithe from' [NJB], 'to tithe' [Lns; REB]. The active voice is also translated as passive: 'to be paid tithes by' [NIC]. The perfect tense indicates the enduring nature of Melchizedek's priesthood [Alf, Mil, NIC]; it implies that the action is still relevant [Hwt, Lns, NIGTC, NTC, TNTC, WBC, Wst]. This verb does not imply a demand by Melchizedek, but only that Abraham voluntarily gave him the tenth [Lns, Mil, NTC].

QUESTION—What relationship is indicated by δέ 'but on the other hand'?

It states the contrast with the preceding verse [Alf, EGT, Mil, NIGTC]. The two actions of this verse imply that Melchizedek's priesthood was of a different kind than the Levitical priesthood [Blm, HNTC].

QUESTION—What relationship is indicated by the participial form γενεαλογούμενος 'being descended'?

The present tense indicates customary action [Alf]: who regularly does not have his genealogy traced from them.

1. With the definite article ὁ 'the (one)', it is attributive [HNTC, Lns, Mil, NIC; KJV, NAB, NASB, NRSV, TNT]: the one being descended.
2. It indicates concession [WBC; NIV, REB, TEV]: although he is not descended from them. The concession is implied by translating the two following verbs as contraexpectations, 'yet/but he received a tenth . . . and blessed . . .' [WBC; NIV, TEV].

QUESTION—To what does ἐξ αὐτῶν 'from them' refer?

It refers to the sons of Levi [Mil, My; TEV] and their genealogy [Alf, EGT, GNC, ICC, Lg, Lns, NCBC, NIGTC, TH, WBC, Wst]; it refers to priests [TNT].

and has-blessed the-(one) having the promises.

QUESTION—Why is this clause mentioned?

It further indicates Melchizedek's exalted position [My, WBC]. Abraham recognized Melchizedek's superiority by accepting a blessing from him [NIC].

QUESTION—What relationship is indicated by καί 'and'?

It connects two coordinate actions, receiving a tenth and blessing [Alf, Mil; all versions]: he has received a tenth and he has blessed. It introduces a new development in the discussion [NIGTC].

QUESTION—What is implied by εὐλόγηκεν 'he has blessed'?

It indicates an official action by an authorized person of superior position to the recipient [EBC, HNTC, NIC, Wst]. The perfect tense implies that the action is still relevant [Hwt, Lns, NIGTC, NTC, WBC, Wst], that Melchizedek's status is permanent [NIC].

QUESTION—What does the present tense of the participle τὸν ἔχοντα 'the one having' indicate?

It designates Abraham as the possessor of the promises [Alf, EGT, ICC]. The phrase points to Abraham's status as the possessor of the promises [NIGTC].

QUESTION—What is implied by the plural ἐπαγγελίας 'promises'?

It refers to repetitions of the original promise that through Abraham all families of earth would be blessed [Blm]. The definite article and the lack of any modifier implies that the promise referred to is well-known and needs no further identification [NIGTC]. The reference is to God's act of promising, not to the possession of what was promised [TH].

7:7 And apart-from[a] all contradiction[b] the inferior[c] is-blessed by[d] the superior.[e]

LEXICON—a. χωρίς with genitive object (LN 89.120) (BAGD 2.b.β. p. 890): 'apart from' [LN], 'without' [BAGD, LN, Lns; KJV, NASB, NIV, NLT], 'without expressing' [BAGD], 'beyond' [NIC; NRSV, REB], not explicit [HNTC, Mil, WBC; CEV, NAB, NJB, TEV, TNT].

b. ἀντιλογία (LN 33.445, **33.456**) (BAGD 1. p. 75): 'contradiction' [BAGD, **LN** (33.456); KJV], 'doubt' [BAGD; NIV, TEV], 'contradictory statement' [LN (33.445)], 'dispute' [LN (33.445), Lns, NIC; NASB, NRSV, REB], 'question' [NLT]. The phrase χωρὶς πάσης ἀντιλογίας 'apart from all contradiction' is translated 'it is indisputable that' [NAB, NJB], 'there is no doubt that' [TEV], 'there is no question that' [Mil], 'unquestionably' [HNTC, WBC; TNT], 'everyone agrees' [CEV].

c. ἐλάσσων (LN **87.67**) (BAGD p. 248): 'inferior' [BAGD, Mil, NIC; NJB, NRSV, TNT], 'lesser' [HNTC, LN; NASB, REB], 'lesser person' [NAB, NIV], 'less' [Lns; KJV]. The phrase τὸ ἔλαττον 'the lesser' is translated 'the person of lesser status' [WBC], 'that which is of lesser status' [**LN**]. The phrase τὸ ἔλαττον ὑπὸ τοῦ κρείττονος εὐλογεῖται 'the inferior is blessed by the superior' is translated 'the one who blesses is greater than the one who is blessed' [TEV], 'a person who gives a blessing is greater than the one who receives the blessing' [CEV], 'the person who has the power to bless is always greater than the person who is blessed' [NLT].

d. ὑπό with genitive object (LN 90.1): 'by' [HNTC, LN, Lns, Mil, NIC, WBC; all versions except KJV, TEV], 'of' [KJV]. It indicates agency [Mil].

e. κρείττων (LN 87.28) (BAGD 1. p. 449): 'superior' [Mil, NIC; NJB, NRSV, TNT], 'greater' [HNTC, LN, Lns; CEV, NASB, NLT, REB, TEV], 'greater person' [NAB, NIV], 'one of greater status' [WBC], 'higher in rank' [BAGD], 'more prominent' [BAGD], 'better' [BAGD, LN; KJV]. It refers to status [TH, WBC].

QUESTION—What relationship is indicated by δέ 'and'?

It introduces a new proposition [Alf]. It carries on the argument [Blm]. It expresses the grounds for the comment in the preceding verse [Mil]: Abraham is inferior to Melchizedek, because the inferior is blessed by the superior. It is an explanatory comment [TH], a parenthetical comment on the implications of blessing and being blessed [ICC, WBC]. It expresses a principle which is universally accepted [Mil, TH, TNTC] as simple logic [NTC]. It implies that Melchizedek is superior to Abraham [EGT, GNC, Hwt, My, TNTC].

QUESTION—What relationship is indicated by the neuter gender of ἔλαττον 'inferior' and κρείττονος 'superior'?

It broadens and generalizes the reference [Alf, Blm, EGT, ICC, Mil, My, Wst] especially in a collective reference to persons [ICC, Lns, My, WBC]. With the definite article [WBC] it also directs attention to the qualities indicated by these two words [Lns, WBC].

7:8 and here[a] on-the-one-hand dying[b] men receive tithes,[c]

LEXICON—a. ὧδε (LN **92.35**) (BAGD 2.b. p. 895): 'here' [Lns, Mil; KJV], 'in this case' [LN; NASB], 'in the one case' [BAGD, HNTC, WBC; NIV, NRSV, TNT], 'in the one instance' [REB], 'in our situation' [NIC], not explicit [CEV]. The phrase ὧδε μέν 'here on the one hand' is translated 'whereas' [NAB], 'further' [NJB], 'in the case of the priests' [NLT, TEV]. This word reinforces μέν 'on the one hand' [Mil]. It refers to the Levitical priesthood [Alf, Blm, EGT, Hu, Hwt, Mil, My, Wst], to the author's situation [My, NIC]. It implies that the Levitical priesthood still existed when this letter was written [Alf, My].

b. pres. act. participle of ἀποθνήσκω (LN 23.99) (BAGD 2. p. 91): 'to die' [LN, Lns, Mil; CEV, KJV, NIV, NLT, TEV], 'to be mortal' [BAGD; NRSV], 'to be subject to death' [NAB]. This participle is also translated as an adjective: 'mortal' [BAGD, HNTC, Mil, NIC, WBC; NASB, NJB, TNT]; as a phrase: 'who must die' [REB]. This participle precedes ἄνθρωποι 'men' which it modifies, for emphasis [Alf], to emphasize the idea of mortality [WBC]. The meaning is that the Levitical priests in turn die and leave the priesthood to another person [Blm, EGT, Lns, Mil, NIGTC, WBC].

c. δέκατος: 'tithe'. See this word in 7:4. The plural here refers to the repeated receiving of the tithe [Wst].

QUESTION—Why is this verse mentioned?

It gives another aspect of the superiority of Melchizedek's priesthood [Alf, Blm, EGT, GNC, Mil, My, NIC, Wst], the contrast between the Levitical priests and Melchizedek [NCBC, TH, TNTC, WBC], emphasizing the contrast between mortality and life [NIGTC].

QUESTION—What is implied by ἄνθρωποι 'men'?

There is an implied contrast between this word and Melchizedek [Alf]: on the one hand men . . . on the other hand Melchizedek . . .

QUESTION—What relationship is indicated by the participle ἀποθνήσκοντες 'dying'?

1. It is attributive, describing ἄνθρωποι 'men' [My, NIGTC, NTC, TH; KJV, NIV, NLT, NRSV, REB, TEV]: men who die. (Since ἄνθρωποι 'men' has no definite article, the participle can be attributive without an article.)
2. It is translated as an adjective [HNTC, NIC, WBC; NASB, NJB, TNT]: mortal men.
3. It is translated as a verb [CEV]: all priests die.

on-the-other-hand there[a] (one)-being-testified[b] that he-lives.[c]

LEXICON—a. ἐκεῖ (LN 83.2) (BAGD 2.b. p. 895): 'there' [LN, Lns, Mil; KJV], 'at that place' [LN], 'in that situation' [NIC], 'in that case' [NASB, NJB], 'in the other case' [BAGD, HNTC, WBC; NIV, NRSV, TNT], 'in the other instance' [REB], 'as for Melchizedek' [TEV], not explicit [CEV, NAB, NLT]. This word reinforces δέ 'but on the other hand' [Mil]. This refers to Melchizedek's priesthood [Blm, EBC, EGT, Hu, Hwt, Lns, Mil, My], which was in antiquity [My].

b. pres. pass. participle of μαρτυρέω (LN 33.262) (BAGD 2.a. p. 493): 'to be testified' [BAGD, Mil; NRSV], 'to be witnessed' [BAGD, LN; KJV, NASB], 'to have witness borne' [BAGD, WBC], 'to have witness' [Lns], 'to be attested' [NIC; NJB], 'to be affirmed' [HNTC; TNT], 'to be declared' [NIV], 'we are told' [NLT]. This passive voice is translated as an active: 'Scripture testifies' [NAB], 'scripture affirms' [REB], 'as the scripture says' [TEV], 'Scriptures teach' [CEV]. The testimony is given by scripture [Alf, Blm, Hu, Lns, NIGTC, TH, TNTC, WBC; CEV, TEV, TNT]; by God [NIGTC].

c. pres. act. indic. of ζάω (LN 23.88) (BAGD 1.a.ε. p. 336): 'to live' [BAGD, LN, Lns, Mil, WBC; KJV, NIV, NRSV, TEV], 'to be alive' [NIC; CEV, NJB, REB], 'to be still alive' [HNTC], 'to be still living' [TNT], 'to live on' [NAB, NASB, NLT].

QUESTION—What relationship is indicated by the participle μαρτυρούμενος 'being testified'?

It is attributive, modifying the understood 'one' [HNTC, NIC, TH, TNTC, WBC, Wst; NIV, NJB, REB, TEV]: one who is being testified to.

QUESTION—What is meant by ζῇ 'he lives'?

The reference is to Melchizedek's personal life, not to his priesthood [Alf, Lg(K)]. It does not say that he is still living, but that this is, by its silence, the scriptural testimony about him [Blm, EBC, EGT, GNC, ICC, Mil, NIC, Wst]. As an inference from the scripture, he was believed to be immortal [HNTC]. It means that his priesthood was not affected by his death; he still lives in his antitype, Jesus [Lns].

7:9 and as a-word[a] to-say,

LEXICON—a. ἔπος (LN **33.139**) (BAGD p. 305): 'word' [BAGD, LN]. The phrase ὡς ἔπος εἰπεῖν 'as a word to say' is translated 'so to speak' [BAGD, LN; NAB, NASB, TEV], 'that is' [LN], 'that is to say' [LN], 'one might even say' [Mil; NIV, NRSV], 'we might even say' [NLT], 'one might almost say' [BAGD, WBC], 'we could say' [CEV], 'it could be said' [NJB], 'it might be said' [REB, TNT], 'it might even be said' [HNTC], 'as I may so say' [KJV], 'in a sense' [**LN**], 'to use just the right word' [BAGD], 'to state it plainly' [Lns].

QUESTION—What relationship is indicated by καί 'and'?

It introduces a new idea [EGT] reinforcing Melchizedek's superiority [Mil]. It is a further proof of the superiority of Melchizedek's priesthood [Alf, My]; it indicates the implication of Abraham's giving a tithe to Melchizedek [WBC].

QUESTION—What is meant by this phrase?

This phrase indicates that what follows is unexpected or somewhat strained [Alf, ICC, Mil, TNTC] or exaggerated [NIC], something that is surprising [EBC, NTC, WBC, Wst] or could be misinterpreted [EBC, Wst]. It means that the writer does not wish to press the point strictly [EGT, Lg] or unduly [Blm, Hwt, NIGTC] or literally [Mil, My, WBC], that it must be taken allegorically [Hwt]. It means to use the correct word or a strong expression [Lns]. This phrase modifies the following clause [NIGTC].

through[a] Abraham even[b] Levi the-(one) receiving tithes[c] has-paid-tithes;[d]

LEXICON—a. διά with genitive object (LN 90.4): 'through' [HNTC, LN, Lns, Mil, WBC; NASB, NIV, NLT, NRSV, REB, TNT], 'by' [LN], 'by the agency of' [NIC], 'in' [KJV], 'in the person of' [NAB, NJB]. The phrase δι' Ἀβραὰμ καὶ Λευὶ δεδεκάτωται 'through Abraham even Levi has paid tithes' is translated 'when Abraham paid the tenth, Levi also paid it' [TEV], 'when Abraham gave Melchizedek a tenth, Levi also gave him a tenth' [CEV]. The reference is to Abraham's giving a tithe to Melchizedek [My].

b. καί (LN 89.93): 'even' [LN, Lns, Mil, WBC; NASB, TNT], 'also' [LN; CEV, KJV, TEV], not explicit [NIC; NAB, NIV]. The phrase καὶ Λευί 'even Levi' is translated 'Levi himself' [HNTC; NJB, NRSV, REB].

c. δεκάτη: 'tithe'. See this word in 7:4.

d. perf. pass. indic. of δεκατόω (LN **57.114**) (BAGD p. 174): 'to pay tithes' [BAGD, Mil, NIC; KJV, NASB, NJB, NRSV], 'to pay the tenth' [LN, WBC; NIV, TEV], 'to pay a tenth' [NLT, TNT], 'to give a tenth' [CEV], 'to be tithed' [HNTC, Lns; NAB, REB]. The perfect tense implies that Levi stands before us tithed [Lg(K), Lns], that Abraham's act is of permanent significance [NIGTC], a permanent recognition of Melchizedek's superiority [Mil].

QUESTION—What is the meaning of this clause?

It means that Abraham acted as a representative of all his descendants [HNTC, Hu, Lns, My, NTC, TNTC, WBC, Wst] including Levi [NIC, TH], since he contained in his body the seed of all his descendants [NCBC, NIC]. Therefore Levi (and his descendants [TNTC]) recognized Melchizedek's superiority [NCBC, NIC, TNTC]; Melchizedek's superiority is historically based [WBC].

QUESTION—What is meant by Λευὶ ὁ δεκάτας λαμβάνων 'Levi the one receiving tithes'?

It means that Levi is the head of the tribe; his descendants collected the tithes [Alf, Hwt, Lns, Mil, My, TH; TEV].

QUESTION—What relationship is indicated by the participial form ὁ λαμβάνων 'the one receiving'?

The participle describes Levi [Mil, WBC; all versions except NLT, TEV], Levi's descendants [NLT, TEV]. The present tense implies that the Levitical priesthood was still in operation [Mil].

7:10 for he-was still in[a] the loins[b] of-the father[c] when Melchizedek met[d] him.

LEXICON—a. ἐν with dative object (LN 83.13): 'in' [HNTC, LN, Lns, Mil, NIC, WBC; all versions except CEV]. The phrase ἔτι ἐν τῇ ὀσφύϊ τοῦ πατρὸς ἦν 'he was still in the loins of the father' is translated 'he was still in the body of his ancestor' [NIC; TEV], 'Levi was born later into the family of Abraham' [CEV], 'although Levi wasn't born yet, the seed from which he came was in Abraham's loins' [NLT].

b. ὀσφύς: 'loins'. See this word in 7:5.

c. πατήρ (LN 10.20): 'father' [Lns, Mil; KJV, NAB, NASB], 'forefather' [NIC], 'ancestor' [HNTC, LN, WBC; NIV, NJB, NRSV, REB], 'ancestor Abraham' [TEV, TNT], 'Abraham' [CEV, NLT]. It means 'ancestor' [My, NCBC, NIGTC].

d. aorist act. indic. of συναντάω (LN 13.120) (BAGD 1. p. 784): 'to meet' [BAGD, HNTC, Lns, Mil, WBC; all versions except CEV, NJB, NLT], 'to come to meet' [NIC; NJB], 'to come upon' [LN], 'to meet up with' [LN], not explicit [CEV, NLT].

QUESTION—What relationship is indicated by γάρ 'for'?

It indicates the grounds for saying that Levi paid a tithe to Melchizedek [EGT, GNC, Mil, My, NCBC, WBC; CEV]. Since Levi was still in his father's body, so to speak, he was involved in all that Abraham did [NIGTC]. It implies that Melchizedek was superior to Levi and his descendants [GNC, Lns, NCBC, NIGTC, NTC, WBC]. It shows the honorable position of the Levitical priests over their fellow-Israelites, but their lower position than Melchizedek's [ICC]. It emphasizes the unity of Abraham's race [Wst].

QUESTION—What is meant by the phrase ἐν τῇ ὀσφύϊ τοῦ πατρός 'in the loins of the father'?

It means that Levi had not yet been born [Alf, Mil, My, TH; NLT, TEV].

QUESTION—What is meant by τοῦ πατρός 'of the father'?

It refers to Abraham, the ancestor of Levi [Alf, Mil, My, NIGTC, TH, WBC, Wst; all versions].

QUESTION—To whom does αὐτῷ 'him' refer?

It refers to Abraham [Blm, Mil, TH, WBC; NAB, NIV]: Melchizedek met Abraham.

DISCOURSE UNIT: 7:11–28 [Hwt, WBC; NIV]. The topic is Jesus being a priest like Melchizedek [WBC; NIV], a comparison of the legal and spiritual priesthoods [Hwt].

DISCOURSE UNIT: 7:11–19 [HNTC, Lg, NTC]. The topic is the superior priesthood of Melchizedek [NTC], the replacement of the Levitical priesthood [HNTC] by Christ's eternal priesthood [Lg].

DISCOURSE UNIT: 7:11–17 [Lns]. The topic is the inadequacy of the Levitical priesthood and the consequent necessity of a priest of the order of Melchizedek.

DISCOURSE UNIT: 7:11–14 [EBC, NIC; NJB]. The topic is the royal priesthood of Melchizedek and of Christ [EBC], the imperfection of the Levitical priesthood [NIC], from the Levitical to the Melchizedekian priesthood [NJB].

7:11 If on-the-one-hand therefore/now[a] perfection[b] were/was through[c] the Levitical priesthood,

LEXICON—a. οὖν (LN 89.50): 'therefore' [LN; KJV], 'so' [LN], 'so then' [LN], 'then' [HNTC, LN, Lns, Mil, WBC; NAB, TNT], 'consequently, accordingly' [LN], 'now' [NIC; NASB, NJB, NRSV, REB, TEV], 'and finally' [NLT], not explicit [CEV, NIV]. It is emphatic [TH].

b. τελείωσις (LN **88.38**) (BAGD 1. p. 810): 'perfection' [BAGD, HNTC, **LN**, NIC, WBC; KJV, NAB, NASB, NIV, NJB, NRSV, REB], 'a perfecting' [Mil], 'completion' [Lns]. This entire clause is translated 'Now, if the work of the Levitical priests had been perfect' [TEV], 'if then the Levitical priesthood had fulfilled its purpose' [TNT], 'if the priesthood of Levi could have achieved God's purpose' [NLT], 'if the Levitical priesthood could cause perfection' [**LN**], 'those priests cannot make anyone perfect' [CEV]. The suffix -σις implies a process [NTC]. It refers to the full state of salvation [Blm] and sanctification [Alf, HNTC] and bringing people to God [HNTC, Hwt, ICC, NIC], to establishing an eternal covenant [Hwt], to the removal of sin [EGT, My], to acceptability to God [EBC], to arriving at the intended moral and religious goal [My] of full salvation [GNC], to God's purpose for mankind [TH, WBC]. The law was not perfect because it did not establish a covenant that was eternal and did not provide permanent access to God [TNTC].

c. διά with genitive object (LN 89.76, 90.4) (BAGD A.III.1.d. p. 180): 'through' [BAGD, HNTC, LN, NIC, WBC; NAB, NASB, NIV, NJB, NRSV, REB], 'by' [LN (90.4); KJV], 'by means of' [LN (89.76), Lns, Mil], not explicit [CEV, NLT, TEV, TNT].

QUESTION—What relationship is indicated by εἰ 'if'?

1. It introduces a contrary to fact condition [Alf, Blm, GNC, HNTC, Hu, Lg, Mil, My, NIC, NIGTC, TH, TNTC, WBC, Wst; NAB, NRSV, REB, TEV, TNT].

1.1 It relates to past (or present [Alf, My]) time [Alf, Blm, GNC, Mil, My, NIGTC, TH, Wst; NAB, TEV, TNT]: if perfection had occurred, which it had not.

1.2 It relates to future time [HNTC, Hu, TNTC; NRSV, REB]: if perfection could occur in the future, which it could not.

2. It introduces a condition of fact, leaving the readers to decide whether it is true [Lns; NASB, NJB].

2.1 It relates to past time [NASB, NJB]: if perfection was through the Levitical priesthood.

2.2 It relates to future time [NIV]: if perfection could have been attained.

QUESTION—What relationship is indicated by οὖν 'therefore'?

1. It indicates the conclusion to the preceding line of argument [Alf, HNTC, LN, Lns, Mil, WBC; KJV, NAB, TNT]: therefore. It is a conclusion to

7:5–10 [My], to 6:20 [WBC], to 5:10 [Mil]. It takes up the main line of argument, not from the immediately preceding point [Alf]. It resumes the thought interrupted after 6:20; the Levitical priesthood was not adequate because there was to be a new priest like Melchizedek and not like Aaron [WBC].

2. It indicates a transition to a new topic [Lns, NIC, NIGTC, TH; NASB, NJB, NLT, NRSV, REB, TEV]: now.

for[a] the people[b] were-given-the-law[c] on-the-basis-of[d] it,

LEXICON—a. γάρ (LN 89.23): 'for' [LN, Mil, WBC; KJV, NASB, NIV, NRSV], 'because' [LN], 'indeed' [Lns], 'and' [NJB], not explicit [HNTC, NIC; CEV, NAB, NLT, REB, TEV, TNT].

b. λαός: 'people'. See this word in 7:5. This word is emphatic here by its word order [Alf]. It refers to Israel [TH].

c. perf. pass. indic. of νομοθετέω (LN 33.339) (BAGD 1. p. 542): 'the law to be enacted' [LN, Mil], 'the law to be given' [HNTC, LN; NIV, REB, TEV (some use the indefinite form, 'a law' [LN; NIV, NJB])], 'the Law given' [NJB]. This is also translated with 'law' as the object of the verb: 'to receive the law' [BAGD, NIC; KJV, NAB, NASB, NRSV], 'to receive regulations' [WBC], 'the giving of the law' [TNT], 'to be subjected to laws' [Lns]. This clause is also translated 'the Law of Moses says that the priests must be descendants of Levi' [CEV]. The perfect tense implies that the people were still observing the law [Alf, Lns, Wst]; it implies the lasting significance of giving the law [NTC]. The passive voice indicates being furnished with laws [EBC]. It refers to the entire Mosaic legislation [EGT, Hwt, WBC]; it refers only to the laws relative to the priesthood [Lns].

d. ἐπί with genitive object (LN 90.23) (BAGD I.1.b.β. p. 286): 'on the basis of' [BAGD, Mil; NAB, NASB, NIV, REB, TEV], 'with reference to' [LN], 'with respect to' [LN], 'in close connection with' [HNTC], 'under' [NIC; KJV, NRSV], 'closely linked to' [TNT], 'on the score of' [Lns], 'concerning' [WBC], 'on which it was based' [NLT].

QUESTION—What relationship is indicated by γάρ 'for'?

It indicates the reason why perfection could have been expected from the Levitical priesthood [EGT, Lg, Mil]. This sentence is parenthetical [Lg, My, NCBC, NIGTC].

QUESTION—What relationship is indicated by the phrase ἐπ' αὐτῆς 'on the basis of it'?

1. It indicates the grounds for the giving of the law [Alf, EBC, EGT, Lg(K), My, NCBC, NIGTC, TH, Wst]: they were given the law based on the priesthood. It implies that the priestly system is basic to the system of the law [GNC, Hu, Hwt].
2. It means that the law was given under the administration of the Levitical system [NTC; KJV]: they were given the law under the administration of the priesthood.

3. It indicates association with the Levitical system [WBC]: they were given the law in association with the priesthood.
4. It refers to the means by which the people were subjected to the law [Blm]: they were given the law by means of the priesthood.

what need[a] (would-there-be/was-there) still/further for-a-different[b] priest to-arise[c]

LEXICON—a. χρεία (LN 57.40, 71.23) (BAGD 1. p. 885): 'need' [BAGD, HNTC, LN (57.40, 71.23), Lns, Mil, NIC, WBC; all versions except CEV, NJB, NLT], 'necessity' [BAGD]. The phrase τίς ἔτι χρεία 'what need was there/would there be' is translated 'why was it necessary' [NJB], 'why did God need to' [NLT], 'so there needs to be' [CEV].

b. ἕτερος (LN 58.36, 58.37): 'different' [LN (58.36)], 'different kind' [HNTC, Lns, Mil, WBC; NJB, TEV], 'other' [LN (58.37)], 'another' [NIC; KJV, NASB, NIV, NRSV], 'another kind' [REB, TNT]. The phrase ἕτερον ἀνίστασθαι ἱερέα 'for a different priest to arise' is translated 'to appoint a priest' [NAB]. It means a different kind [Alf, EGT, Hwt, Lg, Lns, Mil, My, NIC, NIGTC, NTC, TH].

c. pres. pass. infin. of ἀνίστημι (LN **13.81**) (BAGD 2.c. p. 70): 'to arise' [BAGD, HNTC, LN, Lns, NIC, WBC; NASB, NJB, NRSV, REB, TNT], 'to rise' [KJV], 'to rise up' [BAGD], 'to appear' [BAGD, LN, Mil; TEV], 'to come' [BAGD; NIV], 'to come into existence' [**LN**], 'to be' [CEV]. This verb is also translated actively with God as the subject: 'to send' [NLT], 'to appoint' [NAB]. It implies appearing on the scene [NIGTC]. This infinitive tells what one part of the 'need' was [Lg, My].

QUESTION—What is the function of this question?

1. The question is a strong negative statement [NIGTC], implying the result that did occur because the preceding condition did not occur [Blm, GNC, HNTC, Hu, Mil, NIC, NIGTC, TH, WBC, Wst; NAB, NRSV, REB, TEV, TNT]: there would not have been a need (which there actually was) for a different priest.
2. The question implies what did not occur if the preceding condition did occur [Lns; NASB, NJB]: there was not a need for a different priest.

QUESTION—What relationship is indicated by ἔτι 'still/further'?

1. It refers to time [My; KJV, NIV]: later.
2. It refers to logic [BAGD, Lg(K), Mil, Wst; NASB, NRSV]: further.
3. It is both logical and temporal [NIGTC].

according-to[a] the order[b] of-Melchizedek and not to-be-called[c] according-to[a] the order[b] of-Aaron?

LEXICON—a. κατά with accusative object (LN 89.8): 'according to' [Lns; NAB, NASB], 'in accordance with' [LN], 'in agreement with' [Mil], 'in relation to' [LN], 'after' [NIC; KJV], 'in' [HNTC; NIV, REB, TEV, TNT], 'of' [NJB], 'from' [NLT]. The phrase κατὰ τὴν τάξιν 'according to the order' is translated 'like' [WBC; CEV].

b. τάξις: 'order'. See this word at 5:10.

c. pres. pass. infin. of λέγω (LN 33.131): 'to be called' [LN, NIC; KJV], 'to be spoken of' [NJB], 'to be designated' [Lns, Mil, WBC; NASB], 'to be described as' [HNTC; REB, TNT]; as an active voice: 'to speak of' [NRSV], 'to choose' [NAB], 'to send' [NLT], not explicit [CEV, NIV, TEV]. It implies an appointment [Blm], being designated or spoken of [EGT], being named [TH]. It refers to the designation in Psalm 110.4 [My].

QUESTION—What is οὐ 'not' connected with?

1. It is connected with the following prepositional phrase [Alf, EGT, Lg, Lns, My, NIGTC, Wst]: not according to the order of Aaron.
2. It is connected with the infinitive λέγεσθαι 'to be called' [ICC, WBC]: not to be called.

QUESTION—What is the infinitive λέγεσθαι 'to be called' related to?

1. It is related to the second phrase introduced by κατά 'according to' [Alf, EGT, HNTC, Mil, NIC; KJV, NAB, NASB, TNT]: to be called according to the order of Aaron. It is parallel to the preceding infinitive ἀνίστασθαι 'to arise' [WBC]. It tells what the second 'need' was [Lg].
2. It is related to both phrases introduced by κατά 'according to' [NJB, NRSV, REB]: to speak of another priest . . . rather than . . .

7:12 For the priesthood being-changed,[a] by necessity[b] (there)-occurs[c] also a-change[d] of-law.

LEXICON—a. pres. pass. participle of μετατίθημι (LN 13.64) (BAGD 2.a. p. 513): 'to be changed' [BAGD, HNTC, Mil; CEV, KJV, NASB, NLT, TEV, TNT], 'to be changed to' [LN], 'to undergo a change' [Lns], 'to be altered' [WBC]. This participle is also translated as a phrase: 'when there is a change of' [NAB, NIV], 'when there is a change in' [NRSV]; as a phrase: 'any change in' [NJB], 'a change of' [REB], 'with the change' [NIC]. It implies a complete setting aside of the law [My] by fulfillment in Christ [Lns]; it means only 'change' [NIGTC]. The present tense leaves open the time of the action [Lns]; it indicates a process [NTC]; it indicates action at the same time as the verb γίνεται 'occurs' [Wst].

b. ἀνάγκη (LN 71.38) (BAGD 1. p. 52): 'necessity' [BAGD, Lns, Mil; KJV, NASB], 'inevitability' [LN]. The phrase ἐξ ἀνάγκης 'by necessity' is translated 'necessarily' [BAGD, NIC, WBC; NAB, NRSV]; the phrase ἐξ ἀνάγκης γίνεται 'by necessity there occurs' is translated 'must mean' [NJB, REB], 'there must be' [HNTC; CEV, NIV], 'there has to be' [TEV], 'it is necessary that there should be' [TNT]. It refers to a logical necessity [NIGTC, TH], a necessity arising from the human condition [Blm].

c. pres. pass. (deponent = act.) of γίνομαι (LN 13.107): 'to occur' [LN, Lns], 'to happen' [LN], 'to take place' [NIC; NASB], 'to be made' [KJV], 'to be' [Mil, WBC; CEV, NAB, NLT, NRSV].

d. μετάθεσις (LN **13.52**) (BAGD 2. p. 511): 'change' [BAGD, HNTC, LN, Lns, Mil, NIC; all versions], 'alteration' [WBC], 'transformation'

[BAGD, LN]. The phrase μετάθεσις γίνεται 'occurs a change' is translated 'be changed' [CEV, NLT]. It implies a complete setting aside of the law [GNC, ICC, Lns, My, NIC] by fulfillment in Christ [GNC, Lns]; it means only 'change' [NIGTC]. The suffix -σις indicates a process [NTC].

QUESTION—What relationship is indicated by γάρ 'for'?

It connects the idea in 7:11 that a change in the priesthood is needed with the requirement that the law also must be changed [Mil, My, Wst]. It is connected with the parenthetical clause in 7:11 referring to the giving of the law [Alf, NCBC]. It begins the first argument that the appointment of a Melchizedekian priest shows the inadequacy of the Levitical priesthood [Lg]. It introduces a reason for the topic in the context [Blm]. It introduces the proof that there was in fact a change in the priesthood [Blm]; this change has taken place [Hwt, Lns, NIGTC], is now taking place [EGT, HNTC]. It tells how the change will occur [NTC]. The reference is to a change in the type of priesthood [EBC].

QUESTION—What relationship is indicated by the participle μετατιθεμένης 'being changed'?

1. It is temporal [HNTC, Hu, WBC, Wst; CEV, NAB, NASB, NIV, NLT, NRSV, TEV]: when it is changed.
2. It is conditional [Alf, EGT, Mil; TNT]: if it is changed.
3. It expresses an accompanying action [Lns, NIC]: with the change.
4. It expresses the reason for changing the law (this is not overtly stated, but seems implied, by Blm, Hwt, Lns, NIGTC): since it is changed.

QUESTION—What is the meaning of νόμου 'of law'?

1. It refers to the whole Mosaic law [Alf, Lg, My, NIGTC, TH].
2. It refers to the various laws concerning the Levitical priesthood [Hu, Lns, TNTC].

7:13 For (he) about[a] whom these-things are-said belongs-to[b] a-different[c] tribe,

LEXICON—a. ἐπί with accusative object (LN 90.23) (BAGD III.1.b.ζ. p. 289): 'about' [BAGD, Mil, WBC; CEV, NLT], 'concerning' [NASB], 'with respect to' [LN], 'with a view to' [NIC], 'to' [LN], 'of' [HNTC, Lns; all versions except NASB]. This preposition here implies the one towards whom Psalm 110:4 pointed [NIGTC].

b. perf. act. indic. of μετέχω (LN **34.31**) (BAGD p. 514): 'to belong to' [BAGD, HNTC, LN, Lns, Mil, NIC, WBC; all versions except CEV, KJV, NAB], 'to pertain to' [KJV], 'to be of' [NAB], 'to come from' [CEV]. This word (by the active voice [NTC]) implies that Christ voluntarily took on human nature [Hu, Hwt, Mil, NIGTC, NTC, Wst]. The perfect tense implies his continued human nature [Alf], his permanent identification with his tribe [Lns], namely the tribe of Judah [Mil], which is involved in the change of priesthood [EGT]; it refers to the historical fact now completed before us [Lg], to the permanent effects of the fact [NTC]; it refers merely to the past event, like an aorist tense [ICC].

c. ἕτερος: 'different'. See this word in 7:11.

QUESTION—What relationship is indicated by γάρ 'for'?

By showing that a change of priesthood has occurred [NIGTC], it further confirms that the law has been changed [Alf, Blm, EBC, EGT, Hwt]. It states the grounds for the comment in 7:11 that a different kind of priest is needed [Mil, My(D), NCBC, WBC]. It is the first proof of the comment in 7:12 [My].

QUESTION—To whom does 'he' refer?

It refers to Jesus [NJB, TEV, TNT], the Lord [CEV]: Jesus, about whom these things are said.

QUESTION—To what does ταῦτα 'these things' refer?

1. It refers to the promise made in Psalm 110:4 [Alf, EGT, GNC, Hu, Lg, Lns, My, NIGTC, TH, WBC] (and restated in the present context [Lns]) concerning his eternal Melchizedekian priesthood [Blm]: the things in Psalm 110 (and here).
2. It refers to 7:11 [TNTC].

from[a] which no-one has-officiated-at[b] the altar;[c]

LEXICON—a. ἀπό with genitive object (LN 90.15): 'from' [HNTC, LN, Lns, Mil, NIC, WBC; CEV, NASB, NIV, NRSV, TNT], 'of' [KJV, NAB, NJB, REB, TEV], not explicit [NLT]. It indicates source [Alf, EGT, Lg, Mil].

b. perf. act. indic. of προσέχω (LN **68.19**) (BAGD 1.c. p. 714): 'to officiate at' [BAGD, Mil, WBC; NAB, NASB], 'to serve at' [HNTC; NIV, NLT, NRSV, REB], 'to serve as a priest at' [CEV], 'to come to serve at' [TNT], 'to do service at' [NJB], 'to minister at' [NIC], 'to give attendance at' [KJV], 'to attend' [Lns], 'to give oneself continuously to' [**LN**], 'to continue to give oneself to' [LN], 'to continue to apply oneself to' [LN]. The phrase προσέσχηκεν τῷ θυσιαστηρίῳ 'has officiated at the altar' is translated 'served as a priest' [TEV]. It means to apply oneself to something [Alf]. The perfect tense refers to the historical fact now completed before us [Lg], to the permanent effects of membership in a different tribe [Lns], to the continuation of the fact [Mil, NIGTC].

c. θυσιαστήριον (LN 6.114) (BAGD 1.a. p. 366): 'altar' [BAGD, HNTC, LN, Mil, NIC, WBC; all versions except TEV], 'sacrificial altar' [Lns], not explicit [TEV]. It refers to the altar where sacrifices were burned [Lns, NIGTC, WBC].

QUESTION—What is meant by the phrase προσέσχηκεν τῷ θυσιαστηρίῳ 'has officiated at the altar'?

It means to hold the priestly office [HNTC, Hu], to perform priestly functions [Hwt, My] regularly [Wst].

7:14 for (it is) evident[a] that from[b] Judah[c] our Lord arose,[d]

LEXICON—a. πρόδηλος (LN 28.60) (BAGD p. 704): 'evident' [Lns; KJV, NASB, NRSV], 'clear' [NAB, NIV], 'very clear' [LN], 'quite clear' [TNT], 'perfectly clear' [WBC], 'obvious' [HNTC, Mil], 'very obvious'

[LN], 'beyond all doubt' [REB], 'well known' [TEV], 'known to all' [BAGD, NIC], 'everyone knows' [CEV, NJB]. The phrase πρόδηλον γάρ 'for it is evident' is translated 'what I mean is' [NLT]. It is emphatic [Blm, Hu, Mil, WBC] by the prefixed προ- 'fore-', meaning that something is perfectly well known or conspicuous [Blm, Hu, My, NTC, TNTC, WBC, Wst].

b. ἐκ with genitive object (LN 90.16): 'from' [HNTC, LN, Mil, NIC, WBC; all versions except KJV, TEV], 'out of' [Lns; KJV], 'of' [TEV]. The phrase ἐξ Ἰούδα 'from Judah' is emphatic by forefronting [My, WBC].

c. Ἰούδας (LN 93.173, 93.174) (BAGD 1.b. p. 379): 'Judah' [BAGD, HNTC, LN, Lns, Mil, NIC, WBC; KJV, NASB, NIV, NJB, NRSV, REB], 'the tribe of Judah' [CEV, NAB, NLT, TEV, TNT]. The reference is to the tribe of Judah [Alf, My, WBC]. It does not necessarily imply that Jesus had a human father [HNTC].

d. perf. act. indic. of ἀνατέλλω (LN **10.35**) (BAGD 2. p. 62): 'to arise', 'to rise' [NAB], 'to spring' [HNTC, Lns, NIC; KJV], 'to be sprung' [REB], 'to come' [CEV, NJB, NLT], 'to be a descendant' [**LN**], 'to descend' [Mil; NIV, TNT], 'to be descended' [BAGD, WBC; NASB, NRSV], 'to be an offspring' [LN], 'to be born a member' [TEV]. The meaning 'to arise' has messianic implications in OT scripture [Hu, Hwt, Mil, My, NIC, WBC]. The perfect tense implies that Jesus' human origin has permanent effects [NIGTC], was an acknowledged fact [Hwt].

QUESTION—What relationship is indicated by γάρ 'for'?

It indicates an explanation of the preceding comment (in 7:12–13 [Mil]) [EBC, Lns, Mil, My, NIGTC, WBC; CEV].

QUESTION—To whom does ὁ κύριος ἡμῶν 'our Lord' refer?

This refers to Jesus [EBC, Lns, My, NIGTC, TNTC, WBC]. Ἡμῶν 'our' refers to the writer and his readers [Lns].

with-reference-to[a] which tribe Moses[b] spoke[c] nothing concerning[d] priests.

TEXT—Instead of ἱερέων 'priests' some manuscripts have ἱερωσύνης 'priesthood'. GNT does not deal with this variant; only Blm, KJV, and NLT read 'priesthood'.

LEXICON—a. εἰς with accusative object (LN 90.23): 'with reference to' [Mil; NASB], 'in relation to' [WBC], 'in connection with' [HNTC; NRSV], 'concerning' [LN], 'regarding' [NAB], 'in regard to' [Lns; NIV], 'of' [NIC; KJV], 'to' [REB]. The phrase εἰς ἣν φυλὴν οὐδὲν Μωϋσῆς ἐλάλησεν 'with respect to which tribe Moses spoke nothing' is translated 'a tribe which Moses did not mention at all' [NJB], 'and Moses did not mention this tribe' [TEV], 'Moses never mentioned Judah' [NLT], 'Moses said nothing in connection with this tribe' [TNT]. This whole phrase is translated 'Moses never said that priests would come from that tribe' [CEV]. The meaning is 'with reference to' [Alf, EGT, My]; it indicates the direction of the thought [EGT]; it refers to speaking to (this tribe) [EBC].

b. Μωϋσῆς (LN 33.59, 93.266): 'Moses' [HNTC, LN (33.59, 93.266), Lns, Mil, NIC, WBC; all versions], 'the Law of Moses, the Law given through Moses, the Law' [LN (33.59)]. The meaning is the Pentateuch [GNC, TH].

c. aor. act. indic. of λαλέω (LN 33.70): 'to speak' [LN, Mil; KJV, NASB], 'to say' [HNTC, LN, NIC, WBC; CEV, NAB, NIV, NRSV, TNT], 'to utter' [Lns], 'to mention' [NJB, NLT, TEV], 'to make reference' [REB]. The aorist tense with 'Moses' as the subject of this verb suggests a specific event—the blessing of Levi, Deut. 33:7–11 [NIGTC, TH], or the giving of the Law [TH].

d. περί with genitive object (LN 89.6, 90.24): 'concerning' [LN (89.6, 90.24), Mil, WBC; KJV, NASB], 'about' [HNTC, LN (89.6); NAB, NIV, NRSV, TNT], 'with regard to' [LN (89.6)], 'in relation to' [LN (89.6)], 'pertaining to' [Lns], 'in connection with' [NIC; NLT], 'when dealing with' [NJB], 'in speaking of' [REB], 'when he spoke of' [TEV], not explicit [CEV].

QUESTION—To what does the phrase εἰς ἣν φυλήν 'with respect to which tribe' refer?

It refers to the tribe of Judah [Mil].

QUESTION—What is the phrase περὶ ἱερέων 'concerning priests' connected with?

It is connected with ἐλάλησεν 'he spoke' [Mil]: he spoke concerning priests.

DISCOURSE UNIT: 7:15–28 [EBC, GNC; NLT, TEV]. The topic is Christ's superior priesthood [EBC], the legitimacy and superiority of Christ's priesthood [GNC], another priest, like Melchizedek [TEV], Christ's likeness to Melchizedek [NLT].

DISCOURSE UNIT: 7:15–19 [EBC, NIC; NJB]. The topic is the superiority of the new priesthood [NIC], the superiority of Christ's priesthood because of his life [EBC], the abrogation of the old law [NJB].

7:15 And it-is still all-the-more[a] very-clear,[b]

LEXICON—a. περισσότερος (LN 78.31) (BAGD 3. p. 651): 'all the more' [LN], 'more abundantly' [Lns]. The phrase περισσότερον κατάδηλόν 'all the more very clear' is translated 'clearer' [NIC; CEV, NAB, NASB, REB], 'much clearer' [HNTC], 'more abundantly clear' [Mil; TNT], 'more obvious' [WBC], 'far more evident' [KJV]; the phrase περισσότερον ἔτι κατάδηλον 'still all the more very clear' is translated 'even more evident' [BAGD; NLT], 'even more clearly evident' [NJB], 'even more clear' [NIV], 'even more obvious' [NRSV], 'even plainer' [TEV]. It is used as an adverb modifying the following κατάδηλον: 'very clear' [NIGTC].

b. κατάδηλος (LN **32.20**) (BAGD p. 410): 'very clear' [LN], 'very evident' [LN], 'self-evident' [Lns], 'easily understood' [LN]. The phrase περισσότερον κατάδηλόν 'all the more very clear' is translated 'clearer'

[BAGD]. The phrase περισσότερον ἔτι κατάδηλόν ἐστιν 'it is still all the more very clear' is translated 'the matter becomes very easy to understand' [**LN**]. This word is made stronger by the prefix κατα- [Alf, EGT, ICC, Mil, My, Wst].

QUESTION—Why is this verse mentioned?

It adds new information, an irresistible conclusion [NIGTC]; it states another proof that the priesthood of Christ is superior to the Levitical priesthood [Blm, NIC], that the law is to be changed [Alf, Blm, My] since the priesthood is changed [My]; it implies the inadequacy of the Levitical priesthood [Lg, Mil, NIC] as implied by the appointment of a Melchizedekian priest [Lg].

QUESTION—To what does 'it' refer?

1. It refers to the superiority of Christ's priesthood [GNC, TH], the ineffectiveness of the Levitical priesthood [Hu, TH].
2. It refers to the change of the law [Alf, EGT, ICC, Mil].
3. It refers to the superiority of Christ's priesthood and that the law is to be changed [Blm].
4. It refers to the change of the law and the ineffectiveness (the temporary character [Hwt], the change [My]) of the Levitical priesthood [EBC].
5. It refers to the author's argument (in 7:11–13 [Lns]) [HNTC, Lns, TH, Wst; NAB, NIV]: the argument is much clearer.
6. It refers to Christ's fulfillment of what Melchizedek was symbolically [WBC].

if/since[a] according-to[b] the likeness[c] of-Melchizedek (a) different[d] priest arises,[e]

LEXICON—a. εἰ (LN 89.30, 89.65, 90.26) (BAGD III. p. 219): 'if' [BAGD, HNTC, LN (89.65, 90.26), Lns, NIC, WBC; NAB, NASB, NIV, NJB, TNT], 'when' [CEV, NRSV], 'since' [BAGD, LN (89.30); Mil], 'because' [LN (89.30)], 'that' [LN (90.26); REB], 'for that' [KJV], 'from the fact that' [NLT], not explicit [TEV].

b. κατά with accusative object: 'according to'. See this word in 7:11.

c. ὁμοιότης (LN **64.3**) (BAGD p. 567): 'likeness' [**LN,** Lns, Mil, WBC; NAB, NASB], 'similitude' [KJV], 'fashion' [NIC]. The phrase κατὰ τὴν ὁμοιότητα 'according to the likeness' is translated 'of the type' [NJB], 'similar to' [**LN**], 'in the same way as' [BAGD], 'like' [CEV, NIV, NLT, REB, TEV], 'resembling' [HNTC; NRSV], 'corresponding' [TNT]; this phrase is emphatic by forefronting [My]. The likeness to the quality of Melchizedek rather than the person of Christ is the point of the argument here [Lg, NIGTC].

d. ἕτερος: 'different'. See this word in 7:11. The phrase ἱερεὺς ἕτερος 'different priest' is emphatic by word order [NIGTC].

e. pres. pass. indic. of ἀνίστημι: 'to arise'. See this word in 7:11. The present tense indicates the certain fulfillment of God's purpose [Wst].

QUESTION—What relationship is indicated by εἰ 'if, since, that'?

1. It indicates the condition under which the matter is still clearer [HNTC, Lns, NIC, TH, WBC, Wst; NAB, NASB, NIV, NJB, TNT]. It is a condition implying an actual fact [Lns, WBC, Wst].

1.1 The time of the appearing is indefinite [HNTC; NAB, NASB, NIV, NJB, TNT]: if he arises.

1.2 The time of the appearing is past [Lns, TH, WBC, Wst]: if he has arisen.

1.3 The time of the appearing is future [NIC]: if he will arise.

2. It indicates when the matter is still clearer [CEV, NRSV]: it is still clearer when a different priest arises.

3. It indicates the reason why the change is still clearer [Alf, GNC, Hu, Mil, My; KJV, NLT, REB, TEV]. The εἰ 'if' makes the statement conditional [Mil, NIGTC] (hypothetical [Hu]) in form but referring to a realized fact [Hu, Mil], a reason [NIGTC].

3.1 The time is indefinite [Mil; KJV]: because he arises.

3.2 The time is past [GNC, Hu; REB, TEV] as the present tense indicates [GNC]: because he has arisen.

7:16 who has-arisen[a] not according-to[b] (a) law of-a-fleshly[c] commandment[d]

LEXICON—a. perf. act. indic. of γίνομαι (LN 13.48, 85.7): 'to arise', 'to appear' [LN (85.7)], 'to come' [NIC], 'to become (a priest)' [LN (13.48), Lns, Mil; NAB, NASB, NIV, NLT, NRSV], 'to be (a priest)' [NJB], 'to come to be (a priest)' [LN (85.7)], 'to be made (a priest)' [KJV, TEV], 'to be appointed' [CEV]. The phrase ὃς γέγονεν 'who has arisen' is translated 'he does so' [WBC], 'a priest' [HNTC]. The phrase ὃς γέγονεν κατά 'who has arisen according to' is translated 'he owes his priesthood to' [REB], 'whose priesthood does not depend on' [TNT]. The reference is to becoming a high priest [Blm, EGT, Hu, NIGTC, TNTC; all versions except REB, TEV]. The perfect tense indicates the permanence of the priesthood [GNC, Lns, NIGTC, NTC].

b. κατά with accusative object (LN 89.4, 89.8) (BAGD II.5.a.δ. p. 407): 'according to' [Mil, NIC], 'in accordance with' [BAGD, LN (89.8)], 'in accord with' [Lns], 'with regard to' [LN (89.4)], 'on the basis of' [NASB, NIV], 'because of' [BAGD; CEV], 'in virtue of' [HNTC; NAB, NJB], 'by virtue of' [WBC], 'after' [KJV], 'through' [NRSV], 'by' [NLT, TEV].

c. σάρκινος (LN **9.13, 26.8**) (BAGD 2. p. 743): 'fleshly' [BAGD, Lns], 'human' [**LN** (9.13, 26.8); TEV], 'carnal' [BAGD; KJV], 'belonging to the realm of the flesh' [BAGD], 'concerning the flesh' [HNTC], 'relating to descent' [REB], 'concerning physical descent' [WBC; NAB, NRSV], 'physical descent' [Mil], 'as to his ancestry' [NIV]; 'made by people' [**LN** (9.13)], 'of people' [LN (9.13)], 'natural' [LN (26.8)], 'earthly' [NIC; TNT]. The phrase κατὰ νόμον ἐντολῆς σαρκίνης 'according to a law of a fleshly commandment' is translated 'on the basis of a law of physical requirement' [NASB], 'because of his ancestors' [CEV], 'by meeting the old requirements of belonging to the tribe of Levi' [NLT]. It indicates physical descent [GNC, Mil, NCBC, NIC, NIGTC, NTC, TH, WBC] and such external matters [GNC, HNTC, My, NIC, Wst]; it refers to the earthly and passing sphere of things [GNC, NCBC, NIC]; it implies matters external and weak [Lg, NIGTC]. It is contrasted with the following ἀκατάλυτος 'indestructible' [TNTC].

d. ἐντολή (LN 33.330) (BAGD 2.a.α. p. 269): 'commandment' [HNTC, LN, Lns, NIC; KJV, NAB], 'order' [LN], 'law' [BAGD], 'regulating' [Mil]. The phrase νόμον ἐντολῆς 'a law of a commandment' is translated 'a law' [NJB], 'a regulation' [NIV], 'a legal requirement' [NRSV], 'a legal ordinance' [WBC], 'a system of rules' [REB], 'a system of commandments' [TNT], 'rules and regulations' [TEV], 'requirements' [NLT], not explicit [CEV] The regulation concerned being descended from a particular person [TH].

QUESTION—Why is this verse mentioned?

It defines the similarity of Christ to Melchizedek [EGT, Mil, My, WBC] and makes a double contrast between the Levitical priesthood and Christ's; the Levitical being according to law (an outward restraint [Wst]) and relating to the flesh, while Christ's is according to power (an inward force [Wst]) and relating to indissoluble life [EGT, Mil, TNTC, WBC, Wst].

QUESTION—To whom does ὅς 'who' refer?

It refers to the 'different priest' in the preceding verse [WBC].

QUESTION—What is meant by νόμον ἐντολῆς σαρκίνης 'a law of a fleshly commandment'?

Νόμος 'law' refers to a norm or standard [Wst] (to the Mosaic system as a whole [NIGTC, TH]), and ἐντολῆς 'commandment' refers to the ordinances concerning the Levitical priesthood [My, NIGTC, TH]: the norm/the Mosaic system expressed in the commandment. It means a law (the rule of an outward ordinance [Alf]) which is based on the present fleshly state which is passing away [Alf, Blm] and is to be terminated [Blm], regulations concerning ancestry and the realm of human physical nature [EBC], earthly ceremonies and the requirements concerning the Levitical priesthood [Hwt, ICC, Lns], concerning descent from Levi [Hu].

QUESTION—How are the two nouns related in the genitive construction νόμον ἐντολῆς 'a law of a commandment'?

1. The law consists of a commandment [HNTC].
2. The law contains a commandment [My].
3. The law is expressed in a commandment [Lns, Mil, Wst; NAB].

but according-to[a] (the) power of-life indestructible.[b]

LEXICON—a. κατά with accusative object: 'according to'. See this word in the preceding part of this verse.

b. ἀκατάλυτος (LN **13.47**) (BAGD p. 30): 'indestructible' [BAGD, WBC; NASB, NIV, NJB, NRSV], 'indissoluble' [Lns, Mil, NIC], 'endless' [BAGD; KJV], 'which has no end' [TEV], 'which cannot be destroyed'

[NAB, NLT], 'that cannot be destroyed' [REB], 'that nothing can destroy' [HNTC; TNT], 'that can never end' [CEV], 'that cannot be brought to an end' [**LN**], 'that cannot be caused to finish' [LN]. It is emphatic by word order [Lns, NIGTC]. It describes Christ's whole life [Wst]; it refers to the life which is inherent in Christ's Melchizedekian priesthood [Lg, My] received in his resurrection and exaltation [Lg, WBC]. It is life which death cannot destroy [NIGTC].

QUESTION—How are the two nouns related in the genitive construction δύναμιν ζωῆς ἀκαταλύτου 'power of life indestructible'?

1. It refers to the energy inherent in Christ's eternal priesthood [Alf].
2. 'Life indestructible' describes the quality of the power [Lns]: indestructible, living power.
3. The power is expressed in the life [Mil].

7:17 For it-is-witnessed,[a] that "You (are) a-priest into[b] the age according-to[c] the order[d] of-Melchizedek."

TEXT—Instead of the passive voice μαρτυρεῖται 'it is witnessed', some manuscripts read μαρτυρεῖ 'he/it witnesses'. GNT does not deal with this variant. Only Blm, CEV, KJV, NAB, and NLT translate this verb as an active voice (and CEV, NAB, and NLT probably stylistically and not by accepting the active form of the verb).

LEXICON—a. pres. pass. indic. of μαρτυρέω (LN 33.262) (BAGD 2.a.p. 493): 'to be witnessed' [BAGD, LN; NASB], 'to have witness borne' [BAGD; Mil, WBC], 'to be attested' [Lns; NJB, NRSV], 'to be affirmed' [HNTC], 'to be declared' [NIV]; as an active voice: 'to testify' [KJV (different text), NAB], 'to affirm' [TNT], 'to say' [CEV, NLT, TEV]. This verb is also translated as a phrase: 'here is the testimony' [REB], 'God's testimony is' [NIC].

b. εἰς with accusative object (LN 67.95, 84.22): 'into' [LN (84.22)], 'for' [Lns]. The phrase εἰς τὸν αἰῶνα 'into the age' is translated 'forever' [HNTC, LN (67.95), Mil, NIC, WBC; all versions]. This phrase is the important point of the clause [Alf, EGT, Mil, My, NIGTC, TNTC].

c. κατά with accusative object: 'according to'. See this word in 7:15.

d. τάξις: 'order'. See this word in 7:11.

QUESTION—What relationship is indicated by γάρ 'for'?

It indicates the grounds for the preceding comment [Alf, EBC, EGT, Mil, My, NIGTC, NTC].

QUESTION—Who is the implied actor of the verb μαρτυρεῖται 'it is witnessed'?

1. It is Scripture that witnesses [EGT, Hwt, Mil, NIGTC, TH; CEV, NAB, NJB, TEV, TNT].
2. It is God who witnesses [NIC, NTC] through the scripture [Lns, NTC].
3. It is the psalmist who witnesses [NLT].

QUESTION—Who is the object of the witnessing?

It is the 'different priest' of 7:15 [Alf], Christ [Lg, My]: the different priest is witnessed to.

QUESTION—What relationship is indicated by ὅτι 'that'?

1. It introduces the quotation [Lg, My, NIGTC, WBC]: it is witnessed, "You are a priest . . ."
2 It means 'that' [WBC]: it is witnessed that you are a priest . . .

DISCOURSE UNIT: 7:18–25 [Lns]. The topic is three convincing contrasts.

7:18 For on-the-one-hand there-occurs[a] (an) annulment[b] of-(a)-preceding[c] commandment[d] on-account-of[e] its (being) weak[f] and useless[g]

LEXICON—a. pres. pass. (deponent = act.) indic. of γίνομαι (LN 13.107): 'to occur' [LN, Lns], 'to take place' [Mil], 'to happen' [LN], 'to be' [WBC; KJV, NASB, NRSV], not explicit [CEV, NLT]. This verb is also translated 'we have' [NIC].

b. ἀθέτησις (LN 13.36, **76.24**) (BAGD 1. p. 21): 'annulment' [BAGD, LN (76.24), WBC], 'disannulling' [Lns, Mil; KJV], 'abrogation' [NRSV], 'cancellation' [NIC], 'removal of' [LN (13.36)], 'setting aside' [NASB]. This word is also translated a verb phrase: 'to be set aside' [**LN**; NIV, NLT, TEV, TNT], 'to be put aside' [CEV], 'to be abolished' [NJB], 'to be repealed' [REB], 'to be annulled' [HNTC; NAB]. It indicates complete cancellation [EBC, My, NIGTC, Wst], to be declared invalid [GNC]. It means discounted for gaining perfection [TNTC]. The suffix -σις indicates a process [NTC]. The agent is God [Lns].

c. pres. act. participle of προάγω (LN 13.114) (BAGD 2.b. p. 702): 'to precede' [Lns], 'to be foregoing' [HNTC, Mil], 'to go before' [BAGD; KJV], 'to come before' [BAGD], 'to happen previously' [LN], 'to happen before' [LN], 'to occur formerly' [LN], not explicit [CEV]. This participle is translated as an adjective: 'former' [WBC; NAB, NASB, NIV], 'earlier' [LN (76.24); NJB, NRSV, REB], 'previous' [NIC; TNT], 'old' [NLT, TEV]. It implies a connection between the old system and the new [EBC, Wst]. It is emphatic by forefronting [My], with a subtle implication of being temporary and unsatisfactory [My, NTC], preparatory [EBC, Wst], to be succeeded by something better [TNTC].

d. ἐντολή (LN 33.330) (BAGD 2.a.α. p. 269): 'commandment' [HNTC, LN, Lns, Mil, NIC, WBC; KJV, NAB, NASB, NJB, NRSV, TNT], 'command' [CEV], 'law' [BAGD], 'regulation' [NIV], 'requirement' [NLT], 'rule' [TEV], 'enactment' [Mil]; translated as a plural: 'rules' [REB]. This is the commandment previously mentioned concerning the priesthood [Alf, GNC, Hu, Lns, My, NIC, NIGTC, NTC, TH, TNTC, WBC, Wst]. It refers to the entire Mosaic law [Blm, EBC].

e. διά with accusative object (LN 89.26): 'on account of' [LN], 'because of' [LN, Lns, Mil, WBC; NAB, NASB, NJB], 'by reason of' [LN], not explicit [CEV]. This preposition is also translated as a conjunction:

'because' [HNTC, NIC; NIV, NLT, NRSV, TEV, TNT], 'for' [KJV], 'as' [REB].

f. ἀσθενής (LN 79.69) (BAGD 2.a. p. 115): 'weak' [BAGD, HNTC, LN, NIC; CEV, NIV, NLT, NRSV, TEV, TNT], 'feeble' [BAGD], 'ineffective' [REB]. This neuter adjective has the sense of a noun [Alf, NIGTC] and is translated 'weakness' [Lns, Mil, WBC; KJV, NAB, NASB, NJB]. It was weak, being unable to give spiritual vitality (justification before God [Blm]) to those who obeyed it [HNTC, TNTC]; it was the people who were weak [WBC].

g. ἀνωφελής (LN **65.50**) (BAGD 1. p. 77): 'useless' [BAGD; CEV, NIV, NLT, REB, TEV], 'ineffectual' [NRSV], 'unprofitable' [HNTC, NIC; TNT], 'of no special benefit' [**LN**], 'without advantage' [LN]. This neuter adjective has the sense of a noun [Alf, NIGTC] and is translated 'uselessness' [WBC; NAB, NASB], 'ineffectiveness' [NJB], 'unprofitableness' [Lns, Mil; KJV]. It was useless because it was law and not love [HNTC], useless in being unable to give constant approach to God [Hwt, TNTC], unable to bring spiritual cleansing [Hwt, WBC], outmoded when Christ's priesthood had been established [GNC]. This word and ἀσθενής 'weak' are similar in meaning [TH].

QUESTION—What relationship is indicated by γάρ 'for'?

It indicates the grounds for the preceding comment [Alf, NCBC, TH, WBC, Wst]. This verse and the following one repeat the preceding argument [Blm] and give a reason for a change in the law and the priesthood [Blm, ICC, My]; they state the result of the displacement of the old system by the new [EGT], the displacement of the law concerning physical descent [Mil], the result of Christ's being proclaimed a priest of the order of Melchizedek [Hwt]. They continue the topic of 7:15 [TNTC, Wst].

QUESTION—What relationship is indicated by μέν 'on the one hand'?

1. Its parallel is the δέ 'on the other hand' in 7:19 [Blm, EGT, GNC, Mil, My(D), TH, TNTC, WBC, Wst; NASB]: on the one hand . . . on the other hand.
2. It is elliptical, implying an understood contrast to the permanence indicated by the reference to an indissoluble life in 7:16 [Alf].

QUESTION—How are the two nouns related in the genitive construction ἀθέτησις ἐντολῆς 'an annulment of a commandment'?

'Commandment' tells what is annulled [GNC, HNTC, Hu; NAB, NIV, NJB, REB, TEV, TNT]: the commandment is annulled.

QUESTION—What relationship is indicated by the phrase 'on account of its being weak and useless'?

It indicates the reason why the former commandment was annulled [Alf, Blm, EBC, EGT, GNC, HNTC, Hu, Hwt, Lns, Mil; NAB, NASB, NIV, NJB, NLT, NRSV, REB, TEV, TNT]: it was annulled because it was weak and useless.

7:19 **—for the law perfected[a] nothing—**

LEXICON—a. aorist act. indic. of τελειόω (LN 88.38) (BAGD 1. p. 809, 2.e.α. p. 810): 'to perfect' [HNTC, LN, WBC], 'to make perfect' [BAGD, LN, Mil, NIC; CEV, KJV, NASB, NIV, NJB, NLT, NRSV, TEV], 'to bring to perfection' [NAB, REB], 'to complete' [BAGD], 'to make complete' [Lns], 'to bring to an end' [BAGD], 'to finish' [BAGD], 'to accomplish' [BAGD], 'to fulfill (one's) purpose' [TNT].

QUESTION—What relationship is indicated by γάρ 'for'?

It explains the comment in the preceding verse that the law was weak and useless [Alf, EBC, Lns, Mil, Wst]. Some treat this clause as parenthetical [NASB, NIV, NRSV, TNT], other consider the whole verse to be parenthetical [Alf, EBC, GNC, Lg(K), Lns, Mil, Wst].

QUESTION—What is meant by the law perfecting nothing?

It means that the law was useless for its proper object, which was the expiation of sins [Blm, ICC], redemption [GNC], complete access to God [EBC, HNTC, ICC, Mil], a right relationship to God through heart-cleansing [WBC].

but/and[a] (a) bringing-in[b] of-(a)-better[c] hope[d] through[e] which we-draw-near[f] to-God.

LEXICON—a. δέ (LN 89.124): 'but' [LN, WBC; KJV, NAB, NJB], 'and' [HNTC, Mil, NIC; NIV, REB, TEV, TNT], 'and now' [NLT], 'and on the other hand' [NASB], 'on the other hand' [LN, Lns; NRSV], 'at the same time' [CEV].

b. ἐπεισαγωγή (LN **68.10**) (BAGD p. 284): '(a) bringing in' [BAGD, Lns; KJV, NASB], '(a) bringing in thereupon' [Mil], '(a) bringing in its place' [Mil], 'introduction' [BAGD, LN, NIC, WBC; NRSV]. The phrase ἐπεισαγωγὴ κρείττονος ἐλπίδος 'a bringing in of a better hope' is translated 'a better hope is introduced' [BAGD; NIV, REB], 'a better hope has been introduced' [HNTC], 'a better hope has supervened' [NAB], 'a better hope has been provided' [TEV], 'a better hope has been brought in' [TNT], 'a better hope has taken its place' [NLT], 'this commandment is replaced by something better' [NJB], 'we are given a much better hope' [CEV]. The agent is God [Lns, Mil, TH].

c. κρείττων (LN **65.21**) (BAGD 1. p. 449): 'better' [BAGD, HNTC, **LN**, Lns, Mil, NIC, WBC; all versions], 'superior' [LN], 'preferable' [BAGD]. It emphasizes quality [NTC]; it implies contrast as well as superiority [NIGTC]. It was better as being effective [ICC], in looking toward mankind's final goal and in opening the priesthood to all believers [HNTC], giving full access to God [Hwt, NIC], the permanent as better than the transient [Hu].

d. ἐλπίς (LN 25.61, 25.62) (BAGD 2.b. p. 253): 'hope' [BAGD, HNTC, LN (25.61), Lns, Mil, NIC, WBC; all versions], 'basis for hope' [LN (25.62)], 'reason for hope' [LN (25.62)], 'what is hoped for' [LN (25.61)]. The phrase ἐλπίδος δι' ἧς ἐγγίζομεν 'hope through which we draw near' is translated 'the hope that brings us close' [NJB]. It refers to a confidence concerning the future [GNC, Lns] that transforms the present [GNC], to the thing hoped for [Lns, NIGTC, TH], which in effect is Christ [NIGTC, NTC], Christ's atoning blood [Lns].

e. διά with genitive object (LN 89.76): 'through' [HNTC, LN, Mil, WBC; NAB, NASB, NRSV, REB, TEV, TNT], 'by' [Lns, NIC; KJV, NIV]. This preposition is also translated by a phrase: 'and it can' [CEV], 'and that is how' [NLT].

f. pres. act. indic. of ἐγγίζω (LN 15.75) (BAGD 1. p. 213): 'to draw near' [BAGD, HNTC, LN, Mil, WBC; NAB, NASB, NIV, NLT, REB, TNT], 'to draw nigh' [Lns; KJV], 'to come near' [BAGD, LN; TEV], 'to approach' [BAGD, LN, NIC; NRSV], 'to bring close' [CEV, NJB]. It is a strong word, implying the superiority of the new law over the old [Blm]. The plural 'we' includes the readers as well as the author [NIGTC]. The present tense implies present access [WBC].

QUESTION—What relationship is indicated by δέ 'but, and'?

1. It is connected with 7:18 [Alf, GNC, HNTC, Lg(K), Lns, Mil, NIC, NIGTC, TNTC, WBC, Wst; NASB, NIV, NJB, NRSV, TNT].

1.1 It indicates a contrast [GNC, Lns, NIGTC, TNTC, WBC, Wst; NASB, NJB, NRSV]: there has occurred an annulment of the former commandment, but a better hope has been introduced.

1.2 It indicates an additional thought [Alf, HNTC, Lg(K), Mil, NIC; NIV, REB, TNT]: there has occurred an annulment of the former commandment and a better hope has arisen.

2. It indicates a contrast with the immediately preceding clause [KJV]: the law made nothing perfect, but the bringing in of a better hope did make perfect.

QUESTION—To what does κρείττονος ἐλπίδος 'better hope' refer?

The 'better hope' is better in contrast with the 'preceding commandment' of 7:18 [Alf, EBC, My, TH, TNTC, Wst]. What is hoped for is better than what the law could provide [TH]. It is the hope of salvation [Blm], the removal of all sins [Lns].

QUESTION—What relationship is indicated by the clause 'through which we draw near to God'?

It describes the function of the 'better hope' [all versions except KJV, REB]: through this better hope we draw near to God.

DISCOURSE UNIT: 7:20–28 [HNTC, NTC]. The topic is the superior priesthood of Jesus [HNTC, NTC].

DISCOURSE UNIT: 7:20–25 [NJB]. The topic is the unchangeability of Christ's priesthood.

DISCOURSE UNIT: 7:20–22 [EBC, Lg, NIC, NTC]. The topic is a superior priesthood by the divine oath [EBC, NIC, NTC], the new covenant is superior because Jesus is its guarantee [Lg].

7:20 And in-accordance-with[a] as-much-as[b] (it was) not without[c] oath-taking;[d]

LEXICON—a. κατά with accusative object (LN 89.8) (BAGD II.5.a.δ. p. 407): 'in accordance with, in relation to' [LN]. The phrase καθ' ὅσον 'in accordance with as much as' is translated 'inasmuch as' [KJV, NASB], 'insofar as' [BAGD, Lns, NIC, WBC], 'in proportion as' [Mil], 'how important' [HNTC]. This entire phrase is translated 'this has been confirmed by an oath' [NAB], 'this was confirmed with an oath' [NRSV], 'and it was not without an oath' [NIV], 'moreover this was not done without an oath' [TNT], 'in addition, there is also God's vow' [TEV], 'God himself made a promise' [CEV], 'God took an oath that Christ would always be a priest' [NLT], this entire phrase is omitted [NJB, REB].

b. ὅσος (LN 78.52) (BAGD 3. p. 586): 'as much as, to the degree that, to the same degree' [LN]. The phrase καθ' ὅσον 'in accordance with as much as' is translated 'to the degree that' [BAGD].

c. χωρίς with genitive object (LN 89.120) (BAGD 2.b.β. p.890): 'without' [HNTC, LN, Lns, Mil, WBC; KJV, NASB, NIV], 'without making use of' [BAGD], 'without expressing' [BAGD], 'apart from' [LN], 'unaccompanied by' [NIC]. It expresses manner [Mil].

d. ὁρκωμοσία (LN **33.463**) (BAGD p. 581): 'oath-taking', 'taking an oath' [BAGD], 'the taking of an oath' [HNTC, Mil], 'the swearing of an oath' [LN, NIC, WBC], 'oath' [BAGD; KJV, NAB, NASB, NIV, NLT, NRSV, TNT], 'vow' [TEV], 'sworn statement' [Lns], 'promise' [CEV]. It emphasizes the act of taking the oath [NIGTC, TH, Wst]. The reference is to God's oath about Christ's priesthood [GNC]. The oath-swearing implies the unchangeability of God's purpose [NTC, Wst].

QUESTION—What relationship is indicated by καί 'and'?

It begins a further proof of the superiority of Christ's priesthood [Alf, Blm, My]. It introduces an additional point [Lns, NIGTC, TH, Wst], an additional proof of the superiority of the new priesthood [Mil, NTC].

QUESTION—What is the implied reference of this clause?

'Not apart from oath-taking' is a litotes, which implies a strong affirmation [Lns, NIGTC]: it was definitely with the swearing of an oath.

1. It refers to Christ's becoming a priest [Blm, Hwt, Mil, My, NIGTC, WBC] or the mediator of a better covenant [Alf, Blm, EGT]: it was not without oath-taking that Christ became a priest/mediator.
2. It refers to disannulling and bringing in a new priesthood [Lns]: it was not without oath-taking that the old order was disannulled and a new priesthood was brought in.

QUESTION—What is this clause connected with?

This clause is connected with 7:22, and the rest of this verse and 7:21 form a parenthesis [Alf, Blm, EGT, GNC, ICC, Lns, Mil, My, NIC, NIGTC, WBC, Wst; KJV, NASB]: for insofar as it was not without oath-taking . . . in the same way Christ is mediator of a better covenant. This clause and 7:22 form a comparison [GNC, WBC].

for they on-the-one-hand without[a] oath-taking[b] have become priests,

LEXICON—a. χωρίς with genitive object: 'apart from'. See this word above.

b. ὁρκωμοσία: 'oath-taking'. See this word above.

QUESTION—What relationship is indicated by γάρ 'for'?

It indicates an explanation [Blm, ICC, Lns, Mil, WBC] of the superiority of Christ's priesthood [Mil], a confirmation that Christ's priesthood was confirmed by an oath [EGT, WBC] and a contrast with the Levitical priesthood, which involved no such oath [WBC]. This verse and the following one form a parenthesis [Alf, Blm, EGT, GNC, ICC, Lns, Mil, My, NIC, WBC; KJV, NASB].

QUESTION—What relationship is indicated by οἱ μέν 'they on the one hand'?

Oἱ is used as a pronoun, 'they' [EBC, Lg, Mil; NASB], referring to the Levitical priests [EBC, My, NIGTC, NTC, WBC, Wst; KJV, NAB, NIV, NJB], followed by ὁ δέ 'he on the other hand' in 7:22 [EBC, Mil, Wst; NASB, NIV, NJB], referring to Jesus [EBC, Mil, My, NTC, WBC; KJV, NAB].

QUESTION—What is implied by the periphrastic perfect tense formation εἰσὶν γεγονότες 'they have become'?

1. It implies receiving and possessing the office [EGT, Lg(K), Wst]: they received and possess. It includes the Levitical system from its beginning to the time when this epistle was written [Hu, My].
2. It implies the eternally continuing state of Christ's priesthood [EBC].
3. It implies the beginning of the state of being priests [NIGTC].
4. The two words are to be taken separately [Lns]: they are (priests), having become such.
5. The periphrastic form is merely stylistic [ICC, NIC].

7:21 but he with[a] oath-taking[b] through[c] the-(one) saying to[d] him,

LEXICON—a. μετά with genitive object (LN 89.78): 'with' [HNTC, LN, Lns, Mil, NIC, WBC; KJV, NASB, NIV, NJB, NRSV, TNT], 'through' [LN], 'by means of' [LN; TEV]. The phrase ὁ δὲ μετὰ ὁρκωμοσίας 'but he with oath-taking' is translated 'but for this priest an oath was sworn' [REB]. This entire phrase is translated 'unlike Jesus to whom God said' [NAB], 'only to Jesus did he say' [NLT].

b. ὁρκωμοσία: 'oath-taking'. See this word in 7:20.

c. διά with genitive object (LN 90.4): 'through' [HNTC, LN, WBC; NASB, TNT], 'by' [LN, Mil, NIC; KJV, NJB], 'by means of' [Lns], 'because of' [NRSV]. The phrase διὰ τοῦ λέγοντος 'through the one saying' is translated 'when God said' [NIV, TEV], 'in the words addressed' [REB]. This prepositional phrase indicates the agent [NIC], the means of Christ's appointment [Mil], where and how the oath is located [EGT].

d. πρός with accusative object (LN 90.58): 'to' [HNTC, LN, Mil, NIC, WBC; all versions except KJV], 'unto' [KJV], 'regarding' [Lns]. It means 'to' [NIGTC].

QUESTION—What is ὁ δέ 'but he' connected with?

The ὁ is used as a pronoun 'he' [Alf, EBC, Mil; NIV, TNT], referring to Christ [EBC, HNTC, Mil, My; TEV]. It is connected with the understood phrase 'is/was made a priest' [Lns, Mil, My, NIGTC; NIV, TEV, TNT]: he on the other hand is a priest.

QUESTION—To whom does τοῦ λέγοντος 'the one saying' refer?

It refers to God [Alf, EGT, Lns, My, NIGTC, TH, WBC, Wst; NAB, NIV, TEV]. The present tense of this participle implies the timelessness of Scripture [NIGTC], the continuing effectiveness of God's voice [Wst].

"(The) Lord swore[a] and not will-change-(his)-mind,[b] 'You (are) (a) priest into[c] the age'"—

TEXT—Some manuscripts add κατὰ τὴν τάξιν Μελχισέδεκ 'according to the order of Melchizedek' at the end of this clause. GNT omits this phrase with an A decision, indicating that the text is certain. This phrase is included by My, KJV, and NAB.

LEXICON—a. aorist act. indic. of ὀμνύω (LN 33.463) (BAGD p. 566): 'to swear' [BAGD, HNTC, LN, Lns, Mil, NIC, WBC; KJV, NAB, NASB, NIV, NRSV, REB, TNT], 'to swear an oath' [NJB], 'to take an oath' [BAGD; NLT], 'to make an oath' [LN], 'to promise' [CEV], 'to make a solemn promise' [TEV].

b. fut. pass. (deponent = act.) indic. of μεταμέλομαι (LN **31.59**) (BAGD p. 511): 'to change one's mind' [BAGD, **LN,** Mil, NIC, WBC; CEV, NASB, NIV, NRSV], 'to think differently' [LN], 'to retract' [NJB], 'to take (something) back' [TEV], 'to go back on one's word' [HNTC; REB, TNT], 'to break one's vow' [NLT], 'to repent' [Lns; KJV, NAB]. It has the meaning of the middle voice: 'will not repent himself' [Lns]. This verb reinforces God's promise [NIGTC, WBC].

c. εἰς with accusative object (LN 67.95, 84.22): 'into' [LN (84.22)], 'for' [Lns]. The phrase εἰς τὸν αἰῶνα 'into the age' is translated 'forever' [HNTC, LN (67.95), Mil, NIC, WBC; all versions].

7:22 in-accordance-with[a] as-much-as[b] also Jesus has-become guarantor[c] of-a-better[d] covenant.[e]

LEXICON—a. κατά with accusative object (LN 89.8) (BAGD II.5.a.δ. p. 407): 'in accordance with' [LN], 'by' [Lns, Mil; KJV]. The phrase κατὰ τοσοῦτο 'in accordance with as much as' is translated 'just so far' [BAGD, WBC], 'to that extent' [NIC], 'so much the more' [NASB], 'thus' [NAB], 'so' [TNT], 'accordingly' [NRSV], 'because of this oath' [NIV], 'because of God's oath' [NLT]. This entire clause is translated 'in the same way, God's oath shows how superior is the covenant which Jesus guarantees' [REB], 'so much better, then, is the covenant of which the guarantor is Jesus' [HNTC], 'this difference, then, also makes Jesus the guarantee of a better covenant' [TEV], 'the very fact that it occurred with the swearing of an oath makes the covenant of which Jesus is the guarantee all the greater' [NJB], 'this means that Jesus guarantees us a better agreement with God' [CEV].

b. τοσοῦτος (LN 78.52): 'as much as' [LN], 'so much' [Lns; KJV], 'so much as this' [Mil], 'to the same degree' [LN].

c. ἔγγυος (LN **70.8**) (BAGD p. 214): 'guarantor' [HNTC, **LN**, NIC, WBC; TNT], 'guarantee' [BAGD, LN, Mil; NAB, NASB, NIV, NJB, NRSV, TEV], 'surety' [Lns; KJV]. This noun is also translated as a verb: 'to guarantee' [CEV, NLT, REB]. The noun means both surety and mediator [Blm, NIGTC, NTC]. In Jesus' person certainty is given that God has made a better covenant [Alf, Lg, My, Wst], that the covenant is valid [Hwt, Lg, Wst], that it will not fail [EGT, GNC, Hu, Mil, NIC, TH, WBC], that God's plan of salvation has become a reality [GNC]. Jesus is a guarantor to mankind that God will fulfill his covenant [EBC, Lns, NIC, NTC, TNTC, WBC], and a guarantor of mankind to God [NTC] that those who abide in him are acceptable [EBC, NIC].

d. κρείττων (LN 65.21) (BAGD 1. p. 449): 'better' [BAGD, HNTC, LN, Lns, Mil, NIC, WBC; all versions except NJB, REB], 'preferable' [BAGD], 'superior' [LN; REB], 'greater' [NJB]. The new covenant is 'better' because it supersedes the old covenant and accomplishes what the old covenant could not accomplish [EGT], because it is effective [WBC], because the priesthood of Jesus is permanent and unchangeable and because he is its guarantor [HNTC].

e. διαθήκη (LN 34.44, 57.124) (BAGD 2. p. 183): 'covenant' [BAGD, HNTC, LN (34.44), Mil, NIC, WBC; all versions except CEV, KJV], 'pact' [LN (34.44)], 'decree' [BAGD], 'testament' [LN (57.124), Lns; KJV], 'agreement' [CEV]. The meaning is a covenant [Lg], a testamentary will [Alf], a dispensation [Blm], the arrangement making a reality of God's purpose of salvation [GNC].

QUESTION—What relationship is indicated by the phrase κατὰ τοσοῦτο 'in accordance with as much as'?

It indicates the same proportion as the difference between the oath and no oath [Alf, Lns], the superiority of the permanent new covenant over the transitory old covenant [EGT].

QUESTION—What does the perfect tense of γέγονεν 'has become' indicate?

It implies having become and still being so [EGT].

QUESTION—What is the significance of the use of the name Ἰησοῦς 'Jesus'?

It is emphatic [NIGTC] by being placed last in its clause [Alf, HNTC, Lns, Mil, NCBC, NIC, NTC, TNTC, Wst], by being used by itself [TH]; the use of the human name emphasizes Christ's human nature [HNTC], Christ's saving work [NTC, Wst], the fact that it is as mankind's perfect representative that Christ has become the surety of the covenant [TNTC].

DISCOURSE UNIT: 7:23–25 [EBC, Lg, NIC]. The topic is the superiority of Christ's priesthood's because of its permanence [EBC, NIC], Christ's permanent priesthood [Lg].

7:23 And they on-the-one-hand have become many[a] priests on-account-of[b] to-be-prevented[c] by-death to-continue;[d]

LEXICON—a. πλείων (LN 59.1) (BAGD II.1.a. p. 689): 'many' [LN, Mil, NIC; all versions except CEV, NASB, TNT], 'more' [Lns], 'a lot' [CEV]. The phrase πλείονές εἰσιν γεγονότες 'have become many' is translated 'existed in greater numbers' [BAGD; NASB], 'became in large numbers' [HNTC], 'there were great numbers' [TNT]. The meaning is 'many' [NIGTC, NTC, TH, WBC, Wst], the comparative form of the adjective being used for the positive form [WBC]. It refers to the succession of priests, not to many priests serving at the same time [Blm, EBC, EGT, HNTC, Hu, Lg, My, TH, Wst]. This word is the principal emphasis of the clause, in contrast with Christ's permanent priesthood [Alf, WBC, Wst]. This word here implies incompleteness [WBC], inferiority [Blm].

b. διά with accusative object (LN 89.26): 'on account of' [LN; NJB], 'because of, by reason of' [LN], 'in consequence of' [Lns], 'because' [HNTC, Mil, NIC, WBC; all versions except CEV, NIV, NLT], 'since' [NIV], not explicit [CEV, NLT]. This preposition indicates a reason [Mil], the reason why the number of priests increased [NTC].

c. pres. pass. infin. of κωλύω (LN 13.146) (BAGD 1. p. 461): 'to be prevented' [BAGD, HNTC, LN, Lns, Mil, WBC; NAB, NASB, NRSV, TNT], 'to be hindered' [BAGD, LN], 'to be suffered' [KJV], not explicit [TEV]. This passive verb is also translated as active with death as the subject: 'to prevent' [NIC; NIV, REB], 'to put an end to' [NJB]. The meaning is 'prevented' [NIGTC]. The phrase διὰ τὸ θανάτῳ κωλύεσθαι παραμένειν 'on account of to be prevented by death to continue' is translated 'and all of them have died' [CEV], 'when one priest died, another had to take his place' [NLT]. The present tense indicates repetition [Lns].

d. pres. act. infin. of παραμένω (LN **68.11**) (BAGD 2. p. 620): 'to continue' [Lns, NIC; KJV, NASB], 'to continue in office' [BAGD, Mil, WBC; NIV, NRSV, REB], 'to continue one's work' [LN; TEV], 'to remain in office' [HNTC; NAB, TNT], not explicit [CEV, NLT]. The present tense indicates repetition [Lns].

QUESTION—What relationship is indicated by καί 'and'?

It introduces a new element in the discussion [EGT, Mil, TH]: and in addition. It begins further proof of the superiority of Christ's priesthood [Alf, Blm, EBC, EGT, Hwt, Mil, NTC, Wst].

QUESTION—To whom does οἱ μέν 'they on the one hand' refer?

It refers to the Levitical priests [Alf, EGT, Lns, Mil, Wst]; οἱ is used as a pronoun 'they' [Alf, Lg(K), Lns, Wst; KJV]. It is contrasted by ὁ δέ 'he on the other hand' in 7:24 [Mil].

QUESTION—What is meant by εἰσιν γεγονότες 'have become'?

1. How the two words are related.
1.1 It is the periphrastic perfect indicative [NIC, NIGTC] as an alternative to the regular perfect tense form [Blm].
1.2 The two words together refer to a state [KJV, NAB, NASB, NIV, NJB, REB]: there were/have been many priests.
1.3 The two words are separate, meaning 'are' and 'having become', the perfect participle being connected with the following prepositional phrase [Lns]: they are more, having become priests on account of being prevented by death from continuing.
2. What the tense implies.
2.1 It implies that there were Levitical priests when this epistle was written [GNC, Hu, NIGTC].
2.2 It implies that the Levitical priesthood had ceased [NTC].

QUESTION—To whom does ἱερεῖς 'priests' refer?

1. It refers to priests in general [Alf, Blm, EBC, EGT, GNC, HNTC, Hu, Hwt, Mil, NTC, TH, WBC; all versions].
2. It refers to the high-priests [Lg, My, NTC, TNTC].

QUESTION—What is the implied predicate of παραμένειν 'to continue'?

1. It refers to continuing in their priesthood [Alf, Blm, EGT, Hu, ICC, Lg(K), My(D), NIC, NIGTC, NTC, TH, TNTC, WBC, Wst; NAB, NIV, NRSV, REB, TEV, TNT]: from continuing in their priesthood.
2. It refers to continuing to live [Lg, Mil, My]: from continuing to live.

7:24 he on-the-other-hand on-account-of[a] him to-remain[b] into[c] the age has the priesthood unchangeable;[d]

LEXICON—a. διά with accusative object: 'on account of'. See this word in 7:23.

b. pres. act. infin. of μένω (LN 13.89) (BAGD 1.c.α. p. 504): 'to remain' [BAGD, HNTC, LN, Lns; NAB, NJB, NLT, REB, TNT], 'to abide' [Mil; NASB], 'to continue' [LN, NIC, WBC; KJV, NRSV], 'to continue to exist' [LN], 'to be still in existence' [LN], 'to live' [NIV], 'to continue to live' [BAGD], 'to live on forever' [TEV], 'never to die' [CEV]. It refers to remaining in life [Alf, Mil, My].

c. εἰς with accusative object: 'into'. See this word in 7:21.

d. ἀπαράβατος (LN **13.61**) (BAGD p. 80): 'unchangeable' [BAGD, Lns; KJV], 'unchanging, not changing, never to change' [LN], 'unalterable' [Mil], 'untransferable' [NIC], 'inviolable' [Mil], 'permanent' [BAGD, WBC; NIV], 'perpetual' [NJB, REB], 'which does not pass away' [NAB]. This adjective is also translated as an adverb: 'permanently' [NASB, NRSV]. The phrase ἀπαράβατον ἔχει τὴν ἱερωσύνην 'he has the priesthood unchangeable' is translated 'his priesthood never changes' [**LN**], 'his priesthood will never end' [NLT], 'and his work as priest does not pass on to someone else' [TEV], 'he has a priesthood which cannot pass to another' [HNTC; TNT], 'he will be a priest forever' [CEV]. It means ‘unchangeable’, not possible to be changed [Alf, EBC, EGT, GNC, Hwt, Lg, Lns, Mil, My, NCBC, NTC, TH, TNTC, Wst]; it means that it is not to be passed on to others [Blm, ICC, NIC]; it means both of the preceding [Hu]; it means that it is permanent [NIGTC, WBC].

QUESTION—To whom does ὁ δέ ‘he on the other hand’ refer?

It refers to Jesus [Alf, ICC, NCBC, TH, Wst; NAB, NASB, NIV, REB, TEV]; ὁ is used as a pronoun ‘he’ [Alf, Lg(K), Lns, TH, Wst; NASB, NRSV, TNT]. It is slightly emphatic [TH].

QUESTION—How is the adjective ἀπαράβατον ‘unchangeable’ related to the noun ἱερωσύνην ‘priesthood’?

1. The adjective is in a predicate relationship to the noun [Alf, Lg(K), Mil, My] (it is translated as an adverb ‘unchangeably’ [NASB, NRSV]): he has the priesthood (and it is) unchangeable.
2. The adjective is translated with attributive meaning (which violates Greek grammar).

2.1 As an attributive adjective [Lns; KJV, NIV, NJB, REB]: an unchangeable priesthood.

2.2 As a relative clause [HNTC, NIC; NAB]: a priesthood which is permanent, or cannot be passed to another. The emphasis is on permanence [WBC].

7:25 therefore[a] also he-is-able to-save[b] into[c] the complete/forever the-(ones) approaching[d] to-God through[e] him,

LEXICON—a. ὅθεν (LN 89.25) (BAGD 3. p. 555): ‘therefore’ [BAGD, NIC; NAB, NIV, NLT], ‘wherefore’ [KJV], ‘whence’ [Lns], ‘hence’ [BAGD; NASB], ‘consequently’ [NRSV], ‘it follows, then’ [NJB], ‘that is why’ [REB], ‘so’ [TNT], ‘and so’ [HNTC, WBC; TEV], ‘for this reason’ [Mil], ‘since’ [LN], not explicit [CEV]. It introduces the consequence (the conclusion [EBC, TH, WBC]) of the preceding comment [Alf, EBC, Lg, TH] concerning Christ’s eternal priesthood [EGT, Lns, Mil, My, WBC, Wst].

b. pres. act. infin. of σῴζω (LN 21.27) (BAGD 2.a.α. p. 798): ‘to save’ [BAGD, HNTC, LN, Lns, Mil, WBC; all versions except NJB], ‘to bring to salvation’ [BAGD]. The phrase σῴζειν εἰς τὸ παντελὲς δύναται ‘he is able to save completely/forever’ is translated ‘he is able to bring complete and final salvation’ [NIC], ‘that his power to save is absolute’ [NJB]. It means to rescue from sin [Alf, My] and secure eternal blessedness [My]. The present tense indicates continuity [WBC, Wst].

c. εἰς with accusative object (**LN 67.95**, **78.47**, 84.22) (BAGD 3. p. 229): ‘into’ [LN (84.22)], ‘to’ [Lns, Mil; KJV]. The phrase εἰς τὸ παντελές ‘into the complete’ is translated, ‘completely’ [BAGD, **LN** (78.47), Mil; NIV, REB], ‘fully’ [BAGD], ‘absolutely’ [BAGD, WBC], ‘wholly’ [BAGD], ‘forever’ [BAGD, **LN** (67.95); CEV, NASB], ‘always’ [NAB], ‘now and always’ [TEV], ‘once and forever’ [NLT], ‘for all time’ [BAGD, HNTC; NRSV, TNT].

d. pres. pass. (deponent = act.) of προσέρχομαι (LN 15.77) (BAGD 2.a. p. 713): 'to approach' [BAGD, HNTC, LN, Mil, NIC, WBC; NAB, NRSV, REB], 'to come to' [BAGD, Lns; NIV, NJB, NLT, TEV, TNT], 'to come unto' [KJV], 'to go to' [BAGD], 'to come near to' [LN], 'to draw near to' [NASB], 'to move toward' [LN]. The phrase τοὺς προσερχομένους δι' αὐτοῦ τῷ θεῷ 'the ones approaching to God through him' is translated 'the people he leads to God' [CEV].

e. διά with genitive object (LN 90.4): 'through' [HNTC, LN, Lns, Mil, NIC, WBC; all versions except CEV, KJV], 'by' [LN; KJV]. It expresses means [Mil, TH], agent [TH].

QUESTION—What is καί 'also' connected with?

It is connected with the whole clause [Alf, My]: it is also true that he is able to save. It indicates that the statement is the natural effect of the preceding comment [My].

QUESTION—What is meant by εἰς τὸ παντελές 'completely/forever'?

1. It refers to degree [Alf, Blm, EBC, EGT, GNC, Lg, Mil, My, NCBC, NTC, TH, Wst; KJV, NIV, NJB, REB]: completely.

1.1 It refers to the degree of salvation [Alf, Blm, EBC, Lg, Mil, My, NTC, TH; KJV, NIV, REB]: he is able to save completely.

1.2 It refers to the degree of Christ's ability to save [NJB]: he is fully able to save.

2. It refers to time [HNTC, ICC, NIGTC, TNTC; NAB, NASB, NRSV, TEV, TNT]: forever/always.

2.1 It means that he is forever or always able to save [HNTC, ICC, NCBC, TNTC; NAB, NRSV, TEV, TNT], which is how long he remains a priest [HNTC, ICC, TNTC].

2.2 It means that the salvation he provides is forever [HNTC, NIGTC; NASB].

3. It refers to both of the above.

3.1 It refers to 1 and 2 above [Hwt, NIC, WBC].

3.2 It refers to 1.1 and 2 above [GNC, Hu].

3.3 It refers to 1.2 and 2.1 above [Lns].

QUESTION—What is meant by δι' αὐτοῦ 'through him'?

It indicates approach to God through Christ in contrast with those who approach through the Levitical priesthood [Alf, EGT].

always[a] living for[b] the to-intercede[c] on-behalf-of[d] them.

LEXICON—a. πάντοτε (LN 67.88) (BAGD p. 609): 'always' [BAGD, LN; CEV, NASB, NIV, NRSV, REB, TNT], 'at all times' [BAGD], 'ever' [Lns, Mil; KJV], 'continually' [WBC], 'continuously' [NIC], 'forever' [HNTC; NAB, NJB, NLT, TEV].

b. εἰς with accusative object (LN 89.57): 'for', 'for the purpose of' [LN], 'in order to' [LN, WBC], 'to' [HNTC, Lns, Mil, NIC; all versions]. It expresses purpose [Mil, NTC, TH, WBC, Wst].

c. pres. act. infin. of ἐντυγχάνω (LN 33.169, 33.347) (BAGD 1. p. 270): 'to intercede' [LN (33.347), Lns, Mil, NIC, WBC; NIV, NJB], 'to make intercession' [KJV, NAB, NASB, NRSV], 'to appeal' [BAGD], 'to plead' [HNTC, LN (33.169); NLT, REB, TEV], 'to petition' [LN (33.169)], 'to speak' [CEV], 'to turn to God' [TNT]. It refers to Christ's full work of mediation [Alf, Blm], the confident pleas of an advocate [HNTC, Hwt], not of a suppliant [HNTC, Lns]. Christ's victorious presence at God's right hand constitutes his effective intercession [EBC, Hu].

d. ὑπέρ with genitive object (LN 90.36): 'on behalf of' [HNTC, LN, Mil; NLT, REB, TNT], 'for the sake of' [LN], 'for' [LN, Lns, NIC, WBC; all versions except NLT, REB, TNT].

QUESTION—What relationship is indicated by the participial form ζῶν 'living'?

It indicates a reason [Alf, EGT, HNTC, Mil, My, NIC, NIGTC, NTC, WBC, Wst; all versions]: he is able to save because he lives.

QUESTION—Who is the implied receiver of the interceding?

It is God [TH].

DISCOURSE UNIT: 7:26–28 [EBC, Lg, Lns, NIC; NJB]. The topic is the superiority of Christ's priesthood because of his better sacrifice [EBC], because of the character of Jesus [NIC], Christ's sacrifice of himself for mankind's sins [Lg], our appropriate high priest [Lns], the perfect high priest [NJB].

7:26 For such[a] (a) high-priest was-fitting[b] also for-us,

LEXICON—a. τοιοῦτος (LN 64.2, 92.31) (BAGD 2.a.β. p. 821): 'such' [BAGD, HNTC, LN (64.2), Lns, WBC; all versions except TEV, TNT], 'just such' [Mil], 'like that' [LN (64.2)], 'like this' [NIC], 'of this kind' [LN (92.31)], 'of such a kind' [BAGD, LN (92.31); TNT], 'the kind of' [NLT], 'such as this' [BAGD, LN (92.31)]. This entire phrase is translated 'Jesus, then, is the High Priest that meets our needs' [TEV], 'Jesus is the high priest we need' [CEV].

b. imperf. act. indic. of πρέπω (LN 66.1) (BAGD p. 699): 'to be fitting' [BAGD, LN; NAB, NASB, NRSV], 'to be suited' [REB], 'to be suitable' [BAGD], 'to be appropriate' [WBC], 'to be seemly' [BAGD], 'to be right' [LN], 'to be becoming' [Lns; KJV]. The phrase ἡμῖν ἔπρεπεν 'was fitting for us' is translated 'suited our case' [NIC], 'was suited to our condition' [HNTC], 'was suited to our need' [Mil], 'met our need' [NJB], 'does meet our need' [TNT], 'meets our need' [NIV], 'meets our needs' [TEV], 'we need' [CEV, NLT]. It relates to the serious needs of mankind [Hu]. It implies that no other kind of priest would meet the needs [TNTC]. The imperfect tense implies the continuation of the propriety [Lns].

QUESTION—What relationship is indicated by γάρ 'for'?

1. It indicates an additional reason for Christ to be such a high priest [Alf, Blm, EBC, Lg, Mil, My, NIC] because of his better sacrifice [EBC].
2. It summarizes the preceding points [Lns, NTC, WBC], the γάρ introducing the expansion of the preceding [Lns].

3. It begins a description of the general character of Christ's high priesthood [Wst].

QUESTION—What is τοιοῦτος 'such' connected with?

1. It refers to the preceding descriptions and is further amplified by the following phrases [Alf, Hu, Hwt, Lg, Lns, Mil, My, NIGTC, NTC, TNTC], as γάρ 'for' indicates [Hu, Mil, NIGTC, TNTC]: a high priest such as has been described.
2. It refers primarily to the following verse [EGT, WBC]: a high priest who does not have need to offer sacrifice.
3. It looks both backward and forward [Wst].

QUESTION—What relationship is indicated by καί 'also'?

It introduces emphasis [Hu, Lg, Lns, My, WBC, Wst], emphasizing the verb [WBC, Wst], and implies a climax [Alf]: in addition, even this.

QUESTION—What is implied by ἡμῖν 'for us'?

It is emphatic by forefronting [Alf, EGT]. It includes both the author and his readers [NIGTC] but only Christians [TNTC, Wst].

holy,[a] innocent,[b] undefiled,[c]

LEXICON—a. ὅσιος (LN 88.24) (BAGD 1.b. p. 585): 'holy' [BAGD, LN, Lns, Mil, NIC; all versions], 'devout' [HNTC, WBC]. It implies piety toward God [Alf, ICC, NCBC, NIC, NIGTC], being pleasing to God [TH]; it refers to duties toward God [Blm, Lg], inner purity [Blm, NTC]; it implies the appropriate character for separation to God [EBC], personal holiness [EGT, Hu, Hwt, Mil, My, TNTC, Wst] and relationship to God [EGT, Hu, Hwt, Mil, My], participation in God's holiness [HNTC, NTC] and without sin [NTC]. This and the two following adjectives are essentially synonymous [Lns].

b. ἄκακος (LN **88.2**) (BAGD p. 29): 'innocent' [BAGD, HNTC, LN; CEV, NAB, NASB, NJB, REB, TNT], 'innocent of evil' [Mil], 'without fault' [LN], 'without anything bad' [Lns], 'blameless' [NIV, NLT, NRSV], 'guileless' [BAGD, **LN**; WBC], 'harmless' [KJV]. The phrase ἄκακος, ἀμίαντος 'innocent, undefiled' is translated 'free from guile and defilement' [NIC], 'he has no fault or sin in him' [TEV]. This word implies absence of vice or of suspicion of evil [Alf, EBC, EGT, HNTC, Hu, Hwt, Lns, Mil, My, NIC, NIGTC] (personal holiness [Hu]) in relationship to mankind [EGT, Hu, Hwt, Lg, My, Wst], to purity of heart [HNTC]; it refers to duties toward persons and inner purity [Blm].

c. ἀμίαντος (LN 53.36) (BAGD 2. p. 46): 'undefiled' [BAGD, HNTC, LN, WBC; KJV, NAB, NASB, NRSV, REB], 'untainted' [LN], 'uncontaminated' [NJB], 'unstained' [TNT], 'unstained by sin' [NLT], 'without a stain' [Lns], 'spotless' [Mil], 'pure' [BAGD; NIV], 'faultless' [CEV]. It implies absence of legal or moral pollution [Alf], moral and spiritual flawlessness [HNTC, Hu, Hwt, Mil, NCBC, NTC] in relation to himself [Hu, My], fitness to appear before God [EGT], fitness for priestly service

[Lg], free from anything (any cultic impurity [NIC, WBC]) that would disqualify him for his service [NIC, NIGTC, Wst].

QUESTION—Why is this and the following phrases mentioned?

They carry forward the description of τοιοῦτος 'such' [Alf] in summation of the preceding comments [Hu]: such a high priest; namely, holy, etc.

separated[a] from[b] the sinners

LEXICON—a. perf. pass. participle of χωρίζω (LN **63.29**) (BAGD 2.c. p. 890): 'to be separated' [BAGD, HNTC, LN, Mil, NIC, WBC; NAB, NASB, NRSV, TNT], 'to be withdrawn' [Lns], 'to be set apart' [NIV, NJB, NLT, REB, TEV]. This participle is also translated as an adjective: 'separate' [KJV], 'different' [BAGD]. This clause is translated 'not at all like us sinners' [CEV]. The perfect tense implies a continued state following the event of his exaltation [EBC, Wst].

b. ἀπό with genitive object (LN 89.122): 'from' [HNTC, LN, Lns, Mil, NIC, WBC; all versions except CEV], not explicit [CEV].

QUESTION—What does this phrase refer to?

1. It refers to Christ's difference from other persons by the sinlessness of his earthly life [Blm, EGT, Hu, Hwt, Lns, Mil, NIC, NTC].
2. It refers to Christ's priesthood in heaven, away from contact with sinners [Alf, EBC, GNC, HNTC, ICC, Lg, My, NCBC, TH, WBC].
3. It means both of the above [NIGTC].

QUESTION—What is implied by the definite article in the phrase τῶν ἁμαρτωλῶν 'the sinners'?

It refers to the whole race of sinners [Alf]: separated from the sinners in general.

and having-become higher[a] than-the heavens,

LEXICON—a. ὑψηλότερος (LN **83.50**) (BAGD 1. p. 850): 'higher' [Lns, Mil; KJV, NAB], 'higher than' [LN], 'above' [**LN**]. The phrase ὑψηλότερος τῶν οὐρανῶν γενόμενος 'having become higher than the heavens' is translated 'raised to greater heights than the heavens' [BAGD], 'raised above the heavens' [TEV], 'raised up above the heavens' [NJB], 'raised high above the heavens' [REB], 'exalted above the heavens' [HNTC; NASB, NIV, NRSV, TNT], 'exalted high above the heavens' [NIC], 'exalted even higher than the heavens' [WBC], 'Jesus is honored above all beings in heaven' [CEV], 'he has been given the highest place of honor in heaven' [NLT].

QUESTION—What does this phrase refer to?

It refers to Christ's exalted dignity in heaven [Blm, Hu] and on earth [Blm].

7:27 who (does) not have throughout[a] day (a) need, just-as[b] the high-priests, first to-offer-up sacrifices for[c] his-own sins, then (for) the (sins) of-the people;

LEXICON—a. κατά with accusative object (LN 89.90) (BAGD ii.2.c. p. 406): 'throughout' [LN]. The phrase καθ' ἡμέραν 'throughout day' is translated 'daily' [BAGD, HNTC, NIC, WBC; KJV, NASB, REB, TNT], 'every day' [BAGD; NJB, NLT, TEV], 'each day' [CEV], 'day after day' [LN; NAB, NIV, NRSV], 'day by day' [Lns, Mil]. This phrase refers to the sacrifice of the day of atonement, but repeated in some sense in the priests' daily offerings [Alf, NIC], the high priest's daily offerings [Blm, HNTC] as mentioned in Lev. 6:13 [HNTC].

b. ὥσπερ (LN 64.13) (BAGD 2. p. 899): 'just as' [BAGD, LN], 'as' [HNTC, LN; KJV, NJB, REB, TNT], 'like' [Lns, Mil, NIC, WBC; NASB, NLT], 'unlike' [NAB, NIV, NRSV], 'not like' [TEV], not explicit [CEV].

c. ὑπέρ with genitive object (LN 90.36) (BAGD 1.b. p. 838): 'for' [HNTC, LN, Lns, Mil, NIC, WBC; all versions], 'on behalf of' [LN], 'in order to atone for' [BAGD], 'to remove' [BAGD].

QUESTION—Why is this verse mentioned?

It is the principal point to which the preceding comments are leading [EGT, Mil], describing the work of the high priest who is mentioned in the preceding verse [Lns, Mil, WBC].

QUESTION—What is implied by this clause?

1. It means that Christ did not need to offer up daily the sin-offerings that the high priests made yearly [Alf, EGT].
2. It means that Christ did not need to make a daily sacrifice for his own sins nor for those of the people [Blm].
3. It means that Christ did not need to offer a sacrifice for his own sins [EBC, Hu], nor to continue offering a sacrifice for the sins of the people following his own sacrifice [EBC, Hwt]. Two references are combined; 'daily' refers to the daily priestly routine, while the reference to the sacrifice for sins refers to the annual day of atonement [Hu, Hwt, ICC, Lg, My, NCBC, NIGTC].
4. It implies that in some sense the high priests were responsible for the daily sacrifices [Mil, Wst].

QUESTION—What relationship is indicated by the verb ἔχει 'he has'?

The indicative mood (the aorist tense [Lns]) indicates that the author is referring to an actual situation [Alf, Lns].

QUESTION—What is the phrase καθ' ἡμέραν 'throughout day' connected with?

1. It is connected with οὐκ ἔχει ἀνάγκην 'does not have need' [GNC, ICC, Lns, TNTC, Wst]: he has no daily need to offer up sacrifices.
2. It is connected with ἀναφέρειν θυσίας 'to offer up sacrifices' [HNTC, Mil, NIC, WBC; all versions except KJV, NASB]: he does not have need to offer up sacrifices daily.

QUESTION—What is the phrase ὥσπερ οἱ ἀρχιερεῖς 'just as the high priests' connected with?

It is connected with ἔχει ἀνάγκην 'he has no need' [Alf, ICC, Mil, TNTC]: he does not have the need that the high priests have.

for this he-did once-for-all[a] having-offered-up[b] himself.

LEXICON—a. ἐφάπαξ (LN 60.67, 60.68) (BAGD 2. p. 330): 'once for all' [BAGD, HNTC, Lns, Mil, NIC, WBC; CEV, NAB, NASB, NIV, NLT, NRSV, REB, TNT], 'once and for all' [LN (60.68); NJB, TEV], 'once and never again' [LN (60.68)], 'once' [LN (60.67); KJV]. This word is stronger than merely 'once' [Alf, Lns, NIC, NIGTC, TH], implying complete finality [EBC, Hu, TH, TNTC, WBC] in contrast with καθ' ἡμέραν 'daily' [EGT, WBC], and implying the abolition of every other system of sacrifices [Hu], the end of the Levitical system [NTC]. It modifies ἐποίησεν 'he did' [Alf, My]; it is explained by the following ἑαυτὸν ἀνενέγκας 'having offered up himself' [EGT].

b. aorist act. participle of ἀναφέρω; 'to offer up'. See this word above.

QUESTION—What relationship is indicated by γάρ 'for'?

It indicates grounds for the preceding thought [Blm, Mil, TH].

QUESTION—To what does τοῦτο 'this' refer?

It refers to offering up a sacrifice for the sins of the people [Alf, EGT, HNTC, ICC, Lns, My, NIGTC, TH, WBC].

QUESTION—What relationship is indicated by the participial form ἀνενέγκας 'having offered up'?

The aorist tense refers to the one act [NIGTC].

1. It is temporal [Alf, HNTC, TH; all versions except NJB] (but probably implying means as well as a reference to time [Ed]): when he offered up himself.
2. It expresses means [Lg(K), Lns, Mil, My, Wst; NJB]: by offering up himself.

7:28 For the law appoints[a] men (as) high-priests having weakness,[b]

LEXICON—a. pres. act. indic. of καθίστημι (LN 37.104) (BAGD 2.b. p. 332): 'to appoint' [BAGD, HNTC, LN, Mil, NIC, WBC; all versions except KJV, NAB, NLT], 'to designate' [LN], 'to establish' [Lns], 'to make' [BAGD; KJV], 'to set up' [NAB]. The phrase ὁ νόμος γὰρ ἀνθρώπους καθίστησιν ἀρχιερεῖς 'the law appoints men as high priests' is translated 'those who were high priests under the law of Moses' [NLT]. The present tense implies that the Levitical priesthood was still operating when this epistle was written [Hu].

b. ἀσθένεια (LN 74.23) (BAGD 1.c. p. 115): 'weakness' [BAGD, LN, Lns, WBC; CEV, NJB, NRSV, REB, TNT], 'human weakness' [NLT], 'limitation' [LN], 'infirmity' [Mil; KJV], 'frailty' [NIC]. The phrase ἔχοντας ἀσθένειαν 'having weakness' is translated 'who are weak' [NAB, NASB, NIV], 'who are frail' [HNTC], 'who are imperfect' [TEV]. It here includes a sinful condition [NTC], sin [WBC], liability to sin and being subject to death [Alf], the common frailty of humankind [EBC, HNTC, Wst] plus the individual imperfections of each priest [HNTC, Wst], inability to do what is needed [TH].

QUESTION—What relationship is indicated by γάρ 'for'?

1. It indicates the reason for the difference mentioned in the preceding verse [Alf, Lg, Mil, My].
2. It summarizes the preceding argument [ICC] (the principal theme of the epistle thus far [Hu]) with another contrast [GNC, HNTC, Lns, NCBC, NIGTC, NTC, TNTC, WBC, Wst].

QUESTION—What is implied by the position of ἀνθρώπους 'men'?

It is emphatic [Lg(K)], contrasting with υἱόν 'Son' in the following phrase [Alf]

QUESTION—What relationship is indicated by the participial form ἔχοντας 'having'?

1. It is attributive, describing the men/high priests [Alf, EGT, HNTC, Lns, NIC; all versions except REB, TNT]: who have weakness.
2. It is concessive [Mil, TH]: although they have weakness.

QUESTION—What is the participial phrase ἔχοντας ἀσθένειαν 'having weakness' connected with?

1. It is connected with ἀνθρώπους 'men' [EBC, HNTC, My, NCBC, NIC, NTC, TNTC, WBC; NAB, NIV, NJB, REB, TEV, TNT]: men who have weakness.
2. It is connected with ἀρχιερεῖς 'high priests' [EGT, GNC, Mil; CEV, NRSV]: priests who have weakness.

but the word[a] of-the oath-taking[b] the-(one) after[c] the law (appoints) (a) Son into[d] the age perfected.[e]

LEXICON—a. λόγος (LN 33.98) (BAGD 1.b.α. p. 478): 'word' [BAGD, LN, Lns, Mil, WBC; KJV, NAB, NASB, NRSV], 'statement' [LN], 'command' [BAGD], 'promise' [TEV]. This singular noun is translated as a plural: 'words' [HNTC; REB, TNT]. The phrase ὁ λόγος τῆς ὁρκωμοσίας 'the word of the oath-swearing' is translated 'the sworn word' [NIC], 'the promise on oath' [NJB], 'the oath' [NIV], 'with an oath' [NLT], 'God's promise' [CEV].

b. ὁρκωμοσία: 'oath-taking'. See this word in 7:20.

c. μετά with accusative object (LN 67.48): 'after' [HNTC, LN, NIC, WBC; NAB, NASB, NIV, NJB, NLT], 'since' [KJV], 'later than' [Mil; CEV, NRSV, TEV, TNT], 'subsequent to' [Lns]. The phrase τῆς μετά 'the one after' is translated 'which supersedes' [REB].

d. εἰς with accusative object: 'into'. See this word and the phrase εἰς τὸν αἰῶνα 'into the age' in 7:21.

e. perf. pass. participle of τελειόω (LN 88.38) (BAGD 2.a. p. 809, 3. p. 810): 'to be perfected' [BAGD, HNTC, LN; TNT], 'to be made perfect' [LN, Mil, NIC, WBC; all versions except CEV, KJV, TNT], 'to be completed' [BAGD], 'to be made complete' [Lns], 'to be brought to one's goal' [BAGD], 'to be brought to accomplishment' [BAGD], 'to be consecrated' [BAGD; KJV]. This passive verb is also translated actively: 'and he is the perfect high priest' [CEV]. It is emphatic by its final position [WBC]. It refers to moral perfection [EGT]; it means having accomplished God's plan of salvation and being exalted to God's right hand [GNC], the whole process of preparing the Son to be mediator in heaven [WBC] by his earthly life [Wst]; it means enabled to do all that he should do [TH], being enabled to expiate the sins of mankind [Blm]. The perfect tense indicates action completed in the past and continuing into the present [GNC], permanence [NTC, Wst]. The passive voice implies that God is the agent [NTC].

QUESTION—How are the two nouns related in the genitive construction ὁ λόγος τῆς ὁρκωμοσίας 'the word of the oath-taking'?

None of the commentaries deal with this point. The possibilities include:

1. 'Oath-taking' is in apposition to 'word': the word which consisted of oath-taking.
2. 'Oath-taking' is the contents of the 'word': the word which expresses the oath.
3. The 'oath-taking' is a part of the 'word': the oath-taking included in the word..
4. 'Oath-taking' describes 'word': the oath-taking word.

QUESTION—What is the attributive prepositional phrase τῆς μετὰ τὸν νόμον 'the one after the law' connected with?

It is connected with ὁρκωμοσίας 'oath-taking' [Alf, EGT, Mil, My, NTC, Wst] as indicated by the genitive case of the article [Alf, EGT, Wst]: the oath-swearing which was after the law. This prepositional phrase implies that the preceding system has been superseded [Lns, My, TH, Wst].

QUESTION—What is implied by υἱόν 'Son' without a definite article?

It indicates the nature of sonship [EGT, Lg(K), Lns, TH], in contrast with the preceding plural noun ἀνθρώπους 'men' [EGT, Hu, Wst]: one whose nature is sonship. It implies the close relationship between the Son and God [Hu, Lns]. The singular noun 'Son' is also contrasted with the high priests [My(D)].

QUESTION—What relationship is indicated by the participial form τετελειωμένον 'perfected'?

1. It is attributive, describing the Son [EGT, HNTC, Lns, Mil, WBC; all versions except NAB, NASB]: who is perfected.
2. It expresses a reason [Mil]: because he is perfected.

QUESTION—What relationship is indicated by the phrase εἰς τὸν αἰῶνα 'forever'?

It emphasizes the permanent effectiveness of the priestly work [WBC]. It is connected with the participle τετελειωμένον 'perfected' [Alf, Hwt, Lns, Mil, NCBC]: perfected forever.

DISCOURSE UNIT: 8:1–10:39 [EBC]. The topic is a new and better covenant.

DISCOURSE UNIT: 8:1–10:18 [Lns, NIC, NTC, Wst]. The topic is Jesus' sacrificial work described in six comparisons [Lns], Jesus as high priest and sacrifice [NTC], the fulfillment of Christ's priestly work [Wst], covenant, sanctuary, and sacrifice [NIC].

DISCOURSE UNIT: 8:1–9:28 [Hwt, NIGTC; NJB]. The topic is Christ's ministry [Hwt], fulfillment [NIGTC], the superiority provided by Christ regarding worship, sanctuary, and mediation [NJB].

DISCOURSE UNIT: 8:1–13 [GNT, Lg, Mil, NTC, TNTC, WBC, Wst; CEV, NIV, NLT, TEV]. The topic is Jesus being our high priest [NLT, TEV], the high priest of a new and better covenant [GNT; NIV], Christ's priesthood as heavenly king and mediator of the new covenant [Lg], a better promise [CEV], the old covenant replaced by a better covenant [Mil], a general view concerning Christ's high-priestly work [Wst], Jesus as high priest and sacrifice, part 1 [NTC], the minister of the new covenant [TNTC], sanctuary and covenant [WBC].

DISCOURSE UNIT: 8:1–7 [EBC, NCBC, NIC]. The topic is Christ's more excellent ministry [EBC], the priest in the heavenly sanctuary [NCBC], priesthood and promise [NIC].

DISCOURSE UNIT: 8:1–6 [GNC, HNTC, Hwt, NIGTC, Wst; NAB, NASB]. The topic is the new sanctuary [Wst], a better ministry [NASB], the ministry of the true high priest [GNC], Christ's heavenly ministry [NIGTC; NAB], Christ as high priest in the true holy of holies [Hwt], priesthood and cultus [HNTC].

DISCOURSE UNIT: 8:1–5 [Lg; NJB]. The topic is the new priesthood and sanctuary [NJB], Christ's heavenly high-priesthood [Lg].

DISCOURSE UNIT: 8:1–2 [Lns, NTC]. The topic is the preamble [Lns], the heavenly sanctuary [NTC].

8:1 Now (as the) principal-point[a] with-respect-to[b] the-(things) being-said, we-have such[c] (a) high-priest,

LEXICON—a. κεφάλαιον (LN **33.12**) (BAGD 1. p. 429): 'principal point' [NJB], 'main point' [BAGD, HNTC, LN, Lns; NAB, NASB, NLT, NRSV, REB], 'chief point' [Mil; TNT], 'point' [NIV], 'whole point' [TEV], 'summary' [**LN**], 'sum' [NIC; KJV], 'crowning affirmation' [WBC]. The phrase κεφάλαιον δὲ ἐπὶ τοῖς λεγομένοις 'now as the principal point with respect to the things being said' is translated 'what I mean is that' [CEV]. Thus forefronted it is definite without the article [Alf, EGT, Lns, NTC, Wst]. Without the article it refers to a principal point [Lg, My]. It means the point [ICC, NTC, TNTC], the principal point [Alf, Blm, EBC, EGT, HNTC, Hwt, NIGTC, TH, Wst], a principal point [Lg, My], the entire point [TEV], the culmination [NCBC], the summary and a new chief point [GNC]. Since he is not summarizing what he has been saying, but passes to a new point, it is usually taken to mean that he is now reaching the main point in the argument and this crowning affirmation is that Christ is performing his priestly ministry in heaven [WBC].

b. ἐπί with dative object (LN 90.23) (BAGD II.1.b.β. p. 287): 'with respect to' [LN], 'with reference to' [LN], 'to' [BAGD, WBC], 'in' [LN, Lns, Mil; NAB, NASB, NRSV, TNT], 'of' [HNTC, NIC; KJV, NIV, NJB, TEV], not explicit [NLT, REB]. It implies the idea of lying upon or over (the things being said) [Alf, EGT, Lg(K)], in respect to [Blm, My], in the case of [Wst], concerning [ICC, NIGTC], in addition to [WBC].

c. τοιοῦτος (LN 64.2, 92.31) (BAGD 2.a.γ. p. 821): 'such' [HNTC, LN (64.2), Lns, WBC; KJV, NAB, NASB, NIV, NRSV, TEV, TNT], 'just such' [Mil], 'of such a kind' [BAGD, LN (92.31)], 'such as this' [BAGD, LN (92.31)], 'of a kind such as this' [LN (92.31)], 'of this kind' [LN (92.31)], 'of exactly this kind' [NJB], 'this kind of' [NIC; REB], 'like that' [LN (64.2)], not explicit [CEV, NLT]. It is emphatic by forefronting [Alf]. It refers to what follows [Alf, EBC, EGT, Lns, My, WBC, Wst]; it refers to the preceding comments [HNTC, Mil, NIGTC].

QUESTION—What relationship is indicated by δέ 'now'?

It introduces a transition to a different point [Lns, Mil]. It indicates a subordinate development [NIGTC].

QUESTION—What does the present tense of the participle τοῖς λεγομένοις 'the things being said' indicate?

It refers to the present discussion [Alf, Lg, My, NIGTC, NTC]; to the discussion now beginning [Lns]; both to what precedes and to what follows [TH]. He is referring to the whole discussion about Christ's priesthood, which is still going on [Wst].

who sat-down[a] at[b] (the) right-hand[c] of-the throne of-the Majesty[d] in[e] the heavens,

LEXICON—a. aorist act. indic. of καθίζω (LN 17.12) (BAGD 2.a.α. p. 390): 'to sit down' [BAGD, LN, Lns, Mil; NIV, NLT, TNT], 'to sit' [CEV, TEV], 'to take one's seat' [HNTC, NIC, WBC; NAB, NASB, NJB, REB], 'to be seated' [NRSV], 'to be set' [KJV]. The aorist tense refers to taking the seat [Lg(K), Mil, Wst]. This word implies a completed work [EBC]. It implies honor [NTC, TNTC], Christ's preeminence [EGT] over the OT priests [Alf, Blm, TNTC] by his being seated [Alf, Blm, EBC, TNTC] and by his being in heaven [Blm, EGT].

b. ἐν with dative object (LN 83.23) (BAGD I.1.c. p. 258): 'at' [BAGD, HNTC, LN, Lns, Mil, NIC, WBC; all versions except KJV], 'on' [KJV].

c. δεξιός (LN 82.8, 87.36) (BAGD 2.a. p. 174): 'right hand' [BAGD, HNTC, LN (87.36), Lns, Mil, NIC, WBC; KJV, NAB, NASB, NIV, NRSV, REB, TNT], 'right side' [LN (82.8, 87.34); CEV], 'right' [LN (82.8); NJB, TEV], 'a special place of honor' [LN (87.36)] 'the place of honor, at God's right hand' [NLT]. It refers to the place of highest honor [EBC, TH], implying Christ's majesty [EGT, Wst], his privilege, and authority [Hu, Wst].

d. μεγαλωσύνη (LN 12.5) (BAGD p. 497): 'Majesty' [BAGD, HNTC, LN, Lns, Mil, NIC, WBC; all versions except NJB, TEV], 'divine Majesty'

[NJB], 'Divine Majesty' [TEV], 'Majestic One' [LN], 'God' [NLT]. It means God [BAGD, LN, TH, WBC]. The idea of majesty is also expressed by expressing his place of honor: 'God's great throne' [CEV].

e. ἐν with dative object (LN 83.13): 'in' [HNTC, LN, Lns, Mil, NIC, WBC; all versions].

QUESTION—Why is this clause mentioned?

It describes the area of Christ's ministry [Mil] in heaven [WBC].

QUESTION—How are the two nouns related in the genitive construction δεξιᾷ τοῦ θρόνου 'the right hand of the throne'?

1. Most commentaries and versions are indefinite, but they presumably refer to sitting on a separate throne to the right of God's throne [EBC, GNC, ICC, Lg, Lns, Mil, NTC, TNTC].
2. The throne is figurative and implies full participation in God's glory and power [NIGTC, Wst]. 'Throne' means simply God's presence [NIGTC].

QUESTION—To what does τῆς μεγαλωσύνης ἐν τοῖς οὐρανοῖς 'the Majesty in the heavens' refer?

It is a reverent reference to God [EBC, GNC, Hu, NIC, NTC].

QUESTION—What is the phrase ἐν τοῖς οὐρανοῖς 'in the heavens' connected with?

'The heavens' refers to God's dwelling place [EBC].

1. It is connected with τῆς μεγαλωσύνης 'the Majesty' [EBC, GNC, Hu, NIC]: the Majesty in the heavens.
2. It is connected with ἐκάθισεν 'he sat down' [Mil, My]: he sat down in the heavens.

8:2 a minister[a] of-the holy-things[b]/sanctuary—that-is/and of-the true[c] tabernacle,[d]

LEXICON—a. λειτουργός (LN 35.23) (BAGD 2. p. 471): 'minister' [BAGD, HNTC, Mil, NIC; KJV, NAB, NASB, NJB, NRSV, REB], 'ministrant' [Lns], 'ministering priest' [WBC], 'servant' [LN]. This noun is also translated as a verb: 'to minister' [NLT], 'to serve' [NIV, TNT], 'to serve as the priest' [CEV], 'to serve as high priest' [TEV]. It is almost synonymous with 'high priest', with the emphasis on worship [WBC]. It implies work [WBC]. It refers to one who performs a public service [HNTC, Lns] with religious implications [HNTC, NCBC], a ministry in holy things [TNTC]. It refers to Christ in his function as a servant [EBC], to Christ's priesthood [Lg, TH] as a sacrificing priest [My], to his ministry of intercession to God for his children [Hwt], to his priestly ministry in heaven [WBC].

b. ἅγιος (LN 88.24) (BAGD 2.b. p. 10): 'holy' [LN]. This plural form is translated as a singular: 'sanctuary' [BAGD, HNTC, Mil, NIC, WBC; all versions except CEV, NLT, TEV], 'Holy Place' [Lns], 'Most Holy Place' [CEV, TEV], 'sacred tent' [NLT]. The phrase τῶν ἁγίων refers to the sanctuary as a whole [EBC, GNC, ICC, NCBC, NIGTC, TH, WBC, Wst], to the innermost room of the sanctuary, the holy of holies [Alf, Blm, EGT, TNTC, Wst], to the heavenly holy of holies [Hu, Hwt].

c. ἀληθινός (LN 70.3) (BAGD 3. p. 37): 'true' [BAGD, LN, Lns, NIC, WBC; all versions except CEV, REB, TEV], 'real' [HNTC, LN, Mil; CEV, REB, TEV]. It indicates reality in contrast with a copy [EBC, Lg(K), My, NCBC, NIC, NIGTC, TH, Wst], the antitype in heaven [Blm, EGT, Hwt, My, NIGTC, TH, Wst]. It describes only σκηνῆς 'the tabernacle' [Lg, Lns]. It implicitly describes τῶν ἁγίων 'the sanctuary' as well as σκηνῆς 'tabernacle' (by implied adjustment of the form [My]) [Blm, EGT, My; REB]. This word is emphatic by word order [NIGTC].

d. σκηνή (LN 7.17) (BAGD p. 754): 'tabernacle' [BAGD, Lns, Mil, WBC; KJV, NAB, NASB, NIV], 'tabernacle tent' [LN], 'tent' [BAGD, HNTC, LN, NIC; NJB, NRSV, REB, TEV, TNT], 'tent, the place of worship' [NLT], 'tent of worship' [CEV]. It refers to the tabernacle [GNC]; it is the same thing as τῶν ἁγίων 'the sanctuary' [Hu].

QUESTION—Why is this clause mentioned?

It is in apposition with and identifies ἀρχιερέα 'high priest', in 8:1 [Mil], indicating the capacity in which Christ took his seat at God's right hand [My].

QUESTION—What relationship is indicated by καί 'that is/and'?

1. It is explanatory, connecting two descriptions of one item [HNTC, Hu, ICC, Lg, My, NIC, NIGTC, NTC, TH, WBC; NIV, REB, TEV, TNT] as the following singular ἥν 'which' implies [WBC]: the sanctuary; that is, the true tabernacle. The phrase 'and of the true tabernacle' is a fuller expression of 'the sanctuary' [Lg(K)].
2. It connects two items [Alf, Blm, Lns, Mil; KJV, NAB, NASB, NJB, NRSV]: the sanctuary and the true tabernacle.

QUESTION—How are the two genitives, τῶν ἁγίων 'the sanctuary' and τῆς σκηνῆς 'the tabernacle', related to λειτουργός 'minister' in the construction τῶν ἁγίων λειτουργὸς καὶ τῆς σκηνῆς τῆς ἀληθινῆς 'a minister of the sanctuary and of the true tabernacle'?

The genitives tell where the ministry is done [Mil, NCBC, NTC, WBC; NASB, NIV, NRSV, REB, TEV, TNT]: he ministers in the sanctuary and/which is in the true tabernacle.

which the Lord pitched,[a] not man.

LEXICON—a. aorist act. indic. of πήγνυμι (LN **45.2**) (BAGD 2. p. 656): 'to pitch' [Mil, NIC, WBC; KJV, NASB], 'to set up' [BAGD, HNTC, LN; CEV, NAB, NIV, NJB, NRSV, REB, TNT], 'to erect' [LN, Lns], 'to put up' [**LN**; TEV]. This active verb is also translated as passive with the tent as subject: 'to be built' [NLT]. This is the regular word for setting up a tent [Alf].

QUESTION—Why is this clause mentioned?

1. It indicates the sense of ἀληθινή 'true' [Lns]: true because pitched by the Lord.

2. It identifies the true tabernacle [Mil]: the true tabernacle, the one which the Lord pitched.

QUESTION—To whom does ὁ κύριος 'the Lord' refer?

It refers to God the Father [Alf, EBC, HNTC, My, NIGTC, NTC, TH].

QUESTION—What relationship is indicated by ἄνθρωπος 'man' without the definite article?

1. It is indefinite [Alf, TH; NJB, NRSV]: no person pitched it.
2. It is qualitative, referring to human nature [NIC; TEV]: no human being pitched it.

DISCOURSE UNIT: 8:3–6 [Lns, NTC]. The topic is the two ministries compared [Lns], Jesus the mediator [NTC].

8:3 For every high-priest is-appointed[a] for-the purpose-of[b] offering both gifts[c] and sacrifices;[d]

LEXICON—a. pres. pass. indic. of καθίστημι (LN 37.104) (BAGD 2.b. p. 390): 'to be appointed' [BAGD, HNTC, LN, Lns, Mil, NIC, WBC; NAB, NASB, NIV, NRSV, REB, TEV, TNT], 'to be designated' [LN], 'to be constituted' [NJB], 'to be ordained' [KJV], 'to be required' [NLT], 'must' [CEV].

b. εἰς with accusative (LN 89.57): 'for' [Lns], 'for the purpose of' [LN], 'in order to' [LN]. The phrase εἰς τὸ προσφέρειν 'for the purpose of offering' is translated 'to offer' [HNTC, Mil, NIC, WBC; all versions except TEV], 'to present' [TEV]. This prepositional phrase states the purpose of the appointment [Mil].

c. δῶρον (LN 57.84): 'gift' [HNTC, LN, Lns, Mil, NIC, WBC; all versions except TEV], 'offering' [TEV].

d. θυσία (LN 53.20) (BAGD 2.a. p. 366): 'sacrifice' [HNTC, LN, Lns, Mil, NIC, WBC; all versions except TEV], 'animal sacrifice' [TEV], 'offering' [BAGD].

QUESTION—What relationship is indicated by γάρ 'for'?

1. It indicates the reason for the implied thought that we do have a high priest in heaven [Blm].
2. It indicates the reason Christ is ministering in the heavenly tabernacle [EBC, Mil]: he is ministering in the heavenly tabernacle because offering a sacrifice is characteristic of the high priest. It proves that Christ's ministry can be carried out only in a heavenly sanctuary [Lg].
3. It introduces a development of 8:1, that high priests offer sacrifices [TH]. It recapitulates and supports the comment of 8:1–2 [NIGTC].
4. It refers back to (recapitulates [HNTC]) the reference in 5:1 that the high priest offers sacrifices [HNTC, Hu, NCBC, NTC, TNTC, WBC] to specify the need for Christ to have an offering [WBC].

QUESTION—To what do the δῶρα καὶ θυσίας 'gifts and sacrifices' refer?

1. They are the atoning sacrifices, both of blood and without blood [Blm].
2. They are the various sacrifices offered by the priests [GNC, TH].

hence[a] (it is/was) necessary[b] (for) this-one also to-have something which he-may-offer.

LEXICON—a. ὅθεν (BAGD 3. p. 555): 'hence' [HNTC, Lns; NAB, NASB, NRSV, REB], 'therefore' [BAGD; NIC], 'wherefore' [KJV], 'and so' [NIV, NJB, TEV], 'that is why' [Mil], 'this being the case' [WBC], not explicit [CEV, NLT, TNT].

b. ἀναγκαῖος (LN 71.39) (BAGD 1. p. 52): 'necessary' [BAGD, HNTC, LN, Lns, Mil; NASB, NIV, NRSV]. This adjective is translated as a noun: 'of necessity' [KJV, REB], 'the necessity' [NAB]. The phrase ἀναγκαῖον ἔχειν 'it is necessary to have' is translated 'must have' [BAGD, NIC; NJB, TEV, TNT], 'had necessarily to have' [WBC], 'needed to have' [CEV], 'must make (an offering)' [NLT].

QUESTION—What relationship is indicated by ὅθεν 'hence'?

It indicates the logical conclusion (the result [Mil]) of the preceding clause [EGT, Hu, Hwt, Lns, Mil, NCBC, NIGTC].

QUESTION—What is the implied verb with ἀναγκαῖον 'necessary'?

1. 'It is' is implied [EGT, Lg, Lns, Mil], referring to the logic rather than to actual time [EGT, Lns]: it is necessary.
2. 'It was' is implied [EBC, HNTC, Hwt, My, NIGTC, Wst], referring to the historical event of Christ's sacrifice [EBC, HNTC, Hwt, My, Wst]: it was necessary. Christ does not continue to offer his blood in heaven [HNTC].

QUESTION—To what does τι ὃ προσενέκῃ 'something which he may offer' refer?

The singular τι 'something' indicates that he offered only a single sacrifice [Hu]; it implies the mysterious nature of the offering [Wst]. It is intentionally indefinite since what it refers to was mentioned in 7:27 [My, NIGTC, TNTC] and is only incidental here [My, NIGTC]. What it refers to is not stated here, but is identified later [Lg, Lns, NTC, TH]. It refers to Christ's blood [EGT, TH], offered on earth [EBC, EGT] but forever effective (continually being offered [EGT]) in heaven [Alf]. Christ enters the heavenly tabernacle with his blood [Lg(K)]. Christ offered his body [My], i.e., himself [Blm, GNC, HNTC, Hu, Hwt, NIC, TNTC, WBC, Wst]. His sacrifice is heavenly in its meaning rather than earthly [GNC].

QUESTION—What is indicated by the tenses of the two instances of the verb προσφέρω 'to offer'?

The present tense of the first occurrence implies the repetition of offering the sacrifices in the earthly tabernacle; the aorist tense of the second occurrence implies the once-for-all nature of Christ's sacrifice [GNC, Hu, Hwt, Lns, NCBC, NIC, NIGTC, NTC, WBC, Wst].

8:4 If therefore on-the-one-hand he-were on[a] earth, not-even would-he-be (a) priest,

TEXT—Instead of οὖν 'therefore' some manuscripts have γάρ 'for'. GNT does not deal with this variant. Only Blm, Lg(K), and KJV read 'for'.

LEXICON—a. ἐπί with genitive object (LN 83.46): 'on' [HNTC, LN, Lns, NIC, WBC; all versions], 'upon' [LN, Mil].

QUESTION—What relationship is indicated by οὖν 'therefore'?

1. It indicates the conclusion that Christ's ministry must be in heaven rather than on earth (and is thus superior to the Levitical priesthood [TNTC]) [EGT, GNC, HNTC, Hu, Hwt, Lns, My, TNTC], since the Levitical priesthood has been established by God to officiate on earth [HNTC, Hu, Hwt]. It continues the thought of 8:2 [My].
2. It indicates the result of the fact that Christ is not of the tribe of Judah, as mentioned in 7:14 [Mil].
3. If γάρ 'for' is read instead of οὖν 'therefore', it indicates the reason Christ is a priest in the heavenly tabernacle rather than the earthly one [Blm]: he is a priest in heaven, because if he were on earth he would not be a priest.

QUESTION—What relationship is indicated by μέν 'on the one hand'?

It indicates the first part of a contrast which is carried out by δέ 'on the other hand' in 8:6 [Mil, NIGTC]: on the one hand, on earth . . . ; on the other hand, in heaven. . . .

QUESTION—What is implied by the imperfect tense of the two instances of ἦν '(if) he-were'?

This clause is a contrary-to-fact condition [Lns, Mil, NIGTC, NTC, WBC, Wst]: if he were on earth (which he is not) he could not be a priest (which in fact he is).

1. They indicate a continuing state when the epistle was written [Alf, EGT, Mil, My, NIGTC, Wst]: if he were now continually on earth, he would not be a priest. The implication is that God cannot establish two competing priesthoods [NIGTC].
2. They refer to Christ's earthly life [Blm]: if he were/had been on earth (instead of being in heaven), he would not have been a priest.

QUESTION—What is indicated by οὐδὲ ἦν 'he would not even be'?

Οὐδέ 'not even' modifies ἦν 'be' [Lg].

1. It is emphatic, negating the state [Alf, Lg(K), TH]: he would *not even be* a priest.
2. It contrasts ἱερεύς 'priest' with ἀρχιερεύς 'high priest' in 8:3 [EGT, NIGTC, Wst]: he would not even be a *priest*, much less a *high priest*.

being the-(ones) offering the gifts according-to[a] law;

TEXT—Some manuscripts add τῶν ἱερέων 'the priests' or ἱερέων 'priests' following ὄντων 'being'. GNT does not deal with this variant; Blm, HNTC, KJV, NAB, NRSV, REB, TEV, TNT add '(the) priests', but all except Blm and KJV almost certainly do so only to clarify the sense without accepting the Greek addition.

LEXICON—a. κατά with accusative object (LN 89.8): 'according to' [HNTC, Lns, Mil; KJV, NASB, NRSV, TNT], 'in accordance with' [LN], 'prescribed by' [WBC; NIV, REB], 'laid down by' [NJB], 'required by' [NLT, TEV]. The phrase κατὰ νόμον 'according to law' is translated 'which the law prescribes' [NAB], 'prescribed' [NIC], 'the Law appoints' [CEV].

QUESTION—What relationship is indicated by the participle ὄντων 'being'?

It indicates reason [Alf, Lg(K), Lns, Mil, My, WBC, Wst; all versions] and is emphatic [Alf, My]: he would not be a priest because there already are those who offer the gifts.

QUESTION—What does the present tense of the participle ὄντων 'being' indicate?

It indicates continuation [WBC] at the time when the epistle was written [Alf]: since there are always priests.

QUESTION—What does the present tense of the participle προσφερόντων 'offering' indicate?

It indicates repeated offering [Lns]: those who repeatedly offer. This participle refers to the Levitical priests [NIGTC].

QUESTION—What is the phrase κατὰ νόμον 'according to law' connected with?

1. It is connected with προσφερόντων 'offering', indicating manner [HNTC, Lns, Mil, NCBC; KJV, NASB, NRSV, TNT]: offering in the way the law prescribes.
2. It is connected with τὰ δῶρα 'the gifts' [NIC, TH, WBC, Wst; NAB, NIV, NJB, REB, TEV]: the gifts which the laws prescribes. The use of the definite article relates this noun back to δῶρα 'gifts' in 8:3 [NIGTC].

QUESTION—What is indicated by the absence of the article with νόμον 'law'?

It is qualitative [EGT, Wst], referring to the authoritative character of the law [Wst]: according to law. It is nevertheless definite [Alf, HNTC, NTC, TH]: according to *the* law. It refers to the Mosaic Law [NIGTC].

8:5 who serve[a] (a)/(in-a) copy[b] and shadow[c] of-the heavenly[d] (things),

LEXICON—a. pres. act. indic. of λατρεύω (LN 53.14) (BAGD p. 467): 'to serve' [BAGD, HNTC, Lns, Mil, WBC; CEV, KJV, NASB, NIV, NLT], 'to perform a service' [TNT], 'to maintain the service' [NJB], 'to minister' [NIC; REB], 'to worship' [LN], 'to offer worship' [NAB, NRSV]. The phrase οἵτινες λατρεύουσιν 'who serve' is translated 'the work they do as priests' [TEV]. It refers to the aspect of serving [Alf, EGT, Lns], priestly service or worship [NIC]. The present tense implies that the Levitical priesthood was still in existence [Hu].

b. ὑπόδειγμα (LN 58.59) (BAGD 2. p. 844): 'copy' [BAGD, Mil, NIC; CEV, NAB, NASB, NIV, NLT, TEV, TNT], 'model' [HNTC, LN; NJB], 'example' [LN; KJV], 'sketch' [Lns; NRSV]. The phrase ὑποδείγματι καὶ σκιᾷ 'model and shadow' is translated 'shadowy suggestion' [WBC], 'shadowy symbol' [REB]. It means a suggestive representation [Alf], a sketch or exemplar [Blm, Hu, Lns, My], an outline [EGT, ICC, My], a copy [Lg, My], the earthly copy of the heavenly reality [NIGTC]. It is still something substantial [NTC].

c. σκιά (LN 58.65) (BAGD 2. p. 755): 'shadow' [BAGD, HNTC, LN, Lns, Mil, NIC; all versions except NJB, REB], 'foreshadow' [LN], 'foreshadowing' [BAGD], 'reflection' [NJB], 'faint prototype' [LN]. The shadow presupposes a corresponding reality behind it [Hu, NIGTC, TNTC]. It is synonymous with ὑπόδειγμα 'copy' [NIGTC]; it implies a reflection of something [NTC].

d. ἐπουράνιος (LN 1.12) (BAGD 2.a.β. p. 306): 'heavenly' [LN, Lns; KJV], 'heavenly thing' [BAGD, Mil; NASB, TNT], 'heavenly reality' [NIC; NJB], 'heavenly place' [HNTC], 'heavenly (sanctuary)' [WBC; NAB, NRSV, REB], 'what is in heaven' [NIV, TEV], 'the real one in heaven' [CEV, NLT], 'in heaven' [LN]. It refers to heavenly things in general but implies the tabernacle [TNTC], the heavenly sanctuary [Alf, Lg(K), My], heavenly relationships [Lg], the divine presence and heavenly realities [Wst].

QUESTION—What relationship is indicated by οἵτινες 'who'?

This relative pronoun calls attention to the class of persons referred to [Alf, EGT, ICC, Lg(K), Lns, Mil, Wst]: that is, those who serve. It is qualitative [Mil, Wst].

QUESTION—What relationship is indicated by καί 'and' in the phrase ὑποδείγματι καὶ σκιᾷ 'model and shadow'?

1. It indicates a coordinate relationship [Hu]: they serve both a model and a shadow.
2. It is a hendiadys where 'shadow' modifies 'model' [ICC, TH, WBC; REB]: they serve a shadowy symbol.

QUESTION—What relationship is indicated by the two dative nouns ὑποδείγματι καὶ σκιᾷ 'model and shadow'?

1. They indicate what is being served [Alf, EGT, HNTC, ICC, Lns, Mil, My, WBC; NASB, NJB]: they serve a model and shadow.
2. They indicate the place where they serve [EBC, NIC, NIGTC; NAB, NIV, NRSV, REB]: they serve in a model and shadow.
3. They indicate the means by which the priest serves [BAGD (p. 467)]: they serve by means of the holy objects which are a model and shadow.

QUESTION—How are the two dative nouns and the genitive adjective related in the genitive construction ὑποδείγματι καὶ σκιᾷ τῶν ἐπουρανίων 'model and shadow of the heavenly things'?

1. The genitive τῶν ἐπουρανίων 'of the heavenly things' expresses the source of the 'model and shadow' [Mil]: the heavenly things which are the source of the model and shadow.
2. The genitive τῶν ἐπουρανίων 'of the heavenly things' may be objective, but none of the commentaries mention this possibility: they serve something that foreshadows the heavenly things.

just-as[a] Moses was-warned[b] being-about to-erect[c] the tent,[d]

LEXICON—a. καθώς (LN 64.14): 'just as' [LN; NASB, NJB, TNT], 'even as' [Lns, Mil, WBC], 'as' [HNTC, NIC; KJV], 'this is why' [NIV, REB], 'for' [NAB, NRSV], not explicit [CEV, NLT]. The phrase καθώς κεχρημάτισται Μωϋσῆς 'just as Moses was warned' is translated 'it is the same as it was with Moses. God told him' [TEV].

b. perf. pass. indic. of χρηματίζω (LN 28.39) (BAGD 1.b.α. p. 885): 'to be warned' [NAB, NIV, NRSV], 'to be warned by God' [NASB, NJB], 'to be instructed' [HNTC; TNT], 'to be instructed by God' [REB], 'to be told' [CEV], 'to be admonished' [Mil], 'to be admonished by God' [WBC], 'to be admonished of God' [KJV], 'to be made known' [LN] 'to have God's message made known' [LN], 'to have a message from God revealed' [LN], 'a revelation to be given' [BAGD]. This passive verb is also translated as an active voice: 'to receive divine direction' [Lns], 'to give a warning' [NLT]. The phrase κεχρημάτισται Μωϋσῆς 'Moses was warned' is translated 'the oracle said to Moses' [NIC]. It refers to a command from God [Alf, EGT, Lns]. It includes instructions [Hwt, NIGTC, NTC], communications, and warnings [Hwt]. It is an authoritative word [TNTC, Wst] which must be obeyed [TNTC]. The perfect tense implies that the things referred to were still in existence [Alf], that the message stands valid permanently [NIC, NTC, Wst]. The implied speaker is God [EGT, Hu, ICC, Mil, NIGTC, NTC, TH, WBC, Wst].

c. pres. act. infin. of ἐπιτελέω (LN **45.2**) (BAGD 2. p. 302): 'to erect' [BAGD, LN, NIC, WBC; NAB, NASB, NRSV, TNT], 'to set up' [**LN**], 'to put up' [LN; REB], 'to construct' [Lns, Mil], 'to build' [NIV, NJB, NLT, TEV], 'to make' [HNTC; CEV, KJV]. It refers to the act of constructing as a whole [Alf, EGT, My, NIGTC].

d. σκηνή (LN 7.17) (BAGD p. 754): 'tent' [BAGD, LN, NIC; CEV, NRSV, REB, TNT], 'Tent' [HNTC; NJB], 'Sacred Tent' [TEV], 'tabernacle tent' [LN], 'tabernacle' [Mil, WBC; KJV, NAB, NASB, NIV], 'Tabernacle' [Lns; NLT].

QUESTION—What relationship is indicated by καθώς 'just as'?

It introduces the support for the preceding argument [NIGTC]. This and the following clause show the appropriateness of the terms 'model and shadow' [Blm, ICC, Mil]: they are a model and shadow, just as God's words to Moses indicate.

QUESTION—What relationship is indicated by the participial form μέλλων 'being about'?

It is temporal [all versions]: Moses was warned when he was about to erect the tent.

QUESTION—What relationship is indicated by the verb phrase μέλλων ἐπιτελεῖν 'being about to build'?

1. It implies anticipated action [all versions except NJB]: being about to erect the tent.
2. It implies an intended action [WBC]: intending to erect the tent.
3. It implies being destined by a divine message [Wst; NJB]: being destined to erect the tent.

for "See-to-it,"[a] he-says, "you-shall-make[b] everything according-to[c] the pattern[d] the-(one) having-been-shown[e] to-you on[f] the mountain;"

LEXICON—a. pres. act. impera. of ὁράω (LN 30.45) (BAGD 2.b. p. 578): 'to see to it' [Lns], 'to see to it that' [BAGD, LN, NIC; NIV, REB], 'to see that' [HNTC, Mil; KJV, NAB, NASB, NJB, NRSV, TNT], 'to pay attention to' [LN], 'to concern oneself with' [LN], 'to be sure' [CEV, NLT, TEV], 'to look' [WBC]. It is used to strengthen the following command ποιήσεις 'you shall make' [Lns].

b. fut. act. indic. of ποιέω (LN 42.29) (BAGD I.1.a.α. p. 680): 'to make' [BAGD, LN, Lns, Mil, NIC, WBC; all versions except NJB, TNT], 'to fashion' [LN], 'to do' [HNTC; TNT], 'to work' [NJB]. The future indicative has imperative force [EGT].

c. κατά with accusative object (LN 89.8) (BAGD II.5.b.α. p. 407): 'according to' [Lns, NIC, WBC; all versions except CEV, NJB, TNT], 'in accordance with' [BAGD, HNTC, LN, Mil; TNT], 'exactly like' [CEV], 'to' [NJB]. It indicates manner, referring to ποιήσεις 'you shall make' [Mil].

d. τύπος (LN **58.58**) (BAGD 5.a. p. 830): 'pattern' [BAGD, HNTC, LN, Mil, NIC, WBC; all versions except NJB, NLT], 'model' [**LN**], 'design' [BAGD; NJB, NLT], 'type' [Lns]. It indicates a scale model [NIC].

e. aorist pass. participle of δείκνυμι (LN 33.150) (BAGD 1.a. p. 172): 'to be shown' [BAGD, HNTC, LN, Lns, Mil, NIC, WBC; all versions], 'to be made known' [BAGD].

f. ἐν with dative object (LN **83.47**) (BAGD I.1.b. p. 258): 'on' [BAGD, HNTC, LN, NIC, WBC; all versions except KJV], 'in' [Lns, Mil; KJV]. It indicates location, referring to the participle δειχθέντα 'shown' [Mil].

QUESTION—What relationship is indicated by γάρ 'for'?

It indicates the grounds for the preceding statement [Alf]: Moses was warned, for this is what God said to him.

QUESTION—Who is the implied actor of φησίν 'he says'?

It is God [Alf, EGT, ICC, Mil, My, NIGTC, TH, WBC, Wst]: God said to him.

DISCOURSE UNIT: 8:6–13 [Lg; NJB]. The topic is Christ's priestly service being more excellent than that of the old covenant [Lg], Christ the mediator of a better covenant [NJB].

8:6 but/on-the-other-hand now he-has-obtained[a] a-more-excellent[b] ministry,[c]

LEXICON—a. perf. act. indic. of τυγχάνω (LN 90.61) (BAGD p. 829): 'to obtain' [HNTC, Lns, Mil; KJV, NAB, NASB, NRSV, TNT], 'to attain' [BAGD, WBC], 'to receive' [NIC; NIV], 'to experience' [BAGD, LN], 'to gain, to find' [BAGD]. This active voice is also translated as a passive: 'to be given' [NJB, NLT, REB, TEV], 'to be appointed' [CEV]. It implies achievement and victory [Hu]; it is neutral and is not explicitly expressing effort [NIGTC]. The perfect tense implies that it is still in effect [Lns, TH, WBC].

b. διάφορος (LN **35.25**, 58.40) (BAGD 2. p. 191): 'more excellent' [BAGD, LN (**35.25**), Lns, Mil; KJV, NAB, NASB, NRSV], 'more different' [LN (58.40)], 'better' [NIC], 'superior' [REB, TEV], 'far superior' [NLT, TNT], 'in a much better way' [CEV]. The phrase διαφορωτέρας ὅσῳ 'more excellent by as much as' is translated 'as superior as' [WBC; NIV], 'as far superior as' [HNTC; NJB].

c. λειτουργία (LN **35.25**) (BAGD 1. p. 471): 'ministry' [HNTC, LN, Mil, NIC, WBC; all versions except CEV, TEV], 'ministration' [Lns], 'priestly work' [TEV], 'service' [BAGD]. This noun is also translated as a verb phrase: 'to serve as a priest' [CEV].

QUESTION—What relationship is indicated by νυνὶ δέ 'but now, on the other hand'?

It answers to εἰ μέν 'if on the one hand' in 8:4 [ICC, Lg, Mil, My, NIGTC, WBC]: now on the other hand.

QUESTION—What relationship is indicated by νυνί 'now'?

1. It is logical [Alf, EGT, HNTC, Hu, ICC, Lg, Mil, My, WBC, Wst] marking the contrast with εἰ μέν 'if on the one hand' in 8:4 [NIGTC]: as the situation is. It has temporal implications as well [Hu, NIGTC]. It emphasizes the contrast between the old and the new order [Hu].
2. It is temporal [Blm, GNC, TH]: as things now are. It has logical implications as well [TH]

QUESTION—What relationship is indicated by διαφορωτέρας λειτουργίας 'a more excellent ministry'?

It contrasts with the thought of 8:5 [My]. It means superior to earthly priests [Alf, NIC], to the Levitical ministry [Blm, Hu, Hwt, Lg, NTC, WBC].

by-as-much-as/just-as[a] he-is also mediator[b] of-a-better[c] covenant,[d]

LEXICON—a. ὅσος (LN **78.52**) (BAGD 3. p. 586): '(by) as much as' [**LN**, Lns; NASB], 'just as' [NAB, TEV, TNT], 'to the degree that' [BAGD, LN], 'to the same degree that' [**LN**], 'to that degree' [NRSV], 'by how much' [KJV], 'in proportion as' [Mil], 'inasmuch as' [NIC], 'for' [NLT, REB], 'and' [CEV].

b. μεσίτης (LN 31.22) (BAGD p. 507): 'mediator' [BAGD, HNTC, LN, Lns, Mil, NIC, WBC; all versions except CEV, NLT, TEV], 'one who guarantees' [NLT]. The phrase ἐστιν μεσίτης 'he is mediator' is translated 'which he arranged between God and his people' [TEV], 'he has given us much assurance' [CEV]. It refers to one who arbitrates between two parties [Alf, Blm, EBC, EGT, HNTC, Lns, Mil, TH, TNTC, Wst; TEV], in this case between God and mankind [EBC, HNTC; TEV]. The mediation is unilateral, Christ acting for God to mankind [Lns, NIGTC]. It implies the accomplishing of salvation [GNC].

c. κρείττων (LN 65.21) (BAGD 1. p. 449): 'better' [BAGD, HNTC, LN, Lns, Mil, NIC; all versions except NIV, NJB], 'superior' [LN, WBC; NIV, NJB], 'preferable' [BAGD]. It is emphatic by word order [WBC].

d. διαθήκη (LN 34.43) (BAGD 2. p. 183): 'covenant' [BAGD, HNTC, LN, Mil, NIC, WBC; all versions except CEV], 'testament' [Lns], 'agreement' [CEV].

QUESTION—What relationship is indicated by ὅσῳ 'by as much as'?

1. It indicates difference of degree [Alf, GNC, HNTC, Hwt, Lg, Lns, Mil, TH, WBC; KJV, NASB, NIV, NJB, NRSV]: to the degree that.
2. It indicates a comparison [NIGTC; NAB, TEV, TNT] between Christ's ministry and the new covenant [NIGTC]: just as.
3. It indicates reason [REB]: because.

QUESTION—What relationship is implied by καί 'also'?

It introduces the second half of the comparison [NIGTC], a fact previously acknowledged in 6:7 [Alf]: he is also mediator.

QUESTION—What relationship is indicated by κρείττονος διαθήκης 'better covenant'?

It means better than the Mosaic covenant [Blm, Hu].

QUESTION—How are the two nouns related in the genitive construction κρείττονος διαθήκης μεσίτης 'mediator of a better covenant'?

Μεσίτης 'covenant' is an objective genitive [Alf], telling what he mediates [Alf, Hu, ICC]: he mediates a better covenant. The covenant is between God and mankind [Alf].

which[a] is-enacted[b] upon[c] better[d] promises.

LEXICON—a. ὅστις (LN 92.18): 'which' [LN, Mil; KJV, NASB, NJB, NRSV], 'one of a kind that' [Lns], 'because' [TEV, TNT], 'for' [HNTC], 'seeing that' [WBC], 'and' [NIV], not explicit [CEV, NLT]. The phrase ἥτις νενομοθέτηται 'which is enacted' is translated as a participle: 'enacted' [NIC], 'founded' [NAB], 'established' [REB]. It is qualitative [Mil], it characterizes [Lg(K), Lns, My], identifies [Alf] and also introduces an implied reason [Alf, EGT, Mil]; it is causal [WBC].

b. perf. pass. indic. of νομοθετέω (LN **33.339**) (BAGD 2. p. 542): 'to be enacted' [Mil, NIC; NASB, NRSV], 'to be established' [KJV, REB, TNT], 'to be founded' [NAB, NIV, NJB], 'to be based' [NLT, TEV], 'to be drawn up' [WBC], 'to be given as law' [**LN**], 'to be enacted as law' [LN], 'to be legally enacted' [BAGD], 'to be legally secured' [HNTC], 'to be given legal force' [Lns]. It implies that the covenant referred to was also in some sense a law [Blm, Hu, Lg(K), My]. The perfect tense implies that it is still in force [Lns, TH]. The actor is God [ICC, WBC].

c. ἐπί with dative object (LN 89.13) (BAGD ii.1.b.γ. p. 287): 'upon' [Mil; KJV], 'on' [HNTC; NAB, NASB, NIV, NJB, NLT, REB, TEV], 'on the basis of' [BAGD, LN, NIC, WBC; TNT], 'on the score of' [Lns], 'through' [NRSV]. It introduces the grounds (the conditions [Alf, Wst]) upon which the better covenant is based [Alf, Blm, My, WBC, Wst].

d. κρείττων (LN 65.21) (BAGD 1. p. 449): 'better' [BAGD, HNTC, LN, Lns, Mil, NIC, WBC; all versions except TEV]. This adjective is also translated as a genitive phrase: 'of better things' [TEV]. It refers to the promises which are mentioned in the following verses [Alf, Blm, EGT, GNC, HNTC, ICC, My, NCBC, NIC, NIGTC, Wst]. It includes also the true sabbath rest and the heavenly Jerusalem [GNC]; it does not include these things [My]. It is emphatic by word order [WBC]. See this word at 1:4; 6:9; 7:7, 19, 22.

QUESTION—Why is this clause mentioned?

1. It further describes διαθήκη 'covenant' [Alf, Lns, Mil, NIC; KJV, NAB, NASB, NJB, NRSV, REB], but also implying the reason [Alf]: a better covenant, (which is) enacted. . . .
2. It makes an additional comment concerning διαθήκη 'covenant' [NIV]: and it is enacted. . . .
3. It expresses the reason why (how [Blm]) the new covenant is better [Blm, EBC, HNTC, NTC, WBC; TEV, TNT]: a better covenant because it is enacted. . . .

QUESTION—What is ἥτις 'which' connected with?

Its antecedent is διαθήκη 'covenant' [Hu; all versions].

QUESTION—To what does κρείττοσιν ἐπαγγελίαις 'better promises' refer?

1. It refers to what is promised [GNC, TNTC; TEV].
2. It refers to the promises themselves [Alf, Blm, EGT, HNTC].

DISCOURSE UNIT: 8:7–13 [GNC, HNTC, Hwt, Lns, NTC, Wst; NAB, NASB]. The topic is the promise of a new covenant [GNC], God's new covenant [NTC, Wst; NASB], the inadequacy of the old covenant [HNTC], the two covenants [Hwt; NAB], a comparison of the two testaments [Lns].

8:7 For if that first (covenant) were faultless,[a]

LEXICON—a. ἄμεμπτος (LN 88.317) (BAGD p. 45): 'faultless' [BAGD, HNTC, Lns, Mil, NIC; all versions except CEV, NIV, TEV], 'blameless' [BAGD, LN], 'without blame' [LN], 'irreproachable' [WBC]. This entire clause is translated 'for if there had been nothing wrong with that first covenant' [NIV], 'if there had been nothing wrong with the first covenant' [TEV], 'if the first agreement with God had been all right' [CEV]. The use of this word does not imply that the old covenant had positive faults [Blm, EBC, HNTC, Hu, TH, TNTC, Wst], but only that it could not fully accomplish what was needed [Blm, EBC, EGT, HNTC, Hu, Hwt, Mil, NIGTC, TH, Wst]; the fault was with mankind's experience in it [TNTC, Wst].

QUESTION—Why is this verse mentioned?

This verse is a contrary-to-fact condition [Lns, Mil, NIGTC, NTC, WBC] relating to a timeless proposition [Lns], to an existing situation [NIGTC]. It begins the argument to show that the old covenant was imperfect [Alf], that the new covenant is superior [Blm], that the introduction of a new covenant implies the inadequacy of the preceding one [Blm, EBC, HNTC, Hu, Hwt,

ICC, NIC]; it begins the justification of the reference to 'better' in 8:6 [My], the justification of the establishment of a better covenant [EGT, Mil], as the γάρ 'for' indicates [Mil]. The introductory γάρ 'for' relates the following verses to the preceding 8:1–6 [NIGTC].

QUESTION—To what does ἡ πρώτη ἐκείνη 'that first (covenant)' refer?

It refers to the covenant at Mount Sinai [GNC, WBC], to the covenant referred to in 8:1–5 [NIGTC].

not for-a-second (covenant) a-place[a] would-be-being-sought.[b]

LEXICON—a. τόπος (LN 80.1) (BAGD 1.f. p. 823): 'place' [LN, Lns, Mil, NIC; KJV, NIV], 'room' [LN], 'occasion' [BAGD, WBC; NASB]. This entire clause is translated 'there would have been no place for a second one' [NAB], 'there would have been no need for a second one' [TEV], 'there would not have been any need for another one' [CEV], 'there would have been no need for a second covenant to replace it' [NLT], 'there would have been no need to look for a second one' [NRSV], 'there would have been no occasion to look for a second to replace it' [REB], 'there would have been no room for a second one to replace it' [NJB], 'there would have been no desire for a second to take its place' [HNTC], 'God would not have been seeking a place for a second' [TNT]. It refers to a place in history [Alf], in the history of redemption [NTC].

b. imperf. pass. indic. of ζητέω (LN 25.9, 57.59): 'to be sought' [LN (57.59), Lns, Mil, NIC, WBC; KJV, NASB, NIV], 'to be desired' [LN (25.9)], 'to be tried to obtain' [LN (57.59)], 'to be attempted to get' [LN (57.59)]. It refers to anxious desire and expectation [Blm]. The imperfect tense implies continual searching from the past [Mil] even while the first covenant was in force [Wst]. The actor is God [My, NIGTC].

QUESTION—To what does δευτέρας 'second (covenant)' refer?

It refers to the new covenant [WBC] mentioned in the following quotation from Jeremiah 31:31–34 [GNC]. Δευτέρας 'second' is emphatic by forefronting [Alf, Lg]. It was needed because God had revealed a new aspect of his plan of redemption [WBC].

QUESTION—What is implied by ἐζητεῖτο τόπος 'a place would be being sought'?

It implies that God was seeking an opportunity to establish a second covenant [Lg, NIGTC] for which he already had a place [Lg].

QUESTION—How are the noun τόπος 'place' and the genitive adjective δευτέρας 'second (covenant)' related?

Δευτέρας 'second (covenant)' tells for what a place was being sought [Lns]: a place for a second covenant.

DISCOURSE UNIT: 8:8–13 [EBC, NCBC, NIC]. The topic is the old covenant superseded [EBC, NIC], the old and new covenants [NCBC].

8:8 For finding-fault[a] with-/to-them he-says,

TEXT—Instead of the accusative αὐτούς '(finding fault) with them,' some manuscripts read the dative αὐτοῖς, which can mean either '(finding fault) with them' or '(he says) to them'. GNT reads αὐτούς with a B decision, indicating that this reading is almost certain. Αὐτούς is clearly read by BAGD, Mil, NIGTC, Wst; αὐτοῖς is clearly read by Alf, Blm, EGT, GNC, Hu, Lg, My, WBC. Since μέμφομαι 'to find fault' can take either the dative or accusative case as its object, it cannot be determined precisely which form some translations are rendering.

LEXICON—a. pres. mid. (deponent = act.) participle of μέμφομαι (LN **33.431**) (BAGD p. 502): 'to find fault' [BAGD, HNTC, Mil, NIC, WBC; all versions], 'to fault' [Lns], 'to blame' [LN].

QUESTION—What relationship is indicated by γάρ 'for'?

It introduces the proof that a second covenant is contemplated [Alf, EBC, ICC, My, NCBC], the grounds for implying that the old covenant was faulty [EGT, Mil, My, NIGTC]; the phrase "it is being sought" is implied preceding 'for' [Alf, Blm, ICC].

QUESTION—What relationship is indicated by the participial form μεμφόμενος 'finding fault'?

The actor is God [Blm, EBC, GNC, HNTC, Hu, Hwt, Lns, Mil, NIC, NIGTC, NTC; NIV, NJB, NRSV, REB, TEV, TNT].

1. It expresses the grounds for what follows [Mil; NRSV]: because he finds fault, he says.
2. It expresses a separate action [NIV, NJB]: he found fault and said.
3. It expresses the implication of what God says [TNT]: he finds fault, saying.

QUESTION—What is the pronoun αὐτούς/αὐτοῖς 'with/to them' connected with?

Μεμφόμενος 'finding fault' can take either the dative or the accusative form [ICC, Lg]; λέγει 'he says' can take only the dative form.

1. It is connected with μεμφόμενος 'finding fault' [Alf, EBC, EGT, GNC, HNTC, Hwt, ICC, Lns, Mil, NCBC, NIC, NIGTC, NTC, Wst; all versions except CEV, NLT]: finding fault with them, he says.
2. It is connected with λέγει 'he says' [Blm, Hu, Lg, My, WBC; CEV, NLT]: finding fault with it, he says to them. The fault is with the old covenant [Blm, Hu, Lg(K), WBC; CEV, NLT].

QUESTION—Who is the implied speaker of λέγει 'he says'?

The speaker is God [EBC, EGT, GNC, HNTC, Hu, Lns, Mil, My, NIC, Wst; all versions except KJV, TNT]. The present tense makes the following quotation contemporary with the readers [WBC].

“‘Behold, days[a] come,’ says (the) Lord, ‘and I-will-accomplish[b] over[c] the house[d] of-Israel and over[c] the house[d] of-Judah a-new[e] covenant,[f]

LEXICON—a. ἡμέρα (LN 67.178) (BAGD 4.b. p. 347): ‘day’ [HNTC, LN, Lns, Mil, NIC; KJV, NAB, NASB, NJB, NLT, NRSV, TEV], ‘time’ [BAGD, WBC; CEV, NIV, REB, TNT].

b. fut. act. indic. of συντελέω (LN **13.88**, 68.22) (BAGD 2. p. 792): ‘to accomplish’ [LN (13.88, 68.22)], ‘to bring to accomplishment’ [BAGD], ‘to consummate’ [Lns], ‘to bring into existence’ [LN (**13.88**)], ‘to bring about’ [Mil], ‘to conclude’ [HNTC; REB, TNT], ‘to effect’ [NASB], ‘to establish’ [WBC; NRSV], ‘to draw up’ [TEV], ‘to make’ [NIC; CEV, KJV, NAB, NIV, NJB, NLT].

c. ἐπί with accusative object (LN 37.9): ‘over’ [LN], ‘with’ [HNTC, Mil, NIC, WBC; all versions], ‘in regard to’ [Lns]. It implies motion upon its object [Alf, Mil].

d. οἶκος (LN 11.58) (BAGD 1. p. 561): ‘house’ [HNTC, Lns, Mil, NIC, WBC; all versions except CEV, NLT, TEV], ‘people’ [LN; CEV, NLT, TEV], ‘nation’ [BAGD, LN], ‘descendants’ [BAGD].

e. καινός (LN 28.33, 58.71) (BAGD 3.b. p. 394): ‘new’ [BAGD, HNTC, LN (28.33, 58.71), Lns, Mil, NIC, WBC; all versions]. It means new in character [EGT], new in quality [WBC], different in kind [HNTC], better than the previous one [NIGTC]. It refers to a new manner of presenting God’s law, not new in content [WBC].

f. διαθήκη: ‘covenant’. See this word in 8:6.

QUESTION—What is the meaning of ἔρχονται ‘(days) come’?

It is a prophetic present tense [Blm, Hu]: days will come.

QUESTION—How are the two phrases, λέγει ‘he says’, and λέγει κύριος ‘says the Lord’ related?

Λέγει ‘he says’ introduces the quotation, which makes λέγει κύριος ‘says the Lord’ redundant but that is included since it was part of the quotation [NIGTC]. By using the latter phrase, Jeremiah indicates that he was consciously uttering an oracle from God [Mil].

QUESTION—What relationship is indicated by καί ‘and’?

1. It introduces a temporal concept [Blm, EGT, HNTC, Hu, Mil, NIC, NIGTC, WBC; all versions]: when I will complete.
2. It introduces an explanation of what precedes [Alf]: days come; that is, the time that I will complete.
3. It introduces an additional thought [Lns]: days come, and I will complete.

QUESTION—How are the two (indeclinable) genitive nouns Ἰσραήλ ‘Israel’ and Ἰούδα ‘Judah’ related to the noun οἶκον ‘house’ in the two phrases ‘house of Israel’ and ‘house of Judah’?

The two genitive nouns identify the ‘house’ in each phrase [TH]: the house which is the tribe of Israel and the house which is the tribe of Judah. These two phrases include the entire OT people of God [EGT]; they imply a reconciliation between the two houses [Hu, Mil, NTC, TNTC, Wst] but imply the inclusion of Gentiles as well [NTC].

8:9 not according-to[a] the covenant[b] which I-made with-their fathers[c]

LEXICON—a. κατά with accusative object (LN 89.8) (BAGD II.5.b.α. p. 407): 'according to' [KJV], 'in accordance with' [BAGD, LN], 'similarly to' [BAGD], 'like' [HNTC, Lns, Mil, NIC, WBC; all versions except KJV]. It expresses manner [Mil] and means different in quality [Alf]. This prepositional phrase modifies συντελέσω 'I will accomplish' in 8:8 [Mil].

b. διαθήκη: 'covenant'. See this word in 8:6.

c. πατήρ (LN 10.20) (BAGD 1.b. p. 635): 'father' [HNTC, Lns; KJV, NAB, NASB, TNT], 'forefather' [BAGD, LN, Mil, NIC, WBC; NIV, REB], 'ancestor' [BAGD, LN; CEV, NJB, NLT, NRSV, TEV], 'progenitor' [BAGD].

QUESTION—What is implied by this phrase?

It indicates that the new covenant is to be different from the former one [Alf, EBC, EGT, Hwt, My, Wst] and better in quality [Alf, My], contrasted with the former one [EBC].

QUESTION—What relationship is indicated by the dative phrase τοῖς πατράσιν 'with their fathers'?

It indicates the fathers as the recipients of God's unilateral provision of the covenant [Alf, Lns, My, Wst].

on[a] (the) day of-me taking-hold-of[b] their hand to-lead-out[c] them from[d] (the) land of-Egypt,

LEXICON—a. ἐν with dative object (LN 83.47): 'on' [LN, NIC; NASB, NRSV, TEV, TNT], 'in' [Lns, Mil; KJV], not explicit [NAB, NJB]. The phrase ἐν ἡμέρᾳ 'on the day' is translated 'when' [HNTC; CEV, NIV, NLT, REB], 'at the time when' [WBC].

b. aorist mid. (deponent = act.) participle of ἐπιλαμβάνομαι (LN 18.2) (BAGD 1. p. 295): 'to take hold of' [BAGD, LN, Mil], 'to grasp' [BAGD, LN], 'to take' [HNTC, Lns, NIC, WBC; all versions]. It implies parental care and tenderness [Blm].

c. aorist act. infin. of ἐξάγω (LN 15.174) (BAGD 1. p. 271): 'to lead out' [BAGD, HNTC, LN, Lns, WBC; CEV, KJV, NASB, NIV, NLT, NRSV, REB, TEV], 'to lead forth' [Mil; NAB], 'to bring out' [BAGD, NIC; NJB, TNT], 'to bring forth' [LN]. This infinitive expresses the purpose of taking them by the hand [Mil].

d. ἐκ with genitive object (LN 84.4): 'from' [LN; NAB], 'out from' [LN], 'out of' [LN, Mil], 'of' [HNTC, Lns, NIC, WBC; all versions except NAB].

QUESTION—What is meant by ἐν ἡμέρᾳ 'on the day'?

It refers to a specific time but not a single day [NIGTC, Wst].

QUESTION—What relationship is indicated by the participial form ἐπιλαβομένου μου 'of me taking hold of'?

It is temporal [Blm, HNTC, Mil, My, NIGTC, WBC; KJV, NASB, NIV, NRSV, REB, TNT]: when I took hold of their hand. It implies careful leading [TH], God's initiative [TNTC], and the helplessness of the people until God intervened for them [TNTC]. It refers to the Mosaic covenant [My]. This phrase translates a Hebraistic idiom [Alf, Blm, EGT], a Hellenistic idiom [ICC], from the Septuagint [Alf, ICC]; it is irregular Greek which the author of Hebrews would never have written on his own [Alf]; the proper form would be either an articular infinitive phrase τοῦ ἐπιλαβεῖν με 'of my taking up' or a temporal clause introduced by ὅτε 'when'.

because they continued[a] not in[b] my covenant,[c] and-I disregarded[d] them,' says (the) Lord;

LEXICON—a. aorist act. indic. of ἐμμένω (LN **68.11**, 85.55) (BAGD 2. p. 255): 'to continue' [LN (**68.11**), NIC; KJV, NASB, NRSV], 'to remain' [LN (85.55), Lns], 'to stay' [LN (85.55)], 'to abide' [HNTC; REB, TNT], 'to remain faithful' [WBC; NIV, NLT], 'to be faithful' [TEV], 'to stand firm in' [Mil], 'to persevere in' [BAGD, Mil]. The phrase οὐκ ἐνέμειναν ἐν 'they continued not in' is translated 'they broke' [CEV, NAB, NJB].

b. ἐν with dative object (LN 83.13): 'in' [LN, Mil, NIC; KJV, NASB, NRSV], 'to' [WBC; NIV, NLT, TEV], 'by' [HNTC; TNT], 'by the terms of' [REB], not explicit [CEV, NAB, NJB].

c. διαθήκη: 'covenant'. See this word in 8:6.

d. aorist act. indic. of ἀμελέω (LN 30.50) (BAGD p. 44): 'to disregard' [LN, Mil, NIC], 'not to regard' [KJV], 'to have no concern for' [NRSV], 'to neglect' [BAGD, LN, Lns], 'to be unconcerned about' [BAGD], 'to pay no attention to' [TEV], 'not to care' [NASB], 'to cease to care for' [HNTC; CEV, TNT], 'to grow weary of' [NAB], 'to turn away from' [WBC; NIV], 'to turn one's back' [NLT], 'to abandon' [NJB, REB]. It is a strong term, meaning to turn away or to abandon [EBC]. The aorist tense indicates one historical act [Mil].

QUESTION—What is implied by this phrase?

It means that both parties to the covenant abandoned it, with the result that it became null and void [EGT]. It implies that God revoked the covenant [Hwt].

QUESTION—What relationship is indicated by ὅτι 'because'?

1. It indicates the reason for the preceding thought [Alf, Hwt, My; KJV, NAB, NASB, NIV, NRSV], the reason why God found fault with them and planned to make a new and different covenant [Lns]; it governs the rest of this verse [Alf].
2. It indicates the reason why God disregarded them [TEV]: they did not continue in the covenant, so I disregarded them.
3. It includes aspects of both 1 and 2. [Mil].

QUESTION—What is implied by the phrase αὐτοὶ οὐκ ἐνέμειναν 'they did not continue'?

It implies the opposite of continuing [Blm, TNTC]: they violated my covenant.

QUESTION—What is implied by αὐτοί 'they' and κἀγώ 'and I' ?

They form an emphatic contrast ('I' is emphatic [Mil]) [EBC, Lg(K), My, TNTC, Wst]: *they* did not continue, and *I* disregarded them. God includes both the people and himself [Lg].

QUESTION—What relationship is indicated by καί 'and'?

It introduces a result [Mil, My]: and as a result I disregarded them.

8:10 'because this (is) the covenant[a] which I-will-covenant[b] for-the house[c] of-Israel after[d] those days,' says (the) Lord,

LEXICON—a. διαθήκη: 'covenant'. See this word in 8:6.

b. fut. mid. (deponent = act.) indic. of διατίθεμαι (LN **34.43**) (BAGD 1. p. 189): 'to covenant' [Mil], 'to make' [HNTC, LN, NIC, WBC; all versions except CEV], 'to decree' [BAGD], 'to ordain' [BAGD], 'to draw up' [Lns], 'to arrange' [Mil], 'my new agreement' [CEV].

c. οἶκος: 'house'. See this word in 8:8. The phrase τῷ οἴκῳ Ἰσραήλ 'for the house of Israel' is translated 'with Israel' [REB].

d. μετά with accusative object (LN 67.48): 'after' [HNTC, LN, Lns, Mil, WBC; KJV, NAB, NASB, NIV, NRSV, REB, TNT]. The phrase μετὰ τὰς ἡμέρας ἐκείνας 'after those days' is translated 'when those days have come' [NJB], 'in the days to come' [TEV], 'in days to come' [NIC], 'the time will come' [CEV], 'on that day' [NLT].

QUESTION—What relationship is indicated by ὅτι 'because'?

1. It indicates the reason for saying a 'new' covenant [Alf, EGT, GNC, Mil, My]: I say 'new', because. . . .
2. It indicates the result of the preceding comment [Lns]: therefore this is the covenant. . . .
3. It is transitional to the following comment [TH]: now this is the covenant.

QUESTION—What is implied by αὕτη 'this'?

It introduces emphatically the description of the new covenant [My]; *this* is the covenant. The emphasis is upon the kind of covenant it will be [TH].

QUESTION—What relationship is indicated by the dative phrase τῷ οἴκῳ Ἰσραήλ 'for the house of Israel'?

It indicates that God alone is the author of the covenant [Wst].

QUESTION—What is meant by 'the house of Israel'?

It has its wider sense, both Israel and Judah, and implies a reunion of the two houses [Alf, EBC, HNTC, Mil, My, Wst], including Gentile believers as well [NTC, TNTC].

QUESTION—What is meant by 'after those days'?

1. It refers to the time after the days when God 'disregarded' the people of Israel [Alf, Mil], after the Mosaic dispensation has been done away with [Blm, Mil], when the days mentioned have arrived which were mentioned in 8:8 [EGT, Lns, My], in 8:9 [Mil]..
2. It refers to the Christian era [TNTC].
3. It refers to an undefined future [EBC, TH].
4. It refers to the period immediately preceding Christ's triumph [Wst].

5. It refers to an eschatological future [GNC].

giving[a] my laws into[b] their mind[c]

LEXICON—a. pres. act. participle of δίδωμι (LN 85.33) (BAGD 1.b.β. p. 193): 'to give' [BAGD, Lns], 'to plant' [NJB], 'to put' [HNTC, LN, Mil, NIC, WBC; KJV, NASB, NIV, NLT, NRSV, TEV, TNT], 'to place' [NAB], 'to set' [REB], 'to send' [BAGD]. This clause is combined with the following one and translated 'I . . . will write my laws on their minds and hearts' [CEV].

b. εἰς with accusative object (LN 84.22): 'into' [LN, Mil; KJV, NASB], 'in' [HNTC, NIC, WBC; all versions except CEV, KJV, NASB], 'on' [CEV], 'upon' [Lns].

c. διάνοια (LN 26.14) (BAGD 1. p. 187): 'mind' [BAGD, HNTC, LN, Lns, Mil, NIC, WBC; all versions except REB], 'understanding' [BAGD; REB]. It refers to the inner being [EGT, My, NTC], the intellect [Hwt, Mil], the source of thinking [Lns, Mil, Wst]. It emphasizes the inward character of the new covenant [My, TNTC].

QUESTION—What is meant by this phrase?

It implies making the meaning of the laws understood [Blm; NLT].

QUESTION—What relationship is indicated by the participial form διδούς 'giving'?

1. It is connected with διαθήσομαι 'I will covenant' earlier in this verse [Alf, My, Wst], expressing the means by which the covenant is implemented [Wst]: I will make a new covenant with them by putting my laws into their mind.
2. It is a new independent clause [Blm, EGT, HNTC, ICC, Lns, Mil, NIC, WBC; all versions].

2.1 An ellipsed verb 'I am' or 'I shall be' is implied [Blm, ICC]: I am/shall be giving.

2.2 No ellipsed verb is implied [ICC]; the participle is used as a finite verb parallel to the following ἐπιγράψω 'I will write' [Lns]: I will give.

and upon[a] their hearts[b] I-will-write them;

LEXICON—a. ἐπί with accusative plural or genitive singular object (LN 83.46): 'upon' [HNTC, LN, Mil; NAB, NASB], 'on' [LN, Lns, NIC, WBC; CEV, NIV, NJB, NLT, NRSV, REB, TEV, TNT], 'in' [KJV].

b. καρδία (LN 26.3) (BAGD 1.b.γ. p. 404): 'heart' [BAGD, HNTC, LN, Lns, Mil, NIC, WBC; all versions], 'inner self, mind' [LN]. It is the center of human personality [HNTC, Lns], the inner being [NTC], the seat of the moral character [Wst], the center of the affections [Hwt, Mil, TNTC] and the will [Hwt]. It emphasizes the inward character of the new covenant [HNTC, NCBC]. It is accusative plural [ICC, TH; all versions]: upon their hearts. It is genitive singular [Alf, EGT, Hu, Mil, NIGTC, Wst]: upon their heart.

QUESTION—What is meant by this clause?

It means to experience inwardly what God requires [Blm]. This and the preceding clause indicate that obedience to the new commandment will come from the heart [NCBC; NLT].

and I-shall-be to-them as[a] God, and they shall-be to-me as[a] people;

LEXICON—a. εἰς with accusative object (LN 13.51) (BAGD 8.a.β. p. 230): 'as'. It equals a predicate nominative [BAGD] (= 'be their God…be my people'). The phrase εἰμὶ εἰς 'to be as' is translated 'to become' [LN, Mil], 'to be' [HNTC, Lns, NIC, WBC; all versions].

QUESTION—What is meant by this clause?

1. It means 'I shall be (become [Mil]) their God and they shall be (become [Mil]) my people' [EBC, HNTC, Hu, Lns, Mil, NIC, NTC, WBC; all versions except KJV].
2. It means 'I shall be to them a God and they shall be to me a people' [EGT; KJV].
3. It means 'I shall be to them for a God and they shall be to me for a people' [Alf].

QUESTION—What is implied by this clause?

It implies protection and blessing by God and obedience and worship by the people [Blm]. It implies that God had freely chosen Israel [TH]. It expresses the result of the preceding comment [Lns; NJB]. Both αὐτοῖς 'to them' and μοι 'to me' are emphatic [TNTC].

8:11 and by-no-means[a] will-they-teach each-one his fellow-citizen[b] and each-one his brother[c] saying, "Know[d] the Lord,"

TEXT—Instead of πολίτην 'fellow citizen' some manuscripts read πλησίον 'neighbor'. GNT reads πολίτην 'fellow citizen' with an A decision, indicating that the reading is certain. KJV presumably reads πλησίον 'neighbor', since this is the reading of the Textus Receptus; others who translate 'neighbor' doubtless read πολίτην 'fellow citizen' in their text.

LEXICON—a. οὐ μή (LN 69.5): 'by no means' [LN], 'in no way' [Mil], 'certainly not' [LN], 'not' [HNTC, Lns; KJV, NAB, NASB, NRSV, REB], 'neither' [NIC], 'no longer' [Mil, WBC; NIV]. The phrase καὶ οὐ μὴ διδάξωσιν ἕκαστος 'and by no means will each one teach' is translated 'no man shall teach' [TNT], 'they will not need to teach' [NLT], 'not one of them will have to teach' [CEV], 'none of them will have to teach' [TEV], 'there will be no further need for each to teach' [NJB]. The phrase οὐ μή indicates an emphatic negation [Lg(K), Mil, WBC].

b. πολίτης (LN **11.68**) (BAGD 2. p. 686): 'fellow citizen' [BAGD, LN, Lns, Mil, WBC; NAB, NASB, REB], 'fellow townsman' [BAGD], 'neighbor' [HNTC, NIC; NIV, NJB, NLT, TNT], 'friend' [TEV], 'another' [CEV]; different text: 'neighbor' [KJV]. The phrase ἕκαστος τὸν πολίτην αὐτοῦ 'each one his fellow citizen' is translated 'one another' [NRSV].

c. ἀδελφός (LN 10.49, 11.57, 11.89): 'brother' [HNTC, LN (10.49, 11.89), Lns, Mil, NIC, WBC; KJV, NAB, NASB, NIV, NJB, REB, TNT], 'fellow countryman' [LN (11.57)], 'neighbor' [LN; TEV], 'family' [NLT], not explicit [CEV]. The phrase καὶ ἕκαστος τὸν ἀδελφὸν αὐτοῦ λέγων 'and each one his brother, saying' is translated 'or say to each other' [NRSV]. This word refers to a more special relationship than πολίτης 'fellow citizen' [Wst].

d. aorist act. impera. of γινώσκω (LN 28.1): 'to know' [HNTC, LN, Lns, Mil, NIC, WBC; all versions except NJB], 'to learn to know' [NJB]. This word implies to become acquainted with [Mil], a personal experience and relationship [TH, Wst], to acquire knowledge [NTC].

QUESTION—Why is this verse mentioned?

The initial καί coordinates this clause to the preceding characteristic of the new covenant [Mil].

1. It states the next characteristic of the better covenant [Alf, EBC, EGT, Hwt, Lns, Mil, NTC, Wst], which is universal knowledge of God [Alf, EBC, EGT, Hwt, Lns, NTC, Wst], the universality of the new covenant [Mil].
2. It states the result of putting God's laws into the people's hearts [My].

QUESTION—What is meant by οὐ μὴ διδάξωσιν 'by no means will they teach'?

It means that there will be no need for the people to teach each other [Alf, Blm, EBC, Mil, My, NTC, WBC; TEV], to urge others to know the Lord [Hu]. It does not mean that there will be no need for teachers; it means that the former need for a prophet's message to be passed along from those who heard him to others would no longer be necessary, for God's word would be available to all [Lns].

QUESTION—What is meant by the phrase "saying, 'Know the Lord'"?

It illustrates what they will not need to teach [Blm]: they shall not have to teach people to know the Lord. Knowledge of God will be so universal that the teaching will not be needed [Blm]. The participle λέγων 'saying' is appositional to διδάξωσιν 'they will teach'.

because they-all shall-know[a] me, from[b] small[c] to[d] great[e] of-them,

LEXICON—a. fut. act. indic. of οἶδα (LN 28.1): 'to know' [HNTC, LN, Mil, NIC, WBC; all versions], 'to be acquainted with' [Lns]. This verb implies inward experiential knowledge [Mil], the possession of knowledge [NTC].

b. ἀπό with genitive object (LN 84.3): 'from' [HNTC, LN, Lns, Mil, NIC, WBC; all versions except CEV, REB], not explicit [CEV, REB].

c. μικρός (LN 78.9, 79.125) (BAGD 1.b. p. 521): 'small' [HNTC, LN (79.125), Lns; TNT], 'little' [BAGD, LN (78.9, 79.125)]. This adjective is translated as a superlative: 'least' [Mil, NIC, WBC; all versions except CEV, REB, TNT]. The phrase ἀπὸ μικροῦ ἕως μεγάλου αὐτῶν 'from small to great of them' is translated 'no matter who they are' [CEV], 'great and small' [BAGD], 'high and low alike' [REB].

d. ἕως with genitive object (LN 84.19) (BAGD II.3. p. 335): 'to' [HNTC, LN, Lns, Mil, NIC, WBC; all versions except CEV, REB], 'up to' [LN].

e. μέγας (LN 78.2, 79.123, 87.22) (BAGD 2.a.α. p. 497): 'great' [BAGD, HNTC, LN (78.2, 79.123, 87.22), Lns; TNT], 'large' [LN (79.123)], 'big' [LN (79.123)], 'important' [LN]. This adjective is translated as a superlative: 'greatest' [Mil, NIC, WBC; all versions except CEV, REB, TNT].

QUESTION—What relationship is indicated by ὅτι 'because'?

It indicates the reason for the preceding comment [Mil, My]. It means that knowledge of God (understanding of the details of the law [EGT]) (personal experience of God [Hwt]) will not be limited to a few privileged persons [EBC, EGT, Hu]; no privileged class of intermediaries or teachers will be necessary for access to God [EGT, Mil, TNTC, Wst].

QUESTION—What is meant by the phrase 'from small to great of them'?

It implies universality [EGT, GNC, Mil], young and old [My], from children to theologians [Lns], no limitation of status [TH], with no distinction based on age, status, or personal qualities [Mil, TNTC, Wst].

8:12 because I-will-be merciful[a] to-their unrighteousnesses[b] and their sins by-no-means[c] will-I-remember[d] still.'"[e]

TEXT—Some manuscripts add καὶ τῶν ἀνομιῶν αὐτῶν 'and their lawlessnesses' following τῶν ἁμαρτιῶν αὐτῶν 'their sins'. GNT does not mention this variant. Only Blm, Lg (evidently), My, and KJV add this phrase.

LEXICON—a. ἵλεως (LN **88.77**) (BAGD p. 376): 'merciful' [BAGD, HNTC, LN, Lns, Mil, NIC; KJV, NASB, NRSV, TNT], 'gracious' [WBC]. The phrase ἵλεως ἔσομαι 'I will be merciful' is translated 'I will forgive' [NAB, NIV, NJB, NLT, TEV], 'I shall pardon' [REB], 'I will treat with kindness' [CEV]. It means that God will not punish them [Lns], he will forgive them [My, NIC]. It does not imply that this is a new quality of God [TNTC]. This word properly refers to persons [Alf, Blm]; therefore the following phrase ταῖς ἀδικίαις αὐτῶν 'to their unrighteousnesses' stands for the unrighteous persons [Blm].

b. ἀδικία (LN 88.21) (BAGD 1. p. 18): 'unrighteousness' [LN, Lns; KJV], 'unjust deed' [LN], 'wicked deed' [REB], 'wickedness' [NIV], 'iniquity' [Mil, NIC, WBC; NASB, NRSV], 'evildoing' [NAB], 'wrongdoing' [BAGD, HNTC; NLT, TNT], 'misdeed' [BAGD], 'guilt' [NJB], 'sin' [TEV]. This plural is translated as a singular: 'unrighteousness' [Mil]. This noun is also translated as a predicate adjective: 'wicked' [CEV]. The plural here refers to individual acts [My].

c. οὐ μή: 'by no means'. See this phrase in 8:11.

d. aorist pass. (deponent = act.) subj. of μιμνῄσκομαι (LN 29.7, 29.16) (BAGD 1.c. p. 522): 'to remember' [BAGD, HNTC, LN (29.7, 29.16), Lns, Mil, NIC, WBC; all versions except CEV, NJB], 'to call to mind'

[NJB], 'to recall' [LN (29.7, 29.16)], 'to think about again' [LN (29.7)]. The negative form 'by no means will I remember' is translated 'I will forget' [CEV].

e. ἔτι (LN 67.128) (BAGD 1.b.β. p. 315): 'still' [LN], 'yet' [LN], 'any more' [Mil]. The phrase οὐ μὴ ἔτι 'by no means still' is translated 'never again' [BAGD, WBC; NLT], 'no more' [HNTC, NIC; all versions except CEV, NJB, TEV], 'no longer' [TEV], 'not any longer' [Lns], 'never more' [NJB], not explicit [CEV].

QUESTION—What relationship is indicated by ὅτι 'because'?

1. It explains the spiritual basis of the new covenant [TNTC]. It states why everyone should worship God [Blm].
2. It indicates the grounds for the comment that everyone would know God [Mil, My]; it states God's forgiveness of sins as the basis for the preceding promises [EBC, EGT, Hwt].

QUESTION—What relationship is indicated by καί 'and'?

It coordinates the two aspects of the forgiveness, in the persons and in God's mind [Mil].

QUESTION—What is meant by the clause 'and their sins I will by no means remember still'?

It means to forgive their sins [Blm], to forgive completely [TNTC], to let their sins go unpunished [BAGD, TH].

8:13 By/In[a] saying, "New," he-has-made-old[b] the first;

LEXICON—a. ἐν with dative object (LN 67.33, 89.76) (BAGD III.1.b. p. 260): 'by' [HNTC, LN (89.76), Mil; NIV, NJB, REB, TEV, TNT], 'by means of' [LN (89.76)], 'in' [Lns, NIC; NRSV], 'when' [LN (67.33); CEV, NLT], 'while' [BAGD]. The phrase ἐν τῷ λέγειν 'by/in saying' is translated 'in that he says' [BAGD (by implication), WBC], 'in that he saith' [KJV], 'when he says' [NAB], 'when he said' [NASB]. It is instrumental [NIGTC, TH]; it is temporal [NTC].

b. perf. act. indic. of παλαιόω (LN **67.103**) (BAGD 1. p. 606): 'to make old' [HNTC, LN, NIC; KJV, TEV], 'to declare old' [Lns], 'to be old' [NJB], 'to make out of date' [**LN**], 'to be out of date' [CEV], 'to make obsolete' [NASB, NIV, NLT, NRSV, TNT], 'to treat as obsolete' [BAGD, Mil, WBC], 'to pronounce obsolete' [REB], 'to declare obsolete' [NAB]. It means that it is shown as antiquated [Blm]. The perfect tense indicates the permanent effect of God's statement [NIGTC], a past event with continuing effects [NTC, TH, TNTC], a continuing state [Alf], the completed act [Lg].

QUESTION—Why is this verse mentioned?

It forms a transition to the following contrasting parallel [Alf]. It expresses the result of the preceding comments [My, NCBC]. It is a comment on the quotation from Jeremiah [TNTC], on the final words of 8:8 [NIGTC], on the word καινήν 'new' in 8:8 [GNC, Mil, WBC].

QUESTION—Who is the speaker of the quotation?

The speaker is God [Alf, Mil, My, NIGTC, NTC, WBC, Wst; NASB, TEV].

QUESTION—What is the meaning of this clause?

It means that by speaking of a new covenant, God has declared (it is implied [TNTC]) that the first covenant is old [EGT, TNTC, WBC; NJB], outmoded [Blm, EBC, GNC; NAB, REB], that he has treated it as obsolete [Hu, Mil], and has thus actually resulted in making it old [Alf, HNTC, ICC, Mil, TH, Wst; KJV, TEV], obsolete [Hwt, NIC, WBC; NASB, NIV, NRSV, TNT].

now[a] the-(thing) being-made-old[b] and growing-old[c] (is) near to-disappearance.[d]

LEXICON—a. δέ (LN 89.94): 'now' [Lns, Mil; KJV], 'and' [HNTC, LN, NIC, WBC; all versions except KJV, NASB, NLT], 'but' [NASB], not explicit [NLT]. It introduces an added truth [Lns]; it indicates a transition from a specific statement to a general truth [Alf, NIGTC].

b. pres. pass. participle of παλαιόω (LN **67.103**) (BAGD 1. p. 606): 'to be made old' [LN], 'to be made out of date' [**LN**], 'to be declared old' [Lns], 'to be treated as obsolete' [BAGD]. This passive participle is translated intransitively: 'to be old' [CEV, NJB], 'to become old' [TEV], 'to grow old' [NIC], 'to be out of date' [NLT], 'to be obsolete' [WBC; NIV, NRSV], 'to become obsolete' [Mil; NAB, NASB, REB, TNT], 'to be antiquated' [HNTC], 'to decay' [KJV]. The present tense implies a gradual action [TNTC, Wst].

c. pres. act. participle of γηράσκω (LN 67.105) (BAGD p. 158): 'to grow old' [BAGD, LN, Mil; NAB, NASB, NRSV, REB], 'to become old' [LN; TNT], 'to wax old' [KJV], 'to be aging' [HNTC; NIV, NJB], 'to age' [NIC], 'to become aged' [Lns], 'to be outdated' [WBC], 'to become worn out' [TEV], 'to be useless' [CEV], not explicit [NLT]. It implies decay [ICC]. The present tense implies a continuing action. Both this and the preceding participle παλαιούμενον 'being made old' are governed by one article, showing that both participles describe the same thing; it is both declared old by God and is becoming aged [Lns].

d. ἀφανισμός (LN **13.98**) (BAGD p. 124): 'disappearance' [BAGD, LN], 'destruction' [BAGD]. The phrase ἐγγὺς ἀφανισμοῦ 'is near to disappearance' is translated 'has nearly disappeared' [HNTC], 'is close to disappearing' [NAB], 'is not far from disappearing' [TNT], 'is ready to disappear' [NASB, NJB], 'will soon disappear' [**LN**, NIC, WBC; CEV, NIV, NRSV, TEV], 'will shortly disappear' [REB], 'is near to extinction' [Mil], 'will soon cease to exist' [**LN**], 'is ready to be put aside' [NLT], 'is ready to vanish away' [KJV], 'is near to vanishing away' [Lns]. It implies abolition [EGT]. The disappearance began with the utterance of the prophecy [Alf, Hwt, Lns].

QUESTION—What is the meaning of this clause?

It means that since the first covenant is antiquated, it will soon disappear [EBC, Hu, NCBC] and be replaced by a new and perfect one [Blm]. This clause states a general principle which is applicable to other circumstances as well [Lns]. It states the author's own conclusion [Mil]. The antiquated condition existed when Jeremiah made his prophecy [Lns, My, NTC, Wst].

1. It implies that the Levitical priesthood was still in existence when this epistle was written [GNC, Hu, Hwt].
2. Nothing can be deduced concerning the continuation of worship under the old covenant when this epistle was written [Lns, NCBC, NIC], but the first covenant must by now have lost its force [My].

DISCOURSE UNIT: 9:1–12:29 [Lg]. The topic is the superiority of the new covenant mediated by Christ.

DISCOURSE UNIT: 9:1–10:18 [Lg]. The topic is fellowship with God, produced by the new covenant.

DISCOURSE UNIT: 9:1–28 [Mil; NASB]. The topic is the superiority of the sacrifice that brought in the new covenant over the sacrifices in the old covenant [Mil], the old and the new covenants [NASB].

DISCOURSE UNIT: 9:1–22 [GNT; CEV, TEV]. The topic is the earthly and the heavenly sanctuaries [GNT], earthly and heavenly worship [TEV], the tent in heaven [CEV].

DISCOURSE UNIT: 9:1–14 [TNTC; NJB]. The topic is the greater glory of the new covenant [TNTC], Christ entering the heavenly sanctuary [NJB].

DISCOURSE UNIT: 9:1–12 [Lns]. The topic is a comparison of the two tabernacles.

DISCOURSE UNIT: 9:1–10 [EBC, GNC, Hwt, Lg, NCBC, NTC, WBC, Wst; NAB, NIV, NLT]. The topic is the earthly sanctuary [NTC], description of the old ritual [GNC], the institutions of the first covenant [NCBC], the old sanctuary and its ritual [EBC], the sanctuary and priests of the old covenant [Wst], the worship in the old covenant [NAB], the old rules about worship [NLT], worship in the earthly tabernacle [NIV], the ministry of the first tabernacle [Hwt], the nature of the Mosaic sanctuary pointing to imperfect communion with God [Lg], the need for new cultic action [WBC].

DISCOURSE UNIT: 9:1–5 [HNTC, NIC, NTC]. The topic is the institution of the old covenant [HNTC], the sanctuary under the old covenant [NIC, NTC].

9:1 Now[a] on-the-one-hand also/even the first (covenant) had regulations[b] of-worship[c] and the holy-place,[d] which was earthly.[e]

TEXT—Some manuscripts omit καί 'also/even'. GNT includes καί in brackets with a C decision, indicating that the committee had difficulty in deciding whether to include this word. 'Also/even' is omitted by Hwt, WBC, and it is not translated by CEV, NAB, NIV, REB, TEV, TNT, although in some of these the omission may be stylistic rather than textual.

LEXICON—a. οὖν (LN 89.127, 91.7): 'now' [Lns; NIC, WBC; NASB, NIV, NLT, NRSV], 'then' [LN (91.7); KJV], 'to resume' [Mil], 'but' [LN (89.127)], not explicit [HNTC; CEV, NAB, NJB, REB, TEV, TNT]. It picks up the thought from 8:5 [Alf, Mil], in which Moses was directed concerning building the tabernacle [Alf]; it picks up the thought from before the quotation from Jeremiah [TH]; it indicates continuation [Blm]. The phrase μὲν οὖν 'now on the one hand' is merely transitional [Lns, WBC]; it indicates continuation [Blm, WBC] and inference [Blm], linking what follows with the preceding [Lg(K)]; it indicates a resumption of the discussion of the old covenant from 8:7 [NIGTC]. It implies that the old tabernacle was exalted [My].

b. δικαίωμα (LN 33.334) (BAGD 1. p. 198): 'regulation' [BAGD, HNTC, LN, WBC; NAB, NASB, NIV, NLT, NRSV, TNT], 'ordinance' [Lns, Mil, NIC; KJV, REB], 'requirement' [LN], 'rule' [CEV, TEV], 'law' [NJB]. It implies the force of right underlying the regulation [Alf, Mil] by its relationship to δίκαιος 'righteous'. It implies their origin from God [EGT, Mil, My, NTC].

c. λατρεία (LN **53.14**) (BAGD p. 467): 'worship' [BAGD, HNTC, LN, Mil, NIC; CEV, NAB, NIV, NJB, NLT, NRSV, TEV, TNT], 'cultic worship' [WBC], 'divine worship' [NASB], 'divine service' [Lns; KJV, REB], 'rule for worship' [**LN**]. The reference is to the liturgical forms [TH].

d. ἅγιος (LN 7.18) (BAGD 2.a.β. p. 10): 'Holy Place' [Lns], 'sanctuary' [BAGD, HNTC, LN, Mil, NIC, WBC; all versions except CEV, NLT, TEV], 'tent for worship' [CEV], 'sacred tent' [NLT]. The phrase τὸ ἅγιον κοσμικόν 'the holy place, which was earthly' is translated 'a place made for worship' [TEV]. The phrase τὸ ἅγιον 'the holy place' refers to the entire sanctuary [ICC, Lg, Lns, NIGTC, WBC, Wst]. It is the tent in the wilderness [NIC]. The definite article τό indicates that this sanctuary was well-known to the readers [NIGTC, TH]; it indicates the particular sanctuary in which the priests served [TNTC].

e. κοσμικός (LN **1.40**) (BAGD 1. p. 445): 'earthly' [BAGD, HNTC, WBC; NAB, NASB, NIV, NRSV, REB, TNT], 'worldly' [KJV]. This adjective is also translated as a phrase: 'on earth' [LN; CEV, NLT], 'on this earth' [NJB], 'in the world' [Lns], 'of this world' [NIC], 'suitable to this world' [Mil]. It implies belonging to this world [Alf, EBC, HNTC, Hu, Hwt, My, NIC, NIGTC, TH, TNTC, WBC], suitable to this world [EGT], external and material [ICC, TH], transitory [Hwt, My, WBC, Wst] and imperfect [Hwt, My, WBC]. It implies a contrast with the new heavenly covenant [HNTC, Hu, Lg, Mil, My, NCBC, NIGTC, NTC, WBC], a contrast with the heavenly sanctuary [Hu, TNTC, WBC]. It is emphatic by its position [EGT, ICC]. Since the definite article is not repeated before this word, it is something of an afterthought—'the sanctuary, one belonging to this world' [HNTC, Lg, NIGTC; REB, TNT] in a predicative sense [Lns, NIGTC, WBC, Wst] like a relative clause preceded by a comma [WBC]—i.e., a nonrestrictive relative clause.

QUESTION—What relationship is indicated by μέν 'on the one hand'?

1. Μέν (Μὲν οὖν [Lg, Wst]) is balanced by δέ 'on the other hand' in 9:6 [Alf, EGT, Mil, My, Wst], in 9:11 [Blm, TH]. It implies a limitation in comparison with the new covenant which is to be described later [Lg].
2. It is not related to a following δέ 'on the other hand' [Lns, NIGTC]; nor does it imply a limitation but rather emphasizes the greatness of the first tabernacle [Lns].

QUESTION—What is meant by καί 'also/even'?

1. It means the first covenant as well as the new one [Alf, Blm, ICC, Lg, My, NIGTC, TH, Wst; NJB]: the first covenant also, as well as the new one.
2. It emphasizes the fact that the first covenant did have such regulations [EGT, Mil, NCBC, Wst; NASB, NRSV]: even the first covenant had regulations.

QUESTION—What is implied by the imperfect indicative verb εἶχε '(it) had'?

1. It merely means that the regulations of the first covenant were instituted in the past from the present writer's point of view [EGT, GNC, HNTC, Hu, Lns, Mil, Wst].
2. It relates to the entire period of the old covenant [NTC].
3. It implies that the first covenant was no longer in effect [Alf, EBC, ICC, Lg, My], made antiquated by God [Lg, My] in Jeremiah's prophecy [My], even if it was still being observed [Alf].

QUESTION—How are the two nouns related in the genitive construction δικαιώματα λατρείας 'regulations of worship'?

Λατρείας 'worship' is an objective genitive, telling what was regulated [Lns, Mil, NIGTC, NTC, Wst; NJB, REB], or a genitive telling what the regulations were related to [Blm, HNTC, Hu, ICC, Lns, My, WBC; NAB, NIV, NRSV, TEV]: regulations governing/related to worship.

9:2 For (a) tent/tabernacle[a] was-prepared,[b] the first (one),[c]

LEXICON—a. σκηνή (LN 7.17) (BAGD p. 754): 'tent' [BAGD, HNTC, LN, Mil, NIC; CEV, NJB, NLT, NRSV, REB, TEV, TNT], 'tabernacle' [Lns, Mil, WBC; KJV, NAB, NASB, NIV], 'tabernacle tent' [LN]. It refers to a tent or tabernacle of two compartments [Blm, EGT, Hu, Hwt, Lns, NIGTC, NTC, TNTC, WBC]; it refers to two tents [EBC, HNTC, Lg, Mil, My, NIC, Wst]. It is emphatic by word order [NTC].

b. aorist pass. indic. of κατασκευάζω (LN 77.6) (BAGD 3. p. 418): 'to be prepared' [Mil; NASB], 'to be furnished' [BAGD, Mil], 'to be fitted up' [Lns], 'to be made ready' [LN], 'to be set up' [NIC, WBC; NIV, REB], 'to be put up' [TEV], 'to be constructed' [NAB, NRSV, TNT], 'to be made' [HNTC; KJV], not explicit [CEV, NLT]. This passive verb is also translated as a stative: 'to be' [NJB]. It refers to setting up or establishing [Alf, Lg(K), TNTC, Wst]. It includes both erecting and furnishing the tabernacle [EBC, NIGTC].

c. πρῶτος (LN **60.46**) (BAGD 1.d. p. 726): 'first' [HNTC, LN, Lns, NIC; KJV, NJB, NRSV] (referring to the outer tent) [LN], 'outer' [BAGD;

NAB, NASB, REB, TEV, TNT], 'fore-tent' [Mil], 'front compartment' [WBC], 'first room' [NIV, NLT], 'first part' [CEV]. It refers to the part which was first entered [Alf, Blm, EGT, Hu, Hwt, ICC, Lg, Mil, My, NIGTC, TH, TNTC, WBC, Wst].

QUESTION—What relationship is indicated by γάρ 'for'?

It introduces the description of the first covenant (the earthly sanctuary [Alf, My]) [Alf, Lns, My], an explanation (an expansion [NIGTC, TH] and justification [Wst]) of the preceding statement [Mil, NIGTC, TH, Wst].

QUESTION—What is the significance of the lack of a definite article with σκηνή 'tent/tabernacle'?

1. It is identified by the following ἡ πρώτη 'the first' [EGT, Lg, NTC, Wst]; it is made definite by the following description even though it has no article [Alf, My]

1.1 It is general [Lg, My]: tent/tabernacle.

1.2 It is indefinite [EGT, Wst]; a tent/tabernacle.

2. It is the equivalent of a proper name and therefore is definite even without the article [Blm]: the tent/tabernacle.

3. It implies that this is new information and that σκηνή 'tent/tabernacle' here does not have the same meaning as in 9:1 [NIGTC].

QUESTION—How is ἡ πρώτη 'the first one' related to other phrases?

1. It relates to what precedes [Alf, EGT, Lns, Mil, NIC; NAB, NASB, NRSV, TEV]: the tabernacle, that is, the outer one.

2. It relates to what follows [Blm, EBC, NIGTC, WBC; KJV, NIV, NJB, REB, TNT]: in the first tent were. . . . It is emphatic by position [NIGTC].

in[a] which (were) both the lampstand[b] and the table and the setting-forth[c] of-the loaves-of-bread,[d]

LEXICON—a. ἐν with dative object (LN 83.13): 'in' [HNTC, LN, Lns, Mil, NIC, WBC; all versions except CEV, REB, TNT], 'within' [LN]. The phrase ἐν ᾗ 'in which' is translated 'where were' [TNT], 'to contain' [REB], 'were kept there' [CEV].

b. λυχνία (LN 6.105) (BAGD p. 483): 'lampstand' [BAGD, HNTC, LN, Mil, NIC, WBC; all versions except KJV], 'candelabrum' [Lns], 'candlestick' [KJV].

c. πρόθεσις (LN 53.26) (BAGD 1. p. 706): 'setting-forth, presentation' [BAGD]. The phrase ἡ πρόθεσις τῶν ἄρτων 'the setting-forth of the loaves of bread' is translated 'the showbread' [Lns, NIC; KJV, NAB], 'the sacred bread' [NASB], 'the sacred loaves of bread' [CEV], 'the loaves of holy bread on the table' [NLT], 'the consecrated bread' [WBC; NIV], 'the bread of the presence' [HNTC; NRSV, REB, TNT], 'the loaves of permanent offering' [NJB], 'the bread offered to God' [TEV], 'with its loaves set forth' [Mil], 'the table for the sacred bread' [BAGD]. The phrase ἄρτοι τῆς προθέσεως 'bread of the presentation' (similar to, but not identical to ἡ πρόθεσις τῶν ἄρτῶν 'the setting-forth of the bread' of this verse) is translated 'the consecrated bread, bread offered to God' [LN

(53.26)]. This word refers to the bread on the table [Alf, Lns, NIGTC]; it refers to the act of setting forth the bread [Lg, My].

d. ἄρτος (LN 5.8) (BAGD 1.b. p. 110): 'loaf of bread' [LN], 'loaf' [Mil; NJB], 'bread' [HNTC, WBC; NASB, NIV, NRSV, REB, TEV, TNT], 'consecrated bread' [BAGD].

QUESTION—What is the significance of the definite article with 'lampstand', 'table', and 'setting-forth'?

It indicates that these objects were well-known to the readers [NIGTC, TH] and that they were unique objects [TH].

QUESTION—What relationship is indicated by the phrase ἡ πρόθεσις τῶν ἄρτων 'the setting-forth of the loaves of bread'?

1. It is a third item in the list [Alf, EGT, Hwt, Lns, NIC, NIGTC, NTC, TNTC; all versions except TEV, TNT]: the lampstand and the table and the setting-forth.
2. It is a hendiadys with the preceding ἡ τράπεζα 'the table' [Hu, ICC, Mil, NIC, WBC]; it indicates what was on the table [HNTC, Hu, ICC, Mil, WBC; NLT, TEV, TNT]: the table with the setting-forth of the loaves . . .
3. 'Η πρόθεσις 'the setting-forth' is actually 'the table' [BAGD, EBC] in spite of the occurrence of τράπεζα 'table' immediately preceding it [BAGD]: the table with the loaves on it.

QUESTION—How are the two nouns related in the genitive construction ἡ πρόθεσις τῶν ἄρτῶν 'the setting-forth of the bread'?

The genitive τῶν ἄρτῶν 'of the bread' tells what was set forth [Alf]: the bread was set forth.

which is-called "Holy-things";[a]

LEXICON—a. ἅγιος (LN 7.18, **7.35,** 88.24) (BAGD 2.b. p. 10): 'holy' [LN (88.24)]. This neuter plural form ἅγια is translated 'holy' [HNTC], 'Holy Place' [Lns, WBC], 'the Holy Place' [BAGD, LN (**7.35**), Mil, NIC; all versions except KJV], 'sanctuary' [LN (7.18)], 'the sanctuary' [KJV]. This word is neuter plural, referring to the Holy Place [Alf, EBC, EGT, Hu, ICC, Lg, Lns, My, NIC, NTC, WBC] in contrast with the Holy of Holies [Lg, Lns, My]; it is feminine singular, modifying σκηνή 'tent/tabernacle' [HNTC]. The absence of the article indicates the character of the tent/tabernacle [Alf, Lg(K), My, Wst]. This word is regarded as a proper name and is definite even without the article [Blm, NIGTC]. The plural refers to the sanctuary with all its furnishings [Wst].

QUESTION—To what does ἥτις 'which' refer?

It refers to the σκηνή 'tent/tabernacle' [Alf, HNTC, Mil, My]: which tent/tabernacle is called 'Holy things'. It is qualitative, emphasizing the nature of the sanctuary [EGT, Mil, Wst]. It is synonymous with the simple relative pronoun, not qualitative [NIGTC].

9:3 and/but after[a] the second curtain[b] (a) tent/tabernacle[c] the-(one) being-called Holy-things[d] of-Holy-things,[d]

LEXICON—a. μετά with accusative object (LN **83.56**) (BAGD B.I. p. 510): 'after' [Lns, Mil; KJV], 'beyond' [HNTC, LN; NJB, REB, TNT], 'behind' [BAGD, **LN**, NIC, WBC; CEV, NAB, NASB, NIV, NLT, NRSV, TEV]. The sense is 'after entering' [Alf, Blm] or behind the second curtain [Alf, EBC, Hwt, ICC, Lns, My, NIC, WBC].

b. καταπέτασμα (LN 6.160) (BAGD p. 416): 'curtain' [BAGD, LN, NIC, WBC; CEV, NIV, NLT, NRSV, REB, TEV, TNT], 'veil' [HNTC, LN, Lns, Mil; KJV, NAB, NASB, NJB], 'drape' [LN]. It refers to the curtain which separated the Holy Place from the Most Holy Place [Alf, Blm, EBC, EGT, GNC, HNTC, Hu, ICC, NIC, NTC, TNTC, WBC]. It is called the second curtain to distinguish it from the curtain at the entrance to the Holy Place from the outside court [Alf, EBC, GNC, Hu, ICC, My, NIC]. The definite article implies that this second curtain was known to the readers [NIGTC]

c. σκηνή: 'tent/tabernacle'. See this word in 9:2. The absence of a definite article implies that this is new information [NIGTC].

d. ἅγιος (LN **7.35**) (BAGD 2.b. p. 10): 'holy'. The phrase Ἅγια Ἁγίων 'Holy things of holy things' is translated 'Holy of Holies' [BAGD, HNTC, LN, Lns], 'the Holy of Holies' [Mil, NIC; NAB, NASB, NJB, NRSV, TNT], 'the Most Holy Place' [WBC; NIV, REB, TEV], 'the holiest of all' [KJV]. It is an idiom from Hebrew style that implies a superlative [Alf, EGT, Hu, My, NIGTC, TH, WBC]. It was the place of atonement [GNC].

QUESTION—What relationship is indicated by δέ 'and/but'?

1. It indicates continuation [Mil; KJV, NASB], introducing an additional point [NIGTC].
2. It indicates a contrast with the preceding statement [Alf].

QUESTION—What relationship is indicated by σκηνή 'tent/tabernacle' without a definite article?

1. It is considered definite even without the article [Alf, EGT, Mil, NIC; KJV, NAB, REB, TEV, TNT].
2. It is indefinite, and defined by the following phrase [EBC, HNTC, Lns, WBC; NASB, NIV, NJB, NRSV].

QUESTION—What relationship is indicated by the participial form ἡ λεγομένη 'the one being called'?

It is equivalent to a (restrictive [Mil; KJV, NASB, NJB]) relative clause [EGT, Mil, NIGTC; KJV, NASB, NJB]; in other words, it is an attributive participle.

9:4 having[a] a-golden incense-altar[b] and the ark[c] of-the covenant[d] covered-around[e] on-all-sides[f] with-gold,

LEXICON—a. pres. act. participle of ἔχω (LN 90.27): 'to have' [HNTC, Lns, NIC; KJV, NASB, NIV], 'to contain' [LN, WBC], not explicit [CEV].

This participle is also translated as a phrase: 'here were' [REB], 'in it were' [TEV, TNT], 'in which were' [NAB], 'in it stood' [NRSV], 'to which belonged' [Mil; NJB], 'in that room were' [NLT]. It is the equivalent of a relative clause [KJV, NIV], i.e., an attributive participle. It means 'containing' [WBC; NAB, NRSV, TEV, TNT] or related in some way [Alf, Mil; NJB, REB].

b. θυμιατήριον (LN **6.116**) (BAGD p. 365): 'incense altar' [LN, Mil, NIC; REB], 'altar of incense' [BAGD, HNTC, **LN**, Lns, WBC; NAB, NASB, NIV, NJB, NRSV], 'altar for burning incense' [TNT], 'altar for the burning of incense' [TEV], 'altar that was used for burning incense' [CEV], 'censer' [KJV]. It refers to the altar of incense [EBC, HNTC, Hwt, Lg, Lns, Mil, My, NCBC, NIC, NIGTC, NTC, TH, WBC; all versions except KJV], which was located outside the Holy of Holies but was intimately connected with the Holy of Holies [EBC, EGT, GNC, HNTC, Hu, Hwt, Lg, Lns, Mil, TNTC, Wst]. It refers to the censer [Blm; KJV]. Its descriptive adjective χρυσοῦν 'golden' is emphatic by its word order [My].

c. κιβωτός (LN **6.139**) (BAGD 2. p. 432): 'ark' [BAGD, HNTC, Lns, Mil, NIC, WBC; all versions except CEV, TEV], 'Covenant Box, chest, coffer' [LN], 'box' [LN; TEV]. The phrase κιβωτὸν τῆς διαθήκης 'ark of the covenant' is translated 'sacred chest' [CEV].

d. διαθήκη (LN 34.44) (BAGD 3. p. 183): 'covenant' [HNTC, LN, Mil, NIC, WBC; all versions except CEV], 'testament' [Lns], 'compact' [BAGD], 'contract' [BAGD], not explicit [CEV].

e. perf. pass. participle of περικαλύπτω (LN 79.115) (BAGD p. 647): 'to be covered around' [LN, Mil], 'to be covered' [BAGD, HNTC, LN; NAB, NASB, NLT, TEV, TNT], 'to be overlaid' [Lns, NIC; KJV, NRSV], 'to be plated' [NJB, REB]. The phrase περικεκαλυμμένην πάντοθεν χρυσίῳ 'covered around on all sides with gold' is translated 'gold-covered' [WBC; CEV, NIV]. The perfect tense indicates a continuing state. This participle is in a predicative relation to κιβωτόν 'ark', 'the ark, overlaid with gold' [HNTC, Lns, Wst; all versions except NIV]. Some treat it as attributive, 'the gold-covered ark' [NIV, WBC], but this violates Greek grammar.

f. πάντοθεν (LN **83.8**) (BAGD p. 608): 'on all sides' [BAGD, Mil; NASB, NLT, NRSV], 'all over' [HNTC, **LN**; NJB, REB, TNT], 'all around' [NIC], 'all' [TEV], 'round about' [KJV], 'entirely' [BAGD, Lns; NAB], 'everywhere' [**LN**], 'within and without' [Mil]. It means both outside and inside [Blm, My, TNTC, WBC].

QUESTION—Where was the golden incense altar located?

Most commentaries bring up the problem that in Exod. 30:6 it appears that the incense altar was not inside the Holy of Holies with the ark, but in the first part of the tabernacle in front of the curtain that led into the Holy of Holies. Various solutions are discussed and most admit that they must speculate. Perhaps the author was being imprecise and was not concerned with exact details of the furniture [NIGTC]. Perhaps this is because there is a special connection between the altar of incense and the Holy of Holies, since only one day of the year the high priest entered the Holy of Holies bringing incense from the incense altar [NIC, NTC]. Or, although located outside the curtain, it was closely connected to the Holy of Holies and could be considered as part of the furniture of the inner room [Hu, TNTC].

QUESTION—How are the two nouns related in the genitive construction τὴν κιβωτὸν τῆς διαθήκης 'the ark of the covenant'?

The genitive τῆς διαθήκης 'of the covenant' tells what the ark contained [Lns, NIC, NIGTC, TH]: the ark containing the covenant.

in[a] which (was) (the) golden jar[b] having[c] the manna and the rod[d] of-Aaron the-(one) having budded[e] and the tablets[f] of-the covenant,[g]

LEXICON—a. ἐν with dative object (LN 83.13): 'in' [HNTC, LN, Lns, Mil, NIC, WBC; KJV, NAB, NASB, NJB, NRSV, REB, TNT], 'inside' [CEV, NLT]. The phrase ἐν ᾗ 'in which' is translated 'this ark contained' [NIV], 'and containing' [TEV].

b. στάμνος (LN **6.125**) (BAGD p. 764): 'jar' [BAGD, HNTC, LN, Mil, WBC; all versions except KJV, NRSV], 'urn' [NIC; NRSV], 'pot' [Lns; KJV].

c. pres. act. participle of ἔχω (LN 90.27): 'to have' [KJV], 'to contain' [HNTC, LN, Lns, Mil, WBC; NAB, NJB, NLT, REB, TNT], 'to hold' [NASB, NRSV], 'to be filled with' [CEV]. The phrase ἔχουσα τὸ μάννα 'having the manna' is translated 'with the manna in it' [TEV], 'with manna' [NIC], 'of manna' [NIV]. It is the equivalent of a relative clause [KJV], i.e., an attributive participle. It means 'containing' [Alf, HNTC, Hu, Lns, Mil, WBC; all versions].

d. ῥάβδος (LN 6.218) (BAGD p. 733): 'rod' [BAGD, LN, Lns, NIC, WBC; KJV, NAB, NASB, NRSV], 'staff' [BAGD, HNTC, Mil; NIV, NLT, REB, TNT], 'branch' [NJB], 'stick' [BAGD, LN; TEV], 'walking stick' [CEV].

e. aorist act. participle of βλαστάνω (LN **23.195**) (BAGD 2. p. 142): 'to bud' [BAGD, Lns, NIC; KJV, NASB, NIV, NRSV, REB], 'to grow buds' [NJB], 'to sprout' [BAGD, HNTC, LN, Mil; CEV, TNT], 'to sprout leaves' [**LN**; NLT, TEV], 'to blossom' [WBC; NAB]. This participle is the equivalent of a relative clause [EBC, GNC, HNTC, Lns, Mil, NIC, NTC, WBC; all versions], i.e., an attributive participle. The sprouting was God's proof of Aaron's exclusive right to the priesthood [GNC, HNTC, ICC, NIC].

f. πλάξ (LN **6.61**) (BAGD p. 666): 'tablet' [BAGD, LN, Mil, NIC; NAB, NLT, NRSV, REB], 'stone tablet' [HNTC, WBC; NIV, TEV, TNT], 'flat stone' [BAGD; CEV], 'table' [BAGD, Lns; KJV, NASB, NJB].

g. διαθήκη: 'covenant', 'testimony' [NIC]. See this word above.

QUESTION—To what does ἐν ᾗ 'in which' refer?

It refers to κιβωτόν 'ark' [Blm, EBC, EGT, GNC, HNTC, ICC, Lg, My, NIC, NIGTC; CEV, NAB, NIV, NLT, TEV, TNT]: in the ark.

QUESTION—How are the two nouns related in the genitive construction ἡ ῥάβδος 'Ααρών 'the rod of Aaron'?

The genitive 'Ααρών 'Aaron' indicates the possessor of the rod [CEV, NLT]: the rod which belonged to Aaron.

QUESTION—How are the two nouns related in the genitive construction αἱ πλάκες τῆς διαθήκης 'the tablets of the covenant'?

The genitive τῆς διαθήκης 'of the covenant' tells what was written on the tablets [Mil; CEV, NLT, TEV]: the tablets with the covenant written on them. It refers to the tablets containing the Decalogue [HNTC, Hu, ICC, Lns, Mil, NCBC, NTC], which was a summary of God's covenant with the people [ICC].

9:5 and above[a] it cherubim[b] of-glory[c] overshadowing[d] the mercy-seat;[e]

LEXICON—a. ὑπεράνω with genitive object (LN **83.49**) (BAGD p. 840): 'above' [BAGD, HNTC, **LN**, Lns, NIC, WBC; all versions except CEV, KJV, NJB], 'over' [LN, Mil; KJV], 'on top of' [CEV, NJB].

b. Χερούβ (LN **6.99**) (BAGD p. 881): 'cherub' [BAGD, HNTC, Lns, Mil, NIC, WBC; all versions except CEV, NJB, TEV], 'winged creature' [LN; NJB, TEV], 'creature with wings' [CEV]. They symbolize all that is best in created beings by their combination of characteristics which no one creature possesses [EGT].

c. δόξα (LN 14.49, 79.18) (BAGD 1.a. p. 203): 'glory' [LN (79.18), Lns, NIC; KJV, NAB, NASB, NRSV], 'Glory' [Mil], 'the Glory' [HNTC, WBC; NIV], 'God's glory' [REB], 'radiance' [BAGD], 'splendor' [BAGD, LN (79.18)], 'brightness' [BAGD, LN (14.49)]. This noun is also translated as an adjective: 'glorious' [CEV, NJB, NLT]; as a phrase: 'representing God's presence' [TEV], 'who revealed God's glory' [TNT]. It refers to God's glory [Lg, NCBC, NTC, Wst], God's presence [NIGTC, TH, TNTC, WBC]. This is the Shekinah glory in which God appeared between the cherubim [Alf, GNC, Mil, NIC]. This word is a synonym for God [HNTC].

d. pres. act. participle of κατασκιάζω (LN **14.62**) (BAGD p. 418): 'to overshadow' [BAGD, HNTC, **LN**, Lns, Mil, NIC, WBC; NAB, NASB, NIV, NJB, NRSV, REB], 'to shadow' [KJV], 'to cast a shadow upon' [LN], 'to be opened out above' [CEV]. This participle is also translated as a phrase: 'with their wings spread over' [TEV], 'and their wings overshadowed' [TNT], 'and their wings were stretched out over' [NLT]. It means to cast a shadow upon something [Alf].

e. ἱλαστήριον (LN **40.13**) (BAGD p. 375): 'mercy-seat' [BAGD, Lns, Mil, NIC; KJV, NASB, NRSV], 'throne of mercy' [NJB], 'atonement cover' [NIV], 'place of atonement' [WBC], 'place where sins are forgiven' [**LN**], 'place where sins were forgiven' [TEV], 'place of forgiveness' [LN], 'place of mercy' [CEV], 'place of reconciliation' [TNT], 'place of expiation' [HNTC; NAB, REB], 'the ark's cover, the place of atonement' [NLT]. It refers to the great golden cover of the ark of the covenant [HNTC, Wst] (although it was not part of the ark itself [Wst]), upon which the sacrificial blood of the day of atonement was sprinkled [Alf, Blm, EBC, EGT, GNC, Hu, Hwt, ICC, Lg, Mil, My, NCBC, NIC, NIGTC, NTC, TH, TNTC, WBC].

QUESTION—To what does αὐτῆς 'it' refer?

It refers to the ark [Alf, Blm, EBC, EGT, Hwt, Mil, My, NIGTC, NTC, TH, WBC, Wst; CEV, NAB, NIV, NLT, REB, TEV]: above the ark.

QUESTION—How are the two nouns related in the genitive construction Χερουβὶν δόξης 'cherubim of glory'?

The genitive noun δόξης 'of glory' means that the cherubim reveal God's glory [TNT], they belong to God's glory [Lns], they represent God's presence [Blm; TEV] denoting God's government over the universe [Blm]. They were associated with God's presence [EBC, Mil], they support God's glory [Alf, My, NIC], they were associated with the place where God's glory was manifested [EGT, Hu].

QUESTION—What relationship is indicated by the participial form κατασκιάζοντα 'overshadowing'?

1. This participle is evidently in a predicate relationship to Χερουβίν 'cherubim' and the present tense indicates a continuing state, but none of the commentaries mention this: the cherubim, overshadowing the mercy-seat.
2. It is attributive [My]: the cherubim which overshadowed the mercy-seat.

concerning[a] which-things it-is[b] not now to-speak[c] in-regard -to[d] part.[e]

LEXICON—a. περί with genitive object (LN 90.24): 'concerning' [LN, Lns], 'about' [LN, WBC; CEV, NJB], 'of' [HNTC, LN, Mil; KJV, NAB, NASB, NRSV, TNT]. The phrase περὶ ὧν 'concerning which things' is translated 'these things' [NIC; NIV, NLT], 'these' [REB], 'everything' [TEV].

b. pres. indic. of εἰμί (LN **71.1**) (BAGD I.7. p. 223): 'to be', 'to be possible' [BAGD, HNTC, LN, NIC; TNT]. The phrase οὐκ ἔστιν 'it is not' is translated 'it is not in order' [Lns], 'this is not the time' [NJB]. The phrase οὐκ ἔστιν λέγειν 'it is not to speak' is translated 'we cannot speak' [Mil, WBC; KJV, NAB, NASB, NRSV], 'we cannot discuss' [NIV], 'we need not discuss' [REB], 'we cannot explain' [NLT], 'is not the time' [CEV, TEV]. This idiom means that it was not opportune [Alf], it was not the time [EBC, Lns], it was not the place [TH], it was not possible [NIGTC], the author did not have time [HNTC, ICC, Mil, TNTC], it was not his purpose [Hwt], there was no need [Hu], he could not now [EGT, NIC], he was not going to discuss in detail [Blm].

c. pres. act. infin. of λέγω (LN 33.69): 'to speak' [HNTC, LN, Lns, Mil, WBC; KJV, NAB, NASB, TNT], 'to talk' [LN], 'to discuss' [NIV, REB], 'to explain' [NLT, TEV]. The phrase λέγειν κατὰ μέρος 'to speak in regard to part' is translated 'to go into detail' [CEV, NJB].

d. κατά with genitive object (LN **63.16**, 89.4) (BAGD II.3.b. p. 406): 'in regard to' [LN (89.4)], 'in relation to' [LN (89.4)]. The phrase κατὰ μέρος 'in regard to part' is translated 'in detail' [BAGD, HNTC, LN (**63.16**), Mil, WBC; all versions except KJV, NJB, NLT], 'one by one' [NIC], 'particularly' [KJV]; not explicit [Lns; NLT].

e. μέρος (LN 63.14) (BAGD 1.c. p. 506): 'part' [LN].

DISCOURSE UNIT: 9:6–10 [HNTC, NIC]. The topic is the insufficiency of the old covenant [HNTC], a temporary ritual [NIC].

9:6 Now these-things thus furnished,[a] on-the-one-hand into[b] the first tent/tabernacle[c] through[d] every (time)/continually the priests enter[e] completing[f] the service.[g]

LEXICON—a. perf. pass. participle of κατασκευάζω (LN 77.6) (BAGD 3. p. 418): 'to be furnished' [BAGD, Mil], 'to be made ready' [LN], 'to be prepared' [NASB], 'to be fitted up' [Lns], 'to be set up' [NIC], 'to be arranged' [WBC; NIV], 'to be in place' [NLT], 'to be ordained' [KJV]. The phrase τούτων οὕτως κατεσκευασμένων 'these things thus furnished' is translated 'these were the arrangements for worship' [NAB], 'under this arrangement' [REB], 'under these arrangements' [HNTC; TNT], 'under these provisions' [NJB], 'such preparations having been made' [NRSV], 'this is how those things have been arranged' [TEV], 'this is how everything was' [CEV].

b. εἰς with accusative object (LN 84.22): 'into' [LN, Lns, Mil, NIC, WBC; CEV, KJV, NAB, NIV, NJB, NRSV, TEV], 'in' [NLT], not explicit [HNTC; NASB, REB, TNT].

c. σκηνή: 'tent/tabernacle'. See this word in 9:2.

d. διά with genitive object (LN **67.15**, 67.140) (BAGD A.II.1.a. p. 179): 'through', 'throughout' [LN (67.140)]. The phrase διὰ παντός 'through every time/continually' is translated 'always' [BAGD; KJV], 'continually' [BAGD, HNTC, Mil, NIC, WBC; NASB, NRSV, REB, TNT], 'constantly' [BAGD, Lns; NAB], 'regularly' [LN (67.15); NIV, NJB, NLT], 'periodically' [LN (67.15)], 'every day' [TEV], 'each day' [CEV]. It means at any time without prescribed limits [Alf], continually [EGT, TH, TNTC], constantly [ICC, NIGTC], regularly [EBC, NTC], day after day [Hu, My].

e. pres. indic. of εἴσειμι (LN 15.93) (BAGD p. 232): 'to enter' [HNTC, LN, Mil, WBC; NASB, NIV, REB, TNT], 'to go into' [BAGD, Lns, NIC; CEV, KJV, NAB, NJB, NRSV, TEV], 'to go in' [BAGD; NLT]. The present tense refers to the ancient time being referred to [Lns, Wst], not to the present time of the writer [Lns, NIGTC]; it is timeless [Blm, EGT, TNTC] implying repetition [TNTC], but includes the time of the writer [Blm, Wst]. It indicates that the temple worship was still continuing [Hu, My]; it does not necessarily indicate that it was continuing [GNC, Lg]. It is translated as present tense [Alf, Blm, EGT, GNC, HNTC, Hu, Lg, Lns, Mil, My, NIC, TH, TNTC; NASB, NJB, NRSV, REB, TEV, TNT]; as past tense [WBC; CEV, KJV, NAB, NIV, NLT].

f. pres. act. participle of ἐπιτελέω (LN 68.22) (BAGD 2. p. 302): 'to complete' [LN], 'to finish' [LN], 'to perform' [BAGD, WBC; NAB, NASB, NLT, TEV], 'to accomplish' [LN, Mil; KJV], 'to do' [CEV], 'to carry on' [NIV], 'to carry out' [HNTC; NJB, NRSV, TNT], 'to attend to' [Lns]. This participle is also translated as a phrase: 'in the performance of' [REB], 'in the discharge of' [NIC].

g. λατρεία (LN 53.14) (BAGD p. 467): 'service' [Lns, Mil; NAB], 'service of God' [KJV], 'duty of one's service' [HNTC; TNT], 'worship' [BAGD, LN], 'act of worship' [NJB], 'divine worship' [NASB], 'sacred office' [NIC], 'ritual function' [WBC], 'duty' [CEV, REB, TEV], 'ritual duty' [NRSV], 'religious duty' [NLT], 'ministry' [NIV]. The reference is to all of the daily care [Blm], including care of the lampstand, offering incense [EGT, My, TNTC], and the weekly replacing of the showbread [Alf, EBC, GNC, HNTC, Hu, Hwt, ICC, Lns, Mil, NCBC, NIC, NIGTC, NTC, WBC, Wst].

QUESTION—What relationship is indicated by δέ 'now?

It is transitional, introducing a new point [Alf, Lns, Mil, NIGTC].

QUESTION—What is the phrase τούτων οὕτως κατεσκευασμένων 'these things thus furnished' connected with?

It refers to the preceding verses [GNC, My, NIGTC, TH, WBC], to the mention in 9:2 of a tabernacle being prepared [Hu, Mil]: the things previously mentioned being thus furnished.

QUESTION—What relationship is indicated by the participial form κατεσκευασμένων 'furnished'?

The perfect tense implies completion and a continuing state [Alf, EGT, Lns, My, NIGTC, NTC, Wst]: furnished and continuing so. It implies continuing at the time of the author [My].

1. The participle is temporal [EGT, Mil, WBC, Wst; KJV, NASB, NIV, NLT]: after they were furnished, the priests enter.
2. The participle indicates the circumstances under which the priests enter [Alf, HNTC; CEV, NJB, REB, TNT]: with these things thus arranged, the priests enter.

QUESTION—What relationship is indicated by the participial form ἐπιτελοῦντες 'completing'?

The present tense implies repeated action, but none of the commentaries mention this: repeatedly completing their service.

1. The participle is temporal [HNTC, WBC; NLT, TNT]: when they are completing their service.
2. The participle indicates purpose [Mil; CEV, NIV, NJB, NRSV, TEV]: in order to complete their service.

9:7 But into[a] the second once during-the year only the high-priest,

LEXICON—a. εἰς with accusative object: 'into'. See this word in 9:6.

QUESTION—What relationship is indicated by δέ 'but'?

It indicates a contrast with the preceding comment involving the priests and the Holy Place [EBC, GNC, Mil, NIGTC; all versions].

QUESTION—To what does δευτέραν 'second' refer?

It refers to the Holy of Holies [Alf, Hu, WBC; NLT], the second tent [EBC], the second part of the tent [CEV], the inner tent [GNC].

QUESTION—How is the genitive noun ἐνιαυτοῦ 'year' related to ἅπαξ 'once' in the genitive construction ἅπαξ τοῦ ἐνιαυτοῦ 'once during the year'?

It is a genitive expressing time within which [NIGTC]: once within the year.

QUESTION—To what does ἅπαξ τοῦ ἐνιαυτοῦ 'once during the year' refer?

It refers to the Day of Atonement [Alf, Blm, EBC, EGT, GNC, HNTC, Hu, Hwt, ICC, Lg, Lns, Mil, My, NCBC, NIC, NIGTC, NTC, TH, TNTC, WBC], but to at least two (three [EGT, HNTC]) entrances on that occasion [Alf, Blm, EBC, EGT, Hwt, Lg, Lns, Mil, My, NCBC, NIC, NIGTC, NTC, Wst].

QUESTION—What is the implied verb of this clause?

1. It is present tense 'enters' or 'goes into' [HNTC, Hu, Mil, NIC; NASB, NJB, NLT, NRSV, REB, TEV, TNT]: the high priest enters.
2. It is past tense 'entered' or 'went in' [WBC; CEV, KJV, NAB, NIV].

QUESTION—To whom does ὁ ἀρχιερεύς 'the high priest' refer?

It is generic, referring to high priests in general [NIGTC].

not without[a] blood which he-offers[b] on-behalf-of[c] himself and the sins-of-ignorance[d] of-the people,

LEXICON—a. χωρίς with genitive object (LN 89.120) (BAGD 2.b.β. p. 890): 'without' [BAGD, LN, Lns, Mil, NIC, WBC; KJV, NASB, NIV, NRSV]. The phrase οὐ χωρίς 'not without' is translated 'with' [NAB], 'always with' [NLT], 'and that only with' [HNTC], 'who takes in' [NJB], 'he always takes' [TNT], 'each time he carried' [CEV], 'he takes with him' [REB, TEV].

b. pres. act. indic. of προσφέρω (LN 15.192, 57.80) (BAGD 2.a. p 720): 'to offer' [BAGD, HNTC, Lns, Mil, NIC, WBC; all versions except NJB, TEV], 'to offer to God' [TEV], 'to make an offering' [NJB], 'to present' [BAGD, LN (57.80)], 'to bring to' [LN (15.192, 57.80)]. It is translated as a present tense [Alf, GNC, HNTC, Hwt, Lg, Lns, Mil, NIC; NASB, NRSV, REB, TEV, TNT]; as a past tense [WBC; KJV, NAB, NIV].

c. ὑπέρ with genitive object (LN 90.36) (BAGD 1.a.γ. p. 838, 1.b. p. 838): 'on behalf of' [LN, Mil; TEV], 'in behalf of' [BAGD], 'for' [BAGD, HNTC, LN, Lns, NIC, WBC; all versions except NLT, TEV], 'for the sake of' [BAGD, LN], 'to cover (his own sins)' [NLT].

d. ἀγνόημα (LN **88.302**) (BAGD p. 11): 'sin of ignorance' [HNTC, NIC; TNT], 'sin committed in ignorance' [BAGD, Mil, WBC; NASB, NIV, NLT], 'ignorance' [Lns], 'sin committed unintentionally' [NRSV], 'sin committed without meaning to' [CEV], 'sin which someone has committed without knowing he was sinning' [**LN**; TEV], 'fault of inadvertence' [NJB], 'inadvertent sin' [REB], 'sin' [NAB], 'error' [KJV]. This noun is also translated as a verb phrase: 'to sin through ignorance' [LN]. It refers to sins committed unwittingly [Lns, NCBC, NIGTC, NTC, TH, Wst], to more than merely sins committed unwittingly [Alf], to all except presumptuous sins [Blm, GNC, HNTC, Hu]. It refers to sins in general [Hwt, ICC], to the universal guilt of the human race [Mil]. This word is emphatic by word order [NIGTC].

QUESTION—What is implied by the phrase οὐ χωρὶς αἵματος 'not without blood'?

It is a double negative, implying a strong positive statement [NIGTC, TH]: he surely takes blood.

QUESTION—What is the meaning of ἑαυτοῦ 'himself'?

1. It means 'himself' [Alf, EBC, EGT, HNTC, Hu, Lg, Lns, Mil, My, NIC, NIGTC, TNTC, WBC, Wst; all versions except NJB]: in behalf of himself. It means for himself as high priest to enable him to act for the people [Lns, Mil]. The implied meaning, however, is for his own sins [NIGTC].
2. It means 'his own' [CEV, NJB, NLT]: in behalf of his own (sins of ignorance).

9:8 this the Holy Spirit showing,[a] not-yet to-be-revealed[b] the way of-the holy (things),[c] the first tent/tabernacle[d] still having (a) standing,[e]

LEXICON—a. pres. act. participle of δηλόω (LN 28.42) (BAGD p. 178): 'to show' [HNTC, NIC, WBC; NAB, NIV, TNT], 'to reveal' [BAGD, LN (28.42); NLT], 'to make known' [LN (28.42)], 'to signify' [KJV, NASB], 'to indicate' [Lns; NRSV, REB], 'to teach' [TEV], 'to say' [CEV], 'to make plain' [LN (28.42)], 'to make clear' [BAGD, LN (33.152), Mil], 'to make evident' [LN (33.152)], 'means us to see' [NJB]. It refers to showing by the arrangement by which no one could enter the Holy of Holies except the high priest only once a year [Alf]. The present tense implies the Holy Spirit's continuing action [TNTC]; it merely implies the continuing significance of the OT passages mentioned [NIGTC].

b. perf. pass. infin. of φανερόω (LN 28.36) (BAGD 1.b. p. 852): 'to be revealed' [BAGD; NAB, TNT], 'to be disclosed' [WBC; NASB, NIV, NRSV], 'to be made known, to be fully known' [LN], 'to become known' [BAGD], 'to be made manifest' [Lns; KJV], 'to be open' [HNTC], 'to be opened' [Mil; TEV], 'to be opened up' [NIC; NJB, REB], not explicit [CEV, NLT]. It is a stylistic variant for the preceding δηλοῦντος 'showing' [NIGTC]. It means to be disclosed [EGT]. This infinitive expresses indirect discourse [Lns, Mil, NTC] and is in apposition with τοῦτο 'this' [Lns]. The perfect tense implies that the Holy Spirit was indicating this throughout the entire period of the tabernacle arrangement

[Lns]; it implies the long-term exclusion from the heavenly sanctuary under the tabernacle ritual [NIGTC].

c. ἅγιος (LN 88.44): 'holy' [LN]. The phrase τῶν ἁγίων 'the holy things' is translated 'the sanctuary' [HNTC; NAB, NRSV, REB, TNT], 'the real sanctuary' [WBC], 'the holy place' [Lns, NIC; NASB, NJB], 'the Most Holy Place' [CEV, NIV, NLT, TEV], 'the holiest' [Mil], 'the holiest of all' [KJV]. This phrase refers to the true sanctuary [Lg], to the true holy places in heaven [Alf, TH], to the presence of God in heaven [Hwt, ICC, My, NIGTC, WBC] as 'the holiest of all' [Hwt]. It refers to the earthly Holy of Holies, implying that full access to God (the final Holy Place [Lns]) was not yet completed [EBC, GNC, Hu, Lns, NIC]. It includes the Holy of Holies, symbolic of the presence of God, as well as the Holy Place [Wst].

d. σκηνή: 'tent/tabernacle'. See this word in 9:2.

e. στάσις (LN **13.72**) (BAGD 1. p. 764): 'standing' [BAGD], 'position' [Lns], 'existence' [BAGD, LN], 'continuance' [BAGD]. The phrase ἐχούσης στάσιν 'having a standing' is translated 'was in existence' [HNTC; TNT], 'was standing' [KJV, NAB, NIV], 'is standing' [NASB, NRSV], 'stands' [Mil, NIC; NJB, REB, TEV], 'exists' [Mil], 'had cultic status' [WBC], 'was still the place of worship' [CEV], 'were still in use' [NLT]. The phrase indicates having a standing, hence to continue to exist [Blm, ICC, My]; it means retaining its status [Hwt, NIC, TNTC, WBC], continuing to have an appointed place in worship [EGT, Hu, Lg(K), Wst].

QUESTION—To what does τοῦτο 'this' refer?

1. It refers to what follows [Alf, Blm, Lg, Lns, Mil, My; NASB]: showing this; namely, that the way. . . . This word is emphatic by its position [Lns, Mil, My], indicating that the principal point of the reference to the tabernacle has now been reached [Mil].
2. It refers to what precedes [HNTC, NIC, TH, WBC; all versions except KJV, NASB]: by the preceding situation the Holy Spirit is showing . . .

QUESTION—What relationship is indicated by the genitive absolute participle δηλοῦντος 'showing'?

1. It indicates the purpose of the pattern stated in 9:7 [EBC, EGT, My, TNTC]: this happened in order for the Holy Spirit to show that ordinary people did not have access to God under the old dispensation. The Holy Spirit is considered to be the author of the temple ritual [EGT].
2. It expresses the Holy Spirit's interpretation of the ritual just mentioned [Alf, Lns, Mil; all versions except KJV, NASB].

QUESTION—What is implied by μήπω 'not yet'?

It implies the expectation that the way would later be opened [Hu].

QUESTION—How are the noun and the adjective related in the genitive phrase τὴν τῶν ἁγίων ὁδόν 'the way of the holy things'?

The genitive phrase τῶν ἁγίων 'of the holy things' indicates where the way leads to [Alf, EBC, HNTC, ICC, Lg, Lns, Mil, My, NIGTC, NTC, TH,

WBC; all versions]: the way into the holy things. The reference is to the possibility and right to enter, not a physical path [Mil].

QUESTION—To what does πρώτης 'first' refer?

It means the first dispensation, which was under the first temple [Blm], the tabernacle set up by Moses [NTC], the first tabernacle as a whole [EBC, Hu, Hwt, NIC, NIGTC; CEV, NJB, NRSV] and the successive temples which followed the original one [NIC], the fore-tent of the tabernacle [Alf, EGT, GNC, HNTC, Lg, Mil, My, TNTC, WBC, Wst; NASB, REB, TEV, TNT] but as representing the entire tabernacle as the center of worship [Wst; NLT].

QUESTION—What relationship is indicated by the genitive absolute participle ἐχούσης 'having'?

It is temporal [Alf, EBC, HNTC, Hu, Hwt, Lns, Mil, NIC, WBC, Wst; all versions]: while the first tabernacle had a standing.

9:9 which (is) (a) parable[a] for[b] the current[c] time,[d]

LEXICON—a. παραβολή (LN 33.15, **58.63**) (BAGD 1. p. 612): 'parable' [LN 33.15, Mil, NIC], 'symbol' [BAGD, HNTC, LN (**58.63**); NAB, NASB, NJB, NRSV, TEV, TNT], 'figure' [LN (33.15), Lns; KJV], 'allegory' [LN 33.15], 'illustration' [WBC; NIV, NLT]. This noun is also translated as an adjective: 'symbolic' [REB]. This entire clause is translated 'this also has a meaning for today' [CEV].

b. εἰς with accusative object (LN 67.117, 67. 119, 90.23): 'for' [LN (67.117); CEV, KJV, NASB, NIV, NJB], 'concerning, with respect to' [LN (90.23)], 'with reference to' [Mil], 'with a bearing on' [NIC], 'regarding' [Lns], 'pointing to' [HNTC, WBC; NLT, REB, TNT], 'which points to' [TEV], 'to' [LN (67.119)], 'of' [NAB, NRSV]. It means 'in reference to' [Alf, EGT, My].

c. perf. act. participle of ἐνίστημι (LN 67.41, 67.63) (BAGD 1. p. 266): 'current', 'present' [BAGD, HNTC, LN (67.41), Lns, NIC, WBC; all versions except CEV, KJV], 'to be then present' [KJV], 'to be imminent' [LN (67.63)], 'to be impending' [LN (67.63)]. The phrase τὸν καιρὸν τὸν ἐνεστηκότα 'the current time' is translated 'today' [CEV]. The perfect tense has present meaning [Lns].

d. καιρός (LN 67.1, 67.78, 67.145) (BAGD 1. p. 394): 'time' [BAGD, HNTC, LN (67.1, 67.78), NIC, WBC; all versions except CEV], 'period of time' [BAGD], 'period' [Lns], 'occasion' [LN (67.1)], 'age, era' [LN (67.145)]. It refers to a period of time [Alf].

QUESTION—What is the meaning of this clause?

1. 'The current time' means the time when the epistle was written [Alf, Blm, GNC, HNTC, Hu, ICC, Lns, NIGTC, WBC]. It implies that the OT ritual was continuing when this epistle was written [HNTC].

1.1 It means that the temple veil emphasized the contrast between the limited access to God under the OT ritual and the full access now available through Christ [NIC].

1.2 It means that the outer tabernacle, as a symbol of the old covenant, represented an obstruction to entrance into the most holy place, as a figure of heavenly things to which access is now available through Christ's work [Alf, GNC].

1.3 It means that the earthly sanctuary is a symbol of the situation under the old covenant which was still existing when the epistle was written [HNTC].

1.4 It means that the presenting of gifts and sacrifices in the OT ritual was a parable which indicated the need for forgiveness of sins [Hu].

2. 'The current time' means 'the time then present' [EGT, Lg, Mil, My, Wst; KJV].

2.1 It means that the outer tent (the veil [NIC]) was a parable of the OT dispensation, showing that access to God had not yet been opened [EGT; NIC].

2.2 It means that the earthly tabernacle, a symbol of the heavenly tabernacle, was a symbol for that time [Hwt].

QUESTION—To what does ἥτις 'which' refer?

1. It refers to the outer tabernacle [Alf, Blm, EGT, ICC, Lg, Lns, Mil, My, NCBC, WBC], which was a symbol of the old dispensation [Blm, EGT].
2. It refers to the earthly tabernacle as a whole [NTC] as a type of the heavenly tabernacle [NIGTC].

QUESTION—What verb is to be supplied in this clause?

1. The verb 'is' is to be supplied [Alf, Blm, Lg(K), My; all versions except KJV]: which is a parable.
2. The verb 'was' is to be supplied [KJV]: which was a parable.

according-to[a] which both gifts[b] and sacrifices[c] are-offered[d] not being-able with-regard-to[e] conscience to-perfect[f] the-(one) worshipping,[g]

LEXICON—a. κατά with accusative object (LN 89.8): 'according to' [Mil, NIC, WBC], 'in accord with' [Lns], 'in accordance with, in relation to' [LN], 'in' [KJV, NAB], 'during' [NRSV], 'for' [NLT], 'by' [CEV], 'under' [NJB], not explicit [NIV, REB, TEV, TNT]. The phrase καθ' ἥν 'according to which' is translated 'accordingly' [NASB].

b. δῶρον (LN 57.84) (BAGD 2. p. 211): 'gift' [HNTC, LN, Lns, Mil, NIC, WBC; all versions except REB, TEV], 'present' [LN], 'offering' [BAGD; REB, TEV].

c. θυσία (LN 53.20) (BAGD 2.a. p. 366): 'sacrifice' [BAGD, HNTC, LN, Lns, Mil, NIC, WBC; all versions except TEV], 'animal sacrifice' [TEV], 'offering' [BAGD].

d. pres. pass. indic. of προσφέρω: 'to be offered'. See this word in 9:7. The present tense refers to the continuation of the action during the OT Levitical system [Alf, Lg(K)].

e. κατά with accusative object (LN 89.4): 'with regard to, in relation to' [LN], 'as regards' [NIC], 'as pertaining to' [KJV], 'as touching' [Mil], 'in' [NASB, NJB]. The phrase κατὰ συνείδησιν 'according to conscience' is translated 'as far as conscience is concerned' [Lns], 'so far as his conscience is concerned' [WBC], 'inwardly' [TNT]; the phrase κατὰ συνείδησιν τελειῶσαι 'according to conscience to perfect' is translated 'give a clear conscience' [REB], 'give a perfectly clear conscience' [HNTC], 'make inwardly perfect' [TNT], 'to make our consciences clear' [CEV], 'to cleanse the consciences' [NLT]. The phrase κατὰ συνείδησιν τὸν λατρεύοντα 'according to conscience the one worshipping' is translated 'the conscience of the worshiper' [NAB, NIV, NRSV], 'the worshiper's heart' [TEV].

f. aorist act. infin. of τελειόω (LN 88.38) (BAGD 2.e.α. p. 810): 'to perfect' [LN; NRSV], 'to make perfect' [BAGD, LN, Mil, NIC; KJV, NAB, NASB, TEV, TNT], 'to bring to perfection' [NJB], 'to bring decisive purgation' [WBC], 'to clear' [NIV], 'to bring to the goal' [Lns], 'to cleanse' [NLT], 'to make clean' [CEV].

g. pres. act. participle of λατρεύω (LN 53.14) (BAGD p. 467): 'to worship' [LN], 'to render the worship' [Lns], 'to do service' [KJV], not explicit [CEV]. The participial phrase τὸν λατρεύοντα 'the one worshipping' is translated 'the worshiper' [BAGD, HNTC, Mil, NIC, WBC; NAB, NASB, NIV, NRSV, REB, TEV, TNT], 'any worshiper' [NJB], 'the people who bring them' [NLT]. The reference is to the people in general, not the priests [Alf, NIC, Wst]; it includes both priests and people [GNC, My, WBC]; it includes only priests and high priests [NIGTC].

QUESTION—Why is this clause mentioned?

It tells how the outer tabernacle is the symbol mentioned in the preceding clause [Lns].

QUESTION—To what does ἥν 'which' refer?

1. It refers to παραβολή 'parable' in the preceding clause [Alf, EGT, Lg(K), Lns, Mil, NCBC, NIC]: according to which parable.
2. It refers to the tabernacle [Hu, My]: in which tabernacle were offered.
3. It refers to the outer tent of the tabernacle [WBC].

QUESTION—To what does the feminine participle δυνάμεναι 'being able' refer?

It refers to both δῶρα 'gifts' and θυσίαι 'sacrifices' [Alf, Blm, Mil, My, NIGTC]; it is feminine in gender in agreement with the nearer (and more important [Blm]) noun [Alf, Blm, NIGTC]: both gifts and sacrifices which are not able to perfect the worshiper. The two nouns include the various expiatory sacrifices [Blm].

9:10 only on-the-basis-of[a] foods and drinks and various washings,[b]

LEXICON—a. ἐπί with dative object (LN 37.9, 90.23) (BAGD II.1.b.γ. p. 287): 'on the basis of' [BAGD, WBC], 'over' [LN (37.9)], 'about' [LN (90.23); CEV], 'concerning, with respect to, with reference to, in' [LN (90.23)], 'in addition to' [Lns, NIC], 'along with' [Mil]. The phrase μόνον ἐπί 'only on the basis of' is translated 'which stood only in' [KJV], 'but can only cleanse in matters of' [NAB], 'since they relate only to' [NASB], 'since they have to do only with' [TEV], 'since they were concerned only with' [HNTC; TNT], 'for that old system deals only with' [NLT], 'they are concerned only with' [REB], 'they are only a matter of' [NIV], 'they are connected with' [NJB], 'but deal only with' [NRSV]. This preposition introduces the items comprising the gifts and sacrifices [Alf].

b. βαπτισμός (LN 53.31, 53.41) (BAGD p. 132): 'washing' [BAGD, LN (53.31), Mil; KJV, NASB, NJB], 'washing rites' [HNTC], 'ritual washing' [NAB, NLT, TNT], 'ceremonial washing' [WBC; NIV], 'ceremony for washing oneself' [CEV], 'ablution' [NIC], 'purification ceremonies' [TEV], 'rite of cleansing' [REB], 'baptism' [LN (53.41), Lns; NRSV]. It includes the requirement for the high priest to bathe before (and after [NCBC]) the Day of Atonement ritual, but also other washing rites for the people, to remove defilement [NCBC, NIC]. It refers to washings prescribed for the people [Alf, Blm], priests, and/or Levites [Blm].

QUESTION—How is this phrase related to the preceding clause?

1. The entire phrase.

1.1 It states what the offering of the gifts and sacrifices mentioned in 9:9 relate to [EBC, GNC, HNTC, Hu, Lg(K), NCBC, NIGTC, NTC, TNTC; all versions except NAB]: they relate only to matters of food, drink, and washings.

1.2 It states the area in which the offerings mentioned in 9:9 are effective [EGT, WBC; NAB]: they can cleanse only in matters of food, drink, and washings. It relates to defilement caused by eating or drinking prohibited things or by neglecting the prescribed washings [EGT].

1.3 It tells what was included in the gifts and sacrifices [Alf, ICC]: gifts and sacrifices consisting of food, drinks, and washings. It is a disparaging comment [ICC].

2. Beginning with ἐπί 'on the basis of'. This phrase mentions items additional to the gifts and sacrifices mentioned in 9:9 [Lns, Mil, My, NIC, Wst]: gifts and sacrifices, in addition to food, drinks, and washings. Μόνον 'only' is connected with δικαιώματα σαρκός 'regulations of flesh' [Lns, My].

QUESTION—To what does βρώμασιν καὶ πόμασιν 'food and drink' refer?

1. It refers to food and drink dealt with in the Mosaic law [Blm, ICC, My, NIC], forbidden or permitted [Blm, ICC, My, TH, Wst]. The reference is deprecatory [ICC]: merely such things.

2. It refers to offerings of food and drink [NCBC].

regulations[a] of-flesh[b] being-imposed[c] until[d] (the) time of-(the)-new-order.[e]

TEXT—Instead of δικαιώματα 'regulations' some manuscripts read καὶ δικαιώματα or καὶ δικαιώμασιν 'and regulations'. GNT omits καί with an A decision, indicating that the text is certain. Only KJV adds 'and'.

LEXICON—a. δικαίωμα (LN 33.334) (BAGD 1. p. 198): 'regulation' [BAGD, HNTC, LN, WBC; NAB, NASB, NIV, NLT, NRSV, TNT], 'requirement'

[LN], 'ordinance' [Lns, Mil, NIC; KJV, REB], 'rule' [CEV, NJB, TEV]. This word is in apposition with δῶρα καὶ θυσίαι 'gifts and sacrifices' in 9:9 [Alf, ICC, Lns].

b. σάρξ (LN 8.4) (BAGD 2. p. 743): 'flesh' [Lns; NAB], 'body' [HNTC, LN; NASB, NRSV], 'physical body' [BAGD], 'physical things' [CEV], 'outward life' [NJB], 'human order' [WBC]. This noun is also translated as an adjective: 'fleshly' [Mil], 'material' [NIC], 'carnal' [KJV], 'external' [NIV, NLT, REB, TNT], 'outward' [TEV]. It means external [EBC, GNC, Hu, ICC, NCBC], material as contrasted with spiritual [Alf, GNC, TNTC]. It means related to the physical body [HNTC, Hwt, Lns, My], related to human life [WBC]. It is in contrast with the conscience [Lns, NIGTC, TH].

c. pres. mid. (deponent = act.) participle of ἐπίκειμαι (LN **13.73**, **76.17**) (BAGD 2.c. p. 294): 'to be imposed' [BAGD, Mil, NIC, WBC; KJV, NAB, NASB, NRSV], 'to be in force' [HNTC, LN (**76.17**); NJB, REB, TNT], 'to be obligatory' [Lns], 'to exist' [LN (**13.73**)], 'to be in effect' [NLT], 'to last' [CEV], 'to apply' [NIV, TEV]. It is parallel to δυνάμεναι 'being able' in 9:9 [Lg].

d. μέχρι with genitive object (LN 67.119) (BAGD 1.b. p. 515): 'until' [BAGD, HNTC, LN, Mil, NIC, WBC; all versions], 'up to' [Lns].

e. διόρθωσις (LN **62.5, 62.6**) (BAGD p. 199): 'new order' [BAGD, LN (**62.5**); NAB, NIV, REB, TEV, TNT], 'right order' [Lns], 'the establishing of a new order' [LN (**62.6**)], 'reformation' [HNTC, NIC; KJV, NASB], 'correction' [WBC], 'when all things would be set right' [Mil]. This noun is also translated as a verb: 'to set things right' [NJB, NRSV]. The phrase καιροῦ διορθώσεως 'the time of the new order' is translated 'the time comes to change them for something better' [CEV], 'their limitations can be corrected' [NLT]. It refers to the reality, the new covenant, which would replace the shadow, the old covenant [Alf, Blm, EGT]. This new order was already in effect through Christ's sacrifice [Alf, Blm, EBC, GNC, Lns, Mil, NIC, TNTC], it was inaugurated by Christ [NIGTC], it relates to the messianic times [EGT, NTC], but the old regulations will not vanish completely until the final "universal restoration" mentioned in Acts 3:21 [HNTC].

QUESTION—How is this phrase related to what precedes?

1. It describes the offerings mentioned in 9:9–10a [Mil, NIC; all versions except KJV]: the gifts and sacrifices, along with food, drink, and washings, are only material ordinances.
2. It describes the offerings mentioned in the first phrase of this verse [Blm, WBC]: food, drink, and washings are only material ordinances.

QUESTION—How are the two nouns related in the genitive construction δικαιώματα σαρκός 'regulations of flesh'?

1. 'Flesh' states the area within which the regulations apply [Lg, Lns, Mil; CEV, NAB, NASB, NJB, NRSV]: regulations governing the physical area of life.

2. 'Flesh' describes the ordinances [KJV, NIV, REB, TEV, TNT].
2.1 They relate to the flesh [KJV]: carnal regulations.
2.2 They deal with physical rather than spiritual matters [NIV, NLT, REB, TEV, TNT]: external regulations.

QUESTION—How are the two nouns related in the genitive construction καιροῦ διορθώσεως 'time of the new order'?

'New order' identifies the 'time' referred to [Lns, Mil; NJB, NRSV, TEV]: the time when the new order is instituted. The absence of articles emphasizes the character of the age [Wst].

QUESTION—What relationship is indicated by the participial construction ἐπικείμενα 'being imposed'?

It is attributive to δικαιώματα 'regulations' [NJB, TEV]: regulations which were imposed.

DISCOURSE UNIT: 9:11–28 [Hwt, NTC, WBC, Wst; NAB, NIV, NLT]. The topic is a more detailed description of the better ministry [Hwt], the sacrifice of Jesus [NAB], Christ, the perfect sacrifice [NLT], the sacrificial blood of Jesus [NTC; NIV], full cleansing through Christ's blood [WBC], Christ's high-priestly atonement under the new covenant [Wst].

DISCOURSE UNIT: 9:11–15 [Lg]. The topic is perfect communion with God through Christ's perfect mediation.

DISCOURSE UNIT: 9:11–14 [EBC, GNC, HNTC, NCBC, NIC, NTC]. The topic is Christ's blood [EBC], Christ's definitive work [GNC], the cultus of Christ [HNTC], Christ's eternal redemption [NCBC, NIC], our conscience cleansed by Christ's blood [NTC].

9:11 But Christ having-come[a] (as) high-priest of-the good (things) having-come-to-be[b]

TEXT—Instead of γενομένων 'having come to be' some manuscripts read μελλόντων 'being about to come to be'. GNT reads 'having come' with a B decision, indicating that this reading is almost certain. Γενομένων 'having come to be' (referring to the past) is read by EBC, GNC, Hu, Mil, NCBC, NIC, NIGTC, NTC, TH, TNTC, WBC, Wst, CEV, NAB, NIV, NLT, NRSV, REB, TEV, and TNT; Μελλόντων 'being about to come to be' (referring to the future) is read by Alf, Blm, EGT, HNTC, Hwt, ICC, Lg, Lns, My, KJV, NASB, and NJB.

LEXICON—a. aorist mid. (deponent = act.) participle of παραγίνομαι (LN **15.86**, 85.7) (BAGD 2. p. 613): 'to come' [LN (**15.86**); all versions except NASB, NLT], 'to appear' [BAGD, HNTC, LN (85.7), Mil, NIC, WBC; NASB], 'to make a public appearance' [BAGD], 'to arrive' [Lns], 'to become' [NLT]. It means to come [Hu, Lns]. It implies having arrived [EGT], having appeared in history [Alf, Lg], to be present [Wst]. It refers to Christ's work as a whole [Alf]. It refers to Christ's appearing as high priest [TH], to his entrance into heaven [NIGTC]

b. aorist mid. participle of γίνομαι (LN 13.48): 'to come to be' [NAB], 'to come to pass' [Mil, NIC], 'to come' [WBC; NLT, NRSV], 'to become' [LN], 'to be already here' [NIV, TEV, TNT], 'to be now here' [CEV], 'already in being' [REB]; different text: [HNTC, Lns; KJV, NASB, NJB].

QUESTION—What relationship is indicated by δέ?

It introduces a contrast with the preceding comments concerning the ineffectiveness of the Levitical offerings [Alf, EGT, Mil, My, NCBC, NIGTC, TH, WBC, Wst; KJV, NASB, NJB, NRSV, REB, TEV, TNT].

QUESTION—What is implied by the use of 'Christ' instead of 'Jesus' in this clause?

1. 'Christ' is used as a name now well-known to Christians and not as a title, 'the Messiah'; it implies the fulfillment of type and prophecy [Alf].
2. It emphasizes his unique priesthood, as 'the Messiah' [HNTC, Lns, NTC]. It amounts to a title [NIGTC, NTC, Wst]. It is emphatic by word order [NIGTC].

QUESTION—What relationship is indicated by the participial form παραγενόμενος 'having come'?

1. It is temporal [Mil, WBC; NAB, NASB, NIV, NRSV]: when Christ came.
2. It states a separate action [HNTC, Lns, NIC; CEV, NLT, REB, TEV]: Christ has come and . . .

QUESTION—What relationship is indicated by the nominative case of ἀρχιερεύς 'high priest'?

It describes the office in which Christ appeared [Alf, ICC, Mil, My, NIGTC, NTC, WBC, Wst; CEV, NAB, NASB, NIV, NJB, NLT, NRSV, TEV]: Christ having appeared as high priest.

QUESTION—How are the noun and the participial phrase related in the genitive construction ἀρχιρεὺς τῶν γενομένων/μελλόντων ἀγαθῶν 'high priest of the good things having come to be'?

1. If γενομένων 'having come to be' is read, the participial phrase tells what the high priest accomplished [Mil]: the high priest accomplished good things.
2. If μελλόντων 'being about to come' is read.
2.1 The participial phrase states the object of Christ's high-priesthood [Alf, EGT]: high priest with reference to the coming good things.
2.2 The participial phrase tells what results from Christ's high-priesthood [Blm]: high priest who causes good things to occur.
2.3 The participial phrase tells what belongs to Christ [Lns]: the coming good things that belong to Christ.

QUESTION—To what does ἀγαθῶν 'good things' refer?

1. If γενομένων ἀγαθῶν 'good things having come to be' is read, it refers to the eternal redemption [Mil], to all the blessings Christ has gained for his people [EBC, GNC, NIGTC, NTC, TH, TNTC], to decisive cleansing and full access to God [WBC], to the fulfillment of the promises in the new covenant, but which will have their ultimate fulfillment later [Hu, Wst].

The aorist tense of the participle refers to the cross and what began there with its full realization in the future [EBC].

2. If μελλόντων ἀγαθῶν 'good things being about to come' is read, it refers to the future from the author's point of view, the future inheritance Christians look forward to [Alf, Lg, Lns], commencing in this world and completed in the future world [Blm, ICC], the full realization of salvation in the future [My]. It refers to the good things under the new covenant [EGT].

through/by-means-of[a] the greater and more-perfect[b] tent/tabernacle[c] not hand-made,[d]

LEXICON—a. διά with genitive object (LN 84.29, 89.76, 90.8): 'through' [LN (84.29, 89.76, 90.8), Mil, NIC, WBC; NAB, NASB, NIV, NJB, NRSV], 'by' [KJV], 'by means of' [HNTC, LN (90.8), Lns], 'with' [LN (90.8); Mil]. The phrase διὰ τῆς σκηνῆς 'through the tent/tabernacle' is translated 'the tent of his priesthood is' [REB], 'the tent in which he serves is' [TEV], 'he is priest in the tent' [TNT], 'he also went into a tent' [CEV], 'he entered that sanctuary' [NLT].

b. τέλειος (LN **79.129**) (BAGD 1.a.α. p. 809): 'more perfect' [BAGD, HNTC, LN, Mil, NIC, WBC; all versions except CEV, NLT, NRSV], 'perfect' [NLT], 'more complete' [BAGD, Lns], 'perfect' [NRSV]. The phrase μείζονος καὶ τελειοτέρας 'greater and more perfect' is translated 'much better' [CEV]. This comparative adjective does not imply the possibility of another still more perfect tabernacle, but simply follows the author's general theme that the new covenant is 'better'; however, none of the commentaries mention this point.

c. σκηνή: 'tent/tabernacle'. See this word in 9:2.

d. χειροποίητος (LN 42.32) (BAGD p. 881): 'hand-made' [Lns], 'made with hands' [Mil, NIC, WBC; KJV, NASB, NRSV, TNT], 'made by hands' [NAB], 'made by human hands' [BAGD, LN; NJB, NLT, REB, TEV], 'made with human hands' [HNTC], 'made by humans' [CEV], 'man-made' [LN; NIV]. The phrase οὐ χειροποιήτου 'not hand-made' implies that it was made by the God [Alf, EGT, My, NIGTC], belonging to the future age [Alf]. It means not made by human hands [Blm, NCBC], not manufactured [ICC], not of the present creation nor of the visible world [NIGTC]. It means not even made by God's hand [Lns].

QUESTION—What relationship is indicated by διά 'through/by means of'?

1. It indicates means [Blm, EBC, EGT, HNTC, Lns, Mil, NCBC, Wst; KJV]: Christ is high priest by means of the greater and more perfect tabernacle. Because he was high priest in the heavenly tabernacle, not the earthly one, he was able to get these wonderful results [EGT].
2. It indicates location [Alf, My, NIC, NIGTC, NTC, TH, WBC; NAB]: Christ has passed through the greater and more perfect tabernacle. He passed from one end to the other end of the tent [TH]. He passed through the great and perfect tent to enter the heavenly Holy of Holies [NIC].

QUESTION—To what tabernacle does this clause refer?

1. The tabernacle referred to is the heavens [Alf, HNTC, NIC, WBC], God's dwelling place [Alf, WBC], the lower parts of the heavens [My], the exterior parts of the heavenly holy of holies [Blm], the very presence of God [GNC, ICC, NTC], the true tabernacle [NIC], the heavenly sanctuary [Lg, Mil, NCBC].
2. It is the union of redeemed persons in Christ, through which Christ ministers [Wst].

this is, not of-this creation,[a]

LEXICON—a. κτίσις (LN 42.35) (BAGD 1.b.β. p. 456): 'creation' [LN, Lns, NIC; NAB, NASB, NIV, NJB, NRSV], 'created order' [NJB], 'created world' [HNTC; NLT, TNT], 'material creation' [Mil], 'world' [BAGD; CEV], 'belonging to this created world' [REB], 'a part of this created world' [TEV], 'ordinary building' [WBC], 'building' [KJV]. It refers to the present created order [ICC].

QUESTION—What is the meaning of this phrase?

It means that it is of heavenly rather than earthly materials [Blm], that it does not belong to this world at all [EGT, Lg(K), NCBC, TH], that it is not a part of the material creation [Mil, My, NIC, WBC].

QUESTION—What is this phrase connected with?

It is in apposition with οὐ χειροποιήτου 'not hand-made' [Alf] and further describes it [Mil, NCBC]: not hand-made, that is, not of this creation.

9:12 neither through[a] **blood of-goats and calves but through**[a] **his-own blood**

LEXICON—a. διά with genitive object (LN 89.76, 90.8): 'through' [LN (89.76, 90.80), Mil; NASB], 'by' [HNTC; KJV], 'by means of' [LN (90.8), Lns, WBC], 'by virtue of' [NIC], 'with' [LN (90.8), Mil; NAB, NLT, NRSV, TNT], 'taking with him' [NJB]. The phrase οὐδὲ διὰ . . . διά 'neither through . . . through' is translated 'not by means of . . . by' [NIV], 'he did not take . . . he took' [TEV], 'by offering . . . instead of' [CEV]. This entire phrase is translated 'the blood of his sacrifice is his own blood, not the blood of goats and calves' [REB]. Both instances of this word are instrumental [Alf, EBC, Hu, Lns, Mil, My, NIC, NTC, TH, Wst].

QUESTION—What is implied by the phrase, 'neither through blood of goats and calves'?

It implies that it was not with the items typical of the old covenant [Alf].

QUESTION—What is implied by the plurals τράγων καὶ μόσχων 'goats and calves'?

The plurals are generic [Alf, NIC, Wst]; the repeated annual offering consisted of one of each animal [EGT].

QUESTION—What relationship is indicated by δέ 'but'?

It introduces a strong contrast [Alf, TH, WBC]: not this blood but rather his own blood.

QUESTION—What relationship is indicated by the reference to Christ's blood?
Christ's blood is the ransom [Alf]. 'Blood' refers to his death [Alf, NCBC, TH].

he-entered once-for-all[a] into[b] the holy-things[c]

LEXICON—a. ἐφάπαξ (LN 60.67, 60.68) (BAGD 2. p. 330): 'once for all' [BAGD, HNTC, Lns, Mil, NIC, WBC; CEV, NAB, NASB, NIV, NRSV, REB, TNT], 'once and for all' [LN (60.68); NJB, TEV], 'once for all time' [NLT], 'once' [LN (60.67); KJV], 'one time' [LN (60.67)]. This word contrasts with the OT high priest's entering once each year [Blm, EGT, Hu, Hwt, NIGTC, TNTC, WBC]. It is emphatic [EBC]. It emphasizes that no repetition is necessary [Hu, Lns, WBC] or possible [Lns, WBC].

b. εἰς with accusative object (LN 84.22): 'into' [LN, Lns, Mil, WBC; KJV, NAB, NRSV, TEV]. The phrase εἰσῆλθεν εἰς 'he entered into' is translated 'he entered' [HNTC; NASB, NIV, NJB, TNT], 'he has entered' [NIC; REB].

c. ἅγιος (LN 7.18, **7.35,** 88.24) (BAGD 2.b. p. 10): 'holy' [LN (88.24)]. The neuter plural form ἅγια is translated 'Holy Place' [LN (**7.35**), Lns, NIC; KJV, NASB, NRSV], 'Most Holy Place' [CEV, NIV, NLT, TEV], 'holiest' [Mil], 'sanctuary' [BAGD, HNTC, LN (7.18); NAB, NJB, REB, TNT], 'real sanctuary' [WBC]. It means the holy of holies [GNC, Hu, Hwt], the presence of God [Lg], the inner sanctuary of heaven [My, TH].

QUESTION—What is the meaning of this phrase?
It means that when Christ died on the cross he figuratively entered the Holy of Holies of the temple [NTC].

having-obtained[a] eternal[b] redemption.[c]

LEXICON—a. aorist mid. participle of εὑρίσκω (LN **90.70**) (BAGD 3. p. 325): 'to obtain' [BAGD, Lns, Mil, WBC; KJV, NASB, NIV, NRSV, TEV], 'to procure' [NIC], 'to attain' [LN], 'to achieve' [NAB], 'to win' [NJB], 'to secure' [HNTC; NLT, REB, TNT]. The phrase λύτρωσιν εὑράμενος 'having obtained redemption' is translated 'freed us from sin' [CEV]. The middle voice implies Christ's full involvement in the action [Alf, Mil, Wst], that Christ offered himself [EGT], that he obtained deliverance for himself [Blm, NIGTC, NTC] and for the people [NIGTC]; that is, for the benefit of the people [NTC].

b. αἰώνιος (LN 67.96) (BAGD 3. p. 28): 'eternal' [BAGD, LN, Lns, Mil, NIC, WBC; all versions except CEV, NLT], 'everlasting' [HNTC], 'forever' [CEV, NLT]. This word contrasts with the provisional annual redemption under the old covenant [Blm, EGT, GNC, My, NCBC, Wst]. It is eternal because it is complete and therefore unrepeatable [TNTC]. It has eschatological meaning [WBC].

c. λύτρωσις (LN 37.128) (BAGD 1. p. 483): 'redemption' [BAGD, Mil, NIC, WBC; KJV, NAB, NASB, NIV, NJB, NRSV], 'ransoming' [Lns], 'salvation' [NLT, TEV], 'deliverance' [HNTC, LN; TNT], 'liberation'

[LN; REB]. It indicates liberation [NIGTC, TH], deliverance and the price paid for the redemption [Alf, EBC], that is, Christ's sacrificial death [Alf]. The reference is to final redemption at Christ's return [Alf]. It refers to deliverance from guilt [EGT, Lns, My] and punishment for sin [My].

QUESTION—What relationship is indicated by the aorist participle εὑράμενος 'having obtained'?

1. It indicates the result of Christ's entering the sanctuary [Alf, EGT, Mil, NCBC, NIGTC, NTC, TNTC, WBC, Wst; NLT, NRSV, TEV]: he entered and thus obtained eternal redemption. Redemption was effected by offering his blood in the sanctuary [TNTC]. The initial work of redemption in conquering death was accomplished at the cross, but the full effect of redemption was brought about by his ascension [Wst]. On the basis of his sacrificial blood shed at the cross, he figuratively entered the Most Holy Place to procure redemption for his people forever [NTC].
2. It is temporal [GNC, Hu, Hwt, My, NIC]: he entered after he had obtained eternal redemption. Redemption was secured on the cross before he entered the sanctuary [Hu, NIC].

QUESTION—To whom does the eternal redemption refer?

It refers to the author and his readers [KJV, TEV, TNT]: eternal redemption for us.

DISCOURSE UNIT: 9:13–28 [Lns]. The topic is a comparison of the two kinds of blood.

9:13 For if the blood of-goats and bulls and ashes of-a-heifer sprinkling[a] the-(ones) defiled[b] sanctifies[c] for[d] the purity[e] of-the flesh,[f]

LEXICON—a. pres. act. participle of ῥαντίζω (LN 47.16) (BAGD 1. p. 734): 'to sprinkle' [BAGD, HNTC, LN, Lns, Mil, NIC, WBC; all versions except CEV, NLT], not explicit [NLT]. This active verb is also translated in the passive voice: 'to be sprinkled' [CEV]. The ashes were mixed with water for sprinkling [Blm, EBC, EGT, GNC, HNTC, ICC, Lg].

b. perf. pass. participle of κοινόω (LN 53.33) (BAGD 1.a. p. 438): 'to be defiled' [HNTC, LN, Lns, NIC; NAB, NASB, NRSV, REB, TNT], 'to incur defilement' [NJB], 'to be made unclean' [LN], 'to become unclean' [CEV], 'to be ceremonially unclean' [BAGD; NIV], 'to be ceremonially defiled' [Mil, WBC], 'to be ritually unclean' [TEV], not explicit [NLT]. This participle is translated as an adjective: 'unclean' [KJV]. The perfect tense refers to the state of uncleanness resulting from the defilement [NIGTC, WBC].

c. pres. act. indic. of ἁγιάζω (LN 53.44) (BAGD 2. p. 8): 'to sanctify' [BAGD, Lns, Mil, WBC; KJV, NAB, NASB, NIV, NRSV], 'to have sanctifying power' [NIC], 'to hallow' [HNTC], 'to consecrate' [LN; REB], 'to purify' [TNT]. The phrase ἁγιάζει πρὸς τὴν τῆς σαρκὸς καθαρότητα 'sanctifies for the purity of the flesh' is translated 'may restore their bodily purity' [NJB], 'and this purifies them by taking away their ritual impurity' [TEV], 'will be considered clean' [CEV], 'could cleanse people's bodies from ritual defilement' [NLT]. The meaning here is to purify [NIC], to remove ceremonial defilement [EBC, EGT]. The present tense expresses a general timeless statement [Lns].

d. πρός with accusative object (LN 89.60): 'for' [NASB], 'for the purpose of' [LN], 'as regards' [Lns], 'as far as' [NIC], 'to the extent of' [WBC], 'to' [KJV]. This word implies bringing about [Alf], result [Mil, My; NIV], in reference to [Lg(K)], to the extent of [WBC], in the direction of [EGT].

e. καθαρότης (LN **53.28**) (BAGD p. 388): 'purity' [BAGD; NJB], 'purification' [**LN**], 'purifying' [KJV], 'purging' [WBC], 'cleansing' [NASB], 'cleanness' [Lns]. The phrase πρὸς τὴν τῆς σαρκὸς καθαρότητα 'for the purity of the flesh' is translated 'as far as bodily cleansing is concerned' [NIC], 'so that their flesh is cleansed' [NAB], 'so that their flesh is purified' [NRSV], 'so that they are outwardly clean' [NIV], 'so as to produce an outward purity' [Mil], 'and restore their external purity' [HNTC], 'in order to make them ritually acceptable' [**LN**], 'and free them from ritual uncleanness' [TNT], 'restores their ritual purity' [REB]. This word refers to purity as a quality, not to the action of purifying [Alf].

f. σάρξ (LN 8.63) (BAGD 2. p. 743): 'flesh' [LN, Lns, WBC; KJV, NAB, NASB, NRSV], 'body' [BAGD]. This word is in contrast with the internal concept of conscience [EGT, Hu]. It refers to the person's body [Lns, NIC] as distinct from the inner being [NIC].

QUESTION—What relationship is indicated by γάρ 'for'?

It indicates the grounds for the statement that Christ has obtained eternal redemption [Alf, EGT, ICC, Mil, My, NIGTC]. It further explains and advances the thought [Lns].

QUESTION—What relationship is indicated by the clause introduced by εἰ 'if'?

It expresses the grounds for the conclusion in 9:14 [Alf, Mil, NIGTC, WBC; TEV]: if, as we know it does. It is the first part of an argument from the lesser to the greater [Alf, ICC, NIGTC, NTC, WBC]: if the blood of animals . . . then by how much more the blood of Christ?

QUESTION—To what does τὸ αἷμα τράγων καὶ ταύρων 'the blood of goats and bulls' refer?

It refers to the annual offering on the day of atonement [Alf, TNTC, Wst]. Ταύρων 'bulls' here is more specific than μόσχων 'calves' in 9:12; only the males were offered [Alf]. The blood of goats refers to the day of atonement, but the blood of bulls (both goats and bulls [NCBC, NIC]) refers to other sacrifices [Lns, NCBC, NIC, NIGTC]. The plural refers to the annual repetition of the sacrifice of one of each animal [Hu].

QUESTION—What is implied by the absence of the definite article with σποδός 'ashes'?

This noun has no article, since only portions of the ashes were used for each action [Alf].

QUESTION—What is the participle ῥαντίζουσα 'sprinkling' connected with?

This sprinkling was for ceremonial cleansing after contact with or presence near a dead body [EBC, EGT, GNC, HNTC, Hu, Hwt, ICC, Lg, Lns, Mil, My, NCBC, NIC, NTC, WBC, Wst] and had no connection with the day of atonement [ICC].

1. It is connected only with σποδὸς δαμάλεως 'the ashes of a heifer' [EBC, GNC, HNTC, Hu, Hwt, ICC, Lg, Lns, My, NIC, WBC, Wst; KJV, NAB, NRSV, TNT]; the participle is feminine singular, agreeing with σποδός 'ashes' [Hu]: the ashes of a heifer sprinkling.
2. It is connected with all of the preceding items [NIGTC, TH; NASB, NIV, NJB, REB, TEV]: the blood and the ashes sprinkling.

QUESTION—What relationship is indicated by the participle ῥαντίζουσα 'sprinkling'?

1. It is attributive [HNTC, WBC]: ashes which sprinkle.
2. It expresses means [Mil]: ashes, by sprinkling.

QUESTION—What is the participial phrase τοὺς κεκοινωμένους 'the defiled ones' connected with?

1. It is connected with ῥαντίζουσα 'sprinkling' [GNC, Hu, Hwt, ICC, Lg, Mil, My, NIC, Wst; KJV, NASB, NIV, NJB, TEV]: sprinkling the defiled ones.
2. It is connected with ἁγιάζει 'sanctifies' [HNTC, WBC; NAB, NRSV, REB, TNT]: sanctifies the defiled ones.

QUESTION—How are the two nouns related in the genitive construction τὴν τῆς σαρκὸς καθαρότητα 'the purity of the flesh'?

The genitive noun σαρκός 'flesh' tells what is purified [Mil; NAB, NRSV]: so that the flesh is purified. The reference is to cleansing from ritual defilement [EBC].

9:14 by-how-much more the blood of-the Christ,

QUESTION—Why is this phrase mentioned?

It, together with the final part of this verse, continues the argument from the lesser to the greater [Hu, My, NIC, NIGTC]: if the blood of bulls . . . by how much more the blood of Christ.

QUESTION—What relationship is indicated by πόσῳ 'by how much'?

1. It introduces an exclamation [NIGTC, TH, WBC; NAB, NIV, NRSV, TEV, TNT], a statement [Mil; CEV, NJB, NLT, REB]: by how much more . . . !
2. It introduces a (rhetorical) question [HNTC, Lns, NIC; KJV, NASB]: by how much more . . . ?

QUESTION—What is implied by the phrase 'the blood of Christ'?

It implies Christ's death as a sacrifice [EBC, HNTC, ICC, NIC, NIGTC, TH, TNTC, WBC, Wst].

QUESTION—What is meant by τοῦ Χριστοῦ 'the Christ'?

1. 'The Christ' is used as a title [EGT]: the Christ.
2. It amounts to a personal name [Hu]: Christ.

who through[a] eternal[b] Spirit/spirit[c] offered[d] himself without-blemish[e] to-God,

TEXT—Instead of αἰωνίου 'eternal' some manuscripts read ἁγίου 'holy'. GNT reads αἰωνίου 'eternal' with an A decision, indicating that the text is certain. None of the versions or commentaries reads 'holy'.

LEXICON—a. διά with genitive object (LN 89.76, 90.4): 'through' [LN (89.76, 90.4), Mil, NIC, WBC; all versions except CEV, NLT], 'by' [Lns], 'by the power of' [NLT], 'in' [HNTC], 'as' [CEV]. It introduces the means by which Christ's offered himself [Mil, My, NIGTC]

b. αἰώνιος: 'eternal'. See this word in 9:12. Here it implies the non-earthly aspect of reality more than the temporal [NIGTC].

c. πνεῦμα (LN 12.18, 26.9) (BAGD 5.c.β. p. 676): 'Spirit' [BAGD, LN, Mil, NIC, WBC; all versions except CEV, NAB], 'spirit' [LN, Lns; NAB], 'nature' [HNTC]. This noun is also translated as an adjective: '(as an eternal and) spiritual (sacrifice)' [CEV].

d. aorist act. indic. of προσφέρω (LN 57.80) (BAGD 2.a. p.720): 'to offer' [BAGD, Lns, Mil, NIC, WBC; all versions except NAB, TNT], 'to offer up' [NAB], 'to present to' [BAGD, LN], 'to give' [HNTC; TNT]. The offering occurred on the cross [Alf, EGT, My].

e. ἄμωμος (LN 88.34) (BAGD 1. p. 47): 'without blemish' [BAGD; NASB, NRSV, REB], 'unblemished' [NAB, NIV], 'blemishless' [Lns], 'blameless' [LN; NJB], 'sinless' [CEV], 'without a flaw' [Mil], 'without spot' [KJV], 'faultless, without fault, perfect' [LN], 'as a perfect sacrifice' [NLT, TEV], 'as an unblemished sacrifice' [NIC, WBC], 'as an unblemished offering' [TNT], 'as a spotless self-oblation' [HNTC]. It means to be without defect [Alf, EBC, GNC, Wst], without inward blemish [EGT, NIC], morally perfect [Hu, Hwt, My, NCBC], of a sinless nature [ICC, My, NIGTC, TNTC], perfectly fulfilling God's will [TNTC], a perfect sacrifice [WBC].

QUESTION—Why is this clause mentioned?

It gives the grounds for stating that the blood of Christ can cleanse the conscience [EGT]. It emphasizes the value of Christ's sacrifice [Lns]. It describes why Christ's sacrifice is efficacious [Mil]. The introductory relative pronoun ὅς 'who' has a causal sense, and the clause implies the reason for the effectiveness of Christ's sacrifice [WBC].

QUESTION—To what does the phrase πνεύματος αἰωνίου 'eternal Spirit/spirit' refer?

1. It refers to the Holy Spirit [BAGD (2. p. 28, 5.c.β. p. 676), Blm, EBC, GNC, Lg, Mil, NCBC, NIC, NIGTC, NTC, WBC; all versions except CEV, NAB]. It is definite (made so by the modifier 'eternal' [GNC]) even without the definite article [GNC, NIGTC; KJV, NASB, NIV].
2. It does not refer to the Holy Spirit [Alf, EGT, HNTC, Hwt, ICC, Lns, My, TNTC, Wst; CEV, NAB]. The absence of the definite article emphasizes the quality or nature of 'eternal spirit' [Lns, My, TNTC, Wst] in contrast with his flesh [TNTC]; it is definite even without the article [NAB].

2.1 It refers to Christ's eternal nature [HNTC], his eternal spirit [Hwt], his divine personality [Alf, Lns, Wst] in contrast with his physical body [Lns, My].

2.2 It refers to the spiritual nature of the sacrifice [EGT, ICC; CEV].

QUESTION—What is implied by the phrase ἑαυτὸν προσήνεγκεν 'he offered himself'?

It indicates that the offering was voluntary and premeditated [TNTC, WBC, Wst]. It refers to Christ's death on the cross [EGT, Wst]. The pronoun ἑαυτόν 'himself' preceding the verb is emphatic [Alf] and contrasts with the offering of the blood of animals [EGT].

QUESTION—What is the phrase τῷ θεῷ 'to God' connected with?

It is connected with the whole preceding relative clause [My].

shall-cleanse[a] our/your conscience from[b] dead[c] works[d] for[e] the to-serve[f]/for-the-purpose-of[e] serving[f] (a) living God.

TEXT—Instead of ἡμῶν 'our' some manuscripts read ὑμῶν 'your'. GNT reads ἡμῶν 'our' with a C decision, indicating that the committee had difficulty in making a decision. Ὑμῶν 'your' is read by Blm, EGT, Lns, KJV, and NASB.

LEXICON—a. fut. act. indic. of καθαρίζω (LN 53.28) (BAGD 2.b.α. p. 387): 'to cleanse' [BAGD, LN, Lns, NIC; NAB, NASB, NIV, REB], 'to purify' [BAGD, HNTC, LN; NJB, NLT, NRSV, TEV], 'to purge' [Mil, WBC; KJV], 'to set free' [TNT], 'to make clear' [CEV]. The future tense implies a general reference [NIGTC]; it refers to the personal effect on believers, extending into the future [Lns]. It implies certainty [NTC, TH].

b. ἀπό with genitive object (LN 89.122): 'from' [HNTC, LN, Lns, Mil, NIC, WBC; all versions except CEV], not explicit [CEV]. It implies separation [Mil, NIGTC].

c. νεκρός (LN **65.39**) (BAGD 1.b.β. p. 534): 'dead' [BAGD, HNTC, Lns, Mil, NIC; KJV, NAB, NASB, NJB, NRSV], 'useless' [LN; TEV], 'futile, vain' [LN] 'that lead to death' [WBC; CEV, NIV, NLT], 'which leads to death' [TNT]. The phrase νεκρῶν ἔργων 'dead works' is translated 'deadness of our former ways' [REB].

d. ἔργον (LN 42.11) (BAGD 1.c.β. p. 308): 'work' [HNTC, Lns, Mil, NIC; KJV, NAB, NASB, NRSV], 'act' [LN, WBC; NIV], 'action' [NJB], 'deed' [BAGD, LN; NLT], 'conduct' [TNT], 'ritual' [TEV], 'way' [REB]. This noun is also translated as a verb phrase: 'to do things' [CEV].

e. εἰς with accusative object (LN 89.57): 'for' [Lns], 'for the purpose of' [LN], 'so that' [Mil, NIC, WBC; NIV, NJB, NLT, TEV], 'that' [TNT], 'to' [HNTC; CEV, KJV, NAB, NRSV]. It introduces the purpose of the cleansing [Blm, Hu, ICC, Lg(K), Mil, TH, WBC].

f. pres. act. infin. of λατρεύω (LN 53.14) (BAGD p. 467): 'to serve' [BAGD, HNTC, Lns, Mil; CEV, KJV, NASB, NIV, REB, TEV], 'to worship' [LN, NIC, WBC; NAB, NJB, NLT, NRSV, TNT], 'to perform religious rites' [LN]. The primary meaning is worship [Mil, TH, TNTC], but service for God may be included [Mil].

QUESTION—What relationship is indicated by συνείδησιν 'conscience'?

It is in contrast with σάρξ in 9:13 [NIGTC].

QUESTION—What relationship is indicated by the phrase νεκρῶν ἔργων 'dead works'?

1. It means works that cannot give eternal life [BAGD (1.b.β. p. 534), NCBC], works done apart from God [HNTC], rituals (OT rituals [Lg]) that are useless [Lg; TEV], useless deeds [My, TNTC] because they are polluted with sin and self [TNTC], all false legal observances and human attempts to merit standing before God [Lns].
2. It means works that lead to death [Mil, NTC, WBC; CEV, NIV, NLT, TNT], works that have their origin in sin [Alf], sinful deeds [GNC, Mil] that deny access to God [NIGTC], works that pollute the soul [Blm, EGT, Mil], works that cannot remove sin and guilt [TH].
3. They are 'dead' because the person who does them is dead toward God, they are unproductive, and they end in death [Hu].

QUESTION—What is implied by the absence of the definite article in the phrase θεῷ ζῶντι 'living God'?

1. It is nevertheless considered definite [EGT, HNTC, Hu, Lns, Mil, NIC, WBC; KJV, NAB, NASB, NIV, NJB, NRSV, REB, TEV, TNT]: the living God.
2. It may be qualitative, focusing on God's nature as deity, but none of the commentaries mention this possibility: God as a living God.

DISCOURSE UNIT: 9:15–10:18 [TNTC]. The topic is the mediator.

DISCOURSE UNIT: 9:15–28 [NJB]. The topic is Christ sealing the new covenant with his blood.

DISCOURSE UNIT: 9:15–22 [EBC, GNC, HNTC, NCBC, NIC, TNTC]. The topic is the mediator of the new covenant [EBC, NCBC, NIC], the covenant sacrifice [HNTC], the significance of Christ's death [TNTC], Christ's sacrifice as the basis of the new covenant [GNC].

9:15 And on-account-of[a] this he-is mediator[b] of-(a)-new covenant,[c]

LEXICON—a. διά with accusative object (LN 89.26), (BAGD B.II.2, p. 181): 'on account of, by reason of' [LN], 'because of' [LN, Lns], not explicit [CEV]. The phrase διὰ τοῦτο 'on account of this' is translated 'for this reason' [BAGD, Mil, NIC, WBC; NASB, NIV, NRSV, TEV], 'for this cause' [KJV], 'this makes him' [NJB], 'this is why' [NAB], 'that is why' [NLT, REB], 'therefore' [HNTC; TNT].

b. μεσίτης (LN 31.22, 40.6) (BAGD p. 507): 'mediator' [BAGD, HNTC, LN (31.22, 40.6), Lns, Mil, NIC, WBC; all versions except CEV, NLT, TEV], 'go-between' [LN (31.22)], 'the one who mediates' [NLT], 'the one who arranges' [TEV]. This noun is also translated as a verb: 'to bring' [CEV].

c. διαθήκη (LN 34.44) (BAGD 2. p. 183): 'covenant' [BAGD, LN, Mil, NIC, WBC; all versions except CEV, KJV, REB], 'testament' [Lns; KJV], 'covenant or testament' [HNTC; REB], 'agreement' [CEV].

QUESTION—What relationship is indicated by καί 'and'?

It indicates the result of the preceding comment [Mil]: and as a result he is mediator.

QUESTION—To what does the phrase διὰ τοῦτο 'on account of this' refer?

1. It refers to the preceding thought [Alf, EGT, GNC, HNTC, Hu, Hwt, Lg, Mil, My, NIC, NIGTC, NTC, TNTC, WBC, Wst; NJB, REB, TNT]: because of his sacrifice he is mediator. It refers back to the efficacy of Christ's sacrifice [Alf, EGT].
2. It refers to what follows [ICC, Lns, TH].

2.1 He is mediator in order that the called ones may receive the inheritance [ICC, Lns].

2.2 He is mediator, because his death has enabled the called ones to receive the promise [NAB].

QUESTION—What is the significance of the absence of a definite article with μεσίτης 'mediator'?

1. 'Mediator' is qualitative, emphasizing what Christ is [Alf, EGT, Lns, Mil, NIC, Wst; NAB, REB]: he is mediator.
2. It is nevertheless considered definite [GNC, HNTC, Hu, Hwt, My, NTC, WBC; all versions except NAB, REB]: he is the mediator.

QUESTION—How are the two nouns related in the genitive construction διαθήκης καινῆς μεσίτης 'mediator of a new covenant'?

The genitive διαθήκης καινῆς 'new covenant' tells what Christ mediates [TEV]: he mediates a new covenant. 'Covenant' ('new covenant' [Mil]) is emphatic by forefronting [Mil, My, NIGTC, TNTC, Wst].

in-order-that,[a] death having-occurred for[b] redemption[c] of-the transgressions[d] under[e] the first covenant,[f]

LEXICON—a. ὅπως (LN 89.59) (BAGD 2.a.α. p. 576): 'in order that' [BAGD, HNTC, LN, Lns, WBC; NASB, TNT], 'so that' [LN, Mil, NIC; NJB, NLT, NRSV, TEV], 'that' [KJV, NIV], 'its purpose is' [REB], not explicit [CEV, NAB].

b. εἰς with accusative object (LN 89.57): 'for the purpose of' [LN], 'for' [Lns, Mil, WBC; KJV, NAB, NASB], 'effective for' [NIC], 'as' [NIV], 'to' [CEV, NJB, NLT], 'to bring' [REB], 'to secure' [HNTC; TNT]. The phrase εἰς ἀπολύτρωσιν 'for redemption' is translated 'that redeems' [NRSV], 'which sets people free' [TEV]. It expresses purpose [Lns, Mil, TNTC].

c. ἀπολύτρωσις (LN 37.128) (BAGD 2.a. p. 96): 'redemption' [BAGD, Mil, NIC, WBC; KJV, NASB], 'ransom to set free' [NIV], 'ransoming' [Lns], 'deliverance' [HNTC, LN; NAB, TNT], 'liberation' [LN; REB]. This noun is also translated as a verb: 'to redeem' [NJB, NRSV], 'to set free'

[NLT, TEV], 'to rescue' [CEV]. The use of this word does not imply the actual payment of a debt [HNTC]. It implies full forgiveness [ICC].

d. παράβασις (LN 36.28) (BAGD p. 612): 'transgression' [BAGD, HNTC, LN, Lns, Mil, NIC, WBC; KJV, NAB, NASB, NRSV, TNT], 'sin' [NIV, NJB, NLT, REB], 'wrong' [TEV], 'those who had sinned' [CEV].

e. ἐπί with dative object (LN 67.136, 89.13) (BAGD II.1.b.γ. p. 287, II.2. p. 288): 'under' [HNTC, NIC; all versions except CEV, TEV], 'on the basis of' [LN (89.13), WBC], 'on' [BAGD], 'for' [LN (67.136)], 'during' [LN (67.136)], 'during the time of' [Mil], 'at the time of' [BAGD, Lns], 'while (it) was in effect' [TEV]. The phrase τῶν ἐπὶ τῇ πρώτῃ διαθήκῃ παραβάσεων 'transgressions under the first covenant' is translated 'those who had sinned and broken the old agreement' [CEV].

f. διαθήκη: 'covenant'. See this word above.

QUESTION—What is ὅπως 'in order that' connected with?

It is connected with the latter part of the verse [Alf, HNTC, Hu, Hwt, Mil, NCBC, WBC; NIV, NJB, TEV, TNT]: in order that the ones called may receive the promise.

QUESTION—What is the significance of the lack of a definite article with θανάτου 'death'?

1. 'Death' is indefinite [HNTC, Mil, My, NIC, NIGTC, WBC; NASB, NJB, NRSV, REB, TEV, TNT]: a death has occurred.
2. It is qualitative, emphasizing what it was [KJV]: death has occurred.
3. It refers to Christ's death [Lns; NAB]: his death has occurred.

QUESTION—What is indicated by the participial phrase θανάτου γενομένου 'death having occurred'?

This phrase reflects back to the reference to Christ's death in the preceding verses [WBC]. The aorist tense implies a single act [NTC].

1. It indicates reason [Alf, GNC, HNTC, Hu, Lns, NIGTC; NAB, NASB, NRSV, TEV, TNT]: because a death has occurred, the called ones may receive.
2. It indicates means [Mil; KJV]: by means of death having occurred, the called ones may receive.
3. It is temporal [NIC; NIV, NJB, REB]: now that a death has occurred, the called ones may receive.

QUESTION—How are the two nouns related in the genitive construction ἀπολύτρωσιν τῶν παραβάσεων 'redemption of the transgressions'?

The genitive noun παραβάσεων 'transgressions' tells what the deliverance is from [EGT, GNC, HNTC, Hu, Lns, Mil, NIGTC, Wst; all versions except KJV, NASB]: redemption from the transgressions. The genitive indicates separation [NIGTC]. 'Transgressions' is used figuratively to refer to the persons who committed the transgressions [NTC].

QUESTION—What relationship is indicated by ἐπί 'under'?

1. It implies occurrence 'under the regime of' [Blm, HNTC, Hu, NIC, WBC; all versions except TEV]: transgressions which occurred under the regime of the first covenant.

2. It is temporal [Alf, EGT, Lns, Mil, TH; TEV]: transgressions committed while the first covenant was in effect.
3. It indicates the circumstances [Wst]: transgressions made known in the first covenant.

the-(ones) called[a] might-receive[b] the promise of-the eternal[c] inheritance.[d]

LEXICON—a. perf. pass. participle of καλέω (LN 33.307) (BAGD 2. p. 399): 'to be called' [BAGD, HNTC, LN, Lns, Mil, NIC, WBC; all versions except CEV, NLT], 'to be summoned' [LN], 'to be chosen' [CEV], 'to be invited' [NLT].

b. aorist act. subj. of λαμβάνω (LN 57.55, 57.125): 'to receive' [HNTC, LN (57.125), Lns, Mil, NIC, WBC; all versions except CEV, TNT], 'to obtain' [LN (57.55); TNT], 'to acquire' [LN (57.55)]. This verb is also translated with Christ as the subject: 'he brings' [CEV]. This aorist subjunctive refers to all time in general [Lns].

c. αἰώνιος: 'eternal'. See this word in 9:12.

d. κληρονομία (LN 57.132, 57.140) (BAGD 3. p. 435): 'inheritance' [BAGD, HNTC, LN (57.140), Lns, Mil, NIC, WBC; all versions except CEV, TEV, TNT], 'possession' [LN (57.132); TNT], 'blessings' [CEV, TEV].

QUESTION—To whom does οἱ κεκλημένοι 'the called ones' refer?

The perfect tense indicates a continuing state resulting from a previous call [Lns, My, TNTC].

1. It refers to Christians [GNC].
2. It refers both to Christians (the Hebrew Christians addressed [EGT]) and to those who lived under the OT covenant [EGT, HNTC, Hwt, ICC, Lg, Lns, My].

QUESTION—To what are they called?

1. It has no stated object [Alf, Blm, HNTC, Hu, Hwt, ICC, Lg(K), Lns, Mil, My, NIC, NTC, WBC, Wst; all versions except NJB]: the called ones.
2. They are called to τῆς αἰωνίου κληρονομίας 'the eternal inheritance' [Lg; NJB]: the ones called to an eternal inheritance.

QUESTION—How are the two nouns related in the genitive construction τὴν ἐπαγγελίαν τῆς αἰωνίου κληρονομίας 'the promise of the eternal inheritance'?

1. 'Inheritance' identifies the 'promise' and is what is received [Alf, Blm, EGT, Hu, Hwt, ICC, Lns, Mil, My, NIC, NIGTC, NTC, WBC; NAB, NIV, NRSV, REB]: that they might receive what was promised, namely, the eternal inheritance. It refers to the promised eternal blessings [Blm; TEV], the eternal possession [TNT]. Τὴν ἐπαγγελίαν 'the promise' is forefronted for emphasis [ICC, My].
2. 'Promise' is what is received, and 'the eternal inheritance' gives the content of the promise [HNTC; NJB]: that they might receive the promise, which assured them of the eternal inheritance to come.

DISCOURSE UNIT: 9:16–22 [Lg]. The topic is the necessity for Christ's blood in order to complete the new covenant.

9:16 For where[a] (there is a) testament/will/covenant,[b] (there is a) necessity[c] (for the) death of-the-(one) having-made-the-testament[d] to-be-brought-in;[e]

LEXICON—a. ὅπου (LN 83.5, **89.5**) (BAGD 2.a. p. 576): 'where' [BAGD, HNTC, LN (83.5), Lns, Mil, NIC, WBC; KJV, NASB, NRSV, REB], 'wherever' [NJB], 'when' [NAB, NLT], 'in the case of' [LN (**89.5**); NIV, TEV, TNT], not explicit [CEV].

b. διαθήκη (LN **57.124**) (BAGD 1. p. 183): 'testament' [HNTC, LN, Lns, Mil; KJV, NAB, REB], 'will' [**LN**, Mil; CEV, NIV, NJB, NLT, NRSV, TEV, TNT], 'last will and testament' [BAGD], 'testamentary covenant' [NIC], 'covenant' [WBC; NASB].

c. ἀνάγκη (LN 71.30) (BAGD 1. p. 52): 'necessity' [Lns; NASB], 'necessary obligation, complete obligation, obligation' [LN]. This noun is also translated as an adjective: '(it is) necessary' [Mil, NIC, WBC; NAB, NIV, REB, TEV], '(it is) essential' [HNTC]; as a verb: 'must' [NJB, NRSV, TNT]. The phrase θάνατον ἀνάγκη 'there is a necessity for the death' is translated 'the death . . . must' [BAGD]. The phrase θάνατον ἀνάγκη φέρεσθαι 'there is a necessity for the death to be brought in' is translated 'there must also of necessity be the death' [KJV], 'it is proved that . . . is dead' [NLT], 'must die before it is of any use' [CEV]. It refers to inherent necessity [NIGTC].

d. aorist mid. participle (deponent = act.) of διατίθημι (LN 57.123) (BAGD 3. p. 190): 'to make a will' [BAGD, LN]. The participle τοῦ διαθεμένου 'the one having made the testament/will/covenant' is translated 'the testator' [BAGD, HNTC, Lns, NIC; KJV, NAB, NJB, REB], 'the one who made the will/testament' [Mil], 'the one who made/makes the will' [CEV, NIV, NRSV, TNT], 'the person who made the will' [TEV], 'the person who wrote the will' [NLT], 'the one who made the covenant' [NASB], 'the one who ratifies (the covenant)' [WBC].

e. pres. pass. infin. of φέρω (LN 70.5) (BAGD 4.a.β. p. 855): 'to be brought in' [Lns], 'to be brought forward' [WBC], 'to be established' [BAGD, HNTC, Mil; NJB, NRSV, REB], 'to be confirmed' [NAB], 'to be proved' [NLT, TNT], 'to be registered' [NIC], 'to be shown actually' [LN], 'to be shown that something happened, to be demonstrated that something was real' [LN]. This passive verb is also translated as active: 'to prove' [NIV, TEV]; as a stative verb: 'to be' [KJV, NASB]. It means 'to be implied' [Alf], 'to be brought in' [Blm, Wst], 'to be registered' [GNC], 'to be announced' [ICC, Lg(K), My, NTC], 'to be established' [Hwt, NIGTC], 'to be proved' [My].

QUESTION—What relationship is indicated by γάρ 'for'?

It indicates the grounds for the reference in 9:15 to a death having occurred [Alf, Mil, My, WBC].

QUESTION—What is meant by διαθήκη 'testament/will/covenant'?

1. Here this word refers to a testamentary will [Alf, EBC, GNC, Hu, Hwt, ICC, Lg, My, NIC, NIGTC, NTC, TH, TNTC; all versions except NASB]. The absence of the definite article implies that this is a different kind of διαθήκη than in the preceding verse, where it is a 'covenant' [NIGTC].
2. It refers to a covenant [EGT, WBC, Wst; NASB].

QUESTION—What is meant by θάνατον 'death'?

1. For those who treat διαθήκη as 'will' or 'testament', it refers to the death of the person who made the will [Alf, EBC, GNC, HNTC, Hu, Hwt, ICC, Lg, Lns, Mil, My, NCBC, NIGTC, NTC, TH, TNTC; all versions except NASB]. It is emphatic by forefronting [Alf, My], and is therefore definite without the article [Alf].
2. For those who treat διαθήκη as 'covenant'.

2.1 It refers to the sacrificial death of animals in sealing a covenant [EGT, WBC, Wst].

2.2 It refers to the death of the person who made the covenant [NASB].

9:17 for a testament/will/covenant[a] (is) firm[b] over[c] dead (persons),

LEXICON—a. διαθήκη: 'testament/will/covenant'. See this word in 9:16.

b. βέβαιος (LN 71.15) (BAGD 2. p. 138): 'firm', 'valid' [BAGD, HNTC, Mil, NIC; NASB, TNT], 'certain, sure' [LN], 'made legally secure' [WBC], 'of force' [KJV]. This adjective is also translated as a verb: 'to take effect' [NRSV, REB], 'to come into effect' [NJB], 'to go into effect' [CEV, NLT, TEV], 'to come into force' [NAB], 'to be in force' [Lns; NIV].

c. ἐπί with dative object (LN 89.13, 90.23) (BAGD II.1.b.γ. p. 287): 'over', 'on the basis of' [BAGD, LN (89.13); WBC], 'in view of' [LN (89.13)], 'concerning, with respect to, with reference to' [LN (90.23)], 'in case of' [Lns], 'in the case of' [NAB], not explicit [CEV]. The phrase ἐπὶ νεκροῖς 'over dead persons' is translated 'after men are dead' [Mil; KJV], 'when men are dead' [NASB], 'when somebody has died' [NIV], 'when a death has occurred' [REB], 'when death has taken place' [NIC], 'after death' [HNTC; TNT], 'after a death' [NJB], 'after his death' [TEV], 'at death' [NRSV], 'only after the death of the person who wrote it' [NLT]. This phrase tells the manner in which the testament comes into effect [Mil]. It indicates basis or time [NIGTC]. It expresses accompanying conditions [Wst].

QUESTION—What relationship is indicated by γάρ?

It explains the statement of 9:16 [Alf, Mil, My]. This verse restates (clarifies and expands [WBC]) the thought of 9:16 [NIGTC, TNTC, WBC].

QUESTION—To whom or what does νεκροῖς 'dead' refer?

The plural here has the same sense as the following generic singular διαθέμενος 'the one having made the testament' [NIGTC].

1. It refers to the death of persons making a testament or will [GNC, HNTC, Hu, Hwt, Lns, My, NCBC, NIC, TNTC; CEV, NLT, TEV].

2. It refers to the dead bodies of victims killed to validate covenants [EGT, WBC, Wst].

since[a] not-ever[b] is-it-valid[c] when the-(one) having-made-the-testament[d] is-living.

TEXT—Instead of μήποτε 'not ever' some manuscripts read μὴ τότε 'not then'. GNT reads μήποτε 'not ever' with an A decision, indicating that the text is certain. None of the versions or commentaries read μὴ τότε 'not then'.

LEXICON—a. ἐπεί (LN 89.32) (BAGD 2. p. 284): 'since' [BAGD, HNTC, LN, Lns, Mil, WBC; NJB, NRSV, TNT], 'because' [BAGD, LN], 'for' [BAGD, LN; NASB, TEV], 'otherwise' [KJV], not explicit [NIC; CEV, NAB, NIV, NLT, REB]. It introduces the negative parallel to the preceding clause, not a reason for it [NIGTC].

b. μήποτε (LN 67.10) (BAGD 1. p. 519): 'not ever' [LN, Lns], 'never' [BAGD, HNTC, LN, Mil, WBC; NASB, NIV, TNT], 'not' [CEV, NRSV], 'no' [NAB, NJB, REB]. The phrase μήποτε ἰσχύει 'not ever is it valid' is translated 'it is of no strength at all' [KJV], 'it means nothing' [TEV], 'no one can use the will to get any of the things promised them' [NLT]. It is translated as a question: 'has it ever any force?' [NIC]. This word means 'never' [ICC, My]; it is a strong negative [NIGTC, WBC]. It is not emphatic but softening, with the sense of 'see whether it may not be' [Lg(K)]. The use of μήποτε 'not ever' instead of οὔποτε (same translation) shows that the author expected debate on the validity of a will [NTC].

c. pres. act. indic. of ἰσχύω (BAGD 4. p. 384): 'to be valid' [BAGD, WBC], 'to take effect' [NIV], 'to be in effect' [Lns], 'to go into effect' [CEV], 'to be in force' [Mil; NASB, NRSV], 'to have force' [HNTC, NIC; NAB, NJB, REB, TNT], 'to be of strength' [KJV].

d. aorist mid. (deponent = act.) of διατίθημι: 'to make a will'. See this word in 9:16.

QUESTION—What is the form of this clause?

1. It is a statement [Alf, EGT, HNTC, Hu, ICC, Lg, Lns, Mil, My(D), NIGTC, WBC; all versions]; it is not valid.
2. It is a question [EBC, NIC]: is it valid?

QUESTION—What is the implied subject of ἰσχύει 'it is valid'?

The implied subject is διαθήκη 'testament' [Alf, My; all versions]; the testament is valid.

9:18 From-which[a] not-even the first was-inaugurated[b] without[c] blood;

LEXICON—a. ὅθεν (LN 84.11, 89.25) (BAGD 3. p. 555): 'from which' [LN (84.11)], 'because of (this)' [LN (89.25)], 'therefore' [BAGD, NIC; NASB], 'hence' [BAGD, Lns; NAB, NRSV], 'whereupon' [KJV], 'this is why' [WBC; NIV], 'that is why' [HNTC; NJB, NLT, TEV, TNT], 'for which reason' [Mil], not explicit [CEV, REB].

b. perf. pass. indic. of ἐγκαινίζω (LN 13.84) (BAGD 2. p. 215): 'to be inaugurated' [BAGD, HNTC, Lns, Mil; NAB, NASB, NJB, NRSV, REB,

TNT], 'to be dedicated' [BAGD; KJV], 'to be put into effect' [LN; CEV, NIV], 'to be put into force, to be established' [LN], 'to be ratified' [NIC], 'to be confirmed' [WBC]. This passive verb is also translated as active voice: 'to go into effect' [TEV]. The phrase οὐδὲ χωρὶς αἵματος ἐγκεκαίνισται 'not even was inaugurated without blood' is translated 'even was inaugurated with blood' [NJB], 'blood was required as a proof of death' [NLT]. It refers to the first inauguration of the Mosaic law [Alf]. It means 'to be inaugurated' [Lg(K), My], which means to be introduced in a valid manner [My], 'to ratify' [Blm]. The perfect tense indicates the permanent character [WBC], the enduring effect [Lns] from the time of Moses to the time of the new covenant [NTC], the permanent record in scripture [NIGTC]; it implies that the rites referred to were still existing [Alf, Lg(K)]; it refers merely to the past event, like the aorist tense [EGT].

c. χωρίς (LN 89.120) (BAGD 2.b.β. p. 890): 'without' [BAGD, HNTC, LN, Lns, Mil, NIC, WBC; all versions except NJB, TEV], 'apart from' [LN], 'with the use of' [TEV].

QUESTION—What relationship is indicated by ὅθεν 'from which'?

1. It indicates the conclusion that death is necessary in order to make the will/covenant valid (9:16–17) [Alf, Mil, My, WBC, Wst].
2. It further illustrates the principle that death is necessary to make a will valid (9:15) [Blm, EBC, NTC]. Verses 9:16–17 are parenthetical [NTC].

QUESTION—To what does ἡ πρώτη 'the first' refer?

It refers to the first διαθήκη 'testament/will/covenant' [Blm, EBC, EGT, GNC, Hu, Hwt, ICC, Lg, Lns, Mil, My, NCBC, NIGTC, NTC, TH, TNTC, WBC, Wst; all versions].

1. This word here returns to the meaning 'covenant' [EBC, GNC, HNTC, Hu, Hwt, ICC, Mil, NCBC, NIGTC, NTC, TH; all versions except KJV, NASB]. The author shows that death was necessary for a covenant as well as for a testament/will to become valid [EBC, GNC, HNTC].
2. This word continues to mean 'covenant' [EGT, WBC, Wst; NASB].
3. This word continues to mean 'testament' [KJV].

QUESTION—What is meant by αἵματος 'blood'?

It implies death [EGT, TH], shedding blood in offering a sacrifice [Hu, NIGTC].

9:19 for having-been-spoken every commandment according-to[a] the Law[b] by[c] Moses to-all the people,

LEXICON—a. κατά with accusative object (LN 89.8): 'according to' [Lns, Mil; KJV, NASB], 'in accordance with' [LN, NIC; NRSV], 'in relation to' [LN], 'as set forth in' [REB, TEV], 'of' [HNTC, WBC; NAB, NIV, NJB, TNT]. The phrase πάσης ἐντολῆς κατὰ τὸν νόμον 'every commandment according to the Law' is translated 'all of God's laws' [NLT], 'all that the Law said they must do' [CEV].

b. νόμος (LN 33.55) (BAGD 4.a. p. 543): 'Law' [HNTC, LN, Lns; NASB, NJB, TEV, TNT], 'law' [BAGD, Mil, NIC, WBC; KJV, NAB, NIV, NRSV, REB].

c. ὑπό with genitive object (LN 90.1): 'by' [HNTC, LN, Lns, Mil, NIC, WBC; NASB, NRSV, TNT]. The phrase λαληθείσης ὑπὸ Μωϋσέως 'having been spoken by Moses' is translated 'when Moses had spoken' [KJV], 'when Moses had proclaimed' [NIV], 'when Moses had told' [REB], 'when Moses had read' [NAB], 'after Moses had given' [NLT], 'after Moses had promulgated' [NJB], 'first, Moses proclaimed' [TEV], 'Moses told' [CEV].

QUESTION—What relationship is indicated by γάρ 'for'?

1. It explains the comment in the preceding verse [Alf, Blm, Lns].
2. It indicates the grounds for the preceding verse [Mil, NIGTC].

QUESTI0N—What relationship is indicated by the participial form λαληθείσης 'having been spoken'?

1. It is temporal [Blm, HNTC, Lg(K), Lns, Mil, My, NCBC, NIC, TNTC, WBC, Wst; all versions except TEV]: when it had been spoken.
2. It indicates an action of the same mood as the following verb ἐράντισεν 'he sprinkled' [TEV]: he proclaimed . . . and he sprinkled.

QUESTION—What is the phrase κατὰ τὸν νόμον 'according to the law' connected with?

1. It is connected with ἐντολῆς 'commandment' [EGT, HNTC, TNTC, WBC; NAB, NIV, NJB, REB, TEV, TNT]: every commandment according to the law.
2. It is connected with λαληθείσης 'having been spoken' [Alf, Mil, My, NIC, NIGTC, Wst; KJV, NASB, NRSV]: having been spoken according to the law.

having-taken the blood of-the calves and of-the goats with[a] water and scarlet[b] wool and hyssop,[c]

TEXT—Instead of τῶν μόσχων καὶ τῶν τράγων 'of the calves and the goats' some manuscripts reverse the order of the nouns, and other manuscripts read only τῶν μόσχων 'of the calves'. GNT reads 'of the calves and the goats' with a C decision, indicating that the committee had difficulty in making the decision. 'Goats and calves' is read by NAB; 'calves' is read by EBC, Hu, NIC, WBC, NIV, REB, and TNT.

LEXICON—a. μετά with genitive object (LN 89.109): 'with' [HNTC, LN, Mil, NIC; CEV, KJV, NASB, NRSV, REB, TNT], 'together with' [Lns, WBC; NAB, NIV], 'along with' [NLT], 'mixed with' [TEV], 'and some' [NJB]. It indicates the additional objects used [Mil].

b. κόκκινος (LN 79.29) (BAGD p. 440): 'scarlet' [BAGD, HNTC, LN, Lns, Mil, NIC; all versions except CEV, NAB, TEV], 'crimson' [WBC; NAB], 'red' [BAGD, LN; CEV, TEV].

c. ὕσσωπος (LN 3.26) (BAGD p. 849): 'hyssop' [BAGD, LN, Lns, Mil, NIC, WBC; all versions except CEV, NLT, REB], 'hyssop plant' [CEV], 'branches of hyssop bushes' [NLT], 'marjoram' [HNTC; REB].

QUESTION—What relationship is indicated by the participial form λαβών 'having taken'?

It indicates an action of the same mood as the following verb ἐράντισεν 'he sprinkled' [HNTC, Hwt, Mil, NIC; all versions]: he took the blood and sprinkled with water.

QUESTION—How are the nouns related in the genitive construction τὸ αἷμα τῶν μόσχων καὶ τῶν τράγων 'the blood of the calves and of the goats'?

'Calves' and 'goats' are the source of the 'blood' [Mil].

he-sprinkled both the scroll[a] itself and all the people,

LEXICON—a. βιβλίον (LN 33.52) (BAGD 1. p. 141): 'scroll' [BAGD, HNTC; NIV, NRSV, TNT], 'book' [BAGD, LN, Lns, Mil, NIC, WBC; KJV, NAB, NASB, NJB], 'law book' [REB], 'book of the Law' [CEV, TEV], 'book of God's laws' [NLT]. It refers to the scroll from which Moses had read the commandments [Alf, EGT, ICC], the scroll of the covenant [My].

QUESTION—What is the phrase αὐτὸ τὸ βιβλίον 'the scroll itself' connected with?

It is connected with ἐράντισεν 'he sprinkled' [Alf, Blm, EBC, EGT, GNC, HNTC, Hu, Hwt, ICC, Lns, Mil, My, NIC, NIGTC, NTC, TNTC, WBC, Wst; all versions]: he sprinkled the scroll itself. Αὐτό 'itself' is emphatic [NIGTC].

QUESTION—What relationship is indicated by the phrase πάντα τὸν λαόν 'all the people'?

It does not mean every individual, but the crowd in general [Alf].

9:20 saying, "This (is) the blood of-the covenant[a] which God has-commanded[b] to/for[c] you."

LEXICON—a. διαθήκη: 'covenant'. See this word in 9:16.

b. aorist mid. (deponent = act.) indic. of ἐντέλλομαι (LN 33.329) (BAGD p. 268): 'to command' [HNTC, LN, Mil; NASB, NIV, REB, TEV, TNT], 'to enjoin' [NIC, WBC; KJV, NAB], 'to ordain' [BAGD; NRSV], 'to make' [CEV, NJB, NLT], 'to design' [Lns]. This verb indicates that God has specified the terms of the covenant [EBC].

c. πρός with accusative object (LN 90.58): 'to' [LN, Mil], 'unto' [KJV], 'for' [Lns; NRSV], 'with' [LN; CEV, NJB, NLT], 'on' [NIC], 'upon' [WBC; NAB], not explicit [HNTC; NASB, NIV, REB, TEV, TNT]. It indicates direction [Mil].

QUESTION—What relationship is indicated by the participial form λέγων 'saying'?

It expresses an additional circumstance to the principal verb [Mil, TH]: he sprinkled with water and, in addition, he said. It serves as a speech orienter to the following quotation [Mil]. Moses is speaking here as a participant in the account, not as the author of the OT book [NIGTC].

QUESTION—How are the two nouns related in the genitive construction τὸ αἷμα τῆς διαθήκης 'the blood of the covenant'?

'Covenant' receives the action; the 'blood' seals the 'covenant' [Mil, NIGTC, NTC, TH]: the blood inaugurates the covenant. The definite article with 'blood' indicates that it is the same as the blood mentioned in the preceding verse [Mil].

QUESTION—What is meant by ἐντείλατο πρός 'commanded to/for'?

1. It means that God has commanded them to obey it [HNTC, NIC, NTC, TH, WBC; KJV, NAB, NASB, NIV, REB, TEV, TNT].
2. It means that God has made a covenant with them [Blm, Lns, Mil; CEV, NJB, NLT, NRSV].

9:21 And the tent/tabernacle[a] and all the vessels[b] of-the divine-service[c] likewise[d] he-sprinkled with-the blood.

LEXICON—a. σκηνή (LN 7.17) (BAGD p. 754): 'tent' [BAGD, HNTC, LN, NIC; CEV, NJB, NRSV, REB, TNT], 'tabernacle' [BAGD, Lns, Mil, WBC; KJV, NAB, NASB, NIV], 'tabernacle tent' [LN], 'Sacred Tent' [NLT, TEV].

b. σκεῦος (LN 6.1, 6.118) (BAGD 1.a. p. 754): 'vessel' [HNTC, LN (6.118), Mil, NIC, WBC; KJV, NAB, NASB, NJB, NRSV, REB], 'utensil' [Lns], 'equipment' [BAGD], 'thing' [LN (6.1); TEV, TNT], 'object' [LN (6.1)]. The phrase πάντα τὰ σκεύη 'all the vessels' is translated 'everything' [NIV], 'everything else' [CEV, NLT].

c. λειτουργία (LN 53.13) (BAGD 1. p. 471): 'divine service' [HNTC, NIC; REB], 'divine worship' [Mil], 'worship' [CEV, NAB, NLT, NRSV, TEV, TNT], 'ministry' [KJV, NASB], 'the performance of religious rites' [LN], 'priestly service' [BAGD], 'official service' [Lns]. This noun is also translated as an adjective: 'liturgical' [NJB], 'cultic' [WBC]; this singular noun is translated as a plural: 'ceremonies' [NIV].

d. ὁμοίως (LN 64.1): 'likewise' [LN, Lns, WBC; KJV], 'similarly' [LN], 'in the same way' [HNTC, Mil, NIC; all versions except CEV, KJV, NAB], 'also' [CEV], not explicit [NAB]. This word does not imply 'at the same time' as the event in 9:19–20, since the tabernacle was erected much later [EBC].

QUESTION—How is this verse related to the preceding verses?

1. It relates to the dedication of the Tabernacle at a much later time than the event referred to in 9:19–20 [Alf, Blm, EBC, EGT, Hu, Lg, Lns, Mil, My, NIC, NTC].
2. It appears to be a generalized reference, referring to the first covenant but adding details from other OT passages [NCBC, NIGTC].

QUESTION—How are the two nouns related in the genitive construction τὰ σκεύη τῆς λειτουργίας 'the vessels of the divine service'?

1. The genitive noun 'divine service' tells how the 'vessels' were used [Mil, My; CEV, NIV, NLT, NRSV, TEV, TNT]: the vessels used in divine service.

2. The genitive noun 'divine service' is used adjectivally to describe the 'vessels' [WBC; NJB]: the liturgical vessels.

QUESTION—What relationship is indicated by τῷ αἵματι 'with the blood'?

It indicates means [Mil]: by means of the blood. The definite article indicates that this was the blood of the covenant [Wst].

9:22 And nearly everything is-cleansed[a] by[b] blood according-to[c] the law

LEXICON—a. pres. pass. indic. of καθαρίζω (LN 53.28) (BAGD 2.c. p. 387): 'to be cleansed' [BAGD, HNTC, LN, Lns, Mil, NIC; NASB, NIV, REB], 'to be purified' [BAGD, LN; NAB, NLT, NRSV, TEV, TNT], 'to be made clean' [BAGD, LN], 'to be purged' [WBC; KJV], 'to be sprinkled' [CEV]. The phrase πάντα καθαρίζεται 'everything is cleansed' is translated 'every purification takes place' [NJB]. The present tense shows that it refers to the Mosaic law in general [NIGTC].

b. ἐν with dative object (LN 89.76) (BAGD III.1.a. p. 260): 'by' [LN; NAB, NLT, REB, TEV, TNT], 'by means of' [LN], 'with' [HNTC, Mil, NIC, WBC; CEV, KJV, NASB, NIV, NRSV], 'in connection with' [Lns]. It indicates means [BAGD; Mil], instrument [EGT, Mil], location [WBC, Wst].

c. κατά with accusative object (LN 89.8): 'according to' [HNTC, Lns, NIC, WBC; NAB, NASB, NJB, NLT, TEV], 'in accordance with' [LN], 'in conformity with' [Mil], 'by' [KJV], 'under' [NRSV, REB, TNT]. It expresses manner [Mil]. The phrase κατὰ τὸν νόμον 'according to the law' is translated 'the law requires' [NIV], 'the Law says' [CEV].

QUESTION—What relationship is indicated by καί 'and'?

It introduces two general statements related to (summarizing [WBC]) the preceding specific statements of 9:18–21 [Mil, WBC]. It confirms those statements by a general principle [My].

QUESTION—What is σχεδόν 'almost' connected with?

1. It is connected with πάντα 'everything' [EBC, HNTC, Hu, Hwt, ICC, Lg, Lns, NCBC, NIC, NIGTC, NTC; CEV, KJV, NAB, NIV, NJB, NLT, NRSV, TEV]: almost everything.
2. It is connected with an implied verb 'to say' [Alf, EGT, Lg(K), Mil, My, TNTC, WBC; NASB, REB, TNT]: one may almost say. It is forefronted to relate to the whole first statement [Mil].

and without[a] blood-shedding[b] forgiveness[c] does-not occur.[d]

LEXICON—a. χωρίς with genitive object (LN 89.120) (BAGD 2.b.β. p. 890): 'without' [HNTC, LN, Mil, WBC; all versions except CEV, NJB, TEV], 'without making use of' [BAGD], 'apart from' [Lns, NIC], 'if there is no' [NJB]. This entire phrase is translated 'and sins are forgiven only if blood is poured out' [TEV], 'and no sin can be forgiven unless blood is offered' [CEV].

b. αἱματεκχυσία (LN **23.183**) (BAGD p. 23): 'blood-shedding' [Lns, Mil], 'shedding of blood' [BAGD, NIC; KJV, NAB, NASB, NIV, NJB, NLT, NRSV, REB, TNT], 'outpouring of blood' [HNTC], 'the flow of blood'

[LN], 'the application of blood' [WBC]. This is also translated as a verb phrase: 'blood is offered' [CEV], 'blood is poured out' [TEV], 'blood is caused to flow' [**LN**]. It refers to the blood-shedding in death [Alf, EGT, ICC, Lg(K), My, NTC]; it refers to pouring out the blood on the altar [WBC]; it refers both to the death and to pouring out the blood on the altar [TH, TNTC, Wst].

c. ἄφεσις (LN 40.8) (BAGD 2. p. 125): 'forgiveness' [BAGD, LN, NIC; NAB, NASB, NIV, REB], 'forgiveness of sins' [NLT, NRSV], 'remitting of sins' [TNT], 'remission of sins' [HNTC], 'remission' [Lns, Mil; KJV, NJB], 'definitive purgation' [WBC]. This noun is also translated as a verb: 'to be forgiven' [CEV, TEV]. It refers to the forgiveness of sins [HNTC, ICC, Lns, NTC; NRSV, TNT]; it includes the partial forgiveness provided by the OT sacrifices [TNTC]; it refers to putting away defilement [WBC], to release from the bondage which results in doing wrong [Wst]. It is emphatic by its final position [NIGTC, TH].

d. pres. mid. (deponent = act.) of γίνομαι (LN 13.107): 'to occur' [LN, Lns], 'to happen' [LN], 'to take place' [Mil], 'to be' [HNTC, NIC, WBC; all versions except TEV]. It means 'to take place' [NIGTC]. It implies the operation of God's law [Wst].

QUESTION—How is this clause related to the preceding clause?

1. For some who connect σχεδόν 'almost' with an understood verb 'to say', it is a continuation of what might almost be said [Alf, Mil, My; TNT]: and one might also say that . . .
2. It is primarily a further reference to what occurs 'according to the law' [HNTC, Hwt, ICC, NCBC, TH, TNTC, Wst]: and according to the law . . .
3. It is a general principle which has a broader application than merely under the OT law [Hu, NIC, NIGTC, WBC]: and it is a general truth that . . .

QUESTION—How is this clause related to σχεδόν 'almost' in the preceding clause?

1. It is not governed by σχεδόν 'almost' [HNTC, Lns, NCBC, NIGTC, NTC, WBC, Wst].
2. It is governed by σχεδόν 'almost' [Alf, Hwt, Mil, My].

DISCOURSE UNIT: 9:23–10:39 [REB]. The topic is Jesus as the final sacrifice.

DISCOURSE UNIT: 9:23–10:18 [GNT; CEV, TEV]. The topic is Christ's sacrifice taking away sins [GNT; TEV], Christ's great sacrifice [CEV].

DISCOURSE UNIT: 9:23–28 [EBC, GNC, HNTC, Lg, NCBC, NIC, NTC]. The topic is purification by better sacrifices [NCBC], the perfect sacrifice [EBC, NIC], Christ's perfect sacrifice [NTC], Christ's sacrifice [HNTC], Christ's work as the final answer to sin [GNC], Christ's once-for-all death as the adequate propitiation [Lg].

9:23 **(There was) a-necessity,[a] then/therefore,[b] on-the-one-hand, (for) the copies[c] of-the (things) in[d] the heavens to-be-cleansed[e] by/with-these (things),**

LEXICON—a. ἀνάγκη (LN 71.30) (BAGD 1. p. 52): 'necessity' [Lns], 'obligation, complete obligation, necessary obligation' [LN], 'only' [NJB], '(they) must' [BAGD], '(they) had to' [CEV, NLT, TEV], 'if (they) required' [REB]. This word is also translated '(it was) necessary' [HNTC, Mil, WBC; KJV, NAB, NASB, NIV, NRSV, TNT]. The phrase ἀνάγκη καθαρίζεσθαι 'there was a necessity to be cleansed' is translated 'if (they) are necessarily cleansed' [NIC]. It is emphatic by its word order [NTC, TH]. It was necessary because there was no other way [EBC], the OT law required it [NTC, TH], blood is God's requirement for purification [Wst].

b. οὖν (LN 89.50): 'then' [HNTC, LN, Lns, NIC, WBC; NIV, REB], 'therefore' [LN, Mil; KJV, NASB], 'so' [LN; CEV], 'so then, consequently, accordingly' [LN], 'thus' [NRSV], 'that is why' [NLT], not explicit [NAB, NJB, TEV, TNT]. It introduces the conclusion to the comment in 9:22 (9:18–22 [My, NCBC]) [Alf, EBC, EGT, Mil, NCBC] that blood is necessary for forgiveness [My]. It summarizes the preceding comments [TH]. It picks up the thought from 9:14, 9:15–22 being a parenthesis [TNTC]. It elaborates on the comment in 9:11–12 but presupposes 9:15–22 as well [WBC, Wst]. The first clause is the result of 9:18–22 and the second is the conclusion from the first clause [My]; the first clause is the minor conclusion which introduces the second clause, and the second clause, the major conclusion [Alf, EGT, My]. It is merely transitional in meaning [Lns].

c. ὑπόδειγμα (LN 58.59) (BAGD 2. p. 844): 'copy' [BAGD, HNTC, Lns, Mil, NIC; CEV, NAB, NASB, NIV, NJB, NLT, TEV, TNT], 'example, model' [LN], 'pattern' [KJV], 'sketch' [NRSV], 'imitation' [BAGD], 'symbol' [REB], 'suggestion' [WBC]. It means a copy [Lg(K), Lns], a representation [Alf]. It refers to the earthly tabernacle and its furnishings [Blm, EGT, Hu, My, NTC].

d. ἐν with dative object (LN 83.13): 'in' [LN, Lns, Mil, WBC; CEV, KJV, NASB, NLT]. The phrase ἐν τοῖς οὐρανοῖς 'in the heavens' is translated 'heavenly' [HNTC, NIC; all versions except KJV, NASB].

e. pres. pass. infin. of καθαρίζω: 'to be cleansed'. See this word in 9:22.

QUESTION—What verb is to be supplied in this clause?

1. "Was" is to be supplied [Lg; KJV, NAB, NASB, NRSV, TNT], since the statement relates to the past [Alf, TNTC]: there was a necessity.
2. "Is" is to be supplied [NJB], since the author is speaking universally [My]: there is a necessity.

QUESTION—To what does τῶν ἐν τοῖς οὐρανοῖς 'of the things in the heavens' refer?

It refers to the heavenly tabernacle [Alf, My] and its contents [Alf], the heavenly counterparts to the earthly tabernacle [TNTC].

QUESTION—To what does τούτοις 'these things' refer?

It refers to the things mentioned in 9:19 [TH], to the OT tabernacle and its vessels [NIGTC], to the various purification rites of the OT [My], to the sprinkling of blood (of the bulls and goats [Alf, Blm, Wst]) in the OT ceremonies [Alf, Blm, Mil, Wst]. The plural refers to the plurality of animals sacrificed [Alf].

but the heavenly-things themselves by/with-better[a] sacrifices than[b] these.

LEXICON—a. κρείττων (LN 65.21, 87.28) (BAGD 1. p. 449): 'better' [BAGD, HNTC, LN (65.21, 87.28), Lns, Mil, NIC, WBC; CEV, KJV, NAB, NASB, NIV, NLT, NRSV, TNT], 'still better' [REB], 'much better' [TEV], 'superior' [LN (65.21)], 'greater' [LN (87.28)], 'a higher sort' [NJB].

b. παρά with accusative object (LN 78.29) (BAGD III.3. p. 611): 'than' [HNTC, LN, Lns, Mil, NIC, WBC; KJV, NASB, NIV, NJB, NLT, NRSV, TNT], 'more than, in comparison to' [BAGD], 'beyond' [BAGD, LN], not explicit [CEV, NAB, REB, TEV].

QUESTION—What verb is to be supplied in this clause?

1. It is the same verb as in the first clause, καθαρίζεσθαι 'to be cleansed' [NCBC, NIC, Wst]: to be cleansed by better sacrifices.
2. It is the concept of being consecrated to God's service [My]: to be consecrated by better sacrifices. It refers to the opening of the heavenly sanctuary to access by mankind [My]. The verb is not repeated, probably because the parallel idea for the heavenly realities is not cleansing but the related idea of inauguration.
3. It is the same verb as in the first clause, but with the sense of consecration and inauguration rather than removing impurity [NIGTC].

QUESTION—To what does τὰ ἐπουράνια 'the heavenly things' refer?

This word refers to the same thing as τῶν ἐν τοῖς οὐρανοῖς 'the things in the heavens' in the preceding clause [My, WBC]. The suffix of this adjective indicates that this word means 'related to heaven'.

1. It is not to be taken literally, but simply means the ultimate reality, the spiritual sphere where atonement is completed [GNC, Hwt].
2. It refers to the heavenly worship system by which mankind's conscience is cleansed [HNTC]. It refers to the consciences of the people, who are the temple of God, which need cleansing [NCBC, NIC].
3. It refers to the heavenly sanctuary [Lg, Lns, Mil, My, WBC].
3.1 It needs to be cleansed from the influence of human sin upon it [Lg, Mil, WBC, Wst].
3.2 It needs to be cleansed because, like the earthly sanctuary, it serves sinners; the cleansing does not remove defilement from the sanctuary, but enables it to serve sinners without becoming defiled itself [Lns].
4. It refers to heaven itself [ICC] and the things in it [Alf, EGT], which need cleansing because they are entered by sinful mankind [EGT].

5. It refers to the approach to heaven [Blm]; Christ's sacrifice opened heaven as a sanctuary for mankind [NTC].
6. It refers to spiritual forces of evil beyond the earth [EBC].

QUESTION—To what does κρείττοσιν θυσίαις 'better sacrifices' refer?

It refers to spiritual sacrifices [EGT], the blood of Christ [Blm].

QUESTION—What is implied by the plural θυσίαις 'sacrifices'?

It is a carry-over from the preceding plural sacrifices referred to by τούτοις 'these' [EGT, GNC, Hu, WBC], a generic plural [EBC, Hu, Lg, Lns, My, NIC, NIGTC, Wst], the plural of an abstraction [Alf, EGT]. It means a better kind of sacrifice [TH]; it means that Christ's one sacrifice fulfills the many OT sacrifices [TNTC]. It refers only to Christ's one sacrifice [Alf, EBC, GNC, Hu, Lns, My, NIC, NTC, TNTC, WBC, Wst].

9:24 For not into[a] (a) handmade[b] sanctuary[c] Christ entered, antitypes[d] of-the true,[e]

LEXICON—a. εἰς with accusative object (LN 84.22): 'into' [HNTC, LN, Lns, Mil, NIC; CEV, KJV, NAB, NLT, TEV, TNT], not explicit [WBC; NASB, NIV, NJB, NRSV, REB].

b. χειροποίητος (LN 42.32) (BAGD p. 881): 'handmade' [Lns], 'man-made' [LN; NIV, NJB], 'made with hands' [NIC, WBC; KJV, NASB], 'made by hands' [Mil; NAB], 'made by men's hands' [TNT], 'made by human hands' [BAGD, HNTC, LN; NRSV, REB, TEV], 'built by human hands' [LN], 'made by humans' [CEV], 'earthly' [NLT]. It refers to the earthly OT holy of holies [Alf, Blm]. It is emphatic by its word order [My, Wst].

c. ἅγια (the plural of the adjective ἅγιος) (LN **7.18**. 7.35) (BAGD 2.b. p. 10): 'sanctuary' [BAGD, HNTC, LN (**7.18**), Lns, WBC; NAB, NIV, NJB, NRSV, REB, TNT], 'holy place' [Mil, NIC; NASB], 'Holy Place' [LN (7.35); TEV], 'holy places' [KJV], 'tent' [CEV], 'place of worship' [NLT].

d. ἀντίτυπος (LN **58.69**) (BAGD 2. p. 76): 'antitype' [LN], 'type' [Lns], 'copy' [BAGD, HNTC, NIC; CEV, NAB, NASB, NIV, NLT, NRSV, TEV, TNT], 'representative copy' [Mil], 'model' [NJB], 'figure' [KJV], 'representation' [LN, WBC], 'correspondence' [LN], 'pointer' [REB]. This noun is also translated as a participle: 'corresponding' [**LN**]. It is plural in form to agree with the preceding plural ἅγια 'sanctuary' [Lns]. It implies resemblance [Blm], a copy of the reality in heaven [EBC, GNC, HNTC, ICC, Lns, NTC, TNTC, Wst], a type [EGT, Hu]. It means a copy formed according to the pattern shown to Moses by God [My].

e. ἀληθινός (LN 73.2) (BAGD 3. p. 37): 'true' [BAGD, LN, Lns, Mil, NIC, WBC; KJV, NAB, NASB, NIV, NRSV], 'genuine' [LN], 'real' [HNTC; CEV, NJB, NLT, TEV, TNT]. This adjective is also translated as a noun: 'reality' [REB]. It means 'authentic' [Hu].

QUESTION—Why is this clause mentioned?

It restates what was mentioned in 9:11–12 and has been expanded in the following verses up to now [Alf]. With the two following verses it summarizes and emphasizes the preceding points [NCBC]. It begins further arguments showing the value of Christ's sacrifice [Blm]. It confirms the preceding statement that the needed purification has actually occurred [Lg].

QUESTION—What relationship is indicated by γάρ 'for'?

1. It explains (continues [Alf, Hu], develops [NIGTC]) the preceding reference [EBC] to τὰ ἐπουράνια 'the heavenly things' in 9:23 [Alf, EGT, Hu, Mil, My, NIGTC].
2. It explains why Christ's sacrificial blood was necessary [Lns].
3. It indicates the grounds for the reference to purifying the heavenly things [Wst].

QUESTION—How is the genitive plural ἀληθινῶν 'true' related to the noun in the genitive construction ἀντίτυπα τῶν ἀληθινῶν 'antitypes of the true'?

1. 'True' is an objective genitive, indicating what is copied by the 'antitype': the true (sanctuary) is copied by the (earthly) antitype.
2. The 'antitype' points to the reality [REB]: it points to the real (sanctuary).

but into[a] the heaven itself, now to-appear[b] to-the face[c] of God on-behalf-of[d] us;

LEXICON—a. εἰς with accusative object: 'into'. See this word in the preceding clause.

b. aorist pass. infin. of ἐμφανίζω (LN 24.19) (BAGD 1.a. p. 257): 'to appear' [BAGD, HNTC, Lns, Mil, NIC, WBC; all versions except CEV], 'to become visible' [BAGD], 'to be seen' [LN], 'to be there' [CEV]. It refers to appearing as an advocate for mankind [Blm, HNTC, Hu, My] in a face-to-face relationship between God and Christ [Lg]. It implies a clear sight of what is normally not clear [Wst]. The infinitive expresses purpose [EGT, Mil, NIGTC]; the aorist tense refers to his whole intercession as a fact [Lns, TNTC], as one act [Wst].

c. πρόσωπον (LN 8.18, 85.26) (BAGD 1.b. p. 721): 'face' [BAGD, LN (8.18), Lns, Mil], 'countenance' [BAGD], 'presence' [HNTC, LN (85.26), NIC, WBC; KJV, NASB, NIV, NJB, NRSV, TEV, TNT]. The phrase τῷ προσώπῳ τοῦ θεοῦ 'to the face of God' is translated 'before God' [NAB, NLT, REB], 'with God' [CEV]. It implies full and direct sight [Wst].

d. ὑπέρ with genitive object (LN 90.36): 'on behalf of' [HNTC, LN, WBC; NAB, NJB, NRSV, REB, TEV, TNT], 'in behalf of' [Lns, Mil], 'for the sake of' [LN], 'for' [LN, NIC; KJV, NASB, NIV], 'as our Advocate' [NLT], 'to help' [CEV]. The prepositional phrase ὑπὲρ ἡμῶν 'in behalf of us' is emphatic by its final position in the clause [Lg].

QUESTION—What relationship is indicated by ἀλλά 'but'?

It indicates a strong contrast with the preceding clause [EBC]: not (this), on the contrary (this).

QUESTION—What is meant by αὐτὸν τὸν οὐρανόν 'heaven itself'?

It refers to the heavenly Holy of Holies [My], the uncreated holiest place, where God reveals himself [Alf], the presence of God [TNTC, WBC]; it is not a location [TNTC]. The singular form τὸν οὐρανόν 'heaven' refers to the highest heaven [WBC]; it indicates a definite locality [Wst].

QUESTION—What is implied by νῦν 'now'?

It indicates present activity [EBC, Mil, TNTC, Wst] for each believer [Wst] in the eternal timeless present [HNTC, Lg] as included in the infinitive ἐμφανισθῆναι 'to appear' [Lns]; it refers to Christ's continuing work following his completed work on earth [EBC, EGT, NIGTC] and obtaining his permanent place in heaven [My]. It is emphatic by its word order [ICC].

QUESTION—What relationship is indicated by the phrase τῷ προσώπῳ τοῦ θεοῦ 'the face of God'?

It implies that Christ stands face to face with God with no cloud or veil such as was in the OT sanctuary [EGT, Wst].

9:25 nor in-order-that/that many-times[a] he-should-offer himself,

LEXICON—a. πολλάκις (LN 67.11) (BAGD 1.a. p. 40): 'many times' [BAGD, LN, WBC; CEV, TEV], 'time after time' [HNTC], 'often' [BAGD, Lns; KJV, NASB], 'frequently' [BAGD, Mil], 'repeatedly' [NIC], 'again and again' [NAB, NIV, NJB, NLT, NRSV, REB, TNT].

QUESTION—What verb is to be supplied with οὐδέ 'nor'?

1. If ἵνα 'in order that/that' expresses purpose [Alf, EGT, HNTC, Lns, Mil, NIC, NTC, WBC, Wst; NIV, NLT, NRSV, REB, TEV, TNT].

1.1 The verb 'to be' is to be supplied [HNTC; NRSV].

1.1.1 The past tense [NRSV]: nor was it in order that he should offer himself.

1.1.2 The present tense [HNTC]: nor is he there in order to offer himself.

1.2 A verb of entering is to be supplied [EGT, Lns, Mil, NIC, NTC, WBC, Wst; NIV, TEV, TNT], carried over from this verb in the preceding verse [EGT, Lns, Mil, NIC, NTC, WBC, Wst]: nor did he enter in order to offer himself. He entered heaven [Lns, NTC, WBC; NIV].

1.3 The concept of purpose is to be supplied [REB]: it was not his purpose to offer himself.

2. If ἵνα 'in order that/that' expresses content, the concept of necessity is to be supplied [NJB]: nor was it necessary that he should offer himself.

QUESTION—To what does προσφέρῃ 'he should offer' refer?

1. It refers to Christ's death on the cross [ICC, Lg(K), My, NTC, WBC, Wst]: that he should repeatedly offer himself on the cross.

2. It refers to Christ's offering himself in heaven [Alf, Blm, EBC, Lg, My(D); NAB, NIV, TNT]: that he should repeatedly offer himself in heaven.

just-as[a] the high-priest enters into[b] the sanctuary[c] by[d] year with[e] blood belonging-to-another,[f]

LEXICON—a. ὥσπερ (LN 64.13) (BAGD 2. p. 899): 'just as' [BAGD, LN], 'as' [LN, Mil, NIC; KJV, NAB, NASB, NJB, NRSV, REB, TNT], 'like as' [Lns], 'like' [HNTC, WBC; CEV, NLT], 'the way' [NIV], not explicit [TEV]. It introduces a comparison [Mil].

b. εἰς with accusative object: 'into'. See this word in 9:24.
c. ἅγια (the plural of the adjective ἅγιος): 'sanctuary'. See this word in 9:24.
d. κατά with accusative object (LN 89.90) (BAGD II.2.c. p. 406): 'by', 'every' [BAGD, HNTC; KJV, NIV, TEV, TNT], 'each' [CEV]. The phrase κατ' ἐνιαυτόν 'by year' is translated 'year after year' [LN; NAB, NJB, NLT, NRSV, REB], 'year by year' [Lns, Mil, WBC; NASB], 'annually' [NIC].
e. ἐν with dative object (LN 89.76, 90.10) (BAGD I.4.c.β. p. 259): 'with' [BAGD, HNTC, LN (90.10), Mil, NIC; all versions except CEV, NLT], 'in connection with' [Lns], 'by' [LN (89.76, 90.10)], 'by means of' [LN (89.76)]. The phrase ἐν αἵματι 'with blood' is translated 'bringing blood with him' [WBC], 'to offer blood' [CEV, NLT]. It means to be furnished with [Alf], carrying with him [TH, TNTC, WBC]. It is instrumental [EGT] expressing the means [Mil].
f. ἀλλότριος (LN 92.20) (BAGD 1.a. p. 40): 'belonging to another' [BAGD, LN], 'belonging to someone else' [LN], 'not one's own' [BAGD, HNTC, Lns, Mil, NIC, WBC; NAB, NASB, NIV, NJB, NRSV, REB, TNT], 'of others' [KJV], 'of an animal' [CEV, NLT, TEV].

QUESTION—What is indicated by the present tense of εἰσέρχεται 'he enters'?
1. It may be a timeless reference to the custom under the OT system [NIGTC]: (under the OT ritual) the high priest enters the sanctuary. It does not prove that the Levitical system was still in operation [NIGTC].
2. It refers to present action, implying that the OT Levitical system was still in operation [Hu]: the high priest still enters (yearly) the sanctuary.

9:26 since[a] (otherwise) it-would-have-been-necessary[b] (for) him to-suffer[c] many-times[d] from[e] (the) foundation[f] of-(the)-world;[g]

LEXICON—a. ἐπεί (LN **89.32**) (BAGD 2. p. 248): 'since' [BAGD, **LN**, Lns, Mil], 'because, for' [BAGD, LN], 'for then' [KJV, NRSV, REB, TEV], 'for in that case' [NIC], 'if that had been so' [TNT], 'if that were so' [NAB], 'if that had been necessary' [NLT], 'if he had offered himself every year' [CEV], 'or else' [NJB], 'otherwise' [HNTC, WBC; NASB], 'then' [NIV], 'in view of the fact that' [LN]. The additional concept of 'otherwise' is implied [Alf, Blm, EBC, EGT, Lns, My, Wst]. It introduces the conclusion from the implied contrary-to-fact concept of the preceding verse [Mil, NIGTC, WBC].
b. imperf. act. indic. of the impersonal verb δεῖ (LN 71.34): 'to be necessary' [LN, Lns, WBC], '(he) must' [LN; KJV], 'to have to' [HNTC, NIC; all versions except KJV, NASB], 'to need' [Mil; NASB]. It indicates necessity [Alf, EGT, ICC, Lg(K)], expediency [Blm].
c. aor. act. infin. of πάσχω (LN 24.78) (BAGD 3.a.α. p. 634): 'to suffer' [BAGD, HNTC, LN, Lns, Mil, NIC; all versions except NAB, NLT], 'to die' [NLT], 'to suffer death' [WBC; NAB]. It means to suffer death [EBC, My, NIGTC, TH, TNTC, WBC; NAB].

d. πολλάκις: 'many times'. See this word in 9:25.

e. ἀπό with genitive object (LN 67.131): 'from' [HNTC, LN; NAB], 'from . . . on' [Lns], 'since' [LN, Mil, NIC, WBC; all versions except NAB, NLT, TEV], 'ever since' [NLT, TEV].

f. καταβολή (LN 42.37) (BAGD 1. p. 409): 'foundation' [BAGD, Lns, Mil, NIC, WBC; KJV, NASB, NRSV], 'creation' [HNTC, LN; CEV, NAB, NIV, TEV, TNT]. The phrase καταβολῆς κόσμου 'foundation of the world' is translated 'the world began' [NJB, NLT], 'the world was created' [REB].

g. κόσμος (LN 1.1, 1.39) (BAGD 2. p. 445): 'world' [BAGD, HNTC, LN (1.39), Lns, Mil, NIC, WBC; all versions], 'earth' [LN (1.39)], 'universe' [LN (1.1)].

QUESTION—Why is this clause mentioned?

It carries on the argument from the preceding verse [Alf, My, NIGTC], drawing the conclusion from the unreal comment [NIGTC]. It is a *reductio ad absurdum*, "reduction to an absurdity," showing how absurd the alternative would be if Christ's one sacrifice were not sufficient [Blm, Hu, ICC, My, NIC, NTC]. It is parenthetical [Blm]; it is not parenthetical [My].

QUESTION—What relationship is indicated by the phrase ἐπεὶ ἔδει 'since it would have been necessary'?

It means that the following action would have been necessary if the preceding statement were not true [Alf, BAGD, HNTC, LN, Lns, Mil, NIC, TH, WBC; all versions]: since otherwise it would have been necessary.

QUESTION—How are the two nouns related in the genitive construction καταβολῆς κόσμου 'foundation of the world'?

The objective genitive κόσμου 'world' tells what was founded [TH; NJB, REB]: the world was founded.

but now once-for-all[a] at[b] (the) end[c] of-the ages[d] for[e] removal[f] of-the sin[g] through[h] the sacrifice of him he-has-appeared.[i]

TEXT—Some manuscripts omit the definite article τῆς 'the' before ἁμαρτίας 'sin'. GNT includes the article in brackets, indicating uncertainty about including it, but with no discussion. For most translations and commentaries it cannot be determined whether they include or omit this word; however, it is included by NIC (but with expressed doubt), NIGTC, WBC, Wst; it is included in brackets by Mil; it is omitted by Alf, Blm, EGT, My.

LEXICON—a. ἅπαξ (LN **60.68**) (BAGD 1. p. 80): 'once for all' [Mil, NIC, WBC; NAB, NIV, NRSV, REB, TNT], 'once for all time' [NLT], 'once and for all' [HNTC, LN; CEV, NJB, TEV], 'once' [BAGD, Lns; KJV, NASB]. It means once with no need for repetition [Alf, Wst].

b. ἐπί with dative object (LN 67.33) (BAGD II.2. p. 288): 'at' [BAGD, HNTC, Lns, Mil, NIC, WBC; all versions except CEV, KJV, TEV], 'at the time of, when' [LN], 'in' [KJV], 'near' [CEV]. The phrase ἐπὶ συντελείᾳ τῶν αἰώνων 'at the end of the ages' is translated 'when all ages of time are nearing the end' [TEV]. It expresses time [Lns, Mil].

c. συντέλεια (LN 67.66) (BAGD p. 792): 'end' [BAGD, LN; all versions except NASB, REB], 'consummation' [HNTC, Lns, Mil, NIC; NASB], 'climax' [WBC; REB].

d. αἰών (LN 67.143) (BAGD 2.a. p. 27): 'age' [BAGD, HNTC, LN, Mil, NIC, WBC; NAB, NASB, NIV, NLT, TEV, TNT], 'eon' [Lns], 'era' [LN], 'time' [CEV], 'world' [KJV]. This plural τῶν αἰώνων 'the ages' is translated as a singular: 'the age' [NRSV], 'the last age' [NJB], 'history' [REB].

e. εἰς with accusative object (LN 89.57): 'for' [Lns, WBC], 'for the purpose of' [LN]. It expresses purpose [Lns, WBC].

f. ἀθέτησις (LN **13.36**) (BAGD 2. p. 21): 'removal' [BAGD, LN], 'putting away' [Lns], 'annulling' [WBC]. The phrase εἰς ἀθέτησιν 'for removal' is translated 'to remove' [**LN**; NLT, NRSV, TEV], 'to take away' [NAB], 'to put away' [KJV, NASB], 'to do away with' [Mil, NIC; CEV, NIV, NJB], 'to annul' [HNTC], 'to abolish' [REB]. The phrase εἰς ἀθέτησιν τῆς ἁμαρτίας 'for removal of sin' is translated 'so that sin may be set aside' [TNT]. It implies totally annulling [EBC, TNTC, Wst], but only for those who repent and trust in Christ's atonement [TNTC].

g. ἁμαρτία (LN 88.289): 'sin' [HNTC, LN, Lns, Mil, NIC, WBC; all versions except CEV, NAB], 'the power of sin' [CEV]. This singular noun is translated as a plural: 'sins' [NAB]. This singular noun with the definite article is generic, referring to all sins in general [EGT]. It refers to sin as an abstract principle [Mil, Wst] (but this requires the omission of the definite article, which Mil includes in brackets and Wst includes).

h. διά with genitive object (LN 89.76) (BAGD A.III.1.a. p. 180): 'through' [BAGD, HNTC, LN, Mil; TEV, TNT], 'by means of' [BAGD, Lns], 'with' [BAGD], 'by' [NIC, WBC; all versions except CEV, TEV, TNT], not explicit [CEV]. It expresses means [Mil].

i. perf. mid. indic. of φανερόω (LN 24.19) (BAGD 2.b.β. p. 853): 'to appear' [BAGD, HNTC, LN, Lns, Mil, WBC; KJV, NAB, NIV, NRSV, REB, TEV], 'to make oneself visible' [LN], 'to make one's appearance' [NJB], 'to show oneself, to reveal oneself' [BAGD], 'to offer oneself' [CEV], 'to come' [NLT]. This middle voice is also translated as a passive: 'to be revealed' [TNT], 'to be manifested' [NIC; NASB]. It refers to Christ's earthly incarnation [Alf, Hu, Lg, My, NIGTC]. The perfect tense implies the continuing effects of his appearance [Wst]; it covers the time of Christ's earthly life [Lns].

QUESTION—What is meant by νυνί 'now'?

1. It is logical, not temporal [Alf, EBC, ICC, Lg, Mil, My, NIC, NIGTC, NTC, TNTC, Wst] (although a temporal sense is an underlying concept [NIGTC]), introducing the true situation following an unreal situation [EBC, EGT, NIGTC, NTC]: but as things actually are. It calls attention to what follows [NIGTC]. This word is an emphatic form of νῦν 'now'.
2. It is temporal [TH; TEV]: now, at the close of the ages. The contrast is between the OT times and the author's time [TH].

QUESTION—What is ἅπαξ 'once for all' connected with?

1. It modifies πεφανέρωται 'he has appeared' [HNTC, Lg(K), Lns, Mil, NIC, NTC, WBC, Wst; all versions except NAB]: he has appeared once for all.
2. It modifies εἰς ἀθέτησιν τῆς ἁμαρτίας 'for removal of sin' [NAB]: to remove sin once for all.

QUESTION—What is meant by ἐπὶ συντελείᾳ τῶν αἰώνων 'at the end of the ages'?

1. It refers to the end of time [Alf, ICC, My, NCBC, TH] which includes all time since Christ's earthly ministry [Alf].
2. It refers to the close of the Mosaic dispensation [Blm].
3. It refers to Christ's appearance on earth [EBC, Hu, Lns, NTC, Wst] as inaugurating the final age [Hu, NIGTC], as inaugurating the period of the New Covenant [Mil, NIC, TNTC, Wst], the end of the period of mere symbolism [EGT], the climax of history [EBC]. It was Christ's coming that caused time to be the time of the new order [NIC].

QUESTION—How are the two nouns related in the genitive construction ἀθέτησιν τῆς ἁμαρτίας 'removal of sin'?

The objective genitive τῆς ἁμαρτίας 'of sin' tells what is removed [HNTC, Lns, Mil, NIC, NTC, TH, TNTC, Wst; all versions]: to remove sin.

QUESTION—What is the phrase διὰ τῆς θυσίας αὐτοῦ 'through the sacrifice of him' connected with?

It is connected with the preceding phrase εἰς ἀθέτησιν τῆς ἁμαρτίας 'through the sacrifice of him' [My]: for putting away sin through his sacrifice.

QUESTION—How are the two nouns related in the genitive construction τῆς θυσίας αὐτοῦ 'the sacrifice of him'?

1. The genitive αὐτοῦ is the personal pronoun 'of him' [Alf, EGT, Lg(K), Lns, My, NIC; NAB]; it is subjective and tells who made the sacrifice [EGT, Lg(K), NIC]: he made the sacrifice. Αὐτοῦ is emphatic, 'his own' [NIC]; it is not emphatic [My].
2. The genitive personal pronoun αὐτοῦ 'of him' is treated as a reflexive pronoun 'of himself' (influenced by προσφέρῃ ἑαυτόν 'he should offer himself' in 9:25 [Mil, NIGTC], telling who was sacrificed [EBC, HNTC, Hu, Hwt, Mil, NIGTC, TNTC, Wst; all versions except NAB]: (he) sacrificed himself.

9:27 And in-accordance-with[a] as-much-as[b] it-is-destined[c] to-the men once[d] to-die,

LEXICON—a. κατά with accusative object (LN 89.4, 89.8) (BAGD II.5.b.α. p. 407): 'in accordance with' [LN (89.8)], 'in accord with' [Lns], 'with regard to, in relation to' [LN (89.4, 89.8)]. The phrase καθ' ὅσον 'according to as much as' is translated 'just as' [BAGD, WBC; NAB, NIV, NLT, NRSV, REB], 'as' [HNTC; KJV], 'inasmuch as' [Mil;

NASB], 'since' [NIC; NJB], not explicit [TNT]. This entire clause is translated 'everyone must die once' [TEV], 'we die only once' [CEV].

b. ὅσος (LN 78.52) (BAGD 3. p. 586): 'as much as, to the degree that, to the same degree' [LN], 'the way' [Lns]. The phrase καθ' ὅσον 'in accordance with, as much as' is translated 'just as' [BAGD].

c. pres. mid. (deponent = act.) indic. of ἀπόκειμαι (LN **71.37**) (BAGD 2. p. 93): 'to be destined' [BAGD; NIV, NLT], 'to be appointed' [KJV, NAB, NASB, NRSV], 'to be one's lot' [REB], 'to be necessary' [LN], '(one) must' [**LN**], 'to be reserved' [BAGD, Lns, Mil, WBC], 'to be laid up in store' [NIC], 'to be certain' [BAGD], not explicit [CEV, TEV]. The phrase ἀπόκειται τοῖς ἀνθρώποις 'it is destined to men' is translated 'men are appointed' [TNT], 'it is the lot of men' [HNTC]. The phrase ἀπόκειται τοῖς ἀνθρώποις ἀποθανεῖν 'it is destined to men to die' is translated 'human beings die' [NJB]. It implies being laid up or reserved for some future use [Alf, Blm, Lg(K), Lns, My, TH, TNTC, Wst] by God's decree [My].

d. ἅπαξ (LN 60.67) (BAGD 1. p. 80): 'once' [BAGD, HNTC, LN, Lns, Mil, NIC, WBC; all versions except CEV, NJB, NLT], 'one time' [LN], 'only once' [CEV, NJB, NLT]. It means that people die only once [Alf, Hu]. It indicates finality, 'once for all' [EBC]. It implies that what is destined is not merely to die, but to die once [EGT] and only once [Lns; NJB].

QUESTION—Why is this verse mentioned?

Together with the following verse it gives a comparison of the similarity of the human situation with Christ's [Alf, EGT, HNTC, ICC, Lns, My, NCBC, NIC, NIGTC, NTC, TNTC, WBC, Wst], a reference to the one death for each person and Christ's one death [EBC, GNC, Hu, Hwt, ICC, Mil, My, NIC]: just as people die once, followed by judgment, so Christ offered himself once and will return to save from judgment those who await him. It continues the argument that it was proper that Christ offered himself only once [Blm, My], proving the finality of Christ's work [Hwt, NCBC]; he can return to earth only for a different purpose [HNTC]. These two verses form a parenthesis, although they are an important statement [ICC, TH].

QUESTION—What relationship is indicated by the phrase καθ' ὅσον 'in accordance with as much as'?

It indicates a comparison [Alf, ICC] and grounds or reason [Lg, Mil, My, NIGTC] (but reason only related to ἅπαξ ἀποθανεῖν 'once to die' [My]), measure or degree [Mil].

QUESTION—What relationship is indicated by the definite article in the phrase τοῖς ἀνθρώποις 'the men'?

The article makes the noun generic [Alf, ICC; NIV]: mankind in general.

and after[a] this, judgment,[b]

LEXICON—a. μετά with accusative object (LN 67.48) (BAGD B.II.3. p. 510): 'after' [BAGD, HNTC, LN, Lns, Mil, NIC, WBC; all versions except

CEV, REB]. This entire phrase is translated 'with judgment to follow' [REB], 'and then we are judged' [CEV].

b. κρίσις (LN 30.110) (BAGD 1.a.α. p. 452): 'judgment' [BAGD, LN, Lns, Mil, NIC, WBC; NASB, NIV, NJB, NLT, REB], 'the judgment' [HNTC; KJV, NRSV, TNT]. This noun is also translated as a verb: 'to be judged' [CEV, NAB, TEV]. It has a neutral sense [Alf, ICC, My, NIGTC]. It refers to the action of judging [NTC, Wst].

QUESTION—What is meant by this phrase?

It means that following death the next event is judgment [Alf, Blm, EGT, Hwt, ICC, My].

QUESTION—To what does τοῦτο 'this' refer?

It refers to ἀποθανεῖν 'to die' in the preceding phrase [Mil]: after death.

QUESTION—What verb is to be supplied in this phrase?

1. The verb ἀποκεῖται 'it is destined' is to be supplied [My] from the preceding clause: after this, judgment is destined.
2. The idea of experiencing is to be supplied [WBC]: after this, judgment is to be experienced.
3. The verb 'to come' is to be supplied [Wst; NASB, NJB, TNT]: after this comes judgment.
4. The verb 'to face' is to be supplied [NIV]: after this to face judgment.
5. The verb 'to follow' is to be supplied [REB]: with judgment to follow.
6. The noun κρίσις 'judgment' is translated as a verb: 'to be judged' [CEV, NAB, TEV]: after this be judged.

QUESTION—What is the significance of the lack of the definite article with κρίσις 'judgment'?

1. The noun is qualitative, emphasizing what it is [ICC, Lns, Mil, My, NIC, WBC, Wst; NASB, NIV, NJB]: it is judgment.
2. It is nevertheless treated as definite [HNTC, TNTC; KJV, NRSV, TNT]: it is the (final) judgment (by God).

9:28 Thus the Christ also once[a] having-been-offered[b] for[c] the taking-away[d] sins of-many (persons),

LEXICON—a. ἅπαξ (LN 60.67) (BAGD 1. p. 80): 'once' [BAGD, HNTC, LN, Lns, Mil, WBC; all versions except CEV, NJB, NLT], 'only once' [CEV, NJB, NLT], 'once for all' [NIC]. It means 'once for all' [Alf, EBC].

b. aorist pass. participle of προσφέρω (BAGD 2.a. p. 720): 'to be offered' [BAGD, HNTC, Lns, Mil, NIC, WBC; KJV, NAB, NASB, NRSV, REB, TNT], 'to be offered in sacrifice' [TEV], 'to be sacrificed' [NIV]. This passive verb is also translated as middle voice: 'to offer oneself' [NJB], 'to die as a sacrifice' [NLT], 'to die' [CEV]. The emphasis in this passive voice is the concept of something appointed to him [Alf, Lg, Mil, NIGTC] resulting from outward forces [Wst], to God's purpose [EBC, HNTC, NIGTC, TNTC], with God as the implied agent [NIGTC]; God is not to be represented as the agent [TH, TNTC, Wst]. It refers to Christ's death [Alf, EGT, My], taking upon himself the consequences of sins [EBC]; it refers to Christ's offering himself [Lns, NTC, TH, TNTC, Wst]. Offering as a sacrifice is implied [Blm].

c. εἰς with accusative object (LN 89.57): 'for', 'for the purpose of, in order to' [LN], 'to' [HNTC, Lns, Mil, NIC, WBC; all versions]. It means 'in this respect' [NIGTC].

d. aorist act. infin. of ἀναφέρω (BAGD 3. p. 63): 'to take away' [BAGD; CEV, NAB, NIV, NLT, TEV], 'to bear' [HNTC, Lns, Mil, NIC, WBC; KJV, NASB, NJB, NRSV, REB, TNT], 'to take upon oneself' [BAGD]. It refers to bearing or carrying on oneself [Alf, NIGTC], the expiation of sins [My].

QUESTION—Why is this verse mentioned?

Primarily, it adds to the discussion concerning Christ's work; it also completes the comparison with the situation of mankind in 9:27 [NIGTC, WBC]. This clause states what Christ did because the OT sacrifices could not take away sin [Blm]. The introductory οὕτως 'thus' corresponds to καθ' ὅσον 'according to as much as/just as' in 9:27 [Blm, EBC]; it introduces a comparison involving both parts of 9:27 [EGT].

QUESTION—What relationship is indicated by the articular form ὁ Χριστός 'the Christ'?

It means 'the Christ' as a title [HNTC], as the one identified with mankind and who was God's Christ [Alf], the Messiah [NTC, TH].

QUESTION—What relationship is indicated by the participle προσενεχθείς 'having been offered'?

1. It describes an action parallel to the following verb ὀφθήσεται 'he will appear' [NIC; KJV, NAB, NIV, REB, TEV, TNT]: he was offered and he will appear.
2. It is temporal [Mil, WBC]: after he was offered.
3. It is treated as an attributive participle and translated as the verb of a relative clause [HNTC]: who was offered.

QUESTION—What is the meaning of πολλῶν 'of many'?

1. It indicates people in general [HNTC, NCBC] in contrast with one or a few [NCBC, TH], stressing the idea of plurality without indicating whether all or less than all are included [My]; it is a qualitative reference [Alf] meaning 'all' [Alf, Hu], a Hebraic reference to 'all' [GNC, Hu, TH] influenced by Isa. 53:12 [GNC, Hu, Mil]. It contrasts the 'many' with Christ's one sacrifice [Alf, Hu, NIGTC, TNTC, Wst]: the sins of all people in general.
2. It refers to those who accept Christ's sacrifice [Blm]: the sins of the many who accept his sacrifice.

from[a] (the) second (time) apart-from[b] sin he-will-appear[c] to-the-(ones) awaiting[d] him for[e] salvation.

LEXICON—a. ἐκ with genitive object (LN 67.33): 'from'; not explicit [HNTC, LN, Lns, Mil, NIC, WBC; all versions].

b. χωρίς with genitive object (LN 89.120) (BAGD 2.b.δ. p. 891): 'apart from' [LN, Lns], 'without' [LN; KJV], 'without reference to' [WBC; NASB], 'without any relation to' [BAGD, Mil], 'not to deal with' [HNTC; NLT, NRSV, REB, TEV, TNT], 'not to take away' [CEV, NAB], 'not to bear' [NIV]. The phrase χωρὶς ἁμαρτίας 'apart from sin' is translated 'sin being no more' [NJB], 'sin having been done away with' [NIC]. It expresses manner [Mil].

c. fut. mid./pass. indic. of ὁράω (LN 34.50) (BAGD 1.a.δ. p. 578): 'to appear' [BAGD, HNTC, Mil, NIC, WBC; all versions except CEV, NJB, NLT], 'to become visible' [BAGD], 'to visit' [LN], 'to go to see' [LN], 'to be seen' [LN, Lns], 'to manifest oneself' [NJB], 'to come' [CEV, NLT]. This is the verb which is commonly used for Christ's post-resurrection appearances [Alf, EGT]; it means to become visible to sight [EGT, Lg, My, Wst].

d. pres. mid. (deponent = act.) participle of ἀπεκδέχομαι (LN **25.63**) (BAGD p. 83): 'to await' [HNTC, LN; TNT], 'to await eagerly' [BAGD, Mil; NAB, NASB, REB], 'to await expectantly' [LN], 'to wait for' [CEV, NIV, NJB, TEV], 'to wait eagerly for' [WBC; NLT, NRSV], 'to expect' [Lns], 'to expect eagerly' [**LN**], 'to look for' [NIC; KJV], 'to look forward eagerly' [LN].

e. εἰς with accusative object (LN 89.57): 'for' [Lns, WBC; NASB], 'for the purpose of' [LN], 'in order to' [LN], 'unto' [KJV], 'to bring' [HNTC, Mil; NAB, NIV, NLT, REB, TNT], 'to bring them' [NIC; NJB]. The phrase εἰς σωτηρίαν 'for salvation' is translated 'to save' [CEV, NRSV, TEV]. It expresses purpose [Alf].

QUESTION—What relationship is indicated by the phrase χωρὶς ἁμαρτίας 'apart from sin'?

It means that his dealing with sin was completed, so that his second appearance will not be involved with sin [Alf, BAGD, EBC, EGT, GNC, HNTC, Hu, Hwt, ICC, Mil, My, NCBC, NIC, NIGTC, TH, TNTC, WBC; NASB, NRSV, REB, TEV, TNT]; without having to atone for sins [Blm, NTC, Wst], not to take away sin [NTC; NAB, NIV]. It contrasts with the reference to bearing the sins of many in the preceding clause [My].

QUESTION—What is the phrase εἰς σωτηρίαν 'for salvation' connected with?

It is connected with ὀφθήσεται 'he will appear' [Alf, Blm, EBC, EGT, HNTC, Hu, ICC, Lg, Mil, My, NIC, NIGTC, NTC, TH, WBC, Wst; all versions]: he will appear for salvation. It is contrasted with χωρὶς ἁμαρτίας 'apart from sin' [My].

DISCOURSE UNIT: 10:1–18 [Hwt, Mil, NIGTC, NTC, TNTC, WBC, Wst; NAB, NASB, NIV, NJB, NLT]. The topic is Christ's self-sacrifice for others [TNTC], the true character of Christ's single, personal sacrifice [WBC], Christ's once-for-all sacrifice [NIV, NLT], the superiority of Christ's sacrifice [Hwt; NJB], the permanent sufficiency of Christ's one sacrifice [Wst; NASB], Christ's perfect redemption [Mil], sanctification by Christ's sacrifice [NIGTC], one sacrifice rather than many [NAB], Jesus as both high priest and sacrifice [NTC].

DISCOURSE UNIT: 10:1–10 [Lns; NJB]. The topic is a comparison of the two sacrifices [Lns], the ineffectiveness of the old sacrifices [NJB].

DISCOURSE UNIT: 10:1–4 [EBC, GNC, HNTC, Lg, NCBC, NIC]. The topic is shadow and reality [NCBC, NIC], the law was a mere shadow [EBC], good things [HNTC], the ineffectiveness of the law [GNC] as shown by the repetition of the OT sacrifices [Lg].

10:1 For the law having a shadow[a] of the coming good-things,

LEXICON—a. σκία (LN 14.61) (BAGD 2. p. 755): 'shadow' [BAGD, HNTC, LN, Lns, Mil, NIC; CEV, KJV, NAB, NASB, NIV, NLT, NRSV, REB], 'foreshadowing' [BAGD; WBC], 'reflection' [NJB], 'faint outline' [TEV]. The phrase σκιὰν ἔχων 'having a shadow' is translated 'it foreshadows' [TNT]. It was nothing more than a shadow [Blm, HNTC, Hu, Lns, Mil, Wst; NAB, NASB, NIV], something unsubstantial [EBC, EGT], incomplete [WBC], a dim representation of a reality [NTC]. It refers to the ceremonial cultus of the OT [TNTC]. It is emphatic by forefronting [EGT, Lg(K), WBC].

QUESTION—What is this clause connected with?

It is connected with 9:24–28 [Alf, Mil, My(D)], with 9:25–28 [My], with 9:23–28 [NIGTC], with 8:3–5 and 9:23–26 [WBC], the γάρ introducing the grounds [Mil, My(D)], the recapitulation [WBC]. It restates the thought of 8:5 [Hu]. The introductory γάρ introduces a further explanation of the finality and superiority of Christ's sacrifice to those of the OT [EGT].

QUESTION—To what does ὁ νόμος 'the law' refer?

It refers to the whole OT [EBC, NTC], with particular reference to its sacrificial system [EBC], primarily to its cultic aspect [NIGTC].

QUESTION—What relationship is indicated by the participial form ἔχων 'having'?

It means that the law is not the shadow but that it possesses the shadow [TNTC]. It is emphatic by its word order [Wst].

1. It indicates the reason for the law's inability [Alf, GNC, Mil, NIC, WBC, Wst; NAB, NASB, NIV, NJB, NRSV]: because the law has only a shadow, it can never perfect those who approach.
2. It is translated as a finite verb parallel to the following verb [HNTC; CEV, NLT, REB, TEV, TNT]: the law has only a shadow.

QUESTION—How are the noun and the participial phrase related in the genitive construction σκιὰν τῶν μελλόντων ἀγαθῶν 'a shadow of the coming good things'?

'The coming good things' states the reality of which the law is merely a shadow [Alf]: the law is a shadow; the reality is the coming good things.

QUESTION—To what does τῶν μελλόντων ἀγαθῶν 'the coming good things' refer?

1. It refers to the blessings which are still future but are made certain in Christ [Alf, HNTC, ICC].
2. It refers to future blessings from the point of view of the law, realized by Christ's atonement, but still future as regards the full enjoyment of them [Wst].
3. It refers to things not fulfilled under the old covenant [NIGTC] but which are now realized [TH].
4. It refers to Christ's sacrifice, his present ministry, access to God, and eternal redemption [NCBC, NIC].
5. It refers to the blessings of salvation [NTC, WBC], the Gospel and its spiritual high-priesthood [TNTC].

not the form[a] itself of the things,[b]

LEXICON—a. εἰκών (LN **58.61**) (BAGD 2. p. 222): 'form' [BAGD, HNTC, Mil, WBC; NASB, NRSV], 'image' [Lns, NIC; KJV, NAB, NJB], 'representation' [**LN**], 'pattern' [LN], 'model' [TEV], 'reality' [NLT]. The phrase αὐτὴν τὴν εἰκόνα τῶν πραγμάτων 'the form itself of the things' is translated 'the realities themselves' [NIV], 'the true picture' [REB], 'identical with actual realities' [TNT], 'the good things themselves' [CEV]. It contrasts with σκίαν 'shadow' above [Blm, EBC, ICC], and implies substantiality [EGT] and the full representation (and visible manifestation [Mil]) of the heavenly reality [Blm, EGT, HNTC, Hu, ICC, Lg, Mil], an exact replica [NIC]. It is the New Covenant [Mil].

b. πρᾶγμα (LN 13.105) (BAGD 4.p.697): 'thing' [BAGD, Lns, NIC; CEV, KJV, NAB, NASB, NJB, NLT], 'real thing' [TEV], 'reality' [HNTC, Mil, WBC; NRSV, TNT], 'matter' [BAGD], 'affair' [BAGD], 'event' [LN], 'happening' [LN]. It refers to Christ's atonement and its results [NTC].

QUESTION—How are the two nouns related in the genitive construction τὴν εἰκόνα τῶν πραγμάτων 'the form of the things'?

1. 'The things' is possessive [Lns]: the form that belongs to the things.
2. 'The things' may state what 'the form' is, but none of the commentaries mention this: the form, i.e., the things.

according-to[a] year by-the same sacrifices which they offer[b] into the continuous[c] (time) never is-it-able to-perfect[d] the-(ones) approaching;[e]

LEXICON—a. κατά with accusative object (LN 89.90) (BAGD II.2.c. p. 406): 'according to', 'every' [BAGD], 'from . . . to' [LN]. The phrase κατ' ἐνιαυτόν 'according to year' is translated 'year by year' [Lns, Mil, NIC; KJV, NASB], 'year after year' [HNTC, WBC; all versions except KJV, NASB]. This phrase is forefronted for emphasis [ICC].

b. pres. act. indic. of προσφέρω (LN 57.80): 'to offer' [HNTC, Lns, Mil, NIC; CEV, KJV, NAB, NASB, NJB, REB, TEV], 'to bring to' [LN], 'to present to' [LN]. This active verb is also translated as a passive: 'to be offered' [WBC; NRSV]. The phrase ταῖς αὐταῖς θυσίαις ἃς προσφέρουσιν εἰς τὸ διηνεκές 'by the same sacrifices which they offer into the continuous' is translated 'by a constant repetition of the same sacrifices' [TNT]. It is used impersonally [NIGTC, WBC, Wst] as equivalent to a passive [NIGTC, WBC], not explicit [NIV, NLT, TNT]. The implied subject of this verb is the priests [Alf, Lg, Mil, Wst], the high priests [Lns, My].

c. διηνεκής (LN 67.95) (BAGD p. 195): 'continuous'. The phrase εἰς τὸ διηνεκές 'into the continuous' is translated 'continually' [BAGD, Mil; KJV, NAB, NASB, NRSV], 'continuously' [WBC], 'forever' [BAGD, LN; TEV], 'endlessly' [NIV], 'without end' [NIC], 'repeatedly' [NJB], 'repeated again and again' [NLT], 'for all time' [REB], 'in perpetuity' [Lns], 'for all time' [HNTC], 'by a constant repetition' [TNT], not explicit [CEV].

d. aorist act. infin. of τελειόω (LN **88.38**) (BAGD 2.e.α. p. 810): 'to perfect' [LN; NAB], 'to make perfect' [BAGD, **LN,** Mil; KJV, NASB, NIV, NRSV, TEV, TNT], 'to bring to perfection' [HNTC, NIC; NJB, REB], 'to bring to completion' [Lns], 'to purge decisively' [WBC], 'to provide perfect cleansing' [NLT], 'to free from sin' [CEV]. It refers to moral and spiritual perfection [EBC], arriving at the goal of God's plan [GNC].

e. pres. mid. (deponent = act.) of προσέρχομαι (LN 15.77) (BAGD 2.a. p. 713): 'to approach' [LN; NRSV], 'to approach God' [NIC], 'to come to' [BAGD], 'to come to God' [TEV], 'to come thereunto' [KJV], 'to draw near' [Lns, Mil, WBC; NASB], 'to draw near to worship' [NIV], 'to come to worship' [NLT], 'to worship' [HNTC; NAB, NJB, REB, TNT], not explicit [CEV]. It refers to the worshipers drawing near to God [Alf, EBC, Lg, Mil, My, NIGTC, WBC, Wst].

QUESTION—What is the phrase κατ' ἐνιαυτόν 'according to year' connected with?

1. It is connected with προσφέρουσιν 'they offer' [HNTC, ICC, Lg, Mil, NIC, WBC, Wst; all versions except NASB]: they offer year by year.
2. It is connected with ταῖς αὐταῖς θυσίαις 'by the same sacrifices' [Alf, EGT, Lns, My; NASB]: by the same sacrifices every year.

QUESTION—To what does ταῖς αὐταῖς θυσίαις 'the same sacrifices' refer?

It refers to the sacrifices on the annual day of atonement [Alf, EBC, HNTC, ICC, Lns, Mil, My, TNTC, Wst], as the phrase κατ' ἐνιαυτόν 'according to year' indicates [NIGTC], but it includes the whole system of daily sacrifices as well [NIGTC, TNTC, Wst]. It refers to the rites, not the sacrificed animals [NIGTC].

QUESTION—What is the phrase εἰς τὸ διηνεκές 'into the continuous' connected with?

1. It is connected with προσφέρουσιν 'they offer' [EGT, ICC, Lg, Lns, Mil, My, NIC, WBC; all versions]: they offer continually.
2. It is connected with τελειῶσαι 'to perfect' [EBC, HNTC, Wst]: to perfect for all time. It implies continuous consequences [Wst].

QUESTION—What is the subject of δύναται 'it is able'?

The subject is ὁ νόμος 'the law' [EGT, GNC, HNTC, ICC, Lns, Mil, NIC, NIGTC, Wst; all versions]: the law is not able.

10:2 since[a] not would-they-have-stopped being-offered[b]

LEXICON—a. ἐπεί (LN 89.32) (BAGD 2. p. 284): 'since' [LN, Mil], 'for then' [KJV], 'otherwise' [HNTC, NIC, WBC; NASB, NJB, NRSV], 'for otherwise' [BAGD], 'were matters otherwise' [NAB], 'else' [Lns], 'if it could' [NIV, REB], 'if they could have' [NLT], 'if that were possible' [TNT], not explicit [CEV, TEV].

b. pres. pass. participle of προσφέρω: 'to be offered'. See this word in 10:1.

QUESTION—What is implied by the rhetorical question in this clause?

It is implied that the proposition is true [EBC, Hwt, Lns, NIC, NIGTC, TNTC; NAB, NJB, REB, TEV, TNT]: they would have stopped being offered. It also implies that the OT ritual was being continued when this epistle was written [NIC, NIGTC].

1. It implies the consequence of the understood statement, "if the OT sacrifices could have perfected the worshipers" [Mil, NTC]: if the sacrifices could have perfected the worshipers, then the sacrifices would have stopped being offered.
2. It implies the consequence of the understood statement "if the law could have perfected the worshipers" [Alf, Blm, EBC, EGT, HNTC, Hwt, ICC, Lg(K), Lns, NCBC, NIC, NIGTC, TNTC, WBC, Wst; all versions]: if the law could have perfected the worshippers, then the sacrifices would have stopped being offered.
3. It implies the proof of the comment in 10:1 [Blm, EGT, My].

QUESTION—What relationship is indicated by the participle προσφερόμενοι 'being offered'?

It expresses the object of the preceding verb, telling what was stopped [HNTC, Lns, Mil, NIC, WBC; all versions]: stopped being offered.

because-of[a] the having still[b] no consciousness[c] of-sins, the-(ones) worshiping[d] once[e] cleansed[f]?

LEXICON—a. διά with accusative object (LN 89.26): 'because of' [LN], 'because' [Lns, Mil; NASB, NJB, REB, TNT], 'because that' [KJV], 'for' [NAB, NIV, NLT], 'since' [HNTC, WBC; NRSV], not explicit [CEV, NIV, TEV].

b. ἔτι (LN 67.128): 'still' [LN], 'more' [Lns; KJV], 'any longer' [WBC], not explicit [CEV, NAB, NJB, NLT]. The phrase μηδεμίαν ἔτι 'still no' is translated 'no longer' [HNTC, Mil, NIC; NASB, NIV, NRSV, REB, TNT], 'not any more' [TEV].

c. συνείδησις (LN 28.4) (BAGD 1. p. 786): 'consciousness' [HNTC, Mil, WBC; NASB, NRSV], 'conscience' [Lns, NIC; CEV, KJV, NAB], 'awareness' [NJB], 'sense' [REB, TNT], 'feelings of guilt' [NLT]. The phrase τὸ ἔχειν συνείδησιν 'the having consciousness' is translated 'to be conscious of' [LN], 'to feel guilty' [NIV, TEV], 'their feelings of guilt' [NLT]. It involves responsibility and culpability [Lg].

d. pres. act. participle of λατρεύω (LN 53.14) (BAGD p. 467): 'to worship' [TEV]. The phrase τοὺς λατρεύοντας 'the ones worshiping' is translated 'worshiper' [HNTC, LN, Lns, Mil, NIC, WBC; all versions except TEV]. This participle includes both priests and people [Alf], worshipers in general [WBC].

e. ἅπαξ (LN 60.67, 60.68) (BAGD 2. p. 80): 'once' [LN, Lns, WBC; KJV, NAB, NASB, NJB], 'once for all' [BAGD, Mil, NIC; NIV, NRSV, REB], 'once and for all' [HNTC, LN; TNT], 'once for all time' [NLT], not explicit [CEV, TEV]. The meaning is 'once for all' [Alf, Blm, GNC, Hu, Lg(K), WBC, Wst].

f. perf. pass. participle of καθαρίζω (LN 53.28) (BAGD 2.b.α. p. 387): 'to be cleansed' [BAGD, LN, Lns, Mil, NIC, WBC; NAB, NASB, NIV, NRSV, REB], 'to be made clean' [LN], 'to be purified' [BAGD, HNTC, LN; NJB, NLT, TEV, TNT], 'to be made clear' [CEV], 'to be purged' [KJV]. The perfect tense implies the abiding results of the cleansing [GNC, Hu, Lns, NIGTC, WBC, Wst] rather than upon the act of cleansing [Wst].

QUESTION—How are the two nouns related in the genitive construction συνείδησιν ἁμαρτιῶν 'consciousness of sins'?

'Sins' expresses the content of the 'consciousness' [Lns]: what they were conscious of was sins.

QUESTION—What relationship is indicated by the participle κεκαθαρισμένους 'cleansed'?

1. It indicates reason [TNT]: because in that case they would have been purified.
2. It indicates condition [Mil, NIC]: if they had been cleansed.
3. It is temporal [NJB]: when they had been purified.

10:3 but in[a] them (there is) a-remembrance[b] of-sins according-to[c] year;

LEXICON—a. ἐν with dative object (LN 83.13, 89.76): 'in' [HNTC, LN (83.13), Mil, NIC, WBC; KJV, NASB, NJB, NRSV], 'in connection with' [Lns], 'through' [NAB], 'by' [LN (89.76); REB], not explicit [CEV]. The phrase ἐν αὐταῖς 'in them' is translated 'those sacrifices are' [NIV], 'the sacrifices' [TEV], 'these sacrifices' [TNT], 'those yearly sacrifices' [NLT]. The meaning is 'by means of' [TH].

b. ἀνάμνησις (LN **29.11**) (BAGD p. 58): 'remembrance' [Lns; KJV], 'reminder' [BAGD, HNTC, **LN**, Mil, NIC, WBC; NASB, NIV, NRSV], 'means of remembering' [LN], 'recalling' [NAB]. This noun is also translated as a verb: 'to remind' [CEV, NLT, TEV, TNT], 'to be recalled' [NJB], 'to be brought to mind' [REB]. The sense is a calling to mind [Wst], reminding [My], remembrance [EBC]. It required public notice [ICC]; it did not require public notice [NIGTC]. All those who offered sacrifices under the OT law were reminded of their sins [GNC, HNTC,

ICC, NIGTC, TNTC] by the sacrifices [WBC, Wst], and they were also reminded that God remembered sin [Hu], but reference to God is less likely [NIGTC]. The remembrance occurred on the annual Day of Atonement [Hu]. This word implies a process [NTC]; an action by the people of either repentance or continuing to sin, and action by God of either pardon or punishment [NIC].

c. κατά with accusative object: 'according to'. See this word in 10:1.

QUESTION—What relationship is indicated by ἀλλ' 'but'?

1. It introduces the opposite of what was stated in 10:2 [Alf, Blm, EBC, EGT, HNTC, Lns, Mil, My, NIGTC, Wst; NJB, REB, TEV, TNT]: on the contrary.
2. It is used adverbially in the sense of assent to what has been said [WBC]: really, in them . . .

QUESTION—To what does αὐταῖς 'them' refer?

It refers to the OT sacrifices [Alf, My, NIGTC; all versions] in the course of their being offered [Alf].

QUESTION—How are the two nouns related in the genitive construction ἀνάμνησις ἁμαρτιῶν 'remembrance of sins'?

'Sins' tells what is remembered [Alf; NJB, REB]: sins are remembered.

QUESTION—To what does the phrase κατ' ἐνιαυτόν 'according to year' refer?

It means 'year by year' and refers primarily to the annual Day of Atonement [Alf, EGT, Lns, NCBC, NIC, NIGTC, WBC] but including other sacrifices as well [NIGTC]. It refers to the whole sacrificial system [Wst].

10:4 for blood of bulls and goats (is) unable to-take-away sins.

QUESTION—To what does αἷμα 'blood' refer?

It refers to the blood itself, not merely the death of the animals [NIGTC]. Two kinds of blood are meant: the blood of bulls and the blood of goats [TH].

QUESTION—What relationship is indicated by γάρ 'for'?

It indicates the reason why the OT sacrifices were inadequate [Alf, Blm, EBC, Mil, My, WBC]. The γάρ 'for' confirms the preceding comment [Blm]. This clause explains the statements of 10:1 [WBC].

QUESTION—What is implied by ἀδύνατον 'unable'?

It is a strong word, implying impossibility [EBC, EGT, GNC, HNTC, Hu, Hwt, Lg(K), Lns, Mil, NIC, TH, TNTC, WBC; KJV, NAB, NASB, NIV, NRSV]. It is a moral impossibility [TNTC].

QUESTION—What is implied by ἀφαιρεῖν ἁμαρτίας 'to take away sins'?

It implies complete removal [EBC, Mil], equivalent to forgiveness [TH], removing the guilt [EGT]. It presents a picture of removing a load [WBC, Wst]. The present tense implies a continuing situation [Lns, NIGTC].

QUESTION—What is implied by the reference to 'blood of bulls and goats'?

It refers to the sacrifices on the Day of Atonement [HNTC, Hu, Wst].

DISCOURSE UNIT: 10:5–18 [EBC, Lg]. The topic is one sacrifice for sins [EBC], proof of the effective sanctification obtained through Christ [Lg].

DISCOURSE UNIT: 10:5–10 [GNC, HNTC, NCBC, NIC]. The topic is the old and the new in Psalm 40:6–8 [GNC], Christ's voluntary offering of himself [HNTC], the true offering [NCBC], the new order, which is the reality [NIC].

10:5 Therefore, entering into[a] the world he-says,

LEXICON—a. εἰς with accusative object (LN 84.22): 'into' [HNTC, LN, Lns, Mil, NIC, WBC; all versions].

QUESTION—What relationship is indicated by διό 'therefore'?

It indicates the conclusion from the preceding comment that animal sacrifices were inadequate to take away sin [Alf, EBC, Hwt, Lg, Mil, My, NCBC, NIGTC, TNTC, Wst]. It is based on the OT [Blm]. It governs 10:5–10 [NIGTC].

QUESTION—What relationship is indicated by the participle εἰσερχόμενος 'entering'?

It is temporal [Blm, EGT, HNTC, Mil, NIC, WBC; all versions]: when he was entering.

1. It refers to his life on earth in general [Alf, EGT, Lg(K), Mil, NIGTC].
2. It refers to the time of his coming to earth [HNTC, Hu, Hwt, ICC, Lg, Lns, My, NCBC, NTC, TH].
3. It includes both of the above [TNTC, Wst].

QUESTION—Who is the implied subject of λέγει 'he says'?

The implied subject is Christ [EBC, EGT, GNC, HNTC, Hwt, Lg, Lns, Mil, My, NCBC, NIC, NIGTC, NTC, TH, TNTC, WBC, Wst; CEV, NAB, NASB, NIV, NLT, NRSV, REB, TEV, TNT]: Jesus says. He is speaking to God [EBC, GNC, HNTC; TEV, TNT]. The present tense indicates the permanent record of Scripture, still available to the readers [My, NIGTC, TH].

"Sacrifice and offering[a] not you-desired,[b]

LEXICON—a. προσφορά (LN 53.16) (BAGD 2. p. 720): 'offering' [BAGD, HNTC, LN, Lns, Mil, NIC, WBC; all versions except NJB, NLT], 'cereal offering' [NJB], 'grain offering' [NLT], 'sacrifice' [LN]. It is virtually equivalent in meaning to 'sacrifice' [EBC, NIGTC].

b. aorist act. indic. of θέλω (LN 25.1) (BAGD 4.b. p. 355): 'to desire' [HNTC, LN, Mil, NIC; NAB, NASB, NIV, NRSV, REB], 'to want' [LN, Lns, WBC; CEV, NJB, NLT, TEV, TNT], 'to wish' [LN], 'to like' [BAGD], 'to will' [KJV], 'to take pleasure in' [BAGD].

QUESTION—To what does θυσίαν 'sacrifice' refer?

It refers to animal sacrifices [Alf, EGT, Lns, Wst], bloody sacrifices [My], the peace offering [GNC, NIC]. It is a general reference, but the underlying Hebrew refers to animal sacrifices [EBC].

QUESTION—To what does προσφοράν 'offering' refer?

It is a general reference [Alf, EBC, NIC], but the underlying Hebrew refers to the cereal offering [EBC, EGT, NIC, Wst]. It refers to meat and drink offerings [Lns], to offerings not involving blood [My].

but a-body you-prepared[a] for-me;

LEXICON—a. aorist mid. indic. of καταρτίζω (LN 42.36) (BAGD 2.b. p. 418): 'to prepare' [BAGD, HNTC, Mil, WBC; all versions except CEV, NJB, NLT], 'to give' [CEV, NJB, NLT], 'to create, to make' [LN], 'to fashion' [NIC], 'to fit' [Lns].

QUESTION—To what body does this clause refer?

It refers to Christ's earthly body [Hu].

10:6 whole-burnt-offerings[a] and for[b] sin not you-were-pleased-with.[c]

LEXICON—a. ὁλοκαύτωμα (LN **53.24**) (BAGD 1. p. 564): 'whole burnt offering' [BAGD, HNTC, LN, Lns, Mil, NIC, WBC; NASB, TNT], 'burnt offering' [KJV, NIV, NJB, NRSV], 'whole-offering' [REB], 'offering of animals burned whole' [**LN**], 'animals burned whole on the altar' [TEV], 'animals burned on the altar' [NLT], 'animal sacrifices' [CEV], 'holocaust' [NAB]. It refers to a whole animal burned on the altar [Alf].

b. περί with genitive object (LN 89.6) (BAGD 1.g. p. 645): 'for', 'in relation to, with regard to, concerning' [LN], 'to take away' [BAGD], 'to atone for' [BAGD]. The phrase περὶ ἁμαρτίας 'for sin' is translated 'sin offering' [BAGD, HNTC, Lns, NIC, WBC; NAB, NIV, NRSV, REB, TNT], 'offering for sin' [CEV], 'other offerings for sin' [NLT], 'sacrifice for sin' [Mil; KJV, NASB, NJB], 'sacrifice to take away sins' [TEV]. This phrase refers to sin offerings [Alf, EGT, GNC, Hu, Lg(K), My, Wst].

c. aorist act. indic. of εὐδοκέω (LN 25.87) (BAGD 2.b. p. 319): 'to be pleased with' [LN; CEV, NIV, NLT, TEV], 'to approve' [BAGD, Lns], 'to take pleasure in' [HNTC, LN; NASB, NJB, NRSV], 'to find pleasure in' [TNT], 'to have pleasure in' [Mil, NIC; KJV] [BAGD; WBC], 'to delight in' [BAGD; REB], 'to take delight in' [NAB].

10:7 Then I said, 'Behold, I-have-come'[a]

LEXICON—a. pres. act. indic. of ἥκω (LN 15.84, 85.10) (BAGD 1.c. p. 344): 'to have come' [BAGD, HNTC, NIC, WBC; CEV, NAB, NASB, NIV, NLT, NRSV, REB], 'to be present' [BAGD], 'to be here' [LN (85.10), Lns, Mil; TEV, TNT], 'to arrive' [LN (15.84)], 'to come' [LN (15.84); KJV, NJB]. It indicates a state, with the force of the perfect tense [Mil]. It implies that the speaker had already arrived [NCBC, TNTC]. The speaker is Christ [TH].

QUESTION—Why is this verse mentioned?

It shows that Scripture attested God's purpose which was that, instead of the OT sacrifices, Christ should offer his body to God [HNTC].

QUESTION—What is meant by τότε 'then'?

1. It is temporal [Alf, Blm, EGT, Hwt, Mil, My, TNTC, Wst].

1.1 It refers to the time when God had prepared a body for Christ [Alf, My, TNTC] at the incarnation [TNTC].

1.2 It refers to the time referred to in the preceding quotation from the Psalm [Blm].

1.3 It refers to the time when it was evident that animal sacrifices were not adequate [EGT, Wst].
1.4 It refers to the fullness of time [Hwt].
2. It is circumstantial, referring to the circumstances just referred to [EBC]: (since the OT sacrifices were inadequate,) in those circumstances . . .

—in[a] a-roll[b] of-a-scroll[c] it-stands-written concerning[d] me—

LEXICON—a. ἐν with dative object (LN 83.13): 'in' [HNTC, LN, Lns, Mil, NIC, WBC; all versions except CEV]. The whole clause is translated 'as the Scriptures say' [CEV].

b. κεθαλίς (LN **6.67**) (BAGD p. 430): 'roll' [BAGD, HNTC, Mil; NASB], 'scroll' [LN, NIC; NJB, NRSV], 'section' [LN], 'volume' [Mil; KJV]. The phrase κεφαλίδι βιβλίου 'roll of a scroll' is translated 'the book' [NAB], 'the scroll' [WBC; NIV, REB], 'the bookroll' [Lns], 'the book of the Law' [TEV, TNT], 'the Scriptures' [CEV, NLT]. This phrase refers to the OT Scriptures [Blm, EBC, Hu, Hwt, NIC, TNTC] in the form of scrolls rolled on wooden rods [HNTC], to the books of Moses [NTC, TH, Wst]. The κεθαλίς 'roll' was literally the knob on the head of the wooden roller on which the scroll was rolled [Alf, Blm, EGT, Hu, Hwt, Lg, Lns, Mil, My, NIC, NIGTC, NTC]; it came to mean the scroll itself [EBC, Lg, Lns, Mil, NIC, NIGTC, WBC].

c. βιβλίον (LN 6.64, 33.52) (BAGD 1. p. 1141): 'scroll' [BAGD, LN (6.64)], 'roll' [LN (6.64)], 'book' [BAGD, HNTC, LN (6.64, 33.52), Mil, NIC; KJV, NASB, NJB, NRSV].

d. περί with genitive object (LN 90.24): 'concerning' [LN, Lns, Mil], 'about' [HNTC, LN, WBC; NIV, NLT], 'of' [LN, NIC; all versions except CEV, NIV, NLT], not explicit [CEV].

QUESTION—How is this phrase related to other phrases?

1. It is parenthetical [Alf, EGT, ICC, Lg, Lns, Mil, My, NIC, TH; KJV, NASB, NIV, NRSV], implying that Christ's coming had been written in the Scriptures [EGT, ICC, My] and that Christ acknowledged that what was written was binding on him [EGT], that Christ is consciously fulfilling prophecy [Mil].
2. It authenticates the preceding quotation from the Psalm [HNTC, Hu; NAB, TEV, TNT]: I have come, as it is written.

QUESTION—How are the two nouns related in the genitive construction κεφαλίδι βιβλίου 'roll of the scroll'?

1. The κεφαλίδι 'roll' is the βιβλίου 'scroll' [Alf, Hu, Lg, Lns, My, NTC; NAB, NIV, REB]: the roll, which is the scroll.
2. The βιβλίου 'scroll' indicates the form of the κεφαλίδι 'roll' [NIC, WBC]: the roll in the form of a scroll.

QUESTION—What relationship is indicated by the perfect tense form γέγραπται 'it stands written'?

It indicates the continuing validity of what was written [NTC, TH].

'to-do, God, your will.'"[a]

LEXICON—a. θέλημα (LN 25.2, 30.59) (BAGD 1.c.γ. p. 354): 'will' [BAGD, HNTC, LN (30.59), Lns, Mil, NIC, WBC; all versions except CEV, TNT], 'wish' [LN (25.2)], 'desire' [LN (25.2)], 'what one wants' [CEV, TNT], 'purpose' [LN (30.59)], 'plan' [LN (30.59)].

QUESTION—What is this phrase related to?

It is related to ἥκω 'I have come' [Alf, Lg, Mil, My, NIGTC]: I have come to do your will. It is emphatic [NIGTC].

QUESTION—What relationship is indicated by the genitive articular infinitive τοῦ ποιῆσαι 'to do'?

It indicates purpose [EBC, Lg(K), Mil]: I have come in order to do your will.

QUESTION—How is the nominative articular form ὁ θεός 'God' used?

It is used as a vocative [HNTC, Lns, Mil, TH; all versions]: (oh) God.

10:8 above[a] saying, (quote) "Sacrifices and offerings[b] and whole-burnt-offerings[c] and for[d] sin not you-desired[e] nor were-pleased-with,"[f]

LEXICON—a. ἀνώτερος (LN **61.6**) (BAGD 2. p. 77): 'above' [BAGD, **LN**, Mil; KJV, NASB, NRSV], 'earlier' [BAGD], 'preceding' [**LN**], 'first' [HNTC, NIC; NAB, NIV, NJB, REB, TEV, TNT], 'up at the head' [Lns], 'in the former part of the quotation' [WBC], not explicit [CEV, NLT]. The phrase ἀνώτερον λέγων 'above saying' is translated 'referring to what has just been said' [**LN**]. It refers to what was mentioned in the preceding quotation [EBC, NIC], in 10:5–6 [EGT, GNC], in 10:5 [HNTC], in 10:6 [ICC], in the first part of the quotation [My, NIGTC, TH, WBC]. It refers only to lines 1 and 3 of the quotation ("sacrifice and offering . . ." and "whole burnt offerings and sin offering . . ."), indicating that these are the 'above'—i.e., the 'more important'— lines [Lns].

b. προσφορά: 'offering'. See this word in 10:5.

c. ὁλοκαύτωμα: 'whole burnt offering'. See this word in 10:6.

d. περί: 'for'. See this word and the phrase περὶ ἁμαρτίας 'for sin' in 10:6.

e. aorist act. indic. of θέλω: 'to desire'. See this word in 10:5.

f. aorist act. indic. of εὐδοκέω: 'to be pleased with'. See this word in 10:6.

QUESTION—What is the function of this verse?

It begins the comments on the prophecy quoted above [Alf, Blm, GNC, Hu, Mil, WBC] and explains the significance of the quotation [EGT].

QUESTION—What relationship is indicated by the present participle λέγων 'saying'?

1. It is subordinate to the following finite verb εἴρηκεν 'he said' and thus moves the focus of attention to the quotation in the following verse [NIGTC]. The present tense is used because the quotation is still in effect in Scripture [NIGTC].
2. It is treated as a finite verb parallel to εἴρηκεν 'he said' in the following verse [HNTC; NAB, NIV, NJB, REB, TEV, TNT]: he says . . . then he said.
3. It expresses correspondence [My]: as he was saying . . . so he then said . . .

4. It is temporal [Mil; KJV, NASB, NRSV]: when/after he said. (The fact that the action of this participle precedes the following εἴρηκεν 'he said' even though it is present tense is shown by the introductory τότε 'then' in 10:9.)

QUESTION—What is indicated by the plurals used in naming the various sacrifices in this verse?

1. The plurals generalize the reference to these sacrifices [EBC, My], emphasizing their inadequacy [EBC], the inadequacy of the multiplicity and repetition of these sacrifices [WBC].
2. The plurals here are semantic equivalents to the generic singulars in the preceding mention in 1:5 [NIGTC].
3. They are accommodated to the plural ὁλοκαυτώματα 'whole burnt offerings' [Wst].

which-sort-of-things are-offered according-to[a] law,[b]

LEXICON—a. κατά with accusative object: (LN 89.8): 'according to' [HNTC, Lns, Mil, NIC; NAB, NASB, NRSV], 'in accordance with' [LN; TNT], 'by' [KJV]. The phrase κατὰ νόμον 'according to law' is translated 'as the law prescribes' [WBC], 'the Law teaches' [CEV]. This entire clause is translated 'what the Law lays down as the things to be offered' [NJB], 'although the law prescribes them' [REB], 'although the law required them to be made' [NIV], 'even though all these sacrifices are offered according to the law' [TEV], 'though they are required by the law of Moses' [NLT]. This expresses manner [Mil]. This word here implies 'in accordance with the commands of' [Alf].

b. νόμος (LN 33.55, 33.56, 33.333) (BAGD 3. p. 542): 'law' [LN (33.333), Lns], 'Law' [HNTC], 'the law' [BAGD, Mil, NIC, WBC; KJV, NIV, NLT, NRSV, REB], 'the Law' [LN (33.55); CEV, NASB, NJB, TEV, TNT], 'Scriptures' [LN (33.56)], 'the prescriptions of the law' [NAB].

QUESTION—How is this clause related to the preceding clause?

1. It is parenthetical [HNTC, Mil, NIC, NTC, TH, WBC; NAB, NASB, NLT, NRSV].
2. It is not parenthetical, but rather applies the preceding comment to the levitical system [My, NIGTC; CEV], thus identifying them as inferior [NIGTC].

QUESTION—What relationship is indicated by the indefinite relative pronoun αἵτινες 'which'?

Although it is feminine gender, it refers to all four types of sacrifices [Lns, My, NIGTC].

1. It is used as a simple relative pronoun describing the sacrifices and offerings mentioned in the preceding clause [GNC, NIC, WBC; KJV, NASB, NJB]: which are offered.
2. It is qualitative, classifying its antecedents, focusing on the kind of things they are [Alf, Lg(K), Mil, My]: which sort of things are offered.

3. It makes a statement concerning the sacrifices and offerings [HNTC; CEV, NAB, NRSV]: they are offered.
4. It expresses a concession [EBC, NTC; NIV, NLT, REB, TEV, TNT]: although they are offered.

QUESTION—What is implied by the present tense of προσφέρονται 'are offered'?

It implies that the levitical sacrifices were still being offered [Hu].

QUESTION—What is implied by νόμον 'law' without the definite article?

1. It is nevertheless definite [Alf, GNC, HNTC, Hu, Mil, NIC, NTC; all versions] either with or without the article [Alf, NIGTC]; it refers to the Mosaic law [Alf, GNC, HNTC, Hu, Mil; TNT]: the Law.
2. The absence of the article calls attention to the legal aspect [Wst].

10:9 then he-has-said, "Behold, I-have-come[a] to-do your will."[b]

TEXT—Some manuscripts add ὁ θεός '(oh) God' after ποιῆσαι 'to do'. GNT does not deal with this variant; only Blm (evidently), EGT, KJV, TEV, TNT add 'oh God'.

LEXICON—a. pres. act. indic. of ἥκω: 'to have come.' See this word in 10:7.
b. θέλημα: 'will'. See this word in 10:7.

QUESTION—What is implied by the perfect tense of εἴρηκεν 'he has said'?

It indicates the permanence of what he said [EBC, ICC, Lns, NIC, NTC], that what he has said permanently accomplishes God's will [EGT, Mil].

He-does-away-with[a] the first in-order-that he-may-establish[b] the second,

LEXICON—a. pres. act. indic. of ἀναιρέω (LN **76.22**) (BAGD 1.b. p. 55): 'to do away with' [BAGD, **LN**, NIC, WBC; CEV, TEV], 'to abolish' [BAGD, HNTC, LN; NJB, NRSV, REB, TNT], 'to take away' [Lns, Mil; KJV, NAB, NASB], 'to set aside' [NIV], 'to cancel' [NLT], 'to invalidate' [LN]. It is an emphatic word [EBC, NIGTC], indicating total abolition [EBC, My, NIGTC, TH].
b. aorist act. subj. of ἵστημι (LN **76.21**) (BAGD I.2.a. p. 382): 'to establish' [BAGD, HNTC, **LN,** Lns, Mil, NIC; all versions except CEV, TEV], 'to put into force' [LN], 'to make valid' [BAGD], 'to put in (their) place' [TEV], 'to confirm the validity of' [WBC], 'to replace (the first)' [CEV].

QUESTION—How is this clause related to the preceding clause?

1. It expresses the implication of the preceding quotation [Hu; NAB, REB]: that is, he does away with the first.
2. It indicates the conclusion from the preceding statement [Blm; TEV]: the conclusion is that he does away with the first.
3. It summarizes the two parts of the quotation [NTC].
4. It is parenthetical; it calls attention to the importance of what is said in the following verse [My].
5. It indicates the significance of the preceding quotation as it is attributed to Christ [WBC].
6. It is a general comment on the preceding quotation [TNTC].

QUESTION—Who is the actor of ἀναιρεῖ 'he does away with'?
1. It is God [Mil; TEV]: God does away with the first.
2. It is Christ [Alf, My; CEV, TNT]: Christ does away with the first.

QUESTION—To what do πρῶτον 'first' and δεύτερον 'second' refer?
1. They refer to the first and second covenants [Mil; NAB]: the first covenant . . . the second covenant.
2. They refer to the old sacrifices and Christ's sacrifice [Blm, EBC, GNC, HNTC, Hu, NCBC, NIGTC; TEV, TNT]: the old sacrifices . . . Christ's sacrifice.
3. 'First' refers to the offering of sacrifices and offerings; 'second' refers to doing the will of God [Lns, My, NIC, NTC, TH, WBC, Wst], the latter expressed in Christ's sacrificial death [TH, Wst].
4. They refer to what God does not desire and what he does desire [Alf].

10:10 by[a] which will we-are sanctified[b] through[c] the offering[d] of-the body of-Jesus Christ once-for-all.[e]

LEXICON—a. ἐν with dative object (LN 89.76) (BAGD III.3.a. p. 261): 'by' [HNTC, LN, NIC, WBC; KJV, NAB, NASB, NIV, NRSV, REB], 'by means of' [LN], 'in the fulfillment of' [Mil], 'in connection with' [Lns], not explicit [CEV]. The phrase ἐν ᾧ θελήματι 'by which will' is translated 'because (he) did what God wanted him to do' [TEV, TNT], 'what God wants is' [NLT]. The phrase ἐν ᾧ θελήματι ἡγιασμένοι ἐσμέν 'by which will we are sanctified' is translated 'and this will was for us to be made holy' [NJB]. This preposition here means 'in the course of or fulfillment of' [Alf, My], 'in conformity with' [Blm], 'contained in' [EGT, Lg(K), Wst]; it expresses cause [BAGD, Mil, WBC].

b. perf. pass. participle of ἁγιάζω (LN 88.26) (BAGD 2. p. 8): 'to be sanctified' [BAGD, Lns, Mil, NIC; KJV, NAB, NASB, NRSV], 'to be made holy' [LN, Mil; CEV, NIV, NJB, NLT], 'to be purified from sin' [TEV], 'to be cleansed and set apart for (his) service' [TNT], 'to be consecrated' [HNTC, WBC; REB]. The perfect indicative tense (expressed by this perfect participle plus ἐσμέν 'we are') indicates the permanence of Christ's work [Alf, HNTC, NCBC, NIGTC, NTC, TH], the completed act [Lg(K), NIC], the continuing state of believers [NIGTC]. This verb phrase refers to atonement [Blm, Mil, My], to conversion and being set apart for God [EBC, Lns], and purification [Blm]. It means to be cleansed from sin [EGT, GNC, NIC] and made fit for fellowship with God [EGT, Hwt, NIC].

c. διά with genitive object (LN **89.76**) (BAGD A.III.1.a. p. 180): 'through' [BAGD, HNTC, LN, Mil, NIC, WBC; KJV, NAB, NASB, NIV, NRSV, REB], 'by' [NJB, NLT, TEV], 'by means of' [Lns]. The phrase διὰ τῆς προσφορᾶς τοῦ σώματος 'through the offering of the body' is translated 'and offered (his) body' [TNT], 'because Christ obeyed God and offered himself' [CEV]. It expresses means [Mil, TNTC].

d. προσφορά: 'offering'. See this word in 10:5.

e. ἐφάπαξ: 'once for all'. See this word in 10:5. It is an emphatic word [EBC, Lns, TH] and emphatic by its position [GNC, Lns, NCBC, NIC, NIGTC, TH]. Since it is fully adequate, it is absolutely final [Hu, Lns, NIC, TNTC].

QUESTION—Why is this clause mentioned?

It explains what is meant by doing God's will and the results of Christ's obedience to God's will [Blm, NIGTC] and sums up the preceding argument [NIGTC]. It makes the application of the biblical quotation [WBC].

QUESTION—What is meant by ἐν ᾧ θελήματι 'by which will'?

It refers to the will of God as fulfilled by Christ [NIC, NIGTC, WBC].

QUESTION—What is implied by σῶματος 'body'?

It implies Christ's full incarnate personality [HNTC], his participation in human life [TNTC, WBC]. It emphasizes the reality of Christ's physical death [NTC]. It means simply the offering of himself in his incarnate life [NIC, TH]; it reflects the reference to Christ's body in 10:5 [WBC]; it emphasizes the totality of Christ's work [Wst].

QUESTION—What relationship is indicated by the combination Ἰησοῦ Χριστοῦ 'Jesus Christ', which is not often found in this epistle?

It emphasizes that both the human nature (Jesus) and the divine nature (Christ) were involved in the sanctification [NTC, Wst].

QUESTION—What is ἐφάπαξ 'once for all' connected with?

1. It is connected with προσφορᾶς 'offering' [Alf, Blm, EBC, Hu, ICC, Mil, NCBC, TH, WBC; CEV, NJB, TEV, TNT]: the offering which occurred once for all.
2. It is connected with ἡγιασμένοι ἐσμέν 'we are sanctified' [Lg, Lns, My, NIC, Wst]: we are sanctified once for all.

DISCOURSE UNIT: 10:11–18 [GNC, Lns, NCBC, NIC; NJB]. The topic is the perfect offering and the fulfillment of Jer. 31:31–34 [GNC], the final comparison with regard to the removal of sin [Lns], Christ seated at God's right hand [NCBC], the enthroned high priest [NIC], the efficacy of Christ's sacrifice [NJB].

DISCOURSE UNIT: 10:11–14 [HNTC]. The topic is Christ's unique sacrifice.

10:11 And on-the-one-hand every priest stands according-to[a] day ministering[b] and offering the same sacrifices many-times,

TEXT—Instead of ἱερεύς 'priest' some manuscripts have ἀρχιερεύς 'high priest'. GNT reads 'priest' with an A decision, indicating that the text is certain. Only Alf and My read 'high priest'.

LEXICON—a. κατά with accusative object (LN) (BAGD II.2.c. p. 406): 'from . . . to' [LN], 'every' [BAGD; NJB, TEV], 'each' [CEV]. The phrase καθ' ἡμέραν 'according to day' is translated 'daily' [BAGD, Mil; KJV, NASB, REB], 'day by day' [Lns, NIC; NAB], 'day after day' [HNTC, WBC; NIV, NLT, NRSV, TNT].

b. pres. act. participle of λειτουργέω (LN **53.13**) (BAGD 1. p. 470): 'to minister' [HNTC, Mil, NIC; KJV, NAB, NASB, TNT], 'to perform one's service' [REB], 'to perform one's priestly service' [WBC], 'to do one's work' [CEV], 'to perform one's religious duties' [LN; NIV], 'to perform one's religious rites' [**LN**], 'to carry out religious rites, to do official service' [Lns], 'to perform a public service' (of service performed by priests and Levites in the Temple) [BAGD]. This participle is also translated as a phrase: 'at his duties' [NJB], 'at his service' [NRSV]. The phrase ἕστηκεν λειτουργῶν 'stands ministering' is translated 'performs his services' [TEV], 'stands before the altar' [NLT]. This word refers to all of the priestly functions [EBC].

QUESTION—What relationship is indicated by the introductory καί 'and'?

It introduces a new contrasting pair [Alf, EGT, Hwt, Lg, NCBC, NTC] contrasting the priests who stand and Christ who has sat down [Hwt, Lg]. It advances the argument one step further [EGT, Mil, My, NIGTC, Wst], focusing on the actions of the priest [EGT]. It recapitulates the preceding statements [Hu, Mil]. The contrast is indicated by μέν 'on the one hand' in this verse and δέ 'on the other hand' in the following verse [Mil, NTC, Wst].

QUESTION—What is implied by πᾶς ἱερεύς 'every priest'?

It refers to the priests in general in the course of their ministry [Blm, EBC, HNTC, Hu, Lns, NCBC, NIGTC], including the high priest [Blm, NCBC].

QUESTION—What is implied by ἕστηκεν 'stands'?

It refers to the fact that the priests were required to stand in performing their ministry [Alf, Blm, EBC, HNTC, Hu, Hwt, Lg, Mil, My, NIC, NIGTC, NTC, TNTC, WBC, Wst]. It implies that their task is never finished [GNC, Hu, Hwt, Mil, NIC, NTC, TNTC, WBC, Wst]. It implies humility [Blm], inferiority [My]. The perfect tense of this verb has present tense force [Hu, NTC, WBC]; it may imply that the levitical ritual was still being carried on when the epistle was written [GNC, Hu].

QUESTION—What is the phrase καθ' ἡμέραν 'according to day' connected with?

1. It is connected with ἕστηκεν 'stands' [Lns, Mil; KJV, NASB, NRSV]: he stands daily.
2. It is connected with λειτουργῶν 'ministering' [NIC; CEV, NAB, TEV]: ministering daily.
3. It is connected with both of the above [EBC, HNTC, NIC; TNT]: he stands ministering day after day.
4. It is connected with the clause as a whole [NIV, REB]: every day he stands and ministers.

QUESTION—What relationship is indicated by the participles λειτουργῶν 'ministering' and προσφέρων 'offering'?

The present tenses may imply that the levitical ritual was still being carried on when the epistle was written [GNC, Hu].

1. They indicate the circumstances involved in the priest's position [NTC]: he stands ministering and offering.

2. They are treated as equivalent to parallel finite verbs [NIV, TEV]: he stands and ministers and offers.

QUESTION—What relationship is indicated by the second καί 'and'?

1. It coordinates the actions of the two present participles λειτουργῶν 'ministering' and προσφέρων 'offering' [Mil; KJV]: ministering and offering.
2. It introduces προσφέρων 'offering' as an expansion of λειτουργῶν 'ministering' [NIGTC]: ministering; that is, offering.
3. It indicates that 'offering' is the important part of the 'ministering' [Alf, Lns].

which never are-able to-take-away sins,

QUESTION—What relationship is indicated by the indefinite relative pronoun αἵτινες 'which'?

1. It is qualitative [Alf, Lns, Mil, NIGTC, TNTC, Wst]: the sort of things which. It introduces a nonrestrictive relative clause, describing rather than identifying the sacrifices referred to [Mil].
2. It implies a concession [NTC]: although they never . . .

QUESTION—What is indicated by περιελεῖν 'to take away'?

1. It is emphatic [EGT, Lns, Mil, My, NTC, TNTC, WBC]: to deliver completely.
2. It is not emphatic [ICC, TH].

10:12 this-man on-the-other-hand having-offered one sacrifice for[a] sins into[b] the continuous[c] sat-down at[d] (the) right-(hand)[e] of-God,

LEXICON—a. ὑπέρ with genitive object (LN 90.36) (BAGD 1.b. p. 838): 'for' [HNTC, LN, Lns, Mil, NIC, WBC; all versions except CEV], 'on behalf of' [LN], not explicit [CEV]. The phrase ὑπὲρ ἁμαρτιῶν 'for sins' is translated 'in order to atone for sins' [BAGD]. Here it means 'to deal with' [NIGTC].

b. εἰς with accusative object (LN 67.95, 84.22) (BAGD 2.b. p. 229): 'into' [LN (84.22)], 'for' [BAGD, HNTC, Mil, NIC, WBC; NASB, NIV, NLT, NRSV, REB, TNT], 'throughout' [BAGD], 'in' [Lns]. The phrase εἰς τὸ διηνεκές 'into the continuous' is translated 'forever' [BAGD, LN (67.95); KJV, NAB, NJB, TEV], 'that is good forever' [CEV].

c. διηνεκής (LN 67.95) (BAGD p. 195): 'continuous' [BAGD], 'all time' [HNTC, Mil, WBC; NASB, NIV, NLT, NRSV, REB, TNT], 'evermore' [NIC], 'perpetuity' [Lns]. See b. above [BAGD, LN].

d. ἐν with dative object (LN 83.23, 87.36): 'at' [HNTC, LN (83.23), Lns, Mil, NIC, WBC; all versions except KJV], 'on' [KJV]. The phrase ἐκάθισεν ἐν δεξιᾷ 'sat down at the right' is translated 'to sit at the right hand, to give a special place of honor to' [LN (87.36)].

e. δεξιός (LN 87.36) (BAGD 2.a. p. 174): 'right hand' [HNTC, Mil, NIC, WBC; all versions except TEV], 'right side' [CEV, TEV], 'right' [BAGD], 'the place of honor at God's right hand' [NLT]. See d. above [LN (87.36)].

QUESTION—What relationship is indicated by δέ 'on the other hand'?

It balances the μέν 'on the one hand' in the preceding verse [Lns, Mil, NIGTC]. It indicates a strong contrast with the preceding verse [TH].

QUESTION—What relationship is indicated by the participle προσενέγκας 'having offered'?

1. It is temporal [GNC, Hu, Lg(K), Mil, WBC, Wst; KJV, NIV, NRSV]: after he had offered.
2. It is semantically parallel to the following verb ἐκάθισεν 'sat down' [NIC; NAB, NJB, TEV, TNT]: he offered . . . and sat down.

QUESTION—What is implied by the word order of μίαν 'one'?

It is emphatic by forefronting [EBC, NIGTC]: having offered *one* offering.

QUESTION—What is the phrase εἰς τὸ διηνεκές 'into the continuous, forever' connected with?

1. It is connected with what precedes [EBC, GNC, HNTC, Mil, NIC, TNTC, WBC, Wst; all versions except NAB, NJB]: having offered one sacrifice for sins forever. It means that the sacrifice was effective forever [NIC; TEV].
2. It is connected with the following ἐκάθισεν 'he sat down' [Alf, Blm, EGT, ICC, Lg, Lns, My, NIGTC, TH; NAB, NJB]: he sat down forever.

QUESTION—What is implied by ἐκάθισεν 'he sat down'?

It contrasts with the standing position of the priests [EBC, Hwt, ICC] and implies that Christ's work is completed [EBC, GNC, HNTC, Hu, Hwt, ICC, NCBC, NIC, NTC, TNTC, WBC] and that he has put an end to the Levitical priesthood [NTC], and that God has accepted his sacrifice [NCBC, NIC].

QUESTION—What is implied by the phrase ἐν δεξιᾷ τοῦ θεοῦ 'at the right hand of God'?

It refers to the place of highest honor [EBC, Hu, Lns, NCBC, NIC, NTC, TNTC, WBC; NLT].

10:13 the rest/henceforth[a] waiting until his enemies are-placed (as) a-footstool[b] of-his feet.

LEXICON—a. λοιπός (LN 63.21, 67.134) (BAGD 3.a.α. p. 480): 'rest' [LN (63.21)], 'remaining' [LN (63.21)]. The phrase τὸ λοιπόν 'the rest' is translated 'henceforth' [HNTC, LN, Lns, Mil], 'from henceforth' [KJV], 'thenceforward' [NIC], 'from that time onward' [NASB], 'from now on' [LN], 'since that time' [NIV], 'since then' [NRSV, TNT], 'then' [BAGD, WBC], 'there' [CEV, NLT], 'there now' [TEV], 'now' [NAB], 'where now' [NJB, REB]. It refers to the time following Christ's taking his seat [EBC, Lg(K), My]. It means 'from now on' [NTC, TH]. It means 'in this connection' and indicates that the author is going to continue his reference to the quoted Psalm [NIGTC].

b. ὑποπόδιον (LN 6.117, 37.8) (BAGD p. 847): 'footstool' [BAGD, HNTC, LN, Lns, Mil, NIC; NASB, NLT, NRSV, TEV]. The phrase ὑποπόδιον τῶν ποδῶν 'footstool of the feet' is translated 'footstool' [WBC; KJV, NIV, NJB, REB, TNT], 'under his power' [CEV], 'under the complete control of' [LN (37.8)]. The phrase ὑποπόδιον τῶν ποδῶν αὐτοῦ 'footstool of his feet' is translated 'beneath his feet' [NAB], implying subjugation [Mil]. This word figuratively expresses the position of conquered enemies [Mil].

QUESTION—What relationship is indicated by the participle ἐκδεχόμενος 'waiting'?

It is translated as a finite verb [HNTC; all versions except KJV, NASB] expressing an accompanying fact [Mil]: in addition, now he waits. There is no implication of doubt concerning the outcome; the defeat is certain [Hu, Mil, TNTC]. It implies eager (patient [TH]) expectation [NIGTC, TH].

QUESTION—Who is the implied actor of τεθῶσιν 'are placed'?

The implied actor is God [GNC, Mil, NIGTC, TH, WBC; TEV]: his enemies are placed as a footstool by God.

QUESTION—To whom does οἱ ἐχθροὶ αὐτοῦ 'his enemies' refer?

It includes all evil [EBC], every opposing power [WBC], everyone who opposes Christ's authority [Hu, NTC], Satan and all who reject Christ [Lns]. They include the elect also, who were previously enemies [Alf].

QUESTION—How are the two nouns related in the genitive construction ὑποπόδιον τῶν ποδῶν 'footstool of the feet'?

1. The genitive 'feet' states the purpose of the footstool [HNTC, Lns, Mil, NIC; NASB]: footstool for the use of the feet.
2. The genitive case states what the footstool is under [TEV]: footstool under the feet.

10:14 for by-one offering[a] he-has-perfected[b] into[c] the continuous[d] the-(ones) being-sanctified.[e]

LEXICON—a. προσφορά: 'offering'. See this word in 10:5. Here it refers to Christ's perfect life [Wst] and his atoning death [NIGTC, Wst].

b. perf. act. indic. of τελειόω (LN 88.38) (BAGD 2.e.α. p. 810): 'to perfect' [LN, Mil; KJV, NAB, NASB, NLT, NRSV, REB], 'to make perfect' [BAGD, HNTC, LN; NIV, TEV, TNT], 'to achieve eternal perfection' [NJB], 'to bring to perfection' [NIC], 'to bring to completion' [Lns], 'to purge decisively' [WBC], 'to set free from sin' [CEV]. It implies a condition of perfection [Lg, Mil] from imperfection [Mil], moral purity [Mil], perfect justification and reconciliation to God [Blm], free access to God [NIGTC]. It means the full accomplishment of God's saving purpose [GNC]. The perfect tense implies a continuing result of Christ's act [Mil, NCBC, NIGTC, WBC], an accomplished fact [WBC].

c. εἰς with accusative object: 'into'. See this word and the phrase εἰς τὸ διηνεκές in 10:12.

d. διηνεκής: 'continuous'. See this word in 10:12.

e. pres. pass. participle of ἁγιάζω (LN 88.26) (BAGD 2. p. 8): 'to be sanctified' [BAGD, Lns, Mil, NIC; KJV, NAB, NASB, NJB, NRSV], 'to be made holy' [LN; NIV], 'to be purified from sin' [TEV], 'to be consecrated' [WBC; REB]. This passive participle is also translated as an active voice: 'to consecrate' [HNTC], 'to make holy' [NLT]; as a clause: 'those whom he cleanses and sets apart for his service' [TNT], 'the people he brings to God' [CEV]. It refers to being made holy by faith through the action of the Holy Spirit and resulting in obedience to God [Blm], being cleansed from sin resulting in holy living [Lns], actual sanctification in people's hearts [Mil].

QUESTION—What relationship is indicated by γάρ 'for'?

It indicates the reason for the statement in 10:13 (10:12–13 NIGTC) [EBC, Lns, Mil, NIGTC], the proof of the preceding argument [WBC], of the statement in 10:12 [My]; it sums up the whole preceding argument [NCBC].

QUESTION—What is implied by the word order of μιᾷ 'one'?

It indicates emphasis by forefronting [EBC]: by *one* offering.

QUESTION—Who is the implied subject of τετελείωκεν 'he has perfected'?

The subject is Christ [Alf, EBC, Wst]: Christ has perfected.

QUESTION—What is the implied actor/instrument of the participle τοὺς ἁγιαζομένους 'the ones being made holy'?

1. The implied actor is Christ [HNTC, WBC; TNT]: they are being made holy by Christ.
2. The implied instrument is μιᾷ προσφορᾷ 'one offering' [REB]: they are being made holy by the one offering.

QUESTION—What does the present tense of the participle τοὺς ἁγιαζομένους 'the ones being made holy' indicate?

1. It indicates a continued process of adding to the number of persons who are made holy [TNTC] (cf. "the ones entering the room"): the ones who come, one after the other, and are made holy.
2. It is timeless [EGT, ICC, Mil, My, NIC]: the sanctified ones.
3. It indicates a process of being made holy [Alf, Lns, NCBC, NTC, WBC, Wst]: the ones gradually being made holy. It refers to the entire course of sainthood [Lns].

DISCOURSE UNIT: 10:15–18 [HNTC]. The topic is the final sacrifice.

10:15 And the Holy Spirit testifies to-us;

QUESTION—What relationship is indicated by δέ 'and'?

It indicates transition [Mil, My]. This and the following three verses state the proof that Christ's sacrifice is final [EGT, HNTC, Hu, Hwt, ICC, Lg, My, NCBC].

QUESTION—What does the present tense of the verb μαρτυρεῖ 'he testifies' indicate?

It indicates that the Holy Spirit is speaking now, bringing the text from the past into the present [WBC]. This word is emphatic by its word order [Wst].

QUESTION—To whom does ἡμῖν 'to us' refer?

It refers to Christians in general [Alf, ICC, My, NIGTC, TH], including the author [ICC, NIGTC, TH].

1. It is a dative of indirect object [EBC, My, TH; KJV, NAB, NASB, NIV, NJB, NRSV]: after having said to us.

2. It is a dative of respect or advantage [Alf, EGT, HNTC, Lg(K)]: after having said for us.

for after[a] the to-have-said/having-said,

TEXT—Instead of εἰρηκέναι 'to have said' some manuscripts read προειρηκέναι 'to have said beforehand'. GNT does not deal with this variant. Only Blm, KJV read προειρηκέναι 'to have said beforehand'.

LEXICON—a. μετά with accusative object (LN 67.48) (BAGD B.II.4.b. p. 510): 'after' [BAGD, HNTC, LN, Lns, Mil, NIC, WBC; KJV, NAB, NASB, NJB, NRSV], not explicit [CEV]. The phrase μετὰ γὰρ τὸ εἰρηκέναι 'for after having said' is translated 'first he says' [NIV, NLT, REB, TEV, TNT].

QUESTION—What relationship is indicated by γάρ 'for'?

It indicates the grounds for the preceding comment [Mil, NIGTC].

QUESTION—Who is the implied actor of τὸ εἰρηκέναι 'having said'?

1. The implied actor is the Holy Spirit [NIC; CEV]: after the Holy Spirit had said.
2. The implied actor is God [My, TH]: after God had said.

QUESTION—What is the prepositional phrase μετὰ τὸ εἰρηκέναι 'after having said' connected with?

1. There is nothing to follow it up [EBC, EGT, GNC, TH, WBC; NASB]; however, in sense it is followed by the words of 10:17 [EBC, EGT, ICC, Mil, TH, TNTC, WBC, Wst; all versions except KJV].
2. It is connected with λέγει κύριος 'the Lord says' in the following verse [Blm, Lns, My; NJB]: after having said . . . the Lord says. . . . Although this phrase is a part of the quotation, the author of Hebrews uses it to divide the quotation [Lns, My].
3. It is connected with what precedes [NIGTC]: after the Holy Spirit had spoken in the preceding verses, he witnesses in the following words.

10:16 "'This (is) the covenant[a] which I-will-covenant[b] with[c] them after[d] those days,' says (the) Lord;

LEXICON—a. διαθήκη (LN 34.43, 34.44) (BAGD 2. p. 183): 'covenant' [BAGD, HNTC, LN (34.43, 34.44), Mil, NIC, WBC; all versions except CEV, NLT], 'new covenant' [NLT], 'agreement' [CEV], 'testament' [Lns].

b. fut. mid. (deponent = act.) indic. of διατίθημι (LN 34.43) (BAGD 1. p. 189): 'to covenant' [Mil], 'to make a covenant, to draw up' [Lns], 'to make (a covenant)' [HNTC, LN, NIC, WBC; all versions], 'to decree, to ordain' [BAGD], 'to arrange' [Mil].

c. πρός with accusative object (LN 89.112): 'with' [HNTC, LN, Mil, NIC, WBC; all versions], 'in regard to' [Lns].

d. μετά with accusative object (LN 67.48): 'after' [HNTC, LN, Lns, Mil, WBC; all versions except NJB, TEV]. The phrase μετὰ τὰς ἡμέρας ἐκείνας 'after those days' is translated 'when those days have come'

[NJB], 'in the days to come' [TEV], 'in days to come' [NIC], 'on that day' [NLT], 'when the time comes' [CEV].

QUESTION—What relationship is indicated by this quotation?

It expresses a contrast with the old covenant [NJB]: no, this is the new covenant. It gives the prophecy a universal application [Alf]; it emphasizes the prediction of the new covenant [GNC, NTC]; it shows that by Christ's sacrificial work the new covenant has begun [NTC, WBC].

QUESTION—To what does αὕτη 'this' refer?

It refers to the new covenant described in what follows [TH].

QUESTION—What is indicated by the use of the phrase πρὸς αὐτούς 'with them' instead of τῷ οἴκῳ Ἰσραήλ 'the house of Israel' in the OT text?

It universalizes the reference [My, NIGTC], putting the Israelites into the background [My] and making it applicable to Gentiles as well [NIGTC].

QUESTION—How is the phrase λέγει κύριος 'says the Lord' related to other phrases?

1. It is a part of the quotation [Alf, HNTC, Mil, NIC, WBC; all versions except NJB].
2. It introduces the second part of the quotation [Lns; NJB] although it is also a part of the original quotation [Lns].

'giving[a] my laws upon[b] their hearts[c]

LEXICON—a. pres. act. participle of δίδωμι (LN 85.33) (BAGD 1.b.β. p. 193): 'to give' [BAGD, Lns], 'to put' [HNTC, LN, Mil, NIC, WBC; all versions except CEV, NJB, REB], 'to grant, to send' [BAGD], 'to plant' [NJB], 'to set' [REB], 'to write' [CEV].

b. ἐπί with accusative object (LN 83.46): 'upon' [LN, Lns, Mil; NASB], 'on' [LN; CEV, NJB], 'into' [KJV], 'in' [HNTC, NIC, WBC; NAB, NIV, NLT, NRSV, REB, TEV, TNT].

c. καρδία (LN 26.3): 'heart' [HNTC, LN, Lns, Mil, NIC, WBC; all versions], 'inner self, mind' [LN].

QUESTION—What relationship is indicated by the participle διδούς 'giving'?

1. It is translated as a finite verb [HNTC, Lns, Mil, NIC, WBC; all versions]: I will put my laws in their hearts. It is parallel to the following verb ἐπιγράψω 'I will inscribe' [Lns].
2. It is related to the preceding phrase ἣν διαθήσομαι 'which I will covenant' [My]. It may describe how the new covenant is given: I will make a new covenant by giving my laws in their hearts.

and on[a] their mind[b] I-will-inscribe[c] them,

LEXICON—a. ἐπί with accusative object: 'on' [LN, Lns, NIC, WBC; CEV, NAB, NIV, NLT, NRSV, REB, TEV, TNT], 'upon' [HNTC, LN, Mil; NASB], 'in' [KJV, NJB].

b. διανοία (LN 26.14) (BAGD 1. p. 187): 'mind' [BAGD, HNTC, LN, Lns, Mil, NIC, WBC; all versions except REB], 'understanding' [BAGD; REB], 'intelligence' [BAGD].

c. fut. act. indic. of ἐπιγράφω (LN 33.65) (BAGD 2. p. 291): 'to inscribe' [Lns, WBC], 'to write on' [BAGD, LN, NIC; all versions except KJV, NASB], 'to write in' [BAGD; KJV], 'to write upon' [HNTC, Mil; NASB].

QUESTION—How is this phrase related to the preceding phrases?

1. It may be an added comment: in addition, I will inscribe them on their minds.
2. It may be a doublet, repeating the thought of the preceding phrase: that is, I will inscribe them on their minds.

10:17 and their sins and their lawlessnesses[a] surely not will-I-remember still.'"[b]

LEXICON—a. ἀνομία (LN 88.139) (BAGD 2. p. 72): 'lawlessness' [LN, Lns], 'lawless deed' [BAGD; NASB, NLT, NRSV], 'lawless act' [Mil; NIV, TNT], 'wicked deed' [REB], 'evil deed' [HNTC; CEV, TEV], 'transgression' [BAGD, WBC; NAB], 'iniquity' [Mil, NIC; KJV], 'offence' [NJB].

b. ἔτι (LN 67.128) (BAGD 1.b.β. p. 315): 'still' [LN], 'any longer' [Lns, WBC; TEV], 'any more' [Mil]. The phrase οὐ μὴ ἔτι 'surely not still' is translated 'no more' [HNTC, NIC; all versions except NJB, TEV], 'never again' [BAGD; NLT], 'never more' [NJB], 'no longer' [CEV].

QUESTION—How is this verse related to what precedes?

This verse includes the important point of the quotation [NCBC, NIGTC, TH].

1. It is an unbroken continuation of the preceding quotation [Lns; CEV, KJV, NJB].
2. It is separated from the preceding part of the quotation by an implied phrase such as "he also says" [Alf, HNTC, Mil, NIC, WBC; all versions except CEV, KJV, NJB]. This interpretation is supported by the fact that there is a break in the OT quotation between this and the preceding verse, and this verse carries the point of the quotation [Alf].

QUESTION—What relationship is indicated by the καί 'and' at the beginning of this verse?

It is a part of the quoted text, but here it serves to introduce the second part of the quotation [Alf, NIGTC].

QUESTION—What relationship is indicated by οὐ μή 'surely not' (literally 'not not')?

It indicates an emphatic negative [GNC, WBC]: surely not.

10:18 Now where[a] (there is) forgiveness[b] of-these,

LEXICON—a. ὅπου (LN 92.28) (BAGD 2.a. p. 576): 'where' [BAGD, HNTC, LN, Lns, Mil, NIC, WBC; KJV, NASB, NIV, NRSV, REB, TNT], 'when' [CEV, NJB, NLT, TEV]. This entire phrase is translated 'once these have been forgiven' [NAB]. This word refers to circumstances [GNC, NIGTC, TH] whose result is stated in the following clause [NIGTC].

b. ἄφεσις (LN 40.8) (BAGD 2. p. 125): 'forgiveness' [BAGD, LN; NASB, NRSV], 'pardon' [BAGD], 'remission' [HNTC, Lns, Mil; KJV], 'decisive putting away' [WBC]. The phrase ἄφεσις τούτων 'forgiveness of these' is translated 'these have been forgiven' [NIV, NJB, REB, TEV, TNT], 'these are forgiven' [NIC], 'sins are forgiven' [CEV], 'sins have been forgiven' [NLT]. It denotes forgiveness and complete removal [Mil], decisively putting away [WBC].

QUESTION—What is the function of this verse?

It is the conclusion from the preceding discussion [EGT, GNC, HNTC, Hu, Hwt, Mil, NCBC, NIGTC, TH, TNTC, WBC], the conclusion of the middle portion (chapters 7–10) of the epistle, with the theme of Christ a high priest of the order of Melchizedek [Alf]. It sums up the reason why full pardon is provided under the Gospel [Blm]. It indicates the finality of Christ's sacrifice and anything further is impossible [EBC], unnecessary [GNC, HNTC].

QUESTION—What relationship is indicated by δέ 'now'?

It is transitional [Mil], resumptive [NIGTC]. It introduces the conclusion of the preceding comment [KJV, NASB, TEV]. It introduces an axiomatic fact [Alf, WBC].

QUESTION—How are the two words related in the genitive phrase ἄφεσις τούτων 'forgiveness of these'?

Τούτων 'these' tells what was forgiven [NAB, NIV, NJB, REB, TEV, TNT], referring to the 'sins' and 'lawlessnesses' of the preceding verse [Lns, Mil, My, NIGTC, TH]: where (God) forgives these sins.

(there is) no-longer[a] (an) offering[b] for[c] sin.

LEXICON—a. οὐκέτι (LN 67.130): 'no longer' [HNTC, LN, Lns, Mil, WBC; NASB, NIV, NRSV, TEV, TNT], 'no more' [KJV, NJB], 'no further' [NAB, REB], 'no . . . any longer' [NIC]. This entire clause is translated 'there is no more need to offer sacrifices' [CEV], 'there is no need to offer any more sacrifices' [NLT]. It is temporal [GNC, TH].

b. προσφορά (LN **53.16**) (BAGD 1. p. 720): 'offering' [BAGD, HNTC, **LN**, Lns, Mil, NIC, WBC; KJV, NAB, NASB, NRSV, TEV], 'sacrifice' [LN; NIV]. This singular noun is translated as a plural: 'offerings' [NJB, REB]. The phrase προσφορὰ περὶ ἁμαρτίας 'offering for sin' is translated 'sin offering' [NIC; TNT], 'sin offerings' [NJB], 'to offer sacrifices' [CEV, NLT].

c. περί with genitive object (LN 89.6) (BAGD 1.g. p. 645): 'for' [HNTC, Lns, Mil, WBC; KJV, NAB, NASB, NIV, NRSV, REB], 'to take away' [BAGD; TEV], 'to atone for' [BAGD], 'in relation to, with regard to, concerning' [LN], not explicit [CEV, NLT].

QUESTION—What is implied by οὐκέτι 'no longer'?

1. It refers to a fact [Hu, My, NIC; KJV, NAB, NASB, NIV, NRSV, REB]: there is no longer an offering. This is because it is unnecessary [My].
2. It refers to the absence of need [GNC, Hwt, TNTC, WBC; TEV, TNT]: there is no longer a need for an offering.

3. It refers to an impossibility [Lns, Wst; NJB]: there can be no more offering.

DISCOURSE UNIT: 10:19–13:25 [TNTC, Wst]. The topic is exhortations [TNTC], application of the preceding truths [Wst].

DISCOURSE UNIT: 10:19–13:17 [Lns]. The topic is exhortations to faith and faithfulness [Lns].

DISCOURSE UNIT: 10:19–12:29 [Hu, Hwt, Mil, NIC; NJB]. The topic is exhortation [Hwt, Mil] and application [Mil], the superiority of Christ as the new and living way [Hu], a summons to worship, faith, and perseverance [NIC], persevering faith [NJB].

DISCOURSE UNIT: 10:19–39 [GNT, Hwt, Lg, Mil, NIGTC, NTC, TNTC, WBC, Wst; CEV, NAB, NIV, NLT, TEV]. The topic is exhortation and warning [GNT, Lg, Mil; CEV], exhortations [NTC], final exhortation [NIGTC], exhortation to persevere [NIV, NLT], exhortation to draw near to God [TEV], privileges and responsibilities [Hwt], the believer's position [TNTC], warning of the danger of disloyalty to Christ [WBC], privileges, perils, and encouragement [Wst], recalling the past [NAB].

DISCOURSE UNIT: 10:19–25 [EBC, GNC, HNTC, Lg, Lns, NCBC, NIC, NTC, TNTC; NASB, NJB]. The topic is the right way [EBC], the new and living way [TNTC; NASB], the basis for faithfulness [GNC], faith, hope, and love [HNTC], exhortation to remain faithful [NTC] in view of the second coming of Christ [Lg], drawing near to God [Lns], confidence to enter the sanctuary [NCBC], access to God through Christ's sacrifice [NIC], recalling the past [NAB], the Christian opportunity [NJB].

10:19 Having, therefore, brothers,[a] confidence[b] for[c] the entering[d] of-the holy-things/sanctuary[e] by[f] the blood[g] of-Jesus,

LEXICON—a. ἀδελφός (LN 11.23): 'brother' [HNTC, Lns, Mil, NIC, WBC; KJV, NAB, NASB, NIV, NJB, TNT], 'fellow believer, Christian brother' [LN], 'friend' [CEV, NRSV, REB, TEV], 'dear friend' [NLT]. This word refers to fellow Christians [TH]. It indicates affection [EBC]. It appeals to the unity of believers [NIGTC, NTC]; it implies the fellowship in Christ by believers [Wst]. It indicates a new section [Lns, Mil, NIGTC, TH] when used with οὖν 'therefore' [Mil].

b. παρρησία (LN 25.158) (BAGD 3.b. p. 631): 'confidence' [BAGD, HNTC, Mil; NASB, NIV, NRSV, REB], 'complete confidence' [NJB], 'assurance' [Lns], 'freedom' [Mil, NIC], 'complete freedom' [TEV, TNT], 'boldness' [LN, Mil; KJV], 'courage' [LN; CEV], 'authorization' [WBC]. The phrase ἔχοντες παρρησίαν εἰς 'having confidence for' is translated 'we may with complete freedom pass through the curtain into' [TNT], 'we can boldly enter' [NLT]; the phrase ἔχοντες παρρησίαν . . . ἐν τῷ αἵματι Ἰησοῦ 'having confidence by the blood of Jesus' is translated 'the blood of Jesus makes us free . . . with confidence' [REB], 'the blood of Jesus gives us courage' [CEV]. This word indicates confident trust [ICC, My] to approach God [TH, TNTC], freedom of access [NIGTC, TNTC, WBC], permission for access [WBC], certainty based on Christ's sacrifice [WBC].

c. εἰς with accusative object (LN 89.48, 89.57, 90.23): 'for' [Mil, WBC], 'for the purpose of' [LN (89.57)], 'with the result that, so that as a result' [LN (89.48)], 'concerning, with reference to' [LN (90.23)], 'in regard to' [Lns], 'in' [NJB]. The phrase εἰς τὴν εἴσοδον 'for the entering' is translated 'to enter' [HNTC; CEV, KJV, NASB, NIV, NLT, NRSV, REB], 'to go into' [TEV], 'of access into' [NIC]. It means going into [NIGTC], leading to [EBC]. This word indicates the purpose [Mil], the goal [EBC, EGT, Wst].

d. εἴσοδος (LN 15.87) (BAGD 1. p. 233): 'entering' [BAGD, Mil; NJB], 'entrance' [BAGD, Lns; NAB], 'access' [BAGD], 'free access' [WBC], 'coming' [LN]. It refers to the act of entering [EGT, Mil, My, NTC, WBC], entering by the people [Alf]. It refers to the entrance as a place [Lns], the means of entering [Wst].

e. ἅγιος (LN 7.18, 7.35, 88.24) (BAGD 2.b. p. 10): 'holy' [LN]. The neuter plural τὰ ἅγια is translated 'the sanctuary' [HNTC, LN (7.18), Lns; NAB, NJB, NRSV, REB, TNT], 'the heavenly sanctuary' [WBC], 'the holy place' [BAGD, LN (7.35), NIC; NASB], 'the Most Holy Place' [Mil; CEV, NIV, TEV], 'heaven's Most Holy Place' [NLT], 'the holiest' [Mil; KJV]. It refers to the Most Holy Place [NTC], to heaven [Blm, EGT, Hu] as the true Holy of Holies [Blm, Hu], the heavenly sanctuary as a whole [Lns, NIGTC, WBC], the presence of God [EBC, NIC, TH, TNTC].

f. ἐν with dative object (LN 89.76): 'by' [HNTC, LN, NIC; KJV, NASB, NIV, NRSV], 'by means of' [LN, Mil, WBC; TEV], 'through' [NJB], 'in connection with' [Lns], 'because of' [NLT]. The phrase ἐν τῷ αἵματι Ἰησοῦ 'by the blood of Jesus' is translated 'Jesus has died for us' [TNT], 'the blood of Jesus gives (courage)' [CEV]. This preposition expresses means [Mil, WBC], instrument [NIC, NIGTC, WBC], the grounds of the confidence [Alf, Hu, My]. It means 'in the power of' [Wst].

g. αἷμα (LN 8.64, 23.107) (BAGD 2.b. p. 23): 'blood' [BAGD, HNTC, LN (8.64), Lns, Mil, NIC, WBC; all versions except TEV, TNT], 'death' [LN (23.107); TEV].

QUESTION—What relationship is indicated by οὖν 'therefore'?

It indicates a connection with (the logical consequence of [Hu]) what precedes [EBC, GNC, Hu]. It introduces in brief form what was argued in the preceding passages [Lns, Mil, My, NTC, WBC], a new section [TH]. It introduces the conclusion (the application [TNTC]) from the preceding argument [Mil, NCBC, NIGTC, TNTC], from chapter 5 on [My] and a transition to an exhortation [TH].

QUESTION—What relationship is indicated by the participial form ἔχοντες 'having'?

It indicates reason [HNTC, ICC, Mil, NIGTC, NTC, TNTC, WBC; NAB, NASB, NIV, NRSV], the reason why believers have access to God [NTC]: because we have confidence, let us approach. It is emphatic by forefronting [Alf, Lg(K)]. The present tense implies present reality [TNTC].

QUESTION—What is παρρησίαν 'confidence' related to?

It is related to the phrase εἰς τὴν εἴσοδον 'for the entering' [Alf, Blm, EGT, HNTC, Hu, ICC, Lg, Lns, Mil, NIC, NTC, WBC, Wst; all versions except NAB, NJB]: confidence to enter. The confidence is through the blood [NAB, NJB].

QUESTION—What relationship is indicated by the use of the human name, 'Jesus'?

It emphasizes his true humanity [NTC, WBC] and the validity of his act of redemption [Hu, WBC] by the fact that his name refers to salvation [NTC]; it is emphatic [NIGTC, TH].

10:20 which he inaugurated[a] for-us, a-way[b] new[c] and living[d] through[e] the curtain,[f] this is, his flesh,[g]

LEXICON—a. aorist act. indic. of ἐγκαινίζω (LN 13.84) (BAGD 1. p. 215): 'to inaugurate' [HNTC, Lns; NASB], 'to open' [BAGD; NJB, NRSV, REB, TEV], 'to open up' [NAB, NLT, TNT], 'to open newly' [Mil], 'to establish, to put into effect, to put into force' [LN], 'to make available' [WBC], 'to consecrate' [KJV], 'to dedicate' [NIC], not explicit [CEV]. This active verb is also translated as a passive: 'to be opened' [NIV]. The aorist tense indicates a historic fact [Lns].

b. ὁδός (LN 1.99, 41.16) (BAGD 2.a. p. 554): 'way' [BAGD, HNTC, LN (1.99), Lns, Mil, NIC, WBC; all versions except NAB], 'road' [LN (1.99)], 'path' [NAB], 'way of life, way to live' [LN (41.16)].

c. πρόσφατος (LN **58.73**) (BAGD p. 719): 'new' [BAGD, HNTC, **LN**, Mil, NIC, WBC; all versions], 'newly made' [Lns], 'new and different, recent' [LN]. It implies a recent origin [Alf, EGT, Hwt, Lns, NIC, NTC, WBC, Wst], newly opened [Hwt, Lg, Mil, My, NCBC, TH, TNTC], a new situation [EBC, Lns], qualitatively fresh [ICC, Lns, WBC] and not subject to growing old [Wst], a break with the old system [Hu].

d. pres. act. participle of ζάω (LN 23.88) (BAGD 4.b. p.337): 'to live' [BAGD, HNTC, LN, Lns, Mil, NIC; all versions except CEV, NLT], 'to be alive' [LN]. This participle is also translated as a clause: 'which/that leads to life' [WBC; CEV], 'life-giving (way)' [NLT]. It is in contrast with the mere ceremony of the OT entrance into the sanctuary [Alf]. It is real and effective [Alf, EGT, GNC, Hwt, Lg, My]. It leads to salvation [Blm], to life [WBC]. It is living because it is Christ himself [Lns], because it is related to the living Christ [EBC, Hu, NCBC, NIC, Wst] and to fellowship with him [Wst].

e. διά with genitive object (LN 84.29): 'through' [HNTC, LN, Mil, NIC, WBC; all versions], 'by means of' [Lns]. It refers to location [Alf, Blm, GNC, HNTC, ICC, Lg, My, TH, WBC] and is also instrumental [Lg(K)]; it is only instrumental [Lns].

f. καταπέτασμα (LN 6.160) (BAGD p. 416): 'curtain' [BAGD, HNTC, LN, NIC, WBC; CEV, NIV, NJB, NLT, NRSV, REB, TEV, TNT], 'veil' [LN, Lns, Mil; KJV, NAB, NASB], 'drape' [LN].

g. σάρξ (LN 8.4, 8.63) (BAGD 2. p. 743): 'flesh' [HNTC, LN (8.63), Lns, Mil, NIC, WBC; KJV, NAB, NASB, NJB, NRSV, REB], 'body' [BAGD, LN (8.4); NIV, TEV, TNT], 'Christ himself' [CEV], 'his death for us' [NLT]. It refers to Christ's body [Blm], his life offered in sacrifice [NCBC]. It refers to Christ's flesh [Alf, EGT, GNC] as the curtain before the Holy of Holies [Alf, Blm], as an analogy to the tearing of the curtain in the Temple [GNC]. It represents the curtain, through which he passed, referring to the limitations of Christ's earthly existence [WBC, Wst].

QUESTION—Why is this verse mentioned?

It explains the preceding verse [WBC].

QUESTION—What is ἥν 'which' connected with?

1. It is connected with εἴσοδον 'entering' in the preceding verse [Alf, EGT, ICC, Lg(K), Lns, Mil, My, NIGTC, WBC]: which entering he inaugurated. The following ὁδόν is in apposition with ἥν 'which' [ICC], with εἴσοδον 'entering' in the preceding verse [Mil], amplifying the means of entering [Mil]. It is the direct object of ἐνεκαίνισεν 'he inaugurated' [WBC].
2. It is connected with ὁδόν 'way' [NIC; KJV, NAB, NJB, NRSV, REB]: the way which he has inaugurated.

QUESTION—What relationship is indicated by the phrase ὁδὸν πρόσφατον καὶ ζῶσαν 'a way new and living'?

1. It tells how the entering is accomplished [KJV, NAB, NASB, REB]: our entrance by the new and living way.
2. It is related to ἐνεκαίνισεν 'he inaugurated' [Alf, WBC; TEV].

2.1 It is the direct object of ἐνεκαίνισεν 'he inaugurated' [TEV, TNT]: he inaugurated a new and living way.

2.2 It is a second predicate to ἐνεκαίνισεν 'he inaugurated' [Alf, WBC]: he inaugurated the entrance as a way.

QUESTION—What is the phrase διὰ τοῦ καταπετάσματος 'through the curtain' connected with?

1. It is connected with ἐνεκαίνισεν 'he inaugurated' [HNTC, ICC, WBC, Wst; NAB, NASB, NIV, NRSV, REB]: he inaugurated through the curtain.
2. It is connected with ὁδόν 'way' [EGT, GNC, Lg, Mil, My, WBC; NJB, TNT]: a way through the curtain.
3. It is connected with both of the above [WBC]: he inaugurated a way through the curtain.

QUESTION—What is meant by τοῦ καταπετάσματος 'the curtain'?

1. It is regarded as a barrier of exclusion from God's presence [EGT, GNC, Hu, ICC, Lg, WBC, Wst] which must be passed through [Alf, Blm, EGT, GNC, TH].
2. It is regarded as the means of approach to God [GNC, TNTC].
3. It is regarded as Christ's flesh, which had to be rent so his blood could be shed, thus opening access to God's presence for the people [NCBC].

QUESTION—What is the phrase τοῦτ' ἔστιν τῆς σαρκὸς αὐτοῦ 'this is, his flesh' connected with?

1. It is connected with καταπετάσματος 'curtain' [EBC, EGT, Hu, Hwt, Lns, Mil, My, NIC, NTC; CEV, KJV, NAB, NASB, NIV, NJB] to explain the meaning of the curtain [Mil]: the curtain, that is, his flesh. The genitive phrase τῆς σαρκὸς αὐτοῦ 'his flesh' is in apposition with καταπετάσματος 'curtain' [My].
2. It expresses a parallel to the phrase διὰ τοῦ καταπετάσματος 'through the curtain' [NRSV, TEV]: through the curtain, that is, through his flesh.
3. It is connected with ὁδόν 'way' [HNTC, Wst; REB]: a way, that is, his flesh.
4. It explains the preceding part of the verse as a whole [WBC; TNT]: he inaugurated the way by means of his flesh.

10:21 and a-great[a] priest over[b] the house[c] of-God,

LEXICON—a. μέγας (LN 87.22): 'great' [HNTC, LN, Lns, Mil, NIC, WBC; all versions except KJV, NJB], 'important' [LN], 'high' [KJV, NJB].

b. ἐπί with accusative object (LN 37.9) (BAGD III.1.b.α. p. 288): 'over' [BAGD, HNTC, LN, Lns, Mil, NIC; KJV, NAB, NASB, NIV, NJB, NRSV, TNT], 'set over' [REB], 'in charge of' [WBC; CEV, TEV], 'with responsibility for' [LN], 'to rule over' [NLT]. It refers to administration over [EGT, GNC, HNTC, Hu, Lns, Mil, WBC].

c. οἶκος (LN 7.2) (BAGD 1.a.β. p. 560): 'house' [BAGD, HNTC, LN, Lns, Mil, NIC; CEV, KJV, NAB, NASB, NIV, NRSV, TEV], 'household' [WBC; REB, TNT], 'temple' [LN], 'sanctuary' [LN; NJB], 'people' [NLT]. It refers to the heavenly sanctuary [BAGD, Lg, My, TH], to the heavenly sanctuary and secondarily God's family on earth [Blm], only to God's people [GNC, Hu, Hwt, Lg(K), Lns, NIC, NIGTC, WBC] both in heaven and (primarily [TNTC]) on earth [NIGTC, Wst], people of both the old and the new covenant [Hwt].

QUESTION—What is this phrase connected with?

1. It is a parallel to the participial phrase introduced by ἔχοντες 'having' in 10:19 [Alf, HNTC, Hu, ICC, Lns, Mil, My, NIGTC, WBC; KJV, NAB, NASB, NIV, NRSV], and both are dependent on προσερχώμεθα 'let us approach' in the following verse [HNTC, Hu, Lns, Mil, WBC; KJV, NAB, NASB, NIV, NRSV]. It expresses a second reason [HNTC, Hu, Mil, WBC; NAB, NASB, NIV, NRSV]: since we have confidence to enter the sanctuary and since we have a great priest, let us approach.

2. It is translated as an independent clause [NIC; NJB, REB, TEV, TNT]: we have a great priest.

QUESTION—What relationship is indicated by ἱερέα μέγαν 'great priest'?

1. It refers to the greatness of Christ's priesthood, not his high-priesthood [Alf, EGT, Hu, Lg, Lns, Wst]: great priest. It implies his greatness as Son of God [EGT, Hu], the greatness of his sacrifice, and his resultant glorious exalted position [Hu].
2. It refers to Christ's high-priesthood [EBC, HNTC, ICC, NIC, NIGTC, TH, WBC; KJV, NJB]: high priest. Μέγαν 'great' indicates that he is greater than other priests [NIC] and has accomplished what no other high priest could do [GNC].
3. 'Ιερέα 'priest' means 'high priest', and μέγαν 'great' refers to his exalted position [My; CEV, NLT]: great high priest.

10:22 let-us-approach[a] with[b] (a) true[c] heart in[d] full-assurance[e] of-faith,[f]

LEXICON—a. pres. mid. (deponent = act.) subj. of προσέρχομαι (LN 15.77) (BAGD 2.a. p. 713): 'to approach' [BAGD, LN, Mil, NIC; NRSV, TNT], 'to make one's approach' [HNTC; REB], 'to come to, to go to' [BAGD], 'to come near to' [LN], 'to come near' [CEV, TEV], 'to draw near' [Lns, Mil, WBC; KJV, NAB, NASB, NIV], 'to go in' [NJB], 'to go into (the presence of God)' [NLT]. The present tense implies continual or repeated approaching [EGT, Lns, Mil, WBC]. The first person plural includes the author with his readers [TH].

b. μετά with genitive object (LN 89.78, 89.79, 89.109): 'with' [HNTC, LN (89.78, 89.79, 89.109), Lns, Mil, NIC, WBC; CEV, KJV, NASB, NIV, NLT, NRSV, TEV, TNT], 'having' [LN (89.79, 89.109)], 'in' [LN (89.79); NAB, REB], 'by means of, through' [LN (89.78)]. The phrase προσερχώμεθα μετὰ ἀληθινῆς καρδίας 'let us approach with a true heart' is translated 'so as we go in, let us be sincere in heart' [NJB]. The phrase μετὰ ἀληθινῆς καρδίας ἐν πληροθορίᾳ πίστεως 'with a true heart in full assurance of faith' is translated 'sincerely and fully believing in him' [TNT]. This preposition indicates manner [Mil].

c. ἀληθινός (LN **73.2**) (BAGD 1. p. 37): 'true' [BAGD, LN, Lns, Mil, NIC; KJV, NLT, NRSV], 'sincere' [HNTC, **LN**, WBC; NASB, NIV, NJB, TEV], 'genuine' [LN], 'pure' [CEV]. The phrase ἀληθινῆς καρδίας 'true heart' is translated 'sincerity of heart' [REB], 'utter sincerity' [NAB]. It means faithful and stable [NIGTC], honest and committed [NTC], genuine and sincere [WBC], fully devoted to God [Wst], without hypocrisy or doubt [NCBC].

d. ἐν with dative object (LN 13.8, 89.76, 89.80, 89.119, 90.10): 'in' [HNTC, LN (13.8, 89.119), Lns, NIC, WBC; KJV, NASB, NIV, NRSV], 'with' [LN (13.8, 89.80, 90.10), Mil; CEV], 'in union with, one with, joined closely to' [LN (89.119)], 'while at the same time' [LN (89.80)], 'by' [LN (89.76, 90.10)], 'by means of' [LN (89.76)], 'and' [REB]; the phrase ἐν πληροθορίᾳ πίστεως 'in full assurance of faith' is translated 'and absolute confidence' [NAB], 'and filled with faith' [NJB], 'fully trusting him' [NLT], 'and a sure faith' [TEV]. This preposition expresses manner [Mil], the environment of the approach [TNTC].

e. πληροθορία (LN 31.45) (BAGD p. 670): 'full assurance' [BAGD, HNTC, Lns, Mil, NIC; KJV, NASB, NIV, NRSV, REB], 'confidence' [CEV], 'fullness' [BAGD; WBC], 'certainty' [BAGD], 'complete certainty' [LN], 'firm certainty' [Mil].

f. πίστις (LN 31.85) (BAGD 2.d.α. p. 663): 'faith' [BAGD, HNTC, LN, Lns, Mil, NIC, WBC; CEV, KJV, NASB, NIV, NJB, NRSV, REB, TEV], 'trust' [LN]. This noun is also translated as a verb: 'to trust' [NLT]. It refers to trust in Christ [EBC].

QUESTION—Why is this clause mentioned?

It is an exhortation expressing the desired conclusion from the two preceding participial phrases [HNTC, Hu, NIGTC, TH]: since we have . . . , let us approach.

QUESTION—What is the implied object of προσερχώμεθα 'let us approach'?

1.The implied object is God [Alf, EGT, HNTC, NIC, NIGTC, NTC, TH, WBC; NIV, TEV, TNT], God's presence [Mil]: let us approach God.

2. The implied object is the true sanctuary, heaven [Lns]: let us approach the Sanctuary.

QUESTION—What relationship is indicated by the phrase ἀληθινῆς καρδίας 'a true heart'?

It means a faithful and true disposition [Blm], perfect sincerity [Hwt], an attitude of worship from the inner being [EGT], singleness of purpose [Hu], whole-hearted [ICC]. Together with the following prepositional phrase it expresses the necessary condition for approaching God [Lg].

QUESTION—What is the phrase ἐν πληροφορίᾳ πίστεως 'in full assurance of faith' connected with?

1. It is an added parallel to the preceding phrase μετὰ ἀληθινῆς καρδίας 'with a true heart' [Hu, Hwt, Mil, NIC; NAB, NJB, REB, TEV, TNT]: with a true heart and in full assurance of faith. Both phrases express attitudes which must accompany the approach to God [TH].

2. It further describes the true heart [Lns, My]: with a true heart, in full assurance of faith.

QUESTION—How are the two nouns related in the genitive phrase πληροφορίᾳ πίστεως 'full assurance of faith' ?

1. Πληροφορίᾳ 'full assurance' describes πίστεως 'faith' [Blm, Mil; NAB, TEV, TNT]: fully assured faith.

2. Πίστεως 'faith' produces full assurance [CEV]: assurance that comes from having faith.

2. Πίστις 'faith' tells what they are to be filled with [NJB, NLT]: filled with faith.

QUESTION—What is meant by ἐν πληροφορίᾳ πίστεως 'in full assurance of faith'?

It implies the certainty of access to God through Jesus' blood [Alf, EGT, Hwt], unwavering trust [Hu], with no doubt or hesitation [ICC].

sprinkled[a] (with respect to) the hearts from[b] (an) evil[c] conscience[d]

LEXICON—a. perf. mid./pass. participle of ῥαντίζω (LN 47.16, 53.32, **88.31**, **88.314**) (BAGD 2.b. p. 734): as a passive: 'to be sprinkled' [HNTC, LN (47.16), Lns, Mil; KJV, NIV, NJB, NLT], 'to be sprinkled clean' [NIC, WBC; NAB, NASB, NRSV], 'to be cleansed' [LN (53.32, **88.314**), Mil], 'to be made clean' [LN (88.314)], 'to be purified' [LN (53.32, **88.31**, **88.314**); TEV]; as a middle voice: 'to purify for oneself' [BAGD], 'to keep pure' [CEV]. The phrase ῥεραντισμένοι τὰς καρδίας 'sprinkled with respect to the hearts' is translated 'inwardly cleansed' [REB]. This entire phrase is translated 'with our guilty consciences cleansed' [TNT]. This is a reference to a liturgical act [EGT, ICC, Lns, Wst], to Levitical purification [Alf, Blm] and then to the spiritual sprinkling of the blood of Jesus [Alf, EBC, Hu, Wst].

b. ἀπό with genitive object (LN 89.122): 'from' [HNTC, LN, Lns, Mil, NIC, WBC; all versions except NJB, TNT], 'separated from' [LN], 'free from' [CEV], 'free from any trace of' [NJB], not explicit [NLT].

c. πονηρός (LN 88.314) (BAGD 1.b.β. p. 691): 'evil' [BAGD, Mil, NIC; CEV, KJV, NAB, NASB, NLT, NRSV], 'guilty' [BAGD, LN; NIV, REB, TEV, TNT], 'wicked' [Lns], 'bad' [HNTC; NJB], 'burdened' [WBC]. It refers to the evil of which the conscience is aware [NAB].

d. συνείδησις (BAGD, LN 26.13) (BAGD 2. p. 786): 'conscience' [HNTC, LN, Lns, Mil, NIC, WBC; all versions], 'consciousness' [BAGD].

QUESTION—What is implied by 'sprinkled with respect to the heart'?

It means to be cleansed by the sprinkling [Alf]. It refers to forgiveness of sins [Blm, Hu], deliverance from a guilty conscience [EGT, GNC, HNTC], internal cleansing [GNC, ICC, NIC, NTC, TNTC].

QUESTION—What relationship is indicated by the two participles ῥεραντισμένοι 'sprinkled' and λελουσμένοι 'washed'?

The perfect tenses imply acts (already completed [EGT, GNC, Mil, WBC]) with continuing results [Alf, EGT, GNC, Hu, Mil, NIC, NIGTC, NTC, WBC]. Both participles refer to Christian baptism [HNTC, NIGTC].

1. They are to be taken together, and both are dependent on the verb προσερχώμεθα 'let us approach' [Alf, EGT, ICC, Lns, Mil, NIC, NIGTC, TH, WBC, Wst]: let us approach, sprinkled and washed. The second participial phrase does not add new information [NIGTC].

1.1 They express accompanying circumstances to the verb [HNTC; NRSV, TEV, TNT]: let us approach, sprinkled with respect to the hearts and washed with respect to the body.

1.2 They express a reason [Mil, NIC, WBC]: because we have been sprinkled and washed.

2. The phrase introduced by ῥεραντισμένοι 'sprinkled' is dependent on the preceding verb προσερχώμεθα 'let us approach', and the second phrase introduced by λελουσμένοι 'washed' is dependent on the following verb κατέχωμεν 'let us hold fast' [Hwt, Lg, My]: let us approach, sprinkled . . . ; and washed, let us hold fast. The phrase introduced by ῥεραντισμένοι 'sprinkled' states the condition of fitness for approaching God [Lg].

QUESTION—What do the two participles ῥεραντισμένοι 'sprinkled' and λελουσμένοι 'washed' modify?

Being nominatives, they modify the subject of the verb [Lns]: we . . . sprinkled and washed.

QUESTION—How are the two accusatives τὰς καρδίας 'the hearts' and τὸ σῶμα 'the body' related to the two respective participles ῥεραντισμένοι 'sprinkled' and λελουσμένοι 'washed'?

They tell respectively what is 'sprinkled' and 'washed' [HNTC, Lns, Mil, NIC, NIGTC, WBC; all versions except REB]: sprinkled with respect to the hearts and washed with respect to the body.

QUESTION—What is meant by συνειδήσεως πονηρᾶς 'an evil conscience'?

It means a conscience polluted by the guilt of sin [Alf].

and washed[a] (with respect to) the body[b] with-pure[c] water;

LEXICON—a. perf. mid./pass. participle of λούω (LN 47.12) (BAGD 2.b. p. 481): As a passive: 'to be washed' [HNTC, LN, Lns, Mil, NIC, WBC; all versions except REB], 'to be bathed' [LN]; as a middle: 'to wash for oneself' [BAGD]. The phrase λελουσμένοι τὸ σῶμα 'bathed with respect to the body' is translated 'outwardly washed' [REB]. This is a reference to a liturgical act [EGT, ICC, Lns, Wst], to Levitical purification [Alf, Blm, Hwt], to Christian baptism [Alf, Blm, EBC, EGT, GNC, HNTC, Hu, Hwt, ICC], to moral purity [Blm]. It is a symbol of inner purity [Hwt].

b. σῶμα (LN 8.1): 'body' [LN, Lns, WBC]. This singular noun is translated as a plural: 'bodies' [HNTC, Mil, NIC; CEV, KJV, NAB, NASB, NIV, NJB, NLT, NRSV, TEV, TNT]. It refers to the physical body [NTC], to the whole natural life [Alf].

c. καθαρός (LN 79.48) (BAGD 1. p. 388): 'pure' [BAGD, HNTC, Lns, Mil, NIC; all versions except CEV, REB], 'clean' [BAGD, LN, WBC; CEV, TEV].

QUESTION—What does the washing refer to?

It refers to baptism [Mil, NIC, NTC, TH, TNTC, WBC] as the outward sign of the inner cleansing [WBC] which is the reality, expressed in the preceding phrase, referring to sprinkling [Hu, NTC].

10:23 let-us-hold-fast[a] the confession[b] of-the hope[c] without-wavering,[d]

LEXICON—a. pres. act. subj. of κατέχω (LN 31.48, **33.274**) (BAGD 1.b.β. p. 423): 'to hold fast' [BAGD, HNTC, Lns, Mil, WBC; KJV, NASB, NRSV, TNT], 'to hold tightly to' [CEV, NLT], 'to hold on' [LN (**33.274**); TEV], 'to hold' [NAB, NIV], 'to continue to believe and practice, to continue to follow' [LN (31.48)], 'to retain' [BAGD], 'to maintain' [NIC], 'to be firm' [NJB, REB]. The present tense implies continuation [Lns, WBC].

b. ὁμολογία (LN **33.274**) (BAGD 2. p. 568): 'confession' [BAGD, HNTC, LN, Lns, Mil, NIC; NASB, NRSV, REB], 'profession' [KJV, NAB]. This noun is also translated as a verb phrase: 'we profess' [LN (**33.274**), WBC; NIV, NJB, TEV], 'which we have professed' [TNT], 'that we say is ours' [CEV], 'we say we have' [NLT], 'in which we have told people' [**LN** (33.274)]. It refers to the thing which is confessed [Alf, GNC, Lns], that which is hoped for [Lns]; it is the vital personal witness of the believer [Hu, WBC]; it is a formula summarizing the Christian faith [NIGTC, NTC].

c. ἐλπίς (LN 25.61, 25.62) (BAGD 2.b. p. 253): 'hope' [BAGD, HNTC, LN (25.61), Lns, Mil, NIC, WBC; all versions except KJV], 'what is hoped for' [LN (25.61)], 'the basis for hope' [LN (25.62)], 'the reason for hope' [LN (25.62)], 'faith' [KJV]. It is more comprehensive in meaning than 'faith' [TNTC]. It refers to the thing hoped for [Alf, EGT, GNC, NIGTC, TH, WBC], the future aspects of our faith [GNC, ICC], the hope of final salvation [Blm, EGT], present and future salvation [WBC], the expectation that Christ will fulfill his promises [NTC].

d. ἀκλινής (LN **31.80**) (BAGD p. 30): 'without wavering' [BAGD, **LN**, NIC, WBC; KJV, NASB, NLT, NRSV], 'without swerving' [HNTC], 'unswervingly' [NAB, NIV], 'unbent' [Lns], 'firmly' [LN; TEV], not explicit [CEV]. This adverb is also translated as an adjective: 'unswerving' [REB]; as a phrase: 'and never turn away from it' [TNT], 'without letting that confession waver' [Mil]. The phrase κατέχωμεν ἀκλινῆ 'let us hold fast without wavering' is translated 'let us keep firm' [NJB]. It is emphatic by word order [Lns].

QUESTION—How is this clause related to what precedes?

It expresses a new thought [Mil, WBC], as indicated by the absence of a connecting word (asyndeton) [Mil]. It is the second of three exhortations in 10:22–24 [NCBC, NIC, NIGTC, NTC, TNTC, WBC].

QUESTION—How are the two nouns related in the genitive construction τὴν ὁμολογίαν τῆς ἐλπίδος 'the confession of the hope'?

1. The 'confession' gives 'hope' [NAB]: the confession which gives hope.
2. 'Hope' is the object (the content [NTC]) of 'confession' [EBC, Mil, NTC, WBC; CEV, NIV, NJB, NLT, TEV, TNT]: we confess the hope.
3. 'Hope' is in apposition to 'confession'; both refer to the same thing [NIGTC]: the confession, which is the hope.

QUESTION—What is meant by τῆς ἐλπίδος 'the hope'?

1. The definite article implies 'our hope' [Alf, EBC, NIC].
2. In spite of the definite article, it is translated as an abstraction, 'hope' [Mil].

QUESTION—What relationship is indicated by ἀκλινῆ 'without wavering'?

1. It indicates how we should 'hold the confession fast' [EGT, GNC, HNTC, Hu, ICC, Lns, NTC, TNTC, WBC; NAB, NIV, NJB, REB, TEV, TNT]: let us hold fast without wavering.
2. It indicates how the confession will become by being held fast [Alf, Lg(K), Mil, NCBC, NIC, NIGTC]: so that the confession will be without wavering. The confession will be without wavering if the believers are without wavering [NCBC, NIC].
3. It modifies 'the hope' [TH]: an unwavering hope.

for faithful[a] (is) the-(one) having-promised,[b]

LEXICON—a. πιστός (LN 31.87) (BAGD 1.a.β. p. 664): 'faithful' [BAGD, LN, Lns, Mil, WBC; KJV, NASB, NIV, NRSV], 'trustworthy' [BAGD, HNTC, LN, NIC; NJB], 'dependable' [BAGD, LN], 'reliable' [LN]. This adjective is also translated as a verb phrase describing him: 'to deserve one's trust' [NAB], 'to be trusted' [NLT, REB, TNT]: as a verb with him as the object: 'to trust' [CEV, TEV].

b. aorist mid.(deponent = act.) participle of ἐπαγγέλλομαι (LN 33.286) (BAGD 1.b. p. 281): 'to promise' [BAGD, HNTC, LN, Mil; KJV, NASB, NIV, NRSV], 'to make a promise' [Lns; NAB, NJB], 'to give a promise' [NIC, WBC; TNT], 'to keep a promise' [NLT, TEV], 'to make an agreement' [CEV]. This articular participle is also translated as a phrase: 'the giver of the promise' [REB]. The one who promised is God [Alf, Blm, EBC, GNC, Hu, Hwt, ICC, Lns, My, NCBC, NIC, NIGTC, TH, WBC, Wst; NLT, TEV, TNT].

QUESTION—What relationship is indicated by γάρ 'for'?

It indicates the grounds for exhortation to hold fast the confession of the hope [Blm, EGT, GNC, HNTC, Hu, Hwt, Mil, TNTC, Wst].

10:24 and let-us-consider[a] one-another for[b] stimulation[c] of-love and good[d] works,[e]

LEXICON—a. pres. act. subj. of κατανοέω (LN 30.43) (BAGD 3. p. 415): 'to consider' [BAGD, Lns, Mil; KJV, NAB, NASB, NIV, NRSV], 'to consider carefully' [LN], 'to take thought' [HNTC], 'to be concerned about' [LN], 'to be concerned for' [NJB, TEV], 'to care for' [WBC], 'to think of ways [NLT], to see how' [REB], 'to think how' [TNT], 'to cultivate mutual consideration' [NIC], not explicit [CEV]. It implies considering one's neighbor's circumstances and risks [EGT].

b. εἰς with accusative object (LN 89.57): 'for' [WBC], 'for the purpose of' [LN], 'with a view to' [Mil], 'as regards' [Lns], 'so as to' [HNTC]. The phrase εἰς παροξυσμόν 'for stimulation' is translated 'to provoke' [KJV], 'how to provoke' [NRSV], 'to help one another' [TEV], The phrase ἀλλήλους εἰς παροξυσμόν 'one another for stimulation' is translated 'how to rouse each other' [NAB], 'how to stimulate one another' [NASB], 'how we may spur one another on' [NIV], 'to stir a response' [NJB], 'so as to stimulate' [HNTC]. This preposition expresses purpose [Mil].

c. παροξυσμός (LN **90.55**, **90.55fn12**) (BAGD 1. p. 629): 'stimulation' [WBC], 'encouragement' [BAGD, LN (90.55)], 'incitement' [Mil], 'provocation' [Lns]. This noun is also translated as a verb: 'to stimulate' [HNTC, NIC; NASB, TNT], 'to encourage' [CEV, NLT], 'to arouse' [REB], 'to rouse' [NAB], 'to spur on' [NIV], 'to stir a response' [NJB], 'to provoke to' [KJV, NRSV], 'to help one show' [TEV]. The phrase εἰς παροξυσμόν 'for stimulation' is translated 'in order to encourage' [**LN** (90.55)]. The phrase εἰς παροξυσμὸν ἀγάπης καὶ καλῶν ἔργων 'for stimulation of love and good works' is translated 'to cause people to love and to do good' [LN **(90.55, 90.55 fn12)**]. It has a favorable sense here [Alf, EBC, Hwt, ICC, Lg, Lns, Mil, My, NCBC, NIC, NIGTC, TNTC, WBC].

d. καλός (LN 88.4) (BAGD 2.b. p. 400): 'good' [HNTC, LN, Lns, Mil, NIC, WBC; KJV, NAB, NASB, NIV, NJB, NLT, NRSV, TEV, TNT], 'fine' [LN], 'helpful' [CEV], 'morally good, noble, contributing to salvation' [BAGD], 'praiseworthy' [BAGD, LN]. The phrase καλῶν ἔργων 'good works' is translated 'active goodness' [REB]. This word implies having an attractive appearance [TNTC, Wst].

e. ἔργον (LN 42.11) (BAGD 1.c.β. p. 308): 'work' [Lns, Mil, NIC, WBC; KJV, NJB], 'deed' [BAGD, HNTC, LN; NAB, NASB, NIV, NLT, NRSV], 'act' [LN]. This noun is also translated as a verb: 'to do' [CEV, TEV, TNT]. The good works are those which prove the sincerity of one's faith, especially works of benevolence [Blm].

QUESTION—How is this verse related to the preceding?

It is the third exhortation [Alf, EBC, EGT, GNC, Hu, Hwt, ICC, Lg, Mil, NCBC, NIGTC, NTC, TNTC, WBC] in a series based on the participle ἔχοντες 'having' in 10:19 [Alf]. The exhortations have been to faith (10:22), hope (10:23), and now love [Alf, EGT, GNC, Hu, ICC, Lg, Mil, NTC, WBC]; they refer respectively to God, the world, and the church [Lns].

QUESTION—How are the nouns related in the genitive construction παροξυσμὸν ἀγάπης καὶ καλῶν ἔργων 'stimulation of love and good works'?

'Love' and 'good works' are the goal of the 'stimulation' [Alf, EGT, GNC, HNTC, Lns, Mil, My, NIC, WBC; all versions]: stimulation toward love and good works.

10:25 not forsaking[a] the meeting-together[b] of-ourselves,

LEXICON—a. pres. act. participle of ἐγκαταλείπω (LN **68.36**) (BAGD 2. p. 215): 'to forsake' [BAGD, **LN**, Mil; KJV, NASB], 'to cease, to stop' [LN], 'to discontinue' [WBC], 'to abandon' [BAGD, Lns, NIC], 'to give up' [NIV, TEV], 'to neglect' [NLT, NRSV], 'to stay away from' [REB, TNT], 'to desert' [HNTC], 'to get out of the habit' [CEV]. This active participle is also translated as a middle voice: 'to absent oneself' [NAB, NJB]. It refers to negligence, not apostasy [Alf, Lg].

b. ἐπισυναγωγή (LN **15.128**) (BAGD 1. p. 301): 'meeting together' [NIC, WBC; NIV, NLT, TEV], 'meeting' [BAGD], 'assembling' [**LN**], 'assembling together' [Mil; KJV, NASB], 'assembly' [Lns; NAB], 'gathering' [LN]. This singular noun is translated as a plural: 'assemblies' [NJB], 'meetings' [REB, TNT]. The phrase τὴν ἐπισυναγωγὴν ἑαυτῶν 'the meeting together of ourselves' is translated 'to meet together' [NRSV], 'our meetings when we assemble together' [HNTC], 'to meet for worship' [CEV].

QUESTION—What relationship is indicated by the participial form ἐγκαταλείποντες 'forsaking'?

1. It is an action in addition to (and at the same time as [Mil]) κατανοῶμεν 'let us consider' in the preceding verse [EBC, Mil, NIC; NAB, NIV, NJB, REB, TEV, TNT] (it takes its mood from the preceding verb): and we should not forsake meeting together. It carries on (supports [GNC]) the thought of the preceding verb [EBC, WBC].
2. It is temporal [My]: while not forsaking.

QUESTION—How are the noun and pronoun related in the genitive construction τὴν ἐπισυναγωγὴν ἑαυτῶν 'the meeting together of ourselves'?

1. The genitive ἑαυτῶν 'of ourselves' states to whom the assemblies are related [NJB, REB, TNT].
   1.1 It means 'our assemblies' [REB, TNT].
   1.2 It means 'your own assemblies' [NJB].
2. The genitive ἑαυτῶν 'of ourselves' states who should not forsake [NIC, WBC; NAB, NASB].

QUESTION—To what does τὴν ἐπισυναγωγήν 'the meeting together' refer?

1. It refers to the action of assembling [Alf, Blm, EGT, GNC, Hu, Hwt, Lns, Mil, My, NIC, WBC; KJV, NASB, NIV, NRSV, TEV]: assembling.
2. It refers to the assembled group [ICC, Lg; NAB, NJB, REB, TNT]: the assembly.
3. It refers both to the action of assembling and to the assembly itself [HNTC, Wst].

QUESTION—What relationship is indicated by the prefix ἐπι- in the word ἐπισυναγωγὴν 'meeting together'?

1. The prefixed ἐπι- adds the idea of assembling 'at' a certain place [Lns, Wst].
2. The prefixed ἐπι- implies 'together' [Hwt; KJV, NASB, NIV]: assembling together.
3. The prefixed ἐπι- adds nothing to the meaning [NIC, NIGTC, NTC].

QUESTION—To whom does ἑαυτῶν 'ourselves/yourselves' refer?

1. It means 'ourselves' [HNTC, ICC, Lg(K), Lns, Mil, My, NIC, NTC, WBC, Wst; KJV, NAB, NASB, REB, TNT]. It is emphatic [My]; it is not emphatic [NIGTC].
2. It means 'yourselves' [NJB].

just-as[a] (is the) habit[b] to-some (people),

LEXICON—a. καθώς (LN 64.14): 'just as' [LN], 'as' [HNTC, LN, Lns, NIC, WBC; all versions except CEV], not explicit [CEV].

b. ἔθος (LN 41.25) (BAGD 1. p. 218): 'habit' [BAGD, LN; CEV, NASB, NIV, NRSV], 'custom' [LN, Lns], 'manner' [KJV]. This entire phrase is translated 'as some do' [NAB, NJB, NLT, REB, TNT], 'as some people do' [NLT], 'as some people are regularly doing' [WBC], 'as some are doing' [TEV], 'as some habitually do' [HNTC], 'as some are in the habit of doing' [NIC], 'as indeed some are accustomed to do' [Mil], 'some people have gotten out of the habit of meeting for worship' [CEV].

QUESTION—Why is this clause mentioned?

It expresses the manner of the 'forsaking' in the preceding phrase [Mil]: not forsaking, in the manner of some people.

QUESTION—What is implied by this clause?

It implies carelessness [Alf, Blm], the beginning of apostasy [Lns].

but-on-the-contrary encouraging,[a]

LEXICON—a. pres. act. participle of παρακαλέω (LN 25.150) (BAGD 2. p. 617): 'to encourage' [BAGD, HNTC, LN, Mil, NIC, WBC; all versions except KJV, NLT], 'to encourage and warn' [NLT], 'to offer encouragement' [Lns], 'to urge' [BAGD], 'to appeal to' [BAGD], 'to exhort' [KJV]. It implies strong insistence [NIGTC].

QUESTION—What relationship is indicated by the participial form παρακαλοῦντες 'exhorting'?

It is an additional action parallel to (and at the same time as [Mil]) the preceding μὴ ἐγκαταλείποντες 'not forsaking' [Mil, NIC; NAB, NIV, NJB, REB, TEV, TNT] (it takes its mood from the verb κατανοῶμεν 'let us consider'): but we should encourage. It supports the thought of the preceding verb [WBC].

QUESTION—Who is the implied object of παρακαλοῦντες 'encouraging'?

The implied object is the readers [Alf, Blm, HNTC, Hu, Hwt, Mil, My, NIC, NIGTC, TNTC, WBC; all versions]: encouraging one another.

and by-so-much[a] more[b] in/by-as-much-as[c] you-see the day[d] approaching.[e]

LEXICON—a. τοσοῦτος (LN 78.52) (BAGD 2.b.γ. p. 823): 'so much' [Lns, Mil; KJV], 'as much as, to the degree, to the same degree, to (the) extent' [LN]. The phrase τοσούτῳ μᾶλλον 'by so much more' is translated 'all the more' [WBC; NASB, NIV, NRSV, REB, TEV], 'this all the more' [NAB], 'all the more so' [NIC], 'the more so' [NJB], 'especially' [HNTC; CEV, NLT, TNT].

b. μᾶλλον (LN 78.28) (BAGD 2.a. p. 489): 'more' [LN; all versions except TNT], 'the more' [Lns, Mil, NIC, WBC], 'even more, to a greater degree' [LN]. The phrase τοσούτῳ μᾶλλον ὅσῳ 'by so much more by as much as' is translated 'all the more, since' [BAGD].

c. ὅσος (LN 78.52) (BAGD 3. p. 586): 'as much as, to the degree that' [LN], 'how much' [Lns], 'as' [HNTC, Mil, NIC; KJV, NASB, NIV, NJB, NRSV, TNT], 'because' [NAB, REB], 'since' [WBC; CEV, TEV], not explicit [NLT]. The phrase τοσούτῳ μᾶλλον ὅσῳ 'by so much more by as much as' is translated 'all the more, as' [BAGD].

d. ἡμέρα (LN 67.142, 67.178) (BAGD 3.b.β. p. 347): 'day' [BAGD, LN (67.178), Lns, Mil; KJV, NASB], 'Day' [HNTC, NIC; NAB, NIV, NJB, NRSV, TNT], 'Day of the Lord' [WBC; REB, TEV], 'day of the Lord's coming' [CEV], 'day of his coming' [NLT], 'time, period' [LN (67.142)]. It refers to the day of Christ's return [Alf, Blm, EGT, GNC, Hwt, Lg, Mil, My, NCBC, NIC, TH, TNTC], the day of judgment [Alf, EBC, Hu, Lns, NCBC, NIGTC, NTC, TH].

e. pres. act. participle of ἐγγίζω (LN 67.21) (BAGD 5.b. p. 213): 'to approach' [BAGD, LN, NIC, WBC; KJV, NIV, NRSV], 'to draw near' [HNTC, Lns, Mil; NAB, NASB, NJB, NLT, REB, TNT], 'to come near' [BAGD, LN], 'to come nearer' [TEV], 'to get closer' [CEV].

QUESTION—Why is this clause mentioned?

It reinforces the preceding participial phrase [Mil, My, NIC]: encouraging one another by so much more as you see the day approaching.

QUESTION—To what does the phrase τοσούτῳ μᾶλλον 'by so much more' refer?

It refers to the two preceding participial phrases [Alf]: not neglecting . . . but encouraging, by so much more . . .

QUESTION—What relationship is indicated by ὅσῳ 'in/by as much as'?

1. It implies degree [BAGD, EGT, LN, Lns, Mil]: to the degree that you see the day approaching.
2. It implies reason [WBC; CEV, NAB, REB, TEV]: because you see the day approaching.

QUESTION—What relationship is indicated by the participial form ἐγγίζουσαν 'approaching'?

1. It is a predicate relationship to τὴν ἡμέραν 'the day', stating what the 'day' is doing [HNTC, Lns, Mil, NIC, WBC; all versions except NAB, TEV]: you see the day, that it is approaching.
2. It is translated as the verb of a substantive clause [NAB, TEV]: you see that the day is approaching.

DISCOURSE UNIT:10:26–39 [NASB]. The topic is Christ or judgment.

DISCOURSE UNIT:10:26–31 [EBC, GNC, HNTC, Lg, Lns, NCBC, NIC, NIGTC, NTC, TNTC; NJB]. The topic is the wrong way [EBC], the fearful possibility of judgment [NCBC], apostasy and judgment [GNC, Lg], the sin of apostasy [NIC], the danger of apostasy [HNTC; NJB], warning against apostasy [Lns], another warning [TNTC], warning to take heed [NTC], the consequences of willful sin [NIGTC].

10:26 For we willfully[a] sinning[b] after[c] the receiving[d] the true-knowledge[e] of-the truth,

LEXICON—a. ἑκουσίως (LN **30.64**) (BAGD p. 243): 'willfully' [Mil; KJV, NAB, NASB, NRSV], 'willingly' [Lns], 'intentionally' [BAGD, LN], 'purposely' [**LN**; TEV], 'deliberately' [BAGD, HNTC, LN, NIC, WBC; NIV, NJB, NLT, REB, TNT]. The phrase ἑκουσίως ἁμαρτανόντων ἡμῶν 'we willfully sinning' is translated 'people who decide to sin' [CEV]. It is emphatic by word order [EGT, Hwt, ICC, Lg(K), Lns, Mil, NIGTC, NTC, TH, TNTC, WBC, Wst]. It is the key word in the passage [ICC, TH].

b. pres. act. participle of ἁμαρτάνω (LN 88.289) (BAGD 3. p. 42): 'to sin' [BAGD, LN, Mil, NIC; CEV, KJV, NAB], 'to commit sin' [NJB], 'to persist in sin' [WBC; NRSV, REB], 'to go on sinning' [HNTC, Lns; NASB, TEV, TNT], 'to keep on sinning' [NIV], 'to continue to sin' [NLT]. The present tense refers to continuous sinning [EBC, EGT, HNTC, Lg, Lns, Mil, My, NIGTC, NTC, TH, WBC, Wst; NASB, NIV, NLT, NRSV, REB, TEV, TNT], to a persistent attitude [ICC, Lg(K)], to a state of sin [Alf]. It refers to apostasy and returning to Judaism [Alf].

c. μετά with accusative object (LN 67.48) (BAGD B.II.4.b. p. 510): 'after' [BAGD, HNTC, LN, Lns, Mil, NIC, WBC; all versions].

d. aorist act. infin. of λαμβάνω (LN 31.50): 'to receive' [HNTC, LN, Lns, Mil, NIC, WBC; all versions except CEV, NJB, TEV], 'to accept, to come to believe' [LN]. This active infinitive is translated as a passive: 'to be given' [NJB]. The phrase τὸ λαβεῖν τὴν ἐπίγνωσιν τῆς ἀληθείας 'the receiving the true knowledge of the truth' is translated 'the truth has been made known to us' [TEV], 'to find out about the truth' [CEV]. The aorist tense implies the act receiving [Mil, NIGTC], the act of coming to faith in Christ [NIGTC].

e. ἐπίγνωσις (LN 28.2, 28.18) (BAGD p. 291): 'true knowledge' [LN (28.2)], 'full knowledge' [LN (28.18), Mil, WBC; NLT], 'definite knowledge' [LN (28.18)], 'knowledge about' [LN (28.2)], 'knowledge' [BAGD, HNTC, LN (28.2, 28.18), NIC; all versions except CEV, NAB, TEV], 'realization' [Lns]. The phrase τὴν ἐπίγνωσιν τῆς ἀληθείας 'the true knowledge of the truth' is translated 'the truth' [CEV, NAB]. This word implies a true understanding [Alf, Lg(K), Lns, Mil, NTC, WBC] and active assimilation of the truth of the gospel [Alf, WBC], full knowledge [WBC, Wst], a living knowledge [Alf, Lg(K)] and personal experience [My]. It is more emphatic than the simple γνῶσις 'knowledge' [Wst]; it means no more than the simple γνῶσις 'knowledge' [Hwt, NIGTC].

QUESTION—What relationship is indicated by γάρ 'for'?

It indicates the grounds for the warning expressed in the preceding verse [Blm, EGT, HNTC, Hwt, Lns, Mil]. It is connected with the argument which is completed in 10:18 [NIGTC].

QUESTION—What relationship is indicated by the participle ἁμαρτανόντων 'sinning'?

1. It indicates a condition [Alf, Blm, EBC, EGT, HNTC, Hwt, Mil, My, NIC, NIGTC, NTC, TNTC, WBC; all versions]; it implies contingency, i.e. possibility [Mil]: if we should continue to sin, then there no longer remains a sacrifice for sins.
2. It expresses time [Lns]: when we continue sinning . . .

QUESTION—To whom does ἡμων 'we' refer?

It includes the writer with his readers [EBC, NIGTC, NTC, TNTC, WBC, Wst] in a tactful pastoral reference [NIGTC, Wst]: if we willfully sin.

QUESTION—What is implied by the phrase ἑκουσίως ἁμαρτανόντων 'willfully sinning'?

1. It refers to deliberate apostasy [Blm, EBC, EGT, GNC, Hu, Lg, NIC], the sin from which there is no return [GNC]. It implies true previous conversion [Alf, Hu, Lg, NCBC, NIC]. It can occur only 'after receiving the true knowledge of the truth' [EGT, Hu, Lg]. It implies declaring that Christianity is inadequate [ICC].
2. It refers to persons who have accepted Christian beliefs but have no personal experience with Christ [Hwt].

QUESTION—How are the two nouns related in the genitive construction τὴν ἐπίγνωσιν τῆς ἀληθείας 'the true knowledge of the truth'?

'The truth' states what is known [Mil; TEV]: knowing the truth. This phrase is a description of Christianity [ICC]. The truth referred to is the truth of God [Alf, NTC], Christianity as the absolute truth [EBC, My, NIGTC], the objective revelation [HNTC, NTC, TNTC] of Christ [Wst], the revelation of God's plan of salvation [WBC], Christian teaching [TH], a body of doctrine [TNTC].

(there) no-longer[a] remains[b] a-sacrifice[c] for[d] sins,

LEXICON–a. οὐκέτι (LN 67.130): 'no longer' [LN, Lns, Mil, WBC; NASB, NJB, NRSV, TEV], 'no further' [HNTC, NIC; NAB, REB, TNT], 'no more' [KJV], 'no other' [NLT], 'no' [CEV, NIV].

b. pres. pass. (deponent = act.) indic. of ἀπολείπω (LN **13.74**) (BAGD 2. p. 94): 'to remain' [BAGD, HNTC, Mil; KJV, NAB, NASB, NRSV], 'to exist' [**LN**], 'to continue to exist' [LN], 'to be left' [Lns, NIC; NIV, TNT], 'to be' [WBC; NJB, TEV], 'there can be' [CEV, REB], not explicit [NLT].

c. θυσία (LN 53.20) (BAGD 2.a. p. 366): 'sacrifice' [BAGD, LN, Lns, Mil, NIC, WBC; all versions], 'offering' [BAGD]. The phrase περὶ ἁμαρτιῶν θυσία 'sacrifice for sins' is translated 'sin-offering' [HNTC]. It means a sacrifice to take away sins [NIGTC]. The word is emphatic [NIGTC].

d. περί with genitive object (LN 90.39) (BAGD 1.g. p. 645): 'for' [Lns, NIC, WBC; all versions except NLT, TEV, TNT], 'on behalf of' [LN], 'that will take away' [TEV, TNT], 'that will cover' [NLT], 'to take away' [BAGD], 'to atone for' [BAGD, Mil].

QUESTION—What is the adverb οὐκέτι 'no longer' connected with?

1. It is connected with the verb ἀπολείπεται 'is left' [EGT, Lns, Mil, WBC; NASB, NJB, NRSV, TEV]: no longer is left.
2. It is treated as an adjective and connected with θυσία 'sacrifice' [EBC, HNTC, NIC; KJV, NAB, NIV, NLT, REB, TNT]: no further sacrifice.

QUESTION—What is meant by οὐκέτι ἀπολείπεται 'no longer remains'?

1. It means that if someone has accepted the one sacrifice made by Christ and then rejects it, it has ceased to operate for him and there is no second sacrifice left for him [Alf, EGT, NTC, TH, TNTC, WBC, Wst]; Christ's sacrifice is not repeated [My, NCBC]; there is no other means for forgiveness [Blm, EBC, EGT, Lns]. The apostate has cut himself off from the only means of forgiveness [GNC, Hu, ICC].
2. It means to understand the significance of Christ's sacrifice and to reject it, but without any personal experience with Christ [Hwt].

QUESTION—What is meant by the plural form of ἁμαρτιῶν 'sins'?

1. The plural 'sins' refers to individual experience rather than the idea of 'for sin' in general [Wst]. It is emphatic, emphasizing the fact of sin [Wst].
2. This plural noun is translated as a singular or generic [NAB]: for sin. The phrase is translated 'sin-offering' [HNTC].

10:27 but some[a] fearful[b] expectation[c] of-judgment,[d] and zeal[e] of-fire[f] being-about[g] to-consume[h] the hostile-ones.[i]

LEXICON—a. τις (LN 92.12) (BAGD 2.b.β. p. 820): 'some' [BAGD, Lns], 'something' [LN], 'a certain' [BAGD; KJV, NASB], 'a kind of' [Mil], 'inevitable' [WBC], 'a/an' [HNTC, NIC; NAB, NIV, NRSV, REB], 'the' [NJB], not explicit [CEV, NLT, TEV, TNT]. It is a literary device [Alf, Lg, My, WBC, Wst] adding to the sense of the adjective φοβερά 'fearful' [Alf, Blm, NTC, WBC] and implying 'some one' of the possible fearful expectations [Alf]. The indefinite pronoun heightens the terror [EGT, ICC, Lg, Lns, Mil, My, NIGTC, NTC, Wst].

b. φοβερός (LN 25.255) (BAGD p. 862): 'fearful' [BAGD, LN, NIC; KJV, NAB, NIV, NRSV], 'causing fear' [BAGD, LN], 'frightful' [Lns], 'terrible' [BAGD; CEV, NLT], 'terrifying' [HNTC, Mil, WBC; NASB, REB], 'dreadful' [NJB], 'in fear' [TEV], 'in terror' [TNT]. It implies something frightening [EBC], something causing fear [EGT, Mil, TH]. It means frightful [Alf, Lns], fearful [TNTC], terrible [My]. It is emphatic by word order [GNC, NTC].

c. ἐκδοχή (LN **30.53**) (BAGD p. 239): 'expectation' [BAGD, HNTC, LN, Lns, Mil, NIC, WBC; NAB, NASB, NIV, NLT, REB], 'prospect' [NJB, NRSV], 'looking for' [KJV]. This noun is also translated as a verb: 'to look forward to' [CEV], 'to wait' [TEV, TNT]. It means expectation [EBC, EGT, My], doom or reception of something [Alf].

d. κρίσις (LN 30.110, 38.1, 56.30) (BAGD 1.a.β. p. 452): 'judgment' [BAGD, HNTC, LN (30.110), Lns, Mil, NIC, WBC; all versions], 'condemnation' [LN (56.30)], 'punishment' [LN (38.1)]. It refers to the final Judgment [HNTC, NIGTC; TEV]. It refers to condemnation [Wst], to judgment in a neutral sense, the sense of punishment being conveyed by the context [My].

e. ζῆλος (LN **78.25**) (BAGD 1. p. 337): 'zeal, ardor' [BAGD], 'eagerness' [Lns], 'fury' [HNTC, Mil; NASB, NRSV], 'wrath' [NJB], 'anger' [TNT], 'indignation' [NIC; KJV]. This noun is also translated as an adjective: 'fierce' [LN; REB, TEV], 'furious' [CEV]; as a participle: 'flaming' [NAB], 'raging' [WBC; NIV, NLT]. It refers to God's avenging zeal [NIGTC].

f. πῦρ (LN 2.3) (BAGD 1.b. p. 730): 'fire' [BAGD, HNTC, LN, Lns, Mil, WBC; CEV, NAB, NASB, NIV, NLT, NRSV, REB, TEV]. This noun is also translated as an adjective: 'fiery' [NIC; KJV, NJB]; as a participle: 'burning' [TNT]. It is emphatic by word order [Alf, My]. It is personified [Lg, Lns, Mil, My], as the following action indicates. It is the fire of God's presence [Alf], the fire of judgment [EBC], the wrath of God [Mil].

g. pres. act. participle of μέλλω (LN 67.62) (BAGD 1.c.β. p. 501): 'to be about to' [LN, Lns, NIC], 'to be going to' [Mil], '(it) will surely' [HNTC], '(it) will' [BAGD; NASB, NIV, NLT, NRSV, REB, TEV, TNT], '(it) shall' [KJV], '(it) is' [NJB], not explicit [CEV, NAB]. This verb is also translated as an adjective: 'ready' [WBC]. It means to be destined to [Alf, EGT; NJB], to be on the point of doing [Lg(K), WBC], to be certain to [HNTC]. With the following infinitive, it is merely the equivalent of the future tense [BAGD, NIGTC; KJV, NASB, NIV, NRSV, TEV, TNT].

h. pres. act. infin. of ἐσθίω (LN **20.44**) (BAGD 2. p. 313): 'to consume' [BAGD, HNTC, LN, Mil, NIC, WBC; NAB, NASB, NIV, NLT, NRSV, REB], 'to devour' [KJV, NJB, TNT], 'to destroy' [**LN**; TEV], 'to eat' [Lns], not explicit [CEV]. It implies conscious suffering, not annihilation [Lg].

i. ὑπεναντίος (LN **39.6**) (BAGD p. 838): 'hostile' [LN, Lns]. This adjective is also translated as a noun: 'adversary' [BAGD, HNTC, Mil, NIC, WBC; KJV, NAB, NASB, NRSV], 'enemy' [CEV, NIV, NJB, NLT, REB], 'those who oppose God' [TEV], 'those who oppose him' [TNT]. It refers to enemies [EBC], to those who reject God's Son and his salvation [GNC]. It implies persistent opposition [EGT, Mil].

QUESTION—What verb is implied for this clause?

The verb ἀπολείπεται 'there remains' is implied, carried over from the preceding clause [Alf, EGT, GNC, Hu, Hwt, Lg, Lns, Mil, My, TNTC, Wst; NJB]: there remains some fearful expectation of judgment.

QUESTION—How are the two nouns related in the genitive construction ἐκδοχὴ κρίσεως 'expectation of judgment'?

'Judgment' tells what is expected [Mil; TEV, TNT]: we expect judgment.

QUESTION—What is the phrase καὶ πυρὸς ζῆλος 'and zeal of fire' connected with?

1. It is parallel to ἐκδοχή 'expectation' [HNTC, Lns, Mil; NASB, NRSV]: there remains expectation of judgment, and there remains zeal of fire. This phrase explains what is meant by the preceding comment [Lns, NIGTC].
2. The nominative noun ζῆλος 'zeal' is erroneously translated as a genitive, and this phrase is thus mistakenly made parallel to κρίσεως 'judgment'

[NIC, NTC, WBC; KJV, NIV, NJB, TEV, TNT]: expectation of judgment and expectation of zeal of fire.

QUESTION—How are the two nouns related in the genitive construction πυρὸς ζῆλος 'zeal of fire'?

1. The genitive πυρός 'of fire' describes ζῆλος 'zeal' [EGT, Hu, NIC; KJV, NJB, TNT]: fiery zeal.
2. Ζῆλος 'zeal' describes the genitive noun πυρός 'of fire' [EBC, Mil, TH, WBC; NAB, NIV, REB, TEV]: zealous fire.
3. The genitive πυρός 'of fire' is in apposition with ζῆλος 'zeal' [NIGTC]: zeal, which is expressed as fire.

QUESTION—What relationship is indicated by the participle μέλλοντος 'being about to'?

It is indefinite attributive [HNTC, Hu, Lg(K), NIC; all versions except NAB]: zeal of fire which is about to consume.

QUESTION—What is the genitive participle μέλλοντος 'being about to' connected with?

It is connected with πυρὸς ζῆλος 'zeal of fire' [EGT, HNTC, Hu, NIC; all versions except KJV, NAB].

1. It agrees with the genitive case of πυρός 'zeal' [EGT, Lg], which indicates that it is πυρός 'fire', not ζῆλος 'zeal', that is about to consume the hostile ones [WBC; NAB, NASB, NIV, NRSV, REB, TEV]: fire which is about to devour.
2. It is mistakenly translated as if it agreed with the nominative noun ζῆλος 'zeal' [NIC; NJB, TNT]: zeal which is about to devour.

QUESTION—Who is the implied object of τοὺς ὑπεναντίους 'the hostile ones'?

1. They are hostile against God [EBC, HNTC, Mil, NIC, TH, WBC; NAB, NIV, REB, TNT]: the adversaries of God.
2. They are adversaries of Christ [Lns]: the adversaries of Christ.
3. They are adversaries of the readers [NJB]: your adversaries.

10:28 Anyone[a] having-set-aside[b] (the) law of-Moses, apart-from[c] mercies[d] on-the-basis-of[e] two or three witnesses, dies;

LEXICON—a. τις (LN 92.12) (BAGD 1.a.δ. p. 820): 'anyone' [BAGD, HNTC, LN, Mil, NIC, WBC; all versions except CEV, KJV, TNT], 'someone' [CEV], 'one' [Lns], 'he' [KJV], 'any Jew' [TNT].

b. aorist act. participle of ἀθετέω (LN **76.24**) (BAGD 1.a. p. 21): 'to set aside' [BAGD, HNTC; NASB, TNT], 'to disregard' [NJB], 'to set at naught' [Mil], 'to reject' [**LN**; NAB, NIV], 'to regard as invalid' [LN], 'to declare invalid' [BAGD], 'to despise' [Mil; KJV], 'to disobey' [TEV], 'to refuse to obey' [NLT], 'to violate' [NIC, WBC; NRSV], 'to break' [CEV], 'to flout' [REB], 'to defy' [Lns]. It is a stronger word than 'to disobey' [GNC, TH]; it means denial of the authority and validity of the law [HNTC, TNTC, Wst], willful rejection of the law [ICC], willful disobedience [NIGTC], annulling the law [NTC], thus breaking the covenant [NTC, TH]. The aorist tense treats this action as contemporary with the verb ἀποθνῄσκει 'he dies' [all versions].

c. χωρίς with genitive object (LN 89.120): 'apart from' [LN], 'without' [LN, Lns, Mil, NIC, WBC; all versions except CEV, NJB], not explicit [CEV]. The phrase χωρὶς οἰκτιρμῶν 'without pity' is translated 'ruthlessly' [NJB]. This phrase is omitted by HNTC (probably by accident).

d. οἰκτιρμός (LN 88.80) (BAGD p. 561): 'mercy'. This plural noun is translated as a singular: 'mercy' [LN, Mil, NIC; all versions except CEV, NJB], 'pity' [BAGD, WBC], 'compassion' [Lns], 'tender compassion' [LN], not explicit [CEV]. It refers to merciful feelings by anyone concerned for the guilty person [Alf, Wst]. The plural is merely idiomatic [Lns, NIGTC, WBC, Wst] and does not refer to individual acts of mercy [NIGTC]; it refers to every kind of mercy [Mil].

e. ἐπί with dative object (LN 89.13) (BAGD II.1.b.γ. p. 287): 'on the basis of' [BAGD, LN], 'on the word of' [NJB], 'on the testimony of' [NIC; NAB, NASB, NIV, NLT, NRSV], 'on the evidence of' [HNTC, WBC; REB], 'upon the evidence of' [Mil], 'when judged guilty from the evidence of' [TEV], 'under' [KJV], 'before' [Lns]. The phrase ἐπὶ δυσὶν ἢ τρισὶν μάρτυσιν 'on the basis of two or three witnesses' is translated 'if there are two or three witnesses to give evidence against him' [TNT], 'if two or more witnesses accused someone' [CEV]. This preposition refers to evidence given by witnesses [EGT, ICC]. It implies 'in the presence of' [NTC].

QUESTION—Why is this clause mentioned?

This and the following verse state the argument from the lesser to the greater to show how great the punishment of apostasy will be [Alf, Blm, EBC, GNC, HNTC, Hu, Hwt, Mil, My, NIGTC, WBC]. These verses draw a comparison [Lns].

QUESTION—What relationship is indicated by the participle ἀθετήσας 'having set aside'?

1. It is indefinite attributive [EGT, HNTC, My, NIC, WBC, Wst; all versions except CEV]: anyone who has set aside.
2. It is conditional, stating the grounds for the conclusion in the following verse [Mil; CEV]: if anyone has set aside.
3. It is temporal [Lg(K)]: after anyone has set aside.

QUESTION—What relationship is indicated by the phrase νόμον Μωϋσέως 'law of Moses'?

It refers to the sin of idolatry [Hwt, Lg, My, NCBC, Wst], which involved breaking the covenant [Lg, NCBC], denying the validity of some of God's laws [Hwt]. It refers to the sin of apostasy [HNTC, Hu, My, NCBC, Wst], which rejects the entire law [HNTC]. It refers to certain cases, not to every violation [Alf, HNTC, Hu]. This refers to the ceremonial law [Blm].

1. It is definite [Alf, EBC, EGT, NIGTC], made definite by the following genitive pronoun Μωϋσέως 'of Moses' and referring to the Old Covenant [Mil]: the law of Moses.
2. It is qualitative, referring to what was prescribed by the law of Moses [Wst].

QUESTION—What is the phrase χωρὶς οἰκτιρμῶν 'apart from pity' connected with?

It is connected with ἀποθνήσκει 'he dies' [EGT, Lns, Mil, NIC, WBC; all versions]: he dies without mercy. It emphasizes the certainty of the punishment [EGT]. This phrase is emphatic by word order.

QUESTION—What does the present tense of ἀποθνήσκει 'he dies' indicate?

1. It is a timeless present tense [NIGTC; NAB, NASB]; it refers to the law as it stands, whether or not the law was still in effect [EGT, NIGTC, TH].
2. It indicates an action repeated from time to time [WBC].
3. It refers to past action [KJV, NIV].

10:29 by-how-much, do-you-think, will-he-be-considered-worthy[a] of worse[b] punishment,[c] the-(one) having-trampled-on[d] the Son of-God

LEXICON—a. fut. pass. indic. of ἀξιόω (LN 65.18) (BAGD 1.a. p. 78): 'to be considered worthy' [BAGD], 'to be regarded as worthy of' [LN], 'to be thought worthy' [KJV], 'to be counted worthy' [Lns, Mil], 'to be considered as meriting' [LN], 'to be deemed fit' [NIC], 'to be considered deserving' [BAGD], 'to be deserved' [NRSV, REB], not explicit [NLT]. This passive voice is also translated as an active voice: 'to deserve' [HNTC, WBC; NASB, TNT]. The phrase χείρονος ἀξιωθήσεται τιμωρίας 'he will be considered worthy of worse punishment' is translated 'that a much worse punishment is due' [NAB]. The phrase πόσῳ δοκεῖτε χείρονος ἀξιωθήσεται τιμωρίας 'by how much do you think he will be considered worthy of worse punishment' is translated 'how much more severely do you think a man deserves to be punished' [NIV], 'just think how much worse is the punishment they will deserve' [TEV], 'but it is much worse' [CEV]. This entire phrase is translated 'and you may be sure that anyone who tramples on the Son of God . . . will be condemned to a far severer punishment' [NJB]. The actor of this verb is God [Alf, EGT, Lg, My, NIGTC]. The aorist tense indicates a single act of consideration [Alf].

b. χείρων (LN 65.29) (BAGD p. 881): 'worse' [BAGD, LN, Lns, Mil; CEV, NAB, NRSV, TEV], 'more terrible' [NLT], 'more severe' [BAGD, HNTC, NIC; REB], 'severer' [WBC; NASB, TNT], 'far severer' [NJB], 'sorer' [KJV].

c. τιμωρία (LN **38.6**) (BAGD p. 818): 'punishment' [BAGD, HNTC, LN, Lns, Mil, WBC; all versions except CEV, NIV, REB], 'penalty' [NIC; REB], not explicit [CEV]. This genitive noun is the predicate of the verb ἀξιωθήσεται 'he will be considered worthy' [Mil, NTC].

d. aorist act. participle of καταπατέω (LN 19.52, **88.196**) (BAGD 2. p. 415): 'to trample on' [HNTC, LN (19.52); NJB, NLT, TNT], 'to trample upon' [WBC], 'to trample under foot' [BAGD, Lns, Mil, NIC; NASB, NIV, REB], 'to tread underfoot' [KJV], 'to despise' [LN (88.196); TEV], 'to disdain' [NAB], 'to treat with disdain' [BAGD], 'to treat with complete disdain' [LN (88.196)], 'to show utter disdain' [LN (**88.196**)], 'to spurn' [NRSV], 'to dishonor' [CEV]. The aorist tense looks back on the past life as a single fact [Alf]. This word implies strong disdain [EBC], utter contempt [Blm, Hu, ICC, My, NIC, Wst], outrageous scorn [EGT], strong antagonism [TNTC].

QUESTION—What relationship is indicated by 'by how much'?

It is a dative of degree [HNTC, Mil, NIC, NIGTC, WBC].

1. It introduces a rhetorical question [Alf, EGT, Hu, NIGTC, TH, TNTC, WBC; KJV, NASB, NIV, NRSV]: by how much?
2. It introduces an exclamation [TEV]: by how much!
3. It introduces a statement [HNTC; CEV, NAB, NJB, REB, TNT]: by how much.

QUESTION—What is the dative pronoun πόσῳ 'by how much' connected with?

1. It is connected with the verb ἀξιωθήσεται 'he will be considered worthy' [Mil]: he will be considered worthy by how much?
2. This dative pronoun is erroneously translated as a genitive and connected with the genitive χείρονος τιμωρίας 'worse punishment' [Alf, EGT, HNTC, Hu, Lns, My, NIC, TNTC, WBC; all versions except NAB, NJB]: of how much worse punishment?

QUESTION—What relationship is indicated by δοκεῖτε 'do you think'?

It is parenthetical [Alf, NIGTC, WBC, Wst; KJV], an orienter appealing to the readers' sense of appropriateness [EGT, Hu, Lg, Mil, My, NIGTC], in form giving them the privilege of making the decision, but without indicating any doubt of the appropriate response [EGT, Lg, Mil, My, NIGTC]. The readers are urged to give special thought to this matter [TNTC].

QUESTION—What relationship is indicated by the three participles ὁ καταπατήσας . . . ἡγησάμενος . . . ἐνυβρίσας 'the one having trampled on . . . having considered . . . having insulted'?

They are attributive participles (translated as a compound relative clause) used substantively as the compound subject of the verb ἀξιωθήσεται 'he shall be considered worthy' [Alf, Mil, NIC, WBC; all versions except TEV]: the one having done these things shall be considered worthy of. . . . The one definite article governing all three participles shows that they all describe the same person [Mil, NIGTC, TH, Wst], actually a generic reference, not of one individual [NIGTC]. They indicate a deliberate decision [WBC, Wst] after experiencing Christ's blessings [Wst]. The use of the three participles emphasizes the argument [NIGTC]. The aorist tenses indicate past events [NIGTC]; they summarize a continuing attitude [WBC].

QUESTION—What is implied by the position of the phrase τὸν υἱὸν τοῦ θεοῦ 'the Son of God'?
It is emphatic by its position [NIGTC].

and having-considered[a] common[b] the blood of-the covenant,[c] by[d] which he-was-sanctified,[e]

LEXICON—a. aorist mid. (deponent = act.) participle of ἡγέομαι (LN 31.1) (BAGD 2. p. 343): 'to consider' [BAGD], 'to regard' [LN; NASB], 'to count' [Lns; KJV], 'to treat' [NIC, WBC; NIV, NJB, NLT, TEV, TNT], 'to look upon' [BAGD], 'to think' [LN; NAB], 'to hold a view' [LN], 'to reckon' [Mil], 'to disgrace' [CEV]. The phrase κοινὸν ἡγησάμενος 'having considered common' is translated 'profaned' [HNTC; NRSV, REB]. The aorist tense refers to an action prior to the following verb ἡγιάσθη 'he was sanctified' [Mil]. It involves human judgment and implies conduct resulting from that judgment [NIGTC].

b. κοινός (LN **65.15**) (BAGD 2. p. 438): 'common' [Lns, Mil; NLT], 'something common' [NIC], 'unclean' [BAGD; NASB], 'defiled' [WBC], 'unholy' [Mil], 'an unholy thing' [KJV, NIV], 'as if it were not holy' [NJB], 'ordinary' [NAB], 'a cheap thing' [TEV], 'of little value' [**LN**], 'relatively worthless' [LN], 'of no account' [TNT]. It means to consider Christ's blood as merely the blood of an ordinary person [Alf, Blm, EBC, ICC, Lg(K), NIC, NTC] and consequently of no saving value [Blm, ICC, WBC, Wst]. It means ceremonially unclean [EGT], impure [Lg, My], unclean or unholy [GNC, Lg(K), NIC, TNTC], the opposite of holy [Hu], a cheap thing [TH].

c. διαθήκη (LN 34.44) (BAGD 2. p. 183): 'covenant' [BAGD, HNTC, LN, Mil, NIC, WBC; all versions except CEV], 'pact' [LN], 'testament' [Lns], 'promise' [CEV].

d. ἐν with dative object (LN 89.76): 'by' [HNTC, LN, WBC; NAB, NASB, NRSV, REB], 'by means of' [LN], 'through' [LN], 'with' [Mil, NIC], 'wherewith' [KJV], 'in connection with' [Lns], not explicit [NLT]. The phrase ἐν ᾧ ἡγιάσθη 'by which he was sanctified' is translated 'that sanctified him' [NIV], 'which sanctified him' [NJB], 'which had cleansed him' [TNT], 'which purified them from sin' [TEV], 'that made us holy' [CEV]. It indicates the element in which the action occurred [Alf]. It expresses means [Mil], instrument [NIGTC, WBC]; it indicates where the action occurred [Wst].

e. aorist pass. indic. of ἁγιάζω (LN 53.44, 88.26) (BAGD 2. p. 8): 'to be sanctified' [BAGD, Lns, Mil, NIC; KJV, NAB, NASB, NRSV], 'to be made holy' [LN (88.26)], 'to be consecrated' [BAGD, HNTC, LN (53.44), WBC; REB], 'to be dedicated' [BAGD], 'to be dedicated to God' [LN (53.44)], not explicit [NLT]. This passive voice is also translated as active: 'to make holy' [CEV], 'to sanctify' [NIV, NJB], 'to cleanse' [TNT], 'to purify' [TEV]. The actor is God [NIGTC]. It refers to the initial act [EBC, Wst] of being set apart for God [EBC]. It means to be cleansed from sin [Blm, Hu, Hwt, TH] and set apart for service to God [Blm, Hu, Hwt]. It refers to the application of Christ's blood to the heart resulting in purifying effects [Alf, EGT], to Christ's action upon the life of the person [WBC], to incorporation into Christ [Wst]. The aorist tense indicates an event [Mil, Wst]. In the present situation the person described has not truly received this sanctification [Hu, Hwt, NTC].

QUESTION—How are the two nouns related in the genitive construction τὸ αἷμα τῆς διαθήκης 'the blood of the covenant'?

'The covenant' tells what was established by 'the blood' [Blm, EBC, EGT, Mil, My, NIGTC, TH, TNTC, WBC]: the blood that established the covenant. This phrase refers to the one atoning death of Christ [Hu, Mil], as the definite article with 'blood' indicates [Mil].

QUESTION—To what does ᾧ 'which' refer?

It refers to τὸ αἷμα 'the blood' [Alf, Lg, Mil, NIC, Wst; NAB, TNT]: the blood by which he was sanctified.

and having-insulted[a] the Spirit of-the grace?[b]

LEXICON—a. aorist act. participle of ἐνυβρίζω (LN 33.390) (BAGD p. 270): 'to insult' [BAGD, HNTC, LN, Lns, Mil, WBC; all versions except KJV, NLT, NRSV], 'to insult and enrage' [NLT], 'to do despite unto' [KJV], 'to outrage' [BAGD, NIC; NRSV]. It implies insolent arrogance [EBC, NIGTC, TNTC].

b. χάρις (LN 25.89, 88.66) (BAGD 3.b. p. 878): 'grace' [BAGD, LN (88.66), Mil, NIC, WBC; all versions except REB, TNT], 'divine grace' [Lns], 'graciousness' [LN (88.66)], 'kindness' [LN (88.66)], 'favor' [LN (25.89)], 'good will' [LN (25.89)], 'mercy' [CEV, NLT]. The phrase τὸ πνεῦμα τῆς χάριτος 'the spirit of grace' is translated 'God's gracious Spirit' [REB, TNT], 'the gracious Spirit of God' [HNTC]. It is God's grace [NIGTC].

QUESTION—To whom/what does τὸ πνεῦμα 'the Spirit' refer?

1. The Spirit is regarded as a person [Alf, Blm, EBC, GNC, HNTC, Hu, Hwt, NIC, NIGTC, NTC, TNTC, WBC; all versions]: the Holy Spirit.
2. It refers to the effective principle [Lg]: the principle of grace.

QUESTION—How are the two nouns related in the genitive construction τὸ πνεῦμα τῆς χάριτος 'the Spirit of grace'?

1. 'Grace' indicates what is bestowed by the Holy Spirit [Mil, NTC, TH, TNTC, Wst; CEV, NLT]: the Spirit who bestows grace.
2. The genitive noun χάριτος 'grace' describes τὸ πνεῦμα 'the Spirit' [Alf, NIGTC; REB, TNT]: the gracious Spirit.
3. It is both of the above [Blm, GNC, HNTC].
4. This phrase is the equivalent of 'the Holy Spirit' [My] but emphasizing his gracious nature [ICC].

10:30 For we-know the-(one) having-said, "To-me (is/belongs) vengeance,[a] I will-repay";[b]

TEXT—Some manuscripts add λέγει κύριος 'says the Lord' at the end of this clause. GNT does not deal with this variant. Only Alf, EGT, Lg, My, KJV include this phrase; Blm includes it in brackets in his Greek text.

LEXICON—a. ἐκδίκησις (LN 38.8, 39.33) (BAGD p. 238): 'vengeance' [BAGD, HNTC, Lns, Mil, NIC, WBC; KJV, NAB, NASB, NJB, NLT, NRSV, TNT], 'retribution' [LN (39.33)], 'punishment' [LN (38.8)], 'justice' [REB]. The phrase ἐμοὶ ἐκδίκησις 'to me is vengeance' is translated 'it is mine to avenge' [NIV], 'I will take revenge' [TEV], 'he will punish' [CEV]. It implies certain punishment [Mil].

b. fut. act. indic. of ἀνταποδίδωμι (LN 38.19) (BAGD 2. p. 73): 'to repay' [BAGD, HNTC, LN, WBC; all versions except CEV, KJV, NJB], 'to pay back' [LN; NJB], 'to recompense' [Mil; KJV], 'to give back due return' [Lns], 'to requite' [NIC], 'to cause retribution' [LN], 'to take revenge' [CEV]. The prefixed preposition ἀντι- adds emphasis to the verb [NIGTC, WBC]; the infixed preposition ἀπο- adds the concept of 'due from (God)' [Lns].

QUESTION—Why is this verse mentioned?

It emphasizes the certainty that the sinner will be punished by God [EBC, EGT, HNTC, ICC, Lns, My, NCBC, NIC, WBC, Wst], the reality of the punishment [GNC], the seriousness of the judgment [Hwt].

QUESTION—What relationship is indicated by γάρ 'for'?

It indicates the grounds for the preceding warning [Alf, Blm, Mil, NIGTC]: the punishment will be worse, because God has said . . .

QUESTION—What relationship is indicated by οἴδαμεν 'we know'?

It is a speech orienter. The implied sense is "because God is the one who said" [Mil]. The writer is appealing to his readers' understanding [EBC]. By saying 'we', he includes himself with his readers [Hu, Lns, TH], maintains his readers' interest [NIGTC], and softens the comment [NIGTC].

QUESTION—To whom does τὸν εἰπόντα 'the one having said' refer?

It refers to God [Alf, EBC, EGT, GNC, HNTC, Hu, Hwt, Lns, My, NIGTC, TH, WBC] in a reverential manner [NIGTC]. This aorist participle refers to an action in the past [NIGTC]

QUESTION—What relationship is indicated by ἐμοί 'to me' and ἐγώ 'I'?

The pronoun ἐμοί 'to me' is emphatic and it is emphatic by forefronting [Mil]; the pronoun ἐγώ 'I' is emphatic [NIGTC, WBC] and it is emphatic by forefronting.

and again, "(The) Lord will-judge[a] his people."

LEXICON—a. fut. act. indic. of κρίνω (LN 56.20, 56.30) (BAGD 4.b.α. p. 452): 'to judge' [BAGD, HNTC, LN (56.20), Lns, Mil, NIC, WBC; all versions except NJB], 'to judge as guilty' [LN (56.30)], 'to punish' [BAGD], 'to condemn' [LN (56.30)], 'to vindicate' [NJB].

QUESTION—What relationship is indicated by καὶ πάλιν 'and again'?
It gives emphasis to the following quotation [NIGTC, TH].

QUESTION—What is the purpose of this quotation?
It points to punishment and condemnation [Alf, Blm, EBC, GNC, HNTC, Hu, ICC, Lns, Mil, My, NCBC, NIC, NTC, WBC]. It means that God will vindicate his people against their enemies [Lg].

QUESTION—To whom does τὸν λαὸν αὐτοῦ 'his people' refer?
It refers to people in covenant relation to God in the NT church [Mil].

10:31 Fearful[a] (is) the to-fall/falling-in into[b] hands[c] of-(a/the)-living God.

LEXICON—a. φοβερός (LN **25.255**) (BAGD p. 862): 'fearful' [BAGD, NIC], 'fearful thing' [LN, Mil; KJV, NAB, NRSV], 'frightful' [BAGD, Lns], 'dreadful thing' [NIV, NJB], 'terrible' [BAGD, HNTC], 'terrible thing' [CEV, NLT], 'terrifying' [WBC], 'terrifying thing' [NASB, REB, TEV, TNT]. It is emphatic by its position [WBC].
b. εἰς with accusative object (LN 84.22): 'into' [BAGD, HNTC, LN, Lns, Mil, NIC, WBC; all versions].
c. χείρ (LN 8.30, 37.14) (BAGD 2.a.γ. p. 880): 'hand' [BAGD, HNTC, LN (8.30), Lns, Mil, NIC, WBC; all versions], 'control' [LN (37.14)].

QUESTION—Why is this clause mentioned?
It states the conclusion (a summary [NIGTC, WBC]) of the preceding warnings [Alf, Hu, Mil, My, NCBC, NIGTC, WBC] in an axiomatic form [Alf] and closes the paragraph [Mil, My]. It refers to the unfaithful falling into God's hands for their doom [Alf].

QUESTION—What is meant by 'falling into the hands'?
It means coming under the power of someone [TH]. For sinners, it implies punishment [Blm, EGT, Hwt, ICC, Lns, My, NIGTC, NTC]. The negative implication is carried over from the negative implication of the verb ἐμπεσεῖν 'to fall into' [NIGTC]. The aorist tense of the infinitive indicates a single occurrence [NTC]. The articular infinitive τὸ ἐμπεσεῖν 'the falling' is the subject of the unexpressed verb ἐστιν 'is' [WBC].

QUESTION—What is the significance of the lack of a definite article with χεῖρας 'hands'?
1. It may be qualitative, focusing on what kind of thing it is: hands.
2. It is considered definite [Alf, EGT, HNTC, Lns, Mil, NIC, NTC, WBC; all versions]: the hands. It may be considered definite with no article since the modifying phrase θεοῦ ζῶντος 'living God' is without the definite article.

QUESTION—What is the significance of the lack of a definite article with θεοῦ ζῶντος 'living God'?
Ζῶντος 'living' implies the powerful ability of God's action [Alf, GNC, HNTC, Hu, ICC]; it distinguishes him from dead idols [NTC]. It emphasizes the hopeless situation of God's enemies because of his omnipotence [Blm, EBC], his eternity, or both [Blm].
1. The phrase is qualitative, focusing on God's nature [Alf]: God (as deity).

2. It is considered definite [EGT, HNTC, Lns, Mil, NIC, WBC; all versions]; (θεοῦ 'God' may be definite with or without the article: the living God).

DISCOURSE UNIT: 10:32–39 [EBC, GNC, Lg, NCBC, NIC, NIGTC, NTC, TNTC; NJB]. The topic is choosing what is right [EBC], a call to persevere [NIC, NTC], motives for perseverance [NJB], an exhortation to endure and be faithful [GNC], the need to endure [NCBC], an assurance that blessedness awaits those who endure to the end [Lg], faith between the past and the future [NIGTC], the value of past experience [TNTC].

DISCOURSE UNIT: 10:32–35 [HNTC]. The topic is a reminder of the past.

DISCOURSE UNIT: 10:32–34 [Lns, NTC]. The topic is a reminder of past days [Lns, NTC].

10:32 But remember[a] the former days, in[b] which having-been-illuminated[c] you endured[d] a-great contest[e] of-sufferings,[f]

LEXICON—a. pres. pass. impera. of ἀναμιμνῄσκω (LN 29.9) (BAGD p. 57): 'to remember' [BAGD, HNTC, LN, NIC, WBC; NASB, NIV, NJB, REB, TEV, TNT], 'to recall' [LN; NAB, NRSV], 'to call to remembrance' [Lns; KJV], 'not to forget' [CEV, NLT]. The passive voice is also translated as a middle voice: 'to remind yourselves' [Mil]. The present tense indicates habitual recalling [Lg(K), Mil].

b. ἐν with dative object (LN 67.136): 'in' [Lns, Mil; KJV, NJB, TEV, TNT], 'during, in the course of' [LN]. The phrase ἐν αἷς 'in which' is translated 'when' [HNTC, NIC, WBC; CEV, NAB, NASB, NIV, NLT, NRSV, REB]. It indicates time within which (something occurs) [NIGTC].

c. aorist pass. participle of φωτίζω (LN 14.39) (BAGD 2.b. p. 873): 'to be illuminated' [BAGD, LN; KJV], 'to be enlightened' [HNTC, Lns; NAB, NASB, NRSV, REB], 'to be shined upon' [LN]. This passive participle is translated as an active voice: 'to receive the light' [WBC; CEV, NIV, NJB], 'to receive the light of the Gospel' [Mil], 'to receive the light of God' [TNT], 'to learn about Christ' [NLT]. This participle is translated as a temporal clause: 'after God's light had shone on you' [TEV], 'after your enlightenment' [NIC]. It refers to the enlightenment of the truth which the Gospel had brought [EBC, EGT, My, NTC], the event (as the aorist tense indicates [NIGTC]) of their conversion [Hu, Lg, Mil, NIGTC, NTC, TH, TNTC, WBC], their baptism [Mil, NCBC, NIGTC, NTC, TH]; it does not include baptism [WBC]. The implied actor is God [NIGTC, TH].

d. aorist act. indic. of ὑπομένω (LN 25.175) (BAGD 2. p. 846): 'to endure' [BAGD, LN, Lns, Mil, NIC, WBC; KJV, NAB, NASB, NRSV], 'to put up with' [LN], 'to go through' [CEV], 'to hold out' [BAGD], 'to stand one's ground' [BAGD; NIV], 'to meet and hold firm' [REB], 'to remain' [BAGD], 'to remain steadfast' [HNTC; TNT], 'to remain faithful' [NLT], 'to have to meet' [NJB]. The phrase πολλὴν ἄθλησιν ὑπομείνατε παθημάτων 'you endured a great conflict of sufferings' is translated 'you suffered many things, yet were not defeated by the struggle' [TEV]. This word implies steadfastness [My, NIGTC].

e. ἄθλησις (LN **50.3, 74.13**) (BAGD p. 21): 'contest' [Lns, WBC; NAB, NIV], 'conflict' [LN (50.3), Mil; NASB], 'struggle' [BAGD, HNTC, **LN (50.3)**, NIC; NRSV, TEV, TNT], 'challenge' [**LN** (74.13); NJB], 'fight' [KJV], 'test' [REB]. The phrase πολλὴν ἄθλησιν παθημάτων 'a great contest of sufferings' is translated 'though it was a hard and painful struggle' [TNT], 'in a hard and painful struggle' [HNTC], 'even though it meant terrible suffering' [NLT], 'the hard times' [CEV]. It implies strenuousness [EBC].

f. πάθημα (LN 24.78) (BAGD 1. p. 602): 'suffering' [BAGD, LN, Lns, Mil, NIC, WBC; NASB, NJB, NRSV, REB], 'affliction' [KJV], 'pain' [LN]. This plural noun παθημάτων is translated as a singular: 'suffering' [NAB, NIV, NLT].

QUESTION—Why is this verse mentioned?

Following the preceding warnings it begins words of encouragement [Alf, EBC, EGT, GNC, HNTC, Hu, Mil, My, NCBC, NIC, NIGTC, NTC, TH, WBC], arguments of self-interest [Blm], reminding the readers of their good past [EGT]. The introductory δέ 'but' indicates this contrast [EBC, Mil, My, NIGTC, TH, WBC].

QUESTION—What relationship is indicated by the relative clause beginning with ἐν αἷς 'in which'?

It is nonrestrictive, describing what happened in 'the former days' [Mil].

QUESTION—What relationship is indicated by the participial form φωτισθέντες 'having been illuminated'?

It is temporal [HNTC, Lns, Mil, NIC, WBC; all versions except REB]: after you were illuminated. The aorist tense indicates action prior to the following verb ὑπεμείνατε 'you endured' [Mil].

1. It is connected with what follows [HNTC, Lns, Mil, NIC; all versions except NIV]: after you were illuminated you endured.
2. It is connected with the preceding noun phrase [WBC; NIV]: remember the former days following your illumination.

QUESTION—To what does τὰς πρότερον ἡμέρας 'the former days' refer?

It refers to the time when they first became Christians [Hu], shortly after their conversion [Lns], following their baptism [NCBC]. It implies that they had been Christians for some time [TNTC] and that the events referred to had occurred a good while ago [NTC].

QUESTION—How are the two nouns related in the genitive construction ἄθλησιν παθημάτων 'contest of suffering'?

1. The ἄθλησιν 'contest' is what is endured [BAGD, Blm, GNC, HNTC, ICC, NIC, TNTC, Wst; NIV, NRSV, TNT].

1.1 Παθημάτων 'sufferings' are the contents of the contest [BAGD, ICC, Wst], the objects to be overcome [TNTC]: a contest which consisted of sufferings.

1.2 Παθημάτων 'sufferings' accompany the contest [NIV]: a contest in the face of sufferings.
1.3 Παθημάτων 'sufferings' accompany the contest or are the object of the contest (depending on the meaning of 'with') [Blm, NIC, WBC; NRSV]: a contest with sufferings.
1.4 Παθημάτων 'sufferings' describe the contest [HNTC; TNT]: a painful struggle.
2. Παθημάτων 'sufferings' are what are endured, and ἄθλησιν 'contest' expresses the description of the sufferings [NJB]: sufferings to the extent of a great contest.

10:33 this[a] on-the-one-hand being-made-a-public-spectacle[b] both by-reproaches[c] and by-tribulations,[d]

LEXICON—a. οὗτος (LN 92.29) (BAGD 1.b.δ. p. 597): 'this' [LN]. The phrase τοῦτο μέν . . . τοῦτο δέ 'this on the one hand . . . this on the other hand' is translated 'sometimes . . . sometimes' [BAGD], 'sometimes . . . and sometimes' [NJB, NLT, NRSV], 'sometimes . . . at other times' [CEV, NIV], 'at times . . . at other times' [NAB, TEV], 'sometimes . . . and on other occasions' [WBC], 'partly . . . and partly' [Mil; KJV, NASB], 'partly . . . partly' [Lns], 'not only . . . but' [TNT], 'not only . . . but also' [BAGD, HNTC], 'either . . . or else' [NIC]. This neuter phrase is translated as a masculine: 'some of you . . . while others' [REB]. The meaning of this phrase is 'partly (this) . . . partly (that)' [Alf, Blm, EGT, My], 'as well by . . . as by' [EGT, Mil]. It indicates similarity in the two phrases [Mil, NIGTC, WBC]. It refers to two groups of persons within the Christian community, 'some . . . others' [EBC, NIC, TH, Wst]; it refers to the same group at different times [Hu, ICC, Mil, My, NCBC, TNTC].

b. pres. pass. participle of θεατρίζω (LN **25.201**) (BAGD p. 353): 'to be made a public spectacle' [HNTC, Mil; NASB, TNT], 'to be made a theatrical show' [Lns], 'to be publicly exposed to ridicule' [WBC], 'to be exposed to public (ridicule)' [NLT], 'to be exposed to public shame' [NIC], 'to be exhibited as an object of shame' [**LN**], 'to be shamed publicly' [LN], 'to be put to shame' [BAGD], 'to be publicly exposed' [BAGD; NAB, NIV, NJB, NRSV, REB], 'to be made a gazingstock' [KJV]. The phrase ὀνειδισμοῖς τε καὶ θλίψεσιν θεατριζόμενοι 'being made a public spectacle both by reproaches and tribulations' is translated 'publicly insulted and mistreated' [TEV], 'you were abased and mistreated in public' [CEV]. It implies public situations [Blm, EBC, GNC, ICC, Mil, My, NCBC, TH, TNTC, WBC, Wst].

c. ὀνειδισμός (LN **33.389**) (BAGD p. 570): 'reproach' [Lns, Mil; KJV, NASB], 'taunt' [HNTC], 'insult' [BAGD, LN, NIC, WBC; NAB, NIV], 'humiliation' [NJB], 'abuse' [NRSV, REB], 'ridicule' [NLT]. This noun is also translated as a verb: 'to be taunted' [TNT], 'to be abused' [CEV]. It refers to insulting speech [EBC, EGT, GNC, HNTC, My, NIGTC, WBC]. The dative case expresses manner [Alf].

d. θλῖψις (LN 22.2) (BAGD 1. p. 362): 'tribulation' [BAGD; NASB], 'persecution' [LN, NIC, WBC; NIV, NRSV], 'violence' [NJB], 'suffering, trouble, and suffering' [LN], 'oppression' [BAGD], 'affliction' [BAGD, HNTC, Lns, Mil; KJV], 'trial' [NAB]. This noun is also translated as a verb: 'to be tormented' [REB], 'to be abused' [TNT], 'to be mistreated' [CEV], 'to be beaten' [NLT]. It refers to various forms of persecution [EBC, EGT, GNC, HNTC, My, NIGTC, WBC, Wst]. The dative case expresses manner [Alf].

QUESTION—Why is this verse mentioned?

It specifies the nature of the sufferings referred to in the preceding verse [Alf, EBC, EGT, GNC, My, TNTC, WBC].

QUESTION—What relationship is indicated by the participles θεατριζόμενοι 'being made a public spectacle' and γενηθέντες 'having become'?

The present tense of θεατριζόμενοι 'being made a public spectacle' indicates repeated actions [Lg(K), Lns, Wst]; the aorist tense of γενηθέντες 'having become' indicates a single fact [Lg(K), Wst], the beginning of a state [Lns].

1. They express means [Mil; NASB, NJB]: you endured sufferings by being made . . . and by becoming . . .
2. They are temporal [KJV]: you endured sufferings while you were being made . . . and after you became . . .
3. They express events accompanying the preceding verb ὑπεμείνατε 'you endured' [HNTC, NIC, WBC; NAB, NIV, NRSV, REB, TEV, TNT]: you endured sufferings . . . you were made . . . and you became.

this[a] on-the-other-hand having-become companions[b] of-the-(ones) thus[c] being-treated.[d]

LEXICON—a. οὗτος: 'this'. See this word above.

b. κοινωνός (LN 34.6) (BAGD 1.a.β. p. 439): 'companion' [BAGD; KJV], 'partner' [BAGD, LN, NIC; NRSV], 'associate' [LN; NJB], 'sharer' [BAGD, Mil; NASB]. This plural noun κοινωνοί 'companions' is translated 'in the fellowship of' [Lns], 'you associated yourselves' [HNTC; NAB], 'you shared' [CEV], 'you deliberately shared' [TNT], 'you stood side by side' [NIV], 'you showed solidarity with' [WBC], 'you were ready to join' [TEV], 'stood loyally by' [REB], 'you helped others' [NLT]. The reference is to assisting those who were in distress [Blm].

c. οὕτως (LN 61.9): 'thus' [LN, Lns], 'so' [LN, NIC; KJV, NAB, NASB, NIV, NRSV, REB], 'this way' [Mil], 'in this way' [HNTC, LN, WBC; TEV, TNT], 'in the same way' [NJB], 'the same things' [NLT], not explicit [CEV]. It refers to the manner of suffering mentioned in the preceding phrase [My, NIGTC, Wst].

d. pres. mid. participle of ἀναστρέφω (LN 41.3) (BAGD 2.bδ. p. 61): 'to be treated' [BAGD, HNTC, Mil, NIC, WBC; NASB, NIV, NJB, NRSV, REB, TEV, TNT], 'to be dealt with' [NAB], 'to be used' [KJV], 'to fare'

[Lns], 'to conduct oneself, to behave' [LN], 'to live' [BAGD, LN], 'to suffer' [NLT], 'the sufferings' [CEV].

QUESTION—How is this phrase related to the preceding phrase?

It refers to persons who suffered because they were associated with the persons of the preceding phrase [EBC, EGT, HNTC, ICC, Mil, NCBC, NTC, TH, TNTC, WBC, Wst] and supported and helped them [GNC, HNTC, ICC, Mil, My, NCBC, NTC, TNTC, WBC].

QUESTION—How are the noun and the participial phrase related in the genitive construction κοινωνοί τῶν οὕτως ἀναστρεφομένων 'companions of the ones thus being treated'?

The noun κοινωνοί 'companions' expresses the role relationship to (association with [NAB, NIV, NJB, REB, TEV], sharing with [NASB, TNT]) the other group, τῶν οὕτως ἀναστρεφομένων 'of the ones thus being treated' [Mil; NRSV]: occupying the relationship of companions to those who were being thus treated.

10:34 For both/even[a] with-the prisoners[b] you-sympathized[c]

TEXT—Instead of δεσμίοις 'prisoners', some manuscripts have δεσμοῖς 'bonds' and other manuscripts have δεσμοῖς μου 'my bonds'. GNT reads δεσμίοις 'prisoners' with a B decision, indicating that the text is almost certain. Δεσμοῖς μου 'my bonds' is read by Blm and KJV.

LEXICON—a. καί (LN 89.93, 89.102): 'both' [Lns, Mil], 'even' [LN (89.93); NAB], 'also' [LN (89.93)], 'indeed' [NIC; REB], 'in fact' [WBC], 'not only' [NJB], not explicit [HNTC; all versions except NAB, NJB, REB]. The phrase καὶ . . . καί is translated 'both . . . and' [LN (89.102)]. The meaning of καί in this clause is 'both', introducing the example of the action mentioned in the preceding verse [Alf]; it means 'also' [NIGTC]; it emphasizes the following statement and is not part of a construction 'both . . . and' with the following καί 'and' [Wst].

b. δέσμιος (LN 37.117) (BAGD p. 176): 'prisoner' [BAGD, LN, Lns, Mil; NASB, TEV]; different text [KJV]. The phrase τοῖς δεσμίοις 'the prisoners' is translated 'those in prison' [WBC; NIV, TNT], 'those who were in prison' [HNTC; NAB, NJB, NRSV, REB], 'those who were imprisoned' [NIC], 'those who were thrown into jail' [NLT], 'people in jail' [CEV].

c. aorist act. indic. of συμπαθέω (LN **24.80**, 25.57) (BAGD p. 779): 'to sympathize' [BAGD, Lns; NIV], 'to feel sympathy' [LN (25.57)], 'to have sympathy' [BAGD, LN (25.57)], 'to show sympathy with' [BAGD, Mil], 'to show sympathy' [NASB], 'to manifest (one's) sympathy' [NIC], 'to be sympathetic' [LN (25.57)], 'to have compassion' [KJV, NRSV], 'to be kind to' [CEV], 'to share the sufferings' [**LN**, WBC; REB, TEV], 'to share in the sufferings' [LN (24.80); NJB], 'to suffer with' [HNTC, LN (24.80); TNT], 'to suffer along with' [NLT], 'to join in the sufferings' [NAB]. It refers to having sympathetic feelings [NIGTC, TNTC].

QUESTION—Why is this verse mentioned?

It illustrates and explains the two points made in the preceding verse [Alf, EGT, Hu, Lns, My, TH, TNTC, Wst], as the γάρ 'for' indicates [Hu, Lns, TH]. The introductory καὶ γάρ means 'for indeed' and introduces the proof of the two preceding comments [EGT]. This and the preceding verse form a chiastic structure [My, NIGTC, TNTC, WBC, Wst].

and the seizure[a] of-the-(things) belonging[b] (to) you you-accepted[c] with[d] joy,[e]

LEXICON—a. ἁρπαγή (LN **57.235**) (BAGD 1. p. 108): 'seizure' [HNTC, Mil, WBC; NASB, REB], 'snatching' [Lns], 'plundering' [LN, Mil, NIC; NRSV], 'plunder, robbery' [BAGD], 'confiscation' [NAB, NIV], 'spoiling' [KJV]. This word is also translated as a verb: 'to be stripped' [NJB], 'to be seized' [TEV], 'to be taken away' [CEV, NLT], 'to be confiscated' [TNT]. It refers to violent and unjust seizure [EGT], forcible confiscation [NIGTC] by governmental authorities [NTC], seizure by mob violence [EBC, HNTC].

b. pres. act. participle of ὑπάρχω (LN 57.2, 57.16) (BAGD 1. p. 838): 'to belong to' [LN (57.2)]. The participial phrase τὰ ὑπάρχοντα 'the things belonging' is translated 'belongings' [NJB, TEV], 'the property' [BAGD, LN (57.16), Lns, NIC, WBC; NASB, NIV], 'the possessions' [BAGD, HNTC, Mil; CEV, NRSV, REB, TNT], 'goods' [KJV, NAB], 'all (one) owned' [NLT].

c. aorist mid. (deponent = act.) of προσδέχομαι (LN 31.53) (BAGD 1.b. p. 712): 'to accept' [HNTC, LN, Lns, Mil, WBC; NASB, NIV, NJB, NLT, NRSV, REB], 'to assent to' [NAB], 'to allow' [TNT], 'to let' [CEV], 'to receive' [LN], 'to receive willingly' [BAGD], 'to put up with' [BAGD, NIC], 'to take' [KJV], 'to endure one's loss' [TEV]. It implies accepting [Alf, TH], enduring [Blm].

d. μετά with genitive object (LN 89.79) (BAGD A.III.1. p. 509): 'with' [BAGD, LN, Lns; NJB, NLT]. The phrase μετὰ χαρᾶς 'with joy' is translated 'joyfully' [HNTC, Mil; KJV, NAB, NASB, NIV], 'cheerfully' [NIC, WBC; NRSV, REB, TNT], 'gladly' [CEV, TEV].

e. χαρά (LN 25.123) (BAGD 1. p. 875): 'joy' [BAGD, LN, Lns; NJB].

knowing yourselves to-have a-better[a] and remaining[b] possession.[c]

TEXT—Instead of the accusative pronoun ἑαυτούς 'yourselves', some manuscripts read the dative ἑαυτοῖς 'for yourselves'; other manuscripts read ἐν ἑαυτοῖς 'in yourselves'; two manuscripts have none of the above. GNT reads ἑαυτούς 'yourselves' with an A decision, indicating that the text is certain. 'Εαυτοῖς 'for yourselves' is read by Alf, Blm, Lg, My, and NASB; ἐν ἑαυτοῖς 'in yourselves' is read by KJV.

TEXT—Some manuscripts add ἐν οὐρανοῖς 'in heaven' following ὕπαρξιν 'possession'. GNT does not deal with this variant. Only KJV adds 'in heaven'.

LEXICON—a. κρείττων (LN 65.21, 87.28) (BAGD 1. p. 449): 'better' [BAGD, HNTC, LN (65.21, 87.28), Lns, Mil, NIC, WBC; all versions except TEV], 'much better' [TEV], 'greater, superior to' [LN (87.28)], 'higher in rank, preferable' [BAGD]. It indicates superior quality [WBC].

b. pres. act. participle of μένω (LN 13.89) (BAGD 1.c.β. p. 504): 'to remain' [BAGD, LN], 'to continue to exist, to still be in existence' [LN], 'to last' [BAGD; NIV, NJB], 'to endure' [Mil; KJV], 'to abide' [Lns; NASB], 'to last forever' [CEV], 'to wait in eternity' [NLT]. This participle is translated 'permanent' [NIC, WBC], 'more permanent' [NAB], 'more lasting' [HNTC; NRSV, REB], 'which would last' [TNT], 'which would last forever' [TEV]. By its word order it is emphatic [NIGTC] and both it and the preceding κρείττονα 'better' are given separate identity [Wst; NASB, TEV, TNT]. It indicates stability [WBC].

c. ὕπαρξις (LN 57.16) (BAGD 2. p. 837): 'possession' [NIC; NASB, REB], 'possessions' [BAGD, LN, WBC; NAB, NIV], 'property' [BAGD, Lns], 'that which one has' [BAGD], 'substance' [Mil; KJV]. The phrase ἔχειν ἑαυτοὺς ὕπαρξιν 'yourselves to have a possession' is translated 'you possessed something' [HNTC; TNT], 'you still possessed something' [TEV], 'you yourselves possessed something' [NRSV], 'you owned something' [NJB], 'you had something' [CEV], 'you had things' [NLT]. It indicates wealth or property [Blm]. This noun is singular [Lns]; it indicates their heavenly possession [Lns, WBC], their spiritual blessings [My], their advantages in Christ [TNTC].

QUESTION—What relationship is indicated by the present participle γινώσκοντες 'knowing'?

It indicates reason [GNC, Mil, My, NIC, NIGTC, TH, WBC; CEV, NIV, TEV]: because you know. The present tense refers to repeated realizations when the seizures occurred [Lns], to their assurance at the time of these circumstances [Mil, WBC]. This word implies coming to know through experience [Wst].

QUESTION—What relationship is indicated by ἔχειν 'to have'?

It is a form of indirect statement [Alf, EGT, GNC, HNTC, Hu, ICC, Lg, Lns, Mil, My, NIGTC, TH; all versions]: (knowing) that you have . . .

QUESTION—What is ἑαυτούς/ἑαυτοῖς 'yourselves/for yourselves' connected with?

1. For those who read ἑαυτούς 'yourselves':

1.1 It is the subject of the infinitive ἔχειν 'to have' in an indirect statement [EGT, GNC, HNTC, Hu, Hwt, ICC, Lns, Mil, NIC, NIGTC, TH, WBC; all versions except KJV, NASB]: knowing that you have a better possession.

1.1.1 This pronoun is not emphatic [Hu, ICC, NIGTC, TH, WBC; NAB, NJB, REB, TEV, TNT]; it is reflexive [GNC, NIGTC, WBC], meaning that it reflects the implied 'you' of the participle γινώσκοντες '(you) knowing': knowing yourselves to have, or, knowing that you have. (In the present construction, ἑαυτούς 'yourselves' is required, as the English translation at the beginning of this phrase shows, and it is therefore not emphatic; the unemphatic ὑμᾶς 'you' would be grammatically incorrect.)

1.1.2 This pronoun is emphatic [EGT, HNTC, Lns, Mil, NIC; NIV, NRSV]: knowing that *you yourselves* have . . .

1.2 It is the predicate of the infinitive ἔχειν 'to have' [My(D), Wst]: knowing that you have yourselves for a better possession.

2. For those who read ἑαυτοῖς 'for yourselves' it is a dative of reference [Blm, Lg(K), My; NASB]: knowing that you have for yourselves a better possession.
3. For those who read ἐν ἑαυτοῖς 'in yourselves' it tells where the possessions are [KJV]: you have in yourselves.

DISCOURSE UNIT: 10:35–39 [Lns]. The topic is an appeal not to shrink back.

10:35 Therefore (do) not throw-away[a] your confidence,[b]

LEXICON—a. aorist act. subj. of ἀποβάλλω (LN **13.45**) (BAGD 2. p. 89): 'to throw away' [HNTC, Lns, NIC, WBC; NASB, NIV, NLT, REB, TNT], 'to cast away' [Mil; KJV], 'to surrender' [NAB], 'to lose' [BAGD; NJB, TEV], 'to abandon' [NRSV], 'to let cease' [**LN**], 'to cause to cease' [**LN**], 'to do away with' [LN]. The phrase μὴ ἀποβάλητε 'do not throw away' is translated 'keep on' [CEV]. It has the active sense of casting away [Alf, Hwt, My, TH, TNTC, Wst], letting fall away [My], abandoning [Blm], recklessly rejecting [EBC]. This aorist subjunctive with μή 'not' states a prohibition [Mil, WBC], urging not to begin to throw away [Mil], implying that they had not thrown away [NTC, WBC]; it implies a single act [NIGTC].

b. παρρησία (LN **25.158**) (BAGD 3.b. p. 630): 'confidence' [BAGD, HNTC, NIC; KJV, NAB, NASB, NIV, NRSV, REB, TNT], 'joyful confidence' [Mil], 'confident trust' [NLT], 'assurance' [Lns], 'courage' [LN; TEV], 'fearlessness' [NJB], 'joyousness' [BAGD], 'joyful boldness' [Mil], 'boldness' [LN, WBC]. This noun is also translated as a verb: 'to be brave' [CEV]. It refers to the readers' confident hope [Blm] in God [Hu], toward Christ [My], maintaining their courageous confession [NIC].

QUESTION—What relationship is indicated by οὖν 'therefore'?

It indicates an exhortation based on the reminders of what they had successfully endured [EGT, GNC, Lns, Mil, My, NIGTC, TH, WBC].

QUESTION—What is this type of negative clause?

It is a litotes, a negative implying an opposite strong positive statement [Lns]: by all means hold fast!

which has great recompense;[a]

LEXICON—a. μισθαποδοσία (LN 38.17) (BAGD p. 523): 'recompense' [LN], 'recompense of reward' [KJV], 'reward' [BAGD, HNTC, LN, Mil, NIC, WBC; all versions except KJV, NIV], 'pay-gift' [Lns]. This entire clause is translated 'it will be richly rewarded' [NIV]. This word implies full payment of wages [Blm, Lns, Mil]. It refers to the heavenly inheritance [Hu, My], final salvation [Mil].

QUESTION—Why is this clause mentioned?

It states the reason for not casting away their confidence [EBC, EGT, Lg(K), Lns, NIGTC, NTC, WBC, Wst; NJB, REB, TEV]: because it has. The recompense is not for having the confidence; rather, retaining the confidence will enable them to receive what has already been promised [HNTC]. The word ἥτις 'which' is qualitative [Alf, Lg(K), Lns, Mil, NIGTC], introducing a descriptive comment [Mil]: which is of such a kind as. It introduces a well-known truth [My].

QUESTION—What is indicated by the present indicative ἔχει '(it) has'?

It implies that the reward is presently involved [Alf, EGT], holds within itself [Mil, NIGTC], is imminent [TH], is certain [ICC, WBC], is beginning to be experienced now, even though its fulfillment is in the future [TNTC].

DISCOURSE UNIT: 10:36–39 [HNTC]. The topic is the present need for faith.

10:36 for you-have need[a] of-endurance[b] in-order-that, having-done the will of-God, you-may-receive[c] the promise.[d]

LEXICON—a. χρεία (LN 57.40, 71.23) (BAGD 1. p. 885): 'need' [BAGD, LN, Lns, Mil; KJV, NASB]. This noun is also translated as a verb: 'to need' [NJB, NLT], 'to learn' [CEV]. The phrase ἔχετε χρείαν 'you have need' is translated 'you need' [HNTC, NIC, WBC; NAB, NIV, NRSV, REB, TEV, TNT]. It indicates an absolute necessity [EBC]. This point is emphasized [TNTC]. It may imply a lack [NIGTC, TH, TNTC].

b. ὑπομονή (LN 25.174) (BAGD 1. p. 846): 'endurance' [BAGD, LN, WBC; NASB, NRSV, REB], 'patience' [BAGD, NIC; KJV, NAB], 'fortitude' [BAGD], 'steadfastness' [BAGD, HNTC], 'perseverance' [BAGD, Lns, Mil; NJB]. This noun is also translated as a verb: 'to persevere' [NIV], 'to be patient' [CEV, TEV], 'to be steadfast' [TNT], 'to be able to endure' [LN], 'to continue to do' [NLT]. It is emphatic by forefronting [Alf, HNTC, My]. It refers to active steadfastness [EBC, NCBC], endurance [GNC, Lg, NCBC, TNTC] to the end [Lg]. It is a necessary condition for doing God's will [TH].

c. aorist mid. subj. of κομίζω (LN 57.126) (BAGD 2.a. p. 442): 'to receive' [BAGD, LN, Mil, NIC, WBC; all versions except CEV, NJB, REB], 'to obtain' [HNTC, LN], 'to gain' [NJB], 'to get for oneself' [BAGD], 'to win' [REB], 'to carry off' [BAGD, Lns], 'to be given' [CEV]. It means to get what was promised [ICC], to carry off something as one's own, as the middle voice implies [Lns, Mil, Wst], to appropriate the promise personally [NTC, Wst].

d. ἐπαγγελία (LN 33.288) (BAGD 2.b. p. 280): 'promise' [HNTC, LN, Lns, Mil, WBC; KJV], 'what was promised' [BAGD; NASB, NRSV], 'what one has promised' [NIC; CEV, NAB, NIV, NJB, NLT, REB, TNT], 'what one promises' [TEV]. It refers to what was promised [Alf, EGT, Hu, Lg, Lns, Mil, My, NTC, TH, TNTC, Wst], God's gift of salvation [EBC,

GNC, NTC], eternal life [Lns, My, WBC, Wst]. The one who promised is God [HNTC, Mil, NIC, TH; NAB, NIV, NJB, REB, TEV, TNT].

QUESTION—What relationship is indicated by γάρ 'for'?

1. It introduces the grounds for the preceding exhortation [Alf, Mil, My], the counterpart to the first part of the preceding verse [NIGTC]. This verse looks both to what precedes and to what follows [NIGTC].
2. It introduces an inference from what precedes [WBC].

QUESTION—To what does ὑπομονῆς 'endurance' refer?

1. It is the means for doing the will of God [Hu, Mil]: endurance is required in order to do God's will.
2. It is defined by τὸ θέλημα τοῦ θεοῦ 'the will of God' [GNC, Hwt, My]: endurance is God's will for you.
3. It states the necessary condition for receiving what was promised [ICC]: if you endure you will receive the promise.

QUESTION—What relationship is indicated by ἵνα 'in order that/that'?

1. It indicates the purpose of having endurance [GNC, HNTC, Lg(K), Mil, NIC, TH, TNTC; CEV, NASB, NRSV, REB, TEV]: you need patience in order that you may receive.
2. It indicates the content of ὑπομονῆς 'patience' [NAB]: you need patience to receive.
3. It indicates an anticipated result [ICC, Lns, NIGTC, WBC; NIV, NLT]: you need patience, with the anticipated result of receiving.
4. It indicates a conditional clause [NJB, TNT]: you need endurance if you are to receive. (This rendering is evidently editorial, since condition is not a possible meaning of ἵνα.)

QUESTION—What relationship is indicated by the participle ποιήσαντες 'having done'?

1. It is temporal [Lg(K), Mil, My, NIC, NIGTC, WBC, Wst; KJV, NASB, NIV, NRSV]: after you have done.
2. It indicates means [Lns]: by means of having done.
3. It is parallel to the finite verb κομίσησθε 'you may receive' [Alf, HNTC; NAB, NJB, REB, TEV, TNT]: endurance to do and to receive.

QUESTION—What is indicated by the aorist tense of the participle ποιήσαντες 'having done'?

1. It refers to acts done prior to the verb κομίσησθε 'you may receive' [NIGTC, Wst] in the future [Lg(K), My] under the influence of ὑπομονή 'endurance' [Lg(K)].
2. The action is at the same time as that of the verb κομίσησθε 'you may receive' [Alf].

QUESTION—To what does the phrase τὸ θέλημα τοῦ θεοῦ 'the will of God' refer?

It refers to following Christ [NTC], to being faithful to the end [EGT, NIGTC]. It must precede receiving what was promised [Hwt, TH].

10:37 For yet[a] a-little[b] how-long[c] how-long,[c]

LEXICON—a. ἔτι (LN 67.128) (BAGD 1.c. p. 316): 'yet' [BAGD, LN, Lns, Mil, NIC; KJV, NASB, NRSV], 'still' [BAGD, LN]. The phrase ἔτι μικρὸν 'yet a little' is translated 'a little while longer' [BAGD]. It is temporal [NIGTC].

b. μικρός (LN 67.106, **67.107**) (BAGD 3.e. p. 521): 'little', 'a little' [Lns], 'a little while' [LN (67.106); KJV], 'in a very short while' [LN (67.107)]. The phrase μικρὸν ὅσον ὅσον 'a little how long how long' is translated 'very soon, in a very short while' [LN (67.107)], 'in a very little while' [Mil; NASB, NRSV], 'in just a little while' [NLT], 'a very little while' [NIC]; the phrase ἔτι μικρὸν ὅσον ὅσον 'yet a little how long how long' is translated 'a little while longer' [WBC], 'just a little while longer' [TEV], 'just a very little while longer' [LN (**67.107**)], 'in just a very little while' [NIV], 'in a very little while' [BAGD], 'only a little while now, a very little while' [NJB], 'in a very little time now' [HNTC; TNT], 'very soon' [REB], 'soon' [BAGD], 'just a brief moment' [NAB], 'it won't be very long' [CEV]. The phrase μικρὸν ὅσον ὅσον 'a little how long how long' indicates a very short time [Blm, EBC, Hwt, Lg(K), Lns, My] and emphasizes the shortness of the time [NIGTC]. Μικρὸν 'little' means 'a little while'; it strengthens the sense of the following comment [WBC], as does the double ὅσον [My]; the double ὅσον amounts to a double diminutive [Lg(K)], the equivalent of the superlative [Lg].

c. ὅσος (LN 67.139) (BAGD 1. p. 586): 'as long as' [LN], 'how long' [BAGD], not explicit [KJV]. The phrase ὅσον ὅσον 'how long how long' is translated 'how very, very' [Lns]; the phrase ἔτι μικρὸν ὅσον ὅσον 'yet a little how long how long' is translated 'in a very little while' [BAGD]. It is temporal; it is repeated for emphasis, 'a very little while' [NIGTC].

QUESTION—What relationship is indicated by γάρ 'for'?

It indicates the scriptural grounds for the preceding comment [Alf, EBC, My, NIGTC, WBC], the reason for the need of endurance [WBC]. They must endure since the time is short [Alf], that the Messiah will come in due course [EBC]. It amplifies the comments of the preceding verse [Mil].

the-(one) coming will-have-come[a] and not will-delay;[b]

LEXICON—a. fut. act. indic. of ἥκω (LN 15.84, 85.10) (BAGD 1.c. p. 344): 'to have come' [BAGD, HNTC; TNT], 'to come' [LN (15.84), Lns, NIC, WBC; all versions except NJB, TNT], 'to arrive' [LN (15.84)], 'to be here' [LN (85.10), Mil], 'to be present' [BAGD]. This entire phrase is translated 'for come he certainly will before too long' [NJB].

b. fut. act. indic. of χρονίζω (LN 67.122) (BAGD 1. p. 887): 'to delay' [Lns, Mil, WBC; NAB, NASB, NIV, NLT, NRSV, REB, TEV], 'to make a delay' [NIC], 'to be late' [LN], 'to tarry' [KJV], 'to be long' [HNTC; TNT], 'to linger, to take time, to fail to come for a long time, to stay away for a long time' [BAGD]. This entire clause is translated 'God is coming soon' [CEV]. The future tense adds emphasis [NIGTC].

QUESTION—What is meant by ὁ ἐρχόμενος 'the one coming'?

It refers to the Messiah [Blm, EBC, EGT, GNC, Hu, My, NCBC, NIC, NIGTC, NTC, WBC], Christ [Hwt, ICC, Lns, NIGTC]: the Coming One. It refers to Christ's second coming [Lns, My, WBC], the Messiah's coming to destroy Jerusalem and bring an end to the Jewish state [Blm].

10:38 but my righteous-one[a] shall-live[b] by[c] faith,[d]

TEXT—Some manuscripts omit μου 'my'. GNT does not deal with this variant. 'My' is omitted by Blm, EGT, Lns.

LEXICON—a. δίκαιος (LN 88.12) (BAGD 1.b. p. 195): 'righteous' [BAGD, HNTC, LN, Lns, Mil, NIC, WBC; NASB, NIV, NLT, NRSV, REB, TEV, TNT], 'just' [BAGD, LN; KJV, NAB], 'upright' [BAGD; NJB]. The phrase ὁ δίκαιος 'the righteous one' is translated as a plural: 'righteous people' [TEV], 'the people God accepts' [CEV]. It means the person declared righteous (accepted as righteous [EBC]) by God [EBC, Hu, Lns]. It means the devout person [My], the faithful Christian [WBC], the true believer [Wst], one of God's people [Alf]. The phrase ὁ δίκαιος 'the righteous one' is generic, referring to persons in general [NIGTC, TH; TEV].

b. fut. mid. indic. of ζάω (LN 23.88) (BAGD 2.bβ. p. 336): 'to live' [BAGD, HNTC, LN, Lns, Mil, NIC, WBC; all versions except REB], 'to find life' [REB]. The phrase ἐκ πίστεως ζήσεται 'shall live by means of faith' is translated 'will believe and live' [TEV]. The future tense refers to spiritual life now and continuing into the future [Lns].

c. ἐκ with genitive object (LN 89.77): 'by' [Mil, NIC; all versions except CEV, NJB, TEV], 'by means of, from' [LN], 'through' [HNTC; NJB], 'as a result of' [Lns], 'because of' [CEV].

d. πίστις (LN 31.102) (BAGD 2.a., 2.d.α. p. 663): 'faith' [BAGD, HNTC, LN, Lns, Mil, NIC; all versions except TEV], 'faithfulness' [WBC].

QUESTION—What is meant by this clause?

1. It indicates how the righteous person is to live [Alf, Blm, EBC, GNC, HNTC, Hu, Hwt, ICC, Lns, Mil, My, NCBC, NIC, NIGTC, WBC, Wst; all versions except TEV]: he shall live by means of faith.
2. It indicates that faith results in life [Lns]: the righteous person shall have life as a result of faith.

QUESTION—What relationship is indicated by δέ 'but'?

It is transitional, introducing another aspect of the proposition [Mil, NIGTC, WBC].

QUESTION—To whom does μου 'my' refer?

It is possessive [Mil, My], referring to God [Alf, EBC, My, TH, WBC]: the righteous person who belongs to God.

and if he-should-draw-back,[a] my soul not is-pleased[b] in[c] him.

LEXICON—a. aorist mid. subj. of ὑποστέλλω (LN 68.53) (BAGD 2.a. p. 847): 'to draw back' [BAGD, HNTC, NIC, WBC; KJV, NAB, NJB, TNT], 'to shrink back' [Lns, Mil; NASB, NIV, NRSV, REB], 'to turn back' [CEV,

TEV], 'to turn away' [NLT], 'to withdraw' [LN], 'to cease' [LN], 'to stop' [LN], 'to give up doing' [LN]. It refers to apostasy [WBC].

b. pres. act. indic. of εὐδοκέω (LN 25.87) (BAGD 2.a. p. 319): 'to be pleased', 'to be well pleased' [BAGD], 'to be pleased with' [LN; NIV, TEV], 'to have pleasure in' [Mil, NIC; CEV, KJV, NASB, NLT], 'to take pleasure in' [HNTC, LN, Lns; NAB, NJB, NRSV, REB, TNT]. The phrase οὐκ εὐδοκεῖ ἡ ψυχή μου ἐν αὐτῷ 'my soul is not pleased in him' is translated 'I myself will reject him' [WBC].

c. ἐν with dative object (LN 83.13, 89.5. 90.6): 'in' [HNTC, LN (83.13, 89.5), Lns, Mil, NIC; all versions except NIV, TEV], 'with' [NIV, TEV], 'with regard to, about' [LN (89.5)], 'by' [LN (90.6)].

QUESTION—What relationship is indicated by καί 'and'?

It introduces a contrast [WBC], connecting the preceding affirmative clause to a coordinate negative proposition which is in the form of a litotes, a negative thought implying a strong opposite [Mil]: but my soul is very displeased with him.

QUESTION—Who is the implied subject of the verb ὑποστείληται 'draw back'?

1. The subject is 'he', that is, ὁ δίκαιος 'the righteous one' [Alf, Blm, EGT, GNC, HNTC, Hu, Hwt, ICC, Lg(K), Lns, Mil, My, NIC, NTC, Wst; NAB, NASB, NIV, NJB, TEV, TNT]: if my righteous one should draw back. If he draws back he would cease to be ὁ δίκαιος 'the righteous one' [My].
2. The subject is an implied τις 'anyone' (without manuscript authority) [CEV, KJV, NLT, NRSV, REB]: if anyone should draw back.

QUESTION—To whom does ἡ ψυχή μου 'my soul' refer?

It refers to God [Hwt, ICC, Mil, My, NTC, TH], the equivalent of 'I myself' [NIGTC, WBC]: I myself will not be pleased.

10:39 But we are not of-turning-back[a] into[b] destruction[c] but of-faith[d] into[e] preservation[f] of-soul.[g]

LEXICON—a. ὑποστολή (LN **68.53**) (BAGD p. 847): 'turning back' [Lns], 'shrinking' [BAGD], 'timidity' [BAGD]. This noun is also translated as a phrase: 'them who draw back' [KJV], 'those who draw back' [HNTC, NIC, WBC; NAB, TNT], 'those who shrink back' [Mil; NASB, NIV, NRSV, REB], 'people who turn back' [CEV, TEV], 'the sort of people who draw back' [NJB], 'those who turn their backs on God' [NLT], 'those who are timid' [BAGD]. The phrase ἡμεῖς οὐκ ἐσμὲν ὑποστολῆς 'we are not of turning back' is translated 'we will not cease believing' [LN]. It implies turning away from God and persistent deliberate sin [WBC].

b. εἰς with accusative object (LN 84.22, 89.48) (BAGD 4.e. p. 229): 'into' [BAGD, LN (84.22)], 'to' [BAGD, Lns, Mil; NASB], 'unto' [KJV], 'leading to' [WBC], 'so that' [BAGD], 'and so' [NRSV], 'with the result that, as a result, so that as a result, to cause' [LN (89.48)], 'to' [HNTC,

NIC; CEV, NAB, NIV, NJB, NLT, NRSV, REB, TEV, TNT]. This preposition expresses result here [Alf, Blm, EGT, Mil, NIGTC, TH, WBC].

c. ἀπώλεια (LN 20.31) (BAGD 2. p. 103): 'destruction' [BAGD, LN, WBC; NASB], 'ruin' [BAGD], 'perdition' [Lns, Mil; KJV]. This noun is also translated as a verb: 'to perish' [NIC; NAB], 'to be destroyed' [CEV, NIV]. 'to be lost' [HNTC; NJB, NRSV, REB, TEV, TNT], 'to seal one's fate' [NLT]. It refers to eternal lostness [My], the opposite of salvation [Wst].

d. πίστις (LN 31.85, 31.102) (BAGD 2.d.α. p. 663): 'faith' [BAGD, LN (31.85, 31.102), Lns]. This noun is also translated as a phrase: 'those who have faith' [HNTC; NAB, NASB, NRSV], 'those who are faithful' [WBC], 'the sort who keep faith' [NJB], 'we have faith' [NLT, TEV, TNT], 'we have the faith' [REB], 'those who believe' [Mil, NIC; NIV], 'them that believe' [KJV], 'we will keep on having faith' [CEV]. It implies firmness [NIGTC], steadfastness [WBC].

e. εἰς with accusative object (LN 84.22, 89.48) (BAGD 4.c. p. 229): 'into' [BAGD, LN (84.22)], 'to' [BAGD, Mil; KJV, NASB, REB], 'for' [Lns], 'so that' [BAGD], 'with the result that, as a result, so that as a result, to cause' [LN (89.48)], 'culminating in' [WBC], 'thus' [NIC], 'and so' [NRSV]. This preposition expresses result here [Alf, Blm, EGT, Mil, NIGTC, TH, TNTC, WBC].

f. περιποίησις (LN 57.62) (BAGD 1. p. 650): 'preserving' [BAGD, Mil; NASB], 'preservation' [Lns], 'saving' [BAGD; KJV], 'keeping safe' [BAGD], 'acquisition' [WBC], 'possession' [LN]. This noun is also translated as a verb: 'to preserve' [REB]. The phrase εἰς περειποίησιν ψυχῆς 'into preservation of soul' is translated 'and live' [NAB], 'and obtain life' [HNTC], 'and thus gain our lives' [NIC], 'and are saved' [NIV, TEV], 'until we are saved' [CEV], 'that assures our salvation' [NLT], 'and so are saved' [NRSV], 'until our souls are saved' [NJB], 'and God will save us' [TNT]. It refers to salvation [Blm, Mil]; it indicates possession or gaining [Hu], preserving [TNTC], keeping safe [NIGTC].

g. ψυχή (LN 26.4) (BAGD 1.c. p. 893): 'soul' [BAGD, Lns, Mil; KJV, NASB, NJB], 'being, inner self' [LN], 'life' [WBC; REB]. The soul is the subject of salvation [Alf, Mil]; it refers to life [Hu, NCBC], eternal life [HNTC, Lg, WBC].

QUESTION—Why is this verse mentioned?

It states a positive conclusion to (a summary of [WBC]) the preceding section of the epistle [NIGTC, TH, WBC]. The introductory δέ 'but' indicates a strong contrast with what precedes [GNC, Mil, NIGTC]. This verse makes a personal application of the preceding verse [TH, WBC]; it turns from warning to reassuring [Alf, Mil, NCBC, NTC], encouraging [GNC], but retaining the sense of urgency of the warnings [Mil], in effect an exhortation more urgent than a direct exhortation would be [My]; it expresses strong confidence [EBC, Hu, ICC, My, NIC]; it is a brief commentary on the preceding OT quotation [GNC]. It introduces the following discussion of faith [Blm]. It proves that the preceding warnings are merely hypothetical, not implying the real possibility of falling away [Hwt]. It does not draw a final conclusion concerning the future [NIGTC]. This and the preceding verse form a chiasmus [WBC].

QUESTION—What is indicated by ἡμεῖς 'we'?

It is emphatic [Alf, GNC, Mil, NIGTC, NTC, TH, WBC], both this word itself and by forefronting [Mil, NTC, WBC]: *we* are not . . . It includes the author with his readers [EBC, GNC, Hu, My, NIC, NIGTC, NTC, TNTC, WBC, Wst].

QUESTION—What relationship is indicated by the genitive nouns ὑποστολῆς 'of turning back' and πίστεως 'of faith'?

1. These genitive nouns refer to being among a group [HNTC, NIC, NIGTC, NTC, WBC; NAB, NRSV, REB, TNT], indicating the kind of people referred to [Alf, EGT, Lns, Mil, My, NIC, TH, Wst; NJB, TEV]: not among those who are the sort of people who turn back . . . who preserve their soul. They are genitives expressing a category [Alf].
2. These genitive nouns indicate belonging to ἡμεῖς 'us' [Lg(K)]: turning back does not belong to us; soul preservation belongs to us.

QUESTION—What is implied by the phrase ὑποστολῆς εἰς ἀπώλειαν 'of turning back into destruction'?

It refers to deserting the faith and being destroyed, showing that such persons are not heirs of salvation [Hu].

QUESTION—What relationship is indicated by ἀλλά 'but'?

It is a strong adversative, contrasting the preceding and following phrases [Mil, NIGTC, TH, WBC]: not (this), on the contrary (this).

QUESTION—How are the two nouns related in the genitive construction περιποίησιν ψυχῆς 'preservation of soul'?

The genitive noun ψυχῆς 'soul' tells what is preserved.

1. The soul is preserved [Alf, Lns, Mil, My, NCBC, TNTC; all versions except NAB, REB].
2. Life is preserved [Hu, NIC; NAB, REB].

DISCOURSE UNIT: 11:1–12:29 [NAB]. The topic is examples, discipline, disobedience.

DISCOURSE UNIT: 11:1–12:13 [NIGTC, WBC]. The topic is faith [NIGTC], loyalty to God through persevering faith [WBC].

DISCOURSE UNIT: 11:1–12:3 [Mil]. The topic is encouragement to persevere in faith through examples from the OT and from Jesus.

DISCOURSE UNIT: 11:1–40 [EBC, GNC, GNT, Hwt, Lg, Lns, NCBC, NIC, NIGTC, NTC, TNTC, WBC, Wst; CEV, NAB, NASB, NIV, NJB, NLT, REB, TEV]. The topic is faith [EBC, TNTC; TEV], by faith [NIV], the nature and importance of faith [GNC], the characteristics and triumphs of faith [Hwt], the great faith of God's people [CEV], the faith of people of old [NIC; NAB, REB], heroes of faith [NCBC, NTC], faith on OT times [NIGTC], great examples of faith [NLT], the triumphs of persevering faith [WBC; NASB], the past triumphs of faith [Wst], inspiring examples of believing ancestors [Lg, Lns; NJB].

DISCOURSE UNIT: 11:1–7 [Lg, WBC]. The topic is examples of faith from ancient times to Abraham [Lg], triumphs of faith before the Flood [WBC].

DISCOURSE UNIT: 11:1–3 [EBC, GNC, HNTC, NIC, NTC, TNTC]. The topic is the meaning of faith [EBC], the nature of faith [NIC, TNTC], the definition of faith [NTC], the definition and presupposition of faith [HNTC].

11:1 Now faith is (the) assurance/substance[a] of-being-hoped-for[b] (things),

LEXICON—a. ὑπόστασις (LN 31.84, 58.1) (BAGD 3. p. 847): 'assurance' [LN (31.84); NASB, NRSV], 'confident assurance' [NAB], 'confident assurance of the reality' [Mil], 'confident assurance that something is going to happen' [NLT], 'firm confidence' [Lns], 'trust' [LN (31.84)], 'certainty' [HNTC], 'substance' [LN; KJV], 'firm foundation' [NIC], 'essence, real being' [LN (58.1)], 'realization' [BAGD]. This noun is also translated as a verb phrase: 'to be sure' [NIV, TEV]. The phrase ἔστιν ὑπόστασις 'is the assurance/substance' is translated 'gives substance' [REB], 'celebrates the objective reality' [WBC], 'makes us sure' [CEV]. The phrase ἔστιν πίστις ἐλπιζομένων ὑπόστασις 'faith is the assurance/substance of things being hoped for' is translated 'if we have faith we are sure that our hopes are real' [TNT], 'in faith things hoped for become realized/reality' [BAGD], 'only faith can guarantee the blessings that we hope for' [NJB].

b. pres. pass. participle of ἐλπίζω (LN 25.59) (BAGD 1. p. 252): 'to be hoped for' [BAGD, HNTC, LN, Lns, Mil; KJV, NASB, NRSV], 'to be hoped' [LN]. The passive voice is also translated as an active voice: 'to hope for' [NIC, WBC; CEV, NAB, NIV, NJB, NLT, TEV]; as a noun phrase: 'to our hopes' [REB]. This participle refers to the fulfillment of God's promises [NCBC], the heavenly blessings as the objects of hope [WBC], all of mental and spiritual activity [Wst]. Lacking the definite article, this participle has a broad reference [NTC].

QUESTION—Why is this verse mentioned?

Since πίστις 'faith' is without a definite article here, this verse expresses a description of faith in general [Alf, Lg, My, TNTC, Wst], of religious faith [HNTC], of firm confidence in God's promises [Blm, EBC] that enables the believer to continue steadfastly in his faith [EBC]. It is a description of what true faith does [Hwt, NIGTC], a statement of the nature of faith [Lg(K), Lns], a definition of one aspect of faith [My], a general statement about faith [TNTC]. It states some significant features of faith [EBC]. The introductory δέ is transitional [Lns, Mil, NIGTC, TH] and carries on the discussion of faith in 10:39 [WBC].

QUESTION—What relationship is indicated by ἔστιν 'is' in first position in the sentence?

1. It is emphatic by forefronting [Alf, Hwt, Lg(K), My, WBC], implying a strong affirmation of the following statement [Alf, Hwt, Lg(K), My]: now faith *is*. . . . It implies that faith is a present and continuing reality [EBC]. Its position calls attention to the following characteristics that are mentioned [Lg, Wst].
2. It is merely an unemphatic connective [ICC, Lns].

QUESTION—What is meant by ἐλπιζομένων 'assurance/substance'?

1. It has the subjective sense of 'assurance' [Alf, Blm, EGT, HNTC, ICC, Lg, Lns, Mil, My, NIC, NTC, TH; CEV, NAB, NASB, NIV, NLT, NRSV, TEV, TNT]: faith is the assurance that what is hoped for will come to be.
2. It has the objective sense of 'substance' [BAGD, EBC, GNC, Hu, Hwt, WBC, Wst; KJV, NJB, REB]: faith gives substance to the things that are hoped for. It expresses the tangible reality of future things even though material evidence is not yet present [EBC, WBC]. It indicates something underlying what is visible and guarantees future possession [Hu, Hwt].

(the) conviction/proof[a] of-things[b] not being-seen.[c]

LEXICON—a. ἔλεγχος (LN **72.8**) (BAGD 1. p. 249): 'conviction' [BAGD, Lns, NIC; NAB, NASB, NRSV], 'conviction based on demonstration' [Mil], 'demonstration' [WBC], 'verification' [LN], 'evidence' [LN; KJV, NLT], 'proof' [BAGD, LN], 'proving' [BAGD, HNTC]. This noun is also translated as a verb phrase: 'to be certain' [NIV, TEV], 'to give proof' [CEV]. The phrase πραγμάτων ἔλεγχος 'conviction of things' is translated 'convinces us of realities' [REB], 'prove the existence of the realities' [NJB]. This entire phrase is translated 'we come to know that the unseen things really do exist' [TNT].

b. πρᾶγμα (LN 13.105) (BAGD 4. p. 697): 'thing' [Alf, BAGD, Lns, Mil, My, NIC, NIGTC; KJV, NAB, NASB, NRSV, TEV, TNT], 'what' [HNTC; CEV, NIV, NLT], 'matter, affair' [BAGD], 'event' [LN, WBC], 'happening' [LN], 'reality' [NJB, REB].

c. pres. pass. participle of βλέπω (LN 24.7): 'to be seen' [Alf, HNTC, LN, Lns, Mil, My, NIC, NIGTC; KJV, NASB, NRSV]. This passive participle is translated as an active voice: 'we see' [NAB, NIV, REB]. The phrase οὐ βλεπομένων 'not being seen' is translated 'unseen' [WBC], 'is not seen' [HNTC], 'that are unseen' [NJB], 'we cannot see' [CEV, NLT, TEV].

QUESTION—How is this phrase related to the preceding phrase?

It confirms the preceding phrase rather than adding to it [Hu]. The two phrases are in apposition with each other [WBC] and are essentially synonymous [NIGTC, TH], and the two phrases form a chiasmus [NIGTC]. The preceding phrase refers to past events; this phrase refers to the eschatological future [WBC].

QUESTION—What is meant by ἔλεγχος 'conviction/proof'?

1. It has the subjective sense of 'conviction'. It means vital certainty [Hu], assurance [Lg, My(D), NIC], firm persuasion [Blm] of the reality of unseen things [EGT, My], based on moral evidence [Blm]. It is synonymous with ὑπόστασις 'assurance' above [Lns, NTC].
2. It has the objective sense of proof [Alf, HNTC, Lns, Mil, NCBC, TH, WBC, Wst] or demonstration [Alf, Mil, NCBC, WBC].

QUESTION—To what does οὐ βλεπομένων 'not being seen' refer?

It is broader than the preceding 'things hoped for' and includes the whole realm of what is spiritual and invisible [Alf, TNTC], referring especially to the future [TNTC], the heavenly world [NCBC], excluding what is physically visible [EBC]. The use of the negative οὐ 'not' with the participle rather than the usual μή emphasizes the negative aspect [NTC, WBC]. The genitive noun πραγμάτων 'of things' states the object of the conviction [Lns, Mil, NIC, NTC; NAB, WBC]: the conviction about things.

11:2 For by[a] this the elders[b] were-approved.[c]

LEXICON—a. ἐν with dative object (LN 89.26, 89.76): 'by' [LN (89.76), Mil, NIC; KJV, NASB, NRSV, TEV], 'by means of' [LN (89.76)], 'because of' [LN (89.26); NAB], 'by reason of, on account of' [LN (89.26)], 'because of' [HNTC; NLT], 'for' [NJB, REB, TNT], 'in connection with' [Lns], not explicit [NIV]. The phrase ἐν ταύτῃ 'by this' is translated 'on this account' [WBC]. This clause is translated 'it was their faith that made our ancestors pleasing to God' [CEV]. This preposition indicates the domain [Alf], means [Mil, TH], or instrument [NIGTC]; it indicates reason [NIGTC]; it means 'in respect of' [Lg]; it implies 'in possession of' [My].

b. πρεσβύτερος (LN **67.27**) (BAGD 1.b. p. 699): 'elder' [Mil; KJV], 'man of old' [BAGD, HNTC; NAB, NASB], 'man of the past' [WBC], '(an) ancient (one)' [Lns; NIV], 'ancestor' [BAGD; CEV, NJB, NRSV, TNT]. The plural πρεσβύτεροι is translated 'people of old' [REB], 'people of ancient times' [TEV], 'those of ancient times' [LN], 'men and women of old' [NIC], 'people in days of old' [NLT]. It refers to people of ancient times [Lns, NCBC, WBC], the ancients who are designated as elders [Alf], the ancient religious leaders [EBC], heroes of the past [HNTC], earlier generations in Israel [NIGTC], believers in pre-Christian times [Hu], persons typified by those mentioned in the following verses [GNC], forefathers [GNC, My] of the OT times, implying honor [Hwt, My], the same people mentioned in 1:1 [HNTC, NTC, TH].

c. aorist pass. indic. of μαρτυρέω (LN 33.263) (BAGD 2.b. p. 493): 'to be approved' [BAGD, Lns; NAB], 'to be approved of' [LN], 'to be commended' [NIV], 'to be spoken well of' [BAGD, LN], 'to be made pleasing to' [CEV], 'to be acknowledged' [NJB], 'to be borne witness to' [Mil]. This passive verb is translated as an active voice with ancestors as subject: 'to obtain a good report' [KJV], 'to gain approval' [NASB], 'to receive approval' [NRSV], 'to win approval' [REB, TEV, TNT], 'to receive attestation' [WBC], 'to gain (one's) testimony' [HNTC], 'to establish (one's) record' [NIC]; with God as subject: to give one's approval [NLT]. A good report is implied [Alf, ICC, My, NIGTC].

QUESTION—What relationship is indicated by γάρ 'for'?

1. It indicates the grounds for the preceding description of faith [Alf, EGT, Mil, My]: the foregoing description of faith is warranted, because. . . . The sense is that faith is what God is pleased with and what united people to God [EGT].
2. It indicates the grounds for the preceding statement [Blm, Lg, Lns, WBC] and the transition to the following examples of faith [WBC]: this is the nature of faith, because by possessing it, the ancients were approved.
3. It introduces an illustration of the nature of faith and, in sense, it governs the rest of the chapter [My(D)].
4. It continues the description of what faith does [NIGTC]: because of this kind of faith . . .

QUESTION—What is meant by ταύτῃ 'this'?

It is stronger than the pronoun αὕτη 'it' [Alf, NIGTC]: by *this*. It refers to the faith mentioned in the preceding verse [EBC, GNC, Hu, Lns, Mil, TH, WBC, Wst; CEV, TEV].

QUESTION—Who is the implied actor of ἐμαρτυρήθησαν 'were approved'?

God approved them [Blm, EGT, Hu, Hwt, Lns, Mil, NIGTC, TH, TNTC, WBC; CEV, NAB, NLT, REB, TEV, TNT]. This also includes approval by man [Blm], and Scripture [NIGTC, WBC].

11:3 By-faith we-understand[a] the ages[b] to-have-been-prepared[c] by-(the/a)-word[d] of-God,

LEXICON—a. pres. act. indic. of νοέω (LN **32.2**) (BAGD 1.c. p. 540): 'to understand' [BAGD, **LN**, Lns, Mil, NIC, WBC; all versions except CEV, NAB], 'to perceive' [BAGD, HNTC, LN; NAB], 'to know' [CEV], 'to apprehend' [BAGD], 'to comprehend' [LN]. It refers to intellectual perception [Alf, Lg, Mil], inner perception [My, NTC] and not by the senses [NIGTC], spiritual perception [WBC]. The basis for this understanding is God's written word [WBC]. By using the first person plural the author includes himself with his readers [NTC, WBC].

b. αἰών (LN 1.2) (BAGD 3. p. 28): 'age' [NJB], 'eon' [Lns], 'world' [Mil; KJV, NAB, NASB, NRSV]. This plural noun is translated 'universe' [HNTC, LN, NIC, WBC; NIV, REB, TEV, TNT], 'the entire universe' [NLT], 'world' [BAGD; CEV]. The plural form refers to time and space, and everything that exists under them [Alf], the universe of space and time [NIC, NTC], the visible world existing in time [EGT, Lg(K), My, NIGTC], heaven and earth and everything in them [Lns], the 'ages' [Hwt, Wst], the spiritual and invisible potencies of the phenomenal world [Lg].

c. perf. pass. infin. of καταρτίζω (LN **42.36**) (BAGD 2.a. p. 418): 'to be prepared' [BAGD, Mil; NASB, NRSV], 'to be created' [BAGD, **LN**;

NAB, NJB, TEV], 'to be made' [BAGD, LN; CEV, TNT], 'to be framed' [Lns; KJV], 'to be fashioned' [HNTC, NIC], 'to be formed' [NIV, NLT, REB], 'to be ordered' [WBC]. The perfect tense indicates the ages as having been prepared and now being in that condition [Lg(K), Wst]. It implies being placed in a completed and perfect condition [Mil, My, TNTC], set in proper order [NCBC].

d. ῥῆμα (LN 33.9) (BAGD 1. p. 735): 'word' [HNTC, LN, Mil, WBC; KJV, NAB, NASB, NJB, NRSV, TEV, TNT], 'uttered word' [Lns], 'utterance' [NIC], 'command' [BAGD; CEV, NIV, NLT, REB], 'order, direction' [BAGD]. It refers to spoken words [Alf, Lg(K), Lns, TH], here to God's single utterance which fashioned the universe [HNTC, NIC, Wst], God's dynamic creative force [Hu, Mil], his creative command [WBC], his authoritative command [My, NTC]. The dative case expresses means [Mil, WBC].

QUESTION—Why is this verse mentioned?

It illustrates the statement in 11:1 [NIC]. It indicates that faith is necessary in reference to a past fact recorded in scripture [My]. It supplements the statements in 11:1–2 [WBC]. It is a prerequisite to all that follows in the chapter [NCBC]. This verse is in the form of a three-member chiasmus [NIGTC].

QUESTION—What relationship is indicated by the dative noun πίστει 'by faith'?

Here and throughout this chapter it stands first in its clause, indicating emphasis, and the emphasis is also indicated by the repetition of this word [GNC, WBC].

1. It indicates means [Alf, Lns, Mil, My, Wst]: by means of faith. In the following verses, most versions translate this dative instrumentally.
2. It indicates reason [TH; CEV]: because of faith. In the following verses, NJB sometimes translates this word causally, sometimes instrumentally.

QUESTION—What is indicated by ῥήματι 'word' without a definite article?

1. It is nevertheless considered definite [Alf, EBC, Mil, WBC; KJV, NAB, NASB, NRSV]: the word of God. This is acceptable, since the modifying noun θεοῦ 'of God' is also without the article.
2. It is indefinite [Lg(K); NJB]: a word from God.

so-that[a] the-(thing) being-seen[b] not to-have-come-into-being[c] from[d] appearing-things.[e]

LEXICON—a. εἰς with accusative object (LN 89.48) (BAGD 4.e. p. 229): 'so that' [BAGD, HNTC, Lns, Mil, NIC, WBC; all versions except CEV, NAB], 'with the result that, so that as a result' [LN], 'and that' [NAB], not explicit [CEV]. It expresses actual result [Alf, EGT, GNC, ICC, Lns, Mil, NIGTC, NTC, TH, TNTC, WBC, Wst]; it expresses God's logical purpose [Lg, My]; it expresses both purpose and result [My(D)].

b. pres. pass. participle of βλέπω (LN 24.7): 'to be seen' [LN, Lns, Mil, NIC, WBC; KJV, NASB, NIV, NLT, NRSV], 'to be visible' [HNTC;

NAB]. The phrase τὸ βλεπόμενον 'the thing being seen' is translated 'what we see' [TNT], 'what can be seen' [CEV, TEV], 'the visible' [REB], 'the visible world' [NJB]. This phrase refers to the visible world [Alf, EGT, My, NTC, WBC], the singular presenting it as a unity [EGT, Lns, My, Wst]. It is synonymous with τοὺς αἰῶνας 'the ages' above [NIGTC].

c. perf. act. infin. of γίνομαι (LN 13.80): 'to come into being' [HNTC, NIC; NAB, TNT], 'to come to be' [Lns; NJB], 'to come to exist, to be formed' [LN], 'to be made' [Mil; CEV, KJV, NASB, NIV, NLT, NRSV, TEV], 'to be brought into being' [WBC], 'to come forth' [REB]. The perfect tense indicates permanence [ICC, NTC, TH].

d. ἐκ with genitive object (LN 90.16): 'from' [HNTC, LN, NIC, WBC; NRSV], 'by' [LN], 'of' [KJV, NLT], 'out of' [Lns, Mil; NASB, NIV]. The phrase μὴ ἐκ φαινομένων 'not from appearing things' is translated 'from what we cannot see' [TNT], 'out of what cannot be seen' [CEV, TEV], 'from the invisible' [NJB, REB], 'through the invisible' [NAB]. This phrase is emphatic by forefronting [Lg(K)]. It is causal [NIGTC].

e. pres. pass. (deponent = act.) participle of φαίνομαι (LN 24.18) (BAGD 2.b. p. 851): 'to appear' [BAGD, LN, Lns; KJV, NLT], 'to be visible' [HNTC, Mil, NIC; NASB, NIV, NRSV], 'to become visible' [LN]. The participle φαινομένων 'appearing things' is translated 'anything observable' [WBC]. It refers to outward things perceived by the senses [My]. The plural implies the many elements involved [Wst].

QUESTION—What is μή 'not' connected with?

1. It is connected with γεγονέναι 'to have come into being' [Blm, Lg, Mil, NIC, NTC, WBC; KJV, NASB, NIV]: it did not come into being through things which appear. The negative μή 'not' thus negates the entire clause [Mil, My, WBC].
2. It is connected with ἐκ φαινομένων 'from appearing things'.

2.1 The phrase μή ἐκ φαινομένων means 'not from appearing things' [Alf, GNC, Lns, Wst].

2.2 This phrase means 'from not-appearing/invisible things' [HNTC, ICC, NIGTC, TH, TNTC; CEV, NAB, NJB, NRSV, REB, TEV, TNT].

DISCOURSE UNIT: 11:4–40 [TNTC]. The topic is examples from the past.

DISCOURSE UNIT: 11:4–7 [EBC, GNC, HNTC, NIC, NTC]. The topic is the faith of men before the Flood [EBC, NIC], the faith of Abel, Enoch, and Noah [GNC, HNTC, NTC].

11:4 By-faith Abel offered to God a-better[a] sacrifice than[b] Cain,

LEXICON—a. πλείων (LN **66.11**) (BAGD II.1.b. p. 689): 'better' [LN, NIC; CEV, NASB, NIV, NJB, TEV], 'superior' [Lns], 'more fitting' [**LN**], 'more appropriate' [LN], 'more acceptable' [LN, WBC; NLT, NRSV], 'more excellent' [Mil; KJV], 'greater' [HNTC; NAB, REB, TNT], 'more' [BAGD].

b. παρά with accusative object (LN 78.29) (BAGD III.3. p. 611): 'than' [HNTC, LN, Lns, Mil, NIC, WBC; all versions], 'in comparison to' [BAGD].

QUESTION—Why is this verse mentioned?

It is the second amplification of the definition of faith mentioned in 11:1 [Mil].

QUESTION—What is the phrase παρὰ Κάϊν 'than Cain' connected with?

1. It is connected with 'Abel' [Alf, My; CEV, NIV, TNT]: Abel offered a better sacrifice than Cain did.
2. It is connected with 'sacrifice' [HNTC; NAB, NLT, NRSV, REB, TEV]: a sacrifice better than Cain's sacrifice.

QUESTION—In what respect was it better?

It was better in quality, not in the nature of the sacrifice [Alf, Blm, Hu, Lns, Mil, My, NIGTC, NTC, TH, WBC], the quality being faith [Alf, Blm, EBC, HNTC, Hu, Mil]. It was better because Abel had faith [My, NCBC, NIGTC], because the offering was prompted by faith [EGT, ICC]; the gifts were the evidence of his faith [Lns]. It was better because Abel was righteous [NIC, NTC, TNTC, WBC], was right with God [EBC, Mil], and made his offering in faith [EBC, GNC, Hwt, Lns, Mil, NIGTC, NTC, WBC] as a demonstration of his faith [EBC]. It means that what he offered was better [Wst].

through[a] which he-was-approved[b] to-be righteous,[c]

LEXICON—a. διά with genitive object (LN 89.26, 89.76): 'through' [HNTC, LN (89.76), Mil; NASB, NRSV, TEV], 'by' [LN (89.76), WBC; KJV, NIV], 'by means of' [LN (89.76), Lns], 'because of' [LN (89.26); NAB, REB, TNT], 'on account of, by reason of' [LN (89.26)], not explicit [CEV, NLT]. The phrase δι' ἧς 'through which' is translated 'by virtue of this sacrifice' [NIC], 'and for that' [NJB].

b. aorist pass. indic. of μαρτυρέω (LN 33.263) (BAGD 2.b. p. 493): 'to be approved' [BAGD], 'to be approved of, to be spoken well of' [LN], 'to be well spoken of' [BAGD], 'to be commended' [NIV], 'to be praised' [BAGD], 'to be attested' [NIC; NAB], 'to be acknowledged' [NJB], not explicit [CEV]. This passive voice is translated as an active: 'to attest' [REB], 'to approve' [TNT], 'to show' [NLT], 'to receive attestation' [WBC], 'to receive approval' [NRSV], 'to win approval' [TEV], 'to obtain witness' [KJV], 'to obtain testimony' [Mil; NASB], 'to receive testimony' [HNTC]. This verb is also translated 'testimony was given to him' [Lns]. This approval occurred at the time of his sacrifice [Alf].

c. δίκαιος (LN 34.47, 88.12) (BAGD 1.b. p. 195): 'righteous' [BAGD, LN (34.47, 88.12), Lns, Mil; KJV, NIV, NLT, NRSV], 'a righteous man' [HNTC, NIC; NASB, TEV, TNT], 'a righteous person' [WBC], 'in a right relation with God' [LN (34.47)], 'just' [BAGD, LN (88.12); NAB], 'upright' [BAGD; NJB]. The phrase εἶναι δίκαιος 'to be righteous' is translated 'his goodness' [REB]. The whole phrase is translated 'God was pleased with him' [CEV]. It refers to a righteous man [EGT] and concerns a right attitude of mind which is acceptable to God [TNTC].

QUESTION—To what does ἧς 'which' refer?

1. It refers to faith [Alf, Hu, Lns, My, NIGTC, TH, WBC; NIV, REB, TEV, TNT]: through faith.
2. It refers to Abel's sacrifice [EGT, Hwt, Mil, NIC, Wst; NLT]: through this sacrifice.

QUESTION—Who is the implied actor of ἐμαρτυρήθη 'he was approved'?

The one who approved is God [Alf, Blm, Hu, Mil, My, NIGTC, TH, WBC; REB, TEV, TNT]. It is the testimony given in the OT [My(D), NIGTC, TH].

God testifying[a] with-respect-to[b] his gifts;[c]

LEXICON—a. pres. act. participle of μαρτυρέω (LN 33.262, 33.263) (BAGD 2.b. p. 493): 'to testify' [KJV, NASB], 'to bear witness' [BAGD, NIC; NAB], 'to witness' [LN (33.262)], 'to give testimony' [Lns], 'to give a testimony' [Mil], 'to make acknowledgement of' [NJB], 'to approve' [HNTC, WBC; REB, TEV], 'to approve of' [LN (33.263)], 'to show approval of' [TNT], 'to give approval to' [NRSV], 'to be pleased with' [CEV], 'to speak well of' [LN (33.263); NIV], 'to accept' [NLT]. The approval was shown by God's consuming the gift with fire [Alf, Blm, Mil].

b. ἐπί with dative object (LN 90.23) (BAGD II.1.b.δ. p. 287): 'with respect to, with reference to' [LN], 'in respect to' [Mil], 'to' [NIC; NRSV], 'about' [BAGD, LN; NASB], 'on the basis of' [Lns], 'on account of' [NAB], 'in virtue of' [HNTC], 'of' [WBC; KJV, NIV, NJB, TEV, TNT], 'with' [CEV], 'by accepting' [Mil], not explicit [NLT, REB]. The sense is 'in regard to' [Alf], 'over' [Lg(K)]. It states the basis of what follows [Mil, NIGTC].

c. δῶρον (LN 57.84) (BAGD 2. p. 210): 'gift' [BAGD, HNTC, LN, Lns, Mil, NIC, WBC; CEV, KJV, NAB, NASB, NRSV, TEV, TNT], 'present' [LN], 'offering' [BAGD; NIV, NJB, NLT, REB].

QUESTION—What relationship is indicated by the participle μαρτυροῦντος 'testifying'?

1. It indicates a separate accompanying fact [REB, TNT]: also, God testified.
2. It is temporal, connected with the preceding clause [NIV, NJB]: he was approved to be righteous when God testified.
3. It indicates reason [HNTC, NIC; TEV]: he was approved, because God testified.
4. It expands and states the specifics (the evidence [TH]) of God's testimony [Mil, NIGTC, TH, WBC]: God's testimony, in the fact that God gave testimony regarding his gifts.

QUESTION—What is the implied object of the participle μαρτυροῦντος 'testifying'?

1. The object is the gifts [Alf, Blm, EGT, Mil, NIC, WBC; all versions except NAB]: God testified about the gifts.

2. The object is Abel [HNTC, Lns; NAB]: God testifying to Abel with respect to his gifts.

and through[a] it, having-died[b] he-speaks still.

LEXICON—a. διά with genitive object (LN 89.26, 89.76): ‘through’ [LN (89.76), Mil, NIC; NASB, NRSV, REB, TNT], ‘by’ [LN (89.76), WBC; KJV, NIV, NJB], ‘by means of’ [LN (89.76), Lns; TEV], ‘because of’ [LN (89.26); CEV, NLT], ‘on account of, by reason of’ [LN (89.26)]. The phrase καὶ δι’ αὐτῆς ‘and through it’ is translated ‘therefore’ [NAB], ‘this is why’ [HNTC].

b. aorist act. participle of ἀποθνήσκω (LN 23.99): ‘to die’ [LN, Lns, NIC, WBC; NRSV], ‘to be dead’ [HNTC, Mil; all versions except NRSV]. The implied subject is Abel [NAB]. The aorist tense indicates a single past action [Lns, NIC, WBC; NRSV]. It is translated as a state [HNTC, Mil; all versions except NRSV]: he is dead.

QUESTION—To what does αὐτῆς ‘it’ refer?

It refers to faith [Alf, EBC, EGT, Hu, ICC, Mil, My, NIGTC, TNTC, WBC, Wst; all versions except KJV, NAB]: through faith.

QUESTION—What relationship is indicated by the aorist participle ἀποθανών ‘having died’?

1. It indicates a concession [Blm, EGT, HNTC, Lns, Mil, My, NIGTC, TH, WBC; all versions except KJV, NRSV]: although he died.
2. It is temporal [Lg(K), NIC]: after he died.
3. It indicates an independent proposition [NRSV]: he died.

QUESTION—What is meant by ἔτι λαλεῖ ‘he still speaks’?

1. He speaks by his faith [Blm, EBC, GNC, HNTC, Hu, Lns, Mil, NTC, TH, TNTC, WBC] in the scripture record [ICC, TH, WBC] as an example to us [Blm, HNTC, Hu, ICC, NCBC, NTC, TNTC, WBC]; he speaks of the value of faith [Mil]. The present tense indicates continuing speaking [Mil].
2. It is his blood that speaks [Alf], that spoke crying immediately after his death [EGT], crying to God for vengeance [Lg, My, NIC]; λαλεῖ ‘he speaks’ is a historical present referring to the past [Lg, My].

QUESTION—What is meant by ἔτι ‘still’?

1. It refers to present time [NIGTC, TH]: he still speaks.
2. It has a logical sense, emphasizing the contrast [My]: nevertheless he speaks.

11:5 By-faith Enoch was-translated[a] (so-that/so-as) the not to-see[b] death,

LEXICON—a. aorist pass. indic. of μετατίθημι (LN 15.2) (BAGD 1. p. 513): ‘to be translated’ [BAGD, Lns, Mil, NIC, WBC; KJV], ‘to be taken’ [NRSV], ‘to be taken up’ [BAGD, Mil; NASB, NJB, TEV], ‘to be taken up to heaven’ [NLT], ‘to be taken away’ [HNTC; NAB, TNT], ‘to be taken from this life’ [NIV], ‘to be taken up to another life’ [REB], ‘to be moved, to be moved from one place to another’ [LN], not explicit [CEV]. It indicates being transferred [EBC, EGT] from one location to another

[EGT, Hu, WBC], conveyed from one realm to another [GNC], from earth to heaven [NIGTC, WBC] by God [NIGTC].

b. aorist act. infin. of ὁράω (LN 24.1, **90.79**) (BAGD 5. p. 221): 'to see' [BAGD, HNTC, LN, Lns; KJV, NASB], 'to experience' [BAGD, **LN (90.79)**, Mil, NIC, WBC; NIV, NJB, NRSV], 'to undergo' [LN (90.79)]. The phrase τοῦ μὴ ἰδεῖν θάνατον 'so that/as not to see death' is translated 'without dying' [NAB, NLT], 'without experiencing death' [TNT], 'without passing through death' [REB]. The phrase πίστει Ἑνὼχ . . . τοῦ μὴ ἰδεῖν θάνατον 'by faith Enoch . . . so that/as not to see death' is translated 'it was faith that kept Enoch from dying' [TEV], 'Enoch had faith and did not die' [CEV]. Here it means to experience death [Lns, NIGTC, TH, WBC].

QUESTION—What relationship is indicated by the phrase τοῦ μὴ ἰδεῖν θάνατον 'so that/so as not to see death'?

1. It indicates result [EGT, HNTC, ICC, Lns, WBC; NIV, NRSV]: Enoch was translated so that he did not see death.
2. It indicates purpose [My, NIC; KJV, NASB], God's purpose [My]: Enoch was translated in order that he should not see death.

and "not he-was-being-found[a] because God had-translated[b] him."

LEXICON—a. imperf. pass. indic. of εὑρίσκω (LN 27.27) (BAGD 1.a. p. 325): 'to be found' [BAGD, HNTC, LN, Lns, Mil, NIC; KJV, NASB, NRSV, REB, TNT]. The phrase οὐχ ηὑρίσκετο 'he was not being found' is translated 'he could not be found' [WBC; NIV], 'he was seen no more' [NAB], 'he was no more' [NJB], 'nobody could find him' [TEV], 'his body was never found' [CEV], 'suddenly he disappeared' [NLT]. The imperfect tense implies repeated looking [NTC].

b. aorist act. indic. of μετατίθημι (LN 15.2) (BAGD 1. p. 513): 'to translate' [BAGD, Lns, NIC, WBC; KJV], 'to take' [NAB, NJB, NLT, NRSV, REB], 'to take up' [BAGD; NASB, TEV], 'to take away' [HNTC, Mil; NIV, TNT], 'to take up to heaven' [CEV], 'to move, to move from one place to another' [LN]. It implies being suddenly and supernaturally removed from earth [Hu], taken up to heaven by God [TH].

QUESTION—What relationship is indicated by καί 'and'?

1. It indicates the result of his being taken up [Mil]: as a result he was not being found.
2. It merely introduces the following quotation [TH].

QUESTION—What is the significance of the position of ὁ θεός 'God'?

It is emphatic [NIGTC]: *God* had translated him.

For before[a] the translation[b] he-was-attested[c] to-be-pleasing[d] to God;

LEXICON—a. πρό with genitive object (LN 67.17) (BAGD 2. p. 701): 'before' [BAGD, HNTC, LN, Lns, Mil, NIC, WBC; all versions except CEV], not explicit [CEV].

b. μετάθεσις (LN **15.2**) (BAGD 1. p. 511): 'translation' [BAGD, Lns, Mil, NIC, WBC; KJV], 'removal' [Mil], 'taking up' [BAGD], 'departure'

[LN], 'assumption' [NJB]. The phrase τῆς μεταθέσεως 'the translation' is translated 'his being taken up' [NASB], 'he was taken up' [NAB, NLT], 'Enoch was taken up' [TEV], 'he was taken' [NIV, REB], 'he was taken away' [HNTC; NRSV, TNT], 'God took him up to heaven' [CEV].

c. perf. pass. indic. of μαρτυρέω (LN 33.263) (BAGD 2.b. p. 493): 'to be attested' [NIC; NRSV], 'to have (a) testimony' [KJV], 'to receive the testimony' [Lns], 'to be acknowledged' [NJB], 'to obtain a witness' [Mil; NASB], 'to be well spoken of' [BAGD], 'to be spoken well of, to be approved of' [LN], 'to be approved' [BAGD, WBC; NLT], 'to be commended' [NIV], not explicit [CEV]. This passive verb is translated as an active: 'it is testified that' [HNTC], '(Scripture) testifies that' [NAB], 'it is the testimony (of Scripture) that' [REB], 'scripture says that' [TNT], 'the scripture says that' [TEV]. The perfect tense indicates permanence [EBC], the continued existence of the testimony in Scripture [Alf, ICC, Lg(K), NTC, Wst].

d. perf. act. infin. of εὐαρεστέω (LN **25.93**) (BAGD 1. p. 318): 'to please' [BAGD, LN; CEV, KJV, NJB, NLT, NRSV, REB, TEV, TNT], 'to be pleasing' [BAGD, HNTC, LN, WBC; NASB], 'to become pleasing' [Mil], 'to be well-pleasing' [Lns], 'to give pleasure' [NIC]. This verb is also translated 'as one who pleased' [NIV].

QUESTION—What relationship is indicated by γάρ 'for'?

It introduces the evidence for the preceding statement [Mil]: this is true, the evidence being that . . .

QUESTION—What is the phrase πρὸ τῆς μεταθέσεως 'before the translation' connected with?

This prepositional phrase is forefronted for emphasis [Lns].

1. It is connected with εὐαρεστηκέναι 'to be pleasing' [HNTC, Lns, My(D), NIC, NIGTC, TNTC; NAB, NASB, REB, TEV, TNT]: before he was translated he was pleasing to God.
2. It is connected with μεμαρτύρηται 'he was attested' [Alf, EGT, Hwt, Mil, WBC, Wst; KJV, NIV, NJB, NRSV]: before he was translated he was attested.

11:6 And/but without[a] faith (it is) impossible[b] to-please[c] (him);

LEXICON—a. χωρίς with genitive object (LN 89.120) (BAGD 2.b.γ. p. 890): 'without' [BAGD, HNTC, LN, Lns, Mil, NIC, WBC; all versions], 'apart from' [BAGD, LN].

b. ἀδύνατος (LN 71.3) (BAGD 2.a. p. 19): 'impossible' [BAGD, HNTC, LN, Lns, Mil, NIC, WBC; all versions except CEV, TEV]. The phrase ἀδύνατον εὐαρεστῆσαι 'it is impossible to please' is translated 'no one can please' [CEV, TEV].

c. aorist act. infin. of εὐαρεστέω (LN 25.93) (BAGD 1. p. 318): 'to please' [BAGD, HNTC, LN, Mil; all versions], 'to begin to please' [WBC], 'to be well-pleasing' [Lns], 'to be pleasing to' [BAGD], 'to give someone pleasure' [NIC], 'to cause someone to be pleased, to cause someone to be well disposed toward someone' [LN]. The aorist tense implies doing a single act (here, with the negative, indicating none at all) [Alf], without reference to time [Alf, Mil, My].

QUESTION—Why is this clause mentioned?

It introduces a new stage in the argument [NIGTC]. It is a statement of a general truth, not merely referring to Enoch [Alf, EBC, HNTC, Hu, Hwt, ICC, Mil, My, NIC]. It is emphatic by its position [WBC].

QUESTION—What relationship is indicated by δέ 'and/but'?

1. It introduces an added (interpretive [WBC]) comment concerning faith [HNTC, Lns, Mil, NIC, WBC; NASB, NIV, NJB, NLT, NRSV, TNT]: and apart from faith, it is impossible to please God. It is transitional [Mil].
2. It indicates the grounds for the comment concerning Enoch's faith [TNTC]: Enoch had faith, because apart from faith it is impossible to please God.
3. It indicates a contrast with the preceding comment [Alf; CEV, KJV, NAB, REB]: but apart from faith, it is impossible to please God.

QUESTION—What is the implied object of εὐαρεστῆσαι 'to please'?

The implied object is God [Alf, EBC, EGT, GNC, HNTC, Hu, Hwt, Lns, Mil, My, NIC, WBC; all versions]: to please God.

for it-is-necessary[a] for-the-(one) coming-to[b] God to-believe[c] that he-exists[d]

LEXICON—a. pres. act. indic. of irregular verb δεῖ (LN 71.34): 'it is necessary' [LN, Lns, WBC], '(one) must' [HNTC, LN, Mil, NIC; all versions].

b. pres. pass. (deponent = act.) participle of προσέρχομαι (LN 15.77, 34.23) (BAGD 2.a. p. 713): 'to come to' [BAGD, HNTC, Lns; all versions except CEV, NRSV], 'to come near to' [LN (15.77)], 'to approach' [BAGD, LN (15.77), Mil, NIC, WBC; NRSV], 'to undertake to join with, to seek association with' [LN (34.23)], not explicit [CEV]. The present tense implies habitual coming [Alf]. The coming is for worship [Alf, Blm, EBC, Hwt, Lg, My, TH], service [Alf].

c. aorist act. infin. of πιστεύω (LN 31.35) (BAGD 1.a. β. p. 660): 'to believe' [BAGD, LN, Lns, Mil, NIC, WBC; all versions except TEV, TNT], 'to have faith' [HNTC; TEV, TNT], 'to think to be true' [LN]. The aorist tense refers to the state which motivated the coming [Alf].

d. pres. (act.) indic. of εἰμί (LN **13.69**) (BAGD I.1. p. 223): 'to exist' [BAGD, HNTC, Hu, **LN,** Lns, Mil, NIC, WBC; all versions except CEV, KJV, NASB, NLT], 'to be' [LN; KJV, NASB], 'to be real' [CEV], 'there is a God' [NLT]. The reference is to God's existence [Alf, Blm, EBC, ICC, My, NCBC, NIGTC, TNTC].

QUESTION—What relationship is indicated by γάρ 'for'?

It introduces the grounds for the preceding comment [EGT, Lns, Mil, NCBC]: it is impossible to please God without faith, since it is necessary to believe that God exists in order to come to him.

QUESTION—What is meant by the definite article in the participial phrase τὸν προσερχόμενον 'the one coming to'?

It is a generic singular, referring to anyone who comes [EBC, HNTC, Hu, Hwt; all versions except KJV, NASB]: anyone who comes to God.

and becomes[a] (a) rewarder[b] to-the-(ones) seeking[c] him.

LEXICON—a. pres. pass. (deponent = act.) indic. of γίνομαι (LN 13.48) (BAGD II.1. p. 160): 'to become' [LN, Lns, Mil, WBC], 'to be' [BAGD, NIC; KJV, NASB], not explicit [HNTC; all versions except KJV, NASB].

b. μισθαποδότης (LN **38.18**) (BAGD p. 523): 'rewarder' [**LN**, Mil, NIC, WBC; KJV, NASB], 'recompenser' [BAGD, LN], 'giver of due pay' [Lns]. This noun is also translated as a verb: 'to reward' [HNTC; all versions except KJV, NASB].

c. pres. act. participle of ἐκζητέω (LN 27.35) (BAGD 1. p. 240): 'to seek' [BAGD, HNTC, LN; all versions except CEV, KJV, NIV], 'to seek after' [Lns, Mil], 'to seek out' [NIC, WBC], 'to seek diligently' [KJV], 'to seek earnestly' [NIV], 'to search for' [CEV], 'to make a careful search for' [LN]. Here it implies seeking in order to worship [NIGTC, TH], to devote oneself to God's service [WBC].

QUESTION—How is this phrase related to the preceding phrase?

It is the second part of the clause introduced by ὅτι 'that' [HNTC, Lns, Mil, My, NIC, TH; all versions]: it is necessary to believe that he exists and becomes a rewarder to those who seek him. There is an unexpressed second ὅτι 'that' [HNTC, Mil, NIC; CEV, KJV, NAB, NASB, NIV, NLT, NRSV]: that he exists and that he becomes a rewarder to those who seek him. It is the more important part of the comment [ICC, TH], the consequence of the first part [NIGTC].

11:7 By faith Noah, having-been-warned[a] concerning[b] the-(things) not-yet being-seen,[c]

LEXICON—a. aorist pass. participle of χρηματίζω (LN 28.39) (BAGD 1.b.α. p. 885): 'to be warned' [CEV, NAB, NIV], 'to be divinely warned' [HNTC, Mil, NIC], 'to be warned by God' [NASB, NJB, NRSV], 'to be warned of God' [KJV], 'to be instructed by God' [WBC], 'to be given a revelation or warning' [BAGD], 'a message from God having been revealed, God's message having been made known' [LN]. This passive voice is also translated as an active voice with Noah as subject: 'to hear God's warnings' [TEV], 'to receive God's warning' [TNT], 'to receive divine communication' [Lns]; with God as subject: 'to warn' [NLT]. The phrase χρηματισθεὶς . . . εὐλαβηθείς 'having been warned . . . having been moved by piety' is translated 'took good heed of the divine warning' [REB]. It refers to a divine message of warning [EGT, TH]. The passive voice implies that God is the actor [HNTC, Lns, Mil, NIC, NIGTC, WBC; KJV, NASB, NJB, NLT, NRSV, TEV, TNT].

b. περί with genitive object (LN 89.6, 90.24): 'concerning' [LN (89.6, 90.24), Lns, WBC], 'about' [HNTC, LN (90.24), Mil, NIC; all versions except KJV, NJB], 'of' [LN (90.24); KJV, NJB], 'with regard to, in relation to' [LN (89.6)].

c. pres. pass. participle of βλέπω (LN 24.7): 'to be seen' [LN, Lns, Mil, NIC; KJV, NAB, NASB, NIV, NJB]. The phrase τῶν μηδέπω βλεπομένων 'the things not yet being seen' is translated 'events as yet unseen' [WBC; NRSV], 'the unseen future' [REB], 'things in the future that he could not see' [TEV], 'what he did not yet see' [HNTC], 'events which at the time belonged to the future' [TNT], 'something that had not yet happened' [CEV], 'something that had never happened before' [NLT]. The reference is to the flood [Blm, EGT, Hu, Lns, Mil, My, TNTC], the destruction of corrupt mankind [Mil, My], and subsequent events [Blm, Wst] as the plural implies [My].

QUESTION—What is πίστει 'by faith' connected with?

1. It is connected with κατεσκεύασεν 'he built' [Alf, Blm, EGT, HNTC, Hu, Lns, Mil, My, NIC, NIGTC, WBC; KJV, NAB, NASB, NJB, NLT, NRSV, REB]: by faith he built an ark.
2. It is connected with χρηματισθείς 'having been warned' [TH; CEV, TEV, TNT]: because of his faith he was warned.

QUESTION—What relationship is indicated by the participial form χρηματισθείς 'having been warned'?

1. It is temporal [Mil; NIV, NJB], the aorist tense indicating a prior action [Mil]: when/after he was warned, he built an ark. It also implies the reason he built the ark [Mil].
2. It expresses a independent definite action [TEV, TNT]: he heard God's warnings.
3. This participle plus the following participle εὐλαβηθείς state an action parallel to and preceding the verb κατεσκεύασεν 'built' [REB]: he took good heed to the divine warning and built an ark.

QUESTION—What is implied by the definite article in the participial phrase τῶν μηδέπω βλεπομένων 'the things not yet being seen'?

The definite article refers to specific things [Alf, Wst; NJB, REB] and implies that the readers knew about these things [Lns, My]: the things not yet being seen. The participle is nevertheless treated as indefinite [EBC, EGT, GNC, Hu, Lns, Mil, NIC, NTC, WBC; all versions except NJB, REB]: things not yet being seen.

having-been-moved-with-godly-fear[a] he built[b] an-ark[c] for[d] deliverance[e] of-his household,[f]

LEXICON—a. aorist pass. (deponent = act.) participle of εὐλαβέομαι (LN **36.13**, **53.7**) (BAGD 1. p. 322): 'to be moved with godly fear' [Mil], 'to be filled with godly fear' [Lns], 'to be moved with fear' [KJV], 'to become afraid' [BAGD], 'to revere God' [NAB], 'to be moved by reverent submission' [NIC], 'to listen carefully to what God said' [TNT], 'to take good heed' [HNTC; REB], 'to respect the warning' [NRSV], 'to pay attention' [WBC], 'to obey' [LN (**36.13**); CEV], 'to obey God' [NLT,

TEV], 'to take care' [BAGD; NJB]. This participle is also translated as manner: 'in reverence' [NASB], 'in holy fear' [NIV], 'with reverent regard for (God)' [LN (**53.7**)]. The meaning is to take forethought [Alf, Lg], to have reverential awe [TNTC], to have a reverential regard to God's command [Blm, EBC, EGT, GNC, Hu, My, NIGTC]. It means that he was attentive to God's will [WBC] and means 'obey' with awe and reverence for the one who gave the command [LN (36.13)]. Noah showed his reverence by doing what God commanded and so it is implied that the verb means 'obeyed' here [TH].

b. aorist act. indic. of κατασκευάζω (LN 45.1, 77.6) (BAGD 2. p. 418): 'to build' [BAGD, HNTC, LN (45.1), NIC; all versions except KJV, NASB], 'to construct' [BAGD, LN (45.1), Lns, WBC], 'to prepare' [LN (77.6), Mil; KJV, NASB]. It implies both building and outfitting [Wst].

c. κιβωτός (LN 6.44) (BAGD 1. p. 431): 'ark' [HNTC, Lns, Mil, NIC, WBC; all versions except CEV, TEV, TNT], 'the ark' [BAGD, LN; TNT], 'boat' [LN; CEV, TEV], 'ship' [LN]. The reference is to 'the (well-known) ark' [Alf].

d. εἰς with accusative object (LN 89.57): 'for' [Lns, WBC; NASB], 'for the purpose of' [LN, Mil], 'to' [KJV, NLT], 'that' [HNTC, NIC; CEV, NIV, NJB, NRSV, REB, TNT], not explicit [TEV]. This preposition expresses purpose [Mil].

e. σωτηρία (LN 21.18) (BAGD 1. p. 801): 'deliverance' [BAGD, LN], 'preservation' [BAGD], 'safety' [WBC], 'saving' [Lns, Mil; KJV], 'salvation' [NASB]. This noun is also translated as a verb: 'to save' [HNTC, NIC; CEV, NIV, NJB, NLT, NRSV, REB, TNT], 'to be saved' [NAB, TEV]. It refers to saving from danger [EBC], from drowning [NIGTC].

f. οἶκος (LN 10.8): 'household' [HNTC, LN, Mil, NIC, WBC; NAB, NASB, NRSV, REB, TNT], 'family' [LN, Lns; CEV, NIV, NJB, NLT, TEV], 'house' [KJV]. The reference is to Noah's family [NIGTC].

QUESTION—What relationship is indicated by the participial form εὐλαβηθείς 'having been moved with godly fear'?

1. It describes an action preceding and parallel to the following verb κατεσκεύασεν 'he built' [HNTC, NIC, WBC; NAB, NRSV, REB, TEV, TNT]: he was moved by godly fear and built an ark.
2. It indicates the basis of building [NJB]: he took care to build an ark.
3. It indicates the reason for the following action, the aorist tense referring to the beginning of the action [Mil]: because he began to be moved by godly fear, he built an ark.

through[a] which he-condemned[b] the world,[c]

LEXICON—a. διά with genitive object (LN 89.76, 90.8): 'through' [LN (89.76, 90.8), Mil; REB], 'by means of' [LN (90.8), Lns, NIC], 'by' [HNTC, WBC; KJV, NASB, NIV, NLT, NRSV]. The phrase δι' ἧς 'through which' is translated 'he thereby' [NAB], 'as a result' [TEV], 'in this way'

[CEV]. The phrase δι' ἧς κατέκρινεν 'through which he condemned' is translated 'his faith was a judgment on' [NJB, TNT].

b. aorist/imperf. act. indic. of κατακρίνω (LN 56.31) (BAGD p. 412): 'to condemn' [BAGD, HNTC, LN, Lns, Mil, WBC; KJV, NAB, NASB, NIV, NLT, NRSV], 'to put in the wrong' [NIC; REB]. The phrase κατέκρινεν τὸν κόσμον 'he condemned the world' is translated 'the world was condemned' [TEV], 'the people of the world were judged' [CEV]. The condemnation consisted in Noah's righteous conduct, which contrasted with the unrighteous conduct of others [BAGD, Blm, EGT, GNC, HNTC, ICC, Mil, My, NCBC, WBC]. It is an aorist tense, indicating one act [Alf]; it is an imperfect tense, implying continuation [NIGTC, Wst].

c. κόσμος (LN 9.23, 41.38): 'world' [HNTC, LN (41.38), Lns, Mil, NIC; all versions], 'people of the world' [LN (9.23); CEV], 'the rest of the world' [NLT], 'humanity' [WBC], 'world system, world's standards' [LN (41.38)]. It has a negative reference [NIGTC, TH]; it refers to the disobedient mankind of Noah's day [EBC], sinful humanity [ICC, My], human society hostile to God [NCBC].

QUESTION—To what does ἧς 'which' refer?

1. It refers to Noah's faith [Alf, Blm, EBC, EGT, GNC, ICC, Lg, Lns, Mil, My, NIGTC, NTC, TH, WBC; NIV, NJB, NLT, REB, TNT]: by having faith he condemned the world.
2. It refers to κιβωτόν 'ark' [TNTC, Wst] as the expression of Noah's faith [Wst]: by building the ark he condemned the world.

and of-the righteousness[a] according-to[b] faith he-became an-heir.[c]

LEXICON—a. δικαιοσύνη (LN 88.13) (BAGD 3. p. 197): 'righteousness' [BAGD, HNTC, LN, Lns, Mil, NIC, WBC; KJV, NASB, NIV, NRSV, REB, TEV, TNT], 'justice' [NAB], 'uprightness' [NJB]. This noun is also translated as a verb: 'to please God' [CEV], 'to be made right in God's sight' [NLT]. It refers to God's verdict concerning a person [Lns, TH], to acceptance with God [Blm] by believing God's word and acting accordingly [EBC], a right relationship with God [TH]. It is righteousness in contrast with sin [NIGTC].

b. κατά with accusative object (LN 89.8) (BAGD II.7.c. p. 408): 'according to' [WBC], 'in accordance with' [LN], 'in relation to' [LN], 'of' [BAGD, Lns], 'by' [NLT], 'which is by' [KJV], 'that comes by' [NIV, TEV, TNT], 'that comes through' [HNTC], 'which is according to' [NIC; NASB], 'that is in accordance with' [NRSV], 'which results from' [Mil], 'which comes from' [NJB], 'which comes through' [NAB], 'which comes of' [REB], not explicit [CEV]. The sense is 'which is by' [Alf]. It indicates the norm or measure of faith [WBC].

c. κληρονόμος (LN 57.139) (BAGD 2.b. p. 435): 'heir' [BAGD, LN, Lns, Mil, NIC, WBC; KJV, NASB, NIV, NRSV], 'possessor' [HNTC], 'partaker' [Mil], not explicit [NLT]. The phrase ἐγένετο κληρονόμος 'became an heir' is translated 'inherited' [NAB], 'entered into possession of' [TNT], 'received from God' [TEV], 'was able to claim' [NJB], 'made good his own claim to' [REB], 'Noah was given the blessings' [CEV]. The reference is to possession rather than inheriting [EBC, EGT, ICC, My, NTC, TH].

QUESTION—What relationship is indicated by καί 'and'?

It introduces the second part of the clause [Mil]: through which he condemned the world and became heir.

QUESTION—How are the two nouns related in the phrase δικαιοσύνης κληρονόμος 'heir of righteousness'?

'Righteousness' tells what was inherited [Mil; NAB, NJB, NRSV, REB, TEV, TNT]: he inherited righteousness.

QUESTION—What relationship is indicated by the prepositional phrase κατὰ πίστιν 'according to faith'?

1. It is adjectival, describing 'righteousness' [Alf, HNTC, Hu, Mil, NCBC, NIC, WBC; all versions except CEV, NLT]: the righteousness which is according to faith. It is a righteousness which God bestowed according to the norm of faith [WBC].
2. It is equivalent to the dative of means [NIGTC; NLT]: the righteousness which is obtained by means of faith.

QUESTION—What relationship is indicated by ἐγένετο 'he became'?

Here it means 'to be made (by God)' [NIGTC].

DISCOURSE UNIT: 11:8–22 [WBC]. The topic is triumphs of perseverance in faith in the time of the Patriarchs.

DISCOURSE UNIT: 11:8–19 [EBC, NTC]. The topic is the faith of Abraham and Sarah [EBC], the faith of Abraham [NTC].

DISCOURSE UNIT: 11:8–12 [GNC, HNTC, Lg, NIC]. The topic is the faith of Abraham and Sarah [GNC, NIC], the example of Abraham and Sarah [Lg], the faith of Abraham [HNTC].

11:8 By faith Abraham being-called[a] obeyed to-go-out into[b] (a) place[c]

TEXT—Some manuscripts insert the definite article ὁ 'the' before καλούμενος 'being called'. GNT does not deal with this variant. Only My inserts this article.

LEXICON—a. pres. pass. participle of καλέω (LN 33.312) (BAGD 1.d. p. 399): 'to be called' [LN, Lns, Mil, WBC; KJV, NAB, NASB, NIV, NRSV], 'to be called to a task' [LN], 'to be called upon' [BAGD], 'to be told' [CEV]. This passive participle is also translated as active: 'when God called him' [NLT, TEV]. The phrase καλούμενος ὑπήκουσεν 'being called he obeyed' is translated 'he obeyed the call' [HNTC; NJB, REB], 'he obeyed God's call' [TNT], 'in obedience to the call of God' [NIC].

b. εἰς with accusative object (LN 84.22): 'into' [LN, Lns, Mil, NIC; KJV], 'to' [HNTC; CEV, NAB, NASB, NIV, NLT, TEV, TNT], 'for' [WBC; NJB, NRSV, REB].

c. τόπος (LN 80.1): 'place' [HNTC, LN, Lns, Mil, NIC, WBC; KJV, NAB, NASB, NIV, NRSV], 'country' [NJB, TEV, TNT], 'land' [CEV, NLT, REB]. The absence of the definite article implies uncertainty as to the location [NIGTC].

QUESTION—What relationship is indicated by the participle καλούμενος?

The present tense implies immediate response [EBC, EGT, HNTC, Hu, ICC, Mil, My, NIGTC, NTC, WBC, Wst] as the close connection with ὑπήκουσεν 'he obeyed' also shows [Hu, WBC].

1. It is temporal [EBC, EGT, Hu, ICC, Mil, NTC, TH, WBC, Wst; KJV, NAB, NASB, NIV, NLT, NRSV, TEV]: when/as he was called.
2. With the preceding definite article (ὁ καλούμενος) the meaning is 'the one being called' [My]: Abraham, who was called to go out.

QUESTION—What is the infinitive ἐξελθεῖν 'to go out' connected with?

1. It is related to ὑπήκουσεν 'he obeyed' [Alf, Blm, EBC, Lns, Mil, NIC, NIGTC, WBC; NASB]

1.1 It tells how he obeyed [NASB]: he obeyed by going out.

1.2 It tells what he did in obedience [Alf, EBC, ICC, Lg(K), Lns, Mil, NIC]: his obedience consisted in going out.

1.3 It tells the result of his obedience [Blm, WBC]: he obeyed, with the result that he went out.

2. It is related to καλούμενος 'being called' and tells what he was called to do [HNTC; all versions except NAB, NASB]: being called to go out.
3. It is translated as an independent action [NAB]: he obeyed . . . and he went forth.

which he-was-going[a] to-receive for[b] (an) inheritance,[c]

LEXICON—a. imperf. act. indic. of μέλλω (LN 67.62) (BAGD 1.c.δ. p. 501): 'to be going' [Mil], 'to be about to' [LN], 'to be destined, will certainly' [BAGD]. The phrase ἤμελλεν λαμβάνειν 'he was going to receive' is translated 'he should after receive' [KJV], 'he would later receive' [NIV], 'he was to receive' [HNTC, Lns, NIC, WBC; NAB, NASB, NRSV, REB], 'that God would give him' [NLT]. This entire clause is translated 'which God had promised to give him' [TEV], 'that God had said would be his' [CEV], 'which one day God would give him to be his own' [TNT], 'that was the inheritance given to him and his descendants' [NJB]. The meaning is 'about to' [GNC], 'destined to' [Lg(K)].

b. εἰς with accusative object (LN 89.57): 'as' [HNTC, NIC, WBC; NAB, NIV, NLT, NRSV, REB], 'for' [Lns, Mil; KJV, NASB], 'for the purpose of, to serve as' [LN]. It expresses purpose [Mil].

c. κληρονομία (LN 57.132) (BAGD 2. p. 435): 'inheritance' [Lns, Mil, NIC, WBC; KJV, NASB, NIV, NJB, NLT, NRSV], 'heritage' [NAB], 'possession' [BAGD, HNTC, LN; REB]. The meaning is a possession [NIGTC], a gift (from God) [TH].

QUESTION—Why is this clause mentioned?

It is restrictive, identifying the place referred to in the preceding clause [Mil]: a place that he was going to receive.

and he-went-out[a] not knowing where he-was-going.

LEXICON—a. aorist act. indic. of ἐξέρχομαι (LN 15.40) (BAGD 1.a.β. p. 274): 'to go out' [HNTC, LN, Lns; KJV, NASB], 'to go forth' [Mil, NIC; NAB], 'to go away' [BAGD; REB], 'to go' [NIV, NLT], 'to set out' [WBC; NJB, NRSV], 'to come out' [LN], 'to leave' [CEV], 'to leave home' [TNT], 'to leave one's own country' [TEV].

QUESTION—What relationship is indicated by the participle ἐπιστάμενος 'knowing'?

1. It indicates concession [EBC, GNC, Mil, TH; NIV]: he went out, although he did not know where he was going. This word refers to knowledge of facts (about the place to which he was going) [NIGTC].
2. It is temporal [Wst]: he went out while he did not know where he was going. He did not know until after he had left Haran [Wst].

QUESTION—What relationship is indicated by the clause ποῦ ἔρχεται 'where he was going'?

It is an indirect form of the question "Where is he going?" [Mil]: he did not know to what place he was going.

11:9 By-faith he-sojourned[a] in/into[b] (the) land of-the promise[c] as[d] (a) foreigner/ in-a-foreign-land,[e]

LEXICON—a. aorist act. indic. of παροικέω (LN 85.71, **85.78**) (BAGD 1.c. p. 628): 'to sojourn' [LN (85.78); KJV, NAB, NJB], 'to migrate' [BAGD, WBC], 'to dwell temporarily, to be a foreigner' [LN (85.71)], 'to live as a foreigner' [LN (85.78)], 'to live as an alien' [NASB], 'to live as a stranger' [Mil], 'to live as an outsider' [Lns], 'to stay for a time' [NRSV], 'to make one's home' [NIV], 'to take up residence' [NIC], 'to live' [LN **(85.78)**; CEV, TEV], 'to settle' [HNTC; REB, TNT], 'to reach' [NLT]. The meaning is to dwell temporarily [NTC, TH, Wst], dwell as an alien [EBC, Hu, NIC, NIGTC], dwell as a stranger [Alf, Lg, My, NTC, TNTC] alongside the citizens of the country [Mil]; it means to migrate [WBC]. The aorist tense refers to his life as a whole [Mil].

b. εἰς with accusative object (LN 83.13, 84.22) (BAGD 9.a. p. 230): 'in' [BAGD, HNTC, LN (83.13), Lns, Mil, NIC; all versions except NLT], 'into' [LN (84.22)], 'to' [with παροικέω 'to migrate' [BAGD (1.c. p. 628), WBC], not explicit [NLT]. Here this word implies having entered into and now dwelling in [Blm, EGT, Lg, My], migrated to [NIC].

c. ἐπαγγελία (LN 33.280, 33.288) (BAGD 2.a. p. 280): 'promise' [BAGD, HNTC, LN (33.288), Lns; KJV, NASB], 'agreement' [LN (33.280)]. This noun is also translated as an adjective: 'promised (land)' [BAGD, WBC; CEV, NAB, NIV, NJB]. The phrase τῆς ἐπαγγελίας 'of the promise' is translated 'which had been promised him' [REB], 'which he had been promised' [NIC], 'he had been promised' [NRSV], 'that God promised'

[Mil], ‘that God had promised him’ [NLT, TEV], ‘which God had promised to him’ [TNT].

d. ὡς (LN 64.12; **85.78**) (BAGD III.1.a. p. 898): ‘as’ [BAGD, HNTC, LN (64.12), Lns, Mil, WBC; CEV, KJV, NAB, NASB, NRSV, REB, TEV], ‘like’ [LN (64.12); NIV, NLT, TNT], ‘as though’ [LN (85.78), NIC; NJB].

e. ἀλλότριος (LN 11.74) (BAGD 1.a. p. 40): ‘foreigner’ [LN; NLT, TEV], ‘in a foreign land’ [NASB, NRSV], ‘alien’ [REB], ‘stranger’ [LN; CEV], ‘a stranger in a foreign land’ [TNT], ‘a stranger in a foreign country’ [NIV], ‘a stranger in a strange country’ [HNTC]. This is also translated as a descriptive phrase: ‘in a strange country’ [KJV], ‘in a foreign country’ [NAB], ‘to a foreign land’ [WBC], ‘in a land not his own’ [Mil], ‘not his own’ [Lns]; as an adjective: ‘foreign’ [BAGD]. The phrase ὡς ἀλλοτρίαν ‘as a foreigner’ is translated ‘as though he were a foreigner’ [LN (85.78)], ‘as though it were not his’ [NJB], ‘as though it belonged to others’ [NIC].

QUESTION—How are the two nouns related in the genitive construction γῆν τῆς ἐπαγγελίας ‘land of the promise’?

The genitive noun τῆς ἐπαγγελίας ‘of the promise’ describes the land [BAGD, Mil, NIC, WBC; all versions except KJV, NASB], the land which was attached to the promises [Wst]: the land promised (to him). The noun γῆν ‘land’ without a definite article is made definite by the defining genitive τῆς ἐπαγγελίας ‘of the promise’ [Mil].

QUESTION—What relationship is indicated by the definite article in the noun phrase τῆς ἐπαγγελίας ‘of the promise’?

1. It implies a definite promise previously given [Alf, Lns]: of the (previous) promise.
2. The definite article is not translated [HNTC; KJV, NASB]: of promise.

QUESTION—What relationship is indicated by the phrase ὡς ἀλλοτρίαν ‘as a foreigner/as in a foreign land’?

1. It describes the manner of Abraham’s dwelling (the actual quality [BAGD]) [Alf, BAGD, Blm, EBC, EGT, Lg(K), Lns, Mil, NIC, NIGTC, TH, TNTC; KJV, NAB, NASB, NJB, NRSV]: he sojourned as in a foreign land, a land not his own.
2. It describes Abraham’s personal situation [Hu, Hwt, ICC, Lg; CEV, NLT, REB, TEV, TNT]: he sojourned as a foreigner.
3. It tells where Abraham went [WBC]: as to a foreign land.

living[a] in[b] tents[c] with[d] Isaac and Jacob the fellow-heirs[e] of-the same promise;[f]

LEXICON—a. aorist act. participle of κατοικέω (LN 85.69) (BAGD 1.a. p. 424): ‘to live’ [BAGD, HNTC, LN, WBC; CEV, NIV, NJB, NLT, NRSV, REB, TEV, TNT], ‘to dwell’ [BAGD, LN, Mil; KJV, NAB, NASB], ‘to reside’ [BAGD, LN], ‘to settle down’ [BAGD]. The phrase ἐν σκηναῖς κατοικήσας ‘living in tents’ is translated ‘he became a tent-dweller' [NIC]. It implies settling down [EBC], permanent dwelling [NTC]; it means temporary residence [NIGTC].

b. ἐν with dative object (LN 83.13): 'in' [HNTC, LN, Mil, WBC; all versions].

c. σκηνή (LN **7.9**) (BAGD p. 754): 'tent' [BAGD, HNTC, LN, Mil, NIC, WBC; all versions except KJV], 'tabernacle' [KJV]. It implies a temporary dwelling [EBC].

d. μετά with genitive object (LN 89.108): 'with' [HNTC, LN; KJV, NAB, NASB, NJB, REB], 'along with' [Mil], 'together with, in the company of' [LN], 'as did' [NIC, WBC; NIV, NRSV, TEV, TNT], 'and so did' [CEV, NLT]. This word means 'with' [TH]; it implies similarity of circumstances and motive, not the same time as [Blm].

e. συγκληρνόμος (LN 57.134) (BAGD p. 774): 'fellow heir' [BAGD, LN, Mil, NIC; NASB], 'joint heir with someone' [WBC], 'heir with someone' [KJV, NIV, NJB, NRSV, REB], 'heir' [NAB], 'receiver' [LN], 'one who also receives' [LN], 'who shared' [HNTC], 'who received from God' [TEV]. The phrase τῶν συγκληρονόμων τῆς ἐπαγγελίας τῆς αὐτῆς 'the fellow heirs of the same promise' is translated 'to whom God had also made the same promise' [TNT], 'to whom God gave the same promise' [NLT], 'who were later given the same promise' [CEV].

f. ἐπαγγελία (LN 33.280, 33.288) (BAGD 2.c. p. 280): 'promise' [HNTC, LN (33.288), Mil, NIC, WBC; all versions], 'promise' or 'what was promised' [BAGD], 'agreement' [LN (33.280)].

QUESTION—Why is this phrase mentioned?

It refers to the fact that they did not build permanent abodes for themselves [Alf, Blm, EGT, GNC, HNTC, Hu] because all three patriarchs awaited the same promise [Alf, WBC]; building a house would have implied owning the land [Blm].

QUESTION—What relationship is indicated by the participle κατοικήσας 'living'?

The aorist tense indicates an action at the same time as the preceding aorist verb παρῴκησεν 'he sojourned' [Alf].

1. It states a separate action [NIC; NIV, TEV, TNT]: he sojourned . . . ; he lived in tents.
2. It states the circumstance of the verb παρῴκησεν 'he sojourned' [Mil, WBC]: he sojourned in the circumstance of living in tents.

QUESTION—What relationship is indicated by the phrase ἐν σκηναῖς κατοπικήσας 'living in tents'?

It implies temporariness in contrast with living in a house [Blm, EGT, GNC, HNTC, Hu, Hwt, ICC, Lns, TNTC, WBC, Wst].

QUESTION—How are the two nouns related in the genitive construction τῶν συγκληρονόμων τῆς ἐπαγγελίας 'the joint heirs of the promise'?

'The promise' tells what they were to receive [Mil, NIGTC, TH; REB, TEV, TNT]: heirs to the promise.

11:10 for he-was-waiting-for[a] the city the-(one) having the foundations,[b]

LEXICON—a. imperf. mid. (deponent = act.) of ἐκδέχομαι (LN 30.53, 85.60) (BAGD p. 238): 'to wait for' [BAGD, LN (85.60); CEV, TEV, TNT], 'to await' [LN (85.60)], 'to keep awaiting' [Lns], 'to expect' [BAGD, LN (30.53)], 'to look for' [Mil; KJV, NASB], 'to look forward to' [HNTC, NIC; NAB, NIV, NJB, NRSV, REB], 'to look forward with certainty to' [WBC], 'to look forward confidently to' [NLT]. The prefixed preposition ἐκ- makes the verb intensive [Alf, Hu], adding the idea of certainty [WBC]; it indicates forward direction [NTC]. This word means to wait for [EGT], to look forward to [NIGTC, TH], to expect [BAGD, LN]. The imperfect tense implies continuation in past time [Lg(K), Lns, Mil, NTC, WBC].

b. θεμέλιος (LN 7.41, 7.43) (BAGD 1.b. p. 355): 'foundation' [BAGD, HNTC, LN (7.41), Lns, Mil; KJV, NAB, NASB, NIV, NRSV, REB], 'foundation stone' [LN (7.43)], 'eternal foundations' [NLT], 'permanent foundations' [TEV], 'real foundations' [TNT], 'the true foundations' [NIC]. This noun is also translated as an adjective modifying 'city': 'well-founded' [NJB], 'eternal' [CEV]. It implies permanency [Lns, NIC, WBC]. It means that the city has permanent foundations, more than earthly ones [EBC]. It contrasts with tents, which do not have foundations [EGT, Hu, Lns, My, NIGTC, Wst]. The plural, used here, has no difference in meaning from the singular; nor does the masculine form, used here, differ in meaning from the neuter θεμέλιον 'foundation' [NIGTC].

QUESTION—What relationship is indicated by γάρ 'for'?

It indicates the reason that Abraham lived in the land of promise as a foreigner [Alf, Blm, EBC, GNC, Hu, Mil, My, NIC, NIGTC, WBC, Wst; NLT].

QUESTION—What is the function of the definite article with τὴν πόλιν 'the city'?

1. It makes 'city' definite [Alf, Blm, EBC, EGT, HNTC, Hu, Lg(K), Lns, Mil, NIC, WBC; all versions except KJV, REB]: the city. It refers to the heavenly Jerusalem [Alf, Blm, EBC, EGT, GNC, HNTC, Hu, Hwt, Lg, Lns, My, NIC, NIGTC, WBC].
2. It is omitted from the translation [KJV, NLT, REB]: a city.

QUESTION—What is the function of the definite article in the phrase τούς θεμελίους 'the foundations'?

1. It implies definite foundations [Alf, EGT, Lns, Mil, My, NIC, Wst] which tents did not have [ICC, My]: having the foundations. It implies the true foundations [NIC]; it refers to the foundations of the heavenly city [Alf]. It makes the noun emphatic, implying the eternal foundations [Hu, WBC] appropriate for a city designed by God [WBC].
2. This article is not translated [Blm, HNTC; all versions except NJB]: having foundations.

whose designer[a] and builder[b] (is) God.

LEXICON—a. τεχνίτης (LN 42.53) (BAGD p. 814): 'designer' [WBC; NAB], 'builder' [KJV], 'craftsman' [LN], 'architect' [BAGD, Lns, Mil, NIC; NASB, NIV, NRSV, REB], 'maker' [HNTC]. This noun is also translated as a verb with God as subject: 'to design' [TEV], 'to plan' [CEV]; with the city as subject: 'to be designed' [NJB, NLT, TNT]. It indicates the designer [EBC], the architect [Lg(K)], the planner [Lg, TNTC, Wst].

b. δημιουργός (LN **45.8**) (BAGD p. 179): 'builder' [LN, Mil, NIC; NASB, NIV, NRSV, REB], 'creator' [BAGD; WBC], 'designer' [HNTC], 'craftsman' [BAGD], 'erecter' [Lns], 'maker' [BAGD; KJV, NAB]. This noun is also translated as a verb with God as subject: 'to build' [CEV, TEV]; with the city as subject: 'to be built' [NJB, NLT], 'to be made' [TNT]. It refers to one who does the actual work [EBC], the maker [EGT], the builder [Lg(K)], the one who carries out the plans [Lg, TNTC, Wst].

QUESTION—What relationship is indicated by this clause?

The definite article with 'God', ὁ θεός, shows that 'God' is the subject of the clause, and τεχνίτης 'designer' and δημιουργός 'builder' without the article are predicates [Lns]. 'God' is emphatic by its word order [NIGTC, WBC].

1. It is nonrestrictive, making an added statement concerning the city already identified by the preceding reference [HNTC, Lns, Mil, NIC; all versions except CEV, TEV]: the city which has foundations, whose designer and builder is God.
2. It is restrictive, serving to identify the city [CEV, TEV]: the city that God designed and built.
3. It expresses cause [WBC]: the city has eternal foundations because its designer and builder is God.

11:11 By-faith Sarah also herself barren[a] (she/he)-received[b] ability[c] for[d] deposition[e] of-seed[f] even beyond[g] (the) time[h] of-age,[i]

TEXT—Instead of καὶ αὐτὴ Σάρρα στεῖρα 'Sarah also herself barren', some manuscripts read καὶ αὐτὴ Σάρρα στεῖρα οὖσα 'Sarah also herself being barren', some read καὶ αὐτὴ Σάρρα ἡ στεῖρα 'Sarah also herself the barren one' (some with a change of word order), and some read καὶ αὐτὴ Σάρρα 'Sarah also herself', all of which are in the nominative case. GNT reads καὶ αὐτὴ Σάρρα στεῖρα 'Sarah also herself barren' with a C decision, indicating that the Committee had difficulty deciding between the readings. Καὶ αὐτὴ Σάρρα 'Sarah herself also' is read by Alf, Blm, EGT, HNTC, ICC, My, Wst, CEV, KJV, NAB, NASB, NJB, REB; καὶ αὐτὴ Σάρρα στεῖρα 'Sarah also herself barren' or καὶ αὐτὴ Σάρρα στεῖρα οὖσα 'Sarah also herself being barren' is read by Mil, NIC, TH, WBC; NIV, NLT, NRSV, TEV, TNT; a conjecture, καὶ αὐτῇ Σάρρᾳ 'with Sarah herself', assuming that αὐτή 'herself' is actually the dative αὐτῇ and that Σάρρα 'Sarah' is either indeclinable or else is the dative Σάρρᾳ, is read by EBC, Lns, and NIGTC, although the dative form is supported by no reported manuscript [HNTC] nor by any ancient Church Father [Hu].

TEXT—Some manuscripts add ἔτεκεν 'she gave birth' at the end of this clause. GNT does not deal with this variant. 'She gave birth' is added by only KJV.

LEXICON—a. στεῖρα (LN 23.56) (BAGD p. 766): 'barren' [BAGD, LN, Mil, NIC; NIV, NLT, NRSV], 'sterile' [WBC], 'not able to bear children' [LN], 'incapable of bearing children' [BAGD], 'unable to have children' [TEV, TNT]; this word is omitted by Alf, Blm, EBC, EGT, HNTC, ICC, Lns; CEV, KJV, NAB, NASB, NJB, REB.

b. aorist act. indic. of λαμβάνω (LN 57.125): 'to receive' [HNTC, LN, Lns, Mil, NIC; KJV, NAB, NASB, NRSV, TNT], 'to accept' [LN]. The phrase δύναμιν ἔλαβεν 'received ability' is translated 'to be enabled' [WBC; NIV, REB], 'to be made able' [NJB], 'to make able' [TEV], 'to be able' [NLT], not explicit [CEV]. The source of the receiving was God [ICC, NIGTC] by indirect reverential reference [NIGTC].

c. δύναμις (LN 74.1): 'ability' [LN, Lns; NASB], 'capability' [LN], 'strength' [Mil; KJV], 'power' [HNTC, NIC; NAB, NRSV, TNT].

d. εἰς with accusative object (LN 89.57, 90.23): 'for' [Lns], 'for the purpose of' [LN (89.57)], 'concerning' [LN (90.23)], 'with respect to' [LN (90.23)], 'with reference to' [LN (90.23)]. It indicates direction [Alf].

e. καταβολή (LN **23.49**) (BAGD 1. p. 409): 'deposition'. This noun is translated as a verb: 'to project' [Lns]. The phrase εἰς καταβολὴν σπέρματος 'for deposition of seed' is translated 'to conceive' [HNTC, LN; NAB, NASB, NJB, REB, TNT], 'to conceive seed' [KJV], 'to implant seed' [Mil], 'of procreation' [NRSV], 'to beget a child' [NIC], 'to have a child' [NLT], 'to have a son' [CEV], 'to become a father' [WBC; TEV], 'to establish a posterity' [BAGD].

f. σπέρμα (LN 10.29) (BAGD 1.b. p. 761, 2.b. p. 762): 'seed' [BAGD, Lns, Mil; KJV], 'offspring' [LN], 'descendents, children, posterity' [BAGD].

g. παρά with accusative object (LN 78.29) (BAGD III.3. p. 611): 'beyond' [LN; NASB], 'instead of' [BAGD], 'rather than' [BAGD], 'contrary to' [Lns]. The phrase καὶ παρὰ καιρὸν ἡλικίας 'even beyond the time of age' is translated 'in spite of being past the age' [NJB], 'and that although past the time of life' [HNTC], 'even after the natural season of life' [NIC], 'and was in any case past the time of life' [TNT], 'and past the normal age of child-bearing' [WBC], 'and when she was past age' [KJV], 'though she was past the age' [NAB, REB], 'even though he was past age' [Mil; NIV], 'even though he was too old' [TEV], 'though he was too old' [NRSV], 'even though they were too old' [NLT], 'even when Sarah was too old to have children' [CEV]. This preposition here implies inconsistency with or contrary to [Alf].

h. καιρός (LN 67.78) (BAGD 3. p. 395): 'time' [LN; TNT], 'proper time' [NASB], 'definite time' [BAGD], 'fixed time' [BAGD]. The phrase καιρὸν ἡλικίας 'time of age' is translated 'age-period' [Lns].

i. ἡλικία (LN **67.156**) (BAGD 1.c.α. p. 345): 'age' [BAGD], 'life' [NASB, TNT], 'time of life' [BAGD]; the phrase καὶ παρὰ καιρὸν ἡλικίας 'even beyond the time of age' is translated 'though she was past her prime' [LN].

QUESTION—For those who read στεῖρα 'barren', what relationship is indicated by the phrase καὶ αὐτὴ Σάρρα στεῖρα 'Sarah herself also barren' ?

1. It is a Hebraic circumstantial clause, stating a concession [WBC; NLT, TNT]: although Sarah was barren.
2. It states an additional circumstance to Abraham's age [NIV, NRSV, TEV]: and Sarah was barren.

QUESTION—What relationship is indicated by the phrase καὶ αὐτή 'also herself'?

It is emphatic [Lg, My, TH].

1. It indicates a contrast with Sarah's former incredulity at the promise that she would have a child [Blm, EGT, Hwt, Lg, My, NIC, Wst].
2. It emphasizes her physical condition [ICC]: even in her physical condition.
3. It indicates a transition to and prominence of a new subject [Alf].
4. It is not translated [NAB, NJB].

QUESTION—Who is the implied actor of ἔλαβεν 'she/he received'?

1. The actor is Sarah [Alf, EGT, HNTC, Hu, Hwt, ICC, LN, TNTC; CEV, KJV, NAB, NASB, NJB, REB, TNT]: Sarah received ability.
2. The actor is Abraham [EBC, GNC, Lns, Mil, NIC, TH, WBC; NIV, NRSV, TEV]: Abraham received ability. (This requires that the phrase concerning Sarah be a "nominative absolute," which has no parallel in Hebrews and few, if any, parallels in the entire NT.)
3. The actors are both [NLT]: 'Sarah together with Abraham was able to have a child'.

QUESTION—To whom does the phrase εἰς καταβολὴν σπέρματος 'for deposition of seed' refer?

1. Translated as above [Alf, EBC, EGT, ICC], it properly leaves open the actor to be supplied.

1.1 It refers to the act of deposition of seed in Sarah's body [Alf, EGT, ICC]: the deposition of seed (in Sarah's body by Abraham). It indicates causing the deposited seed to develop [Alf].

1.2 It refers to Abraham's deposition of seed together with Sarah [EBC, Lns; NLT] (reading αὐτή as the dative αὐτῇ 'with her') [EBC, Lns]: the deposition of seed (by Abraham with Sarah).

1.3 It refers to the act of conception [Blm].

1.4 It refers to founding a posterity [My].

2. It is translated with the sense of an infinitive, 'to lay down seed' [BAGD, GNC, HNTC, LN, Mil, NIC, WBC; all versions], which therefore erroneously requires that the actor be the same person as the subject of the preceding verb.

2.1 Sarah is the actor [Blm, EGT, HNTC, Wst; KJV, NAB, NASB, NJB, REB, TNT].

2.1.1 It refers to her power to conceive [Blm, EGT, HNTC; KJV, NAB, NASB, NJB, REB, TNT]: power for Sarah to conceive.

2.1.2 It refers to power for founding a posterity [BAGD, Hu, Hwt]: power to found a posterity.

2.2 Abraham is the actor [GNC, Mil, NIC, TH, WBC; NIV, NRSV, TEV]: power for Abraham to lay down seed.

QUESTION—To whom does καὶ παρὰ καιρὸν ἡλικίας 'even beyond the time of age' refer to?

It refers to the age proper for the deposition of seed [Alf]. It expresses a concession [Mil].

1. It refers to Sarah [Alf, EGT, HNTC, Hu, ICC, Lg(K), TNTC, WBC, Wst; CEV, KJV, NAB, NASB, NJB, REB, TNT]: even though Sarah was beyond the time of age. It further emphasizes Sarah's faith [EGT].
2. It refers to Abraham [EBC, Lns, Mil, NIC; NIV, NRSV, TEV]: even though Abraham was beyond the time of age.
3. It refers to both Sarah and Abraham [GNC; NLT]: even though both were beyond the time of age.

since (she/he)-considered[a] faithful[b] the-(one) having-promised.[c]

LEXICON—a. aorist mid. (deponent = act.) of ἡγέομαι (LN 31.1) (BAGD 2. p. 343): 'to consider' [BAGD, LN, Lns, Mil, WBC; NASB, NIV, NRSV], 'to regard' [HNTC, LN], 'to think' [LN; NAB], 'to reckon' [NIC], 'to know' [TNT], 'to judge' [KJV, REB], 'to believe' [NJB, NLT], 'to have faith' [CEV], 'to trust' [TEV].

b. πιστός (LN 31.87) (BAGD 1.a.α. p. 664, 1.aβ. p. 664): 'faithful' [LN, Lns, Mil, WBC; KJV, NASB, NIV, NJB, NRSV], 'trustworthy' [BAGD, HNTC, LN, NIC], 'worthy of trust' [NAB], 'dependable, reliable' [LN]. This adjective is also translated as a verb phrase: 'to keep faith' [REB], 'to do what one has promised' [CEV], 'to keep one's promise' [NLT, TEV]. The phrase πιστὸν ἡγήσατο 'she/he considered faithful' is translated 'she knew she could trust him' [TNT]. It is emphatic by word order [NIGTC, WBC].

c. aorist mid. (deponent = act.) of ἐπαγγέλλομαι (LN 33.286) (BAGD 1.b. p. 281): 'to promise' [BAGD, HNTC, LN; CEV, KJV, NASB, NRSV, REB, TNT], 'to make a promise' [Lns, WBC; NAB, NIV, NJB], 'to give a promise' [Mil, NIC]. The phrase τὸν ἐπαγγειλάμενον 'the one having promised' is translated 'his promise' [NLT, TEV]. The aorist tense refers to the repeated promises considered as a single event [NIGTC].

QUESTION—Why is this clause mentioned?

It expresses the reason for the preceding comment [Mil].

QUESTION—Who is the actor of the verb ἡγήσατο 'she/he considered'? (See the preceding clause.)

1. The actor is Sarah [Alf, EGT, HNTC, ICC, TNTC; CEV, KJV, NAB, NASB, NJB, REB, TNT]: Sarah considered.

2. The actor is Abraham [EBC, GNC, Lns, Mil, NIC, NIGTC, TH, WBC; NIV, NLT, NRSV, TEV]: Abraham considered.

QUESTION—Who is the actor of τὸν ἐπαγγειλάμενον 'the one having promised'?

The one who promised is God [Alf, EBC, GNC, ICC, Lns, Mil, NIGTC, TH, TNTC, WBC; CEV, NAB, NASB, NLT, REB, TNT].

11:12 Wherefore also/even from[a] one-man[b] there-were-begotten,[c]

TEXT—Instead of ἐγεννήθησαν 'there were begotten' some manuscripts read ἐγενήθησαν 'there became'. GNT does not deal with this variant. Due to similarity of meaning of these two words, it cannot be stated with certainty which word some versions and commentaries read; ἐγεννήθησαν 'there were begotten' is probably or certainly read by Blm, Lns, Mil, TH, WBC, Wst; NASB, NRSV, and ἐγενήθησαν 'there became' by Alf, BAGD, HNTC, ICC, Lg, My, NIC, and by all versions except NASB, NRSV.

LEXICON—a. ἀπό with genitive object (LN 90.15) (BAGD V.4. p. 88): 'from' [BAGD, HNTC, LN, Lns, Mil, NIC, WBC; all versions except CEV, KJV, NASB], 'by' [LN], 'of' [KJV, NASB], not explicit [CEV].

b. εἷς (LN 60.10): 'one man' [HNTC, Mil, NIC; NAB, NASB, NJB, REB, TNT], 'this one man' [WBC; NIV, NLT, TEV], 'one person' [NRSV], 'one' [LN, Lns; KJV], not explicit [CEV]. It implies 'from one person only' [Blm, EBC, Mil], namely Abraham [Blm, EBC, EGT, Hu, ICC, Lns, My, NIC, NIGTC, Wst]. 'One' here is contrasted with the following reference to the multitude of descendants [TNTC, WBC].

c. aorist pass. indic. of γεννάω (LN 23.58) (BAGD 1.a. p. 155): 'to be begotten' [BAGD, LN, Lns], 'to be born' [Mil, WBC; NASB, NRSV]; probably reading γίνομαι (ἐγενήθησαν) 'to become': 'to spring' [KJV], 'to spring (offspring)' [NIC], 'to spring (descendants)' [REB], 'to come (descendants)' [HNTC; NIV, NJB, NLT, TEV, TNT], 'to come forth (descendants)' [NAB]. The phrase ἀφ' ἑνὸς ἐγεννήθησαν 'from one man there were begotten' is translated 'he became the ancestor of many people' [CEV]. The subject of this verb is the descendants implied in the rest of the verse [Alf, EGT].

QUESTION—What relationship is indicated by διό 'wherefore'?

It indicates the result of the faith mentioned in the preceding verse [Alf, EBC, EGT, Hu, Lns, Mil, My, NIGTC, NTC, WBC, Wst].

1. It shows the importance of Sarah's faith [EGT, My, TNTC, Wst].
2. It shows the importance of Abraham's faith [EBC, Mil, NIGTC, NTC].
3. It shows the importance of the faith of both Sarah and Abraham [Alf].

QUESTION—What relationship is indicated by καί 'even/also'?

It indicates that the result stated is self-evident [Mil].

and these-things[a] (from)-(one)-dead,[b]

LEXICON—a. neuter plural of οὗτος (LN 92.29) (BAGD 1.b.γ. p. 597): 'this' [LN], 'that' [Lns], 'that too' [Mil], 'him in this respect' [HNTC; NIV]. This neuter plural ταῦτα 'these things' is translated 'this one' [NRSV], 'he' [WBC], 'him' [KJV], 'him at that' [NASB], 'at that' [BAGD], 'who was himself' [NAB], 'one who' [NIC], 'although' [BAGD]. The phrase καὶ ταῦτα 'and these things' is translated 'though' [TEV], 'a man' [REB], 'who was' [NLT, TNT]. This entire phrase is translated 'and one who already had the mark of death on him' [NJB], 'her husband Abraham was almost dead' [CEV]. The neuter plural used here, ταῦτα 'these things', has the same meaning as the singular τοῦτο 'this thing' [Alf, Blm] and implies 'this man' [Blm]; it is a collective plural [Alf]; the plural refers to two things, the deadness of Abraham and Sarah's unbelief and advanced age [My].

b. perf. pass. participle of νεκρόω (LN 68.48) (BAGD p. 535): 'to be made dead', 'to become dead' [HNTC, Lns], 'to be as good as dead' [BAGD, Mil, NIC; KJV, NAB, NASB, NIV, NRSV, REB, TNT], 'to be practically dead' [TEV], 'to be almost dead' [CEV], 'to be too old to have any children' [NLT], 'to be stopped completely' [LN], 'to be ceased completely' [LN]. It refers to being dead so far as begetting offspring is concerned [Blm, EBC, EGT, My, NIC, WBC], to being impotent [GNC, NIGTC], to being of advanced age [Hu]. The perfect tense implies a permanent condition [Lns, NTC], indicating that a miracle was required [Mil].

QUESTION—What relationship is indicated by the phrase καὶ ταῦτα 'and these things'?

1. It serves to emphasize the following participle νενεκρωμένου 'one dead' [Lg(K), NIGTC]: and indeed as good as dead.
2. It implies a concession [Lns, Mil, TH], indicating that the instance is a special one [Mil]: although as good as dead.

QUESTION—What relationship is indicated by the perfect participle νενεκρωμένου 'dead' ?

1. It is (indefinite) attributive, modifying ἑνός 'one man' [Lns, NIC, NTC; NAB, NJB, TNT]: one man who was as good as dead.
2. It is temporal [Mil]: when he was as good as dead.
3. It makes a statement concerning ἑνός 'one man' [Blm; KJV, NASB, NIV, NLT, NRSV, REB]: and he was as good as dead.
4. It expresses a concession [WBC; CEV, TEV]: although he was as good as dead.

just-as[a] the stars of-the heaven[b] in-the quantity[c]

LEXICON—a. καθώς (LN 64.14): 'just as' [LN], 'so many as' [KJV], 'as many as' [NASB], 'as many even as' [Lns], 'as' [NIV]. The phrase καθὼς τῷ πλήθει 'just as in the quantity' is translated 'just as many as' [Mil], 'as many as' [NRSV, TEV], 'as numerous as' [HNTC, NIC, WBC; NIV, NJB, REB, TNT], 'there are as many of them as there are' [CEV], 'a nation with so many people that, like . . .' [NLT]. This entire phrase and the following phrase are translated 'as numerous as the stars in the sky and the sands of the seashore' [NAB]. This word indicates equal measure [Lg(K)].

b. οὐρανός (LN **1.5**) (BAGD 1.c. p. 594): 'heaven' [BAGD, Lns, WBC; NASB, NJB, NRSV], 'heavens' [REB], 'sky' [HNTC, LN, Mil, NIC; CEV, KJV, NAB, NIV, NLT, TEV, TNT].

c. πλῆθος (LN **59.9**) (BAGD 1. p. 668): 'quantity' [BAGD], 'multitude' [LN, Lns, Mil; KJV], 'number' [BAGD, **LN**; NASB].

QUESTION—What is the function of this phrase?

It indicates the extent of the descendants [HNTC, Lns, Mil, NIC; all versions]: as numerous as the stars. It implies that they would be too many to count.

QUESTION—What is the significance of the definite article in the phrase τῷ πλήθει 'in the quantity'?

1. The definite article indicates reference to the descendants being discussed: the quantity of the descendants.
2. The article is not translated [Lns, Mil; KJV, NASB]: as many in quantity.

and as the innumerable[a] sand the-(one) alongside[b] the shore[c] of-the sea.

LEXICON—a. ἀναρίθμητος (LN **60.6**) (BAGD p. 60): 'innumerable' [BAGD, LN, Mil, WBC; KJV, NASB, NRSV], 'numberless' [TEV], 'unnumbered' [Lns, NIC], 'countless' [HNTC, **LN**; NIV, REB, TNT], 'beyond counting' [LN], not explicit [CEV]. This adjective is also translated as a phrase: 'which cannot be counted' [NJB], 'there is no way to count them' [NLT].

b. παρά with accusative object (LN 83.25) (BAGD III.1.d. p. 611): 'alongside' [LN], 'along' [Mil; CEV], 'beside' [LN], 'by' [LN; KJV, NASB, NRSV], 'on' [BAGD, HNTC, NIC, WBC; NIV, NJB, NLT, REB, TEV, TNT], 'at' [LN], 'of' [Lns].

c. χεῖλος (LN **1.62**) (BAGD 2. p. 879): 'shore' [BAGD, LN, Lns, Mil], 'bank' [BAGD]. The phrase τὸ χεῖλος τῆς θαλάσσης 'the shore of the sea' is translated 'the seashore' [HNTC, NIC, WBC; all versions except CEV], 'the beach' [CEV]. It means 'margin' [Blm].

QUESTION—Why is this phrase mentioned?

It expresses a further comparison [Alf] coordinated with the preceding phrase by καί 'and' [Mil]. It implies that they would be too many to count. It repeats the same point as the preceding phrase [Hu] and thus emphasizes the description [Lns].

QUESTION—What relationship is indicated by ἡ ἀναρίθμητος 'the innumerable' with the definite article?

1. It describes ἡ ἄμμος 'the sand' [Alf, HNTC, Lg(K); NJB, NRSV, REB, TEV]: the grains of sand which are innumerable.
2. The definite article is not translated.

2.1 It indicates the quantity of ἡ ἄμμος 'the sand' [Mil, NIC, WBC; NASB, NIV, TNT]: and as innumerable as the grains of sand.

2.2 It makes a statement concerning ἡ ἄμμος 'the sand' [Lns; KJV]: as the grains of sand are unnumbered.

DISCOURSE UNIT: 11:13–19 [Lg]. The topic is a further look at the Patriarchs, with special emphasis on Abraham's act of faith.

DISCOURSE UNIT: 11:13–16 [GNC, HNTC, NIC]. The topic is the transcendent nature of hope [GNC], seeking a better homeland [HNTC], the city of God as the homeland of the faithful ones [NIC].

11:13 In[a] faith these all died,

LEXICON—a. κατά with accusative object (LN 89.8): 'in' [HNTC, NIC; all versions except CEV, NIV, NLT], 'in accordance with' [LN], 'in accordance with the principle of' [WBC], 'in keeping with' [Lns], 'while still in the way of' [Mil]. The phrase κατὰ πίστιν 'in faith' is translated 'were still living by faith' [NIV], 'but they still had faith' [CEV], 'faithful (ones)' [NLT]. It means to be in keeping with [EGT], consistent with [Alf], in accordance with the principle of [GNC, Hu, Lg, My(D)], under the controlling influence of [GNC, TNTC, Wst].

QUESTION—Why are verses 11:13–16 mentioned?

These verses are an analysis of the tradition of faith, placed here in the middle of the list of examples [WBC]. They are an interpretation of the history of salvation, placed in a prominent position in the central part of the discussion [NIGTC]. They are an elaboration of 11:8–11 [GNC]. They explain more fully the faith of the persons mentioned [Lns, My(D)], developing the concept of the promise and of the city without foundations [NCBC], drawing a conclusion concerning the validity of faith [Mil], giving general observations concerning the faith of the patriarchs mentioned above [My, TNTC].

QUESTION—What relationship is indicated by the phrase κατὰ πίστιν 'in faith'?

This prepositional phrase is emphatic by its position [Hu, Lg(K), WBC].

1. It expresses the manner in which the persons faced death [Mil, NIGTC], whereas the dative πίστει 'by faith' used in other verses indicates means [NIGTC].
2. It is a stylistic difference [EBC, NCBC, NIC] to set this verse apart from the preceding and following datives πίστει 'by faith' [NCBC], but with no difference in meaning [EBC, NCBC, NTC].

QUESTION— To whom does οὗτοι πάντες 'these all' refer?

Πάντες 'all' is somewhat emphatic by its position [NIGTC].

1. It refers to the persons mentioned in the preceding verses [EBC, GNC, Lg, TH], but to all of them [EBC] except Enoch [Lg].
2. It refers only to the four persons mentioned in verses 8–12 [EGT, Hwt, ICC, My, NIC, NTC, WBC, Wst], especially the three patriarchs mentioned [ICC].
3. It refers only to Abraham, Isaac, and Jacob [Alf, Lns, Mil, NCBC].
4. It refers primarily to Abraham and secondarily to Jacob [NIGTC].

not having-received the promises

TEXT—Instead of λαβόντες 'having received' some manuscripts read κομισάμενοι and one manuscript reads προσδεξάμενοι, both of which can also be translated 'having received'. GNT does not deal with this variant. Λαβόντες is clearly read by Alf, Blm, EGT, Lg, Mil, My, NIC, NIGTC, NTC, WBC; κομισάμενοι is clearly read by GNC, Hu, ICC, Wst.

TEXT—Some manuscripts add καὶ πεισθέντες 'and having been persuaded' following ἰδόντες 'having seen'. GNT does not deal with this variant. Only KJV adds 'and having been persuaded'.

QUESTION—What relationship is indicated by the participial form λαβόντες (or the variant reading κομίσαντες) 'having received'?

1. It states an additional fact [HNTC, NIC; NAB, NIV, TEV, TNT]: they did not receive the promises.
2. It states an accompanying fact [NASB, NRSV]: without receiving the promises.
3. It is temporal [NJB]: before receiving the promises.
4. It states a concession [CEV, REB]: although they did not receive the promises.
5. It states a reason [Mil, Wst]: because they had not received the promises. It states one evidence of the faith mentioned [Mil].
6. It (reading κομίσαντες 'having received' [ICC]) indicates the conditions under which they died [Alf, ICC, Lg(K)]: they died under the conditions of not having received the promises.

QUESTION—What is meant by τὰς ἐπαγγελίας 'the promises'?

It means what was promised [Alf, HNTC, NIGTC, TH, WBC], the fulfillment of the promises [WBC], what was hoped for [GNC]. The promises concerned the possession of the land, the founding of a great nation, and the blessing which would come through Abraham's descendants [WBC]. The plural refers to the repetition of the promise at various times [Alf], the repetition to Abraham, Isaac, and Jacob, or to the various items contained in the promise [Lns].

but from-afar[a] having-seen and having-welcomed[b] them,

LEXICON—a. πόρρωθεν (LN **67.46, 83.31**) (BAGD p. 693): 'from afar' [HNTC, Mil, NIC; NAB], 'afar off' [Lns; KJV], 'from a long way off' [LN (**83.31**); TEV], 'from far away' [CEV], 'from a distance' [BAGD, WBC; NASB, NIV, NLT, NRSV], 'in the distance' [TNT], 'in the far distance' [NJB], 'far ahead' [REB], 'far ahead of time' [LN (67.46)], 'long before' [LN (**67.46**)].

b. aorist mid. (deponent = act.) participle of ἀσπάζομαι (LN 33.20, **34.55, 25.130**) (BAGD 2. p. 117): 'to welcome' [BAGD, HNTC, LN (**34.55**); NASB, NIV, NJB, NLT, REB, TEV, TNT], 'to salute' [Lns, WBC; NAB], 'to embrace' [KJV], 'to anticipate with pleasure, to look forward with happiness to what was going to happen' [LN (**25.130**)], 'to greet' [BAGD, LN (33.20), Mil, NIC; NRSV], 'to be glad (just to see)' [CEV].

It refers to welcoming joyfully [My], anticipating joyfully [Blm, ICC, TH] with assurance [ICC].

QUESTION—What relationship is indicated by this phrase?

It states a contrast with the preceding phrase [NIGTC, WBC].

QUESTION—What relationship is indicated by πόρρωθεν 'from afar'?

1. It relates to distance [Alf, BAGD, EGT, HNTC, Hwt, Lg(K), Lns, Mil, My, NIC, TH, TNTC, WBC, Wst; all versions except REB]: from a far distance.
2. It relates to time [LN (67.46), NIGTC; REB]: far ahead of time.

QUESTION—What is πόρρωθεν 'from afar' connected with?

1. It is connected with ἰδόντες 'having seen' [Hwt, Lns, Mil; KJV, NJB, NLT, REB, TNT]: having seen them from afar.
2. It is connected with both ἰδόντες 'having seen' and ἀσπασάμενοι 'having welcomed' [Alf, EGT, HNTC, Lg(K), My, NIC, WBC; NAB, NASB, NIV, NRSV, TEV]: having seen and welcomed from afar.

QUESTION—What relationship is indicated by the participial forms ἰδόντες 'having seen' and ἀσπασάμενοι 'having welcomed'?

The aorist tenses indicate actions prior to ἀπέθανον 'they died' [Lns]. They state additional facts [HNTC, Mil, NIC; NAB, NIV, NJB, NRSV, REB, TNT]: they saw and they welcomed. They give further evidence of the faith of the persons mentioned [Mil].

QUESTION—What relationship is indicated by ἰδόντες 'having seen'?

It refers to an inner awareness by faith of what the promises meant [EBC, Hu].

and having-acknowledged[a] that they-were strangers[b] and pilgrims[c] upon[d] the earth;

LEXICON—a. aorist act. participle of ὁμολογέω (LN 33.275) (BAGD 2. p. 568): 'to acknowledge' [NIC; NAB, REB], 'to acknowledge openly' [TNT], 'to admit' [BAGD, LN; NIV], 'to admit openly' [TEV], 'to agree' [CEV, NLT], 'to confess' [HNTC, LN, Lns, Mil, WBC; KJV, NASB, NRSV], 'to recognize' [NJB]. This confession was made by Abraham at Sarah's death [EGT, ICC, My, NIC, WBC, Wst] and a similar comment was made by Jacob to Pharaoh [ICC, My, NIC]. The aorist tense indicates action prior to ἀπέθανον 'they died' [Lns].

b. ξένος (LN 11.73) (BAGD 2.a. p. 548): 'stranger' [BAGD, HNTC, LN, Lns, Mil, WBC; all versions except NIV, NLT, TEV], 'foreigner' [LN; NLT, TEV], 'alien' [BAGD, NIC; NIV]. It refers to temporary foreign residents [HNTC], strangers [TH].

c. παρεπίδημος (LN 11.77) (BAGD p. 625): 'pilgrim' [Lns, NIC; KJV], 'sojourner' [Mil, WBC], 'nomad' [NJB, NLT], 'temporary resident' [LN], 'foreigner' [CEV, NAB, NRSV, TNT], 'alien' [HNTC, LN], 'alien without fixed abode' [REB], 'stranger' [LN; NIV], 'refugee' [TEV], 'exile' [BAGD; NASB]. It refers to resident aliens [TH], people living in a country to which they do not belong [EBC], people living in a country without rights of citizenship [HNTC]. This word combined with the preceding word ξένος 'stranger' form a hendiadys meaning 'sojourning stranger' [WBC].

d. ἐπί with genitive object (LN 83.46): 'upon' [LN, Mil], 'on' [HNTC, LN, Lns, NIC; all versions], 'in' [WBC].

QUESTION—What is this phrase connected with?

1. It is connected with the preceding part of this verse [HNTC, Lns, Mil, NIC, WBC; KJV, NASB, NIV, NJB, REB, TEV]: . . . and having acknowledged . . .
2. It is connected with the following clause [NAB, NRSV]: by acknowledging . . . they showed that they were seeking a homeland.

QUESTION—What relationship is indicated by the participial form ὁμολογήσαντες 'having acknowledged'?

1. It states an additional fact [HNTC, Mil; NIV, NRSV, REB, TEV, TNT]: they acknowledged. It gives further evidence of the faith of the persons mentioned [Mil].
2. It indicates means [NAB]: by acknowledging . . . , they made clear that they were seeking a homeland.

QUESTION—What relationship is indicated by the present tense εἰσιν translated as a past, 'they were'?

1. It is the indirect form of a statement whose direct form would be 'they are'; the tense of the direct form is retained in the Greek indirect form, but is rendered as a past tense in English.
2. It implies the permanent record of scripture [NIGTC].

QUESTION—What relationship is indicated by τῆς γῆς 'the earth'?

1. It refers to the planet Earth [BAGD, Blm, HNTC, Hu, Lns, NIC, NIGTC; all versions] in contrast to heaven [Blm].
2. It refers to the land in which they were living [EGT, Mil, WBC] as the inclusion of the definite article τῆς 'the' indicates [EGT]: in the land of Canaan.

11:14 for the-(ones) saying such-things make-clear[a] that they-are-seeking[b] (a) homeland.[c]

LEXICON—a. pres. act. indic. of ἐμφανίζω (LN 28.36) (BAGD 2. p. 257): 'to make clear' [BAGD, HNTC; NASB, NRSV, TEV, TNT], 'to make quite plain' [NJB], 'to declare plainly' [KJV], 'to show plainly' [REB], 'to make known' [BAGD], 'to make manifest' [Mil], 'to reveal, to disclose' [LN], 'to show' [NAB, NIV], 'to show clearly' [NIC], 'to show plainly' [WBC], 'to indicate' [Lns], 'it is clear' [CEV]. This verb is also translated as an adverb: 'obviously' [NLT]. The present tense is timeless [Lns]; it is an emphatic reference to a continuing attitude in present time [WBC].

b. pres. act. indic. of ἐπιζητέω (LN 25.9, 27.42) (BAGD 2.a. p. 292): 'to seek' [LN (27.42), Mil, NIC; KJV, NAB, NASB, NRSV], 'to seek earnestly' [Lns], 'to search for' [LN (27.42)], 'to be in search of' [NJB], 'to look for' [HNTC; CEV, NIV, REB, TEV, TNT], 'to look forward to'

[NLT], 'to expect intently' [WBC], 'to desire, to want' [LN (25.9)], 'to wish for' [BAGD]. It means to seek or desire earnestly [My]. It is emphatic by word order [NIGTC]. The present tense is timeless [Lns]; it refers to a habitual attitude [WBC]. The prefixed preposition ἐπι- indicates the direction of the seeking [Alf, EGT].

c. πατρίς (LN 1.81) (BAGD 1. p. 637): 'homeland' [BAGD, HNTC, LN, NIC; NAB, NJB, NRSV], 'homeland of one's own' [WBC; TNT], 'country of one's own' [Mil; NASB, NIV, REB, TEV], 'country' [KJV], 'fatherland' [BAGD, Lns], 'a place to call their own' [CEV], 'a country they can call their own' [NLT]. It refers to a homeland [Hu, NIGTC], an ancestral home [Lg(K)], a fatherland [EGT, GNC, TNTC, Wst], a native land [Lns, NIC], the country of one's origin [HNTC], a country of one's own [EBC, TH], a country for permanent abode [Blm]. It refers to heaven [ICC, NTC].

QUESTION—What relationship is indicated by γάρ 'for'?

1. It indicates the grounds for the preceding comment [Alf, Mil, My, Wst].

1.1 The comment that those mentioned finished their life 'in faith' [Alf, Mil, Wst].

1.2 The comment that those mentioned were strangers and pilgrims [My].

2. It introduces the conclusion from the preceding comment [EBC, EGT, ICC, Lns].

3. It indicates the conclusion from the patriarchs' comments that they were strangers and pilgrims on earth [NIGTC].

QUESTION—To whom does οἱ λέγοντες 'the ones saying' refer?

It refers to the persons who acknowledged that they were strangers and pilgrims [TH], primarily to Abraham and Jacob [NIGTC].

QUESTION—To what does τοιαῦτα 'such things' refer?

It refers to Abraham's and Jacob's comments that they were strangers and pilgrims [NIGTC].

11:15 And if on-the-one-hand they-were-thinking-of[a] that (homeland) from[b] which they-had-gone-out,

TEXT—Instead of the imperfect tense ἐμνημόνευον 'they were thinking', some manuscripts read the present tense μνημονεύουσιν 'they are thinking of'. GNT does not deal with this variant. Only NIC reads the present tense.

LEXICON—a. imperf. act. indic. of μνημονεύω (LN **29.8**) (BAGD 1.a. p. 525): 'to think of' [BAGD; NASB, NIV, NRSV, TNT], 'to keep thinking of' [**LN**], 'to keep thinking about' [LN; TEV], 'to think about again and again' [LN], 'to think back to' [NAB], 'to remember' [Lns], 'to be mindful of' [KJV], 'to have in mind' [HNTC], 'to mean' [BAGD, WBC; NJB, NLT], 'to refer to' [Mil], 'to talk about' [CEV]. The verb ἐμνημόνευον 'they were thinking of' is translated 'their thoughts had been with' [REB].

b. ἀπό with genitive object (LN 90.15): 'from' [HNTC, LN, Lns, Mil, WBC; KJV, NAB, NASB]. The phrase ἀφ' ἧς ἐξέβησαν 'from which they had gone out' is translated 'the one they had left' [NIC], 'they had left' [NIV, REB, TEV], 'they had left behind' [TNT], 'that they had left behind' [NRSV], 'they came from' [NJB, NLT], 'where they had once lived' [CEV].

QUESTION—What relationship is indicated by καί 'and'?

It introduces a further exposition of the preceding statement [Mil, NIGTC].

QUESTION—What relationship is indicated by this clause introduced by εἰ 'if' and the following clause?

1. It is a contrary-to-fact condition and consequence [HNTC, Lns, Mil, NIGTC, NTC, WBC; all versions]: if they were thinking of . . . (which they weren't), they would have opportunity to return (but they didn't return). It is actually a slightly irregular construction, since the apodosis (the second clause) would logically be "they would return." The imperfect tenses indicate that this is a *present* time contrary-to-fact condition, not past time [Lns] (Samuel G. Green, *Handbook to the Grammar of the Greek Testament*, §383,δ); it is related to the present tense ἐμφανίζουσιν 'they make clear' in the preceding verse, and the present tense is continued in v. 16.
2. The following interpretations relate this condition to the past tenses in 11:13 (which would require the aorist tenses in both clauses of this conditional expression). Some commentaries indicate that they are confused about this interpretation [Alf, Lg(K), NTC].

2.1 The imperfect tenses indicate a habitual condition in the past [Alf, EGT, ICC, Lg(K), My, NTC, WBC, Wst]: if they were continually thinking . . . , they would repeatedly have opportunity to return.

2.2 The construction is translated as if the verbs were aorist tense, indicating a condition prior to the time when they 'acknowledged' [HNTC, Mil, NCBC; all versions]: if they had been thinking . . . , they would have had opportunity to return.

3. Reading the present tense μνημονεύουσιν 'they are thinking of', this first clause states a present condition of fact; but it is translated as a past tense [NIC] (presumably to agree with the time of 11:13): they (are) were thinking of. . . .

QUESTION—What is meant by ἐμνημόνευον '(if) they were remembering'?

1. It refers to remembering their former home [Alf, EBC, Hu, ICC, NTC; KJV, TEV]: if they were thinking of their former home.
2. It means that πατρίδα 'homeland' in the preceding verse refers to their former home [BAGD, Lg, Mil, My, NIC, NIGTC, TH, WBC, Wst; CEV, NJB, NLT]: if they meant their former home.

QUESTION—To what does ἐκείνης 'that' refer?

It refers to πατρίδα 'homeland' in the preceding verse [Alf, EBC, EGT, Lns, Mil, NIC, WBC; all versions].

they-would-have opportunity[a] to-return;

LEXICON—a. καιρός (LN 22.45, 67.78) (BAGD 2.a. p. 395): 'opportunity' [BAGD, HNTC, LN (22.45), Lns, Mil, NIC, WBC; all versions except CEV, NLT, TEV], 'chance' [TEV], 'time' [LN (67.78)]. It refers to time [ICC], opportunity [NIGTC, TH]. This entire clause is translated 'they could have gone back at any time' [CEV], 'they would have found a way to go back' [NLT].

11:16 now on-the-other-hand they-long-for[a] (a) better (homeland), this is (a) heavenly (homeland).

LEXICON—a. pres. mid. indic. of ὀρέγω (LN **25.15**) (BAGD p. 579): 'to long for' [BAGD, Mil, NIC, WBC; NIV, NJB, REB, TEV], 'to long for eagerly' [**LN**], 'to be eager for' [HNTC], 'to desire' [KJV, NASB, NRSV], 'to aspire to' [LN, Lns], 'to strive to attain' [LN], 'to search for' [NAB], 'to reach out for' [TNT], 'to look for' [NLT], 'to look forward to' [CEV]. It implies a realistic hope based on God's promise [NIGTC]. The present tense indicates timelessness [WBC].

QUESTION—What relationship is indicated by νῦν 'now'?

It indicates logic, not time [Alf, Blm, EGT, ICC, Lg(K), Lns, My, NIGTC, WBC, Wst]: as the case now is.

QUESTION—To what do κρείττονος 'better' and ἐπουρανίου 'heavenly' refer?

They refer to πατρίδα 'homeland' in the preceding verses [Alf, EBC, HNTC, Hu, Lns, Mil, NIC, NIGTC, NTC, TH, TNTC, WBC; all versions]. The heavenly country is their homeland because it is the home of their heavenly Father [HNTC]; it is the same as the city of God [NIC].

Wherefore God is-not-ashamed-of[a] them, to-be-called[b] their God;

LEXICON—a. pres. mid. (deponent = act.) of ἐπαισχύνομαι (LN 25.193) (BAGD 3. p. 282): 'to be ashamed of' [HNTC, LN, Lns, Mil], 'to be ashamed' [BAGD, NIC, WBC; all versions]. The present tense implies that God now is not ashamed [Alf].

b. pres. pass. infin. of ἐπικαλέω (LN 33.131) (BAGD 1.b.α. p. 294): 'to be called' [BAGD, HNTC, LN, Lns, Mil, NIC, WBC; all versions except CEV, TEV], 'to be named' [LN]. The phrase αὐτοὺς θεὸς ἐπικαλεῖσθαι αὐτῶν 'them to be called their God' is translated 'for them to call him their God' [CEV, TEV]. It explains why God is not ashamed [ICC].

QUESTION—What relationship is indicated by διό 'wherefore'?

1. It introduces the result of the preceding comment [Blm, Mil, Wst] that the patriarchs were seeking a heavenly country [My].
2. It looks forward to the latter part of this verse [NIGTC]: the reason why God is not ashamed . . . is because he has prepared a city for them.

QUESTION—What is meant by οὐκ ἐπαισχύνεται 'he is not ashamed'?

It is a litotes, the negative implying a strong opposite affirmative [Blm, Hu, My]: he is very willing.

QUESTION—What relationship is indicated by αὐτούς 'them'?

1. It is the predicate of ἐπαισχύνεται 'he is ashamed of' [Alf, EGT, HNTC, Lns, Mil, My, Wst]: he is not ashamed of them, not ashamed to be called their God. The infinitive ἐπικαλεῖσθαι 'to be called' is the second predicate [Alf], giving further explanation [My, Wst].
2. It is translated as the subject of the passive infinitive ἐπικαλεῖσθαι 'to be called' but translated as active voice [CEV, TEV]: for them to call him their God.
3. It is not translated [ICC, NIC, WBC; all versions except CEV, TEV]; it is redundant, anticipating the following αὐτῶν 'their' [NIGTC]: he is not ashamed to be called their God.

QUESTION—What relationship is indicated by αὐτῶν 'their'?

It is emphatic by word order; it refers only to Abraham, Isaac, and Jacob and implies belonging to [NIGTC].

for he-has-prepared[a] (a) city for-them.

LEXICON—a. aorist act. indic. of ἑτοιμάζω (LN 77.3) (BAGD 3. p. 316): 'to prepare' [BAGD, LN, Lns, Mil, NIC; all versions except CEV, NJB, REB], 'to make ready' [HNTC, LN, WBC], 'to have ready' [REB], 'to put in readiness' [BAGD], 'to found' [NJB], 'to build' [CEV]. The aorist tense indicates that God has already prepared the city [EBC].

QUESTION—What relationship is indicated by γάρ 'for'?

It indicates the grounds for saying that God is not ashamed to be called their God [Alf, Blm, EGT, ICC, Mil, My, NIGTC, TH]. It is the evidence that God accepted the patriarchs [Wst], the explanation of the preceding comment [Lns].

QUESTION—To what does πόλιν 'city' refer?

It refers to the heavenly Jerusalem [My].

DISCOURSE UNIT: 11:17–22 [GNC, NIC]. The topic is Abraham's offering of Isaac, and the faith of Isaac, Jacob, and Joseph [GNC], more about the patriarchs' faith [NIC].

DISCOURSE UNIT: 11:17–19 [HNTC]. The topic is the testing of Abraham's faith.

11:17 By-faith Abraham offered-up[a] Isaac, being-tested,[b]

LEXICON—a. perf. act. indic. of προσφέρω (LN 57.80): 'to offer up' [HNTC, Mil, NIC; all versions except NIV, TNT], 'to offer up in sacrifice' [WBC], 'to sacrifice' [CEV], 'to offer as a sacrifice' [NIV, NLT, TEV], 'to offer' [Lns], 'to present to' [LN]. It means to offer up as a sacrifice [TH]. The perfect tense refers to the will or endeavor to offer up, and here the offering up is regarded as having the merit of the completed act [Blm]. It implies continuing results of the offering [Alf, Lns, TNTC, Wst] permanently recorded in scripture [Hwt, Lg(K), NIGTC]. The 'offering up' actually took place [Alf, Lg(K), NTC], it was complete from Abraham's point of view [EBC, HNTC, Hu, NIC, WBC, Wst]; the obedience was completed [Mil, My, NTC]. The perfect tense merely refers to a past act [EGT, ICC].

b. pres. pass. participle of πειράζω (LN 27.46) (BAGD 2.b. p. 640): 'to be tested' [HNTC, LN, Mil; CEV, NASB], 'to be put to the test' [BAGD, LN, NIC, WBC; NAB, NJB, NRSV, REB, TNT], 'to be tried' [BAGD, Lns; KJV]. This passive participle is translated as active voice: 'when God tested him' [NIV], 'when God was testing him' [NLT], 'when God put Abraham to the test' [TEV]. It means to be tested legitimately [Blm, My, NTC]. The actor was God [My, NIGTC, TH, WBC], as the passive voice implies [TH, WBC]. The test was that Abraham was commanded to put to death the son in whom the promises were to be fulfilled [EBC, EGT, HNTC, Hu, Hwt]. The present tense implies a continued period of testing [Mil], action at the same time as the verb προσενήνοχεν 'he offered up' [WBC, Wst].

QUESTION—What relationship is indicated by the participle πειραζόμενος 'being tested'?

It is temporal [Alf, Blm, EGT, Lns, Mil, My, NIC, WBC; all versions]: when he was tested.

and the only-(one)[a] he-was-offering-up,[b]

LEXICON—a. μονογενής (LN **58.52**) (BAGD p. 527): 'only' [BAGD, **LN**], 'only son' [HNTC, NIC, WBC; CEV, NAB, NJB, NLT, NRSV, REB, TEV, TNT], 'one and only son' [Mil; NIV], 'only begotten son' [KJV, NASB], 'only-begotten' [Lns], 'unique' [LN]. It implies being unique [EBC]; it means 'only' [EGT, My]; Ishmael is not considered [My, NIC, NIGTC]. Isaac was Sarah's only son [GNC, Hwt], the only son through whom the promises could be completed [GNC, HNTC, Hu, Hwt, My, NCBC, NIC, NTC, TNTC, WBC, Wst]. It is a synonym for 'beloved' [Hwt].

b. imperf. act. indic. of προσφέρω (LN 57.80) (BAGD 2.a. p. 719): 'to offer up' [HNTC; KJV, NASB], 'to be ready to offer up' [NRSV, TNT], 'to be on the point of offering up' [Mil, NIC], 'to be ready to offer' [REB], 'to be ready to sacrifice' [NAB, NLT], 'to be ready to offer as a sacrifice' [TEV], 'to be about to sacrifice' [NIV], 'to offer to sacrifice' [NJB], 'to try to sacrifice' [WBC], 'to offer' [BAGD, Lns], 'to present' [BAGD], 'to present to' [LN], not explicit [CEV]. The imperfect tense implies that the act of offering was begun [Alf, GNC, HNTC, Hu, Lg(K), Mil, My] but not completed [EBC, EGT, GNC, HNTC, Hu, ICC, Lg(K), Mil, NIC, Wst], was attempted [Hwt, NTC, WBC] or ready to be offered [Hwt, TNTC, Wst], was intended [NIGTC, TH, TNTC]. It focuses attention on the action [Lns].

QUESTION—What relationship is indicated by καί 'and'?

1. It expands the preceding clause [ICC, Lns, My, NIC, WBC] in a more specific restatement [NIGTC, WBC], to a climax [Alf, Mil]: indeed, his only son he was offering up.

2. It is translated as a concession to the following participial phrase [TEV, TNT]: yet he was ready to offer his only son.

the-(one) having-received[a] the promises,

LEXICON—a. aorist mid. (deponent = act.) participle of ἀναδέχομαι (LN **90.75**) (BAGD 1. p. 53): 'to receive' [BAGD, **LN**, Mil, NIC; all versions except CEV, NJB, TEV], 'to accept' [Lns, WBC], 'to experience' [LN]. The phrase ὁ ἀναδεξάμενος 'the one having received' is translated 'he who was the recipient of' [HNTC], 'even though he had yet to receive' [NJB]. This entire phrase is translated 'Abraham was the one to whom God had made the promise' [TEV], 'Abraham had been promised' [CEV]. This participle relates to experiencing the event of promising [LN]; it implies accepting and taking to oneself [Alf, Blm, Wst], to embrace in faith [My], to receive hospitably [EGT]. It implies a responsibility for carrying forward the fulfillment of the promises [HNTC, Hu, WBC, Wst].

QUESTION—To whom does this phrase refer?

It refers to Abraham [GNC, Lns, NIGTC, WBC; CEV, NJB, NLT, REB, TEV, TNT]: Abraham, the one who received the promises. This phrase increases the dramatic poignancy of the situation [Hu].

11:18 to/with-regard-to[a] whom it-was-spoken that/*quote* "In/through[b] Isaac descendants[c] shall-be-called[d] to-you,"

LEXICON—a. πρός with accusative object (LN 89.7, 90.25, 90.58): 'to' [LN (90.25, 90.58), Lns, Mil; NASB, NIV, TEV], 'with regard to' [LN (89.7)], 'of' [KJV, NAB, NRSV, REB], 'concerning' [NIC, WBC], 'about' [LN (90.25)]. The phrase πρὸς ὃν ἐλαλήθη 'to/with regard to whom it was spoken' is translated 'he had been told' [NJB], 'though he had been told' [TNT], 'although he had been told' [HNTC], 'Abraham had been promised' [CEV], 'though God had promised him' [NLT].

b. ἐν with dative object (LN 90.56) (BAGD III.3.a. p. 261): 'in' [NIC; KJV, NASB], 'through' [HNTC, Mil, WBC; NAB, NIV, NJB, NLT, NRSV, TEV, TNT], 'through the line of' [REB], 'in connection with' [Lns], 'in relation to, with respect to' [LN], 'because of, on account of' [BAGD], not explicit [CEV].

c. σπέρμα (LN 10.29) (BAGD 2.b. p. 761): 'descendants' [BAGD, HNTC, LN, WBC; NAB, NASB, NLT, NRSV, REB, TEV, TNT], 'children' [BAGD], 'offspring' [LN, NIC; NIV], 'posterity' [BAGD, LN], 'seed' [Lns; KJV]. The phrase κληθήσεταί σοι σπέρμα 'descendants shall be called to you' is translated 'that you are to have your descendants' [Mil], 'you will have the descendants I promised' [TEV], 'your name will be carried on' [NJB]; the phrase ὅτι κληθήσεταί σοι σπέρμα 'that/*quote* descendants shall be called to you' is translated 'that his descendants would come' [TNT], 'that Isaac would continue his family' [CEV]. It means descendants [NIGTC].

d. fut. pass. indic. of καλέω (LN 33.129, 33.131): 'to be called' [LN (33.129, 33.131), Lns, NIC; KJV, NAB, NASB], 'to be named' [HNTC, LN

(33.129, 33.131); NRSV], 'to be reckoned' [NIV], 'to be counted' [NLT], 'to be traced' [REB], not explicit [CEV]. The phrase κληθήσεταί σοι 'shall be called to you' is translated 'that you will have' [WBC].

QUESTION—What relationship is indicated by this clause?

1. It makes an additional comment concerning Isaac [Lns, NIC, WBC; all versions except NIV, TNT].
2. It indicates a concession [HNTC, Mil; NIV, TNT] concerning Abraham's obedience [Mil]: although it had been spoken to him.

QUESTION—To whom does the phrase πρὸς ὅν 'to/with regard to whom' refer?

1. It refers to Abraham [Alf, Blm, EGT, HNTC, ICC, Lns, Mil, My, NIGTC, TNTC, Wst; CEV, NASB, NIV, NJB, NLT, TEV, TNT]: it was spoken to Abraham.
2. It refers to Isaac [Lg(K), NIC, WBC; KJV, NAB, NRSV, REB]: it was spoken with respect to Isaac.

QUESTION—Who is the actor of ἐλαλήθη 'it was spoken'?

The speaker is God [Alf, Lns, NIGTC, WBC; CEV, NIV, NLT, TEV]: it was spoken by God.

QUESTION—What relationship is indicated by ὅτι?

1. It introduces a direct quotation and does not need to be translated into English [Alf, HNTC, ICC, Lns, Mil, My, NIC, NIGTC, WBC; NAB, NASB, NIV, NJB, NRSV, REB, TEV]: it was spoken, "In Isaac. . . ."
2. The quotation is translated as an indirect quotation, and ὅτι is translated as the introductory 'that' [CEV, NLT, TNT]: he had been told that. . . .
3. It is translated as a part of the quotation [KJV]: it was spoken, "That in Isaac. . . ."

QUESTION—What is the function of the quotation in this verse?

The quotation explains (emphasizes [WBC]) the nature of the promises referred to in v. 17 [TNTC, WBC]. It means that it is only through Isaac's descendants that Abraham's descendants will be counted [EBC, ICC, Lns, Mil, NIGTC, NIC, Wst; NLT], be known [Alf, EGT], be traced [REB]. It means that Abraham will have descendants [Blm, GNC, My, WBC; TEV]. It refers to Abraham's name being carried to future generations [NJB, NRSV]. The phrase ἐν 'Ισαάκ 'in Isaac' is emphatic by word order [EBC, Mil, My, Wst].

11:19 having-considered[a] that even from[b] (the) dead God (is/was) able to-raise[c] (people/him),

LEXICON—a. aorist mid. (deponent = act.) participle of λογίζομαι (LN 31.1) (BAGD 2. p. 476): 'to consider' [BAGD, LN, WBC; NASB, NRSV, TNT], 'to reckon' [HNTC, Mil, NIC; REB, TEV], 'to assume' [NLT], 'to be confident' [NJB], 'to be sure' [CEV], 'to account' [KJV], 'to draw a conclusion' [Lns], 'to reason' [NAB, NIV], 'to have an opinion, to be of an opinion, to hold a view' [LN]. It implies inward conviction [WBC].

The middle voice emphasizes Abraham as the actor [WBC]. The aorist tense implies one final action [WBC].

b. ἐκ with genitive object (LN 84.4) (BAGD 1.b. p. 234): 'from' [BAGD, HNTC, LN, Lns, Mil, NIC, WBC; KJV, NAB, NASB, NRSV, REB, TEV], 'away from' [BAGD], 'out from' [LN], 'out of' [BAGD, LN]. The phrase ἐκ νεκρῶν 'from the dead' is translated 'the dead to life' [TNT], 'people to life' [CEV], 'the dead' [NIV, NJB].

c. pres. act. infin. of ἐγείρω (LN 23.94) (BAGD 1.a.β. p. 214): 'to raise' [BAGD, HNTC; all versions except KJV], 'to raise up' [Lns, Mil, NIC, WBC; KJV], 'to raise to life, to make to live again' [LN]. The phrase καὶ ἐκ νεκρῶν ἐγείρειν δυνατός 'even from the dead is/was able to raise' is translated 'even to raise the dead' [NJB], 'could raise the dead' [NIV], 'if Isaac died, God was able to bring him back to life again' [NLT]. The present tense implies raising people in general [Alf, Mil], not merely raising Isaac [Alf, Mil]; it expresses a general truth [WBC].

QUESTION—What relationship is indicated by the participial form λογισάμενος 'having considered'?

1. It indicates the reason for Abraham's action [Alf, EBC, EGT, Hu, ICC, Mil, My, TNTC; CEV, REB]: because he considered. . . .
2. It states an additional fact [HNTC, NIC, WBC; all versions except CEV, KJV, REB]: he considered. . . .

QUESTION—What is the implied verb of the clause introduced by ὅτι 'that'?

1. The implied verb is present tense, with a general reference [Alf, EGT, Lg(K), Lns, Mil, My, NIGTC, Wst; NASB, NRSV]: God is able.
2. The implied verb is past tense [Hwt, ICC, NIC, WBC; CEV, KJV, NAB, NLT, TEV, TNT]: God was able.

2.1 The reference is general [ICC; CEV, NAB, TNT]: God was able to raise people.

2.2 The reference is to raising Isaac [Hwt, WBC; KJV, NLT, TEV].

QUESTION—What relationship is indicated by καί 'even'?

It is emphatic [NIGTC, WBC], emphasizing God's power [NIGTC].

QUESTION—What is the implied object of ἐγείρειν 'to raise'?

1. It is a general reference [EBC, EGT, HNTC, Lns, Mil, My, NIC, NIGTC, Wst; CEV, NAB, NASB, NIV, NJB, NRSV, REB, TNT]: to raise (people) from the dead.
2. It is 'him' [Blm, WBC; KJV], i.e. Isaac [GNC, TH, WBC; NLT, TEV]: to raise him from the dead.

from-which/therefore[a] even in[b] (a) parable[c] he-did-receive-back[d] him.

LEXICON—a. ὅθεν (LN 84.11) (BAGD 3. p. 555): 'from which' [LN; NASB], 'therefore' [BAGD], 'from where' [LN], 'from whence' [KJV], 'from among whom' [BAGD], 'and from death' [NIV], 'hence' [BAGD, Lns], 'and so' [NAB, NJB], 'and as a result' [HNTC], 'and' [NIC; NLT, NRSV, REB, TEV, TNT], 'for this reason' [Mil], 'because of this conviction' [WBC], not explicit [CEV].

b. ἐν with dative object (LN 33.17) (BAGD 1. p. 612): 'in' [HNTC, WBC; KJV, REB, TNT], 'in the way of' [Lns], 'as' [BAGD, NIC; NAB, NASB], also see c. below.

c. παραβολή (LN **33.17**) (BAGD 1. p. 612): 'parable' [Lns], 'figure' [KJV], 'figurative sense' [HNTC], 'type' [BAGD, NIC; NASB], 'foreshadowing' [WBC], 'symbol' [NAB], 'sense' [REB, TNT]. The phrase ἐν παραβολῇ 'in a parable' is translated 'so to speak' [**LN** (33.17); TEV], 'in a sense' [NLT], 'symbolically, allegorically, figuratively' [LN], 'figuratively speaking' [Mil; NIV, NJB, NRSV], 'this was like' [CEV].

d. aorist mid. indic. of κομίζω (LN 57.136) (BAGD 2.b. p. 443): 'to receive back' [BAGD, HNTC, LN, Mil, NIC, WBC; all versions except CEV, KJV, NJB], 'to receive' [KJV], 'to get back' [LN; CEV], 'to bring away' [Lns]. This verb is also translated as a passive voice: 'he was given back' [NJB]. It refers to Abraham's receiving Isaac at his birth [Wst]. The middle voice and the context exclude active effort by Abraham [NIGTC]; the middle voice of this verb implies recovering one's own possession [NTC, WBC].

QUESTION—What relationship is indicated by ὅθεν 'from which'?

1. It indicates source, from the dead [Alf, EGT, GNC, Lg, Wst; KJV, NASB], from death [NIV].
2. It expresses the result of Abraham's faith [Blm, HNTC, Hwt, ICC, Lns, Mil, My, NIGTC, NTC, WBC; NAB, NJB]: and as a result he received.
3. It states an additional fact [NIC; NLT, NRSV, REB, TEV, TNT]: and he received.

QUESTION—What relationship is indicated by the phrase ἐν παραβολῇ 'in a parable'?

1. It describes the manner in which he received him back [Alf, Blm, EBC, GNC, HNTC, Hu, Lg, LN, Mil, My(D), NTC, TH; NIV, NJB, NRSV, REB, TNT].

1.1 He received him back figuratively [EGT, HNTC, Hu, Lg, NTC], not actually from the dead, since he had not died [EGT].

1.2 He received him back in a manner of speaking [Blm, EBC, LN, Mil, TH; NIV, NJB, NRSV, REB, TNT].

1.3 He received him back by the sacrifice of the ram, the ram being the παραβολή 'parable' [Alf].

2. It means 'as a type' [BAGD, Hwt, ICC, Lns, My(D), NIC, NIGTC, WBC; NAB, NASB].

2.1 It is a type of the death and resurrection of Jesus [BAGD, Hwt, Lns, NIC].

2.2 It is a type (a veiled foreshadowing [WBC]) of the resurrection of believers [ICC, NIGTC, WBC], emphasized by the καί 'even' preceding this phrase; the restoration of Isaac is only a type of what will come later [NIGTC].

3. It refers to Isaac's birth, indicating that Abraham received Isaac at his birth 'in a figure' that suggested a future resurrection [Wst].

4. It means 'because he exposed Isaac to danger' [My].

DISCOURSE UNIT: 11:20–22 [EBC, HNTC, Lg, NTC]. The topic is the faith of the patriarchs [EBC, HNTC], the example of faith of Isaac, Jacob, and Joseph [Lg, NTC].

11:20 By-faith also concerning[a] coming-things[b] Isaac blessed[c] Jacob and Esau.

TEXT—Some manuscripts omit καί 'also'. GNT does not deal with this variant. This word is included by Alf, ICC, Lg, Lns, Mil, My, NIC, NIGTC, NTC, WBC, Wst; NASB; it is omitted by Blm, EGT, HNTC, and all versions except NASB, but some versions probably omit it for stylistic reasons although accepting it as part of the Greek text.

LEXICON—a. περί with genitive object (LN 89.6) (BAGD 1.e. p. 644): 'concerning' [HNTC, LN, Lns, Mil; KJV], 'regarding' [NASB], 'in regard to' [Mil; NIV], 'with regard to, in relation to' [BAGD, LN], 'with reference to' [BAGD], 'with respect to' [BAGD, WBC], 'in respect of' [NIC], 'for' [NJB, NRSV, TEV], 'and spoke of' [REB], not explicit [CEV].

b. pres. act. participle of μέλλω (LN 67.62): 'to come', 'to be about to' [LN]. This participle is translated 'things to come' [HNTC, Lns, Mil, NIC; KJV, NASB, REB], 'their future' [WBC; NIV], 'the future' [NRSV, TEV], 'the still distant future' [NJB], not explicit [CEV]. The phrase περὶ μελλόντων 'concerning coming things' is translated 'that were still to be' [NAB], 'for his blessing concerned things to come' [TNT], 'in what God was going to do in the future' [NLT]. It refers to the future in the present world [ICC].

c. aorist act. indic. of εὐλογέω (LN 33.470) (BAGD 2.a. p. 322): 'to bless' [BAGD, HNTC, LN, Lns, Mil, NIC, WBC; KJV, NASB, NIV, NLT, REB, TNT], 'to invoke blessings' [NAB, NRSV], 'to give (one's) blessing' [NJB], 'to promise blessings' [CEV, TEV].

QUESTION—What is καί 'also' connected with?

It is connected with περὶ μελλόντων 'concerning coming things' [Alf, Mil, NIGTC, WBC, Wst]: not only present things but also future things. It adds emphasis to the phrase [ICC, Mil, My, WBC].

QUESTION—What is the phrase περὶ μελλόντων 'concerning coming things' connected with?

The absence of the definite article implies that the reference is to future things as yet unseen [WBC, Wst].

1. It is connected with εὐλόγησεν 'blessed' [Alf, EGT, HNTC, Hu, ICC, Lg, Mil, NIC, NIGTC, WBC; all versions except NLT, REB, TNT]: he blessed concerning coming things.
2. It expresses a separate action [NLT, REB]: he blessed . . . and he spoke of coming things.
3. It states the reason for the blessing [TNT]: he blessed . . . for his blessing concerned coming things.

QUESTION—What is implied by naming Jacob before Esau?

1. It implies that Jacob is more important [Alf, My] as the one in whom the promises were to be fulfilled [Hwt]; it shows that the promise was not according to the order of flesh but according to faith [Hu, NTC], according to God's will [Wst].
2. This was the order in which the two sons received their blessing [NIC].
3. It is both of the above [My].

11:21 By-faith Jacob dying blessed each of-the sons of-Joseph

QUESTION—What relationship is indicated by the participle ἀποθνῄσκων 'dying'?

It is temporal [Alf, Blm, EGT, HNTC, Hu, Lns, Mil, My, WBC, Wst; all versions]: when he was dying. This participle is also translated 'on his deathbed' [NIC]. The present tense implies a process [NIGTC, WBC].

and he-worshiped[a] upon[b] the top[c] of-his staff.[d]

LEXICON—a. aorist act. indic. of προσκυνέω (LN 53.56) (BAGD 2.a. p. 717): 'to worship' [LN, Mil, NIC; CEV, KJV, NASB, NIV], 'to bow in worship' [BAGD, HNTC, Lns, WBC; NLT, NRSV, REB, TNT], 'to bow in reverence' [NJB], 'to worship God' [NAB, TEV]. It refers to an act of thankfulness to God [Blm]. The implied object of worship is God [Blm, WBC; NAB, TEV].

b. ἐπί with accusative object (LN 83.46): 'upon' [LN, Mil; KJV], 'on' [HNTC, LN, NIC, WBC; CEV, NAB, NASB, NIV, NJB, TEV, TNT], 'over' [Lns; NRSV, REB].

c. ἄκρον (LN **79.104**) (BAGD p. 34): 'top' [BAGD, HNTC, LN, Lns, Mil, NIC, WBC; KJV, NASB, NIV, NRSV, REB, TEV, TNT], 'head' [NAB], not explicit [CEV, NJB, NLT].

d. ῥάβδος (LN 6.218) (BAGD p. 733): 'staff' [BAGD, HNTC, Lns, Mil, NIC, WBC; all versions except CEV, TEV], 'rod, stick' [BAGD, LN], 'walking stick' [LN; CEV, TEV]. Another view is that this word means the head of the bed [Blm].

QUESTION—How is this clause related to the preceding clause?

1. It states an additional fact [Blm, EGT, HNTC, Hu, Lns, Mil, My, NIC, WBC; all versions except NJB, NRSV]: he blessed and he worshiped. The introductory καί makes this clause coordinate with the preceding clause [Mil]. This act actually occurred some time earlier than the act of blessing [Alf, Blm, HNTC, Hu, Wst].
2. It is translated as a participial phrase describing Jacob's position as he blessed Joseph's sons [NJB, NRSV]: he blessed them, bowing in reverence.

QUESTION—What is the phrase ἐπὶ τὸν ἄκρον τῆς ῥάβδου αὐτοῦ 'upon the top of his staff' connected with?

1. It is connected with the understood word 'leaning' [HNTC, Mil, My, NIC, NTC, WBC; all versions except NRSV, REB]: he worshiped leaning upon his staff. He supported himself on his staff [ICC].

2. It is connected with προσεκύνησεν translated 'to bow in worship' [Lns; NRSV, REB]: bowing in worship over the top of his staff.

QUESTION—What relationship is indicated by the understood participle 'leaning'?

It is temporal [NIV, NJB]: he worshiped as he leaned.

11:22 By-faith Joseph dying[a] made-mention[b] concerning[c] the exodus[d] of-the sons[e] of-Israel

LEXICON—a. pres. act. participle of τελευτάω (LN 23.102) (BAGD p. 810): 'to die' [BAGD, LN; KJV, NASB]. This participle is translated 'when he was about to die' [NJB, TEV], 'when he was old and dying' [NLT], 'when his end was near' [NIC; NIV, TNT], 'right before he died' [CEV], 'at the end of his life' [NRSV, REB], 'near the end of his life' [NAB], 'as he was nearing the end of his life' [Mil], 'while coming to the end of his life' [WBC], 'as his life was ending' [HNTC], 'when finishing his life' [Lns]. It refers to coming to the close of his life [EGT]; it refers to dying [My, NIGTC, TH].

b. aorist act. indic. of μνημονεύω (LN 29.16, 29.18) (BAGD 1.c. p. 525): 'to make mention' [HNTC, Mil, WBC; KJV, NASB, NRSV], 'to mention' [BAGD, NIC; NJB], 'to speak' [NAB, NIV, REB, TEV], 'to speak confidently' [NLT], 'to refer' [TNT], 'to think of, to keep in mind' [BAGD], 'to remember' [BAGD, LN (29.16), Lns], 'to recall' [LN (29.16)], 'to remember and mention, to remember to mention' [LN (29.18)], not explicit [CEV]. It means to call to mind [ICC], to make mention [My, NIGTC]. It refers to mentioning prophetically [Blm].

c. περί with genitive object (LN 90.24): 'concerning' [LN], 'about' [LN; NIV], 'regarding' [Lns], 'of' [HNTC, LN, Mil, WBC; KJV, NAB, NASB, NLT, NRSV, REB, TEV], 'to' [TNT], 'that' [CEV], not explicit [NIC; NJB].

d. ἔξοδος (LN **15.42**) (BAGD 1. p. 276): 'exodus' [Lns, Mil; NASB, NRSV], 'Exodus' [BAGD, HNTC, LN; NAB, NJB], 'exodus from Egypt' [NIV], 'Exodus from Egypt' [TNT], 'departing' [KJV], 'departure' [**LN**, NIC, WBC], 'departure from Egypt' [REB, TEV]. This noun is also translated as a verb phrase: 'to lead out of Egypt' [CEV], 'God's bringing out of Egypt' [NLT]. With the definite article [NTC] it is the specific term for the Exodus [Alf, NTC, TH]; it implies a triumphant deliverance [TNTC].

e. υἱός (LN 10.30, 11.58) (BAGD 1.b.α. p. 833): 'son' [LN (11.58), Lns, Mil; NASB], 'children' [KJV], 'descendant' [BAGD], 'male descendant' [LN (10.30, 11.58)]. The plural υἱῶν 'sons' is translated 'people' [LN (11.58), NIC; CEV, NLT]. The phrase υἱῶν Ἰσραήλ 'sons of Israel' is translated 'Israelites' [HNTC, WBC; NAB, NIV, NJB, NRSV, TEV, TNT], 'Israel' [REB]. It refers to the descendants of Israel [NIGTC].

QUESTION—What relationship is indicated by the participle τελευτῶν 'dying'?

It is temporal [Alf, HNTC, Lns, Mil, NIC, TH, WBC; KJV, NASB, NIV, NJB, NLT, TNT]: when he was dying.

and gave-orders[a] concerning[b] his bones.[c]

LEXICON—a. aorist mid. indic. (deponent = act.) of ἐντέλλομαι (LN 33.329) (BAGD p. 268): 'to give orders' [BAGD, Lns; NASB], 'to order' [BAGD], 'to give instruction(s)' [WBC; NAB, NIV, NJB, NRSV, REB], 'to give directions' [HNTC, Mil, NIC], 'to leave instructions' [TEV], 'to command' [BAGD, LN; NLT], 'to give commandment' [KJV], 'to say' [TNT], 'to tell' [CEV].

b. περί with genitive object (LN 90.24): 'concerning' [HNTC, LN, Lns, WBC; KJV, NASB], 'about' [LN; NAB, NIV, NJB, NRSV, REB], 'with regard to' [NIC], 'of' [LN], 'about what should be done with' [TEV], 'what was to be done with' [TNT], 'regarding what to do with' [Mil]. This is translated more specifically: 'he commanded them to carry his bones with them when they left' [NLT], 'he told them to take his bones with them' [CEV].

c. ὀστέον (LN 8.61) (BAGD p. 586): 'bone' [BAGD, HNTC, LN, Lns, Mil, NIC; CEV, KJV, NASB, NIV, NLT, TNT], 'body' [TEV], 'burial' [NAB, NRSV, REB]. The phrase τῶν ὀστέων αὐτοῦ 'his bones' is translated 'his own remains' [NJB], 'the burial of his bones' [WBC].

QUESTION—What relationship is indicated by καί 'and'?

It coordinates the following clause with the preceding [Mil]; but in meaning, the following clause is subordinate to the preceding clause [My].

DISCOURSE UNIT: 11:23–31 [WBC]. The topic is the victories resulting from perseverance in faith in the time of Moses.

DISCOURSE UNIT: 11:23–29 [GNC, HNTC, Lg, NTC]. The topic is the faith of Moses and the Israelites [GNC], five instances of the faith of Moses [HNTC], the example of Moses [Lg], Moses's faith [NTC].

DISCOURSE UNIT: 11:23–28 [EBC, NIC].The topic is Moses's faith [EBC, NIC].

11:23 By-faith Moses having-been-born was-hidden for-three-months by[a] his parents,

LEXICON—a. ὑπό with genitive object (LN 90.1): 'by' [HNTC, LN, Lns, Mil, NIC, WBC; NASB, NJB, NRSV], 'of' [KJV]. This preposition is omitted by having the parents be the subject of the verb [CEV, NAB, NIV, NLT, REB, TEV, TNT]: Moses' parents hid him.

QUESTION—What relationship is indicated by the participle γεννηθείς 'having been born'?

It is temporal [Alf, HNTC, Lg(K), Lns, Mil, NIC, WBC; all versions except CEV, NLT]: after he was born. This participle is not translated [CEV, NLT].

QUESTION—What is implied by τῶν πατέρων αὐτοῦ 'his parents'?

This phrase, literally 'his fathers', refers to his parents [Alf, Blm, EBC, EGT, GNC, HNTC, Hu, Hwt, ICC, Lg, Lns, Mil, My, NCBC, NIC, NIGTC, NTC, TH, TNTC, WBC, Wst; all versions].

because they-saw the child (to be) beautiful[a]

LEXICON—a. ἀστεῖος (LN **79.11**) (BAGD 1. p. 117): 'beautiful' [BAGD, HNTC, **LN**, NIC; CEV, NAB, NASB, NRSV, TEV], 'attractive' [LN], 'very lovely' [TNT], 'fair' [Lns], 'uncommonly striking' [WBC], 'well-formed' [BAGD], 'fine' [Mil; NJB, REB], 'proper' [KJV], 'no ordinary' [NIV], 'unusual' [NLT]. It means 'beautiful' [EBC, EGT], uncommonly attractive [Hu, Lns, NTC], fair and graceful [My], of extraordinary appearance [TNTC, WBC], pleasing to God [GNC]. Many commentators think the word implies more than being beautiful; it means that they recognized God's approval [NTC], God's favor [TH, WBC], that God had a special destiny for him [EBC, EGT, GNC, Hu, Mil, My, NIC]. However, another thinks that it does not imply this [Lns].

QUESTION—Why is this clause mentioned?

It expresses a secondary reason; the principal reason was their faith [Blm].

and they-feared not the edict[a] of-the king.

LEXICON—a. διάταγμα (LN **33.326**) (BAGD p. 189): 'edict' [BAGD, WBC; NAB, NASB, NIV, NJB, NRSV, REB], 'decree' [Mil, NIC], 'mandate' [Lns], 'ordinance' [LN], 'order' [HNTC, **LN**; CEV, TEV, TNT], 'commandment' [KJV], 'command' [BAGD, LN]. This whole clause is translated 'they were not afraid of what the king might do' [NLT].

QUESTION—What relationship is indicated by καί 'and'?

1. It is a separate statement parallel to the first clause of the verse [Alf, HNTC, Lns, My, NIC, NIGTC; all versions].
   1.1 It is an additional comment [Alf, HNTC, Lns, My, NIC, NIGTC; all versions except NAB]: he was hidden by his parents; in addition, they did not fear . . .
   1.2 It is translated as the result of hiding him [NAB]: they hid him . . . , resulting in disregarding the king's edict.
2. It is the second part of the clause introduced by διότι 'because' [Mil, WBC, Wst]: because they saw . . . , and did not fear . . .

11:24 By-faith Moses having-become grown-up[a] refused[b] to-be-called[c] son of-(the/a)-daughter of-Pharaoh,

LEXICON—a. μέγας (LN 79.123) (BAGD 2.a.α. p. 497): 'grown up' [BAGD, Lns, Mil, WBC; NAB, NASB, NIV, NJB, NRSV, TEV], 'come to years' [KJV], 'great, big, large' [LN]. The phrase μέγας γενόμενος 'having become grown up' is translated 'when he grew up' [HNTC, NIC; NLT, REB, TNT], 'after he grew up' [CEV]. It means to be an adult person [Alf, BAGD, Blm, EBC, EGT, HNTC, Hu, Hwt, ICC, Lg, LN, Lns, Mil, My, NIC, NIGTC, NTC, TH, TNTC, WBC, Wst; all versions].

b. aorist mid. (deponent = act.) of ἀρνέομαι (LN **31.25**) (BAGD 1. p. 107): 'to refuse' [BAGD, HNTC, **LN,** Lns, Mil, NIC; all versions], 'to disdain' [WBC], 'not to consent to' [LN]. It refers to Moses' renunciation of his former position [Blm, NIGTC]. The aorist tense refers to a specific act [TNTC, Wst]. His intervention in behalf of the Hebrew worker who was being mistreated by his Egyptian overseer constituted his identification of himself with the Hebrews and the consequent denial of his status in the Egyptian court [WBC].

c. pres. pass. infin. of λέγω (LN 33.131) (BAGD II.3. p. 470): 'to be called' [BAGD, HNTC, LN, Lns, Mil, NIC, WBC; CEV, KJV, NASB, NRSV, REB, TEV, TNT], 'to be known as' [NAB, NIV, NJB], 'to be named' [BAGD], 'to be treated as' [NLT]. It refers to having the privileges and position [TH].

QUESTION—What relationship is indicated by the participle γενόμενος 'having become'?

It is temporal [BAGD, EBC, HNTC, LN, Lns, Mil, NIC, WBC, Wst; all versions].

QUESTION—What relationship is indicated by the absence of the definite article with the three nouns υἱός 'son', θυγατρός 'daughter', and Φαραώ 'Pharaoh'?

1. All three (the first and second [NIGTC], the second [Wst], the second and third [My]) are qualitative [My, NIGTC], each focusing on the concept involved rather than on the specific person [Lns, NTC].
2. Φαραώ 'Pharaoh' is without the article as a proper noun [NIGTC].
3. Υἱός 'son' is translated as definite [EBC, HNTC; CEV, KJV, NAB, NASB, NIV, NJB, NLT, TEV, TNT]: the son.
4. Υἱός 'son' is translated as qualitative [Alf, ICC] or indefinite [Alf, EGT, ICC; NRSV, REB]: a son.

11:25 having-chosen[a] rather[b] to-suffer-with[c] the people of-God

LEXICON—a. aorist mid. participle of αἱρέω (LN **30.86**) (BAGD 2. p. 24): 'to choose' [BAGD, **LN**, Lns, NIC, WBC; CEV, KJV, NASB, NIV, NJB, NLT, NRSV], 'to prefer' [HNTC, LN, Mil; REB, TEV, TNT], 'to select' [LN], 'to wish' [NAB]. The middle voice emphasizes Moses's personal involvement [NIGTC, WBC].

b. μᾶλλον (LN 89.126) (BAGD 3.c. p. 489): 'rather' [HNTC, LN, Lns, WBC; all versions except CEV, NLT], 'rather than' [BAGD], 'instead, on the contrary' [LN], not explicit [Mil]. The phrase μᾶλλον . . . ἤ 'rather . . . than' is translated at the beginning of the next clause 'in preference to' [NIC], 'instead of' [CEV, NLT].

c. pres. mid. (deponent = act.) of συγκακουχέομαι (LN **24.84**) (BAGD p. 773): 'to suffer with' [BAGD, **LN**; TEV], 'to suffer together, to join in suffering' [LN], 'to suffer affliction with' [KJV], 'to be ill-treated along with' [NAB], 'to be ill-treated in company with' [NJB], 'to endure ill-treatment with' [NASB], 'to suffer ill-treatment with' [HNTC, Mil], 'to share ill-treatment with' [NRSV], 'to share oppression' [NLT], 'to be basely treated together with' [Lns], 'to be mistreated with' [BAGD; CEV], 'to be mistreated along with' [NIV], 'to share hardship with' [REB], 'to suffer hardship with' [TNT], 'to endure hardship with' [WBC], 'the endurance of hardship with' [NIC]. The present tense indicates continued action [NTC].

QUESTION—What relationship is indicated by the participle ἑλόμενος 'choosing'?

1. Concerning the participial function.
1.1 It is translated as a separate proposition [NIC; CEV, NAB, NIV, NJB, NLT, TEV, TNT]: he chose.
1.2 It states a reason [Blm, Mil, My]: because he chose.
2. Concerning the aorist tense.
2.1 It refers to an action prior to ἠρνήσατο 'he refused' in the preceding verse [Mil]: he refused because he had previously considered.
2.2 It refers to an action at the same time as ἠρνήσατο 'he refused' [Lns, NTC]: he refused at the same time that he considered.

than for-a-while[a] to-have enjoyment[b] of-sin,

LEXICON—a. πρόσκαιρος (LN 67.109) (BAGD p. 715): 'for a while' [LN], 'for a little while' [CEV, TEV, TNT], 'for a season' [KJV], 'for a short time' [NIV], 'lasting only for a time' [BAGD], 'lasting for a period' [Lns], 'temporary' [BAGD, LN, NIC, WBC], 'transitory' [BAGD, Mil; NJB], 'transient' [HNTC; REB], 'passing' [NASB], 'fleeting' [NAB, NLT, NRSV].

b. ἀπόλαυσις (LN **25.115**) (BAGD p. 94): 'enjoyment' [Lns, NIC], 'pleasure' [WBC], 'good time' [CEV]. This singular noun is translated as a plural: 'pleasures' [BAGD, HNTC, Mil; KJV, NASB, NIV, NJB, NRSV, REB, TNT], 'rewards' [NAB]. The phrase ἔχειν ἀπόλαυσιν 'to have enjoyment' is translated 'to enjoy' [LN; NLT, TEV].

QUESTION—What relationship is indicated by the neuter adjective πρόσκαιρον 'for a while'?

It is emphatic by forefronting [Mil].

1. It is used adverbially, modifying ἔχειν 'to have' [LN, Lns; CEV, KJV, NIV, TEV, TNT]: to have enjoyment for a while.
2. It is translated as if it were an adjective agreeing with the feminine noun ἀπόλαυσιν 'enjoyment' [Alf, HNTC, Lg(K), Mil, My, NIC, WBC; NAB, NASB, NJB, NLT, NRSV, REB]: to have temporary enjoyment.

QUESTION—How are the two nouns related in the genitive construction ἁμαρτίας ἀπόλαυσιν 'enjoyment of sin'?

'Sin' is emphatic by forefronting [Mil]. The sin would have been in abandoning his people [EGT, GNC, HNTC, Hwt, ICC, My, NTC], in disobeying God's call [EBC, Hu, NCBC, NIGTC, Wst]; it would have amounted to apostasy [HNTC, Lg, My, NCBC, NIC, NTC].

1. The genitive noun ἁμαρτίας 'sin' tells what is enjoyed [Alf, NTC, Wst; TEV]: to enjoy sin.
2. The genitive noun ἁμαρτίας 'sin' is the source of the enjoyment [EGT, Lg, Mil, My, WBC; CEV]: enjoyment that sin provides.

11:26 having-considered[a] (as) greater riches[b] than-the treasures[c] of-Egypt the reproach[d] of-the Christ;

TEXT—Instead of Αἰγύπτου 'of Egypt' some manuscripts read ἐν Αἰγύπτῳ 'in Egypt'. Neither GNT nor Aland deal with this variant. Only Blm, KJV read 'in Egypt'.

LEXICON—a. aorist mid. (deponent = act.) participle of ἡγέομαι (LN 31.1) (BAGD 2. p. 343): 'to consider' [BAGD, LN, Mil; NAB, NASB, NJB, NRSV, REB, TNT], 'to regard' [LN, WBC; NIV], 'to reckon' [HNTC, NIC; TEV], 'to think' [LN; NLT], 'to hold a view' [LN], 'to look upon' [BAGD], 'to esteem' [KJV], 'to come to esteem' [Lns], 'to know' [CEV]. The aorist tense refers to an act at the same time as the preceding aorist participle ἑλόμενος 'choosing' [Alf], at the same time as the finite verb ἠρνήσατο 'he refused' in 11:24 [NTC].

b. πλοῦτος (LN 57.29) (BAGD 2. p. 674): 'riches' [LN, Lns, Mil; KJV, NAB, NASB], 'wealth' [BAGD, HNTC, LN, NIC, WBC; NRSV, REB, TNT], 'value' [NIV]. The phrase μείζονα πλοῦτον 'greater riches' is translated 'something more precious' [NJB], 'was worth far more' [TEV], 'it was better' [NLT], 'not as wonderful as what he would receive' [CEV].

c. θησαυρός (LN 65.10) (BAGD 2.a. p. 361): 'treasure' [BAGD, HNTC, LN, Lns, Mil, NIC, WBC; all versions], 'wealth, riches' [LN].

d. ὀνειδισμός (LN 33.389) (BAGD p. 570): 'reproach' [BAGD, HNTC, Lns, Mil; KJV, NAB, NASB], 'insult' [LN], 'abuse' [WBC; NRSV], 'suffering' [CEV], 'disgrace' [NIV], 'shame' [TNT], 'stigma' [NIC; REB]. This singular noun is translated as a plural: 'humiliations' [NJB]; as a verb phrase: 'to suffer scorn' [TEV], 'to suffer' [NLT].

QUESTION—What relationship is indicated by the participle ἡγησάμενος 'having considered'?

It is in apposition with the preceding participle ἑλόμενος 'having chosen' [Lns]. It is subordinate to ἑλόμενος 'having chosen' [My].

1. It states the reason for Moses' decision [EGT, ICC, Mil, My, TNTC, Wst; TNT]: because he considered . . .
2. It states an additional proposition [HNTC, NIC, WBC; CEV, NAB, NIV, NJB, NLT, NRSV, REB, TEV]: he considered . . .

QUESTION—What relationship is indicated by the accusative phrase μείζονα πλοῦτον 'greater riches'?

It is emphatic by forefronting [Mil, NTC].

1. It is in apposition with the accusative noun phrase in the following clause, τὸν ὀνειδισμόν 'the reproach' [Lns; NIV]: having considered the reproach (of Christ) as greater riches.

2. It is the predicate of the understood verb εἶναι 'to be' [Mil, NIC; NRSV, TNT]: having considered the reproach (of Christ) to be greater riches.

QUESTION—What relationship is indicated by the genitive noun phrase τῶν θησαυρῶν 'the treasures'?

It is a genitive stating a comparison with μείζονα πλοῦτον 'greater riches' [Alf, EGT, HNTC, Lns, Mil, NIC, WBC; all versions]: greater riches than the treasures (of Egypt).

QUESTION—How are two nouns related in the genitive phrase τῶν Αἰγύπτου θησαυρῶν 'than the treasures of Egypt'?

1. The source of the 'treasures' is Egypt [Mil]: the treasures that come from Egypt.
2. (Different text) The 'treasures' are located in Egypt [Blm; KJV].

QUESTION—What relationship is indicated by the accusative noun phrase τὸν ὀνειδισμόν 'the reproach'?

1. It is the predicate of the participle ἡγησάμενος 'having considered' [Alf, EGT, HNTC, Lns, Mil, NIC, WBC; all versions except NJB, TEV]: having considered the reproach.
2. It is translated as a nominative case and subject of an implied noun clause [NJB, TEV]: having considered that the reproach of Christ was greater riches.

QUESTION—How are two nouns related in the genitive phrase τὸν ὀνειδισμὸν τοῦ Χριστοῦ 'the reproach of Christ'?

1. 'Christ' is the one for whose sake the 'reproach' is suffered [Blm, EBC, EGT, GNC, Lns, NTC, WBC; CEV, NIV, NLT, NRSV, TEV, TNT]: reproach borne by people for the sake of Christ. It is also a participation in Christ's sufferings [Lns].
1.1 Suffered by Moses and the Israelites [Blm, WBC]. Christ is involved with them in their sufferings [EBC].
1.2 Suffered by Moses [EGT, GNC, Lns, NTC] from Pharaoh's court [GNC].
2. Christ is the one who brings the reproach [Mil]: the reproach brought by Christ.
3. 'Christ' is the one who bears the 'reproach' [Alf, HNTC, Hu, ICC, Lg, My, Wst; NAB, NJB, REB] in himself and in his people [Alf, Lg]: the reproach borne by Christ. Christ's reproach is the fulfillment of the following type:
3.1 The type is the reproach suffered by the Israelites [My, Wst] together with Moses [My] from the Egyptians [HNTC, My].
3.2 The type is the reproach suffered by Moses by identifying himself with the Israelites [Hu].
3.3 The type is the reproach suffered by Moses from the Israelites who mistreated him [ICC].
4. 'Christ' is the one to whom the reproach is related [NIC, TH, TNTC, WBC]: the reproach attached to Christ. The reproach that the Israelites

suffered is linked to Christ's sufferings [TNTC]. The reproach that Moses suffered is also related to the sufferings of the Israelites [TH].

for he-was-looking-ahead[a] to[b] the reward.[c]

LEXICON—a. imperf. act. indic. of ἀποβλέπω (LN **30.31**) (BAGD p. 89): 'to look ahead' [WBC; NIV, NLT, NRSV], 'to look forward' [CEV], 'to look away' [Lns], 'to look' [NAB, NASB], 'to fix one's attention on' [**LN**], 'to think about' [LN], 'to have respect' [KJV]. The phrase ἀπέβλεπεν εἰς 'he was looking away to' is translated 'his attention was on' [BAGD], 'he had his eyes fixed on' [NJB], 'his eyes were fixed on' [REB], 'his eyes were fixed upon' [TNT], 'he kept his eyes on' [HNTC; TEV], 'he kept his eyes fixed on' [NIC], 'he kept steadily in view' [Mil]. It means to keep one's eye fixed upon [ICC, NIC], to turn away from one thing to look at another [TNTC] with fixed attention [WBC], to look from the present to the future [Hu, WBC, Wst]. The imperfect tense implies repeated action [NIGTC], a habitual state [WBC, Wst].

b. εἰς with accusative object (LN 84.16): 'to' [LN, Lns, WBC; CEV, NAB, NASB, NIV, NLT, NRSV], 'unto' [KJV], 'toward' [LN], 'on' [HNTC; NJB, REB, TEV], 'upon' [TNT].

c. μισθαποδοσία (LN **38.17**) (BAGD p. 523): 'reward' [BAGD, HNTC, **LN**, Mil, NIC, WBC; CEV, NAB, NASB, NIV, NJB, NRSV], 'great reward' [NLT], 'future reward' [TEV], 'coming reward' [REB], 'due pay-gift' [Lns], 'recompense' [LN], 'recompense of the reward' [KJV], 'reward God would give him' [TNT]. It refers to Moses' reward [HNTC; NIV, TNT], to the eternal reward for believers [Alf, Blm, Lns, My, NIGTC].

QUESTION—What relationship is indicated by γάρ 'for'?

It introduces the reason for the preceding statement [Mil, My, WBC].

11:27 By-faith he-left[a] Egypt, not having-feared[b] the anger[c] of-the king;

LEXICON—a. aorist act. indic. of καταλείπω (LN **15.57**) (BAGD 2.b. p. 413): 'to leave' [BAGD, HNTC, LN, Mil, WBC; all versions except KJV], 'to leave behind' [Lns], 'to forsake' [KJV], 'to abandon' [NIC]. The prefixed κατα- is intensive [Lg(K)]. The singular form refers to Moses alone [Lg].

b. aorist pass. (deponent = act.) participle of φοβέομαι (LN 25.252) (BAGD 1.b.γ. p. 863): 'to fear' [BAGD, HNTC, LN, Lns, WBC; KJV, NAB, NASB, NIV], 'to be afraid' [LN; TNT], 'to be afraid of' [Mil, NIC; CEV, NLT, TEV]. The participial phrase μὴ φοβηθείς 'not having feared' is translated 'without fear of' [NJB], 'with no fear of' [REB], 'unafraid of' [NRSV].

c. θυμός (LN 88.178) (BAGD 2. p. 365): 'anger' [BAGD, LN, Lns, Mil, NIC; CEV, NIV, NJB, NRSV, REB, TEV, TNT], 'wrath' [BAGD, HNTC, LN; KJV, NAB, NASB], 'fury' [LN], 'rage' [BAGD, LN; WBC], not explicit [NLT].

QUESTION—What relationship is indicated by the participle φοβηθείς 'having feared'?

1. Regarding the aorist tense.
1.1 The aorist tense indicates a state prior to the verb κατέλιπεν 'he left' [Mil]: before he left, he did not fear.
1.2 It refers to action at the same time as the main verb [WBC]: when he left, he did not fear.
2. Regarding the function of the participle.
2.1 It expresses an additional fact [HNTC; TNT]: he left Egypt and he was not afraid of the king's anger.
2.2 It states a reason [NIC, NTC]: he left Egypt, but not because he feared the king's anger.
3. It states a concession [Mil]: he left Egypt, although he did not fear the king's anger.

for he-persevered[a] as[b] seeing[c] the unseen-one.[d]

LEXICON—a. aorist act. indic. of καρτερέω (LN **25.178**) (BAGD p. 405): 'to persevere' [BAGD, **LN**, Mil, NIC; NAB, NIV, NRSV], 'to persist' [LN], 'to endure' [KJV, NASB], 'to be steadfast' [Lns], 'to hold to one's purpose' [HNTC; NJB, TNT], 'to be resolute' [REB], 'to refuse to turn back' [TEV], 'to keep right on going' [NLT], not explicit [CEV]. The phrase ὁρῶν ἐκαρτέρησεν 'he endured seeing' is translated 'he kept continually before his eyes' [BAGD, WBC]. It implies long continued endurance [EGT]. It refers to Moses' courage in disobeying the Pharaoh [Blm]. The aorist tense includes the forty years in Midian [EGT, GNC] and subsequent events leading up to the Exodus [GNC].

b. ὡς (LN 64.12): 'as' [HNTC, LN, Lns, Mil; KJV, NASB, REB], 'as if' [NAB], 'as though' [NRSV, TEV], 'like' [NJB, TNT], 'as it were' [WBC], 'because' [NIC; NIV, NLT], not explicit [CEV].

c. pres. act. participle of ὁράω (LN 24.1) (BAGD 1.a.α. p. 577): 'to see' [BAGD, HNTC, LN, Lns, Mil, NIC; all versions except NAB], 'to look on' [NAB], 'to catch sight of' [BAGD], 'to keep one's eyes on' [NLT].

d. ἀόρατος (LN 24.4) (BAGD p. 79): 'unseen' [BAGD], 'what cannot be seen' [LN], 'invisible' [BAGD, LN], 'Invisible' [NJB]. The phrase τὸν ἀόρατον 'the unseen one' is translated 'the Invisible One' [Lns, NIC], 'the one who is invisible' [WBC; NLT], 'him who is invisible' [HNTC; KJV, NIV, NRSV], 'Him who is unseen' [NASB], 'the invisible God' [Mil; CEV, NAB, REB, TEV, TNT]. It refers to God [NIGTC, TH, WBC].

QUESTION—What relationship is indicated by γάρ 'for'?

1. It indicates the reason why Moses left Egypt 'by faith' [Mil, NCBC].
2. It indicates the reason why he did not fear the king's wrath [Blm, ICC, TNTC, WBC].

QUESTION—What relationship is indicated by ὡς 'as'?

It softens the following participle [My, NIGTC, WBC]: seeing, so to speak.

1. He did not actually see God [HNTC, TH; NAB, NRSV, TEV].
2. He did see God [EBC, EGT, NIC; NIV].
3. He saw God with inward vision [ICC, Lg(K), Lns, TNTC].

QUESTION—What relationship is indicated by the participle ὁρῶν 'seeing'?

1. With the preceding ὡς 'as', it expresses the manner of enduring [Alf, HNTC, Lns, Mil (translation); all versions except NIV]: he endured as if he were seeing.
   1.1 It is adverbial, focusing on the action [Alf, Lns; KJV, NAB, NASB, NRSV, TEV]: he endured as if seeing.
   1.2 It is indefinite attributive, focusing on the person [HNTC, Mil (translation); NJB, REB, TNT]: he endured as someone who sees.
2. With the preceding ὡς 'as', it expresses the reason for enduring [EBC, EGT, Mil (discussion), NIC, Wst; NIV]: he endured because he saw.
3. This participle followed by καρτερέω 'to persevere' expresses the quality in which the endurance takes place [BAGD (under καρτερέω), WBC]: he kept continually before his eyes.

11:28 By-faith he-celebrated[a] the Passover and the sprinkling[b] of-the blood,

LEXICON—a. perf. act. indic. of ποιέω (LN 42.7, **90.45**) (BAGD I.1.b.ζ. p. 681): 'to celebrate' [BAGD, HNTC; CEV, REB, TNT], 'to keep' [BAGD, WBC; KJV, NAB, NASB, NIV, NJB, NLT, NRSV], 'to do' [LN (42.7, 90.45)], 'to perform' [LN (42.7, **90.45**)], 'to carry out' [LN (42.7)], 'to attend to' [Lns], 'to make' [LN (90.45)], 'to establish' [TEV], 'to institute' [Mil, NIC]. It refers to celebrating the Passover [Alf, BAGD, EGT, HNTC, Lg, Lns, Wst; all versions except TEV] and the sprinkling of the blood [Lns]; it refers to instituting the Passover [GNC, Hwt, Mil, My, NIC, NTC, TH, WBC; TEV]. The perfect tense implies a continuing institution [Alf, EBC, Hwt, Lns, Mil, My, NIGTC, NTC, TH, WBC] of the Passover only, not the sprinkling of the blood [TH], a perpetual memorial [Mil, NIC, NIGTC, Wst]; it refers to the continuing effects of Moses' celebration [EGT], as an accomplished fact [Lg]; it refers to its permanent record in history [Lg(K)]; it is merely the equivalent of the aorist tense [ICC].

b. πρόσχυσις (LN **47.7**) (BAGD p. 720): 'sprinkling' [BAGD, LN, Mil, NIC; KJV, NASB, NIV, NRSV, REB], 'splashing' [Lns], 'pouring' [**LN**], 'spreading' [WBC], 'affusion' [Mil]. The phrase τὴν πρόσχυσιν τοῦ αἵματος 'the sprinkling of the blood' is translated 'to sprinkle the blood' [HNTC; NJB], 'to sprinkle the lamb's blood' [NAB], 'to sprinkle blood on the doorposts' [NLT, TNT], 'to sprinkle blood on the doors' [TEV], 'to sprinkle the blood of animals on the doorposts' [NLT]. It implies pouring on [Lg(K)].

QUESTION—What is implied by the noun phrase τοῦ αἵματος 'the blood'?

1. With the definite article it refers to a specific sprinkling [HNTC, Lns, Mil, NIC, WBC; NAB, NASB, NJB, TEV]: the sprinkling of the blood.

2. The definite article is not translated [KJV, NIV, NRSV, REB, TNT]: the sprinkling of blood.

in-order-that the-(one) destroying[a] the firstborn(-ones)[b] not should-touch[c] them

or: lest the-(one) destroying[a] should-touch[c] the firstborn-(ones)[b] of-them.

LEXICON—a. pres. act. participle of ὀλοθρεύω (LN **20.34**) (BAGD p. 564): 'to destroy' [LN, Lns, Mil; KJV, NASB]. The participial phrase ὁ ὀλοθρεύων 'the one destroying' is translated 'the Destroyer' [HNTC, **LN**; NJB], 'the destroyer' [NIC; NIV, NRSV], 'the destroying angel' [BAGD, WBC; CEV, NAB, REB], 'the Destroying Angel' [TNT], 'the Angel of Death' [NLT, TEV]. This participle refers to the destroying angel of Passover night [Alf].

b. πρωτότοκος (LN 10.43) (BAGD 1. p. 726): 'firstborn' [BAGD, HNTC, LN, Lns, NIC, WBC; KJV, NAB, NASB, NIV, NRSV, REB, TNT], 'firstborn son' [Mil; CEV, NJB, NLT, TEV]. This neuter plural includes both people and animals [Alf, EGT, NIGTC, NTC, WBC]; both male and female [Alf, NTC].

c. aorist act. subj. of θιγγάνω (LN **20.75**, **24.74**) (BAGD p. 361): 'to touch' [BAGD, HNTC, LN (**24.74**), Lns, Mil, NIC, WBC; all versions except CEV, NLT, TEV], 'to kill' [LN (20.75); NLT, TEV], 'to slay' [LN (20.75)], 'to cause the death of' [LN (**20.75**)]. This active verb is also translated in the passive: 'to be killed' [CEV]. It implies here touching with a hostile intent [BAGD, Mil].

QUESTION—How is this clause related to the preceding clause?

1. It expresses the purpose of both the Passover and the sprinkling of the blood [Alf; NLT].
2. It expresses the purpose of the sprinkling of the blood [ICC; CEV].

QUESTION—What are the noun phrase τὰ πρωτότοκα 'the firstborn ones' and the genitive pronoun αὐτῶν 'of them' connected with?

1. Τὰ πρωτότοκα 'the firstborn ones' is the predicate of ὁ ὀλοθρεύων 'the one destroying', and αὐτῶν 'of them' is the predicate of θίγῃ 'should touch' [Alf, EGT, Lns, Mil, My, NIC, Wst; KJV, NASB, NIV, NRSV]: in order that the one destroying the firstborn ones should not touch them. The verb θιγγάνω 'to touch' takes the genitive case [Lg, NTC]. (Grammatically, those who translate the participle ὁ ὀλοθρεύων 'the one destroying' as a noun, e.g., 'the Destroyer', should not make it govern the accusative τὰ πρωτότοκα 'the firstborn ones', since it would have to be a genitive case. Nevertheless, My, NIC, NIV, NRSV translate τὰ πρωτότοκα 'the firstborn ones' as a genitive, 'of the firstborn'.)
2. Τὰ πρωτότοκα 'the firstborn ones' is the predicate of θίγῃ 'should touch' and αὐτῶν 'of them' is related to τὰ πρωτότοκα 'the firstborn ones' [HNTC, NCBC, NIGTC, WBC; NAB, NJB, NLT, REB, TEV, TNT]: in order that the one destroying should not touch the firstborn ones of them.

The verb θιγγάνω 'to touch' may also take the accusative case [BAGD, NCBC].

DISCOURSE UNIT: 11:29–31 [EBC, NIC]. The topic is the faith of the Exodus generation [EBC], faith at the Exodus and Settlement [NIC].

11:29 By-faith they-passed-through the Red Sea as through[a] dry land,

TEXT—Some manuscripts omit γῆς 'land'. GNT does not deal with this variant. Only Blm, WBC, KJV omit 'land', although WBC adds 'land' in its translation and KJV adds this word in italics.

LEXICON—a. διά with genitive object (LN 84.29) (BAGD A.I.1. p. 179): 'through' [BAGD, LN, Lns, Mil; NASB], 'by' [KJV], 'on' [HNTC, WBC; CEV, NIV, TEV, TNT]. The phrase ὡς διά 'as through' is translated 'as if it were' [NAB, NRSV], 'as though it were' [NIC; REB], 'as though they were on' [NLT], 'as easily as' [NJB].

QUESTION—To whom does διέβησαν 'they passed through' refer?

It refers to the Israelites [Alf, EBC, EGT, Hwt, ICC, Mil, My, NIC, NIGTC, TNTC, WBC], identified as αὐτῶν 'of them' in the preceding clause [Alf, EBC, EGT, ICC, Mil, NIGTC, NTC, WBC, Wst]: the Israelites passed through.

QUESTION—What relationship is indicated by ὡς 'as'?

It indicates manner [HNTC, Lns, Mil, My, NIC, NIGTC; NAB, NJB, NRSV, REB, TEV, TNT]: they passed through as though on dry land.

of-which[a] the Egyptians having-taken[b] (an) attempt[c] they-were-swallowed-up.[d]

LEXICON—a. ὅς (LN 92.27): 'which' [LN, Lns; KJV], 'who, what' [LN]. The phrase ἧς πεῖραν λαβόντες 'of which . . . having taken an attempt' is translated 'when . . . tried to do it' [LN; CEV, TEV, TNT], 'but when . . . tried to do so' [NIV], 'but when . . . tried to do the same' [NIC], 'but when . . . attempted to do so' [WBC], 'while . . . trying to do the same' [NJB], 'when . . . made the attempt' [HNTC], 'when they attempted' [BAGD], 'and when they attempted it' [NASB], 'but when . . . attempted the same thing' [NAB], 'when they attempted to do the same thing' [Mil], 'but when . . . attempted to do so' [NRSV], 'whereas when they attempted the crossing' [REB], 'but when . . . followed' [NLT].

b. aorist act. participle of λαμβάνω (LN **68.58**) (BAGD 1.h. p. 465): 'to take'. The phrase πεῖραν λαβόντες 'having taken an attempt' is translated 'assaying to do' [KJV], 'having undertaken to try' [Lns]. This phrase means to make an experiment [Alf, NIGTC], to make an attempt [ICC, Lg, Mil, WBC], to make a trial [Lg, NIGTC, TH], to experience [NTC, WBC]; it means 'to try' [BAGD].

c. πεῖρα (LN **68.58**) (BAGD 1. p 640): see a. above [BAGD, **LN**], b. above [BAGD].

d. aorist pass. indic. of καταπίνω (LN 20.52) (BAGD 1.c. p. 416): 'to be swallowed up' [HNTC, Lns, Mil, NIC], 'to be drowned' [BAGD, Mil; all versions except REB, TEV], 'to be engulfed' [REB], 'to be destroyed' [LN]; this verb κατεπόθησαν 'they were swallowed up' is translated 'the water swallowed them up' [TEV]. The prefixed preposition κατα- intensifies the verb [WBC].

QUESTION—What relationship is indicated by the genitive feminine singular relative pronoun ἧς 'which'?

1. Its antecedent is τὴν Ἐρυθρὰν Θάλασσαν 'the Red Sea' [Alf, EGT, ICC, Mil, My, NIC, NTC, Wst]: having taken attempt of the Red Sea.
2. Its antecedent is ξηρᾶς (γῆς) 'dry (land)' [Blm, NIGTC]: having taken attempt of dry land.

QUESTION—What relationship is indicated by the participle λαβόντες 'having taken'?

It is temporal [HNTC, Mil, NIC; all versions except KJV, NJB]: when they made an attempt.

DISCOURSE UNIT: 11:30–40 [GNC, Lg]. The topic is the faith of Rahab and many others [GNC], examples of faith from the conquest of Canaan to the Maccabees [Lg].

DISCOURSE UNIT: 11:30–31 [HNTC, NTC]. The topic is faith in Joshua's day [HNTC], faith at Jericho [NTC].

11:30 By-faith the walls of-Jericho fell, having-been-encircled[a] for[b] seven days.

LEXICON—a. aorist pass. participle of κυκλόω (LN **15.146**) (BAGD 2. p. 456): 'to be encircled' [HNTC, Mil, WBC; NAB, NASB, NRSV, REB], 'to be circled' [Lns], 'to be gone around' [LN], 'to be compassed about' [KJV]. This passive participle is also translated as an active voice: 'to march around' [BAGD, NIC; NIV, NJB, NLT, TEV, TNT], 'to walk around' [CEV].

b. ἐπί with accusative object (LN 67.136) (BAGD III.2.b., p. 289): 'for' [HNTC, LN, Lns, Mil, NIC, WBC; all versions except KJV, NLT, REB], 'over a period of' [BAGD], 'on . . . successive' [REB], not explicit [KJV, NLT]. It implies duration of time [Alf, EGT, Lg, Mil, NIGTC, TH, WBC].

QUESTION—What relationship is indicated by the participle κυκλωθέντα 'having been surrounded'?

It is temporal [HNTC, Mil, My, NIC, WBC; all versions]: after they had been surrounded. It also implies the reason for their falling [Mil].

11:31 By-faith Rahab the prostitute[a] not perished-with[b] the-(ones) having-disobeyed,[c]

LEXICON—a. πόρνη (LN 88.275) (BAGD 1. p. 693): 'prostitute' [BAGD, LN, WBC; CEV, NIV, NJB, NLT, NRSV, REB, TEV, TNT], 'harlot' [BAGD, Lns, Mil, NIC; KJV, NAB, NASB], 'whore' [HNTC].

b. aorist mid. indic. of συναπόλλυμι (LN **20.32**) (BAGD p. 785): 'to perish with' [BAGD, **LN**, Lns, Mil, NIC, WBC; KJV, NRSV], 'to perish along with' [NASB], 'to die with' [NLT], 'to be destroyed with' [BAGD, HNTC, LN; TNT], 'to be killed with' [CEV, NIV, NJB, TEV]. The phrase οὐ συναπώλετο 'did not perish with' is translated 'escaped from being destroyed with' [NAB], 'escaped the fate of' [REB].

c. aorist act. participle of ἀπειθέω (LN 31.107, 36.23) (BAGD 2. p. 82): 'to disobey' [LN (36.23); CEV], 'to disobey God' [TEV], 'to be disobedient' [Mil, NIC; NASB, NIV, NRSV], 'to believe not' [KJV], 'to refuse to obey' [NLT], 'to refuse to believe, to refuse to be a believer, to reject the Christian message' [LN (31.107)]. The phrase τοῖς ἀπειθήσασιν 'the ones having disobeyed' is translated 'the disobedient' [BAGD, HNTC], 'the disobedient ones' [Lns], 'the unbelievers' [WBC; NAB, NJB, REB, TNT]. It means disobedient [Hu, Lns, My, Wst] to God [Alf, EBC, EGT, ICC]. It means the same as unbelief [Hu].

having-received[a] the spies[b] with[c] peace.[d]

LEXICON—a. aorist mid. (deponent = act.) of δέχομαι (LN 34.53) (BAGD 1. p. 177): 'to receive' [BAGD, HNTC, LN, Lns, NIC; KJV, NAB, NRSV], 'to welcome' [Mil, WBC; CEV, NASB, NIV, NJB], 'to give a welcome' [NLT, REB, TEV, TNT].

b. κατάσκοπος (LN **27.47**) (BAGD p. 418): 'spy' [BAGD, HNTC, LN, Lns, Mil, NIC, WBC; all versions except TEV], 'Israelite spy' [TEV].

c. μετά with genitive object (LN 89.79) (BAGD A.III.1. p. 509): 'with' [BAGD, LN, Lns; KJV], 'in' [LN; NASB, NRSV], not explicit [WBC]. It indicates manner [Mil, NIC].

d. εἰρήνη (LN 22.42) (BAGD 1.b. p. 227): 'peace' [LN, Lns; KJV, NASB, NRSV]. The phrase μετ' εἰρήνης 'with peace' is translated as an adverb: 'peaceably' [BAGD, HNTC, Mil], 'peacefully' [NAB], 'kindly' [REB], 'friendly' [NLT, TEV, TNT], 'hospitably' [NIC]. The phrase δεξαμένη μετ' εἰρήνης 'having received with peace' is translated 'to welcome' [WBC; CEV, NIV, NJB]. This phrase implies friendliness [ICC], as friends [EGT, Lns].

QUESTION—What relationship is indicated by the participle δεξαμένη 'having received'?

1. It indicates reason [HNTC, My, WBC; CEV, NAB, NIV, NJB, NLT, NRSV, TEV, TNT]: she did not perish because she received the spies.
2. It is temporal [Mil; KJV, NASB]: she did not perish after she received the spies. It also expresses the reason [Mil].

DISCOURSE UNIT: 11:32–40 [NTC, WBC]. The topic is known and unknown heroes of faith [NTC], triumphs in faith in subsequent times [WBC].

DISCOURSE UNIT: 11:32–38 [EBC, NIC]. The topic is the faith exercised by other servants of God [EBC], further examples of faith [NIC].

DISCOURSE UNIT: 11:32–35a [HNTC, NTC]. The topic is the power of faith [HNTC], those who triumphed [NTC].

11:32 And what yet should/do-I-say?

QUESTION—What relationship is indicated by this question?

This rhetorical question is a deliberative question with a subjunctive verb [EGT, Hu, Hwt, ICC, Lns, Mil, NIGTC, NTC]. It is a question of fact with an indicative verb [Alf, Lg(K), My].

1. It is translated in a deliberative sense [HNTC, My, NIGTC; NRSV, REB, TEV, TNT].

1.1 Of obligation [NRSV, TEV]: what yet should I say ?

1.2 Of need [My; NLT, REB, TNT]: need I say more? It implies that there is no need to say more [Hu, My].

1.3 Of intention [HNTC, NIGTC]: am I to say more?

2. It is translated as a future tense [EGT, Lns, Mil, NIC, WBC; KJV, NAB, NASB, NIV, NJB]: what shall I say?

For the time[a] will/would-fail[b] me telling[c] about[d] Gideon, Barak, Sampson, Jephthah, both David and Samuel and the prophets,

TEXT—Instead of Βαράκ, Σαμψών 'Barak, Sampson', some manuscripts read Βαράκ τε καὶ Σαμψὼν καὶ 'Ιεφθάε 'both Barak and Sampson and Jephthah', thus dividing the list into three (two [Alf]) groups instead of two. GNT does not deal with this variant. Only Alf, EGT add these words.

LEXICON—a. χρόνος (LN 67.78) (BAGD p. 888): 'time' [BAGD, HNTC, LN, Lns, Mil, NIC, WBC; all versions except NLT], not explicit [NLT].

b. fut. act. indic. of ἐπιλεὶπω (LN **13.41**) (BAGD p. 295): 'to fail' [BAGD, HNTC, LN, Lns, Mil, NIC, WBC; KJV, NASB, NRSV], 'to run out' [**LN**], 'to begin to come to the end' [LN]. The phrase ἐπιλείψει με ὁ χρόνος 'the time will fail me' is translated 'I have no time' [NAB], 'I do not have time' [NIV], 'there is not time for me' [NJB], 'there would be no time for me' [TNT], 'there isn't enough time' [CEV], 'there isn't enough time for me' [TEV], 'time is too short for me' [REB], 'it would take too long' [NLT].

c. pres. mid. (deponent = act.) of διηγέομαι (LN 33.201) (BAGD p. 195): 'to tell' [BAGD, HNTC, LN, Mil, NIC, WBC; all versions except NJB, NLT, TEV], 'to recount' [Lns], 'to recount the stories' [NLT], 'to relate' [BAGD], 'to speak' [TEV], 'to give an account' [NJB]. It means to relate in detail [EGT], to tell stories [TH].

d. περί with genitive object (LN 90.24): 'about' [LN, Lns, Mil, NIC, WBC; CEV, NIV], 'of' [HNTC, LN; all versions except CEV, NIV].

QUESTION—What relationship is indicated by γάρ?

It indicates the reason for the implied response to the preceding question [Mil]: I won't say more, because the time will fail me.

QUESTION—What relationship is indicated by the future indicative verb ἐπιλείψει 'will fail'?

1. It states a fact [Alf, EGT, HNTC, Lns, Mil, My, NIC; CEV, NASB, NLT]: time will fail me.

2. It is translated as hypothetical [ICC, WBC; KJV, NRSV]: time would fail me.

QUESTION—What relationship is indicated by the masculine accusative participle διηγούμενον 'telling'?

1. It modifies the accusative pronoun με 'me' [NTC] in a predicate relationship: time will fail me in telling.
2. It is temporal [Wst]: time will fail me as I tell.
3. It is conditional [Alf, EGT, Mil, NIC, NIGTC, WBC; NASB]: time will fail me if I tell.
4. It is translated as defining the nominative ὁ χρόνος 'the time' [HNTC, ICC, My; all versions except NASB]: the time to tell will fail.

QUESTION—What is implied by the masculine gender of the participle διηγούμενον 'telling'?

It indicates that the author is a man [Mil, NCBC, NIC, NIGTC, NTC, WBC]. The gender may be merely formal; or if a woman—e.g., Priscilla—wrote this book, she could have used the masculine gender of this participle to conceal her gender [GNC].

QUESTION—What relationship is indicated by the use of τε 'and'?

1. It introduces a new series distinct from the preceding series [ICC, Lns, Wst; KJV, NAB, NASB, NJB, NRSV, REB]: . . . Samson, Jephthah; and of David and Samuel . . .
2. It ties David closely with Samuel [Mil]: both David and Samuel.
3. It distinguishes David from Samuel and the prophets [WBC].
4. It is not translated [HNTC, NIC; CEV, NIV, NLT, TEV, TNT].

11:33 who through[a] faith conquered[b] kingdoms,

LEXICON—a. διά with genitive object (LN 90.8): 'through' [HNTC, LN, Lns, NIC, WBC; KJV, NIV, NJB, NLT, NRSV, REB, TEV], 'by' [NAB, NASB, TNT], 'by virtue of' [Mil], 'by means of, with' [LN]. The phrase διὰ πίστεως 'through faith' is translated 'their faith helped them' [CEV]. It is instrumental [NIGTC]; it is causal [Mil].

b. aorist mid. (deponent= act.) indic. of καταγωνίζομαι (LN **39.52**) (BAGD p. 410): 'to conquer' [BAGD, **LN**, Mil, NIC, WBC; CEV, NAB, NASB, NIV, NJB, NRSV], 'to be victorious over' [LN], 'to overcome, to defeat' [BAGD], 'to overthrow' [HNTC; NLT, REB, TNT], 'to subdue' [Lns, Mil; KJV], 'to fight and win' [TEV]. This verb and all of those in the following list are aorist tense, indicating historical facts [Lns].

QUESTION—To whom does οἵ 'who' refer?

It is a general reference, not limited to those mentioned in the preceding verse [Alf, Hwt, Lg, Mil, My, TH, WBC]. It governs 11:33–34 [ICC].

QUESTION—What is the phrase διὰ πίστεως 'through faith' connected with?

It applies to all of the events mentioned through 11:34 [Alf], through 11:37 [My], through 11:38 [EGT, ICC].

they-worked[a] righteousness,[b]

LEXICON—a. aorist mid. (deponent = act.) of ἐργάζομαι (LN 13.9, 42.41) (BAGD 2.a. p. 307): 'to work' [LN (42.41), Lns; KJV], 'to perform' [NASB], 'to do' [BAGD; CEV, NAB, NJB, TEV], 'to administer' [Mil; NIV, NRSV], 'to rule' [NLT], 'to exercise' [HNTC], 'to practice' [WBC], 'to establish' [NIC; REB, TNT], 'to cause' [LN (13.9)]. The prefixed κατα- adds emphasis [NTC].

b. δικαιοσύνη (LN 88.13) (BAGD 1. p. 196): 'righteousness' [LN, Lns; KJV], 'acts of righteousness' [NASB], 'justice' [BAGD, HNTC, Mil, NIC, WBC; NIV, NLT, NRSV, REB, TNT], 'what is just' [NAB], 'what is upright' [NJB], 'what is right' [TEV], 'right' [CEV].

QUESTION—What is meant by 'working righteousness'?

It means to administer justice [EBC, HNTC, Mil, My, NCBC, NIGTC, NTC, TNTC; NIV, NRSV], to establish and administer just government [WBC], to establish justice [REB, TNT], to practice justice [WBC], to rule righteously [EGT, Hwt, Lns, TH, Wst].

they-obtained[a] promises,

LEXICON—a. aorist act. indic. of ἐπιτυγχάνω (LN 57.60) (BAGD p. 304): 'to obtain' [BAGD, HNTC, LN, Lns, Mil, NIC; KJV, NAB, NASB, NRSV], 'to receive' [NLT, TEV], 'to acquire' [LN], 'to gain' [NIV], 'to attain' [LN, WBC], 'to attain to' [BAGD], 'to earn' [NJB], 'to find . . . come true' [TNT], 'to see fulfilled' [REB]. This clause is translated 'God made promises to them' [CEV].

QUESTION—What is meant by ἐπέτυχον 'obtained'?

1. It means that they obtained the fulfillment of things previously promised [Alf, HNTC, ICC, Lns, Mil, NIC, NIGTC, NTC, TH, WBC, Wst; NIV, NLT, REB, TEV, TNT] and thus the heightened expectation of further fulfillment [Wst].
2. It means that God made promises to them [CEV].
3. It refers both to having promises made and to receiving what was promised [Hu].

QUESTION—To what does ἐπαγγελιῶν 'promises' without a definite article refer?

It refers to what God has promised [NIGTC; REB, TEV, TNT], to promises of land and inheritances [HNTC].

1. It refers to unspecified promises [EGT, Lns, Mil, NIC; KJV, NASB, NRSV]: promises.
2. It is translated as if it had a definite article [HNTC, WBC; NAB, NJB]: the (specific) promises.

they-shut[a] mouths of lions,

LEXICON—a. aorist act. indic. of φράσσω (LN 20.30) (BAGD 1.a. p. 865): 'to shut' [BAGD, LN, Mil, NIC, WBC; NASB, NIV, NLT, NRSV, REB, TEV], 'to close' [BAGD; CEV], 'to stop' [BAGD; KJV], 'to muzzle'

[HNTC], 'to lock' [Lns], 'to keep shut' [NJB], 'to keep from doing harm, to keep from harming' [LN], 'to break' [NAB].

11:34 they-quenched[a] (the) power[b] of-fire,

LEXICON—a. aorist act. indic. of σβέννυμι (LN **14.70**) (BAGD 1. p. 745): 'to quench' [HNTC, Lns, Mil, NIC; KJV, NASB, NIV, NLT, NRSV, REB], 'to extinguish' [BAGD, LN, WBC], 'to put out' [BAGD, **LN**; CEV, NAB, NJB, TEV, TNT].

b. δύναμις (LN 76.1) (BAGD 1. p. 207): 'power' [BAGD, LN, Lns, Mil; NASB], 'strength' [BAGD], 'force' [HNTC, NIC], 'fury' [Mil, WBC; NIV, REB], 'violence' [KJV], 'flames' [NLT]. This noun is also translated as a participle: 'raging' [CEV, NAB, NRSV], 'blazing' [NJB]; as an adjective: 'fierce' [TEV]; as a phrase: 'in all their fury' [TNT].

QUESTION—How are the two nouns related in the genitive construction δύναμιν πυρός 'power of fire'?

1. 'Fire' is the source of the 'power': power which has its source in fire.
2. 'Power' describes 'fire' [CEV, NAB, NJB, NRSV, TEV]: raging fire.

they-escaped[a] mouths[b] of-sword,

LEXICON—a. aorist act. indic. of φεύγω (LN **6.33**, **21.14**) (BAGD 2. p. 855): 'to escape' [BAGD, HNTC, LN **(21.14)**, Lns, Mil, NIC, WBC; all versions except NJB, NLT], 'to escape death' [NLT]. This entire phrase is translated 'they escaped being killed by the sword' [LN **(6.33)**], 'they emerged unscathed from battle' [NJB]. The aorist tense implies fleeing successfully [WBC]

b. στόμα (LN 8.19, 79.109) (BAGD 2. p. 770): 'mouth' [LN (8.19), Lns], 'edge' [BAGD, HNTC, LN (79.109), Mil, NIC, WBC; KJV, NASB, NIV, NLT, NRSV], 'sharp edge, cutting edge' [LN (79.109)], not explicit [CEV, NJB]. The phrase στόματα μαχαίρης 'mouths of sword' is translated 'the devouring sword' [NAB], 'death by the sword' [REB, TNT], 'being killed by the sword' [TEV]. The plural indicates reference to several examples [Alf, EBC, TH, Wst]; it refers to the two edges of a sword [Lns, NIGTC].

QUESTION—How are the two nouns related in the genitive construction στόματα μαχαίρης 'mouths of sword'?

1. 'Mouths' is a part of 'sword': mouths which are a part of the sword.
2. 'Mouths' describes 'sword' [NAB]: the devouring sword.

they-were-strengthened[a] from[b] weakness,[c]

LEXICON—a. aorist pass. indic. of δυναμόω (LN 74.6) (BAGD p. 208): 'to be strengthened' [LN], 'to be made strong' [Mil; KJV, NASB], 'to be given strength' [CEV, NJB], 'to be turned to strength' [NIC; NIV, NLT, REB], 'to be made powerful' [HNTC; NAB], 'to be brought to power' [Lns], 'to be empowered, to be enabled, to be given capability' [LN]. This passive verb is translated as an active voice with 'they' as subject: 'to pass to strength' [BAGD], 'to become strong' [WBC; TEV], 'to win strength' [NRSV]; with faith as subject: 'to make strong' [TNT].

b. πρό with genitive object (LN 89.122): 'from' [HNTC, LN, Lns, Mil; NASB], 'out of' [KJV, NRSV], 'after' [WBC], 'though' [NAB], not explicit [CEV, NIV, NJB, NLT, REB, TEV, TNT]. It has a temporal sense [WBC].

c. ἀσθένεια (LN 23.143) (BAGD 1.b. p. 115): 'weakness' [BAGD, LN, Lns, Mil, NIC, WBC; KJV, NASB, NIV, NLT, NRSV, REB], 'illness' [LN], 'disability' [LN]. This noun is also translated as a participial phrase: 'being weak' [HNTC]; as an adjective: 'weak' [CEV, NAB, NJB, TEV, TNT]. It refers to physical weakness [Alf, HNTC, Mil, My, NCBC, NIC, NIGTC, NTC, TNTC, Wst], power to wage war [TH].

they-became strong[a] in[b] war,[c]

LEXICON—a. ἰσχυρός (LN 76.11, 79.63) (BAGD 1.b. p. 383): 'strong' [HNTC, LN (76.11, 79.63), Lns; NAB, NLT], 'powerful' [LN (76.11); NIV, REB], 'mighty' [BAGD, Mil, NIC, WBC; NASB, NRSV, TEV], 'valiant' [KJV], 'brave' [NJB]. This entire clause is translated 'they became powerful fighters' [TNT], 'they were given power' [CEV].

b. ἐν with dative object (LN 83.13): 'in' [HNTC, LN, Lns, Mil, NIC, WBC; all versions except CEV, TNT], not explicit [CEV, TNT].

c. πόλεμος (LN 39.26, 55.5) (BAGD 1.a. p. 685): 'war' [BAGD, HNTC, LN (55.5), Lns, NIC, WBC; NASB, NJB, NRSV, REB], 'battle' [Mil; NAB, NIV, NLT, TEV], 'fight' [KJV], 'struggle' [LN (39.26)], not explicit [CEV].

they-turned-to-flight[a] camps[b] of-foreigners.[c]

LEXICON—a. aorist act. indic. of κλίνω (LN **15.65**) (BAGD 1.d. p. 436): 'to turn to flight' [BAGD, Lns; KJV], 'to put to flight' [LN, NIC; NASB, NLT, NRSV], 'to put to rout' [REB], 'to rout' [**LN**, Mil, WBC; NIV], 'to defeat' [TEV], 'to turn back' [HNTC; NAB, TNT], 'to drive back' [NJB], 'to cause to run away' [LN], 'to chase away' [CEV], 'to cause to fall' [BAGD]. It means to break a military formation [WBC].

b. παρεμβολή (LN 1.94, 7.22) (BAGD 3. p. 625): 'camp' [LN (1.94)], 'battle line' [BAGD, Lns], 'barracks' [LN (7.22)], 'army' [HNTC, Mil, NIC, WBC; all versions except NAB, NJB], 'invader' [NAB, NJB]. It refers to the army which is in the camp [Alf, Blm, EGT, Lg, Mil, My, NTC, Wst] in battle array [Lg, NTC].

c. ἀλλότριος (LN **39.12**) (BAGD 3. p. 41): 'foreigner' [HNTC; TEV, TNT], 'enemy' [BAGD, LN]. This noun is translated as an adjective: 'foreign' [Mil, NIC, WBC; CEV, NAB, NASB, NIV, NJB, NRSV, REB], 'alien' [Lns; KJV], not explicit [NLT]. It implies enemies [NIGTC, NTC].

11:35 Women received the dead-ones of-them from[a] resurrection;[b]

LEXICON—a. ἐκ with genitive object (LN 89.77) (BAGD 3.f. p. 235): 'from, by means of' [LN], 'by reason of' [BAGD], 'as a result of' [BAGD, Lns,

Mil], 'because of' [BAGD], 'by' [HNTC, NIC, WBC; NASB, NJB, NRSV], 'through' [NAB]. It expresses cause [Alf, NIGTC], reason [Mil].

b. ἀνάστασις (LN 23.93) (BAGD 2a. p. 60): 'resurrection' [BAGD, HNTC, LN, Lns, Mil, NIC, WBC; NAB, NASB, NJB, NRSV]. The phrase ἐξ ἀναστάσεως 'from resurrection' is translated 'raised to life' [REB], 'raised back to life' [TEV], 'raised to life again' [KJV, NIV, TNT], 'back again from death' [NLT], 'back from death' [CEV]. Here it refers to a return to the present earthly life [NIGTC, WBC].

QUESTION—What is this clause connected with?

1. It begins a new series and is connected with what follows [TH; CEV].
2. It stands alone [TNTC].
3. It belongs to what precedes [WBC; NLT, TEV].

QUESTION—To whom does τοὺς νεκρούς 'the dead ones' refer?

It refers to their husbands [NJB], their sons [GNC, HNTC, Hwt, Lns, My, NIGTC, NTC, TNTC, WBC], their children [NIC], their relatives [TH; TEV], their loved ones [CEV, NLT].

DISCOURSE UNIT: 11:35b–38 [HNTC]. The topic is faith under duress.

but others were-tortured,[a] not having-accepted[b] the release,[c]

LEXICON—a. aorist pass. indic. of τυμπανίζω (LN **38.13**) (BAGD p. 829): 'to be tortured' [BAGD, HNTC, LN, Lns, WBC; CEV, KJV, NAB, NASB, NIV, NLT, NRSV], 'to be tortured to death' [NIC; REB, TNT], 'to be beaten to death' [Mil]. This passive voice is also translated as an active voice: 'to submit to torture' [NJB], 'to die under torture' [TEV]. It refers to being stretched on a rack [Alf, EBC, GNC, HNTC, Hu, Hwt, ICC, Lg, Lns, My, NCBC, NIC, NIGTC, TH, Wst], and beaten to death [Alf, EBC, EGT, GNC, Hu, Hwt, ICC, Lg, Lns, My, NCBC, NIC, NIGTC, TH, Wst]. It is a general term referring to being beaten to death [Mil], to various means of torture [Lns].

b. aorist mid. (deponent = act.) participle of προσδέχομαι (LN 31.53) (BAGD 1.b. p. 712): 'to accept' [HNTC, LN, Lns; KJV, NASB], 'to receive' [BAGD, LN; NAB]. The phrase οὐ προσδεξάμενοι 'not having accepted' is translated 'to refuse' [CEV, NIV, NJB, REB, TNT], 'to refuse to accept' [Mil, NIC, WBC; NRSV, TEV], 'to prefer to die rather than turn from God' [NLT].

c. ἀπολύτρωσις (LN 37.128) (BAGD 1. p. 96): 'release' [BAGD, HNTC; NASB, NJB, NRSV, REB], 'the offered release' [WBC], 'deliverance' [LN, Mil, NIC; KJV, NAB], 'ransoming' [Lns], 'liberation' [LN], 'freedom' [TEV]. This noun is also translated as a verb: 'to be released' [CEV, NIV, TNT], 'to be free' [NLT]. The release was conditioned upon denying their faith [Blm, EBC, EGT, HNTC, Hu, ICC, Lns, My, NIC, TNTC, WBC].

QUESTION—What is this clause connected with?

1. It is connected with what precedes [Lns, Mil, NIC, NIGTC, TH; CEV].
2. It is connected with what follows [GNC, HNTC, My, Wst; NLT, TEV].

QUESTION—What relationship is indicated by ἄλλοι δέ 'but others'?
It indicates a change of subject from the preceding [Lns, WBC]; it introduces a new grouping [Wst].

QUESTION—What relationship is indicated by the aorist participial phrase οὐ προσδεξάμενοι 'not having accepted'?
1. It expresses the negative of the alternative [CEV, NAB, NIV, TNT]: they were tortured but they did not accept release.
2. It indicates reason [Mil, TH]: because they did not accept release.
3. It is temporal [WBC, Wst]: after they did not accept release.

in-order-that they-might-experience[a] (a) better[b] resurrection;[c]

LEXICON—a. aorist act. subj. of τυγχάνω (LN **90.61**) (BAGD 1. p. 829): 'to experience' [BAGD, LN], 'to attain' [BAGD, NIC, WBC], 'to gain' [BAGD, Mil; NIV], 'to obtain' [HNTC, Lns; KJV, NAB, NASB, NRSV], 'to win' [REB], not explicit [NLT]. This entire clause is translated 'so that they would rise again to a better life' [NJB], 'in order to be raised to a better life' [TEV], 'in order that they might rise to a better life' [TNT], 'they were sure that they would get a better reward when the dead are raised to life' [CEV].

b. κρείττων (LN 65.21) (BAGD 1. p. 449): 'better' [BAGD, HNTC, LN, Lns, Mil, NIC, WBC; all versions except NLT, REB], 'superior' [LN], 'to a better life' [NLT, REB]. It is qualitative [WBC]. The phrase κρείττονος ἀναστάσεως 'better resurrection' refers to resurrection to a different and better life [Blm], life in the age to come with God [EBC, NIC], eternal life [EGT, My, WBC, Wst], a better state than their enemies [TH], a better state than their present situation [TNTC, Wst].

c. ἀνάστασις: 'resurrection'. See above. It refers to resurrection to eternal life [Hwt, NCBC].

QUESTION—What relationship is indicated by ἵνα 'in order that'?
It introduces the purpose of the preceding clause [Mil, My, TH]: they did not accept release in order that they might gain . . .

11:36 and others received trial[a] of-mockings[b] and scourgings,[c]

LEXICON—a. πεῖρα (LN 68.58) (BAGD 2. p. 640): 'trial' [KJV]. The phrase πεῖραν ἔλαβον 'received trial' is translated 'to experience' [BAGD, HNTC, **LN** (90.63), Mil, NIC, WBC; NASB], 'to endure' [NAB], 'to face' [NIV, REB], 'to have to bear' [NJB], 'to suffer' [NRSV], 'to know what it was' [TNT], 'to undertake to try' [Lns], not explicit [CEV, NLT, TEV].

b. ἐμπαιγμός (LN **33.406**) (BAGD p. 255): 'mocking' [BAGD, Lns, Mil; NASB], 'cruel mocking' [KJV], 'scorn' [BAGD], 'jeer' [NIV, REB]. This plural noun is translated as a singular: 'mocking' [HNTC, NIC; NRSV], 'mockery' [NAB], 'jeering' [WBC]. This noun is also translated as a verb: 'to be pilloried' [NJB], 'to be taunted' [TNT]. The phrase ἐμπαιγμῶν πεῖραν ἔλαβον 'received trial of mockings' is translated 'to be mocked'

[LN; NLT], 'to be made fun of' [CEV]. This word implies insult accompanied by cruelty [Alf].

c. μάστιξ (LN **19.9**) (BAGD 1. p. 495): 'scourging' [Lns, Mil; KJV, NAB, NASB] 'lashing, lash' [BAGD]. This plural noun is translated as a singular: 'scourging' [NIC], 'flogging' [HNTC; NIV, NRSV, REB], 'lashing' [WBC]. This noun is also translated as a verb: 'to be flogged' [NJB, TNT], 'to be beaten with whips' [CEV], 'to be cut open with whips' [NLT]. This noun together with the preceding ἐμπαιγμῶν 'mockings' forms one thought, a hendiadys, implying flogging that was insulting [ICC].

QUESTION—What relationship is indicated by ἕτεροι δέ 'and others'?

1. It introduces a different class of victories of faith [EGT, Hwt, Lg, Lns, Mil, My, Wst].
2. Ἕτεροι is merely used for variety after the preceding ἄλλοι 'others' [NIGTC, NTC] and δέ 'and' introduces a transition [NIGTC].

QUESTION—How are the two genitive nouns related to the other noun in the phrase ἐμπαιγμῶν καὶ μαστίγων πεῖραν 'trial of mockings and scourgings'?

The genitive nouns 'mockings and scourgings' state what the 'trial' consisted of [Blm, Lg, Mil, NIC, TH, TNTC, WBC, Wst; all versions except CEV, KJV, NLT]: trial that consisted of mockings and scourgings.

and in-addition,[a] of-bonds[b] and prison;[c]

LEXICON—a. ἔτι (LN 59.75) (BAGD 2.b. p. 316): 'in addition' [BAGD, LN], 'besides' [LN], 'also' [BAGD, HNTC], 'moreover' [KJV], 'even' [WBC; NAB, NRSV, REB], 'too' [NIC], not explicit [CEV, NLT, TEV, TNT]. The phrase ἔτι δέ 'and in addition' is translated 'besides even' [Lns], 'even more' [Mil], 'yes, also' [NASB], 'or even' [NJB], 'while still others' [NIV]. Ἔτι δέ 'and in addition' indicates rising to a climax [Alf, EGT, ICC, Lg, Lns, Mil, My].

b. δεσμός (LN 6.14, 37.115) (BAGD 1. p. 176): 'bond' [BAGD, LN (6.14), Mil; KJV], 'chain' [HNTC, LN (6.14), NIC, WBC; NAB, NASB, NRSV], 'fetter' [LN (6.14); REB], 'imprisonment' [LN (37.115)]. This plural noun is translated as a singular: 'confinement' [Lns]. This noun is also translated as a verb: 'to be chained' [CEV, NIV, NLT], 'to be chained up' [TNT], 'to be put in chains' [TEV]. It means virtually the same as the following φυλακῆς 'prison' [NIGTC].

c. φυλακή (LN 7.24) (BAGD 3. p. 867): 'prison' [BAGD, LN, Lns, WBC; NJB, TEV], 'imprisonment' [HNTC, Mil, NIC; KJV, NAB, NASB, NRSV], 'prison bar' [REB], 'jail' [LN; CEV], 'dungeon' [NLT]. This noun is also translated as a verb: 'to be put in prison' [NIV], 'to be imprisoned' [TNT]. This and the preceding noun δεσμῶν 'chains' form one idea, a hendiadys, meaning 'captivity' [WBC].

QUESTION— What are the two genitive nouns δεσμῶν 'bonds' and φυλακῆς 'chains' connected with?

They further identify πεῖραν 'trial' in the preceding clause [Lg, NIC, TH, TNTC, WBC, Wst]: trial that consisted of bonds and chains.

11:37 they-were-stoned, they-were-sawed-in-two,[a] they-died by murder[b] of-sword,

TEXT—Some manuscripts add ἐπειράσθησαν 'they were tested' either before or following ἐπρίσθησαν 'they were sawed in two'. GNT rejects this addition with a C decision, indicating that the committee had difficulty making the decision. 'They were sawed in two, they were tested' is read by only Alf, Blm, EGT, Lg, My, KJV, NASB; 'they were tested, they were sawed in two' is read by only Wst.

LEXICON—a. aorist pass. indic. of πρίζω (LN **19.20**) (BAGD p. 701): 'to be sawed in two' [BAGD, HNTC, **LN**, Mil, NIC, WBC; NAB, NASB, NIV, NRSV, REB, TEV, TNT], 'to be sawed in half' [NJB, NLT], 'to be sawn asunder' [Lns; KJV], 'to be cut in two with a saw' [LN].

b. φόνος (LN 20.82) (BAGD p. 864): 'murder' [LN, Lns]. The phrase ἐν φόνῳ μαχαίρης 'by murder of sword' is translated 'by being murdered with the sword' [BAGD]. The phrase ἐν φόνῳ μαχαίρης ἀπέθανον 'they died by murder of sword' is translated 'to be murdered by the sword' [WBC], 'to be slain with the sword' [KJV], 'to be slaughtered with the sword' [Mil], 'to be put to death with the sword' [NASB], 'to be put to death by the sword' [NIV, TNT], 'to be put to death by the edge of the sword' [HNTC], 'to be killed by the sword' [NIC; NJB, NRSV, TEV], 'to be killed with the sword' [NLT], 'to be killed with swords' [CEV], 'to be put to the sword' [REB], 'to be put to death at sword's point' [NAB].

QUESTION—How are the two nouns related in the genitive phrase φόνῳ μαχαίρης 'by murder of sword'?

'Sword' is the source or instrument of the 'murder' [Alf, EBC, Mil, NIGTC, WBC; NIV, NJB, NRSV, TEV, TNT]: murder caused by the sword.

they-went-around[a] in[b] sheepskins,[c] in skins[d] of-goats,[e]

LEXICON—a. aorist act. indic. of περιέρχομαι (LN **15.23**) (BAGD p. 646): 'to go around' [LN; TEV], 'to go about' [HNTC, NIC, WBC; NAB, NASB, NIV, NLT, NRSV, REB, TNT], 'to wander about' [BAGD, Lns, Mil; KJV], 'to wander around' [**LN**], 'to be homeless' [NJB], not explicit [CEV].

b. ἐν with dative object (LN 13.8): 'in' [HNTC, LN, Lns, Mil, NIC, WBC; KJV, NASB, NIV, NLT, REB, TNT]. This preposition is also translated as a phrase: 'clothed in' [NRSV, TEV], 'garbed in' [NAB], 'and wore only' [NJB], 'some had nothing but . . . to wear' [CEV]. This preposition here means 'clothed with' [My].

c. μηλωτή (LN **6.187**) (BAGD p. 518): 'sheepskin' [BAGD, HNTC, **LN**, Mil, NIC, WBC; CEV, KJV, NASB, NIV, TNT], 'skin of sheep' [NAB, NJB, NLT, NRSV, REB, TEV], 'sheep pelt' [Lns], 'fleece' [LN].

d. δέρμα (LN **6.184**) (BAGD p. 175): 'skin' [BAGD, LN; CEV, NAB, NJB, NLT, NRSV, REB, TEV]. The phrase αἰγείοις δέρμασιν 'skins of goats' is translated 'goatskins' [HNTC, **LN**, Lns, Mil, NIC, WBC; KJV, NASB, NIV, TNT].

e. αἴγειος (LN **4.20**) (BAGD p. 21): 'goat' [BAGD, LN]. The phrase αἰγείοις δέρμασιν 'skins of goats' is translated 'goat skins' [BAGD, **LN**].

being-in-need,[a] being-afflicted,[b] being-maltreated,[c]

LEXICON—a. pres. mid. participle of ὑστερέω (LN **57.37**) (BAGD 2. p. 849): 'to be in need' [**LN**], 'to be in want' [LN; NJB], 'to be destitute' [Lns, NIC; KJV, NASB], 'to suffer poverty' [TNT], 'to be poor' [CEV], 'to go without' [BAGD], 'needy' [HNTC; NAB], 'destitute' [Mil, WBC; NIV, NRSV], 'deprived' [REB], 'poor' [TEV], 'hungry' [NLT].

b. pres. pass. participle of θλίβω (LN **22.15**) (BAGD 3. p. 362): 'to be afflicted' [BAGD, Lns, NIC; KJV, NASB], 'to be mistreated' [CEV], 'to be in hardship' [NJB], 'to suffer hardship' [LN], 'to suffer oppression' [TNT], 'to suffer' [**LN**], 'to be troubled' [LN], 'to be distressed' [BAGD], 'afflicted' [Mil; NAB], 'persecuted' [NIV, NRSV, TEV], 'oppressed' [HNTC, WBC; NLT, REB].

c. pres. pass. participle of κακουχέω (LN **88.126**) (BAGD p. 398): 'to be maltreated' [BAGD; NJB], 'to be mistreated' [**LN**], 'to be ill-treated' [NIC; NASB], 'to be basely treated' [Lns], 'to be tormented' [BAGD; KJV], 'to be tortured' [CEV], 'to be caused to suffer' [LN], 'to suffer misery' [TNT], 'to suffer hardship' [HNTC], 'tormented' [NAB, NRSV], 'mistreated' [WBC; NIV, NLT, TEV], 'ill-treated' [Mil; REB].

11:38 of-whom the world[a] was not worthy,[b]

LEXICON—a. κόσμος (LN 9.23): 'world' [HNTC, Lns, Mil, NIC; all versions except NJB, TEV], 'people of the world' [LN], 'humanity' [WBC]. This word refers to human society organized without God [HNTC], in hostility to God [NCBC, NIGTC].

b. ἄξιος (LN 65.17) (BAGD 2.a. p. 78): 'worthy' [BAGD, HNTC, LN, Lns, Mil, NIC, WBC; KJV, NAB, NASB, NIV, NRSV, REB, TNT], 'of comparable value' [LN], 'comparable' [LN]. This entire phrase is translated 'they were too good for the world' [NJB, NLT], 'the world was not good enough for them' [TEV], 'the world did not deserve these good people' [CEV].

QUESTION—To whom does ὧν 'of whom' refer?

It refers to ἕτεροι 'others' in 11:36 [NIGTC], to the persons mentioned in the preceding verse [Alf, Mil, My] as is indicated by the following participle, which refers to those same persons [Alf]. This relative pronoun introduces a parenthetical statement [Mil].

QUESTION—How are the adjective and the pronoun related in the genitive construction ὧν οὐκ ἄξιος 'not worthy of whom (of them)'?

It implies that (the world) did not deserve to possess them [BAGD, My, WBC], it was not fit to have them in it [Alf, EGT, HNTC, Lns, TH], was not fit to be compared with them [TNTC], that human society was unfit for them [NIC], that they were of more value than the rest of mankind [EBC, Hwt, Wst].

wandering[a] in[b] deserts[c] and mountains and caves[d] and the holes[e] of-the ground.[f]

LEXICON—a. pres. mid. participle of πλανάω (LN **15.24**) (BAGD 2.a. p. 665): 'to wander' [HNTC, **LN**, Mil, NIC; CEV, KJV, NASB, NIV, NJB, NLT, NRSV], 'to wander about' [BAGD, LN; NAB, TNT], 'to wander aimlessly' [WBC], 'to wander like a refugee' [TEV], 'to be a refugee' [REB], 'to err about' [Lns].

b. ἐπί with dative object (LN 83.46): 'in' [HNTC, Lns, (ἐν, NIC), WBC; all versions except NLT], 'on, upon' [LN], 'over' [Mil; NLT].

c. ἐρημία (LN 1.86) (BAGD p. 309): 'desert' [BAGD, LN, Lns, Mil, NIC; all versions except TNT], 'wilderness' [LN], 'uninhabited region' [BAGD, WBC], 'uninhabited place' [HNTC], 'lonely place' [TNT].

d. σπήλαιον (LN 1.57) (BAGD p. 762): 'cave' [BAGD, HNTC, LN, Lns, Mil, NIC, WBC; all versions except KJV], 'den' [LN; KJV]. It means a cavern [Blm]; it would be entered horizontally [TH].

e. ὀπή (LN **1.53**) (BAGD p. 574): 'hole' [BAGD, HNTC, **LN**, Lns, NIC; all versions except KJV, NJB], 'opening' [BAGD, LN], 'crevice' [WBC], 'rift' [Mil], 'cave' [KJV]. The phrase ταῖς ὀπαῖς τῆς γῆς 'the holes of the earth' is translated 'ravines' [NJB]. This word refers to caves [Blm]; it refers to something smaller than σπήλαιον 'cave' [NIGTC]. It would be entered by going down [TH].

f. γῆ (LN 1.39): 'ground' [HNTC, Mil, NIC, WBC; CEV, NASB, NIV, NLT, NRSV, REB, TEV, TNT], 'earth' [LN, Lns; KJV, NAB], 'world' [LN].

QUESTION—What relationship is indicated by the participle πλανώμενοι 'wandering'?

1. It states an additional fact [WBC; all versions except NASB]: (in addition) they wandered . . .
2. It makes specific the general reference indicated by περιῆλθον 'they went around' in the preceding verse [Mil]: they went around—i.e., they wandered . . .
3. It is temporal [NIC]: as they wandered . . .

QUESTION—How are the two nouns related in the genitive construction ταῖς ὀπαῖς τῆς γῆς 'the holes of the earth'?

The genitive noun γῆς 'earth' tells where the ὀπαῖς 'holes' are located [HNTC, NIC, WBC; NASB, NIV, NRSV, REB, TEV, TNT]: the holes located in the earth.

DISCOURSE UNIT: 11:39–40 (EBC, HNTC, NIC). The topic is the promise [EBC], the testimony of faith [HNTC], the vindication of faith comes with Christ [NIC].

11:39 And these all, having-been-approved[a] through[b] the faith, (did) not receive[c] the promise,[d]

LEXICON—a. aorist pass. participle of μαρτυρέω (LN 33.263) (BAGD 2.b. p. 493): 'to be approved' [NAB], 'to be approved of, to be spoken well of' [LN], 'to be well attested' [NIC], 'to be commended' [NIV, NRSV], 'to be praised' [BAGD], 'to have witness borne to one' [Mil]. This passive voice is also translated as an active: 'to gain approval' [NASB], 'to receive God's approval' [NLT], 'to obtain a good report' [KJV], 'to receive testimony' [Lns], 'to win testimony' [HNTC], 'to win acknowledgment' [NJB], 'to win God's approval' [REB, TNT], 'to please God' [CEV], 'to receive attestation from God' [WBC], 'to win a record' [TEV]. This word is emphatic [Alf]. The witness is favorable [NIGTC]; it was borne by God [Hwt, NTC, TH, Wst]; it was found in Scripture [My, TH].

b. διά with genitive object (LN 89.26, 89.76): 'through' [LN (89.76), WBC; KJV, NASB, NJB], 'because of' [HNTC, LN (89.26), Mil; CEV, NAB, NLT, REB], 'on account of, by reason of' [LN (89.26)], 'by means of' [Lns], 'by' [TEV], 'for' [NIC; NIV, NRSV, TNT]. It means 'on account of' [EBC, Hwt]. It indicates a reason [Mil], means [NIGTC].

c. aorist act. indic. of κομίζω (LN 90.92) (BAGD 2.a. p. 442): 'to receive' [BAGD, HNTC, Mil, NIC, WBC; all versions except CEV, NAB, TNT], 'to obtain' [NAB, TNT], 'to bring off' [Lns], 'to get for oneself' [BAGD], 'to be given' [CEV], 'to cause to experience in return, to cause to experience in proportion to' [LN]. The aorist tense summarizes the actions of numerous persons [WBC].

d. ἐπαγγελία (LN 33.288) (BAGD 2.b. p. 280): 'promise' [HNTC, LN, Lns; KJV], 'what was promised' [BAGD; NASB, NJB, NRSV, REB], 'what had been promised' [WBC; CEV, NAB, NIV], 'what they had been promised' [NIC], 'what he had promised' [TNT], 'what God had promised' [Mil; TEV], 'all that God had promised' [NLT]. It refers to the promise of eternal salvation [Alf, Hwt, ICC, WBC], the coming of Christ [Blm, NTC, TNTC], the promises realized through Christ [Hu], the promised Messianic blessedness [Lg, Lns, My], the final resurrection and glorification of our bodies [Lns].

QUESTION—What relationship is indicated by καί 'and'?

It introduces a further reason and result [Mil].

QUESTION—To whom does οὗτοι πάντες 'these all' refer?

'These' refers to the heroes of faith mentioned in this chapter [EBC, EGT, GNC, Hu, Hwt, ICC, Lg, My, TH, WBC], and 'all' indicates that none were omitted [EBC]. It includes also the many other unnamed persons who were likewise faithful in the past [GNC, Hu, Lg, Wst].

QUESTION—What relationship is indicated by the participle μαρτυρηθέντες 'having been approved'?

It expresses a concession [Alf, EGT, HNTC, Lg, Lns, Mil, My, NIC, NTC, WBC; NAB, NIV, NJB, NRSV, REB, TEV]: although they had been approved. The passive voice implies God as the actor [WBC].

QUESTION—What relationship is indicated by the definite article in the noun phrase τῆς πίστεως 'the faith'?

1. The definite article implies possession [Alf, EBC, EGT, GNC, HNTC, Hu, Hwt, Mil, My, NIC, NTC, Wst; all versions except KJV]: through their faith.
2. The definite article is not translated [ICC, WBC; KJV]: through faith.

11:40 God having provided[a] something better[b] for[c] us,

LEXICON—a. aorist mid. participle of προβλέπω (LN **30.100, 35.35**) (BAGD p. 703): 'to provide' [BAGD, LN (**35.35**), Mil, NIC, WBC; KJV, NASB, NRSV], 'to provide for' [LN (35.35)], 'to make provision to have' [NJB], 'to have in store' [CEV], 'to plan' [NIV], 'to make a plan' [HNTC; NAB, REB], 'to decide on a plan' [TEV], 'to have a plan' [TNT], 'to have in view' [Lns, Mil], 'to have in mind' [NLT], 'to choose beforehand' [LN (30.100)], 'to choose ahead of time' [LN (**30.100**)], 'to select' [BAGD], 'to select in advance' [LN (30.100)]. The middle voice means to foresee from afar [Alf]; it means to provide something for someone [WBC].

b. κρείττων (LN 65.21, 87.28) (BAGD 1. p. 449): 'better' [BAGD, HNTC, LN (65.21, 87.28), Lns, Mil, NIC, WBC; all versions except TEV, TNT], 'even better' [TEV, TNT], 'superior' [LN (65.21, 87.28)], 'greater' [LN (87.28)].

c. περί with genitive object (LN 90.39): 'for' [Mil; CEV, KJV, NASB, NIV, NJB, NLT, TEV], 'on behalf of' [LN], 'as pertaining to' [Lns], 'including' [HNTC], 'which included' [NAB]; the phrase περὶ ἡμῶν 'for us' is translated 'with us in mind' [WBC; REB, TNT], 'with us in view' [NIC], not explicit [NRSV]. The phrase περὶ ἡμῶν 'for us' is emphatic by word order [Alf, Lns, My] in contrast with οὗτοι πάντες 'these all' in the preceding verse [Alf, My].

QUESTION—What relationship is indicated by the participle προβλεψαμένου 'having provided'?

1. It expresses cause [Lns, Mil, NIC, NTC; CEV, NASB, NJB, NRSV, REB, TEV]: because God had provided.
2. It expresses an additional statement [WBC; NAB, NIV, TNT]: God had provided.

QUESTION—To what does κρεῖττόν τι 'something better' refer?

It refers to the fulfillment of the promise in Christ [Alf, Blm, EBC, My(D), NIGTC], full fellowship with God through the work of Christ [EGT, Mil, NIC], the new covenant with its blessings [GNC, HNTC], the superiority of the Christian revelation [TNTC]. It includes a better high priest, sacrifice, covenant, and country [Hu, Mil, NIC] and other better things mentioned earlier [Mil, NIC, TH].

in-order-that not apart-from[a] us they-should-be-perfected.[b]

LEXICON—a. χωρίς with genitive object (LN 89.120) (BAGD 2.a.α. p. 890): 'apart from' [LN, Lns, NIC; NASB, NRSV], 'without' [BAGD, HNTC, LN, Mil; CEV, KJV, NAB], 'except with' [WBC; NJB], 'only with' [REB, TNT], 'only together with' [NIV], 'only in company with' [TEV], not explicit [NLT].

b. aorist pass. subjunctive of τελειόω (LN 88.38) (BAGD 2.d. p. 810): 'to be perfected' [LN], 'to be made perfect' [HNTC, LN, Mil; KJV, NAB, NASB, NIV, NRSV, TEV], 'to be brought to perfection' [TNT], 'to be brought to completeness' [Lns], 'to be brought to one's goal' [BAGD]. This passive voice is translated as an active voice: 'to reach perfection' [WBC; NJB, REB], 'to attain one's perfection' [NIC], 'to reach the goal of their faith' [CEV], 'to receive the prize at the end of the race' [NLT]. It refers to arriving at the goal of God's saving purposes [GNC].

QUESTION—What is the negative μή 'not' connected with?

1. It is connected with χωρὶς ἡμῶν 'apart from us' [Lns, My, NIGTC, NTC; NIV, REB, TEV, TNT]: not apart from us. Word order favors this connection.
2. It is connected with the verb τελειωθῶσιν 'they should be perfected' [HNTC, ICC, Mil, NIC, WBC, Wst; KJV, NAB, NASB, NJB, NRSV]: they should not be perfected.

DISCOURSE UNIT: 12:1–13:25 [NTC]. The topic is admonitions and exhortations.

DISCOURSE UNIT: 12:1–29 [Hwt, Lg, TNTC, Wst; NIV]. The topic is present endurance motivated by future hope [Hwt], a comprehensive appeal, based on what has preceded [Lg], discipline and its benefits [TNTC], God's discipline of his sons [NIV].

DISCOURSE UNIT: 12:1–13 [GNT, NIGTC, NTC, WBC; CEV, NAB, NLT, REB]. The topic is the Lord's discipline [GNT, NTC], the need for endurance [NIGTC], the display of necessary endurance [WBC], God's treatment of his sons [NAB], God's love proved by his discipline [NLT], faith today [REB], a large crowd of witnesses [CEV].

DISCOURSE UNIT: 12:1–11 [NCBC, TNTC; TEV]. The topic is discipline and endurance [NCBC], the need for discipline [TNTC], God our Father [TEV].

DISCOURSE UNIT: 12:1–4 [NJB]. The topic is the example of Jesus Christ.

DISCOURSE UNIT: 12:1–3 [EBC, GNC, HNTC, Lg, Lns, NIC; NASB]. The topic is Christ our example [EBC; NASB], looking to Jesus as the perfect pattern [GNC], summons to endurance [HNTC, Lg], Jesus the author and completer of the faith [Lns, NIC].

12:1 Wherefore-then we also, having so-great[a] a-cloud[b] of-witnesses surrounding[c] us,

LEXICON—a. τοσοῦτος (LN 59.18) (BAGD 1.a.β. p. 823): 'so great' [BAGD, LN, Lns, Mil, NIC, WBC; KJV, NASB, NRSV], 'such a great' [HNTC; NIV], 'such a large' [LN; CEV], 'such a huge' [NLT], 'this large' [TEV], 'this great' [REB], 'this' [NAB]. The phrase τοσοῦτον ἔχοντες . . . νέφος μαρτύρων 'having so great a cloud of witnesses' is translated 'with all these witnesses to faith . . . in a great cloud' [TNT], 'with so many witnesses in a great cloud' [NJB]. This word is emphatic by word order [EBC, ICC, NIGTC, WBC] and the emphasis is upon quality [WBC].

b. νέφος (LN **11.3**) (BAGD p. 537): 'cloud' [HNTC, Lns, Mil, NIC; all versions except CEV, NLT, TEV], 'host' [BAGD, WBC], 'crowd' [CEV, NLT, TEV], 'large crowd' [LN]. It is emphatic by word order [ICC]. It emphasizes the great number of persons involved [EBC, EGT, My, NIC, NIGTC, NTC, TH, TNTC, Wst], densely compact [My, Wst].

c. pres. mid. (deponent = act.) of περίκειμαι (LN **85.5**) (BAGD 1.b. p. 648): 'to surround' [LN, Mil; NASB, TNT], 'to be around' [LN], 'to lie around' [BAGD]. The middle voice is also translated as active: 'to be compassed about with' [KJV], 'to be surrounded by' [NIC; NAB, NIV, NLT, NRSV]. This participle is also translated as a preposition: 'around' [HNTC, **LN**; REB, TEV], 'all around' [CEV, NJB], 'all about' [Lns], 'about' [WBC].

QUESTION—What relationship is indicated by τοιγαροῦν 'wherefore then'?

It is emphatic [EGT, GNC, Mil, NIGTC]. It joins the preceding references with the following exhortations [Lg, WBC]. It connects specifically with 11:39–40 [WBC].

QUESTION—What is meant by καὶ ἡμεῖς 'we also'?

It is emphatic [Lns, Mil, NIGTC, NTC, TH, WBC]. Καί 'also' means 'in addition' [Alf]; ἡμεῖς 'we' (emphatic [Lg(K)]) joins the writer with his readers [EBC, Hwt, NIGTC, NTC, TNTC, Wst]: we also in addition to those already mentioned.

QUESTION—What relationship is indicated by the participial form ἔχοντες 'having'?

It indicates reason [EGT, Lns, Mil, My, NIGTC, NTC, WBC; KJV, NAB, NASB, NIV, NRSV, TEV]: because we have a great many witnesses, therefore we must run the race.

QUESTION—What is meant by μαρτύρων 'witnesses'?

1. It refers to persons whose lives have been witnesses to the faith [EGT, GNC, Hwt, Lns, My, NIC; NLT] and whose faith was witnessed to by Scripture [EGT]. It does not means 'spectators' who look down upon runners [EGT, GNC, Hwt, Lns, My, NIC] since the witnesses are in heaven and no longer concerned with earthly affairs [Lns]; rather, the runners are to look at these witnesses [Hwt, NIC].
2. It refers to persons who have been witnesses for the faith and who also witness the lives of present believers [Alf, Blm, EBC, HNTC, Hu, ICC,

Lg, Mil, My(D), NCBC, NTC, TH, TNTC, WBC]. It refers both to the great multitude and to the fact that they are looking on from heaven above [Alf, Lg]. They have a unified witness and are approved by God [WBC].

3. It refers to persons who are spectators; the witnesses are like a crowd in a stadium watching the runners [NIGTC].

having-laid-aside[a] every impediment[b] and the easily-ensnaring[c] sin,

TEXT—Instead of εὐπερίστατον 'easily ensnaring' some manuscripts read εὐπερίσπαστον 'easily distracting'. GNT reads εὐπερίστατον 'easily ensnaring' with an A decision, indicating that the text is certain. Εὐπερίσπαστον 'easily distracting' is read by only WBC.

LEXICON—a. aorist mid. (deponent = act.) participle of ἀποτίθημι (LN 85.42) (BAGD 1.b. p. 101): 'to lay aside' [BAGD, HNTC, Mil, WBC; KJV, NAB, NASB, NRSV], 'to put away' [LN, Lns], 'to remove' [LN], 'to get rid of' [Mil, NIC; CEV, TNT], 'to rid oneself of' [BAGD; TEV], 'to throw off' [NIV, NJB, REB], 'to strip off' [NLT].

b. ὄγκος (LN **13.149**) (BAGD p. 553): 'impediment' [BAGD, LN], 'hindrance' [**LN**], 'thing that hinders' [NIV], 'encumbrance' [HNTC, Mil; NAB, NASB, REB, TNT], 'weight' [Lns, NIC; KJV, NRSV], 'excess weight' [WBC], 'weight that slows down' [NLT], 'thing that slows down' [CEV], 'thing that weighs us down' [NJB], 'thing that gets in the way' [TEV]. It is emphatic by word order [EBC, NIGTC, WBC]. This word literally refers to a person's excess weight [Alf, Blm], unnecessary clothing [Blm, HNTC], and here figuratively to any impeding disposition [Blm], to anything that would hinder [EBC, EGT, GNC, Hu, Hwt, Lg(K), My, NCBC, NIC, NTC, TNTC, WBC, Wst]. It includes things that are not sinful in themselves [EBC, EGT, Hu, NIC, NTC], anything superfluous [ICC]. This word refers to clinging to external Judaism [My]. It includes sin [Hu, Lns, My, TNTC], it means sin [NIGTC]. It is clarified by the following καὶ τὴν εὐπερίστατον ἁμαρτίαν 'the easily ensnaring sin' [Hu, Lns, NCBC, TH; NAB] and is nearly synonymous with ἁμαρτίαν 'sin' [ICC, TH].

c. εὐπερίστατος (LN **37.6**) (BAGD p. 324): 'easily ensnaring, obstructing, constricting' [BAGD], 'clinging' [TNT], 'easily hampering' [Lns], 'controlling tightly' [LN], 'which controls so tightly' [**LN**], 'which clings' [NAB], 'which readily clings' [HNTC], 'that clings so closely' [NJB, NRSV], 'which holds on so tightly' [TEV], 'that just won't let go' [CEV], 'that so easily hinders progress' [NLT], 'which so easily entangles' [NASB], 'that so easily entangles' [Mil; NIV], 'which so readily ensnares' [NIC], 'that all too readily restricts' [REB], 'which does so easily beset' [KJV]; different text [WBC]. It means 'which easily surrounds' as a garment [Alf, EGT, My, NCBC], which winds around and hinders [Blm, NCBC], clinging closely [Hwt, ICC]. The prefix εὐ- 'well' is intensive [ICC].

QUESTION—What relationship is indicated by the participial form ἀποθέμενοι 'having laid aside'?

1. It expresses an exhortation preceding and parallel (but subordinate [Lns]) to the following verb τρέχωμεν 'let us run' [EBC, EGT, HNTC, Lg, Lns, Mil, NIC, NIGTC, WBC, Wst; all versions]: let us lay aside . . . and let us run.
2. It expresses means [Lns]: by having laid aside, let us run.

QUESTION—What relationship is indicated by καί 'and'?

1. It introduces another item [Alf, EBC, EGT, HNTC, Mil, Wst; all versions except NAB, TNT]: let us lay aside every weight and the sin that ensnares us.
2. It introduces a specific class of weights [My], implying 'especially' [My(D)], 'in particular' [Blm, Lns, NIGTC]: let us lay aside every weight, especially the sin that ensnares us.
3. It introduces a further identification of ὄγκον 'weight' [NAB]: let us lay aside the encumbrance of sin.

QUESTION—What is meant by the definite article τήν 'the' in the phrase τὴν εὐπερίστατον ἁμαρτίαν 'the easily ensnaring sin'?

1. It is generic, referring to sin in general [ICC, Lns, My, NIC, TNTC, WBC, Wst], to the characteristic tendency of all sin to cling tenaciously [EGT].
2. It is definite [Blm, EBC, HNTC, Mil; all versions except NAB, TNT]: the sin that easily ensnares us.

through[a] patience[b] let-us-run the race[c] lying-before[d] us,

LEXICON—a. διά with genitive object (LN 89.76): 'through' [LN], 'by means of' [Lns], 'with' [HNTC, Mil, NIC, WBC; all versions except CEV, NAB], not explicit [CEV, NAB]. This prepositional phrase implies a distance run [WBC]. This preposition refers here to manner [Mil], to the state by means of which the race is run [Alf], to an attendant circumstance [NIGTC]. This prepositional phrase is emphatic [TH].

b. ὑπομονή (LN 25.174) (BAGD 1. p. 846): 'patience' [BAGD; KJV], 'fortitude' [BAGD], 'endurance' [HNTC, LN, Mil, WBC; NASB, NLT], 'steadfast endurance' [NIC], 'perseverance' [Lns; NIV, NJB, NRSV], 'resolution' [REB], 'firm resolution' [TNT], 'determination' [TEV]. This noun is also translated as a verb: 'to persevere' [NAB], 'to be determined' [CEV].

c. ἀγών (LN **50.4**) (BAGD 1. p. 15): 'race' [BAGD, HNTC, LN, Mil, NIC, WBC; all versions], 'contest' [Lns]. It implies struggle [Blm].

d. pres. mid. (deponent = act.) participle of πρόκειμαι (LN 13.76) (BAGD 3. p. 707): 'to lie before' [BAGD, HNTC, LN, Lns, Mil; TEV, TNT], 'to lie ahead' [LN; NAB, NJB, REB], 'to be ahead' [CEV], 'to be set before' [BAGD; KJV, NASB, NRSV], 'to be marked out' [NIV], 'to be prescribed' [WBC]. This participle is also translated 'for which we are entered' [NIC], 'that God has set before us' [NLT].

QUESTION—What relationship is indicated by the present subjunctive verb τρέχωμεν 'let us run'?

It implies both effort and the possibility of success or failure, and continuing action [NIGTC]. By using the first person plural the author includes himself [Lns, NIGTC].

12:2 looking-away[a] to[b] the originator[c] and perfecter[d] of-the faith, Jesus,

LEXICON—a. pres. act. participle of ἀφοράω (LN **30.31**) (BAGD 1. p. 127): 'to look away' [BAGD, Lns, Mil], 'to look' [KJV, NRSV], 'to fix one's eyes' [BAGD, WBC; NASB, NIV, TNT], 'to have one's eyes fixed' [REB], 'to keep one's eyes fixed' [NIC; NAB, NJB, TEV], 'to keep one's eyes on' [HNTC; CEV, NLT], 'to fix one's attention' [**LN**], 'to think about' [LN]. It implies a firmly fixed gaze [EBC, ICC]. The prefixed preposition ἀφ-'from' implies looking away from present surroundings [Alf, TNTC, WBC], from every distraction [Wst]. The present tense indicates continuing action [Hu, Lns, NIGTC, NTC, WBC, Wst] and action occurring at the same time as τρέχωμεν 'let us run' in the preceding clause [WBC]. This participle indicates the supreme motive for running the race faithfully [Lns]. This first clause is the emphatic part of this verse [NTC], referring to the exercise of faith by Jesus [WBC].

b. εἰς with accusative object (LN 84.16): 'to' [LN, Lns; NRSV], 'toward' [LN], 'unto' [Mil; KJV], 'on' [HNTC, NIC; all versions except KJV, NRSV], 'upon' [WBC].

c. ἀρχηγός (LN 36.6, 68.2) (BAGD 3. p. 112): 'originator, founder' [BAGD, LN (68.2)], 'initiator' [LN (68.2)], 'author' [Lns; KJV, NASB, NIV], 'founding leader' [LN (36.6)], 'pioneer leader' [LN (36.6), Mil], 'pioneer' [NIC; NRSV, REB], 'champion' [WBC]. This noun is also translated as a relative clause: 'who inspires' [NAB], 'who leads us' [CEV], 'who leads us in the way of faith' [TNT], 'who leads us in our faith' [NJB]. The phrase τὸν τῆς πίστεως ἀρχηγὸν καὶ τελειωτήν 'the originator and perfecter of the faith' is translated 'on whom (our) faith depends from beginning to end' [**LN**; TEV], 'on whom our faith depends from start to finish' [NLT], 'who inspires our faith from the beginning to the end' [HNTC]. It describes Christ as the originator of the faith previously described [Lns], the originator of the Christian faith in the believer [EBC, Hwt, Lg, My, NTC], the leader of the believers' faith [NJB, TNT]. It refers to a person who sets an example [EGT, ICC, Mil, My(D), NIGTC], a person who fully exercised faith [WBC, Wst], who precedes others who will follow his example [Alf, Lg, Mil, NCBC, NIGTC, WBC]. It indicates calling forth faith by the promises in the Gospel and furnishing himself as an example [Blm].

d. τελειωτής (LN **68.24**) (BAGD p. 810): 'perfecter' [BAGD, LN, Mil; NASB, NIV, NRSV, REB], 'finisher' [KJV], 'completer' [Lns]. This noun is also translated as a relative clause: 'who perfects' [NAB], 'one who completes' [**LN**], 'who has finished the course' [NIC]. The phrase τῆς πίστεως τελειωτήν 'perfecter of the faith' is translated 'the one who brought faith to complete expression' [WBC], 'who makes our faith complete' [CEV], 'who brings our faith to perfection' [NJB], 'who brings faith to fulfillment' [TNT]. It implies exhibiting faith in its perfect form [EGT, ICC, My(D), NIC, WBC, Wst]; it implies both perfecting faith in his own person and making faith effectual for believers [Alf]; it implies bringing the believer's faith to its intended goal [EBC, GNC, My, NTC, TH, WBC; NJB]. This word means 'completer' [Hwt].

QUESTION—What relationship is indicated by the participle ἀφορῶντες 'looking away'?

It states an additional attendant exhortation [NAB, NIV, NJB, TEV, TNT]: and let us look away to Jesus.

QUESTION—How are the two nouns ἀρχηγόν 'originator' and τελειωτήν 'perfecter' related to the genitive noun πίστεως 'faith'?

1. Concerning the function of the genitive noun πίστεως 'faith'. It is related to both nouns [Alf, EBC, EGT, GNC, Hu, Hwt, ICC, Lg, Lns, Mil, My, NCBC, NIC, NTC, TNTC, WBC, Wst; all versions], as the one definite article τόν for both nouns indicates [WBC].

1.1 Πίστεως 'faith' tells what was originated and perfected [Lns, NTC, TNTC; NAB]: Jesus originated and perfected the faith.

1.2 Πίστεως 'faith' tells in what area the leading and perfecting occurs [NJB, TNT]: (Jesus) leads us and perfects us in our faith.

1.3 Jesus was a champion (ἀρχηγόν 'originator') in the exercise of faith and brought faith to complete expression (τελειωτήν 'perfecter') [WBC].

2. Concerning the relationship of Jesus as 'originator and perfecter' of faith.

2.1 Jesus is described as exercising faith himself, as well as his followers [Alf, Blm, EGT, GNC, Hu, ICC, Lg, Mil, My(D), NCBC, NIC, NIGTC, WBC, Wst].

2.2 Jesus is not described as himself exercising faith, but only as leading his followers to faith [HNTC, Hwt, Lns, My, NTC, TNTC].

QUESTION—What is meant by the noun phrase τῆς πίστεως 'the faith' with the definite article?

1. It means 'our faith' [HNTC, TNTC; CEV, KJV, NAB, NIV, NJB, NLT, NRSV, TEV]. It sums up the whole concept of Christian faith [TNTC].

2. It is translated as 'the faith' [Lns, NIGTC], referring to the faith the author has been speaking of [Alf], the faith described in 11:1 [Lns], the faith of the author and the readers, and less directly to the faith of the OT witnesses mentioned [NIGTC].

3. It is translated as 'faith' [Mil, NIC, WBC; NASB, REB], faith in the absolute and unqualified sense [Hu, NCBC, NIC, WBC, Wst], faith as a principle of action [Mil].

QUESTION—What relationship is indicated by the use of the personal name, 'Jesus'?

It emphasizes his humanity [HNTC, TNTC, WBC, Wst], his earthly life [NTC]; it is emphatic by word order [Mil, NCBC, NIGTC, WBC, Wst].

who for[a] the joy lying-before[b] him endured[c] (a) cross, having-disregarded[d] shame,[e]

LEXICON—a. ἀντί with genitive object (LN 89.24, 89.133) (BAGD 1. p. 73): 'for' [Lns; KJV, NASB, NIV], 'for the sake of' [Mil, NIC; NAB, NJB, NRSV, REB, TNT], 'because of' [LN (89.24); CEV, NLT, TEV], 'instead of' [BAGD, LN (89.133)], 'in place of' [BAGD, HNTC], 'rather than' [WBC]. It means because of [Blm, GNC], for the sake of [EBC, EGT, Hu, NCBC], looking forward to [Alf], in order to reach [ICC].

b. pres. mid. (deponent = act.) of πρόκειμαι (LN **13.76**) (BAGD 2. p. 707, 3. p. 707): 'to lie before' [BAGD, HNTC, LN, Lns, Mil; NAB, TNT], 'to be set before' [BAGD, NIC, WBC; KJV, NASB, NIV, NRSV], 'to lie ahead' [**LN**; NJB, REB], 'to wait for' [TEV], 'to exist later' [LN], 'to be present' [BAGD]. The phrase τῆς προκειμένης αὐτῷ χαρᾶς 'the joy lying before him' is translated 'he knew that later on he would be glad he did' [CEV], 'the joy he knew would be his afterward' [NLT].

c. aorist act. indic. of ὑπομένω (LN 25.175) (BAGD 2. p. 846): 'to endure' [HNTC, LN, Mil, WBC; all versions except NLT, TEV], 'to endure perseveringly' [Lns], 'to bear' [NIC], 'to suffer, to submit to' [BAGD]. The phrase ὑπέμεινεν σταυρόν 'he endured a cross' is translated 'he did not give up because of the cross' [TEV], 'to die on the cross' [NLT].

d. aorist act. participle of καταφρονέω (LN 88.192) (BAGD 2. p. 420): 'to disregard' [BAGD, WBC; NJB, NRSV], 'to be unafraid of' [BAGD], 'to scorn' [LN; NIV], 'to despise' [HNTC, LN, Lns, Mil, NIC; KJV, NASB], 'to have contempt for' [LN], 'to care nothing for' [TNT], 'to think nothing of' [TEV], 'to ignore' [REB]. This participle is also translated as an adjective: 'heedless' [NAB]. The phrase ὑπέμεινεν σταυρὸν αἰσχύνης καταφρονήσας 'endured a cross having disregarded the shame' is translated 'he endured the shame of being nailed to a cross' [CEV], 'he was willing to die a shameful death on the cross' [NLT]. It means to rise above the shame [ICC], to think little of [EBC, Lg(K), Lns, NIC, TNTC] in comparison with the joy that lay ahead [Lns, TNTC], in comparison with obedience to God's will [NIC]; it implies being unafraid in spite of the pain [WBC].

e. αἰσχύνη (LN 25.189) (BAGD 2. p. 25): 'shame' [BAGD, HNTC, LN, Lns, Mil; all versions except NLT, REB, TEV], 'disgrace' [LN, NIC, WBC; REB, TEV]. This noun is also translated as an adjective: 'shameful' [NLT]. It refers to the great indignity of the cross [ICC, TH] and the verbal abuse by the people standing by [TH]; it refers to shame in an abstract sense [Lg(K)].

QUESTION—What relationship is indicated by the phrase ἀντὶ τῆς προκειμένης αὐτῷ χαρᾶς 'for the joy lying before him'?

1. It means 'because of the joy that lay before him', the joy of what his death would accomplish [Alf, Blm, EBC, EGT, GNC, Hu, Hwt, Lg, Lns, Mil, My, NCBC, NIC, NIGTC, NTC, TH, TNTC, Wst; CEV, NAB, NJB, NLT, NRSV, REB, TEV, TNT]: because of the joy that lay beyond his

atoning death. It includes redemption and its blessings for believers [EBC, Lg, Wst], and also the joys of heaven for them [Lg]. It refers to Christ's future glorification and kingship [Blm, Lns, Mil, NTC]. It includes both of the above [GNC, My, NCBC, NIC].

2. It means 'instead of the joy that lay before him' [BAGD, HNTC, WBC].

2.1 It refers to the joy he had before he came to earth [BAGD, HNTC], the joy of his eternal sonship [HNTC]: instead of the joy he already had.

2.2 It refers to the joy that he would have had by being delivered from his impending death; the participle refers to something within his grasp [WBC].

QUESTION—What relationship is indicated by σταυρόν without the definite article?

1. It is qualitative, focusing on the nature of the death [Alf, Blm, Lns, Wst; CEV]: such a thing as death on a cross. It indicates submission to the cross [WBC]. It refers to the death as an ordeal occasioned by opposition from sinners [WBC].
2. It is nevertheless translated as definite [NIC; all versions except CEV]: the cross.

QUESTION—What relationship is indicated by the participle καταφρονήσας 'having disregarded'?

It is translated as an additional statement [Mil; TEV, TNT]: and he disregarded the shame.

QUESTION—What relationship is indicated by αἰσχύνης without the definite article?

1. It is qualitative, focusing on the concept of shame [Alf, Lns].
2. It is nevertheless translated as definite [Mil, NIC, WBC; KJV, NAB, NASB, NJB], referring to the shame associated with the cross [GNC, HNTC, NIC, WBC; all versions except KJV, NASB]: the shame associated with the cross.

and at[a] (the) right[b] of-the throne of-God is-seated.[c]

LEXICON—a. ἐν with dative object (LN 83.47, 87.36): 'at' [HNTC, LN, Lns, Mil, NIC, WBC; all versions except NLT], 'on' [LN], 'beside' [NLT]. The phrase ἐν δεξιᾷ κεκάθικεν 'at the right is seated' means 'to have a special place of honor' [LN].

b. δεξιός (LN 82.8) (BAGD 2.a. p. 174): 'right' [LN; NAB, NJB], 'right side' [LN; CEV, TEV], 'right hand' [BAGD, HNTC, Lns, Mil, NIC, WBC; KJV, NASB, NIV, NRSV, REB, TNT], 'the place of highest honor' [NLT]. It indicates the place of honor [TH].

c. perf. act. indic. of καθίζω (LN 17.12) (BAGD 2.a.α. p. 390): 'to sit' [LN], 'to sit down' [BAGD, LN, Lns, Mil; KJV, NASB, NIV], 'to take one's seat' [HNTC, NIC, WBC; NAB, NJB, NRSV, REB, TNT], 'to be seated' [LN; CEV, NLT, TEV]. The perfect tense indicates the continuing state [Alf, GNC, HNTC, Lg, TH], the permanent result [EBC, Lns, NIC, NIGTC, NTC, WBC, Wst].

QUESTION—How are the two nouns related in the genitive construction δεξιᾷ τοῦ θρόνου 'right of the throne'?

1. It means on the throne, at God's right hand [Alf].
2. It may mean seated on a different seat from God's throne, located at the right side of God's throne.

12:3 For consider[a] the-(one) having-endured[b] such[c] opposition[d] by[e] the sinners against[f] himself,

TEXT—Instead of ἑαυτόν 'himself', some manuscripts read αὐτόν 'him', some read αὐτούς 'them' (or possibly 'themselves'), and others read ἑαυτούς 'themselves'. GNT reads ἑαυτόν 'himself' with a C decision, indicating that the committee had difficulty in deciding between the readings. Αὐτόν 'him' is read by Alf, Blm, EGT; ἑαυτούς 'themselves' is read by HNTC, WBC, Wst (indicating that the sinners hurt themselves by their opposition to Jesus).

LEXICON—a. aorist mid. (deponent = act.) impera. of ἀναλογίζομαι (LN **30.10**) (BAGD p. 57): 'to consider' [BAGD, HNTC, Mil, NIC, WBC; KJV, NASB, NIV, NRSV], 'to consider carefully' [LN], 'to take into consideration' [Lns], 'to think of' [NJB, REB, TEV, TNT], 'to think about' [NLT], 'to keep one's mind on' [CEV], 'to remember' [NAB]. The phrase ἀναλογίσασθε τὸν ὑπομεμενηκότα 'consider the one having endured' is translated 'think of the way he persevered against' [NJB], 'think of what he went through; how he put up with' [TEV]. It means to think about and make a comparison [Alf, Blm, EGT, Hu, Hwt, ICC, Lg, Mil, NCBC, NIC, NTC, TH, TNTC, WBC, Wst]; it means merely to consider thoughtfully [Lns]. The aorist tense indicates a once-for-all action [Wst].

b. perf. act. participle of ὑπομένω (LN 25.175) (BAGD 2. p. 846): 'to endure' [BAGD, HNTC, LN, Mil, WBC; KJV, NAB, NASB, NIV, NLT, NRSV], 'to endure perseveringly' [Lns], 'to persevere' [NJB], 'to bear' [NIC; TNT], 'to submit to' [BAGD; REB], 'to suffer' [BAGD], 'to put up with' [LN; CEV, TEV]. The perfect tense implies continuing results [Alf, EBC, GNC, Hu, Lns, NTC, TNTC, WBC, Wst], completed results [GNC]; it indicates endurance over a period of time [NIGTC]; it is merely the equivalent of the aorist tense, referring to a past event [ICC].

c. τοιοῦτος (LN 92.31): 'such' [Lns, Mil, NIC, WBC; KJV, NASB, NIV, NJB, NRSV, REB], 'of such a kind' [LN], 'so great' [HNTC], 'so much' [TEV], 'many' [CEV], not explicit [NAB, NLT, TNT]. This word emphasizes the extent of Christ's suffering and thus points out the reason for fixing their eyes on Jesus [EGT]. It refers to the cross and the shame previously mentioned [ICC, Lns, My], so much greater suffering than the readers' sufferings [My]; it implies intensity [NIGTC, WBC]; it refers to quality [NTC].

d. ἀντιλογία (LN **39.35**) (BAGD 2. p. 75): 'opposition' [HNTC, Lns, WBC; NAB, NIV, NJB, REB], 'strong opposition' [LN], 'hostility' [BAGD, NIC; NASB, NRSV], 'bitter enmity' [TNT], 'hatred' [TEV], 'defiance'

[**LN**], 'contradiction' [Mil; KJV], 'insults' [CEV]. This noun is also translated as a verb phrase: 'to do terrible things' [NLT]. It indicates opposition in words [EGT, Mil, My, NCBC, Wst], in words and deeds [Alf, Blm, Hu, ICC, Lns, TH, TNTC, WBC]; it refers primarily to the events of the trial of Jesus [HNTC, NCBC], to opposition to Christ as divine Son and Messiah [My].

e. ὑπό with genitive object (LN 90.1) (BAGD 1.b. p. 843): 'by' [BAGD, LN, Lns, Mil; NASB], 'of' [NIC; KJV, NAB, TNT], 'from' [HNTC, WBC; CEV, NIV, NJB, NRSV, REB, TEV], not explicit [NLT].

f. εἰς with accusative object (LN 90.59): 'against' [HNTC, Lns, Mil, NIC, WBC; KJV, NASB, NRSV, TNT], 'to' [LN; NLT], 'toward' [LN]. The phrase εἰς ἑαυτόν 'against himself' is not explicit [CEV, NAB, NIV, NJB, REB, TEV].

QUESTION—What relationship is indicated by γάρ 'for'?

1. It indicates the reason the readers should fix their attention on Jesus [Alf, EGT, My(D)]: fix your eyes on Jesus because he was the object of opposition, as you are.
2. It indicates a confirmation and emphasis of the preceding exhortation [ICC, Lns, My, NIC, NIGTC, TH]: yes, consider him.
3. It indicates the result of making the comparison with Jesus [Wst].

QUESTION—To whom does the participle τὸν ὑπομεμενηκότα 'the one having endured' refer?

It refers to Jesus [Blm, NIGTC, NTC; CEV, TNT]: consider Jesus, who endured . . .

QUESTION—What is the function of the definite article in the noun phrase τῶν ἁμαρτωλῶν 'the sinners'?

1. It indicates the representative class who were involved in Christ's crucifixion [Wst]: by the sinners who were involved.
2. It refers to the group of sinners well-known to the readers [Lns]: by the sinners—you know whom I mean.
3. The definite article is not translated [HNTC, Mil, NIC, WBC; all versions]: by sinners.

in-order-that not you-may-grow-weary[a] in-your souls,[b] fainting.[c]

LEXICON—a. aorist act. subj. of κάμνω (LN **25.291**) (BAGD 1. p. 402): 'to grow weary' [Mil, NIC; NASB, NIV, NRSV], 'to become weary' [WBC; NLT], 'to be weary' [BAGD; KJV], 'to be fatigued' [BAGD], 'to tire' [HNTC], 'to grow tired' [Lns; TNT], 'to grow despondent' [NAB], 'to lose heart' [NJB, REB], 'to become discouraged' [LN; CEV, TEV]. The aorist tense refers to becoming weary [Lns, WBC].

b. ψυχή (LN **26.4**) (BAGD 1.b.γ. p. 893): 'soul' [BAGD, Lns, Mil, NIC], 'inner self' [LN], 'mind' [LN; KJV], 'heart' [**LN**]; the phrase ταῖς ψυχαῖς ὑμῶν 'in your souls' is not explicit [HNTC, WBC; all versions except KJV]. The phrase ἵνα μὴ κάμητε ταῖς ψυχαῖς ὑμῶν ἐκλυόμενοι is translated 'so do not let your hearts become discouraged and give up' [**LN**].

c. pres. mid. participle of ἐκλύω (LN 23.79, 25.288): 'to faint' [Mil; KJV], 'to grow faint' [REB], 'to faint from exhaustion, to become extremely weary, to give out' [LN (23.79)], 'to give up' [LN (25.288); CEV, NLT, TEV], 'to become discouraged' [LN (25.288)], 'to lose heart' [HNTC, NIC, WBC; NASB, NIV, NRSV, TNT], 'to abandon the struggle' [NAB], 'to come to grief' [NJB], 'to relax' [Lns]. The present tense implies gradual action [Lns, Wst].

QUESTION—What relationship is indicated by ἵνα μή 'in order that not'?

1. It introduces the purpose of considering the experience of Jesus [HNTC, Lns, Mil, TNTC, WBC; NASB, NIV, NLT, NRSV]: consider him, in order that you may not become weary.
2. It introduces the possible result to be avoided by considering the experience of Jesus [KJV]: consider him, lest you become weary.
3. It is translated as introducing the result of considering the experience of Jesus [NIC; CEV, NJB, REB, TNT]: consider him, and then you will not grow weary.
4. It is translated as introducing an exhortation resulting from considering the experience of Jesus [NAB, TEV]: consider him, and therefore do not grow weary.

QUESTION—What is the phrase ταῖς ψυχαῖς ὑμῶν 'in your souls' connected with?

1. It is connected with ἐκλυόμενοι 'fainting' [Alf, EGT, Lg, Lns, Mil, My, NTC, WBC, Wst]: fainting in your souls.
2. It is connected with μὴ κάμητε 'you may not become weary' [NIC]: in order that you may not become weary in your souls.
3. It is connected with both of the above [Blm, ICC]: in order that you may not become both weary and fainting in your souls.
4. It is not specifically expressed [HNTC; all versions except KJV].

QUESTION—What relationship is indicated by the participle ἐκλυόμενοι 'fainting'?

1. It states an attendant action [HNTC, Mil, NIC, WBC; CEV, NASB, NIV, NJB, NLT, REB, TEV, TNT]: and lose heart.
2. It may further define κάμητε 'you may become weary': you may become weary; i.e., you may faint.
3. It expresses means [Lns]: by fainting.
4. It indicates manner [NTC]: in a fainting manner.
5. It states an alternative to κάμητε 'you may become weary' [NAB, NRSV]: become weary or lose heart.

DISCOURSE UNIT: 12:4–17 [NASB]. The topic is a father's discipline.

DISCOURSE UNIT: 12:4–13 [Lg, Lns, Mil]. The topic is sufferings as chastisements from God's love [Lg], sons chastised by their father [Lns], the reasonableness of affliction as discipline by a father [Mil].

DISCOURSE UNIT: 12:4–11 [EBC, GNC, NIC]. The topic is discipline [EBC], discipline being for sons [NIC], the purpose of chastening [GNC].

DISCOURSE UNIT: 12:4–8 [HNTC]. The topic is discipline and sonship.

12:4 Not-yet to-the-point-of[a] blood[b] have-you-resisted,[c] struggling[d] against[e] the sin.

LEXICON—a. μέχρις (LN **78.51**) (BAGD 1.c. p. 515): 'to the point of' [BAGD, HNTC, LN, Mil, NIC, WBC; NAB, NASB, NIV, NJB, NRSV, REB, TEV], 'up to the point of' [Lns], 'unto' [KJV], not explicit [CEV, NLT, TNT]. This word expresses degree or measure [WBC].

b. αἷμα (LN 8.64, 23.107) (BAGD 2.a. p. 22): 'blood' [BAGD, LN (8.64), Lns; KJV], 'bloodshed' [HNTC, Mil, WBC; NJB], 'death' [LN (23.107)]. This noun is also translated as a verb phrase: 'to shed blood' [NAB, NASB], 'to shed one's blood' [NIC; NIV, NRSV, REB], 'to be killed' [TEV], 'to give one's life' [NLT], 'to face death' [TNT], 'to be hurt' [CEV]. It refers to death [BAGD].

c. aorist act. indic. of ἀντικαθίστημι (LN **39.18**) (BAGD p. 74): 'to resist' [BAGD, LN, Lns, Mil, NIC, WBC; all versions except NJB, TNT], 'to contend' [HNTC], 'to have to keep fighting' [NJB], not explicit [CEV, NLT, TNT]. The aorist tense indicates a (negative) historical fact [Lns].

d. pres. mid. participle of ἀνταγωνίζομαι (LN **39.31**) (BAGD p. 72): 'to struggle' [BAGD, Mil, WBC], 'to struggle against' [LN], 'to strive' [KJV, NASB], 'to contend' [Lns]. This word is translated as a phrase: 'in the struggle' [REB], 'in your struggle' [**LN**, NIC; NIV, NLT, NRSV, TEV, TNT], 'in your fight' [NAB], 'in the fight' [NJB], 'in your battle' [CEV], 'in your contest' [HNTC]. The present tense implies continuing action [NTC].

e. πρός with accusative object (LN 90.33): 'against' [HNTC, LN, Lns, Mil, NIC, WBC; all versions].

QUESTION—What relationship is indicated by the lack of a connecting word to introduce this clause?

It indicates a new paragraph and a new thought [Lns, Mil; CEV].

QUESTION—What relationship is indicated by οὔπω 'not yet'?

It implies that there was a possible danger in the future [EBC, Wst].

QUESTION—What relationship is indicated by the phrase μέχρις αἵματος 'to the point of blood'?

It refers to the readers' blood being shed [BAGD, My, NTC; NIV, NRSV, REB], in being wounded [Alf, HNTC; CEV] as in a boxing match [Alf], in being killed [EBC, GNC, Hu, Hwt, ICC, Lg, Lns, My, NIC, NIGTC, NTC, TH, TNTC, WBC, Wst; NLT, TEV].

QUESTION—What relationship is indicated by the present participle ἀνταγωνιζόμενοι 'struggling'?

1. It describes an action accompanying ἀντικατέστητε 'you have resisted' [HNTC, LN, Lns, NIC; all versions except KJV]: you have (not) resisted . . . in your struggling.

2. It is temporal [WBC]: while you are struggling.
3. It expresses means or an accompanying action [Mil (translation)]: by/in your struggling.
4. It expresses concession and time [Mil]: although/as you are struggling.

QUESTION—What is meant by the definite article in the phrase τὴν ἁμαρτίαν 'the sin'?

1. It indicates 'sin' personified, as an adversary [Alf, Blm, Hu, Lg, Lns, Mil, My, NTC, TH, WBC, Wst]: against the adversary, sin. This adversary tempts believers to apostasy [My].
1.1 Sin personified refers to the readers' adversaries [TNTC], or any source of hostile opposition [WBC].
1.2 It refers to sin in their adversaries [Lg, Wst].
1.3 It includes sin both in themselves and in their persecutors [Alf, GNC].
2. It refers to the readers' sin [Lg(K)], the sin of unbelief in themselves [EGT], the sin of apostasy [HNTC].
3. It refers to the sin committed by their oppressors [EBC].

DISCOURSE UNIT: 12:5–13 [NJB]. The topic is God's fatherly instruction.

12:5 And you-have-entirely-forgotten[a] the exhortation,[b] which speaks[c] to-you as to-sons,[d]

LEXICON—a. perf. mid.(deponent = act.) indic. of ἐκλανθάνομαι (LN **29.15**) (BAGD p. 242): 'to forget entirely' [LN; NLT], 'to forget altogether' [BAGD, Mil], 'to forget completely' [WBC], 'to forget' [HNTC, Lns, NIC; all versions except NLT]. The prefix ἐκ- is intensive, implying 'completely' [NIGTC]. The perfect tense implies an action with lasting results [NTC].

b. παράκλησις (LN 25.150) (BAGD 1. p. 618): 'exhortation' [BAGD, Mil; KJV, NASB, NRSV, REB], 'encouragement' [BAGD, LN, Lns, WBC], 'word of encouragement' [HNTC, NIC; NIV], 'encouraging text' [NJB], not explicit [CEV]. This singular noun is translated as a plural: 'encouraging words' [NAB, NLT, TEV]. The phrase τῆς παρακλήσεως ἥτις 'the exhortation, which' is translated 'that Scripture which, for your comfort' [TNT]. It indicates conversing [My]. It implies encouragement [EBC, NIGTC, TH, TNTC, Wst], exhortation [Alf, Blm, NIGTC, TNTC, WBC], consolation [Alf, WBC, Wst], rebuke [Blm].

c. pres. mid. (deponent = act.) indic. of διαλέγομαι (LN 33.26) (BAGD 2. p. 185): 'to speak' [BAGD, LN, WBC; KJV, NLT, TEV], 'to address' [LN, NIC; NIV, NRSV, REB], 'to reason' [Lns, Mil]. This verb is also translated as a passive voice: 'to be addressed' [HNTC; NAB, NASB, TNT]. The phrase ἥτις ὑμῖν διαλέγεται 'which speaks to you' is translated 'in which you are addressed' [NJB], 'that the Scriptures say' [CEV]. This verb implies a discourse [Alf]. It means merely to speak [NIGTC].

d. υἱός (LN 9.46, 10.42) (BAGD 1.c.α. p. 833, 1.c.γ. p. 834): 'son' [BAGD, HNTC, LN (9.46, 10.42), Lns, Mil, NIC, WBC; NAB, NASB, NIV, NJB, REB, TNT], 'child' [CEV, KJV, NLT, NRSV, TEV].

QUESTION—What relationship is indicated by the initial word καί 'and'?

1. It introduces a new topic [EGT, ICC, TH; all versions except CEV, NASB].
2. It is closely related to the preceding statement [HNTC, Lns, NIGTC], perhaps implying a result [NIGTC]: and as a result . . .
3. It is both of the above [Mil].
4. It introduces a contrast [CEV]: but you have forgotten.

QUESTION—What is the form of this sentence?

1. It is a statement [Alf, Blm, EGT, HNTC, Hu, Lg(K), LN, Lns, Mil, NIC; CEV, KJV, NAB, NASB, NIV, NRSV, REB]: you have forgotten.
2. It is a question [Hwt, ICC, My, TH, TNTC, WBC, Wst; NJB, NLT, TEV, TNT]: have you forgotten? This question is less severe than a statement would be [Wst].

QUESTION—What relationship is indicated by the relative pronoun ἥτις 'which'?

It is qualitative [Alf], descriptive, indicating the character of the following exhortation [Mil]: which is the kind of exhortation which speaks to you as sons. It indicates that the quotation is known to the readers [My].

QUESTION—Who is the speaker of the verb διαλέγεται 'speaks'?

1. The speaker is the exhortation [Lns, Mil, My, NIC, TNTC; KJV, NAB, NIV, NRSV, REB]: the exhortation which speaks.
2. The speaker is scripture [Hu, Hwt, NIGTC; CEV], which is treated as God's voice [Hu, Hwt]: the scripture which speaks.
3. The speaker is God [WBC, Wst; NLT, TEV] speaking through scripture [WBC, Wst]: which God speaks.

QUESTION—What relationship is indicated by ὡς 'as'?

It indicates a comparison [Mil]. It implies that they are sons [NIGTC, TH].

QUESTION—What is implied by υἱοῖς 'sons' without the definite article?

1. It is translated as indefinite or qualitative [Alf, EBC, HNTC, Lns, Mil, NIC, WBC; all versions except CEV, NLT, TEV]: as sons.
2. It is nevertheless translated as possessive [CEV, NLT, TEV]: as his sons.

"My son,[a] (do) not think-lightly[b] of-(the)-discipline[c] of-(the)-Lord

LEXICON—a. υἱός (LN 9.46, 10.42) (BAGD 1.c.α. p. 833, 1.c.γ. p. 834): 'son' [BAGD, HNTC, LN (9.46, 10.42), Lns, Mil, NIC, WBC; KJV, NASB, NIV, NJB, REB, TNT], 'child' [NLT, NRSV, TEV], not explicit [CEV]; this singular noun is translated as a plural: 'sons' [NAB].

b. pres. act. impera. of ὀλιγωρέω (LN **88.197**) (BAGD p. 564): 'to think lightly of' [BAGD; REB, TNT], 'to make light of' [BAGD, **LN**, Mil; CEV, NIV], 'to regard lightly' [HNTC, WBC; NASB, NRSV], 'to treat lightly' [Lns], 'to look down on, to have contempt for' [LN], 'to disdain' [NAB], 'to despise' [LN, NIC; KJV], 'to scorn' [NJB], 'to ignore' [NLT].

The phrase μὴ ὀλιγώρει 'do not think lightly' is translated 'pay attention' [TEV]. It means to treat as insignificant [TNTC]. It implies ignoring any divine meaning in the discipline [ICC]. The present tense implies continuation [Mil, NTC] (whether now in progress or not).

c. παιδεία (LN 33.226, 36.10, 38.4) (BAGD 1. p. 603): 'discipline' [BAGD, HNTC, LN (36.10), Mil, NIC, WBC; NAB, NASB, NIV, NRSV, REB, TNT], 'instruction' [LN (33.226)], 'correction' [NJB], 'chastening' [KJV], 'punishment' [LN (38.4)]. This singular noun is translated as a plural: 'chastisements' [Lns]. The phrase παιδείας κυρίου 'discipline of the Lord' is translated 'when the Lord disciplines you' [NLT], 'when the Lord corrects you' [TEV], 'when the Lord punishes you' [CEV]. This word implies chastening [Blm, EBC, Hwt] and education [EBC, Hwt]. It is discipline that trains in obedience [GNC, WBC] plus correction and punishment [WBC]. It means moral training [ICC]. It includes unpleasant elements [NIGTC].

QUESTION—What relationship is implied by υἱέ μου 'my son'?

The author intends it as a generic singular applying to the readers [NIGTC, TNTC]; μου 'my' makes the expression more intimate [WBC].

QUESTION—What relationship is indicated by μὴ ὀλιγώρει 'do not think lightly'?

It implies an emphatic opposite [My]: be thankful. It implies that the discipline comes from God [NTC].

QUESTION—How are the two nouns related in the genitive construction παιδείας κυρίου 'discipline of the Lord'?

Κυρίου 'Lord' is the source the 'discipline' [My; CEV, NJB, NLT, TEV]: the discipline that comes from the Lord.

nor faint[a] being-reproved[b] by[c] him;

LEXICON—a. pres. mid. impera. of ἐκλύω (LN **25.288**) (BAGD p. 243): 'to faint' [Mil; KJV, NASB], 'to be discouraged' [**LN**; CEV, NLT, REB, TEV], 'to lose heart' [BAGD, HNTC, LN, NIC, WBC; NAB, NIV, NRSV, TNT], 'to relax' [Lns]. This entire clause is translated 'do not resent his training' [NJB]. The present tense implies continuation, whether already in progress or not.

b. pres. pass. participle of ἐλέγχω (LN 33.417) (BAGD 4. p. 249): 'to be reproved' [HNTC, Lns, NIC; NASB], 'to be corrected' [Mil, WBC], 'to be rebuked' [LN; KJV], 'to be reproached' [LN], 'to be disciplined' [BAGD], 'to be punished' [BAGD, Mil; NRSV]. The phrase ὑπ' αὐτοῦ ἐλεγχόμενος 'being reproved by him' is translated 'when he reproves you' [NAB, TNT], 'when he corrects you' [CEV, NLT, REB], 'when he rebukes you' [NIV, TEV].

c. ὑπό with genitive object (LN 90.1): 'by' [HNTC, LN, Lns, Mil, NIC, WBC; NASB, NRSV], 'of' [KJV].

QUESTION—What relationship is indicated by the participle ἐλεγχόμενος 'being reproved'?

1. It is temporal [HNTC, Lg(K), Lns, NIC, WBC; all versions except NJB]: when you are being reproved.
2. It indicates the reason as well as being temporal [Mil]: because you are being reproved.

12:6 for he-whom (the) Lord loves he-disciplines,[a]

LEXICON—a. pres. act. indic. of παιδεύω (LN 36.10, 38.4) (BAGD 2.b. p. 604): 'to discipline' [BAGD, HNTC, LN (36.10), Mil, NIC, WBC; NAB, NASB, NIV, NLT, NRSV, REB, TNT], 'to train' [NJB], 'to correct' [CEV, TEV], 'to chasten' [KJV], 'to chastise' [Lns], 'to punish' [LN (38.4)]. It refers to God's helpful discipline [NIGTC]. The present tense implies continued activity [NTC].

QUESTION—What relationship is indicated by γάρ 'for'?

It indicates the grounds for the preceding exhortation [Mil].

QUESTION—To whom does ὅν 'he' refer?

1. It is generic [NIGTC, TH]: anyone whom the Lord loves.
2. Its antecedent is υἱέ 'son' in the preceding verse [Mil]: my son whom the Lord loves.

QUESTION—What is indicated by the word order of the relative clause ὃν ἀγαπᾷ 'whom he loves'?

It is emphatic by forefronting [EGT]. It also implies the reason for the disciplining mentioned in the preceding verse [Mil].

and he-punishes[a] **every son**[b] **whom he-accepts."**[c]

LEXICON—a. pres. act. indic. of μαστιγόω (LN 19.9, **38.11**) (BAGD 2.a. p. 495): 'to punish' [BAGD, LN (38.11); NIV, NLT, TEV], 'to bestow corrective punishment' [WBC], 'to chastise' [BAGD, NIC; NJB, NRSV, REB], 'to discipline' [CEV], 'to scourge' [Lns, Mil; KJV, NAB, NASB], 'to whip' [LN (19.9); TNT], 'to lay the rod on' [HNTC]. It means to flog [NIGTC], to strike with a whip [NTC, TH]. The punishment is for the purpose of correcting [WBC].

b. υἱός (LN 10.42): 'son' [HNTC, LN, Lns, Mil, NIC, WBC; KJV, NAB, NASB, NIV, NJB, REB, TNT], 'child' [NLT, NRSV, TEV], not explicit [CEV].

c. pres. mid. (deponent = act.) indic. of παραδέχομαι (LN 31.52) (BAGD 2. p. 614): 'to accept' [BAGD, HNTC, LN (31.52, **34.53**); NJB, NRSV], 'to receive' [BAGD, LN (31.52), Mil, NIC; KJV, NAB, NASB], 'to receive favorably' [WBC], 'to take over as a son' [Lns], 'to welcome' [LN (34.53)], 'to acknowledge' [REB, TNT]. The phrase πάντα υἱὸν ὃν παραδέχεται 'every son whom he accepts' is translated 'everyone he accepts as a son' [NIV], 'everyone he accepts as a child' [TEV], 'those he accepts as his children' [NLT], 'those he calls his own' [CEV]. It means to receive to his heart as a son and cherish [Alf, EGT], to welcome and acknowledge as a son [Mil]. It implies love [WBC]. It refers to being received into God's heavenly kingdom [NIGTC].

QUESTION—What relationship is indicated by δέ 'and'?

It indicates a connection with the preceding clause [NIGTC], a continuation [WBC], and indicates that the clause it introduces is a climax [Alf]. This clause is a parallel to the preceding clause [Alf].

12:7 For[a] discipline[b] you-are-enduring/endure;

TEXT—Instead of εἰς 'for' some manuscripts read εἰ 'if'. GNT does not deal with this variant. Εἰ 'if' is read by only Blm, My, KJV.

LEXICON—a. εἰς with accusative object (LN 89.57): 'for' [Lns, Mil, NIC; NASB], 'for the purpose of' [LN], 'for the sake of' [NRSV, TNT], 'as' [HNTC, WBC; NAB, NIV, REB, TEV]; different text [KJV], not explicit [NLT]. This entire clause is translated 'perseverance is part of your training' [NJB], 'be patient when you are being corrected' [CEV]. It expresses purpose [BAGD, Lg], cause [NTC].

b. παιδεία (LN 36.10, 38.4) (BAGD 1. p. 603): 'discipline' [BAGD, HNTC, LN (36.10), Mil, NIC, WBC; NASB, NIV, NRSV, REB, TNT], 'discipline of God' [NAB], 'divine discipline' [NLT], 'chastening' [KJV], 'chastisement' [Lns], 'training' [LN (36.10); NJB], 'punishment' [LN (38.4); TEV]. This noun is also translated as a verb: 'to be corrected' [CEV]. It refers to discipline [EBC, TNTC, Wst], corrective discipline [WBC], chastisement [Alf, Blm, Lg], training [EGT, Hwt], parental upbringing [TH]. It includes the idea of education [NTC].

QUESTION—What relationship is indicated by ὑπομένετε 'you are enduring/endure'?

1. It is indicative [Alf, EGT, Hwt, ICC, Lns, My(D), NCBC, NIC, NIGTC, Wst; NASB, NJB, NLT]: you are enduring. If it were imperative, the verb would probably have been first in word order [Alf]. The indicative mood is supported by the absence of a connecting word in the following clause [Wst].
2. It is imperative [BAGD, GNC, HNTC, TH, WBC; CEV, NAB, NIV, NRSV, REB, TEV, TNT]: endure.

QUESTION—What relationship is indicated by the word order of the phrase εἰς παιδείαν 'for discipline'?

It is emphatic [EBC].

QUESTION—What is the implied object of ὑπομένετε 'you endure/endure'?

1. The implied object is the trials the readers were suffering [WBC; NAB, NIV, NRSV, TEV]: you are enduring/endure your trials.
2. The object is discipline [CEV, NLT, REB]: you are enduring/endure God's discipline.

as sons[a] God is-dealing-with[b] you.

LEXICON—a. υἱός (LN 10.42): 'son' [HNTC, LN, Lns, Mil, NIC, WBC; all versions except NRSV, TEV], 'child' [CEV, NLT, NRSV, TEV]. This noun without the definite article is qualitative, emphasizing the nature of sonship [WBC].

b. pres. mid. indic. of προσφέρω (LN 15.192, **41.7**) (BAGD 3. p. 720): 'to deal with' [BAGD, HNTC, LN (41.7), Lns, Mil, NIC; KJV, NAB, NASB, TNT], 'to treat' [WBC; CEV, NIV, NJB, NLT, NRSV, REB, TEV], 'to behave toward' [LN (**41.7**)], 'to bring to' [LN (15.192)].

QUESTION—What relationship is indicated by the phrase ὡς υἱοῖς 'as sons'?

It is emphatic by word order.

1. It indicates a relationship [EBC, EGT, GNC, HNTC, NIC, NIGTC, WBC; all versions except KJV, NASB]: as sons. They are real sons [NIGTC, WBC]. It implies that they are God's sons [NJB, TEV].
2. It indicates a comparison [Alf; KJV, NASB]: as with sons.

QUESTION—What relationship is indicated by the position of ὁ θεός 'God' at the end of its clause?

It is emphatic by its position [NIGTC].

For what son[a] (is there) whom a-father (does) not discipline?[b]

LEXICON—a. υἱός 'son'. See this word in the preceding clause.

b. pres. act. indic. of παιδεύω (LN 36.10, 38.4) (BAGD 2.b.β. p. 604): 'to discipline' [BAGD, HNTC, LN (36.10), Mil, NIC, WBC; NAB, NASB, NIV, NLT, NRSV, REB, TNT], 'to chasten' [KJV], 'to chastise' [Lns], 'to train' [LN (36.10); NJB], 'to punish' [LN (36.10); TEV], 'to correct' [CEV].

QUESTION—What relationship is indicated by γάρ 'for'?

It indicates the grounds of (the conclusion from [NIGTC]) the preceding comment [Blm, Mil, NIGTC]: what I said is justified because, since you are children, you should expect discipline.

QUESTION—What relationship is indicated by πατήρ 'father' without a definite article?

1. It is a general reference [Lns, WBC; CEV, KJV, NLT, NRSV]: (any) father.
2. It is qualitative [WBC]: one of the nature of father.
3. It is translated as possessive [HNTC, NIC; all versions except KJV, NRSV]: his (the son's) father.

12:8 But if you-are without[a] discipline,[b] of-which all have-become partakers,[c]

LEXICON—a. χωρίς with genitive object (LN 89.120): 'without' [HNTC, LN, Lns, Mil, WBC; KJV, NASB], 'apart from' [LN]. The phrase χωρίς ἐστε παιδείας 'you are without discipline' is translated 'you are not disciplined' [NIV], 'you do not have that/the discipline' [NRSV, TNT], 'you have no part in the discipline' [NIC], 'you escape the discipline' [REB], 'you were not getting this training' [NJB], 'you are not punished' [TEV], 'God doesn't discipline you' [NLT], 'he doesn't correct you' [CEV]. These two entire clauses are translated 'if you do not know the discipline of sons' [NAB]. This word is emphatic by word order [Wst].

b. παιδεία: 'discipline'. See this word in 12:7.

c. μέτοχος (LN 34.8) (BAGD 1. p. 514): 'partaker' [Lns, Mil; KJV, NASB], 'companion, partner' [LN]. This noun is translated as a participle: 'sharing in, participating in' [BAGD]. The phrase ἧς μέτοχοι γεγόνασιν πάντες 'of which all have become partakers' is translated 'in which all children share' [NRSV], 'in which all sons share' [HNTC, WBC; REB, TNT], 'and everyone undergoes discipline' [NIV], 'as all of you are' [NJB], 'as all his children are' [TEV], 'which is shared by all' [NIC], 'as he does all of his children' [NLT], 'God corrects all his children' [CEV]. This word implies personal acceptance of the discipline [Wst].

QUESTION—What relationship is indicated by this verse?

1. It expresses a condition of fact, indicating an actual possibility [HNTC, Lns, Mil, NIC, NTC, TH, WBC; all versions except NJB] whether fulfilled or not: if you are without discipline, then you are not true sons. It is a strong proposition [NTC]. The writer is thinking of real instances [TH].
2. It is treated as a contrary-to-fact condition [NIGTC; NJB] in view of the wider context [NIGTC]: if you were without discipline, then you would not be true sons. This interpretation violates the rules of Greek grammar; a contrary-to-fact condition would require the imperfect tense ἦν 'were' here and in the following clause.

QUESTION—What relationship is indicated by δέ 'but'?

1. It indicates a contrast with the preceding comment [Mil].
2. It indicates a further step in the author's argument [NIGTC, TH, TNTC].

QUESTION—To whom does πάντες 'all' refer?

1. It refers to all true children of God by faith [Blm, EGT, Hu, Mil, My, NIGTC].
2. It refers to all of God's legitimate sons [NIGTC, TH], but without specifying who they were [NIGTC].
3. It refers to all of the persons mentioned in Chapter 11 [Alf].
4. It refers to children in general [EBC, TNTC, WBC].

QUESTION—What does the perfect tense of the verb γεγόνασιν 'have become' indicate?

It indicates that πάντες 'all' refers to the past history of God's children [Mil], to God's children, not to earthly relationships [My]. It indicates a general truth [WBC]; it indicates that the discipline had permanent effects [Wst].

then[a] you-are illegitimate[b] and not sons.[c]

LEXICON—a. ἄρα (LN 89.46) (BAGD 3. p. 103): 'then' [BAGD, HNTC, LN, Lns, NIC, WBC; CEV, KJV, NASB, NIV, NJB, NRSV, TNT], 'then in that case' [Mil], 'consequently' [LN], 'as a result' [BAGD, LN], 'it means' [NLT, TEV], not explicit [NAB, REB]. It introduces an inference from the preceding [Alf]. It is emphatic [NTC]; it implies tentativeness, indicating that an opposite response is also possible [WBC].

b. νόθος (LN **10.39**) (BAGD p. 541): 'illegitimate' [LN; NLT, NRSV, REB], 'illegitimate child' [BAGD, WBC; NASB, NIV], 'illegitimate offspring' [Mil], 'bastard' [HNTC, **LN**, Lns, Mil, NIC; KJV, NAB, NJB, TEV, TNT]. This entire clause is translated 'then you don't really belong to him' [CEV]. It means born out of wedlock [Hwt, ICC, My, TH].

c. υἱός (LN 10.42) (BAGD 1.c.γ. p. 834): 'son' [BAGD, HNTC, LN, Lns, Mil; KJV, NAB, NASB, NJB, TNT], 'true son' [WBC; NIV, REB], 'trueborn son' [NIC], 'real child' [TEV], 'his child' [NLT, NRSV], not explicit [CEV].

QUESTION—What relationship is indicated by ἐστε 'you are'?

1. It expresses a fact [HNTC, Lns, Mil, NIC; KJV, NAB, NASB, NIV, NRSV, TEV, TNT]: you are. The writer supposes an actual case [ICC] (this is incorrect; it supposes only an actual possibility).
2. The two following interpretations violate the rules of Greek grammar.

2.1 It expresses a possibility [REB]: you must be.

2.2 It is translated as the verb of the consequence of a contrary-to-fact condition [NJB]: you would be.

QUESTION—What relationship is indicated by καί 'and'?

It is explanatory [NIGTC]: illegitimate; i.e., not sons.

DISCOURSE UNIT: 12:9–13 [HNTC]. The topic is divine discipline.

12:9 Furthermore[a] on-the-one-hand we-were-having fathers of-our flesh[b] (as) instructors[c] and we-were-respecting[d] (them);

LEXICON—a. εἶτα (LN 67.44, **89.100**) (BAGD 2. p. 234): 'furthermore' [BAGD, LN (89.100), Lns, Mil; KJV, NASB], 'moreover' [NIV, NRSV], 'then' [BAGD, LN (67.44)], 'then again' [WBC], 'again' [HNTC, NIC; REB], 'besides' [NJB], 'besides this' [LN (**89.100**)], 'if' [NAB], not explicit [CEV, NLT, TEV, TNT]. This word introduces a new argument [Alf, Lns, My, NCBC, NIGTC, WBC, Wst], a new phase of the argument [EGT, Mil], the continuation of the argument [Lg].

b. σάρξ (LN 8.4, **9.12**) (BAGD 4. p. 743): 'flesh' [Lns, Mil; KJV], 'human nature, mortal nature' [BAGD], 'body, physical body' [LN (8.4)], 'physical nature' [LN (9.12)], 'earthly descent' [BAGD]. This noun is also translated as an adjective: 'human' [LN (**9.12**); NIV, NJB, NRSV, REB, TEV, TNT], 'earthly' [HNTC; CEV, NAB, NASB, NLT], 'natural' [NIC, WBC]. This genitive noun means 'natural' [Blm], 'human' in a neutral sense [NIGTC], referring to natural human life [Mil].

c. παιδευτής (LN 33.244, **38.5**) (BAGD p. 603): 'instructor, trainer, teacher' [LN (33.244)], 'chastiser' [Lns], 'corrector' [BAGD] 'punisher, one who punishes' [LN (38.5)]. This noun is also translated as a verb: 'to correct' [KJV, NAB], 'to discipline' [BAGD, HNTC, Mil, NIC, WBC; NASB, NIV, NLT, NRSV, REB, TNT], 'to punish' [LN (**38.5**); NJB, TEV], 'to correct' [CEV]. Here it implies correction through discipline [WBC].

d. imperf. mid. indic. of ἐντρέπω (LN 87.11) (BAGD 2.b. p. 269): 'to respect' [BAGD, LN, Lns, WBC; CEV, NAB, NASB, NIV, NJB, NLT,

NRSV, TEV], 'to show respect' [LN, Mil], 'to pay respect' [NIC], 'to pay due respect' [REB], 'to hold in respect' [HNTC; TNT], 'to give reverence' [KJV]. The imperfect tense indicates continuation in indefinite past time [Lns, Mil, My, NIGTC].

QUESTION—What relationship is indicated by this verse?

It is an argument from the lesser to the greater [HNTC, Hu, Lns, Mil, My, NIGTC, TNTC].

QUESTION—What is indicated by the imperfect tense of the verb εἴχομεν 'we were having'?

It indicates a former continuing state [Alf, Lns, Mil, NIGTC], customary action in the past [WBC]: we formerly were having.

QUESTION—How are the two nouns related in the genitive construction τῆς σαρκὸς ἡμῶν πατέρας 'fathers of our flesh'?

Σάρξ 'flesh' is a genitive of general relationship [Lns], indicating the (earthly [CEV, NLT]) sphere referred to [WBC; CEV, NLT]: our fathers had a general relationship in the sphere of our physical nature.

QUESTION—What relationship is indicated by the two accusative nouns τοὺς πατέρας παιδευτάς 'the fathers as instructors'?

Τοὺς πατέρας 'the fathers' is the object of the verb εἴχομεν 'we were having', and παιδευτάς 'instructors' is in apposition with 'fathers' [Alf, Mil]: we were having the fathers as instructors. The reference to 'fathers' is not intended to exclude mothers as well [Lns; NRSV].

QUESTION—What relationship is indicated by καί 'and'?

1. It may be merely a connective [Alf, Blm, EGT, HNTC, Hwt, ICC, Mil, My, NIC, NTC, Wst; all versions except NIV, NJB]: and we respected them.
2. It introduces a result [EBC, TNTC, WBC; NIV, NJB]: and as a result we respected them.
3. It introduces a contraexpectation [GNC, Lns]: and yet we respected them.

QUESTION—What relationship is indicated by ἐνετρεπόμεθα 'we were respecting'?

1. It refers to respecting our human fathers, with no further specification [Alf, Blm, GNC, HNTC, Hwt, ICC, Lns, Mil, NIC, WBC; all versions except NIV, NJB]. It implies respecting them in spite of their disciplining us [GNC, Lns].
2. It implies respecting our human fathers because they disciplined us [TNTC; NIV, NJB].
3. It refers to heeding their discipline [My].

on-the-other-hand/and not much more/rather[a] shall-we-be-subject[b] to-the father[c] of-the spirits[d] and shall-live?[e]

LEXICON—a. μᾶλλον (LN 78.28, 89.126) (BAGD 2.a. p. 489): 'more' [HNTC, LN (78.28), Mil, NIC; NIV, TEV], 'rather' [BAGD, Lns; KJV, NASB], 'even more, to a greater degree' [LN (78.28)], 'all the more' [NAB, NLT], 'but rather, instead' [LN (89.126)]. The phrase πολὺ μᾶλλον 'much more/rather' is translated 'even more readily' [REB], 'all the more readily' [NJB], 'isn't it even better' [CEV]. The phrase οὐ πολὺ μᾶλλον ὑποταγησόμεθα 'shall we not much more be subject' is translated 'should we not be even more willing to be subject' [NRSV], 'should we not be even more willing to submit' [TNT].

b. fut. mid./pass. indic. of ὑποτάσσω (LN 36.18, 37.31) (BAGD 1.b.β. p. 848): 'to be subject to' [LN (37.31), Lns; NASB, NRSV], 'to subject oneself' [BAGD, Mil], 'to be in subjection' [KJV], 'to be subjected, to be subordinated' [BAGD], 'to submit' [HNTC; NAB, NIV, NJB, NLT, REB, TEV, TNT], 'to be submissive' [NIC], 'to obey' [BAGD, LN (36.18)], 'to let correct' [CEV]. By the first person plural here and in the following verb ζήσομεν 'we shall live' the author associates himself with his readers [NIGTC, NTC].

c. πατήρ (LN 10.14, 58.64) (BAGD 3.b. p. 635): 'father' [BAGD, LN (10.14, 58.64)], 'Father' [HNTC, Lns, Mil, NIC; all versions], 'spiritual father' [LN (58.64)]. It refers to God [Alf, Lg, My, NIGTC, TNTC].

d. πνεῦμα (LN 26.9) (BAGD 4.b. p. 675): 'spirit' [BAGD, HNTC, LN, Lns, Mil, NIC; KJV, NAB, NASB, NJB, NRSV], 'our spirit' [NIV], 'spirit being' [BAGD], 'spiritual nature, inner being' [LN]. This noun is also translated as an adjective: 'spiritual' [CEV, REB, TEV, TNT], 'heavenly' [NLT]. It refers to human personality as animated by God [HNTC, Mil] through the new birth [Mil].

e. fut. act. indic. of ζάω (LN 23.88) (BAGD 2.b.α. p. 336): 'to live' [BAGD, LN, Lns, Mil; KJV, NAB, NASB, NIV, NRSV, TEV], 'to live forever' [NLT], 'to earn life' [NJB], 'to gain life' [HNTC, NIC; TNT], 'to attain life' [REB], 'to be given true life' [CEV]. It refers to eternal life [Alf, BAGD, EBC, GNC, My, NIGTC, NTC], to possessing the true life that makes us God's sons, beginning now and extending into eternity [Lns].

QUESTION—What relationship is indicated by this clause?

It states a contrast with the preceding clause [Mil, NTC].

1. It is a deliberative question [Lns, NIGTC, TNTC, WBC; CEV, KJV, NAB, NASB, NLT, NRSV, REB, TNT]: should we not be subject . . . and live? It implies an exhortation [WBC]. It assumes that the response is affirmative [TNTC, WBC; KJV], as the introductory οὐ 'not' implies [WBC].
2. It is translated as a strong exhortation [NIV, NJB, TEV]: we should be subject . . .

QUESTION—What relationship is indicated by μᾶλλον 'more/rather'?

1. It indicates a greater degree [HNTC, Mil, NIC, NTC, WBC; CEV, NAB, NIV, NJB, NLT, TEV]: all the more.
2. It indicates a contrast [BAGD, Lns, My; KJV, NASB]: instead.

QUESTION—How are the two nouns related in the genitive construction τῷ πατρὶ τῶν πνευμάτων 'the father of the spirits'?

The genitive τῶν πνευμάτων 'of the spirits' states what the father-relationship governs [Blm, GNC, HNTC, Hu, Hwt, ICC, Lg, My, NIGTC,

TNTC, WBC, Wst]: father as the source of the spirits. It means that God regenerates our spirits in salvation [Blm, GNC]. It means that God is the author of spiritual (and eternal [Hwt]) life [Hwt, ICC, My, NIC, TNTC]. It means that God has a general relationship of father to us [Lns].

QUESTION—What is meant by τῶν πνευμάτων 'the spirits'?

It is in contrast with τῆς σαρκὸς ἡμῶν 'our flesh' [EGT, GNC, HNTC, TH].

1. It is generic and refers to spirits in general [Alf, Lg, Lns, NIGTC, WBC, Wst; KJV, NAB, NASB, NJB, NRSV]. It includes both angelic and human spirits [Lns].
2. It is possessive and refers to our spirits [Blm, EGT, GNC, HNTC, Hu; NIV].
3. It refers to spiritual (and eternal [Hwt]) life [Hwt, ICC, My, TNTC].
4. It is used as an adjective to describe the father [EBC; CEV, NLT, REB, TEV, TNT]: our spiritual father.

QUESTION— What relationship is indicated by καί 'and'?

It introduces the result [Blm, My, NIGTC, TH, WBC; NJB, REB, TNT]: and so earn life.

12:10 For they on-the-one-hand for[a] a-few days[b] according-to[c] the-(thing) seeming-good[d] to-them were-disciplining,[e]

LEXICON—a. πρός with accusative object (LN 67.106) (BAGD III.2.b. p. 710): 'for' [BAGD, HNTC, LN, Lns, Mil, NIC, WBC; all versions except NAB], 'to prepare us for' [NAB]. This word here refers to duration of time [ICC, Lg]; it means 'in reference to' [Lg(K)]. It indicates a nearer purpose [Mil].

b. ἡμέρα (LN 67.178) (BAGD 4.b. p. 347): 'day' [LN, Lns, Mil, NIC; KJV]. The phrase ὀλίγας ἡμέρας 'a few days' is translated 'a short time' [BAGD, HNTC, WBC; CEV, NASB, NRSV, REB, TEV, TNT], 'a little while' [NIV], 'a short life' [NJB], 'a few years' [NLT], 'the short span of mortal life' [NAB].

c. κατά with accusative object (LN 89.8): 'according to' [Lns, Mil; NJB], 'in accordance with' [LN], 'after' [KJV], 'as' [HNTC, NIC; all versions except KJV, NJB, NLT], not explicit [NLT].

d. pres. act. participle of δοκέω (LN 25.7) (BAGD 3.a p. 202): 'to seem good' [Lns, Mil], 'to seem right' [NAB, TEV, TNT], 'to seem best' [NASB, NRSV], 'to think best' [CEV, NIV, REB], 'to think fit' [NIC], 'to be disposed to, to want to' [LN], 'to choose' [HNTC]. The phrase τὸ δοκοῦν αὐτοῖς 'the thing seeming good to them' is translated 'their own pleasure' [KJV], 'their own lights' [NJB]. The phrase κατὰ τὸ δοκοῦν αὐτοῖς 'according to the thing seeming good to them' is translated 'at their discretion' [BAGD, WBC], 'doing the best they knew how' [NLT].

e. imperf. act. indic. of παιδεύω: 'to discipline'. See this word in 12:7. Here it refers to repeated instances [WBC]. The implied object is the author and his readers [Alf, Blm, EBC, GNC, HNTC, Hwt, ICC, Lg, Mil, My, NIC, TH, WBC; all versions].

QUESTION—Why is this verse mentioned?

It continues the argument of the preceding verse [NTC]; it strengthens the argument by pointing out the contrast between the discipline by earthly fathers and by God [Alf]. The contrast is indicated by οἱ μέν 'they on the one hand' and ὁ δέ 'he on the other hand' [Lns, WBC].

QUESTION—What relationship is indicated by γάρ 'for'?

It indicates the reason (stated specifically in the latter part of this verse) for being subject to God's discipline [EGT, Mil, My, NIGTC]: we should be subject to God, because he disciplines us for our good. It introduces a further explanation [Lns].

QUESTION—To whom does οἱ 'they' refer?

It refers to the earthly fathers [Mil, NIGTC, WBC], parents [Alf].

QUESTION—What relationship is indicated by the phrase πρὸς ὀλίγας ἡμέρας 'for a few days'?

1. It tells how long the disciplining lasted [Alf, Blm, EBC, EGT, HNTC, Hwt, ICC, Lg, Lns, Mil, My, NCBC, NIC, NIGTC, NTC, TH, TNTC, WBC, Wst; all versions except NAB, NJB]: they disciplined for a few days.

1.1 It refers to the brief period of time when we were subject to our earthly father's discipline [Alf, Hwt, Lg, Wst]; i.e., during childhood [EGT, HNTC, Hwt, ICC, Lg, Lns, Mil, NIGTC, NTC, TH]. It includes the idea of purpose [Mil]; it expresses purpose [NAB].

1.2 The phrase 'for a few days' is to be understood in the second part of the verse as well [Blm, HNTC, My], as its forefronted position implies [My]; in the first part it refers to the period of childhood, and in the second part to the brief time of our earthly life [Blm, HNTC]

2. It states the purpose of the disciplining [NAB, NJB]: they disciplined in order to prepare us for the short span of life.

QUESTION—What relationship is indicated by 'according to the thing seeming good to them'?

1. It refers to the earthly fathers' (and mothers' [NTC]) sometimes faulty view of what was proper [Alf, EBC, EGT, Hwt, Lns, My, NIC, NIGTC, NTC, TNTC, WBC, Wst], although they do their best [EBC, Lns, NTC].
2. Earthly fathers' discipline is arbitrary [ICC, Lg(K)]; it may be either good or bad [HNTC].
3. It has a negative sense of arbitrary punishment to promote the earthly fathers' purpose, intended to cause fear rather than improvement [Blm].

on-the-other-hand/but he for[a] the-(thing) being-advantageous[b] for-the-purpose-of[c] the partaking[d] of-his holiness.[e]

LEXICON—a. ἐπί with accusative object (LN 89.13, 89.60) (BAGD III.1.b.η. p. 289): 'for' [HNTC, Lns, Mil, NIC; all versions], 'for the purpose of, for the sake of, in order to' [LN (89.60)], 'on the basis of, in view of' [LN (89.13)], 'to' [BAGD, WBC]. It indicates purpose [Alf], basis [Lns].

b. pres. act. participle of συμφέρω (LN 65.44) (BAGD 2.b.γ. p. 780): 'to be advantageous, to be to someone's advantage' [LN], 'to really profit' [Lns]. The phrase τὸ συμφέρον 'the thing being advantageous' is translated 'our true profit' [NAB], 'our profit' [Mil; KJV], 'profit, advantage' [BAGD], 'our advantage' [NIC, WBC], 'our good' [HNTC; NASB, NIV, NRSV, TNT], 'our own good' [CEV, NJB, TEV], 'our true welfare' [REB], 'right and good for us' [NLT].

c. εἰς with accusative object (LN 89.57): 'for the purpose of, in order to' [LN], 'in order that' [WBC; NRSV], 'so that' [Lns, Mil, NIC; NJB, REB, TEV], 'that' [HNTC; KJV, NAB, NASB, NIV, TNT], 'because' [CEV, NLT]. It indicates purpose [WBC], a more distant purpose in contrast with πρός 'for' as a nearer purpose in the preceding clause [Mil].

d. aorist act. infin. of μεταλαμβάνω (LN 57.129, 90.63) (BAGD 1. p. 511): 'to partake' [Lns], 'to be partakers' [KJV], 'to share' [HNTC; all versions except CEV, KJV, NIV], 'to share in' [BAGD, Mil, WBC; NIV], 'to receive a share in' [NIC], 'to have a share of, to receive a share in' [LN (57.129)], 'to receive one's share, to receive' [BAGD], 'to experience' [LN (90.63)]. The phrase τὸ μεταλαβεῖν τῆς ἁγιότητος αὐτοῦ 'the partaking of his holiness' is translated 'he wants us to be holy, as he is' [CEV].

e. ἁγιότης (LN **88.25**) (BAGD p.10): 'holiness' [BAGD, HNTC, LN, Lns, Mil, NIC; all versions except CEV], 'holy character' [BAGD, WBC]. It refers to God's divine life [ICC]; it is an essential qualitative attribute of God's character [Lns, Mil, NIGTC, WBC]. It refers to positive holiness of life [NIC].

QUESTION—To whom does ὁ δέ 'but he' refer?

It refers to God [NIGTC, TH, WBC].

QUESTION—What relationship is indicated by the contrasted phrases in this verse?

They imply a different quality in the two kinds of discipline [EBC].

1. 'According to the thing seeming good thing to them' is contrasted with 'for the thing being advantageous' (i.e., 'for our benefit') [Mil, My, NIGTC, TNTC, WBC, Wst].

1.1 The phrase 'for a few days' is contrasted with 'for the partaking of his holiness' in a chiastic structure combining both sets of contrasts [Mil, Wst].

1.2 The phrase 'for a few days' is unemphatic and belongs to both 'according to the thing seeming good to them' and 'for the thing being advantageous' (i.e., 'for our benefit'), as its forefronted position implies [My].

2. The phrase 'for a few days', indicating a short time, is contrasted with the great purpose implied in the phrase 'for the thing being advantageous' (i.e., 'for our benefit') [Alf]; and the earthly fathers' purpose, 'according to the thing seeming good to them' is contrasted with God's purpose, 'for the partaking of his holiness' [Alf].

QUESTION—Who is the implied object of τὸ συμφέρον 'the thing being advantageous' and the implied actor of τὸ μεταλαβεῖν 'the partaking'?

Both references are to the author and his readers [Alf, Blm, EBC, GNC, HNTC, Hwt, Lns, Mil, My, NCBC, NIC, TH, WBC; all versions]: for our advantage, that we may partake . . .

QUESTION—What relationship is indicated by the phrase 'for the partaking of his holiness'?

It expresses purpose [EBC, NTC, WBC], contemplated result [Lns]. It means to make us partakers of his holiness [Alf, HNTC, WBC], to produce a holy character like his [HNTC, TH, TNTC], as a gift through his discipline [WBC]. It explains the preceding phrase, 'for the thing being advantageous' (i.e., 'for our benefit') [Blm, EGT, ICC, TH].

12:11 Now all discipline[a] at[b] the-(time) being-present,[c] on-the-one-hand, (does) not seem[d] to-be of-joy[e] but of-grief,[f]

LEXICON—a. παιδεία (LN 33.226, 36.10, **38.4**) (BAGD 1. p. 603): 'discipline' [BAGD, HNTC, LN (36.10), Mil, NIC, WBC; all versions except CEV, KJV, TEV], 'chastening' [KJV], 'chastisement' [Lns], 'instruction' [LN (33.226)], 'punishment' [LN (38.4)]. This noun is also translated as a verb: 'to be punished' [TEV], 'to be corrected' [CEV]. This phrase refers to both human and divine discipline [Alf, Hwt, My, NIGTC, NTC, Wst]; it refers only to divine discipline [Lns, Mil], which is most likely to cause grief and misunderstanding [Mil].

b. πρός with accusative object (LN **67.16**) (BAGD III.2.b. p. 710): 'at' [HNTC, LN, WBC; all versions except KJV, NASB, NLT], 'for' [BAGD, Lns, Mil, NIC; KJV, NASB], 'while' [NLT]. It means 'during' [Alf].

c. pres. act. participle of πάρειμι (LN **67.37**, 85.23) (BAGD 1.b. p. 624): 'to be present' [LN (85.23)]. The phrase τὸ παρόν 'the time being present' is translated 'the present' [BAGD, LN (67.37), Lns, Mil; KJV], 'the moment' [BAGD; NASB], 'the time' [HNTC, LN (**67.37**); CEV, NIV, NJB, NRSV, REB, TEV, TNT], 'the time being' [NIC], 'the actual time' [WBC], 'the time it is administered' [NAB], 'while it is happening' [NLT]. It refers to the time while enduring the discipline [Blm, My].

d. pres. act. indic. of δοκέω (LN 31.30) (BAGD 2.a. p. 202): 'to seem' [HNTC, LN, Lns, Mil, WBC; all versions except CEV, NJB, NLT], 'to appear' [LN, NIC], 'to have the appearance' [BAGD], 'to be' [CEV, NJB, NLT]. It implies a mistaken impression [Blm, My, Wst], a superficial impression [WBC].

e. χαρά (LN 25.124) (BAGD 1. p. 875 twice): 'joy' [BAGD], 'cause for joy' [LN; NAB], 'reason for gladness' [LN], 'something to make us glad' [TEV], 'a matter for joy' [NJB], 'a matter of joy' [Lns, Mil], 'fun' [CEV]. This genitive noun is also translated as an adjective: 'joyful' [NASB], 'joyous' [KJV], 'enjoyable' [NLT], 'pleasant' [BAGD, HNTC, NIC, WBC; NIV, NRSV, REB, TNT]. This noun is a genitive of quality, the equivalent of the adjective 'joyous' [Blm, Mil, NIGTC, WBC].

f. λύπη (LN 25.273) (BAGD p. 482): 'grief, pain, affliction' [BAGD], 'cause for grief' [NAB], 'a matter for grief' [NJB], 'a matter of grief' [Lns, Mil], 'sorrow' [BAGD, LN], 'sadness, distress' [LN], 'something to make us sad' [TEV]. This genitive noun is also translated as an adjective: 'painful' [HNTC, NIC, WBC; CEV, NIV, NLT, NRSV, REB, TNT], 'sorrowful' [NASB], 'grievous' [KJV]. This noun is a genitive of quality, the equivalent of the adjective 'grievous' [Mil, NIGTC, WBC].

QUESTION—What relationship is indicated by δέ 'now'?

It resumes the argument by introducing a comment which is generally recognized as true [Alf]; it introduces the summing up of the comments from 12:4 [Mil, NIGTC] (from 12:5 [ICC]) and a contrast with 12:10b [NIGTC].

QUESTION—What relationship is indicated by μέν 'on the one hand' in this clause plus δέ 'on the other hand/but' in the following clause?

They serve to contrast the two expressions of time [Lns, Mil]: at the time being present, on the one hand; and later, on the other hand.

QUESTION—What relationship is indicated by ἀλλά 'but'?

It is a strong adversative contrast [Mil].

on-the-other-hand/but later[a] it-yields[b] peaceable[c] fruit[d] of-righteousness[e] to-the-(ones) trained[f] through[g] it.

LEXICON—a. ὕστερος (LN 67.50) (BAGD 2.a p. 849): 'later' [BAGD, LN, NIC, WBC; NAB, NJB, NRSV, TEV], 'later on' [Lns, Mil; NIV], 'afterward' [KJV, NLT], 'afterwards' [HNTC; NASB, REB, TNT], 'thereafter' [BAGD], not explicit [CEV]. It refers to the time after the discipline has been ended [My, NTC], the period of enjoying the benefits of the discipline [Blm, WBC], the time at the end of earthly life [Hu].

b. pres. act. indic. of ἀποδίδωμι (LN 38.16) (BAGD 1. p. 90): 'to yield' [BAGD, HNTC, Lns, Mil, NIC, WBC; KJV, NASB, NRSV], 'to produce' [NIV, TNT], 'to bear' [NJB], 'to reward, to recompense' [LN], 'to bring forth' [NAB], 'to be' [NLT], not explicit [CEV]. The phrase τοῖς δι' αὐτῆς γεγυμνασμένοις ἀποδίδωσιν 'it yields to the ones trained through it' is translated 'those who have been trained by it reap' [REB], 'those who have been disciplined by such punishment reap' [TEV]. This phrase refers to discipline insofar as it is administered properly [Alf]; it refers only to divine discipline [Hwt, My]. It implies receiving its proper return [Wst], receiving a reward [NIGTC].

c. εἰρηνικός (LN **25.249**) (BAGD p. 228): 'peaceable' [KJV], 'peaceful' [BAGD, HNTC, LN, Lns, Mil, NIC; NASB, NRSV, TEV], 'peaceful life' [REB], 'quiet' [NLT]. This adjective is also translated as a noun: 'of peace' [NAB, NIV, TNT], 'in peace' [NJB], 'which consists of peace' [WBC]; as a verb: 'to be at peace' [CEV]. It means that it is to be enjoyed in peace [Alf]; it means that it brings with it peace of soul [My]. It refers to the peace of mind and peace with God resulting from proper discipline [Blm, EGT, Lns]; it refers to the rest that comes when the conflict is over [Hu]. It implies the resolution of the struggle involved in present sufferings [GNC]. It is in contrast with the pain of the discipline [Hwt, ICC] and also blissful [ICC].

d. καρπός (LN 43.15) (BAGD 1.a. p. 404; 2.a. p. 405): 'fruit' [BAGD, LN, Lns, Mil, WBC; KJV, NAB, NASB, NJB, NRSV], 'harvest' [HNTC, LN, Mil, NIC; NIV, NLT, REB], 'reward' [TEV], 'lives' [TNT], not explicit [CEV]. It implies outcome or result [ICC, TH]. It is a metaphor for the final part of the process of discipline [NIGTC].

e. δικαιοσύνη (LN 88.13) (BAGD 2.b. p. 196): 'righteousness' [BAGD, HNTC, LN, Lns, Mil, NIC, WBC; KJV, NASB, NIV, NRSV], 'righteous life' [TEV], 'right living' [NLT], 'uprightness' [BAGD; NJB], 'upright life' [REB], 'goodness' [TNT], 'justice' [NAB]. This noun is also translated as a verb: 'to do right' [CEV]. It is emphatic by word order [Lg(K), NIGTC, TNTC, Wst]. It refers to ethical conduct [Mil, NIGTC, TH], moral purity [My], godliness [Blm]. It refers to a relationship with God [ICC, NIGTC]. It is the righteousness of Christ, received by the believer when he stands before his Lord in heaven [Hu].

f. perf. pass. participle of γυμνάζω (LN **36.11**) (BAGD p. 167): 'to be trained' [BAGD, HNTC, LN, Mil, NIC, WBC; NAB, NASB, NIV, NLT, NRSV, REB, TNT], 'to be disciplined' [**LN**; TEV], 'to be exercised' [Lns; KJV]. This passive voice is also translated as active: 'to learn to obey' [CEV], 'to undergo' [NJB]. The perfect tense implies the enduring effect [Lns, NIGTC], the continuing training [EBC, NTC], the result of the discipline [Mil].

g. διά with genitive object (LN 89.76): 'through' [LN, Mil], 'by' [HNTC, NIC, WBC; CEV, NASB, NIV, NRSV, REB, TEV], 'by means of' [LN, Lns], 'under' [TNT]. The phrase δι' αὐτῆς 'through it' is translated 'thereby' [KJV], 'in its school' [NAB], 'in this way' [NLT].

QUESTION—What relationship is indicated by this clause?

It forms the summary and conclusion of the section, as the introductory 'therefore' in the following verse indicates [TH].

QUESTION—How are the adjective and the two nouns related in the genitive construction καρπὸν εἰρηνικὸν . . . δικαιοσύνης 'peaceable fruit of righteousness'?

1. The adjective εἰρηνικόν 'peaceable' modifies καρπόν 'fruit' [Alf, EGT, GNC, HNTC, Hu, Hwt, ICC, Lg, Lns, Mil, My, NIC, TNTC, Wst; KJV, NASB, NRSV, TEV]: peaceable fruit.

1.1 The 'peaceable fruit' is 'righteousness' [Alf, Blm, Hwt, ICC, Lg, Lns, Mil, My, Wst]: the peaceable fruit which is righteousness.

1.2 'Righteousness' is the source of the 'peaceable fruit' [TNTC]: the peaceable fruit, whose source is righteousness.

2. The adjective εἰρηνικόν 'peaceable' is translated as a noun parallel to the following genitive noun δικαιοσύνης 'righteousness', with both 'peaceable' and 'righteousness' equally related to 'fruit' [EBC, NIGTC, NTC, TH, WBC; NAB, NIV, NJB, REB, TNT]: the fruit of peace and righteousness.

2.1 The 'fruit' consists of peace and righteousness [NIGTC, WBC]. Εἰρηνικόν 'peaceable' indicates that the fruit consists of peace [NIGTC, WBC]. Δικαιοσύνης 'righteousness' is a genitive of content, stating what is contained in the 'fruit' [NIGTC]; it is a genitive of apposition, stating what the 'fruit' actually is [WBC].

2.2 The 'fruit' is a peaceful and upright life [REB].

QUESTION—To what does αὐτῆς 'it' refer?

It refers to παιδεία 'discipline' earlier in this verse [Alf, EGT, NIGTC, WBC]: through discipline.

DISCOURSE UNIT: 12:12–29 [TEV]. The topic is instructions and warnings.

DISCOURSE UNIT: 12:12–17 [EBC, GNC, NCBC, NIC, TNTC]. The topic is a further admonition [NCBC] to be "up and doing" [NIC], to live a Christian life [EBC], to live in holiness and faithfulness [GNC], to avoid moral inconsistency [TNTC].

12:12 Wherefore the weakened[a] hands[b] and the paralyzed[c] knees[d] strengthen,[e]

LEXICON—a. perf. mid. participle of παρίημι (LN **23.174**) (BAGD 2.a. p. 627): 'to be weakened' [BAGD, LN], 'to droop' [BAGD, HNTC, NIC, WBC; NAB, NRSV, REB, TNT], 'to hang down' [KJV], not explicit [CEV]. This participle is also translated as an adjective: 'weak' [**LN**; NASB], 'listless' [BAGD], 'weary' [NJB], 'tired' [NLT, TEV], 'limp' [Lns], 'feeble' [NIV], 'unnerved' [Mil]. It refers to inability to accomplish anything [EBC], to the listlessness of defeat [EGT].

b. χείρ (LN 8.30): 'hand' [HNTC, LN, Lns, Mil, WBC; all versions except CEV, NIV, REB], 'arm' [NIC; NIV, REB], not explicit [CEV]. 'Hand' stands for 'arm', as a part for the whole [NTC].

c. perf. mid. participle of παραλύω (LN **23.170**) (BAGD p. 620): 'to be paralyzed' [**LN**, Lns, NIC], 'to be weakened' [BAGD, WBC], 'to be lame' [LN], 'to tremble' [NJB, TEV], 'to shake' [CEV, REB], 'to fail' [HNTC]. This participle is translated as an adjective: 'feeble' [KJV, NASB], 'weak' [NAB, NIV, NRSV, TNT], 'wobbly' [Mil], 'shaky' [NLT]. It means incapable of healthy motion [Alf], weak [EBC].

d. γόνυ (LN 8.47) (BAGD p. 165): 'knee' [BAGD, HNTC, LN (8.47), Lns, Mil, NIC, WBC; all versions except NLT], 'leg' [NLT].

e. aorist act. impera. of ἀνορθόω (LN **25.152**) (BAGD p. 72): 'to strengthen' [BAGD, NIC, WBC; NAB, NASB, NIV], 'to revive the grip of' [Mil], 'to lift up' [KJV], 'to steady' [NJB], 'to brace' [REB], 'to brace up' [Mil], 'to stiffen' [HNTC], 'to straighten out' [Lns]. This verb is translated differently for its reference to the hands and to the knees: 'to lift up . . . to strengthen' [NRSV, TEV, TNT], 'to stiffen . . . to straighten' [HNTC], 'to stand up straight . . . to stop from shaking' [CEV], 'to take a new grip . . . to stand firm' [NLT]. The expression means 'to become more determined and encouraged' [LN (**25.152**)]. It means to restore for the purpose of renewing the spiritual conflict [EGT].

QUESTION—Why is this clause mentioned?

It states an exhortation based on the preceding arguments [Blm, EBC, HNTC, Hu, Mil, NTC, TNTC, Wst] concerning the benefits of discipline [Hwt, Mil], based on the preceding encouraging view of trials [EGT, GNC] whose severity has resulted in discouragement [Hwt, Lns]. It is an exhortation pointing out that their sufferings show that they are sons of God [My], that they should become encouraged [GNC, Hwt] and receive the needed strength for their circumstances [GNC]. The introductory διό 'wherefore' connects this clause to the preceding discussion [TNTC]; it introduces the concluding exhortation [WBC]; it gives emphasis to the following words [TH].

QUESTION—To whom does the exhortation of this clause refer?

All the readers need the encouragement, and the readers are urged to strengthen their own arms and knees [EGT, GNC, HNTC, Hwt, ICC, Lns, Mil, My, NIC, NTC, TH, WBC; NAB, NIV, NRSV, REB], but with concern for the weak persons among them [WBC]; some weaker ones need special help from others [NIGTC, Wst].

QUESTION—What is meant by the figures 'weakened hands' and 'paralyzed knees'?

They refer to the effects of mental distress on the physical body [Blm, Hu]; they imply giving way to listless despair [ICC, Mil]; they imply being unable to act because of being exhausted [TNTC]; they imply being exhausted and discouraged [WBC]. Both participles are in the perfect tense, implying lasting effects [NTC]. They imply that the readers are acting as if they were spiritually paralyzed [EBC]. The use of the definite articles in these two phrases implies that the readers knew in general to whom the author was referring [NIGTC]. The reference to 'hands' refers to ability for conflict, and the reference to 'knees' refers to power for progress [Wst].

12:13 and make straight[a] paths[b] for-your feet,

LEXICON—a. ὀρθός (LN **41.30**, **79.88**) (BAGD 1.b. p. 580): 'straight' [BAGD, HNTC, LN (**41.30**, **79.88**), Lns, Mil, NIC; all versions except NIV], 'level' [NIV]. This entire clause is translated 'and move in a straight direction with your feet' [WBC], '(and) live a right life' [LN (**41.30**)]. It means 'in a straight line' [NIGTC]; it means 'level', all unevenness in the path removed [NTC]; it means both straight and with impediments removed [TNTC, Wst].

b. τροχιά (LN **41.30**—see a. above) (BAGD p. 828): 'path' [BAGD, HNTC, Lns, Mil, NIC; all versions]. It is emphatic by word order [WBC]. It refers figuratively to the readers' thoughts [Lns].

QUESTION—What is meant by this verse?

It is addressed to all the members [HNTC, ICC, TH, WBC]. It is addressed to the leaders [Mil].

1. It is an exhortation to walk in such a correct way that a plain path will be made for those who follow [Alf, EGT, NIGTC].
2. It is an exhortation to live in a way pleasing to God so that those who are lame will be healed [GNC, Hu, Hwt, Lns, WBC], so that those who are lagging behind will recover [HNTC, ICC], to prevent any of the members from wandering away [ICC, Mil].
3. It is an exhortation to avoid everything that would impede their own Christian walk [Blm].

QUESTION—What is meant by τροχιὰς ὀρθὰς ποιεῖτε 'make straight paths'?

1. It means to construct straight paths [HNTC, Lns, NIC; KJV, NASB, NIV, NRSV].
2. It means to straighten crooked paths [EBC; NAB, NJB, TNT].
3. It means to walk in a straight path [WBC; REB, TEV].

QUESTION—What is meant by the dative phrase τοῖς ποσίν ὑμῶν 'your feet'?

1. It means to provide straight paths for their feet [Alf, EGT, GNC, HNTC, Lns, Mil, Wst; KJV, NAB, NASB, NIV, NRSV, TNT].
2. It means to move in a straight direction with their feet [My, WBC].

in-order-that not the lame[a] may-be-dislocated,[b] but rather may-be-healed.[c]

LEXICON—a. χωλός (LN 23.175) (BAGD p. 889): 'lame' [BAGD, HNTC, LN, Lns, Mil, NIC, WBC; CEV, KJV, NASB, NIV, NRSV, TEV], 'weak and lame' [NLT], 'injured' [NJB], 'weakened' [REB]. The neuter noun phrase τὸ χωλόν 'the lame' is translated 'your halting limbs' [NAB]. The clause ἵνα μὴ τὸ χωλὸν ἐκτραπῇ 'in order that the lame may not be dislocated' is translated 'then lameness will not cause your limb to be dislocated' [TNT]. This phrase refers to a lame foot [LN, TH; TEV], a lame leg [BAGD], a lame limb [HNTC, Wst; NAB, NASB, NJB, REB], lame joints [NIC], the spiritually lame people [Lns, Mil, My, NIC, WBC, Wst]; it figuratively refers to those in the church who were wavering between Christianity and Judaism [Alf, Mil].

b. aorist pass. subj. of ἐκτρέπω (LN **23.178**, 31.65) (BAGD p. 246): 'to be dislocated' [BAGD, HNTC, NIC, WBC; NAB, TNT], 'to be wrenched' [**LN**], 'to be sprained' [LN (23.178)], 'to be disabled' [NIV, TEV], 'to be maimed' [NJB], 'to be put out of joint' [NASB, NRSV, REB], 'to be further put out of joint' [Mil], 'to get turned off wrong' [Lns], 'to be turned from' [BAGD, LN (31.65)], 'to be turned out of the way' [KJV], 'to be avoided' [BAGD]. This passive verb is also translated as active: 'to stumble and fall' [NLT], 'to get worse' [CEV]. It refers to dislocation [EBC, Mil, NCBC, NIGTC, TH, TNTC, WBC, Wst]; it means to be turned out of the way [EGT, Hu, My].

c. aorist pass. subj. of ἰάομαι (LN 23.136) (BAGD 2. p. 368): 'to be healed' [BAGD, LN, NIC, WBC; CEV, KJV, NAB, NASB, NIV, NRSV, TEV], 'to be cured' [BAGD, HNTC, LN, Lns; TNT], 'to get better' [NJB], 'to regain (its) former powers' [REB], 'to be restored to (its) former strength' [Mil], 'to become strong' [CEV].

QUESTION—Why is this clause mentioned?

It states the purpose of the preceding proposition [Mil].

DISCOURSE UNIT: 12:14–13:25 (NIGTC, WBC; REB). The topic is straight paths [NIGTC], orientation for life as Christians in a hostile world [WBC], the fruit of righteousness [REB].

DISCOURSE UNIT: 12:14–29 [GNT, Mil, NIGTC, WBC; CEV, NAB, NIV, NLT]. The topic is final warnings [NIGTC], warning against refusing God [NIV], warning against turning from God [CEV], warning not to reject God's grace [GNT], warning about the danger of refusing God's gracious word [WBC], a warning of the penalties for disobedience [NAB], an exhortation to partake of God's holiness and a warning against apostasy [Mil], a call to listen to God [NLT].

DISCOURSE UNIT: 12:14–17 (HNTC, Lg, Lns; NJB). The topic is a warning based on Esau's rejection [HNTC, Lns], counteracting tendencies toward apostasy by striving for union and holiness [Lg], the punishment of unfaithfulness [NJB].

12:14 Pursue[a] peace with[b] all (persons) and the holiness[c] without[d] which no-one shall-see the Lord,

LEXICON—a. pres. act. impera. of διώκω (LN 15.158, 68.66) (BAGD 4.b. p. 201): 'to pursue' [BAGD, HNTC, LN (15.158), Lns, Mil, NIC, WBC; NASB, NRSV], 'to strive for' [BAGD; NAB], 'to strive toward' [LN (68.66)], 'to seek' [NJB], 'to seek after' [BAGD], 'to aim at' [REB], 'to aspire to' [BAGD]. 'to follow' [KJV]. The phrase εἰρήνην διώκετε 'pursue peace' is translated 'make every effort to live in peace' [NIV], 'make it your aim to be at peace' [TNT], 'try to be at peace' [TEV], 'try to live at peace' [CEV], 'try to live in peace' [NLT]. It implies earnest pursuit [WBC, Wst]. The present tense implies continued activity [NTC].

b. μετά with genitive object (LN 83.9, 90.42, 90.60) (BAGD A.II.3.b. p. 509): 'with' [BAGD, HNTC, LN, Lns, Mil, NIC; all versions], 'along with' [WBC].

c. ἁγιασμός (LN **53.44**) (BAGD p. 9): 'holiness' [BAGD, HNTC, WBC; KJV, NAB, NJB, NRSV, TNT], 'sanctification' [BAGD, Lns, Mil, NIC; NASB], 'consecration' [BAGD, LN] 'a holy life' [REB], 'a clean life' [CEV], 'a clean and holy life' [NLT]. This noun is also translated as a verb phrase: 'to be holy' [NIV] 'to try to live a holy life' [TEV]. It refers to the process of becoming holy [Alf, Lns, Mil, NTC], a state of holiness [GNC], consecration to God [ICC, NCBC, TH], being set apart for God [EBC, HNTC], being pure in heart [EBC, EGT, HNTC, NIC] and being consecrated by the Holy Spirit [HNTC], drawing near to God with a cleansed conscience [EGT], practical holiness of life [NIC], moral purity [Mil, My]. Here it is limited to abstaining from fornication [Blm]. It is the gift of Christ through his atonement [WBC].

d. χωρίς with genitive object (LN 89.120) (BAGD 2.b.γ. p. 890): 'without' [HNTC, LN, Lns, Mil, WBC; all versions except CEV, NLT], 'without possessing' [BAGD], 'apart from' [LN, NIC], 'apart from the presence of' [BAGD]. This word is also translated as a phrase: 'if you don't' [CEV], 'for those who are not holy . . .' [NLT].

QUESTION—What is implied by the absence of a connecting word at the beginning of this clause?

It implies the beginning of a new section [Mil, NIGTC].

QUESTION—What relationship is indicated by εἰρήνην διώκετε μετὰ πάντων 'pursue peace with all'?

Εἰρήνην 'peace' is emphatic by word order [NIGTC, WBC].

1. It means to strive to be at peace with other people [Alf, EBC, EGT, HNTC, Hu, NIGTC, NTC, TH, TNTC]: seek to be at peace with other people.
2. It means to seek peace as other people are or should be doing [ICC, Mil, WBC]: seek peace along with other people. 'Peace' here is salvation [WBC].

QUESTION—To whom does πάντων 'all' refer?

1. It refers to all the people in the congregation [HNTC, Lns, Mil], fellow believers [Alf, Hwt, ICC, Lg(K), My(D), NCBC, NIGTC, WBC].
2. It refers to all people everywhere [EBC, Hu, My, TH, Wst].

QUESTION—What relationship is indicated by the noun phrase τὸν ἁγιασμόν 'the holiness' with the definite article?

1. It refers to a specific holiness [EGT, HNTC, Hu, Lns, Mil, NIC, WBC; NAB, NASB, NJB, NRSV]: the holiness without which. . . . The definite article indicates that 'holiness' is a familiar term [Wst].
2. The article is not translated [LN; CEV, KJV, NLT, REB, TEV, TNT]: consecration.

2.1 It means 'a holy life' [CEV, NLT, REB, TEV].

2.2 The article is used but not translated because τὸν ἁγιασμόν 'the holiness' is a specific following the general term εἰρήνην 'peace' [Alf].

3. It is translated as a verb [NIV]: to be holy.

QUESTION—To what does οὗ 'which' refer?

1. It refers only to ἁγιασμόν 'holiness' in the preceding clause [EBC, EGT, Hu, Lns, Mil, NCBC, NIC, TNTC, WBC; NAB, NASB, NIV, NJB, NLT, NRSV, TNT], as the masculine gender indicates [Mil]: without the holiness.
2. It refers to both peace and holiness [NTC] (although the relative pronoun is singular and masculine—or neuter): without peace and holiness.

QUESTION—What relationship is indicated by ὄψεται 'shall see'?

It refers to an event yet unfulfilled [TNTC].

1. It refers to innermost union [My].
2. It means to get to see [Lns].

QUESTION—To whom does τὸν κύριον 'the Lord' refer?

1. It refers to God the Father [Alf, Hwt, ICC, WBC].

2. It refers to Christ [Wst].

12:15 seeing-to-it[a] lest (there-should-be) anyone falling-away[b] from[c] the grace of-God,

LEXICON—a. pres. act. participle of ἐπισκοπέω (LN **30.46**, **35.39**) (BAGD 1. p. 299): 'to see to it' [BAGD, LN (**35.39**), NIC; NAB, NASB, NIV, NRSV, TNT], 'to take heed' [REB], 'to look diligently' [KJV], 'to watch' [WBC], 'to look at, to take care' [BAGD], 'to be concerned' [LN (**30.46**)], 'to guard against' [LN (**30.46**); TEV], 'to be careful' [NJB], 'to make sure' [CEV], 'to give careful attention to, to consider carefully' [LN (30.46)], 'to exercise care' [HNTC], 'to exercise oversight' [Lns], 'to exercise insight' [Mil], 'to look after . . . to watch out' [NLT]. This participle carries an imperative force because of its dependence on the imperative διώκετε 'pursue' in the preceding verse, and the present tense implies continuing effort [WBC]. It governs the three following clauses, each introduced by μή τις 'lest any', in this and the next verse [WBC]. This participle plus the following μή 'lest' implies apprehension [WBC]. The reference is to the entire congregation [HNTC, NIGTC, NTC, WBC, Wst], urging care for themselves and for others [Blm, EBC, GNC, Lns, Mil, NTC], assuming that some members are to be watchful lest others lose their faith [NIGTC].

b. pres. act. participle of ὑστερέω (LN 13.21) (BAGD 1.a. p. 849): 'to fall away' [HNTC; NAB, TNT], 'to fall back' [Mil], 'to fall short' [NIC], 'to come short' [NASB], 'to drop away' [Lns], 'to turn back' [TEV], 'to fail' [KJV], 'to fail to attain, to not attain, to be behind in' [LN], 'to be excluded' [BAGD], 'to be deprived' [NJB]. The phrase ὑστερῶν ἀπό 'falling away from' is translated 'to miss' [NIV], 'to fail to obtain' [NRSV], 'to forfeit' [WBC; REB], 'to miss out on' [CEV, NLT]. The present tense implies continuing action [TNTC, Wst]. This verb refers to failing to utilize (to attain [NIC]) the grace given by God [Blm, EBC, NIC], failing to reach the intended blessings [EGT], falling behind in the race and failing to finish [Hu, Lns, Mil], turning one's back on God's grace [My]. It implies apostasy [Hu, WBC]. The phrase ὑστερῶν ἀπό 'falling away from' implies being excluded by one's own fault [WBC], falling back from something specific [Wst].

c. ἀπό with genitive object (LN 89.122): 'from' [HNTC, LN, Lns, Mil; NAB, TEV, TNT], 'separated from' [LN], 'of' [NIC; KJV, NASB, NJB].

QUESTION—Why is this verse mentioned?

It expresses a general thought, which is followed by specific examples [Blm]. It is addressed to all the believers [EGT, My]. It is connected with (it is an amplification of [My]) the preceding verse [Hu, My, WBC], since this verse is introduced by a participle, not a finite verb [Hu, WBC].

QUESTION—What relationship is indicated by the participle ἐπισκοποῦντες 'seeing to it'?

1. It states an action accompanying (dependent on [WBC]) the verb διώκετε 'pursue' in the preceding verse [Mil, WBC]: and all the while seeing to it.
2. It is translated as an independent action [HNTC, NIC; all versions except KJV]: see to it.

QUESTION—What relationship is indicated by the nominative participle ὑστερῶν 'falling away'?

It modifies τις 'anyone'.

1. It is an indefinite attributive participle [REB]: lest there be anyone who is falling away.
2. It is either indefinite attributive or a predicate modifier of τις 'anyone' [Mil]: lest there be anyone falling away.
3. With an understood ᾖ 'should be', it is translated as a finite verb [Blm, EGT, Lg(K), Lns, NIC, WBC; NAB, NASB, NIV, NRSV, TNT]: lest anyone should be falling away.
4. It is translated as if it were in the accusative case as the predicate of ἐπισκοποῦντες 'seeing to it' [TEV]: guard against turning back.

QUESTION—How are the two nouns related in the genitive construction τῆς χάριτος τοῦ θεοῦ 'the grace of God'?

'God' is the source and bestower of the 'grace' [Blm, HNTC, TNTC]: the grace given by God.

lest any root[a] of-bitterness[b] growing[c] up[d] should-cause-trouble[e]

LEXICON—a. ῥίζα (LN 3.47, 89.17) (BAGD 1.b. p. 736): 'root' [BAGD, HNTC, LN (3.47), Lns, Mil, NIC, WBC; KJV, NAB, NASB, NIV, NJB, NRSV], 'root of unbelief' [NLT], 'plant' [TEV], 'weed' [REB], 'source, cause, reason' [LN (89.17)]. The phrase ῥίζα πικρίας 'root of bitterness' is translated 'bitterness' [TNT]. The phrase ῥίζα πικρίας ἄνω φύουσα 'root of bitterness growing up' is translated 'don't let anyone become bitter' [CEV]. This word means metaphorically a 'shoot' [NIGTC].

b. πικρία (LN 79.40, 88.201) (BAGD 1. p. 657): 'bitterness' [BAGD, LN (79.40, 88.201), Lns, Mil; KJV, NASB, NJB, NRSV], 'bitter resentment' [LN (88.201)]. This noun is also translated as an adjective: 'bitter' [BAGD, HNTC, WBC; CEV, NAB, NIV, NLT, TEV], 'bitter, noxious' [REB]; as a clause: 'which produces bitter fruit' [NIC].

c. pres. act. participle of φύω (LN **23.191**) (BAGD p. 870): 'to grow' [BAGD, LN, WBC; NIV, NJB, REB, TEV], 'to spring' [HNTC, Lns, Mil, NIC; KJV, NAB, NASB, NRSV, TNT], 'to rise' [NLT], 'to come' [BAGD].

d. ἄνω (LN **84.25**) (BAGD 2. p. 77): 'up' [BAGD, HNTC, **LN**, Lns, Mil, NIC, WBC; all versions except CEV, NJB], 'upwards' [LN], not explicit [CEV, NJB].

e. pres. act. subj. of ἐνοχλέω (LN **22.24**) (BAGD p. 267): 'to cause trouble' [BAGD, HNTC, LN, Lns, Mil, WBC; CEV, NASB, NIV, NRSV, TNT], 'to make trouble' [NJB], 'to trouble' [NIC; KJV], 'to corrupt by its poison' [NLT], not explicit [NAB].

QUESTION—To what does the phrase ῥίζα πικρίας 'root of bitterness' refer?

1. It refers to a person who introduces evil into the group [EGT, HNTC, Hu, Hwt, Lg(K), Lns, Mil, My, TH, Wst].
2. It refers to any person or thing which results in bitterness [TNTC].
3. It refers to unbelief [NLT].
4. It refers to apostasy or heresy, figuratively described as a poisonous weed in a garden [Blm].

QUESTION—How are the two nouns related in the genitive phrase ῥίζα πικρίας 'root of bitterness'?

1. Πικρίας 'bitterness' expresses a quality [ICC] describing ῥίζα 'root' [BAGD, NIGTC; NAB, NIV, NLT, REB, TEV]: a bitter root.
2. Πικρίας 'bitterness' tells what the root produces [BAGD, EBC, My, NIC, TNTC, Wst]: a root that bears bitter fruit.
3. It is both of the above [WBC].
4. Πικρίας 'bitterness' is the origin and character of the root [Alf]: a root whose source and character is bitterness.
5. Πικρίας 'bitterness' is the 'root' [Lns]: a root, namely, bitterness.
6. This phrase as a whole expresses a quality [CEV, TNT]: bitterness.

QUESTION—What relationship is indicated by the participle θύουσα 'growing'?

1. It modifies ῥίζα 'root' and is an attributive participle [TEV]: a bitter root that grows up.
2. It expresses means [Mil]: by springing (up).
3. It is translated as the finite verb of its clause [HNTC, NIC, WBC; NAB, NJB, NRSV, TNT]: a root that should spring.

QUESTION—What is the subject of ἐνοχλῇ 'should cause trouble'?

1. The subject is the immediately preceding phrase [Blm, EGT, ICC, NIC, WBC; all versions except NAB, REB]: lest any root of bitterness should cause trouble.
2. It is both of the preceding phrases introduced by μή 'lest' [Alf, My]: lest anyone falling away . . . ; i.e., lest any root of bitterness should cause trouble.

QUESTION—What is the implied object of ἐνοχλῇ 'should cause trouble'?

1. This verb is translated as a causative [HNTC, Lns, Mil, My, WBC; NASB, NIV, NJB, NRSV, TEV, TNT]: should cause trouble.
   - 1.1 Without an expressed object [HNTC, Lns, Mil, WBC; NASB, NIV, NJB, NRSV, TEV, TNT]: should cause trouble.
   - 1.2 The implied object is the congregation [My]: should cause trouble to the congregation.
2. This verb is translated as a transitive and the implied object is 'you' [Alf, EGT, NIC; KJV], 'the rest' [REB]: should cause trouble for you/for the rest.

and through[a] it many[b] should-be-defiled;[c]

TEXT—Instead of δι' αὐτῆς 'through it' some manuscripts read διὰ ταύτης 'through this'. GNT does not mention this variant. 'Through this' is read by Blm, ICC.

TEXT—Some manuscripts insert οἱ 'the' before πολλοί 'many'. GNT does not mention this variant. Οἱ πολλοί 'the many' is read by Alf, BAGD, EGT, ICC, Lg, My, Wst.

LEXICON—a. διά with genitive object (LN 89.76, 90.8, 90.44): 'through' [LN (89.76, 90.8), NIC, WBC; NAB, NRSV], 'with' [TEV], 'by' [HNTC; NASB, NLT], 'by means of' [LN (90.8), Lns], 'because of, on account of' [LN (90.44)], not explicit [CEV, NIV, NJB, REB, TNT]. The phrase δι' αὐτῆς 'through it' is translated 'thereby' [KJV], 'by this means' [Mil].

b. πολύς (LN 59.1) (BAGD I.2.a.β. p. 688): In the plural: 'many' [HNTC, LN, Lns, Mil, NIC; KJV, NAB, NASB, NIV, NLT, NRSV], 'large number' [NJB], 'the rest' [CEV, REB], 'the whole community' [WBC]; with the definite article: 'the majority, most' [BAGD]. It refers to the entire congregation [Alf, EGT];

c. aorist pass. subj. of μιαίνω (LN 88.260) (BAGD 2. p. 520): 'to be defiled' [BAGD, HNTC, LN, WBC; KJV, NASB], 'to become defiled' [NAB, NRSV], 'to be morally defiled' [Mil], 'to be contaminated' [Lns], 'to be corrupted' [NLT], not explicit [CEV]. The passive voice is also translated as active: 'to defile' [NIV], 'to contaminate' [REB], 'to spoil' [TNT], 'to cause trouble with its poison' [TEV], 'to poison' [NJB]. The aorist tense suggests finality [NTC]. It refers to becoming unfit for fellowship with God [EGT]; it refers to apostasy [GNC]. The defilement would come from association and imitation [Alf].

QUESTION—What relationship is indicated by καί 'and'?

It introduces the result of the preceding thought [Mil].

QUESTION—To what does δι' αὐτῆς 'through it' refer?

It refers to ῥίζα πικρίας 'root of bitterness' in the preceding clause [Lns; NIV, REB, TEV, TNT]: through the root of bitterness.

12:16 lest (there-should-be) any immoral[a] (person) or worldly[b] (person) as[c] Esau,

LEXICON—a. πόρνος (LN 88.274) (BAGD p. 693): 'immoral' [HNTC; CEV, NASB, NJB, NLT, NRSV, REB, TEV, TNT], 'sexually immoral person' [LN], 'sexually immoral' [NIV], 'one who practices sexual immorality' [BAGD], 'fornicator' [BAGD, Lns, Mil, NIC; KJV, NAB], 'apostate' [WBC]. It means literally 'fornicator' [Alf, Blm, EBC, EGT, HNTC, Hu, Mil, My, NIC, NIGTC, TH, Wst] but with suggestions of spiritual unfaithfulness [NIGTC]; it has the spiritual sense [Lns, WBC], explained by the following βέβηλος 'godless' [Lns], implying apostasy [WBC].

b. βέβηλος (LN 88.115) (BAGD 2. p. 138): 'worldly' [LN; TNT], 'worldly minded' [NJB, REB], 'godless' [LN; NAB, NIV, NLT, NRSV], 'ungodly' [CEV], 'irreligious' [BAGD, NIC], 'unspiritual' [HNTC; TEV], 'secular'

[WBC], 'profane' [Lns, Mil; KJV]. It means not being spiritually minded [EBC], having no appreciation of divine matters [Alf, Blm, Wst] and treating sacred things with contempt [Blm, Hu, TH].

c. ὡς (LN 64.12): 'as' [LN; KJV], 'like' [HNTC, LN, Lns, Mil, NIC, WBC; all versions except KJV].

QUESTION—Why is this clause mentioned?

It is the third warning [NTC, WBC] governed by ἐπισκοποῦντες 'seeing to it' in the preceding verse [EBC, ICC, Lns, NIGTC, WBC]. It reinforces the preceding exhortation [GNC]. It continues the amplification of the exhortation to pursue holiness in 12:14 [My, WBC].

QUESTION—What is the phrase ὡς Ἠσαῦ 'as Esau' connected with?

1. It is connected with both πόρνος 'immoral' and βέβηλος 'worldly' [Blm, HNTC, Hu, ICC, Lns, NCBC, WBC; CEV, NRSV]: any immoral or worldly person like Esau. The emphasis is on βέβηλος 'worldly' [ICC], which is introduced by the connective ἤ 'or' and explains what was meant by πόρνος 'immoral' [Lns]. 'Worldly' is a general term for which πόρνος 'immoral' is a specific [Blm].
2. It is connected with only βέβηλος 'worldly' [EBC, EGT, Hwt, Mil, My, NIC, NTC, Wst; NIV, NJB, REB]: a worldly person as Esau. 'Immoral' is to be taken literally as the sin to be avoided in 13:4, and this is not the way the OT describes Esau [NTC].

QUESTION—What relationship is indicated by the phrase ὡς Ἠσαῦ 'as Esau'?

1. It means 'similar to' [HNTC, NIC, WBC; all versions except KJV]: like Esau.
2. It means 'as an example' [NCBC]: as, for example, Esau.

who in-exchange-for[a] one meal[b] sold[c] his-own birthright.[d]

LEXICON—a. ἀντί with genitive object (LN **57.145**) (BAGD 3. p. 74): 'in exchange for' [BAGD, Mil], 'for' [HNTC, **LN**, Lns, NIC; all versions], 'in place of' [LN], 'rather than' [WBC]. It indicates price [My], an exchange [NIGTC]. It implies 'for the sake of' [WBC].

b. βρῶσις (LN **23.22**) (BAGD 3.a. p. 148): 'meal' [HNTC, LN, Lns, Mil; all versions except KJV], 'helping of food' [NIC], 'dish of food' [WBC], 'food' [BAGD], 'morsel of meat' [KJV].

c. aorist mid. indic. of ἀποδίδωμι (LN 57.186) (BAGD 4.b. p. 90): 'to sell' [HNTC, LN, Mil, NIC; all versions except NLT], 'to trade' [NLT], 'to give up' [BAGD, WBC], 'to give away' [Lns]. It means 'to sell' [Alf].

d. (neuter plural) πρωτοτόκια (LN **10.44**) (BAGD p. 726): 'birthright' [BAGD, HNTC, LN, Mil, NIC; KJV, NAB, NASB, NJB, NRSV, REB, TNT], 'primogeniture' [Lns], 'inheritance rights as the oldest son' [NIV], 'birthright as the oldest son' [NLT], 'inheritance rights as the older son' [WBC], 'rights as the older son' [TEV], 'rights as the firstborn' [**LN**], 'rights of being the firstborn' [LN], 'future blessing' [CEV].

QUESTION—Why is this clause mentioned?

It states one part of the comparison with Esau [Mil]; it explains calling Esau βέβηλος 'worldly' [Wst].

QUESTION—What relationship is indicated by μιᾶς 'one'?

It is emphatic [HNTC, ICC, Mil, NIGTC, TH; all versions except KJV, NAB] by its word order [NIGTC, WBC]: for only *one* meal he sold his birthright.

QUESTION—What relationship is indicated by the reflexive pronoun ἑαυτοῦ 'his own'?

It is emphatic [NIGTC]; it intensifies the perverse unworthiness of the action [Alf, WBC]; it emphasizes the significance of Esau's birthright [Lns].

12:17 for you-know that afterwards[a] also,[b] wanting[c] to-inherit[d] the blessing[e] he-was-rejected,[f]

LEXICON—a. μετέπειτα (LN **67.44**) (BAGD p. 514): 'afterwards' [BAGD, HNTC, LN, Mil; NASB, NJB, REB, TNT], 'afterward' [Lns; KJV, NAB, NIV, NLT, TEV], 'later' [**LN**, NIC; CEV, NRSV], 'later on' [WBC]. It refers to the time after Isaac had given the blessing to Jacob [NIGTC].

b. καί (LN 89.93): 'also' [LN], 'even' [LN, Lns, Mil; NASB], not explicit [HNTC, NIC, WBC; all versions except NASB]. This word implies a second point in the story [ICC, NIGTC]; it puts emphasis on Esau's responsibility in the matter [Alf]; it emphasizes the verb ἀπεδοκιμάσθη 'he was rejected' [My].

c. pres. act. participle of θέλω (LN 25.1): 'to want' [HNTC, LN, Lns, Mil; all versions except KJV, NASB], 'to wish' [LN, NIC, WBC], 'to desire' [LN; NASB]. The phrase θέλων κληρονομῆσαι 'wanting to inherit' is translated 'when he would have inherited' [KJV].

d. aorist act. infin. of κληρονομέω (LN 57.138) (BAGD 2. p. 435): 'to inherit' [HNTC, LN, Lns, Mil, NIC, WBC; KJV, NAB, NASB, NIV, NRSV], 'to obtain' [BAGD; NJB], 'to receive' [TEV], 'to acquire, to come into possession of' [BAGD], 'to claim' [REB, TNT], not explicit [CEV, NLT].

e. εὐλογία (LN 88.70) (BAGD 3.a.α. p. 322, 3.b.α. p. 323): 'blessing' [BAGD, HNTC, LN, Lns, Mil, NIC, WBC; all versions], 'act of blessing' [BAGD], 'benefit' [LN]. It is the specific blessing for the first-born son [My, NIGTC, WBC, Wst], distinct from the birthright [NIGTC, NTC, Wst]; it is the birthright-blessing [NIV, NJB].

f. aorist pass. indic. of ἀποδοκιμάζω (LN 30.117) (BAGD 2. p. 91): 'to be rejected' [BAGD, HNTC, LN, Lns, Mil, NIC, WBC; all versions except CEV, TEV], 'to be turned back' [TEV], 'to be regarded as not worthy' [LN], not explicit [CEV].

QUESTION—What relationship is indicated by γάρ 'for'?

It introduces the reason for the preceding warning [Alf, Mil, WBC] and also for 12:14–15 [WBC], the reason for the preceding conclusion that Esau was a profane person [Mil]; it introduces the comment showing how important Esau's birthright was and how significant was his treatment of it [Lns].

QUESTION—What relationship is indicated by the participle θέλων 'wishing'?

It indicates the specific time referred to by μετέπειτα 'afterwards' [Mil].

1. It is temporal [Alf, GNC, HNTC, Lns, Mil, NIC, WBC; KJV, NASB, NIV, NJB, NRSV, TNT]: when he wished.
2. It indicates concession [EGT; REB]: although he wished.
3. It is translated as an independent thought contrasted with the following clause [NAB, TEV]: he wanted to inherit . . . but he was rejected.

QUESTION—Who is the implied actor of ἀπεδοκιμάσθη 'he was rejected'?

1. His father rejected him [HNTC, My, NIGTC, Wst] as the first-born son [HNTC], at God's leading [My].
2. God rejected him [Hwt, ICC, Lns, NTC, WBC].
3. Both his father and God rejected him [Alf].

QUESTION—What is the implied object of the rejection in ἀπεδοκιμάσθη 'he was rejected'?

Esau's request was rejected [Blm].

1. He was rejected from receiving the blessing [Alf, NTC] of the first-born, which had already been given to Jacob [HNTC, Hwt, Lns, My, NIGTC, WBC, Wst]. It was really God's blessing [WBC].
2. He was rejected from receiving the inheritance [Lns].

for a-place[a] of-repentance[b] he-found[c] not

LEXICON—a. τόπος (LN **71.6**, 80.1) (BAGD 2.c. p. 823): 'place' [LN (80.1), Lns; KJV, NASB], 'way' [NJB, TEV, TNT], 'way open' [REB], 'chance' [BAGD, LN (71.6); NRSV], 'opportunity' [BAGD, HNTC, LN (71.6), Mil, NIC, WBC; NAB], 'possibility' [BAGD, LN (**71.6**)]. The phrase τόπον οὐχ εὗρεν 'a place he found not' is translated 'he could bring about no' [NIV], 'there was nothing he could do' [CEV], 'It was too late for' [NLT]. This word refers to means [Blm], opportunity [TH].

b. μετάνοια (LN 41.52) (BAGD p. 512): 'repentance' [BAGD, LN, Lns, Mil, WBC; KJV, NASB, NLT], 'change of mind' [NIC; NIV, REB]. This noun is also translated as a verb: 'to repent' [NRSV]; as a phrase: 'to alter his choice' [NAB], 'to reverse the decision' [NJB], 'to get the decision changed' [HNTC], 'to undo what he had done' [TNT], 'to change what he had done' [TEV], 'to change things' [CEV]. It is emphatic by word order [WBC].

c. aorist act. indic. of εὑρίσκω (LN **13.17**) (BAGD 3. p. 325): 'to find' [**LN**, Lns, Mil, NIC, WBC; KJV, NASB, NJB, NRSV, REB, TEV, TNT], 'to discover, to attain to' [LN], 'to bring about' [NIV], 'to have' [BAGD, HNTC; NAB], 'to do' [CEV], not explicit [NLT].

QUESTION—What relationship is indicated by γάρ 'for'?

It introduces the reason why 'he was rejected' [Mil].

QUESTION—What is meant by μετανοίας τόπον 'a place of repentance'?

1. It means an opportunity for Esau to repent [Alf, Lg(K), Lns, Mil, NIGTC, WBC; KJV, NASB, NLT, NRSV], to change his mind [Mil, NTC; REB], to change what he had done [Alf, EBC, EGT, GNC, Hu, Hwt, LN (13.17), Mil, Wst; NAB, TEV, TNT], to restore his rights as first-born [Wst], to get the decision changed [HNTC, ICC, Lns, NIC, Wst; NJB].
2. It means an opportunity for Esau to change his father's mind [BAGD (3. p. 325), Blm, Lg, My; CEV], his father's decision [TH].

although with[a] tears having-sought[b] it.

LEXICON—a. μετά with genitive object (LN 89.109) (BAGD A.III.1. p. 509): 'with' [HNTC, LN, Lns, Mil, NIC, WBC; all versions except REB, TEV], 'having' [LN], 'in' [BAGD; TEV], 'to the point of' [REB]. The phrase μετὰ δακρύων 'with tears' is translated as a verb: 'to cry' [CEV], 'to weep bitter tears' [NLT]. This phrase is emphatic by word order [ICC]. It expresses the manner of seeking [Mil].

b. aorist act. participle of ἐκζητέω (LN 27.35) (BAGD 1. p. 240): 'to seek' [HNTC, LN, Lns; NAB, NIV, NRSV, TNT], 'to seek for' [NASB], 'to seek carefully' [KJV], 'to seek diligently' [WBC], 'to seek out, to search for' [BAGD], 'to look for' [TEV], 'to plead for' [NJB], 'to beg for' [Mil, NIC; REB], 'to beg' [CEV], not explicit [NLT]. It is intensive [NIGTC, NTC, WBC], as the prefixed preposition ἐκ- indicates [NTC].

QUESTION—What relationship is indicated by the participle ἐκζητήσας 'having sought'?

It is concessive [EGT, HNTC, Lns, Mil, NIC, WBC; all versions], as the preceding καίπερ 'although' makes clear: although he sought. The implied object is God [NIGTC].

QUESTION—To what does αὐτήν 'it' refer?

1. It refers to εὐλογίαν 'blessing' [Lg(K), Lns, Mil, NIC, NTC, WBC, Wst; NAB, NIV, NRSV]: he sought the blessing.
2. It refers to μετανοίας 'repentance' [Alf, Blm, GNC, Hwt, ICC, Lg, NIGTC, TH]: he sought repentance.
3. It refers to both of the above [Hu]: he sought repentance and the blessing.
4. It refers to both the 'blessing' and a change of the decision concerning the blessing [HNTC].

DISCOURSE UNIT: 12:18–29 (TNTC; NJB). The topic is the two covenants [NJB], the benefits of the new covenant [TNTC].

DISCOURSE UNIT: 12:18–24 (EBC, GNC, Lg, Lns, NCBC, NIC; NASB). The topic is the earthly Mount Sinai and the heavenly Mount Zion [EBC, NIC], the contrast between Sinai and Zion [NASB], the glory of the Christian's status [GNC], the hope that lies before believers [NCBC], our obligation to seek for union and sanctification because of the nature of the New Covenant [Lg], the Holy City and the assembly to which believers have come [Lns].

DISCOURSE UNIT: 12:18–21 (HNTC). The topic is Sinai and the Old Covenant.

12:18 For not you-have-come-to[a] a-(thing)-being touched[b] and burned[c] with-fire, and darkness[d] and gloom[e] and storm,[f]

TEXT—Following or preceding ψηλαφωμένῳ 'a thing being touched' some manuscripts add ὄρει 'mountain'. GNT omits this word with a B decision, indicating near certainty. Ὄρει 'mountain' is added by Blm, Lg, My, CEV, KJV, NAB, NIV, and NLT, although CEV, NAB, NIV, and NLT probably add this word by implication from the context without accepting the textual addition.

LEXICON—a. perf. act. indic. of προσέρχομαι (LN 15.77) (BAGD 1. p. 713): 'to come to' [BAGD, Lns, Mil, NIC, WBC; CEV, NASB, NIV, NJB, NLT, NRSV, REB, TEV], 'to come unto' [KJV], 'to stand before' [TNT], 'to come near to' [LN], 'to draw near to' [HNTC; NAB], 'to approach' [BAGD, LN]. The perfect tense implies coming to and remaining [GNC, Lns], as the Israelites came [Hu; TEV]; it implies lasting results [NIGTC, NTC, WBC, Wst].

b. pres. pass. participle of ψηλαφάω (LN 24.76) (BAGD p. 892): 'to be touched' [BAGD, LN, Lns, Mil, NIC, WBC; CEV, KJV, NASB, NIV, NRSV], 'to be felt' [LN; TNT], 'to be handled' [BAGD, LN]. This participle is also translated as an adjective: 'tangible' [REB], 'physical' [NLT], 'touchable' [NAB]; as a phrase: '(thing) known to the senses' [NJB], as a relative clause: 'what is tangible' [HNTC], 'what you can feel' [TEV]. The present tense implies repeated touching [Alf]. The absence of the definite article emphasizes its tangible nature [Lns].

c. perf. pass. participle of καίω (LN 14.63) (BAGD 1.a. p. 396): 'to be burned' [LN], 'to burn' [BAGD, NIC; KJV, NIV], 'to be lit' [BAGD], 'to be set ablaze' [Lns], 'to be ablaze' [Mil], 'to blaze' [HNTC]. The phrase κεκαυμένῳ πυρί 'burned with fire' is translated 'blazing fire' [WBC; NAB, NASB, NJB, NRSV, REB, TEV, TNT], 'flaming fire' [CEV, NLT]. The perfect tense implies being lighted by something unseen [NIGTC].

d. γνόφος (LN **14.53**) (BAGD p. 163): 'darkness' [BAGD, HNTC, LN, NIC, WBC; NASB, NIV, NLT, NRSV, REB, TEV, TNT], 'enveloping darkness' [Mil], 'blackness' [KJV], 'gloom' [NJB], 'murk' [Lns]. The phrase καὶ γνόφῳ καὶ θυέλλῃ 'and darkness and gloom' is translated 'nor gloomy darkness' [NAB], 'dark cloud or storm' [CEV].

e. ζόφος (LN **14.57**) (BAGD 1. p. 339): 'gloom' [BAGD, HNTC, **LN**, NIC, WBC; NASB, NIV, NLT, NRSV, REB, TEV, TNT], 'murky gloom' [Mil], 'darkness' [BAGD, LN; KJV], 'total darkness' [NJB], 'blackness' [Lns].

f. θύελλα (LN **14.6**) (BAGD p. 365): 'storm' [BAGD, NIC; CEV, NAB, NIV, NJB, TEV, TNT], 'windstorm' [LN], 'strong wind' [**LN**], 'whirlwind' [BAGD, LN, WBC; NASB, NLT, REB], 'tempest' [HNTC,

Lns, Mil; KJV, NRSV], 'squall' [LN]. It is a whirlwind [NTC], a strong windstorm [TH].

QUESTION—Why is this verse mentioned?

1. This and the following verses through 12:24 form a contrast between the Old and the New Covenants [Mil, NIGTC, TNTC], with fear characterizing the Old Covenant and grace the New [Wst].
2. This and the following verses point out that the phenomena connected with Mount Sinai were visible and tangible [NCBC, WBC].
3. This and the following verses through 12:29 point out that the greater the privileges, the greater is the responsibility [Wst].

QUESTION—What relationship is indicated by γάρ 'for'?

It connects this clause (and through 12:24 [Lns, My(D), WBC]) with the preceding unit, introducing the reason for the preceding warning [Alf, Blm, EGT, WBC] in 12:15 [Blm], in 12:14–17 [WBC], in 12:14 [Mil, My]. It brings out the connection with sanctification of Christians in 12:14 and the sanctification required of the Israelites before they could approach Mount Sinai to receive the Law [Hwt]. It relates 12:18–24 with the general condition of the readers as expressed in 12:14–17 [NIGTC].

QUESTION—What is the implied reference of προσεληλύθατε 'you have come to'?

It refers to their approach to God [Alf, NIGTC, TH, WBC]. The οὐ 'not' negating this verb is emphatic by its first position in the clause [NTC, WBC] (but its position is obligatory).

1. It implies arrival [EBC, GNC, Lns, Mil, NIC, WBC, Wst; NJB, NRSV, REB].
2. It implies approaching [HNTC, TH; NAB].

QUESTION—To what does ψηλαφωμένῳ 'a thing being touched' refer;

1. It implies something tangible in general [EBC, HNTC, Hwt, ICC, Lg, Mil, NCBC, NIC, NIGTC, Wst; NJB, NRSV], perceptible to the senses [WBC]. The indirect reference, however, is to Mount Sinai [EBC, Hu, Hwt, ICC, Lns, Mil, NIC, NIGTC, NTC, TH, WBC; TEV].
2. It refers specifically to a mountain [Alf, Blm, Lg, My; KJV, NAB, NASB, NIV], Mount Sinai [Alf, BAGD, Lns, My; REB, TNT], that could not be touched [NAB].

QUESTION—What relationship is indicated by the participle ψηλαφωμένῳ 'a thing being touched'?

1. It implies that it could be touched [Blm, EBC, HNTC, Hwt, ICC, Mil, NCBC, NIC, NIGTC, Wst; KJV, NRSV, TEV, TNT].
2. It implies that it was in fact touched [Alf, Lg, Lns, My].

QUESTION—How are the participle and noun related in the dative construction κεκαυμένῳ πυρί 'burned with fire'?

1. Πυρί 'fire' tells the instrument of the burning [Alf, Blm, EGT, HNTC, Mil, My, NCBC, NIC; KJV, NIV]: burned with fire.
2. Κεκαυμένῳ 'burned' describes πυρί 'fire' [Lg, Lns, Wst; NAB, NASB, NJB, NRSV, REB, TEV, TNT]: burning fire.

QUESTION—How are the two participles ψηλαφωμένῳ 'a thing being touched' and κεκαυμένῳ 'burned' related?

1. They refer to the same thing [Alf, Blm, Mil, My, NCBC, NIGTC, Wst; KJV, NIV, REB, TNT]: a thing being touched and burned.
2. Ψηλαφωμένῳ 'a thing being touched' is the general term and κεκαυμένῳ 'burned' is one of the specific examples mentioned [NJB, NCBC]: a thing being touched; e.g., something burned.
3. They refer to different things [Lns; NAB, NASB]: a thing being touched, and a thing burned.

QUESTION—How is the phrase καὶ γνόφῳ καὶ ζόφῳ καὶ θυέλλῃ 'and darkness and gloom and storm' related to other phrases?

The repeated καὶ 'and' emphasizes the enumeration [EGT, Mil, NIGTC, WBC]; the omission of the articles indicates emphasis on the nature of the items mentioned [EGT, Lns, Mil, NTC].

1. It is a separate and additional item following ψηλαφωμένῳ καὶ κεκαυμένῳ πυρί 'a thing being touched and burned with fire' [Alf, HNTC, Lns, Mil, My, WBC, Wst; KJV, NAB, NASB, NIV, NJB, NRSV]: . . . is being burned with fire, and to darkness and gloom and storm.
2. It is a further description of the preceding phrase [NIGTC; REB, TNT]: fire, with its darkness, gloom, and storm.

12:19 and to-sound[a] of-trumpet and voice[b] of-words,

LEXICON—a. ἦχος (LN **14.75**) (BAGD 1. p. 349): 'sound' [BAGD, LN; CEV, KJV, NRSV], 'blast' [HNTC, Lns, Mil, NIC, WBC; NAB, NASB, NIV, NJB, NLT, REB, TEV]. This noun is also translated as a participle: 'blaring' [TNT].

b. φωνή (LN 14.74, 33.103) (BAGD 1. p. 870): 'voice' [LN (33.103); KJV, NAB, NIV, NRSV], 'sound' [BAGD, HNTC, LN (14.74), Lns, Mil, NIC, WBC; NASB]. The phrase φωνῇ ῥημάτων 'voice of words' is translated 'oracular voice' [REB, TNT], 'the sound of a voice' [TEV], 'the sound of a voice speaking' [NJB], 'heard a voice speak' [CEV], 'a voice with a message' [NLT].

QUESTION—How are the two nouns related in the genitive construction σάλπιγγος ἤχῳ 'sound of trumpet'?

The absence of the definite articles stresses the nature of these two words [NTC].

1. The genitive noun 'trumpet' is the source of the 'sound' [NIV, NJB, REB]: sound which comes from a trumpet.
2. The dative noun ἤχῳ describes 'trumpet' [TNT]: blaring trumpet.

QUESTION—How are the two nouns related in the genitive construction φωνῇ ῥημάτων 'voice of words'?

The absence of the definite articles stresses the nature of these two words [NTC].

1. The genitive noun 'words' tells the content of the 'voice' [GNC, Hu; CEV, NAB, NIV, NJB, NLT]: a voice speaking words.
2. The genitive noun 'words' tells the source of the 'voice' [NRSV]: a voice which has its source in words.
3. The genitive noun 'words' describes 'voice' [REB, TNT]: oracular voice.

which the-(ones) having-heard begged[a] a-word[b] not to-be-added-to[c] them,

LEXICON—a. aorist mid. (deponent = act.) of παραιτέομαι (LN 33.163) (BAGD 2.c. p. 616): 'to beg' [BAGD, Mil, NIC, WBC; all versions except KJV], 'to entreat' [KJV], 'to make entreaty' [Lns], 'to plead for, to ask for' [LN]. The phrase παρῃτήσαντο μὴ προστεθῆναι αὐτοῖς λόγον 'begged a word not to be added to them' is translated 'refused to hear any more' [HNTC].

b. λόγος (LN 33.98) (BAGD 1.b.α. p. 478): 'word' [LN, Lns; NRSV], 'speaking' [BAGD], 'message, statement' [LN]. The phrase μὴ προστεθῆναι αὐτοῖς λόγον 'a word not to be added to them' is translated 'not to hear another word' [TEV], 'that no further word should be spoken to them' [NASB], 'that no further word be spoken to them' [NIV], 'that no more should be said to them' [NJB], 'that not a word more should be spoken to them' [Mil], 'that the word should not be spoken to them any more' [KJV], 'that no further message be given to them' [WBC], 'that they should not have to hear any more' [TNT], 'that nothing further might be said' [NIC], 'to hear no more' [REB], 'that they be not addressed to them' [NAB], 'to stop' [CEV], 'to stop speaking' [NLT].

c. perf. act. infin. of προστίθημι (LN 59.72) (BAGD 1.a. p. 719): 'to be added' [BAGD, LN, Lns]. The phrase προστεθῆναι λόγον 'a word to be added to' is translated 'to speak a further message to' [BAGD].

QUESTION—Why is this relative clause mentioned?

It expresses the result of the preceding phrase, φωνῇ ῥημάτων 'voice of words' [NIC, WBC; NAB, NASB, NIV, NJB, NRSV, TEV]: a voice of words such that as a result those who heard begged. . . .

QUESTION—What is ἧς 'which' connected with?

Its antecedent is φωνῇ 'voice' [Alf, Mil, My, NTC, Wst; KJV, NASB]: a voice, which voice they who heard begged. . . .

QUESTION—What relationship is indicated by the genitive pronoun ἧς 'which'?

It is the genitive predicate of οἱ ἀκούσαντες 'the ones having heard' [Alf, Lns, My, NTC]: they who heard which (i.e., it).

QUESTION—What relationship is indicated by λόγον 'word'?

It is the subject of the infinitive προστεθῆναι 'to be added' [Alf, EGT, ICC, Lg(K), Lns, Mil, My, NIGTC, WBC; KJV, NAB, NASB, NIV, NJB, NRSV]. It refers to the contents of the message [Lns].

1. It refers to additional words [Alf, EGT, Lg(K), Lns, Mil, My, NIGTC, WBC; NASB, NIV, NJB, NRSV, TNT]: that no further word be added.

2. It refers to the words previously spoken [NAB]: that the preceding words not be addressed to them. It is translated 'the word', presumably referring to the preceding ῥημάτων 'words' [KJV].

QUESTION—To what does αὐτοῖς 'to them' refer?

It refers to οἱ ἀκούσαντες 'the ones having heard' [Alf, My]: a word not to be added to the persons who had heard.

12:20 for not they-were-bearing/they-could-bear[a] the-(thing) being commanded,[b]

LEXICON—a. imperf. act. indic. of φέρω (LN 25.176, **31.55**) (BAGD 1.c. p. 855): 'to bear' [HNTC, Lns, Mil, NIC, WBC; NASB, NIV, NJB, REB, TEV, TNT], 'to bear to hear' [NAB], 'to bear patiently, to put up with' [BAGD], 'to endure' [BAGD, LN (25.176); KJV, NRSV], 'to accept' [LN (**31.55**)], 'to obey' [CEV]. The phrase οὐκ ἔφερον 'they were not bearing' is translated 'to stagger back' [NLT].

b. pres. pass. participle of διαστέλλω (LN 33.323) (BAGD p. 188): 'to be commanded' [LN; KJV, NIV], 'to be enjoined' [Lns], 'to be ordered' [LN]. The phrase τὸ διαστελλόμενον 'the thing being commanded' is translated 'command' [BAGD, NIC, WBC; CEV, NAB, NASB, REB], 'God's command' [NLT], 'order' [TNT], 'severe injunction' [Mil], 'order that was given' [HNTC; NJB, NRSV], 'order which said' [TEV]. The prefixed δια- adds emphasis [Mil]. It is passive voice and indicates that which was commanded [Alf, Blm, EBC, ICC, Lg(K), Lns, Mil, My, NIGTC, Wst]; it is middle voice and refers to the voice which commanded [Lg]. The command was given by God [TH; NLT]. The present tense adds to the fearful aspect [EBC], implies a continuing echoing of the command in their ears [HNTC, Wst].

QUESTION—What relationship is indicated by γάρ 'for'?

It introduces the reason for the fear expressed in the preceding clause [Alf, Mil, My, NIGTC]. It also introduces an implied threat of death if the command is violated [NIGTC].

QUESTION—What relationship is indicated by the imperfect indicative οὐκ ἔφερον 'they were not bearing/they could not bear'?

1. It means that they were unable to bear [Alf, EGT, HNTC, Lns, Mil, NIC, NIGTC, TH, WBC, Wst; all versions except NLT].
2. It means that they did not bear [Lg(K), My; NLT].

"If-even[a] (an) animal[b] should-touch the mountain, it-shall-be-stoned";[c]

TEXT—Some manuscripts add ἢ βολίδι κατατοξευθήσεται 'or it shall be shot down with a missile' following λιθοβοληθήσεται 'it shall be stoned'. GNT does not deal with this variant. Only KJV accepts this addition.

LEXICON—a. κἂν (LN 89.73) (BAGD 2. p. 402): 'if even' [HNTC, Mil, WBC; all versions except CEV, KJV, TNT], 'and if so much as' [KJV], 'even if . . . just' [BAGD], 'even if' [LN, NIC], 'even though' [LN]. The phrase κἂν θηρίον θίγῃ 'if even an animal should touch' is translated 'if a beast even touch' [Lns], 'even an animal which touched' [TNT], 'any animal' [CEV].

b. θηρίον (LN 4.3) (BAGD 1.a.α. p. 361): 'animal' [LN, WBC; CEV, NAB, NIV, NLT, NRSV, REB, TEV, TNT], 'wild animal' [BAGD], 'beast' [HNTC, Lns, Mil, NIC; KJV, NASB, NJB].

c. fut. pass. indic. of λιθοβολέω (LN 20.79) (BAGD 2. p. 474): 'to be stoned' [HNTC, Lns, Mil, NIC, WBC; KJV, NASB, NIV, NJB], 'to be stoned to death' [BAGD, LN; NAB, NLT, NRSV, REB, TEV, TNT]. The passive voice is also translated as active: 'to kill' [CEV]. Stoning to death is implied [TH].

QUESTION—What relationship is indicated by κἄν 'if even'?

1. It indicates a conditional clause [EGT, GNC, HNTC, Lns, Mil, NTC, TH; all versions except TNT].
2. It is translated as introducing a relative clause [TNT]: the thing being commanded, that even an animal should be stoned.

QUESTION—What is κἄν 'if even' connected with?

1. It is connected with θηρίον 'animal', emphasizing that nothing whatever, not even an animal, must touch the mountain [Alf, BAGD, Blm, EGT, GNC, HNTC, Hu, Mil, My, NTC, TH, WBC; all versions]: if even an animal touches the mountain.
2. It is translated as referring to θίγῃ 'should touch' [Lns]: if an animal even touches the mountain.

12:21 and, so fearful[a] was the-(thing) being-revealed,[b] Moses said, "I am terrified[c] and trembling."[d]

LEXICON—a. φοβερός (LN 25.255) (BAGD p. 862): 'fearful' [BAGD, LN, NIC; NAB], 'causing fear' [BAGD, LN], 'frightful' [BAGD, Lns], 'frightening' [CEV], 'terrible' [BAGD; KJV, NASB, NJB], 'terrifying' [Mil; NIV, NRSV, TEV, TNT], 'appalling' [HNTC; REB], 'awesome' [WBC]. This word is also translated as a verb: 'to be frightened' [NLT]. It implies profound dread [WBC].

b. pres. pass. participle of φαντάζω (LN **24.26**) (BAGD p. 853): 'to be revealed'. The phrase τὸ φανταζόμενον 'the thing being revealed' is translated 'appearance' [Lns, Mil], 'sight' [BAGD, HNTC, **LN**, NIC; all versions except NAB, NJB], 'whole scene' [NJB], 'spectacle' [BAGD, LN, WBC; NAB]. It refers to the visible form in which God manifested himself to the Israelites [My].

c. ἔκφοβος (LN 25.256) (BAGD p. 247): 'terrified' [BAGD, HNTC, LN, Lns, WBC; NAB, NLT], 'very frightened' [LN], 'full of fear' [NASB], 'filled with fear' [NIC], 'extremely afraid' [Mil], 'afraid' [NJB, TEV]. The phrase ἔκφοβος καὶ ἔντρομος 'fearful and trembling' is translated 'to tremble with fear' [NIV, NRSV, TNT], 'to shudder with fear' [REB], 'to shake with fear' [CEV], 'to exceedingly fear and quake' [KJV].

d. ἔντρομος (LN **25.261**) (BAGD p. 269): 'trembling' [BAGD, HNTC, **LN**, NIC, WBC; NAB, NASB, NJB, NLT, TEV], 'quaking' [Lns], 'extremely fearful' [LN]. This adjective is also translated as a verb: 'to tremble' [Mil; NIV, NRSV, TNT], 'to shake' [CEV], 'to shudder' [REB], 'to quake' [KJV].

QUESTION—Why is this verse mentioned?

It states a further indication of the awesomeness of the occasion [EBC, EGT].

QUESTION—What relationship is indicated by καί 'and'?

It stands for ἀλλὰ καί with the sense of 'nay' [Blm].

QUESTION—What relationship is indicated by Μωϋσῆς εἶπεν 'Moses said'?

It is an implied concession [Blm, EBC, ICC, NIC]: even Moses said.

QUESTION—How is Μωϋσῆς εἶπεν . . . ἔντρομος 'Moses said . . . trembling' related to what precedes?

1. It is connected to the preceding verse (coordinating the people's plea and Moses' fear [Mil]) by the initial καί 'and'; the intervening clause is parenthetical [Alf, Blm, Lg, Lns, Mil, My, NIGTC, Wst] indicating the reason for Moses' statement: the people pled . . . and (so fearful was the appearance) Moses said. . . . This interpretation is supported by the absence of ὅτι 'that' before Μωϋσῆς εἶπεν 'Moses said' [Lg(K)].
2. It expresses the result of the first clause [HNTC, Hu, NIC, WBC; KJV, NAB, NASB, NIV, NJB, NRSV, REB, TEV, TNT]: it was so fearful (that) as a result Moses said. . . .

QUESTION—How are the two adjectives ἔκφοβος 'fearful' and ἔντρομος 'trembling' related?

1. The two adjectives state two concepts [Alf, EGT, HNTC, Lns, Mil, NIC, WBC; KJV, NAB, NASB, NJB, NLT, TEV]: fearful and trembling.
2. The adjective ἔκφοβος 'fearful' states the content/cause of ἔντρομος 'trembling' [CEV, NIV, NRSV, REB, TNT]: trembling with fear.
3. They reinforce each other [LN]; καὶ ἔντρομος 'and trembling' is added for rhetorical effect [ICC, NIGTC, TH].

DISCOURSE UNIT: 12:22–24 (HNTC). The topic is Zion and the new covenant.

12:22 On the contrary, you-have-come-to Mount Zion and (the) city of-(the)-living God,

QUESTION—Why is this verse mentioned?

This and the next two verses state a contrast with the preceding [Alf], with 12:18–21 [NIGTC], with 12:18–19 [My], in specific contrast with 12:18, οὐ προσεληλύθατε 'you have not come to' [WBC]: you have not come to . . . , on the contrary, you have come to Mount Zion.

QUESTION—What is implied by the verb προσεληλύθατε 'you have come to' indicate?

The perfect tense indicates a continuing state resulting from past action [EBC, GNC, Lns, Mil].

1. This verb implies conversion [GNC, Hu, Hwt, NIC] and indicates that they have already entered a permanent place [NTC], their eternal relationship with God [EGT]. It implies communion with God [NIGTC].
2. This verb indicates that they have drawn near to Mount Zion but have not yet fully arrived [HNTC, My, NCBC].

QUESTION—What relationship is indicated by the absence of the definite articles with all of the nouns in this and the next two verses?

1. It indicates emphasis on the characteristics and qualities of these nouns [EBC, NTC].
2. It gives conciseness to the statement [TNTC].

QUESTION—To what does Σιὼν ὄρει 'Mount Zion' refer?

It refers to the heavenly Mount Zion [Blm, My, NIGTC, NTC, TH], the spiritual Zion as the place of God's presence and his people's home [EGT, Lns, My, NTC, Wst], in contrast with Mount Sinai [TH]. It stands for Jerusalem (as the home of God's people [EBC]), and it is also the same as the following πόλει θεοῦ ζῶντος 'city of the living God' [EBC, GNC, HNTC, Hu, My, NIGTC, NTC, TNTC, WBC] (the preceding καί 'and' having the sense of 'even' [NIGTC, WBC]) and also Ἰερουσαλὴμ ἐπουρανίῳ 'heavenly Jerusalem' [EBC, EGT, GNC, HNTC, Hu, Lns, My, NIGTC, NTC, TNTC].

QUESTION—How are the two nouns related in the genitive construction πόλει θεοῦ ζῶντος 'city of the living God'?

1. Θεοῦ 'of God' states who lives in the city [EGT, My, NIC, NTC, Wst]: the city where God dwells.
2. Θεοῦ 'of God' states to whom the city belongs [WBC]: the city which belongs to God.

to-heavenly Jerusalem, and to-myriads[a] of-angels in-festal-gathering/of-angels, a-festal-gathering[b]

LEXICON—a. μυριάς (LN **60.8**) (BAGD 2. p. 529): 'myriad' [BAGD, HNTC, Lns, NIC; NAB, NASB, REB], 'countless' [**LN**], 'innumerable' [LN; NRSV], 'innumerable company' [WBC; KJV], 'innumerable host' [Mil], 'mighty host' [TNT], 'very many' [LN], 'thousands' [NLT, TEV], 'thousands upon thousands' [CEV, NIV], 'millions' [NJB].

b. πανήγυρις (LN **51.4**) (BAGD p. 607): 'festal gathering' [HNTC; NAB, NRSV], 'festal assembly' [Lns, Mil], 'festal array' [NIC], 'festival gathering' [BAGD], 'festivity, celebration' [LN], 'joyous festival' [**LN**], 'joyous assembly' [TNT], 'joyful assembly' [NIV, NLT], 'joyful gathering' [TEV], 'general assembly' [KJV, NASB], 'full concourse' [REB]. This noun is also translated as a verb phrase: 'to come to celebrate' [CEV], 'to gather for the festival' [NJB]. It refers to a joyful gathering [Alf, Blm, EBC, GNC, Lg(K), My, NTC, WBC] in order to celebrate a festival [WBC].

QUESTION—How is the phrase Ἰερουσαλὴμ ἐπουρανίῳ 'heavenly Jerusalem' related to other phrases?

It is in apposition to πόλει 'city', identifying it [Alf, Blm, ICC, Lns, My, TH, WBC]: the city of the living God, that is, the heavenly Jerusalem. Ἐπουρανίῳ 'heavenly' refers to all three of the items preceding this word; it is placed last for rhetorical effect [NIGTC].

QUESTION—What is ἀγγέλων 'of angels' related to?

The fact that καί 'and' is used consistently to introduce the items in this series favors either 1. or 2. below. [ICC, Lg(K), Lns, Mil, NIGTC].

1. It is related to the preceding μυριάσιν 'myriads' and the following πανηγύρει 'festal gathering' [EBC, GNC, HNTC, Hu, ICC, Lns, Mil, NIC, NIGTC, NTC, TNTC, WBC, Wst; NAB, NIV, NJB, NRSV]: to myriads of angels in festal gathering, and the assembly of the firstborn.
2. It is related to the preceding μυριάσιν 'myriads', and the following πανηγύρει 'festal gathering' is in apposition to it [WBC]: myriads of angels; that is, a festal gathering, and to an assembly of the firstborn.
3. With the following πανηγύρει 'festal gathering', it identifies the preceding μυριάσιν 'myriads' [Alf, Blm, Lg]: to myriads; that is, the festal host of angels and the assembly of the firstborn.
4. It is related only to the preceding μυριάσιν 'myriads' [Alf, EGT, My; KJV, NASB, REB, TEV, TNT]: to myriads of angels, to a festal gathering and assembly.

12:23 and to-(the)-assembly[a] of-firstborn-ones registered[b] in[c] heaven

LEXICON—a. ἐκκλησία (LN 11.32, 11.33, 11.78): 'assembly' [HNTC, LN (11.78), NIC, WBC; NAB, NLT, NRSV, REB], 'gathering' [LN (11.78)], 'church' [LN (11.32, 11.33), Lns, Mil; KJV, NASB, NIV, NJB, TNT], 'congregation' [LN (11.32), Mil], not explicit [CEV, TEV]. This word implies being bound together in inner unity [My]. It refers to God's people [NIGTC, Wst], to the redeemed people [WBC], to NT believers [Hu] on earth [Alf], both on earth and in heaven [EBC].

b. perf. pass. participle of ἀπογράφω (LN **33.42**) (BAGD 2. p. 89): 'to be registered' [BAGD, LN], 'to be enrolled' [HNTC, Lns, Mil, NIC; NAB, NASB, NRSV, REB], 'to be enrolled as a citizen' [NJB], 'to be recorded' [BAGD], 'to be inscribed permanently' [WBC], 'to be written' [**LN**; KJV, NIV, TEV, TNT]. This verb is also translated as a relative clause: 'whose names are written' [CEV, NLT]. It refers to the church on earth [Alf, Hwt, ICC], persons assured of heavenly citizenship but not yet in heaven [Alf, Hwt], believers both living and dead [Wst]. The perfect tense emphasizes permanence [Hu, Lns, NIGTC, NTC, WBC].

c. ἐν with dative object (LN 83.13): 'in' [HNTC, LN, Lns, Mil, NIC, WBC; all versions except NJB], 'of' [NJB].

QUESTION—How is this phrase related to what precedes?

1. It is another item in addition to the preceding [Alf, EBC, GNC, Hu, ICC, Lg, Lns, Mil, NIC, NIGTC, NTC, TNTC, WBC, Wst; NAB, NIV, NJB, NRSV]: and also to the assembly.
2. It further describes πανηγύρει 'festal gathering' [Blm, EGT, HNTC, My, TH; KJV, NASB, REB, TEV, TNT]: to a festal gathering and assembly.

QUESTION—How are the two nouns related in the genitive construction ἐκκλησίᾳ πρωτοτόκων 'assembly of firstborn ones'?

The ἐκκλησίᾳ 'assembly' is made up of πρωτοτόκων 'firstborn ones' [Alf].

QUESTION—To whom does πρωτοτόκων 'firstborn ones' refer?

1. It refers to the author's readers [NTC], the church on earth [Mil], all Christians [Alf, GNC, Hu, Lg, Lns, TH, TNTC, Wst] both living and dead [Wst], so designated because of their heavenly inheritance [Alf, GNC, Hu, Lg, Lns, NTC, TH, Wst]. The term implies the dignity of their position [Lg].
2. It includes those who in every age have lived in faith in Christ [Blm, NIC, WBC], both living and dead [NIC], looking forward to their completed company in heaven [WBC]; it is the same as the δικαίων τετελειωμένων 'righteous ones perfected' in the following phrase [Blm].
3. It refers to the OT saints, who are already in heaven [My].
4. It refers to the angels in heaven [EGT, HNTC], who were created before mankind [HNTC].

QUESTION—What relationship is indicated by the participial form ἀπογεγραμμένων 'registered'?

It is attributive to πρωτοτόκων 'firstborn ones' [Alf, HNTC, Mil, NIC; all versions except NAB, NJB]: firstborn ones who are registered. What is registered in heaven is the names of the firstborn [TH; NIV, TEV, TNT], indicating being counted among those who are justified by God [Lns].

and to-judge God of-all/to-God judge of-all and to-spirits[a] of-righteous-ones[b] perfected[c]

LEXICON—a. πνεῦμα (LN 26.9) (BAGD 2. p. 675): 'spirit' [HNTC, LN, Lns, Mil, NIC, WBC; all versions], 'life-spirit' [BAGD], 'soul' [BAGD]. It refers here to the spirit apart from the body [Alf, Blm, EGT, Hu, Lns, My, Wst] awaiting the final resurrection [Alf, EGT, GNC, Hu], awaiting the resurrection body [EGT, Hu, My]. It refers to the spiritual part of the person [GNC]. It emphasizes the spiritual nature of the person's new state [EBC, HNTC].

b. δίκαιος (LN 88.12) (BAGD 1.b. p. 195): 'righteous one' [Lns], 'righteous' [LN, NIC; NRSV], 'righteous man' [HNTC, Mil; NASB, NIV], 'righteous person' [WBC], 'just' [BAGD, LN], 'just man' [KJV, NAB], 'upright' [NJB], 'good man' [REB, TNT], 'good person' [CEV, TEV], 'the redeemed' [NLT]. It means having lived a faithful life [HNTC]. They are 'righteous' because of Christ's sacrifice [TNTC], because they lived in the faith that God approves, including people under both covenants [WBC].

c. perf. pass. participle of τελειόω (LN 88.38) (BAGD 2.d. p. 810): 'to be perfected' [LN], 'to be made perfect' [HNTC, LN, Mil, WBC; all versions], 'to be brought to completion' [Lns], 'to be brought to one's goal, to be brought to an end' [BAGD]. This passive participle is also translated as an active voice: 'to attain perfection' [NIC]. It means that the persons referred to have died [BAGD, Hu, Lns, WBC], have been admitted to the final goal, the state of glory [Blm, GNC, Hwt, Lns, My, NIC, WBC], have the enjoyment of the Lord's presence although they have not yet experienced the resurrection [Hu, Lg], have been perfected by Christ's atonement [ICC, NCBC, NTC, WBC, Wst], have all of God's plan for them completed [TNTC, Wst]. The perfect tense implies permanence [Lns, NTC, WBC].

QUESTION—How are the two nouns κριτῇ 'judge' and θεῷ 'God' related?

Κριτῇ 'judge' is emphatic by forefronting [WBC].

1. Θεῷ 'God' is in apposition to κριτῇ 'judge' [EBC, EGT, HNTC, Hu, Hwt, ICC, Lg, Lns, Mil, My, NTC, TNTC, WBC, Wst]: to a judge who is God of all. The author is here concerned with the concept of a judge [HNTC]; θεῷ πάντων 'God of all' implies God's rights over humankind [WBC].
2. Κριτῇ 'judge' is in apposition to θεῷ 'God' [Alf, Blm, GNC; all versions]: to God who is judge of all.

QUESTION—How is the genitive πάντων 'all' related to κριτῇ 'judge' or θεῷ 'God'?

1. If 1. in the preceding question is accepted, πάντων 'all' tells who is judged: God who judges all.
2. If 2. in the preceding question is accepted, πάντων 'all' tells who is ruled by God: the judge who is God over all.

QUESTION—To what does πάντων 'all' refer?

It is masculine [Alf, ICC, Lg, Lns, Mil, My, NTC, WBC; NIV, TEV, TNT]: all persons.

1. It refers to the Christian community [Lg].
2. It refers to all people [ICC, Lns, Mil, My, NTC].

QUESTION—To whom does πνεύμασι δικαίων τετελειωμένων 'spirits of righteous ones perfected' refer?

1. It refers to both OT and NT saints [EGT, Hu, Hwt, Lg, NCBC, NTC, TH, WBC].
2. It refers to Christians who have died [My].
3. It refers to OT saints [GNC, NIC].

QUESTION—How are the nouns related in the genitive construction πνεύμασι δικαίων 'spirits of righteous ones'?

It may be partitive, 'spirits' which are the inner natures of the 'righteous persons'.

QUESTION—What relationship is indicated by the participial form τετελειωμένων 'perfected'?

It is attributive to δικαίων 'righteous ones' [Alf, HNTC, Lns, NIC; NJB, TNT]: righteous ones who have been perfected.

12:24 and to-(the)-mediator[a] of-(a)-new covenant,[b] Jesus,

LEXICON—a. μεσίτης (LN 31.22) (BAGD p. 507): 'mediator' [BAGD, HNTC, LN, Lns, Mil, NIC, WBC; KJV, NAB, NASB, NIV, NJB, NRSV, REB], 'go-between' [LN], 'one who mediates' [NLT]. The phrase διαθήκης νέας μεσίτῃ 'mediator of a new covenant' is translated 'who arranged the new covenant' [TEV], 'through whom the new covenant has been made' [TNT], 'who makes God's new agreement with us' [CEV].

b. διαθήκη (LN 34.43, 34.44) (BAGD 2. p. 183): 'covenant' [BAGD, HNTC, LN (34.44), Mil, NIC, WBC; all versions except CEV], 'testament' [Lns], 'agreement' [CEV], 'decree' [BAGD].

QUESTION—What relationship is indicated by this verse?

It is the climax of 12:18–24 and the rhetorical climax of the entire epistle [NIGTC].

QUESTION—What is indicated by the absence of the definite article with the nouns in this verse?

It indicates a qualitative emphasis [Lns].

QUESTION—What is implied by νέας 'new'?

1. It means fresh [Alf], recent [EBC, Lg, NTC, TNTC, Wst], new in time [EGT, Hwt, Lns, My] and different in quality [Hwt, Lns], in vigor [Lg].
2. It means the same as καινῆς 'new' which is used elsewhere [GNC, Hu, NIGTC, WBC].

QUESTION—How are the two nouns related in the genitive construction διαθήκης νέας μεσίτῃ 'mediator of a new covenant'?

The genitive noun διαθήκης 'covenant' tells what is mediated [TEV, TNT]: he mediates a new covenant.

QUESTION—What is implied by the use of the personal name 'Jesus'?

It emphasizes the person of Jesus [Alf, Lg], his humanity [HNTC, WBC], his full work of redemption [NTC]. It is used in anticipation of the following reference to his blood [EGT]. It is emphatic by its word order [ICC, NIGTC, WBC].

and to-blood of-sprinkling[a] speaking[b] (a)-better-thing/better[c] than[d] Abel.

TEXT—Instead of παρὰ τὸν Ἅβελ 'than Abel', with the masculine article modifying 'Abel', some manuscripts read παρὰ τὸ Ἅβελ 'than the (blood of) Abel', the neuter article modifying the understood noun αἷμα 'blood'. GNT does not deal with this variant. The masculine article τόν 'the' is clearly read by Alf, Blm, EGT, ICC, Lg(K), Lns, Mil, My, NIC, NIGTC, TH, TNTC, Wst; the neuter article τό 'the' is clearly read by WBC.

LEXICON—a. ῥαντισμός (LN 47.16) (BAGD p. 734): 'sprinkling' [BAGD, LN, Lns; KJV], 'purifying' [NJB]. This genitive noun is translated as an adjective: ‘sprinkled’ [HNTC, Mil, NIC, WBC; CEV, NAB, NASB, NIV, NLT, NRSV, REB, TEV], ‘shed’ [TNT].

b. pres. act. participle of λαλέω (LN 33.70) (BAGD 1. p. 463): ‘to speak’ [LN, Lns, Mil, WBC; KJV, NAB, NASB, NIV, NRSV], ‘to say’ [LN, NIC; CEV, REB, TNT], ‘to tell’ [HNTC, LN], ‘to plead’ [NJB], ‘to promise’ [TEV]. The present tense implies continuing significance [NIGTC], continued speaking [WBC].

c. κρείττων (LN 65.21, 87.28) (BAGD 3. p. 450): ‘better’ [BAGD, LN (65.21, 87.28); NASB], ‘something better’ [Lns, Mil, NIC], ‘better word’ [NIV, NRSV], ‘greater, superior to’ [LN (87.28)], ‘superior’ [LN (65.21)]; this singular adjective is translated as a plural: ‘better things’ [HNTC; KJV, REB], ‘far better things’ [TNT], ‘much better things’ [CEV, TEV], not explicit [NLT]. This adjective is also translated as an adverb: ‘more eloquently’ [NAB], ‘more effectively’ [WBC], ‘more insistently’ [NJB].

d. παρά with accusative object (LN 78.29) (BAGD III.3. p. 611): ‘than’ [HNTC, LN, Lns, Mil, NIC, WBC; all versions], ‘more than, in comparison to’ [BAGD], ‘beyond’ [BAGD, LN]. It introduces a comparison [Mil, NIC].

QUESTION—What relationship is indicated by καί ‘and’?

1. It introduces a further item [Alf, HNTC, Lns, Mil; all versions except REB, TNT]: and to blood of sprinkling.
2. It is translated as a relative pronoun modifying Ἰησοῦ ‘Jesus’ [REB, TNT]: Jesus, whose sprinkled blood speaks.

QUESTION—How are the two nouns related in the genitive construction αἵματι ῥαντισμοῦ ‘blood of sprinkling’?

The phrase refers to Jesus’ atoning blood [GNC, HNTC, Hwt, Lns, My, TNTC] by which we were redeemed [Alf], by which the new covenant was established [EGT, NIC].

1. The genitive noun ῥαντισμοῦ ‘of sprinkling’ tells what is done with the blood [Alf, HNTC, Hwt, Mil, TNTC, WBC; NAB, NASB, NIV, NRSV, REB, TEV]: the sprinkled blood. It is sprinkled on the conscience of persons who come to God through Jesus [Alf, Hwt].
2. The genitive noun ῥαντισμοῦ ‘of sprinkling’ tells what happened to the blood [TNT]: the shed blood.
3. The genitive noun ῥαντισμοῦ ‘of sprinkling’ tells what the blood accomplishes [Lns, My, NIC, TH; NJB]: the purifying blood. It cleanses spiritually [My, NIC].

QUESTION—What relationship is indicated by the participle λαλοῦντι ‘speaking’?

1. It is attributive to the dative noun αἵματι ‘blood’ [HNTC, Mil, NIC, NTC; all versions except REB, TNT]: blood which speaks. . . . Λαλοῦντι ‘speaking’ is used for rhetorical effect [WBC].
2. It may be in predicate relationship to αἵματι ‘blood’, telling what the ‘blood’ is doing: to the blood, speaking better things.

QUESTION—What is implied by κρεῖττον 'better'?

It is 'better' than Abel's blood; Abel's blood called for vengeance (in Gen. 4:10 [EBC]), while Christ's blood speaks of atonement and pardon [Blm, EBC, GNC, HNTC, Hu, Hwt, ICC, Mil, My, NCBC, NIC, NIGTC, NTC, WBC, Wst; NLT], in the new covenant [HNTC].

QUESTION—What does κρεῖττον 'better' modify?

1. It is the predicate of λαλοῦντι 'speaking' [Blm, EBC, GNC, HNTC, Hwt, Lns, Mil, NIC, NTC; KJV, NIV, NRSV, REB, TEV, TNT]: speaking a better thing than Abel.
2. It is adverbial, modifying λαλοῦντι 'speaking' [ICC, Lg(K), My, WBC, Wst; NAB, NASB, NJB]: speaking more effectively than Abel.

QUESTION—What relationship is indicated by the phrase παρὰ τὸν Ἅβελ 'than Abel'?

1. It means 'than the blood of Abel' [Blm, EBC, EGT, GNC, HNTC, Hu, ICC, Lns, Mil, NIC, NTC, TNTC, WBC; all versions]. (Whether 1.1 or 1.2 below is read cannot be determined for several versions and commentaries.)

1.1 It means 'than Abel's blood spoke' [EBC, GNC, HNTC, ICC, Lns, Mil, WBC; NAB, NASB, TEV]. Christ's blood speaks of redemption, which Abel's blood could not achieve [WBC].

1.2 It could mean '(better) than Abel's blood was'.

2. It means 'than Abel' [Lg(K), My, NIGTC, Wst]: (speaking better) than Abel (spoke).

DISCOURSE UNIT: 12:25–29 (EBC, GNC, HNTC, Lg, Lns, NCBC, NIC; NASB). The topic is an unshakeable kingdom [EBC], the unshaken kingdom [NASB], a final warning [NCBC], a warning against rejection [GNC], the fear of the Lord [HNTC], the guilt of apostasy compared with the blessings of the New Covenant [Lg], an exhortation to be grateful [Lns], an exhortation to heed God's voice [NIC].

12:25 Take-care[a] not to-refuse[b] the-(one) speaking;

LEXICON—a. pres. act. impera. of βλέπω (LN 27.58) (BAGD 6. p. 143): 'to take care' [BAGD; TNT], 'to be careful' [WBC; TEV], 'to beware of' [LN], 'to see to it' [BAGD, Mil, NIC; NASB, NIV, NLT], 'to see' [HNTC, Lns; KJV, NRSV, REB], 'to make sure' [CEV, NJB], 'to watch out for' [LN], 'to pay attention to' [LN], not explicit [NAB]

b. aorist mid. (deponent = act.) infin. of παραιτέομαι (LN **36.27**) (BAGD 2.a. p. 616): 'to refuse' [BAGD, Lns, Mil; KJV, NASB, NIV, NRSV], 'to refuse to listen' [NJB], 'to refuse to listen to' [**LN**], 'to refuse to hear' [HNTC, NIC; NAB, REB, TEV, TNT], 'to refuse to obey' [LN], 'to reject' [BAGD], 'to spurn' [Mil], 'to disregard' [WBC]. The phrase μὴ παραιτήσησθε 'not to refuse' is translated 'to obey' [CEV, NLT]. This subjunctive verb expresses the content of the warning verb βλέπετε 'take heed' [WBC]. It implies willful refusal to listen [WBC].

QUESTION—What relationship is indicated by this clause?

This admonition is a litotes, implying a strong affirmation [Lns, Mil]: be sure to accept what God is saying. The absence of an introductory word to connect it to the preceding thought makes it more forceful [Alf, ICC, My, Wst]. It is connected with the preceding clause by the repeated verb λαλέω 'to speak' [GNC, Hu, Mil, NCBC, WBC], but the absence of a connecting word indicates that this clause is a new admonition [Mil].

QUESTION—Who is the implied speaker of τὸν λαλοῦντα 'the one speaking'?

The speaker here is the speaker in the two following clauses [NIGTC, TH]. The present tense implies continued speaking [NTC, WBC].

1. The implied speaker is God [EGT, Hwt, ICC, Lg, Lns, My, NTC, TNTC], speaking through Christ's blood [Lns].
2. The implied speaker is God speaking in Jesus [Alf, Lg(K), Wst]. The reference is to the 'blood of sprinkling' which 'speaks' in the preceding verse [Alf].
3. The implied speaker is Jesus [Blm, HNTC; TNT] speaking from heaven [HNTC].

for if those-people (did) not escape,[a] having-refused[b] the-(one)-warning[c] on[d] earth,

LEXICON—a. aorist act. indic. of ἐκφεύγω (LN 21.14) (BAGD 2.a. p. 247): 'to escape' [BAGD, HNTC, LN, Lns, WBC; CEV, KJV, NASB, NIV, NLT, NRSV, TEV, TNT], 'to escape judgment' [Mil], 'to escape punishment' [NAB, NJB], 'to find an escape' [REB]. The phrase ἐκεῖνοι οὐκ ἐξέφυγον 'those people did not escape' is translated 'there was no escape' [NIC]. This is a litotes implying that they surely received judgment [Mil]. The reference is to escaping justice [Blm], punishment by God [Alf, Hu, My, NTC], judgment [NIC], judgment on their apostasy [Mil], the consequences of their lack of faith [Wst]. It intentionally has no expressed object [ICC].

b. aorist mid. (deponent = act.) participle of παραιτέομαι: 'to refuse'. See this word in b. above.

c. pres. act. participle of χρηματίζω (LN **28.39**) (BAGD 1.a. p. 885): 'to warn' [Mil, WBC; NASB, NIV, NRSV], 'to make a divine message known' [**LN**], 'to give the divine message' [TEV], 'to make known God's message, to reveal a message from God' [LN], 'to impart a revelation or injunction or warning' [BAGD], 'to address' [NIC], 'to speak' [CEV, KJV]. The phrase τὸν χρηματίζοντα 'the one warning' is translated 'as God spoke to them' [NAB], 'God when he spoke through Moses' [TNT], 'the voice of their divine instructor' [HNTC], 'him making divine communication' [Lns], 'a warning' [NJB], 'the oracle speaking' [REB], 'Moses the earthly messenger' [NLT]. This word refers to an utterance from God [Alf, Hu, Lns, Mil], to conveying God's will to people [Blm], here containing a warning [Mil]; it is never used with a human being as the speaker [WBC].

d. ἐπί with genitive object (LN 83.46): 'on' [HNTC, LN, Lns, Mil, NIC, WBC; all versions except CEV, NLT], 'upon' [LN], 'at' [CEV], not explicit [NLT].

QUESTION—What relationship is indicated by the clause introduced by γάρ 'for'?

It indicates the grounds for the following exhortation [Mil].

QUESTION—What relationship is indicated by the clause introduced by εἰ 'if'?

1. It indicates a condition of fact which was true [ICC, Lns, Mil, NIGTC, NTC, TH]: if, as was the case, those people did not escape.
2. It indicates grounds [WBC]: since those people did not escape, how much more we will not escape.

QUESTION—To whom does ἐκεῖνοι 'those people' refer?

It refers to the Israelites [Hu, Lns, NIC, NTC, TNTC, Wst; NAB], to all people of the OT dispensation [NIGTC]. This word is emphatic [GNC].

QUESTION—What relationship is indicated by the participle παραιτησάμενοι 'having refused'?

1. It is temporal [HNTC, Lg(K), Lns, Mil, WBC, Wst; CEV, NAB, NASB, NIV, NRSV]; it also expresses reason [Mil]: when/because they refused. The aorist tense indicates action prior to the punishment [Mil, WBC].
2. It is conditional [NIGTC]: if they refused.
3. It is translated as attributive [NIC; KJV, NJB, REB, TEV, TNT]: who refused. (But this interpretation would require the definite article with this participle [Alf].)

QUESTION—Who is the implied speaker of τὸν χρηματίζοντα 'the one warning'?

The speaker here is the same as the one who speaks 'from heaven' [WBC].

1. The implied speaker is God [Alf, EBC, Hu, Hwt, Lg, Lns, Mil, My, NIC, NIGTC, WBC].
2. The implied speaker is God speaking through Moses [GNC, My(D)].
3. The implied speaker is Moses [Blm, HNTC, ICC, NCBC; NLT]. The participle here indicates 'the man who had divine authority to issue orders' [ICC].

QUESTION—What relationship is indicated by the participial phrase τὸν χρηματίζοντα 'the one warning'?

1. It is attributive [Lns, Mil, WBC; KJV, NIV, NRSV, TEV]: the one having warned.
2. It is translated as temporal [NIC; NAB, TNT]: when God warned them. (But this would require the absence of the definite article.)

QUESTION—What is the phrase ἐπὶ γῆς 'upon earth' connected with?

It refers to Mount Sinai [Alf, EBC, EGT, GNC, Lns], to the sphere of the old covenant [WBC]. This phrase is emphatic by forefronting [My, NIC, NIGTC, WBC] to contrast with the following ἀπ' οὐρανῶν 'from heaven' [NIC, WBC].

1. It is connected with τὸν χρηματίζοντα 'the one warning' [HNTC, Hu, Lns, Mil, My, NCBC, NIC, NIGTC, TNTC, WBC; all versions except NJB]: the one warning on earth.
2. It is connected with ἐκεῖνοι 'those people' [Wst; NJB]: people who on earth refused . . .
3. It is connected with ὄντα 'being' understood [Blm]: Moses, who warned, who was from earth.

much more[a] we the-(ones)-turning-away[b] from the-one from[c] heaven,

TEXT—One ancient manuscript omits the article οἱ 'the-(ones)' governing the participle ἀποστρεφόμενοι 'turning away'. GNT does not deal with this variant. Only WBC specifically omits this article, although other commentaries and versions ignore it in their translation.

LEXICON—a. μᾶλλον (LN 78.28) (BAGD 2.b. p. 489): 'more' [LN, Mil; KJV], 'more surely' [BAGD], 'even more, to a greater degree' [LN], not explicit [Lns]. The phrase πολὺ μᾶλλον ἡμεῖς 'much more we' is translated 'how much less will we' [WBC; NIV], 'how much less shall we escape' [HNTC; TEV], 'much less shall we escape' [NASB], 'how much less will we escape' [NRSV], 'how shall we possibly escape' [NJB], 'still less shall we escape' [REB], 'still less will there be any escape for us' [NIC], 'how much greater punishment will be ours' [NAB], 'what chance have we of escaping' [TNT], 'how terrible our danger' [NLT], 'do you think you can possibly escape?' [CEV]. Ἡμεῖς 'we' is emphatic [GNC, Lns, Mil].

b. pres. mid. participle of ἀποστρέφω (LN **34.26**) (BAGD 3.a. p. 100): 'to turn away' [LN, Lns, Mil; KJV, NAB, NASB, NIV, NJB, TEV], 'to turn one's back on' [HNTC; TNT], 'to refuse to hear' [NIC], 'to refuse to obey' [CEV], 'to reject' [BAGD, WBC; NLT, NRSV, REB]. It is stronger than the preceding παραιτησάμενοι 'having refused' [Blm]. It is almost synonymous with 'to apostatize' [GNC]. The present participle implies a real danger [WBC].

c. ἀπό with genitive object (LN 89.122): 'from' [HNTC, LN, Lns, Mil, NIC, WBC; all versions]. The prepositional phrase ἀπ' οὐρανῶν 'from heaven' refers to the sphere of the new covenant [WBC] and indicates the location of the speaker only, not the readers [Wst].

QUESTION—What verb is to be understood in this phrase?

The verb 'to escape' is to be understood [Alf, Blm, GNC, HNTC, Hu, Lns, Mil, My, NIC, NIGTC, Wst; all versions except NAB, NIV], in the future tense here [NIGTC]: much more shall we not escape.

QUESTION—What relationship is indicated by the participial phrase οἱ ἀποστρεφόμενοι 'the ones turning away'?

It is emphatic by word order [NIGTC].

1. It is attributive to ἡμεῖς 'we' [Alf, Mil, Wst; NASB]: we who turn away. It implies an action going on but not completed [Wst].

2. The following versions ignore the definite article which make this participle attributive, except for WBC, which accepts the textual omission of the definite article.

2.1 It is translated as a conditional participle [HNTC, Hu, NIC, NIGTC, NTC, WBC; all versions except NASB]: if we turn away from.

2.2 It is translated as temporal [Lns]: when turning away.

QUESTION—What participle is to be understood in the phrase τὸν ἀπ' οὐρανῶν 'the one from heaven'?

The participle χρηματίζοντα 'warning' is to be understood [Alf, HNTC, Lns, Mil, My, NIC, NIGTC, NTC, WBC; all versions] (from the preceding phrase): the one warning from heaven. 'Heaven' here is the dwelling place of God [Alf, GNC].

QUESTION—Who is the implied speaker of the understood τὸν χρηματίζοντα 'the one warning'?

1. The implied speaker is God [EBC, Hu, ICC, Lg, Lns, My, NCBC, NIC, NIGTC, WBC], speaking through the exalted Christ from the heavenly kingdom [Alf, GNC, Lg(K), Mil, My(D)]. The fact that it is God who speaks both 'on earth' and 'from heaven' indicates that the emphasis is upon the two modes of revealing God, not on different persons [EBC, Hu, Lg, My, Wst].

2. The implied speaker is Jesus [Blm, HNTC, NTC]

2.1 The meaning is 'warning through Christ' [HNTC].

2.2 However, ὄντα 'being' should be understood [Blm]: Christ, who is from heaven, warning.

12:26 of-whom the voice then[a] shook the earth,

LEXICON—a. τότε (LN 67.47) (BAGD 1.a. p. 823): 'then' [BAGD, HNTC, LN; KJV, NAB, NASB, TNT], 'then indeed' [REB], 'at that time' [Lns, Mil, NIC, WBC; NIV, NRSV, TEV], 'that time' [NJB]. This is also translated specifically: 'when God spoke the first time' [CEV], 'when God spoke from Mount Sinai' [NLT].

QUESTION—To what does this clause refer?

This verse and the two following verses demonstrate the superiority of the new covenant [Hwt]. This clause refers to the literal shaking of the earth at Mount Sinai [Alf, EBC, GNC, HNTC, Hu, ICC, Lns, My, NCBC, NIC, NTC, TNTC, WBC]. The verb used here, ἐσάλευσεν 'shook', is used of violent shaking of the earth [Wst].

QUESTION—To whom does οὗ 'of whom' refer?

1. It refers to God [Alf, GNC, HNTC, Hu, Mil, My, NIGTC, TH; CEV, NLT, TNT], the same as the person referred to by τὸν χρηματίζοντα 'the one warning' [Mil, NIGTC] and τὸν λαλοῦντα 'the one speaking' in the preceding verse [Mil, NIGTC, Wst]: God's voice shook the earth.

2. It is Christ, the one who also spoke from Sinai [Blm].

but now he-has-promised,

QUESTION—To what does νῦν 'now' refer?

It has a temporal [Lg(K), NIGTC, WBC] and a logical sense [Lg(K)]: now/as the case now stands. It implies an expectation of occurrence in the near future [GNC], the time of the fulfillment of God's promise [Lg], the Christian era [Wst]. It indicates a contrast with the preceding τότε 'then' [Mil, NCBC, NIGTC, NTC, TH, WBC, Wst].

QUESTION—Who is the implied actor of ἐπήγγελται 'he has promised'?

God is the actor [Alf, EGT, Lg, My, NIGTC, WBC; TNT], the same as the antecedent of the preceding οὗ 'of whom' [Lg]: God has promised. This passive voice has middle meaning [Alf, EGT, ICC, Lg]; it is the middle voice [My, NTC]; it is the middle voice with active meaning [NIGTC, WBC]. The perfect tense implies continuing validity [GNC, Lns, NIGTC, NTC, TH, WBC].

saying, "Yet once[a] I will-shake[b] not only the earth but also the heaven."

LEXICON—a. ἅπαξ (LN 60.67, 60.68) (BAGD 1. p. 80): 'once' [BAGD, LN (60.67)], 'once more' [HNTC, Mil, NIC; all versions except CEV, NLT, REB], 'once again' [Lns, WBC; CEV, NLT, REB], 'one time, once and for all, once and never again' [LN (60.68)]. The implication is 'once more' [Alf, EGT] and implies the finality of the manifested occurrence [EGT, TNTC], once more only [Lg(K)].

b. fut. act. indic. of σείω (LN **16.7**) (BAGD 1. p. 746): 'to shake' [BAGD, HNTC, LN, NIC, WBC; all versions], 'to rock' [Lns], 'to cause to quake' [Mil]. This verb is stronger than σαλεύω 'to shake', which is used in the first clause of this verse [Mil]; these two verbs are essentially synonymous [ICC, NIGTC].

QUESTION—To what does this clause refer?

It contrasts the two shakings [NIGTC]. It refers to the great final subjection of all the earth under God's rule [Alf], God's decisive intervention at the last of the age [EBC], the overthrow of the earthly nations [WBC], the final judgment at the last times [GNC, Hu, WBC] and the completion of salvation [Hu, WBC], the return of Jesus [ICC, My]. It refers to the great and total change which the Gospel would accomplish [Blm]. It refers to heaven and earth passing away at the last times [HNTC, Hwt]; 'heaven and earth' implies the whole created order [Hu, TH]. It implies that a heavenly order would take over from the ruins of the old order [Hwt].

QUESTION—What relationship is indicated by the participle λέγων 'saying'?

The speaker is God [NIGTC, NTC].

1. It may repeat the sense of ἐπήγγελται 'he has promised' as an apposition: he has promised; i.e., he has said.
2. It may specify the means of making the promise: he has promised by saying.

QUESTION—What relationship is indicated by οὐ μόνον . . . ἀλλὰ καί . . . 'not only . . . but also . . . '?

It strengthens the contrast [Alf, Blm, GNC, Lns, NIGTC, TH, WBC], putting emphasis on the shaking of 'heaven' also by its word order [GNC, NIGTC, WBC].

QUESTION—To what does the shaking of the earth in this clause refer?

1. It refers to the ruin of earthly powers [Alf, WBC].
2. The earth shook at Christ's death and at his resurrection, but also the preaching of the gospel shook the world; and earth and heaven will shake at Christ's return [NTC].

QUESTION—To what does the shaking of heaven refer?

The inclusion of 'heaven' adds to the sense of finality [TNTC].

1. It refers to shaking the material sky above the earth [Alf, Lns].
2. Heaven will shake at Christ's return [NTC].

12:27 Now the "Yet once" indicates[a] the removing[b] of-the (things)-being shaken as[c] (things)-created,[d]

LEXICON—a. pres. act. indic. of δηλόω (LN 28.42, **33.152**) (BAGD p. 178): 'to indicate' [BAGD, HNTC, Lns; NIV, NJB, NRSV], 'to signify' [KJV], 'to denote' [Mil; NASB], 'to mean' [CEV, NLT, TNT], 'to show' [NAB], 'to show plainly' [TEV], 'to portend' [NIC], 'to point to' [WBC; REB], 'to make clear' [LN (**33.152**)], 'to make evident' [LN (33.152)], 'to make known, to make plain, to reveal' [LN (28.42)]. The implied subject is scripture [NIGTC].

b. μετάθεσις (LN 15.2) (BAGD 1. p. 511): 'removing' [KJV, NASB, NIV], 'removal' [BAGD, HNTC, Mil, NIC, WBC; NJB, NRSV, REB], 'departure' [LN], 'change' [Lns], not explicit [NLT]. This word is also translated as a verb: 'to be removed' [CEV, TEV, TNT], 'to pass away' [NAB]. The suffix -σις implies a process [NTC]. It means 'removal' [EBC, WBC], set aside and replaced [TH]; it means 'change' [Lns]. It includes all opposition to God's rule [WBC].

c. ὡς (LN 64.12) (BAGD III.1.a. p. 898): 'as' [BAGD, LN, Lns, Mil, NIC, WBC; KJV, NASB], 'like' [LN], 'that is' [HNTC; NIV, NRSV], 'since these are' [NJB], 'of' [REB], not explicit [CEV, NLT]. It indicates manner [Lns].

d. perf. pass. participle of ποιέω (LN 42.29) (BAGD I.1.aβ. p. 681): 'to be created' [BAGD, HNTC; all versions except KJV], 'to belong to the created order' [NIC], 'to be made' [LN, Lns, Mil; KJV]. This genitive participle is also translated 'of these things having been made' [WBC], 'the things on earth' [NLT]. It refers to all the created order [EGT, Hwt], including earth and the visible heaven [Hwt, Wst]. The perfect tense implies still existing [Lns, NIGTC, WBC]. The actor of the action is God [Mil].

QUESTION—What relationship is indicated by δέ 'now'?

It introduces a comment [Blm, GNC, Lns, My, TNTC] or explanation [Mil, NTC, WBC] about the preceding statement.

QUESTION—What relationship is indicated by the phrase τὸ ἔτι ἅπαξ 'the "yet once"'?

The neuter definite article τό 'the' makes a substantive of the phrase τὸ ἔτι ἅπαξ 'yet once' [Blm, EBC, Lns, Mil, My, NTC; NAB, NASB, NRSV]. It means 'the words "Yet once"' [Alf, GNC, HNTC, Hu, NIC, TH, TNTC, Wst; KJV, NIV, NJB, REB, TEV, TNT], which are the basis of the author's argument [Alf, EBC]. It introduces the quotation [NIC, NIGTC, WBC]. It implies finality, with no other occurrence following [Alf, EBC, Mil, My, NIGTC, Wst], once for all [Blm]. It implies a future event [GNC, Mil], the final judgment [GNC], the bringing in of the new heavens and new earth [Mil].

QUESTION—What relationship is indicated by the two participial phrases τῶν σαλευομένων 'the things being shaken' and (in the following clause) τὰ μὴ σαλευόμενα 'the things not being shaken'?

They imply that temporal things, including heaven and earth, the entire material universe, will be shaken to pieces [NIC], must give way to eternal things [EGT]; both the upper and lower parts of the visible universe will be removed from their places [NIGTC].

1. They refer to actual shaking [HNTC, Lns; NAB, NJB, Wst]: the things which are shaken . . . the things which are not shaken.
2. They refer to the possibility of being shaken [EBC, Hu, Lg, Mil, NTC, WBC; NASB, NIV]: the things which can be shaken . . . the things which cannot be shaken. These participles are used here with the sense of verbal adjectives (which would imply possibility) [EBC].
3. The first refers to actual shaking; the second refers to the possibility of being shaken [Alf, My, NIC; CEV, KJV, NRSV, REB, TEV, TNT]: the things which are shaken . . . the things which cannot be shaken.

QUESTION—What relationship is indicated by the phrase ὡς πεποιημένων 'as things created'?

It is a parenthetical comment [ICC, WBC] in apposition to τῶν σαλευομένων 'the things being shaken' [WBC].

1. It implies that this is what they are [EBC, HNTC, Hu, Lns, NIGTC, NTC, WBC, Wst; CEV, NAB, NIV, NRSV, REB, TEV, TNT]: they are created things.
2. It implies a reason [My; NJB]: since they are created things.
3. It describes the quality of the things, which are temporary [Mil, TNTC] and the purpose of their being created [Mil]: with the quality of created things, created to be only temporary.

QUESTION—To what does τῶν σαλευομένων 'the things created' refer?

This participle here implies 'made by God, but intended to be temporary' [Mil]; it refers to the earthly creation [Alf, Blm, Hwt, My] including the physical heaven [My], which are therefore temporary [Blm]. The author means that the OT dispensation was similarly intended to be abolished so that a new dispensation could be introduced [Blm, Hu, Hwt].

in-order-that the-(things) not being-shaken might-remain.[a]

LEXICON—a. aorist act. subj. of μένω (LN 13.89): 'to remain' [HNTC, LN, Lns, Mil, WBC; all versions except CEV, NLT], 'to continue to exist, to still be in existence' [LN], 'to endure' [NIC], 'to last' [CEV], 'to be left' [NLT]. It means to remain permanently after the shaken things are removed [Alf, Blm]. The aorist tense implies finality [Alf]. It refers to the stability and unchangeable character of God's kingdom and those who share in the kingdom [WBC].

QUESTION—Why is this clause mentioned?

It refers to the final consummation of redemption and the new heaven and earth [Hu]; it refers to the whole course of the Christian age [Wst].

1. It states the purpose (God's purpose [ICC, Lns, My]) of τὴν μετάθεσιν 'the removing' of the things that are/can be shaken [EBC, EGT, ICC, Lg(K), Lns, Mil, My, Wst]: removing in order that . . .
2. It states the purpose of ὡς πεποιημένων 'as things created' [Lg]: as things created in order that . . .
3. It states the contemplated result of ἔτι ἅπαξ 'yet once' [Lns]: yet once with the intended result that . . .

QUESTION—To what does τὰ μὴ σαλευόμενα 'the things not being shaken' refer?

Unshakeable things are necessarily eternal [TNTC]; it refers to God's heavenly kingdom [Hwt], the Christian order [ICC]. This new order is already present and will survive after the shaking [ICC].

12:28 Therefore, receiving (an) unshakeable[a] **kingdom let-us-have**[b] **grace**[c]**/ thankfulness,**[c]

TEXT—Instead of the present subjunctive ἔχωμεν 'let us have' some manuscripts read the present indicative ἔχομεν 'we have'. GNT does not deal with this variant and none of the versions or commentaries accept the indicative form.

LEXICON—a. ἀσάλευτος (LN **13.31**) (BAGD 2. p. 114): 'unshakeable' [HNTC, Lns, Mil, NIC; NAB, NJB, REB, TNT], 'that cannot be shaken' [BAGD, WBC; CEV, NIV, NRSV, TEV], 'which cannot be shaken' [NASB], 'which cannot be moved' [KJV], 'that cannot be destroyed' [NLT], 'unchangeable' [LN], 'unshaken' [BAGD], 'enduring' [**LN**]. It means that it is unshakeable [EBC, GNC], immoveable [EGT, Wst].

b. pres. act. subj. of ἔχω (LN 57.1): 'to have' [LN, Mil; KJV], 'to hold fast to' [NAB], 'to hold on to' [HNTC], 'to show' [NASB], not explicit [Lns, NIC, WBC; CEV, NIV, NJB, NLT, REB, TEV, TNT].

c. χάρις (LN 33.350, 88.66) (BAGD 5. p. 878): 'grace' [HNTC, LN (88.66), Mil; KJV, NAB], 'thanks' [LN (33.350)], 'gratitude' [NASB]. The phrase ἔχωμεν χάριν 'let us have grace' is translated 'let us give thanks' [NIC; NRSV, REB], 'let us be thankful' [BAGD, WBC; NIV, NLT, TNT], 'let us be grateful' [Lns; TEV], 'let us therefore be grateful' [NJB], 'we should be grateful' [CEV]. It refers to the grace of the Holy Spirit [Blm].

QUESTION—What relationship is indicated by διό 'therefore'?

1. It introduces the conclusion from the shaking referred to in the preceding verse [Alf, Blm, EGT, ICC, Mil].
2. It states the conclusion from the fact that what is unshakeable is God's kingdom [My].

QUESTION—What relationship is indicated by the participle παραλαμβάνοντες 'receiving'?

The present tense implies a continuing process of receiving [HNTC, NCBC, NIGTC, NTC, WBC, Wst] continuing into the future [WBC]; it refers to the future, but is a certainty [My]. The implied source of the receiving is God [Mil, Wst].

1. It indicates reason [HNTC, Mil, My, NTC, WBC; NASB, NIV, NRSV, TEV]: because we are receiving.
2. It indicates manner [Lns]: as receiving.
3. It is translated as attributive [EGT; NAB, TNT] (but this would require the definite article): we who are receiving.
4. It is translated as an independent verb [NIC; NJB, REB]: we are receiving.

QUESTION—To what does βασιλείαν ἀσάλευτον 'unshakeable kingdom' refer?

Βασιλείαν 'kingdom' is emphatic by word order [WBC]. It refers to God's eternal kingdom [Blm, EBC, GNC, HNTC, Hu, Lns, My, NCBC] in contrast with earthly kingdoms [EBC].

QUESTION—To whom does χάριν 'grace/thankfulness' refer?

1. It refers to God [BAGD, EBC, EGT, HNTC, My, NIGTC, WBC, Wst; NAB, REB].
1.1 It refers to God's grace [EBC, EGT, HNTC; NAB]: let us have God's grace.
1.2 It refers to thankfulness, and the implied object is God [BAGD, My, NIGTC, WBC, Wst; REB]: let us be thankful to God.
2. There is no expressed referent [Alf, Blm, GNC, Hu, Hwt, ICC, Lg, Lns, Mil, NIC, NTC; all versions except NAB, REB].
2.1 It refers to having grace [Blm, Mil; KJV]: let us have grace.
2.2 It refers to having thankfulness [Alf, GNC, Hu, Hwt, ICC, Lg, Lns, NIC, NTC; CEV, NASB, NIV, NJB, NLT, NRSV, TEV, TNT]: let us be thankful.

through[a] which let-us-serve[b] acceptably[c] (to)-God with[d] piety[e] and awe;[f]

TEXT—Instead of the present subjunctive λατρεύωμεν 'let us be serving', some manuscripts read the aorist subjunctive λατρεύσωμεν 'let us serve', and other manuscripts read the present indicative λατρεύομεν 'we serve'. GNT does not deal with this variant. The distinction in translation between the present and aorist subjunctive is generally not clear, unless the Greek word is given. The present indicative λατρεύομεν 'we serve' is read by only Lns and NRSV.

TEXT—Instead of εὐλαβείας καὶ δέους 'piety and awe' some manuscripts read δέους καὶ εὐλαβείας 'awe and piety', others read εὐλαβείας καὶ αἰδοῦς 'piety and reverence', and others read αἰδοῦς καὶ εὐλαβείας 'reverence and piety'. GNT does not deal with this variant. The similarity of meaning and translation of these words makes it difficult to determine which reading many versions and commentaries accept; however, εὐλαβείας καὶ δέους 'piety and awe' is probably read by almost all; αἰδοῦς καὶ εὐλαβείας 'reverence and piety' is clearly read by only Blm.

LEXICON—a. διά with genitive object (LN 89.76): 'through' [LN, Mil, WBC; NAB], 'by' [NASB, NRSV], 'by means of' [LN], not explicit [CEV, NLT]. The phrase δι' ἧς 'through which' is translated 'whereby' [Lns; KJV], 'and so' [HNTC; NIV, REB], 'and' [NIC; TEV], 'and in gratitude' [TNT]. The phrase δι' ἧς λατρεύωμεν 'through which let us serve' is translated 'and use our gratitude to worship' [NJB].

b. pres. act. subj. of λατρεύω (LN 53.14) (BAGD p. 467): 'to serve' [BAGD, Lns, Mil; KJV], 'to worship' [HNTC, LN, WBC; CEV, NIV, NJB, NLT, REB, TEV], 'to bring worship' [NIC], 'to offer worship' [NAB, NRSV, TNT], 'to offer service' [NASB].

c. εὐαρέστως (LN **25.94**) (BAGD p. 319): 'acceptably' [HNTC, Mil; KJV, NIV], 'in an acceptable manner' [BAGD, WBC], 'pleasingly, pleasing to' [LN], '(that) he can accept' [TNT], 'in a way that will please him' [TEV], 'in a way that pleases' [**LN**], 'in the way that pleases him' [NJB], 'in a well-pleasing way' [Lns], 'as he would be worshiped' [REB]. This adverb is also translated as an adjective: 'acceptable' [NIC; NAB, NASB, NRSV]; as a verb: 'to please' [CEV, NLT].

d. μετά with genitive object (LN 89.79, 89.123): 'with' [HNTC, LN (89.79, 89.123), Mil, NIC, WBC; KJV, NASB, NIV, NLT, NRSV, REB, TEV], 'combined with' [LN (89.79, 89.123)], 'together with' [Lns], 'in' [LN (89.79); NAB, NJB, TNT], not explicit [CEV]. This prepositional phrase amplifies εὐαρέστως 'acceptably' [My].

e. εὐλάβεια (LN 53.7) (BAGD p. 321): 'piety', 'reverence' [HNTC, LN, Lns, Mil; all versions except CEV, NLT], 'humble reverence' [NIC], 'awe' [BAGD], 'reverent awe' [ICC], 'fear' [WBC], 'holy fear' [NLT], 'great honor' [CEV]. It means 'godly fear' [Blm]. (There is some uncertainty concerning this and the following word because of the textual problem mentioned above.)

f. δέος (LN **53.59**) (BAGD p. 175): 'awe' [BAGD, HNTC, **LN**, Lns, Mil, NIC, WBC; all versions except CEV, KJV, NJB], 'fear' [BAGD; NJB]; 'godly fear' [KJV], 'respect' [CEV].

QUESTION—To what does the relative pronoun ἧς refer?

1. It refers to χάριν meaning 'grace' [EGT, HNTC, Mil]: through which grace.

2. It refers to χάριν meaning 'thankfulness' [Alf, Lns, NIGTC, NTC, TH, WBC; NJB, TNT]: through which thankfulness.

QUESTION—What relationship is indicated by λατρεύωμεν 'let us serve'?

1. It states an exhortation [Alf, HNTC, My, NIGTC, NTC, TH, TNTC, WBC, Wst; NIV, NJB, NLT, REB, TEV, TNT]: let us serve.
2. It refers to an enabling [EGT, Mil; KJV, NAB, NASB]: we may serve.
3. Reading the indicative λατρεύομεν 'we serve', it states a fact [Lns; CEV, NRSV]: we serve.

QUESTION—What is the phrase τῷ θεῷ '(to) God' connected with?

1. It is connected with λατρεύωμεν 'let us serve' [Alf, EGT, HNTC, Lns, Mil, My, NIC, WBC; KJV, NASB, NIV, NRSV]: let us serve God acceptably.
2. It is connected with εὐαρέστως 'acceptably' [NIGTC, TH; CEV, NAB, NLT]: let us serve in a manner acceptable to God.
3. It is connected with both λατρεύωμεν 'let us serve' and εὐαρέστως 'acceptably' [GNC, NTC; NJB, REB, TEV, TNT]: let us worship God in a manner acceptable to him.

QUESTION—What relationship is indicated by the phrase μετὰ εὐλαβείας καὶ δέους 'with piety and awe'?

1. It describes the manner of serving [My; NAB, NJB, TNT]: in a pious and awesome manner.
2. It expresses means [NJB]: by means of piety and awe.
3. It refers to accompanying qualities [Lns, Mil]: together with piety and awe.
4. It expresses the result [GNC]: resulting in piety and awe.

QUESTION—How are the two nouns related in the phrase εὐλαβείας καὶ δέους 'piety and awe'?

It forms a hendiadys [NIGTC]: pious awe. They overlap appreciably in meaning [TH].

12:29 for moreover our God (is) (a) consuming[a] fire.

LEXICON—a. pres. act. participle of καταναλίσκω (LN 20.48) (BAGD p. 414): 'to consume' [BAGD, HNTC, LN, Lns, Mil, NIC, WBC; KJV, NAB, NASB, NIV, NJB, NLT, NRSV], 'to consume completely, to destroy completely' [LN], 'to destroy' [CEV, TEV], 'to devour' [REB]. This participle is translated 'all-devouring' [TNT]. The prefixed κατα-intensifies the sense [NTC].

QUESTION—Why is this clause mentioned?

It simply states one aspect of God's character [Lg, NIGTC] and indicates that what the OT said about God is still true under the new covenant [TH, WBC, Wst]; his character is unchangingly righteous [TNTC]. It states an additional reason (it recapitulates the reason [Mil]) for the preceding comment [Alf, EGT, Mil], the reason why the readers should have godly fear toward God [Blm, Hwt, My] because of God's character [WBC]; it indicates that God must not be trifled with [EBC, NCBC]. It indicates the importance of not rejecting God's voice [WBC], of holding fast to God's promises for, if we are unfaithful, we will be destroyed [TH]. It warns against accepting heretical doctrines [Hwt]; it warns of the terrible consequences of abandoning the new covenant [Hu]. This clause forms the close of the epistle proper [ICC].

QUESTION—What is meant by καί 'moreover'?

1. It is emphatic (but only in combination with γάρ 'for' [NIGTC, NTC]) [Mil, NIGTC, NTC, Wst], urging careful attention [Mil]. It emphasizes the description of God [My]: for our God is also a consuming fire.
2. It has lost its force here [WBC].

QUESTION—What is meant by πῦρ καταναλίσκον 'consuming fire'?

It is the holy fire of wrath [HNTC, ICC], of righteousness that can punish [My], that consumes everything unworthy of himself [NIC], everything unfit for his presence [Wst], but also all that is base in his servants [Wst]; it implies the ability to bring utter destruction [Blm].

DISCOURSE UNIT: 13:1–25 [Hu, Hwt, Lg, Mil, NTC, TNTC, WBC, Wst; NAB, NIV, NLT]. The topic is additional exhortations [NTC], conclusion [Lg], concluding advice [TNTC; NLT], final exhortations [Hwt, Mil; NIV], final exhortations, requests, and greetings [Hu], final blessing, exhortation, and greetings [NAB], life in the confessing community [WBC].

DISCOURSE UNIT: 13:1–21 [NIC]. The topic is final exhortation and prayer.

DISCOURSE UNIT: 13:1–19 [GNT, NIGTC; CEV, NJB, TEV]. The topic is service that pleases God [GNT; CEV], how to please God [TEV], final instructions [NIGTC], appendix [NJB].

DISCOURSE UNIT: 13:1–14 [NASB]. The topic is the changeless Christ.

DISCOURSE UNIT: 13:1–6 [EBC, HNTC, Hwt, Lg, Lns, Mil, NCBC, NIC, NTC, WBC; NJB]. The topic is love [EBC], Christian attitudes [HNTC], practical Christian duties [Hwt], pastoral precepts [WBC], communal obligations [NTC], practical admonitions [NCBC], ethical injunctions [NIC], moral exhortations [Lg], exhortation to let Christian virtues continue [Lns], exhortation that ethical precepts have social implications [Mil], final recommendations [NJB].

DISCOURSE UNIT: 13:1–4 [GNC]. The topic is a call to live ethically.

DISCOURSE UNIT: 13:1–3 [TNTC]. The topic is exhortations dealing with social life.

13:1 Let-remain[a] the brotherly-love.[b]

LEXICON—a. pres. act. impera. of μένω (LN 68:11) (BAGD 1.c.β. p. 504): 'to remain' [LN], 'to continue to remain' [Lns], 'to continue' [BAGD, HNTC, LN, Mil, WBC; KJV, NASB, NJB, NLT, NRSV], 'to keep on' [LN (68.11); CEV, NIV, TEV], 'to never cease' [REB, TNT], 'to endure' [NIC]. This verb is also translated as an adverb: 'always' [NAB]. It refers here to the continuance of what is already going on [Alf, Blm, EGT, HNTC, Hwt, ICC, Lg, Lns, Mil, My, NCBC, NIGTC, TNTC, WBC], as the present tense indicates [Lns, TH]. The present tense refers to continuous action [TH]. It implies the possibility of neglecting this love [TNTC, Wst].

b. φιλαδελφία (LN **25.34**) (BAGD p. 858): 'brotherly love' [BAGD, NIC, WBC; KJV], 'love for the brethren' [Mil], 'love of the brethren' [NASB], 'love of brother *or* sister' [BAGD], 'love among fellow-Christians' [HNTC], 'love for one's fellow believer, affection for a fellow believer' [LN], 'fraternal affection' [Lns], 'mutual love' [NRSV]. This noun is also translated as a verb phrase: 'to love each other like brothers' [NJB], 'to love each other as brothers' [NIV], 'to love one another as brothers in Christ' [TNT], 'to love one another as fellow believers' [**LN**], 'to love one another as Christians' [TEV], 'to love one's fellow Christians' [NAB, REB], 'to love each other with true Christian love' [NLT], 'to be concerned about each other as the Lord's followers should' [CEV]. It refers to the love between Christians [Alf, Blm, EBC, GNC, HNTC, Hu, My, NIGTC, TNTC, Wst], since Christians considered each other as brothers and sisters [HNTC, Hu, NTC, TH, WBC]. It includes showing kindness and offering help [Lns].

QUESTION—How is this clause related to what precedes?

The absence of a connecting word indicates that this clause begins a new section [Mil]. However, there is a connection with what precedes [NIGTC]. It expresses an admonition [Lns, Mil, My, NTC, TNTC, WBC]: (I urge that) brotherly love be continued.

13:2 (Do) not neglect[a] the hospitality,[b]

LEXICON—a. pres. mid. (deponent = act.) impera. of ἐπιλανθάνομαι (LN 29.17) (BAGD 2. p. 295): 'to neglect' [BAGD, LN, Mil, WBC; NAB, NASB, NRSV, REB], 'to forget' [HNTC, NIC; NIV, NLT, TNT], 'to be forgetful' [Lns; KJV], 'to forget to do' [LN], 'to overlook' [BAGD, LN]. The phrase μὴ ἐπιλανθάνεσθε 'do not neglect' is translated 'to remember' [TEV], 'to remember always' [NJB], 'to be sure' [CEV]. The present tense implies continuation.

b. φιλοξενία (LN 34.57) (BAGD p. 860): 'hospitality' [BAGD, HNTC, LN, Mil, NIC; NAB, REB], 'hospitality to strangers' [WBC; NASB, NRSV], 'friendliness to strangers' [Lns]. This noun is also translated as a verb phrase: 'to entertain strangers' [KJV, NIV], 'to welcome strangers' [NJB], 'to welcome strangers in your homes' [CEV, TEV], 'to open your homes to welcome strangers' [TNT], 'to show hospitality to strangers' [NLT]. This is one aspect (one manifestation [Hwt, NCBC, WBC]) (the practical result [NTC]) of φιλαδελφία 'brotherly love' mentioned in the preceding verse [Alf, Hwt, Lns, Mil, NCBC, NTC, WBC]; it is closely related to φιλαδελφία 'brotherly love' and is an evidence of it [Blm].

for through[a] this some have-been-unaware[b] having-received-as-guests[c] angels.

LEXICON—a. διά with genitive object (LN 89.76): 'through' [HNTC, LN], 'by' [NIC; NASB, NJB, NRSV, REB, TNT], 'by means of' [LN, Mil, WBC; NAB]. The phrase διὰ ταύτης 'through this' is translated 'thereby' [Lns; KJV], 'by so doing' [NIV], 'by doing this' [CEV], 'some who have done this have . . .' [NLT].

b. aorist act. indic. of λανθάνω (LN **28.14**) (BAGD p. 466): 'to be unaware', 'to be unaware of' [LN], 'not to know' [LN], 'without knowing it' [BAGD, **LN**, WBC; CEV, NAB, NASB, NIV, NJB, NRSV, TEV, TNT], 'without realizing it' [Mil, NIC; NLT]. This verb is also translated as an adverb: 'unawares' [HNTC, Lns; KJV, REB].

c. aorist act. participle of ξενίζω (LN 34.57) (BAGD 1. p. 547): 'to receive as a guest', 'to treat as a guest' [LN], 'to welcome' [TEV], 'to welcome as guests' [CEV], 'to show hospitality' [LN], 'to entertain' [HNTC, Lns, Mil, NIC, WBC; all versions except CEV, TEV].

QUESTION—Why is this clause mentioned?

It states the grounds for the preceding exhortation [Mil]. It refers to a possible result, not the reason for doing so [HNTC, ICC]. It is an encouragement [Hwt]. It implies possible blessing from guests [EBC, Hwt, Lns, NIC, WBC], not the anticipation of actual angels as guests [EBC, Hwt, Lns, NIC]. It suggests that it is better to treat guests as if they might be angels than to risk treating worthy persons unworthily [TNTC].

QUESTION—To what does ταύτης 'this' refer?

It refers to φιλοξενίας 'hospitality' [Alf, ICC, NIC]: through hospitality.

QUESTION—What relationship is indicated by the participial phrase ἔλαθον ξενίσαντες 'have been unaware having received as guests'?

This phrase is a classical Greek idiom [EGT, ICC, Lns, NIC, NIGTC, NTC]. The participle contains the principal idea [BAGD, EGT, HNTC, LN, Lns, Mil, NIC, WBC; all versions] and the finite verb adds an adverbial sense [Lns, Mil, NIGTC, NTC, WBC].

13:3 Remember[a] the prisoners[b] as[c] bound-with[d] (them),

LEXICON—a. pres. mid. (deponent = act.) impera. of μιμνῄσκομαι (LN 29.16) (BAGD 1.c. p. 522): 'to remember' [BAGD, HNTC, LN, Lns, NIC, WBC; all versions except NAB, NJB, NLT], 'to be mindful of' [NAB], 'to keep in mind' [NJB], 'to think of, to be concerned about, to care for' [BAGD], 'to not forget' [NLT]. It implies remembering in order to give caring help [Hu, My, TH]. The present tense implies continuation [Lns, NIC, NIGTC, TH, WBC].

b. δέσμιος (LN 37.117) (BAGD p. 176): 'prisoner' [BAGD, LN, Lns, WBC; NAB, NASB], 'those in prison' [HNTC; NIV, NLT, REB, TNT], 'those who are in prison' [NJB, NRSV, TEV], 'those who are imprisoned' [NIC], 'them that are in bonds' [KJV], 'the Lord's people who are in jail'

[CEV]. The reference is to those who were imprisoned because of their Christian faith [Lns, Mil, TNTC].

c. ὡς (LN 64.12): 'as' [LN, Lns; KJV], 'like' [LN], 'as if' [WBC; NAB, NIV, REB, TNT], 'as though' [HNTC, NIC; NASB, NJB, NLT, NRSV, TEV], not explicit [CEV]. It expresses comparison [Lg].

d. perf. pass. participle of συνδέω (LN **37.116**) (BAGD p. 785): 'to be bound with' [KJV], 'to be in prison with' [LN; NASB, NJB, NRSV, TEV], 'to be imprisoned with' [HNTC; TNT], 'to share (someone's) imprisonment' [NIC; NAB], 'to be (someone's) fellow prisoner' [WBC; NIV], 'to be made (one's) fellow prisoner' [Lns], 'to be there with' [REB], 'to be there' [NLT]. This participle is also translated as a noun: 'fellow-prisoner' [BAGD]; as a verb phrase: 'to be concerned for them' [CEV].

QUESTION—What relationship is indicated by the participial phrase ὡς συνδεδεμένοι 'as bound with'?

1. It indicates manner, as the ὡς 'as' implies [Alf, Blm, EBC, EGT, HNTC, ICC, NIC, NTC, WBC; all versions].
2. It indicates reason [Wst].

the-(ones)-being mistreated[a] as/because[b] you-yourselves also being in[c] (the) body.[d]

LEXICON—a. pres. pass. participle of κακουχέω (LN 88.126) (BAGD p. 398): 'to be mistreated' [LN, WBC; NIV, NLT], 'to be maltreated' [BAGD; REB], 'to be ill-treated' [LN, NIC; NASB], 'to be badly treated' [NJB], 'to be disgracefully treated' [Lns], 'to be tormented' [BAGD], 'to be caused to suffer' [LN], 'to be tortured' [NRSV]. This passive voice is also translated as an active voice: 'to suffer' [HNTC; CEV, TEV], 'to suffer adversity' [KJV], 'to suffer hardship' [TNT]. The participle is also translated as an adjective: 'ill-treated' [NAB]. This word is a more general term, with the preceding reference to prisoners being a specific example [My]. The reference is to those who were mistreated because of their Christian faith [WBC].

b. ὡς (LN 64.12): 'as' [LN, Lns; KJV, NAB], 'like' [LN], 'as if' [WBC; NIV, TNT], 'as though' [NRSV, TEV], 'since' [NASB, NJB], 'because' [NIC], 'for' [HNTC; REB].

c. ἐν with dative object (LN 83.13): 'in' [LN, Lns, NIC; KJV, NASB, NJB]. The phrase ὡς καὶ αὐτοὶ ὄντες ἐν σώματι 'as you yourselves also being in the body' is translated 'as if you yourselves were suffering' [NIV], 'as if you yourselves were suffering bodily' [WBC], 'as though you were suffering as they are' [TEV], 'as if you too shared their lot' [TNT], 'as though you yourselves were being tortured' [NRSV], '(be as mindful of the ill-treated) as of yourselves, for you may yet suffer as they do' [NAB], 'for you are vulnerable too' [REB], 'for you too have bodies' [HNTC] 'as though you feel their pain in your own bodies' [NLT], 'but imagine that you there with them' [CEV].

d. σῶμα (LN 8.1) (BAGD 1.b. p. 799): 'body' [BAGD, LN, Lns, NIC; KJV, NASB, NJB, NLT].

QUESTION—What is this phrase connected with?

This phrase is a second predicate of μιμνῄσκεσθε 'remember' in the preceding clause [HNTC, NIC; NAB, TEV, TNT]: remember the prisoners and remember the ones being mistreated.

QUESTION—What relationship is indicated by the participial phrase ὡς ὄντες 'being'?

1. It indicates manner [Alf, Lns, WBC; CEV, KJV, NAB, NIV, NLT, NRSV, TEV, TNT]

1.1 It means to consider themselves actually being mistreated [Alf, Lns; KJV, NAB].

1.2 It means to act as if they were mistreated, although they are not [NTC, WBC; NIV, NRSV, TEV, TNT].

2. It indicates reason [HNTC, NIC, TNTC, Wst; NASB, NJB, REB]: because you also are mistreated.

3. It combines both manner and reason [NAB]: be mindful as of yourselves, because you may suffer mistreatment.

4. It expresses an expansion of the exhortation to remember those who are mistreated [TH]: consider what it means to suffer.

QUESTION—What relationship is indicated by the phrase ἐν σώματι 'in (the) body'?

1. It refers to being in a physical body (as the absence of the definite article implies [NTC]) [EBC, EGT, HNTC, Lns, NIGTC, NTC, Wst; KJV, NASB, NJB] in this earthly life [GNC, Hu, Hwt, ICC, Lg(K), My, NCBC, NIC], subject to physical ills [NIGTC, TNTC] and therefore subject to the possibility of incurring a similar situation [Alf, Blm, EBC, EGT, GNC, HNTC, Hu, Hwt, ICC, Lg(K), Lns, My, NIGTC, TNTC, Wst; NAB, REB].

2. It implies being in the place of [WBC; NIV, NRSV, TEV, TNT]: (as if) you yourselves were (suffering).

3. It includes both 1. and 2. above [WBC].

4. It means, since the readers know what such suffering is like [Mil].

DISCOURSE UNIT: 13:4–6 [TNTC]. The topic is exhortations affecting private life.

13:4 Marriage (must be) honored[a] in[b] all and the marriage-bed[c] undefiled,[d]

LEXICON—a. τίμιος (LN 87.6) (BAGD 1.c. p. 818): 'honored' [HNTC, LN; NAB, NIV, NJB, REB, TEV], 'honorably esteemed' [NIC], 'respected' [BAGD, LN, WBC; TNT], 'honorable' [Lns; KJV]. This word is also translated as a verb phrase: 'to hold in honor' [BAGD, Mil; NASB, NRSV], 'to give honor to' [NLT], 'to have respect for' [CEV]. It is emphatic by its forefronted position [NIGTC, WBC]; it has an imperatival implication [WBC].

b. ἐν with dative object (LN 83.9, 90.6): 'in' [HNTC, Lns, Mil; KJV, NAB], 'among' [LN (83.9), NIC; NASB], 'by' [LN (90.6), WBC; NIV, NJB, NRSV, REB, TEV, TNT], not explicit [CEV, NLT].

c. κοίτη (LN **23.62**) (BAGD 1.b. p. 440): 'marriage bed' [BAGD, Mil, NIC, WBC; NAB, NASB, NIV, NRSV], 'bed' [HNTC, Lns; KJV], 'sexual life' [**LN**], 'marriage relations' [LN], 'marriage bond' [REB], 'marriages' [NJB]. The phrase ἡ κοίτη ἀμίαντος 'the marriage bed undefiled' is translated 'its vows faithfully kept' [TNT], 'husbands and wives must be faithful to each other' [TEV], 'remain faithful to one another in marriage' [NLT], 'always be faithful to your partner' [CEV]. It refers to sexual intercourse [EBC, HNTC, ICC, NIGTC] within marriage [ICC, NIGTC].

d. ἀμίαντος (LN 53.36) (BAGD 1. p. 46): 'undefiled' [BAGD, HNTC, LN, Lns, WBC; KJV, NAB, NASB, NJB, NRSV], 'unpolluted' [NIC], 'untainted' [LN], 'inviolate' [REB], 'pure' [BAGD, Mil; NIV]. It is the negative of and expounds τίμιος 'honored' in the preceding phrase [Lns]; it has an imperatival implication [WBC]. It is emphatic by its position [NIGTC, WBC] and refers to the spiritual aspect [NIGTC].

QUESTION—What relationship is indicated by the phrase τίμιος ὁ γάμος 'marriage must be honored'?

1. It means that marriage must be held in honor [EGT, HNTC, Hwt, NCBC, NIC, NIGTC, NTC, TNTC, WBC; KJV, NAB, NASB, NIV, NJB, NRSV, REB, TNT].
2. It means that spouses must remain true to their marriage vows [Lns; CEV, NLT, TEV].
3. It means that marriage must not be considered spiritually inferior to celibacy [EBC, GNC].
4. Supplying an understood indicative verb, it means that marriage is honorable [KJV].

QUESTION—What is the implied verb of this clause?

1. An exhortation (a command [HNTC]) is implied [Alf, BAGD, Blm, EBC, EGT, HNTC, Hu, ICC, Lns, Mil, My, NCBC, NIC, NIGTC, NTC, TH, WBC, Wst; all versions except KJV] as is implied by the following γάρ 'for' [Hu, NIC, WBC, Wst], by the hortatory context [Hu, WBC, Wst], and by the forefronted position of τίμιος 'honored' [Mil]: marriage should be honored.
2. A statement is implied [KJV]: marriage is honorable.

QUESTION—What relationship is indicated by the phrase ἐν πᾶσιν 'in all'?

1. It refers to persons [Blm, Hu, ICC, LN, NCBC, NIC, NTC, TH, TNTC, WBC; all versions except CEV, NAB, NLT].
1.1 It refers to agency [ICC, LN, NTC, TH, WBC; NIV, NJB, NRSV, REB, TEV, TNT]: by all persons.
1.2 It refers to location [Blm, Hu, NCBC, NIC, TNTC; NASB]: among all persons.
2. It refers to aspects [Alf, EBC, HNTC, Lg, Lns, Mil, My, NIGTC, Wst; NAB].

2.1 It refers to areas [Alf, HNTC, Lg, Lns, Mil, My, NIGTC]: in every respect.
2.2 It refers to manner [NAB]: in every way.
2.3 It refers to circumstances [EBC]: in every circumstance.
2.4 It refers to both respects and circumstances [Wst]: in every respect and every circumstance.

QUESTION—What relationship is indicated by καί 'and'?
1. It introduces a negative coordinate proposition [Mil, NIGTC].
2. It implies an inference [EGT]: and thus let the marriage bed be undefiled.

QUESTION—What relationship is indicated by the phrase ἡ κοίτη ἀμίαντος 'the marriage bed undefiled'?
1. It means that the marriage relationship must not be defiled by adultery [Blm, GNC, Hu, Hwt, NCBC, NIGTC, NTC, TH] or any other illicit sexual acts [Mil, WBC]. This exhortation is a specific instance of the preceding exhortation [NIGTC].
2. It means that marriage relationships must not be considered defiling [EBC].
3. Supplying an understood indicative verb, it means that marriage relationships are not defiling [KJV].

for fornicators[a] and adulterers[b] God will-judge.[c]

TEXT—Instead of γάρ 'for' some manuscripts read δέ 'but'. GNT does not deal with this variant. Only Blm, EGT, KJV read 'but'.

LEXICON—a. πόρνος (LN 88.274) (BAGD p. 693): 'fornicator' [BAGD, HNTC, Lns, Mil, NIC; NAB, NASB, NRSV, REB], 'sexually immoral person' [LN], 'sexually immoral' [WBC; NIV, NJB], 'those who are immoral' [CEV, NLT, TEV, TNT], 'whoremonger' [KJV]. It refers to those who commit sexual sins in general [NCBC, NIC, TH], to those who engage in sexual relationships (both heterosexual and homosexual [Hu]) outside of marriage [Hu, WBC], referring primarily to those who violate another person's marriage by fornication, incest, or sodomy [ICC]. This plus the following word include all who engage in any improper sexual activity [WBC].

b. μοιχός (LN 88.277) (BAGD 1. p. 526): 'adulterer' [BAGD, HNTC, LN, Lns, Mil, NIC, WBC; all versions except TEV, TNT], 'those who commit adultery' [NLT, TEV], 'those who are adulterous' [TNT], 'anyone who is unfaithful in marriage' [CEV]. It refers to those who violate their own marriage vows [Hu, ICC, NCBC, NIC, TH, WBC].

c. fut. act. indic. of κρίνω (LN 56.20, 56.30) (BAGD 4.b.α. p. 452): 'to judge' [BAGD, HNTC, LN (56.20), Lns, Mil, NIC, WBC; all versions except CEV, NJB, REB], 'to come under (someone's) judgment' [NJB], 'to condemn' [LN (56.30)], 'to punish' [CEV]. The phrase κρινεῖ ὁ θεός 'God will judge' is translated 'God's judgment will fall on' [REB]. It refers to the final judgment [Alf, My, WBC] and implies condemnation [Alf, Blm, My, TH].

QUESTION—What relationship is indicated by γάρ 'for'?

It indicates the grounds for the preceding exhortation [Mil, NIGTC, NTC, TH, TNTC].

QUESTION—What relationship is indicated by the word order of ὁ θεός 'God'?

It is emphatic by its final position [EBC, EGT, ICC, My, NIGTC, NTC, WBC, Wst].

DISCOURSE UNIT: 13:5–6 (GNC). The topic is the security of the believer.

13:5 Not-loving-money[a] the way-of-life[b] (should be),

LEXICON—a. ἀφιλάργυρος (LN 25.109) (BAGD p. 126): 'not loving money, not greedy' [BAGD], 'not loving wealth' [LN], 'without money-love' [Lns], 'free from love of money' [Mil], 'free from the love of money' [HNTC, NIC, WBC; NASB, NIV, NRSV, TEV], 'without covetousness' [KJV]. This entire clause is translated 'do not love money' [NAB], 'do not live for money' [REB], 'don't fall in love with money' [CEV], 'stay away from the love of money' [NLT], 'put avarice out of your lives' [NJB], 'do not let your life be ruled by the love of money' [TNT]. It is used imperatively [WBC]. It is emphatic by its position [WBC].

b. τρόπος (LN **41.10**) (BAGD 2. p. 827): 'way of life' [BAGD, LN, Mil, NIC], 'manner of life' [LN], 'life' [HNTC, LN, WBC; NIV, NJB, NRSV, TEV, TNT], 'behavior' [**LN**], 'conduct' [BAGD, Lns], 'character' [BAGD; NASB], 'turn of mind' [BAGD], 'conversation' [KJV], not explicit [CEV, NAB, NLT]. This noun is also translated as a verb: 'to live for' [REB]. It implies disposition [Blm, EGT, Lg(K)], the way of life [Hwt, TH] and thought [Hwt], character [Wst], mores [ICC].

QUESTION—What is the implied verb of this clause?

An exhortation is implied [Alf, Blm, HNTC, LN, Lns, Mil, My, NIC, WBC, Wst; all versions]: you should be not loving money.

being-content[a] with-the possessions;[b]

LEXICON—a. pres. mid. participle of ἀρκέω (LN 59.46) (BAGD 2. p. 107): 'to be content' [BAGD, HNTC, NIC, WBC; all versions except CEV, NLT, TEV], 'to be contented' [Lns], 'to be satisfied' [Mil; CEV, NLT, TEV], 'to be sufficient, to be adequate, to be enough' [LN].

b. pres. act. participle of πάρειμι (LN **57.17**) (BAGD 2. p. 624): This plural is translated 'possessions' [BAGD, LN], 'what (one) has' [BAGD], 'what you have' [HNTC, **LN**, Mil, WBC; all versions except KJV, NJB], 'whatever you have' [NJB], 'such things as you have' [KJV], 'things at hand' [Lns], 'the things which are available' [NIC]. It refers to earthly possessions [My]; it refers to the present condition [Blm].

QUESTION—What relationship is indicated by the participle ἀρκούμενοι 'being content'?

It describes an additional aspect of the exhortation [HNTC; NASB]: also, be content. It is used imperatively [Mil, NIC, NIGTC, WBC] and is translated as a finite verb [Mil, NIC, WBC; KJV, NAB, NIV, NJB, NRSV, REB, TEV, TNT]. It is translated with an understood imperative verb ἔστε 'be' [My]: be being content. The plural is used since the general sense refers to the readers in general [Lns, NIC].

for he-himself has-said, "Not not/by-no-means[a] will-I-abandon[b] you

LEXICON—a. οὐ μή (LN 69.5) (BAGD D.1.a., b. p. 517; 6.d. p. 591): 'by no means' [LN], 'in no way . . . ever' [Mil], 'in no wise' [Lns], 'certainly not' [BAGD, LN], 'never' [BAGD, HNTC, NIC, WBC; all versions except CEV, NJB], 'not' [CEV, NJB].

b. aorist. act. subj. of ἀνίημι (LN **35.54**) (BAGD 2. p. 69): 'to desert' [BAGD, LN; NAB, NASB, TNT], 'to leave' [HNTC; CEV, KJV, NIV, NRSV, REB, TEV], 'to abandon' [NIC], 'to let go of' [Lns], 'to fail' [WBC; NJB, NLT], 'to fail to uphold' [Mil].

QUESTION—What relationship is indicated by γάρ 'for'?

It indicates the (strongest [Blm]) reason for the contentment (for not loving money [EBC]) urged in the preceding phrase [Blm, EBC, HNTC, Mil, NCBC, TNTC, WBC], the reason for the two preceding exhortations [NIGTC].

QUESTION—Who is the implied actor of εἴρηκεν 'he has said'?

The implied speaker (implied in αὐτός 'himself' [Blm, NIGTC, TH] which is emphatic [WBC]) is God [Alf, Blm, EGT, ICC, Lg, Lns, My, NIC, NIGTC, TH, WBC, Wst; NAB, NIV, NJB, NLT, REB, TEV, TNT]: God has said. The perfect tense implies that what God has said still stands [Lns, Mil, NIGTC, WBC].

QUESTION—What relationship is indicated by αὐτὸς εἴρηκεν 'he himself has said'?

It introduces what is not an exact OT quotation [Blm, Hwt, NIC, WBC] but is similar to several passages [Hwt, NIGTC, NTC, TH, TNTC, WBC, Wst]. It refers to the general sense of God's OT declarations [Blm] and had possibly become a proverbial expression [GNC, Hwt, Lg, My, NTC, Wst]. It was used for consolation [Blm]. It is adapted from Deut. 31:5 [EGT], 31:6 [GNC, HNTC, Mil], 31:8 [NCBC]. It is a quotation from a lost translation of the Greek OT [EBC].

QUESTION—What relationship is indicated by the repeated combinations of negatives in this and the following clause?

It indicates a strong negative assertion [ICC, Lg, Mil, NIGTC, NTC, WBC]: I will by no means . . . nor will I by any. . . . It is a litotes, implying a strong positive affirmation [Mil]: I will surely care for you!

nor not not/by-any-means[a] will-I-forsake[b] you,"

LEXICON—a. οὐ μή (LN 69.5) (BAGD D.1.a., b., p. 517; 6d. p. 591): 'by no means' [LN], 'in no way . . . ever' [Mil], 'certainly not' [BAGD, LN], 'never' [BAGD; NIV, NLT, TEV], not explicit [HNTC; CEV, KJV, NAB, NJB, NRSV, REB, TNT]. The phrase οὐδ' οὐ μή 'nor by any means' is translated 'nor in any wise' [Lns], 'nor ever' [NASB], 'never' [NIC, WBC].

b. aor. act. subj. of ἐγκαταλείπω (LN **35.54**) (BAGD 2. p. 215): 'to forsake' [BAGD, HNTC, LN, NIC, WBC; KJV, NAB, NASB, NIV, NLT, NRSV, TNT], 'to abandon' [BAGD, Lns, Mil; TEV], 'to desert' [BAGD; CEV, NJB, REB]. This verb functions here as the result of the preceding verb ἀνῶ 'I will abandon' [Lns].

13:6 so-that[a] being-courageous[b] us to-say/we say,

LEXICON—a. ὥστε (LN 89.52) (BAGD 2.a.β. p. 900): 'so that' [BAGD, LN, Lns, Mil; KJV, NASB], 'so' [LN, NIC, WBC; NIV, NRSV, REB], 'and so' [NJB], 'so then, so accordingly, as a result' [LN], 'therefore' [HNTC, LN], 'thus' [NAB], 'then' [TEV], 'that is why' [NLT, TNT], not explicit [CEV]. It introduces a result [BAGD, Lns, Mil, NIGTC, NTC, WBC], a conclusion [TH].

b. pres. act. participle of θαρρέω (LN 25.156) (BAGD p. 352): 'to be courageous, to be full of courage' [LN], 'to have courage' [LN, NIC], 'to take courage' [REB], 'to be of good courage' [Lns], 'to be bold' [LN; TEV], 'to make one feel like' [CEV]. This participle is also translated as a phrase: 'with confidence' [BAGD, HNTC, Mil, WBC; NAB, NIV, NJB, NLT, NRSV]; as an adverb: 'confidently' [NASB, TNT], 'boldly' [KJV].

QUESTION—What relationship is indicated by the participle θαρροῦντας 'being courageous'?

It indicates manner [Alf, EBC, HNTC, Hu, Lg(K), Mil, My, NIGTC, TH, TNTC, Wst; all versions]: confidently.

QUESTION—What is meant by the phrase ἡμᾶς λέγειν 'us to say'?

The ἡμᾶς 'us' links the writer with his readers [EBC, NTC].

1. It indicates actuality [Alf, EGT, HNTC, Lns, My, Wst; NASB, NIV]: we say.
2. It indicates possibility (supplying an understood δύνασθαι 'to be able' [NIGTC, WBC]) [EBC, Hu, Mil, NIC, NIGTC, TH, WBC; KJV, NAB, NJB, NLT, NRSV, REB, TNT]: we can say.
3. It is translated as an exhortation [TEV]: let us say.

"(The) Lord (is) helper[a] to-me, and not will-I-fear; What will-do to-me man?"

LEXICON—a. βοηθός (LN **35.11**) (BAGD 2. p. 144): 'helper' [BAGD, HNTC, LN, Lns, Mil, NIC, WBC; all versions except CEV, NJB]. The phrase κύριος ἐμοὶ βοηθός 'the Lord is helper to me' is translated 'with the Lord on my side' [NJB], 'the Lord helps me' [CEV].

QUESTION—To whom does κύριος 'Lord' refer?

It refers to God the Father [Alf, GNC, HNTC, NIC, NIGTC, TNTC]. In first position it contrasts with ἄνθρωπος 'man' in final position [EGT, Mil].

QUESTION—What is indicated by the possessive adjective ἐμοί 'to me'?

It is emphatic [Mil]: the Lord is *to me* a helper.

QUESTION—What relationship is indicated by the phrase καὶ οὐ φοβηθήσομαι 'and I will not fear'?

It states the result of the preceding comment [Mil; NLT]: the Lord is my helper; therefore I will not fear.

QUESTION—What is implied by the question τί ποιήσει μοι ἄνθρωπος 'What will man do to me?'

1. It is a direct question [Alf, Blm, EBC, HNTC, Hu, Hwt, Lg(K), Lns, Mil, My, NIC, NIGTC, NTC, TH, WBC, Wst; all versions except KJV]: I will not fear; what will man do to me?
2. It is a rhetorical question [Mil, NIGTC, NTC, TH], implying a (strong [NIGTC]) negative response that man can do nothing to harm me [Mil, NIGTC, NTC, TNTC].
3. It is a statement [KJV]: I will not fear what man will do to me.

QUESTION—What is implied by the future tense of ποιήσει 'will do'?

1. It refers to future possibility [Alf, EBC, Lns, Mil, Wst; KJV, NASB]: what will man do.
2. It implies ability [HNTC, Hu, NIC, NTC, WBC; all versions except KJV, NASB]: what can man do.

QUESTION—What is meant by ἄνθρωπος 'man' without the definite article?

It is emphatic by word order [NIGTC].

1. It is qualitative [Alf, EBC, HNTC, Hu, Hwt, Lns, Mil, NIC, NTC, TH, WBC, Wst; all versions except NRSV, TEV]: anyone of human nature.
2. It is indefinite [Lg(K), My; NRSV, TEV]: any person.

DISCOURSE UNIT: 13:7–19 (WBC). The topic is communal directives.

DISCOURSE UNIT: 13:7–17 (Hwt, Lg, Lns, Mil, NTC). The topic is necessary religious duties [Hwt], ecclesiastical duties [NTC], special warnings concerning the readers' inclination to apostasy [Lg], exhortation to go to Jesus outside the camp [Lns], exhortation not to disown their leaders' teachings and to break with persons holding Judaistic teachings [Mil].

DISCOURSE UNIT: 13:7–16 (HNTC, NCBC; NJB). The topic is faithfulness [NJB], warning against false teaching [HNTC], additional warnings [NCBC].

DISCOURSE UNIT: 13:7–9 (GNC, TNTC). The topic is a summons to be faithful and a warning against heretical teaching [GNC], exhortations affecting religious life [TNTC].

DISCOURSE UNIT: 13:7–8 (EBC, NIC, NTC). The topic is Christian leadership [EBC], examples to follow [NIC], urging to remember leaders [NTC].

13:7 Remember[a] the-(ones) leading[b] you,

LEXICON—a. pres. act. impera. of μνημονεύω (LN **29.7**) (BAGD 1.a. p. 525): 'to remember' [BAGD, HNTC, LN, NIC; all versions except CEV], 'to continue to remember' [WBC], 'to keep in mind' [Mil], 'to keep calling to mind' [Lns], 'not to forget' [CEV]. It implies remembering so as to imitate (the leaders) [Alf, Blm, EGT, Lg(K), My, NCBC], so as to learn from (the leaders) [NIGTC]. It is emphatic [WBC]. The present tense implies continuation [NIGTC, TNTC, WBC].

b. pres. mid. (deponent = act.) of ἡγέομαι (LN **36.1**) (BAGD 1. p. 343): 'to lead' [BAGD, LN; NASB], 'to guide' [BAGD], 'to have the rule over' [KJV]. This participle is also translated as a noun: 'leader' [HNTC, **LN**, Lns, Mil, WBC; CEV, NAB, NIV, NJB, NLT, NRSV, REB, TNT], 'guide' [NIC], 'former leader' [TEV], 'master' [**LN**]. It refers to their Christian leaders [Alf], those who first guided them into faith [Blm, Hwt; NLT], the founders of the church [ICC, Mil, NCBC, NIC, NTC, TNTC] including the apostles [Hwt, Mil, My]; it refers to Peter and Paul [Lns].

QUESTION—To whom does τῶν ἡγουμένων ὑμῶν 'the ones leading you' refer?

1. It refers to past leaders [Alf, Blm, EBC, EGT, GNC, HNTC, Hu, Hwt, ICC, Lg(K), Lns, Mil, My, NIC, NIGTC, NTC, TNTC, WBC, Wst; all versions except KJV], the original leaders [EBC], who had died [Blm, EGT, Hu, Hwt, ICC, Lg(K), Lns, My, NIC, NIGTC, NTC, TNTC, WBC, Wst; NAB, TEV, TNT], but some may still be alive [NCBC]: those who led you.
2. It refers to present leaders [KJV]: those who lead you.

who[a] spoke to-you the word of God,

LEXICON—a. ὅστις (LN 92.18) (BAGD 2.b. p. 587): 'who'. This plural is translated 'those who' [NIC; NRSV], 'as those who' [WBC], 'such as' [Mil], 'who were such as' [Lns], 'they' [HNTC], 'who' [BAGD, LN; all versions except NRSV], 'whoever' [LN];. It emphasizes the kind of persons they were [Alf, BAGD, Lg(K), Lns, Mil, NTC, TNTC] and also implies cause [Lns, Mil, NTC]; it focuses on the persons referred to [EGT, ICC].

QUESTION—What is indicated by the aorist tense of ἐλάλησαν 'spoke'?

It indicates that the speaking was completed in the past [Alf, GNC, Lg(K), NTC, WBC].

of-whom considering[a] the outcome[b] of-the conduct[c] imitate[d] the faith.

LEXICON—a. pres. act. participle of ἀναθεωρέω (LN **30.28**) (BAGD 2. p. 54): 'to consider' [BAGD, HNTC, Mil, NIC, WBC; KJV, NAB, NASB, NIV, NRSV], 'to think of' [NLT, TNT], 'to think back on' [**LN**; TEV], 'to reflect upon' [LN], 'to reflect on' [NJB], 'to keep before (oneself)' [REB], 'to view carefully' [Lns], 'to remember' [CEV]. The present tense implies continuation [NIGTC, WBC], repetition [Wst].

b. ἔκβασις (LN **67.68, 89.39**) (BAGD p. 238): 'outcome' [BAGD, HNTC, LN (**89.39**), Mil, NIC; NIV, NJB, NRSV, REB], 'end' [BAGD, LN (**67.68**); KJV], 'result' [BAGD; NASB], 'issue' [Lns], 'accomplishment' [WBC]. The phrase ὧν . . . τὴν ἔκβασιν τῆς ἀναστροφῆς 'of whom . . . the outcome of the conduct' is translated 'how their lives ended' [NAB], 'how they lived and died' [TEV], 'the way they lived and died' [TNT], 'what kind of lives they lived' [CEV], 'the good that has come from their lives' [NLT]. It means the result [NTC, TNTC], the successful outcome [GNC, WBC] of the leaders' faith [NCBC, WBC], the achievement of their daily conduct [Hu]. The outcome was death [Alf, Blm, Hwt, ICC, Lg, Lns, Mil, My, NIGTC] by martyrdom [ICC, Lg, My].

c. ἀναστροφή (LN 41.3) (BAGD p. 61): 'conduct' [BAGD, WBC; NASB], 'behavior' [BAGD], 'way of life' [BAGD, Mil; NIV, NRSV], 'manner of life' [Lns, NIC], 'life' [HNTC, LN; CEV, NJB, NLT, REB], 'conversation' [KJV]. It refers to life in its moral aspect in human relations [Wst].

d. pres. mid. (deponent = act.) impera. of μιμέομαι (LN 41.44) (BAGD p. 522): 'to imitate' [BAGD, HNTC, LN, Lns, Mil, NIC, WBC; NAB, NASB, NIV, NRSV, TEV, TNT], 'to take as (one's) model' [NJB], 'to follow' [KJV], 'to follow the example' [REB]. The phrase μιμεῖσθε τὴν πίστιν 'imitate the faith' is translated 'have faith like theirs' [CEV], 'trust the Lord as they do' [NLT]. It refers to holding the same faith as the leaders referred to [Blm, EBC, EGT], to imitating their example [ICC]. The present tense implies continuation [NIGTC].

QUESTION—What is ὧν 'of whom' connected with?

It is connected with τῆς ἀναστροφῆς 'the conduct' [EGT, Mil, My]: whose conduct. It is also connected with τὴν πίστιν 'the faith' [My].

QUESTION—What is the participle ἀναθεωροῦντες 'considering' related to?

1. It is governed by the following imperative verb μιμεῖσθε 'imitate' [HNTC, Lns, Mil, NIC; all versions].
2. It is governed by the preceding imperative μνημονεύετε 'remember' [NTC, WBC].

QUESTION—What relationship is indicated by the participle ἀναθεωροῦντες 'considering'?

1. It states an additional exhortation and is translated as an imperative verb [HNTC, Mil, NIC, NIGTC, TH; CEV, NAB, NIV, NLT, NRSV, REB, TEV, TNT]: consider.
2. It is temporal [NJB]: as you consider.

13:8 Jesus Christ yesterday and today the same and into the ages.[a]

LEXICON—a. αἰών (LN **67.87**, 67.143) (BAGD 1.b. p. 27): 'age' [LN (67.143)], 'eon' [Lns], 'eternity' [BAGD]. The phrase εἰς τοὺς αἰῶνας 'into the ages' is translated 'forever' [HNTC, Mil, NIC, WBC; all versions], 'in perpetuity, to eternity' [BAGD], 'eternally' [BAGD, LN (**67.87**)]. The phrase ἐχθὲς καὶ σήμερον καὶ εἰς τοὺς αἰῶνας 'yesterday and today and forever' is translated 'in the past, in the present, and in the future' [**LN** (67.87)], 'past and present and future, always, eternally' [LN (67.87)]. This phrase emphasizes Christ's unchanging nature [EBC, HNTC].

QUESTION—How is this phrase related to other phrases?

It assumes Christ's eternal unchanging character [GNC, Lg, Lns, My]; it implies Christ's unfailing reliability [Hu]; it implies the unchangeableness of the gospel message delivered by the former leaders [WBC].

1. It is an independent comment not overtly connected with what precedes or follows [GNC, HNTC, NIC, NIGTC, Wst; all versions except NLT, REB]. It expresses a reflection following a pause [Wst].
2. It forms a transition from the preceding to what follows [Alf, Hwt, TH, WBC] and is therefore connected with both [Blm, EGT, Hu, ICC, Lg, TH]. It states the object of the former leaders' faith and the grounds for the statement that follows [Mil, WBC]: their faith was in the unchanging Jesus Christ; therefore don't follow false teachings!
3. It states the grounds for the following exhortation [My; NLT, REB]: Christ is always the same; therefore don't follow teachings which are opposed to his nature.
4. It is connected with the preceding verse [My(D)]: imitate those leaders' faith, since Jesus is always the same.

QUESTION—What is the significance of the use of the full title, 'Jesus Christ', which is rare in this epistle?

It is emphatic by word order [NIGTC, WBC]; it adds solemnity to the declaration [EBC]. 'Jesus' is his personal name [Alf]; 'Christ' refers to him as the Anointed One [Alf], to his unchangeable nature and person [Blm].

QUESTION—To what does ἐχθές 'yesterday' refer?

1. It refers to the time of the leaders mentioned in the preceding verse [Alf, Hu, Lns, WBC]. It is the time Christ was the source of those leaders' faith [Hu], when Paul and Peter preached Christ to the readers [Lns], when those leaders died [Alf].
2. It refers to the time of Christ's atoning work [GNC, NIC, NTC, TNTC], proclaimed to the readers by persons who heard him [NTC].
3. It includes both the time of Christ's atoning work and the time of the leaders mentioned in the preceding verse [ICC].
4. It stands for the past in general [EBC, EGT, HNTC, Wst]. It is a general rhetorical comment [My].

QUESTION—To what does σήμερον 'today' refer?

1. It refers to the present in general [EBC, EGT, HNTC, Hu, WBC, Wst].
2. It refers to the time of the author and his readers [Alf].
3. It refers to Christ's present work of intercession for us [GNC, Lns, NIC, NTC, TNTC].

QUESTION—What is ὁ αὐτός 'the same' connected with?

It is connected with both the preceding and the following phrases [NIGTC, NTC, TH]: the same yesterday and today and forever. It is emphatic by its position [TH].

QUESTION—To what does the phrase εἰς τοὺς αἰῶνας 'forever' refer?

It is emphatic [Lg(K), NIC, NIGTC, WBC; NASB].

1. It refers to Christ's eternal high priesthood [NIGTC, NTC, WBC], his future intercession for believers [NIC], the quality of redemption [WBC], a future consummation [TNTC].
2. It refers to the unending future [EBC, HNTC]; it includes the two preceding concepts, ἐχθὲς καὶ σήμερον 'yesterday and today' [TNTC, Wst] and goes beyond them [Wst].

QUESTION—What is indicated by the use of καὶ . . . καὶ 'and . . . and'?

It indicates an increasing emphasis [Mil]: not only for time, but even for eternity.

DISCOURSE UNIT: 13:9–16 (EBC, NIC). The topic is Christian sacrifice [EBC], the true Christian sacrifices [NIC].

13:9 By-teachings[a] various[b] and strange[c] (do) not be-led-astray;[d]

LEXICON—a. διδαχή (LN 33.224, 33.236) (BAGD 2. p. 192): 'teaching' [BAGD, HNTC, LN (33.224, 33.236), Mil, NIC, WBC; CEV, NAB, NASB, NIV, NRSV, REB, TEV, TNT], 'doctrine' [LN (33.236), Lns; KJV, NJB], 'idea' [NLT]. This plural noun has a negative implication [NIGTC, WBC].

b. ποικίλος (LN 58.45) (BAGD 1.,3. p. 683): 'various' [BAGD, Mil, WBC], 'various kinds' [HNTC, LN], 'diversified' [LN], 'varied' [NASB], 'varicolored' [Lns], 'all kinds' [NAB, NIV, NRSV, TEV, TNT], 'any kind' [CEV], 'all sorts' [NIC; NJB, REB], 'divers' [KJV], not explicit [NLT]. It implies a variety of teachings [EBC, EGT, NIGTC, NTC] that are changing and unreliable [Hu], understood as false by their very variety [Lns], here with a negative sense [Hu]. The word is not intrinsically negative [TH]. This adjective strengthens the negative implication of διδαχαῖς 'teachings' [NIGTC].

c. ξένος (LN 28.34) (BAGD 1.a. p. 548): 'strange' [BAGD, HNTC, Lns, Mil, NIC, WBC; all versions except NLT, REB], 'strange, new' [NLT], 'outlandish' [REB], 'unknown' [LN]. It means that they were strange [EGT, Hu], of foreign origin [NTC, WBC], and contradictory to Christian truth [EGT, Hu, My, NIGTC, NTC, TH, TNTC, WBC]; it means that they were not well-known to the author [HNTC].

d. pres. pass. impera. of παραφέρω (LN **31.75**) (BAGD 2.b. p. 623): 'to be led astray' [**LN**; NJB], 'to be led away' [WBC], 'to be misled' [LN], 'to be fooled' [CEV], 'to be carried away' [BAGD, HNTC, Mil, NIC; NAB, NASB, NIV, NRSV, TNT], 'to be carried aside' [Lns], 'to be swept off (one's) course' [REB], 'to be carried about' [KJV], 'to be attracted' [NLT]. This passive verb is also translated actively: 'to lead from the right way' [TEV]. The prefixed preposition παρα- implies 'out of the proper course' [Alf]. The present tense with μή 'not' exhorts not to be carried off continuously, now or ever [Lns], or from time to time [WBC]; it implies a present danger [Wst] but that they were not yet being carried away [Lns]; it implies that some from time to time were being carried away [NTC], and that they should stop being carried away [Hu, Mil].

QUESTION—To what does the phrase διδαχαῖς ποικίλαις καὶ ξέναις 'teachings various and strange' refer?

It refers to teachings differing within themselves and all of them differing from the truth in Christ [Blm]; they include Judaizing teachings [Blm, Wst], the law of Moses in general as necessary for salvation [My]. They are connected with βρώματα 'foods' [ICC, Lg]; they are related to syncretistic gnostic ideas and possibly have Essene associations [NIC]. This phrase has negative implications [WBC]. It is emphatic by word order [Lns, WBC].

QUESTION—How are the two adjectives related in the phrase διδαχαῖς ποικίλαις καὶ ξέναις 'teachings various and strange'?

1. They are two distinct descriptions of διδαχαῖς 'teachings' [Alf, Hu, Lns, Mil, Wst; KJV, NASB]: various and strange teachings.
2. They form a hendiadys [NIGTC, WBC], combining into one description [EBC, HNTC, NIC, NIGTC, NTC, WBC; all versions except KJV, NASB]: all kinds of strange teachings.

for (it is) good (for) the heart[a] to-be-strengthened[b] by-grace,[c] not by-foods[d]

LEXICON—a. καρδία (LN 26.3): 'heart' [LN, Lns, Mil, NIC, WBC; KJV, NAB, NASB, NIV, NRSV], 'soul' [HNTC; TNT], 'inner self, mind' [LN], not explicit [CEV]. This noun is also translated as an adjective: 'inner' [NJB, REB, TEV], 'spiritual' [NLT]. This word refers to the human soul [Blm], the inner life as a whole [EBC, ICC, WBC], the center of one's religious life [GNC].

b. pres. pass. infin. of βεβαιόω (LN 28.44, 31.91) (BAGD 1. p. 138): 'to be strengthened' [BAGD, HNTC, Mil, NIC, WBC; NAB, NASB, NIV, NRSV], 'to receive strength' [CEV, TEV], 'to gain strength' [REB], 'to rely for strength' [NJB], 'to be made firm' [BAGD, Lns], 'to be confirmed' [LN (28.44)], 'to be established' [KJV], 'to be established in belief' [LN (31.91)]. This passive verb is also translated actively: 'to strengthen' [TNT]. The phrase βεβαιοῦσθαι τὴν καρδίαν 'the heart to be strengthened' is translated 'your strength comes from God' [NLT]. The present tense implies that the author is now making it firm [Lns].

c. χάρις (LN 88.66) (BAGD 3.b. p. 878): 'grace' [BAGD, HNTC, LN, Lns, Mil, NIC, WBC; KJV, NASB, NIV, NJB, NRSV], 'God's grace' [TEV, TNT], 'the grace of God' [NAB, REB], 'God's undeserved kindness' [CEV], 'God's special favor' [NLT]. It is God's grace [Alf, HNTC, NCBC, NIC, NTC, TH, TNTC, WBC].

d. βρῶμα (LN 5.1, 5.7) (BAGD 1. p. 148): 'food' [BAGD, LN (5.1), Mil, WBC; CEV, NAB, NASB], 'solid food' [LN (5.7)], 'ceremonial food' [NIV], 'prescribed food' [HNTC], 'meat' [Lns; KJV], 'ceremonial rules about food' [NLT], 'food regulations' [NIC], 'regulations about food' [NRSV, TNT], 'rules about food' [REB], 'by obeying rules about foods' [TEV]. This plural noun is also translated as a singular: 'food' [NJB]. It refers to solid food in contrast to milk [Mil].

QUESTION—Why is this clause mentioned?

It states the reason for holding to the true and simple teachings [Blm, Mil], for not being led astray [Lns, WBC]. It indicates that the human soul cannot be strengthened by material food [HNTC].

QUESTION—What relationship is indicated by the dative noun χάριτι 'grace'?

It is emphatic by word order [Lns, Wst] and forms a contrast with the following βρώμασιν 'foods' [Mil, NIGTC, TNTC].

1. It is instrumental [HNTC, Lns, Mil, NIC, WBC; NAB, NASB, NIV, NRSV]: by grace.
2. It is translated as source [REB, TEV]: from grace.

QUESTION—To what does βρώμασιν 'foods' refer?

It is a specific area of the strange teachings just mentioned above [Blm, My]. It is emphatic by word order [Lns].

1. It refers to actual foods [Alf, EBC, EGT, HNTC, Hu, ICC, Lns, Mil, My, NCBC, NTC, TNTC, WBC, Wst; KJV, NASB, NJB] It means 'foods' in general [KJV, NASB, NJB]. It refers to foods eaten or not eaten as a matter of conscience [Alf]. It means 'prescribed food' [HNTC], ceremonial food [EBC, NTC, WBC; NIV], sacrificial meals [EBC, EGT, ICC], Jewish cultic meals [WBC, Wst], pagan cult meals [ICC]. It refers to certain foods in a setting of Judaism [Hu], Jewish festival meals [Lns]. It refers to foods which were eaten (and the whole system of Jewish observances which were followed [Mil]) as a means of justification [Lg, Mil, My, NCBC].
2. It means 'regulations about food' [GNC, NIC, TH; NLT, NRSV, REB, TNT], possibly including sacrificial meals [NIC]: they have not been profited by regulations about food.
3. It means 'obeying rules about food' [TEV]: they have not been profited by obeying rules about food.

in[a] which the-(ones) walking[b] (have) not been-benefited.[c]

LEXICON—a. ἐν with dative object (LN 13.8, 89.5): 'in' [LN (13.8, 89.5)], 'in connection with' [Lns], 'through' [NASB], 'with' [WBC], 'with regard to' [LN (89.5)], 'from' [Mil]. This entire clause is translated 'which have not benefited those who observe them' [NRSV], 'which have never benefited those who observed them' [REB], 'which never helped anyone who followed them' [TNT], 'which have never brought any advantage to those who follow them' [NIC], 'which have not profited them that have been occupied therein' [KJV], 'which are useless to those who take them as a standard for living' [NAB], 'which are of no value to those who eat them' [NIV], 'those who obey these rules have not been helped by them' [TEV], 'those who have lived by them have not been benefited' [HNTC], 'which has done no good to those who concentrate on it' [NJB]. This preposition means here 'in the observance of' [Alf].

b. pres. act. participle of περιπατέω (LN 41.11) (BAGD 2.a.δ. p. 649): 'to walk, to conduct oneself' [BAGD], 'to walk about' [Lns], 'to live'

[BAGD, HNTC, LN], 'to go about doing, to behave' [LN], 'to be thus occupied' [NASB]. The phrase ἐν οἷς περιπατοῦντες 'in which walking' is translated 'to be occupied therein' [KJV], 'to be preoccupied with' [Mil], 'to observe them' [NRSV, REB], 'to follow them' [NIC; NLT, TNT], 'to concentrate on it' [NJB], 'to take them as a standard of living' [NAB], 'to obey these rules' [TEV], 'to eat them' [CEV, NIV]. The participial phrase οἱ περιπατοῦντες 'the ones walking' is translated 'their adherents' [WBC]. It implies continual preoccupation [Mil]. It refers to the people of God under the OT dispensation [Alf]; it refers to persons other than the readers [NTC].

c. aorist pass. indic. of ὠφελέω (LN 35.2) (BAGD 1.a. p. 900): 'to be benefited' [BAGD, Lns, WBC; NASB], 'to be aided' [BAGD], 'to be helped' [BAGD, LN; TEV]. The passive voice is also translated as an active voice: 'to help' [CEV, NLT, TNT], 'to benefit' [HNTC; NRSV, REB], 'to profit' [KJV], 'to derive benefit' [Mil], 'to bring an advantage' [NIC], 'to do good' [NJB], 'to be of value' [NIV], 'to be useful' [NAB].

QUESTION—How is this clause related to the preceding clause?

1. It is nonrestrictive, making a further statement concerning βρώμασιν 'foods' [HNTC, Mil, NIC, WBC; all versions except NAB]: . . . foods, they have not profited. It implies the reason why the heart is not strengthened by foods [Mil].
2. It is restrictive, identifying which foods are being referred to [Lns; NAB]: foods which have not profited.

QUESTION—What is the prepositional phrase ἐν οἷς 'in which' connected with?

Its antecedent is βρώμασιν 'foods' [Mil, NIGTC, Wst]: by foods.

1. It is connected with οἱ περιπατοῦντες 'the ones walking' [Alf, ICC, Lg(K), Mil, My, NCBC, NIC, TH, TNTC, WBC, Wst]: the ones walking in which/in them.
2. It is connected with ὠφελήθησαν 'have not been profited' [Lns]: they have not been profited in them.
3. It is connected with both of the above [NIGTC]: foods by which those whose manner of life centers on them are not profited.

DISCOURSE UNIT:13:10–16 [GNC, TNTC]. The topic is Christ's sacrifice and Christians' spiritual sacrifices [GNC], concerning the Christians' new altar [TNTC].

13:10 We-have an altar[a] from[b] which the-(ones) serving[c] the tabernacle[d] (do) not have authority[e] to-eat.

LEXICON—a. θυσιαστήριον (LN 6.114) (BAGD 2.d. p. 367): 'altar' [BAGD, HNTC, LN, Mil, NIC, WBC; all versions], 'altar of sacrifice' [Lns].

b. ἐκ with genitive object (LN 90.16) (BAGD 1.a. p. 234): 'from' [BAGD, HNTC, LN, Lns, Mil, NIC, WBC; all versions except CEV, KJV, TEV], 'out of' [BAGD]. The phrase ἐξ οὗ 'from which' is translated 'whereof' [KJV], 'where' [CEV]. Its sense is partitive, 'a part of which' [ICC].

c. pres. act. participle of λατρεύω (LN 53.14) (BAGD p. 467): 'to serve' [BAGD, HNTC, Lns, Mil, WBC; KJV, NAB, NASB, NJB], 'to minister at' [NIV], 'to officiate in' [NRSV, TNT], 'to perform religious rites' [LN], 'to worship' [LN], 'to carry out the worship in' [NIC]. The participial phrase οἱ λατρεύοντες 'the ones serving' is translated 'the priests' [NLT, REB], 'the priests who serve in' [CEV, TEV].

d. σκηνή (LN 7.17) (BAGD p. 754): 'tabernacle' [Mil, WBC; KJV, NAB, NASB, NIV], 'Tabernacle' [BAGD, Lns], 'tabernacle tent' [LN], 'Temple' [NLT], 'Tent of Testimony' [BAGD], 'Tent' [HNTC; NJB], 'sacred tent' [REB], 'tent' [LN, NIC; NRSV, TNT], 'the place of worship' [CEV], 'Jewish place of worship' [TEV]. It refers to the Jewish tabernacle [Alf].

e. ἐξουσία (LN 76.12) (BAGD 1. p. 277): 'authority' [Lns], 'right' [BAGD, HNTC, Mil, NIC, WBC; all versions], 'power' [LN].

QUESTION—How is this verse connected with the preceding clause?

The mention of 'foods' in 13:9 leads to a contrast between the levitical service and the Christian faith and worship [NIGTC]. It expresses a contrast with the preceding verse [Mil, NCBC]. It contrasts the Jewish place of worship with the altar of the Christians, but also implies a contrast with food rules and the Christians sacrifice of praise (13:15) and doing good (13:16) [TH]. It states the grounds for the comment regarding οὐ βρώμασιν 'not foods' in the preceding verse [My].

QUESTION—What is implied by this verse?

1. It implies that Christians do eat (figuratively [Hu, NIGTC]) from their altar [My]—i.e., share in Christ's sacrifice, [Alf, Blm, HNTC, Hu, NIC, WBC, Wst], share in the benefits of Christ's sacrifice [GNC, Lg, My] and communion with Christ [Lg]; it emphasizes that Judaism and Christianity are incompatible [My, NIGTC].
2. It implies that the Christian sacrifice does not involve eating [Hwt, ICC, Lns, Mil, TH].

QUESTION—What is indicated by the position of ἔχομεν 'we have'?

It is emphatic by word order [NIGTC, WBC], perhaps reminding the readers of their present possession of blessings [NIGTC]; it implies a contrast with what some others do not have [Wst]. The phrase ἔχομεν θυσιαστήριον 'we have an altar' is emphatic and states the important point of the passage [WBC].

QUESTION—To what does θυσιαστήριον 'altar' refer?

1. It is the cross on which Christ died [Alf, EBC, Hu, Hwt, Lg, My, NTC, Wst], referring to Christ's sacrifice there [Hu, Hwt, Mil, NIC, NIGTC, WBC, Wst]. This word is not emphatic here [Alf].
2. It refers to Christ who died on the cross of Calvary [HNTC].
3. It refers to the benefits received by those who serve Christ [TNTC].

QUESTION—What relationship is indicated by the relative clause introduced by ἐξ οὗ 'from which'?

1. It is nonrestrictive, not identifying the altar but making a comment about it [Mil (comment); KJV, NASB]: we have an altar; from it . . .
2. It is restrictive, identifying the altar [HNTC, Lns, Mil, WBC; NAB, NIV, NRSV, TNT]: we have an altar from which . . .

QUESTION—To whom does οἱ τῇ σκηνῇ λατρεύοντες 'the ones serving the tabernacle' refer?

1. It refers to the Jewish priesthood [Alf, Blm, GNC, Hu, Lns, Mil, NIGTC, TH, WBC, Wst] and worshipers [Alf, Blm, HNTC, NIGTC, WBC], to Jewish worshipers in general [EBC, Hwt, My, NCBC, NIC, NTC, TNTC], to either the priests or the worshipers in general [ICC, Lg].
2. It refers to Christian worshipers; the Christian sacrifice is not eaten [EGT].

QUESTION—What is meant by τῇ σκηνῇ 'the tabernacle'?

1. It means to serve the tabernacle [Alf, EGT, HNTC, Lns, My, NTC, WBC; KJV, NAB, NASB, NJB].
2. It means to serve in the tabernacle [EBC, NIC; NIV, NRSV, TEV, TNT].

QUESTION—What relationship is indicated by the word order of φαγεῖν 'to eat'?

It is emphatic by its word order [ICC, WBC].

13:11 For of-which animals[a] the blood for[b] sin is-brought-into into[c] the sanctuary[d] through[e] the high-priest,

TEXT—The phrase περὶ ἁμαρτίας 'for sin' is omitted by some manuscripts. GNT does not deal with this variant. Only Alf and My omit this phrase.

LEXICON—a. ζῷον (LN **4.2**) (BAGD 2. p. 341): 'animal' [BAGD, HNTC, **LN**, Lns, Mil, NIC, WBC; all versions except KJV], 'beast' [KJV], 'living creature' [LN].

b. περί with genitive object (LN 89.6) (BAGD 1.g. p. 645): 'for' [Lns, WBC; KJV], 'concerning, with regard to, in relation to' [LN], 'to take away, to atone for' [BAGD]. The phrase περὶ ἁμαρτίας 'for sin' is translated 'as a sin offering' [NIC; CEV, NAB, NIV, REB], 'as an offering for sin' [HNTC; NASB, TNT], 'as a sacrifice for sin' [NLT, NRSV], 'as a sacrifice for sins' [TEV], 'to take away sin, to atone for sin' [Mil], 'for the rite of expiation' [NJB]. This prepositional phrase expresses the purpose of the verb εἰσφέρεται 'is brought into' [Mil].

c. εἰς with accusative object (LN 84.22): 'into' [HNTC, LN, Lns, Mil, NIC, WBC; all versions except CEV], not explicit [CEV].

d. ἅγιος (LN 7.18, 7.35, 88.24) (BAGD 2.b. p. 10): 'holy' [LN (88.24)]. The neuter plural noun ἅγια is translated 'sanctuary' [BAGD, HNTC, LN (7.18), Mil; KJV, NAB, NJB, NRSV, REB, TNT], 'Sanctuary' [Lns], 'holy place' [LN (7.35), NIC; NASB], 'Holy Place' [LN (7.35); NLT], 'Most Holy Place' [WBC; NIV, TEV], not explicit [CEV]. Τὰ ἅγια here refers to the Holy of Holies [Alf, GNC, My, NIGTC].

e. διά with genitive object (LN 90.4): 'through' [LN], 'by' [HNTC, LN, Lns, Mil, NIC, WBC; KJV, NAB, NASB, NJB, NRSV, REB], not explicit [CEV, NLT]. Here it implies agency [Mil, WBC, Wst], 'acting for' the people or for God [Lg(K)].

QUESTION—Why is this verse mentioned?

It has a loose connection with the preceding verse [NIGTC]. It leads from a general principle to the specific example, the Day of Atonement ceremony [EBC]; it connects Jesus' sacrifice with that sin-offering [HNTC]. It states the proof of the privileges of Christians [Wst]; it (with the following verse, which contains the principal point [My]) gives the grounds of the preceding verse [Lg, Mil, My, WBC]; it states the reason why those who serve the tabernacle could not eat from the Christians' altar [Alf, Lns, WBC], namely, because the sin-offering was not eaten [Alf, Lns]; thus neither do Christians literally partake of Christ's body [Hwt, ICC, Lns].

QUESTION—What relationship is indicated by this relative clause?

1. It is restrictive, identifying the animals referred to [HNTC, Mil, NIC; NAB, NASB, NJB, NRSV, REB]: the animals whose blood . . .
2. It is nonrestrictive, making a comment about the animals [EGT; KJV]: the animals, whose blood . . .

QUESTION—What does the relative pronoun ὧν 'of which' modify?

It modifies ζῴων 'animals' [NIGTC]: of which animals.

QUESTION—What does the present tense of εἰσφέρεται 'is brought into' indicate?

It is a timeless present [NIGTC]: is (at whatever time) brought into. It is used because the OT is still available [TH].

of-these the bodies are-burned[a] outside[b] the camp.

LEXICON—a. pres. pass. indic. of κατακαίω (LN 14.66) (BAGD p. 411): 'to be burned' [HNTC, LN, Lns, NIC, WBC; all versions], 'to be entirely burned' [Mil], 'to be burned up' [BAGD, LN], 'to be consumed' [BAGD]. The prefixed preposition κατα- emphasizes burning completely [NTC].

b. ἔξω with genitive object (LN 83.20) (BAGD 2.a. p. 279): 'outside' [BAGD, HNTC, LN, Mil, NIC, WBC; all versions except KJV], 'outside of' [Lns], 'without' [KJV].

QUESTION—What is implied by the word order of τούτων 'of these'?

It is emphatic by word order [WBC, Wst].

1. It is inserted to make clear that this clause refers to ζῴων 'animals' in the preceding clause [NIGTC]: of the animals . . . of these animals.
2. Its position emphasizes the fact that the bodies of these animals are burned entirely [Mil]: it is *these* animals whose bodies are burned.
3. Its emphatic use places the weight of the construction on its clause [WBC].

QUESTION—What relationship is indicated by the use of ἔξω τῆς παρεμβολῆς 'outside the camp'?

It is emphatic by its final position [NIGTC].

1. It refers to the time of the wilderness wanderings of the Israelites [Alf, EBC, GNC, Lg(K), My, NIGTC, TH].
2. It represents the Jewish community in general [Mil].

13:12 Wherefore Jesus also, in-order-that he-might-sanctify[a] the people[b] through[c] his-own blood, suffered[d] outside[e] the gate.[f]

LEXICON—a. aorist act. subj. of ἁγιάζω (LN 88.26) (BAGD 2. p. 8): 'to sanctify' [BAGD, Lns, Mil, NIC; KJV, NAB, NASB, NJB, NRSV], 'to make holy' [LN, Mil; CEV, NIV, NLT, TNT], 'to purify from sin' [TEV], 'to consecrate' [HNTC, WBC; REB]. It means to set aside for God [EBC] and make acceptable to God through being cleansed from guilt [Hu], cleansed in conscience [NIC]; it means to cleanse from sin [GNC] or make atonement [GNC], to equip the people to worship God acceptably [NIGTC], to make them fit to enter God's presence [TH, WBC].

b. λαός (LN 11.12): 'people' [HNTC, Lns, Mil, NIC, WBC; all versions except NLT], 'his people' [NLT], 'people of God, God's people' [LN]. It refers here to God's people [EBC, NTC, TH], the true Israel [Wst], the people of the new covenant [GNC].

c. διά with genitive object (LN 89.76): 'through' [LN, Mil, WBC; NASB, NIV], 'by' [HNTC; NAB, NLT, NRSV, REB, TNT], 'by means of' [Lns, NIC], 'with' [KJV, NJB, TEV], not explicit [CEV].

d. aorist act. indic. of πάσχω (LN 24.78) (BAGD 3.a.β. p. 634): 'to suffer' [BAGD, HNTC, LN, Lns, Mil, NIC; all versions except NAB, NLT, TEV], 'to suffer and die' [NLT], 'to suffer death' [WBC], 'to die' [NAB, TEV]. It implies death [NIC, NIGTC, TH, WBC]. By this word the author emphasizes the humanity of Jesus [HNTC].

e. ἔξω with genitive object: 'outside'. See b. in the preceding clause.

f. πύλη (LN 7.48) (BAGD 1. p. 729): 'gate' [BAGD, HNTC, LN, Lns, Mil, NIC; KJV, NAB, NASB, NJB, REB, TNT], 'city gate' [WBC; CEV, NIV, NLT, NRSV], 'city' [TEV]. It refers to the gate of Jerusalem [Mil, My, NIGTC]. It is figurative, meaning 'outside of Judaism' [Mil].

QUESTION—What is the function of this verse?

It states the conclusion (result [NIGTC]) from the preceding comment [Alf, EBC, Mil, My, NCBC, NIC, NTC]; that is, the fact that Jesus is the antitype of the sin-offering of the Day of Atonement [Alf, EBC, My]. In addition, καί 'also' introduces a comparison with the preceding comment [Mil].

QUESTION—What is indicated by the use of the personal name 'Jesus'?

It points to Jesus in his humanity as he suffered for us [EBC, WBC, Wst]. It is emphatic [NIGTC, WBC], and is given without an accompanying title in this reference to his humiliation [NIGTC].

QUESTION—Why is the clause introduced by ἵνα 'in order that' mentioned?

It states the purpose of Jesus' suffering [EBC, Mil].

QUESTION—What relationship is indicated by the prepositional phrase διὰ τοῦ ἰδίου αἵματος 'through his own blood'?

It expresses means [EBC, NIC], agency [NIGTC], contrasting with the preceding reference to animals' blood [TH]. It emphasizes the fact that Christ did not need a sacrificial victim, since he himself was the sacrifice [EBC, Mil, My] (as indicated by ἰδίου 'his own' [My], which is emphatic [TH]) and the officiating priest [Mil, WBC]. 'Blood' refers to death here [EBC].

QUESTION—What relationship is indicated by the prepositional phrase ἔξω τῆς πύλης 'outside the gate'?

It makes a comparison between Jesus' death and the sin-offering on the Day of Atonement [Blm, EBC, GNC, HNTC, Lg(K), WBC], and also implies the rejection of Jesus by the Jewish authorities [EBC], by the Jewish people [WBC]. It implies being outcast and condemned as a criminal [EGT, WBC].

13:13 Therefore let-us-go-out to[a] him outside[b] the camp bearing[c] his reproach;[d]

LEXICON—a. πρός with accusative object (LN 84.18): 'to' [HNTC, LN, Lns, Mil, NIC, WBC; all versions except KJV], 'unto' [KJV].

b. ἔξω with genitive object: 'outside'. See this word in the preceding verse.

c. pres. act. participle of φέρω (LN 15.187, 25.176, **90.64**) (BAGD 1.c. p. 855): 'to bear' [HNTC, LN, Lns, Mil, NIC, WBC; all versions except CEV, TEV, TNT], 'to bear patiently' [BAGD], 'to carry' [LN (15.187)], 'to experience' [LN (**90.64**)], 'to undergo' [LN (90.64)], 'to endure, to put up with' [BAGD, LN (25.176)], 'to share' [CEV, TEV, TNT]. It means to put up with something unpleasant [NIGTC].

d. ὀνειδισμός (LN 33.389) (BAGD p. 570): 'reproach' [BAGD, HNTC, Lns, Mil; KJV, NASB], 'insult' [LN; NAB], 'abuse' [NRSV], 'disgrace' [WBC; CEV, NIV, NLT, TNT], 'stigma' [NIC; REB], 'shame' [TEV], 'humiliation' [NJB]. This word refers here to Christ's cross [Blm].

QUESTION—Why is this clause mentioned?

The introductory word τοίνυν is emphatic by its position [TH]. It implies that the exhortation it introduces is a logical conclusion from what precedes [TNTC]. This verse is the heart of the conclusion the author is drawing [TNTC].

1. It states the conclusion drawn from the preceding comments [My, NCBC, NTC, WBC].
2. It makes a comparison between the situation of Christ in his humiliation and the situation which the readers are urged to accept [NIGTC].
3. It states a change from references to history to an exhortation for action [TH].

QUESTION—What is meant by ἐξερχώμεθα πρὸς αὐτόν 'let us go out to him'?

The present tense implies immediate effort [Wst], repeated actions, whenever the readers are required to bear the reproach of Jesus [Lns]. By using the first person plural the author includes himself [Lns, NIGTC, TH].

1. It means to come out from Judaism and the Old Covenant [My, NIGTC, TNTC, WBC].
2. It means to come to the same mind as that which Christ had in his sufferings, to think on his sufferings for us, and to be prepared to endure whatever we may suffer for his sake [Blm].

QUESTION—What is indicated by the repeated ἐξ 'out' in the two words ἐξερχώμεθα . . . ἔξω 'let us go out outside'?

It emphasizes the idea of going 'outside' [EBC].

QUESTION—To what does ἔξω τῆς παρεμβολῆς 'outside the camp' refer?

The three-fold use of the phrase 'outside the camp/gate' makes it emphatic [Mil]; it ties together verses 11–13 [WBC].

1. It refers to leaving Judaism [EBC, GNC, HNTC, Hu, Hwt, Lg, Mil, NIC, TNTC, Wst]: outside of Judaism. It also refers to separating themselves from the sinful values of un-Christian society [Hu].
2. It means going to Jesus, who had been rejected by Judaism and was 'outside the camp' [NIC, WBC].
3. It implies living an unsettled and insulted life [ICC].

QUESTION—What relationship is indicated by the participle φέροντες 'bearing'?

It expresses an action accompanying the action of the verb [Mil; NJB, NRSV, TEV, TNT]: let us go forth . . . and let us bear his reproach.

QUESTION—What is meant by τὸν ὀνειδισμὸν αὐτοῦ φέροντες 'bearing his reproach'?

1. It means to be prepared to suffer the same kind of abuse that Christ suffered [GNC, Hwt, TNTC, WBC].
2. It means to share the shame that Christ bore [Hu, NTC] which resulted from the manner of his death [TH].
3. It means to share the rejection which Christ experienced [EBC].
4. It means to share in the shame of being associated with the crucified Christ [Mil, NIGTC] and to bear humiliation in the way that Jesus bore it [NIGTC].

QUESTION—How are the noun and pronoun related in the genitive construction τὸν ὀνειδισμὸν αὐτοῦ 'his reproach'?

1. The genitive pronoun αὐτοῦ 'his' tells who bore the reproach [EBC, Lns, Mil (translation), WBC; NAB, NIV, NRSV, REB]: he bore the reproach. It is emphatic by its position [WBC].
2. The genitive pronoun αὐτοῦ 'his' is possessive [Mil (discussion)]; it tells to whom the reproach was attached [NIC].

13:14 for we-have not here (a) remaining[a] city, but we-seek-for[b] the-(one) coming.[c]

LEXICON—a. pres. act. participle of μένω (LN 13.89) (BAGD 1.c.β. p. 504): 'to remain, to continue to exist, to be still in existence' [LN], 'to continue' [LN, Lns, Mil; KJV], 'to endure' [NIV], 'to last' [HNTC; NAB, NASB, NRSV, REB], 'to last forever' [CEV]. This participle is also translated as an adjective: 'permanent' [BAGD, NIC, WBC; NJB, TEV, TNT]. The phrase οὐ...ἔχομεν μένουσαν πόλιν 'we have not a remaining city' is translated 'this world is not our home' [NLT].

b. pres. act. indic. of ἐπιζητέω (LN 25.9, 27.42) (BAGD 2.a. p. 292): 'to seek for' [HNTC, Mil], 'to seek' [LN (27.42), Lns; KJV, NAB, NASB], 'to be a seeker' [REB], 'to search for' [LN (27.42)], 'to look for' [NIC; NIV, NJB, NRSV, TEV, TNT], 'to look forward to' [NLT], 'to desire' [LN (25.9)], 'to wish for' [BAGD], 'to expect intently' [WBC], 'to wait for' [CEV]. It implies earnest endeavor [EBC], striving for something which is at present unobtainable [TH]. The prepositional prefix ἐπι- intensifies the verb [NIGTC]. The present tense indicates an habitual attitude [WBC].

c. pres. act. participle of μέλλω (LN 67.62) (BAGD 2. p. 501): 'to come' [BAGD, HNTC, NIC, WBC; all versions except CEV, NJB, TNT], 'to be about to' [LN], 'to be yet to be' [NJB], 'to be about to come' [Lns], 'to be yet to come' [TNT]. This participle is also translated as an adjective: 'future' [BAGD, Mil]; as a phrase: 'for such a city' [CEV]. It implies the future [TH].

QUESTION—Why is this clause mentioned?

It states (reinforces [EBC]) the reason for going out to Christ [Alf, EBC, My(D), WBC], for being prepared to suffer for Christ's sake [Blm], for being willing to bear Christ's reproach [Hwt, My, WBC]. It states a central theme of this epistle [NIGTC].

QUESTION—To whom does ἔχομεν 'we have' refer?

It refers to Christians [My, NIGTC].

QUESTION—What relationship is indicated by ὧδε 'here' ?

It refers to a place [Alf], meaning 'here on earth' [EBC, Hwt, LN (83.1), Mil, My, NIGTC, WBC, Wst; CEV, NLT], the present world order [Hu, ICC].

QUESTION—What relationship is indicated by ἀλλά 'but'?

It indicates an antithesis between the two concepts expressed by ἔχομεν 'we have' and ἐπιζητοῦμεν 'we seek for' [NIGTC].

QUESTION—What relationship is indicated by the participial phrase τὴν μέλλουσαν 'the one coming'?

It modifies πόλιν 'city', understood from the preceding phrase [Alf, Hu, Hwt, Lg(K), NIC, NIGTC, NTC, WBC; all versions]: the coming city. It is the heavenly city [EBC, NIC], heavenly Jerusalem [Alf, Blm, EGT, GNC, WBC]. The definite article implies that τὴν μέλλουσαν 'the coming (city)' was well-known to the readers [NIGTC].

1. With the definite article it is definite [Alf, Hu, Hwt, Lg(K), Lns, Mil(translation), NIC, WBC, Wst; all versions except KJV, NAB]: the city which is to come.
2. The definite article is not translated [HNTC, Mil (commentary); KJV, NAB]: a city which is to come.

DISCOURSE UNIT: 13:15–19 (NASB). The topic is sacrifices that please God.

13:15 Through[a] him therefore let-us-offer-up (a) sacrifice[b] of-praise through[c] all (time) to-God,

TEXT—Some manuscripts omit οὖν 'therefore'. GNT includes this word in brackets with a C decision, indicating that the committee had difficulty in making the decision. This word is omitted by CEV, NAB, NJB, NLT, and REB, but it is not clear whether the omission is because of the manuscript omission or is merely stylistic.

LEXICON—a. διά with genitive object (LN 90.4): 'through' [HNTC, LN, Lns, Mil, NIC, WBC; all versions except CEV, KJV, NLT], 'by' [KJV], not explicit [CEV]. The phrase δι' αὐτοῦ 'through him' is translated 'with Jesus' help' [NLT], 'in the name of Jesus' [CEV]. It expresses agency [Mil], mediation [NIGTC, WBC]. This prepositional phrase is emphatic by forefronting [Alf, EBC, EGT, Hu, Hwt, My, NIGTC, NTC, TH, WBC, Wst]; it is linked with this entire phrase [TH].

b. θυσία (LN 53.20) (BAGD 2.b. p. 366): 'sacrifice' [BAGD, HNTC, LN, Lns, Mil, NIC, WBC; all versions], 'offering' [BAGD]; the phrase θυσίαν αἰνέσεως 'sacrifice of praise' is translated 'praise-offering' [BAGD]. This noun without a definite article is translated 'the sacrifice' [KJV], 'our sacrifice' [TNT].

c. διά with genitive object (LN 67.86, 67.140) (BAGD A.II.1.a. p. 179): 'through', 'throughout' [LN (67.140)]. The phrase διὰ παντός 'through all' is translated 'always' [BAGD, LN (67.86); TEV], 'constantly' [BAGD, LN (67.86), Lns], 'continually' [BAGD, HNTC, LN (67.86), Mil, NIC, WBC; KJV, NAB, NASB, NIV, NLT, NRSV, REB], 'unending' [NJB], 'never cease' [TNT], 'keep (offering)' [CEV]. This phrase means throughout life [Alf], under all circumstances [EBC, Hu], continually [EGT, Hu, Hwt, My, NTC, TNTC, Wst].

QUESTION—What relationship is indicated by οὖν 'therefore'?

It indicates a conclusion from the preceding argument [Mil], from verses 8–14 [My], from verses 10–14 [Alf], from the whole argument, especially verses 10–12 [Blm].

QUESTION—To whom does αὐτοῦ 'him' refer?

It refers to Jesus [Alf, Blm, EBC, GNC, HNTC, Hu, Hwt, ICC, Mil, My, NCBC, NIC, NIGTC, TNTC, WBC, Wst; NIV, REB, TEV, TNT]: through Jesus.

QUESTION—What is indicated by the present tense of the verb ἀναφέρωμεν 'let us offer up'?

It indicates continuing action [Lg(K)]: let us be offering up.

QUESTION—How are the two nouns related in the genitive construction θυσίαν αἰνέσεως 'sacrifice of praise'?

The genitive noun αἰνέσεως 'praise' identifies the sacrifice [EBC, NIGTC, WBC; CEV, TEV]: a sacrifice, which is praise. This phrase is the term for a thank-offering in the OT law [Alf, Lg].

this is, fruit[a] of-lips confessing[b] his name.

LEXICON—a. κάρπος (LN 3.33, 42.13, 43.15) (BAGD 2.c. p. 405): 'fruit' [BAGD, LN (3.33, 43.15), Lns], 'harvest' [LN (43.15)], 'activity' [LN (42.13)]. This noun with no definite article is translated as a definite noun, 'the fruit' [HNTC, Mil, NIC, WBC; KJV, NAB, NASB, NIV, NJB, NRSV], 'the offering' [TEV], 'the tribute' [REB], not explicit [CEV, NLT]. The phrase τοῦτ' ἔστιν καρπὸν χειλέων 'this is, fruit of lips' is translated 'praise that springs from lips' [TNT].

b. pres. act. participle of ὁμολογέω (LN 33.221) (BAGD 5. p. 568): 'to confess' [HNTC, LN (33.274), Lns; NIV, NRSV, TEV], 'to confess thankfully' [Mil], 'to declare' [LN (33.74)], 'to acknowledge' [NIC; NAB, NJB, REB, TNT], 'to praise' [BAGD, WBC], 'to give thanks' [KJV, NASB], 'to proclaim the glory of' [NLT]. The phrase ὁμολογούντων τῷ ὀνόματι αὐτοῦ 'confessing his name' is translated 'in the name of Jesus' [CEV]. It means to praise [NIGTC].

QUESTION—Why is this phrase included?

It explains what is meant by the preceding phrase, θυσίαν αἰνέσεως 'sacrifice of praise' [Blm, EGT, Hu, ICC, Mil, My, NIC, NIGTC, NTC, WBC].

QUESTION—How are the two nouns related in the genitive construction καρπὸν χειλέων 'fruit of lips'?

The genitive noun χειλέων 'lips' tells what is offering (what is the source of [TNTC; TNT]) the 'fruit' [Lg(K), TH, TNTC; TEV, TNT]: fruit offered by lips. This phrase is a figure implying 'speech' [WBC].

QUESTION—What relationship is indicated by the participle ὁμολογούντων 'confessing'?

1. It is attributive [HNTC, Mil, My, NIC, WBC; all versions except KJV].

1.1 It modifies χειλέων 'lips' [HNTC, Mil, My, NIC, NTC, WBC; all versions except KJV, NJB]: lips that confess his name.

1.2 It modifies 'of those' understood [NJB]: lips of those who confess his name.

2. Since neither the noun nor the participle have a definite article, it could be a predicate usage, stating what the lips are doing (Alf, Blm, EGT, KJV may imply this meaning by translating simply as a participle): fruit of lips, (and they are) confessing his name.

QUESTION—What relationship is indicated by the phrase ὁμολογούντωντῷ ὀνόματι αὐτοῦ 'confessing his name'?

It means to acknowledge him as Lord [TEV].

QUESTION—What relationship is indicated by τῷ ὀνόματι αὐτοῦ 'his name'?

It refers to God's revealed personality [ICC, Lns], revealed in Jesus [Lns]; it refers to God's nature, hence to God himself [TH].

QUESTION—To whom does αὐτοῦ 'his' refer?

It refers to God [Alf, Lg, Lns, Mil, My, NIGTC, TH]: God's name.

13:16 And the doing-good[a] and sharing[b] forget[c] not;

LEXICON—a. εὐποιΐα (LN **88.7**) (BAGD 1. p. 324): 'doing good' [Lns; NASB], '(the) doing of good' [BAGD], 'good works' [NJB], 'good deeds' [NAB], 'acts of kindness' [WBC]. This noun is also translated as a verb: 'to do good' [HNTC, LN, Mil; KJV, NIV, NLT, NRSV, TEV], 'to be kind' [TNT], 'to do deeds of kindness' [NIC], 'to show kindness' [REB], 'to help' [CEV]. It refers to acts of kindness [WBC].

b. κοινωνία (LN 34.5, 57.98) (BAGD 2. p. 439): 'sharing' [LN (57.98); NASB], 'sharing (one's) resources' [NJB], 'generosity' [BAGD, WBC; NAB], 'fellow-feeling, altruism' [BAGD], 'fellowship' [LN (34.5), Lns]. This noun is also translated as a verb phrase: 'to share' [HNTC], 'to share with others' [NIV, TNT], 'to share what one has' [NLT, NRSV], 'to share what one has with others' [NIC; REB], 'to share one's possessions with others' [Mil; CEV], 'to help one another' [TEV], 'to communicate' [KJV]. It means sharing one's means with needy persons [Alf, Hu, Hwt, ICC, Lg, Mil, My, Wst], with needy Christians [WBC]. This term has nearly the same meaning as the preceding εὐποιΐας 'doing good' [NIGTC], but strengthens it [Blm], describes it [NTC, TH], clarifies it [WBC], is more specific [EBC, TNTC], forms virtually a hendiadys with it [NIGTC]. The two nouns are combined in thought under one definite article [Lns, Wst]. It means faithful fellowship, communion of hearts [Lns].

c. pres. mid. (deponent = act.) of ἐπιλανθάνομαι (LN 29.14, 29.17) (BAGD 2. p. 295): 'to forget' [HNTC, LN (29.14, 29.17), Lns, Mil, NIC; CEV, KJV, NIV, NLT, TEV, TNT], 'to neglect' [BAGD, LN (29.17), WBC; NAB, NASB, NRSV, REB], 'to overlook' [BAGD, LN (29.17)]. The phrase μὴ ἐπιλανθάνεσθε 'neglect not' is translated 'keep doing' [NJB] and is a litotes, implying an emphatic 'be remembering' [Lns, Mil].

QUESTION—What relationship is indicated by δέ 'but/and'?

It introduces an additional coordinate necessity [Mil], the necessity of praising God with one's life in addition to praising him with one's lips [Alf]; it introduces two additional examples of Christians' sacrifices [EBC].

for with-such[a] sacrifices God is-well-pleased.[b]

LEXICON—a. τοιοῦτος (LN 64.2, 92.31) (BAGD 2.a.β. p. 821): 'such' [BAGD, LN (64.2), Lns, WBC; KJV, NASB, NIV, NLT, NRSV, REB], 'such as these' [Mil], 'like that' [LN (64.2)], 'of such a kind, of this kind'

[LN (92.31)], 'of that kind' [NAB], 'these are' [HNTC; NJB, TEV, TNT], 'this is like' [CEV]. It refers to the preceding εὐποιΐας 'doing good' and κοινωνίας 'sharing' [My, Wst].

b. pres. pass. indic. of εὐαρεστέω (LN 25.93) (BAGD 2.b. p. 318): 'to be well-pleased' [Lns, Mil; KJV], 'to be pleased' [HNTC, LN, WBC; NAB, NASB, NIV], 'to be satisfied' [BAGD]. The passive voice is also translated as active with sacrifices as the subject: 'to please' [CEV, NJB, TEV, TNT], 'to be pleasing to' [NLT, NRSV], 'to give pleasure to' [NIC]; with God as the subject: 'to be pleased' [HNTC], 'to approve' [REB].

QUESTION—What relationship is indicated by γάρ 'for'?

It indicates the grounds for the two preceding exhortations [Mil].

QUESTION—What relationship is indicated by the dative phrase τοιαύταις θυσίαις 'with such sacrifices'?

1. It indicates means [NAB, NJB, NRSV, TEV, TNT]: by means of such sacrifices.
2. It indicates reason [NIGTC, NTC, WBC]: because of such sacrifices.
3. It expresses the basis [HNTC, Lns, Mil; KJV, NASB, NIV]: with such sacrifices.

QUESTION—What is the significance of the final position of ὁ θεός 'God'?

It is emphatic [NTC].

DISCOURSE UNIT: 13:17–25 (TNTC). The topic is final words.

DISCOURSE UNIT: 13:17–19 (GNC, HNTC, NCBC; NJB). The topic is obedience to church leaders [GNC; NJB] and a request for prayer [GNC], respect for authority [HNTC], respect for leadership [NCBC].

DISCOURSE UNIT: 13:17 (EBC, NIC). The topic is Christian obedience [EBC], submission to guides [NIC].

13:17 Obey the-(ones) leading[a] you and submit,[b]

LEXICON—a. pres. mid. (deponent = act.) participle of ἡγέομαι (LN 36.1, 37.58) (BAGD 1. p. 343): 'to lead' [BAGD, Lns], 'to guide' [BAGD], 'to take the lead' [LN (36.1)], 'to have the rule over' [KJV], 'to rule over, to govern' [LN (37.58)]. The phrase τοῖς ἡγουμένοις 'the ones leading' is translated 'master' [LN (36.1)], 'leader' [HNTC, LN (36.1), Mil, WBC; all versions except KJV, NLT], 'spiritual leader' [NLT], 'guide' [NIC]. It refers to current leaders [EBC, EGT, GNC, Hu, Hwt, Mil, NCBC, NIGTC, TH].

b. pres. act. impera. of ὑπείκω (LN **36.18**) (BAGD p. 838): 'to submit' [BAGD, HNTC, LN, Lns, Mil, NIC, WBC; KJV, NASB, NIV, NRSV, REB], 'to give way' [NJB], 'to follow one's orders' [TEV], 'to do what one says' [CEV, NLT, TNT]. It implies yielding trustfully [EGT], yielding when the leaders' rule is at variance with the readers' will [Alf, Lns], being submissive to the wishes of the leaders [Wst]. It is a stronger (more specific [TH]) word than the preceding πείθω 'obey' [NIGTC, TH], but refers to the same activity [TH].

QUESTION—What is meant by the verb πείθεσθε 'obey'?

It refers to obeying specific injunctions [Wst]. The present tense implies habitual action [WBC]: regularly obey.

QUESTION—What is the implied predicate of the verb ὑπείκετε 'submit'?

1. A direct object is implied [LN; KJV]: submit yourselves.
2. An indirect object is implied [EBC, GNC, HNTC, Hwt, Mil, My, NIC, WBC; all versions except KJV].
2.1 Submit to them [EBC, HNTC, My, NIC; NAB, NASB, NJB, NRSV].
2.2 Submit to their authority [GNC, Hwt, Mil, WBC; NIV, REB, TEV, TNT].

for they-themselves watch[a] over[b] your souls[c] as[d] going-to-render[e] (an) account,[f]

LEXICON—a. pres. act. indic. of ἀγρυπνέω (LN **35.41**) (BAGD 2. p. 14): 'to watch' [Lns, Mil; CEV, KJV, NJB, NLT], 'to keep watch' [WBC], 'to keep watch (over)' [BAGD, NIC; NAB, NASB, NIV, NRSV], 'to watch without resting' [TEV], 'to care for' [BAGD, **LN**], 'to take care day and night' [TNT], 'to take care of, to look after' [LN], 'to be tireless in (one's) care' [REB], 'to guard' [BAGD], 'to be vigilant' [HNTC]. It implies great diligence [Blm], constant vigilance [GNC].

b. ὑπέρ with genitive object (LN 90.24, 90.36): 'over' [Lns, Mil, NIC; CEV, NAB, NASB, NIV, NJB, NLT, NRSV, TEV], 'for' [LN (90.36), WBC; KJV, REB], 'on behalf of' [HNTC, LN (90.36)], 'for the sake of' [LN (90.36)], 'concerning, about' [LN (90.24)], 'of' [TNT].

c. ψυχή (LN 23.88) (BAGD 1.c. p. 893, 1.f. p. 894): 'soul' [BAGD, Lns, Mil, NIC; KJV, NASB, NJB, NLT, NRSV, TEV], 'life' [LN], 'eternal life' [WBC]. The phrase τῶν ψυχῶν ὑμῶν 'your souls' is translated 'you' [HNTC; CEV, NAB, NIV, REB, TNT]. It is the center of life that is more than physical [BAGD]; it implies immortality [Alf].

d. ὡς (LN 64.12): 'as' [HNTC, LN, Lns, Mil, WBC; KJV, NAB, NASB, NIV, REB], 'because' [NJB], 'since' [TEV], 'for' [TNT], 'in the knowledge that' [NIC], 'and' [CEV, NLT, NRSV]. It implies being conscious of [ICC], intent or purpose [WBC].

e. fut. act. participle of ἀποδίδωμι (LN 90.46) (BAGD 1. p. 90): 'to render' [HNTC, Mil, NIC; NAB, REB], 'to give' [BAGD, LN, WBC; KJV, NASB, NIV, NJB, NRSV, TEV], 'to give duly' [Lns], 'to make' [LN]. The phrase λόγον ἀποδώσοντες 'going to render an account' is translated 'they are responsible to God for you' [TNT], 'they must answer to God' [CEV], 'they are accountable to God' [NLT]. The future tense refers to future time [HNTC, Lns, Mil; NASB] when the leaders' work is finished [Lns], to future anticipation [NIGTC]; it indicates purpose [NTC, WBC], necessity [NIC, NIGTC; KJV, NAB, NIV, NJB, REB, TEV].

f. λόγος (LN 57.228) (BAGD 2.a. p. 478): 'account' [BAGD, HNTC, LN, Lns, Mil, NIC, WBC; all versions except CEV, NLT, TNT], 'reckoning' [BAGD].

QUESTION—What relationship is indicated by γάρ 'for'?

It indicates the reason for submitting to the leaders [EBC, Mil, NCBC, WBC].

QUESTION—What is the significance of the word αὐτοί 'themselves'?

It is emphatic [Alf, EBC, Lns, Mil, WBC, Wst] and also is emphatic by forefronting [WBC]: they themselves and none other. It gives emphasis to the leaders' authority [WBC], to the leaders' obligations [Wst]; it implies that these leaders are concerned for the readers' interests [ICC].

QUESTION—What is meant by ὑπὲρ τῶν ψυχῶν ὑμῶν 'over your souls'?

1. It refers to the readers with regard to their salvation [Alf, Hwt, My, WBC], their spiritual well-being [EBC, NIGTC]: over your spiritual welfare.
2. It refers to them as persons [GNC, HNTC, Hu, TH, TNTC, Wst; NAB, NIV, REB, TNT]: over you.

QUESTION—What relationship is indicated by ὡς 'as'?

1. It indicates manner [HNTC, Lns, My; KJV, NAB, NASB, NIV, REB]: in a manner appropriate to.
2. It indicates reason [Mil, NIC, TH; NJB, TEV, TNT]: because.

QUESTION—What relationship is indicated by the participle ἀποδώσοντες 'rendering'?

1. It states an attendant fact [NIC; NJB, NRSV, TEV, TNT]: and they will hand over an account.
2. It is translated as an attributive participle [Blm, HNTC, Mil, My, WBC; KJV, NAB, NASB, NIV, REB]: as those who will hand over an account. With ὡς 'as', it expresses motive or purpose [WBC].

QUESTION—Who is the implied object of ἀποδώσοντες 'rendering'?

The implied object is God [EBC, EGT, My, NIGTC, TH, WBC; CEV, NLT, TEV, TNT] and to Christ at his return [My]: handing over to God (and to Christ).

QUESTION—To what does λόγον 'account' refer?

The time referred to is the Judgment Day [Blm, Hwt], the return of Jesus [Hwt].

1. It refers to the leaders' care [EGT, NCBC, NIC, TH, TNTC, WBC; TEV]: an account of their care.
2. It refers to the readers' souls [NJB]: an account of your souls.

in-order-that with[a] joy they-may-do this and not sighing;[b]

LEXICON—a. μετά with genitive object (LN 89.79) (BAGD A.III.1. p. 509): 'with' [BAGD, HNTC, LN, Lns, Mil, NIC, WBC; KJV, NAB, NASB, NRSV]. The phrase μετὰ χαρᾶς τοῦτο ποιῶσιν 'with joy they may do this' is translated 'their work will be a joy' [NIV], 'make this a joy to them' [TNT], 'make this a joy for them to do' [NJB], 'see that their work brings them happiness' [REB], 'they will do their work gladly' [TEV], 'give them reason to do this gladly' [NLT], '. . . they will do their work. Make them happy' [CEV]. This word here indicates manner [NIC, TNTC, WBC].

b. pres. act. participle of στενάζω (LN 25.143) (BAGD p. 766): 'to sigh' [BAGD, LN, NIC; NRSV], 'to groan' [BAGD, LN, Lns, Mil, WBC]. This participle is also translated as a noun: 'grief' [HNTC; KJV, NASB, NJB], 'sadness' [TEV], 'pain and grief' [REB], 'burden' [NIV, TNT], 'sorrow' [NAB, NLT]; as an adjective: 'sad' [CEV]. The sighing would be if the readers disobeyed [Alf, HNTC, Hwt, ICC, Lg(K), Lns, My], if the leaders had to give a negative account [NIGTC], if they followed false doctrines [ICC].

QUESTION—What relationship is indicated by ἵνα 'in order that'?

1. It indicates purpose (contemplated result [Lns]) [Lns, Mil] of obeying their leaders [My, Wst]: obey them in order that . . .
2. It is used imperatively [WBC]: let them do this.

QUESTION—To what does μετὰ χαρᾶς 'with joy' refer?

1. It refers with joy over their obedience [My].
2. It refers to joy in keeping watch [NIGTC; NIV, NJB, REB, TEV].

QUESTION—To what does τοῦτο 'this' refer?

It refers to the leaders' watching over the souls of the readers [Alf, Blm, EBC, EGT, GNC, Hwt, ICC, Lg, Lns, My, Wst]: that they may watch over you with joy.

QUESTION—What relationship is indicated by the participle στενάζοντες 'sighing'?

It expresses manner [EGT, HNTC, Lns, Mil, My, NIC, TH, TNTC, WBC; KJV, NAB, NASB, NRSV, TEV]: do it in a sighing manner.

for this (is/would-be) unprofitable[a] for-you.

LEXICON—a. ἀλυσιτελής (LN **65.49**) (BAGD p. 41): 'unprofitable' [Mil, WBC; KJV, NASB], 'not profitable' [HNTC], 'no advantage' [REB], 'of no advantage' [LN; NIV], 'not of any advantage' [**LN**], 'unadvantageous' [Lns], 'of no help' [BAGD; TEV], 'without special benefit' [LN], 'not of any special benefit' [**LN**], 'not for one's benefit' [NLT], 'not any good' [NIC], 'harmful' [NAB, NRSV]. This entire clause is translated 'that would not do you any good' [TNT], 'you yourselves would be the losers' [NJB], 'otherwise, they won't be able to help you at all' [CEV]. It is a litotes [Blm, ICC, Lns, My], an understatement [Lg, Mil, NCBC, NIGTC], implying a strong positive meaning, hurtful [NIGTC], causing punishment from God [My].

QUESTION—To what does τοῦτο 'this' refer?

1. It refers to grieving over the readers [Alf, EBC, Hwt, Lg, Mil, My], over their spiritual decline [Hu]: if they would have to grieve over you.

2. It refers to failing to submit to the leaders [GNC], giving the leaders reason to complain about them [Blm]: if they would have to complain about you.

QUESTION—What is the implied verb in this clause?

1. The indicative mood is implied [Alf, Blm, Lns; KJV] (which is the form commonly left understood): this is unprofitable.
2. A conditional form is implied [BAGD, HNTC, LN, Mil, NIC, WBC; all versions except KJV]: this would be unprofitable.

DISCOURSE UNIT: 13:18–25 (Hwt, Lg, Lns, Mil). The topic is conclusion [Lns], final exhortations and benedictions [Hwt], final greetings and benediction [Mil], personal communications [Lg].

DISCOURSE UNIT: 13:18–21 (NTC). The topic is prayers and benediction.

DISCOURSE UNIT: 13:18–19 (EBC, NIC). The topic is prayer [EBC], request for prayer [NIC].

13:18 Pray for[a] us;

LEXICON—a. περί with genitive object (LN 90.39) (BAGD 1.f. p. 644): 'for' [BAGD, HNTC, Lns, Mil, NIC, WBC; all versions], 'on behalf of' [LN]. It implies purpose [Mil].

QUESTION—How is this verse related to other verses?

It is not connected with the preceding verse, but is connected with the following verse [NIGTC].

QUESTION—What relationship is indicated by the present tense of προσεύχεσθε 'pray'?

It indicates continued action [EBC, HNTC, ICC, Lns, NIGTC, NTC, WBC; TEV, TNT]: keep on praying. It also implies that the readers had been praying for the writer [EBC, NIGTC, WBC].

QUESTION—What relationship is indicated by the first person plurals of the verbs and participle in this verse?

1. They refer to the author only [Blm, EBC, EGT, GNC, HNTC, Hwt, ICC, Lg, My, NIC, NTC]: pray for me.
2. They refer to the author and his companions [Alf, Lns, Mil, NIGTC, TNTC, WBC, Wst] pray for me and my companions. The author is included among τοῖς ἡγουμένοις 'the ones leading' in the preceding verse [WBC].

for we-are-convinced[a] that we-have (a) good[b] conscience,

LEXICON—a. pres. pass. indic. of πείθω (LN **31.46**, 33.301) (BAGD 2.b., 3.a., p. 639): 'to be convinced' [BAGD, LN (31.46, 33.301), Mil, NIC, WBC], 'to be sure' [BAGD, HNTC, LN (**31.46**); NASB, NIV, NJB, NRSV, REB, TEV, TNT], 'to be persuaded' [LN (33.301), Lns], 'to be confident' [NAB], 'to be certain, to believe' [BAGD], 'to trust' [KJV], not explicit [CEV, NLT].

b. καλός (LN 88.4) (BAGD 2.b. p. 400): 'good' [LN, Lns; KJV, NAB, NASB], 'morally good' [BAGD], 'clear' [HNTC, Mil, NIC, WBC; CEV, NIV, NJB, NLT, NRSV, REB, TEV, TNT].

QUESTION—What relationship is indicated by γάρ 'for'?

It indicates the grounds for the preceding request [Mil, NTC, Wst].

QUESTION—Why is the clause ὅτι καλὴν συνείδησιν ἔχομεν 'that we have a good conscience' mentioned?

It states the basis for requesting prayer [Blm, Hwt, ICC, Lg, My]: I trust I merit your prayer by having a good conscience. It refers to the author's conduct toward the readers [WBC]; it means that his conduct in relation to them can bear the examination by God and by people [Hu], that he has fulfilled his responsibility well [NIC]. It implies that some persons (his enemies [Lg]) may have had doubts about him [Blm, EBC, EGT, GNC, HNTC, Hwt, ICC, Lg, Mil]; some have objected to his abolishing the Levitical order [NTC]; Palestinian Christians have objected to the Pauline character of his teaching [My]; some Jewish teachers had spoken ill of him [Blm].

in[a] everything desiring[b] to-conduct-ourselves[c] well.[d]

LEXICON—a. ἐν with dative object (LN 89.5): 'in' [HNTC, LN, Lns, Mil, NIC, WBC; all versions except CEV, REB, TEV], 'in the case of, with regard to' [LN], 'at' [TEV]; the phrase ἐν πᾶσιν 'in everything' is translated 'always' [CEV, REB].

b. pres. act. participle of θέλω (LN 25.1): 'to desire' [LN, Mil, NIC; NASB, NIV, NRSV], 'to want' [HNTC, LN, Lns; NLT, TEV, TNT], 'to wish' [LN; NAB], 'to will' [KJV], 'to be determined' [NJB], 'to strive' [WBC]. This participle is translated 'and our desire is' [REB], 'to try' [CEV]. It implies an earnest wish [Wst], a firm determination [EBC].

c. pres. mid. infin. of ἀναστρέφω (LN 41.3) (BAGD 2.b.α. p. 61): 'to conduct oneself' [BAGD, LN, Lns, Mil; NASB], 'to behave' [HNTC, LN, NIC; NJB], 'to live' [LN, Mil; CEV, KJV, NIV, NLT], 'to act' [WBC; NAB, NRSV], 'to do' [REB, TEV, TNT].

d. καλῶς (LN 88.4) (BAGD 2. p. 401): 'well' [Lns], 'commendably' [BAGD, WBC], 'rightly' [HNTC; NAB], 'right' [CEV], 'honorably' [Mil, NIC; NASB, NIV, NJB, NLT, NRSV], 'honestly' [KJV], 'what is right' [REB, TNT], 'the right thing' [TEV], 'in a manner free from objection' [BAGD], not specific [LN].

QUESTION—What is meant by ἐν πᾶσιν 'in everything'?

It is emphatic by word order [WBC].

1. It refers to circumstances [HNTC; TNT]: in all circumstances.
2. It refers to events [Alf, Blm, GNC, Lns, NIC, NIGTC, Wst; KJV, NAB, NASB, NJB, NRSV]: in all things.
3. It refers to manner [EBC, Lns, Mil, WBC; NIV]: in every way.
4. It is temporal [REB, TEV]: at all times.

QUESTION—What relationship is indicated by the participle θέλοντες 'desiring'?

1. It states an additional proposition [NIV, NJB, REB]: and we desire . . .
2. This participial phrase specifies the area of the good conscience [Lg, Lns, Wst]: have a good conscience in the fact of desiring to live well.
3. It states a reason [HNTC, Mil, My, NIC, WBC; TEV, TNT]: because we desire to live well.

13:19 And more-abundantly[a] I-urge[b] (you) to-do this,

LEXICON—a. περισσοτέρως (LN 78.31) (BAGD 1. p. 651): 'more abundantly', 'all the more' [NASB, NRSV], 'so much the more' [BAGD], 'the more' [Lns], 'the more earnestly' [HNTC, Mil, NIC], 'even more earnestly' [TEV], 'more greatly' [LN], 'very particularly' [NJB], 'the rather' [KJV]. This comparative adverb is also translated as a positive degree: 'particularly' [NIV], 'especially' [WBC; CEV, NAB, NLT], 'specially' [REB]; as a superlative degree: 'most earnestly' [TNT]. It is emphatic rather than comparative in meaning [Hu, NIGTC, WBC]; it is comparative [NTC].

b. pres. act. indic. of παρακαλέω (LN 33.168): 'to urge' [Lns, Mil, WBC; NASB, NIV, NRSV], 'to beseech' [KJV], 'to beg' [NIC; TEV, TNT], 'to entreat' [HNTC], 'to appeal to, to ask for earnestly, to ask earnestly' [LN], 'to ask' [NAB, NJB, REB], 'to request' [LN], 'to want' [CEV], 'to need' [NLT].

QUESTION—What relationship is indicated by δέ 'and'?

It introduces a coordinate exhortation [Mil]; it connects this verse with the preceding verse [TH], stating a new step in the author's appeal [NIGTC].

QUESTION—To what does τοῦτο 'this' refer?

It refers to the author's request for prayer [Alf, Hu, Mil, NIGTC, TH, WBC; CEV, NIV, NLT, REB, TEV, TNT] for his restoration to them [NAB, NJB, TEV]: I urge you to pray.

in-order-that/that more-quickly[a] I-may-be-restored[b] to-you.

LEXICON—a. τάχέως (LN 67.110) (BAGD 2.a. p. 806): 'more quickly, faster' [BAGD], 'the more quickly' [Lns, NIC], 'sooner' [WBC], 'the sooner' [HNTC, Mil; KJV, NASB, REB, TNT], 'all the sooner' [NJB], 'very soon' [NAB, NRSV]. This comparative adverb is also translated as a positive degree: 'quickly' [LN], 'soon' [CEV, NIV, NLT, TEV]. Its sense is positive rather than comparative [Hu]; it is comparative [WBC].

b. aorist pass. subj. of ἀποκαθίστημι (LN **15.74**) (BAGD 3. p. 92): 'to be restored' [BAGD, HNTC, Lns, Mil, NIC, WBC; KJV, NAB, NASB, NIV, NRSV, REB], 'to be sent back' [LN]. This passive verb is translated as intransitive: 'to come back' [NJB, NLT], 'to visit again' [CEV]; with God as subject: 'to bring back' [TNT], 'to send back' [TEV]. Action by God is implied [TH] by the passive voice [NIGTC].

QUESTION—What relationship is indicated by ἵνα 'in order that/that'?

1. It indicates the purpose of τοῦτο ποιῆσαι 'to do this' [Alf, GNC, HNTC, Hu, Lns, Mil, NIC, WBC; NIV, NLT, REB, TNT]: do this, in order that I may be restored to you.
2. It indicates the content of the requested prayer [ICC, NIGTC, NTC; CEV, NAB, TEV]: pray (asking) that I may be restored to you.

DISCOURSE UNIT: 13:20–25 (EBC, GNT, NCBC, NIGTC; NASB, NJB). The topic is conclusion [EBC], conclusion and final greetings [NIGTC], benediction and final greetings [GNT, NCBC], benediction [NASB], epilogue: news, good wishes, and greetings [NJB].

DISCOURSE UNIT: 13:20–21 (EBC, GNC, HNTC, NIC, WBC; TEV). The topic is doxology [EBC], closing doxology [WBC], prayer and doxology [NIC], a concluding prayer [GNC, HNTC; TEV].

13:20 And/now the God of-the peace, the-(one) having-brought-up/again from[a] dead-ones the shepherd of-the sheep the-great-one by[b] blood of eternal covenant, our Lord Jesus,

LEXICON—a. ἐκ with genitive object (LN 84.4): 'from' [HNTC, LN, Lns, Mil, NIC, WBC; all versions], 'out from, out of' [LN].

b. ἐν with dative object (LN 89.76): 'by' [LN, NIC; NAB, NJB, NRSV, TEV, TNT], 'by means of' [LN], 'through' [LN; KJV, NASB, NIV, NLT, REB], 'by virtue of' [Mil, WBC], 'because of' [Mil], 'with' [HNTC], 'in connection with' [Lns], not explicit [CEV]. It is instrumental [Alf, NIC, NTC], implying by virtue of [Alf, EGT, My], in the power of [Alf], on the basis of [Hu], equipped with [ICC]. It is causal [WBC].

QUESTION—Why is this verse mentioned?

This and the following verse form the proper conclusion to the epistle [Hu, WBC]; they sum up the epistle [Lns, WBC]. Although formally addressed to the readers, it is an appeal to God [Lns]. The introductory δέ 'and/now' introduces a transition to a new aspect [Mil]; it connects this prayer to the preceding comments [NIGTC, WBC].

QUESTION—How are the two nouns related in the genitive construction ὁ θεὸς τῆς εἰρήνης 'the God of peace'?

The genitive noun 'peace' tells what is bestowed by God [Blm, Hu, Hwt, Lns, Mil, NIGTC, NTC, TH, WBC, Wst; CEV], what God produces [My], what God promotes [TNTC]. 'Peace' here refers to the general well-being of the whole person [EBC, NCBC, NIGTC] and salvation [NCBC, NIGTC], an end to all difficulties [EGT], the security brought through Christ's triumph over the powers of evil [ICC]; it is related to the tension between the church and its leaders [Alf, My, WBC]. It refers to the peace between mankind and God through Christ's death [Hu]. With the definite article here it refers to the divine peace given to believers [Lns].

QUESTION—What is meant by the participle ἀναγαγών 'having brought up/again'?

This participle refers to an action in the past [HNTC, Lns, Wst; all versions].

1. It means 'having brought up' [EBC, EGT, HNTC, ICC, My, Wst; NAB, NASB] from a lower to a higher place [NIGTC].
2. It means 'having brought again' [Lns, Mil; KJV, NLT].
3. It means 'having brought back' [Lg(K), NIC; NIV, NRSV, REB].
4. It means 'having brought out' [WBC].

QUESTION—How are the two nouns related in the genitive construction τὸν ποιμένα τῶν προβάτων τὸν μέγαν 'the shepherd of the sheep the great one'?

'Shepherd' implies care for his people [EBC]; 'great' sets him above other shepherds [EBC, Hu, Mil, WBC], and is made prominent by its position with a repeated article after the noun [Mil].

1. 'Shepherd' is the role-relationship to the genitive noun 'the sheep' [Mil]: he relates to the sheep as a shepherd.
2. 'The sheep' receive the action of shepherding: he shepherds the sheep.

QUESTION—What is the phrase τὸν ποιμένα τῶν προβάτων τὸν μέγαν 'the shepherd of the sheep the great one' connected with?

It is connected with τὸν κύριον ἡμῶν Ἰησοῦν 'our Lord Jesus' [Alf, Blm, EBC, GNC, HNTC, Hu, ICC, Lns, Mil, NIC, TNTC, WBC; NAB, NASB, TEV, TNT], as the agreement in case indicates: the great shepherd . . . our Lord Jesus.

QUESTION—What is the phrase ἐν αἵματι διαθήκης αἰωνίου 'the blood of an eternal covenant' connected with?

1. It is connected with ὁ ἀναγαγών 'the one having brought up' [Alf, Blm, EGT, Hu, ICC, Lg(K), Lns, Mil, My(D), NIC, WBC, Wst; KJV, NASB, NIV, NJB, NRSV, REB]: having brought up by the blood . . .
2. It is connected with τὸν ποιμένα τῶν προβάτων τὸν μέγαν 'the shepherd of the sheep the great one' [Lg, My; NLT, TEV, TNT]: (he is) the great shepherd . . . by the blood of an eternal covenant.

QUESTION—How are the two nouns related in the genitive construction αἵματι διαθήκης αἰωνίου 'blood of an eternal covenant'?

The genitive noun phrase 'eternal covenant' tells what the 'blood' accomplished [Alf, Mil, My, TH, WBC; NJB, NLT, TEV]: the blood that sealed the covenant. The adjective 'eternal' is emphatic by its word order [ICC].

QUESTION—What is indicated by the absence of the definite article with the nouns αἵματι 'blood' and διαθήκης 'covenant'?

1. The absence of the article with both nouns emphasizes their quality [Lns, Wst].
2. They are nevertheless treated as definite [Alf, Blm, HNTC, ICC, Mil, NIC, WBC; all versions except NJB, REB]: the blood of the eternal covenant.
3. 'Blood' is made definite, 'covenant' is not [Lg(K), My(D); NJB, REB]: the blood of an eternal covenant.

4. 'Blood' is not definite, 'covenant' is [NTC]: blood of the eternal covenant.

QUESTION—What is indicated by the phrase τὸν κύριον ἡμῶν Ἰησοῦν 'our Lord Jesus'?

The title τὸν κύριον 'the Lord' emphasizes the sovereignty of Jesus [Alf, NTC] and the personal name Ἰησοῦν 'Jesus' refers to his humanity and earthly ministry [NTC]. 'Our Lord Jesus' is emphatic by its final position [EBC, GNC, Lns, NCBC, NIGTC, NTC]; 'the great' is emphatic by its position [NIGTC, NTC].

13:21 may-he-equip[a] you in/with[b] every good (thing) for[c] the doing[d] his will,

TEXT—Before ἀγαθῷ 'good' some manuscripts insert ἔργῳ 'work'. GNT omits this word with an A decision, indicating that the text without the addition is certain. This word is included by Alf, Blm, EGT, Lg, My, KJV.

LEXICON—a. aorist act. optative of καταρτίζω (LN 75.5) (BAGD 1.b. p. 417): 'to equip' [HNTC; NASB, NIV, NLT, TNT], 'to equip perfectly' [Mil], 'to fit out' [Lns], 'to fit' [NIC], 'to provide' [TEV], 'to make complete' [BAGD, WBC; NRSV], 'to furnish' [NAB], 'to furnish completely, to make adequate, to cause to be fully qualified' [LN], 'to prepare' [NJB], 'to make someone ready' [CEV], 'to make perfect' [KJV, REB]. The aorist tense indicates a completed action.

b. ἐν with dative object (LN 13.8, 89.5, 90.10) (BAGD IV.1.b. p. 261): 'in' [LN (13.8, 89.5), Lns, NIC; KJV, NASB, NJB, NRSV, REB], 'with' [HNTC, LN (13.8, 90.10), Mil, WBC; NAB, NIV, NLT, TEV, TNT], 'with regard to' [LN (89.5)], 'by' [LN (90.10)], 'as far as . . . is concerned' [BAGD], not explicit [CEV].

c. εἰς with accusative object (LN 89.57): 'for' [NIV, NLT], 'for the purpose of, in order to' [LN]. The phrase εἰς τὸ ποιῆσαι 'for the doing' is translated 'so that you may do' [Mil; NRSV, REB, TNT], 'that you may do' [NAB], 'in order to do' [TEV], 'to do' [HNTC, Lns, NIC, WBC; KJV, NASB, NJB].

d. aorist act. infin. of ποιέω (LN 42.7, 90.45) (BAGD I.1.c.α. p. 682): 'to do' [BAGD, HNTC, LN (42.7, 90.45), Lns, Mil, NIC, WBC; KJV, NAB, NASB, NIV, NJB, NLT, NRSV, REB, TEV, TNT], 'to keep' [BAGD], 'to carry out' [LN (42.7)], 'to accomplish' [LN (42.7)]. The phrase τὸ ποιῆσαι τὸ θέλημα 'the doing his will' is translated 'to obey him' [CEV]. The aorist tense indicates a completed action.

QUESTION—What is the subject of καταρτίσαι 'may he equip'?

The subject is ὁ θεός 'God' in the preceding verse [Blm, HNTC, Hu, ICC, Lns, Mil, NCBC, NIC, NTC, TNTC, WBC, Wst; all versions]: may the God of peace equip you.

QUESTION—What is meant by ἐν 'in/with'?

1. It refers to an area [Alf, Blm, EBC, EGT, GNC, Lns, NIC, WBC; KJV, NASB, NJB, NRSV, REB, TEV].

1.1 It refers to the area of the equipping [Blm, EBC, GNC, Lns, WBC; KJV, NASB, NRSV, REB, TEV]: equip you in every good thing.
1.2 It refers to the area of doing God's will [EGT, NIC; NJB]: to do God's will in every good thing.
2. It refers to what is given [HNTC, Hwt, ICC; NAB, TEV]: equip you with every good thing.
3. It expresses the means [Mil, TNTC]: equip you by means of every good thing.

QUESTION—To what does ἀγαθῷ 'good' refer?
It refers to an inner endowment from God that enables the believer to do God's will [WBC].

doing[a] in[b] us the pleasing[c] (thing) before[d] him through[e] Jesus Christ,

TEXT—Instead of ἡμῖν 'us' some manuscripts read ὑμῖν 'you'. GNT reads ἡμῖν 'us' with an A decision, indicating that 'us' is certain. 'You' is read by Alf, Blm, EGT, ICC, Lg, Lns, My, CEV, KJV, NAB, and NLT.

LEXICON—a. pres. act. participle of ποιέω (LN 42.7, 90.45) (BAGD I.1.b.ε. p. 681): 'to do' [BAGD, HNTC, LN (42.7, 90.45), Lns; CEV, TEV, TNT], 'to bring about' [BAGD], 'to bring to pass' [NIC], 'to effect' [NJB], 'to carry out' [LN (42.7); NAB], 'to accomplish' [BAGD, LN (42.7), Mil, WBC], 'to work' [KJV, NASB, NIV, NRSV], 'to create' [REB], 'to produce' [NLT].
b. ἐν with dative object (LN 83.13): 'in' [HNTC, LN, Lns, Mil, NIC, WBC; all versions except CEV, NRSV], 'among' [NRSV], not explicit [CEV].
c. εὐάρεστος (LN 25.94) (BAGD 1. p. 318): 'pleasing' [BAGD, HNTC, WBC; NAB, NASB, NIV, NLT, NRSV, REB, TNT], 'pleasing to' [LN], 'well-pleasing' [Lns, Mil; KJV], 'acceptable' [BAGD; NJB]. The phrase τὸ εὐάρεστον ἐνώπιον αὐτοῦ 'the pleasing thing before him' is translated 'what pleases him' [CEV, TEV], 'whatever gives him pleasure' [NIC].
d. ἐνώπιον (LN 90.20) (BAGD 3. p. 270): 'in the sight of' [LN, Lns, Mil; KJV, NASB, NRSV], 'in the opinion of, in the judgment of' [BAGD, LN], 'to' [HNTC, WBC; NAB, NIV, NJB, REB, TEV, TNT], not explicit [NIC; CEV, NLT, TEV].
e. διά with genitive object (LN 90.4): 'through' [HNTC, LN, Lns, Mil, NIC, WBC; all versions except CEV], 'by' [LN], not explicit [CEV].

QUESTION—What relationship is indicated by the participle ποιῶν 'doing'?
The present tense implies continuing action [Lns]. It modifies the preceding ὁ θεός 'God' [NIGTC, NTC].
1. It more specifically defines καταρτίσαι 'may he equip' [My]: may he equip you; that is, may he do . . .
2. It indicates result [Mil]: may he equip you, and so he accomplishes . . .
3. It is temporal [NIC]: may he equip you as he brings to pass . . .
4. It is translated as an additional exhortation [HNTC, NTC; NAB, NIV, REB, TEV, TNT]: may he equip you, and may he do . . .

QUESTION—What is the phrase διὰ Ἰησοῦ Χριστοῦ 'through Jesus Christ' connected with?

1. It is connected with ποιῶν 'doing' [HNTC, ICC, Lns, Mil, My, NIC, NIGTC, NTC, TNTC, WBC; NAB, NJB, REB, TEV]: doing through Jesus Christ.
2. It is connected with the entire clause [EGT, Lns], but especially with καταρτίσαι 'may he equip' [EGT]: may he equip us/you through Jesus Christ.

to-whom (be/is) the glory[a] into[b] the ages of-the ages, amen.

TEXT—Some manuscripts omit τῶν αἰώνων 'of the ages'. GNT includes this phrase in brackets with a C decision, indicating that the committee had difficulty in making a decision. These words are omitted by Alf, EBC, My, WBC, and NAB.

LEXICON—a. δόξα (LN 33.357, 87.4, 87.23): 'glory' [HNTC, LN (87.23), Lns, Mil, NIC, WBC; all versions], 'praise' [LN (33.357)], 'honor' [LN (87.4)], 'greatness' [LN (87.23)].

b. εἰς with accusative object (LN 67.95, 84.22): 'into' [LN (84.22)]. The phrase εἰς τοὺς αἰῶνας τῶν αἰώνων 'into the ages of the ages' is translated 'forever and ever' [HNTC, LN (67.95), Mil, NIC; all versions except NAB], 'forever more' [BAGD], 'for the eons of the eons' [Lns]; εἰς τοὺς αἰῶνας 'into the ages' is translated 'forever' [WBC; NAB].

QUESTION—To whom does ᾧ 'to whom' refer?

1. It refers to Jesus Christ [EGT, GNC, Lg, Lns, My, NTC, TH; CEV, REB, TEV], since Jesus Christ is the nearer referent [EGT, GNC, My, NTC]: to Jesus Christ be the glory.
2. It refers to God the Father [Alf, HNTC, Hu, ICC, My(D), NCBC, NIC, NIGTC, WBC, Wst], since God is the principal subject of the sentence [My(D), NCBC, NIC, Wst]: to God be the glory.

QUESTION—What form of the verb 'to be' is implied in this clause?

The imperative mood ἔστω [My] 'be' or optative εἴη [ICC] 'may (the glory) be' is understood [Alf, HNTC, ICC, Mil, My, NIC, TH, WBC; KJV, NAB, NASB, NIV, NJB, NRSV, REB, TEV, TNT]: to whom be the glory.

QUESTION—What relationship is indicated by the phrase ἡ δόξα with the definite article?

1. With the definite article, it is definite [Alf, Lns, Mil, My, NIC; NASB, NRSV, TEV]: the glory. It refers to the glory due to him [My].
2. The definite article is not translated [HNTC, ICC, WBC; KJV, NAB, NIV, NJB, REB, TNT]: to him be glory.

DISCOURSE UNIT: 13:22–25 (EBC, GNC, HNTC, NIC, NTC, WBC; TEV). The topic is postscript [NIC], postscript and final benediction [GNC], final exhortations [EBC], final greetings [HNTC, NTC], final words [TEV], personal note [WBC].

DISCOURSE UNIT: 13:22–23 (NIC). The topic is personal notes.

13:22 And/Now I-urge[a] you, brothers,[b] bear-with[c] the word[d] of-the exhortation,[e]

LEXICON—a. pres. act. indic. of παρακαλέω (LN 33.168) (BAGD 2. p. 617): 'to urge' [BAGD, Lns, WBC; NASB, NIV, NJB, NLT], 'to appeal to' [BAGD, LN; NRSV], 'to exhort' [BAGD], 'to entreat' [HNTC, Mil], 'to beseech' [KJV], 'to beg' [CEV, NAB, REB, TEV, TNT], 'to request' [LN], 'to encourage' [BAGD]. This indicative verb is also translated 'please' [NIC]. It includes appeal and encouragement [EBC]. It implies the authority of a church leader [WBC].

b. ἀδελφός (LN 11.23): 'brother' [HNTC, Lns, Mil, NIC, WBC; KJV, NAB, NASB, NIV, NJB, TNT], 'brother and sister' [NRSV], 'fellow believer, Christian brother' [LN], 'friend' [CEV, NLT, REB, TEV].

c. pres. mid. (deponent = act.) impera. of ἀνέχομαι (LN 31.54) (BAGD 2. p. 66): 'to bear with' [Lns; NAB, NASB, NIV, NRSV, REB], 'to bear patiently with' [HNTC, Mil; TNT], 'to accept' [LN], 'to receive' [LN], 'to listen willingly' [BAGD, WBC], 'to listen patiently to' [TEV], 'to pay close attention' [CEV], 'to listen carefully to' [NLT], 'to take kindly' [NJB], 'to suffer' [KJV], 'to put up with' [NIC]. It means 'to bear with' [GNC, My, Wst]. This word implies that the author feels that the readers may not welcome the epistle [NCBC], may object to its length [ICC, NIC].

d. λόγος (LN 33.51, 33.98) (BAGD 1.a.ζ. p. 478): 'word' [BAGD, HNTC, LN (33.98), Lns, Mil, NIC, WBC; KJV, NAB, NASB, NIV, NJB, NRSV, TNT], 'treatise' [LN (33.51)], 'message' [LN (33.98); TEV], 'what I have said' [CEV], not explicit [NLT, REB]. With the definite article, it refers to the present epistle [NJB], the author's message to them [NIC; NIV].

e. παράκλησις (LN 25.150) (BAGD 1. p. 618): 'exhortation' [BAGD, HNTC, Mil, NIC, WBC; KJV, NASB, NIV, NRSV, TNT], 'urging' [Lns], 'encouragement' [LN; NAB, NJB, TEV], 'appeal' [REB], not explicit [NLT]. This noun is also translated as a verb: 'to encourage' [CEV]. It refers to exhortation [Hu, NIGTC, NTC], to encouragement [NCBC], to both exhortation and encouragement [EBC, WBC].

QUESTION—What relationship is indicated by δέ 'and/now'?

It is transitional, introducing a coordinating comment [Mil, NIGTC].

QUESTION—What is indicated by ἀδελφοί 'brothers'?

It helps introduce a new point and renews the readers' attention [NIGTC]; it implies a note of gentleness [WBC].

QUESTION—How are the two nouns related in the genitive construction τοῦ λόγου τῆς παρακλήσεως 'the word of exhortation'?

The genitive noun παρακλήσεως 'exhortation' states the contents of τοῦ λόγου 'the word' [Mil]: the word containing the exhortation. This phrase refers to the epistle as a whole [Alf, My, NIC, NIGTC, WBC]; it is a common idiom to describe a sermon [WBC].

for even/also through[a] (a) few[b] (words) I-have-written[c] to-you.

LEXICON—a. διά with genitive object (LN 84.29) (BAGD A.III.1.b. p. 180): 'through' [LN (67.106, 84.29)], 'in' [NIC; KJV]. This preposition expresses means [Alf, NIC], manner [WBC].

b. βραχύς (LN 59.4) (BAGD 3. p. 147): 'few' [LN]. The phrase διὰ βραχέων 'through a few words' is translated 'briefly' [BAGD, HNTC, LN (67.106), Lns, Mil, WBC; NASB, NJB, NRSV], 'rather briefly' [NAB], 'in this brief letter' [NLT], 'in few words' [NIC; KJV], 'only a short letter' [CEV, NIV], 'this letter is not very long' [TEV], 'this is after all a short letter' [REB], 'it is only a short letter' [TNT]. This adjective modifies 'words' understood [Alf, NIC, NTC, Wst; KJV]. It means 'few' in comparison with what might have been written [Alf, EBC, Hu, Wst], in comparison with what he could say later in personal contact [GNC], in view of the importance of the subject [GNC, Lns, Mil, NIGTC], in view of his full thoughts on the subject [Lg].

c. aorist act. indic. of ἐπιστέλλω (LN 33.49) (BAGD p. 300): 'to write' [BAGD, HNTC, Lns, Mil, WBC; CEV, NAB, NASB, NIV, NJB, NRSV, TEV, TNT], 'to write a letter' [LN; KJV], 'to send a letter' [NIC], 'to send a letter to' [LN], 'to say' [NLT], not explicit [REB]. The aorist tense is epistolary [ICC, Lg(K), Lns, NIC, NTC], referring to what will have been a past action when it is read [NTC]. It refers to writing a letter [BAGD, Hu, Hwt, Lg, LN, My, NIC, NTC], to instructing by a letter [NIGTC].

QUESTION—What relationship is indicated by γάρ 'for'?

It indicates the reason for the preceding comment [Mil, My, NIGTC, Wst]: bear with this word because I have written briefly. It implies the possibility that the hearers would think the homily was too long [WBC, Wst].

QUESTION—What relationship is indicated by καί 'even/also'?

1. It adds emphasis [Mil, NTC, WBC]: for indeed.
2. It introduces an additional fact [My]: for also.

QUESTION—What relationship is indicated by the phrase διὰ βραχέων 'through a few'?

It refers to the brevity of the letter as a whole [EBC, EGT, GNC, HNTC, Hu, Hwt, ICC, Lns, Mil, My, NCBC, NIC, NIGTC, NTC, WBC; all versions]: 'in a few words'. It is merely a literary convention [NIGTC, WBC].

13:23 Know[a] our brother Timothy released,[b]

TEXT—Some manuscripts omit ἡμῶν 'our'. GNT does not deal with this variant. Only Alf, Blm, and KJV omit this word.

LEXICON—a. pres. act. impera. of γινώσκω (LN 28.1) (BAGD 6.a.β. p. 161): 'to know' [BAGD, LN, Lns, NIC, WBC; CEV], 'to let someone know' [NAB], 'to want someone to know' [HNTC, Mil; NIV, NJB, NLT, NRSV, TEV, TNT], 'to take notice' [NASB]. This verb is also translated with a phrase: 'I have news for you' [REB].

b. perf. pass. participle of ἀπολύω (LN 37.127) (BAGD 2.b., 3. p. 96): 'to be released' [HNTC, LN, Mil, WBC; NASB, NIV, REB, TNT], 'to be set free' [NIC; NAB, NJB, NRSV], 'to be set at liberty' [KJV], 'to be let out of prison' [TEV], 'to be dismissed' [BAGD]. This passive verb is translated actively: 'to leave' [Lns], 'to take one's leave, to depart, to go away' [BAGD], 'to be out of jail' [CEV, NLT].

QUESTION—What is the mood of the verb γινώσκετε 'know'?

1. It is imperative mood [Alf, EBC, EGT, GNC, HNTC, Hu, Hwt, ICC, Lg, Mil, My, NIC, NIGTC, TH, WBC, Wst; all versions except CEV]: Know . . .
2. It is indicative mood [Lns; CEV]: You know . . .

QUESTION—What is meant by ἡμῶν 'our'?

It is inclusive [NIGTC, WBC]: your brother and mine.

QUESTION—What is meant by ἀπολελυμένον 'released'?

This participle is translated as a noun clause (of indirect discourse [Alf, EGT, HNTC, Hwt, Lns, Mil, NIC, NIGTC, NTC, WBC, Wst; all versions]) describing Timothy's situation [Alf, EGT, HNTC, Hu, Hwt, ICC, Lg, Lns, Mil, My, NCBC, NIC, NIGTC, NTC, WBC, Wst; all versions]. The participle is used where an infinitive could be used [Alf, Lg(K)]. The perfect tense implies that Timothy has been released and is now in a released state [Lns].

1. Timothy is released [ICC, Mil; all versions] from prison [EBC, EGT, HNTC, Hu, Hwt, Lg, My, NCBC, NIC, NIGTC, NTC, TH, TNTC, WBC, Wst; CEV, NLT, TEV], not necessarily from prison [ICC].
2. Timothy is dismissed [Alf].
3. Timothy has departed on a mission [Lns].

with[a] whom, if soon[b] he-should-come,[c] I-shall-see[d] you.

LEXICON—a. μετά with genitive object (LN 89.108): 'with' [HNTC, LN, Mil, NIC, WBC; KJV, NASB, NIV], 'together with, in the company of' [LN], 'in company with' [Lns]. The phrase μεθ' οὗ 'with whom' is translated 'he will be with me' [NAB, NJB, NRSV, REB], 'I will have him with me' [TEV], 'I will bring him with me' [CEV, NLT, TNT].

b. ταχέως (LN 67.110) (BAGD 2.b. p. 807): 'soon' [BAGD; NAB, NASB, NIV, NLT], 'soon enough' [HNTC; TEV], 'fairly soon' [NIC], 'very soon' [WBC], 'without delay' [BAGD], 'shortly' [KJV], 'quickly' [BAGD, LN], 'in time' [CEV, NJB, NRSV, REB, TNT]. The phrase ἐὰν τάχιον ἔρχηται 'if soon he should come' is translated 'as soon as he comes' [Lns, Mil]. This comparative form τάχιον has its comparative meaning [Wst]; it means 'very speedily' [My, WBC]; it has the meaning of the positive degree, 'soon' [EGT, NIGTC].

c. pres. mid. (deponent = act.) of ἔρχομαι (LN 15.81): 'to come' [HNTC, LN, Lns, Mil, NIC, WBC; KJV, NASB, NLT, NRSV, TNT], 'to arrive' [NIV]. The phrase ἐὰν ἔρχηται 'if he should come' is translated 'if he is able to join me' [NAB], 'if he gets here' [CEV].

d. fut. mid. (deponent = act.) of ὁράω (LN 24.1, **34.50**) (BAGD 1.a.α. p. 578): 'to see' [HNTC, LN (24.1), Lns, Mil, NIC; all versions except CEV, TNT], 'to come to see' [TNT], 'to go to see' [LN (34.50)], 'to visit' [BAGD, LN (**34.50**), WBC; CEV].

QUESTION—What relationship is indicated by the phrase ἐὰν τάχιον ἔρχηται 'if soon he should come'?

The construction implies uncertainty [NTC, TNTC].

1. It means if Timothy will reach the author in time [Alf, GNC, HNTC, Hu, Hwt, ICC, Lns, My, NIGTC, NTC, TH, WBC; all versions except KJV, NASB].
2. It means that the author expects to go to where Timothy was [EBC].
3. It means that the author expects Timothy to go to the readers of the epistle [EGT].

13:24 Greet[a] all the-(ones) leading[b] you and all the saints.[c]

LEXICON—a. aorist mid. (deponent = act.) impera. of ἀσπάζομαι (LN 33.20) (BAGD 1.a. p. 116): 'to greet' [HNTC, LN, Mil, NIC, WBC; NASB, NIV, NRSV, REB], 'to send greetings to' [LN], 'to give one's greetings to' [CEV, NLT, TEV], 'to give one's warm greetings to' [TNT], 'to salute' [Lns; KJV]. This verb is also translated 'greetings to' [BAGD; NAB, NJB], 'remember me to' [BAGD]. It indicates warm cordiality [WBC]. The aorist tense implies that the action is to be completed.

b. pres. mid. (deponent = act.) of ἡγέομαι (LN 36.1, 37.58) (BAGD 1. p. 343): 'to lead' [BAGD, LN (36.1), Lns], 'to guide' [BAGD, LN (36.1)], 'to direct' [LN (36.1)], 'to have the rule over' [KJV], 'to rule over, to govern' [LN (37.58)]. The participial phrase τοὺς ἡγουμένους 'the ones leading' is translated 'leaders' [HNTC, Mil, WBC; all versions except KJV], 'guides' [NIC]. The present tense with the definite article gives a substantive sense, referring to activity characterizing the persons as 'leaders'.

c. ἅγιος (LN 11.27, 88.24): 'saint' [Lns, Mil, WBC; KJV, NASB, NRSV], 'holy' [LN (88.24)]. The phrase οἱ ἅγιοι 'the saints' is translated 'the people of God' [NAB], 'God's people' [HNTC, LN (11.27); NIV, REB, TEV, TNT], 'the Lord's people' [CEV], 'God's holy people' [NIC; NJB], 'believers' [NLT]. It refers to true believers [Lns], people dedicated to God for his service [EBC], people who belong to God in a special way [TH].

QUESTION—What is indicated by the repeated πάντας 'all'?

It is emphatic [Wst]. It indicates that there were no exceptions [EBC, Hu, NCBC]; it includes all the leaders [Hu, ICC, Lg, WBC] and all the saints [GNC, Hu, ICC, Lg]; 'all the saints' implies the existence of several house churches [WBC]. The three repetitions of 'all' in this and the following verse implies concern for each member of the church [NIGTC].

The-ones from[a] Italy greet[b] you.

LEXICON—a. ἀπό with genitive object (LN 90.15) (BAGD IV.1.b. p. 87): 'from' [HNTC, LN, Lns, Mil, NIC, WBC; CEV, NASB, NIV, NLT, NRSV, REB], 'of' [KJV]. The phrase οἱ ἀπὸ τῆς Ἰταλίας 'the ones from Italy' is translated 'the believers from Italy' [TEV], 'God's holy people in Italy' [NJB], 'the Italians' [BAGD], 'our Italian friends also' [TNT].

b. pres. mid. (deponent = act.) of ἀσπάζομαι (LN 33.20) (BAGD 1.a. p. 116): 'to greet' [BAGD, HNTC, LN, WBC; NASB], 'to send greetings' [BAGD, Mil; CEV, NIV, NJB, NLT, NRSV], 'to send (one's) greetings' [NIC; TEV, TNT], 'to send greetings to' [LN], 'to wish to be remembered' [BAGD], 'to salute' [Lns; KJV]. This verb is translated 'greetings' [REB].

QUESTION—Who are οἱ ἀπὸ τῆς Ἰταλίας 'the ones from Italy'?

Expressions of this type normally refer to natives of a place [EGT]. Here the reference is to fellow-Christians [TH].

1. Here it refers to persons from Italy who were in another place with the author [EGT, Lns, Mil, My, NCBC, NIGTC, NTC, WBC].
2. The reference is ambiguous [Hwt, ICC, Lg, NIC, TNTC, Wst].

13:25 The grace[a] (be) with[b] all of-you.

TEXT—Some manuscripts add ἀμήν 'amen' at the end of this verse. GNT omits 'amen' with an A decision, indicating that the text is certain. 'Amen' is added by Alf, Blm, EGT, and KJV.

TEXT—In some manuscripts a subscription in one of several forms is added at the close of this verse. GNT does not deal with this addition. The clause Πρὸς Ἑβραίους ἐγράφη ἀπὸ Ἰταλίας διὰ Τιμοθέου 'To Hebrews was written (or 'It was written to Hebrews') from Italy through Timothy' is included by Blm, EGT; this clause, translated 'written to the Hebrews from Italy by Timothy', is read by KJV; the phrase Πρὸς Ἑβραίους 'to Hebrews' is read by Alf.

LEXICON—a. χάρις (LN 25.89, 88.66) (BAGD 2.c. p. 877): 'grace' [BAGD, EGT, HNTC, LN (88.66), Mil, NIC, WBC; KJV, NAB, NASB, NIV, NJB, NRSV, TNT], 'God's grace' [NLT, REB, TEV], 'the divine grace' [Lns], 'kindness' [LN (88.66)], 'favor' [BAGD, LN (25.89)], 'good-will' [LN (25.89)]. This noun is also translated as a verb: 'to be kind' [CEV]. It refers to God's grace [Alf, Hu, Mil, NIGTC, TH, TNTC, WBC], what God has done for people through Christ [EBC, Hu]; it is the grace of Christ [Wst].

b. μετά with genitive object (LN 90.60) (BAGD A.II.1.c.γ. p. 509): 'with' [BAGD, HNTC, LN, Lns, Mil, NIC, WBC; all versions except CEV], 'to' [LN; CEV].

QUESTION—What relationship is indicated by the position of πάντων 'all' before ὑμῶν 'of you'?

It is emphatic, emphasizing every individual [Alf].

www.ingramcontent.com/pod-product-compliance
Lightning Source LLC
LaVergne TN
LVHW020514100826
845148LV00010B/1232

* 9 7 8 1 5 5 6 7 1 2 0 9 8 *